Text, Cases and Materials on Medical Law and Ethics

Text, Cases and Materials on Medical Law and Ethics presents a valuable collection of materials relating to often controversial areas of the law. Comprising extracts from statutes, cases and scholarly articles alongside expert author commentary and guidance which signposts the key issues and principles, this book is an ideal companion to this increasingly popular subject.

Fully revised, this new edition incorporates expanded content, including:

● updated coverage of consent and decision-making, including the *Montgomery v Lanarkshire Health Board* (2015) judgment;
● the impacts of the EC directive for clinical trials and GDPR on the research use of patient data; and
● discussion of other recent developments in the case law, including the 2017 Charlie Gard litigation, the 2016 Privy Council decision in *Williams v Bermuda* on negligence causation, and the UK Supreme Court judgment in *A & B v SS for Health* (2017) on funding for patients from Northern Ireland seeking terminations elsewhere in the UK.

Providing a comprehensive and up-to-date resource on this topical area of the law, this textbook is an invaluable reference tool for students of medical law as well as those studying medicine.

Marc Stauch, MA (Oxon), Dr jur (Göttingen) is a Lecturer and Research Fellow at Leibniz University of Hannover.

Kay Wheat, BA is Reader in Law at Nottingham Trent University.

Text, Cases and Materials on Medical Law and Ethics

SIXTH EDITION

Marc Stauch and Kay Wheat

Routledge
Taylor & Francis Group

LONDON AND NEW YORK

Sixth edition published 2019
by Routledge
2 Park Square, Milton Park, Abingdon, Oxon, OX14 4RN

and by Routledge
711 Third Avenue, New York, NY 10017

Routledge is an imprint of the Taylor & Francis Group, an informa business

First edition published by Cavendish Publishing 1998
Fifth edition published by Routledge 2015

British Library Cataloguing-in-Publication Data
A catalogue record for this book is available from the British Library

Library of Congress Cataloging-in-Publication Data
Names: Stauch, Marc, author. | Wheat, Kay, author.
Title: Text, cases and materials on medical law and ethics / Marc Stauch, Kay Wheat.
Description: Sixth edition. | Milton Park, Abingdon, Oxon ; New York, NY : Routledge, [2019] | Includes bibliographical references and index.
Identifiers: LCCN 2018017199 | ISBN 9781138051263 (hbk) | ISBN 9781138051287 (pbk) | ISBN 9781315168326 (ebk)
Subjects: LCSH: Medical laws and legislation—England. | Medical care—Law and legislation—England. | Medical ethics. | LCGFT: Casebooks (Law)
Classification: LCC KD3395 .S73 2019 | DDC 344.4204/1—dc23
LC record available at https://lccn.loc.gov/2018017199

ISBN: 978-1-138-05126-3 (hbk)
ISBN: 978-1-138-05128-7 (pbk)
ISBN: 978-1-315-16832-6 (ebk)

Typeset in Goudy
by Apex CoVantage, LLC

Printed and bound by CPI Group (UK) Ltd, Croydon, CR0 4YY

Outline contents

Detailed contents

Acknowledgements

Grateful acknowledgement is made to all the authors and publishers of copyright material which appears in this book, and in particular to the following for permission to reprint material from the sources indicated:

Cambridge University Press for extracts from Keown, John, *Abortion, Doctors and the Law: Some Legal Aspects of the Legal Regulation of Abortion in England from 1803 to 1982* (1988), © 1988 Cambridge University Press, reproduced with permission; Maclean, Alasdair, *Autonomy, Informed Consent and Medical Law: A Relational Challenge* (2009), © 2009 Alasdair Maclean, published by Cambridge University Press, reproduced with permission.

Michael Cavadino for extracts from *Mental Health Law in Context: Doctors' Orders* (Dartmouth, 1989), pp 138–41, reproduced by permission of the author.

Routledge/Taylor and Francis for extracts from Lamb, David, *Organ Transplants and Ethics* (1990), © 1990 David Lamb; Fennell, Phil, *Treatment without Consent: Law, Psychiatry and the Treatment of Mentally Disordered People Since 1845* (1996), © 1996 Phil Fennel, reproduced by permission of Taylor and Francis Books UK; Stone, D., *Confidentiality, Access to Health Records and the Human Rights Act 1998*, in Garwood-Gowers, Austen, et al., *Healthcare Law: The Impact of the Human Rights Act 1998* (Cavendish Publishing, 2001); Harris, J, *The Value of Life: Introduction to Medical Ethics* (1985).

Wiley-Blackwell for extracts from Davies, ACL, 'This Time, it's for Real: The Health and Social Care Act 2012' (2013) 76(3) MLR 564; Dworkin, G, 'The law relating to organ transplantation in England' (1970) 33 MLR 353; Hursthouse, R, *Beginning Lives* (1987), © 1987 Rosalind Hursthouse; Fortin, J, 'Legal protection for the unborn child' (1988) 51(1) MLR 54–83; Keown, J, 'The ashes of AIDS and the phoenix of informed consent' (1989) 52(6) MLR 790–800; Fox, Marie and McHale, Jean, 'In whose Best Interests? (1997) 60(5) MLR 700–709; Thomson, JJ, 'A Defence of Abortion' (1971) 1(1) *Philosophy and Public Affairs* 47–66.

Oxford University Press for extracts from Skegg, PDG, *Law, Ethics and Medicine: Studies in Medical Law* (1998), pp 40, 110–112; Culver, CM and Gert, B, *Philosophy in Medicine: Conceptual and Ethical Issues in Medicine and Psychiatry* (1982), pp 66, 146; Grubb, Andrew (ed), *Principles of Medical Law*, 2nd edn (2004); Downie, RS, 'Traditional Medical Ethics and Economics in Health Care: A Critique' in Mooney, Gavin and McGuire, Alistair (eds), *Medical Ethics and Economics in Health Care* (1989), pp 40–55.

The British Medical Journal for extracts from Wilkinson, S and Garrard, E, 'Bodily integrity and the sale of human organs' (1996) 22 Journal of Medical Ethics 334.

Harper Collins/Fourth Estate for extracts from Dworkin, R, *Life's Dominion: An Argument About Abortion and Euthanasia* (1993), © 1993 Ronald Dworkin; Glover, J et al., *Report to the European Commission on Reproductive Technologies, Fertility and the Family* (1989), London: Fourth Estate.

Princeton University Press for extracts from Robertson, John A, *Children of Choice: Freedom and the New Reproductive Technologies* (1994), © 1994 Princeton University Press. Reprinted by permission of Princeton University Press.

Lexis Nexis for extracts from *Re T* [1997] 1 All ER 906.

Thompson Reuters for extracts from the Australian Law Journal and Reports, *Secretary of Health v JWB & SMB* (1992) 66 ALJR 30; *HL v HK* (2005) 40 EHRR 32 (European Human Rights Reports).

Every effort has been made to trace and contact copyright holders prior to publication. If notified, the publisher will undertake to rectify any errors or omissions at the earliest opportunity.

Table of cases

Table of legislation

Table of statutory instruments

Table of treaties and EU legislation

Abbreviations

A	The Atlantic Reporter
AC	Appeal Cases
ALJR	Australian Law Journal Reports
All ER	All England Law Reports
ALR	Australian Law Reports and Personal Injuries and Quantum Reports
Am J Law & Med	American Journal of Law and Medicine
Aust Torts Rep	Australian Torts Reports
BMJ	British Medical Journal
BMLR	Butterworths Medico-Legal Reports
British J of Obstet and Gyn	British Journal of Obstretrics and Gynaecology
Cal App	Californian Appellate Cases
Cal Rptr	Californian Reporter
Ch	Chancery Division/Chapter
CLJ	Cambridge Law Journal
Cox	Cox's Criminal Cases
Cr App R	Criminal Appeal Reports
Crim LR	Criminal Law Review
CSIH	Court of Session Inner House
DLR	Dominion Law Reports
EHRR	European Human Rights Reports
EMLR	Entertainment and Media Law Reports
Eur J Mental Health L	European Journal of Mental Health Law
F	Federal Reporter
Fam Law	Family Law
Fam	Family Division
FCR	Family Court Reports
Fem Leg Stud	Feminist Legal Studies
FLR	Family Law Reports
IRLR	Industrial Relations Law Reports
J Mental Health L	Journal of Mental Health Law
J Soc Wel L	Journal of Social Welfare Law
JETL	Journal of European Tort Law
JLS	Journal of Law and Society
JME	Journal of Medical Ethics
JPIL	Journal of Personal Injury Law
KB	King's Bench Law Reports
LGR	Local Government Reports
Lloyd's Rep Med	Lloyd's Law Reports: Medical
LQR	Law Quarterly Review
Mass	Massachusetts Supreme Judicial Court Reports
Med L Rev	Medical Law Review

Med LR	Medical Law Reports
MLR	Modern Law Review
NBR	New Brunswick Reports
NE	North Eastern Reporter
NJ	New Jersey Supreme Court Reports
NLJ	New Law Journal
Nott LJ	Nottingham Law Journal
NSWLR	New South Wales Law Reports
NW	North Western Reporter
NYS	New York Supplement
NZLR	New Zealand Law Reports
OJLS	Oxford Journal of Legal Studies
OR	Ontario Reports
Pa D & C	Pennsylvania District and County Reports
PIQR	Personal Injuries and Quantum Reports
Proc Roy Soc Med	Proceedings of the Royal Society of Medicine
QB	Queen's Bench Law Reports
RTR	Road Traffic Reports
S Ct	Supreme Court Reporter
SC	Session Cases
SCR	Canada Law Reports: Supreme Court
SJ	Solicitor's Journal
SLT	Scots Law Times
SW	South Western Reporter
Texas L Rev	Texas Law Review
US	United States Supreme Court Reports
USLW	United States Law Week
VR	Victorian Reports
WLR	Weekly Law Reports
WWR	Western Weekly Reports

Part 1

General principles

Chapter 1

Introduction to ethics

This chapter will examine the ways in which ethical issues are part of the practice of medicine. In this first section we will look, briefly, at a number of ethical theories and concepts and the ways in which they might relate to medicine. Next, we consider the doctor–patient relationship and the way in which medicine has given rise to particular ways of describing this relationship and its ethical implications. Although it is by no means a clear-cut dichotomy, generally it can be said that many of the problems in medical ethics, and certainly many of the conflicting opinions, are based upon the debate between paternalism and the patient's right to autonomy. First, the view that paternalism is central to the doctor–patient relationship means that because of the doctor's superior knowledge and his ethical obligation to do good, the medical view of what is best for the patient should prevail. The opposing view is that the patient has a right to autonomous decision-making and that this should not be overridden by 'doctor knows best'. Later in the chapter we will study these two different ways of looking at the doctor–patient relationship, question whether it is helpful to use either of these models as frameworks for medical decision-making, and look at alternatives. Finally, we will look at justice and fairness in the allocation of treatment between competing patients when resources dictate that not all can be treated, and at the distribution of healthcare resources on a national level.

However, although the current chapter looks at general principles, when appropriate, ethical problems in particular areas of medical practice will be examined in other chapters.

1.1 Why study ethics?

Why should ethics be so important in medicine? In other fields of activity, such as commerce, ethics plays a small role. As long as business is operated on the right side of the law, little consideration is given to whether it is practised ethically. Although many may protest, for example, that 'it isn't fair' for large supermarkets to put small shops out of business, the 'ethics' of this plays a minor role in the general discourse about such matters, which is much more likely to be concerned with convenience and consumer choice. That is not to say that it is not relevant. It is simply that the language of ethics has not permeated the world of business in the way in which it has the practice of medicine. The reason may be that much of medicine is about issues of life and death: for example, abortion, infertility treatment, the threat to life through negligent treatment, or insufficiency of health resources, the treatment of the terminally ill and so on. Perhaps the heart of the doctor–patient relationship is this: the doctor does things to the body of the patient, thereby invading his physical integrity. This is neither good nor bad in itself, but is instrumentally good if the likely effect is the cure or amelioration of the patient's condition, and if it is done with the real consent and co-operation of the patient. However, in so far as it can be ascertained, it must be done in the patient's best medical interests. If there is no real consent, or if the treatment is unsuitable or negligently carried out, then it could be regarded as a violation of the patient's physical integrity.

Although, as we shall see, there is some argument that the doctor–patient relationship has been wrongly accorded this special status, there is no doubt that since the time of ancient Greece, it has given rise to ethical codes prescribing the extent of the doctor's duties:

Mason, JK and Laurie, GT, *Mason and McCall Smith's Law and Medical Ethics*[1]

The Hippocratic Influence
Hippocrates remains as the most famous figure in Greek philosophical medicine but he was not alone and it is probable that the Oath predates his own school. It therefore indicates a prevailing ethos rather than a

---

1 Oxford: OUP, 8th edn, 2011.

professorial edict and it is still regarded as the fundamental governance of the medical profession . . . the Oath lays down a number of guidelines. First, it implies the need for co-ordinated instruction and registration of doctors – the public is to be protected, so far as is possible, from the dabbler or the charlatan. Secondly, it is clearly stated that a doctor is there for the benefit of his patients – to the best of his ability he must do them good and he must do nothing which he knows will cause harm. . . . Thirdly, euthanasia and abortion are proscribed; the reference to lithotomy probably prohibits mutilating operations (castration) but has been taken by many to imply the proper limitation of one's practice to that in which one has expertise. Fourthly, the nature of the doctor–patient relationship is outlined and an undertaking is given not to take advantage of that relationship. Finally, the Oath expresses the doctrine of medical confidentiality.

What is the study of ethics about? The purpose of ethics is to try and find principles for living good lives. It will be seen that there is much overlap between ethical theories, and within each, there are contradictions and tensions. Words such as 'equality', 'rights' and 'liberty' all sound good, and we all like to think that we approve of these things. However, in deciding what we mean by them we may find that we are making all sorts of value judgments and interpretations which suit the end we would like to achieve.

1.1.1 Universalisation and relativism

A fundamental starting point in discussions about ethics is universalisation. This means that one must seek principles that can apply to everyone. Peter Singer describes the way this has permeated ethical thinking:

Singer, P, *Practical Ethics*[2]

From ancient times, philosophers and moralists have expressed the idea that ethical conduct is acceptable from a point of view that is somehow universal. Kant developed this idea into his famous formula: 'Act only on that maxim through which you can at the same time will that it should become a universal law.' Kant's theory has itself been modified and developed by RM Hare, who sees 'universalisability' as a logical feature of moral judgments. The 18th century British philosophers Hutcheson, Hume and Adam Smith appealed to an imaginary 'impartial spectator' as the test of a moral judgment . . . Utilitarians from Jeremy Bentham to JJC Smart take it as axiomatic that in deciding moral issues 'each counts for one and none for more than one'; while John Rawls, a leading contemporary critic of utilitarianism, incorporates essentially the same axiom into his own theory by deriving basic ethical principles from an imaginary choice in which those choosing do not know whether they will be the ones who gain or lose by the principles they select. . . .

This does not mean that a particular ethical judgment must be universally applicable. . . . What it does mean is that in making ethical judgments we go beyond our own likes and dislikes. From an ethical point of view the fact that it is I who benefit from, say, a more equal distribution of income and you, say, who lose by it, is irrelevant. Ethics requires us to go beyond 'I' and 'you' to the universal law, the universalisable judgment, the standpoint of the impartial spectator or ideal observer, or whatever we choose to call it.

Can we use this universal aspect of ethics to derive an ethical theory which will give us guidance about right and wrong? . . . The problem is that if we describe the universal aspect of ethics in bare, formal terms, a wide range of ethical theories, including quite irreconcilable ones, are compatible with this notion of universality; if, on the other hand, we build up our description of the universal aspect of ethics so that

---

2 Cambridge: CUP, 1979.

it leads us ineluctably to one particular ethical theory, we shall be accused of smuggling our own ethical beliefs into our definition of the ethical – and this definition was supposed to be broad enough, and neutral enough, to encompass all serious candidates for the status of 'ethical theory'.

As Singer says, the principle of universalisation has appealed to many and it cannot be said to belong to any particular theory.

See Hart's criticism of Mill, at **1.3.2** →

Nevertheless, it is arguable that we approach ethical problems from the standpoint of a white Western man. Increasingly, therefore, there are thinkers who want to move away from this and explore the issues from the perspective of women or of people from different cultures.

We commenced this section with the suggestion that ethical principles should be universal. Some would argue that this does not address the way in which cultural differences might give rise to different ethical norms:

Beauchamp, TL and Walters, L, *Contemporary Issues in Bioethics*[3]

[Cultural] relativists defend their position by appeal to anthropological data indicating that moral rightness and wrongness vary from place to place and that there are no absolute or universal moral standards that could apply to all persons at all times. They add that rightness is contingent on cultural beliefs and that the concepts of rightness and wrongness are therefore meaningless apart from the specific contexts in which they arise . . . . patterns of culture can only be understood as unique wholes and that moral beliefs about normal behaviour are thus closely connected in a culture to other cultural characteristics, such as language and fundamental political institutions.

Similarly, some feminists have taken the view that the language of moral philosophy is male-centred, and dominated by an undue reverence for 'reason'. This is particularly pertinent to medical ethics, as the medical profession has traditionally been dominated by men, particularly in its upper reaches. It has been said that the traditional approach to medical ethics reinforces the practice of patriarchal medicine and the patriarchal institutions within society (for example, by Susan Sherwin).[4] Some feminist writers have spoken of the need for an 'ethics of care', whereby the emotions have an important role to play in ethical theories.[5] Beauchamp and Childress describe the care ethic as follows:

Beauchamp, TL and Childress, JF, *Principles of Biomedical Ethics*[6]

Having a certain emotional attitude and expressing the appropriate emotion in action are morally relevant factors, just as having the appropriate motive for an action is morally relevant. The person seems morally deficient who acts from rule-governed obligations without appropriately aligned feelings such as worry when a friend suffers. In addition to expressing their feelings in their responses, agents also need to attend to the feelings of persons toward whom they act. Insight into the needs of others and considerate attentiveness to their circumstances often come from the emotions more than reason.

In the history of human experimentation, for example, those who first recognised that some subjects of research were being brutalised, subjected to misery, or placed at unjustifiable risk were persons who

---

3 Belmont, CA: Wadsworth Publishing, 1982.
4 See 'Feminist and medical ethics: two different approaches to contextual ethics', in Bequaert Holmes, H and Purdy, LM, *Feminist Perspectives in Medical Ethics*, Bloomington, IN: Indiana UP, 1992.
5 See Gilligan, C, *In a Different Voice: Psychological Theory and Women's Development*, Cambridge, MA: Harvard UP, 1982.
6 Oxford: OUP, 2001.

were able to feel compassion, disgust, and outrage through insight into the situation of these research subjects. They exhibited emotional discernment and sensitivity to the feelings of subjects, where others lacked comparable responses. This emphasis on the emotional dimension of the moral life does not reduce moral response to emotional response. Caring also has a cognitive dimension, because it involves insight into and understanding of another's circumstances, needs, and feelings. As Hume pointed out, emotions motivate us and tell us much about a person's character, but human understanding directs us in choosing a path of action.

The care ethic, however, has its weaknesses, in that it is arguable that it is not sufficient as a moral theory. Beauchamp and Childress comment as follows:

Beauchamp, TL and Childress, JF, *Principles of Biomedical Ethics*[7]

On at least some occasions we need an impartial judgment to arbitrate between conflicting moral judgments or feelings. Many who endorse the ethics of care do not want to exclude all impartial judgments and considerations of justice and the public good. But the problem remains about the extent to which this approach can successfully incorporate these moral notions without losing much of its critical thrust and uniqueness. The ethic of care, as Gilligan and others have defended it, recognises that two perspectives exist, but can they be made *coherent*? . . .

Some feminists [eg Susan Sherwin] have sharply criticised the ethics of care, despite its feminist origins, on the grounds that it attends to women's experiences as givers of care in traditional roles of self-sacrifice, but often neglects their oppression. . . .

. . . without a broader framework, the ethics of care is too confined to the *private* sphere of intimate relationships and may serve to reinforce an uncritical adherence to traditional social patterns of assigning caretaker roles to women.

THINK POINT

Do you agree that the emphasis on 'care' sets up a potential conflict between rationalism and emotions which is unnecessary and unhelpful in deciding on what is the ethically correct thing to do?

Pattinson states that it is clear that moral 'pluralism' ie that there are different moral standpoints, does in fact exist as a matter of fact. For example, we shall see when issues such as abortion are discussed, even within a fairly homogeneous western society, there are very different views on this. However, Pattinson regards this as not being particularly problematic.

Pattinson, SD, *Medical Law and Ethics*[8]

Even in largely secular societies some level of moral consensus is actually quite common. If it were not, no stable polity could exist. It should therefore be no surprise that English legal doctrine actually encompasses many moral values shared by the majority of the population. Indeed, a more widespread developed-world

---

7 Ibid.
8 London: Sweet & Maxwell, 2006.

consensus can be seen in international instruments such as the Helsinki declaration and the innumerable human rights instruments that pepper the international area. These instruments proclaim the universal nature of moral values such as respect for patient autonomy and the democratic process. This still, however, leaves ethical disagreement on many of the issues raised by medical law. ...

... Even *if* moral relativism is to be rejected in favour of objectivism, there are many different variations of moral objectivism.

This brings us to examining some of the different theories.

1.1.2 Consequences v deontological absolutes

One way of deciding whether an action is ethically right or wrong is to look at the consequences of *this* act; or we might consider it important to look at the consequences of translating this act into an ethical proposition about what should be done generally, ie, by framing an ethical principle which will produce the best consequences. So, for example, we might make a rule about keeping promises which is generally a good thing to do, even though in some circumstances the consequences of breaking a promise may be better than keeping it. Another way is to ask whether the act or principle would be right or wrong *regardless of its consequences*. This leads to a somewhat crude distinction between theories which judge the moral correctness of an action by its consequences alone, and those which state there are certain principles, rights or whatever, which are inviolable, whatever the consequences. However, it is by no means a neat division. With varying degrees of success, most consequentialists try to incorporate certain things such as respect for individual rights into their theories. Those who believe in the paramountcy of absolute values cannot disregard consequences entirely. Advocates of certain principles such as the sanctity of life (one of those so-called inviolable principles) may oppose, say, the withdrawal of nutrition from a permanently unconscious patient. However, they may argue that one of the reasons for their view is the 'slippery slope' argument, which says that once a certain course of action is carried out (as here), then the next step will be to withdraw food from a patient who is gravely disabled, but not unconscious. This argument is an appeal to consequentialism.

See Chapter 12 →

1.1.2.1 Consequentialism

The theory that the rightness of a course of action is to be judged by its consequences is an attractive one and it is tempting to embrace this view as being self-evidently right. Human actions have outcomes. We believe that we need to know what these are in order to decide what is the right thing to do. However, a moment's reflection will make us realise that while it may be correct, as it stands, it is full of holes. First, consequences for whom? If we are looking at types of medical treatment or the allocation of health resources we must ask whether we are looking at these sorts of patients or society as a whole? What sorts of consequences are going to be relevant? If the consequences of treating these patients may be that they will live, but live in pain or be dependent upon others for their most basic needs, is this right?

The most well-known consequentialist view is that of utilitarianism. This theory, of whom Jeremy Bentham was one of the earliest exponents, states that ethical principles should produce the greatest happiness for the greatest number of people, and 'happiness' is defined by means of pleasure. The rightness of a decision is judged by deciding whether it produces, on balance, more pleasure than pain. When we consider the treatment of, say, very seriously disabled new-born children, we might discount treating them because they will live (we believe) painful lives. But we also tend to think that there is more to life than the pursuit of pleasure and the avoidance of pain. JJC Smart has put forward the example of the 'pleasure machine'.[9] This is a machine that can be connected to the brain to give pleasure, without the 'inconvenience' of the means of obtaining pleasure, for example from books, sex, sport and so on. Once we acknowledge the absurdity of this and realise that we do not pursue pleasure as such, but an infinite number of pursuits, the pain–pleasure dichotomy is not so attractive. We tend to think that to be human is to be more than the repository of the sensations of pleasure and pain. Although the most well-known utilitarian philosopher, John Stuart Mill, referred to the maximising of pleasure, and described utilitarianism as the 'happiness' theory, he was aware that this might be interpreted as pandering to selfish and, perhaps, base, tastes. Mill tried to deal with this by distinguishing between different kinds of pleasure:

Mill, JS, *Utilitarianism*[10]

It must be admitted . . . that utilitarian writers in general have placed the superiority of mental over bodily pleasures chiefly in the greater permanency, safety, uncostliness, etc, of the former – that is, in their circumstantial advantages rather than in their intrinsic nature. And, on all these points, utilitarians have fully proved their case, but they might have taken the other, and, as it may be called, higher ground, with entire consistency. It is quite compatible with the principle of utility to recognise the fact that some *kinds* of pleasure are more desirable and more valuable than others. It would be absurd that while, in estimating all other things, quality is considered as well as quantity, the estimation of pleasures should be supposed to depend on quantity alone.

Singer describes his own version of utilitarianism, which he claims springs from the universal aspect of ethics. He argues that from this starting point one must look to the interests of others as having equal validity to those of oneself. This means that one must choose a course of action that is most likely to maximise the interests of all those affected. This is utilitarianism, and, Singer says, if we want to go beyond utilitarianism then we need to be provided with good reason for doing this.[11]

Critics of utilitarianism have pointed out that the theory can be upheld and still permit an awful lot of wrongdoing. In other words, the great majority of society can be wealthy and healthy, but a small minority may live in appalling circumstances, with no access whatsoever to basic facilities, such as healthcare. This is a powerful argument and has led theorists to distinguish between 'act' utilitarianism and 'rule' utilitarianism. Pattinson sums this up as follows:

Pattinson, SD, *Medical Law and Ethics*[12]

Faced with the objection that utilitarianism rides roughshod over widely accepted moral norms and requires endless utility evaluation, another version appeared requiring us to adopt rules that *generally* achieve the best utility balance. . . . Standard act-utilitarianism can have a difficult time considering the consequences of every act. Imagine a doctor faced with a number of patients in need of life-saving donations of organs and tissue in circumstances where there is a suitable but unwilling potential 'donor' from whom such tissue can be removed relatively safely. For an act-utilitarian set on maximising utility, the permissibility of removing some tissue . . . to save the lives of four patients will depend on the overall utility balance of so doing. The utility of saving four patients' lives [could be] high enough that in some

---

9 See Smart, JJC and Williams, B, *Utilitarianism: For and Against*, Cambridge: CUP, 1993.
10 London: Routledge, 1997 [1863].
11 Singer, P, *Practical Ethics*, Cambridge: CUP, 1979, p 12.
12 London: Sweet & Maxwell, 2006.

circumstances the disutility of using an unwilling 'donor' could be outweighed ... According to supporters of rule-utilitarianism, adopting rules that track the best utility balance, rather than evaluating all individual acts, avoids the need for such calculations and the possibility of concluding that removing these organs is permissible.

THINK POINT

Do you think that rules can be framed that would satisfy both utilitarians and their opponents?

Although Mill does incorporate concepts such as justice into his form of utilitarianism, is this not coming perilously close to maintaining that there are ideals or principles which are worthy and must be supported regardless of the consequences? Consequentialist theories do not have to be utilitarian, ie, the maximisation of happiness or welfare can be replaced by some other concept of what is good. For example, one may try to incorporate some role for distributive justice. This may be possible, but it is not necessarily part of a consequentialist theory, which may lead us to conclude that judging actions by consequences alone is an insufficient guide to ethical behaviour.

Utilitarianism, however, is an attractive theory when one considers certain specific issues such as the doctor's obligation of confidentiality, where the obligation can be justified on the basis that patients would be less than candid when consulting a doctor if they had doubts that the information would be kept confidential. The fact that the obligation can be broken if it is in the public interest to do so is also an appeal to consequentialism.

See Chapter 5 →

It is also arguable that when looking at the provision of healthcare throughout society some form of consequentialist approach is best. Individual treatment decisions may not fare so well under a consequentialist approach, although, for example, Jonathan Baron favours utilitarianism for medical decision-making in general because, he argues, it is all about risks and trade-offs.[13]

1.1.2.2 Deontology/absolutism

Having recognised the inadequacies of consequentialism, John Mackie considers alternatives:

Mackie, JL, *Ethics: Inventing Right and Wrong*[14]

... we could reject the consequentialist structure, and develop a moral system built not round the notion of some goal that is to be attained, but rather round the notions of rules or principles of action or duties or rights or virtues, or some combination of these – in a very broad sense, some kind of deontological system. Of course a consequentialist theory will usually give some place to items of all these sorts, but a subordinate place: a utilitarian takes virtues, for example, to be good just because and in so far as they tend to issue in behaviour that increases the general happiness. But in a deontological theory actions of the kinds held to be virtuous are seen as being intrinsically obligatory or admirable, and goodness of character too may be seen as having intrinsic value; actions and characters may have a merit of their own not wholly derived from what they bring about.

---

13 Baron, J, *Against Bioethics*, London: MIT, 2006.
14 Harmondsworth: Penguin, 1977.

The term 'deontology' comes from *deon* – the Greek word for 'duty'. Probably the most well-known exponent of this is Immanuel Kant:

Paton, HJ, *The Moral Law: Kant's Groundwork of the Metaphysics of Morals*[15]

> *A human action is morally good, not because it is done from immediate inclination – still less because it is done from self-interest – but because it is done for the sake of duty.*
>
> . . .
>
> An action – even if it accords with duty and is in that sense right – is not commonly regarded as morally good if it is done solely out of self-interest. We may, however, be inclined to attribute moral goodness to right actions done solely from some immediate inclination – for example, from a direct impulse of sympathy or generosity. In order to test this we must *isolate* our motives: we must consider first an action done solely out of inclination and *not* out of duty, and then an action done solely out of duty and *not* out of inclination. . . . The goodness shown in helping others is all the more conspicuous if a man does this for the sake of duty at a time when he is fully occupied with his own troubles and when he is not impelled to do so by his natural inclinations.
>
> Kant's doctrine would be absurd if it meant that the presence of a natural inclination to good actions (or even of a feeling of satisfaction in doing them) detracted from their moral worth. . . . He would have avoided the ambiguity if he had said that a man shows moral worth, not in doing good from inclination, but in doing it for the sake of duty. It is the motive of duty, not the motive of inclination, that gives moral worth to an action.

Just as happiness was central to Mill's view, it plays a significant role in Kant's philosophy: 'the natural end which all men seek is their own happiness'. However, this happiness will only be produced, says Kant, if human beings, as rational beings, make rules to govern their own lives and the lives of others, and have reverence for the moral law. Crucial to Kant's philosophy is the maxim that no one should be treated merely as a means to an end, but always, as well, as an end in themselves. As we shall see, this Kantian rule is particularly pertinent to issues such as medical research and organ donation.[16]

Beauchamp and Walters comment on deontological theories as follows:

Beauchamp, TL and Walters, L, *Contemporary Issues in Bioethics*[17]

> As an example of differences in utilitarian and deontological thinking, consider a survey conducted by researchers K Ann Coleman Stolurow and Dale W Moeller. Stolurow and Moeller were interested in the frequency with which x-rays are routinely used as part of dental checkups. They conducted a telephone survey of dental offices in the Boston area and found that in 95% of the offices surveyed x-ray procedures are customarily ordered in connection with the initial investigation of new patients, and that in nearly half of those offices the procedures employed involve full-mouth x-rays to obtain accurate information. These researchers misrepresented themselves over the telephone as new residents in the Boston area inquiring about available dental services and they asked a series of specific questions that followed a prepared written survey instrument wholly undisclosed to the dentists or their offices. This misrepresentation apparently contributed significantly to the accuracy of the results, because the data obtained showed a

---

15 London: Hutchinson University Library, 1948.
16 Baron, J, *Against Bioethics*, London: MIT, 2006.
17 Belmont, CA: Wadsworth Publishing, 1982.

frequency of dental x-ray use far greater than that reported by an earlier study in which the researchers did not conceal their purposes.

This use of deception raises ethical issues of whether the researchers violated the moral rights of the participants or unjustifiably invaded privacy. Many act utilitarians would likely consider this study justifiable: there are public benefits of obtaining accurate information about dental x-rays. The information, for instance, might form the basis on which the American Dental Association would refocus its ongoing efforts to reduce unnecessary x-ray exposure, from lessening dosage levels to cutting down on the frequency of exposure. . . . A deontologist, by contrast, may find indefensible the deception and invasion of privacy essential to the conduct of the study. In any event, the deontologist will not frame the moral problem exclusively in terms of a weighing of consequences.

We also talk about absolutism, ie the belief in absolute values which can be regarded as inviolable, regardless of what they may bring about in any given set of circumstances. For example, it could be said that torture is *always* wrong. This is illustrated by the prohibition on torture in the Declaration of Tokyo, issued by the World Medical Association:

Declaration of Tokyo 1975 (revised 2006), World Medical Association

1 -The doctor shall not countenance, condone or participate in the practice of torture or other forms of cruel, inhuman or degrading procedures, whatever the offence of which the victim of such procedures is suspected, accused or guilty, and whatever the victim's beliefs or motives, and in all situations, including armed conflict and civil strife . . .

This implies that under no circumstances could torture ever be justified, but it is by no means clear that we can be sure about this. Simmonds gives the following example:

Simmonds, NE, *Central Issues in Jurisprudence*[18]

. . . if a madman had hidden a nuclear device which was set to destroy the whole of South East England at a pre-set time, we might feel justified in torturing him if this really was the only way of discovering the location of the bomb so as to defuse it.

The sanctity of life principle might also be said to be an absolute, but, again, this is questionable. Most people accept the fact that innocent people's lives will be lost in the cause of a just war. In medicine, the right of people to refuse life-saving treatment is respected, even though it conflicts with the sanctity of life principle, and, as we shall see, many doctors believe that it is right not to treat a person if the treatment will not 'benefit' him, even if his death will result because of this.

See Chapter 12 →

This idea that principles can be weighed up against each other depending upon the circumstances is attractive and is reflected in the writings of Ronald Dworkin, who describes the role principles have in legal decision-making.[19] As we shall see, this 'weighing up' of different principles is frequently a feature of medical law cases.

---

18 London: Sweet & Maxwell, 1986.
19 See *Taking Rights Seriously*, London: Duckworth, 1977.

1.1.3 Rights, duties and liberties

When considering absolutist theories, we questioned whether there was, for example, a right not to be tortured which could never be overridden. It leads us to try to get to grips with what we mean by rights. Rights are often described in terms of the corresponding duties which go with them. The jurist WN Hohfeld was a well-known exponent of this, incorporating into his scheme the role of liberties and powers:

Simmonds, NE, *Central Issues in Jurisprudence*[20]

The idea of strict correlativity between rights (ie, claim-rights) and duties is a controversial one, and the controversy is important for two quite different sets of reasons, which we may summarise as follows:

1   If rights are strictly correlative to duties, then a person has established legal rights only in so far as there are established duties corresponding to those rights. The law on this account has a static appearance: it could be represented as a long list of duties. If, on the other hand, it makes sense to talk of established rights without established correlative – we may think of the law as imposing duties, and perhaps creating new duties, in order to protect established rights. On this account, there may at any one time be established legal rights which are inadequately protected by legal duties: such rights provide a legal reason for creating new legal duties. Seen from this perspective, the law is not static but has an inner dynamic of its own. It is not a long list of duties that is added to whenever moral and policy considerations make this desirable: new duties may be recognised as a response to specifically legal considerations, in the attempt to give better legal protection to established legal rights.

2   Politicians and others make frequent use of the concept of rights. People are said to have rights of this and that kind, and rights are generally regarded as a 'good thing'. But if rights (in this case moral, rather than legal, rights) are correlative to duties, such claims are always open to the question 'on whom do the correlative duties rest?' People are much more willing to assert the existence of rights to various amenities than they are to ascribe specific duties. Moreover, if rights are correlative to duties, we may feel that they are not necessarily an unqualified good: for if rights entail duties, they entail greater restrictions on freedom. If therefore we believe that freedom is a 'good thing' we will not wish to see an unlimited expansion in people's rights (meaning, I repeat, 'claim-rights').

Kant distinguished between perfect and imperfect duties. Paton gives examples of these:

Paton, HJ, *The Moral Law: Kant's Groundwork of the Metaphysics of Morals*[21]

A perfect duty is one which admits of no exception in the interests of inclination. Under this heading the examples given are the ban on suicide and on making a false promise in order to receive a loan. We are not entitled to commit suicide because we have a strong inclination to do so, nor are we entitled to pay our debt to one man and not to another because we happen to like him better. In the case of imperfect duties the position is different: we are bound only to adopt the maxim of developing our talents and of helping others, and we are to some extent entitled to decide arbitrarily which persons we will help. There is here a certain 'latitude' or 'playroom' for mere inclination.

In terms of medicine, this could be translated as follows. Doctors are under a perfect duty to be just in the way in which they decide who to treat. They have only an imperfect duty to provide

---

20 London: Sweet & Maxwell, 1986.
21 London: Hutchinson University Library, 1948.

medical treatment to everyone who requests it. Under the Hohfeldian scheme, there is no right to medical treatment, only the right to be considered in accordance with just criteria. In the next chapter we refer to the European Social Charter of 1961, which enshrines the 'right to protection of health, and the right to social and medical assistance'. However, as we shall see, in the context of the provision of medical treatment, the clinical discretion of the doctor as to the provision of treatment is paramount.

We might look for perfect duties in medical law, or we might consider the question the other way round and ask whether there are any absolute rights. Ronald Dworkin argues that there is a right to be treated with equal respect. Are mentally impaired people to be treated with the same respect as the non-impaired? There are a number of controversial cases where mentally impaired young women have been sterilised for contraceptive purposes even though there was little likelihood of them becoming pregnant.[22] Were they being treated with the same respect as non-impaired women?

The principle of self-determination is frequently asserted in medical law and ethics. It could be said that there is an absolute right to self-determination as long as the person has the capacity to make decisions. We often talk of people being competent to make decisions. Problems may arise in deciding whether the person is competent, but once it is established then the right to physical integrity seems to be inviolable. But could the right still be overridden – for example, in an emergency? As we shall see, this 'right' is overridden when the doctor has no time to consult with, for example, an unconscious patient: he will successfully raise the defence of necessity to an action in battery. However, is it arguable that the right to self-determination has not been overridden at all because the patient was incapable of exercising it? In English law the foetus has no legal 'rights'. We will examine this later, in relation, in particular, to abortion and women who refuse Caesarean section operations, even though the refusal may gravely risk their own lives and the survival of the foetuses. Does the foetus have no rights because it cannot enforce them? If this were the case, then children and the seriously mentally disordered would not have rights, but we often speak about the rights of children and the mentally ill. In one of the sterilisation cases referred to above it was said that a woman's 'right' to reproduce meant nothing to her (*Re B (A Minor) (Wardship: Sterilisation)*[23]). Because of the dangers of dismissing rights in this way, it might be preferable to consider the rights of the incompetent in terms of the duties others have towards them. With regard to children, Carl Wellman states:

Wellman, C, *An Approach to Rights: Studies in the Philosophy of Law and Morals*[24]

> The moral right to freedom of movement contains several other associated elements, but let me mention only one – the State's moral duty to enforce the parental duty of non-interference with the child's freedom of movement. Although this duty is very limited in scope, it can be of crucial importance in extreme cases. Imagine that a parent keeps a young child restrained in a crib so much of the time that the child has no opportunity to learn to walk . . . Under such circumstances, the State would have a moral obligation to intervene in the family and force the parent to cease and desist from such grossly unjustified interference with the freedom of movement of the child. Although this moral duty of the State begins as merely a duty regarding the child, in due course it grows into a moral duty to the child when the child becomes capable of claiming State intervention vis à vis the parent.

---

22 See *Taking Rights Seriously*, 1977, London: Duckworth.
23 [1988] AC 199.
24 Dordrecht: Kluwer Academic, 1997.

Wellman goes on to examine the right of the child to protection. In medical law the tension between granting the child the freedom it needs to develop and the protection it may need will be apparent when we look at the ability of the child to consent to treatment.

See Chapter 3

Liberty and equality are two other general ethical concepts that are open to a number of different interpretations. In Mill's philosophy they are interdependent. Mill stresses that the liberty of the individual is paramount, and his liberty to pursue his own choices has to be no more than the equal liberty of everyone else. He can only be restrained from any activity which interferes with the liberty of others:

Mill, JS, On Liberty[25]

The object of this essay is to assert one very simple principle, as entitled to govern absolutely the dealings of society with the individual in the way of compulsion and control, whether the means used be physical force in the form of legal penalties or the moral coercion of public opinion. That principle is that the sole end for which mankind are warranted, individually or collectively, in interfering with the liberty of action of any of their number is self-protection. That the only purpose for which power can be rightfully exercised over any member of a civilised community, against his will, is to prevent harm to others. His own good, either physical or moral, is not a sufficient warrant.

Mill's principle is reflected in the right to self-determination.

1.1.4 Respect for persons

We have referred to Dworkin's equal respect for persons, but do we know what we mean by a person? This may sound like a silly question, but if we pose the question in a different way and ask what we mean by respect for human life it is not an easy one to answer.[26]

Harris asks when human life begins to matter morally and examines the potentiality argument which says that human life begins when the human egg is fertilised, ie when there is the potential for human life:

Harris, J, The Value of Life: Introduction to Medical Ethics[27]

There are two sorts of difficulty with the potentiality argument which are jointly and severally fatal to it. The first is that the bare fact that something will become X (even if it will inevitably become X, which is far from being the case with the fertilised egg and the adult human being) is not a good reason for treating it now as if it were in fact X. We will all inevitably die, but that is, I suppose, an inadequate reason for treating us now as if we were dead.

The second difficulty is that it is not only the fertilised egg that is potentially a human being. To say that a fertilised egg is potentially a human being is just to say that if certain things happen to it (like implantation), and certain other things do not (like spontaneous abortion), it will eventually become a human being. But the same is also true of the unfertilised egg and the sperm. If certain things happen to

25 Harmondsworth: Penguin, 1859 [1982].
26 There are those who argue that respect for life generally is what matters, so that animals should be treated with respect, and this has relevance to medical research and the development of xenotransplantation (animal to human): see Ch 11, and see Singer, P, Animal Liberation, New York: Random House, 1990.
27 London: Routledge & Kegan Paul, 1985.

the egg (like meeting a sperm) and certain things happen to the sperm (like meeting an egg) and thereafter certain other things do not (like meeting a contraceptive), then they will eventually become a new human being.

It is sometimes objected that it is only the fertilised egg that has all the necessary potential present in one place, so to speak, and it is this that is crucial. It is only when the egg has been fertilised, so the argument goes, that a new unique entity exists that itself has all the potential necessary to become a new human being. This seems plausible enough until we remember that something had the potential to become that fertilised egg; and whatever had that potential, had also the potential to become whatever it is that the fertilised egg has the potential to become!

If then we ignore the first difficulty with the potentiality argument, and concede that we are somehow morally required to actualise all human potential, we are all in for a highly exhausting time. And it is clear that if we put the maximal effort into procreation that this imperative demands, our endeavours will ultimately be self-defeating.

Harris goes on to say that what we really value is *a person*:

Harris, J, *The Value of Life: Introduction to Medical Ethics*[28]

. . . a person will be any being capable of valuing its own existence. Apart from the advantage of its simplicity, this account has two other major advantages. The first is that it is value- and species-neutral. It does not imply that any particular kind of being or any particular mode of existence is more valuable than any other so long as the individual in question can value its mode of existence. Once this threshold is crossed, no individual is more of a person or more valuable than any other. This concept of the person sets out to identity which individuals and which forms of life have the sort of value and importance that makes appropriate and justifies our according to them the same concern, respect and protections as we grant to one another. And it tries to do so without begging any questions as to the sort of creatures that will be found to qualify.

The second advantage is that it is capable of performing the two tasks we require of a concept of a person. These are that it should give us some grasp of why persons are valuable and make intelligible the moral difference between persons and other beings. The second task is that it should enable us, in principle, to tell persons from non-persons.

On this concept of the person, the moral difference between persons and non-persons lies in the value that people give to their own lives. The reasons it is wrong to kill is that to do so robs that individual of something they value, and of the very thing that makes possible valuing anything at all. To kill a person not only frustrates their wishes for their own futures, but frustrates every wish a person has. Creatures that cannot value their own existence cannot be wronged in this way, for their death deprives them of nothing that they can value.

Of course non-persons can be harmed in other ways, by being subjected to pain for example, and there are good reasons for avoiding subjecting any sentient creatures to pain if this can be avoided.

THINK POINT

It is important to note that Harris is talking about the *capacity* to value one's own existence, so a new-born child would have that capacity. However, would a foetus also have the capacity?

---

28 Ibid.

1.1.5 Justice

By now it will be apparent that the language of morals can slip easily between rights, duties and liberties. The concept of 'justice' is no less an elusive concept. Although its importance usually lies in the realm of politics, it can be relevant both to the wider issues of allocating health resources on a national basis, and when deciding which patients to treat when local resources are limited. This will be examined further at the end of this chapter and in Chapter 2.

See 1.6 and
◀ Chapter 2

1.2 The doctor–patient relationship

1.2.1 Beneficence

Doctors are generally regarded as having a positive duty to do good, and as being unique in this regard.[29] However, it is by no means clear that this is the case. Referring to the duty of the doctor as going beyond what can reasonably be expected of everyone else, Downie comments:

Downie, RS, 'Traditional medical ethics and economics in healthcare: a critique'[30]

[A main ingredient in a code of medical or other professional ethics] consists of some generalised exhortations to care for patients, which can be summed up by saying that the medical and perhaps all the professions are governed to a much greater extent than other jobs by the principle of benevolence. Indeed, Gillon (1986) goes so far as to describe the doctor's duty as one of supererogatory benevolence, in that it goes beyond what can reasonably be expected of the rest of us.

A short way to dispose of this claim might be to argue that it confuses conceptual points about the definition of the aims of a profession with moral duties; definitional 'oughts' have been confused with moral 'oughts'. Thus, it sounds like a high ideal to say that the doctor ought to care for the health or the welfare of his patient, but in fact this is simply a definition of the job of a doctor. The shepherd *qua* shepherd ought to care for his sheep, the gardener *qua* gardener ought to care for his flower beds and grass, and the pilot *qua* pilot ought to aim at transporting his passengers with safety. These are just definitions of occupations in terms of their aims. Of course, one might say that the person who happens to be a doctor ought to do the best he can as a doctor. Yes, and the person who happens to be a gardener ought to do the best he can for his flower beds. We all ought to work hard in our respective spheres. In other words, if medical ethics is made to seem grander than ordinary morality it is because a conceptual claim has become confused with a perfectly ordinary moral claim.

An argument of this kind is usually thought by doctors to be too superficial. They reply that patients are vulnerable and that healthcare must be delivered through the uniquely special doctor–patient relationship. But that uniquely special relationship requires a special morality to protect it, and so we need medical ethics as traditionally understood.

Yet what is uniquely special about the doctor–patient relationship? What emerges after any attempt to answer this question is that it is difficult to find a set of necessary and sufficient conditions, which justify the description 'uniquely special' of the doctor–patient relationship. Note to begin with that there is no one relationship which is *the* doctor–patient relationship. For example, an anaesthetist might see a patient once before an operation, but adding this to the anaesthetist's function during an operation hardly creates a 'relationship', and in any case it is certainly different from the 'relationship' which a community

---

29 See Gillon, R, *Philosophical Medical Ethics*, Chichester: John Wiley, 1985.
30 Mooney, G and McGuire, A (eds), *Medical Ethics and Economics in Health Care*, Oxford: OUP, 1998.

health doctor might have with the population who live in a given geographical area. But even waiving this objection and concentrating on certain typical sorts of doctor–patient relationships we cannot easily say what is *uniquely* special about them. Certainly, patients are lacking in information and power when, say, a coronary artery bypass operation is prescribed, but so are most of us when the garage mechanic prescribes an engine transplant! In each case most of us must trust in the knowledge, skills, and good faith of our helpers. Perhaps car engines are not so important as our bodies, but then we also commit the latter to the care of airline pilots and taxi drivers. Again, doctors may have access to our bodies; but teachers, clergymen, and advertisers have access to our minds and can influence to varying degrees our very perceptions of our own identities. The conclusion seems to be that if there are uniquely defining conditions of the doctor–patient relationship they are likely to be trivial and not special in the sense of important, and if there are special or important features they are likely to be shared with a variety of occupations such as the lifeboat service, the police, the clergy, teachers, and many others, some of which are 'professions' and some not. It seems more profitable, then, to drop the whole idea of uniquely special features of the doctor–patient relationship and to draw attention to 'family resemblances' between that relationship and a whole variety of others.

To argue, as I have done, that there is nothing uniquely special about the doctor–patient relationship certainly weakens the claim that there is a need for a special sort of morality. But it does not dispose of it entirely. I wish now to argue that medical ethics as traditionally understood is actually harmful to healthcare, and that the need is really to drop the traditional approach and to reassert the claims of ordinary morality (Downie and Calman, 1987).

The first respect in which traditional medical ethics has been harmful to healthcare concerns the distortions it has created in the doctor–patient relationship. For example, traditional codes are expressed in terms of the duties of the doctor, and while this has certainly inspired an idealistic practice it has also created a professional ethos of elitism and paternalism. Thus, generations of medical students have been given the impression that there is an esoteric set of rules – 'medical ethics' – which govern their professional activities. It is easy to extrapolate from this to the conclusion that such a code is different from and superior to ordinary morality. Doctors are not as other men; other men are guided by right and wrong, but doctors have medical ethics. For example, in ordinary life the assumption, if not the reality, is that people speak the truth to each other, but this is not an assumption of those governed by medical ethics; for medical ethics says that the first responsibility of the doctor is to the well being of his patient, and it is generally thought to follow that it is up to the doctor to decide how far, in his opinion, a patient's well being will be furthered by telling the truth. Medical ethics in this respect distorts the doctor–patient relationship, for any true human relationship must have sincerity as its necessary condition, and that condition is discouraged by the attitude built into traditional medical ethics: benevolence (if that is what it is) has swamped sincerity. This criticism might be summed up by saying that the duties of doctors should not be regarded, as they are in the tradition, as duties of benevolence, but rather as duties correlative to the *rights of patients*. To give this emphasis to the doctor–patient relationship is to cut out the distortion caused by the tradition. Indeed, an emphasis on rights – consumer rights, social and political rights, human rights of all kinds – is one moral characteristic of our time.

A second criticism which can be made of the tradition is that its fraternal, inward-looking nature discourages frank and open co-operation with other caring professions. For example, nurses and social workers are not part of the fraternity, so it has been a matter for debate how far they should be admitted into the inner counsels. One consequence of this is inefficiency in the delivery of healthcare due to uncertainty or lack of co-operation among all the members of a healthcare team. Where objectives are not shared and discussed among the caring professions there is a diminution of job satisfaction, friction, and a consequent damage to patient care. For example, one member of a team, a nurse, say, may not know how much a patient has been told or what the overall prognosis is. It is then difficult for the nurse to be fully supportive of the patient. This is not good morality.

A third respect in which the traditional approach to medical ethics is deficient is that it suggests that morality is about selected issues, rather than that it is all-pervasive. The discussion of medical ethics has tended to highlight the dramatic issues which happen to be topical at any one time. Although euthanasia, abortion, resuscitation, surrogate motherhood, and human experimentation are undoubtedly important matters, their prominence has obscured the fact that, not just once but many times in the course of a working day, moral stances, value judgments and decisions will result in actions considered to be right or wrong by the doctor. This is partly, but only partly, due to the uncertain nature of medical diagnosis and prognosis. The doctor, lacking certainty, must estimate what in his opinion is for the total good of the patient. This concept of 'total good' is not just a matter of technical expertise but involves values. For example, let us imagine a 70 year old man who wants to be allowed home soon after an operation. The doctor's judgment here will involve technical expertise, but will also involve economic and value judgments of a total good, including knowledge of the home circumstances and many other factors. Again, whether we do a job only moderately well when we are capable of doing it better is a question of morality, of deciding which direction we want to take. Allowing ourselves to become professionally socialised into routinised working patterns which keep things going but diminish patients' dignity and freedom requires as much a moral justification as a sociological explanation. These moral demands are all-pervasive and inescapable in healthcare.

Fourth, the traditional distinction between 'medical ethics' and 'private morality' suggests that one can deal with moral questions in a professional context without examining personal values and convictions. But I am arguing that it follows from the inescapable and all-pervasive nature of morality that we encounter moral problems in our personal lives which are not fundamentally different from those we may have to explore in our working environment. Whatever values we may feel to be important to us as individuals are almost certainly influencing and directing the decisions that we make as professional healthcare workers. If we have or lack the skills which allow us to approach moral dilemmas in a rational and methodical way in ordinary life, this will affect how we attempt to solve moral problems in a professional context. In other words, morality is 'indivisible'.

On the other hand, this fundamental assumption about the 'indivisibility' of morality does not lead to a rejection of the very special place that the maintenance of acceptable professional standards of behaviour must have in the work of people whose primary responsibility is to care for vulnerable fellow men and women. The potential harm that can come to people who are in some ways and by definition dependent on the knowledge and skills of others will undoubtedly heighten the moral concern in situations which, outside the professional context, might not be perceived as quite so threatening or acute. For example, a critical or sarcastic remark, which might be acceptable in ordinary circumstances, could be devastating to a sick person.

Another aspect of the 'indivisibility' of morality is that hospitals and other healthcare organisations ought not to be immune to general attitudinal changes in society. Moral dilemmas arise frequently from the attempts which the professions make or do not make to accommodate social change. Likewise, what professional people do, or often more pertinently what they would refuse to do, reflects the moral standards of their society in the same way in which actions of the individual doctor or nurse, psychologist or speech therapist, social worker or dietician reflect his or her standards of personal morality. The dilemmas created by social change can be obscured by an emphasis on medical ethics traditionally understood as a product.

A fifth criticism of traditional medical ethics is that it tends to underestimate the fact that medical decisions ought to be made in the real world of technological and economic facts. This point is much stressed in the papers of Mooney and McGuire, and Jennett . . . Traditionally medical ethics tends to be seen in terms of pure moral absolutes – the doctor must do all that is medically possible for his (or her) patient regardless of the cost. I am asserting that in the real world compromises must be made. As an example of compromise we can point to renal dialysis. It is not helpful to say that there is an absolute value on human life if there are two patients who would benefit from dialysis but facilities for treating only one. The moral requirement here is to reflect on the scientific and economic facts of the cases as well as the quality of life of the potential recipients. This point can be expressed in the form of a distinction between compromising our consciences, which is wrong, and conscientious compromises, which consist in making the moral best of a bad job in the light of scientific and economic constraints. This distinction is compatible with the view that in some circumstances no compromises should be made.

These five criticisms of traditional medical ethics . . . suggest that an enlightened medical ethics will be in terms of a 'process' – the process of applying the principles of everyday morality to the scientific and economic complexities of patient care. Moral decisions in medicine are what can be called 'consequential' or 'resultant' in that they arise out of the professional, economic, and legal facts of given cases. Ethics is no substitute for a good diagnosis of the problem, skillfully carried out treatment or clearly communicated information, but equally in doing these things the doctor is at the same time engaging in moral and economic activity.[31]

However, it may be arguable that there is a difference between a doctor and others who provide vital services. It might be said that if a doctor were to refuse to treat in an emergency, he would be the subject of moral condemnation in a way that, say, an off-duty fireman, who refused to help in a rescue, would not. It is important to remember that here we are talking about moral, not legal, obligations. In the UK, a doctor has no legal obligation to stop at the scene of an accident and treat the injured. If he does, then he is obliged to treat with reasonable skill and care and he may be liable in negligence. The position of a non-medically qualified volunteer who assists at the scene of an accident is exactly the same – it is simply that the standard of care is different. The legal duty not to harm is the same for doctor and lay person alike. Is the doctor's moral obligation different? Harris suggests it is not:

See Chapter 6 →

Harris, J, *The Value of Life: Introduction to Medical Ethics*[32]

We believe . . . that we should rescue trapped miners and other victims of accidents, or those shipwrecked, or the victims of hijackers of other hostage-takers; and, not least, those who can be rescued only by medical care. Some of these rescues can be performed by anyone who is on hand; others require all sorts of expertise from that of potholers, sailors, miners, engineers, firemen and so on, to specialised military personnel and those with medical skills. Very often, those of us who lack these skills can best help, and thus discharge our obligation to those at risk, by keeping well out of the way. All of this is perhaps obvious enough, but it helps us to see two important features of the obligation of healthcare professionals. The first is that *there is nothing special about their obligation in particular*. Just as there is no special category of person whose unique and first obligation it is to refrain from inflicting death, injury or suffering on the rest of us, so there is no one who is specially required, morally speaking, to undertake rescues.

It is also illuminating to consider the duty of beneficence in terms of Kant's perfect/imperfect duties. Kant considers generosity or beneficence as imperfect duties, which an individual has no right to demand, as he has a right, for example, to demand justice.

---

31 Mooney, G and McGuire, A (eds), *Medical Ethics and Economics in Health Care* (Oxford: Oxford Medical Publications, OUP, 1988).
32 London: Routledge & Kegan Paul, 1985.

Of course, the doing of 'good' may, in the short term, necessitate the infliction of pain. Beauchamp and McCullough describe the 'balancing exercise' that may arise as follows:

Beauchamp, TL and McCullough, LB, *Medical Ethics: The Moral Responsibilities of Physicians*[33]

The basic roles and concepts that give substance to the principle of beneficence in medicine are as follows: the positive benefit the physician is under obligation to seek is the cure of disease and injury if there is a reasonable hope of cure; the harms to be avoided, prevented, or removed are the pain and suffering of injury and disease. In addition, the physician is enjoined from doing harm. This consideration, too must be included in the beneficence model because physician interventions themselves can inflict unnecessary pain and suffering on patients. The Hippocratic texts hold that inflicting pain and suffering is permissible in those cases in which the physician is attempting to reverse a threat to health, eg, administering an emetic after the accidental ingestion of a poison. Inflicting such pain and suffering on a patient in order to eliminate a deadly substance from the body is justified because the patient is on balance benefited. When the patient cannot be benefited by further intervention, the inflicted pain and suffering is unnecessary and to be avoided. Thus, in its first formulation in Western medical ethics, the beneficence model of moral responsibility adapts the principle of beneficence to patient care by providing a medically oriented account of how to balance goods over harms.

The rosy-spectacled view of the special role of beneficence is questioned by Pellegrino and Thomasma:

Pellegrino, ED and Thomasma, DC, *For the Patient's Good: The Restoration of Beneficence in Health Care*[34]

According to the Hippocratic Oath, the physician promises to 'follow that system of regimen which according to my ability and judgment I consider for the benefit of my patients'. Nowhere in the Hippocratic corpus is there any provision for the patient's view of things. In fact, in one place the relationship is described as being between 'one who orders and one who obeys'.

We shall see that this traditional principle, however, may be tempered to take into account the wishes of the patient.

The work of a doctor in the late twentieth century is often highly technical in nature, depending upon pharmacy, engineering, computer technology and so on. It might be argued that this diminishes the particular duty of beneficence in some way. Beauchamp and McCullough suggest that it does not:

Beauchamp, TL and McCullough, LB, *Medical Ethics: The Moral Responsibilities of Physicians*[35]

In the history of medicine, the physician has primarily functioned in care-giving and comforting roles, with beneficence serving as the moral foundation of these roles. As medical science exploded in the 20th century, medicine was transformed into a more scientific and technical enterprise. Beneficent intervention remains, as ever, the moral foundation of the physician's role, a role powerfully augmented by medical

---

33 Englewood Cliffs, NJ: Prentice-Hall, 1984.
34 Oxford: OUP, 1988.
35 Englewood Cliffs, NJ: Prentice-Hall, 1984.

science and technology. These remarkable new capacities created some moral problems in medicine, especially problems concerning the physician's authority, but they did not destroy medicine's tradition of beneficence.

But is this confidence that the traditional role of the physician has not been undermined misplaced? Much of the research which leads to treatment at the disposal of the physician has not been developed by physicians at all. Developments in genetics are a case in point. Once opportunities for genetic manipulation, for example, have been unleashed, how much power does the physician have to resist them?

The principle of beneficence is at work when we consider the doctrine of 'double effect'. Imagine a gravely ill patient in the last stages of terminal cancer. The patient is in pain and only a substantial dose of morphine will relieve the pain. However, such a large dose will also hasten the patient's death. As far as the law is concerned, this is not homicide, and, as far as medical ethics is concerned, the principle of beneficence means that the doctor's only intention is to do good, ie relieve pain. The fact that death would also be hastened does not undermine the beneficent motive of the doctor. However, as we shall see, there are aspects of medical law where the principle of beneficence is undermined. First, in medical research patients may be subjected to randomised clinical trials (RCTs). This means that some patients will not be receiving any treatment at all but, unknown to them, will be given placebos, so that the researchers can compare their progress with that of the patients who are given drug treatment. It is arguable that this can never be consistent with the principle of beneficence unless the principle is interpreted as meaning beneficence towards patients in the sense of a *general* benefit to the sick. Similarly, it is accepted that doctors may breach their duty of confidentiality in respect of an individual patient in the wider public interest. In these circumstances, it can be argued, the principle of beneficence is only upheld if it is equated with some form of consequentialism.

See Chapter 12 ➤

See Chapter 10 ➤

1.2.2 Non-maleficence

The traditional duty to do good has been accompanied by the obligation to do no harm – *primum non nocere* (first, do no harm). This can be described in terms of Kant's perfect/imperfect duties distinction, ie the obligation not to harm people is a perfect duty whereas the obligation to good is restricted in that it would be impossible to fulfil a duty to benefit everyone and is therefore am imperfect duty.[36]

 See Chapter 12 ➤

This principle might, for example, be used to justify the 'acts and omissions' distinction in the law relating to euthanasia. As we shall see, in the case of a very seriously ill patient, a doctor may not be obliged to continue to treat that patient. In other words, he can withdraw or omit to treat, and remain within the confines of the law. This is because the doctor may decide that the treatment is not benefiting the patient. That is consistent with the principle of beneficence because the doctor will say that the treatment is not, or would not, benefit the patient. The omission to treat is acceptable. However, the doctor is not legally permitted to give the patient a lethal injection to bring about death, even when 'natural' death is very close, as, it is argued, it would infringe the principle of non-maleficence. But it is arguable that the lethal injection would not be harmful as it might be the kindest way of treating a patient who is terminally ill and in great pain.

---

36 See Gillon, R, *Philosophical Medical Ethics*, Chichester: John Wiley, 1985, p 81.

1.2.3 The nature of illness

Why is it necessary to consider this? It could be said that the presence of 'illness' or 'disease' is a straightforward factual matter. However, it is interesting to try and formulate a definition. Culver and Gert review the medical literature and select a number of definitions:

Culver, CM and Gert, B, *Philosophy in Medicine: Conceptual and Ethical Issues in Medicine and Psychiatry*[37]

Some past definitions of 'disease'

There have been many attempts to set out a formal definition of 'disease', but among physicians only rarely has a distinction among 'disease', 'illness', 'injury' and related terms been recognised. Consequently, 'illness' is often used interchangeably with 'disease', and injuries are regarded merely as a subclass of diseases. What most of the following authors have intended to define is what we call a malady, so that in addition to diseases they have included injuries, illnesses, headaches and the like in their definitions. By not realising what they have done, however, they have often been misled by some particular feature of the term 'disease'.

Some definitions are general, vague, and too inclusive. Thus, a pathology textbook (Peery and Miller, 1971) states:

> Disease is any disturbance of the structure or function of the body or any of its parts; an imbalance between the individual and his environment; a lack of perfect health.

This seems to offer three separate but equivalent definitions. According to the first definition, clipping nails and puberty are diseases, as well as a symptomatic *situs inversus* (right-left reversal of position of bodily organs) and being tied to a chair. The second definition is too vague to be of any use, and the third is circular. A textbook on internal medicine (Talso and Remenchik, 1968) says:

> . . . disease may be defined as deprivation or lack of ease, a discomfort or an annoyance, or a morbid condition of the body or of some organ or part thereof.

There are similar problems here. Two separate definitions are offered. The first is too sweeping and would include inflation, quarrelsome in-laws, poor television reception, and ill-fitting shoes, while the second is circular and depends on the phrase 'morbid condition', which is merely a synonym for 'disease'.

Most texts on medicine and pathology make no attempt to define disease, which is appropriate enough since the exercise is irrelevant to their purposes. Thus, it might be said in defence of the above attempts that they were probably not meant to be taken very seriously.

One cluster of definitions which is meant to be taken seriously utilises a dynamic metaphor in which a person is pictured as constantly interacting and adapting to changes in his environment; disease then corresponds to a failure in that adaptation. An early expression of this definition is found in White's 1926 book, *The Meaning of Disease*:

> Disease can only be that state of the organism that for the time being, at least, is fighting a losing game whether the battle be with temperature, water, micro-organisms, disappointment or what not. In any instance, it may be visualised as the reaction of the organism to some sort of energy impact, addition or deprivation.

Thus, one wrestler held down by another is suffering a disease. A more modern version is found in Engel's 1962 book, *Psychological Development in Health and Disease*:

> When adaptation or adjustment fail and the pre-existing dynamic steady state is disrupted, then a state of disease may be said to exist until a new balance is restored which may again permit the effective interaction with the environment.

---

37 New York: OUP, 1982.

Aside from the ambiguities and the question begging inherent in 'adaptation' and 'balance', the emphasis in this definition (and the preceding one) on the deterioration of a previously more normal state seems to rule out all congenital and hereditary diseases . . .

JG Scadding (1959, 1963, 1967) has written a series of papers on the definition of disease. In the most recent of these, he offers the following 'formal definition':

A disease is the sum of the abnormal phenomena displayed by a group of living organisms in association with a specified common characteristic or set of characteristics by which they differ from the norm for their species in such a way as to place them at a biological disadvantage.

Scadding's definition is an improvement over those previously cited. He explicitly introduces the notion of deviation from a norm for a species which, though it does not deserve the prominence he gives it, is necessary for understanding the essential elements of the concept of malady. His 'biological disadvantage' criterion also points in the right direction but is too vague. Kendell, in a recent paper (1975), interprets 'biological disadvantage' as meaning decreased fertility or longevity. But this does not work. Even Kendell recognises that his revision of Scadding's definition leaves one with the 'rather disconcerting' result that a condition such as psoriasis would not qualify as a disease.

Several recent authors have also correctly identified aspects of disease. Spitzer and Endicott (1978) include in their definition of 'a medical disorder' that it is intrinsically associated with distress, disability, or certain types of disadvantage. We think this definition is on the right track. Goodwin and Guze (1979) consider as a disease 'any condition associated with discomfort, pain, disability, death, or an increased liability to these states, regarded by physicians and the public as properly the responsibility of the medical profession . . .'

Note the concluding phrase 'regarded by physicians and the public as properly the responsibility of the medical profession'. Is 'illness' that which a doctor thinks should be treated? A doctor faced with a hypochondriac may well form the conclusion that the symptoms complained of are imagined and that the person is not ill, and therefore no treatment is given regardless of the fact that the patient may have some organic disorder, which would be treated by another doctor who did not know about the hypochondria. This may sound simplistic, but consider treatment for infertile people. Are they ill? Or diseased? The answer is no, but they receive 'treatment' because doctors think that they should. It may be argued that it is society which decides what conditions merit treatment and what do not, but does that underestimate the power of information and medical technology, concentrated as it is, if not in the hands of doctors exclusively, in the hands of medical science? Society did not demand heart transplants until the first operation had been performed.

THINK POINT

There is evidence that genes which 'cause' things such as baldness may be isolated and eradicated. This would be a 'medical' procedure. Would it mean that baldness would become an illness?

1.2.4 The medical humanities movement

A similar move away from the scientific emphasis that is so much a part of Western medicine is the medical humanities movement. It has been around in the USA for some time, but only for the past four or five years has it found a voice in the UK. The journal Medical Humanities, published by the Journal of Medical Ethics, aims to promote this:

Greaves, D, and Evans, M, 'Editorial'[38]

> ... [medical humanities] is a second generational response to the shortcomings of a medical culture dominated by scientific, technical and managerial approaches ... [there are] two main formulations of medical humanities ... [t]he first is concerned with complementing medical science and technology through the contrasting perspective of the arts and humanities, but without either side impinging on the other. The second aims to refocus the whole of medicine in relation to an understanding of what it is to be fully human; the reuniting of technical and humanistic knowledge and practice is central to this enterprise.

It is not clear how far the first of these aims is particularly related to medicine unless it is to point up the statement often made: 'medicine is not an exact science'. This relates particularly to the role played by patient psychology in the development of illness and recovery. The second formulation might be a way of moving to what is often described as patient-centred medicine, which seeks to emphasise all the non-medical components of medical decision-making, and in particular emphasises communication skills in the doctor–patient relationship.[39] We should also think back to the universalisation/moral relativism debate and how this might relate to this approach. Similarly, we are about to discuss the opposing stances of paternalism and autonomy and conclude that this might be a false dichotomy and that collaborative decision-making takes the best of both these worlds. The 'medical humanities' approach can embrace this.

See Chapter 3

See Chapter 4

It is useful to consider these sorts of approaches when making decisions about a patient's capacity to make medical decisions and what might be in the best interests of a patient who lacks capacity.

1.3 The case for paternalism

1.3.1 Introduction

In this and the following sections, we will look at the arguments which may be advanced, respectively, in favour of a paternalistic approach to medicine, and in favour of the primacy of patient autonomy. These two theories are described by Pellegrino and Thomasma:

Pellegrino, ED and Thomasma, DC, *For the Patient's Good: The Restoration of Beneficence in Health Care*[40]

> The first, inherited from the Enlightenment, stresses the liberty and autonomy of the individual. It gathered strength in the 19th century in response to the depreciation of personal worth that accompanied the Industrial Revolution. This theory grounds ethics in rights, duties and obligations. The second theory stresses social utility rather than individual autonomy. Ironically, it too gained ascendancy during the Industrial Revolution to counter the social atomism of a purely individualistic ethic. This theory stresses

---

38 (2000) 26(1) J Med Ethics: Medical Humanities.
39 See, for example, Evans, RG, 'Patient centred medicine: reason, emotion, and human spirit? Some philosophical reflections on being with patients' (2003) 29(1) J Med Ethics: Medical Humanities 8.
40 Oxford: OUP, 1988.

social good, rules of conduct, and social accountability. Mill laid the foundation for such theories when he proposed the principle of autonomy, on the one hand, and the principle of utility, on the other.

Applied to physician – patient relationship, the first theory imposes on the physician the obligation of respect for the patient's self-determination. The second theory requires that the physician act to maximise benefits and goods even if this might demand acting without the patient's consent. It sanctions overriding the patient's autonomous decision if that decision is not judged by the physician to be in the patient's or society's good.

When considering the respective positions of the paternalist and the anti-paternalist, it is important to consider two things. First, as we shall see, the consent of the patient is necessary before any medical treatment can take place. This might be said to reflect the anti-paternalist view. The patient can refuse simple life-saving treatment and there is no mechanism for imposing it upon him. However, at least in English law, the arbiter of what the patient needs to know before he consents or refuses is the doctor. It might be said that this reflects a paternalist viewpoint. Secondly, the patient must be competent, ie have sufficient mental capacity to make a treatment decision. The doctor will decide whether the patient is competent. If he lacks competence, he may be treated in his 'best interests'. When reading the following, keep these points in mind.

1.3.2 What is paternalism?

When we considered the principle of beneficence, we noted that it is a one-sided principle: the doctor is *doing good to/for the patient*. Beneficence does not mean the same as paternalism (the recognition of the patient's right to self-determination may be part of beneficence), but a narrower view of beneficence is compatible with paternalism. The paternalistic doctor 'knows best' and regards himself as being the best judge as to what is for the patient's own good. It is interesting to consider the duty of beneficence in relation to the parent–child relationship (the term paternalistic meaning to act like a father): although the parent may be said to have a duty of non-maleficence towards his child, does he have a positive duty to do good?

John Harris distinguishes paternalism from moralism:

Harris, J, *The Value of Life: Introduction to Medical Ethics*[41]

When healthcare professionals accept that their first duty is to act always in the best interests of their patients they are in effect saying that they are concerned for the welfare of their patients and that this is in no way inconsistent with manifesting 'respect for persons'. Welfare is not here used as a technical term – it means what it usually means, 'the state or condition of doing or being well', which will include things like happiness, health and living standards.

An initial problem is that concern for the welfare of others is compatible both with paternalism and with moralism. Briefly, paternalism is the belief that it can be right to order the lives of others for their own good, irrespective of their own wishes or judgments. The characteristic cry of the paternalist is: 'Don't do that, it isn't good for you.' *Moralism*, on the other hand, is the belief that it can be right to order the lives of others so that 'morality' may be preserved. The characteristic cry of the moralist is: 'Don't do that, it's wicked.'

Both the paternalist and the moralist are genuinely concerned for the welfare of others. They argue that it cannot be in your interest, nor can it be conducive to your being in a state of doing or being well, if you either do what isn't good for you or act immorally. Despite the genuineness of this moral concern, both paternalism

41 London: Routledge & Kegan Paul, 1985.

and moralism involve treating the agent as an incompetent. They deny the individual control over her own life and moral destiny and treat her as incompetent to run her own life as she chooses. While both involve genuine concern for the welfare of others, neither can lay claim to demonstrating respect for their wishes.

But although Harris is right in saying that we are not respecting the wishes of the person whom we exhort to do good, or refrain from doing bad, we would nevertheless argue that we are entitled to do it. If you intervene to prevent another from picking someone's pocket, you are certainly not respecting the pickpocket's wishes, but you are not wrong to do this. Cannot we say the same thing about paternalism? The paternalist's argument would be that, although you are not respecting the patient's wishes when he says he does not want a life-saving operation and you go ahead and perform it anyway, nevertheless you are not wrong to save his life.

Hart describes paternalism as the protection of people against themselves, and maintains that, although respect for individual autonomy is very much a part of modern life, there has been a general decline in the belief that we are the best judges of our own best interests. Referring to the libertarian views of JS Mill, Hart says:

Hart, HLA, *Law, Liberty and Morality*[42]

[There is] an increased awareness of a great range of factors which diminish the significance to be attached to an apparently free choice or to consent. Choices may be made or consent given without adequate reflection or appreciation of the consequences; or in pursuit of merely transitory desires; or in various predicaments when the judgment is likely to be clouded; or under inner psychological compulsion; or under pressure by others of a kind too subtle to be susceptible of proof in a law court. Underlying Mill's extreme fear of paternalism there perhaps is a conception of what a normal human being is like which now seems not to correspond to the facts. Mill, in fact, endows him with much of the psychology of a middle-aged man whose desires are relatively fixed, not liable to be artificially stimulated by external influences; who knows what he wants and what gives him satisfaction or happiness; and who pursues these things when he can.

As far as medicine is concerned, this argument states that paternalism is justified when, in the judgment of the doctor, the patient does not exhibit sufficient of the features of Hart's middle-aged man. The patient may be too young; the patient may have limited intelligence or limited education or may have a volatile personality given to acts of impetuosity. The doctor, on the other hand, is educated, impartial, knowledgeable and has only the best interests of the patient at heart. This grading of patients – and in consequence the way in which a doctor is entitled to regard them – is reflected in some of the case law (see, for example, the case of *Sidaway v Board of Governors of the Bethlem Royal Hospital and the Maudsley Hospital*[43] where Lord Diplock[44] states that an educated judge would 'naturally' want to ask questions about the risks of medical treatment before he consented to it).

See Chapter 3

1.3.2.1 Strong and weak paternalism

It is arguable that the above view, ie that some patients do not have sufficient education, etc, to make valid decisions, does not support paternalism in any form, but only where the patient's views are disregarded because of the circumstances, or something in the patient's own character.

---

42 Oxford: OUP, 1963.
43 [1985] AC 871.
44 See further Ch 3.

Writers sometimes refer to the difference as that between 'strong' and 'weak' (or 'limited') paternalism.

Childress describes the justification for limited paternalism as follows:

Childress, JF, *Who Should Decide? Paternalism in Health Care*[45]

The principle of limited paternalism

Parents sometimes override their children's wishes in order to protect them. . . . This example from familial relations yields two conditions that are frequently invoked to justify medical paternalism: (1) the defects, encumbrances, and limitations of a person's decision-making and acting; and (2) the probability of harm to that person unless there is intervention.

If the second condition – probable harm – is held to be sufficient to justify paternalism, apart from the person's incapacity for decision-making, we have extended or strong paternalism. According to this position, paternalistic interventions can be justified when a patient's risk-benefit analysis is unreasonable even though he is competent and his wishes, choices, or actions are informed and voluntary. If, however, the first set of conditions is held to be necessary, we have limited or weak paternalism, which allows paternalistic interventions only when a person's wishes, choices, or actions are defective because of incompetence, ignorance, or some internal or external constraint.

. . .

If these two conditions are jointly necessary for justified active paternalism, and if only limited paternalism is justified, we are able to express both the principle of beneficence and the principle of respect for persons. In limited paternalism, agents meet the needs of other persons without insulting them. . . .

Since both of these conditions are necessary to justify paternalistic acts, it is possible to start with either one. An apparent reason to start with prevention or removal of harm, or provision of benefit, is that this consideration frequently triggers paternalistic actions. In the order of experience, perception of risk to the patient, apart from intervention, usually precedes and provokes an assessment of the patient's competence to decide. . . . In view of customary medical practice, there are two good reasons for beginning with the patient's incompetence as a necessary condition for justified paternalism. First, to begin with the prevention or removal of harm may appear to give this condition priority and may play into the hands of strong paternalists. Second, even though in practice there may be little interest in the patient's competence unless there are risks, from a moral point of view the assessment of the patient's competence should be somewhat independent of the risks. Otherwise, strong paternalism could masquerade as weak paternalism, since – the argument might go – no competent person would knowingly and voluntarily accept some risks.

Culver and Gert put forward two examples of paternalism, one of which they maintain is justified, the other not:

Culver, CM and Gert, B, *Philosophy in Medicine: Conceptual and Ethical Issues in Medicine and Psychiatry*[46]

Case 8–1

Mr K was brought to the emergency room by his wife and a police officer. Mrs K had confessed to her husband earlier that evening that she was having an affair with one of his colleagues. He had become acutely agitated and depressed and, after several hours of mounting tension, told her he was going to kill himself so 'you'll have the freedom to have all the lovers you want'. She became frightened and called the police because there were loaded guns in the house and she knew her husband was an impulsive man.

---

45 Oxford: OUP, 1982.
46 New York: OUP, 1982.

In the emergency room Mr K would do little more than glower at Dr T, his wife, and the officer. He seemed extremely tense and agitated. Dr T decided that for Mr K's own protection he should be hospitalised but Mr K refused. Dr T therefore committed Mr K to the hospital for a 72-hour emergency detention.

How could Dr T attempt to justify his paternalistic commitment of Mr K? He could claim that by depriving Mr K of his freedom, there was a great likelihood that he was preventing the occurrence of a much greater evil: Mr K's death, or serious injury. Dr T could further claim that in his professional experience the overwhelming majority of persons in Mr K's condition who were hospitalised did subsequently recover from their state of agitated depression and acknowledge the irrational character of their former suicidal desires.

Note that Dr T need not claim that self-inflicted death is an evil of such magnitude that paternalistic intervention to prevent it is always justified. Rather, he could claim that it is justified in Mr K's case on several counts. First, Mr K's desire to kill himself seems irrational; while one may explain his desire, using psychodynamic concepts, he appears to have no adequate reason for killing himself. An adequate reason would be a belief on his part that his death would result in the avoiding of great evil(s) or the attaining of great goods for himself or others (his statement to his wife ['You'll have . . . all the lovers you want'] sarcastically expresses an altruistic reason which, even if taken literally, would not be an adequate reason for his suicide). Second, there is evidence that he suffers from a condition that is well known to be transient. Third, the violation of a moral rule (deprivation of freedom) which Dr T has carried out results in Mr K's suffering a much lesser evil than the evil (death) which Mr K may perpetrate on himself.

But it is not sufficient justification for Dr T merely to show that the evils prevented for Mr K by his paternalistic action outweigh the evils caused to Mr K; he must also be willing to publicly advocate the deprivation of Mr K's freedom in these circumstances. That is, he must be willing to advocate to all rational persons that in these circumstances everyone may be deprived of his freedom for a limited period of time. We believe that, accepting the case as described, not only could Dr T advocate to all rational persons that Mr K may be deprived of his freedom but also that, if they accepted the facts of the case and the conditions of public advocacy, all rational persons would agree with Dr T's judgment completely. Thus, Dr T's paternalistic behaviour is strongly justified.

By contrast, Culver and Gert consider the following:

Case 8–2

Mrs R, a 29 year old mother, is hospitalised with symptoms of abdominal pain, weight loss, weakness, and swelling of the ankles. An extensive medical workup is inconclusive, and exploratory abdominal surgery is carried out which reveals a primary ovarian cancer with extensive spread to other abdominal organs. Her condition is judged to be too far advanced for surgical relief, and her life expectancy is estimated to be at most a few months. Despite her oft-repeated requests to be told 'where I stand and what I face', Dr E tells both the patient and her husband that the diagnosis is still unclear but that he will see her weekly as an outpatient. At the time of discharge she is feeling somewhat better than at admission, and Dr E hopes that the family will have a few happy weeks together before her condition worsens and they must be told the truth.

Dr E's behaviour is clearly paternalistic: he has deceived Mrs R for what he believes is her benefit; he knows that he is violating the moral rule against deception without her consent; and he views her as someone who is competent to give or refuse valid consent to being told the truth.

Dr E could attempt to justify his paternalistic act by claiming that the evil – psychological suffering – he hoped to prevent by his deception is significantly greater than the evil, if any, he caused by lying. While this might be true in this particular case, it is by no means certain. By his deception, Dr E is depriving Mrs R and her family of the opportunity to make those plans that would enable her family to deal more adequately with her death. In the circumstances of this case as described, Mrs R's desire to know the truth is a rational one; in fact, there is no evidence of any irrational behaviour or desires on her part. This contrasts sharply to Mr K's desire to kill himself, which is clearly irrational. Furthermore, although we regard Mr K's desire not to be deprived of freedom, considered in isolation, as a rational one, we would not consider it rational for one to choose a high probability of death over the loss of a few days of freedom.

Arguably, we can see a weak form of paternalism operating when we consider our attitude to organ donation and non-therapeutic medical research. It is unlawful in the UK to sell a non-regenerative organ for transplant. Similarly, we prevent anything other than modest payments for those who undergo non-therapeutic research (ie healthy volunteers). Many people who would not regard themselves as paternalists in the context of medical treatment might support these prohibitions on the basis that it is offensive for there to be a 'trade' in human organs or for people to sell their bodies for the purposes of research. However, is this not a form of paternalism, albeit one based upon the principle of non-maleficence (as opposed to paternalism in relation to medical treatment which is based upon the principle of beneficence)?

See Chapter 11 ➡️

1.3.3 Paternalism and the sanctity of life principle

Both Mill and Kant would accept the sanctity of life principle as this stems from the inherent value of the individual. The duty of beneficence has this principle at its heart. A paternalist might argue that the doctor's duty to do good and to uphold the sanctity of life principle will, on occasion, justifiably, override patient autonomy. For example, in Chapter 3 we look at several cases where the courts have had to consider the refusal by women of consent to Caesarean section operations to deliver their children. It has been held that the women's refusals must be respected, even if there is a strong likelihood that both mother and foetus will not survive. However, there is an argument that the principle of the sanctity of life might, in certain circumstances, override the woman's refusal.

1.3.4 Paternalism and the doctor's duty of beneficence

It might be said that it is bad for those involved in healthcare to be forced to stand helpless in the face of a refusal of life-saving treatment and witness an unnecessary death. This view might be illustrated by the role of doctors and other healthcare workers in the treatment of suicide attempts. Someone who attempts to take their own life can be treated without their consent. From what arises the right to override the patient's wish to die? Is it because the true wishes of the patient may not be known (it could be a 'cry for help' or an accident), or is it because of the dominance of the sanctity of life principle? It should be noted that health authorities have been held liable when a patient has committed suicide while under their care, if there has been inadequate supervision. Again, arguably, this is about sanctity of life and beneficence: it is inappropriate that hospitals should be places of avoidable and self-inflicted deaths; they are places for healing and the saving of lives.

See Chapter 3 ➡️

1.3.5 Paternalism and a duty to oneself?

In Culver and Gert's example of the patient at risk of suicide, it was assumed that paternalism would eventually give way to autonomy. Is there a sustainable ethical argument that one has a duty to oneself to live and to live a healthy life, and, therefore, treatment against one's wishes may be justifiable? It will be recalled that the intuitionist philosopher, WD Ross, said that one of the intuitively good principles was the duty of self-improvement.

Similarly, Kant, whose moral philosophy stated that human life is intrinsically valuable, puts duty before 'natural inclinations'. For example, he thought suicide permissible only if it was to avoid moral degradation. This was based upon the principle that only human beings can uphold the moral law and, therefore, for as long as they are not morally degraded, they have a duty to do that. Would this justify medical paternalism on the basis that the patient has a duty to live a healthy life and if, in the opinion of his doctors, he is not doing so, he must be treated against his will?

1.4 The case for patient autonomy

Paternalism has an old-fashioned ring to it. Two American academics, Pellegrino and Thomasma, comment as follows:

Pellegrino, ED and Thomasma, DC, *For the Patient's Good: The Restoration of Beneficence in Health Care*[47]

The sources of . . . resistance to medical paternalism are many: the political and ethical philosophy of individual rights; the higher educational level of today's public; the latter's awareness of the powers and dangers of medical technology; a distrust of experts; the rise of consumerism; and the moral challenges of the Vietnam War, the civil rights movement, and the campus revolts of the '60s and early '70s. The convergence of these forces has been powerful enough to erode the 2,500 year old tradition of medical status contained in beneficent authoritarianism.

1.4.1 Autonomy

It is in the assertion that the right to autonomous medical decision-making is paramount that Mill's libertarian philosophy is most evident: the only justification for imposing medical treatment on a patient against his will is to prevent harm to others (in the section on utilitarianism and autonomy we will consider whether non-consensual medical treatment may ever by justified on the basis that it will prevent harm to others, but let us assume for the present that it will not). Beauchamp and McCullough describe the autonomy principle as being an extension of the right to individual sovereignty to limit the authority of the state:

Beauchamp, TL and McCullough, LB, *Medical Ethics: The Moral Responsibilities of Physicians*[48]

Individual sovereignty needs protection for two reasons. First, there is a danger of imbalance in power between the individual and the State (or other parties) in favour of the latter. Individual rights provide a corrective to this imbalance by ensuring that individuals as individuals will be given due consideration and respect. Second, conflicts arise between an individual's perception of his or her best interests and another's perception of those interests. Rights of individual sovereignty protect an individual's freedom to choose his or her best interests.

Much of the debate surrounding the principle of autonomy concerns the right of a patient to refuse life-saving treatment. Earlier we considered how far there may be an obligation to prevent suicide. It is interesting to note that it has been said that the liberty to commit suicide may be

---

47 Oxford: OUP, 1988.
48 Englewood Cliffs, NJ: Prentice-Hall, 1984.

seen as 'an index of high civilisation', because the act goes against the most basic of our instincts, that of self-preservation.[49]

1.4.2 The right to self-determination

Is the principle of autonomy equivalent to the right to self-determination? Is this 'right' really a liberty in the sense that there is no claim against anyone in the Hohfeldian sense? Certainly, the right to self-determination could not be relied upon to impose duties on others to provide medical treatment.

There is some debate as to whether autonomy is part of the right to privacy. Wellman considers the issue:

Wellman, C, _An Approach to Rights: Studies in the Philosophy of Law and Morals_[50]

> ... how is this right [to privacy] related to personal autonomy? A tempting hypothesis is that autonomy is located within one portion of this right because one of the constitutionally protected areas of privacy is that of private decisions. Thus, even though the right to privacy is not the liberty-right to make and act on private decisions, it includes the claim-right that others not interfere with these private decisions, for any such interference would be an invasion of a protected area of privacy. I very much doubt, however, that this direct and essential connection between privacy and autonomy has ever been recognised by the courts. For one thing, the expression 'a private decision' is conspicuous by its absence from the opinions in the privacy cases, even in _Roe_ [v _Wade_] and _Quinlan_ that centre on the abortion decision and the decision to refuse medical treatment, respectively. Moreover, this interpretation misrepresents the reasoning of the courts. The argument in _Roe_ is not that the abortion decision is constitutionally protected because it is a private decision, but that it is encompassed by the right to privacy because it involves the exercise of one of the fundamental liberties recognised in the US Constitution. Hence, the emphasis is upon how fundamental, not how personal and private, the decision is.

1.4.3 The political approach and the rejection of 'social control'

Those who support the overriding importance of the autonomy principle are lent support by the way in which psychiatry was used in the former Soviet Union, where some political dissidents were diagnosed as being 'psychiatrically ill' and compulsorily detained in hospital. The writer Thomas Szasz, whose work is considered further in Chapter 9, cites this abuse of medicine in a number of his publications.[51] The argument is that illness is a value-laden concept and any form of paternalism runs the risk of doctors branding patients with 'illness' and subsequent treatment. It is easy to see how this abuse can take place with something as nebulous as mental illness, but could this sort of abuse take place in respect of other forms of illness? Perhaps alcoholism, for example, could be so regarded, and 'imperfections' such as baldness might be categorised as illnesses.

1.4.4 Utilitarianism and autonomy

It is interesting to consider the interaction of these two concepts, because both were embraced in the philosophy of JS Mill. His libertarian views imply that one must be free to pursue a conception

---

49 See Alvarez, A, _The Savage God: A Study of Suicide_, London: Weidenfeld & Nicolson, 1971.
50 Dordrecht: Kluwer Academic, 1997.
51 See, for example, Szasz, TS, _Law, Liberty and Psychiatry: An Inquiry into the Social Uses of Mental Health Practices_, London: Routledge & Kegan Paul, 1974.

of life that is conducive to human flourishing. However, is there one conception of the good life and, if not, how do we maximise welfare? Similarly, if one is looking at the consequences of actions, if the exercise of one's autonomy adversely affects other people, then are not the two principles incompatible? In the context of refusal of life-saving treatment, it may be said that the right to self-determination is in conflict with utility because the consequences of the refusal may be bad for the family left behind: the loss of a breadwinner (the family is now dependent upon society for support) and the infliction of grief. It is arguable that this reflects one of the deficiencies in the utilitarian approach: it allows only a limited role for basic rights. Alternatively, it could be said that subjecting people to violation of their physical integrity has worse consequences for society than does respecting their bodily integrity. If this argument were accepted, respect for autonomy would be an essential element of any utilitarian account of medical ethics.

1.4.5 Rationality

Giving effect to autonomy in relation to medical treatment presupposes that the patient is competent to make decisions about such treatment. Do these decisions have to be rational? GEM Anscombe[52] gives an interesting example of having a reason for doing something. She cites the example of a man who wants a saucer of mud. He is asked whether he wants it to study its chemistry, whether he finds mud aesthetically pleasing, whether he has a practical use for it and so on; he answers all questions in the negative: he just wants a saucer of mud for no reason. Surely we would want to conclude that he does not want a saucer of mud at all. By analogy, there would have to be reasons for making decisions about medical treatment. However, these can be and, as we shall see, often are, bizarre. Do we conclude that, because of this, the patient lacks decision-making capacity? As we shall see from examining the case law in Chapter 3, the answer is 'no'. Decision-making capacity may be present despite the fact that a patient holds a number of strange and, apparently unsupportable, beliefs. Perhaps the correct view is that if these beliefs are genuinely held, and form part of the patient's 'world view', then they should be respected. In other words, unlike the man who wants the saucer of mud for no reason whatsoever, the patient has reasons that *make sense to him* and, as such, should be respected.

1.4.6 Autonomy and beneficence

Even the most ardent proponent of the principle of autonomy would accept that it would be wrong to deny someone medical treatment because they were incapable of consenting. If it were otherwise, no mentally incompetent patient would ever receive treatment. However, the argument would be that in the cases of children and adults lacking capacity, such treatment is not contrary to the principle of autonomy because they are not autonomous human beings. Similarly, people suffering from certain forms of mental disorder may be compulsorily detained and treated for that disorder without consent, and it is argued that this is carried out to *restore* their autonomy, and therefore entirely consistent with the principle.

See Chapter 9

1.4.7 Autonomy – a step too far?

Charles Foster has written a provocative book in which he challenges the current ascendancy of the 'autonomy' approach. He acknowledges that the pre-eminence of the concept has roots in a valid objection to the unacceptable face of paternalism, but believes that this has gone too far.

---

52 See *Intention*, Oxford: Blackwell, 1963.

Foster C, *Choosing Life, Choosing Death: The Tyranny of Autonomy in Medical Ethics and Law*[53]

> Autonomy grew up as a street fighter, and was blooded in some genuinely noble battles against medical paternalism. But like so many rulers with this sort of pedigree, it has quickly forgotten its democratic roots, and grown fat and brutal in power.

Foster argues that the emphasis on autonomy is also illustrated by the paramountcy of clinical judgement in medical decision-making, ie noting that this is an example of doctors being able to rely on the importance of their *own* autonomy. He refers to the rare condition of body dysmorphia, whereby some people experience pain and distress in the belief that one or more appendage is alien to them:

> The law steadfastly refuses to impose on doctors (other than by contract) any obligation to perform any particular medical treatment. Also, a doctor can choose with whom he enters into a doctor–patient relationship . . .
>
> Since Patient X cannot demand of Doctor Y that procedure Z be performed by Y, can X legitimately complain that his autonomy rights are affected? Since these rules are designed (inter alia) to protect the autonomy rights of Y, that is a complaint that autonomy will be slightly embarrassed to support . . .
>
> Autonomy in the medico-legal arena is (rightly) much more concerned with preventing unwanted violations than in guaranteeing a right to positive benefits. For that reason it has little to say about the vexed business of resource allocation: it is happy to acknowledge that that is the province of other principles. Likewise, it is slow to accept the brief from the patient with body image disorder who begs the surgeon, in autonomy's own language, to remove the objectively normal but subjectively horrific limbs.

Undoubtedly there is an argument that emphasis on autonomy alone or paternalism alone impoverishes medical ethics and that both these can be accommodated within a coherent framework.

1.5 Paternalism v autonomy – a false dichotomy?

Using the principle of beneficence, the paternalist will justify treating patients against their will, or withholding information from them which is 'bad for them'. We have seen that, even within the philosophy of autonomy, there may be justified intervention, although the advocate of autonomy would argue that the patient in those cases is not truly autonomous. However, when we look at decision-making capacity, we will find that it is by no means easy to decide whether someone has sufficient capacity to make truly autonomous decisions. It might be thought that this adds fuel to the argument of the paternalists. However, it is arguable that precisely because it can be difficult to assess capacity, it is all the more important to guard against the paternalist declaring someone incapable in order to do what he thinks is best for them. These difficulties might make us wonder whether the traditional opposition of paternalism and autonomy might not give way to something which recognises the best in each of them. Some writers have endeavoured to find a more conciliatory approach, which accommodates both models.

1.5.1 Collaborative decision-making

Pellegrino and Thomasma say that there can never be a single model to describe the doctor–patient relationship adequately. They state that the principle of respect for persons leads to two moral duties:

Pellegrino, ED and Thomasma, DC, *For the Patient's Good: The Restoration of Beneficence in Health Care*[54]

The first is to respect the self-determination or autonomy of others. The second . . . is to help restore that autonomy or help establish it when it is absent. Looked at in this way, beneficence is seen to be a direct consequence of a fundamental moral principle and the guiding duty of medicine. If this is true, then the autonomy model is necessarily incomplete. So, too, is the paternalistic model.

In this regard, other writers have suggested that it would be preferable for medical decision-making to be conceived of as a kind of collaborative effort:

Teff, H, 'Consent to medical procedures: paternalism, self-determination or therapeutic alliance'[55]

It has been argued that the pursuit of a therapeutic alliance, in the sense of a genuine collaborative effort, is desirable in so far as it can facilitate a beneficial outcome. Quite apart from the fact that for many medical conditions there is either no specific remedy or the effectiveness of treatment is unknown, the doctor cannot intuitively know precisely what constitutes health or well being for a particular patient. The optimum 'outcome' is not necessarily to be equated with the technically successful result of a given operation, but may embrace a prognosis of the patient's subsequent medical and psychological condition and ability to function, as well as other social and financial considerations where relevant.

When medical procedures, especially invasive ones, are contemplated, doctor–patient relationships are often fraught with uncertainty and ambiguity. There is no *a priori* reason to assume that a doctor or surgeon possesses the kind of psychological or moral insight that would enable him to decide unaided what is most appropriate. The relative importance which patients attach, for example, to quality as against length of life, and to physical integrity or appearance as against diminution of pain, may reflect personal values, circumstances and priorities of which the surgeon, in particular, is initially unaware and may never become sufficiently apprised. It is apparently common practice in English hospitals for the information deemed relevant to patient consent to be provided by 'the most junior and inexperienced doctor, who will not perform the operation and who knows nothing of the likely complications'. . .

1.5.2 A fiduciary relationship

That the doctor–patient relationship might be a fiduciary relationship has yet to be accepted by the English courts (see, for example, the judgment of Lord Scarman in *Sidaway v Board of Governors of the Bethlem Royal Hospital and the Maudsley Hospital*).[56] However, some commentators

---

54 Oxford: OUP, 1988.
55 (1985) 101 LQR 450.
56 [1985] AC 871.

have suggested that this may be a plausible analysis of the relationship. What is a fiduciary relationship? Peter Bartlett describes it as follows:

Bartlett, P, 'Doctors as fiduciaries: equitable regulation of the doctor–patient relationship'[57]

A fiduciary relationship attracts the attention of equity. The term apparently arose in the 19th century, when a variety of relationships held by equity to be 'on trust' were no longer necessarily flowing from 'trusts' themselves in any meaningful sense. With this motley origin, it is not surprising that fiduciary relationships themselves differ widely in the duties equity imposes on them. Consider the examples of lawyers and trustees. Certainly, one would expect a duty of undivided loyalty to the beneficiary or client in each case, and one would not expect the fiduciary to make a profit from the relationship outside that expressly authorised. There are equally firm differences, however. Unless inconsistent with his or her duty to the court, the lawyer acts on the instructions of the client, even when the instructions do not reflect the lawyer's view of the client's best interest. Trustees, by comparison, act in the beneficiary's best financial interest in any event. Where the beneficiary is in a relatively weak position in the control of the trust, the client is in control of the legal matter.

This has led a number of scholars to argue that it is inappropriate to think of the application of fiduciary relationships as a class at all, but rather specific relationships attracting specific collections of fiduciary duties . . .

Further flexibility is introduced through the distinction between fact-based and status-based fiduciary obligations, the latter being based in relationships traditionally recognised by equity and attracting a broader array of fiduciary obligations, and the former based in specific fact situations and attracting only some fiduciary obligations. The advantage of this approach is that the courts may perceive an increased flexibility to extend obligations beyond the traditional fiduciary situations to offer specific equitable remedies in specific situations, without setting broad precedent.

Is it arguable that the fiduciary model could remove the paternalism – autonomy divide? For example, could the relationship of trust justify paternalistic treatment as long as the doctor was totally candid with the patient? But there may be an inherent problem here: if the doctor is candid and the patient refuses the treatment, then the 'fiduciary' nature of the relationship does not assist in resolving the problem. However, it is clear that aspects of the doctor–patient relationship can be fiduciary in nature, such as the duty of confidentiality and, while the English courts have been reluctant to accept the model in the context of access to medical records, a fiduciary duty may be applicable.

See Chapter 5 →

| **THINK POINT**

| We will see that when we consider the treatment of children, the current approach of the courts is that some young people under the age of 16 are capable of making decisions about their own medical treatment, but are not capable of refusing treatment that their doctors wish them to have. How do you regard this in the light of the discussion we have just had on paternalism and autonomy?

---

57 (1997) Med L Rev 193.

1.6 Justice in the allocation of health resources

The foregoing sections have considered the treatment of patients when they have not wanted treatment, or where the patients' medical conditions have not been fully revealed to them, or where treatment information has been withheld or restricted. A scenario we have not yet considered consists of a patient requiring treatment, and being refused, or a doctor ready and willing to treat a patient, but unable to do so because of lack of resources.

Most of us would agree that resources should be distributed fairly, or in accordance with justice. However, this bland statement gets us nowhere unless we decide the basis of a fair distribution. Concepts of justice often present three different models for distribution. First, resources may be distributed in accordance with merit. This would mean that the most deserving persons, for example, in terms of moral worth or contribution to society, would receive healthcare as a matter of priority. Secondly, resources may be distributed 'equally'. However, this presupposes that we have a test for deciding whether the persons concerned are equal. Certainly they are entitled to equal respect and consideration, but that in itself may not be enough. This tempts us to adopt the third model, which is that resources be distributed in accordance with need.

Our ethical dilemmas have previously been about the nature of the doctor–patient relationship in a one-to-one sense. Now we are looking at the relationship between the doctor and many of his patients. Does this undermine the cosy beneficence model, where the doctor's only concern is to do his best for the patient?

Newdick comments on the issue of clinical freedom and the Hippocratic duty to act in the best interests of patients:

Newdick, C, *Who Should We Treat? Rights, Rationing, and Resources in the NHS*[58]

'Waste' is not a neutral word. Governments, health service managers, doctors, patients, and citizens may each have differing ideas about how resources should be spent. Used as a way of insisting that individual patients receive only the best treatment, it does not undermine the Hippocratic duty to do the best for patients. Many say that doctors should never compromise their clinical commitment to the individual. But this notion may positively increase the costs of treatment by highlighting the many excellent, but expensive, new treatments that become available. By contrast . . . health economists stress the need to distribute national resources efficiently and give 'waste' a different meaning. This approach emphasises the clinical benefits to whole communities, rather than to individuals, and could modify the relationship between doctors and patients. . . . The Bristol Inquiry . . . said: 'Against a background of constrained resources, it may not always be right for the individual doctor treating a particular patient to insist on having his, or her way, if the price to be paid is to limit or impair the care available for other patients.'

Clearly, this idea seeks to change the clinical commitment each clinician has to his, or her patient in the interests of patients as a whole. This changes the traditional Hippocratic ideal and its implications are crucial to the health service we can expect in the future.

It is highly likely in practice that many doctors will frequently have to choose who to treat, or who to treat as a matter of priority, and that this will mean that he is not doing his best for those who are not treated, or not treated in a timely fashion. Some doctors have been frank about these issues and have suggested to their patients that a ballot takes place to decide

---

58 Oxford: Clarendon Press, 2005.

on priority. In the late 1980s the Journal of Medical Ethics reported on the research of Drs Parsons and Lock:

'Editorial'[59]

Who shall die?

Parsons and Lock, disturbed by increasingly inadequate funds for dialysis and transplantation, asked 25 British nephrologists to reject 10 out of 40 realistically described patients, ticking their reasons for rejection from a checklist under the categories of age, marital status, home facilities, underlying disease, and additional disease. All the nephrologists completed the questionnaire except for one who felt unable to accept any of the reasons suggested as valid grounds for rejection. Their responses make important reading. Interestingly, of the 10 patients most generally rejected, 'we found that at least six of them had been successfully treated by our own unit'; and not one of the patients was rejected by all the respondents.

Accepting for the time being that such choices must in practice be made, whereby some individuals are to be allocated life-saving resources while others with the same problem are to be refused them (microallocation or triage) it may be worthwhile distinguishing different criteria upon which such choices might conceivably be made. Perhaps the one most commonly used in practice is that favoured by many of the respondents, notably the medical or technical criterion, whereby triage is based on the probability of successful medical outcome. In clear cases this criterion seems unproblematic; for example, other things being equal, a doctor faced with two patients needing blood transfusion and only enough blood for one would surely be not merely absurd but downright wicked to transfuse the patient with an incompatible blood group when the other's blood group matched that of the available blood. The criterion for proper choice here is quite clearly likelihood of medical success.

The first of the criteria, the probability of successful medical outcome, seems, as the editorial states, unproblematic. However, the example given of the blood transfusion is perhaps too simplistic. It is beyond doubt that in this example there is one, and only one, ethical choice. Indeed, there is no ethical dilemma here at all. Many predictions of 'successful medical outcome', however, might be covert value judgments. From time to time the newspapers report cases of smokers being refused heart surgery. Hospitals are at pains to point out that the refusal is not because they are smokers, but because the cardiac specialists state that the surgery will not be a lasting success if the patient, who has no plans to give up smoking, continues to smoke. However, might, at least in part, these decisions be based on other factors?

'Editorial'[60]

A second criterion for selection might be the candidates' value or disvalue to society; thus those respondents who rejected patients positive for Australia antigen on grounds of the risk to other patients and staff of potentially lethal hepatitis were explicitly or implicitly using this social criterion, as were any respondents who wished to stop treatment on the grounds that resources are being drained by the heavily handicapped and homeless from other less demanding patients.

There may be concern about the restriction on treatment in the cases of elderly people. Doctors may well find it easier to justify this on the basis of successful medical outcome. Is age a good reason for refusing treatment? The following are some of the arguments explored by Harris for and against:

---

59 (1980) 6 JME 171.
60 (1980) 6 JME 171.

Harris, J, *The Value of Life: Introduction to Medical Ethics*[61]

The anti-ageist argument

All of us who wish to go on living have something that each of us values equally, although for each it is different in character, for some a much richer prize than for others, and we none of us know its true extent. This thing is of course 'the rest of our lives'. So long as we do not know the date of our deaths, then for each of us the 'rest of our lives' is of indefinite duration. Whether we are 17 or 70, in perfect health or suffering from a terminal disease, we each have the rest of our lives to lead. So long as we each fervently wish to live out the rest of our lives, however long that turns out to be, then if we do not deserve to die, we each suffer the same injustice if our wishes are deliberately frustrated and we are cut off prematurely. Indeed there may well be a double injustice in deciding that those whose life expectation is short should not benefit from rescue or resuscitation. Suppose I am told today that I have terminal cancer with only approximately six months or so to live, but I want to live until I die, or at least until I decide that life is no longer worth living. Suppose I then am involved in an accident and because my condition is known to my potential rescuers and there are not enough resources to treat all who could immediately be saved I am marked among those who will not be helped. I am then the victim of a double tragedy and a double injustice. I am stricken first by cancer and the knowledge that I have only a short time to live and I'm then stricken again when I'm told that because of my first tragedy a second and more immediate one is to be visited upon me. Because I have once been unlucky I'm now no longer worth saving.

The point is a simple but powerful one. However short or long my life will be, so long as I want to go on living it then I suffer a terrible injustice when that life is prematurely cut short. Imagine a group of people all of an age, say a class of students all in their mid-20s. If fire trapped all in the lecture theatre and only 20 could be rescued in time should the rescuers shout 'youngest first!'? Suppose they had time to debate the question or had been debating it 'academically' before the fire? It would surely seem invidious to deny some what all value so dearly merely because of an accident of birth. It might be argued that age here provides no criterion precisely because although the lifespans of such a group might be expected to vary widely, there would be no way of knowing who was most likely to live longest. But suppose a reliable astrologer could make very realistic estimates or, what amounts to the same thing, suppose the age range of the students to be much greater, say 17 to 55. Does not the invidiousness of selecting by birth-date remain? Should a 17 year old be saved before a 29 year old or she before the 45 year old and should the 55 year old clearly be the last to be saved or the first to be sacrificed?

Our normal intuitions would share this sense of the invidiousness of choosing between our imaginary students by reason of their respective ages, but would start to want to make age relevant at some extremes, say if there were a 2 day old baby and a 90 year old grandmother. We will be returning to discuss a possible basis for this intuition in a moment. However, it is important to be clear that the anti-ageist argument denies the relevance of age or life expectancy as a criterion absolutely. It argues that even if I know for certain that I have only a little space to live, that space, however short, may be very precious to me. Precious, precisely because it is all the time I have left, and just as precious to me on that account as all the time you have left is precious to you, however much those two timespans differ in length. So that where we both want, equally strongly, to go on living, then we each suffer the same injustice when our lives are cut short or are cut further short.

It might seem that someone who would insist on living out the last few months of his life when by 'going quietly' someone else might have the chance to live for a much longer time would be a very selfish person. But this would be true only if the anti-ageist argument is false. It will be true only if it is not plausible to claim that living out the rest of one's life could be equally valuable to the individual whose life it is irrespective of the amount of unelapsed time that is left. And this is of course precisely the usual situation when individuals do not normally have anything but the haziest of ideas as to how long it is that they might have left.

---

61 London: Routledge & Kegan Paul, 1985.

I think the anti-ageist argument has much plausibility. It locates the wrongness of ending an individual's life in the evil of thwarting that person's desire to go on living and argues that it is profoundly unjust to frustrate that desire merely because some of those who have exactly the same desire, held no more strongly, also have a longer life expectancy than the others. However, there are a number of arguments that pull in the opposite direction and these we must now consider.

The fair innings argument

One problem with the anti-ageist argument is our feeling that there is something unfair about a person who has lived a long and happy life hanging on grimly at the end, while someone who has not been so fortunate suffers a related double misfortune, of losing out in a lottery in which his life happened to be in the balance with that of the grim octogenarian. It might be argued that we could accept the part of the anti-ageist argument which focuses on the equal value of unelapsed time, if this could be tempered in some way. How can it be just that someone who has already had more than her fair share of life and its delights should be preferred or even given an equal chance of continued survival with the young person who has not been so favoured? One strategy that seems to take account of our feeling that there is something wrong with taking steps to prolong the lives of the very old at the expense of those much younger is the fair innings argument.

The fair innings argument takes the view that there is some span of years that we consider a reasonable life, a fair innings. Let's say that a fair share of life is the traditional three score and 10, 70 years. Anyone who does not reach 70 suffers, on this view, the injustice of being cut off in their prime. They have missed out on a reasonable share of life; they have been short-changed. Those, however, who do make 70 suffer no such injustice, they have not lost out but rather must consider any additional years a sort of bonus beyond that which could reasonably be hoped for. The fair innings argument requires that everyone be given an equal chance to have a fair innings, to reach the appropriate threshold but, having reached it, they have received their entitlement. The rest of their life is the sort of bonus which may be cancelled when this is necessary to help others reach the threshold.

The attraction of the fair innings argument is that it preserves and incorporates many of the features that made the anti-ageist argument plausible, but allows us to preserve our feeling that the old who have had a good run for their money should not be endlessly propped up at the expense of those who have not had the same chance. We can preserve the conclusion of the anti-ageist argument, that so long as life is equally valued by the person whose life it is, it should be given an equal chance of preservation, and we can go on taking this view until the people in question have reached a fair innings.

There is, however, an important difficulty with the fair innings argument. It is that the very arguments which support the seeing of the threshold at an age which might plausibly be considered to be a reasonable lifespan, equally support the setting of the threshold at any age at all, so long as an argument from fairness can be used to support so doing. Suppose that there is only one place available on the dialysis programme and two patients are in competition for it. One is 30, and the other 40 years of age. The fair innings argument requires that neither be preferred on the grounds of age since both are below the threshold and are entitled to an equal chance of reaching it. If there is no other reason to choose between them we should do something like toss a coin. However, the 30 year old can argue that the considerations which support the fair innings argument require that she be given the place. After all, what's fair about the fair innings argument is precisely that each individual should have an equal chance of enjoying the benefits of a reasonable lifespan. The younger patient can argue that from where she's standing, the age of 40 looks much more reasonable a span than that of 30, and that she should be given the chance to benefit from those 10 extra years.

This argument generalised becomes a reason for always preferring to save younger rather than older people, whatever the age difference, and makes the original anti-ageist argument begin to look again the more attractive line to take. For the younger person can always argue that the older has had a fairer innings, and should now give way. It is difficult to stop whatever span is taken to be a fair innings collapsing towards zero under pressure from those younger candidates who see their innings as less fair than that of those with a larger share.

But perhaps this objection to the fair innings argument is mistaken? If 70 years is a fair innings it does not follow that the nearer a span of life approaches 70 years, the fairer an innings it is. This may be revealed by considering a different sort of threshold. Suppose that most people can run a mile in seven minutes, and that two people are given the opportunity to show that they can run a mile in that time. They both expect to be given seven minutes. However, if one is in fact given only three minutes and the other only four, it's not true that the latter is given a fairer running time: for people with average abilities four minutes is no more realistic a time in which to run a mile than is three. Four minutes is neither a fair threshold in itself, nor a fairer one than three minutes would be.

Nor does the argument that establishes seven minutes as an appropriate threshold lend itself to variation downwards. For that argument just is that seven is the number of minutes that an average adult takes to run a mile. Why then is it different for lifespans? If three score and ten is the number of years available to most people for getting what life has to offer, and is also the number of years people can reasonably expect to have, then it is a misfortune to be allowed anything less, however much less one is allowed, if nothing less than the full span normally suffices for getting what can be got out of life. It's true that the 40 year old gets more time than the 30 year old, but the frame of reference is not time only, but time normally required for a full life.

This objection has some force, but its failure to be a good analogy reveals that two sorts of considerations go to make an innings fair. For while living a full or complete life, just in the sense of experiencing all the ages of man, is one mark of a fair innings, there is also value in living through as many ages as possible. Just as completing the mile is one value, it is not the only one. Runners in the race of life also value ground covered, and generally judge success in terms of distance run.

What the fair innings argument needs to do is to capture and express in a workable form the truth that while it is always a *misfortune* to die when one wants to go on living, it is not a tragedy to die in old age; but it is on the other hand, both a tragedy and a misfortune to be cut off prematurely. Of course, ideas like 'old age' and 'premature death' are inescapably vague, and may vary from society to society, and over time as techniques for postponing death improve. We must also remember that while it may be invidious to choose between a 30 and a 40 year old on the grounds that one has had a fairer innings than the other, it may not be invidious to choose between the 30 and the 65 year old on those grounds.

If we remember, too, that it will remain wrong to end the life of someone who wants to live or to fail to save them, and that the fair innings argument will only operate as a principle of selection where we are forced to choose between lives, then something workable might well be salvaged.

While 'old age' is irredeemably vague, we can tell the old from the young, and even the old from the middle-aged. So that without attempting precise formulation, a reasonable form of the fair innings argument might hold; and might hold that people who had achieved old age or who were closely approaching it would not have their lives further prolonged when this could only be achieved at the cost of the lives of those who were not nearing old age. These categories could be left vague, the idea being that it would be morally defensible to prefer to save the lives of those who 'still had their lives before them' rather than those who had 'already lived full lives'. The criterion to be employed in each case would simply be what reasonable people would say about whether someone had had a fair innings. Where reasonable people would be in no doubt that a particular individual was nearing old age *and* that that person's life could only be further prolonged at the expense of the life of someone that no reasonable person would classify as nearing old age, then the fair innings argument would apply, and it would be justifiable to save the younger candidate.

In cases where reasonable people differed or it seemed likely that they would differ as to whether people fell into one category or the other, then the anti-ageist argument would apply and the inescapable choice would have to be made arbitrarily.

But again it must be emphasised that the fair innings argument would only operate as a counsel of despair, when it was clearly impossible to postpone the deaths of all those who wanted to go on living. In all other circumstances the anti-ageist argument would apply.

One influential proposal for allocating healthcare resources fairly has been by means of calculating QALYs (quality distinguished life year).[62] John Harris describes this approach as follows:

Harris, J, 'QALYfying the value of life'[63]

1 What are QALYs?

It is important to be as clear as possible as to just what a QALY is and what it might be used for. I cannot do better than let Alan Williams, the architect of QALYs, tell you in his own words:

> The essence of a QALY is that it takes a year of healthy life expectancy to be worth one, but regards a year of unhealthy life expectancy as worth less than one. Its precise value is lower the worse the quality of life of the unhealthy person (which is what the 'quality adjusted' bit is all about). If being dead is worth zero, it is, in principle, possible for a QALY to be negative, ie, for the quality of someone's life to be judged worse than being dead.
>
> The general idea is that a beneficial healthcare activity is one that generates a positive amount of QALYs, and that an efficient healthcare activity is one where the cost-per-QALY is as low as it can be. A high priority healthcare activity is one where the cost-per-QALY is low, and a low priority activity is one where cost-per-QALY is high.

The plausibility of the QALY derives from the idea that given the choice, a person would prefer a shorter healthier life to a longer period of survival in a state of severe discomfort and disability. The idea that any rational person would endorse this preference provides the moral and political force behind the QALY. Its acceptability as a measurement of health then depends upon its doing all the theoretical tasks assigned to it, and on its being what people want, or would want, for themselves.

Harris subsequently became involved in a debate with John McKie et al. about the application of QALYs (a series of articles was published in (1996) 22 JME 204–21). Part of the debate centred on John Rawls's famous 'veil of ignorance' argument in A *Theory of Justice*.[64] Rawls was attempting to find a system of distributive justice while accepting the proposition that people tend to be self-interested rather than altruistic. The scenario he envisages is as follows. Imagine that you are one of a number of people who are aware of the way in which the so-called laws of economics work, but do not know their place in society. So, for example, you may be rich and powerful, or you may be unemployed with no resources whatsoever. Behind this 'veil of ignorance' you are asked to agree a set of principles which will govern the way in which the benefits and burdens in society are distributed. Assume, too, that you are motivated by self-interest. Rawls argues that, because you do not know your position in society, you will take care to ensure that conditions for those at the bottom of the pile are as good as possible. Rawls's theory is open to the objection that it assumes that the self-interested person will choose to play safe in this way. It can be argued that those behind the veil might choose to take a gamble. McKie et al. state that QALYs would be chosen by those behind the veil of ignorance because QALYs maximise utility. In other words, they take a wider view of self-interest. Harris states that they would not, because the persons behind the veil, ie typical human beings, are cautious risk-averse persons, who would weigh the downside more than the upside. This is a difficult dispute to resolve. Does it depend upon the view one takes of human psychology, and will there not always be at least two views?

Harris also maintains that the problem with the QALY approach is that a person's life is valued more even if the difference in life expectation is very small. For example, the patient who

---

62 See, for example, *The Measurement of Health*, published by the Office of Health Economics in 1985; and Williams, A, 'The value of QALYs' (1985) Health and Social Services Journal.
63 (1987) 13 JME 117.
64 Oxford: OUP, 1972.

would survive for just two days more than another would be preferred. McKie et al. acknowledge this, but point out that Harris's insistence upon treating all needy patients equally means that the patient who would survive for 30 years if treated, and the patient who would survive for two days if treated, would be regarded as equally deserving of that treatment. Is the Harris–McKie debate another example of utility versus absolutism? On the basis of the former, at least the traditional way of looking at utilitarianism, some pretty ruthless decisions could be made about healthcare rationing. So, for example, the denial of treatment to anyone over 75 years old would provide more resources for younger people who would be in the majority. The utilitarian response would be that such a rule would morally impoverish society, leaving many people to suffer a painful and distressing old age, a spectacle which, far from being good for the majority of younger people, would make them positively unhappy.

Both Harris and McKie agree that any form of resource allocation which creates social divisiveness is wrong. But if the wider issues relating to health are examined, there is a great deal of evidence that poverty and health are inextricably linked. See, for example, Black et al., *Inequalities in Health: The Black Report*.[65] The latter produced evidence on the link between health and wealth, and reported that life expectancy at birth was seven years higher in social class one (professional) than in social class five (manual). There is therefore a cogent argument in favour of a redistribution of health resources to redress the imbalance. Furthermore, it points up the fact that 'healthcare' decisions are strongly linked to economic policy and social justice.

THINK POINT

When we are looking at allocation of healthcare resources at a 'macro' level, is a utilitarian approach appropriate, whereas it is not appropriate at the 'micro' level of looking at the treatment of individual patients?

Summary of key points

1   Medical ethics particularly highlights the issue of universalisation and how far this can be said to apply when, even within one society, there are many social and cultural attitudes.
2   One of the key distinctions in ethics is between consequentialist ethical theories and those that support absolute duties.
3   The doctor–patient relationship is traditionally said to give rise to special ethical obligations relating to doing good and not doing harm. However, it is questionable as to how far this is the case.
4   Another key distinction which is particularly pertinent in the context of medical ethics is the distinction between treating patients paternalistically and respecting their right to autonomous decision-making, although it is arguable that there is room within medical ethics for both these concepts.
5   Justice is a key ethical concept and is particularly relevant to the allocation of healthcare resources.
6   When we are looking at patients and doing what is best for them, are we really only concerned with 'persons' and what exactly is a 'person'?

---

65 Harmondsworth: Penguin, 1982.

Further reading

Blackburn, S, *Being Good: A Short Introduction to Ethics*, Oxford: Oxford University Press, 2001.

Campbell, AV, *The Body in Bioethics*, Abingdon: Routledge-Cavendish, 2009.

Hope, T, *Medical Ethics: A Very Short Introduction*, Oxford: Oxford University Press, 2005.

Miola, J, *Medical Ethics and Medical Law: A Symbiotic Relationship*, Oxford: Hart, 2007.

Pence, GE, *Classic Cases in Medical Ethics: Accounts of the Cases that have Shaped and Defined Medical Ethics, with Philosophical, Legal, and Historical Backgrounds*, New York: McGraw-Hill Higher Education, 2008.

Singer, P, *Writings on an Ethical Life*, London: Fourth Estate, 2000.

Chapter 2

Healthcare in England and Wales

2.1 Background

2.1.1 The international framework

The UK is committed under international law to the promotion of its citizens' health and the prevention of disease. The key aspirations to this end are contained in the European Social Charter of 1961 (as revised in 1996), which is an offshoot from the scheme of political and civil rights found in the 1950 European Convention for the Protection of Human Rights and Fundamental Freedoms and is overseen by the same body, the Council of Europe. Articles 11 and 13 of the Social Charter provide as follows:

Article 11 – The right to protection of health

With a view to ensuring the effective exercise of the right to protection of health, the Parties undertake, either directly or in co-operation with public or private organisations, to take appropriate measures designed *inter alia*:

1   to remove as far as possible the causes of ill health;
2   to provide advisory and educational facilities for the promotion of health and the encouragement of individual responsibility in matters of health;
3   to prevent as far as possible epidemic, endemic and other diseases, as well as accidents.

Article 13 – The right to social and medical assistance

With a view to ensuring the effective exercise of the right to social and medical assistance, the Parties undertake:

1   to ensure that any person who is without adequate resources and who is unable to secure such resources either by his own efforts or from other sources, in particular by benefits under a social security scheme, be granted adequate assistance, and, in case of sickness, the care necessitated by his condition;
2   to ensure that persons receiving such assistance shall not, for that reason, suffer from a diminution of their political or social rights . . .

2.1.2 National provisions

Unlike the position in respect of the European Convention on Human Rights, the failure by a state to protect these 'social rights' will not allow one of its citizens to complain to the European Court of Human Rights. However, the broad commitment on this country's part to the goal of access to healthcare for all is clear, and, in fact, predates the salient international law: it is found in the existence and operation of the National Health Service (NHS), which was established in 1948. They key feature of the NHS is that it was set up, and remains, free at the point of use. The current scheme is set out in the National Health Service Act 2006:

National Health Service Act 2006 c. 41

1 Secretary of State's duty to promote health service

1   The Secretary of State must continue the promotion in England of a comprehensive health service designed to secure improvement –
    a   in the physical and mental health of the people of England, and
    b   in the prevention, diagnosis and treatment of illness.

2   The Secretary of State must for that purpose provide or secure the provision of services in accordance with this Act.

3   The services so provided must be free of charge except in so far as the making and recovery of charges is expressly provided for by or under any enactment, whenever passed.

1A Duty as to improvement in quality of services

1   The Secretary of State must exercise the functions of the Secretary of State in relation to the health service with a view to securing continuous improvement in the quality of services provided to individuals for or in connection with –

a   the prevention, diagnosis or treatment of illness, or

b   the protection or improvement of public health.

2   In discharging the duty under subsection (1) the Secretary of State must, in particular, act with a view to securing continuous improvement in the outcomes that are achieved from the provision of the services.

3   The outcomes relevant for the purposes of subsection (2) include, in particular, outcomes which show –

a   the effectiveness of the services,

b   the safety of the services, and

c   the quality of the experience undergone by patients.

4   In discharging the duty under subsection (1), the Secretary of State must have regard to the quality standards prepared by NICE under section 234 of the Health and Social Care Act 2012.

1B Duty as to the NHS Constitution

1   In exercising functions in relation to the health service, the Secretary of State must have regard to the NHS Constitution.

2   In this Act, 'NHS Constitution' has the same meaning as in Chapter 1 of Part 1 of the Health Act 2009 (see section 1 of that Act).

1C Duty as to reducing inequalities

In exercising functions in relation to the health service, the Secretary of State must have regard to the need to reduce inequalities between the people of England with respect to the benefits that they can obtain from the health service.

1D Duty as to promoting autonomy

1   In exercising functions in relation to the health service, the Secretary of State must have regard to the desirability of securing, so far as consistent with the interests of the health service –

a   that any other person exercising functions in relation to the health service or providing services for its purposes is free to exercise those functions or provide those services in the manner that it considers most appropriate, and

b   that unnecessary burdens are not imposed on any such person.

2   If, in the case of any exercise of functions, the Secretary of State considers that there is a conflict between the matters mentioned in subsection (1) and the discharge by the Secretary of State of the duties under section 1, the Secretary of State must give priority to the duties under that section.

1E Duty as to research

In exercising functions in relation to the health service, the Secretary of State must promote –

a   research on matters relevant to the health service, and

b   the use in the health service of evidence obtained from research.

1F Duty as to education and training

1 The Secretary of State must exercise the functions of the Secretary of State under any relevant enact-ment so as to secure that there is an effective system for the planning and delivery of education and training to persons who are employed, or who are considering becoming employed, in an activity which involves or is connected with the provision of services as part of the health service in England.

2 Any arrangements made with a person under this Act for the provision of services as part of that health service must include arrangements for securing that the person co-operates with the Secre-tary of State in the discharge of the duty under subsection (1) (or, where a Special Health Authority is discharging that duty by virtue of a direction under section 7, with the Special Health Authority).

3 In subsection (1), '*relevant enactment*' means –

a section 63 of the Health Services and Public Health Act 1968,

b this Act,

c the Health and Social Care Act 2008,

d the Health Act 2009, and

e the Health and Social Care Act 2012.

1G Secretary of State's duty as to reporting on and reviewing treatment of providers

1 The Secretary of State must, within one year of the passing of the Health and Social Care Act 2012, lay a report before Parliament on the treatment of NHS healthcare providers as respects any matter, including taxation, which might affect their ability to provide healthcare services for the purposes of the NHS or the reward available to them for doing so.

2 The report must include recommendations as to how any differences in the treatment of NHS health-care providers identified in the report could be addressed.

3 The Secretary of State must keep under review the treatment of NHS healthcare providers as respects any such matter as is mentioned in subsection (1).

4 In this section –

a '*NHS healthcare providers*' means persons providing or intending to provide healthcare services for the purposes of the NHS, and

b '*healthcare services for the purposes of the NHS*' has the same meaning as in Part 3 of the Health and Social Care Act 2012.

2 Secretary of State's general power

1 The Secretary of State may –

a provide such services as he considers appropriate for the purpose of discharging any duty imposed on him by this Act, and

b do anything else which is calculated to facilitate, or is conducive or incidental to, the discharge of such a duty. . . .

In addition to the formal legislation, there is also policy documentation on healthcare provision, most notably the NHS Constitution:

The NHS Constitution[1]

1 The NHS provides a comprehensive service, available to all irrespective of gender, race, disability, age, sexual orientation, religion, belief, gender reassignment, pregnancy and maternity or marital or civil

---

1 London: DoH, 2010, www.dh.gov.uk.

partnership status. The service is designed to diagnose, treat and improve both physical and mental health. It has a duty to each and every individual that it serves and must respect their human rights. At the same time, it has a wider social duty to promote equality through the services it provides and to pay particular attention to groups or sections of society where improvements in health and life expectancy are not keeping pace with the rest of the population.

2   Access to NHS services is based on clinical need, not an individual's ability to pay. NHS services are free of charge, except in limited circumstances sanctioned by Parliament.

3   The NHS aspires to the highest standards of excellence and professionalism – in the provision of high-quality care that is safe, effective and focused on patient experience; in the people it employs, and in the support, education, training and development they receive; in the leadership and management of its organisations; and through its commitment to innovation and to the promotion, conduct and use of research to improve the current and future health and care of the population. Respect, dignity, compassion and care should be at the core of how patients and staff are treated not only because that is the right thing to do but because patient safety, experience and outcomes are all improved when staff are valued, empowered and supported.

4   The NHS aspires to put patients at the heart of everything it does. It should support individuals to promote and manage their own health. NHS services must reflect, and should be coordinated around and tailored to, the needs and preferences of patients, their families and their carers. Patients, with their families and carers, where appropriate, will be involved in and consulted on all decisions about their care and treatment. The NHS will actively encourage feedback from the public, patients and staff, welcome it and use it to improve its services.

5   The NHS works across organisational boundaries and in partnership with other organisations in the interest of patients, local communities and the wider population. The NHS is an integrated system of organisations and services bound together by the principles and values reflected in the Constitution. The NHS is committed to working jointly with other local authority services, other public sector organisations and a wide range of private and voluntary sector organisations to provide and deliver improvements in health and well being.

6   The NHS is committed to providing best value for taxpayers' money and the most effective, fair and sustainable use of finite resources. Public funds for healthcare will be devoted solely to the benefit of the people that the NHS serves.

7   The NHS is accountable to the public, communities and patients that it serves. The NHS is a national service funded through national taxation, and it is the Government which sets the framework for the NHS and which is accountable to Parliament for its operation. However, most decisions in the NHS, especially those about the treatment of individuals and the detailed organisation of services, are rightly taken by the local NHS and by patients with their clinicians. The system of responsibility and accountability for taking decisions in the NHS should be transparent and clear to the public, patients and staff. The Government will ensure that there is always a clear and up-to-date statement of NHS accountability for this purpose.

The NHS is a vast public healthcare system (the largest organisation in Europe), as the following statistics illustrate: in 2002/03 total expenditure was £55.8 billion; in 2007/08 it was £102 billion; in 2008/09 £110 billion and in 2015/16 it was £116.4 billion. Expenditure therefore more than doubled in the 12 years from 2002/2003. Nevertheless, the NHS has remained the focus of continued and deeply felt public concern and debate, and the service has, from time to time, been the subject of important reforms. The major controversies have centred on achieving accountability within the NHS in relation to cost of provision and quality of care.

An issue that has recently generated debate is the question of 'top-up' payments to pay for drugs that are not available on the NHS because of cost. The NHS decided that it would be possible for patients in this situation to continue to receive their normal NHS care but pay for the particular drug or drugs not funded by the NHS.[2] A lot of the controversy is generated by the fact that usually these are cancer drugs. Emily Jackson discusses some of the arguments for and against this. For example, in favour of top-ups is the argument that people are entitled to the NHS care anyway and it seems churlish to deny them this if they want to pay something extra. The argument against points to the creation of a two-tier health service, one for the poor and one for the better-off. Jackson concludes that with the current developments in pharmaceuticals, top-ups are inevitable, but she describes as 'frankly absurd' the proposal that one way of dealing with the distastefulness of differential treatments being provided on the same hospital ward is to deliver the treatments on separate sites.[3] Jackson is surely right here, given that most of these patients will be seriously ill and this sort of fragmented care cannot be good therapy. How far she is right in saying that top-ups are going to be an inevitable feature of the NHS remains to be seen.

We shall next give a little more detail of the structure of the NHS and will then be looking at some of the regulatory mechanisms which have been set up in order to ensure that the NHS delivers both efficient and high-quality care, and how professional regulation operates. The main focus of the remainder of the chapter, however, will be on how far, in law, the individual citizen enjoys a right to obtain the particular treatment he needs.

THINK POINT

Later in this chapter we look at judicial review cases where patients have challenged the health-care decisions within the NHS. Consider now how a patient might be successful within the legal confines of a judicial review action.

2.2 Structure of healthcare in the UK

2.2.1 National Health Service

In economic terms, healthcare as a commodity has the clear potential for generating an anti-competitive market situation, given that the demand for services is in the hands of the same profession (doctors making patient referrals) as is responsible for its supply.

In a drive to make the NHS more competitive and better serve the interests of patients, under John Major the Conservative Government had experimented with an 'internal market' within the health service. Under this system (set out in the National Health Service and Community Care Act 1990) NHS management and funding were organised on the principle of separating the 'purchasers' and 'providers' of care. The former were local health authorities and GP fund-holders (it should be noted that GPs are not employees of the NHS, but are self-employed contractors), responsible for assessing the health needs of their local populations or patients and for purchasing the best possible care for them. Providers, such as hospitals, ambulance and community services, were intended to compete among each other for 'contracts' with purchasers to provide the required care services.

---

2 See, eg: www.telegraph.co.uk/health, 12 May 2009.
3 Jackson, E, 'Top-up payments for expensive cancer drugs: rationing, fairness and the NHS' (2010) 73(3) MLR 399.

However, on assuming office in 1997, the incoming Labour Government quickly signalled its intent to introduce major changes into the NHS. These were highlighted in the Government White Paper, *The New NHS: Modern, Dependable*, Cm 3807.[4] The Labour Government was committed to abolishing the internal market and replacing it with a system of integrated care based on partnerships between NHS bodies and other local agencies. However, that is not to say that the Government was not keen to decentralise the NHS where it could, and proposed the setting up of NHS Foundation Trusts to be run by local managers, staff and members of the public. The intention was to free up the efficient trusts from over-regulation, and they were set up by the Health and Social Care (Community Health and Standards) Act 2003. Following the election of a Conservative Government in May 2010, more change was proposed, culminating in the Health and Social Care Act 2012 (HSCA), which came into force in April 2013.

The HSCA is a further step along the road leading to the NHS operating as a market player. The Department of Health justified further reforms as follows.

Health and Social Care Act 2012, overview factsheet[5]

Case for change

1   The Government is committed to the NHS's founding principles. However, there is a broad consensus that standing still will not protect the NHS. Modernisation is essential for three main reasons.

2   Rising demand and treatment costs. The pressures on the NHS are increasing, in keeping with health systems across the world. Demand is growing rapidly as the population ages and long term conditions become more common; more sophisticated and expensive treatment options are becoming available. The cost of medicines is growing by over £600m per year.

3   Need for improvement. At its best, the NHS is world leading, but there are important areas where the NHS falls behind those of other major European countries. If we had cancer survival rates at the average in Europe, we would save 5,000 lives a year.

4   State of the public finances. Whilst the Government has protected the NHS budget, this is still among the tightest funding settlements the NHS has ever faced. Simply doing the same things in the same way will no longer be affordable in future.

Key legislative changes

5   The provisions in the Act are designed to meet these challenges, by making the NHS more responsive, efficient and accountable. They draw on the evidence and experience of 20 years of NHS reform.

6   Clinically led commissioning (Part 1). The Act puts clinicians in charge of shaping services, enabling NHS funding to be spent more effectively. Previously clinicians in many areas were frustrated by negotiating with primary care trusts to get the right services for their patients. Supported by the NHS Commissioning Board, new clinical commissioning groups will now directly commission services for their populations.

7   Provider regulation to support innovative services (Parts 3 and 4). The Act enshrines a fair playing field in legislation for the first time. This will enable patients to be able to choose services which best meet their needs, including from charity or independent sector providers, as long as they meet NHS costs. Providers, including NHS foundation trusts, will be free to innovate to deliver quality services. Monitor will be established as a specialist regulator to protect patients' interests.

8   Greater voice for patients (Part 5). The Act establishes new Healthwatch patient organisations locally and nationally to drive patient involvement across the NHS.

---

4 London: TSO, 1997, and *Executive Summary*, London: DoH, 1997.
5 London: DoH, June 2012, www.gov.uk/government publications.

9   New focus for public health (Parts 1 and 2). The Act provides the underpinnings for Public Health England, a new body to drive improvements in the public's health.

10 Greater accountability locally and nationally (Parts 1 and 5). The Act sets out clear roles and responsibilities, whilst keeping Ministers' ultimate responsibility for the NHS. It limits political micro-management and gives local authorities a new role to join up local services.

11 Streamlined arm's-length bodies (Parts 7–10). The Act removes unnecessary tiers of management, releasing resources to the frontline. It also places NICE and the Information Centre in primary legislation.

The HSCA came into force in April 2013 and the following guidance was issued by the Department of Health.[6]

The health and care system explained

The new health and care system becomes fully operational from 1 April to deliver the ambitions set out in the Health and Social Care Act. NHS England, Public Health England, the NHS Trust Development Authority and Health Education England will take on their full range of responsibilities.

Locally, clinical commissioning groups – made up of doctors, nurses and other professionals – will buy services for patients, while local councils formally take on their new roles in promoting public health. Health and wellbeing boards will bring together local organisations to work in partnership and Healthwatch will provide a powerful voice for patients and local communities.

The role of the Department of Health in the new system

The Department of Health's purpose is to help people live better for longer. We lead, shape and fund health and care in England, making sure people have the support, care and treatment they need, with the compassion, respect and dignity they deserve. The new and changing health and care organisations work together with the Department to achieve this common purpose.

We enable health and social care bodies to deliver services according to national priorities and work with other parts of government to achieve this. We set objectives and budgets and hold the system to account on behalf of the Secretary of State.

The Secretary of State for Health has ultimate responsibility for ensuring the whole system works together to meet the needs of patients and the public and reflect their experiences.

What the changes to the health and care system mean for patients and local communities

Most people do not notice any immediate difference to how they get the care they need: they will still contact their GP when unwell, or their local council with ongoing social care needs, and they will continue to receive healthcare free at the point of need just as before. However, some important underlying changes have been made to how the health and care system is run.

These changes are about giving local communities and patients more say in the care they receive and doctors and nurses more freedom to shape services to meet people's needs, to improve the quality of the support, care and treatment we all receive.

For instance:

- greater direct control over planning and commissioning means that doctors, nurses and other health and care professionals can better shape what kind of support, care and treatment is available locally

---

6 London: DoH, 26 March 2013, www.gov.uk/governmentpublications.

- more emphasis on preventing illness and helping people stay independent in older age or disability means we can improve everyone's long term health and wellbeing
- more power devolved to local groups and organisations means that communities now have more influence than ever over how their local health services support them
- opening up to a wider range of healthcare providers, including independent and charitable organisations, means that there will be more choice for patients and greater pressure on services to improve.

How health and care organisations will work together locally

- Clinical Commissioning Groups (CCGs) are made up of doctors, nurses and other professionals who use their knowledge of local health needs to plan and buy services for their local community from any service provider that meets NHS standards and costs – these could be NHS hospitals, social enterprises, voluntary organisations or private sector providers. This means better care for patients, designed with knowledge of local services and commissioned in response to their needs.
- Health and wellbeing boards in every area ensure that services work together to respond to communities' needs and priorities. They will involve people and community organisations, including elected representatives, in deciding what services the community needs – this will inform CCGs and local authorities when they commission services.
- Local Healthwatch, which are represented on health and wellbeing boards, give patients and communities a voice in decisions that affect them. Local Healthwatch will report their views and concerns to Healthwatch England so that issues can also be raised at a national level.
- Local authorities commission care and support services and have a new responsibility to protect and improve health and wellbeing. They use their knowledge of their communities to tackle challenges such as smoking, alcohol and drug misuse and obesity. Working together with health and care providers, community groups and other agencies, they prevent ill health by encouraging people to live healthier lives.

How health and care organisations will work together nationally

- NHS England supports NHS services nationally and ensures that money spent on NHS services provides the best possible care for patients. It funds local clinical commissioning groups to commission services for their communities and ensures that they do this effectively. Some specialist services will continue to be commissioned by NHS England centrally where this is most efficient. Working with leading health specialists, NHS England brings together expertise to ensure national standards are consistently in place across the country. Throughout its work it promotes the NHS Constitution and the Constitution's values and commitments.
- Public Health England provides national leadership and expert services to support public health and works with local government, the NHS and other key partners to respond to health protection emergencies.
- The NHS Trust Development Authority supports NHS Trusts to improve so they can take advantage of the benefits of foundation trust status when they are ready.
- Health Education England makes sure the healthcare workforce has the right skills and training to improve the care patients receive. It supports a network of Local Education and Training Boards that plan education and training of the workforce to meet local and national needs.
- The National Institute for Health and Care Excellence (NICE) provides guidance to help health and social care professionals deliver the best possible care for patients based on the best available evidence. NICE involves patients, carers and the public in the development of its guidance and other products.
- The National Institute for Health Research (NIHR) and its clinical research networks form a health research system in which the NHS supports outstanding individuals, working in world class facilities, conducting leading edge research focused on the needs of patients and the public.

- The Health and Social Care Information Centre supports the health and care system by collecting, analysing and publishing national data and statistical information and will deliver national IT systems and services to support health and care providers.
- NHS Blood and Transplant manages the safe supply of blood to the NHS as well as organ donation and transplants across the UK.
- The NHS Litigation Authority resolves fairly all claims made against its scheme members, helping the NHS to learn from them to improve patient safety.
- The NHS Business Services Authority carries out a range of support services to the NHS, patients and the public, including payments for community pharmacists filling prescriptions and dentists carrying out NHS treatment.

How the interests of people using health and care services are protected

As the new system brings more freedom for those who plan, commission and provide services, new and existing health and care regulators will safeguard the interests of patients and the wider public.

- The Care Quality Commission (CQC) measures whether services meet national standards of quality and safety, ensuring that people are treated with dignity and respect. Healthwatch England works as part of the CQC.
- Monitor protects and promotes the interests of people using health services by making sure that NHS services are effective and offer value for money. Licensing providers of healthcare will be one of the main tools Monitor will use to do this.
- The Health Research Authority works to protect and promote the interests of patients and the public in health research.
- The Medicines and Healthcare Products Regulatory Agency makes sure that medicines and medical devices work and are safe to use.
- The Human Tissue Authority regulates human tissue, such as donated organs, to ensure it is used safely and ethically, and with proper consent.
- The Human Fertilisation and Embryology Authority regulates fertility treatment and the use of embryos in research.
- Most health and social care professionals must be registered with one of the independent regulators, such as the General Medical Council, who help protect patients and public by ensuring that professional standards are met.

Davies argues that these reforms are incompatible with the requirements of accountability for the provision of a public service, and that accountability is undermined in three principal ways. Firstly, it is undermined by the creation of clinical commissioning groups (CCGs) that are not subject to ministerial intervention. Secondly, she argues that the accountability of CCGs themselves is already diminished as they go to private sector organisations for assistance in things such as the commissioning process itself, rather than employing experts. Thirdly, she proposes that because the new system is more heavily regulated, particularly in the field of competition law, some aspects of NHS activity will be taken out of the control of the Department of Health all together.

Davies, ACL, 'This time, it's for real: the Health and Social Care Act 2012'[7]

Creeping privatisation?
During the passage of the Bill through Parliament, a key focus of political and public debate was whether it facilitated or indeed represented the privatisation of the NHS, a claim hotly denied by the government. It

---

7 (2013) 76(3) MLR 564.

is clear that the NHS has not been privatised in the straightforward sense of being transferred from public to private ownership. The NHS Commissioning Board and CCGs are public bodies, and at least initially, the vast majority of the NHS budget will continue to be spent on buying services from NHS providers. The 'privatisation' claim relates instead to the possibility that the Act might encourage greater use of private firms in the NHS, primarily but not exclusively as service providers. Although this is ostensibly a more modest development, opponents fear that the growing involvement of private firms will eventually result in full privatisation of the NHS 'by the back door' without proper public debate. Again, this is highly problematic from the perspective of accountability, not least because there is considerable public opposition to the privatisation of the NHS.

Despite substantial continuity between the 2012 reforms and pre-existing government policy, the Act does contain various elements that may encourage greater private sector involvement. First, the Act makes it much more difficult for commissioners who are opposed to private sector involvement to allow this to influence their commissioning activities. A private provider which is qualified (in that it holds a licence and is willing to provide services at tariff prices) will be able to complain to Monitor as the economic regulator of the NHS if it is excluded from a tendering exercise for the provision of NHS services because such an exclusion would probably breach the commissioner's duties to refrain from anti-competitive practices. And well-informed and assertive patients may be able to vote with their feet: commissioners will not be allowed to deny them the option of using a qualified private provider if it can offer treatment more quickly than the local NHS hospital. Second (subject to the discussion of commissioning support), the Act seeks to give a greater role to GPs in decision-making. While many GPs are passionate supporters of the NHS as a public service, some support a greater role for the private sector and may be able to promote this within their CCGs. More worryingly, some GPs are involved in the running of private firms that supply services to the NHS. This gives rise to a significant concern about conflicts of interest when particular GPs might stand to benefit from their CCG's commissioning decisions. Third, the Act's failure regime may be an indirect encouragement to greater private sector involvement. A number of NHS Trusts and Foundation Trusts are in serious financial difficulties. The Act seeks to facilitate the 'normal' market process of going out of business whilst ensuring that there is continuity in the provision of services to patients. This may make it more likely that providers are allowed to fail, instead of being propped up by emergency funding from the Department of Health. In these circumstances, there is an opportunity for private firms to take over the running of the hospital. There are already a few examples of this.

Nevertheless, there are three important limitations on private sector involvement in NHS provision. Two stem from the Act itself, and the third is more practical. First, the obligation on NHS providers to refrain from anti-competitive practices cuts both ways: while commissioners will be limited in their capacity to favour NHS bodies, they will also be limited in their capacity to favour private firms. NHS providers may need to become more astute in making complaints to Monitor in order to ensure that the playing field is kept level. Second, the tariff pricing regime offers some protection to NHS providers because it prevents private firms from engaging in the predictable but highly damaging strategy of undercutting them on price (which would either lead to reductions in quality or to the destruction of NHS services followed by an increase in private sector prices). Of course, the efficacy of this as a safeguard will depend on how Monitor calculates the tariff and on how extensive it becomes in terms of the services to which tariff prices apply. And third, there are significant barriers to entry into the healthcare market. Although there is a private market for healthcare in the UK, it is dwarfed by the NHS and private firms would have to engage in significant investment in order to increase their involvement. Even taking over a failing NHS hospital – which offers a private firm access to facilities and a workforce – is likely to require a substantial resource commitment.

While much of the public debate focused on the use of private firms to provide services to patients on behalf of the NHS, it is important to note that this is not the only example relevant to claims about 'creeping privatisation'. As discussed above, private firms are also becoming involved in providing 'commissioning support' to CCGs. Even the public sector CSSs being set up by the NHS Commissioning Board are due to be privatised in 2016. As a result, there is already private involvement on the purchasing side and this is likely to increase. Another possible example of 'creeping privatisation' is the removal by the 2012 Act of the limit on the provision of treatment to private patients by NHS Foundation Trusts. Given pressures on the NHS budget, it seems likely that hard-pressed Foundation Trusts will seek to expand their role in treating private patients as a means of generating extra income. While it might be argued that this money would be used to subsidise NHS activities (since Foundation Trusts are not profit-making) and would therefore benefit the NHS, critics fear that it would absorb hospital facilities and distract staff from their core NHS duties. However, it may be more difficult for Foundation Trusts to compete effectively in the private market than some have supposed. As Scott *et al* note, Foundation Trusts have some advantages over their private competitors, notably their ability to treat patients with complex medical needs, but private hospitals score highly in other ways, such as the provision of better 'hotel' services.

To sum up, private sector involvement in the NHS is nothing new, and has remained at relatively low levels because of the substantial practical barriers to market entry in the healthcare sector. However, the 2012 Act has created highly favourable conditions for greater private participation, most obviously through the creation of legal avenues of redress for private firms if commissioners seek to restrict their involvement in the NHS. And because (as argued in the previous section) competition in the NHS is becoming a technical rather than a political matter, it is indeed possible that there may be gradual privatisation in the NHS without proper public debate.

THINK POINT

Do you think that the Health and Social Care Act 2012 is compatible with the NHS Constitution?

2.2.2 The private sector

The private sector is subject to statutory regulation pursuant to the Health and Social Care Act 2008. This provides for the Care Quality Commission, a statutory authority set up under the Act, to operate a system of registration and inspection in respect of private hospitals and residential care homes, and is designed to ensure that patients are offered a suitable standard of care. Moreover, as well as being vulnerable, like their NHS counterparts, to malpractice actions brought in negligence, private hospitals can also be sued for breach of contract.

See Chapter 6 →

2.3 Regulating the quality of healthcare

One perennial concern in relation to the NHS is ensuring that minimum standards are maintained throughout the service in terms of all aspects of provision and care. Clearly, this is also an important way of reducing the expenditure of resources on the fighting and settling of malpractice suits brought by dissatisfied patients (a subject dealt with at length in Chapter 6). In this section, we shall first consider the role of a number of agencies, which oversee and influence the implementation of decision-making within the service at the 'macro level' (although the proliferation of these in themselves undermine the above suggestion that expenditure can be significantly reduced), before moving on to address the mechanisms to regulate and provide redress in the context of individual treatment decisions (the 'micro level'). In respect of the latter, there is the possibility for complaints to be brought by aggrieved patients either through the complaints system of the NHS or, where unprofessional conduct on the part of a particular member of the NHS medical staff is alleged, through the latter's professional licensing body – in the case of a doctor, the General Medical Council (GMC).

2.3.1 The 'macro' level: the role of regulatory bodies

Ironically, at the same time as the NHS has absorbed more and more of the national budget, and successive governments have grappled with trying to make it 'more efficient' and to cut down bureaucracy, there has been a growth in concerns about improving patient 'safety' and setting up risk management procedures which processes inevitably militate against a reduction in costs. In its 1997 White Paper, *The New NHS – Modern, Dependable*, Cm 3807,[8] the Government introduced the concept of 'clinical governance', involving the increased use of risk-management techniques and 'evidence-based medicine' 'to assure and improve clinical standards at local level throughout the NHS'. A central role in this initiative was given to two complementary organisations, the National Institute for Clinical Excellence (NICE), and the Commission for Health Improvement (CHI), whose work has since been subsumed within the portfolio of the Care Quality Commission.

NICE began its work as a Special Health Authority on 1 April 1999, pursuant to the National Institute for Clinical Excellence (Establishment and Constitution) Order 1999, SI 1999/220, and became responsible for disseminating 'best practice' guidance to healthcare professionals working within the NHS. The Institute responded to the inquiry into the Bristol heart surgery scandal, in which it was revealed that inept cardiac surgery on children at a Bristol hospital had led to a significant number of extra deaths and disabilities among patients.[9] The response outlined its role as advising on management of disease, use of technologies, drawing up guidelines in these areas, and advising on clinical audit. The latter is important, as one of the failings highlighted by the Bristol Inquiry was that there was no adequate process to alert the hospital to their worrying levels of poor outcomes and morbidity. A network of other organisations grew up (eg the National Patient Safety Agency, and the National Clinical Assessment Authority) to regulate and to improve standards, described by the Department of Health as 'arm's length' bodies to indicate their degree of independence from the department. However, the plethora of these organisations causes overlap and confusion, and there have been proposals to 'reconfigure' them.[10] Since 1 April 2005, NICE has joined with the Health Development Agency to become the new National Institute for Health and Clinical Excellence (also to be known as NICE) and was re-established under s 232 of the Health and Social Care Act 2012. It is now the National Institute for Health and Care Excellence, to reflect the widening of its remit to include social care, but the acronym 'NICE' remains. NICE has three main functions: it produces evidence-based guidance and advice for health, public health and social care practitioners; develops quality standards and performance metrics for those providing and commissioning health, public health and social care services, and provides information for commissioners, practitioners and managers in the fields of health and social care. NICE uses QALYs to inform its recommendations. See Chapter 1 (1.6).

NICE guidelines can be controversial as the process of approval of, say a new drug, can be lengthy, and, without approval, patients will not receive it. Unsurprisingly, pharmaceutical companies also have an interest in approval by NICE and have challenged refusals, eg *R (on the*

8 London: DoH, 1997.
9 Bristol Royal Infirmary Inquiry, *The Report of the Public Inquiry into Children's Heart Surgery at the Bristol Royal Infirmary 1984–1995: Learning from Bristol*, Cm 5207, London: DoH, 2001 – 'The Kennedy Report'.
10 See *Reconfiguring the Department of Health's Arm's Length Bodies*, London: DoH, 2004.

application of Bristol-Myers Squibb Pharmaceuticals Ltd) v National Institute For Health & Clinical Excellence.[11]

Keith Syrett discusses challenges to NICE decisions by way of judicial review:

Syrett, K, 'Nice work? Rationing, review and the legitimacy problem in the new NHS'[12]

. . . [NICE] may be seen as having two functions. First, it is intended to address the problem of so-called 'postcode prescribing' by reducing 'unacceptable variations in performance and practice' across different regions of the NHS. The controversy which this issue may generate is illustrated by the case of *R v North West Lancashire Health Authority ex p A, D and G*, in which three transsexuals successfully challenged a decision to refuse funding for gender reassignment surgery. It was submitted that 34 out of 41 other authorities made some provision for funding such surgery and that a policy which effectively amounted to a 'blanket ban' in one locality would therefore have the effect that entitlement to treatment would depend upon where the patient lived. The Government's hope is that, by acting as 'a single, national focus for appraisal of significant new and existing interventions' whose recommendations are expected to be followed countrywide, variations – and therefore challenges – of this type will become less frequent as the Institute renders decision-making in the NHS more acceptable by bringing 'greater certainty, greater clarity and greater confidence'.

However, such optimism may be premature because it is clear that NICE has a second role in making 'tough choices' on the allocation of resources. Indeed, notwithstanding assertions to the contrary, the establishment of NICE – especially its technology appraisal function – appears to mark 'the beginning of explicit national rationing' in the NHS. This is significant because it has been powerfully argued that explicit resource allocation decisions are inherently more unstable than decisions which can be presented as based upon clinical necessity, even if these are in reality dictated by resource considerations. The greater visibility of the process thus increases the potential for conflict. This may already be seen in the responses to certain Institute decisions. Refusal to authorise the use of an intervention has been opposed by patients and their representatives. On the other hand, approval has been contested by professionals seeking to preserve their clinical and managerial discretion with the consequence that geographical variations in access to treatment have tended to persist. Elsewhere, patients requiring other services have lost out as resources are diverted to fund 'NICE-approved' interventions. The controversy generated has been manifested in media campaigns, Parliamentary debate and threats of legal action.

The range of interests which may be affected by NICE determinations renders some level of opposition a near-certainty.

In addition to the workings of the above organisations, it should also be noted that a statutory duty to achieve quality in healthcare is imposed directly upon NHS bodies by s 45 of the Health and Social Care (Community Health and Standards) Act 2003 (replacing s 18 of the Health Act 1999).

The Freedom of Information Act 2000 is also relevant to 'macro' level regulation. This came into force on 1 January 2005 and provides for a public right of access to information held by public bodies. Information for which disclosure is not provided could be obtained under the Act, but note that (*inter alia*) a request for information can be refused if it would be disproportionately expensive to answer (s 12), the request is vexatious (s 14) and there is a long list of exemptions which include commercial interest, that the information relates to health and safety or is confidential, or if the information is accessible by other means. There is also a public interest exemption.[13]

See Chapter 5 ➡

---

11 [2009] EWHC 2722 (Admin).
12 [2002] 10 Med L Rev 1.
13 See Part II of the Act, and See Ch 5 for a discussion of public interest considerations and what 'confidential information' might be.

2.3.2 The 'micro' level: NHS complaints and discipline

A system to deal with complaints brought by patients in respect of their treatment is an important alternative to formal litigation in the courts. The current system (in place since 2009) has two stages. The first stage, known as local resolution, involves complaining to the hospital or trust and getting hold of a copy of the complaints procedure. NHS organisations have a complaints manager designated to deal with these. If the patient is still not satisfied then the matter can be referred to the Parliamentary and Health Service Ombudsman, who is independent of the NHS and government. Officers from the Patient Advice and Liaison Service (PALS) are available in all hospitals. They offer confidential advice, support and information on health-related matters to patients, their families and their carers. The Independent Complaints Advocacy Service (ICAS) is a national service that supports people who wish to make a complaint about their NHS care or treatment.

It may become apparent as the result of a complaint (or, indeed, in the course of a malpractice action) that the conduct of a particular medical professional is deserving of censure. In this regard, there are two parallel systems for disciplining the professional concerned. First, disciplinary procedures internal to the NHS may be invoked. However, with regard to these there has been much disquiet because of their time-consuming and costly nature (an estimated £40 million caused just by delay) and, in consequence, a new national disciplinary framework was devised which came into force on 1 June 2005.[14]

See Chapter 6

It should also be noted that there is a duty of candour that is contained in the Health and Social Care Act 2008 (Regulated Activities) Regulations 2014.[15] The duty applies to all healthcare professionals, and is not confined to medical treatment but also to those providing care e.g. in a nursing home. The duty means that when something has gone wrong with the patient's treatment or care, they must tell the patient it has happened; apologise; if there is a remedy or support to put matters right this should be offered; and an explanation of the short and long term effects of what has happened (in all these cases, where appropriate, communication with their carer, patient advocate or family). The duty also extends to being honest with colleagues, employers and external bodies, including a duty to co-operate in investigations. The apology does not mean an admission of legal liability.

2.3.3 Professional regulation and discipline

Of even greater consequence for professionals, their conduct may be investigated by the responsible governing and licensing body for their profession. In respect of doctors this is the GMC,[16] and the equivalent body for nurses is the Nursing and Midwifery Council (NMC) (there are also two general regulatory bodies for healthcare professionals: the Professional Standards Authority for Health and Social Care and the Health and Care Professions Council, which regulate 15 other bodies of healthcare professionals such as physiotherapists – a further extension of government's apparently insatiable appetite for regulatory bodies in the field of healthcare, this time provoked by the Harold Shipman case). Self-regulatory organisations have a long tradition of enunciating and administering the standards of professional practice to which their members are required to adhere, and their power to discipline and, ultimately, to 'strike off' the register the names of those found guilty of serious misconduct has been codified in statute. In the case of the GMC, the relevant provisions are found in Pt V of the Medical Act 1983 (as amended).

Erasure from the register is clearly a very serious sanction for professionals, in that, henceforth (unless they succeed at some future date in having their names restored to it), they will be

---

14 See *Maintaining High Professional Standards in the Modern NHS*, London: DoH, 2005.
15 SI 2014/2936.
16 See: www.gmc-uk.org.

deprived of their professional livelihoods. In so far as a doctor is unhappy with the decision of the GMC in this matter, he or she may appeal (pursuant to s 40 of the 1983 Act) to the Privy Council. A case in point, in which the meaning of 'serious professional misconduct' under s 36 of the Act was considered, is that of *McCandless v GMC*:[17]

McCandless v GMC

Lord Hoffmann: Dr David McCandless, a general practitioner in Deeside, appeals against a determination and direction of the Professional Conduct Committee of the General Medical Council. At a hearing on 16 March 1995 the Committee found that he was guilty of serious professional misconduct and directed that his name should be erased from the Register of Medical Practitioners.

The charges alleged errors in his diagnoses of three patients and failure to refer them to hospital. Two subsequently died and the other was found on her eventual admission to hospital to be seriously ill. It is not necessary to go further into the details because Mr Mitting, who appeared for Dr McCandless, accepted that the Committee's findings of fact were not open to any material dispute. He also accepted that in each case Dr McCandless had been negligent. The chairman of the Committee gave the following brief reasons for its finding that he had been guilty of serious professional misconduct:

> Dr McCandless, the Committee take a very serious view of the evidence which they have heard about the poor standard of medical care which you provided to all three patients in this case. The care which you provided fell deplorably short of the standard which patients are entitled to expect from their general practitioners.

Mr Mitting submits that these reasons reveal an error of law by the Committee. He says that the Committee applied the wrong test for what amounts to serious professional misconduct. It thought that it was enough that the treatment given to the three patients fell 'deplorably short' of the standard which would reasonably be expected. Mr Mitting says that poor treatment is not enough. The doctor may nevertheless have been doing his best. He may have been overworked or just not particularly good at the job. But 'serious professional misconduct' means, he said, conduct which is morally blameworthy. This cannot be determined simply by deciding whether the treatment measured up to an objective standard. One has to look at why the doctor gave the treatment which he did. If it fell short of a reasonable standard because he was, for example, too lazy or drunk to examine the patient properly, then he would be guilty of misconduct. But not if he made an honest mistake.

Their Lordships think that some support can be found for Mr Mitting's submission in old cases on the meaning of 'infamous conduct in a professional respect' – the words which were used in 19th century Medical Acts and which continued to be used until replaced by the words 'serious professional misconduct' in the Medical Act 1969...

[However,] ... the authorities on the old wording do not speak with one voice and ... they are of little assistance in the interpretation of the new. Secondly, although there remains the single disciplinary offence now styled 'serious professional misconduct', the possible penalties available to the Committee, which used to be confined to the ultimate sanction of erasure, have been extended to include suspension and the imposition of conditions upon practice. This suggests that the offence was intended to include serious cases of negligence. Thirdly, the public has higher expectations of doctors and members of other self-governing professions. Their governing bodies are under a corresponding duty to protect the public against the genially incompetent as well as the deliberate wrongdoers. Fourthly, the meaning of the new wording has been authoritatively stated by this Board in *Doughty v General Dental Council* [1988] AC 164, p 173 in objective terms:

> ... judged by proper professional standards in the light of the objective facts about the individual patients ... the dental treatments criticised as unnecessary [were] treatments that no dentist of reasonable skill exercising reasonable care would carry out.

---

17 [1996] 1 WLR 167.

> This test appears to their Lordships to be, *mutatis mutandis*, equally applicable to treatment by doctors . . .
> Once it is accepted that seriously negligent treatment can amount to serious professional misconduct, then it seems to their Lordships that the appeal must fail. The eminent medical practitioners who sat on the Committee came to the conclusion that Dr McCandless' treatment of his three patients fell deplorably short of the standard to which patients are entitled to expect from general practitioners. In the circumstances, it is scarcely surprising that they concluded that Dr McCandless was guilty of serious professional misconduct. Their Lordships can see no basis for interfering with that conclusion. Nor can they see any ground for interfering with the Committee's decision that the offences merited the penalty of erasure from the register.

Subsequently, in *Roylance v GMC (No 2)*,[18] it was confirmed that, provided there was 'a link with the profession of medicine', serious professional misconduct could extend beyond clinical conduct (that is, the doctor's own carrying out of medical work). The appellant was the chief executive officer of the NHS Trust in Bristol at the centre of the Bristol heart surgery scandal, with responsibility for the particular hospital at which the incompetent cardiac surgeons worked. The GMC struck him off after finding that he had been made aware of concerns about the mortality rate in paediatric cardiac surgery at the hospital and had failed to take adequate action to prevent the surgeons concerned from carrying out operations.

In *John Walker-Smith v General Medical Council*,[19] it was held that the Fitness to Practise Panel of the GMC had erred in making a finding of serious professional misconduct and that Walker-Smith's name should be removed from the register of medical practitioners. The doctor concerned had been undertaking what were described by him as 'investigations' on children who had been referred to the hospital with symptoms of intestinal disease. He subsequently published a paper suggesting a link between the triple vaccine for measles, mumps and rubella (MMR) and the intestinal conditions and autism. The GMC's allegation was that this was a piece of research for which he did not have ethics committee approval and that the children had received treatment that was not clinically appropriate. Mitting J found that the panel's decision was flawed in that it did not address the expert evidence put forward on behalf of the doctor, and, indeed that the panel had misstated it. Furthermore, the reasons given for the panel's decision did not justify its conclusion. Both the finding of serious misconduct and the decision to erase from the register were quashed. Interestingly, the judge did go on to say that there was no respectable body of opinion that supported a link between the MMR vaccine and intestinal disease and autism.

In *R (On the application of Campbell) v GMC*[20] the issue was whether mitigating factors were relevant to a decision as to whether conduct amounted to serious misconduct. The Court of Appeal held that such an approach was flawed; personal mitigating factors were only relevant to the second stage of the procedure, ie the appropriate sanction to be imposed.

In *Luise Schodlok v GMC*,[21] the Court of Appeal allowed an appeal from a High Court decision upholding a fitness to practise panel's decision that her fitness to practise was impaired due to four findings of serious misconduct and six findings of non-serious misconduct. The appeal was successful because the panel seemed to have taken into account all the findings of misconduct despite that fact that, taking into account the GMC's publication *Good Medical Practice* (May 2006 edition), and the guidance in the Privy Council case of *Roylande v GMC*,[22] only serious misconduct could give rise to an impairment.

---

18 [2000] 1 AC 311.
19 [2012] EWHC 503 (Admin).
20 [2005] 1 WLR 3488.
21 [2015] EWCA Civ 769.
22 [2000] 1 AC 311.

In 2002 the Government announced a number of reforms to the GMC, including a new role of regularly revalidating a doctor's licence to practise (to ensure that his practice remains up to date and of a high standard).[23] The GMC has subsequently set up a new system of dealing with complaints, the key feature of which is the separation of functions. The proposal is that the fitness to practise procedures will be divided into two stages: investigation and adjudication. This is to avoid the traditional criticism of certain professional regulatory bodies who could be accused of acting as police, prosecution and judiciary when dealing with their own members. There is also a proposed new validation procedure whereby doctors will require a licence to practise which will be renewed every five years (due to operate from 2012). The new procedures were due to come into force in April 2005. However, the revalidation procedure is based upon fitness to practise in the sense of being medically competent and does not specifically deal with non-clinical misconduct. In consequence, this issue was highlighted by the publication of the Fifth Report on the Harold Shipman case[24] and, following publication, it was decided that the government's Chief Medical Officer should review the new procedures and the April 2005 launch was postponed. The Health and Social Care Act 2008 set up the Office of the Health Professions Adjudicator (OHPA) which was to be the new, independent body set up to ensure clear separation between the investigation of fitness to practise cases by the GMC and the process of determining whether a professional's 'fitness to practise' is impaired. In December 2010, following a consultation exercise, the new Government decided not to proceed with OHPA and to repeal the relevant legislative provisions.

THINK POINT

Do you agree that, regardless of whatever method is appropriate, it is right to separate the functions of a professional body into investigatory and adjudicatory?

Like other employees of the NHS, doctors and other healthcare professionals can be disciplined by their employer under the express and implied terms of their contracts. The Supreme Court case of *Chhabra v West London Mental Health NHS Trust*[25] concerned this issue of contractual terms when considering disciplinary action against a doctor. The appellant doctor was employed by the trust as a consultant psychiatrist. It was alleged that she breached patient confidentiality by discussing patients and reading medical reports on a train. Under the trust's disciplinary policy, which implemented a national framework, a case manager appointed a case investigator to prepare a report. The doctor was concerned that the Human Resources (HR) Director should not be involved in the investigation, and the trust gave an undertaking that he would not be. Despite this, the investigator communicated with the HR Director and made changes, suggested by him, to her report. After reading the report, the case manager proposed to convene a conduct panel to consider a charge of gross misconduct on the basis of matters covered in the report and another allegation that had not been part of the investigator's remit. The doctor objected and a report into the further allegation was made, which exonerated the doctor. The SC held that while it was within the case manager's discretion to put such a matter before the conduct panel, the irregularities here were such that there was no evidence to support gross misconduct. In consequence there was a breach of contract in two respects. Firstly, the trust had breached its contract with the doctor when the HR Director had continued to

23 See *Reform of the GMC: A Paper for Consultation*, London: DoH, 2002.
24 *The Fifth Report, Safeguarding Patents: Lessons from the Past – Proposals for the Future*, London: Shipman Inquiry, 2004.
25 [2013] UKSC 80.

take part in the investigation and, secondly, the trust's actions constituted a breach of the obligation of good faith.

2.3.4 The role of criminal law

Of course, the disciplinary mechanisms with which we have so far been concerned operate alongside, and independently of, the sanctions provided by the legal system in relation to doctors and other persons who, by their conduct, inflict harm upon others. In Chapters 3 and 6 we shall be focusing upon the civil remedies, in the torts of battery and negligence respectively, available to patients in relation to maltreatment they receive during medical care. However, it is important to note that the criminal law may also be of relevance in some cases. In this regard, where a patient is injured, or simply handled non-consensually, a doctor could in theory be prosecuted for an offence, either in battery at common law, or under the Offences Against the Person Act 1861. Where the patient actually dies, then a charge of murder or manslaughter may be brought, depending on the *mens rea* of the doctor. The former charge, in particular, is a possibility in certain cases of euthanasia.

Although it is generally very rare for criminal charges to be preferred against doctors (it usually not thought to be in the public interest for prosecutions to be brought), the fact that ultimately doctors do not belong to any special category of citizen – and must answer for the serious consequences of deficient conduct – was illustrated by the conviction for manslaughter of an anaesthetist in *R v Adomako*:[26]

R v Adomako[27]

Lord Mackay of Clashfern LC: The conviction arose out of the conduct of an eye operation carried out at the Mayday Hospital, Croydon on 4 January 1987. The appellant was, during the latter part of that operation, the anaesthetist in charge of the patient.

The operation was carried out by two surgeons supported by a team of five nurses and a theatre sister. Anaesthesia commenced at about 9.45 am . . .

At approximately 11.05 am a disconnection occurred at the endotracheal tube connection. The supply of oxygen to the patient ceased and this led to cardiac arrest at 11.14 am. During this period the appellant failed to notice or remedy the disconnection.

The appellant first became aware that something was amiss when an alarm sounded on the Dinamap machine, which monitors the patient's blood pressure. From the evidence it appears that some four and a half minutes would have elapsed between the disconnection and the sounding of this alarm. When this alarm sounded the appellant responded in various ways by checking the equipment and by administering atropine to raise the patient's pulse. But at no stage before the cardiac arrest did he check the integrity of the endotracheal tube connection. The disconnection itself was not discovered until after resuscitation measures had been commenced.

For the prosecution it was alleged that the appellant was guilty of gross negligence in failing to notice or respond appropriately to obvious signs that a disconnection had occurred and that the patient had ceased to breathe. In particular the prosecution alleged that the appellant had failed to notice at various stages during the period after disconnection and before the arrest either occurred or became inevitable that the patient's chest was not moving, the dials on the mechanical ventilating machine were not operating, the disconnection in the endo-tracheal tube, that the alarm on the ventilator was not switched on and that the patient was becoming progressively blue. Further the prosecution alleged that the appellant had

---

26 [1994] 5 Med LR 27.
27 [1994] 5 Med LR 27 (Lord Mackay of Clashfern LC, Lords Keith, Goff, Browne-Wilkinson and Woolf).

noticed but failed to understand the correct significance of the fact that during this period the patient's pulse had dropped and the patient's blood pressure had dropped.

Two expert witnesses gave evidence for the prosecution. Professor Payne described that standard of care as 'abysmal' while Professor Adams stated in that in his view a competent anaesthetist should have recognised the signs of disconnection within 15 seconds and that the appellant's conduct amounted to 'a gross dereliction of care'.

On behalf of the appellant it was conceded at his trial that he had been negligent. The issue was therefore whether his conduct was criminal . . .

. . . [I]n my opinion the ordinary principles of the law of negligence apply to ascertain whether or not the defendant has been in breach of a duty of care towards the victim who has died. If such breach of duty is established the next question is whether that breach of duty caused the death of the victim. If so, the jury must go on to consider whether that breach of duty should be characterised as gross negligence and therefore as a crime. This will depend on the seriousness of the breach of duty committed by the defendant in all the circum-stances in which the defendant was placed when it occurred. The jury will have to consider whether the extent to which the defendant's conduct departed from the proper standard of care incumbent upon him, involving as it must have done a risk of death to the patient, was such that it should be judged criminal.

It is true that to a certain extent this involves an element of circularity, but in this branch of the law I do not believe that is fatal to its being correct as a test of how far conduct must depart from accepted stand-ards to be characterised as criminal. This is necessarily a question of degree and an attempt to specify that degree more closely is I think likely to achieve only a spurious precision. The essence of the matter which is supremely a jury question is whether, having regard to the risk of death involved, the conduct of the defend-ant was so bad in all the circumstances as to amount in their judgment to a criminal act or omission . . .

In my view the summing up of the learned judge in the present case was a model of clarity in analysis of the facts and in setting out the law in a manner which was readily comprehensible by the jury. The sum-ming up was criticised in respect of the inclusion of the following passage ([1991] 2 Med LR 291):

> Of course you will understand it is not for every humble man of the profession to have all that great skill of the great men in Harley Street but, on the other hand, they are not allowed to prac-tise medicine in this country unless they have acquired a certain amount of skill. They are bound to show a reasonable amount of skill according to the circumstances of the case, and you have to judge them on the basis that they are skilled men, but not necessarily so skilled as more skill-ful men in the profession, and you can only convict them criminally if, in your judgment, they fall below the standard of skill which is the least qualification which any doctor should have. You should only convict a doctor of causing a death by negligence if you think he did something which no reasonably skilled doctor should have done.

The criticism was particularly of the latter part of this quotation in that it was open to the meaning that if the defendant did what no reasonably skilled doctor should have done it was open to the jury to convict him of causing death by negligence. Strictly speaking this passage is concerned with the statement of a necessary condition for a conviction by preventing a conviction unless that condition is satisfied. It is incorrect to treat it as stating a sufficient condition for conviction. In any event I consider that this passage in the context was making the point forcefully that the defendant in this case was not to be judged by the standard of more skilled doctors but by the standard of a reasonably competent doctor. There were many other passages in the summing up which emphasised the need for a high degree of negligence if the jury were to convict and read in that context I consider that the summing up cannot be faulted. For these rea-sons I am of the opinion that this appeal should be dismissed . . .

[Lords Keith, Goff, Browne-Wilkinson and Woolf agreed.]

In *R v Amit Misra, R v Rajeev Srivastava*[28] two doctors who had been convicted of manslaughter by gross negligence appealed. One of their arguments (the other related to the admission of fresh evidence) was that the offence lacked certainty and therefore was incompatible with Articles 7 and 6 of the European Convention on Human Rights. The Court of Appeal rejected this argument, stating that the requirement for legal certainty of an offence was sufficient rather than absolute certainty and the European Convention had not changed this. The question for the jury to decide was whether the behaviour was grossly negligent and consequently criminal and this was a question of fact.

In *R v Honey Maria Rose*,[29] an optometrist appealed against a conviction of gross negligence manslaughter, following a routine eye test and examination on a seven-year-old boy. Five months after the examination the boy was taken ill and died of acute hydrocephalus. Up until this time his condition was treatable, and the optometrist admitted that her failure to examine the back of the eye was a breach of duty of care. If this had taken place, the evidence was that the swelling of the optic nerve would have been seen, its significance noted and the appropriate referral would have been made. The judge's direction was that the risk of death caused by the failure to conduct a full examination was reasonably foreseeable. The appeal was upheld on the basis that the test of foreseeability in gross negligence manslaughter required proof of a 'serious and obvious risk of death', rather than failure to carry out routine tests, which would have revealed fatal conditions, but where a 'serious and obvious risk of death' was not apparent.

THINK POINT

Should individual practitioners be prosecuted, or is it preferable that, say, the NHS Trust should be liable to a criminal sanction, instead?

2.4 Access to healthcare

2.4.1 Background – scarcity of NHS resources and setting priorities

Demand for NHS resources has always outstripped supply:

Timmins, N, *NHS 50th Anniversary: A History of the NHS*[30]

The new service uncovered a vast well of unmet need. GPs of the time recall women with prolapsed uteruses, who had been unable to afford the hospital treatment, suddenly pouring into the surgery, along with men with huge hernias held in by trusses. Bevan, who had declared the NHS would 'lift the shadow from millions of homes', had been right.

But there was also some abuse as GPs were inundated with people wanting wigs, or free cotton wool for padding, and free surgical spirit and aspirin. 'One would think the people saved up their illness for the first free day', one GP complained and Bevan himself, when the service had been running for 18 months, declared: 'I shudder to think of the ceaseless cascade of medicine which is pouring down British throats at the present time.'

---

28 [2004] EWCA Crim 2375.
29 [2017] EWCA Crim 1168.
30 London: DoH, 1996, p 3.

Nonetheless, the NHS transformed healthcare – and not just for the poor, who were spared the indignity of means tests, but also for the middle classes, who no longer faced the fear of bills. It did so too for doctors. 'I used to charge 1/6d for a consultation,' one Clydeside GP recalled. 'They laid the money on the desk as they came in. It was all rather embarrassing. I used to charge 2/6d to 7/6d for a visit, the highest rate for foremen and undermanagers. We'd send out the bills, but about a quarter would be bad debts and some you simply didn't bill because you knew they couldn't pay. The NHS thankfully got rid of all that.'

In doing so, however, the service instantly faced the first of the great financial crises which were periodically to mark its history. Spending in the first nine months proved two thirds higher than expected. The sea of unmet need, the sheer difficulty of predicting in advance the costs of the new service, the rising expectations it generated and the costs of medical advance had all combined to blow the early budgets.

If this sounds familiar it is because it is the history of health services the world over. Take medical advance. The first antibiotic – penicillin – had become available, for troops, during the war. But the year 1948 saw new types of penicillin developed. Streptomycin, the first drug to successfully tackle tubercular meningitis – TB in the forties was a major scourge – became available. In both Britain and America, other new antibiotics were developed.

Clearly, pressures on NHS resources are not simply a consequence of inefficiencies in the way the service is run (the issue that various governmental reforms have sought to address). Rather, in the light of constant advances in medical technology, they are to be regarded as inherent and inescapable in nature. It might be thought that it is the high-tech procedures and relatively short-term drugs for, say, cancer, that swell the NHS budget. The availability of drugs to treat heart disease, and an ageing population, mean that many people are routinely prescribed these drugs for many years of their lives. Of course, it is not so easy to separate these out because, for example, a heart bypass operation, which is normally very successful, will mean that the patient will subsequently be dependent upon, say, statins that control blood cholesterol for the rest of their lives. On the other hand, a lot of healthcare expenditure will be on routine treatment of, in particular, children and the elderly and is not driven by technology.

However, the NHS Constitution and other policy documents might not contain sufficient detail to confer a set of enforceable rights upon patients. What, then, are the available legal mechanisms through which a patient may challenge the denial of NHS treatment?

2.4.2 Judicial review

Given the public status of the health service, and the constituent bodies within it (that is, health authorities, NHS Trusts, etc), a decision not to provide some given treatment may be susceptible to challenge in public law. This means that such a decision, if viewed as *Wednesbury* unreasonable,[31] can be quashed by the courts. Lord Diplock in *Council of Civil Service Unions v Minister for the Civil Service*,[32] described the power of judicial review in the following terms:

Lord Diplock: It applies to a decision which is so outrageous in its defiance of logic or of accepted moral standards that no sensible person who had applied his mind to the question to be decided could have arrived at it. Whether a decision falls within this category is a question that judges by their training and experience should be well equipped to answer, or else there would be something badly wrong with our judicial system.[33]

---

31 See *Associated Provincial Picture Houses v Wednesbury Corp* [1947] 2 All ER 680.
32 [1985] AC 374.
33 At 410.

The test has been slightly refined since the Human Rights Act 1998 came into force, in as much as, where Convention Rights are engaged, the courts should look at the degree of interference with those rights when deciding to question the exercise of an administrative discretion on grounds of *Wednesbury* unreasonableness.[34]

In the course of a number of actions brought in judicial review, however, the courts have shown themselves to be unwilling to interfere with decisions of NHS bodies in relation to the treatment of individual patients. In so doing, judges have recognised that the NHS has limited resources and that it is not for them to assume the role of organisers and arbiters of hospital waiting lists.

One of the first cases in which patients invoked judicial review in an attempt to assert a direct right to receive specified healthcare was that of *R v Secretary of State for Social Services et al., ex p Hincks and Others*.[35] It concerned the obligation of the Secretary of State to provide medical services under s 3(1) of the National Health Service Act 1977 (now the National Health Service Act 2006) and, in particular, whether it imposed an absolute duty on the Secretary of State to provide services regardless of available funding. The wording of the Act (identical in the 2006 Act) is that he should provide services 'to such extent as he considers necessary to meet all reasonable requirements'. Four people who had been on the waiting list for orthopaedic surgery sought a declaration that the Secretary of State was in breach of his duty when plans for additional orthopaedic services at a hospital could not be carried out because of lack of funding. The argument was that, as the additional services had been halted for financial reasons, it was not open to the Secretary of State to argue that he did not consider the additional services necessary. In refusing the declaration, the Court of Appeal stated that the Secretary of State has to have regard to the money made available to him.

In some cases, the lives of patients can be seen to be at stake:

R v Central Birmingham HA, ex p Walker, R v Secretary of State for Social Services and another, ex p Walker[36]

David Barber Walker was a premature baby who needed a heart operation. He had been cared for in hospital since his birth and was not in any immediate danger. His operation had been postponed on a number of occasions because of a shortage of specially trained nurses in the intensive care unit where he would have to go after the operation. His mother applied for leave to apply for judicial review of the decision to postpone the operation, seeking certiorari to quash the decision to postpone on the ground that it had been arrived at unlawfully and unreasonably, and mandamus to require the authority to carry out the operation. MacPherson J refused to allow the application.

The applicant's appeal to the Court of Appeal (Sir John Donaldson MR, Nicholls LJ and Caulfield J) was dismissed:

Sir John Donaldson MR: It is not for this court, or indeed any court, to substitute its own judgment for the judgment of those who are responsible for the allocation of resources. This court could only intervene where it was satisfied that there was a *prima facie* case, not only of failing to allocate resources in the way in which others would think that resources should be allocated, but of a failure to allocate resources to an extent which was *Wednesbury* unreasonable, if one likes to use the lawyers' jargon, or, in simpler words, which involves a breach of a public law duty ... Even then, of course, the court has to exercise a judicial discretion. It has to take account of all the circumstances of the particular case with which it is concerned.

---

34 See *R v Ministry of Defence, ex p Smith* [1996] 1 All ER 257.
35 (1980) 1 BMLR 93.
36 (1987) 3 BMLR 32.

A later case which considered the meaning of s 3(1) of the NHS Act 1977, and the scope of a health authority's duty to provide medical services, was *R v Sheffield HA, ex p Seale*:

R v Sheffield HA, ex p Seale J[37]

Julie Anne Seale sought in vitro fertilisation treatment from the respondent health authority. She was refused it on the grounds that, at 37 years of age, she was outside the age range within which the authority provided such treatment. The decision was challenged on three heads:

> **Auld J:** The first is illegality. As I understand his submission, it is that as the Secretary of State has given no directions or imposed no limitations on the provision of *in vitro* fertilisation, and it is not for the district health authority, once it has committed itself to providing such a service, to restrict that provision . . . [if there is a chance] of the treatment being effective. . . .
>
> It is not arguable, in my view, that [a district health authority] is bound, simply because it has undertaken to provide such a service, to provide it on demand to any individual patient for whom it may work, regardless of financial and other constraints upon the authority. Accordingly, I reject as unarguable any submission based on illegality here.
>
> In my view it is clear that if the Secretary of State has not limited or given directions as to the way in which such a service, once undertaken, should be provided; the authority providing it is entitled to form a view as to those circumstances and when they justify provision and when they do not.
>
> The second argument . . . [is that the decision] is irrational because it is not founded on any sustainable, clinical approach. . . . I cannot, nor could the court when deciding the matter as a substantive issue, if it came to that, form a view as to the rightness or wrongness of competing medical views on the effective cut-off date for the utility of such treatment. The decision letter does not say that the treatment cannot be effective after the age of 35, but merely that it is 'generally less effective in women aged over 35 years'.
>
> If that is so, can Mr Straker challenge the decision as irrational on the basis that it is absurd to apply the age of 35 years as a blanket cut-off point, taking no account of individual circumstances? His submission is that every case should be considered individually. . . . I cannot say that it is absurd for this authority, acting on advice that the efficacy of this treatment decreases with age and that it is generally less effective after the age of 35, to take that as an appropriate criterion when balancing the need for such a provision against its ability to provide it and all the other services imposed upon it under the legislation.

The application was refused. (On the provision of fertility treatment generally, see further Chapter 7.)

Seale is a useful decision as it shows a slightly less resolute approach being taken to resource allocation issues compared with cases such as *Walker*. Christopher Newdick has commented on the case as follows:

Newdick, C, 'Resource allocation in the NHS'[38]

Although the application was refused on its merits the case distinguishes between 'critical', and other, illnesses. If critical illness necessitates an individual clinical decision of the case the *Wednesbury* test of

---

37 (1994) 25 BMLR 1.
38 (1997) 23 (2–3) Am J Law & Med 291.

> managerial reasonableness is presumably limited to other areas of elective or optional healthcare. Note how uncomfortably this approach to clinical merits sits with *Collier*. This case is useful on its own facts for identifying that some care may fall into a category in which a clinical assessment is necessary. It says nothing however, about the components of such a decision, who is responsible for making it, or where the line should be drawn.

It does not, of course, follow from the fact that the patient may sometimes be entitled to have his or her own circumstances and condition clinically assessed, that treatment need actually be provided. Indeed, as a corollary of the general ethical obligation on doctors to act in their patients' best interests, it may be that in a particular case no doctor will be found who is willing to carry it out, for example, where it involves serious side effects for the patient and is believed to be of little or no therapeutic benefit. Certainly, the fact that the patient, where competent, wishes to receive the treatment will usually be a strong indicator that such treatment is in his best interests. Nevertheless, there will be exceptions, especially where terminal illness has been diagnosed, and claims for treatment brought on behalf of incompetent patients may also present difficulties.

A well-known case, which raised issues of this nature, as well as the question of how far financial considerations should play a part in the deliberations of the treatment provider, was that of *R v Cambridge HA, ex p B (A Minor)*. A ten-year-old girl was refused the resources for further remedial treatment. She was suffering from acute myeloid leukaemia. The doctors responsible for her care believed that no further treatment could be usefully given to her beyond palliative care. Her father sought further medical treatment by chemotherapy with a view to a second bone marrow transplant. Taking into account clinical judgement, the nature of the treatment requested and its very low chances of success (it was described by the doctors as 'experimental'), the health authority declined the father's request. He sought judicial review of the health authority's decision, which was granted by Laws J at first instance. The authority appealed:

R v Cambridge HA, ex p B (A Minor)[39]

> **Sir Thomas Bingham MR:** First, [the judge] took the view that Dr Zimmern as the decision maker had wrongly failed to have regard to the wishes of the patient, as expressed on behalf of the patient by her family. . . .
>
> It seems to me that the judge's criticism entirely fails to recognise the realities of this situation . . .
>
> [Dr Zimmern] was put under perfectly legitimate, but very obvious, pressure by the family to procure this treatment and he was responding to that pressure. . . . To complain that he did not in terms say that he had regard to the wishes of the patient as expressed by the family, is to shut one's eyes to the reality of the situation with which he was confronted.
>
> The second criticism that is made is of the use of the expression 'experimental' to describe this treatment . . .
>
> The plain fact is that, unlike many courses of medical treatment, this was not one that had a well tried track record of success. It was, on any showing, at the frontier of medical science. That being so, it does not, in my judgment, carry weight to describe this decision as flawed because of the use of this expression.
>
> The third criticism that is made by the judge is of the reference to resources. . . .
>
> . . . Difficult and agonising judgments have to be made as to how a limited budget is best allocated to the maximum advantage of the maximum number of patients. That is not a judgment which the court

---

39 (1995) 23 BMLR 1 (Sir Thomas Bingham MR, Sir Stephen Brown P, Simon Brown LJ).

can make. In my judgment, it is not something that a health authority such as this authority can be fairly criticised for not advancing before the court.

...

The fourth criticism which the judge made was that the authority had wrongly treated the problem which they faced as one of spending £75,000 when, in the first instance, the treatment only involved the expenditure of £15,000. . . . It is, of course, true that if the first stage were unsuccessful, then £15,000, or even less than £15,000, would be the maximum that the authority would end up spending. It would not, however, be reasonable for the authority to embark on this expenditure on that basis since, quite plainly, they would have to continue if, having expended the £15,000, it proved successful and the call for the second stage of the treatment came. It was, therefore, an inescapable decision whether they should embark on this process at all.

The treatment was subsequently paid for by an anonymous benefactor, although B eventually died, in March 1996. She did, however, survive well beyond the six to eight weeks' estimate that the health authority had originally given her to live.

Richard Mullender has commented upon the case as follows, stating the Laws J did refer to the 'right to life', although the Court of Appeal did not expressly refer to this:

Mullender, R, 'Judicial review and the rule of law'[40]

. . . While the bulk of the judge's analysis concerns the right to life, he, nonetheless, states that the same result can be reached by applying *Wednesbury* and identifies four forms of unreasonableness manifested by the health authority: viz, failure to consider the wishes of B's family, wrongly characterising the treatment sought as 'experimental', failure to explain the priorities that led to the decision not to provide it, and an inaccurate estimate of its cost.

In contrast to the judgment of Laws J, the right to life plays no part in that of Bingham MR, notwithstanding his observing both that 'our society is one in which a very high value is put on human life' and that 'no decision affecting human life . . . can be regarded with other than the greatest seriousness'. While, in the light of these comments, the Master of the Rolls' decision not to invoke the right to life might seem surprising, his not doing so can be explained by his commitment to the principle that, in judicial review proceedings, judges must merely scrutinise the lawfulness of a public body's decision and must not adjudicate upon its merits – a commitment to which he gives emphatic expression thus: '. . . we have one function only, which is to rule upon the lawfulness of decisions. That is a function to which we should strictly confine ourselves.' It is, hence, unsurprising to find him basing his decision not on the right to life, but, rather, on the ground of *Wednesbury* unreasonableness, which specifies a modest standard of review and, thus, leaves public bodies with broad scope for making discretionary decisions. The interpretation placed by Bingham MR on *Wednesbury* diverges radically from that of Laws J: he rescinds the judge's quashing order, identifying as unsustainable all four of the grounds on which the latter found the health authority's denial of treatment to be unreasonable.

The case was decided some time before the Human Rights Act came into force. The application of European Convention rights is considered below.

The maintenance by a health authority of a policy directly opposed to Department of Health Circulars and advice will – in the absence of the clearest justifying reasons – fail the *Wednesbury* test. This was established in the case of *R v North Derbyshire HA, ex p Fisher*:

---

40 (1996) 112 LQR 182.

R v North Derbyshire HA, ex p Fisher[41]

Kenneth Fisher, who suffered from the relapsing/remitting form of multiple sclerosis, challenged the refusal of his health authority, North Derbyshire, to finance his treatment with a new form of drug therapy, beta-interferon, which he had been assessed as suitable to receive by doctors at the NHS trust in Sheffield where he was being treated. North Derbyshire's refusal reflected the view of its own experts that beta-interferon (which was expensive) was of unproven therapeutic benefit, which conflicted with the terms of an NHS Circular, EL (95) 97, in which the NHS Executive asked health authorities to assist in implementing the use of the drug:

> **Dyson J**: [The] lawfulness [of the authority's policy] must be judged in accordance with *Wednesbury* principles against the background of national policy which was set out fully and firmly in the guidance to be found in the Circular. The respondents had to have regard to that national policy. They were not obliged to follow the policy, but if they decided to depart from it, they had to give clear reasons for so doing, and those reasons would have been susceptible to a *Wednesbury* challenge ... Moreover, if the respondents failed properly to understand the Circular, then their policy would be as defective as if no regard had been paid to the policy at all. It is accepted on behalf of the respondents that they were under a duty to give serious consideration to each aspect of the Circular. Mr Seys Llewellyn submits that the respondents' policy was an honest and conscientious way of managing the introduction into the NHS of the new drug, and was at least consistent with the Circular.
>
> In my judgment the policy was plainly not in accordance with the Circular. The Circular asked for purchasing authorities and providers:
>
> To develop and implement local arrangements to manage the entry of such drugs into the NHS ... and in particular to initiate a continued prescribing of beta-interferon through hospitals.

One of the key aims was to 'target the drug appropriately at patients who were most likely to benefit from treatment'. In other words, the Circular was giving guidance as to how most effectively beta-interferon could be introduced into the NHS as a drug to be prescribed to treat patients ... I do not consider that the respondents' policy could at any time have fairly been described as a reasonable way of giving effect to the Circular. The respondents, like others, no doubt honestly and conscientiously believed that the efficacy of beta-interferon had not been sufficiently tested. The assumption that underpinned the Circular was that it had been sufficiently tested ... This is not a case in which a health authority departed from the national policy because there were special factors which it considered exceptionally justified departure. ... The respondents did not take the Circular into account and decide exceptionally not to follow it. They decided to disregard it altogether throughout 1996, because they were opposed to it. That is something which in my judgment they were not entitled to do.

Similarly, in *R v North West Lancashire HA, ex p A, D and G*, the application for judicial review was successful due to another example of a somewhat cavalier attitude of a health authority. Three transsexuals brought an action in judicial review after the respondent health authority refused to fund their gender reassignment surgery. While the health authority had accepted that transsexualism is an illness capable of being dealt with by surgical intervention, the policy formulated to deal with it was based upon the belief of the authority's public health consultant that transsexualism should be dealt with by way of psychiatric intervention only. There was nothing unlawful, in principle, about the authority's policy of according cases of transsexualism lower priority and refusing gender reassignment surgery save in exceptional cases, but here there could be no exceptional circumstances, and that was irrational. As Buxton LJ noted:

---

41 [1997] 8 Med LR 327.

R v North West Lancashire HA, ex p A, D and G[42]

Buxton LJ: [A]s the evidence in this application demonstrated . . . there is a strong and respectable body of medical opinion that considers gender reassignment procedures to be effective in suitable and properly selected cases . . . I emphasise that the mere fact that a body of medical opinion supports the procedure does not put the health authority under any legal obligation to provide the procedure: the standard here is far removed from the *Bolam* approach in cases of medical negligence. However, where such a body of opinion exists it is in my view not open to a rational health authority simply to determine that a procedure has no proven clinical benefit while giving no indication of why it considers that that is so . . .

I am therefore driven to the conclusion that the health authority has not demonstrated that degree of rational consideration that can reasonably be expected of it before it decides in effect to give no funding at all to a procedure supported by respectable clinicians and psychiatrists, which is said to be necessary in certain cases to relieve extreme mental distress.

R (on the application of David Tracey) (Appellant) v (1) Cambridge University Hospital NHS Foundation Trust (2) Secretary of State for Health (Respondents) & Equality & Human Rights Commission (Intervener)[43] concerned the use of Do Not Attempt Cardio-Pulmonary Resuscitation (DNACPR) notices. In cases of terminally ill patients, these notices are put with the patient notes and, if the patient goes into cardiac arrest, there will be no attempt to resuscitate. The appellant challenged the use of two such notices placed on the medical file of his terminally ill wife who was hospitalised following a road traffic accident, and also the lawfulness of the first respondent NHS trust's non-resuscitation policy. The basis of the application was that the trust had not told the patient or her family about the non-resuscitation policy in such a way as they could challenge it; the trust's policy was defective because it was confusing as to whether the final decision rested with the patient or, if incapable, their family; and the trust's failure to consult with the patient before signing the first notice was a breach of her rights under the European Convention on Human Rights 1950 Article 8. The judicial review application had been refused by the judge at first instance on the basis that there had been some consultation with the patient's daughter and that it was not in the public interest to undertake a further, more detailed inquiry, given that the Article 8 point was academic because the imposition of the first notice had not caused any harm before its revocation, and that there was not enough evidence to consider whether the trust's non-resuscitation policy was defective.

The Court of Appeal allowed the appeal on the basis that the arguments were not just academic but of general importance, in that one of the contentions was that it was unlawful for the second respondent, the Secretary of State, not to have a national policy in relation to DNACPR notices. Permission to apply for judicial review had been granted for that claim, and nothing had emerged during the fact-finding hearing that impinged upon its strength or weakness.

R (on the application of Ann Marie Rogers) v Swindon NHS PCT (Respondent) & Secretary of State for Health (Interested Party)[44] concerned a challenge to the decision of the PCT not to fund the drug Herceptin to all women with early stage breast cancer, save in 'exceptional circumstances'. The PCT claimed that this had nothing to do with cost. In consequence, the court could readily find that the policy was irrational, as once the cost factor had been discounted, the only criterion would then relate to the legitimate clinical needs of the patient and, since the PCT had not stipulated and could not stipulate what sorts of circumstances would be 'exceptional', it meant that they did not envisage offering anyone this treatment. A policy adopted by a PCT

---

42 Auld, Buxton and May LJJ [1999] Lloyd's Rep Med 399 (CA).
43 [2014] EWCA Civ 33; see also the substantive decision at [2014] 822, discussed in Ch 12.
44 [2006] EWCA Civ 392 (CA).

must genuinely recognise the possibility of an individual meeting its criteria; since there was no conceivable way of distinguishing between eligible individuals, the policy was irrational. A finding of irrationality was also made in R (on the application of Otley) v Barking and Dagenham NHS Primary Care Trust.[45] The applicant had cancer and had responded badly to the treatments available. Through her own research, she found a drug that was licensed in the USA and other countries. She paid for five cycles and had an excellent response, with no side effects. Her local trust had a policy of funding treatments in exceptional circumstances, and her doctor applied to the local trust for funds to pay for a further five cycles, but this was refused. The judge at first instance did not find that the policy was irrational, but that the decision to refuse funding was, as the trust had failed to take into account the fact that the applicant had no other options.

In R (on the application of AC) v Berkshire West Primary Care Trust[46] the applicant was a male-to-female transsexual who was suffering from psychological stress following hormone treatment to stimulate breast growth that had not had the effect she desired. She asked for funding from her local PCT for breast augmentation. The trust had a policy of funding breast reduction in female-to-male transsexuals but not male-to-female (this was not absolute, as the trust's policy was that in 'exceptional circumstances', augmentation was not ruled out altogether). The difference was justified on the basis that there was insufficient evidence to show that breast augmentation was sufficient to prevent distress, while breast reduction in female-to-male transsexuals was positively required because very few men display significant breasts, whereas female body shape varies a great deal. Significantly, the trust generally ruled out breast augmentation for both men in a transsexual situation and non-transsexual women who were distressed by the small size of their breasts. The application failed on general judicial review principles in that both the judge at first instance and the Court of Appeal held that the trust was entitled to conclude that there was insufficient evidence to show that augmentation was effective. Interestingly, the trust argued that a policy that allowed breast augmentation for transsexuals but not for women generally would be sex discrimination. The applicant argued that transsexualism was sui generis and did not give rise to discrimination. The Court of Appeal favoured the argument advanced by the trust that, on general principles, it would not be fair to permit augmentation for transsexuals but not for non-transsexual women.

The relationship of the newly created clinical commissioning groups (CCGs) and their relationship with the National Institute for Health and Care Excellence (NICE) was examined in R (on the application of Rose) v Thanet Clinical Commissioning Group.[47] The court had to consider the status of NICE guidelines in relation to the decisions of clinical commissioning groups. The patient was a young woman who had severe Crohn's disease and was undergoing medical treatment (gonadotoxic therapy) that was likely to render her infertile and cause her to suffer early onset of the menopause. She sought to have oocyte cryostorage, an assisted reproductive technique. There were a number of different guidelines issued by NICE during the relevant period of time, which reflected differing views of the effectiveness of this technique, and the application failed. However, the key issue of principle for the court was whether the CCG could take a different view to that of NICE. Following the ruling in the case of Fisher (see above), Jay J held that CCGs could not legitimately disagree with NICE on matters concerning the current state of medical science. The CCG could not lawfully disagree with the medical or scientific rationale for NICE's recommendation in relation to oocyte cryopreservation. It would perhaps have been open to the CCG to refuse the treatment by operating a requirement of exceptional circumstances in order for the treatment to be approved, but a refusal on scientific grounds would

45 [2007] EWHC 1927 (Admin).
46 [2011] EWCA Civ 247.
47 [2014] EWHC 1182 (Admin).

have been unlawful. Another basis on which the courts have proven willing to quash decisions by health authorities in judicial review is that of procedural irregularity. Thus, in *R v North and East Devon HA, ex p Coughlan*[48] the Court of Appeal held that the respondent authority's planned closure of the severely disabled applicant's care home, contrary to an earlier promise that it would be her home for life, was an unlawful breach of her legitimate expectations. This can be contrasted with the case of *R (on the application of Haggerty and Others) v St Helen's Borough Council*[49] where a similar complaint was made about the closure of a local authority home for the elderly which service was being taken over by a private contractor, but where the application failed on the basis that there had been no promise of 'a home for life'. See also the case of *R v North and East Devon HA, ex p Pow*[50] in which a decision to close a hospital was set aside by the High Court (Moses J) due to the health authority's failure to engage in the required consultation process beforehand, and contrast this with *R (on the application of Val Compton (on behalf of Community Action For Savernake Hospital)) v Wiltshire Primary Care Trust*,[51] where a hospital closed after an extensive consultation exercise and the action in judicial review failed.

In *R (on the application of Save our Surgery Ltd) (Claimant) v Joint Committee of Primary Care Trusts (Defendant) & Newcastle upon Tyne Hospitals NHS Foundation Trust (Interested Party)*,[52] it was held that a consultation process had been sufficiently unfair as to make it unlawful. It concerned a proposal by a group of experts that fewer centres providing paediatric cardiac surgery were needed, as better and safer results would be achieved if the expertise were concentrated in fewer, larger centres. The conclusions involved the allocation of various sub-scores on the application of a number of criteria. These were not published in the subsequent consultation documentation, and Davies J held that the sub-scores were a material consideration, and that when a request was made for disclosure of the scores, disclosure should have been made.

In *R (on the application of SB (A child by his father & litigation friend)) v NHS England*,[53] the court held that a decision of NHS England not to fund treatment was irrational. The patient, aged seven, was severely autistic and also had a rare metabolic condition, phenylketonuria (PKU), which affected his ability to digest protein. | As a result, his body did not break down an amino acid (phenylalanine) which had an adverse effect upon his cognitive function, and also high levels of phenylalanine put him at risk of ongoing brain damage. A drug (brand name Kuvan) significantly ameliorated the effects of PKU. The case centred on the policy of NHS England not to commission Kuvan for routine use in children over the age of four, so an application was made on the child's behalf under the individual funding request procedure (IFR), where there is a requirement that there are 'exceptional clinical circumstances' such that the patient was 'significantly different clinically to the group of patients with the condition in question and at the same stage of progression of the condition' and 'likely to gain significantly more clinical benefit than others in the group of patients with the condition in question and at the same stage of progression of the condition'. The evidence was that dietary treatment would normally be sufficient to control the effects of PKU but, because of his autism and its effect on his behaviour, the child in this case would not comply with dietary treatment. Andrews J found that the evidence that Kuvan was clinically effective in such cases was overwhelming, and quashed the decision to refuse funding.

Another individual funding request (IFR) case is *S (A Child) (By her Father & Litigation Friend M) v NHS England*.[54] This concerned a 17-year-old claimant who suffered from narcolepsy (a sleep

---

48 [2001] QB 213.
49 [2003] EWHC 803.
50 (1997) 39 BMLR 77, QBD.
51 [2009] EWHC 1824 (Admin).
52 [2013] EWHC 439 (Admin).
53 [2017] EWHC 2000 (Admin).
54 [2016] EWHC 1395.

disorder which results in daytime sleepiness and nighttime sleep disturbance) and cataplexy (a disorder of the muscles which results in weakness, which, in this case, caused the claimant's knees to buckle). She was described as academically very bright and good at games but, as a result of her conditions, she had fallen behind with school work, her sporting interests and had found socialising difficult because of being incapable of engaging friends in the normal way. The 'usual' treatment had not proved effective. The IFR concerned a drug, brand name Xyrem, used to treat both narcolepsy and cataplexy, which provided a chance of normalising her life. The decision turned on whether there were exceptional clinical circumstances. The policy states that exceptionality requires more than a failure of the usual treatment. The case was fraught with procedural comings and goings, but Collins J concluded that it was a case of exceptionality because the patient was not just failing to respond to the usual treatment; her condition was actually deteriorating. Quite rightly, he rejected the argument that because of her academic and other potential, this satisfied the exceptionality requirement: every child will need to do their best since otherwise their future life will be severely blighted. This is however a non-clinical factor" (para 31). To have decided otherwise would have been to condone elitism in the allocation of treatment.

In *Re N (An Adult) (Court of Protection: Jurisdiction)*,[55] the Supreme Court considered the power of the Court of Protection (see Chapter 4, where the case is considered further), to order a clinical commissioning group (CCG) to arrange and fund a care plan concerning the wishes of the parents of an adult child who lacked decision-making capacity. They wanted the care plan to include arrangements for visits to the family home, but the CCG was unwilling to implement on the basis that it would not be in his best interests. The court held that the Court of Protection did not have the power to order the CCG to do that because patients with capacity could not insist upon a course of treatment that was not on offer, and the same would apply to someone acting on behalf of an incapacitated person.

As to the division of responsibility between NHS and local authorities in the provision of nursing care in social settings and healthcare settings, see the Supreme Court case of *R (on the application of Forge Care Homes Ltd) & Ors v Cardiff & Vale University Health Board & Ors*.[56]

On a similar note, the case of *National Aids Trust (Claimant) v NHS Commissioning Board (NHS England) (Defendant) & (1) Secretary of State for Health (2) Local Government Association (Interested Parties)*[57] considered whether NHS England had the power to commission an anti-retroviral drug that could be used on a preventative basis for those at high risk of contracting HIV. Under consideration were the provisions of the National Health Service Act 2006, ss 1(1) and 1H(2), and the National Health Service Commissioning Board and Clinical Commissioning Groups (Responsibilities and Standing Rules) Regulations 2012. It was held that NHS England did have the power due to commission such a drug because of the combined effect of 'healthcare services' and 'treatment' that meant that preventative services were included.

So far, we have been looking at cases in which the judicial review applications have been made against the bodies (usually health authorities) directly responsible for providing or funding treatment. However, this is not the only possibility. In particular, given the increasing tendency for treatment targets and priorities to be set centrally by the Department of Health, the latter too may find its decisions challenged where a link can be shown between such central guidance and the denial of some particular treatment 'on the ground'. This is illustrated by the lengthy attempt by the drug manufacturer Pfizer to overturn the government's refusal to approve, other than in exceptional circumstances, the prescription of the drug Viagra (otherwise known as Sildenafil). In *R v Secretary of State for Health, ex p Pfizer*[58] the NHS circular in which this advice was

---

55 [2017] UKSC 22.
56 [2017] UKSC 56.
57 [2016] EWHC 2005 (Admin).
58 [1999] Lloyd's Rep Med 289.

contained (HSC 1998/158) was successfully challenged by Pfizer. Collins J held that this guid-ance imposed an unreasonable fetter upon the discretion of GPs (the circular stated that the 'exceptional circumstances' in which the drug could be prescribed had to be cleared with the NHS in advance of prescription). Further, it was in breach of the European Transparency Direc-tive 89/105/EEC. Following this judgment the government took steps to remedy the situation by issuing regulations pursuant to the National Health Service Act 1977 by adding Viagra to the schedule of drugs where availability is limited.[59] Pfizer mounted a second challenge on the ground that this was still in breach of the directive because this states that the criteria to exclude services in such a situation must be available and transparent (Article 7(3)). Pfizer's argument was that the government's statement to the European Commission, ostensibly justifying the decision, only referred to cost and did not explain how the treatment of erectile dysfunction should be compared with that for other non-life-threatening conditions. The Court of Appeal (*R (on the Application of Pfizer Ltd) v Secretary of State for Health*[60]) held that the directive did not require such a statement of competing priorities and therefore there was no breach.[61]

An aspect of the provision of healthcare is the extent to which patients are entitled to require the NHS to fund medical treatment in other Member States of the EU. Although at the time of writing, the UK is going through the process of leaving the EU, it is not yet known what the terms of exit will be, so it is worth briefly mentioning this. It brings into play Article 49 of the EC Treaty as it relates to prohibition on restrictions on freedom to provide services and Article 22 of Council Regulation 1408/71 which provides that a person, who is a national of a Member State and is insured under the legislation of the Member State and members of his family residing with him, who is 'authorised by the competent institution to go to the territory of another Member State to receive there the treatment appropriate to his condition', may do so at the expense of the competent institution. Clearly, there could be serious implications for those who wish to seek medical treatment in other EU Member States to avoid waiting lists. In *R (on the application of Yvonne Watts) v (1) Bedford Primary Care Trust (2) Secretary of State for Health*[62] it was held by the Court of Appeal that Article 49 applied but that a reference would be made to the European Court of Justice for a ruling on the correct interpretation of Article 22 on such as case as this. The decision of the ECJ was that pursuant to Article 22 of the Council Regula-tion, a patient could go to another Member State to receive medical treatment and be reim-bursed the cost where there would, on an objective medical assessment of his medical circumstances, be an unacceptable delay before treatment could be provided in the UK. The Court acknowledged that waiting lists could be an acceptable way of managing the supply of healthcare as long as they were managed on the basis of predetermined clinical priorities: *R (on the application of Watts) v Bedford Primary Care Trust.*[63]

2.4.3 European Convention on Human Rights

In *R v North West Lancashire HA, ex p A, D and G*,[64] considered above, the applicants for judicial review were successful at first instance and the Court of Appeal. However, although the Euro-pean Convention was canvassed before the courts because it was decided shortly before the Human Rights Act 1998 Act came into force, the Court of Appeal was robust in rejecting what

---

59 Sch 11, National Health Service (General Medical Services) Regulations 1992 (as amended).
60 [2002] EWCA Civ 1566).
61 See Syrett, K, 'Impotence? Judicial Review in an Era of Explicit NHS Rationing' (2004) 67 (2) MLR 289.
62 [2004] EWCA Civ 166.
63 (C-372/04) (2006) ECR I-4325 (ECJ).
64 [1999] Lloyd's Rep Med 399.

it termed 'unfocused recourse' to the ECHR, and decided the case on the basis of English law principles. As Auld LJ commented:

> **Auld LJ**: As to the European Convention of Human Rights, it is not yet part of our domestic law and is relevant only, in an appropriate case, to the Court's consideration of rationality. Mr Blake indicated that the purpose of his fairly detailed submissions and references to Strasbourg jurisprudence was merely to show that transsexualism is a sufficiently serious condition 'to raise human rights problems'. Such an unfocused recourse to that jurisdiction, whether before or after the statutory absorption of part of the Convention into the law of England and Wales, is not helpful to the Court. Indeed, it is positively unhelpful, cluttering up its consideration of adequate and more precise domestic principles and authorities governing the issues in play. Thus, the deployment of generalised propositions from the ECHR that a person's sexual identity is of sufficient importance to attract the protection of the right to respect for private and family life under Article 8, or that a denial of medical treatment may, if sufficiently serious, amount to 'inhuman or degrading treatment' under Article 3, contributes nothing to resolution of the issues here (see, eg, *Rees v United Kingdom* (1988) 9 EHRR 56; *Cossey v United Kingdom* (1991) 13 EHRR 622; and the dissenting opinion of Judge Pettiti in *B v France* (1992) 16 EHRR 1, pp 40–41). It is common ground in this case that transsexualism is an illness; the issues are whether the Authority's policy for the public funding of treatment of it properly reflects that and whether it makes proper provision for consideration of each application for treatment on its individual merits.
>
> In any event, Article 8 imposes no positive obligations to provide treatment . . . As Hidden J observed, in rejecting similar submissions below:
>
>> The Convention does not give the applicants rights to free healthcare in general or to gender reassignment surgery in particular. Even if the applicants had such a right it would be qualified by the respondent's right to determine healthcare priorities in the light of its limited resources.

It may be somewhat different in cases where life-saving treatment is at issue and the patient's right to life under Article 2 of the ECHR is engaged. However, as Butler-Sloss P noted in *NHS Trust A v M, NHS Trust B v H*,[65] it is clear that the positive obligation upon a state to safeguard life is not an absolute one. In that case, her Ladyship held that, in so far as it accords with respectable medical opinion, a decision to withhold life-sustaining treatment considered not to be in the patient's best interests, would not breach the article. For a general examination of the role of judicial review in the light of the Human Rights Act 1998, see the judgment of Lord Walker in *R (on the application of Pro-Life Alliance) v BBC*[66] in particular examining the concepts of 'proportionality' and 'margin of appreciation'.

See Chapter 12

On the other hand, what does seem clear is that in cases where decisions by health authorities not to fund treatment impinge upon the fundamental interests of patients, the court will subject it to a greater degree of scrutiny in order to be satisfied that it passes the *Wednesbury* test. Phil Fennell, commenting upon the view of the ECHR expressed by the Court of Appeal in *R v North West Lancashire HA, ex p A, D and G*, has argued:

Fennell, P, 'Substantive review of decisions to refuse treatment'[67]

> An array of arguments based on the European Convention of Human Rights and EU law was given short shrift by their Lordships, their preferred approach being through principles of English administrative law.

---

65 [2001] Fam 348.
66 [2003] UKHL 23.
67 (2008) 8 Med L Rev 129.

Although the Court of Appeal judges were unanimous in holding that no Convention rights were engaged here, they nevertheless approached the question from the point of view that a fundamental interest was at stake. Therefore the decision-makers had to substantially consider their decision, and the courts would scrutinise carefully that decision to ensure that they have weighed their justification for interfering with that interest against the importance of the interest. 'Careful scrutiny' may differ in intensity from the 'anxious scrutiny' which has been held appropriate in cases where Convention Rights are engaged. Nevertheless, the basic approach remains as described by Lord Woolf MR in *R v Lord Saville of Newdigate ex p A* [1999] 4 All ER 860, where he said:

> [W]hen a fundamental right such as the right to life is engaged, the options open to a reasonable decision-maker are curtailed. They are curtailed because it is unreasonable to reach a decision which contravenes or could contravene a human right unless there are sufficiently significant countervailing considerations. In other words it is not open to the decision-maker to risk interfering with fundamental rights in the absence of compelling justification. Even the broadest discretion is constrained by the need for there to be countervailing circumstances to justify interference with human rights. The courts will anxiously scrutinise the strength of the countervailing circumstances and the degree of interference with the human right involved and then apply the test accepted by Lord Bingham MR in *R v Ministry of Defence ex p Smith* [1996] 1 All ER 257, p 263.

In other words where Convention Rights are engaged, the courts will apply a sliding scale in judging whether to intervene on substantive grounds with the exercise of an administrative discretion on grounds of *Wednesbury* unreasonableness. The more substantial the interference with human rights posed by the decision which is subject to challenge, 'the more the court will require by way of justification before it is satisfied that the decision is reasonable'.

In *R v North West Lancashire HA, ex p A, D and G*,[68] where a 'fundamental interest' rather than a human right was at stake, it was said that a similar sliding scale operated:

> The more important the interest of the citizen that the decision affects, the greater will be the degree of consideration that is required of the decision-maker. A decision that, as is the evidence in this case, seriously affects the citizen's health will require substantial consideration, and be subject to careful scrutiny by the court as to its rationality. That will particularly be the case in respect of decisions which involve the refusing of any, or any significant, treatment in respect of an identified and substantial medical condition.

THINK POINT

Do you think that the reference to a 'fundamental interest' is a useful development in judicial review, or do you think that there is no significant difference between a fundamental interest and a Convention right?

---

68 *Per* Buxton LJ [1999] Lloyd's Rep Med 399, p 412.

2.4.4 Private law remedies

2.4.4.1 Breach of statutory duty

Rather than bringing a claim in judicial review, could a claimant challenge a decision over healthcare resource allocation in private law? Jonathan Montgomery addresses the possibility here of an action being maintained for breach of statutory duty, but sees little scope for the successful use of this tort in relation to the National Health Service Act 1977 (and note that the same considerations could apply to s 45 of the Health and Social Care (Community Health and Standards) Act 2003 – see above):

Montgomery, J, *Health Care Law*[69]

> In an action for the tort of breach of statutory duty, it is alleged that damage has been caused . . . due to the failure to perform a statutory duty which exists for the benefit of the aggrieved individual, and which parliament intended to be enforceable, . . . by that individual. Thus, patients denied services could argue that the NHS body responsible had failed to perform its statutory obligations and had harmed them. . . . However, the courts have shown themselves to be reluctant to permit actions for the breach of duties to provide welfare services, and it is unlikely that such an action could be brought under the NHS Act 1977.
>
> The House of Lords has noted that there has been no case in which statutory social welfare schemes, established for the benefit of the public at large, have been held to give rise to a private law action for damages. Against this authority, there was a suggestion in *R v Ealing DHA ex p Fox* that a specific duty to provide services for discharged mental patients could be spelt out from the provisions of s 3(1) of the NHS Act 1977. It was not necessary for the judge in this case to consider this point, as such a duty was explicitly set out in s 117 of the Mental Health Act 1983. Consequently, it would be dangerous to rely on his comment.
>
> It is possible that the courts will prove themselves less reticent where the statutory duties are more specific, because it is easier to show that the individual was entitled to expect a service to be provided. Thus, a failure to provide after-care services under the Mental Health Act 1983, s 117, might more readily form the basis of an action for breach of statutory duty. There, it will be clear that the individual patient, who has now been discharged, should be receiving help. It is not a general duty owed to the public, but a specific one owed to an identified individual. It may also be possible to use the action for breach of statutory duty where patients are promised specific services after an assessment of their needs, and are then not given them because the relevant authority failed to execute their decision. However, this sort of failure may be more amenable to a claim in negligence.

2.4.4.2 Negligence and health resources

Patients who are denied treatment might also attempt to argue that a health authority or trust has acted carelessly towards them and they have suffered injury as a result. General principles of the law of tort would be applied and the action framed as a malpractice suit (see further Chapter 6). To the extent that treatment is provided, then it is apparent that lack of resources cannot be used as an excuse for failure to reach the requisite standard of care: see *Wilsher v Essex AHA*[70] and *Bull v Devon AHA*.[71] However, it is unlikely that an action in negligence would lie where, due to lack of resources, a decision is taken not to treat in the first place. Certainly, where the NHS body simply refused to make a given facility available, it is difficult to see how any duty of care would arise between it and the patient.

---

69 Oxford: OUP, 2003.
70 [1987] QB 730, CA.
71 [1993] 4 Med LR 117.

Summary of key points

1   The National Health Service, established in 1946, provides a comprehensive healthcare system which is free at the point of delivery. Its structure has changed on a number of occasions over the years and it is always vulnerable to further structural change by new governments because of its ever-increasing costs. Changes in medicine, technology and an ageing population are the main causes for this. The Health and Social Care Act 2012 is a highly significant step along the road towards a market-drive NHS, and it remains to be seen whether this will fundamentally change the way in which healthcare provision is funded.

2   Regulation of the quality of healthcare consists of internal processes within the NHS which have proliferated as medical litigation has increased. There are bodies that are concerned with risk management and patient safety and NICE will also certify (or refuse to certify) new drugs and other treatments for use in the NHS which makes it a target for judicial review.

3   Complaints about quality of care can be dealt with through the NHS complaints system, and, in serious cases, applications can be made to the professional bodies that regulate healthcare professions, such as the General Medical Council.

4   Patients cannot demand any treatment they wish but, when certain treatments are denied them, eg new and expensive drugs, the patient can ask for the decision to be judicially reviewed.

5   Since the passing of the Human Rights Act 1998 and the incorporation of most of the European Convention on Human Rights into English law, the judicial review test has been slightly modified to accommodate cases where judicial review has been sought on the ground that one or more of the Convention rights have been interfered with, but on the whole, the courts take a cautious approach to judicial review applications.

 Further reading

Jackson, E, 'Top-up payments for expensive cancer drugs: rationing, fairness and the NHS' (2010) 73 Modern Law Review 399.

Newdick, C, *Who Should We Treat? Rights, Rationing, and Resources in the NHS*, Oxford: Clarendon, 2005.

Rhodes, R, Battin, M, and Silvers, A, *Medicine and Social Justice: Essays On The Distribution Of Health Care*, Oxford: Oxford University Press, 2005.

Stirton, R, 'The Health and Social Care Act 2008 (Regulated Activities) Regulations 2014: a litany of fundamental flaws? (2017) 80(2) Modern Law Review 299.

Chapter 3

Consent to treatment

Chapter contents

3.1 Introduction

3.1.1 Background

The requirement that a patient must give a valid consent to medical treatment and its corollary, that it is the patient's prerogative to refuse treatment, even at the cost of his life, are issues at the heart of medical law. It is necessary, therefore, to examine the essential elements which have to be satisfied in order for a patient to give a valid consent. However, the boundaries and basis of consent also need to be considered: most significantly, asking the patient to consent presupposes that they are autonomously capable of deciding about the treatment they are willing to undergo. In this regard, it has no relevance to those with serious mental disabilities, who lack the necessary mental capacity (ie, understanding) to make such decisions – the rules dealing with the latter are looked at in Chapter 4. Similarly, our discussion of the position of children will be deferred until then.

> **See Chapter 4** →

The present chapter has the following structure. After next considering the ethical underpinnings of consent, we shall, in section 3.2, begin our analysis of the general legal framework by examining the doctor's potential liability if consent is absent (and occasionally even if it is present); we also look there at the rules as to the form and scope of consent. By contrast, section 3.3 addresses some exceptional situations, where (at least, arguably) treatment may proceed without consent. In section 3.4, we then move on to examine what is actually required for a patient to give a valid consent, in terms of capacity, voluntariness, and information. Each of these elements has its complexities, not least the informational requirement, where English law distinguishes between non-disclosures that found an action in battery, and those where the proper cause of action is negligence. In section 3.5 we conclude by looking at the latter type of action, which typically concern a doctor's failure to disclose risks attached to the treatment, and what it is the patient must show in order to obtain compensation.

3.1.2 Ethical considerations – autonomy and paternalism

In Chapter 1 we looked at the conflict between the patient's right to autonomous decision-making and medical paternalism, and nowhere is this more apparent than in the issue of consent to treatment. Medical treatment, involving as it does an invasion of the patient's body, takes a prima facie harmful form: its delivery invariably involves a degree of physical restraint and often also entails exposure to harm, or the risk thereof, of a serious nature. This being so, a struggle may ensue between the doctor, who believes that, in the long run, the risks and harm are a price worth paying and the patient, who would rather not be interfered with, even if this makes further debility and premature death more likely. The debate between 'paternalism' and 'patient autonomy' is essentially about whose view should prevail in such circumstances.

> **See Chapter 1** →

It will be recalled that Mill's libertarian philosophy is particularly relevant to the issue of consent:

Mill, JS, *On Liberty*[1]

> [T]he only purpose for which power can be rightfully exercised over any member of a civilised community, against his will, is to prevent harm to others. His own good, either physical or moral, is not a sufficient warrant. He cannot rightfully be compelled to do or forbear because it will be better for him to do so, because it will make him happier, because, in the opinions of others, to do so would be wise, or even right.

> **See Chapter 1** →

---

1 Harmondsworth: Penguin, 1982 [1859].

This approach finds close parallels in the Kantian view that persons are ends in themselves, not simply means to the ends of other people. On this view, the failure to respect autonomy represents a breach of the duty of respect we owe to others in view of their inherent dignity as rational agents. Sometimes Kant's view of autonomy (as well as that of Mill) has been criticised for involving an overly atomised conception of the individual, but in the following extract Alasdair Maclean defends it against such a charge:

Maclean, A, *Autonomy, Informed Consent and Medical Law: A Relational Challenge*[2]

It is important to recognise that any valuable or useful conception of autonomy grounded in moral personhood and respect for that personhood – both for the actor and for others – must allow and coexist with influences, constraints and obligations arising from the relationships that envelop us. Reducing individuals to isolated atomistic existences undermines the concept of autonomy . . .

Kant's view of autonomy, for all of its problems . . . is essentially relational. Wholly self-regarding decision-making, even if possible, falls foul of both the universalisability formulation and the ends/means formulation of Kant's imperative. To live in the context of a social existence means that, in making decisions, the individual should take into account the impact of the decision on at least those others who exist in a close relationship with the individual. The impact on society of a rule that requires only self-regard in making decisions would be as great in severing the social bonds as a rule that permits lying. When applied in the context of healthcare, this universal rule would impose on patients a duty to at least take into account the impact of their decision on those others that exist in close relationships with them. There is no reason why this could not be included as a rule of consent.

There are also consequentialist reasons in favour of the need for consent, in terms of the dangers of not having such a rule. These were noted by an American court in the striking case of *McFall v Shimp*,[3] in which a patient required a bone marrow donation to avoid almost certain death. The procedure for donation was virtually risk-free and, if a donation from a suitable donor went ahead, the prognosis was excellent. The patient's cousin had volunteered for a compatibility test, but when the test showed him to be a suitable donor, he declined to undergo further tests or to donate the bone marrow. The patient sought an injunction to compel his cousin to make the donation:

Flaherty J: The common law has consistently held to a rule which provides that one human being is under no legal compulsion to give aid or to take action to save that human being or to rescue. A great deal has been written regarding this rule which, on the surface, appears to be revolting in a moral sense. Introspection, however, will demonstrate that the rule is founded upon the very essence of our free society. It is noteworthy that counsel for the plaintiff has cited authority which has developed in other societies in support of the plaintiff's request in this instance. Our society, contrary to many others, has as its first principle, the respect for the individual, and that society and government exist to protect the individual from being invaded and hurt by another. Many societies adopt a contrary view which has the individual existing to serve the society as a whole. In preserving such a society as we have it is bound to happen that great moral conflicts will arise, and will appear harsh in a given instance. In this case, the Chancellor is being asked to force one member of society to undergo a medical procedure which would provide that part of that individual's body would be removed from him and given to another so that the other could live. Morally, this decision rests with the defendant, and, in the view of the court, the refusal of the defendant

2 Cambridge: CUP, 2009.
3 10 Pa D & C (3d) 90 (1978).

is morally indefensible. For our law to compel the defendant to submit to an intrusion of his body would change every concept and principle upon which our society is founded. To do so would defeat the sanctity of the individual, and would impose a rule which would know no limits, and one could not imagine where the line would be drawn.

On the other hand, the situation may be felt to be different where the therapy stands to benefit the patient whose consent is at issue: here a doctor could, perhaps, be forgiven for believing that the principle of autonomy should be sacrificed in the best interests of the patient. Indeed, as we saw in Chapter 1, even a strong libertarian such as Mill accepted a limited form of paternalism when it was necessary to intervene temporarily to restore autonomy. However, this is not, perhaps, true paternalism: if autonomy has to be restored, then arguably it could not have been exercised in the first place. More problematic are cases where a patient reaches a decision out of step with

their own autonomy considered in the long term; here a temporary, paternalistically motivated, intervention would arguably also serve the patient's overall autonomy interest. Alisdair Maclean discusses this type of problem as follows:

Maclean, A, *Autonomy, Informed Consent and Medical Law: A Relational Challenge*[4]

I argued [earlier] that respect for the patient's autonomy did not permit overriding that person's autonomy in order to protect his or her future autonomy. It might be argued that this is fine as far as defining a general position but that paternalism may still be justifiable in the short term to prevent irrational harm if such decisions are made on a case-by-case basis. The problem with this argument is that it is impossible to isolate cases in this way. As soon as such cases occur they begin to create a more general position and it becomes natural to use each case as a precedent for a new situation with slightly different circumstances so that such a casuistic approach soon starts to resemble a general principle.

This may not completely defeat the casuistic, consequentialist approach if sufficient safeguards can be established to prevent the slippery slide into a general principle. However, overriding a person's decision may undermine their confidence in the security of their autonomy. Once one's decision-making has been overridden it implies that the same could happen again, which is problematic – especially when it is a decision that actually matters and the stakes are high – since it threatens to undermine the whole value of autonomy . . .

A further point supporting a non-paternalist position arises from the risk of bad luck. Even with the best will in the world things sometimes go badly. Most, if not all, medical interventions carry some risk, often of quite serious consequences. Since the patient will have to live with those consequences it should be the patient who controls whether or not the treatment is undergone.

Perhaps for these reasons, the law does not accept paternalism in any form as a permissible argument for imposing treatment upon capable (or competent) patients. At least this is true for adults; as we shall see in Chapter 4, one situation, where the law is prepared to be paternalistic relates to children who purport to refuse treatment with serious implications for their continued life or health; this attitude is captured in the *dictum* of Ward J in *Re E (A Minor) (Wardship: Medical Treatment)*[5] that 'a court should be slow to let a child martyr himself'.

Conversely, paternalism continues to have legal relevance as providing one justification for an upper limit on what may lawfully be consented to. We shall consider this issue in more detail shortly, under 3.2.1.3.

---

4 See n 2 above.
5 [1993] 1 FLR 386.

3.2 The legal framework

3.2.1 The protection of bodily integrity

The importance of bodily inviolability is entrenched in the law of Western societies. Every student of medical law is familiar with the statement made by Cardozo J in *Schloendorff v New York Hospitals:*[6]

> **Cardozo J:** Every human being of adult years and sound mind has a right to determine what shall be done with his own body; and a surgeon who performs an operation without his patient's consent, commits an assault . . .

As we shall see below, the English courts have generally also emphasised the primacy of patient autonomy or self-determination and its effect of blocking the doctor's right (and his duty) to invade the patient's bodily integrity so as to treat the patient. This is so, notwithstanding that the treatment might be regarded as in the latter's best interests. In *Airedale NHS Trust v Bland,*[7] Lord Goff commented:

> **Lord Goff of Chieveley:** [I]t is established that the principle of self-determination requires that respect must be given to the wishes of the patient, so that if an adult patient of sound mind refuses, however unreasonably, to consent to treatment or care by which his life would or might be prolonged, the doctors responsible for his care must give effect to his wishes, even though they do not consider it to be in his best interests to do so . . . To this extent, the principle of the sanctity of human life must yield to the principle of self-determination . . . and, for present purposes perhaps more important, the doctor's duty to act in the best interests of his patient must likewise be qualified.

In so far as the doctor proceeds to treat without consent, he will potentially be liable both in civil and criminal law.

3.2.1.1 Civil law: battery

As regards the position in tort, a valid consent to medical treatment is required because, without it, the doctor will be committing a trespass to the person, ie a battery. The term 'battery' conjures up images of violence and indeed, in *Wilson v Pringle,*[8] the Court of Appeal suggested that the touching must be 'hostile' in order to constitute a battery. However, the reason for this requirement was the need to eliminate actions in battery as a result of things such as physical contact in crowded streets; the court was thus prepared to adopt a very wide view of hostility so as not to confine it to acts of ill will. In fact, the view in *Wilson v Pringle* was later doubted by the House of Lords in *Re F (Mental Patient: Sterilisation).*[9] There, Lord Goff dealt with the problem of contact in crowded spaces, by stating that there could simply be no liability for physical contact which is generally acceptable in the ordinary conduct of everyday life.

As regards medical treatment, it is clear that this does not fall within such an exception. This is already reflected in early case law, such as *Cull v Royal Surrey County Hospital,*[10] which

---

6 (1914) 105 NE 92.
7 [1993] AC 789.
8 [1986] 2 All ER 440.
9 [1990] 2 AC 1.
10 (1932) 1 BMJ 1195.

concerned a patient who had consented to a medical abortion; the surgeon proceeded during the operation to perform a hysterectomy on the basis that her uterus was in a diseased state, making it dangerous for her to become pregnant again. The patient, who had not given consent to the hysterectomy, was successful in her battery action.

3.2.1.2 Criminal law: maim and statutory assault offences

Besides being a tort, battery is also a crime, albeit in the latter context the term used for it is 'assault'.[11] In fact, given the nature of non-consensual surgical procedures, it is clear more serious offences than a bare assault may be committed: these include, in cases of non-consensual surgery, the statutory offences of wounding and assault causing grievous bodily harm contrary to ss 18 and 20 of the Offences Against the Person Act 1861. At least this is so in theory, although in practice the DPP is likely to regard charges as not being in the public interest. It is also interesting to contemplate the relevance of the old common law offence of maim. Skegg comments as follows:

Skegg, PDG, *Law, Ethics and Medicine: Studies in Medical Law*[12]

In practice, the common law offence of maim has long been supplanted by statutory offences. But it has not been expressly abolished, and a judge has made an extra-judicial statement which suggests that there is at least a theoretical possibility of the offence of maim applying to operations in which a kidney is removed from a healthy living donor, for transplantation into a person who is in need of it. It is therefore desirable to consider the extent to which the offence of maim would apply to medical procedures, and the related issue of whether consent would be effective to prevent liability.

The authorities have long distinguished between acts which permanently disable and weaken a man, rendering him less able in fighting; and acts which simply disfigure. The former are maims, which fall within one category rather than the other . . .

The fact that a particular injury has in the past been classified as a maim need not be decisive in any future case. Changes in military practice, or increased medical knowledge, could lead to certain injuries ceasing to be regarded as maims, and other injuries coming to be regarded as maims . . .

Most medical procedures do not permanently disable a person and render that person less able in fighting. They therefore fall outside even the potential scope of any offence of maim. This is as true of the removal of a healthy kidney for transplantation as it is of the removal of a diseased appendix. But even if a medical procedure did come within the potential scope of an offence of maim, it would not follow that a doctor would commit an offence of maim in going ahead with it. Just as the infliction of a maim was some-times permitted in self-defence, so a maiming operation would not amount to the offence of maim if there was a good reason for it. Hence, even if castration could still be regarded as coming within the potential scope of maim, it would be justified if performed for a therapeutic purpose.

As Skegg alludes to in this extract, the patient's consent by itself is not always enough to prevent the commission of a crime. This is because the law, for essentially paternalistic reasons, imposes in many situations an upper limit upon the degree of bodily harm to which a person may consent: see *R v Brown et al*.[13] In other words, a person's autonomy to waive his right to bodily integrity is limited.

---

11 The confusion is added to by the fact that in civil law there is a separate tort of assault, which arises from putting another in reasonable fear of a battery.
12 Oxford: Clarendon Press, 1984.
13 [1993] 2 All ER 75.

We shall look further at the situations where consent will fail to provide a defence to maim, or one of the more modern statutory offences, under 3.2.1.3 below. But why, it may be asked in relation to medical treatment, should consent ever be regarded as making a difference? After all, many forms of treatment (such as amputation or radical surgery) will occasion harm well above the normally permitted limit. In *Airedale NHS Trust v Bland*,[14] Lord Mustill addressed this issue as follows:

> **Lord Mustill:** 1. *Consent to bodily invasion.* Any invasion of the body of one person by another is potentially both a crime and a tort. At the bottom end of the scale consent is a defence both to a charge of common assault and to a claim in tort. The concentration in most discussions of this topic on this end of the scale has tended to divert attention from the fact that whatever the scope of the civil defence of *volenti non fit injuria* there is a point higher up the scale than common assault at which consent in general ceases to form a defence to a criminal charge. The precise location of this point is at present under consideration by another Committee of your Lordships' House in *Reg v Brown (Anthony)* . . . and I need not explore it here, but that the point exists is beyond question. If one person cuts off the hand of another it is no answer to say that the amputee consented to what was done.
>
> 2. *Proper medical treatment.* How is it that, consistently with the proposition just stated, a doctor can with immunity perform on a consenting patient an act which would be a very serious crime if done by someone else? The answer must be that bodily invasions in the course of proper medical treatment stand completely outside the criminal law. The reason why the consent of the patient is so important is not that it furnishes a defence in itself, but because it is usually essential to the propriety of medical treatment. Thus, if the consent is absent, and is not dispensed with in special circumstances by operation of law, the acts of the doctor lose their immunity.

3.2.1.3 Situations where consent may be insufficient

As just noted, it is apparent that there are certain procedures in respect of which consent is no defence at criminal law. Usually, problems will not arise in relation to medical procedures because these are almost always therapeutic, and thus clearly in the public interest. However, there are a number of interventions which are not therapeutic, and whose acceptability may sometimes be more contentious. The issue of consent to non-therapeutic research and to organ donation will be considered later in Chapters 10 and 11, respectively, which focus on those topics; even more starkly, a person cannot consent to a procedure resulting in his own death. However, two other categories of borderline therapeutic/ non-therapeutic, procedure are considered here.

See Chapters ← 10 and 11

See Chapter ← 12

The first relates to (sometimes radical) surgery carried out for psychological rather than somatic therapeutic reasons. The best-known example is of gender reassignment surgery, which is normally carried out when the patient has exhibited serious and continuing manifestations of the personality of someone of the opposite sex, and is psychologically disturbed by being 'in the wrong body'. Such operations are nowadays regarded as fairly routine, and are performed under the NHS as well as privately. It is thus highly unlikely that a challenge to their legality would succeed; indeed, in its 2003 ruling in *Bellinger v Bellinger*,[15] the House of Lords appears to have taken for granted the lawfulness of this type of surgery. More controversial, on the other hand, remain cases of so-called 'body dysmorphic disorder', where patients suffer from a powerful

---

14 See n 7 above.
15 [2003] 2 All ER 593.

psychological urge to have healthy parts of their body amputated. In 2000, a considerable media storm followed revelations that a surgeon in Falkirk, Scotland, had performed two amputations on such patients, and his health authority subsequently refused to allow further operations of this kind. Tracey Elliott suggests though that, at least in some circumstances, such surgery may be ethically and legally justifiable:

Elliott, T, 'Body dysmorphic disorder, radical surgery and the limits of consent'[16]

These operations generally provoke strong reactions of incredulity, disquiet and even disgust when we learn of them, because we find it difficult to understand why individuals should wish to transform normal, healthy bodies into ones with impairments. Such patients challenge our beliefs with regard to bodily integrity by asserting that they will not feel physically 'whole' until they have had a limb removed, beliefs which are so far removed from what we regard as the norm, that we are suspicious of them and of their motives. Given the maiming nature of the surgery which these 'wannabes' request, questions of diagnosis and treatment must be approached with a great deal of care, and the question of how best to treat such individuals raises a number of ethical difficulties. I suggest that, in the case of a very few 'wannabes', provided that they have capacity to consent, are properly informed about the risks of surgery, all other treatments have proved to be unsuccessful, and a full medical and psychiatric assessment has been undertaken, then amputation may be an appropriate treatment to relieve their suffering.

As to the question of whether a surgeon amputating a healthy limb would commit a criminal offence, a study of the so-called 'medical exception' to the general rule that consent is not a defence to the causing of bodily harm reveals that the limits of the exception are uncertain. The courts have stated that 'proper' or 'reasonable' medical treatment which is consented to by a competent adult is lawful, but have not ruled what the proper limits of surgical intervention are. The term 'surgery' covers a wide variety of procedures. In most cases it will be relatively easy to justify these procedures as being in the public interest, since they are performed for therapeutic reasons. Given that the removal of healthy body parts in gender reassignment surgery in order to treat a severe psychological condition is lawful; might not healthy limb amputation be regarded as being justified upon a similar basis? ... I suggest that provided that surgery is conducted by appropriately qualified medical practitioners upon adults who have capacity, and who have consented to the procedure, the matter could be regulated by the civil law, and by the medical profession. This would strike an adequate balance between the protection of patients and the public and respect for individual autonomy.

As Elliott also notes, at a lower level, it could be said that even straightforward instances of cosmetic surgery, such as nose reshaping, often lack a legitimating goal, in terms of clear therapeutic benefit. On the other hand, here, where the social consensus is broadly favourable to such interventions, their *de facto* legality (subject to patient consent) cannot really be doubted.

The second main category of surgical procedures of borderline legality concerns circumcisions carried out for cultural or religious reasons. In most cases, the recipients of such surgery will be infant minors, who, lacking capacity, are unable to consent for themselves. The question of whether their parents may consent for them depends on how far the surgery may be regarded as in their interests; so the question here is whether, in principle, it can be? Dealing first with female circumcision, this is often a drastic procedure, which results in pain, discomfort, sexual and child-birthing difficulties. As a result of a number of well-publicised cases, this was criminalised by the Prohibition of Female Circumcision Act 1985, a provision subsequently re-enacted with increased penalties (of up to 14 years' imprisonment) by the Female Genital Mutilation Act 2003.

However, it is apparent that, even in the male, circumcisions, when undergone for religious or cultural reasons, are non-therapeutic, yet they are carried out almost without question. Although failure to be circumcised may inhibit family relationships; it is also said that it is a practice which results in diminished sexual enjoyment. Christopher Price points out that, historically, the practice has been seen as a means of counteracting excessive lust (twelfth century), and as a preventive for masturbation (nineteenth century England). He also notes that the medical profession justifies carrying out such operations on the basis that they will be performed anyway, and therefore are better done in a clinical setting. He notes that the Bradford Royal Infirmary provide such a service under the NHS. However, he suggests on a number of grounds that the practice should be outlawed:

Price, C, 'Male circumcision: an ethical and legal affront'[17]

Rejoicing in our multicultural society does not mean that we should be blind to practices, whatever their source and motive, which are themselves abusive and discriminatory of others, directly and inevitably diminishing the freedoms, human rights, integrity and dignity of others . . .

The UN Convention on the Rights of the Child makes the position clearer in respect to circumcision. Article 24(3) provides: 'States Parties shall take all effective and appropriate measures with a view to abolishing traditional practices prejudicial to the health of children.' Some have sought to argue that this provision was only aimed at female circumcision; but this argument cannot hold when the Convention is read with the interpretative provisions of the Vienna Convention on the Law of Treaties 1969.

Referring to the conflict with religious freedom, Price states:

Customary international law provides that an individual's exercise of his freedoms can legitimately be restrained when so to exercise them is to damage or deny those freedoms to another. Thus, Art 9(2) of the European Convention on Human Rights provides:

Freedom to manifest one's religion or beliefs shall be subject only to such limitations as are prescribed by law and are necessary in a democratic society in the interests of public safety, for the protection of public order, health or morals, or *for the protection of the rights and freedoms of others*

[emphasis added].

The Convention thus distinguishes between the unfettered right to freedom of thought, and the more restricted right to manifest one's religion.

. . . Non-therapeutic circumcision is clearly discriminatory, unethical and illegal. Its prehistoric origins, and its kinship with subincision and other forms of penile mutilation, show its essential barbarity . . .

Recently, in *Re B and G (Children) (No 2)*, Sir James Munby P (*obiter*) described the different legal position on male and female circumcision as a 'curiosity', and suggested the explanation is simply that 'in 2015 the law . . . is still prepared to tolerate non-therapeutic male circumcision performed for religious or even for purely cultural or conventional reasons, while no longer being willing to tolerate FGM in any of its forms'.[18]

THINK POINT

Do you think the criminal law has a valid role in limiting the kinds of treatment that may be performed, even with consent, and, if so, where should the line be drawn?

---

17 (1997) Bulletin of Medical Ethics (May) 13.
18 [2015] EWFC 3. Where though parents disagree if a male child should be circumcised, the court is unlikely to approve this as part of its wardship jurisdiction: see *Re L and B (Children)* [2016] EWHC 849 (Fam).

3.2.2 The form of consent

3.2.2.1 Express consent

In both the NHS and in private healthcare, the patient will be required to sign a consent form. There is a standard form that covers most forms of medical treatment, although modified types of form are used in certain treatments such as sterilisations (however, in *Taylor v Shropshire Health Authority*,[19] the precise nature of the consent form was described as 'pure window dressing' and the failure to have a specialised consent form at the time was not an indication of negligence).

By signing the form, it may be thought that the patient is confirming that he has received an explanation of the medical procedures and cannot later deny this. However, in *Chatterton v Gerson*,[20] Bristow J stated:

> **Bristow J:** I should add that getting the patient to sign a pro forma expressing consent to undergo the operation 'the effect and nature of which have been explained to me', as was done here in each case, should be a valuable reminder to everyone of the need for explanation and consent. But it would be no defence to an action based on trespass to the person if no explanation had in fact been given. The consent would have been expressed in form only, not in reality.

This approach has been endorsed by the appeal courts (for example, by Lord Donaldson MR in *Re T (Adult: Refusal of Treatment)*)[21] and is acknowledged by the Department of Health in its *Reference Guide to Consent for Examination or Treatment*,[22] which gives general guidance to NHS doctors and other healthcare workers:

> 32. The validity of consent does not depend on the form in which it is given. Written consent merely serves as evidence of consent: if the elements of voluntariness, appropriate information and capacity have not been satisfied, a signature on a form will not make consent valid.

The *Reference Guide* goes on to state that the completion of a consent form will, however, be good practice where a significant invasive procedure, such as surgery, is contemplated.

With respect to NHS treatment, there are different consent forms depending on whether the patient is a capable adult, a person with parental responsibility consenting for a minor, etc. The present model NHS consent form for capable adults (Consent form 1), which was introduced in 2002, is shown below.

3.2.2.2 Implied and presumed consent

As we saw above, a signed consent form will not necessarily show that the patient really consented. Conversely, consent may be deemed to have occurred despite the absence of any consent form. Indeed, purely oral consent, at least as regards minor procedures, is commonplace in day-to-day medical practice. Sometimes, the consent may simply be implied – in the absence of words – by the patient's conduct, as in *O'Brien v Cunard Steamship Co*,[23] in which a ship's passenger who held out her arm to be vaccinated was subsequently unable to succeed in battery against the doctor.

---

19 [1998] Lloyd's Rep Med 395.
20 [1981] QB 432.
21 [1992] 3 WLR 782.
22 London: DoH, 2nd edn, 2009.
23 28 NE 266 (1891).

[NHS organisation name]
consent form 1

Patient agreement to investigation
or treatment

Patient details (or pre-printed label)

Patient's surname/family name................................

Patient's first names ....

Date of birth ....

Responsible health professional.................................

Job title ....

NHS number (or other identifier)................................

◻ Male   ◻ Female

Special requirements ....
(eg other language/other communication method)

To be retained in patient's notes

Patient identifier/label

Name of proposed procedure or course of treatment (include brief explanation if medical term not clear) ....

....

....

Statement of health professional (to be filled in by health professional with appropriate knowledge of proposed procedure, as specified in consent policy)

I have explained the procedure to the patient. In particular, I have explained:

The intended benefits ....

....

....

Serious or frequently occurring risks ....

....

....

Any extra procedures which may become necessary during the procedure

❑ blood transfusion..

❑ other procedure (please specify) ....

....

I have also discussed what the procedure is likely to involve, the benefits and risks of any available alternative treatments (including no treatment) and any particular concerns of this patient.

❑ The following leaflet/tape has been provided ....

This procedure will involve:

❑ general and/or regional anaesthesia   ❑ local anaesthesia   ❑ sedation

Signed:..   Date .. ..
Name (PRINT) ....   Job title ....

Contact details (if patient wishes to discuss options later) ....

Statement of interpreter (where appropriate)

I have interpreted the information above to the patient to the best of my ability and in a way in which I believe s/he can understand.

Signed ....   Date ....
Name (PRINT) ....

Top copy accepted by patient: yes/no (please ring)

Statement of patient

Patient identifier/label

Please read this form carefully. If your treatment has been planned in advance, you should already have your own copy of page 2 which describes the benefits and risks of the proposed treatment. If not, you will be offered a copy now. If you have any further questions, do ask – we are here to help you. You have the right to change your mind at any time, including after you have signed this form.

I agree to the procedure or course of treatment described on this form.

I understand that you cannot give me a guarantee that a particular person will perform the procedure. The person will, however, have appropriate experience.

I understand that I will have the opportunity to discuss the details of anaesthesia with an anaesthetist before the procedure, unless the urgency of my situation prevents this. (This only applies to patients having general or regional anaesthesia.)

I understand that any procedure in addition to those described on this form will only be carried out if it is necessary to save my life or to prevent serious harm to my health.

I have been told about additional procedures which may become necessary during my treatment. I have listed below any procedures **which I do not wish to be carried out** without further discussion. ....
....
....
....

Patient's signature .... Date..............................
Name (PRINT) ....

A witness should sign below if the patient is unable to sign but has indicated his or her consent. Young people/children may also like a parent to sign here (see notes).

Signature .... Date ....
Name (PRINT) ....

Confirmation of consent (to be completed by a health professional when the patient is admitted for the procedure, if the patient has signed the form in advance)

On behalf of the team treating the patient, I have confirmed with the patient that s/he has no further questions and wishes the procedure to go ahead.

Signed:... Date .. ..
Name (PRINT) .... Job title ....

Important notes: (tick if applicable)

☐ See also advance directive/living will (eg Jehovah's Witness form)

☐ Patient has withdrawn consent (ask patient to sign /date here) ....

Guidance to health professionals (to be read in conjunction with consent policy)

What a consent form is for

This form documents the patient's agreement to go ahead with the investigation or treatment you have proposed. It is not a legal waiver – if patients, for example, do not receive enough information on which to base their decision, then the consent may not be valid, even though the form has been signed. Patients are also entitled to change their mind after signing the form, if they retain capacity to do so. The form should act as an *aide-memoire* to health professionals and patients, by providing a check-list of the kind of information patients should be offered, and by enabling the patient to have a written record of the main points discussed. In no way, however, should the written information provided for the patient be regarded as a substitute for face-to-face discussions with the patient.

The law on consent

See the Department of Health's *Reference guide to consent for examination or treatment* for a comprehensive summary of the law on consent (also available at www.doh.gov.uk/consent).

Who can give consent

Everyone aged 16 or more is presumed to be competent to give consent for themselves, unless the opposite is demonstrated. If a child under the age of 16 has "sufficient understanding and intelligence to enable him or her to understand fully what is proposed", then he or she will be competent to give consent for himself or herself. Young people aged 16 and 17, and legally 'competent' younger children, may therefore sign this form for themselves, but may like a parent to countersign as well. If the child is not able to give consent for himself or herself, some-one with parental responsibility may do so on their behalf and a separate form is available for this purpose. Even where a child is able to give consent for himself or herself, you should always involve those with parental responsibility in the child's care, unless the child specifically asks you not to do so. If a patient is mentally competent to give consent but is physically unable to sign a form, you should complete this form as usual, and ask an independent witness to confirm that the patient has given consent orally or non-verbally.

When NOT to use this form

If the patient is 18 or over and is not legally competent to give consent, you should use form 4 (form for adults who are unable to consent to investigation or treatment) instead of this form. A patient will not be legally competent to give consent if:
- they are unable to comprehend and retain information material to the decision and/or
- they are unable to weigh and use this information in coming to a decision.

You should always take all reasonable steps (for example involving more specialist colleagues) to support a patient in making their own decision, before concluding that they are unable to do so. Relatives **cannot** be asked to sign this form on behalf of an adult who is not legally competent to consent for himself or herself.

Information

Information about what the treatment will involve, its benefits and risks (including side-effects and complications) and the alternatives to the particular procedure proposed, is crucial for patients when making up their minds. The courts have stated that patients should be told about 'significant risks which would affect the judgement of a reasonable patient'. 'Significant' has not been legally defined, but the GMC requires doctors to tell patients about 'serious or frequently occurring' risks. In addition if patients make clear they have particular concerns about certain kinds of risk, you should make sure they are informed about these risks, even if they are very small or rare. You should always answer questions honestly. Sometimes, patients may make it clear that they do not want to have any information about the options, but want you to decide on their behalf. In such circumstances, you should do your best to ensure that the patient receives at least very basic information about what is proposed. Where information is refused, you should document this on page 2 of the form or in the patient's notes.

Implied consent should not, however, be confused with the concept of 'presumed consent'. The latter does not concern whether and, if so, to what, the patient actually consents, but whether, hypothetically (ie if the question were asked of them), it may be assumed they would do so. Accordingly, the concept is not relevant in respect of patients who are in a position to provide consent: here, assumptions (on the part of doctors) as to their wishes will be unnecessary and potentially highhanded. Instead, presumed consent may have a role to play in justifying the treatment of those not (currently) able to consent for themselves. As such, it is considered further in Chapter 4 below.

See Chapter 4

3.2.3 The scope of consent

3.2.3.1 What was consented to?

Difficulty may arise in relation to deciding exactly what it was to which the patient consented. In the case of *Mohr v Williams*,[24] the defendant tried to argue that the fact that the patient had consented to the operation on her right ear was relevant to the lawfulness of the operation he proceeded to carry out on her other ear. In other words, the suggestion was that the patient had consented to 'an ear operation'. This, however, was rejected by the judge, who found that there was no basis for interpreting the consent in this wide fashion; indeed as he noted, the diseased condition of the patient's left ear was not discovered in the course of an authorised examination of that ear, but in the course of an examination which had not been authorised.

As we have seen, in the model consent form used by the NHS the patient acknowledges that other (unconsented to) procedures will only be carried out if it is necessary to save his life or to prevent serious harm to his health. Even so, it may be queried how far this amounts to a true consent: it is a standard form, which most patients will feel they are unable to object to, so there could be said to be an element of coercion here. How many patients, about to undergo surgery, are likely to delete or alter a standard consent form? Although, it is clearly desirable that there be a legal basis for doctors to perform additional procedures that are necessary in the patient's vital interests, arguably this lies more naturally in the doctrine of necessity, rather than in trying to stretch patient consent. More generally, the disturbing consequences of unduly wide consent forms are illustrated in the case of *Breen v Baker*,[25] where a woman consented to surgery which she believed would be dilatation and curettage, but was subsequently given a total hysterectomy. There was found to be no battery because the consent form stated: 'I agree to leave the nature and extent of the operation to be performed to the discretion of the surgeon.'

Admittedly, the model NHS consent form is much more carefully drafted. Thus, apart from procedures immediately required to safeguard life/prevent serious harm, the form assumes that the patient will be alerted to additional procedures which may become necessary, and have the opportunity to list those he would not wish to take place. Of course, whether the patient has this opportunity in practice will depend on what was actually said to him (and if he knew in essence what was to happen). In *Williamson v East London and City HA and Others*[26] the claimant underwent surgery following problems with silicone breast implants, and the operation that was eventually performed was a subcutaneous mastectomy. The consent form originally referred to a 'replacement breast prosthesis and right open capsulotomy', procedures less radical than a mastectomy. It seems that after the signing of the form, in a pre-operative examination the surgeon found that the more radical surgery was required: thereupon the hospital altered the consent

---

24 (1905) 104 NW 12.
25 (1956) *The Times*, 27 January.
26 [1998] Lloyd's Rep Med 6.

form, but it was not further signed by the claimant. The claimant successfully recovered against the surgeon in the tort of negligence: it was found that the latter was in breach of duty by not having explained what was proposed to the claimant, and that the consent form was not altered in her presence. Here, it is arguable that battery would have been the more appropriate cause of action.

A recent, interesting case in this area is *Border v Lewisham and Greenwich NHS Trust*,[27] which related to oral consent in the context of 'emergency' AE treatment given to a patient who had suffered *inter alia* a broken right arm. The duty doctor wished, as standard emergency procedure, to insert an IV cannula, and therefore chose her left arm for this; but the patient alerted him that it was also unsuitable due to other recent treatment, meaning there was a heightened risk of infection. However, the doctor proceeded anyway.

After an infection arose, leading to permanent injury, the patient sued in negligence. At first instance legal argument was largely directed to whether it was responsible practice for the doctor to run that risk, and only on appeal did the claimant expressly raise the issue of lack of consent. In this regard Richards LJ noted (at para 21):

> In a medical emergency, when the patient is incapable of giving consent, a doctor may proceed without consent provided that he or she is acting in the patient's best interests (see, for example, *St George's Healthcare NHS Trust v S* . . .) On the evidence, however, this was not such a case of medical emergency. The claimant was in the emergency room – the resuscitation room – but she was fully conscious and capable of giving or withholding her consent. The judge was therefore wrong to regard the issue of consent as unimportant.

In the circumstances, the Court of Appeal found the failure to obtain the patient's clear consent was at least a negligent breach of duty, but it refused leave to the claimant to amend her claim to one of battery (which it felt – at this late stage – would be unfair to the doctor).

We shall be looking further at the patient's right to information, and the remedies in battery and/or in negligence where this right is breached, in section 3.5 below.

3.2.3.2 The person carrying out treatment

The model NHS consent form requires the patient to acknowledge that the procedure need not be carried out by any particular doctor. There are examples of patients in America who have successfully sued following surgery carried out competently and in accordance with the patient's consent, but performed by a different doctor to that expected by the patient.[28] However, it is implied by the form that if the procedure is not carried out by this doctor, it will be carried out by *a* doctor. As discussed by Kennedy and Grubb, controversy surrounds the issue of treatment by medical students, or even nurses:

Kennedy, I and Grubb, A, *Medical Law: Text with Materials*[29]

> There are at least two factual situations . . . which do give rise to legal difficulties if the patient is unaware that the person is a student.
>
> First, a student may, in fact, examine (ie, touch) a patient solely so as to acquire knowledge or experience for himself. The touching plays no part in the care of the patient. In such a circumstance, the consent given by the patient is probably invalid since the identity of the person touching affects the nature of what is being done to the patient, ie, training rather than caring.

---

27 [2015] EWCA Civ 8.
28 See, eg, *Perna v Pirozzi* 457 A 2d 431 (1983).
29 London: Butterworths, 2nd edn, 1994.

> Secondly, a student may touch a patient as part of the patient's care. Does the lack of awareness by the patient of the identity of the person touching (identity being status here) affect the validity of the patient's consent? . . . It could be said that the difference between a lay person and a doctor is material whereas the difference between a medical student (presumably supervised) and a doctor is not. In our view, unless the patient suffered harm and could establish that the medical student was negligent, an English court would reject any claim by a patient.

In the case of *R v Richardson*[30] the Court of Appeal held that there had been a valid consent to treatment by a dentist when, unbeknown to the patient, the dentist had been suspended from practice by the General Dentist Council, and her conviction for assault was, therefore, quashed. There it was accepted that she was practising unlawfully following her suspension. However, this fraud was said not to vitiate the consent to treatment because it had not induced a mistaken belief as to the identity of the person carrying out the treatment, nor had it induced a mistaken belief about the nature and quality of the treatment. The Court of Appeal rejected the Crown's submission that the concept of 'identity' should be extended to cover qualifications or attributes of the dentist. If this were the case, it would distort the everyday meaning of the word 'identity'.

This decision can be contrasted with that of *R v Tabussum*,[31] where the Court of Appeal held that there had not been a valid consent and the defendant's conviction for indecent assault was upheld where he had asked women to take part in a breast cancer survey to enable him to prepare a computer software package for doctors. The three complainants had agreed to the defendant showing them how to self-examine for breast lumps, which involved the removal of their clothes and the defendant touching their breasts. The central issue was that the women believed him to be a doctor. The defendant had no medical qualifications, but he was a scientist with experience in the field of breast cancer, and he denied that he had ever represented himself to be medically qualified. He denied that he had any sexual motive, and the Court of Appeal said that, in any event, this was irrelevant.

Clearly, when the Court of Appeal considered the case of *Tabussum*, it had to try and distinguish it from *Richardson*. The court regarded *Richardson* as being decided solely on the question of identity and not the nature and quality of the acts. In *Tabussum*, the consent was given to touching 'for medical purposes'. This consent was valid as to the nature of the acts but, as the women said they would not have consented if they had known he was not medically qualified, the consent was not valid as to the quality. It is hard to reconcile these two cases when they both turned on 'qualifications and attributes'. Further, the disparity is highlighted by the fact that, in the case of *Richardson*, there was a deliberate unlawful act, whereas, at least on the defendant's evidence, in *Tabussum* the defendant was doing exactly what he had told the women concerned.

3.3 Qualifications on the need for consent

As previously discussed, the law usually privileges the autonomy interests of (capable adult) patients over and above the paternalistic inclinations of doctors to treat them in (what the doctor regards as) their best interests.[32] It does so by making the patient's consent a necessary

---

30 (1998) 43 BMLR 21.
31 [2000] 2 Cr App R 328.
32 See, eg, the *dictum* of Lord Goff in the *Bland* case, at n 7, above.

condition for the propriety and lawfulness of medical treatment. However, there are some exceptional circumstances in which treatment may occur without consent. These exceptions exist both (arguably) at common law and under statute.

3.3.1 The 'four state interests' at common law

In the first place it might be argued that a patient's refusal of certain forms of treatment can exceptionally be overridden at common law in order to uphold broader interests on the part of the state. The American courts have adverted to such interests. Thus, in the New Jersey case *In the Matter of Claire Conroy*,[33] four state interests with potential for limiting patient rights were identified. These were preserving life, preventing suicide, safeguarding the integrity of the medical profession, and protecting innocent third parties:

> **Schrieber J**: The State's interest in preserving life . . . may be seen as embracing two separate but related concerns: an interest in preserving the life of the particular patient, and an interest in preserving the sanctity of life . . .
>
> While both of these State interests in life are certainly strong, in themselves they will usually not foreclose a competent person from declining life-sustaining medical treatment for himself. This is because the life that the State is seeking to protect in such a situation is the life of the same person who has competently decided to forgo the medical intervention; it is not some other actual or potential life that cannot adequately protect itself . . .
>
> It may be contended that in conjunction with its general interest in preserving life, this State has a particular legislative policy of preventing suicide . . . [However] this State interest in protecting people from direct and purposeful self-destruction is motivated by, if not encompassed within, the State's more basic interest in preserving life. Thus, it is questionable whether it is a distinct State interest worthy of independent consideration.
>
> In any event, declining life-sustaining medical treatment may not properly be viewed as an attempt to commit suicide. Refusing medical treatment merely allows the disease to take its natural course; if death were eventually to occur, it would be the result, primarily, of the underlying disease, and not the result of a self-inflicted injury . . .
>
> The third State interest that is frequently asserted as a limitation on a competent patient's right to refuse medical treatment is the interest in safeguarding the integrity of the medical profession. This interest is not particularly threatened by permitting competent patients to refuse life-sustaining medical treatment. Medical ethics do not require medical intervention in disease at all costs . . .
>
> Moreover, even if doctors were exhorted to attempt to cure or sustain their patients under all circumstances, that moral and professional imperative, at least in cases of patients who were clearly competent, presumably would not require doctors to go beyond advising the patient of the risks of forgoing treatment and urging the patient to accept the medical intervention . . .
>
> The fourth asserted State interest in overriding a patient's decision about his medical treatment is the interest in protecting innocent third parties who may be harmed by the patient's treatment decision. When the patient's exercise of his free choice could adversely and directly affect the health, safety, or security of others, the patient's right of self-determination must frequently give way. Thus, for example, the courts have required competent adults to undergo medical procedures against their will if necessary to protect the public health . . . or to prevent the emotional and financial abandonment of the patient's minor children: *Application of President and Directors of Georgetown College Inc* 331 F 2d 1000, . . ., cert denied, 377

---

33 486 A 2d 1209 (1985).

US 978 . . . (1964) (ordering mother of seven month old infant to submit to blood transfusion over her religious objections because of the mother's 'responsibility to the community to care for her infant'); *Holmes v Silver Cross Hospital* 340 F Supp 125 . . . (1972) (indicating that patient's status as father of a minor child might justify authorising blood transfusions to save his life despite his religious objections).

The categorisation of the four state interests in *Conroy* has been endorsed in a number of subsequent US authorities, and was adopted by Thorpe J (as he then was) in the English High Court in *Secretary of State v Robb*.

Secretary of State v Robb[34]

The respondent, a prison inmate with a personality disorder, went on hunger strike. The application concerned the question of whether it was lawful for his doctors and nurses to abstain from force feeding him in such circumstances:

Thorpe J: The only reference to the duty of the Home Office in modern authority is the briefest passage in the speech of Lord Keith of Kinkel in *Airedale NHS Trust v Bland* [1993] 1 All ER 821, p 861; [1993] AC 789, p 859, in which he said:

. . . the principle of the sanctity of life . . . is not an absolute one. It does not compel a medical practitioner on pain of criminal sanctions to treat a patient, who will die if he does not, contrary to the express wishes of the patient. It does not authorise forcible feeding of prisoners on hunger strike. It does not compel the temporary keeping alive of patients who are terminally ill where to do so would merely prolong their suffering.

There have been much fuller developments in other common law jurisdictions, particularly in the United States, and all counsel have drawn attention to and relied upon a number of decisions, all of which consider the right of the individual to refuse nutrition in differing circumstances. I will refer only to recent decision in the United States that is directly concerned with adult prisoners on hunger strike. The most recent, and for me the most helpful, is the decision of the Supreme Court of California, *Thor v Superior Court* 5 Cal 4th 725 (1993). That authority upheld a decision at first instance that the prison authorities failed in their application for an order authorising force feeding of a quadriplegic prison inmate who had determined to refuse food and medical treatment necessary to maintain his life. The conclusion of the court was that the right of self-determination prevailed, but the court recognised that the right of self-determination was not absolute and that there were four specific state interests that might countervail. They were specifically: (i) preserving life; (ii) preventing suicide; (iii) maintaining the integrity of the medical profession; and (iv) protecting innocent third parties . . .

These decisions are obviously relevant and helpful in reaching a decision as to how the law stands in this jurisdiction. I consider specifically the four countervailing state interests that were set against the individual's right of self-determination.

The first, namely the interest that the state holds in preserving life, seems to me to be but part and parcel of the balance that must be struck in determining and declaring the right of self-determination. The principle of the sanctity of human life in this jurisdiction is seen to yield to the principle of self-determination. It is within that balance that the consideration of the preservation of life is reflected.

The second countervailing State interest, preventing suicide, is recognisable, but seems to me to be of no application in cases such as this where the refusal of nutrition and medical treatment in the exercise of the right of self-determination does not constitute an act of suicide.

---

34 [1995] Fam 127.

> The third consideration of maintaining the integrity of the medical profession is one that I find hard to recognise as a distinct consideration. Medical ethical decisions can be acutely difficult and it is when they are at their most acute that applications for declaratory relief are made to the High Court. I cannot myself see that this is a distinct consideration that requires to be set against the right of self-determination of the individual.
>
> The fourth consideration of protecting innocent third parties is one that is undoubtedly recognised in this jurisdiction, as is evidenced by the decision of Sir Stephen Brown P in *Re S (Adult: Refusal of Medical Treatment)* [1992] 4 All ER 671; [1993] Fam 123 . . .

Admittedly, Thorpe J (as indeed Schrieber J had done in *Conroy*) here distances himself from the proposition that these state interests – at any rate, the first three – would actually justify overriding a patient's competent refusal in a given case; it appears more that the interests are acknowledged in order to be dismissed. Thus in the *Robb* case itself, the court confirmed the legality of allowing the prisoner to starve himself to death.

Nevertheless, arguably matters are not quite so straightforward as they may here appear. Accordingly, in the following, we briefly consider each putative state interest in turn.

3.3.1.1 Preservation of life

As a general rule, as we have seen, the state's interest in preserving life is regarded as subordinate to the patient's autonomous decision to refuse life-saving treatment. This has been reiterated on many occasions by the courts. In *Re T (An Adult: Medical Treatment)*, Lord Donaldson MR adverted to the conflict between the sanctity of life, which the state will wish to uphold, and the patient's right to self-determination, as follows:

> **Lord Donaldson MR:** This situation gives rise to a conflict between two interests, that of the patient and that of the society in which he lives. The patient's interest consists of his right to self-determination – his right to live his own life how he wishes, even if it will damage his health or lead to his premature death. Society's interest is in upholding the concept that all human life is sacred and that it should be preserved if at all possible. It is well established that in the ultimate the right of the individual is paramount.[35]

Nevertheless, one group of cases that may arguably be understood, at least partly, in terms of the state's special interest in preserving life relates to refusal of life-saving treatment by 'mature minors' (ie older children, of eg 14 and above, who may be judged capable to make decisions about even highly significant medical interventions). As already alluded to, and discussed further in Chapter 4, in such cases the courts have consistently held that, while the child may be able to consent to treatment, he cannot refuse it at serious cost to his health or life.[36]

3.3.1.2 Prevention of suicide

The interest of the state in preventing suicide was considered by the California Court of Appeal in the case of *Bouvia v Superior Court*.[37] Elizabeth Bouvia was a severely disabled quadriplegic, almost totally immobile, and entirely dependent upon others for all her needs. In addition, she was in continual and severe pain. Mentally, however, she was intelligent and aware. She was

---

35 See n 21 above.
36 See in particular *Re W (A Minor) (Medical Treatment)* [1992] 3 WLR 758, discussed in Ch 4.
37 179 Cal App 3d 1127 (1986).

spoon fed, but found it difficult to take sufficient food orally because of nausea. It was, therefore, decided to feed her by nasogastric tube. She sought a court order that such 'treatment' could be refused (see Chapters 9 and 12 on feeding as treatment), and her right to self-determination was upheld. Associate Justice Beach reviewed the Californian authorities and the Presidential Commission for the Study of Ethical Problems in Medicine and Biomedical and Behavioural Research, and concluded:

> **Beach J**: It is . . . immaterial that the removal of the nasogastric tube will hasten or cause Bouvia's eventual death. Being competent she has the right to live out the remainder of her natural life in dignity and peace. It is precisely the aim and purpose of the many decisions upholding the withdrawal of life support systems to accord and provide as large a measure of dignity, respect and comfort as possible . . .
>
> Overlooking the fact that a desire to terminate one's life is probably the ultimate exercise of one's right to privacy, we find no substantial evidence to support the [trial] court's conclusion [that Bouvia's refusal of tube feeding amounted to a suicide attempt] . . . As a consequence of her changed condition, it is clear she has now merely resigned herself to accept an earlier death, if necessary, rather than live by feedings forced upon her by means of nasogastric tube. Her decision to allow nature to take its course is not equivalent to an election to commit suicide with real parties aiding and abetting therein . . .
>
> Moreover, the trial court seriously erred by basing its decision on the 'motives' behind Elizabeth Bouvia's decision to exercise her rights. If a right exists, it matters not what 'motivates' its exercise. We find nothing in the law to suggest the right to refuse medical treatment may be exercised only if the patient's motives meet someone else's approval. It certainly is not illegal or immoral to prefer a natural, albeit sooner, death than a drugged life attached to a mechanical device.

These issues relating to positive acts of killing and omissions to treat will be examined further in Chapter 12. Consider, however, what difference (if any) it would have made if Elizabeth Bouvia had stated categorically that she was refusing food, not because it was difficult for her to swallow, but because she wished to die? On the analysis of Beach J, the motives are irrelevant. However, if that is the case, why was he at pains to point out that she did not intend to kill herself? In the English case of *Ms B v An NHS Trust Hospital*,[38] where a capable patient wished to have her artificial ventilation discontinued, Butler-Sloss P accepted Lord Goff's *dictum* in *Airedale NHS Trust v Bland*, that 'in cases of this kind, there is no question of the patient having committed suicide'.[39]

If, on the other hand, the patient requires life-saving treatment as the result of *self-inflicted* injuries, it is arguable that a doctor may treat him, despite his refusal to consent. As Skegg has written:

Skegg, PDG, *Law, Ethics and Medicine: Studies in Medical Law*[40]

> Where someone has done something in an apparent attempt to kill himself, doctors will often be justified in taking action to avert the consequences of the action. Prior to the abolition of the offence of suicide, there was no difficulty in explaining the legal basis for a doctor acting to prevent a person from attempting to commit suicide, or to avoid death resulting from such an attempt. Suicide was a felony, so the doctor was simply exercising the general liberty to prevent a felony. [*R v Duffy* [1967] 1 QB 63, p 67] . . . However, since the enactment of the Suicide Act 1961 it has continued to be accepted that doctors are sometimes free – sometimes, indeed, under a duty – to prevent patients from committing suicide.

---

38 [2002] EWHC Fam 429.
39 See n 7 above.
40 Oxford: Clarendon Press, 1984.

> In some cases, the person who has apparently attempted to commit suicide will be suffering from a mental disorder which prevents the giving or withholding of consent. But in many cases the person will have a sufficient understanding to give, or withhold, consent. This is so, even though the act will often result from a passing impulse or temporary depression, rather than from a rational and fixed decision. If restrained and given assistance, the majority are glad that their action did not result in death. Hence, even if it is accepted that a person should not be prevented from carrying out a calm or a reasoned decision to terminate his own life, there is an overwhelming case for intervention where there is reason to believe that, if given help, the person will be glad he did not kill, or seriously injure, himself. Doctors are constantly intervening in these circumstances and there can be little doubt that, were their conduct to be questioned, the courts would hold it justified.

In fact, there are some cases where it has been held that there is not merely a right (in terms of having immunity from a battery suit), but may even be a duty in negligence on another party to prevent suicide. In *Selfe v Ilford and District Hospital Management Committee*[41] damages were recovered from the defendant mental hospital after the patient made a further suicide attempt after being admitted following a drug overdose, and in *Kirkham v Chief Constable of Greater Manchester Police*[42] the Court of Appeal upheld the claim of a widow of a prisoner who killed himself while on remand in custody. The police had failed to pass on to the prison authorities details of the prisoner's suicidal tendencies. More recently, it has been held that, under certain circumstances, the failure to prevent a patient's suicide may in addition infringe his right to life under Article 2 of the European Convention on Human Rights.[43]

The above decisions concerned persons 'of unsound mind' (which arguably equates to a lack of capacity, as discussed below in section 3.4.1). However, in *Reeves v Commissioner of Police of the Metropolis*[44] the House of Lords held that the police owed a duty of care to take reasonable steps to prevent the suicide of a 'sane' prisoner. The state of mind of the prisoner was irrelevant to the establishment of such a duty. Admittedly *Reeves*, as well as the other cases, related to the failure to prevent/restrain a person's initial self-harming behaviour. But it would arguably be odd if, having imposed a duty at that stage, the law were to deny such a right (and *a fortiori* the duty) to treat of those subsequently rendering medical assistance. In *R (on the Application of Pretty) v Director of Public Prosecutions*,[45] the Divisional Court stated that Article 2 ECHR does not require the state to take positive steps to force life on the unwilling, but nor does it mean that the state is *positively obliged* to stand by and allow someone to take his own life. The clear implication of the court's reasoning is that such intervention would be lawful. But in the subsequent High Court decision of *Re W (Adult: Refusal of Treatment)*,[46] Butler-Sloss P held that the prison authorities were debarred from treating a capable prisoner whose self-inflicted wounds were in danger of causing fatal septicaemia. As noted in Chapter 12, in a recent case, doctors at a Norfolk hospital similarly felt obliged to allow a young suicidal woman, who attended hospital after overdosing on painkillers, to die, given her refusal of life-saving countermeasures.[47]

---

41 (1970) 114 SJ 935.
42 [1990] 2 WLR 987.
43 See *Savage v South Essex Partnership NHS Foundation Trust* [2008] UKHL 74, and *cf Rabone v Pennine Care NHS Trust* [2012] UKSC 2, discussed in Ch 9, section 9.7.2.3.
44 [1999] 3 All ER 897.
45 (2001) 151 NLJ 1572 (Div Ct); the point was not considered further when *Pretty* reached the House of Lords.
46 [2002] EWHC Fam 901.
47 See the discussion of the Wooltorton case in Ch 12, section 12.3.4.

THINK POINT

Following the last case, it was reported that the patient's parents were contemplating legal action against the hospital for its failure to intervene. Summarise the arguments they might be able to use in bringing such a claim.

3.3.1.3 Protecting the integrity of the medical profession

As regards the state interest in protecting the integrity of the medical profession, Schrieber J suggested in *Conroy* that this will not justify overriding a refusal of treatment. However, a different rule would seem to apply in the context of *withdrawing* treatment initiated previously. In the case of *Brophy v New England Sinai Hospital*[48] a Massachusetts court held that a hospital need not compromise its own principles by withdrawing feeding from a patient in PVS, who had made it clear he would not wish to survive in such a state, but should permit his transfer to another hospital sympathetic to this course. A similar approach can be found in the decision of the English High Court in *Ms B v An NHS Trust Hospital*,[49] in which the patient wished her life-sustaining ventilation to cease. The clinicians treating her had come to like and respect her and could not bring themselves to disconnect the ventilator. The court accepted evidence from a professor of intensive care medicine from another trust that, in his opinion, the patient should be transferred to another hospital which would be willing to accede to her request.

A further controversial question is whether, on related institutional grounds, the state could justify the force-feeding of prisoners on hunger-strike. In *Secretary of State v Robb*[50] Thorpe J suggested the answer was no, albeit the case was principally concerned with the absence of a *duty* on the authorities to intervene. In fact, arguably such an intervention may be permitted exceptionally to protect the integrity of the judicial system. This was at least hinted at in *R v Collins and Ashworth Hospital Authority, ex p Brady*, which concerned the convicted Moors murderer, Ian Brady, who was on hunger strike and who, by way of judicial review, challenged the decision of the hospital to force-feed him. The case was principally about capacity and about the application of the Mental Health Act (MHA) 1983, and is considered further in Chapters 4 and 9, but one of the submissions on behalf of the hospital was that, whatever the statutory position, the patient's right of self-determination is not absolute and can be overridden on public interest grounds. The judge declined to make a finding in this respect, as he found that the patient lacked capacity and that the provisions of the MHA 1983 justified force feeding, but he said, nevertheless:

See Chapters 4 and 9

> **Maurice Kay J:** It would be a disappointment to me if I were constrained by authority from finding in favour of [the hospital] on this issue. My impression is that I would not be. Moreover, it would seem to me to be a matter for deep regret if the law has developed to a point in this area where the rights of a patient count for everything and other ethical values and institutional integrity count for nothing.[51]

---

48 497 NE 2d 626 (1986).
49 See n 38 above.
50 See n 34 above.
51 [2000] Lloyd's Rep Med 355.

3.3.1.4 Protection of innocent third parties

It must be said that the purported limitation on treatment refusals 'to protect innocent parties', adverted to in the US *Conroy* case, is of dubious validity. While public health arguments may, in the right circumstances, result in the overriding of a patient's refusal of treatment, in the UK this would have to be by express statutory provision: see section 3.3.2. The cases referred to in *Conroy* relating to the emotional and financial abandonment of children are not in accordance with US or UK law: there is no principle which regards the parents as a means to the ends of their children. While the welfare of the child is paramount in English law, the necessary protection is given, not by compelling parents to care for their children (except financially), but by removing the children from the parents. It is unthinkable that a parent would be ordered to undergo a blood transfusion on the ground that her children would be motherless if she died.

Similarly, the case of *Re S (Adult: Refusal of Medical Treatment)*,[52] referred to by Thorpe J in *Robb* as instancing such a state interest, is also suspect. The case concerned the refusal of a pregnant woman to submit to a Caesarean necessary to save the life of her foetus and her own life. As discussed in Chapter 8, subsequent authorities have distanced themselves from the decision to override the patient's refusal (whether or not she was capable) there.[53]

3.3.2 Statutory exceptions to the need for consent

In addition to the common law rules discussed above, there are some statutory exceptions to the need normally to obtain a person's consent prior to giving medical treatment and care. The two most important categories of patient, whose consent may be so dispensed with, namely the mentally incapacitated and the mentally ill, will be the subject of Chapters 4 and 9, respectively. Until 2016, there was also a power given to local authorities (under section 47 of the National Assistance Act 1948) to remove to a place of safety of those who, through age or infirmity, were no longer able to care for themselves. However, this power, which was increasingly viewed as unnecessary, in the light of alternative provision in mental capacity and mental health legislation for treating vulnerable adults, was abolished when the Care Act 2014 entered force.[54]

Lastly, a patient who suffers from an infectious disease which may pose risks to the health of the community at large may be compulsorily detained and subject to health measures pursuant to Part 2A of the Public Health (Control of Disease) Act 1984 (as amended by the Health and Social Care Act 2008). Section 45G of the amended Act, which entered force in April 2010, provides:

45G Power to order health measures in relation to persons

1   A justice of the peace may make an order under subsection (2) in relation to a person ('P') if the justice is satisfied that –

   a   P is or may be infected or contaminated,

   b   the infection or contamination is one which presents or could present significant harm to human health,

   c   there is a risk that P might infect or contaminate others, and

   d   it is necessary to make the order in order to remove or reduce that risk.

---

52 [1993] Fam 123.
53 See Ch 8, section 8.4.3.
54 See s 46 of the 2014 Act.

2   The order may impose on or in relation to P one or more of the following restrictions or requirements –

a   that P submit to medical examination;

b   that P be removed to a hospital or other suitable establishment;

c   that P be detained in a hospital or other suitable establishment;

d   that P be kept in isolation or quarantine;

e   that P be disinfected or decontaminated;

f   that P wear protective clothing;

g   that P provide information or answer questions about P's health or other circumstances;

h   that P's health be monitored and the results reported;

i   that P attend training or advice sessions on how to reduce the risk of infecting or contaminating others;

j   that P be subject to restrictions on where P goes or with whom P has contact;

k   that P abstain from working or trading.

In contrast to the pre-amendment position, the power to make such an order is not limited to cases where the person suffers from a pre-defined 'notifiable disease'; it is enough that he has a contamination or infection that presents or could present a significant risk to human health.[55] At the same time, though, the justification for such compulsory measures is now more clearly the protection of others; in this regard, as appears analogously from s 45E of the Act, the measures at issue may not include treatment for the affected person's own benefit (including vaccination). Instead, the latter's consent here remains necessary.[56]

3.4 The elements to a valid consent

The essential elements to a valid consent to treatment can be summed up as follows:

a   the patient must have sufficient understanding, variously described as mental capacity or mental competence, to make the decision;

b   the patient must consent to (or refuse) the treatment of his own free will, with no duress or undue influence; and

c   the patient must have been given sufficient information about the proposed treatment.

We shall address each of these requirements in turn.

3.4.1 Capacity to consent

In its 1995 report, *Mental Incapacity*, the Law Commission identified three possible alternative approaches to capacity. These are the 'status', 'outcome' and 'functional' approaches. The status approach is most easily explained in relation to children. This would simply state that a person, eg a child under a certain age, lacked capacity and there would be no examination of other issues such as the person's understanding. The Law Commission rejected this in relation to adult patients as being contrary to a policy of encouraging self-determination.

---

55 The concept of a 'notifiable disease' remains relevant in the context of the reporting duties imposed on doctors and others for monitoring the incidence of certain infectious diseases. A list of them is contained in the Health Protection (Notification) Regulations 2010, SI 2010/659.

56 For further information on the new public health regime, see the DoH's 2010 health protection legislation guidance, available at: www.dh.gov.uk/en/Publicationsandstatistics/Publications/PublicationsPolicyAndGuidance/DH_114510.

The 'outcome' approach was described by the Law Commission as follows:

Law Commission, *Mental Incapacity*[57]

> 3.4 An assessor of capacity using the 'outcome' method focuses on the final content of an individual's deci-
> sion. Any decision which is inconsistent with conventional values, or with which the assessor disagrees,
> may be classified as incapable. This penalises individuality and demands conformity at the expense of
> personal autonomy. A number of our respondents argued that an 'outcome' approach is applied by many
> doctors; if the outcome of the patient's deliberations is to agree with the doctor's recommendations then
> he or she is taken to have capacity, while if the outcome is to reject a course which the doctor has advised
> then capacity is found to be absent.

Again, the Law Commission rejected this approach. It must, in fact, be arguable that such an
approach would make a nonsense of the whole issue of consent to treatment. To take an outcome approach would mean that the patient's consent would only be required when a doctor
did not recommend a type of treatment, but described a number of alternatives to a patient
inviting him to decide which to choose. In any situation when there was one recommendation
only, a patient who refused it would be deemed to lack capacity, and the treatment could go
ahead on the ground that it was in the best interests of the patient to treat him without consent. Not only does it undermine the way in which we have traditionally approached
capacity, it would destroy the very basis of the need to obtain a valid consent to treatment at all.

See Chapter 4 →

Accordingly, the Law Commission recommended the 'functional' approach. Here, the assessor asks whether an individual is able, at the time when a particular decision has to be made, to
understand its nature and effects. The Commission favoured this view not least because it is
reflected in the approach the courts have taken. Most notably, in the well-known case of *Gillick
v West Norfolk and Wisbech AHA*,[58] the House of Lords, in the context of deciding that girls under
the age of 16 would sometimes be able to consent to the provision of contraceptive advice and
treatment, had seen the understanding of the particular girl as key. In his speech, Lord Scarman
stated:

> **Lord Scarman:** It will be a question of fact whether a child seeking advice has sufficient understanding of
> what is involved to give a consent valid in law. Until the child achieves the capacity to consent, the paren-
> tal right to make the decision continues save only in exceptional circumstances . . . When applying these
> conclusions to contraceptive advice and treatment it has to be borne in mind that there is much that has
> to be understood by a girl under the age of 16 if she is to have legal capacity to consent to such treatment.
> It is not enough that she should understand the nature of the advice which is being given: she must also
> have a sufficient maturity to understand what is involved.

Following *Gillick*, the threshold of capacity needed to consent to medical treatment is sometimes
referred to as 'Gillick-competence'. Even so, until the 1990s, there remained surprisingly little
authority on the definition of capacity to consent to medical treatment in general. Subsequently,
further guidance was given by the High Court in *Re C (Adult: Refusal of Treatment)*, a striking
case in a number of ways.

---

57 Report No 231, London: HMSO, 1995.
58 [1986] 1 AC 112; the decision is considered in detail in Ch 4, below.

Re C (adult: refusal of treatment) (1994)[59]

The patient was an elderly man, diagnosed as suffering from paranoid schizophrenia. He had been a patient in Broadmoor special hospital for 30 years. One of his delusional beliefs was that he had been a great doctor who had never failed to cure a patient. He also believed that he had the ability to cure damaged limbs. Following an injury to his foot in 1993, he was diagnosed as suffering from gangrene and the doctors at the local general hospital considered that, unless his foot was amputated, because of the highly toxic nature of gangrene, he was 85% likely to die.

Mr C objected to amputation and made an application to the court for an injunction restraining the health authorities from amputating his foot then *or at any time in the future*. Consent to treatment, other than treatment for the mental disorder, is required even if the patient is mentally ill, as long as he has the necessary capacity,[60] so in this case the decision would turn on C's capacity, regardless of his long history as a patient suffering from what is generally regarded as serious mental illness. Thorpe J held that there is a rebuttable presumption in favour of capacity. C's evidence was that he did not believe the gangrene would kill him, that he had been born into the world with four complete limbs and he intended to go out with those limbs, and that he did not believe that God wanted him to have his foot amputated:

> **Thorpe J**: [Counsels'] submissions divide over the definition of the capacity which enables an individual to refuse treatment. Mr Gordon argues for what he calls the minimal competence test, which he defines as the capacity to understand in broad terms the nature and effect of the proposed treatment. It is common ground that C has the legal capacity to initiate these proceedings without a next friend, within the terms of RSC Ord 80. Mr Gordon contends that the capacity to refuse treatment is no higher and is equally no higher than the capacity to contract. I reject that submission. I think that the question to be decided is whether it has been established that C's capacity is so reduced by his chronic mental illness that he does not sufficiently understand the nature, purpose and effects of the proffered amputation.
>
> I consider helpful Dr Eastman's analysis of the decision making process into three stages: first, comprehending and retaining treatment information, second, believing it and, third, weighing it in the balance to arrive at choice. The Law Commission has proposed a similar approach in para 2.20 of Law Commission Consultation Paper No 129, *Mentally Incapacitated Adults and Decision Making*. Applying that test to my findings on the evidence, I am completely satisfied that the presumption that C has the right of self-determination has not been displaced. Although his general capacity is impaired by schizophrenia, it has not been established that he does not sufficiently understand the nature, purpose and effects of the treatment he refuses. Indeed, I am satisfied that he has understood and retained the relevant treatment information, that in his own way he believes it, and that in the same fashion he has arrived at a clear choice.

The prevalence of paternalism in English medical law had been dealt a blow: the patient's beliefs can be more important than medical opinion (it is also interesting to note that Mr C did, in fact, respond to more conservative treatment).

The approach in *Re C* was subsequently approved by the Court of Appeal in the case of *Re MB (Medical Treatment)*,[61] which concerned a pregnant woman who refused a Caesarean section after panicking due to 'needle phobia'. The High Court granted a declaration that it would be lawful to carry out the operation because, on the evidence, the patient was suffering from a

---

59 [1994] 1 WLR 290.
60 See s 63 of the MHA 1983, discussed in Ch 9.
61 [1997] 2 FLR 426, CA.

temporary impairment to her mental functioning and was, therefore, not capable. This decision was upheld by Court of Appeal:

Butler-Sloss LJ (delivering the judgment of the court)

Conclusions on capacity to decide

. . . (1) Every person is presumed to have the capacity to consent to or to refuse medical treatment unless and until that presumption is rebutted . . .

. . . (4) A person lacks capacity if some impairment or disturbance of mental functioning renders the person unable to make a decision whether to consent to or to refuse treatment. That inability to make a decision will occur when:

a   the patient is unable to comprehend and retain the information which is material to the decision, especially as to the likely consequences of having or not having the treatment in question;

b   the patient is unable to use the information and weigh it in the balance as part of the process of arriving at the decision. If, as Thorpe J observed in *Re C* . . . a compulsive disorder or phobia from which the patient suffers stifles belief in the information presented to her, then the decision may not be a true one. As Lord Cockburn CJ put it in *Banks v Goodfellow* (1870) LR 5 QB 549, p 569:

> . . . one object may be so forced upon the attention of the invalid as to shut out all others that might require consideration.

(5) The 'temporary factors' mentioned by Lord Donaldson MR in *Re T* (confusion, shock, fatigue, pain or drugs) may completely erode capacity but those concerned must be satisfied that such factors are operating to such a degree that the ability to decide is absent.

(6) Another such influence may be panic induced by fear. Again, careful scrutiny of the evidence is necessary because fear of an operation may be a rational reason for refusal to undergo it. Fear may also, however, paralyse the will and thus destroy the capacity to make a decision.

This approach has been applied in a number of subsequent authorities.[62] Indeed, the common law test has now received statutory endorsement in terms of the definition of 'lack of capacity' (the obverse of capacity) contained in the Mental Capacity Act 2005. This provides, in ss 2 and 3, as follows:

Mental Capacity Act 2005

2 People who lack capacity

1   For the purposes of this Act, a person lacks capacity in relation to a matter if at the material time he is unable to make a decision for himself in relation to the matter because of an impairment of, or a disturbance in the functioning of, the mind or brain.

2   It does not matter whether the impairment or disturbance is permanent or temporary.

3   A lack of capacity cannot be established merely by reference to –

a   a person's age or appearance, or

b   a condition of his, or an aspect of his behaviour, which might lead others to make unjustified assumptions about his capacity . . .

---

62 See, eg, *St George's Healthcare NHS Trust v S* [1999] Fam 26, CA; *Re W (Adult: Refusal of Treatment)* (n 46 above).

3 Inability to make decisions

1   For the purposes of section 2, a person is unable to make a decision for himself if he is unable –
     a   to understand the information relevant to the decision,
     b   to retain that information,
     c   to use or weigh that information as part of the process of making the decision, or
     d   to communicate his decision (whether by talking, using sign language or any other means).
2   A person is not to be regarded as unable to understand the information relevant to a decision if he is able to understand an explanation of it given to him in a way that is appropriate to his circumstances (using simple language, visual aids or any other means).
3   The fact that a person is able to retain the information relevant to a decision for a short period only does not prevent him from being regarded as able to make the decision.
4   The information relevant to a decision includes information about the reasonably foreseeable consequences of –
     a   deciding one way or another, or
     b   failing to make the decision.

As will be apparent, the wording of these provisions owes much to the decision in *Re MB*, in particular (one gloss is s 3(1)(d), which allows patients who have capacity in principle, but no means of giving expression to it – ie they are 'locked in' as may happen in rare cases of Guillain Barré syndrome – to be treated as though incapacitated).

Even so, in practice, the assessment of capacity may be far from straightforward. Such an assessment by its nature requires one person (the assessor) to form a judgment about the 'interior', ie cognitively not directly accessible, mental state of another. The importance in this context of cultural awareness on the part of the assessor was highlighted by Michael Gunn, when examining the Consultation Paper which preceded the Law Commission's Report on *Mental Incapacity*:

Gunn, M, 'The meaning of incapacity'[63]

It is clearly the case that capacity is a value-laden concept. Undoubtedly, the approach recommended by the Law Commission is one very much within the tradition of Western cultures. Care must therefore be taken in its application to people from other cultures. More specifically, any person assessing the competence of another individual must be aware of their own values so that assumptions and decisions are not made which are unjustifiable. It is the values of the person being assessed which must be respected. The assessor needs to be able to identify where her values vary from those of the person being assessed. Values cannot be removed from any assessment, but assessors of capacity can be educated to be aware of their own values and thus to take care in assessing capacity not to be prejudiced when meeting someone with a different value base.

In the context of medical treatment, it will fall in the first instance to the doctors, at the point of treatment, to make the assessment. The law, as noted above, attempts to provide assistance by directing them to focus separately on such elements as the patient's 'understanding', 'retention', and 'ability to weigh' treatment information.

Nonetheless, as we shall see below, such concepts remain relatively open-textured and fluid.

---

63 (1994) 2 Med L Rev 8.

3.4.2 Assessing capacity

3.4.2.1 The ability to understand and retain information

As we have seen, those caring for the patient must be satisfied that he comprehends or understands the treatment information. The latter must be able to act in an autonomous manner and, as a first step, this requires the ability to identify and process information relevant to his situation. If radical mistake or confusion besets this process, he will be prevented from making a considered decision. Arguably, however, the notion of 'understanding' can be manipulated to facilitate a finding of incapacity.[64] The question has also been raised – in the context of 'mature minors' (although there is no reason to suppose that the position will differ for adults) – as to whether the requirement of 'understanding' means that the patient must actually understand the nature of the information about the treatment and its consequences, or merely that he is capable of understanding:

Kennedy, I and Grubb, A, *Medical Law: Text with Materials*[65]

If the test of understanding is *actual understanding* . . . then whether or not the girl understands *and therefore is competent* to consent may turn on what she is told. Indeed, this seems to have been Lord Donaldson's approach in *Re R* . . . If the girl is not given certain information she may not understand enough, but this would not be the product of any lack of competence but merely that she decided in relative ignorance. It would be an unsatisfactory state of law if doctors could by controlling the information given to a patient thereby grant or deny her competence . . . It must, therefore, be the law that competence is determined by reference to the unvarying conceptual standard of capacity or ability to understand.

A further question relates to whether the patient must have 'first hand' experience in relation to the matters he is required to understand. The answer to this is clearly 'no', as illustrated in *Ms B v An NHS Trust Hospital*.[66] Here the patient was paralysed from the neck downwards, with no prospects of recovery. However, she could be admitted to a spinal rehabilitation unit with a view to rehabilitation into the community. She had declined to participate in this and wanted the ventilator which kept her alive to be disconnected. Dame Butler-Sloss, President of the Family Division, found her to have capacity and, therefore, to be able lawfully to refuse treatment. However, expert evidence on behalf of the trust, which wanted her to go ahead with the rehabilitation, was given by a spinal injuries consultant, who stated that as the patient had not gone through the rehabilitation process she did not have the information necessary to make her decision. This was, rightly, roundly rejected by the President when she said: 'Even in issues of the utmost significance and gravity people, including patients, have to make decisions without experience of the consequences and his requirement is unrealistic.'

As regards the retention of information, an important factor will be the stability of the patient's mental profile. Thus, a fluctuating mental state as in the *Re R* case may impede retention, as can temporary factors such as pain and exhaustion. However, it is important that the latter are stringently defined; there have been some cases, which concern the refusals of Caesarean sections, when, in the course of labour, difficulties have arisen which have put the life of woman and/or foetus at risk. Here, there could be a temptation to use a blanket argument that

---

64 See Lee, S, 'Towards a jurisprudence of consent', in *Oxford Essays in Jurisprudence*, Oxford: Clarendon, 1987, who argues that few adults could meet Lord Scarman's criteria in relation to a child's understanding, set out in the *Gillick* case (see n 58 above).

65 See n 29 above. The case of *Re R (A Minor) (Wardship: Consent to Medical Treatment)* [1991] 3 WLR 592, referred to here, concerned a 15-year-old girl with a fluctuating mental state, who was refusing antipsychotic drugs: see further Ch 4, below.

66 See n 38 above.

the labour process itself has produced temporary factors which have inhibited understanding and/or retention: see, in particular, the judgment of Johnson J in *Rochdale Healthcare (NHS) Trust v C*,[67] where he held that the patient was incapable due to the stress and pain of labour.

In *Re MB (Medical Treatment)*,[68] the Court of Appeal took the opportunity to criticise the evidential basis for Johnson J's finding in the *Rochdale* case. This is not to deny that, on the facts of a given case, there may indeed be evidence of special factors temporarily disruptive of capacity. In *Re MB* itself, the patient's needle phobia was such a factor.

3.4.2.2 Belief and its effect upon understanding

In *Re C (Adult: Refusal of Treatment)*,[69] Thorpe J treated the patient's ability to believe the treatment information as a distinct element in the test of capacity. Subsequently, however, in *Re MB*, belief was not accorded separate mention, and nor is it adverted to by the new statutory test in s 3 of the Mental Capacity Act 2005. The reason is the difficulty, conceptually, of keeping understanding and belief distinct in this context:[70] to mention belief separately is arguably merely a way of emphasising that the patient must appreciate that the information *pertains to him* (as opposed merely to understanding it abstractly in the way, say, one might follow the plot of a novel).

Accordingly, where a patient has certain delusional beliefs in relation to treatment information, one may sometimes be justified in concluding that he is unable to 'understand' it. In this regard, the Court of Appeal suggested in *Re MB* that 'a misperception of reality (eg the blood is poisoned because it is red) . . . will be more readily accepted to be a disorder of the mind'.[71] It is important to note that what is at issue here are beliefs about the empirical world, where agreed standards exist for demonstrating their falsehood (by contrast, religiously grounded beliefs, even if of a minority order and regarded by most as wrong-headed, will provide no basis for inferences as to their holder's mental capacity).

An American case, which illustrates a fundamental misperception of reality on the part of the patient, is *State of Tennessee v Northern*:[72]

Todd J: On 24 January 1978 the Tennessee Department of Human Services filed this suit alleging that Mary C Northern was 72 years old, with no available help from relatives; that Miss Northern resided alone under unsatisfactory conditions as a result of which she had been admitted to and was a patient in Nashville General Hospital; that the patient suffered from gangrene of both feet which required the removal of her feet to save her life; that the patient lacked the capacity to appreciate her condition or to consent to necessary surgery . . .

In the present case, this court has found the patient to be lucid and apparently of sound mind generally. However, on the subjects of death and amputation of her feet, her comprehension is blocked, blinded or dimmed to the extent that she is incapable of recognising facts which would be obvious to a person of normal perception. For example, in the presence of this court, the patient looked at her feet and refused to recognise the obvious facts that the flesh was dead, black, shrivelled, rotting and stinking.

The record also discloses that the patient refuses to consider the eventuality of death which is or ought to be obvious in the face of such dire bodily deterioration.

---

67 [1997] 1 FCR 274.
68 See n 61 above.
69 See n 59 above.
70 See also *Local Authority X v MM* [2007] EWHC 2003 (Fam), where Munby J suggested that the need for belief was subsumed within the more general requirements of understanding and ability to weigh the information in the balance.
71 See n 61 above; and see the facts of *An NHS Trust v T (Adult: Refusal of Medical Treatment)* [2004] EWHC 1279 (Fam).
72 563 SW 2d 197 (1978).

> As described by the doctors and observed by this court, the patient wants to live and keep her dead feet, too, and refuses to consider the impossibility of such a desire. In order to avoid the unpleasant experience of facing death and/or loss of feet, her mind or emotions have resorted to the device of denying the unpleasant reality so that, to the patient, the unpleasant reality does not exist. This is the 'delusion' which renders the patient incapable of making a rational decision as to whether to undergo surgery to save her life or to forgo surgery and forfeit her life.
>
> …If, as repeatedly stated, this patient could and would give evidence of a comprehension of the facts of her condition and could and would express her unequivocal desire in the face of such comprehended facts, then her decision, however unreasonable to others, would be accepted and honoured by the courts and by her doctors. The difficulty is that she cannot or will not comprehend the facts.

Accordingly, the court found that the patient was incapable (see also the decision of the English High Court in *Norfolk and Norwich Healthcare (NHS) Trust v W*,[73] where a patient, who was admitted to hospital in labour, denied that she was pregnant).

More difficulties may arise in cases where a treatment decision by a patient is based upon a mixture of rational and delusional beliefs. An example is provided by the case of *Re SB (Capacity to Consent to Termination)*,[74] decided by the Court of Protection under the Mental Capacity Act 2005. Here the pregnant patient, who suffered from bipolar disorder and had latterly been detained under the Mental Health Act 1983, wished to have an abortion. Her capacity to consent was doubted by her treating psychiatrists, her husband and her mother, who asserted that SB's initial desire to have the child had changed after she discontinued her medication (due to concerns about the side effects for the foetus); she had then formed the delusional belief that her husband and mother would not support her after the birth. However, having heard the evidence of SB herself, Holman J was of the clear view that she retained capacity:

> **Holman J**: 42. During the course of her evidence today the patient has identified a considerable number of discrete reasons for her desire for a termination. They certainly include that she perceives that she receives no support from her family and that they will not function as a family. She says that she does not see a future in the relationship with her husband; it is not stable nor productive; he does not have the same ambitions as she has, or for a child. Let us assume that all of those reasons are influenced by delusion or paranoia. She gives many other reasons for her desire for a termination. She refers again and again to her current position that she is a compulsorily detained patient to which she objects. It is perfectly true . . . that many detained patients who become pregnant choose to carry their babies to term. The view of this particular patient is that 'in the situation that I am in, the idea of me having a baby is crazy'. That situation includes the fact that she is currently compulsorily detained. She says, 'I am extremely unhappy where I am. Imagine being unhappy and being pregnant.' That seems to me to be a perfectly understandable position for a detained patient to take, even though it is not one that all detained patients would take. She referred to the fact that staff at the hospital have frequently said to her, 'Why not give it up for adoption?' Her reaction is, 'Why should I have a child just to give it up?' She said she is very worried about her ability to bring up a child. Since it is so strongly said that she has for 8 years suffered from a lifelong, relapsing bipolar disorder, it is entirely rational that she has that worry.
>
> 43. She has said, not only today, but on a number of other recent occasions, that she feels suicidal at the prospect of having to carry this child to term. She says that if there is no termination she will seek to kill herself or the baby. It may be that those suicidal thoughts are in some way bound up with her illness. But if,

---

73 [1996] 2 FLR 613.
74 [2013] EWHC 1417 (COP).

indeed, she does feel them (and I have no reason to suppose that she expresses them simply to threaten or blackmail me or others) then it seems to me to be entirely rational for her to consider and decide that it is preferable for her to seek and undergo a termination before being driven to attempting suicide.

44. It seems to me, therefore, that even if aspects of the decision making are influenced by paranoid thoughts in relation to her husband and her mother, she is nevertheless able to describe, and genuinely holds, a range of rational reasons for her decision. When I say rational, I do not necessarily say they are good reasons, nor do I indicate whether I agree with her decision, for section 1(4) of the Act expressly provides that someone is not to be treated as unable to make a decision simply because it is an unwise decision. It seems to me that this lady has made, and has maintained for an appreciable period of time, a decision. It may be that aspects of her reasons may be skewed by paranoia. There are other reasons which she has and which she has expressed. My own opinion is that it would be a total affront to the autonomy of this patient to conclude that she lacks capacity to the level required to make this decision. It is of course a profound and grave decision, but it does not necessarily involve complex issues. It is a decision that she has made and maintains; and she has defended and justified her decision against challenge. It is a decision which she has the capacity to reach. So for those reasons I conclude that it has not been established that she lacks capacity to make decisions about her desired termination, and I will either make a declaration to that effect or dismiss these proceedings.

Arguably, as in this case, where the patient's beliefs concern future events, circumspection is called for before concluding that these are delusional. In *Re C (Adult: Refusal of Treatment)*[75] the English High Court upheld a treatment refusal, based on similarly 'mixed' beliefs, including some that pertained to the future. Here it should normally be enough that the patient is free of delusion as to the information about his condition and the proposed treatment. Unless the circumstances are such that a given outcome must be reasonably regarded as objectively certain (eg death in the case of a refused blood transfusion), the patient may be told that he has, say, only a 5 per cent chance of survival without treatment, but it is still not delusional for him to believe he will fall into the 5 per cent category.

3.4.2.3 Weighing treatment information in the balance

As noted, the second main requirement, to have capacity, is that the patient is able to 'weigh' the treatment information. One aspect of this is that the patient must be capable of acting volitionally in the light of the information. There have in fact been a number of cases where, although capable, in intellectual terms, of 'understanding', patients have been found incapable due to an impediment in their will. This may be true, for example, in the case of a person suffering from a compulsive disorder. In *Re W (A Minor) (Medical Treatment)*[76] the Court of Appeal took the view (without deciding the issue) that a 17-year-old girl suffering from anorexia nervosa was probably incapable. One of the symptoms of the condition is that the patient wants to decide herself when to eat:

Lord Donaldson MR: [I]t is a feature of anorexia nervosa that it is capable of destroying the ability to make an informed choice. It creates a compulsion to refuse treatment or only to accept treatment which is likely to be ineffective. This attitude is part and parcel of the disease and the more advanced the illness, the more compelling it may become. Where the wishes of the minor are themselves something which the doctors reasonably consider need to be treated in the minor's own best interests, those wishes clearly have a much reduced significance.

---

75 See n 59 above.
76 See n 36 above.

In the case of *B v Croydon Health Authority*,[77] a 24-year-old woman with a compulsion to self-harm had been detained under the Mental Health Act 1983. She subsequently suffered serious weight loss after refusing further sustenance. Thorpe J held that she was capable, but authorised her force-feeding under the 1983 Act. On appeal, the Court of Appeal was clearly doubtful as to B's capacity:

Hoffmann LJ: I am bound to say that I have some difficulty with the judge's conclusion [that B had capacity at common law]. Reading the letter which Ms B wrote to the hospital at the end of March 1994 and the transcript of her evidence given before the judge on 23 June 1994, I am as impressed as the judge was by her intelligence and self-awareness. It is however this very self-awareness and acute self-analysis which leads me to doubt whether, at the critical time, she could be said to have made a true choice in refusing to eat. In her letter she said: 'My basic need is to be understood why I feel the need to punish myself and at present this is by not eating.' In evidence she said:

> Q. Are you being told that you may die if you are not tube fed? A.... They told me ... that they were doing that to save my life.
> Q. Did you understand what they were telling you? A. I found it difficult to believe because I felt quite well.
> Q. Yes. Did you want to die? A. There are times when you feel so despondent that you do not care whether you live or die but I think deep down I don't. I certainly didn't intend to lose weight. I didn't want to allow myself – I've always enjoyed my food so by denying myself something I endured it as a punishment, but it was never meant as a slow suicide attempt or anything like that.
> Q. Do you think you are running risks in what you are doing? A. (Pause). I understand now that with severe loss of weight, as the weight just goes less and less, it does put stress on your heart and risk of heart attack. It is not always easy to believe when you are feeling quite fit really.
> Q. Looking at the matter today, do you appreciate that you are running some risks in what you are doing? A. Today I understand why they wanted to tube feed me and I understand that my weight – I can accept that my weight was getting out of hand.
> Q. Yes. A. I understand that. As much as some days you just wouldn't – you're crying inside for help but you are so stuck in the routine and self-punishment and that, it's almost like a habit you can't break.
> Q. Yes. A. and sometimes you just want somebody to come and break it.
> Q. Yes; how? A. I don't know how.

I find it hard to accept that someone who acknowledges that in refusing food at the critical time she did not appreciate the extent to which she was hazarding her life, was crying inside for help but unable to break out of the routine of punishing herself, could be said to be capable of making a true choice as to whether or not to eat.

Subsequently, in *R v Collins and Ashworth Hospital Authority, ex p Brady*,[78] it was found that Ian Brady's inability to weigh up the treatment information meant that he lacked capacity:

Maurice Kay J: . . . [N]otwithstanding the fact that he is a man of well above average intelligence, he has engaged in his battle of wills in such a way that, as a result of his severe personality disorder, he has eschewed the weighing of information and the balancing of the risks and needs to such an extent that . . . his decisions on food refusal and force feeding have been incapacitated.

---

77 [1994] 2 WLR 294; the case is further discussed in Ch 9.
78 See n 51 above.

3.4.2.4 Must there be 'reasons' for the patient's choice?

Generally, as we have seen, even where the consequences of so doing are likely to be very grave, the patient with sufficient understanding may refuse treatment, provided he is capable of balancing the risks of refusal against his other needs. Carrying out this sort of balancing exercise might, on the face of it, require the patient to provide reasons for those needs, and, if necessary, reasons for preferring those needs to taking the recommended medical treatment. However, in *Re T (Adult: Refusal of Treatment)*,[79] Lord Donaldson MR stated that, 'the patient's right of choice exists whether the reasons for making that choice are rational, irrational, unknown or even non-existent'. The denial that the patient need have any reasons for his decision in fact stems from remarks by Lord Templeman in *Sidaway v Board of Governors of the Bethlehem Royal Hospital and the Maudsley Hospital*,[80] and it was reiterated by Butler-Sloss LJ in *Re MB (Medical Treatment)*:

> **Butler-Sloss LJ** (speaking for the Court): A mentally competent patient has an absolute right to refuse to consent to medical treatment for any reason, rational or irrational, or for no reason at all, even where that decision may lead to his or her own death.[81]

The reference to non-existent reasons raises some interesting questions, which we examined in Chapter 1.[82] It will be recalled that when we there discussed 'rational' decision-making, we concluded that if the decision fitted in with the patient's world view, then it should be respected. If this subjective test is adopted, then genuinely held beliefs that fit in with an internally coherent body of thought will not disqualify the patient from decision-making, even if the 'internal coherence' contains a number of bizarre beliefs which can be clearly shown to be unsustainable, for example, Mr C's belief in the *Re C* case that he had once been a successful doctor. Ian Kennedy favours this approach:

See Chapter 1 ←

Kennedy, I, 'Consent to treatment: the capable person'[83]

> [I]f the beliefs and values of the patient, though incomprehensible to others, are of long standing and have formed the basis for all the patient's decisions about his life, there is a strong argument to suggest that the doctor should respect and give effect to a patient's decision based on them. That is to say that the doctor should regard such a patient as capable of consenting (or refusing). To argue otherwise would effectively be to rob the patient of his right to his own personality which may be far more serious and destructive than anything that could follow from the patient's decision as regards a particular proposed treatment.

As discussed earlier, the courts are clearly right not to insist that a capable refusal *must* be a rational one (in according with the patient's best interests, objectively considered). For one thing this would rule out refusals based upon religious grounds, which are in practice regarded as among the most respectable reasons for refusing treatment. Indeed, concentration on the rational/irrational raises the image of a neat dichotomy, which is misleading. Aside from religious grounds (which are in fact best described as 'non-rational')[84] many of the factors which influence

---

79 See n 21 above.
80 [1985] AC 871.
81 See n 61 above.
82 See Ch 1, 1.4.5 above.
83 In Dyer, C (ed), *Doctors, Patients and the Law*, Oxford: Blackwell Science, 1992.
84 See Stauch, M, 'Rationality and the refusal of medical treatment: a critique of the recent approach of the English courts' (1995) 21 JME 162.

decisions about medical treatment are difficult to categorise. Thus, is a patient's fear of the pain involved in a given operation irrational?

In *Re JT (Adult: Refusal of Medical Treatment)*[85] Wall J found that an adult patient who suffered from mental disability involving learning difficulties and severe behavioural disturbances, such as to have been compulsorily detained under the MHA 1983, had capacity to refuse renal dialysis, without which she would certainly die. He referred to the *Re C* three-stage test, and, upon the evidence, found it to be satisfied. The patient had said that she objected to dialysis and wanted to die. The judge seemed to be particularly impressed with the evidence of the patient's brother who had said that her refusal was 'anything but a flash in the pan' and that, although the family had tried very hard to persuade her to go ahead with the treatment, they now accepted her decision and supported her. However, there is nothing in the case to indicate why she took this view, for example fear of pain. It may well be that in *Re JT* a significant factor was the need for some degree of co-operation on the patient's part in treatment such as dialysis, which is given while the patient is conscious, and which takes some time to complete. Clearly, the patient in that case was not going to co-operate, but, of course, that should be irrelevant as far as capacity is concerned.

In fact, arguably, identifying the reason or reasons for refusal of treatment will be an essential step at the initial stage of deciding if the patient has capacity. Thus, in practice, despite the radical rhetoric of decisions such as *Re MB*, it appears that judges will subject the patient's reasons for refusing treatment to considerable scrutiny. An example is provided by *Ms B v An NHS Trust Hospital*,[86] where the question related to whether the paralysed patient was competent to refuse life-sustaining ventilation. Dame Elizabeth Butler-Sloss P (interestingly, the same judge as in *Re MB*) carefully chronicled the evidence before her relating it to Ms B's reasons:

> **Butler-Sloss P:** [39] [Ms B] provided two written statements and gave oral evidence for about an hour and a half. She gave a clear account of her wishes and her feelings. She made it clear in her written and oral evidence that she had never changed her view that she wanted the ventilator withdrawn . . .
>
> [47] She was asked by Mr Francis QC, for the Hospital, whether it was her wish to die, or not to remain alive in her present condition, she replied:
>
>> 'The latter. . . . Given the range of choices, I would want to recover and have my life back, or significant enough recovery to have a better quality of life. I am not convinced from the evidence that that is going to happen, and I find the idea of living like this intolerable.'
>>
>> 'My view [about rehabilitation] is that it offers me no real opportunity to recover physically, that, in actual fact, it will be more teaching me to live with my disability and to make use of the technologies available and that sort of thing, working with the carers. But, actually, I will not recover in any way. That is not acceptable to me.'
>
> [48] She was asked by Mr Francis whether the independence gained through rehabilitation would be of value to her, and said,
>
>> 'I think it is an improvement, certainly. Whether it is sufficient for me or not is where we probably disagree. I don't think it is sufficient, but I can see that it offers opportunities for communication. . . . I think it does make a difference to quality of life, but I do not think it is sufficient for me to want to pursue it.'

Ms B was found to have capacity to refuse further ventilation.

---

85 [1998] 1 FLR 48.
86 See n 38 above.

Nowadays such decisions fall to be made within the interpretative framework of the Mental Capacity Act 2005, including the principles (set out in s 1) that an adult is generally presumed to have capacity, and that the unwisdom of their decision is not without more a ground for denying this. Accordingly, in asking for the patient's reasons, the court should clearly not require ones that would be endorsed by persons at large; but the reasons should at least be intelligible by reference to that patient's personality and attitudes as expressed in their lifestyle up until that point. A poignant, but it is submitted correct, decision in this regard is the 2015 Court of Protection case of *Kings College NHS Foundation Trust v C*,[87] which, like the *Ms B* case, involved a dispute as to capacity to refuse life-saving treatment.

Here, as the Court of Protection noted, the patient, C, had lived an unconventional life 'characterised by impulsive and self-centred decision making without guilt or regret. . . . [and] revolving largely around her looks, men, material possessions and "living the high life"'. Following a diagnosis of breast cancer and faced with financial impoverishment after the breakdown of a relationship, she had taken an overdose of Paracetamol and now required kidney dialysis to survive. However, C refused this on the basis that she did not wish to live on without her 'sparkle' and become old and poor.

In finding the trust had failed to establish lack of capacity, MacDonald J commented:

> **MacDonald J**: [97] . . . [O]thers in society may consider C's decision to be unreasonable, illogical or even immoral within the context of the sanctity accorded to life by society in general. None of this however is evidence of a lack of capacity. The court being satisfied that, in accordance with the provisions of the Mental Capacity Act 2005, C has capacity to decide whether or not to accept treatment C is entitled to make her own decision on that question based on the things that are important to her, in keeping with her own personality and system of values and without conforming to society's expectation of what constitutes the 'normal' decision in this situation (if such a thing exists). As a capacitous individual C is, in respect of her own body and mind, sovereign.

THINK POINT

How far may the criteria for capacity, from the case law and the MCA 2005, still allow paternalistically inclined doctors (and judges) to 'reason backwards' and find patients, who refuse clearly beneficial treatment, incapable?[88]

3.4.3 Consent must be voluntary

The case of *Freeman v Home Office*[89] concerned a prisoner who had been injected with certain drugs, apparently for the treatment of a personality disorder. It gave rise to a number of issues: did the prisoner, as a matter of fact, consent to this treatment, and, more interestingly, could it be argued that a prisoner could not give a valid consent to treatment by a prison medical officer where the officer was not acting in his capacity as a doctor but as a disciplinarian. As to the

---

87 [2015] EWCOP 80.
88 See Maclean, A, 'Advance directives and the rocky waters of anticipatory decision-making' (2008) 16 Med L Rev 1.
89 [1984] QB 524.

judge's finding of fact in respect of whether consent had been given, the Court of Appeal refused to disturb this. On the wider point of doctor *qua* disciplinarian, Sir John Donaldson MR stated:

> **Sir John Donaldson MR**: Counsel for the plaintiff submitted that such were the pressures of prison life and discipline that a prisoner could not, as a matter of law, give an effective consent to treatment in any circumstances. This is a somewhat surprising proposition since it would mean that, in the absence of statutory authority, no prison medical officer could ever treat a prisoner. The answer of counsel for the plaintiff was in part that outside medical officers could be brought in, but I am not persuaded that this would reduce the pressures, whatever they may be ...
>
> The judge expressed his view on this aspect of the argument by saying ([1983] 3 All ER 589, p 597 ...):
>
>> The right approach, in my judgment, is to say that where, in a prison setting, a doctor has the power to influence a prisoner's situation and prospects, a court must be alive to the risk that what may appear, on the face of it, to be a real consent is not in fact so.
>
> I would accept that as a wholly accurate statement of the law. The judge said that he had borne this in mind throughout the case. The sole question is therefore whether, on the evidence, there was a real consent.

Although *Freeman* endorses the need for particular vigilance when a patient may be in a vulnerable situation, on the evidence in this case, the patient was being administered drugs 'because of his obvious hostility and cantankerous behaviour'. The question arises whether this was treatment at all? The patient had been told that the drugs would 'make him feel like a new man', but there is a very clear indication that the drugs would make him a much easier prisoner to deal with. Arguably, a rather complacent view of the medical interests of prison inmates was also taken in the American case of *Thor v Superior Court*,[90] in which the Supreme Court of California stated:

> There is no reason to believe that the prison environment, with its possible inadequacy of medical and related support services for ill or injured prisoners, inherently jeopardises the voluntariness of a prisoner's decision to forgo life-sustaining treatment. Any individual who suffers a debilitating or life-threatening disease or injury inevitably faces choices in medical decision making affected or even dictated by his life circumstances, and the prison environment (although in some respects unique) is simply one such circumstance in the individual's personal calculus.

Commenting upon the *Thor* case, Ian Kennedy wrote as follows:

Kennedy, I, 'Commentary on *Thor v Superior Court*'[91]

> Medical law as it relates to those in prison is a distinctly murky world. The California Supreme Court could perhaps be excused for not examining in any detail the tensions between the conflicting claims which arise. The impression which is left, however, is one of too great a willingness to defer to the needs of security over the claims of the prisoner, whether to refuse or, just as important, to obtain medical treatment. English law sadly is no less murky. There is, of course, the statement by Lord Keith in the course of his speech in *Bland* [[1993] 1 All ER 821] that concern for the principle of the sanctity of life 'does not authorise forcible feeding of prisoners on hunger strikes'. But the wider questions of the refusal of medical treatment

---

90 5 Cal 4th 725 (1993).
91 (1994) 2 Med L Rev 224.

by prisoners, their ability to gain access to treatment and the involuntary treatment of them with, for example, psychotropic drugs are greatly under examined. One obvious reason is the inability to obtain reliable information. The instant case should serve as a reminder that such an examination is long overdue. [See now, *Health Care of Detainees in Police Stations*, 1994, London: BMA].

Nonetheless, even within the normal setting of patient care (that is, general hospital or GP's surgery), it might be argued that there remains an inherent risk of coercive behaviour on the part of doctors. The issue is discussed by Culver and Gert as follows:

Culver, CM and Gert, B, *Philosophy in Medicine: Conceptual and Ethical Issues in Medicine and Psychiatry*[92]

Valid consent requires the absence of any coercion by the doctor or the medical staff. Coercion involves any threat of sufficient force that no rational person would reasonably be expected to resist it ... A threat of this kind means that the person being threatened has been deprived of his freedom and so has an excuse for doing what he has been coerced to do. We do not regard strong recommendations, forcefully given, as coercive. To extend the term 'coercion', so that any pressure by a doctor on a patient to accept the doctor's recommendations would count as coercive, and hence in need of justification, seems to us undesirable. We wish to allow doctors considerable leeway in supporting their views. Patients often have irrational fears that must be overcome, so we do not want to set unrealistic limits. But, given the tremendous authority of doctors and the vulnerable position of patients, no threats of lack of care should be allowed.

Culver and Gert may be right in stating that 'strong recommendations' are not coercive (in the sense of amounting to duress), but given the power imbalance between doctor and patient, and the likelihood of the latter enjoying reduced autonomy due to illness, does the doctor exercise undue influence?

The question of undue influence, here exercised by a relative, was one of the issues considered in the important case of *Re T (Adult: Refusal of Medical Treatment)*.

Re T (adult: refusal of medical treatment)[93]

The 20-year-old patient, who was pregnant, was admitted to hospital after a road accident. The patient's mother was a devout Jehovah's Witness, although the patient herself was not of the faith. Shortly after being visited by her mother she informed doctors that she did not want a blood transfusion. She asked doctors if there were alternative treatments and was told that there were. Prior to a Caesarean section she signed a form refusing blood transfusions, but was not told that one might be necessary to save her life or prevent serious injury. After the stillbirth of her baby, the patient's condition deteriorated, and the judge at first instance granted a declaration that it would be lawful to administer a blood transfusion:

> **Lord Donaldson MR:** A special problem may arise if at the time the decision is made the patient has been subjected to the influence of some third party. This is by no means to say that the patient is not entitled to receive and indeed invite advice and assistance from others in reaching a decision, particularly from members of the family. But the doctors have to consider whether the decision is really that of the patient. It is wholly acceptable that the patient should have been persuaded by others of the merits of such a decision and have decided accordingly. It matters not how strong the persuasion was, so long as it did not overbear the independence

---

92 New York: OUP, 1982.
93 See n 21 above.

of the patient's decision. The real question in each such case is: does the patient really mean what he says or is he merely saying it for a quiet life, to someone else or because the advice and persuasion to which he has been subjected is such that he can no longer think and decide for himself? In other words, is it a decision expressed in form only, not in reality?

When considering the effect of outside influences, two aspects can be of crucial importance. First, the strength of the will of the patient. One who is very tired, in pain or depressed will be much less able to resist having his will overborne than one who is rested, free from pain and cheerful. Second, the relationship of the 'persuader' to the patient may be of crucial importance. The influence of parents on their children or of one spouse on the other can be, but is by no means necessarily, much stronger than would be the case in other relationships. Persuasion based upon religious belief can also be much more compelling and the fact that arguments based upon religious beliefs are being deployed by someone in a very close relationship with the patient will give them added force and should alert the doctors to the possibility – no more – that the patient's capacity or will to decide has been overborne. In other words the patient may not mean what he says.

Lord Donaldson MR acknowledged that awareness of the possibility of undue influence should not preclude genuine consultation by the patient with others, particularly family members. However, given that the doctors will rarely be privy to these consultations, it is hard to see how they could have sufficient evidence of undue influence, unless this was revealed to them by the patient. It is arguable that the decision in this case should have revolved more around the genuineness of the consent in relation to the information given by the doctors to the patient (that is, risk of death, possibility of no alternative treatment and so on) and/or on the possible temporary incapacity of the patient, rather than on the issue of undue influence.

The position in *Re T* can be contrasted with that in *The Centre for Reproductive Medicine v U*,[94] where the consent of a man who was described as able, intelligent and educated, with a responsible job and in good health could not be said to have been obtained under duress. He and his wife were undergoing treatment for infertility. He had withdrawn his consent to the posthumous use of his sperm and unfortunately died unexpectedly soon afterwards. The allegation was that the clinical practice manager had pressurised him into the withdrawal. On the evidence, she had clearly warned about the implications of posthumous insemination and would have halted the treatment for further consultation and counselling to take place. At first instance, it was found that the husband had succumbed to the pressure placed on him by the manager, but held that something more than pressure had to be shown; the independence of the patient's decision had to be overborne and that had not taken place in this case. The Court of Appeal upheld the decision.

3.4.4 Informing the patient

Earlier we looked at capacity in terms of the patient's ability to process and act upon information relating to his proposed treatment. Clearly, however, this presupposes something to 'bite upon' in terms of the actual data to be processed: in other words, the patient must also have been provided with information about the treatment in question. It is not uncommon to encounter the expression 'informed consent' as a synonym for consent following the provision to the patient of

---

94 [2002] EWCA Civ 565.

appropriate information. However, this expression has a number of interpretations (depending on differing views as to what is 'appropriate' and in what legal context) and should be approached with caution.

In fact, as regards the validity of consent to medical treatment, the patient need be informed only as to the latter's nature and purpose. As long as he knows this, much of the further detail can be left out: it does not matter, for example, that a treatment risk that the patient was not informed of later materialises (it is important, however, to keep in mind that we are here considering the validity of the patient's consent so as to negate a subsequent action in battery, and not whether a doctor may have been *negligent* in not giving certain additional information: as to which, see section 3.5 below).

The distinction between the 'basic' information required for a valid consent – as opposed to the further disclosure of treatment risks (failing which an action may lie in negligence) – was articulated by Bristow J in *Chatterton v Gerson*:[95]

> **Bristow J**: In my judgment, once the patient is informed in broad terms of the nature of the procedure which is intended, and gives her consent, that consent is real, and the cause of the action on which to base a claim for failure to go into risks and implications is negligence, not trespass. Of course, if information is withheld in bad faith, the consent would be vitiated by fraud. Of course, if by some accident, as in a case in the 1940s in the Salford Hundred Court, where a boy was admitted to hospital for tonsillectomy and due to administrative error was circumcised instead, trespass would be the appropriate cause of action against the doctor, though he was as much the victim of the error as the boy. But in my judgment it would be very much against the interests of justice if actions which are really based on a failure by the doctor to perform his duty adequately to inform were pleaded in trespass.

This approach, of limiting 'trespass' or battery to cases where the patient has, in effect, been deliberately misled or told nothing, was initially employed by US courts (see, eg, *Canterbury v Spence*)[96] and was endorsed by the House of Lords in *Sidaway v Board of Governors of the Bethlem Royal Hospital and the Maudsley Hospital and Others*.[97] In fact, it is now adopted throughout the common law world. In the case of *Reibl v Hughes*,[98] Laskin CJ in the Supreme Court of Canada commented as follows:

> **Laskin CJ**: I can appreciate the temptation to say that the genuineness of consent to medical treatment depends on proper disclosure of the risks which it entails, but in my view . . . a failure to disclose the attendant risks, however serious, should go to negligence rather than to battery. Although such a failure relates to an informed choice of submitting to or refusing recommended and appropriate treatment, it arises as the breach of an anterior duty of due care, comparable in legal obligation to the duty of due care in carrying out the particular treatment to which the patient has consented. It is not a test of the validity of consent.

However, despite its undoubted pedigree, principled reasons for parcelling up the patient's right to information into, on the one hand, that going to the 'nature' of the treatment, and, on the other, that concerning risks, remain elusive.[99] As Laskin CJ acknowledges, a failure to disclose

---

95 See n 20 above.
96 464 F 2d 772 (1972).
97 See n 80 above.
98 (1980) 114 DLR (3d) 1.
99 Indeed, in many civil law jurisdictions, such as Germany, no distinction is drawn between the two types of information: a failure to disclose risks will equally vitiate consent.

the latter may also seriously impede a patient's autonomous decision-making. Another problem is the requirement that the relevant information need only be in 'broad terms', which may be felt to confer too much discretion upon judges. As Andrew Grubb notes:

Grubb, Andrew (ed), *Principles of Medical Law*[100]

> 3.97 The information needs to state in 'broad terms' what is to be done to the patient and why. However, this information need not descend into minute, or indeed any, real detail. In practice, judges have considerable leeway in determining what information is relevant to the 'nature and purpose' of a procedure and what is co-lateral to that and, therefore, immaterial to the reality of the patient's consent. For example, it may be enough that the patient knows that a diagnostic procedure of a certain type is to be undertaken, such as a biopsy, and what that involves in terms of contact with the patient and incision. Even if the doctor had been speaking in terms of a particular biopsy such as a muscle biopsy, knowledge of this will be sufficient to amount to a real consent to a bone biopsy carried out at the same time [see *Brushnett v Cowan* [1991] 2 Med LR 271 . . .].

In *Davis v Barking, Havering and Brentwood HA*,[101] the High Court considered the case of a woman who signed a consent form to undergo a general anaesthetic, but who, subsequently, received a caudal block (ie an injection of anaesthetising drug into part of the body to interrupt nerve function), and who suffered some damage as a result of this. McCullough J rejected the argument that the failure to obtain consent to this procedure amounted to a battery:

> **McCullough J**: If one is to treat the administration of an injection for analgesic purposes while the patient is generally anaesthetised (eg, the caudal block given to Mrs Davis) as something requiring separate consent, why should separate consent not also be sought for an injection of, for example, morphine to provide analgesia when the patient begins to come round from the general anaesthetic?
> . . . And once this degree of sectionalisation is accepted, how long will it be before the court is invited to say that separate consent should be sought for separate steps in the surgical procedure itself? A sectionalised approach of this kind would encourage – indeed necessitate – what has been called the 'deplorable' prospect of actions being brought in trespass rather than in negligence.

An interesting, related issue concerns the carrying out of unauthorised tests on specimens of bodily fluids or tissue, but where consent to the taking of specimens was given. This is particularly relevant to HIV testing. In April 1994 a number of Harrods' staff had tests carried out on their blood samples without explicit consent (some were also carried out in the face of an express refusal of consent). In the light of this sort of reasoning, would a battery be found to have taken place here? Unfortunately, there has been no judicial consideration of the issue, and expert opinions have differed. The British Medical Association took advice from Michael Sherrard QC and Ian Gatt, who formed the view the explicit consent is necessary, as did Kennedy and Grubb and Gordon Langley QC, while Leo Charles QC, advising the Central Committee for Hospital Medical Services, advised that explicit consent was not necessary.

Commenting upon the difference of opinion, with reference to the 'broad nature of the treatment' test in *Chatterton v Gerson*, John Keown states:

---

100 Oxford: OUP, 2nd edn, 2004.
101 [1993] 4 Med LR 85.

Keown, J, 'The ashes of AIDS and the phoenix of informed consent'[102]

The doctor who tells the patient that a sample of blood is to be taken for 'tests' has surely discharged this duty. The fact that he does not inform the patient that one of the tests is for HIV does not alter the general nature of the procedure as part of a process of therapeutic diagnosis.

The Sherrard opinion's invention of a distinction between 'routine' and 'non-routine' tests, a distinction which apparently turns on the seriousness of the consequences of a positive result suffers not only from vagueness (what is meant by 'seriousness' and does the requirement to inform extend to other tests and treatments?) but is unsupported by authority or argument, as are the opinion's assertions of an implied representation by the doctor that he will only do 'routine' tests without express consent, and that this representation vitiates the uninformed patient's consent. Curiously, the most copious use of authority in the opinion is its lengthy quotation from the *dissenting* opinion of Lord Scarman in *Sidaway*. Whereas it is understandable that a distinction could be made between 'therapeutic' and 'non-therapeutic' testing (an example of the latter being where the sample is taken purely as part of a research programme) such as to render the latter a procedure of a different nature to the former, a distinction between 'routine' and 'non-routine' seems to be insupportable.

No less insupportable, with respect, is Kennedy and Grubb's analogy between the removal of a sample of blood for HIV testing and off-the-ball kicks and punches on the sports field, an analogy which can hardly be described as obvious.

It is one thing to say that a person cannot, as a matter of public policy, consent to the deliberate infliction of bodily harm without good reason (and hence to regard off-the-ball kicks and punches as assaults). It is quite another to extend this reasoning to touchings which involve no infliction, deliberate or otherwise, of bodily harm.

Not only is no relevant authority cited to warrant such an extension, but the supporting argument that consent should be required because of the possible far-reaching implications of the test presumably entails the conclusion that on those, doubtless many, occasions when a doctor takes a sample from a patient to perform a test which may have far-reaching implications (such as for cancer) the doctor is guilty of battery if he does not obtain the patient's specific consent to it.

A second argument advanced by Kennedy and Grubb is that *Chatterton* in fact supports their case. They argue that although the doctor need only inform the patient in broad terms of the nature of the procedure, the 'procedure' is not merely the use of the syringe to obtain a blood sample, but to obtain a blood sample for an HIV test. Merely to have assented to a particular touching will not necessarily amount to consent if there is no comprehension of the quality of the touching. In support of this argument they cite the case of *Flattery* (as explained by Dunn LJ in *Sidaway*) and state that it is clear that a woman who consents to sexual intercourse, knowing it is sexual intercourse but believing it is being done as a surgical operation, has not given a valid consent to the intercourse because she is unaware of the underlying quality of the touching . . .

In sum, *Chatterton* merely requires the patient to be informed in broad terms of the nature of the procedure. The doctor who tells his patient that blood is to be removed for testing, even though he does not say that it is to be tested for HIV, has surely satisfied this requirement.

More generally, an important factor in the courts' eagerness to stress the distinction between battery and negligence is that otherwise a doctor would theoretically be guilty of a criminal offence, as well as a breach of civil law, if he were found to have battered the patient in failing to give sufficient information. Although such a case would be highly unlikely to be prosecuted (as public policy generally militates against imposing criminal liability upon the doctor), a residual stigma carries over to the civil, battery action. An illustration of the judicial unwillingness

---

102 (1989) 52 MLR 790.

so to stigmatise a doctor, provided the latter was acting in good faith, may be seen in *Williamson v East London and City HA and Others*.[103] Here, the evidence showed that a patient had not been told that her right breast was to be removed (instead she believed that the operation would replace her silicone breast implant, which had ruptured). Nonetheless, any reference in the judgment to the tort of battery is conspicuously absent: instead Butterfield J awarded the claimant £20,000 for the 'negligent failure on the part of the defendants to acquire her consent to the operative procedure'.[104]

However, while rare, there are cases where doctors have been found to have battered their patients. One example is the Canadian case of *Allan v Mount Sinai Hospital*,[105] in which an anaesthetic injection was given in the patient's left arm, after she had specifically requested that it not be given there. There are also a few English authorities. As noted above, an early example is *Cull v Royal Surrey County Hospital*,[106] in which a patient had consented to an abortion but received a sterilisation in addition. A battery was also found in *Devi v West Midlands RHA*,[107] where the patient, who consented to a repair to a perforation in her uterus, was sterilised by the surgeon, who believed it to be in her best interests. One area where the courts will clearly protect patients is against deliberate deceptions practised upon them by medical professionals acting in bad faith. Thus, in *Appleton v Garrett*,[108] where a dentist represented falsely to his patients that they needed dental treatment and then carried out unnecessary treatment, the court had no hesitation in finding a battery.

Recently, in *Shaw v Kovac*[109] the claimant attempted to persuade the Court of Appeal to recognise 'wrongful invasion of autonomy' as a further, distinct form of action and/or head of damages where the patient receives insufficient information about treatment risks. However, this was rejected by the Court, which noted the lack of legal authority as well as any obvious policy justification for countenancing such an extra award (on top of the existing availability of damages in negligence – see Part 3.5 below).

I **THINK POINT**

What of cases where the doctor fails to obtain the patient's consent by mistake (eg the patient's apparent consent is vitiated by incapacity, or the doctor confuses two patients and performs the procedure intended for one on the other). Should these sound in battery or negligence?

3.5 The duty to disclose in negligence

3.5.1 Introduction

As we have just seen, for his consent to be regarded as valid or 'real' (so as to preclude a subsequent action in *battery* against the doctor), the patient need receive only a relatively low amount of information, viz. as to the 'nature and purpose' of the treatment. However, even where a

---

103 See n 26 above.
104 See also *Connolly v Croydon Health Services NHS Trust* [2015] EWHC 1339 (QB).
105 (1980) 109 DLR (3d) 634.
106 See n 10 above.
107 (1981) CA Transcript 491.
108 [1997] 8 Med LR 75.
109 [2017] EWCA Civ 1028.

patient has been told this much, he will in some cases still be entitled to claim in *negligence* against the doctor: in particular, he may allege that the doctor failed, in breach of his duty, to disclose a given risk or side-effect of the treatment. We shall be examining medical negligence as a topic in its own right in Chapter 6, but, given the close link between warnings of risks and patient autonomy (does a patient who is ignorant of some serious risk or side-effect of treatment choose autonomously, even if he knows its 'purpose'?), it is useful to deal with the extent of the specific duty on the part of doctors to give such warnings here.

3.5.2 The standard of care in relation to disclosing treatment risks

3.5.2.1 The doctrine of 'informed consent'

The legal question here is, what standard of care does the law impose upon doctors, at the time of obtaining consent, as regards disclosure of risks, side-effects and alternative treatment options? It is in this context that the doctrine of 'informed consent' (in its strict usage: as indicated above, the expression is not always used with sufficient precision) offers one possible answer. The doctrine, which was originally American, but has since found widespread acceptance in other parts of the common law world, defines the doctor's duty to disclose risks by reference to the reasonable patient's desire and need to know of them. For this reason, the approach is also often termed 'the prudent patient test'.

This approach received its classic exposition in the decision of the US Court of Appeals, District of Columbia circuit, in *Canterbury v Spence*:[110]

> **Robinson J**: There are, in our view, formidable obstacles to acceptance of the notion that the physician's obligation to disclose is either germinated or limited by medical practice. To begin with, the reality of any discernible custom reflecting a professional consensus on communication of option and risk information to patient is open to serious doubt. We sense the danger that what in fact is no custom at all may be taken as an affirmative custom to maintain silence, and that physician witnesses to the so called custom may state merely their personal opinions as to what they or others would do under given conditions. We cannot gloss over the inconsistency between reliance on a general practice respecting divulgence and, on the other hand, realisation that the myriad of variables among patients makes each case so differing that its omission can rationally justified only by the effect of its individual circumstances. Nor can we ignore the fact that to bind the disclosure obligation to medical usage is to arrogate the decision on revelation to the physician alone. Respect for the patient's right of self-determination on particular therapy demands a standard set by law for physicians rather than one which physicians may or may not impose upon themselves . . .
>
> In our view, the patient's right of self-decision shapes the boundaries of the duty to reveal. That right can be effectively exercised only if the physician's communications to the patient, then, must be measured by the patient's need, and that need is the information material to the decision. Thus the test for determining whether a particular peril must be divulged is its materiality to the patient's decision: all risks potentially affecting the decision must be unmasked. And to safeguard the patient's interest in achieving his own determination on treatment, the law must itself set the standard for adequate disclosure.

---

110 See n 96 above.

However, as the court noted, a difficulty with the prudent patient test is in deciding whether it is objective or subjective:

> **Robinson J:** Of necessity, the content of the disclosure rests in the first instance with the physician. Ordinarily it is only he who is in a position to identify particular dangers; always he must make a judgment, in terms of materiality, as to whether and to what extent revelation to the patient is called for. He cannot know with complete exactitude what the patient would consider important to his decision, but on the basis of his medical training and experience he can sense how the average, reasonable patient expectably would react . . .
>
> From these considerations we derive the breadth of the disclosure of risks legally to be required. The scope of the standard is not subjective as to either the physician or the patient; it remains objective with due regard for the patient's informational needs and with suitable leeway for the physician's situation. In broad outline, we agree that '[a] risk is thus material when a reasonable person in what the physician knows or should know to be the patient's position would be likely to attach significance to the risks or cluster of risks in deciding whether or not to forgo the proposed therapy'.

While this retains elements of an objective approach (based around the *reasonable* patient), in another common law jurisdiction, Australia, the courts later adopted an amended definition of 'material risk', whose effect is to create a fully subjective approach. This occurred in the Australian High Court decision of *Rogers v Whitaker*, which concerned a patient who had been almost completely blind in her right eye after a childhood injury. Nearly 40 years later she was referred to an eye surgeon who said that removal of the scar tissue would considerably improve the appearance of the eye and might also restore some sight. He failed to warn her that, as a result of surgery, there was a risk (one in 14,000) of her developing sympathetic ophthalmia in her left, good eye. Unfortunately, this risk materialised, leaving the patient totally blind in the left eye and with none of the hoped-for improvement in the right eye. In finding the surgeon in breach of his duty to warn, Mason CJ stated:

> **Mason CJ:** A risk is material if, in the circumstances of the particular case, a reasonable person in the patient's position, if warned of the risk, would be likely to attach significance to it *or if the medical practitioner is or should reasonably be aware that the particular patient, if warned of the risk, would be likely to attach significance to it* [emphasis added].[111]

3.5.2.2 The position in the UK

Until 2015, the UK position, in terms of how far 'informed consent' was part of the law, was not entirely clear. Although the courts, particularly in England, increasingly adverted to the need for doctors to advise patients of 'significant risks that would affect the judgement of a reasonable patient'[112] – an approach also reflected in GMC and Department of Health professional guidance),[113] as a matter of strict precedent there remained the spectre of the 1985 House of Lords decision in *Sidaway v Bethlem Royal Hospital*.[114] In that case their Lordships, by a 4:1 majority

---

111 (1992) 109 ALR 625.
112 *Per* Lord Woolf MR in *Pearce v United Bristol Health Care Trust* [1999] PIQR P53, cited with approval by Lord Steyn (*obiter*) in *Chester v Afshar* [2004] UKHL 41.
113 See, eg, *Consent: patients and doctors making decisions together* (GMC, London, 2008).
114 See n 80 above.

(Lord Scarman gave a strong dissent on the issue), had appeared to reject 'informed consent' in favour of a more cautious *Bolam*-based approach (in which it was primarily left to the doctor, exercising responsible judgement, to decide what risks to disclose).[115]

Matters came to a head in the 2013 Scottish case of *NM v Lanarkshire Health Board*,[116] where the Inner House (the Scottish appellate court) relied on the majority *Sidaway* judgment in holding that the defendant doctor had been entitled, in her clinical discretion, to withhold information from the claimant on the higher risk of delivering her child naturally (as opposed to by Caesarean section). The claimant appealed to the UK Supreme Court and it is the latter's decision (*Montgomery v Lanarkshire Health Board*), which now confirms definitively the application of 'informed consent' in UK law.

Montgomery v Lanarkshire Health Board[117]

Mrs Montgomery sought damages on behalf of her son for the serious injuries which he sustained during his birth at the defendant hospital in 1999. She was a small woman expecting a large baby, giving rise to a risk – from natural delivery – of shoulder dystocia (the inability of the baby's shoulders to pass through the pelvis). She alleged that a consultant at the hospital had negligently failed to advise her of this risk, and of the lower risks involved in alternative delivery by Caesarean section.

The Scottish courts – basing themselves on the majority House of Lords reasoning in *Sidaway* – dismissed her claim, and Mrs Montgomery appealed to the UK Supreme Court:

Lord Kerr and Lord Reed: [74] The Hippocratic Corpus advises physicians to reveal nothing to the patient of her present or future condition, "for many patients through this cause have taken a turn for the worse" (*Decorum*, XVI). Around two millennia later, in *Sidaway's* case Lord Templeman said that "the provision of too much information may prejudice the attainment of the objective of restoring the patient's health" (p 904); and similar observations were made by Lord Diplock and Lord Bridge. On that view, if the optimisation of the patient's health is treated as an overriding objective, then it is unsurprising that the disclosure of information to a patient should be regarded as an aspect of medical care, and that the extent to which disclosure is appropriate should therefore be treated as a matter of clinical judgment, the appropriate standards being set by the medical profession.

[75] Since *Sidaway*, however, it has become increasingly clear that the paradigm of the doctor-patient relationship implicit in the speeches in that case has ceased to reflect the reality and complexity of the way in which healthcare services are provided, or the way in which the providers and recipients of such services view their relationship. One development which is particularly significant in the present context is that patients are now widely regarded as persons holding rights, rather than as the passive recipients of the care of the medical profession. They are also widely treated as consumers exercising choices: a viewpoint which has underpinned some of the developments in the provision of healthcare services. In addition, a wider range of healthcare professionals now provide treatment and advice of one kind or another to members of the public, either as individuals, or as members of a team drawn from different professional backgrounds (with the consequence that, although this judgment is concerned particularly with doctors, it is also relevant, *mutatis mutandis*, to other healthcare providers). The treatment which they can offer is now understood to depend not only upon their clinical judgment,

---

115 An approach sometimes known (especially in the USA) as the 'prudent doctor test' by way of contrast with the informed consent / 'prudent patient test' that centres on the informational needs of the patient.

116 [2013] CSIH 3.

117 [2015] UKSC 11.

but upon bureaucratic decisions as to such matters as resource allocation, cost-containment and hospital administration: decisions which are taken by non-medical professionals. Such decisions are generally understood within a framework of institutional rather than personal responsibilities, and are in principle susceptible to challenge under public law rather than, or in addition to, the law of delict or tort.

[76] Other changes in society, and in the provision of healthcare services, should also be borne in mind. One which is particularly relevant in the present context is that it has become far easier, and far more common, for members of the public to obtain information about symptoms, investigations, treatment options, risks and side-effects via such media as the internet (where, although the information available is of variable quality, reliable sources of information can readily be found), patient support groups, and leaflets issued by healthcare institutions. . . .

[77] These developments in society are reflected in professional practice. The court has been referred in particular to the guidance given to doctors by the General Medical Council, who participated as interveners in the present appeal. One of the documents currently in force (*Good Medical Practice* (2013)) states, under the heading "The duties of a doctor registered with the General Medical Council":

> "Work in partnership with patients. Listen to, and respond to, their concerns and preferences. Give patients the information they want or need in a way they can understand. Respect patients' right to reach decisions with you about their treatment and care."

[78] Another current document (*Consent: patients and doctors making decisions together* (2008)) describes a basic model of partnership between doctor and patient:

> "The doctor explains the options to the patient, setting out the potential benefits, risks, burdens and side effects of each option, including the option to have no treatment. The doctor may recommend a particular option which they believe to be best for the patient, but they must not put pressure on the patient to accept their advice. The patient weighs up the potential benefits, risks and burdens of the various options as well as any non-clinical issues that are relevant to them. The patient decides whether to accept any of the options and, if so, which one." (para 5). . . .

[80] In addition to these developments in society and in medical practice, there have also been developments in the law. Under the stimulus of the Human Rights Act 1998, the courts have become increasingly conscious of the extent to which the common law reflects fundamental values. As Lord Scarman pointed out in *Sidaway's* case, these include the value of self-determination . . . As well as underlying aspects of the common law, that value also underlies the right to respect for private life protected by article 8 of the European Convention on Human Rights. The resulting duty to involve the patient in decisions relating to her treatment has been recognised in judgments of the European Court of Human Rights, such as *Glass v United Kingdom (2004) 39 EHRR 15* . . .

[81] The social and legal developments which we have mentioned point away from a model of the relationship between the doctor and the patient based upon medical paternalism. They also point away from a model based upon a view of the patient as being entirely dependent on information provided by the doctor. What they point towards is an approach to the law which, instead of treating patients as placing themselves in the hands of their doctors (and then being prone to sue their doctors in the event of a disappointing outcome), treats them so far as possible as adults who are capable of understanding that medical treatment is uncertain of success and may involve risks, accepting responsibility for the taking of risks affecting their own lives, and living with the consequences of their choices.

[82] In the law of negligence, this approach entails a duty on the part of doctors to take reasonable care to ensure that a patient is aware of material risks of injury that are inherent in

treatment. This can be understood, within the traditional framework of negligence, as a duty of care to avoid exposing a person to a risk of injury which she would otherwise have avoided, but it is also the counterpart of the patient's entitlement to decide whether or not to incur that risk. The existence of that entitlement, and the fact that its exercise does not depend exclusively on medical considerations, are important. They point to a fundamental distinction between, on the one hand, the doctor's role when considering possible investigatory or treatment options and, on the other, her role in discussing with the patient any recommended treatment and possible alternatives, and the risks of injury which may be involved.

[83] The former role is an exercise of professional skill and judgment: what risks of injury are involved in an operation, for example, is a matter falling within the expertise of members of the medical profession. But it is a *non sequitur* to conclude that the question whether a risk of injury, or the availability of an alternative form of treatment, ought to be discussed with the patient is also a matter of purely professional judgment. The doctor's advisory role cannot be regarded as solely an exercise of medical skill without leaving out of account the patient's entitlement to decide on the risks to her health which she is willing to run (a decision which may be influenced by non-medical considerations). Responsibility for determining the nature and extent of a person's rights rests with the courts, not with the medical professions.

[84] Furthermore, because the extent to which a doctor may be inclined to discuss risks with a patient is not determined by medical learning or experience, the application of the *Bolam* test to this question is liable to result in the sanctioning of differences in practice which are attributable not to divergent schools of thought in medical science, but merely to divergent attitudes among doctors as to the degree of respect owed to their patients.

[85] A person can of course decide that she does not wish to be informed of risks of injury (just as a person may choose to ignore the information leaflet enclosed with her medicine); and a doctor is not obliged to discuss the risks inherent in treatment with a person who makes it clear that she would prefer not to discuss the matter. Deciding whether a person is so disinclined may involve the doctor making a judgment; but it is not a judgment which is dependent on medical expertise . . .

[86] It follows that the analysis of the law by the majority in *Sidaway* is unsatisfactory, in so far as it treated the doctor's duty to advise her patient of the risks of proposed treatment as falling within the scope of the *Bolam* test . . . It is unsurprising that courts have found difficulty in the subsequent application of *Sidaway*, and that the courts in England and Wales have in reality departed from it; a position which was effectively endorsed, particularly by Lord Steyn, in *Chester v Afshar*. There is no reason to perpetuate the application of the *Bolam* test in this context any longer.

[87] The correct position, in relation to the risks of injury involved in treatment, can now be seen to be substantially that adopted in *Sidaway* by Lord Scarman, and by Lord Woolf MR in *Pearce*, subject to the refinement made by the High Court of Australia in *Rogers v Whitaker*, which we have discussed . . . An adult person of sound mind is entitled to decide which, if any, of the available forms of treatment to undergo, and her consent must be obtained before treatment interfering with her bodily integrity is undertaken. The doctor is therefore under a duty to take reasonable care to ensure that the patient is aware of any material risks involved in any recommended treatment, and of any reasonable alternative or variant treatments. The test of materiality is whether, in the circumstances of the particular case, a reasonable person in the patient's position would be likely to attach significance to the risk, or the doctor is or should reasonably be aware that the particular patient would be likely to attach significance to it.

[Lords Neuberger, Clarke, Wilson and Hodge agreed with Lord Kerr and Lord Reed, and Lady Hale delivered a short concurring speech.]

3.5.2.3 Disclosure of alternative therapies and information about the treatment providers

An interesting feature of the *Montgomery* decision is that it can also be understood as a case about the doctor's duty to disclose the availability of alternative treatments (carrying fewer risks than the treatment proposed). This aspect was picked up upon by Lady Hale in her concurring speech:

> [108] It is now well recognised that the interest which the law of negligence protects is a person's interest in their own physical and psychiatric integrity, an important feature of which is their autonomy, their freedom to decide what shall and shall not be done with their body (the unwanted pregnancy cases are an example: see *Rees v Darlington Memorial Hospital NHS Trust* [2003] UKHL 52, [2004] 1 AC 309). Thus, as Jonathan Herring puts it in *Medical Law and Ethics* (2012), 4th ed, p 170), "the issue is not whether enough information was given to ensure consent to the procedure, but whether there was enough information given so that the doctor was not acting negligently and giving due protection to the patient's right of autonomy".
>
> [109] An important consequence of this is that it is not possible to consider a particular medical procedure in isolation from its alternatives. Most decisions about medical care are not simple yes/no answers. There are choices to be made, arguments for and against each of the options to be considered, and sufficient information must be given so that this can be done: see the approach of the General Medical Council in *Consent: patients and doctors making decisions together* (2008), para 5, quoted by Lord Kerr and Lord Reed at para 77 and approved by them at paras 83 to 85.
>
> [110] Pregnancy is a particularly powerful illustration. Once a woman is pregnant, the foetus has somehow to be delivered. Leaving it inside her is not an option. The principal choice is between vaginal delivery and caesarean section. One is, of course, the normal and "natural" way of giving birth; the other used to be a way of saving the baby's life at the expense of the mother's. Now, the risks to both mother and child from a caesarean section are so low that the National Institute for Health and Clinical Excellence (NICE clinical guideline 132, [new 2011] [para 1.2.9.5]) clearly states that "For women requesting a CS, if after discussion and offer of support (including perinatal mental health support for women with anxiety about childbirth), a vaginal birth is still not an acceptable option, offer a planned CS".
>
> [111] That is not necessarily to say that the doctors have to volunteer the pros and cons of each option in every case, but they clearly should do so in any case where either the mother or the child is at heightened risk from a vaginal delivery. . . .[118]

Outside the context of management of childbirth, the question of disclosure of comparative risks of other treatments arose in the pre-*Montgomery* High Court decision of *Birch v University College London NHS Foundation Trust*.[119] There the claimant, who suffered a stroke in the course of an angiography, a mildly invasive diagnostic procedure, was not told of the alternative of using MRI-imaging, which carried no risks of a stroke.

In finding the trust liable on the basis of failing to obtain the claimant's properly informed consent, the judge stated:

> **Cranston J:** 74. If patients must be informed of significant risks it is necessary to spell out what, in practice, that encompasses. In this case the defendant informed the patient of the probabilities, the one percent,

---

118 See also the subsequent Court of Appeal decision in *Webster v Burton Hospitals NHS Foundation Trust* [2017] EWCA Civ 62, involving the purely hypothetical failure to discuss such risks with the expectant mother.
119 [2008] EWHC 2237.

and the nature of the harm of this risk becoming manifest, the stroke. But these were the objectively significant risks associated with the procedure which was performed, the catheter angiogram. Was it necessary for the defendant to go further and to inform Mrs Birch of comparative risk, how this risk compared with that associated with other imaging procedures, in particular MRI? No authority was cited to this effect but in my judgment there will be circumstances where consistently with Lord Woolf MR's statement of the law in *Pearce v United Bristol Healthcare NHS Trust* the duty to inform a patient of the significant risks will not be discharged unless she is made aware that fewer, or no risks, are associated with another procedure. In other words, unless the patient is informed of the comparative risks of different procedures she will not be in a position to give her fully informed consent to one procedure rather than another. The difficulty is in delineating, in general terms, the circumstances in which the duty arises to inform of comparative risks. In my judgment, in the special circumstances of Mrs Birch's case, that duty arose.

. . .

77. As a matter of law it is difficult to state in general terms when the duty to inform about comparative risk arises. Suffice to say that in my judgment, in the special circumstances of Mrs Birch's case, Mr Kitchen is correct and there was a duty to discuss the comparative risks of the catheter angiography alongside MRI. There is no dispute that that duty was breached since the defendant concedes that comparative risks were not raised. The smallness of the risk associated with catheter angiography is irrelevant. The fact is that there was no risk of stroke at all from MRI. What should have occurred is that at Queen Square Mrs Birch should have been given a full and fair explanation of this and of the preference for catheter angiography.

78. Mrs Birch's circumstances were unusual. She had been referred to Queen Square by one of its neurologists, but because of a problem with beds she entered a neurosurgical, rather than a neurology, ward. That neurologist, Professor Giovannoni, had specifically recommended an MRI. The Friday night admission notes identified both an MRI and catheter angiography as possibilities for the next day. It was only later that the decision for a catheter angiogram was made. Even then Dr Al-Jeroudi's evidence was that he was suggesting an MRI. Given this background, where two procedures were open for Mrs Birch, she needed to have explained to her the comparative risks . . .

As Cranston J recognises, the duty to inform of alternatives with lower or other risks is not easy to delineate, which raises a potential issue of legal uncertainty. The issue is also complicated by its relationship to the problem of scarce healthcare resources: thus here, the reason Mrs Birch did not receive an MRI scan was that the equipment was booked out with other patients. Similarly, should a patient be informed of a, statistically, marginally safer therapy, which costs twice as much to provide? One approach would be to tie the answer to whether the doctor believes the patient is in a position to make effective use of the information. For example, he would tell the patient about non-NHS-funded treatment, if and only if the patient could afford to obtain it privately. However, such an approach may be accused of being both high-handed (in second-guessing the patient's means and priorities) and discriminatory.

Further, complex questions surround the need for factors pertaining to the treating side to be disclosed. For example, should a doctor tell a patient that he has never performed this operation before? It may be thought that the training of surgeons is such that they will always have assisted and observed before carrying out a surgical procedure and, therefore, they will always have 'done' the operation in various ways before taking responsibility for it. However, this will not be the case when new procedures and techniques are developed, for example keyhole surgery. What sort of disclosure should be made then? It is likely that many patients would be very interested to know that their surgeons had never done this before, particularly if there was alternative treatment (that is, conventional surgery)?

It is also a moot point as to whether there is any obligation to disclose the hospital's success or, crucially, failure rate for the type of treatment proposed. This is particularly pertinent in the light of the GMC proceedings against three doctors at the United Bristol Healthcare Trust.[120] The doctors were found to be in breach of professional standards in continuing to carry out heart operations on babies in the knowledge that the death rates of the children they were treating were well above the average for such operations. The subsequent inquiry into the events chaired by Professor Ian Kennedy[121] recommended, *inter alia*, that:

> 102 Patients are always entitled to know the extent to which a procedure which they are about to undergo is innovative or experimental. They are also entitled to be informed about the experience of the clinician who is to carry out the procedure.

The second part of this may be thought controversial, in that it could lead to patients refusing care from less experienced clinicians (preventing them from gaining experience, and posing logistical problems for the hospital). Also problematic is the Inquiry's recommendation (no 155) that 'patients and the public must be able to obtain information as to the relative performance of the trust and the services and consultant units within the trust'. It is true that many patients would probably regard such knowledge as of considerable interest and value. However, leaving aside arguments over the interpretation of statistics, the information could potentially be highly sensitive politically (in terms of highlighting geographical inequalities). It might even raise the prospect of patients refusing to be treated in certain hospitals altogether.

3.5.2.4 Therapeutic privilege

'Therapeutic privilege' describes the doctor's potential freedom as a matter of conscience, not to disclose information that he believes would be damaging to the patient. The issue was considered in *Canterbury v Spence*,[122] where it was stated that where the patient is likely to become so distraught by medical information that he is incapable of making a rational decision, information may be withheld on the grounds of the doctor's privilege.

In the days when the English courts held to the 'prudent doctor' approach, this issue could be regarded as part of the doctor's general discretion not to disclose risks where this accorded with his clinical instincts. However, now that the informational needs of the particular patient provide the yardstick, recourse to 'therapeutic privilege' to justify non-disclosure in specific instances may become more common. In *Montgomery v Lanarkshire Health Board*[123] Lord Kerr and Lord Reed endorsed the existence of such a privilege in the following passage:

> **Lord Kerr and Lord Reed:** [88] The doctor is however entitled to withhold from the patient information as to a risk if he reasonably considers that its disclosure would be seriously detrimental to the patient's health. The doctor is also excused from conferring with the patient in circumstances of necessity, as for example where the patient requires treatment urgently but is unconscious or otherwise unable to make a decision. It is unnecessary for the purposes of this case to consider in detail the scope of those exceptions.

At the same time, as their Lordships noted, the scope of this exception should be kept carefully in check:

---

120 See GMC *v Wisheart and others* (Decision of the GMC's PCC), 18 June 1998.
121 Command Paper: Cm 52, *Learning from Bristol: the report of the public inquiry into children's heart surgery at the Bristol Royal Infirmary 1984–1995*,
122 See n 96 above.
123 See n 117 above.

Lord Kerr and Lord Reed: [91] . . . [I]t is important that the therapeutic exception should not be abused. It is a limited exception to the general principle that the patient should make the decision whether to undergo a proposed course of treatment: it is not intended to subvert that principle by enabling the doctor to prevent the patient from making an informed choice where she is liable to make a choice which the doctor considers to be contrary to her best interests.

THINK POINT

Is there a danger that, following *Montgomery*, doctors will overburden patients with information about alternative treatment options with fewer risks, and how might the resource implications of this – where those alternatives are more expensive to provide – be managed?

3.5.3 Causation

3.5.3.1 Factual causation

An important consequence of the fact that the law deals with the failure to disclose treatment risks in negligence is that, to succeed in a claim, the patient, besides showing that a given non-disclosure was a breach of duty, must go on to prove causation of damage. As we shall see, when we discuss causation in Chapter 6, the first aspect of causation – the so-called *factual causation* element – requires that, if the defendant had behaved properly (ie not been in breach), the claimant would not have suffered the injury: this is known as the 'but for test'. In the particular context we are addressing here, ie a breach by a doctor of the duty to warn the patient of risks, the latter must establish that, if he had been properly warned, he would not have gone ahead and had the (injurious) treatment.[124]

See Chapter 6

As Alisdair Maclean points out, the effect of this requirement is to limit the protection offered by the law to the patient's autonomy interests:

Maclean, A, *Autonomy, Informed Consent and Medical Law: A Relational Challenge*[125]

[There is an] inconsistency between what the law claims to be the patient's right and what it is prepared to compensate. The law proclaims that the patient can make any decision regardless of reason. However, it is then only prepared to compensate those cases of a failure to disclose where claimants provide credible evidence that they would have made a different decision. To be credible, claimants must provide accessible reasons. This is inconsistent; there is a right to refuse treatment for irrational reasons (or even no reason) but in trying to show causation in a failure-to-disclose case a claimant's purported refusal of treatment must be rational. This arises because of the need to show that the breach of duty caused actual damage. If outcome responsibility were severed from the issue of consent and dealt with separately, the inconsistency would be removed since liability for failure to consent would no longer be dependent on showing that a different decision would have been made and the harm from the risk materialising avoided. Separating consent and outcome responsibility would allow these distinct harms to be dealt with in a less

---

124 By contrast, it is unclear if causation has to be shown in cases of battery. There, where the wrong is the unlawful treatment, the patient will, on one view, recover automatically for all injuries associated with it: see *Chatterton v Gerson* [1981] QB 432, *per* Bristow J (*obiter*), but *cf Abbas v Kenney* [1996] 7 Med LR 47, *per* Gage J (again *obiter*).

125 See n 2 above.

blunt way, which would facilitate a more just response. However, because liability for negligence requires a bad outcome, it cannot entirely separate consent and outcome responsibility.

On the other hand, it may be argued that what is really at issue in such cases is compensation for iatrogenic injury, not the bare insult to autonomy from being exposed unwittingly to the risk of such injury (arguably few patients will care very much that they did not know of a risk, which did not in any event materialise; and in other contexts too, private law does not recognise an interest in not being wrongfully exposed to risk *per se*, where no harm results).

It is apparent that, in resolving the factual causation issue as an evidential matter, the court must determine the truth of assertions by the patient in relation to his own hypothetical conduct. The question of how far it will be guided here by what an objective 'reasonable patient' would have chosen to do in similar circumstances was addressed in *Smith v Barking, Havering and Brentwood HA*.

Smith v Barking, Havering and Brentwood HA[126]

The claimant was a young woman with a serious spinal condition. Without surgery straightaway she would inevitably develop tetraplegia within a matter of months. However, the surgeon who treated her failed to warn her of the 25% risk of immediate tetraplegia attendant on the operation, which unfortunately materialised:

> **Hutchison J**: There was some discussion as to whether the issue of causation should be approached on what was called the objective or the subjective basis – ie, was the question to be resolved by deciding what a reasonable person in the plaintiff's position would have chosen to do, or by deciding what the plaintiff herself would have chosen to do. In support of the former approach I was referred to the Canadian authority of *Reibl v Robert A Hughes* [1980] 2 SCR 880 and in support of the latter to the decision of Hirst J in *Hills v Potter* [1984] 1 WLR 641. Both counsel invited me to accept that in the end the matter must be one for decision on a subjective basis. This must plainly as a matter of principle be right, because the question must be: 'If this plaintiff had been given the advice that she should have been given, would she have decided to undergo the operation or not?'
>
> However, there is a peculiar difficulty involved in this sort of case – not least for the plaintiff herself – in giving, after the adverse outcome of the operation is known, reliable answers as to what she would have decided before the operation had she been given proper advice as to the risks inherent in it. Accordingly, it would, in my judgment, be right in the ordinary case to give particular weight to the objective assessment. If everything points to the fact that a reasonable plaintiff, properly informed, would have assented to the operation, the assertion from the witness box, made after the adverse outcome is known, in a wholly artificial situation and in the knowledge that the outcome of the case depends upon that assertion being maintained, does not carry great weight unless there are extraneous or additional factors to substantiate it. By extraneous or additional factors I mean, and I am not doing more than giving examples, religious or some other firmly held convictions; particular social or domestic considerations justifying a decision not in accordance with what, objectively, seems the right one; assertions in the immediate aftermath of the operation made in a context other than that of a possible claim for damages; in other words, some particular factor which suggests that the plaintiff had grounds for not doing what a reasonable person in her situation might be expected to have done. Of

---

126 [1994] 5 Med LR 285.

> course, the less confidently the judge reaches the conclusion as to what objectively the reasonable patient might be expected to have decided, the more readily will he be persuaded by her subjective evidence.

This subjective approach (looking to what the *particular* patient would have done), which, nevertheless, takes account of objective 'reasonableness' for evidential purposes, was approved in *Chester v Afshar* at the Court of Appeal stage,[127] and has also been accepted in Australia.[128] It may, however, be contrasted with the US and Canadian approach, which is to focus simply on how an objective reasonable patient would have behaved.[129] The latter approach, whose effect is that a patient may lose even if able to prove that he, individually, would have refused the treatment, is on the face of things hard to justify.

3.5.3.2 The problem of legal causation

As noted previously, to establish factual causation the patient must show that, had he known of the risk, he would have declined the course of treatment. However, what of a case where the patient can show they would have initially refused treatment, and hence would have avoided the (random) risk of the injury that occurred, but would ultimately have required that treatment (and, hence, been exposed to the self-same risk) in the future? Such a case creates a problem in terms of so-called *legal* causation.

The Australian High Court was confronted with this problem in *Chappel v Hart*,[130] in which the respondent, Mrs Hart, suffered damage to her vocal cord in the course of throat surgery – a risk that the appellant, in breach of duty, had failed to disclose. The respondent accepted that, had she been warned, she would still have had the surgery, but at a later date. As the minority judges argued, the surgeon's failure had thus merely altered the time and place at which the claimant had been exposed to the risk of injury:

> **Hayne J**: Of course, the respondent did suffer a perforated oesophagus, she did suffer an infection, she did suffer paralysis of the laryngeal nerve. But if she had not attended the hospital on that day, the probabilities are that none of this would have happened. And if the appellant had told her of the risk to her voice, she would not have had the operation when she did. But precisely the same argument would be open if, instead of suffering damage to her voice, as she has, the operating theatre in which her procedure was performed had been struck by lightning, or a runaway truck, and she had been injured. But for the negligent failure to warn she would not have been in harm's way.

However, a majority of the High Court found Dr Chappel liable. Broadly, and without resolving the conceptual problem posed by the minority, it appears to have felt that, since Mrs Hart's injury would almost certainly not otherwise have occurred (ie *factual* causation was present), such injury should on a 'common sense' basis also be attributed to Dr Chappel's failure as a matter of *legal* causation.

Subsequently, in *Chester v Afshar*, the UK House of Lords was required to address exactly the same problem as had vexed the Australian High Court.

---

127 [2002] 3 All ER 552.
128 See *Rogers v Whitaker* (n 111 above); *Rosenberg v Percival* (2001) 75 ALJR 734.
129 See, eg, the Canadian Supreme Court decision of *Arndt v Smith* [1997] 2 SCR 539.
130 (1998) 72 ALJR 1344.

Chester v Afshar[131]

Miss Chester had suffered from progressively worsening back pain for a number of years, and was referred to Mr Afshar, a distinguished consultant neurosurgeon. Although she was apprehensive about operations in general, at consultation the defendant swiftly persuaded her as to the merits of surgery, which he carried out a few days later. Unfortunately, despite being performed with due care, a risk of such surgery, 'cauda equina syndrome' (assessed at 1–2 per cent), materialised, leaving Miss Chester with serious disabilities. The trial judge (Robert Taylor J) found that the defendant had failed to disclose this risk, and that this constituted a breach of duty.

As to causation, the judge found that Miss Chester, if warned, would not have undergone the operation when she did (as she would have wished to seek further medical opinions as to the need for the surgery), albeit she may well have submitted to it in the future. He noted that, 'had she been adequately warned, the operation in question would not have taken place and she would not have suffered damage. In these circumstances, and without more, it seems to me that the necessary causal link is sufficiently established'. The judge accordingly found in favour of Miss Chester, and this was upheld by the Court of Appeal. The defendant appealed to the House of Lords:

Lord Steyn: [13] Counsel for the surgeon submitted that it is contrary to general principles of tort law to award damages when a defendant's wrong has not been proved to have increased the claimant's exposure to risk. He argued that in order to establish causation in a case of a surgeon's failure to warn a patient of a significant risk of injury, the patient must prove both that she would not have consented to run the relevant risk then and there, and that she would not, ultimately, have consented to run the relevant risk ....

[18] ... [I]n the context of attributing legal responsibility, it is necessary to identify precisely the protected legal interests at stake. A rule requiring a doctor to abstain from performing an operation without the informed consent of a patient serves two purposes. It tends to avoid the occurrence of the particular physical injury the risk of which a patient is not prepared to accept ...

[19] ... [I]t is a distinctive feature of the present case that but for the surgeon's negligent failure to warn the claimant of the small risk of serious injury the actual injury would not have occurred when it did and the chance of it occurring on a subsequent occasion was very small. It could therefore be said that the breach of the surgeon resulted in the very injury about which the claimant was entitled to be warned.

Lord Hope agreed:

Lord Hope: [86] I start with the proposition that the law which imposed the duty to warn on the doctor has at its heart the right of the patient to make an informed choice as to whether, and if so when and by whom, to be operated on. Patients may have, and are entitled to have, different views about these matters. All sorts of factors may be at work here – the patient's hopes and fears and personal circumstances, the nature of the condition that has to be treated and, above all, the patient's own views about whether the risk is worth running for the benefits that may come if the operation is carried out ....

[87] To leave the patient who would find the decision difficult without a remedy, as the normal approach to causation would indicate, would render the duty useless in the cases where it may be needed most. This would discriminate against those who cannot honestly say that they would have declined the operation once and for all if they had been warned. I would find that result unacceptable. The function of the law is to enable rights to be vindicated and to

---

131 [2004] UKHL 41.

provide remedies when duties have been breached. Unless this is done the duty is a hollow one, stripped of all practical force and devoid of all content. It will have lost its ability to protect the patient and thus to fulfil the only purpose which brought it into existence. On policy grounds therefore I would hold that the test of causation is satisfied in this case. The injury was intimately involved with the duty to warn.

Lord Walker agreed with Lords Steyn and Hope in dismissing Mr Afshar's appeal. However, Lords Bingham and Hoffmann dissented:

Lord Hoffmann: [29] The burden is on a claimant to prove that the defendant's breach of duty caused him damage. Where the breach of duty is a failure to warn of a risk, he must prove that he would have taken the opportunity to avoid or reduce that risk. In the context of the present case, that means proving that she would not have had the operation.

[30] The judge made no finding that she would not have had the operation. He was not invited by the claimant to make such a finding. The claimant argued that as a matter of law it was sufficient that she would not have had the operation at that time or by that surgeon, even though the evidence was that the risk could have been precisely the same if she had it at another time or by another surgeon. A similar argument has been advanced before this House.

[31] In my opinion this argument is about as logical as saying that if one had been told, on entering a casino, that the odds on the number 7 coming up at roulette were only 1 in 37, one would have gone away and come back next week or gone to a different casino. The question is whether one would have taken the opportunity to avoid or reduce the risk, not whether one would have changed the scenario in some irrelevant detail. The judge found as a fact that the risk would have been precisely the same whether it was done then or later or by that competent surgeon or by another.

[32] It follows that the claimant failed to prove that the defendant's breach of duty caused her loss. On ordinary principles of tort law, the defendant is not liable.

Their Lordships appeared to believe that, allowing recovery by the claimant involved a special departure from the ordinary rules of causation (the disagreement centring on the propriety of such a departure). With respect, it is unfortunate in this regard that the House of Lords failed to distinguish more carefully between *factual* and *legal* causation. It is submitted that, had it done so, it would have been clearer that no radically new principle was involved. There was merely a modest (and justifiable) relaxation of legal causation:[132]

Stauch, M, 'Causation and confusion in respect of medical non-disclosure: *Chester v Afshar*'[133]

It ought to be clear that, in *Chester, factual* causation was present: Mr Afshar's breach, in failing to advise of the risk, had changed the course of events and led to the claimant being injured when, otherwise, she would almost certainly have escaped such injury. As Lord Steyn commented, '. . . but for the surgeon's negligent failure to warn the claimant of the small risk of serious injury the actual injury would not have occurred when it did and the chance of it occurring on a subsequent occasion was very small'. . .

. . . The reason why, once established, factual causation is significant is two-fold. First it prevents the claimant from getting a windfall. It seems right (as the minority in *Chester* suggested, while failing to see

---

132 See now also the Court of Appeal's analysis of *Chester* in *Correia v University Hospital of North Stafford NHS Trust* [2017] EWCA 356, and in *Duce v Worcestershire Acute Hospitals NHS Trust* [2018] EWCA Civ 1307.
133 (2005) 14 Nott LJ 66.

that the claimant fulfilled the relevant condition) to reserve substantial damages for cases where the doctor's conduct has altered the course of events and resulted in injury (when otherwise there would very likely have been no injury). Indeed, this is merely an instance of the general requirement, foundational in the tort of negligence, that the claimant must show 'damage'... [T]he second, more positive reason why proof of factual causation is significant, ... is that it gives rise to a powerful *prima facie* case for compensation: 'if you had behaved properly, I would not have been injured!' Qualifications on liability based upon remoteness/legal causation points are relatively unusual. This is all the more so in cases where the injury intrudes in close temporal proximity to the wrongful act, and was readily foreseeable (both of which were true here) ...

The further question, as to how far the normal legal causation requirement that the defendant's breach created or added to the risk, should be relaxed in this type of case had been exhaustively discussed in *Chappel v Hart*, a recent case from the High Court of Australia with similar facts, as well as in the meticulous judgment of the Court of Appeal in *Chester* itself. In fact there would seem to be good reasons for such a relaxation. Most importantly, as the majority in the House of Lords recognised, the doctor's duty to inform patients of risks would otherwise be very much attenuated ...

This is not to say that, in other non-disclosure cases, a claim may not sometimes fail for lack of legal causation. One situation is where the patient's injury stemmed from a *different* risk to the one which was faultily not disclosed. Admittedly, the few authorities in point are not wholly consistent. Thus in the Scottish decision of *Moyes v Lothian Health Board*[134] the judge appeared to accept that in such circumstances the doctor would remain liable. However, the Court of Appeal's more recent judgment in *Thompson v Bradford*[135] would suggest otherwise. As mentioned earlier, we shall look further at issues of causation in medical negligence cases – both factual and legal – in Chapter 6.

Summary of key points

1   The requirement that capable (or competent) adult patients consent to their medical treatment is a key principle of medical law, and on the face of it shows the law's commitment to patient autonomy over the desire of doctors to treat in the patient's best interests.

2   A doctor who fails to obtain consent will normally be liable to the patient in civil law for the tort of battery and, also, potentially, in criminal law.

3   Generally speaking, consent is both a necessary and sufficient condition for lawful treatment. However, there are exceptions that run in both directions. Thus, some procedures, eg radical surgery with no therapeutic goal, will remain unlawful (in criminal law) despite the patient's consent.

4   Conversely, non-consensual treatment may occasionally be justified on the basis of an overriding public interest. An example is interventions under public health legislation, so far as this is necessary to protect the health of others.

5   It is less clear if there are also bases in common law for treating without consent. A patient's consent presupposes capacity, and the courts in contentious situations (eg where a suicidal person refuses treatment following a suicide attempt) have tended to find that the patient is incapable.

---

134 [1990] 1 Med LR 463; see also *Hepworth v Kerr* [1995] 6 Med LR 139.
135 [2005] EWCA Civ 1439; the facts of the case are discussed in Ch 6, section 6.4.3.

6   In fact the test for capacity, as developed by the courts and now encoded in the MCA 2005, is relatively open-textured. It requires that the patient is able to take in and retain treatment information (believe it), and weigh it in the balance.

7   Besides capacity, two other elements must be present for the patient to give a valid consent. These are voluntariness (ie the patient's decision is free from duress or undue influence) and that the doctor has provided information about the treatment.

8   Even so, only basic information, as to the 'nature and purpose' of the treatment, needs to be given. By contrast, the failure to mention other matters, such as the risks of the procedure, will not affect the patient's consent, though he may be able to bring a subsequent action in negligence.

9   To succeed in such an action, the patient must first show the doctor was in breach of duty by not disclosing the relevant risks. In the past, the English courts allowed doctors significant discretion as to which risks to disclose, but this has now altered in favour of an 'informed consent' standard, centred on the informational needs of the particular patient.

10   In addition, it remains necessary for the patient to prove a causal link between the non-disclosure and the injury he has suffered (through the occurrence of the treatment risk). Generally, this is satisfied by him showing that he would have declined the treatment, had he known of the risk.

Further reading

Dworkin, G, *The Theory and Practice of Autonomy*, Cambridge: Cambridge University Press, 1988.

Elliott, T, 'Body dysmorphic disorder, radical surgery and the limits of consent' (2009) 17 Medical Law Review 149.

Hockton, A, *The law of consent to medical treatment*, London: Sweet & Maxwell, 2001.

Jones, M, 'Informed consent and other fairy stories' (1999) 7 Medical Law Review 103.

Maclean, A, *Autonomy, Informed Consent and Medical Law: A Relational Challenge*, Cambridge: Cambridge University Press, 2009.

Pattinson, S, 'Consent and informational responsibility' (2009) 35 Journal of Medical Ethics 176.

Laing, JM, 'Delivering informed consent post-*Montgomery*: implications for medical practice and professionalism' (2017) 33 Journal of Professional Negligence 128.

Clark, T, and Nolan, D, 'A critique of *Chester v Afshar*' (2014) 34 Oxford Journal of Legal Studies 659.

Chapter 4

Treating the incapable patient

4.1 Introduction

There can be no doubt that patients who lack capacity should nevertheless receive medical treatment. However, difficulties arise when considering the legal framework in which treatment decisions are made, and the criteria used to decide on the suitability of treatment.

The treatment of the incapable patient will be considered in later chapters in relation to particular forms of treatment (for example, organ donation; medical research; and where the patient is terminally ill or gravely incapacitated). In this chapter we will concentrate on the basic legal framework and general principles, making particular reference to so-called non-therapeutic areas relating to the control of fertility by sterilisation and abortion.

The chapter deals with adults and children separately. They are governed by separate legal regimes, and, also, in the case of children, there has always been surrogate decision-making in the form of parental consent. However, this can result in conflicts between the rights and interests of parents and those of incapable children.

We are referring to patients who are 'incapable' but some of the extracts refer to 'incompetent' patients; this was the more common terminology a few years ago, and, indeed, earlier editions of this book employed it. However, with the passing of the Mental Capacity Act it is more appropriate to use language to reflect this.

As far as incapable adults are concerned, until recently this area was governed entirely by the common law. There is now a statutory scheme under the Mental Capacity Act 2005, but, as case law under the common law will still influence decision-making under the Act, it is helpful to explain the earlier common law situation.

4.2 Incapable adults

4.2.1 Common law

4.2.1.1 Necessity and common law

At common law the treatment of incapable patients, ie without consent, was potentially a battery. However, the common law developed the defence of necessity (latterly developed into the language of best interests) to avoid the unpalatable consequences of a doctor being civilly and criminally liable in such circumstances. Although the defence of necessity could only be successfully invoked if the treatment was in the best interests of the patient, the defence of necessity was frequently used to refer to emergency treatment carried out on unconscious patients, while the best interests defence tended to be referred to when dealing with patients who are permanently lacking in capacity, whether emergency cases or not. It must be stressed, however, that there was no strict dichotomy and, arguably, the distinction is meaningless.

The defence of necessity, therefore, must necessarily entail the doctor acting in the best interests of the patient. The difference lies in the nature of the treatment. In an emergency, the treatment must be confined to that which is necessary to preserve life and limb, when it is impossible to obtain consent. However, the best interests test applied to all forms of medical treatment carried out on permanently incapable patients.

The nature of necessity was examined in the case of *Re F (Mental Patient: Sterilisation)*:

Re F (Mental Patient: Sterilisation)[1]

Lord Goff: Upon what principle can medical treatment be justified when given without consent? We are searching for a principle upon which, in limited circumstances, recognition may be given to a need, in the interests of the patient, that treatment should be given to him in circumstances where he is (temporarily or permanently) disabled from consenting to it. It is this criterion of a need which points to the principle of necessity as providing justification . . .

The distinction I have drawn between cases of emergency, and cases where the state of affairs is (more or less) permanent, is relevant in another respect. We are here concerned with medical treatment, and I limit myself to cases of that kind. Where, for example, a surgeon performs an operation without his consent on a patient temporarily rendered unconscious in an accident, he should do no more than is reasonably required, in the best interests of the patient, before he recovers consciousness. I can see no practical difficulty arising from this requirement, which derives from the fact that the patient is expected before long to regain consciousness and can then be consulted about longer term measures. . . .

But where the state of affairs is permanent or semi-permanent, as may be so in the case of a mentally disordered person, there is no point in waiting to obtain the patient's consent. The need to care for him is obvious; and the doctor must then act in the best interests of his patient, just as if he had received his patient's consent so to do. Were this not so, much useful treatment and care could, in theory at least, be denied to the unfortunate. It follows that, on this point, I am unable to accept the view expressed by Neill LJ in the Court of Appeal . . . that the treatment must be shown to have been necessary.

Lord Goff referred to the Canadian case of *Marshall v Curry*,[2] where a patient brought an action in battery against a surgeon who had removed a diseased testicle during the course of a hernia operation. The surgeon tried to argue that it was necessary to remove the testicle because it seriously threatened the health of the patient. In other words, though couched in terms of necessity, the defence, in reality, was that it was in the best interests of the patient to perform this operation. The court held that the removal of the testicle was necessary and that it would have been unreasonable to put the procedure off to a later date. This is a somewhat troubling decision, and was not followed in a later Canadian case. In *Murray v McMurchy*,[3] the patient was a woman who had been sterilised without her consent in the course of a Caesarean section. The defence was that the condition of her uterus was such as to make it dangerous for her to go through another pregnancy. The court held that it would have been reasonable to postpone this operation in order to seek her consent.

4.2.1.2 Common law and the role of the court

It may seem odd, but in English law, until the enactment of the Mental Capacity Act 2005 there was no mechanism whereby someone could be sanctioned to make decisions about medical treatment on behalf of an adult patient. However, this was not always the case. Incapable adults once had protection: there was an inherent power in the courts (known as the *parens patriae* jurisdiction) to act on behalf of the incapacitated adult in very much the same way as minors are still protected today. This is the jurisdiction extant in the Canadian legal process referred to by La Forest J in the judgment in *Re Eve*.[4] However, the royal warrant by which this power was

---

1 [1990] 2 AC 1, at 73.
2 (1933) 3 DLR 260.
3 (1949) 2 DLR 442.
4 [1986] 2 SCR 388.

delegated to the courts was revoked shortly after the Mental Health Act 1959 came into force because it was believed that the Act made all necessary provision for mental patients. However, while the original Mental Health Act 1983 (since amended) provided for the appointment of a guardian in respect of the patient's financial affairs, no such power was provided for in respect of the personal welfare or health of the patient. *Re F (Mental Patient: Sterilisation)*[5] concerned the sterilisation of a mentally impaired woman aged 36, but said to have an overall mental age of four or five. The case is considered in further detail below but, on the subject of the court's role and its inherent declaratory jurisdiction, only Lord Griffiths dissented from the view that an application to the court remains within the discretion of the doctors concerned:[6]

See Chapter 9

> **Lord Griffiths**: I cannot agree that it is satisfactory to leave this grave decision with all its social implications in the hands of those having the care of the patient with only the expectation that they will have the wisdom to obtain a declaration of lawfulness before the operation is performed. In my view the law ought to be that they must obtain the approval of the court before they sterilise a woman incapable of giving consent and that it is unlawful to sterilise without that consent. I believe that it is open to your Lordships to develop a common law rule to this effect . . .

Similarly, in the earlier case of *Re B (A Minor) (Wardship: Sterilisation)*,[7] only Lord Templeman took the view that court approval should always be obtained. However, in the Australian High Court's decision in *Department of Health v JWB and SMB*,[8] although the judges did not express the view that it is mandatory to apply to the court in the case of a therapeutic sterilisation, in the case of a non-therapeutic sterilisation (that is, a sterilisation carried out where the physical health of the patient does not demand it), the court held that it required prior court approval. Although this case and the case of *Re B* concerned children, it is arguable that exactly the same view should be taken in the case of an incapable adult.

Most of the cases using the declaratory jurisdiction have been brought by the healthcarers involved with the patient. However, it was used in the case of *Re S (Hospital Order: Court's Jurisdiction)*[9] to decide a dispute between the wife and the mistress of an elderly Norwegian who had become incapable following a stroke. Both wife and mistress wanted to care for him. The court held that the declaratory jurisdiction could be used by anyone with a genuine and legitimate interest in obtaining a decision on a serious justiciable issue. The dispute in this case was found to be such an issue (see also *Re S (Adult's Lack of Capacity: Carer and Residence)*).[10]

In *Re F (Adult: Court's Jurisdiction)*,[11] the facts concerned a mentally impaired 18-year-old woman (T). It was agreed that she lacked capacity to make decisions, particularly about the place where she should live. She had been in local authority care, initially with the consent of her parents, but consent to further placement was withdrawn. The local authority sought declarations that it could keep her in similar accommodation and restrict and supervise her contact with her family (previously, she had been neglected and sexually exploited when she had been living at home). An application for guardianship under the MHA 1983 had already been rejected by the Court of Appeal on the basis that she did not satisfy the definition of mental impairment under the Act. However, having reached the age of 18, the wardship jurisdiction was no longer

---

5 [1990] 2 AC 1.
6 At p 70.
7 [1988] AC 199.
8 (1992) 66 ALJR 300.
9 [1995] 3 All ER 290.
10 [2003] EWHC 1909 (Fam).
11 [2000] 2 FLR 512.

available to the court. The Court of Appeal (*Re F (Mental Health Act: Guardianship)*)[12] held that the common law could 'fill the gap' in the statutory framework. Now, of course, the Mental Capacity Act does this job but it is worth noting the flexibility of the common law.

4.3 The Mental Capacity Act 2005

4.3.1 History

We have seen that the common law provided the legal framework for decision-making in cases of incapacitated patients until very recently. However, the need for a legal framework of protection for vulnerable, mentally incapacitated adults had been highlighted by the Law Commission in its report, *Mental Incapacity*, Report no 231.[13] In December 1997, the government published a Green Paper which was closely based upon the Law Commission's report. In 1999, the White Paper, *Making Decisions: the Government's Proposals for Making Decisions on Behalf of Mentally Incapacitated Adults*, Cm 4465,[14] was published. Subsequently there was the draft Mental Incapacity Bill, the draft Mental Capacity Bill (the change of emphasis reflecting the criticisms that 'incapacity' was too negative) and, finally, this resulted in the passing of the Mental Capacity Act 2005. The Act does not apply only to patients as it is used to make decisions about residence or other aspects of personal welfare; it applies to anyone who is incapacitated who has attained the age of 16.

The MCA only applies in England and Wales.

4.3.2 Current scheme

4.3.2.1 Principles

The Mental Capacity Act contains a number of key principles.

Mental Capacity Act 2005

1 The principles

1   The following principles apply for the purposes of this Act.
2   A person must be assumed to have capacity unless it is established that he lacks capacity.
3   A person is not to be treated as unable to make a decision unless all practicable steps to help him to do so have been taken without success.
4   A person is not to be treated as unable to make a decision merely because he makes an unwise decision.
5   An act done, or decision made, under this Act for or on behalf of a person who lacks capacity must be done, or made, in his best interests.
6   Before the act is done, or the decision is made, regard must be had to whether the purpose for which it is needed can be as effectively achieved in a way that is less restrictive of the person's rights and freedom of action.

---

12 [2000] 1 FLR 192.
13 London: HMSO, 1995.
14 London: HMSO, 1999.

These principles reflect a presumption of capacity and the need to help people acquire capacity, and the need to respect actions and wishes which are not necessarily wise, on the basis that we all make unwise decisions, and not to acknowledge this might be regarded as the unacceptable face of paternalism. When there is no capacity, decisions must be taken in the best interests of the person concerned and in a way that least restricts the liberty of the person concerned. Although we are here concerned with patients and medical treatment, the Act applies to all decisions such as where someone lives, what sort of clothes they wear, who they wish to socialise with, and so on.

4.3.2.2 Powers of attorney and advance decisions

Powers of attorney are documents that enable someone to give powers to third parties to make decisions on their behalf. Prior to the Mental Capacity Act it was possible to give someone an 'enduring power of attorney', ie it would continue to be valid if the donor of the power lost capacity. The Mental Capacity Act replaced this with 'lasting powers of attorney' (see s 9 and Sch 1) which widen the remit of the power to cover personal care and treatment. Existing enduring powers of attorney are still valid, and can still be registered, but no new enduring powers can be created. The Public Guardian heads the administrative function of the Court of Protection (see below) and, *inter alia*, maintains a register of lasting powers of attorney.

The Act also provides for advance decision-making either in oral or written form and these are dealt with in Chapter 12.

See Chapter 12

4.3.3 Human rights and the deprivation of liberty safeguards

These provisions, contained in ss 4A and 4B and Sch A1 of the Mental Capacity Act 2005, which were inserted by the Mental Health Act 2007, have their origins in a mental health case but they apply to anyone who is having medical treatment or general care, eg in a hospital, residential or nursing home, who is deprived in some way of their liberty.

See Chapter 9

Under the Mental Health Act 1983 there is a provision whereby patients do not have to be detained under compulsory powers in order to receive treatment for mental disorder; they are regarded as informal patients. As they are informal patients, they do not have any right to go to a Mental Health Review Tribunal because they are not detained, ie they are free to leave hospital. It is entirely understandable that patients who are mentally disordered and who also have the capacity to consent to treatment would prefer to have treatment for mental disorder by consenting to it, rather than by having it imposed upon them. However, the difficulty that can arise concerns the patient who does not have capacity. Informal admission under the Mental Health Act 1983, s 131, fell to be considered by the House of Lords in the case of *R v Bournewood Community and Mental Health NHS Trust, ex p L*.[15] An autistic patient had been 'informally' admitted to a mental health unit. The psychiatrist felt that formal detention was unnecessary unless the patient resisted treatment. The trust argued that he was an informal patient under s 131 because he had chosen not to leave the hospital. The House of Lords held that it had clearly been intended that patients lacking the capacity to consent could be admitted under s 131. Their Lordships relied heavily on the findings of the Percy Commission, which reported prior to the 1959 Mental Health Act and which had envisaged such admissions as avoiding the stigmatisation of such patients with the label of having been 'sectioned'. Such patients would be admitted for treatment 'in their own best interests'. As we have seen, although this is prior to the Mental

---

15 [1998] 3 All ER 289.

Capacity Act of 2005, treatment given 'in the best interests of the patient' was well established by common law. The House of Lords was therefore suggesting that the doctrine of necessity would apply. The case was brought before the European Court of Human Rights. The court held that the patient had been 'detained', and that therefore he was entitled to safeguards that were Article 5 compatible:

HL v United Kingdom[16]

. . . .

Alleged violation of article 5(1) of the convention

. . .

89 It is not disputed that in order to determine whether there has been a deprivation of liberty, the starting point must be the specific situation of the individual concerned and account must be taken of a whole range of factors arising in a particular case such as the type, duration, effects and manner of implementation of the measure in question. The distinction between a deprivation of, and restriction upon, liberty is merely one of degree or intensity and not one of nature or substance.

90 The Court observes that the High Court and the majority of the House of Lords found that the applicant had not been detained during this period while the Court of Appeal and a minority of the House of Lords found that he had. Although this Court will have regard to the domestic courts' related findings of fact, it does not consider itself constrained by their legal conclusions as to whether the applicant was detained or not, not least because the House of Lords considered the question from the point of view of the tort of false imprisonment rather than the Convention concept of 'deprivation of liberty' in Art.5(1), the criteria for assessing those domestic and Convention issues being different.

In this latter respect, considerable emphasis was placed by the domestic courts, and by the Government, on the fact that the applicant was compliant and never attempted, or expressed the wish, to leave. The majority of the House of Lords specifically distinguished actual restraint of a person (which would amount to false imprisonment) and restraint which was conditional upon his seeking to leave (which would not constitute false imprisonment). The Court does not consider such a distinction to be of central importance under the Convention. Nor, for the same reason, can the Court accept as determinative the fact relied on by the Government that the regime applied to the applicant (as a compliant incapacitated patient) did not materially differ from that applied to a person who had the capacity to consent to hospital treatment, neither objecting to their admission to hospital. The Court recalls that the right to liberty is too important in a democratic society for a person to lose the benefit of Convention protection for the single reason that he may have given himself up to be taken into detention, especially when it is not disputed that that person is legally incapable of consenting to, or disagreeing with, the proposed action.

91 Turning therefore to the concrete situation as required by the Ashingdane judgment, the Court considers the key factor in the present case to be that the healthcare professionals treating and managing the applicant exercised complete and effective control over his care and movements from the moment he presented acute behavioural problems on July 22, 1997 to the date he was compulsorily detained on October 29, 1997.

More particularly, the applicant had been resident with his carers for over three years. On July 22, 1997, following a further incident of violent behaviour and self-harm in his day-care centre, the applicant was sedated before being brought to the hospital and subsequently to the IBU, in the latter case supported

---

16 (2005) 40 EHRR 32, ECJ.

by two persons. His responsible medical officer (Dr M) was clear that, had the applicant resisted admission or tried to leave thereafter, she would have prevented him from doing so and would have considered his involuntarily committal under s3 of the 1983 Act: indeed, as soon as the Court of Appeal indicated that his appeal would be allowed, he was compulsorily detained under the 1983 Act. The correspondence between the applicant's carers and Dr M reflects both the carer's wish to have the applicant immediately released to their care and, equally, the clear intention of Dr M and the other relevant health-care professionals to exercise strict control over his assessment, treatment, contacts and, notably, movement and residence: the applicant would only be released from the hospital to the care of Mr and Mrs E as and when those professionals considered it appropriate. While the Government suggested that 'there was evidence' that the applicant had not been denied access to his carers, it is clear from the above-noted correspondence that the applicant's contact with his carers was directed and controlled by the hospital, his carers visiting him for the first time after his admission on November 2, 1997.

Accordingly, the concrete situation was that the applicant was under continuous supervision and control and was not free to leave. Any suggestion to the contrary was, in the Court's view, fairly described by Lord Steyn as 'stretching credulity to breaking point' and as a 'fairy tale'.

92 The Court would therefore agree with the applicant that it is not determinative whether the ward was 'locked' or 'lockable' (the evidence before the House of Lords and the Commissioner appearing to differ in this respect). In this regard, it recalls that the applicant in the Ashingdane case was considered to have been 'detained' for the purposes of Art.5(1)(e) even during a period when he was in an open ward with regular unescorted access to the unsecured hospital grounds and unescorted leave outside the hospital.

93 Considerable reliance was placed by the Government on the above-cited HM v Switzerland judgment, in which it was held that the placing of an elderly applicant in a foster home, to ensure necessary medical care as well as satisfactory living conditions and hygiene, did not amount to a deprivation of liberty within the meaning of Art.5 of the Convention. However, each case has to be decided on its own particular 'range of factors' and, while there may be similarities between the present and the HM case, there are also distinguishing features. In particular, it was not established that HM was legally incapable of expressing a view on her position, she had often stated that she was willing to enter the nursing home and, within weeks of being there, she had agreed to stay. This combined with a regime entirely different to that applied to the present applicant (the foster home was an open institution which allowed freedom of movement and encouraged contacts with the outside world) allows a conclusion that the facts of the HM case were not of a 'degree' or 'intensity' sufficiently serious to justify the conclusion that she was detained.

The Court also finds a conclusion that the present applicant was detained consistent with the above-cited judgment on which the Government also relied. That case turned on the specific fact that the mother had committed the applicant minor to an institution in the exercise of her parental rights, pursuant to which rights she could have removed the applicant from the hospital at any time. Although the Government noted that the hospital retained responsibility for the present applicant following his release in 1994, the fact that the hospital had to rely on the doctrine of necessity and, subsequently, on the involuntary detention provisions of the 1983 Act demonstrates that the hospital did not have legal authority to act on the applicant's behalf in the same way as Mr Nielsen's mother.

94 The Court therefore concludes that the applicant was 'deprived of his liberty' within the meaning of Art.5(1) of the Convention from July 22, 1997 to October 29, 1997.

The court did state that whether someone was detained had to be decided on the basis of the specific situation under consideration. This is important because the decision has serious implications for those mentally incapacitated patients and their carers where the patient is not in a place which is registered to take detained patients but in, say, a residential care home. As far as those informal patients in psychiatric hospitals are concerned who lack capacity it is possible that they will be formally detained or discharged.

Following on from this decision, the Mental Health Act 2007 amended the Mental Capacity Act so that such patients could be lawfully deprived of their liberty when it was appropriate to do so.

Mental Capacity Act 2005

4A Restriction on deprivation of liberty

1   This Act does not authorise any person ('D') to deprive any other person ('P') of his liberty.
2   But that is subject to –
    a   the following provisions of this section, and
    b   section 4B.
3   D may deprive P of his liberty if, by doing so, D is giving effect to a relevant decision of the court.
4   A relevant decision of the court is a decision made by an order under section 16(2)(a) in relation to a matter concerning P's personal welfare.
5   D may deprive P of his liberty if the deprivation is authorised by Schedule A1 (hospital and care home residents: deprivation of liberty).

4B Deprivation of liberty necessary for life-sustaining treatment etc

1   If the following conditions are met, D is authorised to deprive P of his liberty while a decision as respects any relevant issue is sought from the court.
2   The first condition is that there is a question about whether D is authorised to deprive P of his liberty under section 4A.
3   The second condition is that the deprivation of liberty –
    a   is wholly or partly for the purpose of –
        i   giving P life-sustaining treatment, or
        ii   doing any vital act, or
    b   consists wholly or partly of –
        i   giving P life-sustaining treatment, or
        ii   doing any vital act.
4   The third condition is that the deprivation of liberty is necessary in order to –
    a   give the life-sustaining treatment, or
    b   do the vital act.
5   A vital act is any act which the person doing it reasonably believes to be necessary to prevent a serious deterioration in P's condition.

The safeguards apply to anyone aged 18 and over who: suffers from a mental disorder or disability of the mind – such as dementia or a profound learning disability; lacks the capacity to give informed consent to the arrangements made for their care and/or treatment; for whom deprivation of liberty (within the meaning of Art 5 of the ECHR) is considered after an independent assessment to be necessary in their best interests to protect them from harm. The safeguards cover patients in hospitals, and people in care homes registered under the Care Standards Act 2000, whether placed under public or private arrangements and they require a hospital or care home to apply to a supervisory body for authorisation for deprivation of liberty if it finds that a person lacking capacity is being deprived of that liberty or risks being so deprived. The supervisory body is either a local authority or an NHS primary care trust. The upshot of these provisions is that, unless there is a court authorisation, a person can only be deprived of liberty by the 2005

Act where: the deprivation is authorised in accordance with the deprivation of liberty procedures (DOLS) set out in Sch A1 to the 2005 Act; or the deprivation is carried out because it is necessary in order to give life-sustaining treatment, or to carry out a vital act to prevent serious deterioration in the person's condition, while a decision as respects any relevant issue is sought from the court (the other circumstances where the deprivation is permitted is when it is authorised by an order of the Court of Protection under s 16(2)(a) of the 2005 Act). Section 39A and Sch A1 of the Act provide for independent mental capacity advocates to be appointed in cases where the person has no one else with whom they might consult about the person's best interests.

Although it can be seen that the safeguards are designed to protect the interests of an extremely vulnerable group of patients/service users, they have attracted some sharp criticism:

Jones, R, *Mental Health Act Manual*[17]

The Mental Capacity Act 2005 (MCA) is amended by the 2007 Act to provide for a procedure that can be used to authorise the deprivation of liberty of a mentally incapacitated person. The new procedure, which is intended to sit alongside the powers of compulsion set out in the [Mental Health Act 1983 (MHA)], represents the Government's response to the finding of the European Court of Human Rights in *HL v United Kingdom* (the 'Bournewood' case). The Government could have achieved its objective by making minor amendments to the MHA. Instead, a procedure has been created that is hugely complex, voluminous, badly drafted, overly bureaucratic and difficult to understand, and yet provides mentally incapacitated people with minimum safeguards. If that were not enough, the nature of the relationship between the MHA and the MCA in so far as it relates to the detention of patients is far from clear. This is not surprising given that the two Acts had different sponsoring Government Departments and pursue different policy agendas, one being capacity based and the other focussing on risk. By legislating for parallel legislative regimes, Parliament has created a recipe for confusion which will inevitably result in a lack of consistent practice throughout England and Wales.

Jones is suggesting that because the mental health regime is about protecting people from harm (including harm to oneself), there is a different approach to the capacity cases. However, it is not clear that this is the case, as, without treatment in their best interests, there is potential for a great deal of harm. Presumably Jones is arguing that, a better way of dealing with this would have been to enable informal patients to have their cases reviewed by Mental Health Review Tribunals as is the case with people who are compulsorily detained under the Act. However, the deprivation of liberty safeguards apply to *all* patients whose liberty is restricted and to those who are confined to, say, residential homes, and some might argue that for them to be reviewed under a Mental Health Act procedure stigmatises them. However, there could have been mechanisms for distinguishing the two procedures and arguably Jones is right in preferring the simpler approach.

The safeguards apply to any form of deprivation of liberty, not just being in a locked unit, so actions such as tying patients/service users to chairs, for example, are a deprivation of liberty and, while it might be appropriate to prevent them going outside unsupervised, tying them to a chair might be regarded as too restrictive of their liberty.

Jones is right in referring to these as minimum safeguards because there is no effective 'policing' of the system, and it would not be surprising if many privately owned units did not comply at all.

In G *v* E, the Court of Appeal examined the operation of the safeguards. The appellant brought an action in the Court of Protection alleging that there had been a breach of Article 5

---

17 London: Sweet and Maxwell, 11th edn, 2008.

in respect of her brother who had severe learning difficulties, lacked capacity but was not mentally ill. For some time he had lived with his former foster parent, but the local authority removed him from that home to a residential unit without going through the process required by the Mental Capacity Act. The judge at first instance found that this amounted to a breach of his rights under Article 5. However, the judge decided that, despite this, it was open to the court to go on to consider what was in his best interests and, in this case, it was that he remain in the residential unit. The Court of Appeal held that the safeguards did indeed 'plug' the Bournewood gap and that they complied with Article 5. The court went on to uphold the first instance decision.

G v E[18]

Sir Nicholas Wall P

57 . . . We accept Mr. Gordon's submission – indeed, we understand it to be common ground – that the safeguards against arbitrary detention contained in ECHR Article 5 apply to persons lacking capacity. It is our view that MCA 2005 provides a 'procedure prescribed by law' for depriving such persons of their liberty.

58 . . . [W]e do not think that ECHR Article 5 imposes any threshold conditions which have to be satisfied before a best interests assessment under DOLS can be carried out.

59 With great respect, we think that one of the fallacies in Mr. Westgate's argument is that the European jurisprudence derives exclusively from the fact that in the cases which have reached the ECtHR, the issue has involved alleged mental illness and detention in a psychiatric hospital. In such a case, as the Mental Health Act 1983 requires, a psychiatric opinion that a given person requires detention is essential to justify it. In the instant case, E does not suffer from a psychiatric condition, and is not mentally ill. The evidence of impairment was essentially paediatric . . . In these circumstances, psychiatric evidence is unlikely to be of material assistance at the diagnostic stage.

60 . . . [Incapacitated patients] are, of course, 'of unsound mind' within ECHR Article 5, but in our judgment it plainly does not follow either that they are mentally ill, or that ECHR Article 5 requires psychiatric evidence as a threshold to the deprivation of their liberty. Indeed, learning difficulties often lie outside the expertise of the psychiatrist, but firmly within that of the psychologist.

61 Indeed, in the common case, where the adult concerned is suffering from a chronic condition, expert evidence, in our experience is usually provided by a psychologist or, as here, by a paediatrician. Provided there is credible expert evidence upon which the court can be satisfied that the individual concerned lacks capacity that, in our judgment, is sufficient. It would simply be unreal to require psychiatric evidence in every case, quite apart from the fact that it would, in some cases, be irrelevant. To require such evidence would, in our judgment, make MCA 2005 unworkable.

. . .

64 We also agree with Mr. Gordon that the justification of detention in a case under MCA 2005 is not a medical decision but a decision for the court, to be made in the best interests of the person whom it is sought to detain.

The court's reference to threshold conditions means that, unlike cases of mental illness, there was no need to provide any psychiatric assessment of the person's learning disability, given that it was accepted by all that he lacked capacity and, therefore, the court could move straight to a decision as to what is in his best interests. The court accepted that evidence from elsewhere, eg

---

18 [2010] EWCA Civ 822.

a psychologist, may be necessary to establish lack of capacity, but no evidence was necessary to show that they needed to be deprived of liberty; only that the restrictions placed upon them were in their best interests.

In the context of Article 5(1) of the European Convention, there is an important distinction between a deprivation of liberty and a restriction upon liberty. In *Austin v UK*,[19] the European Court had to consider this in the situation of 'kettling', a police tactic to contain demonstrators by keeping them behind a police cordon. The majority decision of the court held that this was not a deprivation of liberty but a justifiable restriction upon the liberty of the demonstrators in the interest of averting a real risk of injury or damage.

The case of *A Local Authority v H*[20] concerned the assessment of capacity, but it also provides an illustration of particular circumstances that result in deprivation of liberty in the case of someone who was nevertheless able to hold down two jobs. H was 29 years old; she had mild learning difficulties and atypical autism, and had, from a very early age, exhibited a high degree of sexualisation. She narrated a history of her willingness to have sex with anyone, including strangers and groups of men. She could not manage her finances and had incurred substantial debts. She was admitted to a psychiatric hospital as a voluntary patient but was subsequently detained compulsorily following bizarre and highly sexualised behaviour in hospital. Hedley J found that she lacked capacity to determine where she lived, her care and support arrangements, contact and finances. At the time of the hearing, she was living in private accommodation in contract with the local authority. A minimum of one-to-one supervision was provided at all times whether in or out of the property (she had two part-time jobs and one-to-one supervision occurred at her places of work). Hedley J found that the regime constituted a deprivation of liberty that should be authorised because although it consisted of 'considerable incursions into personal autonomy and freedom', it was justified in terms of her personal and sexual safety and in terms of life skills.

It fell to the Supreme Court, in *Cheshire West and Chester Council v P and Surrey County Council v P*, to consider deprivation of liberty, again in the context of living arrangements for mentally incapacitated people. P had cerebral palsy and Down's syndrome and had lived with his mother until, due to her ill health, she was unable to care for him any more. At this point the local social services authority obtained orders from the Court of Protection that it was in P's best interests to live in local authority accommodation. He lived in a bungalow which he shared with two other residents. The bungalow was continually staffed and, in addition, P received 98 hours of one-to-one support per week. He went out to a day centre and various social events, and saw his mother, who lived close by. He needed help with all the activities of daily living. He wore incontinence pads and, because he had a history of pulling off pieces of these and putting them in his mouth, he wore a 'body suit' to prevent this. He could be difficult and required interventions to deal with this. The judge at first instance held that, as P could do nothing without support and assistance, this amounted to a deprivation of liberty. The Court of Appeal allowed the appeal by developing the concept of 'relative normality' and held that it was wrong to compare him to someone whose capacity was unimpaired, and for whom the control and supervision would constitute a deprivation of liberty. The Supreme Court unanimously allowed the appeal:

Cheshire West and Chester Council v P and Surrey County Council v P[21]

Lady Hale: 51. In the case of P, the Court of Appeal should not have set aside the decision of the judge for the reasons they gave. Does it follow that the decision of the judge should be restored? In my view it does. In paragraph 46 of his judgment, he correctly directed himself as to the three components of a deprivation

---

19 (2012) 55 EHRR 14.
20 [2012] EWHC 49 (COP).
21 [2014] UKSC 19.

of liberty derived from Storck; he reminded himself that the distinction between a deprivation of and a restriction of liberty is one of degree or intensity rather than nature or substance; and he held that 'a key factor is whether the person is, or is not, free to leave. This may be tested by determining whether those treating and managing the patient exercise complete and effective control of the person's care and movements' (para 46(5)). It is true that, in paragraph 48, he summarised the further guidance given by the Court of Appeal in P and Q, including the relevance of an absence of objection and the relative normality of the person's life, which in my view are not relevant factors. But when he considered the circumstances of P's life at the Z house, he remarked (para 58) upon the very great care taken by the local authority and the staff of Z House to ensure that P's life was as normal as possible, but continued (para 59):

> 'On the other hand, his life is completely under the control of members of staff at Z House. He cannot go anywhere or do anything without their support and assistance. More specifically, his occasionally aggressive behaviour, and his worrying habit of touching and eating his continence pads, require a range of measures, including at time physical restraint, and, when necessary, the intrusive procedure of inserting fingers into his mouth whilst he is being restrained'.
>
> In my view, in substance the judge was applying the right test, derived from *HL v United Kingdom*, and his conclusion that 'looked at overall, P is being deprived of his liberty' (para 60) should be restored.

The second case to be considered by the Supreme Court concerned two sisters, referred to as MIG and MEG, who had learning disabilities. MIG was more severely impaired than her sister; she had difficulty with her sight and hearing, and could not cross the road unaided. Her comprehension and communication skills were limited. MEG had better skills, but she had autistic traits and exhibited challenging behaviour. Both sisters had been neglected and ill-treated when they were living with their mother, and social services had intervened. At the time of the hearing, MEG was 17 and living in an NHS unit for learning-disabled adolescents. She had been in foster care but that had not been successful due to her severe aggressive outbursts. Her care needs were only met by continuous supervision and control, and she did not leave the unit alone. MEG was taking tranquillising medication. She attended a further education unit along with her sister and, because of her better cognitive skills, she had a better social life. MIG was living with a foster mother to whom she was devoted and who provided her with what was described as 'intensive support'. MIG was not on any medication. At first instance the judge found that the living arrangements were in the sisters' best interests and did not amount to a deprivation of liberty and the Court of Appeal stressed the relative normality of their lives, comparing their lives with the circumstances in which they had lived at home. The Supreme Court, by a majority of four to three, upheld the appeal.

Lady Hale: 52 Wilson LJ found MEG's case difficult and only reached the conclusion that she had not been deprived of her liberty after 'protracted thought': [2012] Fam 170, para 34. He relied upon the small size of the adolescent home, her lack of objection to life there, her attendance at the educational unit; her good family contact; and her fairly active social life. It is, however, very difficult to see how her case can be distinguished from that of P, who also enjoyed all of those features. She did not require the sort of restraint which P required because of his incontinence pads, but she did sometimes require physical restraint and she received medication to control her anxiety. Above all, the staff did exercise control over every aspect of her life. She would not be allowed out without supervision, or to see people whom they did not wish her to see, or to do things which they did not wish her to do.

53 MIG's case was different in one important respect. She was living in an ordinary family home, and also going out to attend an educational unit, and enjoying good family contact. Both Parker J and Wilson LJ were

concerned that if these arrangements constituted a deprivation of liberty for which the state was responsible, then so too would HL's placement with his foster carers: but no-one had suggested this – indeed, the restriction on contact with them was one of the features relied upon in concluding that the hospital had deprived HL of his liberty. But the court was not called upon to confront that issue. The reality is that MIG's situation is otherwise the same as her sister's, in that her foster mother and others responsible for her care exercised complete control over every aspect of her life. She too would not be allowed out without supervision, or to see anyone whom they did not wish her to see, or to do things which they did not wish her to do.

54 If the acid test is whether a person is under the complete supervision and control of those caring for her and is not free to leave the place where she lives, then the truth is that both MIG and MEG are being deprived of their liberty. Furthermore, that deprivation is the responsibility of the state. Similar constraints would not necessarily amount to a deprivation of liberty for the purpose of article 5 if imposed by parents in the exercise of their ordinary parental responsibilities and outside the legal framework governing state intervention in the lives of children or people who lack the capacity to make their own decisions.

55 Several objections may be raised to the conclusion that both MIG and MEG are being deprived of their liberty. One is that neither could survive without this level of supervision and control: but that is to resurrect the comparison with other people sharing their disabilities and to deny them the same concept of liberty as everyone else. Another is that they are both content with their placements and have shown no desire to leave. . . . As HL 40 EHRR 761 shows, compliance is not enough. Another possible distinction is that, if either of them indicated that they wanted to leave, the evidence was that the local authority would look for another placement: in other words, they were at least free to express a desire to leave.

56 In the end, none of these suggested distinctions is satisfactory. Nor, in my view, should they be. It is very easy to focus upon the positive features of these placements for all three of the appellants. The local authorities who are responsible for them have no doubt done the best they could to make their lives as happy and fulfilled, as well as safe, as they possibly could be. But the purpose of article 5 is to ensure that people are not deprived of their liberty without proper safeguards, safeguards which will secure that the legal justifications for the constraints which they are under are made out: in these cases, the law requires that they do indeed lack the capacity to decide for themselves where they should live and that the arrangements made for them are in their best interests. It is to set the cart before the horse to decide that because they do indeed lack capacity and the best possible arrangements have been made, they are not in need of those safeguards. If P, MIG and MEG were under the same constraints in the sort of institution in which Mr Stanev was confined, we would have no difficulty in deciding that they had been deprived of their liberty. In the end, it is the constraints that matter.

Policy

57 Because of the extreme vulnerability of people like P, MIG and MEG, I believe that we should err on the side of caution in deciding what constitutes a deprivation of liberty in their case. They need a periodic independent check on whether the arrangements made for them are in their best interests. Such checks need not be as elaborate as those currently provided for in the Court of Protection or in the Deprivation of Liberty safeguards (which could in due course be simplified and extended to placements outside hospitals and care homes). Nor should we regard the need for such checks as in any way stigmatising of them or of their carers. Rather, they are a recognition of their equal dignity and status as human beings like the rest of us.

Lords Carnwath, Hodge and Clarke dissented in the cases of MIG and MEG on the basis that the sisters' circumstances were no more intrusive or confining than was required for their protection and well-being. They also expressed concerned that no one would regard it as a proper use of language to describe them, happily living in a domestic setting, as being deprived of their liberty. MIG and MEG may have had their liberty restricted compared with an unimpaired person, but that was not the same as a deprivation. Arguably, the minority view could be taken as expressing concern about stigmatisation of the impaired people and, in particular, their carers, which is the stance that Lady Hale particularly denied to be the case. Arguably, the distinction between restricted liberty and deprivation of liberty is a dangerous one in the context of mental incapacity. It can work well in the context of public safety, such as in *Austin*, but where vulnerability is concerned (and all people who lack capacity are vulnerable to some degree and/or in some situations) it could be used to undermine the safeguards that were necessitated by *HL*.

It may be recalled that the European Convention requirements impose positive obligations upon the state. This was considered by the Court of Appeal in *Secretary of State for Justice v (1) Staffordshire County Council (2) SRK (by his Litigation Friend, SK) (3) RK (4) Irwin Mitchell Trust Corp.*[22] As a result of receiving damages for personal injury, K received 24-hour care which was managed by the Irwin Mitchell Trust Corporation, which had been appointed by the Court of Protection to act as K's representative ('deputy' in the language of the MCA; see below under 'Procedural Matters'). The deputy informed the local authority that, due to the accommodation arrangements, there may be a deprivation of liberty and a welfare order was applied for, and granted by the Court of Protection as, although these were private care arrangements, there were insufficient procedural safeguards to satisfy the state's positive obligations under Article 5. The Secretary of State appealed on the basis that the criminal and civil law, and enforceable obligations on public bodies in respect of vulnerable people, were sufficient to satisfy this. The Court of Appeal dismissed the appeal on the basis that the operation of the law relied upon by the Secretary of State, was dependent upon wrong-doing being brought to the attention of the state; there was no process of assessment and review of such private care to provide the necessary safeguards.

4.3.4 Decision-making criteria

4.3.4.1 The therapeutic/non-therapeutic distinction

Most medical procedures performed on mentally incapable patients will be carried out to cure or ameliorate the effects of disease and disorder. However, this will not always be the case. In the case of medical research on healthy volunteers, and the control of fertility (see below), there is no physical or mental disorder which is being treated. It is common to refer to these latter cases as instances of non-therapeutic 'treatment'. Of course, they are not really 'treatment' cases at all.

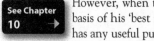

However, when the patient is incapable and the procedure is being carried out on the basis of his 'best interests', the English courts have questioned whether the distinction has any useful purpose.

The validity of making such a distinction was accepted by the Australian High Court in the case of *Secretary, Department of Health and Community Services v JWB and SMB*. However, although accepting that there is a distinction, all seven judges acknowledged that it was not easy to draw the line. Brennan J suggests the following distinguishing factors:

Secretary, Department of Health and Community Services v JWB and SMB[23]

Brennan J: It is necessary to define what is meant by therapeutic medical treatment. I would define treatment (including surgery) as therapeutic when it is administered for the chief purpose of preventing, removing or ameliorating a cosmetic deformity, a pathological condition or a psychiatric disorder,

22 [2016] EWCA Civ 1317
23 (1992) 66 ALJR 300.

provided the treatment is appropriate for and proportionate to the purpose for which it is administered. 'Non-therapeutic' medical treatment is descriptive of treatment which is inappropriate or disproportionate having regard to the cosmetic deformity, pathological condition or psychiatric disorder for which the treatment is administered and of treatment which is administered chiefly for other purposes.

In the Canadian case of *Re Eve*, the distinction was crucial to the decision of the court. The case concerned a 24-year-old woman suffering from extreme expressive aphasia, which is a condition inhibiting the patient from communicating thoughts and feelings. She was described as being mildly to moderately retarded. It was accepted that she may be able to carry out the physical aspects of child care, but due to her severe lack of communication skills she would not make a suitable mother in the wider sense. As a result of what was described as a close relationship with a male student at the school for retarded adults that she attended, her mother became concerned and wished her daughter to be sterilised:

Re Eve[24]

La Forest J: . . . [I]t is difficult to imagine a case in which non-therapeutic sterilisation could possibly be of benefit to the person on behalf of whom a court purports to act, let alone one in which that procedure is necessary in his or her best interest. And how are we to weigh the best interests of a person in this troublesome area, keeping in mind that an error is irreversible? Unlike other cases involving the use of the *parens patriae* jurisdiction, an error cannot be corrected by the subsequent exercise of judicial discretion. That being so, one need only recall Lord Eldon's remark . . . that 'it has always been the principle of this court, not to risk damage to children which it cannot repair' to conclude that non-therapeutic sterilisation may not be authorised in the exercise of the parens patriae jurisdiction.

McQuaid J was, therefore, right in concluding that he had no authority or jurisdiction to grant the application.

In the case of *Re B (A Minor) (Wardship: Sterilisation)*, the distinction was rejected. The child in this case was 17 years old and described as having the mental age of a five or six-year-old. She was in the care of the local authority, and, when it was thought that she was exhibiting signs of some sexual appetite, it applied to the High Court for leave for her to be sterilised. The case eventually reached the House of Lords:

Re B (A Minor) (Wardship: Sterilisation)[25]

Lord Hailsham of St Marylebone LC: We were also properly referred to the Canadian case of *Re Eve* . . . I find, with great respect [La Forest J's] conclusions . . . that the procedure of sterilisation 'should never be authorised for non-therapeutic purposes' (my emphasis) totally unconvincing and in startling contradiction to the welfare principle which should be the first and paramount consideration in wardship cases. Moreover, for the purposes of the present appeal I find the distinction he purposes to draw between 'therapeutic' and 'non-therapeutic' purposes of this operation in relation to the facts of the present case above as totally meaningless, and, if meaningful, quite irrelevant to the correct application of the welfare principle.

. . . To say that the court can never authorise sterilisation of a ward as being in her best interests would be patently wrong. To say that it can only do so if the operation is 'therapeutic' as opposed to

24 [1986] 2 SCR 388.
25 [1988] AC 199.

'non-therapeutic' is to divert attention from the true issue, which is whether the operation is in the ward's best interests, and remove it to an area of arid semantic debate as to where the line is to be drawn between 'therapeutic' and 'non-therapeutic' treatment.

Clearly, there is a good argument that the courts should not be fettered by having no discretion to consider 'wider' issues, but, by implication, adopting the therapeutic/non-therapeutic distinction means that these wider issues can be considered, even though, as, in *Re Eve*, non-therapeutic treatment of a certain nature is rejected.

The case of *R v Human Fertilisation and Embryology Authority, ex p Blood*[26] concerned the legality of using the sperm of the woman's deceased husband after his death. The argument before the court was about the application of the Human Fertilisation and Embryology Act 1990. However, it was accepted that at least some of the sperm was taken from the man before his death.[27] Surprisingly, the Court of Appeal passed little comment on the common law, despite the fact that the procedure was non-therapeutic, carried out without consent and, therefore, probably constituted a battery. However, consider the position if the patient would have wished for his sperm to be taken in this way and used after his death (as his widow tried to argue): would it mean that the 'battery' would be transformed into something done in his best interests? Consider also the 'substituted judgment' test, dealt with below.

See Chapter 7 →

The case of *S v S* concerned two disputed cases of paternity. The parents of the children had agreed that blood samples be taken from the children in question for the appropriate tests to be carried out. The Official Solicitor had argued that the blood tests could not be carried out unless it was in the interests of the children. The effect of this decision has been reversed by s 82(3) of the Child Support, Pensions and Social Security Act 2000 which amends s 21(3) of the 1969 Act and allows the court to order the taking of a blood sample for the purposes of resolving paternity disputes where the custodial parent objects; but the general approach of the court can still be applied.

The implications of this are considered further below. But would it be possible to argue that the child has an interest in knowing the identity of his father and, therefore, this 'procedure' would be 'therapeutic' in the sense that it would have psychological benefits for the child? Arguably it would not. It is pure speculation as to the outcome of the paternity dispute and its effect upon the child and, therefore, whether it would make him *feel* better is unascertainable. However, this raises a crucial factor in the concept of the 'therapeutic' – the making life better for the person concerned. It must be remembered that we are not talking here about patients. The healthy volunteer in a research programme is not a patient. The mentally handicapped person whom it is proposed to sterilise because she may become pregnant is not a patient (she may or may not live in a hospital, but her residence there would not be because of gynaecological disorder). That is not to say that these procedures may never be carried out, but the decision is not a medical decision. It is arguable that it is important to label the procedure as 'non-therapeutic' so as not to lose sight of this.

However, might the converse be the case? We consider below a number of cases where sterilisations have been carried out on women for the purposes of 'managing menstruation'. These have been regarded as 'therapeutic' because the purpose was not to render the women sterile. By describing them thus, it could be said that the distinction might be used to mask a real 'non-therapeutic' intention.

---

26 [1997] 2 WLR 806.
27 See Ch 11 for a discussion of the rights anyone may have when tissue is removed from a dead body.

THINK POINT

Leaving aside procedures that are obviously non-therapeutic, such as research on healthy volunteers, do you think that the use of the 'best interests' criterion has made the therapeutic/non-therapeutic distinction irrelevant?

4.3.4.2 The 'best interests' test

The Mental Capacity Act 2005 states that one of the principles of the Act is that 'an act done, or a decision made under this Act for or on behalf of a person who lacks capacity must be done, or made, in his best interests' (s 1(5)). Section 4 of the Act deals with the way in which 'best interests' must be determined.

Mental Capacity Act 2005

4 Best interests

1 In determining for the purposes of this Act what is in a person's best interests, the person making the determination must not make it merely on the basis of –
   a   the person's age or appearance, or
   b   a condition of his, or an aspect of his behaviour, which might lead others to make unjustified assumptions about what might be in his best interests.

2 The person making the determination must consider all the relevant circumstances and, in particular, take the following steps.

3 He must consider –
   a   whether it is likely that the person will at some time have capacity in relation to the matter in question, and
   b   if it appears likely that he will, when that is likely to be.

4 He must, so far as reasonably practicable, permit and encourage the person to participate, or to improve his ability to participate, as fully as possible in any act done for him and any decision affecting him.

5 Where the determination relates to life-sustaining treatment he must not, in considering whether the treatment is in the best interests of the person concerned, be motivated by a desire to bring about his death.

6 He must consider, so far as is reasonably ascertainable –
   a   the person's past and present wishes and feelings (and, in particular, any relevant written statement made by him when he had capacity),
   b   the beliefs and values that would be likely to influence his decision if he had capacity, and
   c   the other factors that he would be likely to consider if he were able to do so.

7 He must take into account, if it is practicable and appropriate to consult them, the views of –
   a   anyone named by the person as someone to be consulted on the matter in question or on matters of that kind,
   b   anyone engaged in caring for the person or interested in his welfare,
   c   any donee of a lasting power of attorney granted by the person, and
   d   any deputy appointed for the person by the court, as to what would be in the person's best interests and, in particular, as to the matters mentioned in subsection (6).

> 8   The duties imposed by subsections (1) to (7) also apply in relation to the exercise of any powers which –
>   a   are exercisable under a lasting power of attorney, or
>   b   are exercisable by a person under this Act where he reasonably believes that another person lacks capacity.
> 9   In the case of an act done, or a decision made, by a person other than the court, there is sufficient compliance with this section if (having complied with the requirements of subsections (1) to (7)) he reasonably believes that what he does or decides is in the best interests of the person concerned.
> 10 'Life-sustaining treatment' means treatment which in the view of a person providing healthcare for the person concerned is necessary to sustain life.
> 11 'Relevant circumstances' are those –
>   a   of which the person making the determination is aware, and
>   b   which it would be reasonable to regard as relevant.

An argument that has been canvassed is that there can be occasions when it is sufficient to show that a course of action is not against the interests of the patient:

S v S[28]

> **Lord MacDermott**: In exercising what I have called the ancillary jurisdiction in relation to infants the court must also observe and, if need be, exercise its protective jurisdiction. For instance, if the court were satisfied that – as might possibly be the case on rare occasions – a blood test would prejudicially affect the health of the infant it would, no doubt, exercise its discretion against ordering the test. And, again, if the court had reason to believe that the application for a blood test was of a fishing nature, designed for some ulterior motive to call in question the legitimacy, otherwise unimpeached, of a child who had enjoyed a legitimate status, it would be justified in refusing the application. I need not, however, pursue such instances as they do not arise on these appeals. The point to be made is that the protective jurisdiction, if of the nature I have described, would not ordinarily afford ground for refusing a blood test merely because it might, in revealing the truth, prove the infant's illegitimacy in duly constituted paternity proceedings.

Here, it was found that there were no reasons why the tests should not be carried out, as opposed to there being positive reasons in favour. Instead of examining the reasons for the treatment and how these may be for the positive benefit of the patient, the court would be left to decide whether there was any likelihood of detriment to the patient. In practice, might such a change of emphasis be disadvantageous to the patient?

The House of Lords in *Re F* gave no definition of 'best interests', dealing with the case on its particular facts. The lack of judicial guidance was criticised:

Kennedy, I, 'Patients, doctors and human rights'[29]

> [The best interests test] allows lawyers and courts to persuade themselves and others that theirs is a principled approach to law. Meanwhile, they engage in what to others is clearly a form of '*ad hocery*'. The best interests approach of family law allows the courts to atomise the law, to claim that each case depends on its own facts. The court can then respond intuitively to each case while seeking to legitimate its conclusion

---

28 [1972] AC 24.
29 In Blackburn, R and Taylor, J (eds), *Human Rights for the 1990s: Legal, Political and Ethical Issues*, London: Mansell, 1991, p 90.

by asserting that it is derived from the general principle contained in the best interests formula. In fact, of course, there is no general principle other than the empty rhetoric of best interests; or rather, there is some principle (or principles) but the court is not telling. Obviously the court must be following some principles, otherwise a toss of a coin could decide cases. But these principles, which serve as pointers to what amounts to the best interests, are not articulated by the court. Only the conclusion is set out. The opportunity for reasoned analysis and scrutiny is lost.

This view was supported by Brennan J in his dissenting judgment in the Australian case of:

Department of Health v JWB and SMB[30]

Brennan J:14 .. the best interests approach offers no hierarchy of values which might guide the exercise of a discretionary power to authorise sterilisation, much less any general legal principle which might direct the difficult decisions to be made in this area by parents, guardians, the medical profession and courts. It is arguable that, in a field where the law has not developed, where ethical principles remain controversial and where each case turns on its own facts, the law should not pretend to too great a precision. Better, it might be said, that authority and power be conferred on a suitable repository – whether it be parents or guardians, doctors or the court – to decide these difficult questions according to the repository's view as to the best interests of the child in the particular circumstances of the case. In that way, it can be said, the blunt instrument of legal power will be sharpened according to the exigencies of the occasion. The absence of a community consensus on ethical principles may be thought to support this approach. But it must be remembered that, in the absence of legal rules or a hierarchy of values, the best interests approach depends upon the value system of the decision maker. Absent any rule or guideline, that approach simply creates an unexaminable discretion in the repository of the power.

15 Of course the variable circumstances of each case require evaluation and judicial evaluations of circumstances vary, but the power to authorise sterilisation is so awesome, its exercise is so open to abuse, and the consequences of its exercise are generally so irreversible, that guidelines if not rules should be prescribed to govern it. The courts must attempt the task in the course of, and as a necessary incident in, the exercise of their jurisdiction. That is not to say that the courts should arrogate to themselves the power to authorise sterilisations of intellectually disabled children, but it is to say that it has become the duty of the courts – and, in the present case, specifically the duty of this court – to define the scope of the power to authorise sterilisations of intellectually disabled children and the conditions of exercise of the power, and to determine the repository of the power. The power cannot be left in a state so amorphous that it can be exercised according to the idiosyncratic views of the repository as to the 'best interests' of the child. That approach provides an insubstantial protection of the human dignity of children; it wraps no cloak of protective principle around the intellectually disabled child.

The potentially broad scope of the best interests test is illustrated in the organ transplant cases, where it has been argued that it may be in the best interests of the donor to be treated as an altruistic member of the wider community.

See Chapter 11

In *Re M (Child: Refusal of Medical Treatment)*[31] the patient was a girl of 15 and a half who did not want a heart transplant because she did not want someone else's heart inside her, believing that this would make her 'different'. Dying from heart failure, which was the certain outcome without such a transplant, would not have this effect. Johnson J held that it would be in her best

---

30 (1992) 66 ALJR 300.
31 (1999) 52 BMLR 124.

interests to have the operation, notwithstanding that there were risks attached to the operation itself and thereafter, in terms of rejection in the medical sense and rejection by M of further treatment. There was also the risk that she would, for the rest of her life, resent having had the operation imposed upon her. However, balancing these matters against the certainty of death meant that the best interests test was satisfied.

In *JS v An NHS Trust, JA v An NHS Trust*[32] the High Court had to consider the case of two people, aged 18 and 16 respectively, who were suffering from probable variant CJD. Their parents sought a declaration that they lacked capacity and that the proposed treatment was lawful. This treatment was new and untested on human beings. It involved the giving of an infusion surgically under a general anaesthetic. There was no doubt that the patients lacked capacity but, as the treatment was untested, Dame Butler-Sloss was required to consider the application of the *Bolam* test and whether the treatment was in the patients' best interests. She held that a wider view of best interests should be taken in such a case and that the views of the parents and the effect upon them of a refusal to permit the treatment should be taken into account. The declarations were granted. Clearly in this case there was no alternative treatment available and there was no other hope of ameliorating the effects of this progressive and fatal disease. The experts, however, saw the treatment as offering only a very slim chance of improvement. Nevertheless, it must be right not to deny the patients this opportunity on the basis that it was not in their best interests because it could not be shown to have a good chance of success. See also the judgment of Munby J in the case of *R (on the application of Burke) v GMC*,[33] discussed in Chapter 12.

The case of *Wye Valley NHS Trust v Mr B (by his litigation friend, the Official Solicitor)*[34] concerned a 73-year-old man, with a severely infected leg, who, it was said, would die, perhaps in a matter of days, unless he underwent an amputation. Jackson J found that he did not have capacity, and it then fell to him to decide whether the surgery should take place in his best interests. The judge met with Mr B and formed the view that he was entirely serious about the prognosis, the fact that he was not afraid of dying and that he did not want interference in his condition. The judge also found that there were medical risks involved in the surgery, and that the need for sedation to carry out the surgery would be resisted and would make Mr B distressed that his wishes had not been respected. He would have to co-operate with rehabilitation that would be difficult. However, aside from the difficulties in carrying out the operation and dealing with rehabilitation, Jackson J found that there was a significant risk that his mental health and well-being would be badly affected. The loss of his foot would be a constant reminder that his wishes had been overruled. He had multiple physical and mental difficulties and it may mean that he would have been rehabilitated, only to die. If he did not have the operation, he would receive palliative care so that his last days were as comfortable as possible.

This sensitive approach and decision, must be right in these circumstances.

In *Cambridge University Hospitals NHS Foundation Trust v BF (by her Litigation Friend the Official Solicitor)*[35] the Court of Protection granted a declaration that a 36-year-old woman did not have capacity to consent (or refuse) to a total abdominal hysterectomy as treatment for ovarian cancer, but that is should take place as being in her best interests. She had been expressing fluctuating wishes regarding the proposed surgery, and it was found that these wishes were closely connected to her florid psychosis and the repeated urgings of the 'bad voice'.

---

32 [2002] EWHC 2734.
33 [2004] EWHC 1879.
34 [2015] EWCOP 60.
35 [2016] EWCOP 26.

It was also found that the evidence indicated that it was highly likely that she had a danger-ous malignant tumour. In accordance with section 4(7) of the MCA, MacDonald J considered the views of her parents:

> 64 Finally, I have also borne carefully in mind that BF's parents, who are closest to her and responsible for her care, are clear in their view that it is in their daughter's best interests to undergo surgery to remove her cancer. BF's father was clear that his daughter was "hearing voices" and that he did not think that she could make the decision whether to have the surgery and that the medical professionals should be trusted to do what was best for BF.

See also the case of *A Hospital NHS Trust v (1) CD (by her litigation friend The Official Solicitor (2) A Mental Health NHS Foundation Trust*[36] which has a similar fact pattern.

In *Cheshire & Wirral Partnership NHS Foundation Trust v Z*,[37] the case before the Court of Protection concerned a patient detained under s 3 of the Mental Health Act 1983 (the MHA). Although there is no reference to 'best interests' in the MHA (see Chapter 9), this case effectively decided what was in the best interests of this patient without consideration of her capacity because, as she was detained under the MHA, she could be treated without consent even if she had capac-ity. She had suffered from a very extreme form of anorexia nervosa since the age of 15. Now, aged 46, apart from her eating disorder and the underlying psychological problems, she was developing physical ill health, in particular severe osteoporosis. Her dangerously low weight was such that she was detained under s 3 of the MHA, not, of course, because of her physical condition, but because of her mental disorder and the fact that she posed a danger to herself. Her medical team had three options for treatment. The first was to continue to detain and feed her under restraint. The second was to detain and feed her under sedation. The third was that she should be discharged from the s 3 detention and treated voluntarily. The evidence was that the first option posed a serious risk to her musculoskeletal integrity because of her osteosporosis, and the second option posed a sim-ilarly serious risk of her undergoing respiratory or cardiac arrest because of her overall physical fragility. The third option was held to be the best one for her, as the team had stressed that she could return to hospital at any time, and there was evidence that her mental state improved when not being subjected to enforced treatment. Even though she had a 30-year history of not co-oper-ating with treatment regimes, the third option, it was held, would at least preserve her dignity and autonomy. The use of the last word is interesting as it could imply that she did have capacity.

Another best interests case, *Re IH (Observance of Muslim Practice*,[38] concerned a 39-year-old man suffering from a profound learning disability. Due to this impairment he had no understand-ing of religion and religious observations. The court had to decide whether it was in his best interests, firstly, on the application of the Official Solicitor, to be required to fast during the daylight hours of Ramadan and, secondly, on the application of his father, to be required to have his auxillary and pubic hair trimmed in accordance with Islamic culture and religious practice. The judge held that it was not in his best interests in both cases. In the case of fasting, the judge held that the man had no understanding of the religious significance of the withholding of food and water, and this would upset him and he might become distressed and/or aggressive. There was also concern that it might increase the side effects of his medication. In the case of the trim-ming of hair, again he would not understand why this was being done and, again, it was likely to cause him distress. and/or anger. The trimming of hair is part of the Islamic tradition of 'ritual cleanliness', but the judge held that he would derive no spiritual benefit from this, as he already

---

36 [2015] EWCOP 74.
37 [2016] EWCOP 56.
38 [2017] EWCOP 9.

had an elevated status because of his incapacity. The latter aspect is interesting in that it requires a view to be taken that, without capacity, observance of religious practices is not required because of absence of free will.

In *Re N (An Adult) (Court of Protection: Jurisdiction)*[39] (see below and in Chapter 2) the UK Supreme Court stated that when the Court of Protection was making decisions on behalf of incapacitated adults, the court was limited to what the public authority (in this case, the appropriate clinical commissioning group) would agree to implement, ie there could be no hypothetical proposals advanced as being in the best interests of the incapacitated person that a public authority would then be bound to implement.

As to the general operation of the MCA and DOLS, in 2014, via the process of post-legislative scrutiny, the House of Lords Select Committee made a number of recommendations as to the operation of the MCA. One was that there be an independent body to oversee the functioning of the MCA[40] and the other key finding expressed concerns about the DOLS. The view was that the safeguards do not provide sufficient protection, and that the legislative provisions should be re-drafted. This, and the concern about an increase in the number of applications to local authorities following the *Cheshire West* case, resulted in the Law Commission undertaking consultation on the operation of the Act. The Commission reported in March 2017.[41]

It recommends that there should be increased rights to instruct an independent advocate (at the moment under the MCA there is provision for independent advocates to be available in certain circumstances); a system of inspection and review of the circumstances in which people are deprived of their liberty; the extension of the powers to authorise a deprivation of liberty; extending DOLS to those aged 16 and 17; a simplified version of the best interests assessment which emphasises that, in all cases, arrangements must be necessary and proportionate before they can be authorised. There is also some rather vague reference to human rights, and the fact that protection should be extended to all care settings, including domestic settings on the basis that this would avoid applications to the Court of Protection.

The government issued an interim response in October 2017, which did little more than welcome the report, and confirm the importance of this area of law. In 2018 the Government's final response accepted the vast majority of the recommendations made by the Law Commission,[42] and said there is a pressing need to make the reforms.

Shortly after the Commission's Report was published, the need for change was highlighted when the High Court heard judicial review applications by four local authorities: *R (on the application of (1) Liverpool City Council (2) Nottinghamshire County Council (3) Richmond upon Thames LBC (4) Shropshire Council v Secretary of State for Health (Defendant) & Secretary of State for Communities & Local Government (Interested Party)*.[43] They were asking for a review of the failure of the Secretary of State for Health to provide sufficient funding to enable them to meet their responsibilities under the DOLS regime. As it happened the applications were filed 'out of time', and they were dismissed for that reason, but Garnham J considered the substantive arguments as well. Following the *Cheshire West* case there had been what was described as a 'huge' increase in applications under DOLS. The local authorities argued that the Secretary of State had created an unacceptable risk of illegality. They also argued that there had been a breach of a 2011 policy (the Department for Communities and Local Government: 'New Burdens Doctrine – Guidance Government Departments'), which required central government to justify any new burdens, how much they would cost and the source of the additional funding.

---

39 [2017] UKSC 22.
40 https://publications.parliament.uk/pa/ld201314/ldselect/ldmentalcap/139/139.pdf.
41 www.lawcom.gov.uk/app/uploads/2017/03/lc372_mental_capacity.pdf.
42 https://www.parliament.uk/business/publications/written-questions-answers-statements/written-statement/Commons/2018-03-14/HCWS542.
43 [2017] EWHC 986 (Admin).

This was rejected by Garnham J on the basis that the doctrine had made it clear that local authorities would not be refunded if the actual cost of a service was more than their estimates, and the illegality argument was also dismissed on the basis that it was not the case that the authorities could not afford to comply with these statutory obligations, but that funds would have to be diverted from elsewhere.

Certainly the MCA, s 4, clearly sets out a number of important considerations that must be taken into account when deciding best interests. The MCA Code of Practice expands on s 4 by giving specific examples.[44]

In Scotland, the capacity legislation is different and, in particular, does not employ the concept of best interests, but instead specifies that any act done in connection with the incapacitated adult is for their 'benefit' and the benefit cannot reasonably be achieved without that intervention (Adults with Incapacity (Scotland) Act 2000, s 1(2)). The explanatory notes to the Act state that a 'best interests' approach was developed in the context of the law on children and that this is too protective of adults, where it is more appropriate to give weight to the individual's own views. There are a number of ways of regarding these two approaches. The first is to say that 'best interests' has an objective ring to it, ie the individual is being treated as an objectively 'reasonable' person, whereas 'benefit' is looking at the subjective interests of the patient. This might have been the case before the passing of the Mental Capacity Act, but s 4(6) specifically requires the past and present wishes and feelings and beliefs and values of the person to be taken into account when deciding on best interests. The second way of looking at the two concepts is to see it as a semantic distinction only because it would not be possible to decide that something was in someone's best interests if there were no benefit accruing. However, the House of Lords' approach in S v S,[45] ie that something could be done if 'it were not against someone's interests', arguably belies this.

The Scottish approach essentially reflects the 'substituted judgment' test, to which we will now turn.

4.3.4.3 The 'substituted judgment' test

Is it possible to look at the situation from the point of view of the patient, and to make medical decisions on the basis of what he would have wanted, regardless of what may be thought by others to be good for him? The English courts have not adopted the 'substituted judgment' test used by some American courts (see *Re Eve*).[46] In any event, the test cannot be used when the patient has never had sufficient understanding to form genuine personal opinions on such matters, but is relevant to the status of advance directives.

The 'substituted judgment' test was considered, and rejected, in *Airedale NHS Trust v Bland*:

Airedale NHS Trust v Bland[47]

Lord Goff: I wish however to refer at this stage to the approach adopted in most American courts under which the court seeks, in a case in which the patient is incapacitated from expressing any view on the question whether life-prolonging treatment should be withheld in the relevant circumstances, to determine what decision the patient himself would have made had he been able to do so. This is called the substituted judgment test, and it generally involves a detailed inquiry into the patient's views and preferences: see, for example, *Re Quinlan* 70 NJ 10 (1976) and *Belchertown State School Superintendent v Saikewicz* 373

---

44 Ministry of Justice, *Mental Capacity Act Code of Practice*, 2007, London: TSO.
45 See n 4 above.
46 [1993] 1 All ER 821 at 872.
47 [1957] 1 WLR 582.

Mass 728 (1977). In later cases concerned with PVS patients it has been held that, in the absence of clear and convincing evidence of the patient's wishes, the surrogate decision maker has to implement as far as possible the decision which the incapable patient would make if he was competent. However, accepting on this point the submission of Mr Lester, I do not consider that any such test forms part of English law in relation to incapable adults, on whose behalf nobody has power to give consent to medical treatment. Certainly, in *F v West Berkshire HA* your Lordships' House adopted a straightforward test based on the best interests of the patient ... Of course, consistent with the best interests test, anything relevant to the application of the test may be taken into account; and, if the personality of the patient is relevant to the application of the test (as it may be in cases where the various relevant factors have to be weighed), it may be taken into account, as was done in *Re J (A Minor) (Wardship: Medical Treatment)* [1990] 3 All ER 930; [1991] Fam 33.

It is reasonable to conclude that the views of a patient will not be taken into account if he has never been capable of making an anticipatory decision: his views will be subsumed under the 'best interests' test (see Chapter 12 on advance decisions).

In any event, s 4(6) now effectively incorporates a form of substituted judgment into the criteria.

4.3.4.4 The *Bolam* test

The test set down in *Bolam v Friern Hospital Management Committee*[48] provides that a doctor will not be negligent if he follows a medical practice which is supported by a responsible body of medical opinion, and recent case law indicates that the 'body' of opinion to support the actions of the doctor can be small (see *Defreitas v O'Brien and Another*).[49] This test has been subjected to much criticism on the basis that it results in judicial abstentionism, leaving the standard of care to be set exclusively by a single faction within the medical profession. In the

case of *Re F (Mental Patient: Sterilisation)*,[50] which concerned a non-therapeutic sterilisation, it was held that decisions by doctors in respect of incapable patients should be judged by the *Bolam* test:

Lord Bridge: The common law should be readily intelligible to and applicable by all those who undertake the care of persons lacking the capacity to consent to treatment. It would be intolerable for members of the medical, nursing and other professions devoted to the care of the sick that, in caring for those lacking the capacity to consent to treatment they should be put in the dilemma that, if they administer the treatment which they believe to be in the patient's best interests, acting with due skill and care, they run the risk of being held guilty of trespass to the person, but if they withhold that treatment, they may be in breach of a duty of care owed to the patient. If those who undertake responsibility for the care of incapable or unconscious patients administer curative or prophylactic treatment which they believe to be appropriate to the patient's existing condition of disease, injury or bodily malfunction or susceptibility to such a condition in the future, the lawfulness of that treatment should be judged by one standard, not two. It follows that if the professionals in question have acted with due skill and care, judged by the well-known test laid down in *Bolam v Friern Hospital Management Committee* [1957] 1 WLR 582, they should be immune from liability in trespass, just as they are immune from liability in negligence. The special considerations which apply in the case of the sterilisation of a woman who is physically perfectly healthy or of an operation upon an organ transplant donor arise only because such treatment cannot be considered either curative or prophylactic.

---

48 [1995] 4 Med LR 108.
49 [1990] 2 AC 1.
50 [1990] 2 AC 1 at 31.

In the Court of Appeal, the *Bolam* test had been rejected by Neill LJ, with whom Butler-Sloss LJ agreed:

Re F (Mental Patient: Sterilisation)[51]

Neill LJ: A doctor may defeat a claim in negligence if he establishes that he acted in accordance with a practice accepted at the time as proper by a responsible body of medical opinion skilled in the particular form of treatment in question. This is the test laid down in *Bolam* . . . But to say that it is not negligent to carry out a particular form of treatment does not mean that that treatment is necessary. I would define necessary in this context as that which the general body of medical opinion in the particular speciality would consider to be in the best interests of the patient in order to maintain the health and to secure the well being of the patient. One cannot expect unanimity but it should be possible to say of an operation which is necessary in the relevant sense that it would be unreasonable in the opinion of most experts in the field not to make the operation available to the patient. One must consider the alternatives to an operation and the dangers or disadvantages to which the patient may be exposed if no action is taken. The question becomes: what action does the patient's health and welfare require?

Commenting upon this in the House of Lords, Lord Brandon stated (p 68):

Lord Brandon: With respect to the Court of Appeal, I do not agree that the *Bolam* test is inapplicable to cases of performing operations on, or giving other treatment to, adults incapable to give consent. In order that the performance of such operations on, and the giving of such other treatment to, such adults should be lawful, they must be in their best interests. If doctors were to be required, in deciding whether an operation or other treatment was in the best interests of adults incapable to give consent, to apply some test more stringent than the *Bolam* test, the result would be that such adults would, in some circumstances at least, be deprived of the benefit of medical treatment which adults competent to give consent would enjoy. In my opinion it would be wrong for the law, in its concern to protect such adults, to produce such a result.

While in the context of, say, diagnosis, there is much force in the argument that there should be the same standard of care regardless of whether the patient is capable or incapable, in the context of non-therapeutic treatment the *Bolam* test is not sufficiently rigorous. By its very nature, the decision can only be made on *non-medical* grounds and there is no reason why a doctor should be privileged to make such decisions. Clearly, in certain non-therapeutic cases, the best interests of the patient will be concerned with her best 'social' or 'personal' interests, and the *Bolam* test is far too weak to safeguard these.

The Law Commission considered the relationship of best interests and negligence:

Law Commission, *Mental Incapacity*, Report No 231[52]

3.27 It should be made clear beyond any shadow of a doubt that acting in a person's best interests amounts to something more than not treating that person in a negligent manner. Decisions taken on behalf of a person lacking capacity require a careful, focused consideration of that person as an individual. Judgments as to whether a professional has acted negligently, on the other hand, require a careful, focused consideration of how that particular professional acted as compared with the way in which

---

51 London: HMSO, 1995.
52 [2001] Fam 15.

other reasonably competent professionals would have acted. Lord Mustill, who was both a member of the appellate committee of the House of Lords which decided the case of *Airedale NHS Trust v Bland* and a member of the House of Lords Select Committee on Medical Ethics, said during oral evidence to the latter committee that:

> ... one of the things that is not very good is that the phrase 'best interests' has been put into play without any description of what it means. This, I think, actually increases the difficulties for the doctors rather than helps to solve them. What is at the back of my mind is whether perhaps Parliament could give some more specific definition of ... what are the relevant factors ...

However, it must be noted that the *Bolam* test was not considered in the case of *Re T*, where the Court of Appeal said that the welfare of the child was better served by overriding majority medical opinion (see below). Was this because the *parental* views in the case of a very young child were of greater importance? In the case of an incapacitated adult, would the decision be the same? It is also important to note that, in *Re F*, best interests were rolled up with necessity and it is arguable that this implies a more stringent test than *Bolam*.

Re SL (Adult Patient) (Medical Treatment)[53] concerned a conflict between medical opinion and the opinion of the mother of the incapable adult patient in her care. There were two concerns: that the woman would be become pregnant and that she had heavy periods which caused her distress. The two relevant alternatives were the use of a Mirena coil, which would be contraceptive and which would, at the least, reduce menstrual bleeding, and a hysterectomy which would eliminate all bleeding and render the woman permanently incapable of bearing children. The decision of Wall J was that, although medical opinion favoured the less invasive procedure to be tried first, as the hysterectomy, the procedure favoured by the mother and other relatives, was not ruled out by at least one of the experts, that satisfied the *Bolam* test, and could be carried out in the woman's best interests. Wall J said: 'in my judgment the court is entitled to declare lawful a particular course of treatment if that treatment itself is proper and in the interests of the patient, even if it is not the doctor's first choice'. Furthermore, the *Bolam* test, said the judge, should take into account wider social and emotional factors. These statements, without more, are to be welcomed. Unfortunately, the result in this case was that the judge did not sufficiently take into account the medical evidence. What might be described as a bold resistance to being overly influenced by medical opinion in the event resulted in him endorsing the most medically invasive option, while, at the same time, saying that, since both options satisfied the *Bolam* test, he would make a declaration to that effect and leave the mother to discuss with the doctors what option was to be preferred. The Court of Appeal, in upholding the appeal (not least because it appears that the judge misunderstood some of the medical evidence), endorsed the view that, in considering best interests, the *Bolam* test is incorrect, as a number of medical options can satisfy the *Bolam* test, but the best interests test means that the best option must be chosen. The court also stated that it is for the court to declare what that best option is and not to refer it back to the parties concerned, which must surely be correct, as such cases come before the courts in the first place because of a disagreement between the parties, not on whether treatments are objectively '*Bolam* compatible', but on subjective concerns about the incapacitated person.

---

53 [2000] 2 FCR 452.

Re SL (Adult Patient) (Medical Treatment)[54]

Dame Butler-Sloss: I would suggest that the starting point of any medical decision would be the principles enunciated in the *Bolam* test and that a doctor ought not to make any decision about a patient that does not fall within the broad spectrum of the *Bolam* test. The duty to act in accordance with responsible and competent professional opinion may give the doctor more than one option since there may well be more than one acceptable medical opinion. When the doctor moves on to consider the best interests of the patient he/she has to choose the best option, often from a range of options. As Mr Munby has pointed out, the best interests test ought, logically, to give only one answer.

... the *Bolam* test was, in my view, irrelevant to the judicial decision, once the judge was satisfied that the range of options was within the range of acceptable opinion among competent and responsible practitioners. If it was not, I would hope a surgeon would not operate, even if a declaration *was* given by the court.

In my judgment Wall J was in error in his application of the *Bolam* test to his decision-making process ... He had to declare the lawfulness of the surgical intervention in the context of such an operation being in his judgment in the best interests of the patient. To offer in his judgment the alternatives was not to decide which treatment was the better for S.

The Bolam test, therefore, is not the test as to what is in the best interests of a patient but rather it operates as a form of preliminary filter to exclude treatments and practices that are not accepted within the medical community.

4.3.4.5 Adults and the views of others

In a number of the sterilisation cases we are about to consider, it was argued that the views of the close relatives of the patients were relevant to the final outcome of the cases. However, though taken into account by the courts, as they were in the case of *Re P*, the case concerning a child, the argument that a close relative's views could in any way be determinative has been rejected. In the Canadian case of *Re Eve*,[55] La Forest J stated:

La Forest J: One may sympathise with Mrs E [the adult patient's mother]. To use Heilbron J's phrase, it is easy to understand the natural feelings of a parent's heart. But the *parens patriae* jurisdiction cannot be used for her benefit. Its exercise is confined to doing what is necessary for the benefit and protection of persons under disability like Eve. And a court ... must exercise great caution to avoid being misled by this all too human mixture of emotions and motives.

The relevance of blood ties was considered by the Court of Appeal in the case of *Re S (Hospital Order: Court's Jurisdiction)*. The plaintiff was the patient's cohabitee and the defendant, his son. Hale J held, at first instance (approved in the Court of Appeal), as follows:

Re S (Hospital Order: Court's Jurisdiction)[56]

Hale J: Yet although his relationship to the patient is a close one, and his wishes are of course worthy of respect, he has no more legal right to decide the patient's future than has the plaintiff. Indeed, were this to be a Mental Health Act case, the facts might be such that the plaintiff (rather than the wife) would be the patient's nearest relative for the purposes of s 26 of the Mental Health Act 1983.

---

54 [2000] 2 FCR 452.
55 [1986] 2 SCR 388.
56 [1995] 3 All ER 290, at p 295.

The Mental Capacity Act incorporates the views of others into the statutory scheme. Section 4(7) states that the views of others must be taken into account, if it is practicable and appropriate to consult them, if they have been named by the incapacitated person as someone to be consulted, are engaged in caring for that person, or have been given a power of attorney or have been appointed by the court as a 'deputy' (see below). Letts comments as follows:

Letts, P, 'Mental Capacity Act 2005: the statutory principles and best interests test'[57]

> The requirement for consultation must be balanced against the right to confidentiality of the person lacking capacity. That right should be protected so that consultation only takes place where relevant and with people whom it is appropriate to consult. For example, it is unlikely to be appropriate to consult anyone who the person had previously indicated should not be involved. However, there may be occasions where it is in the person's best interests for specific information to be disclosed, or where the public interest in disclosure may override the person's private interest in maintaining confidentiality. If professionals are involved in the determination of best interests, they will also need to comply with their own duties of confidentiality in accordance with their professional codes of conduct.

The reference to consulting with people specifically vetoed by the incapacitated person might lead us to question Letts' view. Thus, to rule this out might mean that crucial information that could help the decision-maker would not be available. Such a course of action would have to be taken cautiously and sensitively in the light of knowledge of the significance of the information, but could not be ruled out altogether.

In *NHS Trust v K, Another Foundation Trust*,[58] Holman J made a declaration that it was in the best interests of a patient to undergo cancer surgery. She was a 61-year-old woman who suffered from a psychotic disorder and chronic schizophrenia. She had many delusions, which included a belief that she was aged about 20 and had a boyfriend. She denied that she had cancer and denied the existence of obvious symptoms such as bleeding. She had three sons and lived with one of them and her daughter-in-law; she had a close relationship with her other sons and their families. Evidence was given by all three sons to the effect that despite her denial, she needed surgery; she had the normal human desire and motivation to survive, and, if she had capacity, that belief and value would be likely to influence her decision, as referred to in s 4(6)(b) of the Act. There was no dispute that she lacked capacity, and Holman J made declarations to the effect that the surgery and associated procedures should take place. He also stated:

NHS Trust v K, Another Foundation Trust[59]

> **Holman J**: 56 . . . It is my duty to take responsibility for my decision . . . But in reaching that decision I have paid considerable regard to the position and views of the three sons, which I respect. They are not doctors but they know their mother well and each of them would be heavily involved during her recovery and convalescence . . .
>
> 57 Circumstances may change. They may reassess issues, such as the mental state of their mother or her likely post-operative compliance. For that reason, although the operation does not require their consent, there must be a temporary brake upon it if any of them notifies the doctors, making reference to the relevant part of the court order, that he no longer considers that the operation should take place.

---

57 [2005] J Mental Health L 150, p 161.
58 [2012] EWHC 2922 (COP).
59 [2012] EWHC 2922 (COP).

I stress that all these powers of veto or brakes are temporary, not absolute. They would halt the process but would not preclude further consideration by the court (myself if possible) in the light of the changed circumstances.

4.3.4.6 Adults and the role of the court

The MCA applies to all aspects of decision-making on the part of incapacitated patients. Prior to the MCA, the Court of Protection dealt with financial matters; now the Court deals with personal welfare matters too. The powers given to the Court of Protection are contained within Part 2 of the Act. Denzil Lush outlines the new powers.

Lush, D, 'The Mental Capacity Act and the new court of protection'[60]

In brief, the new Court of Protection will be able to:

- make declarations as to whether or not someone has the capacity to make a particular decision; for example, where professionals disagree on whether someone with learning difficulties has the capacity to refuse major heart surgery;
- make declarations as to the lawfulness or otherwise of any act done, or yet to be done in relation to a person;
- make single, one-off orders; for example the sale of a house and the investment of the proceeds of sale;
- appoint a deputy to make decisions in relation to the matter or matters in which a person lacks the capacity to make a decision;
- resolve various issues involving last powers of attorney;
- make a declaration as to whether an advance decision to refuse treatment exists, is valid, or is applicable to a particular treatment.

The power to make declarations is similar to, though slightly wider than, the present declaratory jurisdiction of the Family Division. . . .

Appointing deputies

. . . the Act provides that, when deciding whether it is in a person's best interests to appoint a deputy, the court should have regard to the principles that (a) a decision by the court is to be preferred to the appointment of a deputy to make a decision, and that (b) the powers conferred on a deputy should be as limited in scope and duration as is reasonably practicable in the circumstances.

This is a good illustration of the operation of the principle of the least restrictive alternative, which requires the existence of alternative courses of action to be investigated and compared, and the preferred course of action to be the one that achieves the desired objective in a manner that interferes least with the rights and freedom of action of the person concerned.

In other words, it may be overly paternalistic and intrusive to appoint someone to act as a deputy when more informal approaches to decision-making will suffice. However, given the somewhat open-textured nature of the Act in terms of who makes decisions and who they consult, even on the most cautious assessment it remained questionable whether the 2005 Act is sufficiently robust.

It is not surprising therefore that there has been public concern. Indeed, since its inception the Court of Protection has attracted considerable unpopularity, particularly in relation to

---

60 [2005] J Mental Health L 31, p 36.

closed-door decisions. When these decisions relate to the personal and financial welfare of incapacitated people, it is in the public interest for these decisions to be made in open court (obviously at the same time protecting the identity of the participants). In particular, enforced medical treatment, rightly, needs some public scrutiny. This may well have influenced the decision of Sir Nicholas Wall to hand down an open judgment in the case of *DH NHS Foundation Trust v PS*[61] concerning a woman aged 55 who had learning difficulties and an overwhelming fear of hospitals and medical treatment. She was deemed not to have mental capacity and unable to make a decision about her treatment. He ruled that she could be given a drug in a glass of Ribena at her home and detained afterwards on a ward for treatment of cancer of the uterus. There was nothing suspect about the case; indeed, the application had the support of Mencap, who agreed that this was in the best interests of the patient. But it is essential for the public to be made aware of these cases.[62]

The other point that is important to note is that the creation of the new Court of Protection has removed the inherent jurisdiction of the court to deal with cases where the person is not incapacitated in the strict sense of the word (recall the requirement of 'voluntariness', discussed in Chapter 3). In *A Local Authority v MA NA and SA*[63] it was said:

> the inherent jurisdiction can be exercised in relation to a vulnerable adult who, even if not incapacitated by mental disorder or mental illness, is, or is reasonably believed to be, either (i) under constraint or (ii) subject to coercion or undue influence or (iii) for some other reason deprived of the capacity to make the relevant decision, or disabled from making a free choice, or incapacitated or disabled from giving or expressing a real and genuine consent.[64]

In *Re N (An Adult) (Court of Protection: Jurisdiction)*,[65] the Supreme Court considered the power of the Court of Protection to order a clinical commissioning group (CCG) to arrange and fund a care plan concerning the wishes of the parents of an adult child who lacked decision-making capacity and when the CCG was unwilling to do this. The court declined to make such an order, and went on to consider the powers and ambit of the Court of Protection.

Lady Hale

40 The Court of Protection has extensive case management powers. The Court of Protection Rules do not include an express power to strike out a statement of case or to give summary judgment, but such powers are provided for in the Civil Procedure Rules, which apply in any case not provided for so far as necessary to further the overriding objective. The overriding objective is to deal with a case justly having regard to the principles contained in the 2005 Act (Court of Protection Rules 2007, rule 3(1)). Dealing with a case justly includes dealing with the case in ways which are proportionate to the nature, importance and complexity of the issues and allocating to it an appropriate share of the court's resources (rule 3(3)(c) and (f)). The Court will further the overriding objective by actively managing cases (rule 5(1)). This includes encouraging the parties to co-operate with one another in the conduct of the proceedings, identifying the issues at an early stage, deciding promptly with issues needing a full investigation and hearing and those which do not, and encouraging the parties to use an alternative dispute resolution procedure if appropriate (rule 5(2)(a), (b)(i), (c)(i), and(e)). The court's general powers of case management include a power to exclude any issue from consideration and to take any step or give any direction for the purpose of managing the case and furthering the overriding objective (rule 25(j) and (m)). It was held in *KD and LD v Havering London*

---

61 [2010] EWHC 1217 (Fam).
62 For details of the public concerns, see, eg: www.guardian.co.uk, 2 June 2010.
63 [2005] EWHC 2942 (Fam).
64 *Per* Munby J at para 77.
65 [2017] UKSC 22.

Borough Council [2010] 1 FLR 1393 that the court may determine a case summarily of its own motion, but their power "must be exercised appropriately and with a modicum of restraint".

41 The court is clearly entitled to take the view that no useful purpose will be served by holding a hearing to resolve a particular issue. In reaching such a decision, many factors might be relevant. In a case such as this, for example: the nature of the issues; their importance for MN; the cogency of the parents' demands; the reasons why the CCG opposed those demands and their cogency; any relevant and indisputable fact in the history; the views of MN's litigation friend; the consequence of further investigation in terms of costs and court time; the likelihood that it might bring about further modifications to the care plan or consensus between the parties; and generally whether further investigation would serve any useful purpose.

42 In this case, consideration along those lines would no doubt have produced the following conclusions. The issues had been narrowed. They were important for MN but not as important as the basic question of where he should live. There were good reasons, not least in the history, for thinking that the parents' wishes were impracticable and that the CCG had good reasons for rejecting them. The Official Solicitor supported this. In the light of the length of time the proceedings had already taken, and the modifications to the care plan which had been made in the course of them, it was unlikely that investigation would bring about further modifications or consensus. And it would be disproportionate to devote any more of the court's scarce resources to resolving matters.

43 Case management along these lines does not mean that a care provider or funder can pre-empt the court's proceedings by refusing to contemplate changes to the care plan. The court can always ask itself what useful purpose continuing the proceedings, or taking a particular step in them, will serve but that is for the court, not the parties, to decide.

THINK POINT

Do you think that the Mental Capacity Act 2005 sufficiently protects vulnerable patients?

4.4 Children

There are special considerations that apply to children. Although this chapter is about patients who lack the capacity to consent, some children are able to consent, but, for the sake of completeness, both capable and incapable children will be dealt with below.

4.4.1 Consent to treatment

Although the English age of majority is 18 years, and up until that date minors are still subject to the jurisdiction of the courts, the Family Law Reform Act 1969 provides that minors who have attained the age of 16 may give a valid consent to medical treatment:

Family Law Reform Act 1969

8(1) – The consent of a minor who has attained the age of 16 years to any surgical, medical or dental treatment which, in the absence of consent, would constitute a trespass to his person, shall be as effective as it would be if he were of full age; and where a minor has by virtue of this section given an effective consent to any treatment it shall not be necessary to obtain any consent for it from his parent or guardian.

Just as mental illness without more will not remove capacity, neither will tender years. The case of *Gillick v West Norfolk and Wisbech AHA*[66] had to consider the capacity of children to consent to treatment. In *Gillick*, it was acknowledged that there was no magic in the age of 16, and that younger children may be able to consent to medical treatment, depending on their level of understanding, that is, what is generally known as '*Gillick* competence', or 'Fraser competence' (given that one of the key judgments was given by Lord Fraser and provided guidance on 'competence').

Following concern about the number of under-age pregnancies, the Department of Health and Social Security issued guidance to area health authorities on family planning services containing particular provisions relating to young people. Although it stressed the importance of the parents of children under 16 being involved in the consultation, it went on to say that, in exceptional cases, it was for a doctor to decide whether to prescribe contraception without informing the parents of the child. Mrs Gillick, who had a number of daughters under the age of 16, sought a declaration that the guidance gave advice which was unlawful and which adversely affected parental rights and duties. Woolf J refused the declaration. Mrs Gillick succeeded before the Court of Appeal. The House of Lords allowed the Department of Health and Social Security's appeal by a majority of 3:2:

Gillick v West Norfolk and Wisbech AHA[67]

Lord Fraser: It would, therefore, appear that, if the inference which Mrs Gillick's advisers seek to draw from the provisions [of the FLRA 1969] is justified, a minor under the age of 16 has no capacity to authorise any kind of medical advice or treatment or examination of his own body. That seems to me so surprising that I cannot accept it in the absence of clear provisions to that effect. It seems to me verging on the absurd to suggest that a girl or a boy aged 15 could not effectively consent, for example, to have a medical examination of some trivial injury to his body or even to have a broken arm set. Of course the consent of the parents should normally be asked, but they may not be immediately available. Provided the patient, whether a boy or a girl, is capable of understanding what is proposed, and of expressing his or her own wishes, I see no good reason for holding that he or she lacks the capacity to express them validly and effectively and to authorise the medical man to make the examination or give the treatment which he advises. After all, a minor under the age of 16 can, within certain limits, enter into a contract. He or she can also sue and be sued, and can give evidence on oath. Moreover, a girl under 16 can give sufficiently effective consent to sexual intercourse to lead to the legal result that the man involved does not commit the crime of rape – see *R v Howard* [1966] 1 WLR 13, p 15, when Lord Parker CJ said:

> . . . in the case of a girl under 16, the prosecution, in order to prove rape, must prove either that she physically resisted, or if she did not, that her understanding and knowledge were such that she was not in a position to decide whether to consent or resist . . . there are many girls under 16 who know full well what it is all about and can properly consent.

Accordingly, I am not disposed to hold now, for the first time, that a girl aged under 16 lacks the power to give valid consent to contraceptive advice or treatment, merely on account of her age.

Lord Fraser suggested a five-point test for doctors contemplating whether to provide such a girl with contraceptive advice and treatment without reference to her parents:

---

66 [1986] 1 AC 112.
67 Lords Fraser, Scarman, Bridge, Brandon, and Templeman [1986] 1 AC 112, HL.

> **Lord Fraser**: . . . [T]he doctor will, in my opinion, be justified in proceeding without the parents' consent or even knowledge provided he is satisfied on the following matters: (1) that the girl (although under 16 years of age) will understand his advice; (2) that he cannot persuade her to inform her parents or to allow him to inform the parents that she is seeking contraceptive advice; (3) that she is very likely to begin or to continue having sexual intercourse with or without contraceptive treatment; (4) that unless she receives contraceptive advice or treatment her physical or mental health or both are likely to suffer; (5) that her best interests require him to give her contraceptive advice, treatment or both without the parental consent.

Lord Scarman, in his judgment, emphasised the increasing autonomy of minors as they approach adulthood:

> **Lord Scarman**: . . . I would hold that as a matter of law the parental right to determine whether or not their minor child below the age of 16 will have medical treatment terminates if and when the child achieves sufficient understanding and intelligence to enable him or her to understand fully what is proposed. It will be a question of fact whether a child seeking advice has sufficient understanding of what is involved to give a consent valid in law. Until the child achieves the capacity to consent, the parental right to make the decision continues save only in exceptional circumstances. Emergency, parental neglect, abandonment of the child or inability to find the parent are examples of exceptional situations justifying the doctor proceeding to treat the child without parental knowledge and consent; but there will arise, no doubt, other exceptional situations in which it will be reasonable for the doctor to proceed without the parent's consent.
>
> When applying these conclusions to contraceptive advice and treatment it has to be borne in mind that there is much that has to be understood by a girl under 16 if she is to have legal capacity to consent to such treatment. It is not enough that she should understand the nature of the advice which is being given: she must also have a sufficient maturity to understand what is involved. There are moral and family questions, especially her relationship with her parents; long term problems associated with the emotional impact of pregnancy and its termination; and there are the risks to health of sexual intercourse at her age, risks which contraception may diminish but cannot eliminate. It follows that a doctor will have to satisfy himself that she is able to appraise these factors before he can safely proceed on the basis that she has capacity at law to consent to contraceptive advice and treatment. And it further follows that ordinarily the proper course will be for him, as the guidance lays down, first to seek to persuade the girl to bring her parents into consultation, and, if she refuses, not to prescribe contraceptive advice and treatment unless he is satisfied that her circumstances are such that he ought to proceed without parental knowledge and consent.

Lord Bridge agreed with Lords Fraser and Scarman. Dissenting judgments were given by Lords Brandon and Templeman. Lord Templeman accepted the general principle that consent is a function of understanding, not status, but dissented on the specific matter of contraceptive advice and treatment:

> **Lord Templeman**: The effect of the consent of the infant depends on the nature of the treatment and the age and understanding of the infant. For example, a doctor with the consent of an intelligent boy or girl of 15 could, in my opinion, safely remove tonsils or a troublesome appendix. But any decision on the part of a girl to practise sex and contraception requires not only knowledge of the facts of life and of the dangers of pregnancy and disease but also an understanding of the emotional and other consequences to her family, her male partner and to herself. I doubt whether a girl under the age of 16 is capable of a balanced judgment to embark on frequent, regular or casual sexual intercourse fortified by the illusion that medical science can protect her in mind and body and ignoring the danger of leaping from childhood to adulthood

without the difficult formative transitional experiences of adolescence. There are many things which a girl under 16 needs to practise but sex is not one of them. Parliament could declare this view to be out of date. But in my opinion the statutory provisions discussed in the speech of my noble and learned friend, Lord Fraser of Tullybelton, and the provisions of s 6 of the Sexual Offences Act 1956, indicate that as the law now stands an unmarried girl under 16 is not competent to decide to practise sex and contraception?. . .

The position seems to me to be as follows. A doctor is not entitled to decide whether a girl under the age of 16 shall be provided with contraceptive facilities if a parent who is in charge of the girl is ready and willing to make that decision in exercise of parental rights. The doctor is entitled in exceptional circumstances and in emergencies to make provision, normally temporary provision, for contraception but in most cases would be bound to inform the parent of the treatment. The court would not hold the doctor liable for providing contraceptive facilities if the doctor had reasonable grounds for believing that the parent had abandoned or abused parental rights or that there was no parent immediately available for consultation or that there was no parent who was responsible for the girl. But exceptional circumstances and emergencies cannot be expanded into a general discretion for the doctor to provide contraceptive facilities without the knowledge of the parent because of the possibility that a girl to whom contraceptive facilities are not available may irresponsibly court the risk of pregnancy. Such a discretion would enable any girl to obtain contraception on request by threatening to sleep with a man.

Lord Brandon relied on public policy arguments based upon the criminalisation of acts of sex with girls under the age of 16:

Lord Brandon: The Sexual Offences Act 1956 represents the latest pronouncement of parliament on these matters. Sections 5 and 6 provide, so far as material:

> 5 – It is a felony for a man to have unlawful sexual intercourse with a girl under the age of 13.
>   6(1) – It is an offence . . . for a man to have unlawful sexual intercourse with a girl not under the age of 13 but under the age of 16.

Further, by s 37 and Sched 2, the maximum punishment for an offence under s 5 is imprisonment for life, and that for an offence under s 6 imprisonment for two years. Since the passing of the Act of 1956 the distinction between felonies and misdemeanours has been abolished. For the purposes of this case, however, nothing turns on this change of terminology.

My Lords, the inescapable inference from the statutory provisions of the Acts of 1885 and 1956 to which I have referred is that parliament has for the past century regarded, and still regards today, sexual intercourse between a man and a girl under 16 as a serious criminal offence so far as the man who has such intercourse is concerned. So far as the girl is concerned, she does not commit any criminal offence, even if she aids, abets or incites the having of such intercourse. The reason for this, as explained earlier, is that the relevant statutory provisions have been enacted by parliament for the purpose of protecting the girl from herself. The having of such intercourse is, however, unlawful, and the circumstance that the man is guilty of a criminal offence, while the girl is not, cannot alter that situation.

On the footing that the having of sexual intercourse by a man with a girl under 16 is an unlawful act, it follows necessarily that for any person to promote, encourage or facilitate the commission of such an act may itself be a criminal offence, and must, in any event, be contrary to public policy. Nor can it make any difference that the person who promotes, encourages or facilitates the commission of such an act is a parent or a doctor or a social worker.

[T]o give such a girl advice about contraception, to examine her with a view to her using one or more forms of protection, and finally to prescribe contraceptive treatment for her, necessarily involves promoting, encouraging or facilitating the having of sexual intercourse, contrary to public policy, by that girl with a man.

However, as Lord Brandon himself observed, on this logic Mrs Gillick's desire to have the girl's parents involved would also be problematic, since they too would become accessories to an offence. Moreover, it is interesting to reflect upon the earlier judgment of Lord Brandon in the case of *R v D*,[68] which was cited with approval by both Lords Fraser and Scarman. That judgment clearly implied that a mature child could make decisions about medical treatment. It seems that the nature of the treatment in *Gillick* influenced Lord Brandon to take a restrictive approach.

4.4.2 Refusals of treatment

Although *Gillick* makes it clear that, depending on the nature of the treatment, a child may have the capacity to consent, the case has been interpreted subsequently by the Court of Appeal as relating only to consent and not *refusal*, so that a child's refusal of treatment can still be overridden by his parents or others *in loco parentis*.

The mental health of a 15-year-old girl in the care of the local authority deteriorated and she was placed in an adolescent psychiatric unit. Her condition fluctuated between periods of lucidity and what was described as 'florid psychotic behaviour'. However, she objected to receiving antipsychotic drugs, and the local authority applied under the wardship jurisdiction for leave to administer the drugs regardless of her lack of consent. The judge at first instance (Waite J) decided that if she had the necessary capacity, then her refusal could not be overridden, but, on the facts, decided that she lacked capacity. The Court of Appeal accepted that she was not mentally competent due to the fluctuating nature of her mental illness, but went on to assert, *obiter*, that the wardship jurisdiction could not in any event be ousted by the decision of a *Gillick*-competent child. The basis of the *Gillick* decision was interpreted by Lord Donaldson:

Re R (A Minor) (Wardship: Consent to Treatment)[69]

Lord Donaldson MR (p 21): [C]onsent by itself creates no obligation to treat. It is merely a key which unlocks a door. Furthermore, whilst in the case of an adult of full capacity there will usually only be one keyholder, namely the patient, in the ordinary family unit where a young child is the patient there will be two key holders, namely the parents, with a several as well as a joint right to turn the key and unlock the door. If the parents disagree, one consenting and the other refusing, the doctor will be presented with a professional and ethical, but not with a legal, problem because, if he has the consent of one authorised person, treatment will not without more constitute a trespass or a criminal assault.

If Mrs Gillick was to succeed in her claim to a declaration that the memorandum of guidance issued by the department was unlawful, she had to show that no child under the age of 16 could be a keyholder in respect of contraception advice and treatment or that the parents' key overrode the child's. As Lord Fraser put it ([1985] 3 All ER 402, p 412; [1986] AC 112, p 173): 'She has to justify the absolute right of veto in a parent.' If she was to succeed in her claim against the area health authority, she had also to show that it was under a duty to inform all medical staff employed by it that Mrs Gillick was exercising that right of veto, but in the light of the House's finding that there was no such right, this additional factor can be ignored.

In the instant appeal Mr James Munby QC, appearing for the Official Solicitor, submits that: (a) if the child has the right to give consent to medical treatment, the parents' right to give or refuse consent is terminated; and (b) the court in the exercise of its wardship jurisdiction is only entitled to step into the shoes of the parents and thus itself has no right to give or refuse consent. Whilst it is true that he seeks to modify the effect of this rather startling submission by suggesting that, if the child's consent or refusal of consent

---

68 [1984] AC 778.
69 Lord Donaldson MR, Staughton and Farquharson LJJ [1992] Fam 11, CA.

is irrational or misguided, the court will readily infer that in the particular context that individual child is not competent to give or withhold consent, it is necessary to look very carefully at the *Gillick* decision to see whether it supports his argument and, if it does, whether it is binding upon this court.

The key passages upon which Mr Munby relies are to be found in the speech of Lord Scarman ([1985] 3 All ER 402, pp 423–24):

> ...as a matter of law the parental right to determine whether or not their minor child below the age of 16 will have medical treatment terminates if and when the child achieves a sufficient understanding and intelligence to enable him or her to understand fully what is proposed. It will be a question of fact whether a child seeking advice has sufficient understanding of what is involved to give a consent valid in law?...

...What Mr Munby's argument overlooks is that Lord Scarman was discussing the parents' right '*to determine* whether or not their minor child below the age of 16 will have medical treatment' (my emphasis) and this is the 'parental right' to which he was referring in the latter passage. A right of determination is wider than a right to consent. The parents can only have a right of determination if either the child has no right to consent, ie, is not a keyholder, or the parents hold a master key which could nullify the child's consent. I do not understand Lord Scarman to be saying that, if a child was '*Gillick* competent', to adopt the convenient phrase used in argument, the parents ceased to have an independent right of consent as contrasted with ceasing to have a right of determination, ie, a veto. In a case in which the '*Gillick* competent' child refuses treatment, but the parents consent, that consent enables treatment to be undertaken lawfully, but in no way determines that the child shall be so treated. In a case in which the positions are reversed, it is the child's consent which is the enabling factor and again the parents' refusal of consent is not determinative. If Lord Scarman intended to go further than this and to say that in the case of a '*Gillick* competent' child, a parent has no right either to consent or to refuse consent, his remarks were *obiter*, because the only question in issue was Mrs Gillick's alleged right of veto. Furthermore I consider that they would have been wrong.

One glance at the consequences suffices to show that Lord Scarman cannot have been intending to say that the parental right to consent terminates with the achievement by the child of '*Gillick* competence'. It is fundamental to the speeches of the majority that the capacity to consent will vary from child to child and according to the treatment under consideration, depending upon the sufficiency of his or her intelligence and understanding of that treatment. If the position in law is that upon the achievement of '*Gillick* competence' there is a transfer of the right of consent from parents to child and there can never be a concurrent right in both, doctors would be faced with an intolerable dilemma, particularly when the child was nearing the age of 16, if the parents consented, but the child did not. On pain, if they got it wrong, of being sued for trespass to the person or possibly being charged with a criminal assault, they would have to determine as a matter of law in whom the right of consent resided at the particular time in relation to the particular treatment. I do not believe that that is the law.

The Court of Appeal subsequently considered the status of consent under s 8 of the Family Law Reform Act 1969 in relation to a 16-year-old child's refusal of treatment. It will be seen from the section (see above) that it merely states that there is no need to obtain the consent of a parent or guardian if a child gives consent. However, on the face of it, there is no *obligation* on a doctor to obtain the consent of the child in preference to that of the parent or guardian.

A 16-year-old girl, Miss W, was suffering from anorexia nervosa and was in the care of the local authority in an adolescent residential unit. Her condition deteriorated and the local authority sought authorisation from the court for removal of the girl to a specialist unit for treatment without her consent. As she had attained the age of 16, she resisted the application on the ground that s 8 of the Family Law Reform Act 1969 conferred on her the same right as an adult to refuse treatment without her consent. Although there is some suggestion in the judgments that, because of her condition, Miss W may not have been competent, the essence of the Court of Appeal's decision was that s 8 did not in any event confer an absolute right upon a child, and could be overridden by the court exercising its inherent jurisdiction:

Re W (A Minor) (Medical Treatment)[70]

Lord Donaldson MR (at p 76)

Is s 8 ambiguous?

The wording of sub-s (1) shows quite clearly that it is addressed to the legal purpose and legal effect of consent to treatment, namely, to prevent such treatment constituting in law a trespass to the person, and that it does so by making the consent of a 16 or 17-year-old as effective as if he were 'of full age'. No question of 'Gillick competence' in common law terms arises. The 16 or 17-year-old is conclusively presumed to be 'Gillick competent' or, alternatively, the test of 'Gillick competence' is bypassed and has no relevance. The argument that W or any other 16 or 17-year-old can, by refusing to consent to treatment, veto the treatment notwithstanding that the doctor has the consent of someone who has parental responsibilities, involves the proposition that s 8 has the further effect of depriving such a person of the power to consent. It certainly does not say so. Indeed if this were its intended effect, it is difficult to see why the sub-section goes on to say that it is not necessary to obtain the parents' consent, rather than providing that such consent, if obtained, should be ineffective. Furthermore, such a construction does not sit easily with sub-s (3), which preserves the common law as it existed immediately before the Act which undoubtedly gave parents an effective power of consent for all children up to the age of 21, the then existing age of consent?...

The most promising argument in favour of W having an exclusive right to consent to treatment and thus, by refusing consent, to attract the protection of the law on trespass to the person, lies in concentrating upon the words 'as effective as it would be if he were of full age'. If she were of full age her ability to consent would have two separate effects. First, her consent would be fully effective as such. Second, a failure or refusal to give consent would be fully effective as a veto, but only *because no one else would be in a position to consent*. If it is a possible view that s 8 is intended to put a 16 or 17-year-old in exactly the same position as an adult and there is thus some ambiguity, although I do not think that there is, it is a permissible aid to construction to seek to ascertain the mischief at which the section is directed.

The Latey Committee Report

It is common ground that the Family Law Reform Act 1969 was parliament's response to the *Report of the Committee on the Age of Majority*, Cmnd 3342, 1967. The relevant part is contained in paras 474–84. These show that the mischief aimed at was twofold. First, cases were occurring in which young people between 16 and 21 (the then age of majority) were living away from home and wished and needed urgent medical treatment which had not yet reached the emergency stage. Doctors were unable to treat them unless and until their parents had been traced and this could cause unnecessary suffering. Second, difficulties were arising concerning:

> ... operations whose implications bring up the question of a girl's right to privacy about her sexual life. A particularly difficult situation arises in the case of a girl who is sent to hospital in need of a therapeutic abortion and refuses point blank to enter the hospital unless a guarantee is given that her parents shall not be told about it.

The committee had recommended that the age of majority be reduced to 18 generally. The report, in para 480, records that all the professional bodies which gave evidence recommended that patients aged between 16 and 18 should be able to give an effective consent to treatment and all but the Medical Protection Society recommended that they should also be able to give an effective refusal. The point with

---

70 Lord Donaldson MR, Balcombe and Nolan LJJ [1993] Fam 64, CA.

which we are concerned was therefore well in the mind of the committee. It did not so recommend. It recommended that:

> ... without prejudice to any consent that may otherwise be lawful, the consent of young persons aged 16 and over to medical or dental treatment shall be as valid as the consent of a person of full age. (Original emphasis.)

Conclusion on s 8

I am quite unable to accept that parliament in adopting somewhat more prolix language was intending to achieve a result which differed from that recommended by the committee.

On reflection I regret my use in *Re R* ... of the keyholder analogy because keys can lock as well as unlock. I now prefer the analogy of the legal 'flak jacket' which protects the doctor from claims by the litigious whether he acquires it from his patient who may be a minor over the age of 16, or a '*Gillick*' competent' child under that age or from another person having parental responsibilities which include a right to consent to treatment of the minor. Anyone who gives him a flak jacket (that is, consent) may take it back, but the doctor only needs one and so long as he continues to have one he has the legal right to proceed.

It is interesting to compare Lord Donaldson's interpretation of s 8(3) of the 1969 Act with that of Lord Scarman in *Gillick*. He said that 'sub-s (3) leaves open the question whether the consent of a minor under 16 could be an effective consent', whereas Lord Donaldson interprets it as safeguarding parental rights in cases of minors over 16. In the light of this conflict, it should be noted that in Scottish law a child under the age of 16 has legal capacity to consent to medical treatment if 'he is capable of understanding the nature and possible consequences of the procedure or treatment',[71] and in *Houston, Applicant*[72] the Sheriff's Court confirmed that the child's power to consent could not be overridden by a guardian, even though s 5(1) of the Act provides that the guardian of a person under 16 has the same powers after the passing of the Act as before. It was said that it would be illogical to grant a power to consent to medical treatment if this decision could be overridden by a guardian.

Certainly *Re R* and *Re W* sit rather uneasily with the *Gillick* decision. It is hard to see how, for example, Lord Scarman's wide-ranging approach to the issue of understanding and the gradual attainment of the age of discretion can simply have been constructed to provide the doctor with protection from legal action. On the other hand, the recommendation of the Latey Committee does appear to support Lord Donaldson's view. However, could it not be argued that the committee was leaving the question open, and that the *Gillick* decision has since decided the position? The fact that the Report is over 40 years old is also telling. Not surprisingly, the cases have drawn a large amount of critical comment:

Bainham, A, 'The judge and the competent minor'[73]

[In *Re R*] Lord Donaldson sought to draw a distinction between 'determination' and 'consent', the former being a wider concept than the latter, since it implied a right of veto. In his view, Lord Scarman in *Gillick* was referring to the parent's right to determine whether or not a child should receive medical treatment.... There would, according to this interpretation, be concurrent independent rights in parent and child and it would be open to a doctor to act on either consent?...

---

71 s 2 (4) of the Age of Legal Capacity (Scotland) Act 1991.
72 See [1997] 5 Med LR 237.
73 (1992) 108 LQR 194.

There are fundamental objections to this position. It can only work on the assumption that a doctor is dealing solely with the parent or solely with the child and is unaware of any disagreement between them. Where he is aware of a disagreement then, in the absence of judicial intervention, he must choose between the conflicting views. This is so where the parent is proposing action and the child is objecting, or conversely, where the child is in favour of action and the parent is objecting. If the doctor decides to proceed, or not to proceed, on the basis of the parent's view, he is in reality giving effect to a parental veto over the child's view. He is allowing the parent to 'determine' the matter, and the suggested distinction between 'determination' and 'consent' falls apart. And it is difficult to see how medical personnel seeking to administer drugs with the consent of a parent (or, as here, someone else with parental responsibility) could possibly be unaware of the child's objection. . . .

However Lord Donaldson did not stop there. . . . Section 8(1) of the Family Law Reform Act 1969 provides that where this age has been attained, the child's consent 'to any surgical, medical or dental treatment . . . shall be as effective as it would be if he were of full age' and that 'it shall not be necessary to obtain any consent for it from his parent or guardian'. [Lord Donaldson] adopted a literal interpretation to the effect that, while it was unnecessary for a doctor to secure parental consent in relation to a 16-year-old, there was nothing to preclude him from acting on a parent's consent alone. This flies in the face of the settled interpretation of this provision that it was intended to confer complete autonomy on a young person of this age and that by implication this must outweigh any parental claim to decide.

However, there has also been support for the Court of Appeal's interpretation:

Lowe, N and Juss, S, 'Medical treatment – pragmatism and the search for principle'[74]

[There are] two grounds upon which a child's refusal can be overridden: namely (1) the inability to make an informed judgment, in which case the refusal carries no weight; and (2) where the child is capable of making an informed view, that preference is balanced against the harm to the child's welfare which will ensue if these wishes are observed.

We would support the decisions on either basis because it seems to us wrong for the court to allow a child to refuse treatment that would do him or her irreparable harm. After all, it is perhaps all too easily forgotten that, in the final analysis, a child is still only a child. . . . To those who question how a child can be held able to give a valid consent yet be unable to exercise a power of veto, we would reply that there is a rational distinction to be made between giving consent and withholding it. We must start with the assumption that a doctor will act in the best interests of his patient. Hence, if the doctor believes that a particular treatment is necessary for his patient, it is perfectly rational for the law to facilitate this as easily as possible and hence allow a 'Gillick competent' child to give a valid consent, and also to protect the child against parents opposed to what is professionally considered to be in its best medical interests. In contrast, it is surely right for the law to be reluctant to allow a child of whatever age to be able to veto treatment designed for his or her benefit, particularly if a refusal would lead to the child's death or permanent damage. In other words, the clear and consistent policy of the law is to protect the child against wrong-headed parents and against itself with the final safeguard, as Re W unequivocally establishes, of giving the court the last word in cases of dispute.

On this view, a child may be deemed to be Gillick competent, but still lacking the necessary capacity that an adult would enjoy, to the extent that the outcome of its decision is not deemed to be in its own best interests. However, the support Lowe and Juss seek to derive from the Latey

---

74 (1993) 56 MLR 865.

Committee report – that it sought to prevent 'unnecessary pain and suffering' – is in our view not justified. The pain and suffering at issue was caused, not by 'unacceptable' treatment decisions by minors, but by the fact that – pre-*Gillick* – they had no legal power to make any decisions. The Court of Appeal seems to be substituting the functional view of capacity (at the heart of the later adult case of *Re C (Adult: Refusal of Treatment)*)[75] with a bare 'all or nothing' test: either under or over 18 years of age, either capable or incapable. Whatever view is taken it can be seen that the effect of *Re W*, so far as refusals of treatment are concerned, is to re-establish the very 'status' approach which the House of Lords were at pains to reject in *Gillick* in relation to consent. The 'all or nothing' aspect is illustrated by the train of events during and after the case of *Re E (A Minor) (Wardship: Medical Treatment)*,[76] to which the Lowe and Juss refer in the above article. The patient was 15 and, like his parents, a devout Jehovah's Witness. He was suffering from leukaemia, the treatment of which included blood transfusions. Ward J ordered the carrying out of the treatment, which continued until the boy reached 18. At this point he refused further medical treatment and died.

Re L (Medical Treatment: Gillick Competency)[77] concerned a 14-year-old girl who had suffered extensive burns and, in the course of the essential surgery to treat them, would require blood transfusions. Without treatment she would die an unpleasant death. She was a Jehovah's Witness and refused consent to the transfusions. Sir Stephen Brown, President (as he then was), while noting that counsel's submissions had included a reference to Lord Donaldson's analysis of *Gillick* competence, made his decision on the basis of lack of capacity, as she had limited experience of life and that limited her understanding of 'matters which are as grave as her own present situation'. Arguably, this is just another way of saying that she lacks capacity because she is a child. However, it refers to the grave matters under consideration, and, therefore, she might have sufficient understanding in a less serious situation. Nevertheless, the suggestion might be that, in cases where a religious or similar belief is involved, a child might form views which s/he rejects in adulthood. The difficulty with this approach, however, is that the same argument could be advanced for young adults, or, arguably, all adults.

THINK POINT

Lowe and Juss say that 'a child is still a child'. But although they would support the decision in *Re E (A Minor) (Wardship: Medical Treatment)*[78] above, does not that case demonstrate the inadequacy of the status approach to children, ie one day they are a child and the next they are an adult?

More recently, Gilmore and Herring have revisited Lord Donaldson's approach and sought to interpret it so that it is consistent with the non-status principle of *Gillick*. They examine his assertion that there could be concurrent consents in both parent and child and distinguish between two ways of refusing treatment. Firstly, a child might reject a particular treatment that has been proposed. Secondly a child might refuse all treatment. A child may have the capacity in one of these situations but not in the other, and therefore, in certain circumstances, parent and child may hold concurrent consents:

---

75 [1994] 1 WLR 290.
76 [1993] 1 FLR 386.
77 [1998] 2 FLR 810.
78 [1993] 1 FLR 386.

... a great injustice in both cases was that the children's abilities to refuse treatment were never properly ascertained ... *Re R* and *Re W* could be restricted to the facts in the sense of the children's abilities as disclosed by the expert evidence. Lord Donaldson's reasoning supporting the overriding of a child's refusal could therefore be limited to cases where the child lacks the capacity to refuse all possible treatments.

This is a pleasingly subtle and conciliatory approach.[80]

4.4.3 Children and the rights of parents

In *Gillick*, on the subject of parental rights Lord Fraser said:

Gillick v West Norfolk and Wisbech AHA[81]

Lord Fraser (p 171): In practice most wise parents relax their control gradually as the child develops and encourage him or her to become increasingly independent. Moreover, the degree of parental control actually exercised over a particular child does in practice vary considerably according to his understanding and intelligence and it would, in my opinion, be unrealistic for the courts not to recognise these facts. Social customs change, and the law ought to, and does in fact, have regard to such changes when they are of major importance ...

In times gone by the father had almost absolute authority over his children until they attained majority. A rather remarkable example of such authority being upheld by the court was *In re Agar-Ellis* (1883) 24 Ch D 317 which was much relied on by the Court of Appeal. The father in that case restricted the communication which his daughter aged 17 was allowed to have with her mother, against whose moral character nothing was alleged, to an extent that would be universally condemned today as quite unreasonable. The case has been much criticised in recent years and, in my opinion, with good reason ...

... In *J v C* [1970] AC 668 Lord Guest and Lord MacDermott referred to the decision in *Agar-Ellis* (1883) 24 Ch D 317 as an example of the almost absolute power asserted by the father over his children before the Judicature Act 1873 and plainly thought such an assertion was out of place at the present time: see Lord MacDermott, pp 703–04. In *Reg v D* [1984] AC 778 Lord Brandon of Oakbrook cited *Agar-Ellis* as an example of the older view of a father's authority which his Lordship and the other members of the House rejected. In my opinion, the view of absolute paternal authority continuing until a child attains majority which was applied in *Agar-Ellis* is so out of line with present day views that it should no longer be treated as having any authority. I regard it as a historical curiosity ...

Once the rule of the parents' absolute authority over minor children is abandoned, the solution to the problem in this appeal can no longer be found by referring to rigid parental rights at any particular age. The solution depends upon a judgment of what is best for the welfare of the particular child. Nobody doubts, certainly I do not doubt, that in the overwhelming majority of cases the best judges of a child's welfare are his or her parents. Nor do I doubt that any important medical treatment of a child under 16 would normally only be carried out with the parents' approval. That is why it would and should be 'most

---

79 (2011) 41 Fam Law 715.
80 For a continuation of this discussion, see Cave, E and Wallbank, J, 'Minors' capacity to refuse treatment: a reply to Gilmore and Herring' [2012] Med L Rev 2012, 20 (3) 423 and Gilmore, S and Herring J, 'Children's refusal of treatment: the debate continues' (2012) 42 Fam Law 973.
81 [1986] AC 112.

unusual' for a doctor to advise a child without the knowledge and consent of the parents on contraceptive matters. But, as I have already pointed out, Mrs Gillick has to go further if she is to obtain the first declaration that she seeks. She has to justify the absolute right of veto in a parent. But there may be circumstances in which a doctor is a better judge of the medical advice and treatment which will conduce to a girl's welfare than her parents. It is notorious that children of both sexes are often reluctant to confide in their parents about sexual matters, and the DHSS guidance under consideration shows that to abandon the principle of confidentiality for contraceptive advice to girls under 16 might cause some of them not to seek professional advice at all, with the consequence of exposing them to 'the immediate risks of pregnancy and of sexually transmitted diseases'. No doubt the risk could be avoided if the patient were to abstain from sexual intercourse, and one of the doctor's responsibilities will be to decide whether a particular patient can reasonably be expected to act upon advice to abstain. We were told that in a significant number of cases such abstinence could not reasonably be expected ...

... the doctor will, in my opinion, be justified in proceeding without the parents' consent or even knowledge provided he is satisfied on the following matters: (1) that the girl (although under 16 years of age) will understand his advice; (2) that he cannot persuade her to inform her parents or to allow him to inform the parents that she is seeking contraceptive advice; (3) that she is very likely to begin or to continue having sexual intercourse with or without contraceptive treatment; (4) that unless she receives contraceptive advice or treatment her physical or mental health or both are likely to suffer; (5) that her best interests require him to give her contraceptive advice, treatment or both without the parental consent.

Lord Scarman took a similar view (p 182):

Lord Scarman: Mrs Gillick relies on both the statute law and the case law to establish her proposition that parental consent is in all other circumstances necessary. The only statutory provision directly in point is s 8 of the Family Law Reform Act 1969. Sub-section (1) of the section provides that the consent of a minor who has attained the age of 16 to any surgical, mental or dental treatment which in the absence of consent would constitute a trespass to his person shall be as effective as if he were of full age and that the consent of his parent or guardian need not be obtained. Sub-section (3) of the section provides:

Nothing in this section shall be construed as making ineffective any consent which would have been effective if this section had not been enacted.

I cannot accept the submission made on Mrs Gillick's behalf that sub-s (1) necessarily implies that prior to its enactment the consent of a minor to medical treatment could not be effective in law. Sub-section (3) leaves open the question whether the consent of a minor under 16 could be an effective consent. Like my noble and learned friend Lord Fraser of Tullybelton, I read the section as clarifying the law without conveying any indication as to what the law was before it was enacted. So far as minors under 16 are concerned, the law today is as it was before the enactment of the section ...

The law has, therefore, to be found by a search in the judge-made law for the true principle. The legal difficulty is that in our search we find ourselves in a field of medical practice where parental right and a doctor's may point us in different directions. This is not surprising. Three features have emerged in today's society which were not known to our predecessors: (1) contraception as a subject for medical advice and treatment; (2) the increasing independence of young people; and (3) the changed status of women. In times past contraception was rarely a matter for the doctor: but with the development of the contraceptive pill for women it has become part and parcel of everyday medical practice, as it made clear by the department's *Handbook of Contraceptive Practice*, 1984 revision, particularly para 1.2. Family planning services are now available under statutory powers to all without any express limitation as to age or marital status. Young people, once they have attained the age of 16, are capable of consenting to contraceptive treatment, since it is medical treatment: and, however extensive be parental right in the care and upbringing of children, it cannot prevail so as to nullify the 16-year-old's capacity to consent which is now conferred by statute. Furthermore, women have obtained by the availability of the pill a choice of lifestyle with a degree of independence and of opportunity undreamed of until this generation and greater, I would add, than any law of equal opportunity could by itself effect.

The law ignores these developments at its peril . . .

. . . The principle of the law, as I shall endeavour to show, is that parental rights are derived from parental duty and exist only so long as they are needed for the protection of the person and property of the child. The principle has been subjected to certain age limits set by statute for certain purposes: and in some cases the courts have declared an age of discretion at which a child acquires before the age of majority the right to make his (or her) own decision. But these limitations in no way undermine the principle of the law, and should not be allowed to obscure it.

Let me make good, quite shortly, the proposition of principle . . .

. . . It is abundantly plain that the law recognises that there is a right and a duty of parents to determine whether or not to seek medical advice in respect of their child, and, having received advice, to give or withhold consent to medical treatment. The question in the appeal is as to the extent, and duration, of the right and the circumstances in which, outside the two admitted exceptions to which I have earlier referred, it can be overridden by the exercise of medical judgment . . .

Although statute has intervened in respect of a child's capacity to consent to medical treatment from the age of 16 onwards, neither statute nor the case law has ruled on the extent and duration of parental right in respect of children under the age of 16. More specifically, there is no rule yet applied to contraceptive treatment, which has special problems of its own and is a latecomer in medical practice. It is open, therefore, to the House to formulate a rule. The Court of Appeal favoured a fixed age limit of 16, basing themselves on a view of the statute law which I do not share and upon their view of the effect of the older case law which for the reasons already given I cannot accept. They sought to justify the limit by the public interest in the law being certain. Certainty is always an advantage in the law, and in some breaches of the law it is a necessity. But it brings with it an inflexibility and a rigidity which in some branches of the law can obstruct justice, impede the law's development, and stamp upon the law the mark of obsolescence where what is needed is the capacity for development. The law relating to parent and child is concerned with the problems of the growth and maturity of the human personality. If the law should impose upon the process of 'growing up' fixed limits, where nature knows only a continuous process, the price would be artificiality and a lack of realism in an area where the law must be sensitive to human development and social change. If certainty be thought desirable, it is better that the rigid demarcations necessary to achieve it should be laid down by legislation after a full consideration of all the relevant factors than by the courts, confined as they are by the forensic process to the evidence adduced by the parties and to whatever may properly fall within the judicial notice of judges. Unless and until Parliament should think fit to intervene, the courts should establish a principle flexible enough to enable justice to be achieved by its application to the particular circumstances proved by the evidence placed before them . . .

The modern law governing parental right and a child's capacity to make his own decisions was considered in *Reg v D* [1984] AC 778. The House must, in my view, be understood as having in that case accepted that, save where statute otherwise provides, a minor's capacity to make his or her own decision depends upon the minor having sufficient understanding and intelligence to make the decision and is not to be determined by reference to any judicially fixed age limit . . .

In the light of the foregoing I would hold that as a matter of law the parental right to determine whether or not their minor child below the age of 16 will have medical treatment terminates if and when the child achieves a sufficient understanding and intelligence to enable him or her to understand fully what is proposed. It will be a question of fact whether a child seeking advice has sufficient understanding of what is involved to give a consent valid in law. Until the child achieves the capacity to consent, the parental right to make the decision continues save only in exceptional circumstances. Emergency, parental neglect, abandonment of the child, or inability to find the parent are examples of exceptional situations justifying the doctor proceeding to treat the child without parental knowledge and consent: but there will arise, no doubt, other exceptional situations in which it will be reasonable for the doctor to proceed without the parent's consent.

When applying these conclusions to contraceptive advice and treatment it has to be borne in mind that there is much that has to be understood by a girl under the age of 16 if she is to have legal capacity to consent to such treatment. It is not enough that she should understand the nature of the advice which is being given: she must also have a sufficient maturity to understand what is involved. There are moral and family questions, especially her relationship with her parents; long term problems associated with the emotional impact of pregnancy and its termination; and there are the risks to health of sexual intercourse at her age, risks which contraception may diminish but cannot eliminate. It follows that a doctor will have to satisfy himself that she is able to appraise these factors before he can safely proceed upon the basis that she has at law capacity to consent to contraceptive treatment. And it further follows that ordinarily the proper course will be for him, as the guidance lays down, first to seek to persuade the girl to bring her parents into consultation, and if she refuses, not to prescribe contraceptive treatment unless he is satisfied that her circumstances are such that he ought to proceed without parental knowledge and consent.

Most medical decisions made by parents on behalf of their children will be uncontroversial. However, in certain areas, such as the control of fertility, there can be a real conflict between parental wishes and the interests of the child. Bernard M Dickens examines the concept of parental rights:

Dickens, BM, 'Function and limits of parental rights'[82]

The modern function of parental rights, it is proposed, is not to enforce duties children owe their parents, or simply to enforce against third parties powers of custody and control parents enjoy over their children. It is to permit parents to discharge their duties to their children. These duties are not positively to do good, but to avoid harm. It is obvious that to the extent that ill health and, for instance, illiteracy are considered harm, parents are bound by positive duties to provide healthcare and education. This proposition may be derived from an abundance of case law and legislation. The duty to avoid harm is more elastic, however, since it affords licence to control a child not for its benefit, but in non-beneficial and non-therapeutic ways falling short of causing or risking harm. The issue to be critically addressed is the point at which an exercise of parental choice over a child's management and future is so potentially harmful to the welfare or interests of the child as to require State intervention and possibly a countermanding of parental choice.

Not surprisingly, the courts recognise that there are limits to the rights of a parent. The case of *Re S (A Minor) (Medical Treatment)* is a clear illustration of this. The patient was a young child suffering from T-cell leukaemia, treatable only by chemotherapy which necessitated blood transfusions. The parents of the child were devout Jehovah's Witnesses and therefore were

---

82 (1981) 97 LQR 462.

fundamentally opposed to blood transfusions. The local authority invoked the inherent jurisdiction of the court under s 100 of the Children Act 1989, and sought an order permitting such treatment to be given:

Re S (A Minor) (Medical Treatment[83]

Thorpe J: [T]he test must remain the welfare of the child as the paramount consideration. Specifically, in this case, the choice is not between two medical procedures with similar, if differing, prospects of success. Here the stark choice is between one medical procedure with no prospect of success and one medical treatment with a prospect of success which is put at even.

So, as I put to Mr Daniel in argument: are the religious convictions of the parents to deny their child a 50% chance of survival? Are those convictions to deny him that 50% chance and condemn him to inevitable and early death? Mr Daniel realistically saw that this was an extreme case and one in which it is difficult to pursue the argument that the religious convictions of the parents should deny the child the chance of treatment.

Finally, Mr Daniel invites the court to look ahead to the later years of childhood. If this treatment is applied in the face of parental opposition what would be the difficulties and stresses for S in years to come – parented by parents who believe that his life was prolonged by an ungodly act? Well, that consideration seems to me one that has little foundation in reality. The reality seems to me to be that family reaction will recognise that the responsibility for consent was taken from them and, as a judicial act, absolved their conscience of responsibility.

Parental opposition to clinical decisions was considered in the case of Re C (A Minor).[84] The patient was a 16-month-old baby, suffering from spinal muscular atrophy, and said to be seriously disabled and severely emaciated. For a few weeks before the case came before the court, the child had been ventilated to support her breathing. The opinion of the consultant paediatric neurologist in charge of the child's care was that no further ventilation should take place, and if, following withdrawal of the ventilation, the child should undergo further respiratory arrest, she should not be resuscitated. The evidence was that further respiratory arrest would mean long-term ventilator dependency. The parents of the child, who were religious orthodox Jews, were opposed to this. They agreed that ventilation should be withdrawn, but would not agree that no attempt at resuscitation be made. A second medical opinion was obtained which supported the opinion of the treating doctor. Sir Stephen Brown P held that support of the parents' view would be tantamount to requiring doctors to undertake a course of treatment which they were unwilling to do, and no order would be made to this effect. Clinical judgment, however, will not always prevail, as will be seen from the case of Re T (A Minor) (Wardship: Medical Treatment).[85]

In the case of Re S, above, Thorpe J was considering a case where the treatment objected to (the blood transfusion) carried virtually no risk, and nothing more than inconvenience to the child. What about the case of a parent who refuses to agree to a difficult form of treatment which may be lengthy and painful? This was considered in the case of Re T(A Minor) (Wardship: Medical Treatment). The child was born with a serious liver defect and underwent surgery at the age of three-and-a-half weeks. The operation caused pain and distress and was unsuccessful. The medical prognosis was that without a liver transplant the child would not live more than a couple of years. The mother refused consent to a transplant. The child's father (to whom she was not married) agreed with her. Both parents were described as 'healthcare professionals' with

83 [1993] 1 FLR 376.
84 [1998] 1 Lloyd's Rep Med 1.
85 [1997] 1 All ER 906.

experience of caring for sick children. The mother had moved out of the country at the time of the hearing of the local authority's application for permission for the operation to be carried out. The application had been brought at the behest of the consultants who had treated the child. The judge at first instance granted the application on the basis that it was in the child's best interests for it to be carried out and that the mother was being 'unreasonable'. The Court of Appeal allowed the mother's appeal:

Re T (A Minor) (Wardship: Medical Treatment)[86]

Waite LJ: The law's insistence that the welfare of a child shall be paramount is easily stated and universally applauded, but the present case illustrates, poignantly and dramatically, the difficulties that are encountered when trying to put it into practice. Throughout his clear and able judgment, the judge demonstrated his appreciation of the dilemma to which the case gives rise. Loving and devoted parents have taken, after anxious consideration, a decision to withhold consent to operative transplant treatment. Although it is relatively novel treatment, still unavailable in many countries, doctors of the highest expertise have unanimously recommended it for this child on clinical grounds, taking the view that it involves a relatively minor level of risk which they regard as well worth taking in the child's long term interests (which in this instance include an extension of life itself). The parents' opposition is partly instinctive and (being based on their own awareness of the procedures involved) partly practical. It has sufficient cogency to have led one of the principal medical experts in the field of this operation to say that his team would decline to operate without the mother's committed support.

What is the court to do in such a situation? It is not an occasion – even in an age preoccupied with 'rights' – to talk of the rights of a child, or the rights of a parent, or the rights of the court. The cases cited by Butler-Sloss LJ are uncompromising in their assertion that the sole yardstick must be the need to give effect to the demands of paramountcy for the welfare of the child. They establish that there are bound to be occasions when such paramountcy will compel the court, acting as a judicial parent, to substitute the judge's own views as to the claims of child welfare over those of natural parents – even in a case where the views of the latter are supported by qualities of devotion, commitment, love and reason. The judge, after anxious consideration, reached the conclusion that this case provides such an occasion. Was he right to do so?

Of course if his decision was founded on a correct application of legal principle, it is unassailable, however tempted individual members of an appellate court might be to substitute a judgment of our own. These decisions, not least because they are so difficult and finely balanced, are best left to the discretion of the experienced judges who have the task, often a lonely and worrying one, of weighing the numerous delicate elements (including the view taken of the parties and witnesses) which enable a cumulative picture to be formed of the demands of welfare in a particular case, and taking the momentous decision which the child patient cannot take for himself.

In this instance, however, in agreement with Butler-Sloss LJ, I consider that the judge was betrayed into an error of law by his concern with the need to form a judgment about the reasonableness of the mother's approach. An appraisal of parental reasonableness may be appropriate in other areas of family law (in adoption, for example, where it is enjoined by statute), but when it comes to an assessment of the demands of the child patient's welfare, the starting point – and the finishing point too – must always be the judge's own independent assessment of the balance of advantage or disadvantage of the particular medical step under consideration.

In striking that balance, the judge will of course take into account as a relevant, often highly relevant, factor the attitude taken by a natural parent, and that may require examination of his or her motives.

---

86 [1997] 1 All ER 906.

But the result of such an inquiry must never be allowed to prove determinative. It is a mistake to view the issue as one in which the clinical advice of doctors is placed in one scale and the reasonableness of the parent's view in the other. Had the judge viewed the evidence more broadly from the standpoint of his own perception of the child's welfare when appraised in all its aspects, he would have been bound, in my view, to take significant account of other elements in the case. Those include the parents' ties in country AB, and – crucially – the evidence of Dr P.

No one disputes that in the aftermath of the operation the child would remain in the primary care of the mother. Dr P maintained a very clear view that – even assuming that the operation proved wholly successful in surgical terms – the child's subsequent development could be injuriously affected if his day to day care depended upon the commitment of a mother who had suffered the turmoil of having her child being compelled against her will to undergo, as a result of a coercive order from the court, a major operation against which her own medical and maternal judgment wholeheartedly rebelled.

All these cases depend on their own facts and render generalisations – tempting though they may be to the legal or social analyst – wholly out of place. It can only be said safely that there is a scale, at one end of which lies the clear case where parental opposition to medical intervention is prompted by scruple or is of a kind which is patently irreconcilable with principles of child health and welfare widely accepted by the generality of mankind; and that at the other end lie highly problematic cases where there is genuine scope for a difference of view between parent and judge. In both situations it is the duty of the judge to allow the court's own opinion to prevail in the perceived paramount interests of the child concerned, but in cases at the latter end of the scale, there must be a likelihood (though never of course a certainty) that the greater the scope for genuine debate between one view and another the stronger will be the inclination of the court to be influenced by a reflection that in the last analysis the best interests of every child include an expectation that difficult decisions affecting the length and quality of its life will be taken for it by the parent to whom its care has been entrusted by nature. I too would allow this appeal.

Is the distinction between the 'welfare of the child' approach and the 'reasonableness of the parent' approach one of semantics only? In other words, was the first instance decision that the mother was being unreasonable only another way of saying that she was not acting in the best interests of the child, and that the Court of Appeal was wrong to disturb the decision?

It is also of some concern that the Court of Appeal was relying too heavily upon the judgment of the mother to whom the child's care 'has been entrusted by nature'. Marie Fox and Jean McHale, referring to Butler-Sloss LJ's judgment, comment as follows:

Fox, M and McHale, J, 'In whose best interests?'[87]

. . . a significant feature is the emphasis in the Court of Appeal judgments on the parents' status as health-care professionals, with experience of paediatric care. However it is questionable whether such significance should have been attributed to the parents' profession. It should be noted that, in the context of medical treatment, there is some evidence that healthcare professionals are actively discouraged from treating their families. However, amongst the professional bodies there appears to be uncertainty about the ethics of the practice. While the General Medical Council and United Kingdom Council for Nursing, Midwifery and Health Visiting do not censure health professionals who treat themselves or their family members, the British Medical Association regards such practice as unethical. In *Re T*, however, the Court of Appeal drew an implicit distinction between medical treatment on the one hand and 'caring' on the other. This calls into question whether the same objections apply when health professionals are involved

---

87 (1997) 60 MLR 700.

in caring for their own children, and what weight their views should carry in this context. Pinpointing the divide between treatment and care is a process fraught with difficulties, especially since caring may be entrusted to either professionals or lay persons. Such difficulties become particularly acute where parents are also health practitioners. Significantly, this policy issue was not addressed in *Re T*. In part, the Court of Appeal was able to avoid the issue by downplaying the importance of medical opinion. A striking feature of the judgments is that there is virtually no reference to medical evidence. This is in stark contrast to earlier cases, such as *Re C* and *Re J*, where a wealth of expert evidence was cited. Indeed, in *Re T*, greater weight appeared to be placed on a fact sheet published by the Children's Liver Disease Foundation (which highlighted the general complications of liver transplantation, thus endorsing the parental reservations about treatment) than on the specific medical evidence pertaining to this child. Thus, rather than focusing on the evidence which would have justified treatment, the judges focused on the implications for the carers should treatment be authorised against their will. A further point is that the judgments do not clarify whether the significance of the parents' occupations lies simply in their status as health professionals or is derived from their greater competence as decision makers.

Since the legitimacy of according carers an enhanced decision-making role by virtue solely of their status as healthcare professionals is questionable, we need to explore whether other special features of this case justify the weight accorded to the position of the carers. In this regard Butler-Sloss LJ noted that:

> Some of the objections of the mother, such as the difficulties of the operation itself, turned out . . . to be less important than the mother believed. Underlying those less important objections by the mother was deep-seated concern of the mother as to the benefits to her son of the major invasive surgery and post-operative treatment, the dangers of failure long term as well as short term, the possibility of the need for further transplants, the likely length of life and the impact upon her son of all these concerns.

Thus, the mother's opposition to the procedure is represented as rooted in caring attitudes. Butler-Sloss LJ also refers to 'the enormous significance of the close attachment between the mother and baby'. Yet there are unresolved tensions in this portrayal of the mother. We are given little evidence to support the court's opinion that this mother was exceptionally devoted. Furthermore, even assuming that this representation is accurate, two troublesome issues arise. First, if we accept the court's depiction of her as especially caring, it was surely incumbent upon the judges to examine why she was so reluctant to undertake the care of her son following a procedure which could save his life, particularly in view of her professional expertise in this area. Secondly, there is no exploration of the relationship between caring and reasonableness. It must be doubted whether the decisions of an exceptionally caring parent, even one who is a health professional herself, may automatically be deemed reasonable ones . . .

A further noteworthy point is the manner in which caring was construed as the mother's responsibility rather than that of both the parents. Nowhere in the judgments was the role of the father clearly articulated. In the circumstances this may have been largely because the parents were unmarried so that parental responsibility was vested in the mother alone. Certainly, the effect of the relative marginality of the father was to make it easier for the court to depict the mother as sole carer and then to conflate the interests of mother and child. This occurs most strikingly in the following passage of Butler-Sloss LJ's judgment:

> This mother and child are one for the purpose of this unusual case and the decision of the court to consent to the operation jointly affects the mother and son and it also affects the father. The welfare of this child depends upon his mother.

. . . It may be questioned what the broader implications of this line of reasoning are for the autonomy of the mother in cases where no clinical support exists for her views, with the result that they are not upheld by the court.

> Nevertheless, in this case, construing the mother and child as one permitted the Court of Appeal to minimise the potential conflict between the interests of the woman and child. It effectively allowed the court to encompass within the best interests test the interests of the mother as carer as well as the interests of the child. The problem of disentangling the determination of best interests from the question of who decides is rendered still more intractable by the court's reasoning in this case. Thus, it is significant that when Butler-Sloss LJ considered the consequences of upholding the judge's original order that the child should be returned to England for treatment, her emphasis was upon the difficulties and inconvenience of such an outcome for the mother:
>
> > She will have to comply with the court order; return to this country and present the child to one of the hospitals. She will have to arrange to stay in this country for the foreseeable future . . . If [the father] does not come she will have to manage unaided. How will the mother cope? Can her professionalism overcome her view that her son should not be subjected this distressing procedure? Will she break down? How will the child be affected by the conflict with which the mother may have to cope?
>
> . . . surely the Court of Appeal's approach in this case is exceptional, given that in the Jehovah's Witness cases cited above doctors were prepared to undertake treatment in the face of intransigent parental opposition?

Certainly, there is cause for concern in intertwining the interests of a child and its mother, or indeed a child and its parents. It is difficult to see the difference between *Re T (A Minor) (Wardship: Medical Treatment)*[88] and cases where sincere religious views of caring parents are overridden in the best interests of the child.

In the case of *Re T*, the parents purported to care for their child, despite the potentially tragic consequences of their views holding sway. In a case where the parents simply do not want the child to live, judicial decision-making is more clear cut. The case of *Re B (A Minor) (Wardship: Medical Treatment)*[89] may have been such a case. The child was a newly born Down's syndrome baby who also had an intestinal complaint that required surgery in order for it to survive. The parents refused consent. Their view was that the child would be better off dead. This may have been because they anticipated a poor life ahead for the child, or it may have been the fact that they did not want a Down's syndrome child. In that case, the Court of Appeal authorised the treatment. Templeman LJ described the choice as a stark one between authorising the operation so that the child may live for 20 or 30 years as a mongoloid, or terminating the life of a mongoloid child because she also has an intestinal complaint.[90]

An interesting contrast to this case is *Re SL(Adult Patient) (Medical Treatment)*.[91] The mother of a 29-year-old woman, with severe learning difficulties, made an application to the court for a declaration in respect of the lawfulness of a proposed sterilisation/hysterectomy. It was anticipated that before long the mother would not be able to continue to care for her daughter and that she would have to go and live in local authority sheltered accommodation. The mother feared that, as her daughter was an attractive woman, she might become pregnant, and also that she was distressed by 'heavy' menstrual bleeding. Three medical options were available. The first was a total hysterectomy (this would render her incapable of bearing children and eliminate menstruation); the second, a sterilisation by clipping of the fallopian tubes (a contraceptive

---

88 [1997] 1 All ER 906.
89 [1981] 1 WLR 1421.
90 See Ch 12 for further discussion of this and other cases of gravely incapacitated children.
91 [2000] 2 FCR 452.

measure, but it would do nothing about menstruation); the third by the fitting of a Mirena coil (contraceptive, with the possibility of reducing or even eliminating menstruation). The mother favoured the first option. The medical evidence all pointed to trying the Mirena coil as a first attempt, but one of the experts stated that, in his opinion, a hysterectomy could be justified even if undertaken at the outset. This seemed to influence the judge, Wall J, who decided that it would be in the woman's best interests, even if it was not the doctors' first choice because, first, the court should decide the best interests question and, secondly, the decision satisfied the *Bolam* test because there was a body of opinion that would undertake the hysterectomy at this, the first, stage. The judge then said that as both treatments (the sterilisation was not favoured by anyone) were *Bolam* compliant, he would make a declaration to this effect and leave the mother to discuss with the doctors what was best. This aspect of the case was considered but, here, the issue is the view taken by the Court of Appeal of the mother's wishes. These were based upon the fact that her daughter became very distressed at the time of her periods, regarding herself as being dirty, and the Mirena coil would not necessarily have any effect upon this. Further, the coil itself had to be inserted under general anaesthetic, and had to be replaced every five years, or more frequently if it became dislodged. The woman had a horror of hospitals and much of this would take place when her mother would not be there to help her. These were understandable concerns, but they did not sway the Court of Appeal. As it happens, in this case the coil could be tried first and the more invasive method tried later if it did not work. This is unfortunate because, otherwise, the court could have made it more explicit that the interests of this woman and her mother could not be conflated and that might have been an embarrassing contrast with the decision in *Re T (A Minor) (Wardship: Medical Treatment)*.[92]

See Chapter 4 →

The question of parental rights was considered in the case of *Re P (A Minor)*, when Butler-Sloss J (as she then was) made an order for the termination of a 15-year-old girl's pregnancy in the face of her parents' opposition. The girl already had a baby and resided in a special mother and baby unit. Her parents wanted to care for the second child she was carrying, and her father objected to abortion on religious grounds:

Re P (A Minor)[93]

Butler-Sloss J: I would not like it to be thought that because she says she does not want the child her wishes should be given such paramount importance as to mean that for that reason only she should have an abortion. But where her wishes coincide with the facts that she is in danger of injury to her mental health; that she is undoubtedly – when I consider her interests, as I do, as the first and paramount consideration – unable to fulfil her own growing up as a child at her schooling as a consequence of this second pregnancy; where she is endangering the future of her current child; and where I take into account all the aspects of her actual and reasonably foreseeable environment, I have no doubt that this case comes within s 1(a) of the Abortion Act 1967 . . .

I must take into account in considering the welfare of Shirley – and her welfare is what is paramount in my mind because she is a ward of court – and through her the effect on her son of having this unwanted child, the important aspect of her parents. I was helpfully reminded of what had been said in the House of Lords in *J v C* [1970] AC 668 about the rights and obligations of parents. These parents are in certain difficulties in that they do not have the day to day care of Shirley since she is in care, and they are not able to offer to take over the day to day care of Shirley. In the circumstances, although I must give weight to their feelings as a factor in the case to be taken into consideration, and I must take into account their deeply and

---

92 [1997] 1 All ER 906.
93 (1982) 80 LGR 301.

> sincerely held religious objection, in considering the best interest of the minor as to whether she should have her pregnancy terminated I draw to some extent an analogy with Jehovah's Witnesses and blood transfusions . . . I am satisfied . . . that there is a risk of injury to the mental health of this minor, the factors raised by the grandfather on behalf of himself and his wife – which I have taken into account – cannot weigh in the balance against the needs of this girl so as to prevent the termination which I have decided is necessary in her best interests.

This may be thought to be in stark contrast with the views expressed by Butler-Sloss LJ in the much later case of *Re T(A Minor) (Wardship: Medical Treatment)*[94] considered above. However, even if it had been in issue, the closeness of the parent/child relationship, which was regarded as so important in *Re T*, would not have been relevant here as, unlike the case of a young, sick child, there was no question of this child needing her parents to care for her.

Note that, in *Re P*, the judge had to take into account the provisions of the Abortion Act 1967, where, *inter alia*, there has to be a risk to the health of the pregnant woman. There were, therefore, objective factors that had to be satisfied regardless of the wishes of the child and her parents. However, in abortion cases, it is always arguable that a child who does not want to continue with her pregnancy is going to be mentally damaged if she is compelled to continue it. In the context of other areas of medicine and surgery, however, there have been a number of recent cases where there have been disagreements between the parents, either among themselves or, more often, with the doctors, as to what is the appropriate medical treatment for their children.

See Chapter 8

In *Re J (Child's Religious Upbringing and Circumcision)*[95] the Court of Appeal refused an application by a child's father that the child be circumcised. The child's parents had separated when he was two and a half and the mother had custody. The father applied for a specific issue order under the Children Act 1989. The Turkish father, who was permanently resident in the UK, was a Muslim, but non-practising. Similarly, the child's mother was described as non-practising Church of England. The child went to a secular school. The Court of Appeal upheld the first instance decision that it would not be in the child's best interests, as a non-practising Muslim, to undergo irreversible, non-therapeutic surgery which carried with it pain and the small risk of psychological harm. On the other hand, the same surgery, if agreed by both parents, for religious or cultural reasons, would be lawful.

In *C (HIV Test)*[96] both parents were agreed that they did not wish their baby to be tested for HIV. The mother was HIV positive and had resisted any form of intervention to prevent transmission of the virus to the child, both during pregnancy and afterwards. The clinical view was that, if the child was infected, there were measures which could be taken to manage the condition and that, if the child was not infected, then immediate cessation of breastfeeding would be recommended. The local authority made an application for a specific issue order that the child be tested and this was supported by the Official Solicitor on behalf of the child. The judge at first instance granted the order on the basis that it was in the child's best interests and the Court of Appeal refused leave to appeal, confirming that the wishes of parents could be overruled and approving the judge's evaluation of the medical evidence.

The case of *Re MM (A Child) (Medical Treatment)*[97] concerned a child's treatment for immuno-deficiency by immunoglobin, which doctors recommended. The parents were not prepared to consent to this because treatment received in Russia before the family moved to the UK had

---

94 [1997] 1 All ER 906.
95 (1999) 52 BMLR 82.
96 [1999] 2 FLR 1004.
97 [2000] 1 FLR 224.

been working well and because there had been an early misdiagnosis by the English doctors which had shaken their confidence. In the event, an order was agreed that the immunoglobin treatment be continued, but with the parents closely involved in the decision-making, with liberty for either party to apply to the court for further directions.

The case of Re C (Welfare of Child: Immunisation)[98] was a conjoined case that considered a number of disputes between parents as to whether children should receive the MMR injection which immunised against multiple infectious diseases. There has been some controversy about the safety of the MMR immunisation, and the mothers, with whom the children lived, alleged that it presented unacceptable risks, whereas the fathers argued that there was convincing medical evidence that the benefits outweighed any risks. At first instance the judge made a declaration ordering immunisation of the children. The Court of Appeal upheld the decision on the basis that the judge had properly weighed up the medical evidence, and the court confirmed that there was no general proposition of law that a court would not order non-essential invasive medical treatment in the face of strong opposition from a child's primary carer.

4.4.4 Children and the European Convention on Human Rights

The extraordinary circumstances that brought the case of R v Portsmouth Hospital NHS Trust, ex p Glass[99] before the courts came about through a total breakdown of relationships between the doctors and the patient's relatives, such that a fight broke out in which medical staff were punched, kicked and bitten, and three of the patient's relatives were prosecuted and received prison sentences. The patient, David, aged 12, was severely disabled, both mentally and physically, but his family cared for him devotedly and wanted him to live as long as possible. He was hospitalised several times during the summer of 1998, suffering from breathing and digestive problems. The doctors believed he was dying. In October, they wanted to administer diamorphine to relieve distress, but the child's mother refused to consent to this, fearing that sedation was a prelude to death. The doctors went ahead anyway, and a 'Do Not Resuscitate' order was placed on his medical records without consulting his mother. Visiting relatives made strenuous attempts to revive the child, in the course of which the assaults upon the medical staff took place. The child eventually went home and was successfully treated by the family GP. The trust wrote to the child's mother indicating that any future care should be administered by a hospital in Southampton and that it would only deal with him as an emergency admission. The mother sought judicial review of the trust's decision to administer diamorphine in the face of her refusal. Scott-Baker J dismissed the application for judicial review on the basis that the situation which gave rise to the application had now passed; the child was to be admitted to a different hospital and the judicial review mechanism was too blunt a tool for the sensitive and ongoing problems of the type thrown up in such a case. The Court of Appeal agreed and refused leave to appeal, stating that, if future conflicts of 'a grave nature' arose, then declarations could be sought from the court at the appropriate time, rather than trying to anticipate the 'almost infinite' considerations that might arise in the future. The judgment of the Court, given by Lord Woolf MR, while peppered with reminders that these cases give rise to sensitive issues, declined to comment on the fact that, in the face of a total breakdown of confidence, the trust did not see fit to bring the matter before the court, when the only course of action which seemed open to the family at that crucial time was, literally, to fight for the child's life.

The case went before the European Court of Human Rights and the decision of that Court (Glass v United Kingdom)[100] was that the decision to impose treatment on David in defiance of his mother's

---

98 [2003] EWCA Civ 1148.
99 [1999] Lloyd's Rep Med 367.
100 (2004) 39 EHRR 15.

objections gave rise to an interference with the child's Article 8 rights, and in particular his right to physical integrity. Obviously, there are circumstances in which it is right to impose treatment on a child in the face of a parental refusal of consent, as evidenced by the cases above and, under such circumstances, save in emergency situations, UK law requires doctors to seek the intervention of the courts. In the *Glass* case, failure to do this meant that there had been a breach of Article 8. See also *Royal Wolverhampton Hospitals NHS Trust v E and RB and Others*,[101] where, it was assumed by the judge that, in circumstances of parental/medical disagreement, an application to the court by the trust was in the best interests of the child patient. In *Re S(FC)*[102] the House of Lords considered the balancing exercise which must take place when competing articles of the European Convention are engaged.

Parents are, of course, entitled to use the Human Rights Act 1998 to allege there has been unlawful interference of their Convention rights, but Fortin argues that the phrasing of, in particular, Article 8, encourages parents to argue that these rights are all about protecting adult rights; so, for example, when parents challenge decisions to take their children into care, they focus on their own rights under Article 8. Fortin goes on to examine freedom of the press cases and to look at the balancing act carried out by courts when looking at a child's right to privacy and the freedom of the press.[103] Fortin's main argument is that what she refers to as the paramountcy principle, ie s 1 of the Children Act 1989, which states that the welfare of the child is paramount, is the culprit in this situation:

Fortin, J, 'Accommodating children's rights in a post Human Rights Act era'[104]

> ... there is the assumption that rights and welfare are discrete matters and that therefore issues relating to the child's best interests cannot be introduced in the context of a discussion of his rights. Such a view also underlines the recurring concerns voiced by some family lawyers that by using a rights discourse, those concerned with children's wellbeing would be unable to promote their welfare. Indeed, some of those considering the effect of the HRA on the principles of child law have suggested that a rights-based approach to children's interests might actually conflict with their welfare. But the rights-based approach adopted by the European Convention should surely not be interpreted in manner ignoring the basic premises underpinning rights theories.
> ... a child's welfare cannot be inconsistent with his rights. Consequently any evidence which a court would traditionally consider when assessing how to accommodate the child's welfare must be accommodated *within* arguments about his rights. In other words, there cannot be two categories of evidence, one relating to the child's rights and another to his welfare.

Perhaps Fortin is unhappy with the welfare principle because it acts like a sort of 'super-right' that overrides the rights of the parents, when she prefers a balancing act between respective rights. In other words, there is a risk that the welfare principle in children cases assumes the same role as best interests in adult cases, where it is arguable that subsuming decisions under these phrases results in an insufficient airing of the issues.

4.4.5 Children and the role of the court

Decisions concerning the treatment of children can come before the court via the Children Act 1989 (specific issue orders under s 8), or via the jurisdiction of the High Court. The wardship jurisdiction must be distinguished from the inherent jurisdiction of the High Court. In the

---

101 [2000] 1 FLR 953.
102 [2004] UKHL 47.
103 See Ch 5 for more discussion of this issue in the context of privacy generally.
104 (2006) 69 (3) MLR 299, p 311.

former case parental authority is vested in the court; in the latter the court is dealing only with the particular treatment issue put before it. The inherent jurisdiction of the court may be invoked by local authorities, as the wardship jurisdiction is unavailable to them. Regardless of the nature of the judicial proceedings, the welfare of the child is paramount.

THINK POINT

Do you agree with Lord Donaldson's interpretation of the *Gillick* case when considering treatment refusals by children?

4.5 The control of fertility and the incapable patient

4.5.1 The therapeutic/non-therapeutic distinction

Sterilisation, abortion and enforced contraception of incapable patients raise profound ethical issues. Furthermore, these procedures are inevitably associated with the practice of eugenics carried out by the Nazis during the 1930s and 1940s. However, as Davies points out, the practice was by no means unknown before this:

Davies, M, *Textbook on Medical Law*[105]

> **13.3.1 Historical development of sterilisation**
>
> The debate on sterilising the mentally handicapped has been a long, and as the case law will show, a vociferous one. The debate has as its emotive backdrop the history of late nineteenth and early twentieth centuries. The case law will show that the judiciary of a number of common law jurisdictions are aware of the dark side of this history. Sterilisation for eugenic purposes was not a product of Nazi Germany, although that regime was the most horrific expression of the perversion of the concept of eugenics. The theory that the species could be improved or perfected by a cleansing of the gene pool through selective breeding was introduced by Sir Francis Galton at University College London in 1869. It was not long before a number of US State reformatories were using the concept to justify the sterilisation of what were deemed to be those carrying undesirable traits within society ... One of the best known, and to some most frightening, judicial justifications for the performance of these irreversible operations was found in *Buck v Bell* 274 US 200 (1927). Carrie Buck was described as the 'feeble-minded' daughter of a mother who was herself described (among other things) as 'feeble-minded'. Her proposed sterilisation was challenged on 'due process' grounds as a 'cruel and unusual punishment' under the US Constitution. The Supreme Court's view was that it was not going to be done as a punishment, but as a means to facilitate her freedom within the community. One of the most chilling quotes comes from Mr Justice Oliver Wendell Holmes (p 207):
>
>> We have seen more than once that the public welfare may call upon the best citizens for their lives. It would be strange if it could not call upon those who already sap the strength of the State for these lesser sacrifices, often not felt to be such by those concerned, in order to prevent our being swamped with incapables. It is better for all the world, if instead of waiting to execute degenerate offspring for crime, or to let them starve for their imbecility, society can prevent

---

105 London: Blackstone, 1996, p 262.

those who are manifestly unfit from continuing their kind. The principle that sustains compulsory vaccination is broad enough to cover cutting the fallopian tubes. Three generations of imbeciles are enough.

Although, *Buck v Bell* was decided in the 1920s, the issue has not gone away and the controversy remains. The case of *Re B (A Minor)*,[106] which concerned the sterilisation of a mentally handicapped girl, caused a considerable amount of controversy. Michael Freeman, editor of *Medicine, Ethics and the Law*,[107] in a BBC interview, had described the approval of the sterilisation by the Court of Appeal as 'Nazi-like'. In the House of Lords, Lord Hailsham, no doubt bearing in mind this reaction, had sought from the outset to distinguish this case from the practice of eugenics:

Re B (A Minor)[108]

Lord Hailsham: There is no doubt that, in the exercise of its wardship jurisdiction, the first and paramount consideration is the well being, welfare, or interests (each expression occasionally used, but each, for this purpose, synonymous) of the human being concerned, that is the ward herself or himself. In this case I believe it to be the only consideration involved. In particular there is no issue of public policy other than the application of the above principle which can conceivably be taken into account, least of all (since the opposite appears to have been considered in some quarters) any question of eugenics.

When the case of *Re F (Mental Patient: Sterilisation)* was in the Court of Appeal, Lord Donaldson had taken the view that sterilisation operations were special cases:

Re F (Mental Patient: Sterilisation)[109]

Lord Donaldson p 19: Is sterilisation in a special category?

. . . Mr Munby seeks to persuade us that it is in a special category and in this I think he is right, although I would include in the same category abortion and surgical intervention to enable an incapable adult to donate an organ during lifetime. However, there is a real distinction between medical treatment undertaken with a view to securing abortion or sterilisation and that undertaken for a different purpose, for example the excision of a malignant tumour, which has this incidental result. It is only the former type of treatment which the law regards as being in a special category, probably because of its irreversible and emotive character in the light of the history of our times.

As stated by Lord Donaldson, sterilisation operations can be carried out for exclusively therapeutic purposes, for example when the ovaries or uterus are damaged or diseased. Those operations do not concern us here. The cases we will examine fall into two categories. First, 'social' sterilisations, where it is proposed to render sterile those who, it is said, are simply incapable of understanding parenthood and caring for a child. Secondly, there have been a number of cases where young women have been sterilised to avoid difficulties with menstruation. Can these properly be called 'therapeutic'?

---

106 [1988] 1 AC 199.
107 London: Stevens, 1988.
108 [1988] 1 AC 199 at 202.
109 [1990] 2 AC 1.

4.5.2 Non-therapeutic sterilisations

We have considered above whether there is any meaningful distinction between a therapeutic and a non-therapeutic procedure, and saw that La Forest J in the case of *Re Eve*[110] favoured such a distinction. 'Non-therapeutic' sterilisations are those that might be carried out for reasons relating to whether the woman is fit to be a parent. The problem with this is that it necessarily encompasses issues that do not relate to the woman herself but social circumstances. This is fraught with difficulty because, while a physically impaired mother may need some assistance in bringing up a child, it is highly unpalatable to think of her being told she cannot have children because of this.

One of the first English cases to examine the issue was *Re D (A Minor) (Wardship: Sterilisation)*.[111] The case concerned an 11-year-old child, who suffered from Sotos syndrome, a condition characterised by epilepsy, clumsiness, unusual facial appearance, behavioural problems such as emotional instability and aggression and impairment of mental function. She was described as having an IQ of 80 (described as 'dull normal'), some reading and writing skills, good conversational skills and the understanding of a nine or nine-and-a-half-year old. An application was made to the court under the wardship jurisdiction for authorisation of a sterilisation. The reasons are outlined in the judgment of Heilbron J:

Re D (A Minor) (Wardship: Sterilisation)[112]

Heilbron J (p 330):

The background to the decision to operate

When Mrs B first realised that she had given birth to a handicapped child, she recalled with deep concern that, many years before, she had lived near a family who had the misfortune to have three mentally retarded children, and their plight and their troubled lives had deeply affected her. She and her husband not unnaturally were extremely worried about D's future, as at that time they thought D could never improve, and so even when D was a very young child they decided that when she reached the age of about 18 they would take the necessary steps to prevent her from having any children, and would apply to have her sterilised. From the decision made in those early days Mrs B has never resiled, and she has in consequence, over the years, had several discussions about this operation with Dr Gordon. When D reached puberty by the age of 10 Mrs B's concern increased, and so she discussed the operation once again with Dr Gordon on 7 January 1975. Mrs B said, and I accept, that when she reiterated to Dr Gordon that she would like D sterilised when she was older, the doctor said: 'We can do it now'. This is indeed confirmed by the doctor in his affidavit when he says that rather than wait any longer the decision could be taken then. Mrs B agreed that the operation should be performed. She was very worried lest D might be seduced and possibly give birth to a baby, which might also be abnormal. She had always believed that D would not, or should not, marry and in any event would be incapable of bringing up a child. Her anxieties are genuine and understandable.

Dr Gordon took the view that there was a real risk that D might give birth to an abnormal foetus. I have already referred to some of his other anxieties. As to the possibility of producing an abnormal child, the evidence of Dr Snodgrass and Dr Newton, the well-known consultant psychiatrist called on behalf of the Official Solicitor, confirmed that there was, as Dr Gordon stated, an increased risk of such an eventuality. On the other hand, they pointed out that no one with this particular syndrome had ever been known to have a baby, and it is not therefore possible to make any precise predictions whether or not they are able to do so.

---

110 [1986] 2 SCR 388.
111 [1976] 1 All ER 326.
112 [1976] 2 WLR 279.

At that consultation in January Dr Gordon, with Mrs B's agreement, came to a decision provided that Miss Duncan, the consultant gynaecologist, who is a senior lecturer and gynaecologist to the Sheffield and Northern General Hospital, to whom he referred, concurred in his recommendation that the operation should be performed. Miss Duncan saw and interviewed both D and Mrs B on 7 February 1975, but she did not examine the child, and I think there is little doubt that Miss Duncan did not give very much independent consideration to the wider implications of this operation, but was content in large measure to rely on Dr Gordon's recommendation and assessment of the situation. She did, however, agree to perform the sterilisation, namely a hysterectomy, and I am satisfied that D was booked to enter hospital on 4 May for that operation to be carried out on 6 May. No one else was consulted prior to that decision. It is surprising that Dr T, the child psychiatrist, was not, for, prior to the date of the recommendation, he had on a number of occasions interviewed and examined the child, and his views, as Dr Gordon later agreed in evidence, must have been of considerable importance in evaluating the numerous problems, medical, social, educational and psychiatric, which such a vital decision involved.

Dr Gordon maintains, however, that his recommendation was one which was based on clinical judgment as a doctor, and that he and the gynaecologist should be the sole judges whether or not it should be performed, provided of course that they had the parent's consent.

Despite Dr Gordon's assertion that his decision should be upheld because it was based on his clinical judgment, he nevertheless, in putting forward his grounds for recommending this operation, stated that such reasons or such grounds were of a twofold character, ie, that they were both medical and social. The medical reasons included the possibility that she might give birth to an abnormal child, that her epilepsy might cause her to harm a child, and that the only satisfactory method of birth control was this operation. The social reasons included his opinion that D would be unable in the future to maintain herself save in a sheltered environment, her inability due to epilepsy and other handicaps to cope with a family if she were to marry, without substantial support, the deterioration in her behaviour for which he said there was no known method of improvement and the possibility that she might have to enter an institution as he alleged for social or criminal reasons in the future. Certain persons concerned with D's welfare, however, took a different view. They were the former and present headmaster of her school, Mrs Hamidi and the social worker involved with the family. They believed that an operation for sterilisation in the case of a minor, particularly a girl of 11, being irreversible and permanent, was a matter of grave concern, and so on 26 March Mrs Hamidi wrote on their behalf and on her own to the senior school medical officer, pointing out in detail the conflict between Mrs B and the school and the welfare services in regard to D's attainments and their concern in regard to the proposed operation, which they pointed out could affect the whole of her future.

On 21 April there was a meeting between Dr Gordon and those professionals working with the child and her family, at which Dr Gordon's social and behavioural reasons for performing this operation were seriously challenged. Dr Gordon, however, refused to acknowledge that these views could possibly be wrong or exaggerated or premature. I think Dr Gordon, whose sincerity cannot be challenged, was persuaded by his emotional involvement with Mrs B's considerable problems and anxieties, and his strong personal views in favour of sterilisation – as he stated in his affidavit, 'Sterilisation is now an emotive word, and we must try to change its image' – to form a less than detached opinion in regard to a number of matters which were not in my view in reality matters of clinical judgment, but which were concerned, to a large extent, with grounds which were other than medical. I feel it is a pity that he was not prepared to accept that others, whose duties, training and skills were directed to the assessment and amelioration of many of these problems, had much to contribute in the formulation of a decision of this gravity.

In my judgment Dr Gordon's views as to D's present and future social and behavioural problems were somewhat exaggerated and mistaken. I think in this area his views were clouded by his resentment at what he considered unjustified interference.

In the event Dr Gordon did not accept the alternative views, and he and Miss Duncan refused to defer the operation despite the grave implications for the child. Mrs Hamidi and the others, therefore, wrote to the area administrator of the health authority requesting an urgent and independent review of this decision. The area administrator consulted the local authority's specialist in community medicine (child health) and he later replied saying that she had made a very careful appraisal of the case, but could not interfere. Mrs Hamidi and her colleagues, however, were not daunted and they thereupon consulted solicitors, and in due course these proceedings got under way. It is only right that I should pay tribute to their courage, persistence and humane concern for this young girl.

. . . I am dealing here with the case of this particular young girl, but the evidence, including that which disclosed that Dr Gordon has recommended and Miss Duncan has performed two prior operations of this nature on handicapped children in Sheffield, indicates the possibility that further consideration may need to be given to this topic, consideration which would involve extensive consultation and debate elsewhere.

Dr Gordon's reason for wishing this operation to be performed was, of course, to prevent D ever having a child. He recognised, as did Mrs B, that there are other methods of achieving that objective, but his view was that D could not satisfactorily manage any form of contraception. Mrs B was concerned lest D might be seduced and become pregnant . . .

Mrs B's genuine concern . . . cannot be disregarded. A body of evidence was produced, therefore, to indicate the advantages and disadvantages of various forms of contraception. I shall not, however, burden this judgment with any detailed examination of it, save to say that I do not accept on the evidence Dr Gordon's contention that this young girl, if and when the time arrived, would not be a suitable subject for one of the various methods described by the doctors . . .

It was common ground that D had sufficient intellectual capacity to marry, in the future of course, and that many people of a like kind are capable of, and do so. Dr Gordon agreed that this being so, she and her future husband would then be the persons most concerned in a question of sterilisation, and such an operation might have a serious and material bearing on a future marriage and its consequences.

The purpose of performing this operation is permanently to prevent the possibility of reproduction. The evidence of Professor Huntingford, consultant and professor of obstetrics and gynaecology at the University of London and at St Bartholomew's Hospital and the London Hospital Medical Colleges, was that in his view such an operation was normally only appropriate for a woman who consented to it, possibly at the conclusion of child-bearing, and then only after careful and anxious consideration by her and her husband of many factors and, what is most important, with full knowledge of all its implications.

Professor Huntingford, Dr Snodgrass and Dr Newton were all agreed that such an operation was not medically indicated in this case, and should not be performed. Dr Snodgrass said he was firmly of the view that it was wrong to perform this operation on an 11-year-old, on the pretext that it would benefit her in the future. Dr Newton said:

> In my opinion sterilisation of a child before the age of consent can only be justified if it is the treatment for some present or inevitable disease. In this case, sterilisation is not a treatment for any of the signs or symptoms of Sotos syndrome, from which she suffers. I am totally against this operation being performed on D.

. . . Dr Gordon, however, maintained that, provided the parent or parents consented, the decision was one made pursuant to the exercise of his clinical judgment, and that no interference could be tolerated in his clinical freedom.

The other consultants did not agree. Their opinion was that a decision to sterilise a child was not entirely within a doctor's clinical judgment, save only when sterilisation was the treatment of choice for some disease, as, for instance, when in order to treat a child and to ensure her direct physical well being, it might be necessary to perform a hysterectomy to remove a malignant uterus. Whilst the side effect of such an operation would be to sterilise, the operation would be performed solely for therapeutic purposes. I

> entirely accept their opinions. I cannot believe, and the evidence does not warrant the view, that a decision to carry out an operation of this nature performed for non-therapeutic purposes on a minor, can be held to be within the doctor's sole clinical judgment ...
>
> A review of the whole of the evidence leads me to the conclusion that in a case of a child of 11 years of age, where the evidence shows that her mental and physical condition and attainments have already improved, and where her future prospects are as yet unpredictable, where the evidence also shows that she is unable as yet to understand and appreciate the implications of this operation and could not give a valid or informed consent, but the likelihood is that in later years she will be able to make her own choice, where, I believe, the frustration and resentment of realising (as she would one day) what had happened, could be devastating, an operation of this nature is, in my view, contra-indicated.

Three things, in particular, are noteworthy: first, the apparent lack of concern by the gynaecologist; secondly, the intransigence of Dr Gordon; and, thirdly, the chance way in which the case came before the court. As far as the first two points are concerned, this case was heard in the days before the decision in *Re F (Mental Patient: Sterilisation)* which endorsed the *Bolam* test as the criterion for best interests. However, if the *Bolam* test had been applied, would the combined opinions of Miss Duncan and Dr Gordon have constituted a responsible body of medical opinion for the purposes of the *Bolam* test? Even if two opinions were deemed insufficient, it is likely that, if necessary, other doctors could have been found to endorse their views. On an application of the *Bolam* test (which now has only a preliminary role to play in such cases), would Heilbron J have been able, nevertheless, to reject these opinions on the ground that they were not 'responsible' or that they were 'illogical'? This nicely illustrates the inappropriateness of the *Bolam* test in the best interests context. The third point, ie the arbitrary way in which the case came to court, is indicative of the time at which it was decided, and attitudes have changed somewhat since 1976. It was 12 years later that the sterilisation of a minor came before the House of Lords. The case of *Re B (A Minor) (Wardship: Sterilisation)* (the case of 'Jeanette') concerned a 17-year-old girl. She was a voluntary patient in a local authority residential unit. The facts are outlined in the judgment of Lord Oliver:

Re B (A Minor) (Wardship: Sterilisation) (1988)[113]

Lord Oliver p 207: [Jeanette] suffers from what is described as a 'moderate' degree of mental handicap but has a very limited intellectual development. Her ability to understand speech is that of a six-year-old, but her ability to express herself has been described as comparable to that of a two-year-old child. No cause for her mental handicap has been established but the report of Dr Berney, a consultant psychiatrist who gave evidence before the judge, indicates that her epilepsy and the degree of her mental incapacity suggest an underlying abnormality of the brain. It is not envisaged that she will ever be capable of caring for herself in the community or reach a stage where she could return permanently to her mother's care. She is capable of finding her way round a limited locality, of dressing and bathing herself and performing simple household tasks under supervision and she has been taught to cope with menstruation; but the evidence is that she is unlikely to show an improvement in mental capacity beyond that of a six year old child. She has, in the past, shown evidence of extremes of mood and can become violent and aggressive, a phenomenon associated with premenstrual tension. Since the middle of 1986 there has been prescribed for her a drug known as Danazol to help in controlling her irregular periods and relieving premenstrual tension, whilst her epilepsy is controlled by anti-convulsant drugs. She suffers from obesity and an earlier attempt to

---

113 [1988] 1 AC 199.

treat her outbursts of violence with Microgynon 30 (a combined oral contraceptive) had to be abandoned because it produced a significant increase in weight. Another behavioural feature of significance is her high tolerance of pain. There is evidence that she bites her arm and that if injured she interferes with the process of healing by opening and probing the wounds.

What prompted the application to the court was the consciousness on the part of her mother and officers of the council responsible for her care that she was beginning to show recognisable signs of sexual awareness and sexual drive exemplified by provocative approaches to male members of the staff and other residents and by touching herself in the genital area. There was thus brought to their attention the obvious risk of pregnancy and the desirability of taking urgent and effective contraceptive measures. Although at present she is subject to effective supervision, her degree of incapacity is not such that it would be thought right that she should, effectively, be institutionalised all her life. The current approach to persons of her degree of incapacity is to allow them as much freedom as is consistent with their own safety and that of other people and although the likelihood is that she will, for the foreseeable future, continue to live at the residential institution, she visits her mother and her siblings at weekends and will, inevitably, be much less susceptible to supervision when she goes to an adult training centre. At the same time the risks involved in her becoming pregnant are formidable. The evidence of Dr Berney is that there is no prospect of her being capable of forming a long term adult relationship, such as marriage, which is within the capacity of some less mentally handicapped persons. She has displayed no maternal feelings and indeed has an antipathy to small children. Such skills as she has been able to develop are limited to those necessary for caring for herself at the simplest level and there is no prospect of her being capable of raising or caring for a child of her own. If she did give birth to a child it would be essential that it be taken from her for fostering or adoption although her attitude towards children is such that this would not cause her distress. So far as her awareness of her own sexuality is concerned, she has, as has already been mentioned, been taught to manage for herself the necessary hygienic mechanics of menstruation, but it has not been possible to teach her about sexuality in any abstract form. She understands the link between pregnancy and a baby but is unaware of sexual intercourse and its relationship to pregnancy. It is not feasible to discuss contraception with her and even if there should come a time when she becomes capable of understanding the need for contraception, there is no likelihood of her being able to develop the capacity to weigh up the merits of different types of contraception or to make an informed choice in the matter. Should she become pregnant, it would be desirable that the pregnancy should be terminated, but because of her obesity and the irregularity of her periods there is an obvious danger that her condition might not be noticed until it was too late for an abortion to take place safely. On the other hand, the risks if she were permitted to go to full term are serious, for although it is Dr Berney's opinion that she would tolerate the condition of pregnancy without undue distress, the process of delivery would be likely to be traumatic and would cause her to panic. Normal delivery would be likely to require heavy sedation, which could be injurious to the child, so that it might be more appropriate to deliver her by Caesarean section. If this course were adopted, however, past experience of her reaction to injuries suggests that it would be very difficult to prevent her from repeatedly opening up the wound and thus preventing the healing of the post-operative scar. It was against this background and in the light of the increasing freedom which must be allowed her as she grows older and the consequent difficulty of maintaining effective supervision that those having the care of the minor concluded that it was essential in her interests that effective contraceptive measures be taken. Almost all drugs appear to have a bad effect upon her and the view was formed, in which her mother concurred, that the only appropriate course offering complete protection was for her to undergo sterilisation by occluding the fallopian tubes, a relatively minor operation carrying a very small degree of risk to the patient, a very high degree of protection and minimal side effects. There is, however, no possibility that the minor, even if of full age, would herself have the mental capacity to consent to such an operation. Hence the application to the court.

. . . Your Lordships' attention has, quite properly, been directed to the decision of Heilbron J in *In re D (A Minor) (Wardship: Sterilisation)* [1976] Fam 185, a case very different from the instant case, where the evidence indicated that the ward was of an intellectual capacity to marry and would in the future be able to make her own choice. In those circumstances, Heilbron J declined to sanction an operation which involved depriving her of her right to reproduce. That, if I may say so respectfully, was plainly a right decision. But the right to reproduce is of value only if accompanied by the ability to make a choice and in the instant case there is no question of the minor ever being able to make such a choice or indeed to appreciate the need to make one. All the evidence indicates that she will never desire a child and that reproduction would in fact be positively harmful to her.

Was this operation in Jeanette's best interests? Much of the reasoning behind the court's decision was that the operation was necessary to protect her. Lord Oliver said:[114]

Lord Oliver: My Lords, I have thought it right to set out in some detail the background of fact in which this appeal has come before your Lordships' House because it is, in my judgment, essential to appreciate, in considering the welfare of this young woman which it is the duty of the court to protect, the degree of her vulnerability, the urgency of the need to take protective measures and the impossibility of her ever being able at this age or any later age either to consent to any form of operative treatment or to exercise for herself the right of making any informed decision in matters which, in the case of a person less heavily handicapped, would rightly be thought to be matters purely of personal and subjective choice.

Note that, in the judgment of Lord Oliver, he moves from reference to 'provocative gestures' to the 'risk of pregnancy' without pausing to consider that there is no inevitable progression from one to the other. The somewhat hollow ring of the efficacy of this procedure as a protective measure may be, at least in part, related to the fact that it is at odds with much of the evidence. If Jeanette was so limited in her understanding, and this was stressed by carers and judges alike, then the operation was arguably unnecessary *for precisely this very reason*. She would simply never have the opportunity to have sexual intercourse. The concern that she would not be supervised sufficiently at the adult training centre which she was shortly due to attend is not entirely consistent with the negative assertions about her uncontrolled behaviour:

De Cruz, SP, 'Sterilisation, wardship and human rights'[115]

... since Jeanette could not even be allowed on the streets unsupervised, as she could not understand traffic, she would certainly need close and constant attention for a great deal of the time. Admittedly, provided she was indoors, the supervision need not be quite so intensive or intrusive, once this alarming prospect of pregnancy no longer existed. Yet given the prospect of sexual exploitation, of course, sterilisation would give no protection against rape or sexual abuse. Furthermore, the operation would certainly not free her, as Lord Hailsham seemed to imply, from 'incarceration', nor give her the liberty to satisfy the sexual desires she was experiencing, when she would certainly experience difficulties in relationships with the opposite sex. If anything, the ruling accentuates her vulnerability and, tragically, results in her being treated very differently from 'normal' people, which would undermine all the advances made in the last decade or so in the achievements of mental health groups in their efforts to integrate people with mental disabilities into the community at large.

---

114 At p 210.
115 (1988) Fam Law 6.

Lord Oliver had said that the concern of the court had been about 'what is in the best interests of this unfortunate young woman and how best she can be given the protection which is essential to her future well being so that she may lead as full a life as her intellectual capacity allows'. It is tempting, however, to conclude that the 'full life' was a life which relieved her carers of many of their duties to protect her.

Might someone in Jeanette's position be in need of protection from exploitation from those responsible for her safety? Yet, contrariwise, a sterilisation would effectively and outrageously 'free her up' for exploitation.

In this regard, see the case of *Re LC (Medical Treatment: Sterilisation)*,[116] where an application for authority to perform a sterilisation operation on a 25-year-old mentally impaired woman, came before the court because of her mother's anxiety following an indecent assault upon her by a member of staff at her former residential home. In the event, the operation was not authorised, as the woman was now resident in a home where the care was described as 'of exceptionally high quality', and, on balance, the operation was not justified. While not disputing the correctness of this decision, is it right for the outcome to depend upon the quality of care? If this woman had been in a home where the quality of care was poor, would the operation have been authorised? If so, the woman would have been exposed to a double jeopardy: the imposition of major, invasive and irreversible surgery, together with risk of sexual abuse and exploitation.

It is also questionable that there was any significant likelihood that Jeanette would have become pregnant, as provocative gestures, whatever they may be, are a long way from a willingness to have sexual intercourse.

It is, of course, possible that an incapable patient may not be suited to pregnancy and motherhood. Likewise, in the case of a capable woman there may be circumstances which would mean that pregnancy and motherhood would be similarly undesirable. In such a case would sterilisation be thought to be the only solution, particularly when she was not sexually active, was aged only 17 and her future development was uncertain? Surely, it is highly unlikely that sterilisation would even be considered at that stage in her life. However, it is essential to compare Jeanette with a capable woman, otherwise Jeanette is being treated differently *because of her mental impairment*. The comparison with 'normal' people was made in the dissenting judgment of Brennan J in *Department of Health v JWB and SMB*, where the majority of the High Court of Australia sanctioned a 'non-therapeutic' sterilisation on a 14-year-old girl:

Department of Health v JWB and SMB[117]

Brennan J: 22 . . . a variety of different purposes may appear which many would regard as of significant value in assessing the 'best interests' of an intellectually disabled child. The purposes which fall into this category can be gathered under the broad description of 'preventative': to prevent the risk of a pregnancy which the child could not properly understand and the concomitant risk of parenthood with responsibilities beyond the capacity of the child to discharge.

These risks are an understandable source of anxiety to parents, guardians and others who have a genuine concern for the welfare of an intellectually disabled child. These are risks which create an understandable anxiety in many parents, guardians and others who have a genuine concern for the welfare of a normal child. In the case of a normal female child, it would be wholly unacceptable to permit sterilisation in order to prevent pregnancy or parenthood, though those events might be thought to be tragedies in particular circumstances by reasonable persons concerned with the welfare of the child. Depending on the circumstances, the use – or, *a fortiori*, the exploitation – of the sexual attributes of a female child may entail tragic

---

116 [1997] 2 FLR 258.
117 (1992) 66 ALJR 300.

consequences, yet the risk or even the likelihood of tragic consequences affords no justification for her sterilisation. What difference does it make that the risk is occasioned by an intellectual disability? The answer to this question depends on the view taken of the proposition earlier set out in the Declaration on the Rights of Mentally Retarded Persons: they are entitled to the same rights as other humans to the maximum degree of feasibility. To accord in full measure the human dignity that is the due of every intellectually disabled girl, her right to retain her capacity to bear a child cannot be made contingent on her imposing no further burdens, causing no more anxiety or creating no further demands. If the law were to adopt a policy of permitting sterilisation in order to avoid the imposition of burdens, the causing of anxiety and the creating of demands, the human rights which foster and protect human dignity in the powerless would lie in the gift of those who are empowered and the law would fail in its function of protecting the weak.

23 . . . In any event, though pregnancy be a possibility, sterilisation, once performed, is a certainty. If a non-therapeutic sterilisation could be justified at all, it could be justified only by the need to avoid a tragedy that is imminent and certain. Such a situation bespeaks a failure of care, and sterilisation is not the remedy for the failure. Nor should it be forgotten that pregnancy and motherhood may have a significance for some intellectually disabled girls quite different from the significance attributed by other people. Though others may see her pregnancy and motherhood as a tragedy, she, in her world, may find in those events an enrichment of her life.

Were the alternatives properly explored by the court, and, indeed, by Jeanette's carers? Most forms of contraceptive pill were thought to be unsuitable because of her obesity, although it was argued by the Official Solicitor that insufficient consideration had been given to the use of a progestogen contraceptive pill less likely to have that effect. The prospect of a *daily* dose, however, was daunting to Jeanette's carers, although other drugs were administered to her for her epilepsy, apparently without undue difficulty. In addition, it was thought undesirable for the contraceptive drug to be administered to her for 30 years or more. De Cruz suggests that the decision may have been made in something approaching indecent haste:

De Cruz, SP, 'Sterilisation, wardship and human rights'[118]

Should the Law Lords have deferred the decision, pending further investigation and observation? The Canadian courts took nearly seven years to decide Eve's case, and it took 16 months for the Supreme Court to produce its judgment, after studying a very wide range of expert opinions and the exhaustive research of the Canadian Law Commission. In their desire not to be faced with a jurisdictional problem once Jeanette reached the age of 18, the English Law Lords only took 28 days to decide the case, but their assumptions about her future conduct may well have led them to discount other possibilities too readily.

As far as adult patients are concerned, the leading case is *Re F (Mental Patient: Sterilisation)*.[119] The facts of that case concerned a female mental patient, a woman in her 30s, who had been assessed as having a mental age of a four to five-year-old. She was a voluntary in-patient in a mental hospital where she had formed what was described as a sexual relationship with a male patient. Both hospital staff, and the patient's mother, felt that she would not be able to cope with childbirth, nor with the subsequent rearing of a child, and that it would, therefore, be in her best interests to be sterilised. A declaration was sought from the court that the proposed sterilisation would be lawful. The unanimous decision of the Court of Appeal and the House of Lords was that the operation was in her best interests.

---

118 (1988) Fam Law 6.
119 [1990] 2 AC 1.

In both this case and the case of Jeanette, the mental age of the women concerned was a crucial factor. The crude application of intelligence assessments to social and emotional development is questionable:

Lee, R and Morgan, D, 'Sterilisation and mental handicap: sapping the strength of the State?'[120]

The problem of mental age

If the Law Lords appear to have been woefully uninformed as to the reality of the present life for mentally handicapped women, they are also less than convincing in showing an understanding of their capacities. One of the most persistent criticisms of the decision in the professional press concerned the emphasis ascribed to the criteria of mental age, and the use to which this was put. Having stated that Jeanette had a mental age of five or six, the judgments in *Re B* seem to treat Jeanette as if she were simply a child of that age. Jeanette, like all other handicapped people, would be expected to demonstrate different functional abilities across a whole range of skills. Intelligence testing offers little information as to many of these abilities, and in so far as it leads to labels such as 'mental age of five', it misdescribes the mentally handicapped person in a discriminatory fashion. Jeanette may not read at all, unlike many six-year-olds, but she may consistently outperform most children of that age in terms of socialisation or self-help. In addition, the criterion of 'mental age' was treated as static. Yet, as Woolrych has observed . . . the use of the discredited concept of 'mental age' is disturbing, since current experiences indicate learning potential is dependent on the quality and variety of services available in developing an understanding of issues such as the connection between sex and having babies.

Nor will the concept of mental age shed much light upon Jeanette's biological and emotional state as a 17 year old woman. While it may be difficult to grapple with the concept of a physically mature woman manifesting childlike intelligence in some respects, we must be careful that we do not discount and become repulsed by the notion that this person manifests adult sexual desires. This is a problem facing many parents of mentally handicapped young women.

Can we expect judges to be aware of the controversy which surrounds the notion of mental age? It is used, in part, to justify an irreversible surgical procedure. This procedure eliminates reproductive capacities, infringing what some would claim to be a basic human right. If the courts are to be used to channel issues of controversial ethical dilemmas, and if they are to legitimate their authority to resolve them, then informed judgment is a starting point.

Of course, the cases of *Re B* and *Re F* were decided before the Mental Capacity Act was enacted. In the context of these types of case, it is now essential to look at the provisions of the Act:

Mental Capacity Act 2005

1 The principles

. . .

(6) Before the act is done, or the decision is made, regard must be had to whether the purpose for which it is needed can be as effectively achieved in a way that is less restrictive of the person's rights and freedom of action.

A Local Authority v K (by the Official Solicitor) Mrs K and Mr K A NHS Trust concerned a 21-year-old woman with Down's syndrome and an associated mild/moderate learning disability. Her parents

---

120 (1988) 15 JLS 229.

became concerned that as she grew older, they would not be able to supervise her sufficiently to avoid her engaging in sexual activity, particularly as she was now a student at a specialist college for people with learning disabilities. After expressing concerns to their GP, a contraceptive hormonal implant was inserted into her arm. As a result of this, K became difficult to manage, and the implant was consequently removed. Both insertion and removal were traumatic for K. Her parents then sought advice from a number of gynaecologists and, following a number of consultations and meetings, the local authority issued proceedings, not least because K's parents were considering removing her from the jurisdiction to seek sterilisation abroad. A number of expert opinions were obtained and, at the time of the judgment, the parties were agreed that it was not in K's best interests to receive any form of contraception at that time, as she was not sexually active, nor was she showing any interest in becoming so. The issue was whether a declaration in respect of sterilisation should be made at that time:

A Local Authority v K (by the Official Solicitor) Mrs K and Mr K A NHS Trust[121]

Cobb J: 32 While sterilisation is particularly effective at preventing pregnancy (5 in 1000 lifetime pregnancy risk if Filshie clips are used), I bear in mind that there are potential complications of the procedure too (in 2 out of 1000 cases there is a major complication such as damage to the bowel or bladder).

33 I have sought to achieve the right balance between protection and empowerment as advised by Dr. Rowlands. Having regard in particular to his carefully expressed opinion, it is my judgment that sterilisation would be a disproportionate (and not the least restrictive) step to achieve contraception for K in the future (absent significant change in her circumstances). Plainly risk management is better than invasive treatment, it is less restrictive. Moreover, I am persuaded by Dr. Rowlands that there are less restrictive methods of achieving the purpose of contraception than sterilisation, and that in the event of a need for contraception, these ought to be attempted.

34 It is in K's interests that I should make this declaration now; I do not believe that it is in K's interests that this issue should be left unresolved; plainly it may need to be litigated at some point in the future but only if there has been a significant change in circumstances.

4.5.3 An abuse of human rights?

It was stated in *Re B* that the case was about removing the 'right to reproduce'. Is there such a right? It is often stated that there is: for example, Article 12 of the European Convention on Human Rights enshrines the 'right to marry and found a family':

Freeman, MD (ed), *Medicine, Ethics and the Law: Current Legal Problems*[122]

Why do we have the rights we have and do we have the right to reproduce? One common answer links rights with interests. Such a view was implicit in Bentham and Ihering and is found in such contemporary writers as Feinberg and McCloskey. Thus, Feinberg writes that 'the sort of beings who can have rights are precisely those who have (or can have) interests'. It is an argument often employed by those who believe that animals have rights. It is also one of the arguments employed by Carby-Hall to demonstrate the Jeanette did not have the right to reproduce. She writes: 'A being can truly be said to have an interest in x, the subject of a potential right, if and only if x will benefit him in the sense of furthering some or all of

---

121 [2013] EWHC 242 (COP).
122 London: Stevens, 1988, p 72.

his present or future desires.' She argues that a necessary condition of possession of a right is at least the capacity to possess the relevant concepts and a desire for that right. Jeanette clearly lacked the former and almost certainly the latter. But is this association of rights and interests justifiable? I think not. What this does not answer is how the having of interests establishes the grounds for having rights. Animals have interests. I have an interest in Middlesex winning the County Cricket Championship. In neither would it make sense to talk of rights. Human beings do not have the same interests. Surely this does not justify an unequal distribution of human rights. I agree with Alan White that 'no valid argument can be given either for including or for excluding children, imbeciles (*inter alia*) . . . as holders of rights on the ground that being capable of having a right ensures or necessitates being capable either of having something in one's interest or of being interested in something. Hence, he concludes, 'the question whether animals, etc . . . can or cannot have interests, either in the sense of something being in their interest or in the sense of their being interested in something, is irrelevant to the question whether they can have rights'.

Freeman is trying to resist the argument that Jeanette had no right to reproduce as long as she was unaware of that so called right. Is awareness of such a right relevant to its existence? If you are deliberately locked in a room and are unaware of this, does it mean that up until the point that you wish to leave you have no right to leave the room? Of course, in the cases of Jeanette and F, it was assumed that they would never wish to leave the room, but it is questionable whether that assumption is justified. Further, the assertion that the right to reproduce meant nothing to her belongs to a dangerous species of argument, that is, 'you have no rights because you are incapable of exercising them, or incapable of exercising them in your own best interests'.

It could be said that there is no *right* to reproduce because such a right is unenforceable. It might be better to say that one has a right to *attempt* to reproduce. However, viewed in this language, would it make sense to say that in the cases of Jeanette and F, they had no right to attempt, because that presupposes a decision-making capacity which they may not have had? It is doubtful whether this is correct. Many children are produced unintentionally. If one was only endorsing a right to attempt to reproduce, it may be argued that such an unintentional pregnancy was less valuable than others. Might the better view be that of Raanan Gillon who argues that there is a prima facie right not to be prevented?[123] The right may not be absolute, but it is arguable that it should only be overridden, in the words of Brennan J, 'to avoid a tragedy that is imminent and certain'.

Is it even necessary to consider the issue in the language of rights? It must be the case that a woman, even if mentally impaired, is entitled to the same amount of respect for her human dignity and physical integrity as any other person. There is a strong argument that subjecting her to invasive surgery on the off-chance that she may become pregnant and 'pregnancy does not mean anything to her' is flouting respect for her dignity as a human being.

The cases of Jeanette and F are very different in at least one important respect. In the case of Jeanette, there was no suggestion that she was sexually active, or indeed, that she wished to be (it does not necessarily follow that she did, despite the so-called provocative gestures – again consider her in comparison with a competent woman). In the case of *Re F (Mental Patient: Sterilisation)*, however, it was said that she was having a sexual relationship. In the Court of Appeal Lord Donaldson stated:

---

123 See 'On sterilising severely mentally handicapped people' (1987) 13 JME 59.

Re F (Mental Patient: Sterilisation)[124]

> **Lord Donaldson MR:** The particular problem in this case arises out of a relationship F has formed with another patient, P. This is of a sexual nature and probably involves sexual intercourse or something close to it on about two occasions a month . . . There is no evidence of distress or distaste on the part of F. It is probable that she obtains some physical enjoyment. When asked what has happened she replies, 'Nice'. Dr McDonald does not regard P as having the state of mind to make him criminally liable and Dr McDonald certainly does not regard what is happening as sexual molestation. Professor Bicknell made the point that F is quite strong willed and if she does not want something she will not have it. Therefore, whilst there is no direct evidence whether F is a purely passive participant or obtains active enjoyment, I incline to the latter view. There is also evidence that F enjoys a cuddle with those with whom she has some bond. The attitude of F's carers to her relationship with P has been neither to encourage nor discourage it. Although there has been some criticism that this is equivocal, it is, in my judgment, entirely understandable and appropriate.

Some may argue that F needed protecting from this just as much as Jeanette may have needed protecting from sexual exploitation. However, too much 'protection' may interfere with the right to a private life, which, for example, is protected by Article 8 of the European Convention on Human Rights. Many legal mechanisms and social conventions allow competent individuals a considerable measure of privacy. It is generally accepted that mentally impaired people should be afforded similar access to privacy and the means to enjoy pleasurable intimate activities as far as is possible.[125] At least, this is accepted in principle; the practical considerations of providing the necessary facilities are less well worked out. This was acknowledged in *Re F* by Lord Donaldson MR, p 9: 'There has been a shift from the paternalistic to a much freer approach. Mentally handicapped people have the same needs, feelings and longings as other people, and this is much more frequently acknowledged nowadays than years ago.'

It was argued by the Official Solicitor that the proper course of action was to put an end to the relationship with P, but surely it would have been wrong to deny F the opportunity of sexual enjoyment simply as a contraceptive measure, as this would have been treating her differently from people deemed to have capacity. The desirability of sterilisation as opposed to other forms of contraception, however, does not follow from the desirability of allowing this woman a degree of sexual freedom. What does follow from the case of *Re F* is that there was a real risk of pregnancy from a sexual relationship which, it appeared, was pleasurable and non-exploitative. The question of obtaining the consent of P (on the assumption that he may have been able to give consent) to the use of contraception, or even vasectomy, was not raised. If P was not capable of consenting, would sterilisation of him have been in his best interests? The decision in *Re A (Mental Patient Sterilisation)*[126] was anticipated by G Douglas in *Law, Fertility and Reproduction*.[127]

The case concerned A, a 28-year-old Down's syndrome man, who was described as being on the borderline of significant and severe impairment. Although he was supervised by his mother at the time of the application to the court, she was concerned that, if her ill health meant that he had to go and live in local authority accommodation, he might have a sexual relationship and would not be able to understand the possible consequences, or cope with them if and when they occurred. The mother applied for a declaration that a vasectomy was

---

124 [1990] 2 AC 1 at p 9.
125 See, for example, O'Brien, J and Tyne, A, *The Principle of Normalisation*, London: Campaign for Mentally Handicapped People, 1981.
126 [2000] 1 FLR 549.
127 London: Sweet & Maxwell, 1991.

in his best interests. There was evidence that the man was sexually aware, but the judge refused the declaration. The Court of Appeal rejected the appeal, holding that male sterilisation on non-therapeutic grounds was not in his best interests. The fact of the birth of a child or disapproval of his conduct would have little effect on him. A further application could be made if he was moved to local authority accommodation and his freedom was unacceptably curtailed to avoid the risk of him fathering a child. However, it was said that, in such circumstances, the likely outcome would be that the female concerned would be subject to extra supervision, rather than him. The Court of Appeal might have gone on to say that the female concerned would probably find herself the subject of court proceedings relating to her own sterilisation. From the point of view of sexual equality, the contrast between this and the female sterilisation cases might give rise to an accusation of unfairness, but doubtless on the application of the best interests test the decision in *Re A* is correct.

A difficulty which does arise in this context is that, under s 7 of the Sexual Offences Act 1956, it is an offence to have sexual intercourse with a mental defective (defined as someone with severe impairment of intelligence and social functioning). This may well place obstacles in the way of the sexual liberation of mentally impaired people. It is suggested that the offence, codified over 40 years ago, does not reflect the changes in attitude towards the 'normalisation' of impaired people alluded to above.

Some other sterilisation cases merit attention. In *Re W (A Mental Patient) (Sterilisation)*[128] Hollis J authorised a sterilisation operation in circumstances where there was no evidence that the woman was involved in any sexual activity. In *Re P (A Minor) (Wardship: Sterilisation)*,[129] the application was in respect of a 17-year-old girl, who was described as having the intellectual development of a six-year-old, but with 'normal' sexual libido. Evidence suggested that she was likely to improve in the development of her 'social' skills. It was also said that pregnancy would be disastrous for her because she would be unlikely agree to an abortion, and to take the child away from her would cause her great distress as she had some maternal feelings. Similarly, in *Re X (Adult Patient: Sterilisation)*,[130] in the case of a severely mentally disabled 31-year-old woman, it was found to be in her best interests to be sterilised when she expressed her desire to have a baby, and had a boyfriend. In *B*, it will be recalled, the fact that Jeanette had *no* maternal feelings was of some importance. We are now faced with a situation where the *presence* of maternal feelings is still disastrous. The question again arises: were these two women being treated the same as women with capacity? An important factor in the case of *P* was that the type of operation proposed was considered to be reversible. If it was clear that pregnancy would be a disaster, what was the significance of reversibility, if it was not to regard the surgical procedure in the same light as contraceptive measures?

In *Re S (Medical Treatment: Adult Sterilisation)*,[131] Johnson J refused to grant a declaration that it would be lawful to sterilise a 22-year-old woman. Although it was contended that she was vulnerable to sexual exploitation, the judge regarded this as a 'speculative' risk. The invasive procedure of sterilisation with its attendant risk of fatality could not be justified without an identifiable risk of pregnancy. In *Re SL (Adult Patient) (Medical Treatment)*,[132] the Court of Appeal upheld an appeal against a declaration that it would be lawful to carry out a hysterectomy on a patient when there was a less invasive alternative available. It should also be noted in this case that, although the trial judge had found that there was an identifiable risk of

---

128 [1993] 1 FLR 381.
129 [1989] 1 FLR 182.
130 [1998] 2 FLR 1124.
131 [1998] 1 FLR 944.
132 [2000] 2 FCR 452.

pregnancy, in the Court of Appeal this was doubted by Dame Butler-Sloss P. Certainly, the risk in *SL* was 'speculative' and not identifiable, as the woman concerned was still living at home with her mother who carefully supervised her, and whose concerns were all about what might happen in the future.

In *Re F* Lord Bridge had suggested (at p 52) that doctors may be under a *duty* to carry out a sterilisation operation, even for what we have described as 'non-therapeutic' reasons, if it was in the best interests of the patient. What is to be made of this suggestion? It is arguable that this could never be the case in respect of non-therapeutic sterilisations, in that the doctor's duty arises from the therapeutic context only.

Finally, it should be noted that failure to consider whether hysterectomies performed on two mentally incapacitated patients were in their best interests has resulted in a finding of serious misconduct by the General Medical Council: *Pembrey v* GMC.[133]

4.5.4 Sterilisation to manage menstruation – therapeutic or non-therapeutic?

In *Re Eve*[134] it was said:

> **La Forest J**: I should perhaps add . . . that sterilisation may, on occasion, be necessary as an adjunct to treatment of a serious malady, but I would underline that this, of course, does not allow for subterfuge or for treatment of some marginal medical problem . . . The recent British Columbia case of *Re K* (1985) 19 DLR (4th) 255, is at best dangerously close to the limits of the permissible.

The case of *Re K* concerned the authorisation of a sterilisation operation on a child to prevent menstruation occurring because the child had an aversion to blood. There have been several other cases where sterilisation has been advocated as a suitable way of managing menstruation. For example, in *Re E (A Minor) (Medical Treatment)*[135] and *Re GF (Medical Treatment)*[136] hysterectomies were authorised in both cases where the women, described as severely handicapped, suffered from excessively heavy periods. In *Re E*, the proposed sterilisation was in respect of a 17-year-old girl. Sir Stephen Brown P held that since it was for therapeutic reasons and not to achieve sterilisation, the parents could consent to the operation, and there was no need for the intervention of the court. In *Re GF*, the woman was an adult. Again, Sir Stephen Brown referred to the therapeutic nature of the procedure, stating that, because of this, there was no need for a declaration as to its lawfulness. It is submitted that the removal of court protection in this way is wrong. It was suggested earlier in this chapter that the therapeutic/ non-therapeutic distinction may not always protect the person lacking capacity. Sterilisations carried out for the purposes of 'menstrual management' do achieve sterilisation, even if this was not the purpose. To remove the need for an order of the court is to deny the person valuable protection from non-therapeutic sterilisations being carried out under the guise of 'therapeutic' purposes.

---

133 [2003] UKPC 60.
134 [1986] 2 SCR 388.
135 [1991] 2 FLR 585.
136 [1992] 1 FLR 293.

The dangers of such operations being used for non-medical reasons have been considered by Natasha Cica:

Cica, N, 'Sterilising the intellectually disabled'[137]

Care must . . . be taken in defining when performing a hysterectomy to prevent menstruation may be considered to be 'therapeutic'. It is submitted that four broad principles should govern this category of sterilisation.

1   The procedure should only be described as therapeutic if performed to alleviate or prevent a recognised clinical condition. Merely 'hygienic' purposes should, for the reasons discussed above, be classified as non-therapeutic. The recognised clinical condition may be a physical condition such as a disorder whose symptoms include excessively heavy or painful periods. Or it may be a psychiatric or psychological condition, in which case 'mere' distress or embarrassment would seem to be insufficient. The distress or disturbance suffered by the woman must be sufficiently serious to pose an identifiable danger to her mental health. Again this is necessary to ensure that the woman's best social interests are not confused with her best medical interests . . . .

2   Such a procedure will only be 'therapeutic' if the clinically recognised condition is already present or is virtually certain to arise in the near future. There must be a 'real possibility' that the condition will arise. The less imminent the clinical condition whose treatment is sought by hysterectomy, the more likely the physical, psychiatric or psychological state of the intellectually disabled woman will change and that hysterectomy will not be required.

3   A hysterectomy will only be 'therapeutic' if it is *necessary* for the above purposes, in that it is a treatment of 'last resort'. There must be no alternative, less invasive treatment which would effectively alleviate the condition. The harm done must be proportionate to the risk of harm avoided. Brennan J's notion of 'proportionality' is clearly the guiding principle here.

4   There must be advice from appropriately qualified medical experts that the above conditions are satisfied. Where the health-threatening condition is psychiatric or psychological, expert advice must be given by an appropriately qualified psychiatrist or psychologist. The expert opinions of general practitioners and gynaecologists alone would be insufficient in such cases.

A proposed hysterectomy was declared to be lawful in the case of *Re ZM and OS (Sterilisation: Patient's Best Interests)*,[138] where it was required to be carried out for both contraceptive purposes and for the elimination of menstruation which was painful and caused her great embarrassment. The woman was aged 19, born with Down's syndrome and about to move into a residential unit to achieve more independence. She also had a boyfriend. The procedure was said to be in her best interests, as her periods brought her nothing but pain and discomfort, she would be incapable of looking after a child, and pregnancy and childbirth and the removal of the child would be a catastrophe, as would the emotional and psychological consequences of an abortion.

4.5.5 Abortion and contraception

It was stated in *Re SG (A Patient)*[139] that the provisions of the Abortion Act 1967 are an adequate safeguard for an incapable woman, and there is no need of court authorisation. It is submitted that they are not. In addition, assuming that the woman (although incapable) has

---

137 (1993) 1 Med L Rev 186, p 198.
138 [2000] 1 FLR 523.
139 [1993] 4 Med LR 75.

expressed a wish to have the child, there is something highly distasteful about forcing her to submit to an abortion. While there may be many occasions when an abortion will be the best course of action for an incapable woman, it is suggested that the vigilance necessary in cases of sterilisation should be present when considering the performance of an abortion.[140]

See Chapter 8

In *Re SS (Adult: Medical Treatment)*[141] the court had to consider the case of an adult woman who suffered from schizophrenia and who was detained under the MHA 1983. She was 24 weeks pregnant. Her application to the court sought two declarations: first, that she lacked the capacity to make a decision about the termination of her pregnancy; and, secondly, that it was in her best interests. It was accepted by the Official Solicitor, on her behalf, that she lacked decision-making capacity. As will be seen in Chapter 8, 24 weeks is a significant time in the duration of a pregnancy. Unless certain special conditions apply, terminations cannot take place after this time. Having a termination at such a late time entailed going into labour and giving birth to the unviable foetus. Other factors which were considered relevant by the court were: the woman had already had four children, three of whom lived with the father, the fourth had been given up for adoption; the child would be of mixed race and therefore more difficult to place for adoption; she had expressed a desire for a termination and believed the child to be dead. One psychiatrist who had examined her had to consider the provisions of the Abortion Act 1967 (as amended) and weigh up the likely effect of the baby being removed at birth against the termination of the pregnancy, and concluded that it was not clear that a termination was in her best interests. Another psychiatrist, instructed by the Official Solicitor, reported that the woman had said that she would kill herself if she did not have a termination. The woman's responsible medical officer (under the MHA 1983) considered the matter to be so finely balanced that he did not feel he could express an opinion one way or the other. Wall J held that the correct approach was to assess the various risks but, in this case, because the evidence of the medical experts did not come down on one side or another, then it followed that it could not be said that a termination was in her best interests. It was also said that, because the problem of terminating late pregnancies could arise frequently in psychiatric hospitals, each hospital should have a protocol for dealing with them. Two observations can be made. First, it would have been a late termination, that is later than 24 weeks, and, therefore, different considerations apply as far as complying with the Abortion Act 1967 is concerned. Secondly, the woman had decided that she wanted a termination. Although lacking capacity, her views should be taken into account. If the other matters are finely balanced, there is some merit in saying that her wishes should tilt the balance.

See Chapter 8

4.5.6 The Mental Capacity Act 2005 to the rescue?

We have already suggested that the safeguards within the Mental Capacity Act might not be tough enough to protect vulnerable people from exploitation. We have also highlighted public disquiet about highly sensitive decisions being made about medical treatment and personal welfare behind the closed doors of the Court of Protection.

It is pertinent, therefore, to refer to a recent case where Bodey J was critical of a local authority who wanted a married woman aged 29 with an IQ of 53 to be sedated, taken from her home and have contraception imposed on her against her will. The woman had already had two

---

140 See, eg, the remarks of Lord Donaldson MR in the Court of Appeal in *Re F (Mental Patient: Sterilisation)* [1990] 2 AC 1 at 19.
141 [2002] 1 FCR 73.

children that had been taken into care and the local authority did not believe that she (with or without her husband) was capable of developing the necessary 'parenting skills'.

A Local Authority v Mrs A, by her Litigation Friend, the Official Solicitor, Mr A[142]

Bodey J: 77 It is obvious on the facts of this case, that any step towards long-term court imposed contraception by way of physical coercion, with its affinity to enforced sterilisation and shades of social engineering, would raise profound questions about state intervention in private and family life. Whilst the issue of the use of force has not been argued out at this hearing I cannot, on these facts, presently see how it could be acceptable. Following my views expressed along these lines during the hearing, the Local Authority has so formulated its claim that for the moment anyway I am only asked to declare that it would be in the interim best interests of Mrs A to have contraception, if she consents . . . .

78. . . It is accepted by the Local Authority, that if Mrs A became pregnant, there would be a pre-birth assessment of her and Mr A, and that (whilst it may be possible to speculate) it is impossible to say now what would emerge. It might therefore be concluded that they could with much support bring up a child, or perhaps that a child might be able to be kept within the extended family. Striking a balance of advantage and disadvantage, I do not see that any order at all is justified at this point about contraception. Such an order could only be made on the basis of a gut-feeling that it would be 'kinder' to Mr and Mrs A if Mrs A were to use it, which is not in my judgment an acceptable approach. Even if there were any point in the order sought . . . I certainly do not think the court should intervene at a stage when Mr A has not yet been included in any ability-appropriate discussion or help on the contraception issue; when Mr and Mrs A have not yet had any therapeutic input as a couple about it (as recommended by Dr K), nor about their relationship generally; and when they have not yet had the chance to be helped to understand this judgment. I do not propose therefore to make any order about Mrs A's 'best interests' at this stage. If she were to become pregnant, so be it: matters would take their course in the way I have described, with a pre-birth assessment of Mr and Mrs A's joint parenting abilities and the Local Authority taking such steps on the strength of it as appeared appropriate.

Apart from the last case, all of the cases considered above are prior to the Mental Capacity Act, and some of them go back to the 1970s and 1980s; so it might be said that the very real concerns and implications raised by them have gone away in more cautious and, perhaps, more enlightened times. However, the final case shows that, thanks to the developments in contraceptive techniques, less draconian measures than sterilisation might now be the norm. Nevertheless, the problem and the impetus to solve it coercively (albeit often well-meaningly) remain the same.

THINK POINT

The cases we have examined are all prior to the coming into force of the Mental Capacity Act 2005. Do you think that vulnerable patients are now much better protected under the new legislation?

---

142 [2010] EWHC 1549 (Fam).

Summary of key points

1   Prior to the Mental Capacity Act 2005, decisions about medical treatment for adults who lacked capacity were dealt with under the common law of necessity, but this was interpreted as acting in the best interests of the patient. Those common law cases are still relevant in the interpretation of the Mental Capacity Act 2005.
2   The Mental Capacity Act embraces and develops the concept of best interests and puts it on a statutory footing.
3   The Mental Capacity Act contains provisions (the Deprivation of Liberty Safeguards) that are designed to protect patients, or people in residential units, who might be deprived of liberty because of their mental incapacity.
4   The best interests test can include the substituted judgment test as this forms part of the Mental Capacity Act criteria, but the *Bolam* test does not govern best interests as there can be only one course of action that is in the patient's best interests.
5   Parents can consent to treatment on behalf of their children. The Family Law Reform Act 1969 states that children of the age of 16 can consent to treatment. However, the Court of Appeal has held that until they reach the age of 18 they are still within the jurisdiction of the court, and the same court has held that they cannot refuse treatment in circumstances where doctors and parents wish them to have it.
6   Certain forms of treatment or procedures that might be regarded as 'non-therapeutic' must be scrutinised carefully when carried out on incapable patients. We have given the control of fertility as an example.

 Further reading

Alghrani, A, Case, P and Fanning, J (2016) 24(3) special issue, 'Editorial: The Mental Capacity Act 2005 – ten years on'.

Bartlett, P, *Blackstone's Guide to the Mental Capacity Act*, 2nd edn, Oxford: Oxford University Press, 2008.

Department for Constitutional Affairs, *Mental Capacity Act Code of Practice, 2007*, London: The Stationery Office.

Department of Health and Office of the Public Guardian, *Deprivation of liberty safeguards: A guide for hospitals and care homes*, 2009.

Donnelly, M, 'Best interests, patient participation and the Mental Capacity Act 2005' (2009) 17(1) Medical Law Review 1.

Elliston, S, *Best Interests of the Child in Healthcare*, New York: Routledge-Cavendish, 2007.

Jones, R, *Mental Capacity Act Manual*, 6th edn, London: Sweet & Maxwell, 2014.

Sandland, R, 'Sexual capacity: the management of monsters' (2013) 76(6) Medical Law Review 981.

Chapter 5

Confidentiality, privacy and access to medical records

5.1 Confidentiality – the duty

5.1.1 The ethical obligation

It is not only of academic interest to look at the ethical justifications for the obligation of confidence, it is also important to keep them in mind when examining the circumstances in which the obligation can be lawfully breached, and to consider whether the breaches in question can also be justified on ethical grounds.

As we have seen, the doctrine of utilitarianism assesses the ethics of a course of action on the basis that it will result in the best consequences overall. In the context of confidentiality, therefore, the obligation is justified by the utility of doctors keeping medical information secret. The argument is that if there were no assurance of secrecy, then patients would be reluctant to seek medical advice and treatment, or would be less than frank when doing so. This would, it is argued, have an adverse effect on the health of society. The argument is described by Raanan Gillon:

Gillon, R, *Philosophical Medical Ethics*[1]

Why should doctors from the time of Hippocrates to the present have promised to keep their patients' secrets? If confidentiality is not a moral good in itself what moral good does it serve? The commonest justification for the duty of medical confidentiality is undoubtedly consequentialist: people's better health, welfare, the general good, and overall happiness are more likely to be attained if doctors are fully informed by their patients, and this is more likely if doctors undertake not to disclose their patients' secrets. Conversely, if patients did not believe that doctors would keep their secrets then either they would not divulge embarrassing but potentially medically important information, thus reducing their chances of getting the best medical care, or they would disclose such information and feel anxious and unhappy at the prospect of their secrets being made known.

The utilitarian view is particularly appropriate to confidentiality as it will readily admit that the duty is not absolute and can be breached in certain circumstances. It would be argued that the breach is justified when the utility of disclosure outweighs the utility produced by keeping the confidences. As will be seen, the only legal justification at common law for disclosure is either that the patient has consented, or that it is in the public interest to disclose. The language of the public interest defence has a strong utilitarian flavour: *AG v Guardian Newspapers (No 2)*,[2] *per* Lord Goff:

Lord Goff: . . . although the basis of the law's protection of confidence is that there is a public interest that confidences should be preserved and protected by the law, nevertheless that public interest may be outweighed by some other countervailing public interest which favours disclosure.

As we have already seen, utilitarianism can be contrasted with deontological theories in which duty rather than purpose is the fundamental concept of ethics. Gillon states:

Gillon, R, *Philosophical Medical Ethics*[3]

Deontologists . . . are likely to base their arguments for confidentiality not just (if at all) on welfare considerations but also on the moral principle of respect for autonomy or sometimes on a putatively independent principle of respect for privacy, which is seen as a fundamental moral requirement in itself. Thus, while the

---

1 Chichester: John Wiley, 1986.
2 [1990] AC 109, at 282.
3 See n 1 above.

principle of medical confidentiality is not defended as a moral end in itself, it is defended by utilitarians and deontologists alike as a means to some morally desirable end [such as] the general welfare, respect for people's autonomy, or respect for their privacy.

Ethical issues arising around the area of confidentiality are reflected in the various ethical codes referred to in Chapter 1. The Hippocratic Oath states: 'all that may come to my knowledge in the exercise of my profession or outside of my profession or in daily commerce with men, which ought not to be spread abroad, I will keep secret and will never reveal'. The Declaration of Geneva contains a similar statement.

One grey area surrounds disclosure within the family, ie is a doctor breaching confidences if the disclosure is only made to a spouse? It is here that the interface between law and pragmatism reflects many of the essential difficulties of medical law. What is a doctor to do, say, when faced with a distressed spouse of a terminally ill patient? If the patient has informed the doctor that he does not wish any form of disclosure to the spouse, then although any subsequent conversations with that spouse may be difficult, it is quite clear that the doctor must refuse to discuss his patient's medical condition. However, in the absence of that express request on the part of the patient, under what principle does the doctor justify discussing the patient's medical condition with relatives of the patient? In the case of *Re S (Hospital Orders: Court's Jurisdiction)*,[4] it was held that blood ties conferred no right to determine the course of treatment or care, and this would surely extend to the acquisition of confidential information. It seems that the law does not sanction such disclosure, unless one can argue that there is some form of implied or tacit consent.

5.1.1.1 The General Medical Council's guidance

The General Medical Council (GMC) issues guidance to doctors on their obligations in respect of confidentiality, and much of the guidance is co-extensive with general principles of law,[5] but it must be remembered that guidance issued by the GMC does not purport to be an account of the law. However, there is no doubt that the guidance has persuasive authority (see *W v Egdell*[6]).

5.1.2 The legal obligation of privacy and the European Convention on Human Rights

A rights-based approach might regard the duty of keeping confidences as a respect for the right to privacy. There is no right to privacy in English common law, although in practice much that is private can be protected in other ways, for example, the tort of trespass, nuisance and so on. Furthermore, the European Convention on Human Rights (ECHR), incorporated into English law by the Human Rights Act 1998, protects the right to a 'private life' (Article 8).

What is the difference between a right to privacy and a right to have confidential information protected? The law imposes a number of requirements in order for a cause of action to arise for breach of confidence, and these criteria mean that, for example, press photographers owe no duty of confidence unless the photography takes place in 'confidential circumstances', or there had been a prior agreement not to publish. If neither of these apply, only a right to privacy can offer protection from publication.

---

4 [1995] 3 All ER 290.
5 General Medical Council, *Confidentiality*, London: GMC, 2009.
6 [1990] Ch 359.

Article 8 of the ECHR states:

> 1 Everyone has the right to respect for his private and family life, his home and his correspondence.
> 2 There shall be no interference by a public authority with the exercise of this right except such as is in accordance with the law and is necessary in a democratic society in the interests of national security, public safety or the economic well being of the country, for the prevention of disorder or crime for the protection of health or morals, or for the protection of the rights and freedoms of others.

In *Z v Finland*,[7] the European Court of Human Rights stated:

> The protection of personal data, not least medical data, is of fundamental importance to a person's enjoyment of his or her right to respect for private and family life as guaranteed by Article 8 of the Convention . . . Without such protection, those in need of medical assistance may be deterred from revealing such information of a personal and intimate nature as may be necessary in order to receive appropriate treatment and, even, from seeking such assistance, thereby endangering their own health and in the case of transmissible diseases, that of the community.

The facts were as follows. Mrs Z was the wife of a man who had been accused of attempted manslaughter by raping his victims and knowingly infecting them with the HIV virus. For evidential purposes, it was necessary to obtain evidence from Mrs Z's doctors and to obtain her medical records. The court limited the confidentiality of the trial record to ten years, and in its judgment the court disclosed Mrs Z's identity. It was common ground that there had been a violation of Mrs Z's rights under Article 8; the issue for the European Court to decide was whether this could be justified under Article 8(2). It was accepted that the court action was 'in accordance with the law' so the issue was whether it was 'necessary in a democratic society'. The taking of evidence from the doctors and the obtaining of the medical records was held not to breach Article 8(2). However, limiting confidentiality of the trial record to ten years was a disproportionate interference with her right and the disclosure of her identity was not justified at all. See also *I v Finland*,[8] where the court held that it was fundamental to the right to privacy for states to take positive steps to protect medical confidentiality. See too the case of *Colak v Germany*,[9] which is considered in detail below at 5.2.2.6.

In *MS v Sweden*[10] medical records relating to a woman's gynaecological condition held by a clinic had been requested by, and disclosed to, the social security department dealing with a claim of hers for state industrial injury benefit. She had not been consulted about this, and the European Court held that this clear breach under Article 8(1) was, nevertheless, justified under Article 8(2) on the basis that the needs of the state (to avoid paying funds from the public purse to undeserving cases) were for the economic well-being of the country. It is arguable, however, that it is disproportionate to obtain medical records in this way, without prior reference to the claimant. A more appropriate way of achieving the same end would have been for such claims to be subject to the consent of the claimant to the disclosure of all relevant medical records (the case of MS had, at least in part, given rise to the court action because the records disclosed had contained information about a wholly irrelevant abortion).

---

7 (1998) 25 EHRR 371.
8 (2009) 48 EHRR 31.
9 (07714/01), unreported, March 2009.
10 (1997) 45 BMLR 133.

It might be argued that, given the protection of Article 8, the obligation of confidence is redundant. However, the language of confidentiality is still used by the courts.[11] Further, the limitation placed upon Article 8 by Article 8(2) means that there will be circumstances when there can be justification for breaching Article 8 and these circumstances will frequently be analogous to the justification for breaching confidences so that the legal framework is still pertinent. In *Rose and another v Secretary of State for Health and Another*[12] the claimants, who had been conceived by artificial insemination, were seeking disclosure of non-identifying information about sperm donors and, where possible, information that would actually identify such donors. They had requested such information from the Secretary of State who had declined to provide it, and they had commenced an action for judicial review. They argued, first, that the state had an obligation to provide non-identifying information and, secondly, that the state had an obligation to establish a voluntary contact register similar to the contact register available to adopted children. Scott Baker J held that this information engaged Article 8 because such information went to the heart of their identity, and allowed the case to go forward. However, he declined to make a declaration of incompatibility under the Human Rights Act 1998, leaving it open to a court to decide on the basis of the specific facts before it. He did, however, hint strongly that because the donor semen would have been obtained under circumstances of confidentiality, Article 8(2) limitations would weigh heavily in the balance. A further example is the case of *R (on the application of John Wooder) v Dr Graham Fegetter and the Mental Health Act Commission*[13] where Potter LJ stated that, on the question of the patient's right to information regarding s 58 treatment under the Mental Health Act (MHA) 1983, there was no need to invoke Article 8 as the common law provides the necessary protection. See the judgments of Lords Nicholl and Waler in *OBG & anor v Allan & others*.[14]

5.1.3 The legal obligation of confidentiality

The law of the obligation to keep confidences is not easy to categorise. It is sometimes regarded as an application of equitable principles, sometimes as belonging to the law of tort and/or contract. There is no doubt that the obligation may arise under the law of contract, either expressly or impliedly, but it is clear that it is wider than that. Certainly, as far as medicine is concerned, if it were contract-based only, there would be no legal obligation to keep confidences within the context of National Health Service treatment.[15] There has been much academic debate on the subject:

Gurry, F, *Breach of Confidence*[16]

The jurisdictional basis of the action for breach of confidence has been a source of lingering uncertainty and controversy. Contract, equity and property have at different times each provided the basis on which the courts have granted relief. In some cases, a mixture of these bases has been relied on. Thus, in *Alperton Rubber Co v Manning* Peterson J referred to the defendant's conduct as 'a breach of trust or confidence, and . . . a breach of the implied provision in all contracts of service that the employee will observe the rules of honesty'; and, in *Prince Albert v Strange*, the court founded the defendants' liability first on property, secondly on a 'breach of trust, confidence or contract'.

---

11 See, eg, *A Health Authority v X and others* [2001] EWCA Civ 2014.
12 (2003) 69 BMLR 83.
13 [2002] EWCA Civ 554.
14 [2007] UKHL 21.
15 See *Pfizer Corp v Ministry of Health* [1965] AC 512.
16 Oxford: Clarendon Press, 1984.

The lack of clarity in the law led to a Law Commission inquiry which reported in 1981.[17] The Commission made a number of recommendations, the principal one being that there be a new statutory tort of breach of confidence. No government action has ever been taken on this.

The obligation of confidence, whatever its origin, although not absolute, is free standing, in that the preservation of confidence itself is in the public interest and therefore an end in itself. However, it can conflict with other matters of public interest. It is important to stress that, when conflicts arise, they are conflicts between two competing *public* interests, not between private and public interests:

Scott, R, 'Introduction'[18]

The law of confidentiality, like the law of negligence and the law of nuisance, requires a balance to be struck. The balance will, on both sides, involve public and private interests. The newspapers that wanted to publish extracts from *Spycatcher* had a private commercial interest in doing so. But there was also a public interest in freedom of speech. On the other side there was a public interest in the protection of the secrets of the security service (no private interest since the litigant was the Government). In the *Francome* case, the plaintiff had a private interest in maintaining the privacy of his telephone conversations but, ranged on the same side, there was a public interest that private telephone conversations should not be the subject of eavesdropping. On the other side, the *Daily Mirror* could rely, in aid of its own private interest, on the public interest in the disclosure of alleged wrongdoing. These are examples to make the point that every case where the law of confidentiality is invoked requires the judge to strike a balance between competing interests.

The essential elements of the law of confidentiality can be summarised by the statement in *AG v Guardian Newspapers (No 2)*,[19] *per* Lord Goff:

Lord Goff: I start with the broad general principle (which I do not intend in any way to be definitive) that a duty of confidence arises when confidential information comes to the knowledge of a person (the confidant) in circumstances where he has notice, or is held to have agreed, that the information is confidential, with the effect that it would be just in all the circumstances that he should be precluded from disclosing the information to others . . .

[In addition to] this broad general principle, there are three limiting principles to which I wish to refer. The first limiting principle (which is rather an expression of the scope of the duty) is highly relevant to this appeal. It is that the principle of confidentiality only applies to information to the extent that it is confidential. In particular, once it has entered what is usually called the public domain (which means no more than that the information in question is so generally accessible that, in all the circumstances, it cannot be regarded as confidential) then, as a general rule, the principle of confidentiality can have no application to it . . .

The second limiting principle is that the duty of confidence applies neither to useless information, nor to trivia . . .

The third limiting principle is of far greater importance. It is that, although the basis of the law's protection of confidence is that there is a public interest that confidences should be preserved and protected by the law, nevertheless that public interest may be outweighed by some other countervailing public interest which favours disclosure.

---

17 Law Commission, *Breach of Confidence*, Report No 110, Cmnd 8388, London: HMSO, 1981.
18 Clarke, L (ed), *Confidentiality and the Law*, London: LLP, 1990.
19 [1990] AC 109, pp 281–82.

In *Douglas v Hello! Ltd*,[20] Sedley LJ said (at 1001) that developments in privacy law mean that the new approach to confidentiality focusses upon the protection of human autonomy and dignity.

There can be no doubt that the doctor–patient relationship gives rise to an obligation of confidence which fits clearly into the criteria applied generally in the law. *Hunter v Mann*[21] confirmed such an obligation which was reiterated in *AG v Guardian Newspapers (No 2)*,[22] *per* Lord Keith:

> **Lord Keith:** The law has long recognised that an obligation of confidence can arise out of particular relationships. Examples are the relationships of doctor and patient, priest and penitent, solicitor and client, banker and customer.

The uncontroversial nature of the obligation, therefore, means that generally problems will only arise when decisions have to be made which will breach the obligation and whether the breach can be justified. Indeed, it may be said that the doctor's duty of confidence is over-determined in that it stems both from the quality of the information and from the circumstances in which it is acquired, each of which is independently sufficient. It follows that, although not usually the subject of litigation, there may be difficulties, first, if the information is not *medical* information and, secondly, if it has been imparted in circumstances other than a doctor–patient consultation.

5.1.3.1 The confidential information

The law on confidentiality will protect a variety of types of information, imparted in a variety of different situations. Information acquired in the confidential circumstances of an employment relationship, for example, will be protected, as will that acquired in the course of an intimate domestic relationship. The latter need not be a marriage, nor even a heterosexual relationship. This was examined in the case of *Stephens v Avery*,[23] where it was held that information relating to sexual conduct (in that case, a lesbian relationship) could be the subject of a legally enforceable duty of confidentiality.

The case of *Campbell v Mirror Group Newspapers Ltd*[24] is a good illustration of the way in which 'medical confidentiality' can be wider than that which is engendered in the private consultations between healthcare professionals and patients. Naomi Campbell, a well-known 'supermodel', brought an action against a newspaper that published photographs of her leaving a clinic where she had been receiving treatment, on the basis that this was a breach of her Article 8 right to privacy under the European Convention. The newspaper argued that prohibition of publication breached Article 10 of the Convention, ie freedom of expression. Publication was necessary, it was argued, because she had previously denied having a drug problem, and the photographs showed this to have been a lie. By a majority, the House of Lords found that her privacy had been unjustifiably infringed.

---

20 [2001] QB 967.
21 [1974] QB 767.
22 [1990] AC 109, at p 255.
23 [1988] Ch 449.
24 [2004] 2 AC 457.

Campbell v Mirror Group Newspapers Ltd[25]

Lord Hope:

Was the information confidential?

88 The information contained in the article consisted of the following five elements: (1) the fact that Miss Campbell was a drug addict; (2) the fact that she was receiving treatment for her addiction; (3) the fact that the treatment which she was receiving was provided by Narcotics Anonymous; (4) details of the treatment – for how long, how frequently and at what times of day she had been receiving it, the nature of it and extent of her commitment to the process; and (5) a visual portrayal by means of photographs of her when she was leaving the place where treatment had been taking place.

89 The trial judge drew the line between the first two and the last three elements. Mr Caldecott for Miss Campbell said that he was content with this distinction. So the fact that she was a drug addict was open to public comment in view of her denials, although he maintained that this would normally be treated as a medical condition that was entitled to protection. He accepted that the fact that she was receiving treatment for the condition was not in itself intrusive in this context. Moreover disclosure of this fact in itself could not harm her therapy. But he said that the line was crossed as soon as details of the nature and frequency of the treatment were given, especially when these details were accompanied by a covertly taken photograph which showed her leaving one of the places where she had been undertaking it. This was an area of privacy where she was entitled to be protected by an obligation of confidence ...

98 Where the person is suffering from a condition that is in need of treatment one has to try, in order to assess whether the disclosure would be objectionable, to put oneself into the shoes of a reasonable person who is in need of that treatment. Otherwise the exercise is divorced from its context. The fact that no objection could be taken to disclosure of the first two elements in the article does not mean that they must be left out of account in a consideration as to whether disclosure of the other elements was objectionable. The article must be read as a whole along with the photographs to give a proper perspective to each element. The context was that of a drug addict who was receiving treatment. It is her sensibilities that needed to be taken into account. Critical to this exercise was an assessment of whether disclosure of the details would be liable to disrupt her treatment. It does not require much imagination to appreciate the sense of unease that disclosure of these details would be liable to engender, especially when they were accompanied by a covertly taken photograph. The message that it conveyed was that somebody, somewhere, was following her, was well aware of what was going on and was prepared to disclose the facts to the media. I would expect a drug addict who was trying to benefit from meetings to discuss her problem anonymously with other addicts to find this distressing and highly offensive ...

124 Any person in Miss Campbell's position, assuming her to be of ordinary sensibilities but assuming also that she had been photographed surreptitiously outside the place where she been receiving therapy for drug addiction, would have known what they were and would have been distressed on seeing the photographs. She would have seen their publication, in conjunction with the article which revealed what she had been doing when she was photographed and other details about her engagement in the therapy, as a gross interference with her right to respect for her private life. In my opinion this additional element in the publication is more than enough to outweigh the right to freedom of expression which the defendants are asserting in this case.

Conclusion

125 Despite the weight that must be given to the right to freedom of expression that the press needs if it is to play its role effectively, I would hold that there was here an infringement of Miss Campbell's right to privacy that cannot be justified. In my opinion publication of the third, fourth and fifth elements in the article (see para 88) was an invasion of that right for which she is entitled to damages. I would allow the appeal and restore the orders that were made by the trial judge.

---

25 [2004] 2 AC 457, at p 481.

Information concerning the sexual conduct of a patient, if imparted to a doctor in circumstances of confidentiality, will be protected, even though it is not medical information. The Court of Appeal decision in *R v Wilson*[26] raises this issue. In that case, the defendant appealed against a conviction for actual bodily harm under s 47 of the Offences Against the Person Act 1861. He had been charged as a result of marking his wife's buttocks with his initials by use of a hot knife. This was done with her consent and, it appeared from the case reports, at her specific request. Although the appeal was concerned with the applicability of the decision in *R v Brown*,[27] the implications for medical confidentiality arise from the fact that the matter appears to have come to the attention of the police from a report made to them by her doctor, who became aware of the marks during the course of a medical examination.[28]

If the police were informed of this by the doctor, without the consent of the woman concerned, then here was a potential breach of confidentiality. The fact that the information was not strictly medical would not protect the doctor because, first, on the basis of *Stephens v Avery*, it has the necessary quality of confidence and, secondly, it was imparted in the circumstances of a medical consultation.

In *R v Department of Health, ex p Source Informatics Ltd*,[29] the Court of Appeal had to decide whether disclosure of patient information which had been anonymised breached the obligation of confidence. The company had obtained anonymised patient data from pharmacists and doctors which had been extracted from prescription forms. The information was used to create a database for the use of pharmaceutical companies. The Department of Health produced guidance which stated that disclosure of anonymised patient information still amounted to a breach of confidence. Source Informatics challenged this by way of judicial review. The judge at first instance took the view that the Department of Health was correct. However, the Court of Appeal allowed the appeal, stating that the touchstone as to whether there has been a breach of confidence is the 'conscience' of the discloser. Arguably, as Fennell points out,[30] it is correct that there is no breach, but the reason is that it is not against the patients' interests and not something to do with the good faith on the part of the discloser. Note that, in 1997, the Department of Health published *On the Review of Patient-Identifiable Information* (the 'Caldicott Report'),[31] which made a number of recommendations on how to safeguard confidentiality by the anonymisation of the information, and which provides for so-called 'Caldicott guardians' within the NHS to supervise and take responsibility for information systems.

5.1.3.2 The circumstances in which the information is acquired

It may be that it is not clear that the circumstances are such as to amount to 'confidential' circumstances. The inadvertent acquisition of information, which clearly has the necessary quality of confidence about it, binds the recipient; see Lord Goff's judgment in *AG v Guardian Newspapers (No 2)*.[32]

The case of *R v Wilson* is, again, interesting in relation to this point, as it raises the possibility of a doctor being obliged towards a third party when he acquires confidential information in the context of a medical consultation:

---

26 [1996] 3 WLR 125.
27 [1993] 2 All ER 75.
28 See (1996) *The Times*, 5 March.
29 [2000] 1 All ER 786.
30 (2000) 8 Med L Rev 155.
31 London: DoH, 1997.
32 [1990] AC 109, at p 282.

Wheat, K, 'Can paternalism ever justify a breach of confidence?'[33]

Extension of duty

Another difficult question raised to which there is no clear answer is the position of the husband of the patient in this case. Could it be argued that the doctor owed him a duty of confidence? Further, would it make any difference if he were also a patient of the doctor? To look at the latter question first, if the doctor–patient relationship is to make any difference, then it must be the case that the duty extends to any information obtained about a patient which has the necessary quality of confidence.

It cannot be said with any degree of certainty that this reflects the legal position. Gurry, for example, says that, although the duty is not limited to information acquired directly from the patient but extends to information from other sources, that further information must have been picked up by the doctor by way of his or her position as the patient's doctor. Kennedy and Grubb interpret this as extending to information obtained from third parties who know of the doctor–patient relationship, but pass no comment as to whether it would extend to non-medical information.

Here, the information would not have been obtained by the doctor by virtue of his status as the patient's doctor, but as another patient's doctor, and, although the third party here, namely the wife, would have known about the doctor–patient relationship, the information was not of a medical nature. Given the difficulties, therefore, in arguing that the duty owed is a duty owed *qua* doctor, perhaps it is open to the husband to rely upon the general law of confidentiality and a duty owed to him regardless of him being a patient of the doctor concerned.

. . .

Elements of a breach of confidence action

[Referring to the *Guardian* criteria] [t]here is no difficulty in satisfying the first limb of the test as the information concerned intimate details of a sexual relationship, which will possess the necessary quality of confidence. As to the second limb, although a consultation between doctor and patient will usually impart an obligation of confidence, it is arguable that the circumstances only impart the obligation by the doctor towards the patient . . .

If it is clear from its nature that information is confidential, then a third party should be bound by it (see *Saltman Engineering v Campbell Engineering*),[34] so it is hard to see how the fact that it is not acquired by chance, but in the context of another, different set of confidential circumstances should make any difference.

THINK POINT

What are the essential differences between the legal concepts of privacy and confidentiality?

5.1.4 Statutory obligations of confidence

Good, utilitarian, public health arguments can sometimes justify a specific emphasis on confidentiality via statutory means. An example of this is contained within the National Health Service (Venereal Disease) Regulations 1974, SI 1974/29:

---

33 (1997) 3(3) Health Care Risk Report 12.
34 [1963] 3 All ER 413.

National Health Service (Venereal Disease) Regulations 1974, SI 1974/29

Confidentiality of information

2   Every NHS Trust or NHS Foundation Trust . . . shall take all necessary steps to secure that any information capable of identifying an individual obtained by officers with respect to persons examined or
treated for any sexually transmitted disease shall not be disclosed except:

a   for the purpose of communicating that information to a medical practitioner or to a person
employed under the direction of a medical practitioner in connection with the treatment of
persons suffering from such disease or the prevention of the spread thereof; and

b   for the purpose of such treatment or prevention.

Kennedy and Grubb comment as follows:

Kennedy, I and Grubb, A, *Medical Law*[35]

This regulation was introduced so as to give statutory emphasis to the obligation of confidence in this
area of medical practice.

. . .

A small, but important, point to notice is that the obligation of confidence under the Regulations
applies to any disease which is 'sexually transmitted'. If this is so, a patient who is HIV positive may need
to look to the common law for protection of his confidence if he became infected by some other means
as, for example, if he is a haemophiliac or has otherwise become HIV positive as a result of an infected
blood donation. Alternatively a 'sexually transmitted disease' within the Regulations could be said to be
one usually transmitted through sexual contact but which may be transmitted by other means. Blood, for
example, may be infected with syphilis and transfused into someone who then develops the disease. The
disease remains a 'sexually transmitted disease'. On this analysis HIV infection would be within the Regulations regardless of the means of infection. (See *X v Y* [1988] RPC 379, in which Rose J assumes the latter
to be the case.)

5.1.5 Incapable patients and confidentiality

5.1.5.1 Children

The ability of children to consent to medical treatment was dealt with in Chapters 3 and 4. The
leading case is *Gillick v West Norfolk and Wisbech AHA*,[36] and it is important to remember that
this case was about confidentiality as well as consent. It will be recalled that Mrs Gillick objected
to a DHSS circular which stated that a doctor, acting in good faith, would not be acting unlawfully if he prescribed contraceptives to a girl under the age of 16 and that, exceptionally, this
could be done without informing the child's parents, as the principle of confidentiality applied
between a doctor and a patient under the age of 16.

As we have seen, the *Gillick* case has been subject to a number of interpretations by the
Court of Appeal which have sought to limit its application to one of protection for doctors
acting in good faith, rather than an assertion of a child's right to self-determination when he

---

35 London: Butterworths, 3rd edn, 2000.
36 [1986] AC 112.

has the necessary capacity. Although these later cases *(Re R (A Minor) (Wardship: Medical Treatment)*[37] and *Re W (A Minor) (Medical Treatment)*)[38] were not about confidentiality, they have implications for this area of medical law. In *Re R*, Lord Donaldson said at p 186:

> **Lord Donaldson:** . . . the judges treated *Gillick's* case as deciding that a *'Gillick* competent' child has a right to refuse treatment. In this I consider that they were in error. Such a child can consent, but if he or she declines to do so or refuses, consent can be given by someone else who has parental rights or responsibilities. The failure or refusal of the *'Gillick* competent' child is a very important factor in the doctor's decision whether or not to treat, but does not prevent the necessary consent being obtained from another competent source.

The clear implication of this interpretation is that a doctor, faced with a refusal of medical treatment by a child, is entitled to seek consent from a parent or someone *in loco parentis*. Suppose, however, the child consents to treatment, but requests that his parents are not informed? Two views can be taken of the implications for confidentiality of Lord Donaldson's interpretation of *Gillick*. The doctor is protected if, in good faith, he respects the child's confidence, and he cannot have a duty to disclose. If, however, the doctor discloses the matter to the child's parents (let us say, in the course of another consultation) then one view of Lord Donaldson's interpretation is that he will not be in breach of any duty of confidence owed to the child, because the child's consent to treatment was not based on child autonomy, but on the provision of a 'flak jacket' of legal immunity for the doctor. In other words, the obligation of confidence would be modified in exactly the same way as is the requirement that there be a valid consent. The second view would be that the doctor should respect the child's request, as breaching confidentiality serves no purpose in relation to securing treatment. The latter view is to be preferred, being more consistent with the ethic of confidentiality.

However, if one takes a true autonomy view of *Gillick*, that is that a child may be capable of making decisions about medical treatment so that he can refuse rather than consent, then it must be the case that he is entitled to respect of his medical confidences. It may be argued that the doctor is still under an obligation to inform his parents of what is happening because, although the parents will not be responsible for the consequences of medical treatment which they may have opposed if they had been given the opportunity, they will still have general parental responsibility for the child. On the other hand, it was clear from *Gillick* that some duty of confidentiality was owed. It is no explanation to say, without more, that it depends on the nature of the treatment, because capacity to consent depends upon the understanding by the child of that particular treatment. However, the nature of the treatment may mean there are circumstances where a child is deemed to have sufficient understanding to, say, consent to an abortion. In consequence, even if this conflicts with parental opinion it may be necessary for the parents to be informed of the refusal, and the reasons for it, to enable them to continue to act as parents.

In the context of confidentiality, it is tempting to take the view that *Gillick* was special on its facts, that is contraceptive advice, and that there was a strong element of policy in the decision, to avoid teenage pregnancies, and that the *Gillick* view on consent to other forms of medical

---

37 [1991] 4 All ER 177.
38 [1992] 4 All ER 627.

treatment and advice would not usually involve a co-extensive view on confidentiality. Jonathan Montgomery comments on the situation in the USA:

Montgomery, J, 'Confidentiality and the immature minor'[39]

The American position

American litigation in the field of birth control and abortion for minors proceeds by considering the extent of constitutional rights to privacy. In *Bellotti v Baird* 443 US 662 (1979) the court was asked to strike down a statute requiring parental consent before a minor was entitled to an abortion. Such a statute, said Powell J in giving the judgment of the court, could not be constitutional because it allowed an agency external to the minor herself to have a veto. A permissible system could be built around the 'mature minor rule'. Under that rule, a girl could go to court in order to have the abortion authorised. If she can prove herself sufficiently mature to take the decision herself, the court will automatically uphold her autonomy. If she cannot prove this, but can show that it would be in her best interests to have the abortion, the court must authorise the procedure. Otherwise the court has a discretion. In these latter circumstances the court may decide that it will be in the best interests of the child to inform her parents.

This position is similar to that which now prevails in English law. It differs in that the person who must decide whether the minor is sufficiently mature to take her own decision is, in this country, a doctor and not a judge. Powell J also considered the issue of confidentiality for the immature minor. He held that the Massachusetts statute before him was only constitutionally valid because under it 'every pregnant minor is entitled in the first instance to go directly to the court for a judicial determination without prior parental notice, consultation or consent' (443 US 662, p 649). Translated into the English context, this would mean that a minor is entitled to approach his or her doctor to have that person determine her capacity to consent to the medical procedures without her parents being informed. If she is found not to have that capacity, she must choose between not receiving the treatment or telling her parents, but that is 'her choice, not the doctor's'.

The general principles enunciated in *Gillick* were revisited in *R (on the application of Sue Axon) v Secretary of State for Health and the Family Planning Association*.[40] In 2004, the Department of Health issued guidance to healthcare professionals on giving advice and treatment to people under the age of 16 on sexual matters, including contraception, sexually transmitted diseases and abortion. The guidance provided that in cases where the young person was able to understand the advice and its implications but could not be persuaded to notify his or her parents or let the medical professional notify them, then such advice would remain confidential as long as the young person's physical or mental health would not be likely to suffer and the provision of the advice or treatment was in his or her best interests. The guidance also recommended that doctors follow the criteria set out by Lord Fraser in *Gillick*.

The applicant parent in this case sought judicial review on the basis that the guidance was unlawful because people under the age of 16 were not owed the same duty of confidentiality as those over 16, and that there was a breach of Article 8 of the European Convention that protects private life.

Silber J held that there could not be any exception to the duty of confidence owed to a young person as suggested by the applicant. It was important to recognise that, on the whole, a parent was the best person for guiding and advising a young person under the age of 16, that parents had a duty to protect their children, and that secrecy was destructive of family life, but

---

39 (1987) Fam Law 10.
40 [2006] EWHC 37 (Admin).

it was also the case that those factors do not override the duty of confidentiality owed. In consequence there was no infringement of the Article 8(1) rights of a young person's parents and, even if there was, such interference could be justified under Article 8(2).

5.1.5.2 Incapable adults

The sensitive issues surrounding medical decision-making on behalf of incapable adults has been examined in Chapter 4. Generally, decisions can be taken, and treatment administered, if these are in the patient's best interests. It is arguable that it will always be in the patient's best interests to respect his confidences, unless one or more of the circumstances exist in which confidence can be breached lawfully in respect of a capable adult patient.

THINK POINT

Are patients who lack capacity to make decisions about medical treatment owed the same duty of confidentiality?

5.2 Confidentiality – breaching confidences

The duty of confidence is not absolute and there are circumstances in which medical information can be divulged. This part of the chapter will examine these circumstances.

5.2.1 Consent

It may seem trite to say that confidence can be breached with the consent of the patient, but this fell to be considered by the court in the case of C v C.[41] A doctor had refused to disclose details of the respondent's venereal disease, on the basis that it would have been in breach of his duty of confidentiality, despite the fact that both the divorcing petitioner and the respondent (that is the patient) had requested this:

> **Lewis J:** The question which arises out of these circumstances is: is a doctor, when asked by his patient to give him or her particulars of his or her condition and illness to be used in a court of law, when those particulars are vital to the success or failure of the case, entitled to refuse and in effect to say, 'Go on with your case in the dark and I will tell you in court when I am subpoenaed what my conclusions are'? In the present case the patient asked the doctor to give her this information and asked him also to give the petitioner that same information, with the object of their being placed in a position which would enable them to know whether or not the petitioner had a case against the respondent, in other words, to assist the course of justice. It is, of course, of the greatest importance from every point of view that proper secrecy should be observed in connection with venereal disease clinics, and that nothing should be done to diminish their efficiency or to infringe the confidential relationship existing between doctor and patient. But, in my opinion, those considerations do not justify a doctor in refusing to divulge confidential information to a patient

---

41 [1946] 1 All ER 562.

> or to any named person or persons when asked by the patient so to do. In the circumstances of this case the information should have been given, and in all cases where the circumstances are similar the doctor is not guilty of any breach of confidence in giving the information asked for.

It is also important to remember that consent must be validly obtained. Given the powerful position of a doctor in the doctor–patient relationship, it is of considerable importance that the patient's consent is obtained scrupulously.

5.2.2 Public interest

Gurry, F, *Breach of Confidence*[42]

> The influence of principles based on the public interest is predominant in the action for breach of confidence. The public interest has two principal roles in the action. In the first place, since it is the law of the land that confidences are enforceable obligations, it is, of course, 'in the public interest that when information is received in confidence – for a limited and restricted purpose, as it always is – it should not be used for other purposes'. The public interest requires that confidences, like contracts, 'be held sacrosanct'. In this role, the public interest operates not only in the private sector, to enforce a confider's right to preserve the confidentiality of information which he entrusts to another, but also in the public sphere, where the public interest in national security or joint ministerial responsibility may require a public official or a Cabinet minister to keep confidential information secret.
>
> But the public interest also has an opposing role which sometimes requires that confidences be broken, and that information which the courts would otherwise protect from disclosure be released for various purposes. The opposing public interests which call for the release of confidential information may be the interests of justice itself, or the disclosure of iniquity, and, wherever such a judicially recognised opposing interest is identified it must 'be put into the scales against the public interest in preserving privacy and protecting confidential information'.

The philosopher Richard Hare sums up the picture as follows:

Hare, RM, 'The philosophical basis of psychiatric ethics', in *Essays on Bioethics*[43]

> If, for example [a psychiatrist] has as a patient somebody who he knows will be a great deal of trouble to anybody who is so unwise as to employ him, has he any duty to reveal the fact when asked for a medical certificate? Here, as before, it is obviously no use treating the duty of confidentiality to the patient and the duty of candour to the employer as duties on the same level but ranked in order of priority; for it may depend on the case which duty should have precedence. If the patient is an airline pilot and his condition will cause him to lose control of the plane, we may think the public interest paramount; if he is a bank clerk and is merely going to turn up late to work from time to time, we may think that his condition should be concealed.
>
> . . . At the critical level of moral thinking we are bound to be impartial between the interests of all those affected by our own actions. So at this level, we shall have to give no special edge to our patients, but simply ask, in each case we consider, what action would produce the best results for all those affected, treated impartially . . .

---

42 Oxford: Clarendon Press, 1984.
43 Oxford: Clarendon Press, 1993.

The following are examples of public interests which may outweigh the competing public interest in maintaining confidences.

5.2.2.1 Disclosure to maintain the freedom of the press

As we saw above in the case of *Campbell v Mirror Group Newspapers*[44] there is a public interest in the freedom of the press and other forms of media to investigate and report on matters of legitimate public concern. This was examined in the case of *X v Y*, where the court was unsympathetic to the interests of press freedom, in the face of the protection of the anonymity of patients being treated for AIDS. A health authority sought an injunction restraining a newspaper from publishing the names of two practising doctors who were also being treated for AIDS. The names of the doctors had been given to the newspaper by an employee within the health authority. The issue of freedom of the press was dealt with by Rose J, p 395:

> **Rose J**: I keep in the forefront of my mind the very important public interest in freedom of the press. And I accept that there is some public interest in knowing that which the defendants seek to publish (in whichever version). But in my judgment those public interests are substantially outweighed when measured against the public interests in relation to loyalty and confidentiality both generally and with particular reference to AIDS patients' hospital records ... The deprivation of the public of the information sought to be published will be of minimal significance if the injunction is granted; for, without it, all the evidence before me shows that a wide ranging public debate about AIDS generally and about its effect on doctors is taking place among doctors of widely differing views, within and without the BMA, in medical journals and in many newspapers, including *The Observer, The Sunday Times* and the *Daily Express*. Indeed, the sterility of the defendants' argument is demonstrated by the edition of the second defendant's own newspaper dated 22 March 1987. It is there expressly stated, purportedly quoting a Mr Milligan, that three general practitioners, two of whom are practising (impliedly in Britain), have AIDS. Paraphrasing Templeman LJ in the *Schering* case, the facts, in the most limited version now sought to be published, have already been made available and may again be made available if they are known otherwise than through the medium of the informer. The risk of identification is only one factor in assessing whether to permit the use of confidential information. In my judgment, to allow publication in the recently suggested restricted form would be to enable both defendants to procure breaches of confidence and then to make their own selection for publication. This would make a mockery of the law's protection of confidentiality when no justifying public interest has been shown.[45]

The authority succeeded on the basis that the doctors needed protection just as any other patient did.

In *H (A Healthcare Worker) v Associated Newspapers Ltd and N (A Health Authority)*,[46] a healthcare worker had been diagnosed as HIV positive and, in injunction proceedings, his former employer, a health authority, was permitted to be named in newspaper reports. The judge had concluded that the risk of identification of the worker did not justify preserving the anonymity of the health authority. The Court of Appeal held that disclosure of the identity of the health authority would enable the worker to be identified and that part of the judge's order was set aside. It was also said, however, that to disclose the particular speciality of the worker did not run such a high risk, and to restrain publication of that would be an unnecessary fetter on the freedom of the press.

---

44 [2004] 2 AC 457.
45 [1988] RPC 379 at 395.
46 [2002] EWCA Civ 195.

In *Re S (A Child) (Identification: Restriction on Publication)*[47] the House of Lords held that no injunction should be made restraining the publication by newspapers of the identity of the defendant in a murder trial in order to protect the privacy of her child (not involved in the criminal proceedings). The freedom of the press to report the progress of a criminal trial without any restraint under the Article 10 of the Convention outweighed the child's rights under Article 8.

5.2.2.2 Disclosure to prevent crime

In the case of X *v* Y the health authority unsuccessfully tried to obtain disclosure of the name of the person within the authority who had criminally sold the medical records of the doctors concerned (ie contrary to the Public Bodies Corrupt Practices Act 1889 and the Prevention of Corruption Act 1906). The argument of the authority was based on its alleged duty to prevent crime. The court held that it had no public duty to prosecute crime, and that its real purpose had been to prevent publication, which was prevented on other grounds.[48]

The protection of the public from crime was considered in W *v* Egdell.[49] The patient was a prisoner in a secure hospital following conviction for a number of killings and woundings, and had made an application to a mental health review tribunal with a view to being transferred to a regional unit. Such a step would be a step towards discharge and, therefore, the question arose as to whether the patient was still a danger to the public. His legal advisers sought the opinion of an independent psychiatrist, which, it was hoped, could be produced in support of the application. Dr Egdell, however, formed the view that the patient was still dangerous. In the light of this, the patient's application was withdrawn. However, his case was due to be reviewed under the automatic review process, under s 79(1) of the MHA 1983, and Dr Egdell, realising that his report, commissioned confidentially and independently by the patient's legal advisers, would not be included in the notes, sent a copy to the medical director of the hospital and a further copy to the Home Office. The patient brought an action alleging breach of confidence, but the court upheld the breach on the grounds of the public interest, that is the protection of the public from dangerous criminal acts. The patient failed in his action at first instance and appealed.

W v Egdell[50]

> **Bingham LJ**: The parties were agreed, as I think rightly, that the crucial question was how, on the special facts of the case, the balance should be struck between the public interest in maintaining professional confidences and the public interest in protecting the public against possible violence. Counsel for W submitted that on the facts here the public interest in maintaining confidences was shown to be clearly preponderant. In support of that submission he drew our attention to a number of features of the case, of which the most weighty were perhaps these:
>
> 1   Section 76 of the Mental Health Act 1983 shows a clear parliamentary intention that a restricted patient should be free to seek advice and evidence for the specified purposes from a medical source outside the prison and secure hospital system. Section 129 ensures that the independent doctor may make a full examination and see all relevant documents. The examination may be in private, so that the authorities do not learn what passes between doctor and patient.

---

47 [2004] 3 WLR 1129.
48 At p 399.
49 [1990] Ch 359.
50 [1990] Ch 359, at p 422.

2   The proper functioning of s 76 requires that a patient should feel free to bare his soul and open his mind without reserve to the independent doctor he has retained. This he will not do if a doctor is free, on forming an adverse opinion, to communicate it to those empowered to prevent the patient's release from hospital.

3   Although the present situation is not one in which W can assert legal professional privilege, and although tribunal proceedings are not strictly adversarial, the considerations which have given rise to legal professional privilege underpin the public interest in preserving confidence in a situation such as the present. A party to a forthcoming application to a tribunal should be free to unburden himself to an adviser he has retained without fearing that any material damaging to his application will find its way without his consent into the hands of a party with interests adverse to his.

4   Preservation of confidence would be conducive to the public safety: patients would be candid, so that problems such as those highlighted by Dr Egdell would become known, and steps could be taken to explore and if necessary treat the problems without disclosing the report.

5   It is contrary to the public interest that patients such as W should enjoy rights less extensive than those enjoyed by other members of the public, a result of his judgment which the judge expressly accepted (see [1989] 2 WLR 689, p 714; and [1989] 1 All ER 1089, p 1105).

Of these considerations, I accept (1) as a powerful consideration in W's favour. A restricted patient who believes himself unnecessarily confined has, of all members of society, perhaps the greatest need for a professional adviser who is truly independent and reliably discreet. (2) I also, in some measure, accept, subject to the comment that if the patient is unforthcoming, the doctor is bound to be guarded in his opinion. If the patient wishes to enlist the doctor's wholehearted support for his application, he has little choice but to be (or at least convince an expert interviewer that he is being) frank. I see great force in (3). Only the most compelling circumstances could justify a doctor in acting in a way which would injure the immediate interests of his patient, as the patient perceived them, without obtaining his consent. Point (4), if I correctly understand it, did not impress me. Counsel's submissions appeared to suggest that the problems highlighted by Dr Egdell could be explored and if necessary treated without the hospital authorities being told what the problems were thought to be. I do not think this would be very satisfactory. As to (5), I agree that restricted patients should not enjoy rights of confidence less valuable than those enjoyed by other patients save in so far as any breach of confidence can be justified under the stringent terms of r 81(g).

Counsel for Dr Egdell justified his client's disclosure of his report by relying on the risk to the safety of the public if the report were not disclosed. The steps of his argument, briefly summarised, were these:

1   As a result of his examination Dr Egdell believed that W had a long standing and abnormal interest in dangerous explosives dating from well before his period of acute illness.

2   Dr Egdell believed that this interest had been overlooked or insufficiently appreciated by those with clinical responsibility for W.

3   Dr Egdell believed that this interest could throw additional light on W's interest, also long standing and in this instance well documented, in guns and shooting.

4   Dr Egdell believed that exploration of W's interest in explosives and further exploration of W's interest in guns and shooting might lead to a different and more sinister diagnosis of W's mental condition.

5   Dr Egdell believed that these explorations could best be conducted in the secure hospital where W was.

6   Dr Egdell believed that W might possibly be a future danger to members of the public if his interest in firearms and explosives continued after his discharge.

7   Dr Egdell believed that these matters should be brought to the attention of those responsible for W's care and treatment and for making decisions concerning his transfer and release.

Dr Egdell's good faith was not in issue. Nor were his professional standing and competence. His opinions summarised in (1), (2), (3) and (4) (although not accepted) were not criticised as ill-founded or irrational. Dr Egdell deferred to the greater knowledge of another medical expert relied on by W concerning the regime in a regional secure unit but did not (as I understood) modify his view that the explorations he favoured should take place before transfer . . .

There is one consideration which, in my judgment, as in that of the judge, weighs the balance of public interest decisively in favour of disclosure. It may be shortly put. Where a man has committed multiple killings under the disability of serious mental illness, decisions which may lead directly or indirectly to his release from hospital should not be made unless a responsible authority is properly able to make an informed judgment that the risk of repetition is so small as to be acceptable. A consultant psychiatrist who becomes aware, even in the course of a confidential relationship, of information which leads him, in the exercise of what the court considers a sound professional judgment, to fear that such decisions may be made on the basis of inadequate information and with a real risk of consequent danger to the public is entitled to take such steps as are reasonable in all the circumstances to communicate the grounds of his concern to the responsible authorities. I have no doubt that the judge's decision in favour of Dr Egdell was right on the facts of this case.

The question arises whether this case is different from a case where a dangerous criminal is *at large* and a doctor breaches medical confidentiality to enable him to be taken into custody. It is arguable that there is an important difference. After all, in the *Egdell* case the patient was already the subject of expert medical scrutiny by the doctors at the hospital where he was detained; if those doctors had formed the view that the patient was no longer dangerous (that is, a view contrary to that of Dr Egdell), does not this difference of professional opinion considerably weaken the public interest defence to disclosure? Grubb[51] suggests that it may turn on whether the breaching doctor is basing his view on new facts of which he is aware, and which, without breaching confidence, are not known by the other doctor. If it is merely a difference of opinion based on the same set of facts, then there is a good argument against disclosure.

The public interest defence in the prevention of crime was upheld by the Court of Appeal in the case of *R v Crozier*,[52] where a psychiatrist, instructed by the defendant in an attempted murder case, disclosed his report to the prosecution when he realised that the defence had not produced it in court, when sentence was passed. As a result, the Crown informed the judge of the contents of the report, and the judge quashed the sentence of imprisonment and made a hospital order instead.

There is no doubt that the patient in *W v Egdell*[53] had committed very grave criminal offences. Would fear of less serious offences justify disclosure? Although case law in non-medical areas of confidentiality appears to put all crimes in the same basket (see *Initial Services Ltd v Putterill*[54] and *Malone v Commissioner of Police of the Metropolis (No 2)*),[55] in the *Egdell* case the repeated references to the safety of the public – 'In this case the number and nature of the killings by W must inevitably give rise to the gravest concern for the safety of the public'[56] – strongly suggests that the risk of minor crimes being committed would not sway the court in the same way. Furthermore, the non-medical cases generally concern issues of fraud upon the general public (see *British Steel Corp v Granada Television Ltd*).[57]

51 *Medical Law*, 3rd edn, London: Butterworths, 2000, p 1101.
52 (1990) *The Independent*, 11 May.
53 [1990] Ch 359.
54 [1968] QB 396.
55 [1979] 2 All ER 620.
56 *Per* Sir Stephen Brown P, at p 846.
57 [1981] 1 All ER 417.

It should also be noted that in the *Egdell* case it was said that the risk must be 'real, immediate and serious'.[58] This is important, as it must mean that a doctor acting in good faith and in the genuine belief that there is such a risk will be in breach of confidence if it transpires that the risk did not amount to one that was real, immediate and serious. Should all three of these requirements be satisfied: what of a risk which is real and serious, but unlikely to materialise for some time?

What of past, undetected criminal offences? The *risk* of a crime being committed is different to a past crime gone unpunished, the former only a perceived likelihood of criminal activity, the latter a certainty (on the assumption that the doctor is certain). There is a strong argument to say that non-serious crime should not be disclosed on the basis that the countervailing public interest in maintaining medical confidences outweighs disclosure, as, we suggest, was the case in *Wilson*.

5.2.2.3 Disclosure to prevent civil wrongs

Gurry[59] reviews the case law, and concludes that disclosure of a *proposed* civil wrong would be in the public interest, but doubts whether the disclosure of a past civil wrong would satisfy this, as 'this would serve only to raise quibbling enmities and thus destroy, rather than advance, the public welfare', while in the context of commercial confidences it may be the case that proposed civil wrongs may justify a breach. However, it is hard to envisage the circumstances in which past or future civil wrongs would justify a breach of medical confidences. Medical confidentiality would always override the prevention of civil wrongs because of weightier public interest arguments. In any event, what might be an example of a situation where a doctor would consider breaching confidence to prevent a proposed civil wrong? Perhaps a doctor may consider reporting a patient to his employer if, for example, he has failed to disclose a medical condition on a job application form, for example, psychiatric history (see *O'Brien v Prudential Assurance Co*).[60] It is submitted that this sort of medical busy-bodying would be swiftly condemned by the courts and the GMC.

5.2.2.4 Disclosure for the public good

It might be argued that if no wrong, criminal or civil, has been, or is likely to be, committed, then disclosure could not possibly be justified. However, there is clear authority for the fact that 'the public good' can be sufficient. The Court of Appeal in *Lion Laboratories v Evans and Express Newspapers*[61] authorised the publication of internal documents from the manufacturer of the intoximeter that cast doubt upon the accuracy of the machine, which was widely used in the convictions for drink-driving offences. The court held that the possibility of future wrongful convictions raised a matter of legitimate public interest despite the fact that no wrongdoing was involved.

It is possible to envisage countless examples of revelation of medical information for the public good; for example, the publication of information about new drugs and treatments and breakthroughs in medical research may be in the public good. Release of information about the dangers to public health, for example, of an outbreak of illness caused by contaminated materials would, of course, always be in the public good (indeed, the public health authorities would be under a positive duty to do this). However, in most of these cases there would be no need to name identifiable individuals, so there would be no breach of confidentiality. Nevertheless, if circumstances were such that individuals had to be named, for example a patient at large suffering from a highly dangerous and contagious disease, identification may be necessary.

---

58 *Per* Sir Stephen Brown P, at p 416.
59 *Breach of Confidence*, Oxford: Clarendon, 1984, p 334.
60 [1979] IRLR 140.
61 [1985] QB 526.

In *Woolgar v Chief Constable of Sussex Police*[62] the Court of Appeal had to decide whether police records could be disclosed to a regulatory body. The appellant was a registered nurse and the former matron of a nursing home. She had been investigated by the police following the death of a patient at the home. There were no criminal charges brought, but this, and other matters, were referred to the United Kingdom Central Council for Nursing, Midwifery and Health Visiting (UKCC), which was the regulatory and disciplinary body for the nursing, midwifery and health visiting professions. The normal practice was, that if there has been a police investigation before the UKCC became involved, the UKCC would contact the police and, with the consent of those who have made statements, obtain copies of those statements. The nurse refused permission for her statement to be released. The court accepted that the statement was confidential on the basis that, if no charges were brought, the person making it is entitled to rely upon it remaining undisclosed. However, the court also decided that there was a sufficiently strong countervailing interest in the release of the statement.[63]

Woolgar v Chief Constable of Sussex Police[64]

Kennedy LJ: . . . where a regulatory body such as the UKCC, operating in the field of public health and safety, seeks access to confidential material in the possession of the police, being material which the police are reasonably persuaded is of some relevance to the subject matter of an enquiry being conducted by the regulatory body, then a countervailing public interest is shown to exist which, as in this case, entitles the police to release the material to the regulatory body on the basis that save in so far as it may be used by the regulatory body for the purposes of its own enquiry, the confidentiality which already attaches to the material will be maintained. As Mr Horan said in . . . his skeleton argument:

> A properly and efficiently regulated nursing profession is necessary in the interest of the medical welfare of the country, to keep the public safe, and to protect the rights and freedoms of those vulnerable individuals in need of nursing care.

Putting the matter in Convention terms Lord Lester submitted, and I would accept, that disclosure is necessary in a democratic society in the interests of . . . public safety . . . or . . . for the protection of health or morals, or for the protection of the rights and freedoms of others.

THINK POINT

Consider the facts of the case of *Distillers Co (Biochemicals) Ltd v Times Newspapers Ltd*,[65] discussed below at 5.2.2.8, and consider whether similar facts, giving rise to a breach of medical confidentiality, would be justified for the public good.

5.2.2.5 Disclosure for the protection of third parties

It might be thought that the protection of third parties would come within the ambit of preventing either a criminal or a civil wrong. However, it may be necessary to disclose medical

---

62 [1999] Lloyd's Rep Med 335.
63 Note that the UKCC has now been replaced by the Nursing and Midwifery Council (NMC).
64 [1999] Lloyd's Rep Med 335, CA (Kennedy, Otton and Waller LJJ).
65 [1975] QB 613, at p 266.

information when neither of these apply. The case of *Re C (A Minor) (Evidence: Confidential Information)*[66] concerned the proposed adoption of a one-year-old baby. A day before the hearing, the mother withdrew her consent to the adoption. At an adjourned hearing, the adopting parents' solicitor produced an affidavit sworn voluntarily by the mother's GP, containing evidence of her medical condition and fitness to bring up a child. The mother objected to the admissibility of this evidence as it was a breach of medical confidentiality. She was unsuccessful at first instance, and the case went to the Court of Appeal. Sir Stephen Brown said:[67]

> **Sir Stephen Brown:** It is in fact an unusual case. There is no previous authority which is directly in point, and all the cases which have been cited to the court refer to very different situations. The court is concerned with the proposed adoption of a little child. That is, of course, a very serious matter for the child, as well as being a serious decision for the court to have to make when the mother is withholding her consent. The court should have before it all relevant and significant information which will assist it to make a right decision.
>
> In this case, it is clear that the doctor's affidavit is highly relevant. If it can properly be placed before the judge, then it should be admitted. I consider that this case rests on its own very special facts. Moreover, I have considerable hesitation in reaching a conclusion that there was, in fact, any breach of confidence by the doctor in this case. I observe that it was apparently conceded before the judge that, *prima facie*, there was a breach of confidence. However that may be, in my judgment in this case the doctor was justified in making available her evidence. It may be that it could have been made available to the mother's advisers at an earlier stage, or in some other way, but that is not the issue before this court. In any event, I believe that a judge, if carrying out any balancing exercise, would be fully justified in coming down clearly in favour of admitting this evidence.
>
> It should also be recognised that the disclosure of the material contained in this affidavit was the subject of a restricted disclosure. It was not being made available to the public at large. It was being made available only to the judge who had to decide the application, and to those who were also bound by the confidentiality of the hearing in chambers.
>
> Accordingly, I have no hesitation in reaching the conclusion that the judge was correct to rule that this evidence was admissible and that it should be admitted.

What is of particular interest is the suggestion that the finding at first instance that there had been a breach of confidence, albeit a justified breach, may not have been correct. This was a view supported by both the other appeal judges. This was on the basis that the child was also (or had been) a patient of the doctor. However, in our view this is the wrong approach. To hold that there is no breach is tantamount to saying there was no duty in the first place.

Of course, in all these cases we are looking at *competing* public interests, and the protection of children will frequently justify a refusal of disclosure. In *D v National Society for the Prevention of Cruelty to Children*[68] the mother of a child who, it had been alleged, had been abused by her, brought proceedings in negligence against the NSPCC, following the shock-induced illness she had suffered as a result of the society's inspector's call to her home. She alleged that the society had failed to investigate properly the complaint made against her. The society denied negligence and made an application to the court for an order that there should be no discovery of documents which might reveal the identity of the complainant. The House of Lords held that, in the interests of the proper functioning of a body such as the NSPCC, charged with the duty of protecting

---

66 (1991) 7 BMLR 138.
67 At p 143.
68 [1977] All ER 589.

children against ill-treatment, they should have immunity from disclosure, analogously to the guaranteed anonymity of police informers. The case also upheld the principle of disclosure in the interests of the administration of justice.

Disclosure of medical records for the purposes of vindicating a psychiatrist's reputation was considered in the case of *Re C (a child)*.[69] In the course of care proceedings, at the direction of the court, the mother and her child were assessed at a private clinic run by a psychiatrist who was also the mother's treating clinician. The mother subsequently reported the psychiatrist to the General Medical Council, but the allegations were either withdrawn or not established. She had also made allegations to the press, which the psychiatrist claimed had damaged his reputation, and a colleague of his also made a similar claim. They made an application to the court for disclosure of documents from the care proceedings, including psychiatric and psychological reports on the mother, and documents from the GMC proceedings. The stated purpose for which disclosure was sought was to enable them to discuss the documentation and use it in written material but they would not be passed on to any third party, and the name of the child would be redacted from any written material. The case came before Sir James Munby, President of the Family Division, who rejected the application on the basis that disclosure would

> constitute a massive and wholly unjustifiable breach of the confidentiality which attaches to the materials, impossible to justify by any asserted public interest, let alone by reference to any legitimate interests of [the psychiatrist] and, in the same way and for comparable reasons, a breach of the mother's rights under Article 8 of the Convention (para 74).

In the context of competing public interests, this judgment must be correct. The purpose for which disclosure was required did not become clear until relatively late in the proceedings as, first of all, it appears, disclosure was required because of 'a need for transparency for experts in the Family Court' and that the documents would be disclosed to 'reputable journalists' (para 10). But, as can been seen above, this had been considerably modified by the time of the hearing. However, it was still what was described by the President as extending 'far beyond anything to be found in the practice of the family courts' (para 74).

5.2.2.6 Serious communicable diseases

This is not a separate category of public interest defences, but we are dealing with it separately because of the special concerns about such diseases in the eyes of the general public. It will be recalled that the case of *X v Y* concerned the doctors who were HIV positive, and whose identities were at risk of being revealed by the press. Conditions such as HIV and AIDS throw the issues raised about medical confidentiality and its breach into very sharp relief because they are very serious, can be easily communicated (the added sexual dimension introduces the scope for dilemmas for doctors, when they know their HIV patient is in a sexual relationship and the other party is unaware of the diagnosis), and these factors mean that the balance between public health issues ie protection of confidentiality, and serious risks to the health of others ie disclosure, can be very fine.

Both HIV and AIDS attract huge stigma. This is partly because there is no cure for AIDS and, although it is too soon to say with any certainty, it is still assumed that an HIV positive person will become ill with AIDS sooner or later. However, many other incurable conditions exist, with prognoses far worse than that of someone recently discovered to be HIV positive, who could well live for 20 years with no sign of AIDS, with the prospect of a cure becoming available in the meantime. It is suggested that the stigma is as a result of two things: first, the

---

69 [2015] EWFC 79

fact that it may be transmitted through sexual activity; and, secondly, the fact that someone with no outward manifestations of illness may nevertheless be carrying a lethal virus. It also carries some stigma because of the erroneous belief, amongst some, that it is exclusive to, or caused by homosexual activities and/or drug use. The stigma has been recognised by disability legislation which is currently contained within the Equality Act 2010. Under Sch 1 para 6, a diagnosis of HIV is sufficient for someone to be 'disabled' and to acquire protection from discrimination under the Act. Conditions such as HIV/AIDS also have serious insurance implications. The European Court of Human Rights had to consider the issue in *Colak v Germany*.[70] In January 1993 the applicant's partner informed his doctor that he was suffering from AIDS. He did not tell his partner (the applicant) and told the doctor that he must not reveal this either, even though the applicant was also a patient of the doctor. He died in December 1994 (he was also suffering from cancer, which the applicant was aware of, so this presumably masked the AIDS-related illness). In March 1995 the doctor informed the applicant that her partner had died from AIDS. In April 1995 she was diagnosed as HIV positive. She sued her doctor for failure to inform her of her partner's condition and the judge said that, as the doctor has advised her partner to take steps to prevent the spread of the infection and had reasonably believed that he would follow these steps, there was no liability. On appeal to the Frankfurt Court of Appeal, the court held that there was an error on the part of the doctor in not informing her, but the court accepted expert evidence that it was likely she was already infected with HIV at the time that the doctor became aware of the situation and therefore the claim failed. In the European Court of Human Rights, the applicant claimed violation of Articles 2, 6 and 8. It was held that (1) there had been no violation of Article 2, as an event that does not result in death may only in exceptional circumstances disclose a violation of Article 2, and the German legal system provided adequate remedies in cases where there is a threat to life; and (2) (by six votes to one) there had been no violation of Article 8, again on the basis that the legal system provided sufficient safeguards of privacy.

(The Article 6 claim was brought because of the destruction of medical files which might have assisted in dealing with the issue of whether she was already HIV positive at the time the doctor acquired the relevant knowledge. It was held that there was no violation because the destruction of the applicant's medical files could not have an impact on the outcome of the case, as it occurred only after the conclusion of the civil proceedings and the files had been available to the domestic courts throughout.)

The following is an extract from the commentary on the case in the European Human Rights Law Review:

European Human Rights Law Review (2009) *Case Comment*

Colak v Germany (77144/01): HIV-patient confidentiality

What is perhaps surprising about this judgment is how little regard is paid to a patient's right to confidentiality and right to privacy under art.8. Although the applicant's complaints were dismissed, the Court accepted the Frankfurt Court of Appeal's assessment that the doctor should have informed the applicant of her partner's condition.

This stands in contrast to the recent case of *I v Finland* (2009) 48 E.H.R.R. 31 [and the earlier case of] *Z v Finland* (1998) 25 E.H.R.R. 371, the Court expressed the view that there must be a weighty public interest reason to justify the disclosure of a person's HIV status; in that case, it was helpful to the prosecution of Z's husband, a sexual offender. Of course, both these cases concern the disclosure of

---

70 (07714/01), unreported, March 2009.

the applicants' HIV status to the wider public. The facts of the present case are distinguishable on the grounds that the disclosure (had it been made) would have been a narrow one to a person at obvious risk of infection.

It is very unlikely that this case will provide support to a doctor accused in this country of making an impermissible disclosure. What it does indicate is very different approaches to the issue of patient confidentiality between the United Kingdom and Germany and possible inconsistencies in the Court's own case law.

It will be seen, therefore, that if there is a serious and identifiable risk to a specific individual, such as a spouse or other sexual partner, then disclosure can be made. Recalling the case of *Re C (A Minor) (Evidence: Confidential Information)*,[71] if the partner is also the patient of the doctor, the Court of Appeal suggested there may be no breach (see 5.2.2.5, above).

Whether there could ever be a positive duty to disclose was considered in the Californian case of *Reisner v Regents of the University of California*,[72] see below at 5.2.6.

5.2.2.7 Genetic information

Like HIV and AIDS, genetic information does not fall into a special 'legal' category, but because of its nature it does throw the public interest issues into sharp relief. The availability of genetic testing does not give rise to any particular issues in relation to the patient who has been tested, as the results are available to that patient as in any other form of test, and the information is, of course, confidential. However, if a patient is found to be carrying an abnormal gene, then the chances are that other members of the patient's family will also be carrying the gene. Should they be told about this? The two sides of the debate are well illustrated by the discussion in the following books. Laurie argues that when considering whether to disclose such information to relatives, the factors to be considered are the nature of the genetic condition; whether there is any treatment available for the condition; what is the likelihood of the condition developing and how severe is it likely to be; what further testing needs to be done; the precise nature of the information that it is proposed might be disclosed; the likely reaction of the relative and whether disclosure serves the public interest.[73] A different approach is taken by Gilbar who argues that because of its very nature, genetic information, the family aspects of disclosure must be taken into account and therefore the usual medical confidentiality approach as taken by Laurie is not appropriate.[74] The Gilbar approach was upheld in the Court of Appeal in the case of *ABC v (1) St George's Healthcare NHS Trust (2) South West London & St George's Mental Health NHS Trust (3) Sussex Partnership NHS Foundation Trust*.[75] It concerned the disclosure of genetic information to family members against the wishes of the patient, their father. As the Court of Appeal stated, the circumstances were tragic. In 2007 the father of the claimant had shot and killed her mother. He was detained under the criminal provisions of the Mental Health Act 1983, following a conviction of manslaughter on the grounds of diminished responsibility. In 2009 he was diagnosed as suffering from Huntington's disease, which is a progressive and fatal condition for which there is no cure or treatment to control its development or its symptoms. It is an inherited condition and the child of someone with the condition has a 50 per cent chance of inheriting the disease. The father did not want his daughters to know of the diagnosis, although he had disclosed this to their

---

71 (1991) 7 BMLR 138.
72 See (1997) Med L Rev 250.
73 Laurie, G, *Genetic Privacy: A Challenge to Medico-Legal Norms*, Cambridge: CUP, 2002.
74 Gilbar R, *The Status of the Family in Law and Bioethics: The Genetic Context*, Dartmouth: Ashgate, 2005.
75 [2017] EWCA Civ 336.

brother. In 2010 the claimant gave birth to a child, and subsequently was inadvertently told by a doctor about her father's diagnosis. In 2013 she was diagnosed with the condition. She brought an action claiming that she had been owed a duty of care by the clinicians to disclose her father's condition. Part of her case was a claim for 'wrongful birth' ie if she had known of her father's diagnosis she would have terminated the pregnancy. The judge at first instance had struck out her claim, holding that there was no arguable case that a duty of care was owed, and the claimant appealed.

The arguments of the defendants centred on the obligation of confidentiality; the fact that such a duty of care would give rise to conflicting obligations; that it might result in many claims (the 'floodgates' argument), and that it would distract clinicians from the care of their patients. Although these arguments were not dismissed out of hand, the court held that they were not decisive and that it is arguable that it is fair, just and reasonable to impose such a duty of care, and therefore the claim should not have been struck out. The main reason for the Court of Appeal's decision was the particular character of genetic information.

ABC v (1) St George's Healthcare NHS Trust (2) South West London & St George's Mental Health NHS Trust (3) Sussex Partnership NHS Foundation Trust[76]

Irwin LJ: 43 ... However problematic, and whatever the implications for "third parties", the clinician usually only has knowledge of medical facts about the existing patient. It is only in the field of genetics that the clinician acquires definite, reliable and critical medical information about a third party, often meaning that the third party should become a patient.

44 Although parallel duties and difficulties of disclosure arise in other areas of clinical practice, usually to do with risks posed to others by the condition of the existing patient ... the clinical geneticist is in a different position ... One example would be the diagnosis of a strong genetic disposition to breast cancer. In such circumstances the third party is not a patient, but should become a patient.

Irwin LJ went on to say that other scenarios discussed, such as disclosure of information to former sexual partners, may prove problematic in practice. What is more, they do not comprise a closed class of individuals whose risk is confined to a genetic link to the patient and will usually be contactable.

Again, the issue of genetic information raises the question whether there can be a *positive duty* to disclose medical information, which is considered below at 5.2.6.

5.2.2.8 The administration of justice

In the administration of justice there can be conflicts between the public interest in the protection of confidential information and the public interest in parties being able to seek disclosure of confidential communications to assist the presentation of their own cases and to assist the court in adjudication.[77]

In the course of civil proceedings, ss 33 and 34 of the Supreme Court Act 1981 provide for the discovery of documents during the course of a court action (s 34) and, where appropriate, prior to the commencement of proceedings (s 33). The question as to how far documents discovered in the course of legal proceedings may subsequently be published was considered in *Distillers (Biochemicals) Ltd v Times Newspapers Ltd*.[78] The case concerned the drug Thalidomide and, in

---

76 [2017] EWCA Civ 336.
77 For a very detailed account of this, see McHale, JV, *Medical Confidentiality and Legal Privilege*, London: Routledge, 1993.
78 [1975] QB 613.

proceedings brought by those injured by the drug, certain documents were ordered to be disclosed. One of the claimants' expert advisers entered into an agreement with the defendants to sell them the documentary information. The claimant company sought an injunction to prevent publication. The injunction was granted on the basis that those who disclosed documents were entitled to the court's protection against any use of the documents otherwise than in the action in which they were disclosed. Talbot J said, p 625:

> **Talbot J:** Whilst, as I have said, the public have a great interest in the thalidomide story (and it is a matter of public interest), and any light thrown onto this matter to obviate any such thing happening again is welcome, nevertheless the defendants have not persuaded me that such use as they proposed to make of the documents which they possess is of greater advantage to the public than the public's interest in the need for the proper administration of justice, to protect the confidentiality of discovery of documents. I would go further and say that I doubt very much whether there is sufficient in the use which the defendants have proposed to raise a public interest which overcomes the plaintiffs' private right to the confidentiality of their documents. In any event I consider that the plaintiffs have established their right (this is not really disputed) and have an arguable case for its protection by an injunction.

In this regard see also *Lewis v Secretary of State for Health & Redfern*,[79] where, under its general powers, the court authorised the disclosure of medical records of certain deceased patients to the Redfern Inquiry into human tissue analysis in nuclear facilities in the UK.

To refer back to the 'public good' justification, it is clear from this case that the court found that the proper administration of justice outweighed any public interest in knowing about the history of the drug Thalidomide. Although it is clear that doctors have no immunity from the normal processes of disclosure in court proceedings, in *Hunter v Mann*[80] it was said by Lord Widgery that a doctor who did not wish to answer a question in court because it would involve confidential issues may point this out to the judge, who should advise as to whether it is necessary to answer the question. See also the Canadian Supreme Court case *M(A) v Ryan*,[81] in which it was confirmed that communications between psychiatrist and patient are not absolutely privileged. Limited disclosure could be sufficient protection.

5.2.2.9 Disclosure in the interests of national security

It is highly unlikely that this could apply to medical information. It is enough to note it as a legitimate area of public interest.

5.2.3 Medical research

It might be thought that there are no special considerations in the case of disclosure in research, but it is different, in that it could be argued that by consenting to take part in research, particularly non-therapeutic research, there was an altruistic motive on the part of the research subject which changes the nature of confidentiality. Perhaps the only special aspect of research and confidentiality is that information may well be disclosed, but anonymously. However, this might soon change – see 5.4 below on the proposed EU General Data Protection Regulations.

---

79 [2008] EWHC 2196 (QB).
80 [1974] 1 QB 767.
81 [1997] SCR 157.

5.2.4 Exchange of information amongst healthcare workers

This is a grey area. Although it is included here as a particular example of the way in which confidences may be breached, unauthorised exchange of information amongst healthcare workers may fall foul of the law unless it can be argued that the patient has impliedly consented to this because he knows that he is being cared for by a team of people.

It is instructive, however, to consider into how many pairs of hands medical information may fall. Gillon refers to the investigation by a doctor of a patient's complaint:

Gillon, R, *Philosophical Medical Ethics*[82]

> Dr Siegler was 'astonished to learn that at least 25 and possibly as many as 100 health professionals and administrative personnel at our university hospital had access to the patient's record and that all of them had a legitimate need, indeed a professional responsibility, to open and use that chart'.

Note that this was written in 1986. Is it arguable that the larger these numbers become, the less significant the concept of medical confidentiality becomes? Or does it become even more important to bind those increasing numbers of people to secrecy? The NHS has issued a Code of Practice that suggests the latter.[83]

5.2.5 Breaches of confidence justified by statute law

A number of statutory provisions provide for the disclosure of information, and doctors generally are not exempt. The following are examples and it is not an exhaustive list.

National Health Service Act 2006, s 251

Control of patient information

(1) The Secretary of State may by regulations make such provision for and in connection with requiring or regulating the processing of prescribed patient information for medical purposes as he considers necessary or expedient –

    a   in the interests of improving patient care, or

    b   in the public interest.

(2) Regulations under subsection (1) may, in particular, make provision –

    a   for requiring prescribed communications of any nature which contain patient information to be disclosed by health service bodies in prescribed circumstances –

        i   to the person to whom the information relates,

        ii   (where it relates to more than one person) to the person to whom it principally relates, or

        iii   to a prescribed person on behalf of any such person as is mentioned in sub-paragraph (i) or (ii),

        in such manner as may be prescribed,

    b   for requiring or authorising the disclosure or other processing of prescribed patient information to or by persons of any prescribed description subject to compliance with any prescribed conditions (including conditions requiring prescribed undertakings to be obtained from such persons as to the processing of such information),

---

82 Chichester: John Wiley, 1986.
83 NHS Contractors: *Confidentiality and Disclosure of Information: General Medical Services, Personal Medical Services and Alternative Provider Medical Services Code of Practice*, DoH, 2005.

> c   for securing that, where prescribed patient information is processed by a person in accordance with the regulations, anything done by him in so processing the information must be taken to be lawfully done despite any obligation of confidence owed by him in respect of it,
>
> d   for creating offences punishable on summary conviction by a fine not exceeding level 5 on the standard scale or such other level as is prescribed or for creating other procedures for enforcing any provisions of the regulations.
>
> (3)   Subsections (1) and (2) are subject to subsections (4) to (7).
>
> (4)   Regulations under subsection (1) may not make provision requiring the processing of confidential patient information for any purpose if it would be reasonably practicable to achieve that purpose otherwise than pursuant to such regulations, having regard to the cost of and the technology available for achieving that purpose
>
> ...
>
> (7)   Regulations under this section may not make provision for or in connection with the processing of prescribed patient information in a manner inconsistent with any provision made by or under the Data Protection Act 1998 (c 29).

The regulations that were made under earlier legislation continue to apply in this regard (Health Service (Control of Patient Information) Regulations 2002, SI 2002/1438).

It can be seen that s 251 is wide and vague, but the counter-argument is that this is necessary to enable valuable medical research to be carried out in circumstances where it is not possible to obtain patient consent.

It should be noted that s 19 of the Terrorism Act 2000 creates a criminal offence in respect of failure to disclose information which might be of material assistance in preventing acts of terrorism or in apprehending or securing a prosecution or conviction.

Note the provisions of the Road Traffic Act 1988:

Road Traffic Act 1988, s 172

> (2) – Where the driver of a vehicle is alleged to be guilty of an offence to which this section applies –
>
> a   the person keeping the vehicle shall give such information as to the identity of the driver as he may be required to give by or on behalf of a chief officer of police; and
>
> b   any other person shall if required as stated above give any information which it is in his power to give and may lead to identification of the driver.
>
> In this sub-section references to the driver of a vehicle include references to the person riding a cycle.

The case of *Hunter v Mann*[84] examined the extent to which this requirement was applicable to doctors in relation to the forerunner of the 1988 provision, s 168 of the Road Traffic Act 1972. The relevant part of the provision is identical to the 1988 Act. The question to be answered by the Divisional Court was whether a doctor who failed to comply with the provision under s 172(2) (b), above, in respect of information brought to his knowledge in the course of his professional relationship with a patient, was guilty of an offence under s 172(3). The argument on the part of the doctor was that the relevant words should be given a restricted meaning, so as to exclude confidential information, and those in a special position of confidence such as doctors. Boreham J stated:[85]

---

84   [1974] 1 QB 767.
85   At p 774.

Boreham J: For my part I cannot find any ground for saying that a restricted meaning should be given. I find the words clear and unequivocal. I accept, as Mr Bingham has suggested, that one should assume that Parliament has passed this Act, and this section in particular, with the existing law in mind. Accepting that, then it seems to me that Parliament must have been conscious of the use of very wide words here and if it had been intended to create exceptions, why then it would have been easy enough to do so. It has not been done. Moreover I ask myself the question: if there is to be a restriction how far is it to go? Where is it to stop? I find it impossible to provide an answer to that question.

In these circumstances I am driven to the conclusion that a doctor acting within his professional capacity, and carrying out his professional duties and responsibilities, is within the words 'any other person' in s 168(2)(b).

...

May I say, before leaving this case, that I appreciate the concern of a responsible medical practitioner who feels that he is faced with a conflict of duty. That the defendant was conscious of a conflict and realised his duty, both to society and to his patient, is clear from the finding of the justices, but he may find comfort, although the decision goes against him, from the following. First, that he has only to disclose information which may lead to identification and not other confidential matters; secondly, that the result, in my judgment, is entirely consistent with the rules that the British Medical Association have laid down and from which I have quoted in the course of this judgment.

In the result I have come to the conclusion that the justices were correct and that this appeal, therefore, must be dismissed.

Information must also be disclosed pursuant to the Abortion Regulations 1991, SI 1991/499 for various purposes including the investigation of whether an offence has been committed in relation to abortion, and for bona fide scientific research. Note, too, the provisions of ss 33 and 34 of the Supreme Court Act 1981, which provide for disclosure of documents during the course of litigation considered above.

THINK POINT

If the situation is such that disclosure is permissible in the public interest do you think that this means that disclosure can be made to the public at large?

5.2.6 Might there be a common law duty to disclose?

As we have seen in *Hunter v Mann*,[86] a doctor may have a statutory duty to disclose certain information about a patient. However, might there be circumstances in which a common law duty may arise, as opposed to the common law defence which gives a doctor a *discretion* to disclose? This is illustrated by the case of *Tarasoff v Regents of the University of California*.[87] A patient of a psychologist confided that he intended to kill a girl. The psychologist informed the campus police who briefly detained the man, releasing him on the basis that he appeared to be rational.

---

86 [1974] 1 QB 767.
87 17 Cal 3d 425 (1976).

He subsequently killed the girl, and her parents sued the university for failing to warn them that their daughter was in danger. By a majority, the California Supreme Court upheld their claim:

> **Tobriner J**: . . . the adequacy of the therapist's conduct must be measured against the traditional negligence standard of the rendition of reasonable care under the circumstances . . . In sum, the therapist owes a legal duty not only to his patient, but also to his patient's would-be victim and is subject in both respects to scrutiny by judge and jury . . . Some of the alternatives open to the therapist, such as warning the victim, will not result in the drastic consequences of depriving the patient of his liberty. Weighing the uncertain and conjectural character of the alleged damage done to the patient by such a warning against the peril to the victim's life, we conclude that professional inaccuracy in predicting violence cannot negate the therapist's duty to protect the threatened victim . . .

Justice Clark, dissenting, stated:

> **Clark J**: Overwhelming policy considerations weigh against imposing a duty on psychotherapists to warn a potential victim against harm. While offering virtually no benefit to society, such a duty will frustrate psychiatric treatment, invade fundamental patient rights and increase violence. The importance of psychiatric treatment and its need for confidentiality have been recognised by this court. It is clearly recognised that the very practice of psychiatry vitally depends upon the reputation in the community that the psychiatrist will not tell . . . Assurance of confidentiality is important for three reasons:
>
> **Deterrence from treatment**
>
> First, without substantial assurance of confidentiality, those requiring treatment will be deterred from seeking assistance . . .
>
> **Full disclosure**
>
> Second, the guarantee of confidentiality is essential in eliciting the full disclosure necessary for effective treatment. The psychiatric patient approaches treatment with conscious and unconscious inhibitions against revealing his innermost thoughts . . .
>
> **Successful treatment**
>
> Third, even if the patient fully discloses his thoughts, assurance that the confidential relationship will not be breached is necessary to maintain his trust in his psychiatrist – the very means by which treatment is effected . . .
>
> **Violence and civil commitment**
>
> . . . Although under existing psychiatric procedures only a relatively few receiving treatment will ever present a risk of violence, the number making threats is huge, and it is the latter group – not just the former – whose treatment will be impaired and whose risk of commitment will be increased.

This approach has been followed in Nebraska, where the duty was to third parties generally and not just people known to the patient (*Lipari v Sears, Roebuck & Co*[88]). However, in the Florida Court of Appeals, there was a refusal to impose liability based upon a defendant's failure to control the conduct of a third party (*Boynton v Burglass*[89]). It will be seen in Chapter 6 that the case of *Palmer v Tees HA*[90] displayed a similar reluctance. Thomas is highly critical of the decision in *Tarasoff*:

---

88 497 F Supp. 185 (D Neb 1980).
89 590 So 2d 446.
90 [1999] Lloyd's Rep Med 351.

Thomas, M, 'Expanded liability for psychiatrists: *Tarasoff* gone crazy?'[91]

There are several reasons why United Kingdom decision makers should be sceptical about *Tarasoff's* 'enlightened approach'.

Lack of control over patients

In many cases, a psychiatrist will lack the necessary degree of control over a patient to justify the imposition of a duty. For instance, psychiatrists usually have little control over voluntary patients who do not satisfy the criteria for involuntary commitment ...

Causation problems

... it is not clear that the psychologist's failure to warn the victim in *Tarasoff* could be said to have caused the victim's death. Conspicuously, there is no causation analysis in the *Tarasoff* decision.

... To satisfy [the 'but for'] test, the plaintiff would have to prove that had Ms Tarasoff been warned ... she would have avoided being killed ... The most that can be said is that, due to the psychologist's failure to warn ... [she] lost the opportunity to avoid being harmed ... Based on traditional common law principles of causation, this would be insufficient to establish causation.

Uncertain standard of care

... Mosk J stated that a psychiatrist's prediction of violence stands to be examined against 'conformity to standards of the profession'. Yet, one must wonder what common standards the court is referring to, when no such standards exist within the profession itself. Of course, psychiatry has developed a range of risk assessment tools designed to predict dangerousness. However, it appears that there is little consensus within the profession as to what constitutes reasonable practice ...

Note also the Californian case of *Reisner v Regents of the University of California*,[92] where a doctor was found to have been in breach of a duty of care owed to the sexual partner of a patient who had contracted HIV after receiving a contaminated blood transfusion, which information had been concealed by the doctor concerned. It was said that the patient would have been likely to have warned her sexual partner. However, it was said that third parties who might have become infected by contact with the sexual partner would not be owed a duty of care, on remoteness principles.

5.2.7 To whom should disclosure be made and what should be the extent of that disclosure?

It is well established that even if a breach of confidence may be justified, it may still be actionable if the disclosure goes further than that which is necessary. If, for example, as was alluded to by Bingham LJ, in *W v Egdell*,[93] Dr Egdell had disclosed his report to a newspaper, or commented upon it in a journal article, then this would have been going further than was necessary in the public interest of prevention of crime. The defence of public interest was only available to him in the disclosure to the hospital treating the patient, and the Home Office. Similarly, a doctor who is justified in revealing one aspect of the patient's condition is not thereby justified in revealing other medical information. For example, the revelation that a woman is HIV positive, as we have seen, may occasionally be justified. A doctor who, at the same time, points out that this was

---

91 (2009) J Mental Health L 52 2009.
92 See (1997) Med L Rev 250.
93 [1990] Ch 359 at 419.

discovered in the course of an abortion procedure will be in breach of confidence. However, additional information may be revealed if it is necessary by way of explanation.

The extent of disclosure was the subject of *A Health Authority v X and Others*.[94] The case concerned the release of papers which resulted from a case brought under the Children Act 1989. The health authority sought an order for production of case papers and GP records of two people involved in the case. Munby J had ordered disclosure, subject to express conditions to limit the extent of the disclosure. The health authority appealed against such conditions. One argument advanced on behalf of the health authority was that the NHS would grind to a halt if there were not 'free internal exchange of confidential information'. The Court of Appeal rejected this:

A Health Authority v X and Others[95]

Thorpe LJ: [T]he only real issue in the present appeal is whether the conflict between the private/public interest in the confidentiality of medical records and some other public interest should be decided by the health authority or a judge . . . I accept Mr Pannick's submission that the importance of the resolution of such a conflict requires the independence of a judge. I conclude that the spectres developed by Mr Havers, cost and delay and administrative overload, are no more than speculations which good sense and management can contain.

. . . I conclude that [there was no] error of law or principle that would justify our intervention . . . The judge elected for a cautious approach. In my opinion he was not only entitled but wise to do so.

5.3 Confidentiality – remedies

5.3.1 Detriment

In *AG v Guardian Newspapers (No 2)*[96] there was no clear stance as to whether there is a need for detriment to be shown in private actions for breach of confidence. Lord Goff, for example, left the question open (pp 281–82). Although there are instances where a patient would suffer pecuniary loss as a result of that breach (for example disclosure of a medical condition to an employer which results in dismissal), in many cases no quantifiable loss would result. It is arguable that breach of confidence should be actionable *per se*, or that, if detriment is required, the breach itself is a detriment to the patient in the sense that he has been betrayed.

An interesting point arises if we consider inadvertent disclosure. Up until now we have assumed that the act of disclosure has been deliberate. However, if a confidential medical report were to be carelessly lost in a public place, does the patient have to show that damage has resulted from this? In other words, would the negligence criterion be applied; that is, that damage must have resulted from the non-deliberate act? This will be examined further in relation to damages.

5.3.2 Damages

The rather curious New Zealand case of *Furniss v Fitchett*[97] was decided on negligence principles. The facts were as follows. The marriage of a Mr and Mrs Furniss was under a great deal of strain. Both were patients of Dr Fitchett. Mr Furniss asked the doctor to provide him with a letter

---

94 [2001] EWCA Civ 2014.
95 [2001] EWCA Civ 2014, CA (Thorpe and Laws LJJ, Harrison J).
96 [1990] AC 109.
97 [1958] NZLR 396.

detailing his wife's psychiatric problems, which he did. It was not marked 'confidential' and the doctor did not know how it was to be used. Just over a year later, it was produced in the course of a court hearing – the first time Mrs Furniss had heard of it. She suffered what is oddly described in the law report as 'shock to the injury of her health'. Leaving aside the difficult issue of what sort of injury this is (the judge referred to it as 'physical' injury), the general negligence criteria were applied in awarding her damages.

In *Cornelius v De Taranto*[98] the Court of Appeal upheld the decision of the trial judge that a consultant psychiatrist had breached client confidentiality in disclosing a medico-legal report to the patient's GP and another psychiatrist without first obtaining her consent. The report contained defamatory and hurtful material relating to her mental state. Damages of £3,750 were awarded for injury to feelings.

5.3.3 Injunctions

It is important to remember that the injunction is a discretionary remedy and, in the context of breach of confidence, if the information is already in the public domain, there will be no purpose served by an order preventing further publication: see *AG v Guardian Newspapers (No 2)*.[99]

An injunction at the final trial of the action will rarely be granted if there has been no interim injunction when the proceedings are first issued, because if there has been no prior prevention of publication, then, by the time of trial, the information will either be well and truly in the public domain, or no longer worth suppressing.

The interim injunction, therefore, is the key weapon in a breach of confidence action. It means that publication will be prevented for what may be a long time before trial. The basis upon which such relief would be granted was set out in *American Cyanamid Co v Ethicon Ltd*,[100] and is generally known as 'the balance of convenience test', where the court has to decide whether either party will suffer irreparable harm and, if both will suffer, who will suffer the most.

5.3.4 The dead

The Hippocratic Oath binds a doctor to keep medical confidences after death, but it is not clear whether there is any legal obligation to keep confidences after the death of the person to whom the duty is owed, after the death of the patient. The common law is not clear as the doctor–patient relationship of confidence no longer exists. Some statutes specifically do not apply to deceased persons (the Data Protection Act 1998) and some do (the Access to Health Records Act 1990). However, ethically, it seems clear that if harm can be caused to relatives then disclosure should be prohibited, subject to their being no countervailing ethical factor. Note the case of *Lewis v Secretary of State for Health & Redfern* at 5.2.2.8 in relation to the medical records of deceased persons.

5.4 Confidentiality and the Data Protection Act 1998

The Data Protection Act 1998 was passed to give effect to the European Directive 95/46/EC which requires Member States to implement legislation to protect the right of individuals to privacy with respect to the processing of personal data. As far as medical records are concerned,

---

98 [2002] EMLR 6.
99 [1990] AC 109.
100 [1975] AC 396.

the Act gives patients the right of access to their medical records, subject to exclusions. It also gives patients the right to ask for necessary corrections to be made to those records. Data will be processed in adherence to the 'Data Protection Principles':

European Directive 95/46/EC

1   Personal data shall be processed fairly and lawfully.
2   Personal data shall be obtained only for one or more specified lawful purposes.
3   Personal data shall be adequate, relevant and not excessive.
4   Personal data shall be accurate and up to date.
5   Personal data shall not be kept for longer than necessary.
6   Personal data shall be processed in accordance with rights of data subjects.
7   Measures shall be taken against unauthorised or unlawful processing and accidental loss or destruction.

David Stone outlines the application of the Act to medical records:

Stone, D, 'Confidentiality, access to health records and the Human Rights Act 1998'[101]

The first main purpose of the DPA 1998 is to control the way in which such data are 'processed'. This is a comprehensive term covering almost every conceivable activity in relation to such information. Under s 1(12), processing includes the 'obtaining, recording or holding . . . organisation, adaptation or alteration . . . retrieval, consultation or use . . . disclosure . . . alignment, combination, blocking, erasure or destruction' of data.

A 'data processor' is anybody who does one of these things. It will therefore include hospital staff, GPs and their staff; while a 'data controller' is anybody who determines the purpose for which, or manner in which, the data are processed. This will include NHS organisations and GPs alike. Almost everyone who reads or uses patient records in any way – even putting copies in the post or reading them on screen – will be 'processing' data and will therefore be bound by the provisions of the DPA 1998. This will include not only professional staff but, for example, hospital managers and GP receptionists.

. . . [referring to the first data protection principle] To be 'fair' the data must, in general terms, have been obtained from the patient honestly or in accordance with a legal obligation; the patient must have been told the purposes for which the information is to be processed; and the rules for providing access to the data subject must also have been observed (Sched 1, Pt 2).

The word 'lawfully' is not defined. However, it implies that the processing must not be in breach of any other existing legal restrictions, for example, the common law duty of confidence. This emphasises the point that the DPA 1998 does not replace the common law framework of confidentiality and access, but is an addition to it – albeit a dominant one.

Most importantly, it should be noted that, to be considered fair and lawful, the processing of patient records (as 'sensitive personal data') must meet at least one detailed specific criterion from Sched 2 and at least one from Sched 3. In summary these are:

a   that the patient has given 'explicit consent' to the processing ('explicit' is not defined, but Guidance from the Data Protection Commissioner suggests that it means that the patient's consent must be absolutely clear, that is, that it should cover the specific purpose of the processing); or

101 Garwood-Gowers, A et al., *Healthcare Law: The Impact of the Human Rights Act 1998*. London: Cavendish Publishing, 2001.

b   that the processing is necessary for the purposes of exercising or performing a right or obligation imposed by law; or

c   that it is necessary to protect the vital interests of the patient or another person where consent cannot be given by or on behalf of the patient, or where the data controller cannot reasonably be expected to obtain it or it has been unreasonably withheld; or

d   that the information has already been deliberately made public by the patient; or

e   that the processing is necessary for the purpose of actual or prospective legal proceedings, or for obtaining legal advice, or for the purpose of establishing, exercising or defending legal rights; or

f   that it is necessary for the purposes of 'legitimate interests' pursued by the data controller or the third party to whom the data are to be disclosed, unless disclosure would be unwarranted because it would prejudice the data subject; or

g   that it is necessary for the administration of justice, or for the exercise of statutory functions; or

h   that it is necessary for medical purposes (including preventative medicine, diagnosis, research, care, treatment and management of healthcare services), and is carried out by a healthcare professional (as defined in s 69) or by a person who owes the patient an equivalent duty of confidentiality; or

i   that it is authorised by an Order of the Secretary of State.

For the most part, the processing of patient records will be necessary for medical purposes (Sched 3, para 8), so one can avoid the need for consent in that way. However, one can see areas of uncertainty where important tissues will arise.

...

Potential problems

In practical terms, there are a wide range of everyday situations in a hospital or surgery in which the legal rights and duties of NHS data controllers may not be clear . . . one example would be where a trust has the opportunity to generate income by selling prescribing data to a data collection company. Will the court necessarily agree with the Court of Appeal's view in the *Source Informatics* case [see 5.1.3 above] that anonymisation is sufficient to dispel any common law duty of confidentiality? Or should the process of anonymising prescriptions be deemed 'processing' for the purposes of the DPA 1998, as the Department of Health seemed to be arguing in that case? If so, what would be the position if the patient had explicitly indicated his/her opposition to such a process? Would Art 8 enable a GP to rely on the legitimate interests exception under Sched 2 to the DPA 1998, where the sole purpose of the exercise was commercial and contractual?

Again, the issue of disclosing information capable of identifying the patient has caused difficulties. The increasing sophistication of information technology has facilitated the production of group studies and the creation of national databases to assist with the treatment and prevention of conditions such as cancer. However, with rare conditions such as CJD, the possibility of a patient being identified even by anonymised information can never be completely eliminated as the GMC's guidance recognises. It is likely that where a legitimate public health purpose can be shown here (for example, under the Public Health (Control of Diseases) Act 1984), the conditions of Art 8 will be adjudged to have been met. However, that is not to say that patients will not challenge the disclosure.

Another possible difficulty might arise from relying on an exemption under Scheds 2 and 3 of the DPA 1998 based on a legal obligation. For instance, under s 35A of the Medical Act 1983, the GMC is entitled to demand disclosure of information from any person in order to assist with the performance of the GMC's functions. But what if the patient is specifically asked first, for example, as a matter of courtesy, and explicitly refuses disclosure out of loyalty to the doctor: does the exemption available to the data controller override the patient's views, or would disclosure be unlawful in the terms of the First Data Protection Principle and Art 8?

Similarly, the Secretary of State is empowered by the DPA 1998 to make Orders in respect of disclosure in a variety of circumstances without the date subject's consent. For example, the Data Protection

(Processing of Sensitive Personal Data) Order 2000 [SI 2000/417] allows disclosure of patient records without consent for a range of purposes 'in the substantial public interest', including for the prevention and detection of crime or protecting the public against incompetence or misconduct. The Order falls squarely within Scheds 2 and 3 of the DPA 1998 allowing the disclosure of health records without the a patient's consent; but will such blanket authorisations be considered consistent with the specific reservations set out in Art 8, or will patients be able to challenge them successfully as illegitimate encroachments on the basic principle of right to private and family life?

THINK POINT

Information about patients goes through the hands of many healthcare professionals. Do you think that this makes issues of confidentiality more or less important?

In 2012 the EU Commission proposed a new General Data Protection Regulation to replace the current Directive. This caused some concern amongst researchers, particularly cancer specialists,[102] that doctors would have to obtain explicit consent from each patient in respect of the use of their data. In fact the text was later amended to allow for 'broad' consent to such use for research, subject to this being in accord with 'recognised ethical standards for scientific research'.[103] At the same time, the GDPR contains a significant heightening of the compliance obligations on data controllers who process sensitive data, including health data, and the effect of this on day-to-day healthcare provision remains to be seen. The Regulation is applicable from 25 May 2018.

Regulation (EU) 2016/679 of the European Parliament and of the Council

of 27 April 2016

on the protection of natural persons with regard to the processing of personal data and on the free movement of such data, and repealing Directive 95/46/EC (General Data Protection Regulation)

(General Data Protection Regulation)[104]

Whereas:

. . . (35) Personal data concerning health should include all data pertaining to the health status of a data subject which reveal information relating to the past, current or future physical or mental health status of the data subject. This includes information about the natural person collected in the course of the registration for, or the provision of, healthcare services . . .; information derived from the testing or examination of a body part or bodily substance, including from genetic data and biological samples; and any information on, for example, a disease, disability, disease risk, medical history, clinical treatment or the physiological or biomedical state of the data subject independent of its source, for example from a physician or other health professional, a hospital, a medical device or an in vitro diagnostic test.

---

102 (2014) *The Times*, 26 July.
103 GDPR, Recital 33.
104 http://eur-lex.europa.eu/legal-content/EN/TXT/PDF/?uri=CELEX:32016R0679&from=EN.

... (51) Personal data which are, by their nature, particularly sensitive in relation to fundamental rights and freedoms merit specific protection as the context of their processing could create significant risks to the fundamental rights and freedoms. ... Such personal data should not be processed, unless processing is allowed in specific cases set out in this Regulation, taking into account that Member States law may lay down specific provisions on data protection in order to adapt the application of the rules of this Regulation ... Derogations from the general prohibition for processing such special categories of personal data should be explicitly provided, inter alia, where the data subject gives his or her explicit consent or in respect of specific needs in particular where the processing is carried out in the course of legitimate activities by certain associations or foundations the purpose of which is to permit the exercise of fundamental freedoms.

... (53) Special categories of personal data which merit higher protection should be processed for health-related purposes only where necessary to achieve those purposes for the benefit of natural persons and society as a whole, in particular in the context of the management of health or social care services and systems ..., or for archiving purposes in the public interest, scientific or historical research purposes or statistical purposes, based on Union or Member State law ..., as well as for studies ... in the area of public health. Therefore, this Regulation should provide for harmonised conditions for the processing of special categories of personal data concerning health, in respect of specific needs, in particular where the processing of such data is carried out for certain health-related purposes by persons subject to a legal obligation of professional secrecy ... Member States should be allowed to maintain or introduce further conditions, including limitations, with regard to the processing of genetic data, biometric data or data concerning health. However, this should not hamper the free flow of personal data within the Union when those conditions apply to cross-border processing of such data.

As intimated above, the General Data Protection Regulation 2016/679 contains a number of exemptions to facilitate data processing for researchers. These are further discussed in Chapter 10.

5.5 Access to medical records

5.5.1 Access to medical records – ethical considerations

As a corollary to the duty of confidentiality owed by a doctor to a patient, one could be forgiven for assuming that a patient should have an unfettered right to see his medical records. After all, if a doctor is to be privy to intimate medical information which he has a duty to keep quiet about, but not an absolute duty, then the accuracy of that information should be verifiable at least by the patient concerned. At first sight, it might seem that here there are two discrete patient rights, that is the right to respect for privacy and the right to know what the doctor is placing in the medical records. However, in practice they are intertwined. The patient's right to protection of confidences must surely extend to the right to know that the information concerned is accurate. Further, the utilitarian argument that the patient will be more candid if confidentiality is protected and that such candour is necessary for the patient's health and that of society generally, also sustains the proposition that a patient should have a right to check the accuracy of that information (interestingly, it has been argued that, in order to preserve confidentiality, patients should keep their own medical records[105]).

---

105 See 'Editorial' (1991) 17 JME 115, and the article in the same edition by Gilhooly, M and McGhee, S, 'Medical records: practicalities and principles of patient possession' (1991) 17 JME 235.

On the other hand, if the patient has only a discretionary right (or, indeed, no right at all), then this would usually be justified on paternalistic principles. The types of arguments that are advanced in the cause of paternalism, are, for example, that the patient would not understand the records, that they may frighten or confuse him, the doctor would not be able to make 'frank' comments about the patient and so on. However, are paternalistic principles justifiable in certain circumstances where revelation of the contents of records may damage the patient or others? It will be seen that both common law and statute favour the paternalistic approach.

5.5.2 Access to medical records – the law

5.5.2.1 Statutory provisions: Data Protection Act; Access to Medical Reports Act 1988

The Access to Health Records Act 1990 was passed as a result of the case of *Gaskin v United Kingdom*,[106] where the European Court of Human Rights held that the UK's refusal to grant a right of access by a patient to his health records was in breach of Article 8 of the European Convention. This has been replaced by the Data Protection Act 1998 in all respects except in relation to deceased persons in respect of which a personal representative can apply for access (s 3(1)(f)).

The Data Protection Act 1998 enables data subjects to have access to data held about them:

Data Protection Act 1998, Part II

Rights of data subjects and others

7 –

(1) Subject to the following provisions of this section and to sections 8 and 9, an individual is entitled –
    a   to be informed by any data controller whether personal data of which that individual is the data subject are being processed by or on behalf of that data controller;
    b   if that is the case, to be given by the data controller a description of –
        i   the personal data of which that individual is the data subject;
        ii   the purposes for which they are being or are to be processed; and
        iii   the recipients or classes of recipients to whom they are or may be disclosed;
    c   to have communicated to him in an intelligible form –
        i   the information constituting any personal data of which that individual is the data subject; and
        ii   any information available to the data controller as to the source of those data; and
    d   where the processing by automatic means of personal data of which that individual is the data subject for the purpose of evaluating matters relating to him such as, for example, his performance at work, his creditworthiness, his reliability or his conduct, has constituted or is likely to constitute the sole basis for any decision significantly affecting him, to be informed by the data controller of the logic involved in that decision-taking.
(2) A data controller is not obliged to supply any information under subsection (1) unless he has received –
    a   a request in writing; and
    b   except in prescribed cases, such fee (not exceeding the prescribed maximum) as he may require.

---

106 (1990) 12 EHRR 36.

(3)   A data controller is not obliged to comply with a request under this section unless he is supplied with such information as he may reasonably require in order to satisfy himself as to the identity of the person making the request and to locate the information which that person seeks.

(4)   Where a data controller cannot comply with the request without disclosing information relating to another individual who can be identified from that information, he is not obliged to comply with the request unless –

a   the other individual has consented to the disclosure of the information to the person making the request; or

b   it is reasonable in all the circumstances to comply with the request without the consent of the other individual.

(5)   In subsection (4) the reference to information relating to another individual includes a reference to information identifying that individual as the source of the information sought by the request; and that subsection is not to be construed as excusing a data controller from communicating so much of the information sought by the request as can be communicated without disclosing the identity of the other individual concerned, whether by the omission of names or other identifying particulars or otherwise.

(6)   In determining for the purposes of subsection (4)(b) whether it is reasonable in all the circumstances to comply with the request without the consent of the other individual concerned, regard shall be had, in particular, to –

a   any duty of confidentiality owed to the other individual;

b   any steps taken by the data controller with a view to seeking the consent of the other individual;

c   whether the other individual is capable of giving consent; and

d   any express refusal of consent by the other individual.

(7)   An individual making a request under this section may, in such cases as may be prescribed, specify that his request is limited to personal data of any prescribed description.

(8)   Subject to subsection (4), a data controller shall comply with a request under this section promptly and in any event before the end of the prescribed period beginning with the relevant day.

(9)   If a court is satisfied on the application of any person who has made a request under the foregoing provisions of this section that the data controller in question has failed to comply with the request in contravention of those provisions, the court may order him to comply with the request.

(10) In this section –

–   'prescribed' means prescribed by the Secretary of State by regulations;

–   'the prescribed maximum' means such amount as may be prescribed;

–   'the prescribed period' means forty days or such other period as may be prescribed;

–   'the relevant day', in relation to a request under this section, means the day on which the data controller receives the request or, if later, the first day on which the data controller has both the required fee and the information referred to in subsection (3).

Section 14 entitles the data subject to correct inaccurate information.

The Data Protection (Subject Access Modification) (Health) Order 2000, SI 2000/413 also provides that someone with parental responsibility or appointed by a court to manage someone's affairs cannot obtain access to records if the patient does not wish that information to be disclosed. In addition, access cannot be provided if it identifies another person, other than a healthcare professional, who has not consented to the disclosure, unless it is reasonable to comply with the request without the consent of that other individual. This provision complies with the European Court decision in *Gaskin v United Kingdom*,[107] where records were withheld on the ground

---

107 (1990) 12 EHRR 36.

that the social workers objected or could not be traced. The court found that an absolute prohibition on disclosure was in breach of Article 8. As will be seen, s 7(6) sets out those matters to be considered in relation to 'reasonableness'.

The Access to Health Records Act 1990 and the Data Protection Act 1984 both contained exemptions, enabling data/record holders to withhold access to medical records in certain circumstances. There are now some exemptions within the 1998 Act itself (for example, relating to the detection of crime). The main medical record exemption in respect of the Data Protection Act 1998 is contained within the Data Protection (Subject Access Modification) (Health) Order 2000, SI 2000/413. Basically, this entitles the health professional concerned to withhold patient records if they consider that disclosure would be likely to cause serious harm to the physical or mental health or condition of the data subject or any other person (Article 5(1)). Before deciding whether this exemption applies, a data controller who is not a healthcare professional is obliged to consult the health professional responsible for the clinical care of the data subject or, if there is not such a person, someone with the necessary qualifications or experience. Unlike the Access to Health Records Act 1990, there is no specific provision in the Data Protection Act 1998 for applications by, or on behalf of, child patients, nor for incompetent adults, although it is assumed by the Data Protection (Subject Access Modification) (Health) Order 2000, SI 2000/413 that these applications can be made.

If the record holder forms the opinion that the information may cause serious harm to the health of the patient or another, access may be excluded to the relevant part of the records. Yet again, this reflects medical paternalism. Further, it makes no sense that access should be refused because it may seriously harm the patient. If the patient is refused access on this ground, is not the refusal itself likely to cause harm? Speculation as to what the records may contain could, and probably would, cause considerable anxiety. Even if one accepts the argument that many patients do not want to know about risks of treatment before consent is given, the same argument cannot apply to access. Patients of sound mind, who have gone to the trouble of making an application, should have their requests respected. Harm caused to third parties raises different issues, which would depend upon the identity of the third party, the type and magnitude of the harm and so on.

Roberts v Nottinghamshire Healthcare NHS Trust[108] concerned an application for disclosure of a medical report under s 7(9) of the Data Protection Act 1998. The applicant was detained in a high security psychiatric hospital following the commission of violent offences. His case was due to be reviewed by a Mental Health Review Tribunal and a report had been prepared by the psychologist who had been treating him. He asked for disclosure of the report, but this was refused on the basis that the trust did not intend to rely upon the report but on a report from another psychologist. The court held that the trust had compelling reasons to refuse disclosure and there was no injustice to the applicant because the report would not be used by the trust and he had the opportunity to have his own psychologist's report presented to the tribunal. The reasons for non-disclosure were set out in a closed court with only a special advocate present to hear them. McRae comments as follows:

McRae, L, 'Case Comment, Withholding medical records without explanation: a Foucauldian reading of public interest'[109]

It is not a simple task to reconcile the judgment in *Roberts* with substantive and procedural rights. Rule 39.2(3)(c) of the Civil Procedure Rules 1997 states that a hearing, or any part of it, may be conducted in

---

108 [2008] EWHC 1934 (QB).
109 (2009) Med L Rev 438.

private, if it 'involves confidential information … and publicity would damage that confidentiality'. In reaching this decision, the judge will take into account the requirements of Article 6(1) of the Convention (right to a fair and public hearing). Moreover, 'the decision as to whether to hold a hearing in public or in private must be made by the judge conducting the hearing having regard to any *representations* which may have been made to him' [my emphasis].

In respect of this latter requirement, the judge's decision to hear the exemption relied upon by the defendant in private is baffling. Cranston J suggested that '[f]or the reasons given in Closed Judgment the circumstances here were highly unusual'; yet, one would assume that the more unusual the exemption, the stronger the justification for disclosing it. As it was, Cranston J decided to provide a closed judgment on the sole basis that the NHS Trust had been unwilling up until trial to provide Roberts' solicitors with the exemption it was relying on. In effect, the appropriateness of the exemption was not known *until* the decision to hear the defendant's reasons in private had been reached. Consequently, the justification to 'go private' was borne of the judge's confidence in the defendant's reasons for non-disclosure *apriori*. In an era which is supposed to be increasing the 'transparency' of the administration of justice, this makes the reasoning in *Roberts* dubious.

The Access to Medical Reports Act 1988 confers a right of access to medical reports obtained for employment or insurance purposes. The Act also gives a right for the individual to have access to the report before it is supplied, and provides for the correction by the patient of matters contained in the report. It is important to note that the Act only applies to reports prepared by a medical practitioner who is, or has been, responsible for the clinical care of the individual (s 2(1)). What of the situation where the doctor is nominated by an insurance company or employer, to whom the Act does not apply? Would an obligation of confidence arise? It is submitted that, once the doctor had examined the patient and obtained medical information, without express or implied consent that it would be disclosed, the doctor would owe a duty of confidence. However, would it be easier to conclude that implied consent had been given by attending the medical appointment in the first place? The right under the Act is qualified in the same way as it is under the Data Protection Act 1998. There is a right to apply to the court if access is refused (sub-s (8)).

5.5.2.2 Common law

As has been seen above, there is now a qualified, statutory right of access to medical records, but this does not apply to non-computerised records made prior to 1 November 1991. The common law is still, therefore, of considerable importance. The issue was examined by the Court of Appeal in the case of *R v Mid Glamorgan Family Health Services Authority and Another, ex p Martin*. The facts were as follows. As a young man, the applicant had received psychiatric treatment from doctors employed by the respondents. He had also received assistance from a female social worker, with whom he became infatuated. She was taken off his case, and for some years he had sought access to his medical records, to find out why the social worker had been removed and why he had subsequently been committed under the 1959 Mental Health Act. Access had been refused, on the basis that they were the property of the relevant authority and that disclosure would be damaging to the applicant and to third parties. The applicant's lawyers had responded to the effect that these doctors were in no position to judge whether the applicant would be damaged. Clearly, this was a forceful argument, and it resulted in a compromise offer: the respondents would agree to disclose the records to a medical adviser nominated by him, for that person to decide whether they may be damaging. The offer was refused. The judge at first instance dismissed the application for unmediated disclosure. In the Court of Appeal, the appeal was dismissed:

R v Mid Glamorgan Family Health Services Authority and Another, ex p Martin[110]

Nourse LJ:[111] . . . a public body, in fulfilment of its duty to administer its property in accordance with its public purposes, is bound to deal with medical records in the same way as a private doctor. In that regard the observations of Lord Templeman in *Sidaway* [1985] 1 AC 871, p 904, are pertinent:

> I do not subscribe to the theory that the patient is entitled to know everything nor to the theory that the doctor is entitled to decide everything. The relationship between doctor and patient is contractual in origin, the doctor performing services in consideration for fees payable by the patient. The doctor, obedient to the high standards set by the medical profession, impliedly contracts to act at all times in the best interests of the patient. No doctor in his senses would impliedly contract at the same time to give to the patient all the information available to the doctor as a result of the doctor's training and experience and as a result of the doctor's diagnosis of the patient. An obligation to give a patient all the information available to the doctor would often be inconsistent with the doctor's contractual obligation to have regard to the patient's best interests. Some information might confuse, other information might alarm a particular patient. Whenever the occasion arises for the doctor to tell the patient the results of the doctor's diagnosis, the possible methods of treatment and the advantages and disadvantages of the recommended treatment, the doctor must decide in the light of his training and experience and in the light of his knowledge of the patient what should be said and how it should be said.

These observations provide a sensible basis for holding that a doctor, likewise a health authority, as the owner of a patient's medical records, may deny the patient access to them if it is in his best interests to do so, for example if their disclosure would be detrimental to his health.

It is inherent in the views above expressed that I do not accept that a health authority, any more than a private doctor, has an absolute right to deal with medical records in any way that it chooses. As Lord Templeman makes clear, the doctor's general duty, likewise the health authority's, is to act at all times in the best interests of the patient.

The court also relied on the fact that, although there were a number of statutory rights to access, these were not absolute, and could be wholly or partially excluded in appropriate circumstances. It seems that the Court of Appeal in *Martin* simply accepted the opinion of the consultant psychiatrist and, thence, the respondents' solicitors, that disclosure would be detrimental to the patient. As the above common law *dicta* and legislation show, detriment alone ought to be insufficient.

Is it not the case that the 'serious harm' exception in relation to *the patient*, however stringently applied, is contrary to patient autonomy? Surely if the patient is competent and suitably warned, he should be entitled to run the risk?

A paternalistic approach was taken by the Australian Supreme Court of New South Wales in the case of *Breen v Williams*, where the doctor's right to decide what it would be good for a patient to know was upheld:

---

110 [1995] 1 WLR 110.
111 At p 116.

Breen v Williams[112]

> **Mahoney JA:**[113] ... *prima facie*, a medical file kept by a doctor is the property of the doctor. ...
>
> More difficult questions arise in relation to matters such as those particularly referred to by Dr Cashman in the present case, namely, notes taken by the doctor to record the patient's medical history and her signs and symptoms. In one sense such records are made for the purposes of the patient, the making of them is one of the things which the doctor, by his engagement, may undertake to do. In this sense, the document is created so that there may be a record of what the patient has told the doctor and her signs and symptoms at the time. The record may not merely help in the instant diagnosis and a selection of treatment, it may provide a valuable resource for future purposes. Considered in isolation, a record of this kind, if it were contained in a separate document, would, I think, be the property of the patient.
>
> On the other hand, the doctor may – ... include with the record of the history and the signs and symptoms of the patient, comments and observations which are made and recorded for the purpose of helping the doctor form the diagnosis and the opinion to be formed as to treatment. There may be observations – Dr Williams used the term 'musings' – which, if standing alone, would ordinarily be the property of the doctor and not of the patient. It is the fact that these things are combined in the documents which illustrates the nature of the problem in a case such as this.
>
> The combination of such things: the history, signs and symptoms on the one hand and the 'musings' and other things on the other hand, may be accidental in the sense that the combination of the two in the one record is not inherent in the process of medical knowledge. But the thrust of Dr Williams' evidence is, I think, that such a combination is not accidental. His evidence suggests that the combination of these two things is inherent in the way medical practice is conducted or, at least in the way he conducts his practice. The trial judge accepted this portion of the doctor's evidence.
>
> If the records kept by the doctor be in this form, then, in my opinion, the records remain the property of the doctor ...

This decision does not deny that a patient has a right to know the main contents of his records, what it denies to him is the right to look through them and discover his doctor's comments. The reason given for this is that the doctor will be inhibited when making his notes, and that may not be in the patient's interest. It is easy to see that a doctor may feel restrained from making adverse comments relating to, say, genuineness of symptoms, when, for example, referring a patient to another doctor, if he thought that the patient may see this. However, the suspicions must be based upon factual matters such as an inconsistent history of symptoms, and physical examination failing to accord with alleged symptoms, and surely these are matters which the doctor should discuss openly with his patient. Or is it arguable that there is a risk of losing the patient's trust?

However, in *Breen v Williams* there was a dissenting judgment, by Kirby P, in favour of disclosure, which relied on there being a fiduciary duty owed to the patient. This was following the Canadian Supreme Court decision of *McInerney v MacDonald*.[114] In this case comment was made as follows:

> **La Forest J** (p 421): Information about oneself revealed to a doctor acting in a professional capacity remains, in a fundamental sense, one's own. The doctor's position is one of trust and confidence. The information conveyed is held in a fashion somewhat akin to a trust. While the doctor is the owner of the actual record, the information is to be used by the physician for the benefit of the patient. The confiding of the information to the physician for medical purposes gives rise to an expectation that the patient's interest in

---

112 [1995] 6 Med LR 385.
113 At p 427.
114 (1992) 93 DLR (4th) 415.

and control of the information will continue. The trust-like 'beneficial interest' of the patient in the information indicates that, as a general rule, he or she should have a right of access to the information and that the physician should have a corresponding obligation to provide it.

5.5.2.3 European Convention on Human Rights

Gaskin v UK[115] confirmed the right of a patient to access his medical records. In *MG v UK*[116] the ECtHR held that the right was not absolute and there could be legitimate restriction on access to protect third parties. In *KH and others v Slovakia*[117] it was held that a request to access records did not have to be justified; on the contrary it was for the record holders to show that there are compelling reasons for refusal.

THINK POINT

How might the fiduciary duty argument have changed the decision of the Court of Appeal in *Martin*?

Summary of key points

1 The law relating to confidentiality has been refined since the Human Rights Act 1998 whereby Article 8 of the European Convention on Human Rights, which protects the right to privacy, has become part of domestic law. There are subtle differences between confidentiality and privacy.

2 Neither the right to protection of confidences nor the right to privacy are absolute and they can be breached in the public interest, or with the consent of the patient.

3 A countervailing public interest can arise in a wide variety of cases so although it is often about the risk of serious physical or mental harm to an individual, the protection of a free press or a fair judicial system are also compelling public interests.

4 Unjustified breaches of confidence raise interesting questions as to the precise nature of the damage suffered and how it should be compensated.

5 There is a difference between a healthcare professional being able to justify breaching confidence and being *obliged* to do so.

6 Patients have statutory rights of access to their medical records, and a limited common law right, but there are controversial exceptions to these rights.

 Further reading

Case, P, 'Confidence matters: the rise and fall of informational autonomy in medical law' (2003) 11 Medical Law Review 208.

Michalowski, S, *Medical Confidentiality and Crime*, Aldershot: Ashgate Dartmouth, 2003.

Stanley, P, *The Law of Confidentiality: A Restatement*, Oxford: Hart Publishing, 2008.

Taylor, MJ, 'Legal bases for disclosing confidential patient Information for Public Health: distinguishing between health protection and health improvement' (2015) 23 Medical Law Review 348.

Toulson, RG and Phipps, CM, *Confidentiality*, London: Sweet & Maxwell, 2006.

---

115 (1990) 12 EHRR 36.
116 [2002] 3 FCR 413.
117 App 32881/94, judgment April 2009.

Chapter 6

Medical malpractice

6.1 Introduction

Medical malpractice may be defined, broadly, as any unjustified act or failure to act upon the part of a doctor or other healthcare worker which results in harm to the patient. In this chapter we shall be considering the means, under the civil law, by which a victim of such malpractice may pursue a claim for redress, and the difficulties that lie in his way (the rare instances in which the doctor may also be the subject of criminal liability have been noted in Chapter 2 at 2.3.4).

See Chapter 2 →

First, what form might the patient's claim take? On the face of it, there would seem to be three possibilities – to sue in tort, either in battery or negligence, or to mount an action for breach of contract. In practice, however, it is the second of these, a negligence action, which offers the only appropriate channel for the vast majority of malpractice claims. The first option, battery, which forms the civil analogue to the crime of assault, generally only arises as a possibility in those rare cases where treatment is carried out without any consent at all. It is no use to the patient who, having given such consent, suffers injury, however poor the execution of the treatment subsequently turns out to be.

See Chapter 3 →

As for the third option, breach of contract, the first thing to note is that this will not assist patients treated under the NHS scheme (that is, the large majority of patients in this country), who provide no consideration in return for the services they receive.[1] What, though, of patients treated in the private sector? While it is true that the latter may sue for breach of contract instead of (or as well as) in negligence, in proving a breach they normally have exactly the same task as their NHS counterparts. This is because it is most unlikely that the doctor will have promised expressly to achieve a specific desired outcome (although for an exceptional American case in point, see *LaFleur v Cornelis*[2]); and otherwise, in implying the terms which govern such contracts, the courts have held the standard of skill and care warranted by the private doctor to be identical to the standard of care required to avoid a claim in negligence. In *Thake v Maurice*,[3] a case in which a patient treated privately sued following the failure of his vasectomy, Neill LJ in the Court of Appeal commented:

> **Neill LJ**: I do not consider that a reasonable person would have expected a responsible medical man to be intending to give a guarantee. Medicine, though a highly skilled profession, is not, and is not generally regarded as being, an exact science. The reasonable man would have expected the defendant to exercise all the special care and skill of a surgeon in that speciality; he would not in my view have expected the defendant to give a guarantee of 100% success.

This common law standard of care is also echoed in s 13 of the Supply of Goods and Services Act 1982, which provides that a person who supplies services in the course of a business must carry them out with reasonable care and skill.

Accordingly, in the remainder of this chapter we shall focus upon actions in medical (or 'clinical') negligence. In order for such actions to succeed, a number of basic elements (familiar from the general tort of negligence) must be made out, that is the existence of a duty of care, the fact of its breach, and that legally recognised damage was thereby caused. Each raises particular issues in the context of medical negligence, which we shall consider in turn in sections 6.2–6.4, as well as possible defences for the doctor, in section 6.5. In section 6.6 we then address the

---

1 *Appleby v Sleep* [1968] 2 All ER 265. Similarly, it was confirmed in *Reynolds v The Health First Medical Group* [2000] Lloyd's Rep Med 240, that a patient does not have a contractual relationship with his GP.

2 (1979) 28 NBR (2d) 569 (there a cosmetic surgeon promised to improve the appearance of the patient's nose).

3 [1986] QB 644.

scheme of 'strict liability' that exists for medicinal products, as 'consumer goods'. Overall, it is notorious that medical negligence claims are frequently hard to prove (as well as costly, time-consuming and traumatic for those involved), and we shall conclude, in section 6.7, by considering the issue of law reform in this area.

6.2 The duty of care

6.2.1 The duty to the patient

The patient must establish that the defendant, who may be a doctor, nurse, NHS trust, or a health authority, owed him a legal duty of care. This is, generally speaking, the easiest element to show. As Michael Jones comments:

Jones, M, *Medical Negligence*[4]

Normally, there will be no difficulty in finding a duty of care owed by the doctor to his patient, at least where the claim is in respect of personal injuries, and this is true even where there is a contractual relationship. The practitioner may also owe a duty of care to the patient in respect of pure financial loss. In addition, there are a number of circumstances where a doctor may also owe a duty of care to a third party arising out of the treatment given to the patient, but the incident and extent of such duties is more problematic.

6.2.1.1 Hospital treatment

The case of *Barnett v Chelsea and Kensington Hospital Management Committee*[5] is authority for the proposition that an open accident and emergency unit has a duty to treat or at least assess the patient. The facts arose after three nightwatchmen, who were taken ill after drinking some tea, went to their local hospital's casualty department, but were sent away without being seen by a doctor. Nield J stated:

Nield J: I turn to consider the nature of the duty which the law imposes on persons in the position of the defendants and their servants and agents. The authorities deal in the main with the duties of doctors, surgeons, consultants, nurses and staff when a person is treated either by a doctor at his surgery or the patient's home or when the patient is treated in or at a hospital. In *Cassidy v Ministry of Health* [1951] 2 KB 343, Denning LJ dealt with the duties of hospital authorities and said:

> In my opinion, authorities who run a hospital, be they local authorities, government boards, or any other corporation, are in law under the self-same duty as the humblest doctor. Whenever they accept a patient for treatment, they must use reasonable care and skill to cure him of his ailment. The hospital authorities cannot, of course, do it by themselves. They have no ears to listen through the stethoscope, and no hands to hold the knife. They must do it by the staff which they employ, and, if their staff are negligent in giving the treatment, they are just as liable for that negligence as is anyone else who employs others to do his duties for him. Is there any possible difference in law, I ask, can there be, between hospital authorities who accept a patient for treatment and railway or shipping authorities who accept a passenger for carriage? None

---

4 London: Sweet & Maxwell, 1996.
5 [1969] 1 QB 428.

whatever. Once they undertake the task, they come under a duty to use care in the doing of it, and that is so whether they do it for reward or not.

Here the problem is different and no authority bearing directly on it has been cited to me. It is to determine the duty of those who provide and run a casualty department when a person presents himself at that department complaining of illness or injury and before he is treated and received into the hospital wards. This is not a case of a casualty department which closes its doors and says that no patients can be received. The three watchmen entered the defendants' hospital without hindrance, they made complaints to the nurse who received them and she in turn passed those complaints on to the medical casualty officer, and he sent a message through the nurse purporting to advise the three men. Is there, on these facts, shown to be created a relationship between the three watchmen and the hospital staff such as gives9 rise to a duty of care in the defendants which they owe to the three men?

... In my judgment, there was here such a close and direct relationship between the hospital and the watchmen that there was imposed on the hospital a duty of care which they owed to the watchmen. Thus, I have no doubt that Nurse Corbett and Dr Banerjee were under a duty to the deceased to exercise that skill and care which is to be expected of persons in such positions acting reasonably...

Recently, in *Darnley v Croydon Health Services NHS Trust*[6] the Court of Appeal was required to decide if a duty of care should also be imposed upon a receptionist in an A&E department when giving information on waiting times to persons seeking treatment. In the case in question, the claimant, who attended the department with a head injury, left again after being wrongly told he would need to wait four to five hours to be looked at (in fact there was a system in place for head injury cases to be seen by a triage nurse within 30 minutes). The claimant later suffered serious disability due to the progression of his injury, which he alleged would have been avoided if he had been given the correct information (in which case he would have waited and been seen by the triage nurse).

The Court of Appeal, however, by a majority, held there was no such duty on the receptionist to be careful when giving such information, finding (with reference to the *Caparo* test) that this would not be 'fair, just and reasonable'. In the words of Sales LJ:

Sales LJ: [88] In my judgment, the fair, just and reasonable view is that such information is provided as a matter of courtesy and out of a general spirit of trying to be helpful to the public, as the judge held, and that its provision is not subject to a duty of care in law such that compensation must be paid if a mistake is made. Imposition of such a duty would be likely to lead to defensive practices on the part of NHS trusts to forbid their receptionists to provide any information about likely waiting times, as the judge observed. This reflects the fact that, as noted above, provision of such information is not part of the core function performed by a receptionist. It also indicates that there would be a social cost of imposition of a duty of care, in terms of withdrawal of information which is generally helpful to the public when provided as a courtesy, which is not offset by considerations of justice as between claimant and defendant in this sort of case.

Individual hospital doctors and nurses are unlikely to be sued directly by the injured patient. A legal claim will normally be made against the hospital/NHS trust, as the health professional's employer, who will be vicariously liable. This assumes that the negligent doctor or nurse was an

---

6 [2017] EWCA Civ 151.

employee and was acting in the course of his or her employment. The Department of Health has produced special guidance on handling clinical negligence claims against NHS staff:

Department of Health, *NHS Indemnity – Arrangements for Negligence Claims in the NHS*[7]

Main principles

NHS bodies are vicariously liable for the negligent acts and omissions of their employees and should have arrangements for meeting this liability.

NHS Indemnity applies where:

a   the negligent healthcare professional was:

    i   working under a contract of employment and the negligence occurred in the course of that employment;

    ii   not working under a contract of employment but was contracted to an NHS body to provide services to persons to whom that NHS body owed a duty of care;

    iii   neither of the above but otherwise owed a duty of care to the persons injured;

…Where these principles apply, NHS bodies should accept full financial liability where negligent harm has occurred, and not seek to recover their costs from the healthcare professional involved.

Who is not covered

NHS Indemnity does not apply to family health service practitioners working under contracts for services, for example: GPs (including fundholders), general dental practitioners, family dentists, pharmacists or ' optometrists; other self-employed healthcare professionals, for example, independent midwives; employees of FHS practices; employees of private hospitals; local education authorities; voluntary agencies …

Circumstances covered

NHS Indemnity covers negligent harm caused to patients or healthy volunteers in the following circumstances: whenever they are receiving an established treatment, whether or not in accordance with an agreed guideline or protocol; whenever they are receiving a novel or unusual treatment which, in the judgment of the healthcare professional, is appropriate for that particular patient; whenever they are subjects as patients or healthy volunteers of clinical research aimed at benefiting patients now or in the future.

In certain circumstances the hospital or NHS trust may be directly liable for breaching a duty of care they owe to the patient in negligence. In *Wilsher v Essex AHA*[8] the Court of Appeal suggested that such liability would arise if it were shown that the hospital authorities had filled treatment positions with staff who were unable (through inexperience or otherwise) to cope with the demands made upon them. Direct liability will also arise where the claimant's injury is attributable to some overall failure, of an organisational nature, to provide a safe environment for carrying out treatment. Similarly, in the case of a patient whose treatment is 'farmed out' to a private hospital (an increasing expedient in the drive to cut waiting lists), it is apparent, following M v *Calderdale and Kirklees HA*,[9] that the referring NHS institution remains under a non-delegable duty of care in respect of such treatment.

---

7 Catalogue No 96 HR 0024, London: DoH, 1996.
8 [1987] QB 730, CA.
9 [1998] Lloyd's Rep Med 157.

6.2.1.2 Treatment outside hospital

In relation to general practitioners, who operate outside hospitals, these clearly owe a duty of care to their own patients, that is those who are registered with them. Moreover, by virtue of the National Health Service (General Medical Services) Regulations 1992,[10] Sch 2, para 4(1)(h), such a practitioner is required, pursuant to his statutory contract with the area family health services authority, to treat:

> (h) persons to whom he may be requested to give treatment which is immediately required owing to an accident or other emergency at any place in his practice area, provided that –
>
> i   he is not, at time of the request, relieved of liability to give treatment under para 5; and
>
> ii   he is not, at the time of the request, relieved, under para 19(2), of his obligation to give treatment personally; and
>
> iii he is available to provide such treatment,
>
> and any persons by whom he is requested, and agrees, to give treatment which is immediately required owing to an accident or other emergency at any place in the locality of any FHSA in whose medical list he is included, provided there is no doctor who, at the time of the request, is under an obligation otherwise than under this head to give treatment to that person, or there is such a doctor but, after being requested to attend, he is unable to attend and give treatment immediately required . . .

(Paragraphs 5 and 19(2) of the Schedule relieve the doctor of liability to treat, respectively, in cases where he is elderly or infirm, or another doctor is already present.)

The nature of the duty of care owed in such cases by the practitioner to the patient was considered *obiter* by Stuart-Smith LJ in *Capital and Counties v Hants CC:*[11]

> **Stuart-Smith LJ**: There is no doubt that once the relationship of doctor and patient or hospital authority and admitted patient exists, the doctor or the hospital owe a duty to take reasonable care to effect a cure, not merely to prevent further harm. The undertaking is to use the special skills which the doctor and hospital authorities have to treat the patient. In *Cassidy v Ministry of Health (Fahrni, Third Party)* [1951] 1 All ER 574, p 588, Denning LJ said:
>
> > In my opinion, authorities who run a hospital, be they local authorities, government boards, or any other corporation, are in law under the self-same duty as the humblest doctor. Whenever they accept a patient for treatment, they must use reasonable care and skill to cure him of his ailment.
>
> In *Barnett v Chelsea and Kensington Hospital Management Committee* [1968] 1 All ER 1068, Nield J drew a distinction between a casualty department of a hospital that closes its doors and says no patients can be received, in which case he would by inference have held there was no duty of care, and the case before him where the three watchmen who had taken poison entered the hospital and were given erroneous advice, where a duty of care arose.
>
> Likewise, a doctor who happened to witness a road accident will very likely go to the assistance of anyone injured, but he is not under any legal obligation to do so (save in certain limited circumstances which are not relevant) and the relationship of doctor and patient does not arise. If he volunteers his assistance, his only duty as a matter of law is not to make the victim's condition worse.

---

10 SI 1992/635.
11 [1997] QB 1004.

Subsequently, however, the decision in *Capital and Counties* was distinguished by Lord Woolf MR in *Kent v Griffiths (No 3)*[12] in the context of an ambulance's failure to respond expeditiously to a 999 call made on behalf of a woman who had suffered a serious asthma attack (the ambulance took nearly 40 minutes to complete a journey that should have taken no more than 20 minutes, and the patient in the meantime suffered a cardiac arrest). In holding that a duty of care was owed by the ambulance service, his Lordship commented as follows:

> **Lord Woolf MR**: Here what was being provided was a health service. In the case of health services under the 1977 Act the conventional situation is that there is a duty of care. Why should the position of the ambulance staff be different from that of doctors or nurses? In addition the arguments based on public policy are much weaker in the case of the ambulance service than they are in the case of the police or the fire service. The police and fire services' primary obligation is to the public at large. In protecting a particular victim of crime, the police are performing their more general role of maintaining public order and reducing crime. In the case of fire the fire service will normally be concerned not only to protect a particular property where a fire breaks out but also to prevent fire spreading. In the case of both services, there is therefore a concern to protect the public generally . . . Situations could arise where there is a conflict between the interests of a particular individual and the public at large. But, in the case of the ambulance service in this particular case, the only member of the public who could be adversely affected was the claimant. It was the claimant alone for whom the ambulance had been called.

It remains uncertain how far a similar affirmative duty of rescue (requiring him to assist an ill or injured stranger whom he happens to come across outside his practice) would be imposed upon an individual doctor. This question must now be considered in the light of the courts' obligation, under the Human Rights Act 1998, to develop the common law in line with rights under the European Convention on Human Rights, and in this context, Article 2, safeguarding the right to life may well be relevant. In fact, in one kind of situation, namely where a mentally ill patient commits suicide following failings by the hospital staff responsible for them, it has been held that – besides an action in negligence – the bereaved relatives can sue for infringement of the patient's right to life: see *Savage v South Essex Partnership NHS Foundation Trust*[13] and *Rabone v Pennine Care NHS Trust*.[14] Admittedly, in *Powell v United Kingdom*[15] the ECHR ruled that Article 2 was not applicable to the more typical medical negligence scenario of a patient dying after a doctor's failure to treat adequately a life-threatening physical condition. Possibly other considerations would apply, however, where the doctor simply fails to treat the patient at all.[16]

Related questions arise in respect of examinations carried out by doctors upon persons at the behest of third parties, such as employers or insurance companies. Here the examinee does not become the patient of the doctor in the strict sense: nonetheless, should the latter be placed under a positive duty carefully to diagnose and inform him of any abnormalities (as opposed to having a merely negative duty not to injure him during the examination)? In *X (Minors) v Bedfordshire County Council*[17] Lord Browne-Wilkinson suggested *obiter* that only the negative duty would arise, and this was applied by the Court of Appeal in *Kapfunde v Abbey National*.[18] The latter case, however, was one of pure economic loss, suffered by a job applicant who failed to get

---

12 [2001] QB 36.
13 [2008] UKHL 74.
14 [2012] UKSC 2; see further Ch 9, section 9.7.2.3.
15 (2000) 30 EHRR CD 362.
16 For an instructive Australian decision, in which a doctor, who was in his surgery at the time, was held liable in tort for failing to answer a summons for help from a stranger, see *Lowns v Woods* [1996] Aust Torts Rep 81–376.
17 [1995] 2 AC 633.
18 (1998) 46 BMLR 176.

a job in the light of an unfavourable medical report. By contrast, in the context of physical injury related to a condition negligently overlooked by the examining doctor, it seems likely that a duty would be found. As Andrew Grubb has commented:

Grubb, A (ed), *Principles of Medical Law*[19]

> 5.119 . . . [I]n principle, applying the well-known *Caparo* test, there is no difficulty in holding the doctor liable for *all* the immediate consequences of a failure to exercise reasonable care and skill in the course of the examination. Consequently, he could be liable for failing (carelessly) to diagnose a medical condition which could have been treated or its symptoms alleviated if it had been diagnosed earlier. Injury to the person would be foreseeable and there would be a proximate relationship based upon an implied assumption of responsibility by the doctor. The expectation of both examinee and doctor will usually be that the doctor will perform his professional obligation to the person which would include alerting the person to anything untoward.

6.2.2 The duty in 'wrongful conception/birth' cases

In the past, English law was prepared, in principle, to award damages to parents for the costs of bringing up healthy children who would not have been born but for negligence on the part of a doctor: see, for example, the Court of Appeal's decision in *Thake v Maurice*,[20] where the defendant failed to advise a husband that the vasectomy that he had been given was liable to reverse spontaneously. However, this area of the law was dramatically altered by the decision of the House of Lords in *McFarlane v Tayside Health*.

McFarlane v Tayside Health Board[21]

> Mr McFarlane, who was married with four children, underwent a vasectomy operation at the defendant's hospital and was told that it had been a success and that he and his wife need no longer use contraception. Subsequently, his wife became pregnant by him again and gave birth to a fifth child. In their negligence action against the board, the couple claimed damages both for the physical discomfort suffered by Mrs McFarlane during her pregnancy, and for the financial costs of bringing up the child:
>
> > **Lord Slynn of Hadley**: The doctor undertakes a duty of care in regard to the prevention of pregnancy: it does not follow that the duty includes also avoiding the costs of rearing the child if born and accepted into the family. Whereas I have no doubt that there should be compensation for the physical effects of the pregnancy and birth, including of course solatium for consequential suffering by the mother immediately following the birth, I consider that it is not fair, just or reasonable to impose on the doctor or his employer liability for the consequential responsibilities, imposed on or accepted by the parents to bring up a child. The doctor does not assume responsibility for those economic losses. If a client wants to be able to recover such costs he or she must do so by an appropriate contract.
> >
> > **Lord Steyn**: It is possible to view the case simply from the perspective of corrective justice. It requires somebody who has harmed another without justification to indemnify the other. On this approach the parents' claim for the cost of bringing up Catherine must succeed. But one may also

---

19 Oxford: OUP, 2nd edn, 2004.
20 See n 3 above.
21 [2000] 2 AC 59.

approach the case from the vantage point of distributive justice. It requires a focus on the just distribution of burdens and losses among members of a society. If the matter is approached in this way, it may become relevant to ask commuters on the Underground the following question: 'Should the parents of an unwanted but healthy child be able to sue the doctor or hospital for compensation equivalent to the cost of bringing up the child for the years of his or her minority, ie until about 18 years?' My Lords, I am firmly of the view that an overwhelming number of ordinary men and women would answer the question with an emphatic 'No'. And the reason for such a response would be an inarticulate premise as to what is morally acceptable and what is not. Like Ognall J in *Jones v Berkshire AHA*, 2 July 1986, they will have in mind that many couples cannot have children and others have the sorrow and burden of looking after a disabled child. The realisation that compensation for financial loss in respect of the upbringing of a child would necessarily have to discriminate between rich and poor would, surely appear unseemly to them. It would also worry them that parents may be put in a position of arguing in court that the unwanted child, which they accepted and care for, is more trouble than it is worth. Instinctively, the traveller on the Underground would consider that the law of tort has no business to provide legal remedies consequent upon the birth of a healthy child, which all of us regard as a valuable and good thing.

Lord Millett: . . . I am persuaded that the costs of bringing Catherine up are not recoverable. I accept the thrust of both the main arguments in favour of dismissing such a claim. In my opinion the law must take the birth of a normal, healthy baby to be a blessing, not a detriment. In truth it is a mixed blessing. It brings joy and sorrow, blessing and responsibility. The advantages and the disadvantages are inseparable. Individuals may choose to regard the balance as unfavourable and take steps to forgo the pleasures as well as the responsibilities of parenthood. They are entitled to decide for themselves where their own interests lie. But society itself must regard the balance as beneficial. It would be repugnant to its own sense of values to do otherwise. It is morally offensive to regard a normal, healthy baby as more trouble and expense than it is worth.

Although the Law Lords did not speak with one voice in *McFarlane*, it is apparent that, where a healthy child is born, damages will be limited to the physical pain and discomfort suffered by the mother during pregnancy. By contrast, no duty of care is owed to the parents in respect of the subsequent costs of maintaining a healthy child. Given both the incalculable benefits to the parents involved, and the policy factors adverted to by Lord Steyn, it was felt that such a birth should simply not sound in damages in tort.[22]

An issue left unresolved by *McFarlane* concerned the problem of parents who, in similar circumstances, have a disabled child. This matter was subsequently considered in *Parkinson v St James and Seacroft University Hospital NHS Trust*,[23] in which, after usefully analysing the diverse speeches in *McFarlane*, the Court of Appeal concluded that the additional costs associated with the child's disability were recoverable. As Brooke LJ commented:

Brooke LJ: . . . (iv) The purpose of the operation was to prevent Mrs P from conceiving any more children, including children with congenital abnormalities, and the surgeon's duty of care is strictly related to the proper fulfilment of that purpose; (v) Parents in Mrs P's position were entitled to recover damages in these circumstances for 15 years between the decisions in *Emeh* and *McFarlane*, so that this is not a radical step

---

22 See also the subsequent decision of the Court of Appeal in *Greenfield v Irwin (A Firm)* [2001] 1 WLR 1279.
23 [2001] 3 WLR 376.

forward into the unknown; ... (vii) If principles of distributive justice are called in aid, I believe that ordinary people would consider that it would be fair for the law to make an award in such a case, provided that it is limited to the extra expenses associated with the child's disability. I can see nothing in any majority reasoning in *McFarlane* to deflect this court from adopting this course, which in my judgment both logic and justice demands.

In another case following *McFarlane*, that of *Rees v Darlington Memorial Hospital NHS Trust*, a majority of the Court of Appeal held that, similarly, a disabled mother who gave birth to a healthy child was entitled to recover the extra costs of child care arising out of her disability. This decision was subsequently taken on appeal by the NHS trust to a specially constituted seven-judge House of Lords.

Rees v Darlington Memorial Hospital NHS Trust[24]

Ms Rees underwent a sterilisation, due, *inter alia*, to her concern that her severe visual disability would prevent her from being able to care for a child. The operation was performed negligently and she subsequently became pregnant and gave birth to a healthy son. Essentially, the House of Lords was required to consider three points: (i) should it affirm the principle it had laid down four years before in *McFarlane* that damages would not lie for the maintenance of (healthy) children? If so: (iia) did a case, such as this one, involving a disabled parent, comprise an exception to that principle, as *per* the decision of the majority of the Court of Appeal? And – albeit an *obiter* issue: (iib) had the Court of Appeal been right, in the *Parkinson* case, to treat cases of disabled children as an exception to the *McFarlane* principle?

As to the first point, all seven Law Lords upheld the correctness of the decision in *McFarlane*. In his speech Lord Bingham commented on this aspect as follows:

Lord Bingham: [15] In *McFarlane*'s case, your Lordships' House held unanimously that a negligent doctor is not required to meet the cost of bringing up a healthy child born in these circumstances. The language, and to some extent the legal reasoning, employed by each of their Lordships differed. But, however expressed, the underlying perception of all their Lordships was that fairness and reasonableness do not require that the damages payable by a negligent doctor should extend so far. The approach usually adopted in measuring recoverable financial loss is not appropriate when the subject of the legal wrong is the birth of an unintended healthy child and the head of claim is the cost of the whole of the child's upbringing.

[16] I have heard nothing in the submissions advanced on the present appeal to persuade me that this decision by the House was wrong and ought to be revisited. On the contrary, that the negligent doctor or, in most cases, the National Health Service should pay all the costs of bringing up the child seems to me a disproportionate response to the doctor's wrong. It would accord ill with the values society attaches to human life and to parenthood. The birth of a child should not be treated as comparable to a parent suffering a personal injury, with the cost of rearing the child being treated as special damages akin to the financially adverse consequences flowing from the onset of a chronic medical condition.

On the other hand, a 'gloss' on *McFarlane* was approved by a majority of their Lordships (over the dissents of Lords Steyn and Hope), in the form of permitting a 'conventional award' of £15,000 in such cases to reflect the legal wrong done to claimants in having their wishes to stay childless thwarted.

As to the other issues, the House of Lords reversed, by a bare majority (Lords Steyn, Hope and Hutton dissenting), the decision of the Court of Appeal to award Ms Rees the extra costs of maintaining her

---

24 [2003] UKHL 52.

healthy child in this case: in short, she was entitled to the £15,000 conventional sum, but nothing more. As to the final, *obiter* question of the position in relation to disabled children, this was left unresolved. Lords Bingham and Nicholls were of the view that here too only the conventional sum should lie, and disapproved the contrary decision of the Court of Appeal in *Parkinson*. By contrast, Lords Steyn, Hope and Hutton supported the recovery of extra costs attributable to maintaining a disabled child (albeit in the context of their dissenting view that a disabled parent should also recover). The two remaining Law Lords, Millett and Scott, left the question open.

In his speech, the latter Law Lord addressed the disabled-child issue as follows:

> **Lord Scott:** [145] The question how the *McFarlane* principle should be applied to a case in which the mother is healthy but the child is born with a disability is not one which needs to be resolved on this appeal. In my opinion, however, a distinction may need to be drawn between a case where the avoidance of the birth of a child with a disability is the very reason why the parent or parents sought the medical treatment or services to avoid conception that, in the event, were negligently provided and a case where the medical treatment or services were sought simply to avoid conception. *Parkinson*'s case was a case in the latter category. In such a case, where the parents have had no particular reason to fear that if a child is born to them it will suffer from a disability, I do not think there is any sufficient basis for treating the expenses occasioned by the disability as falling outside the principles underlying *McFarlane*'s case. The striking of the balance between the burden of rearing the disabled child and the benefit to the parents of the child as a member of their family seems to me as invidious and impossible as in the case of the child born without any disability.

As Lord Scott points out, the disability suffered by the child in the *Parkinson* case was incidental to the hospital's negligence – the medical procedure there was designed to render the claimant sterile, not because she was at any special risk of having a disabled child, but simply for family planning purposes. However, another possible scenario is that the specific purpose of the procedure, whose negligent performance is the subject of a claim, was to avoid the birth of a disabled child. An example is *Hardman v Amin*,[25] where the defendant negligently failed to diagnose the claimant's rubella, thereby depriving her of the opportunity to have an abortion (which, it was accepted, she would have taken). As his Lordship implies, recovery should arguably be permitted in the latter type of ('direct disability') case. In this regard it is interesting to note that, in several such cases, the lower courts have awarded quite generous damages to cover the child's maintenance, not simply the extra costs attendant upon its disability.[26]

THINK POINT

Do you think that full damages (including for maintenance) should remain payable in respect of disabled children?

6.2.3 The duty to third parties

Interesting questions arise as to how far a doctor will owe a duty to third parties to whom he personally offers no medical care. Three broad types of scenario may be distinguished. The first

---

25 [2000] Lloyd's Rep Med 498.
26 As well as the *Hardman* case, see *Nunnerley v Warrington HA* [2000] PIQR Q69 and *Lee v Taunton and Somerset NHS Trust* [2001] 1 FLR 419 (but *cf Rand v East Dorset HA* [2000] Lloyd's Rep Med 181).

('dangerous patient cases') is where the third party is injured in a foreseeable way through subsequent contact with one of the doctor's patients. The second ('injured patient cases') is where the third party – typically a close relative – suffers secondary harm through the negligence of the doctor in harming the patient. Third, there are some instances of genetic illness, where it may be argued that a doctor (whose patient has such an illness) is under a duty to warn the patient's relatives of the risk that the latter have the same illness ('genetic disclosure cases').

6.2.3.1 Dangerous patient cases

Suppose that a doctor fails to spot that one of his patients is carrying a contagious disease, and the latter subsequently passes on the infection: does the person he infects have any right of action against the doctor? As a general rule, and in accordance with established principles of tort, a person (A)'s liability for injury caused by another (B) to a third party (C) has tended to depend upon two factors: first, the extent to which B is an involuntary agent in the events which lead to C's injury; and, secondly, the ability on A's part to foresee C's presence in relation to B. Both factors appear to have played a part in the rejection by the Court of Appeal of the claimant's action in the case of *Palmer v Tees HA*.

Palmer v Tees HA[27]

> Mrs Palmer, whose four-year-old daughter, Rosie, was murdered by a psychopath, brought an action against the defendant health authority both in her own name (in respect of the psychiatric illness she suffered) and on behalf of Rosie's estate. Some months prior to committing the murder the psychopath had been treated as an outpatient at the defendant's psychiatric hospital, where he had allegedly told staff that he would kill a child:
>
> > **Stuart-Smith LJ**: [T]he critical decision is that of *Hill v Chief Constable of West Yorkshire* [1989] 1 AC 53 which is a case concerned with personal injury . . .
>
> While there are of course differences between *Hill*'s case and the present, that was a case of the police and not psychiatrists, and the identity of the offender was unknown, the crucial point is that there is no relationship between the defendant and the victim. Mr Sherman relied on the case of *Holgate v Lancashire Mental Hospital Board* [1937] 4 All ER 19. The facts bear a striking resemblance to those in the present case. L was a defective who had been convicted of serious crimes and sentenced to detention during His Majesty's pleasure. In due course he was transferred to the defendant's institution. He was allowed out on licence without any proper inquiry being made, and the licence was subsequently extended. During the period of his extended licence L visited the plaintiff's house and savagely assaulted her. The action was tried by a jury and the report contains the summing-up of Lewis J. It appears to have been assumed that the defendant owed a duty of care to the claimant. The summing-up is concerned only with the issue of want of care . . . The case occurred at a time when the essential elements of a duty of care were much less clearly defined than is the position today. In my judgment the case cannot be reconciled with *Hill* on the question of proximity . . .
>
> An additional reason why in my judgment in this case it is at least necessary for the victim to be identifiable (though as I have indicated it may not be sufficient) to establish proximity, is that it seems to me that the most effective way of providing protection would be to give warning to the victim, his or her parents or social services so that some protective measure can be made. As Mr Moon pointed out, the ability to restrict and restrain a psychiatric patient is subject to considerable restriction under the Mental

---

27 [1999] Lloyd's Rep Med 351, CA.

Health Act 1983 (see particularly section 3) and are not unlimited in time. Moreover treatment, especially drug treatment of the patient, depends on his or her co-operation when an out-patient, and is limited when an in-patient. It may be a somewhat novel approach to the question of proximity, but it seems to me to be a relevant consideration to ask what could the defendant have done to avoid the danger, if the suggested precautions, *ie* committal under section 3 of the Mental Health Act or treatment are likely to be of doubtful effectiveness, and the most effective precaution cannot be taken because the defendant does not know who to warn.

6.2.3.2 Injured patient cases

It is readily apparent that, where a patient is injured or dies as a result of a doctor's negligence, this will have a knock-on effect upon others, in particular the patient's next of kin. The question of the duty of care in the context of breaking bad news to relatives was considered by the Court of Appeal in *Powell and Another v Boldaz and Others*,[28] in which a young boy died after a failure to diagnose Addison's disease:

Stuart-Smith LJ: I turn then to consider whether the pleaded post-death matters can give rise to an action for negligence ... Mr Powers submits that the duty of care arises under the principles enunciated by Lord Bridge of Harwich in *Caparo Industries plc v Dickman* [1990] 2 AC 605, pp 616E–18F, namely where the following three elements are present:

a   foreseeability of damage arising from the relevant act or omission;

b   a sufficient relationship of proximity between the parties;

c   as a matter of legal policy it is fair, just and reasonable that a duty of care should exist.

I propose to consider first whether a sufficient relationship of proximity existed. It must be appreciated that prior to 17 April 1990, although the plaintiffs were patients of the defendants in the sense that they were on their register, the only patient who was seeking medical advice and treatment was Robert. It was to him that the defendants owed a duty of care. The discharge of that duty in the case of a young child will often involve giving advice and instruction to the parents so that they can administer the appropriate medication, observe relevant symptoms and seek further medical assistance if need be. In giving such advice, the doctor obviously owes a duty to be careful. But the duty is owed to the child, not to the parents. As Lord Diplock said in *Sidaway v Governors of Bethlem Royal Hospital* [1985] AC 871, p 890:

> ... a doctor's duty of care, whether he be a general practitioner or consulting surgeon or physician, is owed to that patient and none other, idiosyncrasies and all.

... I do not think that a doctor who has been treating a patient who has died, who tells relatives what has happened, thereby undertakes the doctor–patient relationship towards the relatives. It is a situation that calls for sensitivity, tact and discretion, but the mere fact that the communicator is a doctor, does not, without more, mean that he undertakes the doctor–patient relationship. It is of course possible that the doctor in such a situation may realise that the shock has been so great that some immediate therapy is needed, but even so this situation is probably more akin to the doctor giving emergency treatment to an accident victim, though no doubt it will be a question of fact and degree in each case whether doctor–patient relationships came into existence by the doctor undertaking to treat and heal the person as a patient.

---

28 (1997) 39 BMLR 35.

Nonetheless, it is apparent that, where they actually witness the harm occur, relatives may claim as secondary victims of psychiatric injury, subject to satisfying the control mechanisms in *Alcock v Chief Constable of South Yorkshire Police*.[29] In *Allin v City and Hackney HA*[30] a woman recovered damages for post-traumatic stress disorder caused by being told (falsely) that her baby was dead. Subsequently, in *North Glamorgan NHS Trust v Walters*[31] a series of events, which began when the respondent awoke to find her ten-month-old son suffering a seizure and ended with his life-support being terminated some 36 hours later, was held to be a single 'shocking event', entitling her to recover for her pathological grief reaction. Ward LJ held:

> **Ward LJ**: [34] In my judgment the law as presently formulated does permit a realistic view being taken from case to case of what constitutes the necessary 'event'. Our task is not to construe the word as if it had appeared in legislation but to gather the sense of the word in order to inform the principle to be drawn from the various authorities . . . It is a matter of judgment from case to case depending on the facts and circumstance of each case. In my judgment on the facts of this case there was an inexorable progression from the moment when the fit occurred as a result of the failure of the hospital properly to diagnose and then to treat the baby, the fit causing the brain damage which shortly thereafter made termination of this child's life inevitable and the dreadful climax when the child died in her arms. It is a seamless tale with an obvious beginning and an equally obvious end. It was played out over a period of 36 hours, which for her both at the time and as subsequently recollected was undoubtedly one drawn-out experience.

By contrast, recovery has been denied in cases where, rather than a shock, there is a 'dawning realisation' that one's next of kin will die. Thus, in *Sion v Hampstead HA*[32] the court rejected the claim of a father whose psychiatric injury was caused by watching his son die over a two-week period.

6.2.3.3 Genetic disclosure cases

Recently, the English courts have been faced with a novel form of action brought by relatives of the doctor's patient in respect of the doctor's failure to advise them that their relative has a genetic disorder, which they too may have. Thus, in *Smith v University of Leicester NHS Trust*[33] a mother brought an action on behalf of her children against the defendant, which had treated their second cousin for Adrenomyeloneuropathy (AMN), a genetically determined brain disorder. She claimed its negligent failure to diagnose AMN in the cousin and communicate the diagnosis to the family meant her children – who also suffered from AMN – thereby lost the opportunity to be tested and treated earlier. However, in striking out the claim, McKenna J suggested that '[t]he settled policy of the law is opposed to granting remedies to third parties for the effects of injuries to other people', and held it would not be fair, just and reasonable to impose a duty towards relatives in such cases.

---

29 [1992] 1 AC 310.
30 [1996] 7 Med LR 167.
31 [2002] EWCA 1792.
32 [1994] 5 Med LR 170; see too *Ward v Leeds Teaching Hospitals NHS Trust* [2004] Lloyd's Rep Med 530.
33 [2016] EWHC 817 (QB).
34 [2017] EWCA Civ 336.

Subsequently, though, in *ABC v St George's Health Care NHS Trust*[34] the Court of Appeal found that on the particular facts the existence of such a duty was at least arguable, and quashed the decision of Nicol J to strike out the claim, remitting it to the High Court for trial. The case presents an interesting contrast to the *Smith* case in several respects, some telling in favour of a putative duty, others against. Thus, in *ABC* the claimant was the daughter of the patient, and was at a 50 per cent risk of having inherited Huntingdon's Disease (a progressive and fatal neurological genetic disease that manifests itself in later adulthood) from her father. The latter was a patient in a secure psychiatric unit, to which he was committed after killing the claimant's mother. After diagnosing the disease, the defendant – though it had direct contact with the claimant as part of a counselling arrangement – chose to abide by the father's request that they should not tell her.

See Chapter ◄ 5

Especially this last factor raises difficult issues – considered in more detail in Chapter 5 – of balancing prevention of harm to others against patient confidentiality. In this regard, the Court of Appeal engaged in a careful analysis of various policy factors, which might militate against imposing a duty to breach this in order to warn the relatives. Nonetheless, it ultimately found none of them compelling, particularly as relevant professional guidance to clinicians suggested these were at least ethically permitted (so would have a persuasive defence to an action for breach of confidence) to disclose in such a case. As Irwin LJ commented in his judgment:

> **Irwin LJ:** [31] There can be no doubt as to the difficulty facing clinicians in the situation we are contemplating. It seems to me the difficulty already arises, and indeed is exemplified and emphasised by the professional guidance I have quoted above. I quite accept that the existence of a legal duty to the "third party" as well as to the patient may add to the pressure on the clinician. It will no longer be clear to the clinician which decision will be protective of legal action against him or her. Is it necessarily and inevitably in the public interest that clinicians should be relieved of that pressure? In my view, it is self-evident that there is a public interest in avoiding excessive litigation and in keeping to a minimum what one can call, in shorthand, defensive medicine. However, it seems not necessarily correct, in a situation where patient confidentiality should be waived or, if necessary breached, that the common law should so clearly incentivise obligations in one direction but not the other. It seems to me at least arguable that that may encourage rather than diminish defensive medicine.
>
> [32] The Claimant submits that balancing risks is an inherent part of clinical practice. In such circumstances the imposition of the legal duty advanced here would serve to protect the interests of both parties, and ensure that a proper balancing exercise is performed by the clinician. In my view, this is a properly arguable position.

Finally, albeit in a rather different context, it should be noted that, on grounds of public policy, a doctor will not owe a duty of care to parents in cases where he mistakenly diagnoses child abuse on their part (leading, for example, to the child's temporary removal). As the House of Lords held in *JD v East Berkshire Community Health NHS Trust*,[35] the doctor, provided he acts in good faith, should not be inhibited in the course of his investigations by the prospect of such possible liability: his duty is owed to the child alone.

---

35 [2005] UKHL 23.

6.3 The breach of duty

6.3.1 The standard of care

6.3.1.1 The ordinary professional

The first point to note is that the standard of care against which the doctor will be judged is not going to be that of the ordinary reasonable man who enjoys no medical expertise. Instead, in holding himself out as possessing the special skills of his profession, the doctor is under a duty to conform to the ordinary standards of that profession. In *Bolam v Friern Hospital Management Committee*[36] McNair J put this point as follows:

> **McNair J:** How do you test whether [an] act or failure is negligent? In an ordinary case it is generally said that you judge that by the action of the man in the street. He is the ordinary man. In one case it has been said that you judge it by the conduct of the man on the top of a Clapham omnibus. He is the ordinary man. But where you get a situation which involves the use of some special skill or competence, then the test whether there has been negligence or not is not the test of the man on the top of the Clapham omnibus, because he has not got this special skill. The test is the standard of the ordinary skilled man exercising and professing to have that special skill. A man need not possess the highest expert skill at the risk of being found negligent. It is well established law that it is sufficient if he exercises the ordinary skill of an ordinary competent man exercising that particular art.

It is further apparent, however, that doctors will not be treated as an homogenous group in this context. As Lord Bridge noted in *Sidaway v Governors of Bethlem Royal Hospital:*[37]

> **Lord Bridge:** The language of the *Bolam* test clearly requires a different degree of skill from a specialist in his own special field than from a general practitioner. In the field of neuro-surgery it would be necessary to substitute for Lord President Clyde's phrase 'no doctor of ordinary skill', the phrase 'no neuro-surgeon of ordinary skill'.

The ordinary professional will be expected to keep his knowledge reasonably up to date. What counts as 'reasonable' in this context will again vary with the doctor's degree of specialisation. The doctor is not required to read every article in the medical press. In *Crawford v Board of Governors of Charing Cross Hospital*[38] the Court of Appeal found that there had been no breach of duty when an operative procedure was performed resulting in paralysis, which some months previously had been the subject of an isolated report in *The Lancet*. Nonetheless, the doctor should certainly keep abreast of the most significant developments in his field.[39]

THINK POINT

What of an operation that is so difficult it requires a surgeon of special skill: would there be negligence if such a surgeon were not used, and, if so, would this be of the health authority (relative to its primary duty of care) or of the 'ordinary' surgeon who operated?

---

36 [1957] 1 WLR 582.
37 [1985] AC 871; the reference is to Lord President Clyde's speech in the Scottish case of *Hunter v Hanley* (1955) SC 200.
38 (1953) *The Times*, 8 December.
39 See *Gascoine v Ian Sheridan and Co (A Firm) and Latham* [1994] 5 Med LR 437.

6.3.1.2 Junior doctors

A particular difficulty arises in relation to the level of skill expected of junior medical staff who, *ex hypothesi*, will lack the experience of the ordinary competent doctor. Here, the courts have felt obliged to follow the reasoning in *Nettleship v Weston*,[40] in which a learner driver was held to be subject to the same standard of care as the reasonably competent and experienced driver. Indeed, this principle had already been stated in the early medical negligence case of *Jones v Manchester Corp*,[41] where a patient died after the maladministration of anaesthetic by a doctor qualified for only five months. It was said that 'errors due to inexperience are no defence'. There is an understandably pragmatic aspect to this approach. Courts do not want to apply a sliding scale of standards of care depending upon the subjective attributes of the particular defendant. The liability of junior doctors was subsequently considered by the Court of Appeal in *Wilsher v Essex AHA*.

Wilsher v Essex AHA[42]

The claimant was a premature baby who was treated in the defendant's ante-natal unit. He was given oxygen by two doctors, both inexperienced. They inserted the catheter through which the oxygen was to be administered, into a vein rather than an artery. This is, apparently, a common mistake and was not due to negligence. The position of the catheter can be checked by use of an x-ray. The doctors, however, failed to notice the mistake, and the senior registrar checking their work also failed to notice. The majority of the Court of Appeal confirmed that there should be a uniform standard of care:

> **Glidewell LJ**: In my view, the law requires the trainee or learner to be judged by the same standard as his more experienced colleagues. If it did not, inexperience would frequently be urged as a defence to an action for professional negligence.
>
> If this test appears unduly harsh in relation to the inexperienced, I should add that, in my view, the inexperienced doctor called upon to exercise a specialist skill will, as part of that skill, seek the advice and help of his superiors when he does or may need it. If he does seek such help, he will often have satisfied the test, even though he may himself have made a mistake. It is for this reason that I agree that Dr Wiles was not negligent. He made a mistake in inserting the catheter into a vein, and a second mistake in not recognising the signs that he had done so on the x-ray. But, having done what he thought right, he asked Dr Kawa, the senior registrar, to check what he had done, and Dr Kawa did so. Dr Kawa failed to recognise the indication on the x-ray . . .

As this makes clear, junior doctors are entitled to expect their work to be checked, and, on the facts of the case, were found not to be liable (although the registrar was); indeed, the court suggested that a hospital could be directly liable in negligence if it failed to have a proper system for inspecting the work of junior staff.

Mustill LJ similarly rejected the argument that there should be a subjective standard of care, depending on the doctor's experience:

> **Mustill LJ**: To my mind, this notion of a duty tailored to the actor, rather than to the act which he elects to perform, has no place in the law of tort. Indeed, the defendants did not contend that it could be justified by any reported authority on the general law of tort. Instead, it was suggested that the medical profession is a special case. Public hospital medicine has always been organised so that young doctors and nurses learn on the job. If the hospitals abstained from using

---

40 [1971] 3 All ER 581.
41 [1952] 2 All ER 125.
42 See n 8 above.

inexperienced people, they could not staff their wards and theatres, and the junior staff could never learn. The longer term interests of patients as a whole are best served by maintaining the present system, even if this may diminish the legal rights of the individual patient: for, after all, medicine is about curing, not litigation.

I acknowledge the appeal of this argument . . . Nevertheless, I cannot accept that there should be a special rule for doctors in public hospitals. . . . To my mind, it would be a false step to subordinate the legitimate expectation of the patient that he will receive from each person concerned with his care a degree of skill appropriate to the task which he undertakes, to an understandable wish to minimise the psychological and financial pressures on hard-pressed young doctors.

By contrast Sir Nicolas Browne-Wilkinson VC, dissenting from the majority view, commented as follows:

Browne-Wilkinson VC: . . . [O]ne of the chief hazards of inexperience is that one does not always know the risks which exist. In my judgment, so long as the English law rests liability on personal fault, a doctor who has properly accepted a post in a hospital in order to gain necessary experience should only be held liable for acts or omissions which a careful doctor with his qualifications and experience would not have done or omitted.

Recently, in *FB v Rana*, in which the Court of Appeal applied the majority reasoning from *Wilsher*, Jackson LJ noted the law here makes 'an imperfect compromise [achieving] a balance between the interests of society and fairness to the individual practitioner'.[43] As his Lordship elaborated:

Jackson LJ: [56] From the defendant's point of view, it is harsh to disregard their limitations and to hold them liable for doing that which they could not help doing or for failing to achieve that which they could not achieve. But a claimant is entitled to expect that those whom he or she encounters in the ordinary transactions of life will adhere to certain general standards.

6.3.1.3 Scarce resources and emergencies

Another situation where the courts have insisted on an objective standard of medical care is in the face of arguments based on shortages of healthcare resources. In practice, such a claim is likely to be brought not against an individual doctor, but directly against a health trust or hospital, in respect of institutional negligence – ie arguing that the overall system of care it operated was flawed. A case in point is that of *Bull v Devon HA*,[44] in which one of the claimant's twins was born brain damaged due to the delay in getting the registrar to attend her. The defendants maintained maternity services on different sites, but only employed a single registrar, and the system for calling him over to assist in the delivery had broken down. The Court of Appeal unanimously held the health authority liable. In his judgment Mustill LJ commented:

Mustill LJ: The . . . suggested answer [to the claim of negligence] was on these lines: that hospitals such as the Devon and Exeter were in the dilemma of having to supply a maternity service, and yet not disposing

---

43 [2017] EWCA Civ 334, at para [60].
44 [1993] 4 Med LR 117.

of sufficient manpower to provide immediate cover, the more so since the small number of consultants and registrars had to deal with three different sites. They could not be expected to do more than their best, allocating their limited resources as favourably as possible. . . . I have some reservations about this contention, which are not allayed by the submission that hospital medicine is a public service. So it is, but there are other public services in respect of which it is not necessarily an answer to allegations of unsafety that there were insufficient resources to enable the administrators to do everything which they would like to do.

At the same time, what is at issue here is the provision of a minimum level of care. Over and above this, a degree of disparity in treatment services will be tolerated between different geographical regions and types of hospital. Thus, the fact that a district hospital fails to provide the patient with the level of specialist care he would have received in a university hospital is not itself negligent; the issue will instead be whether, in the light of the patient's condition, it was negligent not to refer him for such specialist care.[45]

An exception to the principle, that a doctor will be judged according to the standard of reasonably experienced doctors in their field, is provided by emergency treatment. Michael Jones has commented as follows on the level of experience expected in the latter context:

Jones, M, *Medical Negligence*[46]

In an emergency it may well be reasonable for a practitioner inexperienced in a particular treatment to intervene, or indeed for someone lacking medical qualifications to undertake some forms of treatment. For example, a bystander who renders assistance at a road accident does not necessarily hold himself out as qualified to do so. He would be expected to achieve only the standard that could reasonably be expected in the circumstances, which would probably be very low. This approach is clearly borne of the emergency since if there was no urgency, the unqualified person who undertakes treatment which is beyond his competence would be held to the standard to be expected of the reasonably competent and experienced practitioner. A person who holds himself out as trained in first aid must conform to the standards of 'the ordinary skilled first aider exercising and professing to have that special skill of a first aider'.

Secondly, in relation to treatment decisions taken in an emergency, a doctor will not be found negligent simply because the reasonably competent doctor would have made a different decision, given more time and information. In the case of *Wilson v Swanson*[47] the Supreme Court of Canada held that there was no negligence when a surgeon had to make an immediate decision whether to operate, and the operation was subsequently found to have been unnecessary. Moreover, the skill itself required in the execution of treatment may be somewhat lower. As Mustill LJ commented in the *Wilsher* case:[48]

Mustill LJ: An emergency may overburden the available resources, and, if an individual is forced by circumstances to do too many things at once, the fact that he does one of them incorrectly should not lightly be taken as negligence.

---

45 See *Ball v Wirral HA* [2003] Lloyd's Rep Med 165.
46 See n 4 above.
47 (1956) 5 DLR (2d) 113.
48 See n 8 above.

> **THINK POINT**
>
> It is sometimes suggested that a doctor who treats in an emergency will only be liable if he actively worsens the patient's situation. Do you think this ought to be the case?

6.3.2 Establishing the breach

6.3.2.1 Accepted practice – the '*Bolam* test'

In determining whether, in a particular case, a doctor has satisfied the appropriate standard of care, the courts will look in the first place to accepted practice within the profession: has the doctor conducted himself in the manner in which other doctors would have conducted themselves in the same circumstances? Of course, medicine is a developing science and new schools of thought as to how best to carry out treatments are constantly emerging. For this reason, the courts do not expect to find uniformity of standard medical practice in any given case. Rather, they ask whether the doctor has conformed with *an* (note the use of the indefinite article) accepted practice within the profession. This approach informed McNair J's direction to the jury in the famous case of *Bolam v Friern Hospital Management Committee*.

Bolam v Friern Hospital Management Committee[49]

The claimant suffered from clinical depression and it was decided to treat him with electro-convulsive therapy (ECT), which involves passing an electric current through the patient's brain to induce a fit. At the time this was fairly novel treatment and doctors differed as to how best to minimise the risk of the patient suffering bone fractures during the fit. At the hospital where Mr Bolam was treated, a system of manual restraint in which nurses held the patient down, but only by the chin, was in use (two other practices adopted elsewhere involved the use of rigid restraint, and relaxant drugs administered following a general anaesthetic, respectively). Unfortunately, in the plaintiff's case the manual restraint was ineffective and he suffered serious pelvic injuries during treatment:

> **McNair J** (directing the jury): Counsel for the plaintiff put it in this way, that in the case of a medical man, negligence means failure to act in accordance with the standards of reasonably competent medical men at the time. That is a perfectly accurate statement, as long as it is remembered that there may be one or more perfectly proper standards; and if a medical man confirms with one of those proper standards then he is not negligent. Counsel for the plaintiff was also right, in my judgment, in saying that a mere personal belief that a particular technique is best is no defence unless that belief is based on reasonable grounds. That again is unexceptional. But the emphasis which is laid by counsel for the defendants is on this aspect of negligence: he submitted to you that the real question on which you have to make up your mind on each of the three major points to be considered is whether the defendants, in acting in the way in which they did, were acting in accordance with a practice of competent respected professional opinion . . . I myself would . . . put it this way: a doctor is not guilty of negligence if he has acted in accordance with a practice accepted as proper by a responsible body of medical men skilled in that particular art.

---

49 See n 36 above.

In effect, before finding a negligent error of clinical judgment, the court must be satisfied – on the basis of the opinions of other doctors (acting as expert witnesses) – that no reasonable doctor would have acted as the defendant doctor. The *Bolam* test was subsequently approved on several occasions by the House of Lords. An example is found in the speech of Lord Scarman in *Sidaway v Governors of Bethlem Royal Hospital*,[50] in which his Lordship articulated the *Bolam* test in the following terms:

> **Lord Scarman**: The *Bolam* principle may be formulated as a rule that a doctor is not negligent if he acts in accordance with a practice accepted at the time as proper by a responsible body of medical opinion even though other doctors adopt a different practice. In short, the law imposes the duty of care, but the standard of care is a matter of medical judgment.

(See also the leading judgment of the same Law Lord in the case of *Maynard v W. Midlands RHA*.[51])

What are the reasons the courts have for attaching such importance to expert medical opinion in deciding if there has been negligence in a medical case? One has already been mentioned: medicine is recognised as not being an exact science; there may, at any given moment, be two or more perfectly respectable ways of dealing with a particular problem. Indeed, one could go further and cite the possibility of competition between different accepted practices as a key element in allowing progress in treatment to be made. *Bolam* itself provides an illustration of this: in the 1950s only one of three schools of thought administered ECT following a general anaesthetic, but nowadays it is invariably done this way. Despite the risks associated with anaesthesia itself, experience ultimately has shown this to be preferable to running the risks of bone fracture associated with either rigid or manual restraint.

Secondly, and more controversially, the courts have arguably also been motivated by the fear of otherwise encouraging an explosion of malpractice litigation and an uncongenial climate for doctors to go about their business of treating patients: as Mustill LJ commented in *Wilsher v Essex AHA*, 'medicine is about curing, not litigation'.[52] This attitude found its most notorious expression in Lord Denning's suggestion (repeated in a number of cases over the years) that an 'error of clinical judgment' could not amount to negligence, a view finally laid to rest in 1981 in the case of *Whitehouse v Jordan*.

Whitehouse v Jordan[53]

> The claimant was born brain damaged, allegedly as a result of the defendant obstetrician's negligence. The latter had made prolonged attempts at normal delivery using forceps before realising this was impossible. The claimant, suing by his mother as next friend, argued that the defendant should have moved more quickly to delivery by Caesarean section.
>
> **Lord Edmund Davies**: .... [T]he principal questions calling for decision are: (a) in what manner did Mr Jordan use the forceps? And (b) was that manner consistent with the degree of care which a member of his profession is required by law to exercise? Surprising though it is at this late stage in the development of the law of negligence, counsel for Mr Jordan

---

50 See n 37 above.
51 [1984] 1 WLR 634, HL.
52 See n 8 above.
53 [1981] 1 WLR 246.

persisted in submitting that his client should be completely exculpated were the answer to question (b), 'Well, at worst he was guilty of an error of clinical judgment'. My Lords, it is high time that the unacceptability of such an answer be fully exposed. To say that a surgeon committed an error of clinical judgment is wholly ambiguous, for, while some such errors may be completely consistent with the due exercise of professional skill, other acts or omissions in the course of exercising 'clinical judgment' may be so glaringly below proper standards as to make a finding of negligence inevitable. Indeed, I should have regarded this as a truism were it not that, despite the exposure of the 'false antithesis' by Donaldson LJ in his dissenting judgment in the Court of Appeal, counsel for the defendants adhered to it before your Lordships.

Thirdly, at least in the past, the highly technical nature of some of the information at issue seems to have led judges to defer to the experts in such cases. Thus, in the Court of Appeal case of *Dwyer v Roderick*,[54] May LJ stated:

May LJ: It would be to shut one's eyes to the obvious if one denied that the burden of [establishing a breach of duty on] something more than the mere balance of probabilities was greater when one was investigating the complicated and sophisticated actions of a qualified and experienced doctor than when one was inquiring into the inattention of the driver in a simple running down action.

However, it could be argued that the courts were too ready to mystify medical matters. As Michael Jones comments:

Jones, M, *Medical Negligence*[55]

Where the case does not involve difficult or uncertain questions of medical or surgical treatment, or abstruse or highly technical scientific issues, but is concerned with whether obvious and simple precautions could have been taken, the question of the practice of experts should be largely irrelevant. The courts do not rely on expert rally drivers, for example, to say whether a motorist was negligent.

Moreover, before any question of complying with accepted practice can arise the court must be satisfied on the evidence presented to it that there is a responsible body of professional opinion which supports the practice. It is always open to the court to reject expert evidence applying the ordinary principles of credibility that would be applied in any courtroom, for example, that the evidence is internally contradictory, or that the witness was acting as an advocate rather than an impartial and objective expert.

In fact, more recently the courts have paid greater attention to the proper circumstances for the application of the *Bolam* test. In the case of *Penney v East Kent HA*[56] it was accepted that where the dispute between the expert witnesses is purely factual in nature (here whether cervical smear slides showed significant abnormalities), the *Bolam* test in fact has no part to play. As Lord Woolf MR commented:

---

54 (1983) 127 SJ 805.
55 See n 4 above.
56 [2000] Lloyd's Rep Med 41; see also *Smith v Southampton University Hospital NHS Trust* [2007] EWCA Civ 387; and *Muller v King's College Hospital NHS Foundation Trust* [2017] EWHC 128 (QB).

Lord Woolf MR: . . . the *Bolam* test has no application where what the judge is required to do is to make findings of fact. This is so, even where those findings of fact are the subject of conflicting expert evidence. Thus in this case there were three questions which the judge had to answer: What was to be seen in the slides? At the relevant time could a screener exercising reasonable care fail to see what was on the slide? Could a reasonably competent screener, aware of what a screener exercising reasonable care would observe on the slide, treat the slide as negative? Thus, logically the starting point for the experts reasoning was what was on the slides. . . . In so far as they were not in agreement, the judge had the unenviable task of deciding as a matter of fact which of the experts were correct as to what the slides showed. This was a task which required expert evidence. However the evidence having been given, the judge had to make his own finding on the balance of probabilities on this issue of fact in order to proceed to the next step in answering the question of negligence or no negligence. Having come to his own conclusion as to what the slides showed, the judge had, therefore, then to answer the 2nd and 3rd questions in order to decide whether the screener was in breach of duty in giving a negative report. Whether the screener was in breach of duty would depend on the training and the amount of knowledge a screener should have had in order to properly perform his or her task at that time and how easy it was to discern what the judge had found was on the slide. These issues involved both questions of fact and questions of opinion as to the standards of care which the screeners should have exercised.

This more critical approach can be seen as part of a general sea change that has occurred in the courts' attitude towards the *Bolam* test in the past few years. This development is discussed further in the next section.

THINK POINT

What of a case where the surgeon's scalpel slips during delicate spinal surgery, leaving the patient paralysed: would the *Bolam* test here be of any application?

6.3.2.2 Impugning accepted practice – 'new *Bolam*'

As discussed above, in the past the *Bolam* test appeared to be framed in such a way as to make compliance with an accepted practice a complete defence: that is to say, provided a doctor could show that what he had done complied with such a practice, he could never be found negligent. However, as the twentieth century approached its close, this interpretation came under increasing attack (from patient pressure groups and academics), not only as failing to adequately protect the interests of injured patients, but as misrepresenting McNair J's original direction. Finally, in the 1997 decision of *Bolitho v City and Hackney HA*, the House of Lords took the opportunity to reaffirm that in every case it is for the court to review an accepted practice (relied on by the defendant) for its reasonableness and that it may sometimes find it wanting.

Bolitho v City and Hackney HA[57]

The infant claimant was being treated in the defendant's hospital for respiratory difficulties following a serious bout of the croup. Overall his condition appeared to be improving, but on the day in question he suffered two acute episodes in which his breathing was temporarily obstructed. On both occasions the nurse observing him summoned the senior paediatric registrar, however, neither the latter nor her senior

---

57 [1998] AC 232.

house officer responded to the calls. The claimant subsequently suffered a third episode, leading to cardiac arrest and brain damage.

It was accepted for the defendant that the failure of its doctors to attend the claimant amounted to a breach of duty. However, it claimed that, even if they had attended, they would not have instigated the one procedure – intubation – which would have saved him. This was a defence based essentially on lack of causation [see further 6.4.2.3 below]; however, to succeed it required the court to accept that the hypothetical failure to intubate in such a case would not itself have been a breach of duty. In this regard, the defendant adduced evidence from a number of expert witnesses to the effect that, faced with a patient with the claimant's medical history and symptoms, they too would not intubate:

> **Lord Browne-Wilkinson:** . . . [I]n my view, the court is not bound to hold that a defendant doctor escapes liability for negligent treatment or diagnosis just because he leads evidence from a number of medical experts who are genuinely of the opinion that the defendant's treatment or diagnosis accorded with sound medical practice. In the *Bolam* case itself, McNair J stated . . . that the defendant had to have acted in accordance with the practice accepted as proper by a 'responsible body of medical men'. Later . . . he referred to 'a standard of practice recognised as proper by a competent *reasonable* body of opinion'. Again, in the passage which I have cited from *Maynard's* case, Lord Scarman refers to a 'respectable' body of professional opinion. The use of these adjectives – responsible, reasonable and respectable – all show that the court has to be satisfied that the exponents of the body of opinion relied upon can demonstrate that such opinion has a logical basis. In particular in cases involving, as they so often do, the weighing of risks against benefits, the judge before accepting a body of opinion as being responsible, reasonable or respectable, will need to be satisfied that, in forming their views, the experts have directed their minds to the question of comparative risks and benefits and have reached a defensible conclusion on the matter.
>
> There are decisions which demonstrate that the judge is entitled to approach expert professional opinion on this basis. For example, in *Hucks v Cole* (1993) 4 Med LR 393 (a case from 1968), a doctor failed to treat with penicillin a patient who was suffering from septic spots on her skin though he knew them to contain organisms capable of leading to puerperal fever. A number of distinguished doctors gave evidence that they would not, in the circumstances, have treated with penicillin. The Court of Appeal found the defendant to have been negligent. Sachs LJ said, at p 397:
>
>> When the evidence shows that a lacuna in professional practice exists by which risks of grave danger are knowingly taken, then, however small the risk, the court must anxiously examine that lacuna – particularly if the risk can be easily and inexpensively avoided. If the court finds, on an analysis of the reasons given for not taking those precautions that, in the light of current professional knowledge, there is no proper basis for the lacuna, and that it is definitely not reasonable that those risks should have been taken, its function is to state that fact and where necessary to state that it constitutes negligence. In such a case the practice will no doubt thereafter be altered to the benefit of patients. On such occasions the fact that other practitioners would have done the same thing as the defendant practitioner is a very weighty matter to be put on the scales on his behalf; but it is not, as Mr Webster readily conceded, conclusive. The court must be vigilant to see whether the reasons given for putting a patient at risk are valid in the light of any well-known advance in medical knowledge, or whether they stem from a residual adherence to out-of-date ideas.
>
> . . . These decisions demonstrate that in cases of diagnosis or treatment there are cases where, despite a body of professional opinion sanctioning the defendant's conduct, the defendant can properly be held liable for negligence (I am not here considering questions of disclosure of risk). In my judgment that is because, in some cases, it cannot be demonstrated to the judge's

satisfaction that the body of opinion relied upon is reasonable or responsible. In the vast majority of cases the fact that distinguished experts in the field are of a particular opinion will demonstrate the reasonableness of that opinion. In particular, where there are questions of assessment of the relative risks and benefits of adopting a particular medical practice, a reasonable view necessarily presupposes that the relative risks and benefits have been weighed by the experts in forming their opinions. But if, in a rare case, it can be demonstrated that the professional opinion is not capable of withstanding logical analysis, the judge is entitled to hold that the body of opinion is not reasonable or responsible.

On the facts, his Lordship (with whose judgment the rest of the House of Lords agreed) held that the hypothetical decision not to intubate the claimant would have been in accord with responsible medical practice:

> **Lord Browne-Wilkinson**: According to the accounts of Sister Sallabank and Nurse Newbold, although Patrick had had two severe respiratory crises, he had recovered quickly from both and for the rest presented as a child who was active and running about. Dr Dinwiddie's view was that these symptoms did not show a progressive respiratory collapse and that there was only a small risk of total respiratory failure. Intubation is not a routine, risk-free process. Dr Roberton described it as 'a major undertaking – an invasive procedure with mortality and morbidity attached – it was an assault'. It involves anaesthetising and ventilating the child. A young child does not tolerate a tube easily 'at any rate for a day or two' and the child unless sedated tends to remove it. In those circumstances it cannot be suggested that it was illogical for Dr Dinwiddie, a most distinguished expert, to favour running what, in his view, was a very small risk of total respiratory collapse rather than to submit Patrick to the invasive procedure of intubation.

It is apparent that, in requiring 'responsible practice' to stand up to logical analysis, Lord Browne-Wilkinson has in mind some form of risk – benefit analysis: the risks inherent in a given procedure must be justified by the benefit it may bring (including the amelioration of any greater risk). However, while this may lead to rejection of practices which entail quite unnecessary risks (that is, those where negligible or no benefit is to be gained from running them, as in *Hucks v Cole*),[58] it remains unclear what a judge is to do when faced with evidence of a practice which, say, exposes the patient to a 1 per cent risk of total paralysis but carries a 90 per cent chance of curing the patient's stiff neck. Is such a practice 'illogical'?[59]

See Chapter 2

In the Court of Appeal in *Bolitho*, Dillon LJ had suggested that before impugning an accepted practice, the court should be satisfied that it was '*Wednesbury* unreasonable'.[60] As we saw in Chapter 2, this test is employed in judicial review proceedings and requires a very high degree of unreasonableness (the practice in question must be perverse or irrational). In so doing, it reflects the courts' reluctance to second guess the decisions of public bodies, which are entrusted with a discretion over how best to implement policy (often involving considerations of finite resources). Such a test would seem an inappropriate basis on which to assess the individual treatment decisions made by doctors, and indeed it finds no place in Lord Browne-Wilkinson's judgment. Nevertheless, arguably the latter's approach is scarcely more favourable to the claimant:

---

58 [1993] 4 Med LR 393.
59 For the view that professional conduct may in fact be impugned as 'illogical' in a number of scenarios, see Mulheron, R, 'Trumping *Bolam*: A critical legal analysis of *Bolitho's* "gloss"?' (2010) 69 CLJ 609.
60 (1993) PIQR P334.

Lord Browne-Wilkinson: I emphasise that in my view it will very seldom be right for a judge to reach the conclusion that views genuinely held by a competent medical expert are unreasonable. The assessment of medical risks and benefits is a matter of clinical judgment which a judge would not normally be able to make without expert evidence. As the quotation from Lord Scarman [from *Maynard v W Midlands RHA*] makes clear, it would be wrong to allow such assessment to deteriorate into seeking to persuade the judge to prefer one of two views, both of which are capable of being logically supported. It is only where a judge can be satisfied that the body of expert opinion cannot be logically supported at all that such opinion will not provide the bench mark by reference to which the defendant's conduct falls to be assessed.

In the years following *Bolitho*, judges following the approach endorsed by Lord Browne-Wilkinson have been cautious. Thus, decisions where a doctor's conduct has been held negligent notwithstanding its compliance with accepted practice remain rare. Nevertheless, one case that seems to have been decided on this basis is *Marriott v West Midlands HA*,[61] in which the trial judge found that, given the risk of neurological deficit, a GP's failure to refer a head injury patient back to hospital for further tests was negligent. As Beldam LJ commented in the Court of Appeal:

Beldam LJ: Having read the evidence of both doctors, I think it is questionable whether either Dr Fell or Dr La Frenais had given evidence from which it was reasonable to infer that their individual approaches were shared by a responsible body of others in their profession. Rather it seems that each was saying what his own approach would have been in the circumstances. It is true that each of them gave evidence of discussing the question with their partners, who (perhaps understandably) did in neither case disagree with their approach. But such evidence fell short of establishing that their views of the appropriate course for Dr Patel to have taken were shared by a body of professional colleagues. However, the judge treated this evidence as if it were evidence of that kind, and she correctly directed herself that it was not open to her simply to prefer the expert evidence of one body of competent professional opinion over that of another where there was a conflict between the experts called by the parties . . . She then subjected that body of opinion to analysis to see whether it can properly be regarded as reasonable. In my view, she was entitled to do so.

Another, albeit factually unusual, example of a court finding a breach of duty despite the defendant's compliance with accepted medical practice is *AB v Leeds Teaching Hospital NHS Trust*.[62] This case centred on the failure of doctors to inform parents that tissue removed from their deceased children for post mortem examinations might subsequently be retained by the hospital. Here, interestingly, the very universality of the practice was regarded as counting against its reasonableness. As Gage J commented:

Gage J: [237] . . . [T]he evidence shows that the practice adopted was blanket practice carried out by virtually all clinicians. In so far as it involved the exercise of a therapeutic judgment it was one which does not appear to have been exercised on a case by case basis. The general view was that such information was unnecessary and likely to be distressing to parents. But there is no evidence that clinicians considered the matter individually with each parent or family. To take an example from the lead claims, although the issue does not arise in their claim, Mr and Mrs Carpenter would, in my judgment, have been quite capable of coping with this information at the time of Daniel's death. In any event, in my opinion, there was very little

---

61 [1999] Lloyd's Rep Med 23.
62 [2004] EWHC 644 (QB).

risk of parents being caused greater distress by being given the additional information. It would have been very simple and easy for a clinician to have provided this information and generally they ought to have done so. If the clinician did not know what was involved in a post-mortem, in my opinion, as Dr Moore said, he ought to have known. In the circumstances, my conclusion is that the practice of not warning parents and in particular a mother that a post-mortem might involve the removal and subsequent retention of an organ cannot be justified as a practice to be adopted in all cases.

6.3.2.3 Departures from accepted practice

Normally, where there is only a single course of treatment recognised by the medical profession (an increasing possibility given the work of the National Institute for Clinical Excellence in disseminating 'best practice' clinical guidelines), it will be practically impossible to demonstrate that the practice is illogical and, hence, not reasonable. Arguably, it could be said, even then, that judges might consider practices in other jurisdictions and find that these were superior and should have been adopted by the medical profession here, but this approach was rejected in *Whiteford v Hunter*.[63]

See Chapter 2

However, how far does the converse apply? That is, will deviation from such practice automatically be regarded as negligent? This issue was addressed in the case of *Clark v MacLennan*.

Clark v MacLennan[64]

The claimant had recently given birth and was suffering from stress incontinence. The gynaecologist performed a corrective operation one month after the birth of the child. The normal practice was not to perform such operations until at least three months after birth, as the condition often spontaneously resolved itself and there would be less likelihood of haemorrhage. A haemorrhage did, in fact, take place, and despite further surgery, the claimant's condition became permanent. Although evidence was that in very special circumstances the operation might be performed early, this was not an exceptional case. In fact, none of the witnesses knew of a case where the operation had taken place earlier than three months. Contrasting this situation where there is more than one approved practice, Peter Pain J stated:

> **Peter Pain J**: Where . . . there is but one orthodox course of treatment and the doctor chooses to depart from that, his position is different. It is not enough for him to say as to his decision simply that it was based on his clinical judgment. One has to inquire whether he took all proper factors into account which he knew or should have known, and whether his departure from the orthodox course can be justified on the basis of these factors.
>
> The burden of proof lies on the plaintiff. To succeed she must show, first, that there was a breach of duty and, second, that her damages flowed from that breach . . .
>
> . . . [C]ounsel for the plaintiff contended that, if the plaintiff could show: (1) that there was a general practice not to perform an anterior colporrhaphy until at least three months after birth; (2) that one of the reasons for this practice was to protect the patient from the risk of haemorrhage and a breakdown of the repair; (3) that an operation was performed within four weeks; and (4) that haemorrhage occurred and the repair broke down, then the burden of showing that he was not in breach of duty shifted to the defendants.

---

63 (1950) 94 SJ 758.
64 [1983] 1 All ER 416.

> It must be correct on the basis of *McGhee v National Coal Board* [1973] 1 WLR 1 to say that the burden shifts so far as damages are concerned. But does the burden shift so far as the duty is concerned? Must the medical practitioner justify his departure from the usual practice?
>
> It is very difficult to draw a distinction between the damage and the duty where the duty arises only because of a need to guard against the damage. In *McGhee's* case it was accepted that there was a breach of duty. In the present case the question of whether there was a breach remains in issue.
>
> It seems to me that it follows from *McGhee* that where there is a situation in which a general duty of care arises and there is a failure to take a precaution, and that very damage occurs against which the precaution is designed to be a protection, then the burden lies on the defendant to show that he was not in breach of duty as well as to show that the damage did not result from his breach of duty.

Peter Pain J's view that, in cases of departure from approved practice, the burden shifts to the defence to establish non-negligence was subsequently doubted, however, by Mustill LJ in the Court of Appeal in *Wilsher v Essex AHA*:[65]

> **Mustill LJ**: . . . [A]lthough the judge [in *Clark v MacLennan*] indicated that he proposed to decide the case on burden of proof . . . this could be understood as an example of the forensic commonplace that, where one party has, in the course of the trial, hit the ball into the other's court, it is for that other to return it. But the prominence given in the judgment to *McGhee* and the citation from *Clark* in the present case suggest that the judge may have set out to assert a wider proposition, to the effect that in certain kinds of case of which *Clark* and the present action form examples, there is a general burden of proof on the defendant. If this is so, then I must respectfully say that I find nothing in . . . general principle to support it.

In the light of this, it may be more accurate to speak in terms of evidential presumptions: the fact, if it is established, that the defendant failed to act in accordance with accepted practice supports a prima facie inference of negligence, which it is then up to the defendant to rebut. Such rebuttal will be more difficult if the accepted practice is universal and is specifically directed against the risk that the defendant, in failing to comply, allowed to materialise. A case in point is that of *Chin Keow v Government of Malaysia*,[66] in which a patient died after the doctor gave her penicillin without checking for the possibility of an allergic reaction. The doctor was unable to give any satisfactory explanation of his failure to observe accepted practice in this regard.

On other occasions, however, the doctor may be able to provide cogent reasons for departing from normal practice. In fact, the importance of giving doctors a certain degree of latitude to try out 'innovative' forms of treatment was noted by Lord Clyde in the pre-*Bolam*, Scottish decision of *Hunter v Hanley*:[67]

> **Lord President Clyde**: . . . [I]n regard to allegations of deviation from ordinary professional practice . . . such a deviation is not necessarily evidence of negligence. Indeed it would be disastrous if this were so, for all inducement to progress in medical science would then be destroyed. Even a substantial deviation from normal practice may be warranted by the particular circumstances. To establish liability by a doctor

---

65 See n 8 above.
66 [1967] 1 WLR 813.
67 See n 37 above.

where deviation from normal practice is alleged, three facts require to be established. First of all it must be proved that there is a usual and normal practice; secondly it must be proved that the defender has not adopted that practice; and thirdly (and this is of crucial importance) it must be established that the course the doctor adopted is one which no professional man of ordinary skill would have taken if he had been acting with ordinary care.

It is important to distinguish here between medical research, which is a planned exercise designed specifically to test a new form of treatment, using control groups and almost always approved by a local ethics committee, and a 'one-off' treatment for a particular patient. We are only concerned at present with the latter situation. There is no doubt that there would be no *automatic* finding of negligence if the treatment was innovative. In *Sidaway*[68] Lord Diplock stated:

Lord Diplock: Those members of the public who seek medical or surgical aid would be badly served by the adoption of any legal principle that would confine the doctor to some long-established, well tried method of treatment only, although its past record of success might be small, if he wanted to be confident that he would not run the risk of being held liable in negligence simply because he tried some more modern treatment, and by some unavoidable mischance it failed to heal but did some harm to the patient. This would encourage 'defensive medicine' with a vengeance.

More recently, in *Simms v Simms and Another*,[69] which concerned the lawfulness of experimental treatment on two young patients dying from variant CJD, Butler-Sloss P commented that, '[t]he *Bolam* test ought not to be allowed to inhibit medical progress'. In short, doctors should not be afraid to try new treatments when existing ones are not working. Such a constraint would inhibit the development of better treatments, contrary to important utilitarian considerations, and would be contrary to trying to do the best for the individual patient (both of these limbs must be satisfied as utility without more would involve using the patient merely as a means to an end).

See Chapter 10

There are two important issues here. First (subject to a possible defence of therapeutic privilege), it is suggested that the patient should be fully apprised of the fact that the treatment is innovative and, accordingly, that there may be side effects or other risks that the doctor does not know about.[70] Secondly, the context in which the treatment is given must be considered. In some cases, established treatments may not have been successful, and the patient will, perhaps, agree to accept a 'long shot' chance of success as a last resort. However, what of the situation where other conventional treatments exist and have not been tried? Certainly, in such a case, the patient should be fully informed about these alternatives, associated risks, likely outcomes and so on, but the question must be raised as to whether novel treatment should be given at all. When would such treatment be in the best interests of *this* patient?

A case in which unjustified 'experimentation' on the part of a doctor was at issue is that of *Hepworth v Kerr*.[71] The claimant was admitted to hospital in 1979 for a mastoid operation. During the course of the operation, the anaesthetist reduced the patient's blood pressure to a very low level for a period of one and a half hours. The purpose was to create a relatively blood-free operating field in the middle ear. The anaesthetist had been using this technique for some years and had carried out around 1,500 cases. However, in the case of this patient the level to which he

---

68 See n 37 above.
69 [2003] Fam 83.
70 On the doctor's general duty in negligence to disclose treatment risks, see Ch 3 above.
71 [1995] 6 Med LR 139.

reduced the blood pressure was 40 mm Hg, when a minimum of 60 mm Hg was strongly indicated in the medical literature. McKinnon J described the defendant as 'plainly negligent':

> **McKinnon J**: As I find, the defendant adopted a new hypotensive anaesthetic technique which, as he knew, had never been attempted routinely before. Other anaesthetists had never gone to such low levels over such long periods. The defendant, as he accepted, was to begin with, at least, plainly experimenting. He expected serious complications such as cerebral or cardiac thrombosis to occur. He was surprised when they did not. He never, however, attempted to embark upon any proper scientific validation of his technique in some 1,500 patients by the time of the plaintiff's operation . . .
>
> I simply cannot, and do not, accept that the defendant was justified in doing what he did without proper scientific validation of his technique.

In 2014, a Medical Innovation Bill, sponsored by Lord Saatchi, was introduced in Parliament. This would originally have given a statutory defence to a negligence claim to doctors who reached a decision to employ innovative therapy in a responsible way and with the patient's informed consent. However, this provision (which arguably added little anyway to the position at common law) was ultimately dropped from the Bill as enacted.[72]

6.3.3 Proof issues

In every case it is for the claimant to show that the defendant was negligent on the *balance of probabilities* (that is, according to the usual civil burden of proof). As we have seen, in relation to the normative question of the *reasonableness* of the defendant's conduct, this makes things very awkward for claimants in cases where medical opinion is divided as to whether such conduct accorded with responsible medical practice or not: see *Maynard v W Midlands RHA*.[73] Following *Bolitho*, it may be said that the onus is squarely on the claimant to show that the conduct in question 'cannot be logically supported at all'.

On other occasions, though, where, as a matter of evidence, it is not clear what such conduct actually consisted of, a claimant may be able to bypass these difficulties by entering a plea of *res ipsa loquitur* (literally 'the thing speaks for itself'). A claimant who enters such a plea alleges that the injury could not have happened *without* negligence and, therefore, throws the ball into the doctor's court to show otherwise. To get this far, he must establish three elements: first, the defendant (either primarily or vicariously) must be in control of the situation prior to injury; secondly, in the ordinary course of events, such injury does not occur; and, finally, the claimant does not have all the facts to show what actually happened (it is the third aspect which gave rise to the principle in the first place, so as to allow a claimant to sue in circumstances where he cannot properly plead specific allegations of negligence).

Tort lawyers have long debated whether the principle means, in effect, that the burden of proof is reversed. The favoured view is that it is not. In the Privy Council decision of *Ng Chun Pui v Lee Chuen Tat*,[74] it was said that *res ipsa loquitur* is no more than the use of a Latin maxim to describe the state of the evidence from which it is proper to draw an inference of negligence. In other words, if the claimant asserts that such an accident would not normally happen without negligence, he is merely inviting a finding of negligence earlier in the proceedings than usual.

---

72 As the *Access to Treatments (Innovation) Act* 2016; see: www.mrc.ac.uk/about/policy/mrc-position-statements/access-to-medical-treatments-innovation-act/.
73 See n 51 above; see also *Ashcroft v Mersey RHA* [1983] 2 All ER 245.
74 [1988] RTR 298.

Two relatively early medical negligence cases in which the principle was invoked are *Roe v Minister of Health*[75] and *Cassidy v Ministry of Health*.[76] In *Roe*, the plaintiffs were paralysed during the course of surgery due to the contamination of their anaesthetic by phenol: the latter had seeped through invisible fissures in the glass storage vessels in which the anaesthetic was stored. Denning LJ commented:

> **Denning LJ:** The judge [at first instance] has said that those facts do not speak for themselves, but I think that they do. They certainly call for an explanation. Each of these men is entitled to say to the hospital: 'While I was in your hands something has been done to me which has wrecked my life. Please explain how this has come to pass.'. . . I approach this case, therefore, on the footing that the hospital authorities and Dr Graham were called on to give an explanation of what has happened.

The defendant was eventually able to establish that, at that time, the danger of such contamination was unknown to science and, accordingly, it had not been negligent to fail to guard against it.

In the *Cassidy* case, the claimant was admitted for surgery to correct Dupuytren's syndrome, which had resulted in the contraction of the third and fourth fingers of his left hand. After surgery, the contraction had spread to his two other fingers. The Court of Appeal held that *res ipsa loquitur* applied. It was Denning LJ again who stated:

> **Denning LJ:** If the plaintiff had to prove that some particular doctor or nurse was negligent, he would not be able to do it. But he was not put to that impossible task: he says:
>
> > I went into the hospital to be cured of two stiff fingers. I have come out with four stiff fingers, and my hand is useless. That should not have happened if due care had been used. Explain it, if you can.

Nevertheless, in subsequent cases the courts tended to vacillate on the question of how far, and in what circumstances, the principle should apply in medical negligence cases. The issue was reconsidered by the Court of Appeal in *Ratcliffe v Plymouth and Torbay HA*.

Ratcliffe v Plymouth and Torbay HA[77]

> In September 1989, the claimant underwent a triple arthrodesis of his right ankle, in one of the defendants' hospitals. He received anaesthetic by way of injection into the spine to relieve post-operative pain. Although the operation itself was a success, he was left with a serious neurological defect on the right side from his waist downwards. The defendant was unable to explain how or why this had come about, but the trial judge found the anaesthetist who gave the injection had exercised proper care, and dismissed the claim.
>
> On appeal, the claimant argued the judge should have accorded greater weight to the *res ipsa loquitur* doctrine:
>
> > **Brooke LJ** [*after reviewing the authorities*]: It is now possible to draw some threads out of all this material, by way of explanation of the relevance of the maxim *res ipsa loquitur* to medical

---

75 [1954] 2 QB 66.
76 [1951] 2 KB 343.
77 [1998] Lloyd's Rep Med 162, CA.

negligence cases: (1) In its purest form, the maxim applies where the plaintiff relies on the 'res' (the thing itself) to raise the inference of negligence, which is supported by ordinary human experience, with no need for expert evidence. (2) In principle, the maxim can be applied in that form in simple situations in the medical negligence field (surgeon cuts off right foot instead of left: swab left in operation site; patient wakes up in the course of surgical operation despite general anaesthetic). (3) In practice, in contested medical negligence cases the evidence of the plaintiff, which establishes the 'res', is likely to be buttressed by expert evidence to the effect that the matter complained does not ordinarily occur in the absence of negligence. (4) The position may then be reached at the close of the plaintiff's case that the judge would be entitled to infer negligence on the defendant's part unless the defendant adduces evidence which discharges this inference. (5) This evidence may be to the effect that there is a plausible explanation of what may have happened which does not connote any negligence on the defendant's part. The explanation must be a plausible one and not a theoretically or remotely possible one, but the defendant certainly does not have to prove that his explanation is more likely to be correct than any other. If the plaintiff has no other evidence of negligence to rely on, his claim will then fail. (6) Alternatively, the defendant's evidence may satisfy the judge on the balance of probabilities that he did exercise proper care. If the untoward outcome is extremely rare, or is impossible to explain in the light of the current state of medical knowledge, the judge will be bound to exercise great care in evaluating the evidence before making such a finding, but it he does so, the *prima facie* inference of negligence is rebutted and the plaintiff's claim will fail. The reason why the courts are willing to adopt this approach, particularly in very complex cases, is to be found in the judgments of Stuart-Smith and Dillon LJJ in *Delaney v Southmead HA* [1995] 6 Med LR 355. (7) It follows from all this that, although in very simple situations the 'res' may speak for itself at the end of the lay evidence adduced on behalf of the plaintiff, in practice the inference is then buttressed by expert evidence adduced on his behalf, and if the defendant were to call no evidence, the judge would be deciding the case on inferences he was entitled to draw from the whole of the evidence (including the expert evidence), and not on the application of the maxim in its purest form.

In the *Delaney*[78] case, referred to here, Stuart-Smith LJ had commented:

Stuart-Smith LJ: [I]f the human body was a machine where it is possible to see the internal workings and which operates in accordance with the immutable laws of mechanics and with arithmetical precision, I think that the [res ipsa loquitur] argument might well be unanswerable. But in spite of the wonders of modern medical science, even at post-mortem not everything is known about an individual human being.

In *Ratcliffe*, the Court of Appeal held that the defendant similarly had defused the force of the *res ipsa loquitur* doctrine by proving he had in fact taken due care, ie on the alternative basis summarised by Brooke LJ in his point (6).[79]

As Brooke LJ notes in points (3) and (4), in medical negligence cases there will invariably be at least some evidence of what occurred, so the doctrine will not apply in its pure form of allowing negligence to be inferred from the simple fact of injury; rather, the claimant's medical

---

78 [1995] 6 Med LR 355.
79 For a case in which the Court of Appeal rejected the defendant's evidence of due care and inferred negligence on the basis of his failure to detect foetal abnormalities on a scan, see *Lillywhite v University College University Hospitals NHS Trust* [2005] EWCA Civ 1466.

experts must first make out a positive case to the judge that, in the circumstances of the particular case (as presented by the evidence), the injury should have been avoided; it is at this point that the defendant comes under the evidential burden to explain matters further. If the defendant fails to do so, then, as the Court of Appeal recently reiterated in *Thomas v Curley*,[80] the judge will be entitled to find negligence.

6.4 Causation

Assuming that the claimant manages to establish that the defendant doctor was 'negligent' (in the sense of having breached his duty of care), it does not follow that he will succeed in his claim in *negligence*. A further, and in this context often very troublesome, hurdle remains for him to negotiate in the form of proving causation. Analytically, causation subdivides into two main stages: first, it must be shown that the defendant's breach of duty was a *factual cause* of the claimant's harm; if so, the law must then also deem it to be the *legal cause* (ie the harm must not be so distant from the defendant's breach or unexpected in nature to qualify as 'too remote'). As we shall see, in the context of medical negligence the first of these aspects, especially, may give rise to great difficulty.

6.4.1 Factual causation: the 'but for' test

For the purposes of the tort of negligence, the crucial question is whether the defendant's breach of duty made a difference to (ie was a necessary condition for) the harmful outcome suffered by the claimant. This is generally resolved by means of the so-called 'but for' test. In the well-known words of Denning LJ in the (non-medical negligence) case of *Cork v Kirby Maclean Ltd*,[81] '[i]f you can say that the damage would not have happened but for a particular fault then that fault is in fact a cause of the damage; but if you can say that the damage would have happened just the same, fault or no fault, then the fault is not a cause of the damage'.

A good illustration of the test's application, in the context of medical negligence, is provided by the case of *Barnett v Chelsea and Kensington Hospital Management Committee*.

Barnett v Chelsea & Kensington Hospital Management Committee[82]

Three nightwatchmen attended the defendant's casualty department complaining of nausea and vomiting after drinking some tea. The casualty doctor on duty negligently failed to see the men and they were sent away untreated. One of them later died from what it transpired were the effects of arsenic poisoning. In the subsequent action brought by the man's widow, the judge, after holding that the defendant owed a duty of care to the deceased and was in breach, continued as follows:

Nield J: It remains to consider whether it is shown that the deceased's death was caused by that negligence or whether, as the defendants have said, the deceased must have died in any event. In his concluding submission Mr Pain submitted that the casualty officer should have examined the deceased and had he done so he would have caused tests to be made which would have indicated the treatment required and that, since the defendants were at fault in these respects, therefore the onus of proof passed to the defendants to show that the appropriate treatment would have failed, and authorities were cited to me. I find myself unable to accept

---

80 [2013] EWCA Civ 117; here the claimant, who had surgery for gallstones, suffered an injury to her bile duct some distance from the operation site.
81 [1952] 2 All ER 402.
82 See n 5 above.

that argument, and I am of the view that the onus of proof remains upon the plaintiff, and I have in mind (without quoting it) the decision cited by Mr Wilmers in *Bonnington Castings Ltd v Wardlaw* [1956] AC 613 . . . However, were it otherwise and the onus did pass to the defendants, then I would find that they have discharged it, as I would proceed to show. There has been put before me a timetable which I think is of much importance. The deceased attended at the casualty department at five or 10 minutes past eight in the morning. If the casualty officer had got up and dressed and come to see the three men and examined them and decided to admit them, the deceased (and Dr Lockett agreed with this) could not have been in bed in a ward before 11 am. I accept Dr Goulding's evidence that an intravenous drip would not have been set up before 12 noon, and if potassium loss was suspected it could not have been discovered until 12.30 pm. Dr Lockett, dealing with this, said: 'If this man had not been treated until after 12 noon the chances of survival were not good.' Without going in detail into the considerable volume of technical evidence which has been put before me, it seems to me to be the case that when death results from arsenical poisoning it is brought about by two conditions; on the one hand dehydration and on the other disturbance of the enzyme processes. If the principal condition is one of enzyme disturbance – as I am of the view it was here – then the only method of treatment which is likely to succeed is the use of the specific antidote which is commonly called BAL. Dr Goulding said in the course of his evidence: 'The only way to deal with this is to use the specific BAL. I see no reasonable prospect of the deceased being given BAL before the time at which he died' – and at a later point in his evidence – 'I feel that even if fluid loss had been discovered death would have been caused by the enzyme disturbance. Death might have occurred later.' I regard that evidence as very moderate, and it might be a true assessment of the situation to say that there was no chance of BAL being administered before the death of the deceased. For those reasons, I find that the plaintiff has failed to establish, on the balance of probabilities, that the defendants' negligence caused the death of the deceased.

The *Barnett* case is instructive for a number of reasons. For one thing it illustrates the inevitably *hypothetical* nature of the factual causation enquiry: the court is required to construct a counter-factual parallel series – ie to speculate as to how things *would have turned out* if the defendant had properly performed his duty. At the same time, the case provides a powerful hint as to why it is that factual causation is often difficult to prove in medical negligence. This is because, in such cases, the claimant – at the time of the doctor's breach – is normally already at risk of suffering an adverse outcome: in the context of a non-treatment case as here, this risk is posed by the illness that led him to seek the doctor's assistance. Here, it is always open to the doctor to argue that the patient's injury was due to the progress of the illness, which, even with all due medical care, could not have been arrested; if that is the case, the risk posed by the doctor's faulty non-treatment will remain just that – it will not have materialised in the sense of playing a necessary part in (ie *causing*) the harm.

As we have seen, it was just this type of argument that Nield J accepted in *Barnett* itself. (It is useful here to contrast the position of defendants in most other negligence scenarios: for example, a negligent motorist is highly unlikely to be able to suggest that the pedestrian whose leg he crushed would have lost the leg in any event through an independent risk materialising.)

THINK POINT

Why could the hospital in *Barnett* not argue that, on any view, the true cause of Mr Barnett's death was the person who put the arsenic in the tea?

6.4.2 Evidential problems in applying the test

The fact that, in medical negligence cases, the court must normally consider the respective role in the patient's injury of two or more independent risks may generate significant evidential uncertainty. The scientific evidence may be unable to distinguish between the respective risks and determine which of them actually materialised. This is already so in non-treatment cases, such as *Barnett*, where the question, as we saw, is whether the underlying illness was sufficient alone for the injury (ie was untreatable from the start), or whether the omission of proper treatment also played a part. Potentially more complicated still are cases where the patient suffers additional (or 'iatrogenic') injury after negligent treatment is actually provided: here a further possible 'candidate' as the cause of injury will be the known risk from such treatment, even where carefully performed.[83]

6.4.2.1 Inability to disentangle the effects of multiple sources of risk exposure – relaxing the 'but for' test?

Outside the medical negligence context, the courts have long allowed recovery on occasion on the basis that the defendant's conduct exposed the claimant to a 'material risk' of the harm he suffered, rather than having to go further and show that it was a 'but for' cause of the harm. A well-known case is *McGhee v National Coal Board*,[84] in which the claimant sued his employer for the dermatitis he contracted following exposure to brick dust at his workplace. Such exposure was not itself negligent, but the defendant had faultily added to it (and hence to the risk of injury) by failing to provide adequate washing facilities. The difficulty lay in determining whether the 'guilty' dust (ie the portion the claimant was exposed to by being unable to wash) had played any causative role. The House of Lords' solution was to assert that, here it was open to a court simply to infer, as a question of fact, that the defendant's breach had materially contributed to the injury. Indeed, in one of the judgments, Lord Wilberforce appeared to go further and suggest that, once the claimant shows the defendant's breach of duty created a risk of harm, the burden of proving that the risk did not materialise and contribute to the harm passes to the defendant.

The question of how far the claimant-friendly approach to resolving such difficulties in *McGhee* should also apply in the field of medical negligence was faced by the House of Lords in *Wilsher v Essex AHA*.

Wilsher v Essex AHA[85]

The claimant baby contracted retrolental fibroplasia (RLF), rendering him virtually blind, after treatment in the defendant's post-natal unit. Owing to a breach of duty by hospital staff, he had been over-saturated with oxygen in the first weeks of his life [on this aspect of the case, see 6.3.1.2 above]. However, whilst this might, according to some of the evidence, have caused or contributed to the RLF, there were four other natural conditions, all of which had affected the baby, and which could equally have had the same effect. The majority of the Court of Appeal found for the claimant on causation on the basis of Lord Wilberforce's speech in *McGhee*; the defendant appealed:

Lord Bridge: The Court of Appeal, although it felt unable to resolve the primary conflict in the expert evidence as to the causation of Martin's RLF, did make a finding that the levels of PO2 which Martin experienced in consequence of the misplacement of the catheter were of a kind capable of causing RLF. . . . [A]ssuming, as I do for the present, that the finding was properly made, it carried the plaintiff's case no further than to establish that oxygen administered to

---

83 See further, Stauch, M, 'Causation, risk and loss of chance in medical negligence' (1997) 17 OJLS 205.
84 [1972] 3 All ER 1008.
85 [1988] AC 1074, HL.

Martin as a consequence of the negligent failure to detect the misplacement of the catheter was one of a number of possible causes of Martin's RLF.

Mustill LJ subjected the speeches in *McGhee v National Coal Board* [1972] 3 All ER 1008 . . . to a careful scrutiny and analysis and concluded that they established a principle of law which he expressed in the following terms:

> If it is an established fact that conduct of a particular kind creates a risk that injury will be caused to another or increases an existing risk that injury will ensue, and if the two parties stand in such a relationship that the one party owes a duty not to conduct himself in that way, and if the first party does conduct himself in that way, and if the other party does suffer injury of the kind to which the risk related, then the first party is taken to have caused the injury by his breach of duty, even though the existence and extent of the contribution made by the breach cannot be ascertained.

Applying this principle to the finding that the authority's negligence was one of the possible causes of Martin's RLF, he held that this was sufficient to enable the court to conclude that the negligence was 'taken to have caused the injury'. Glidewell LJ reached the same conclusion by substantially the same process of reasoning. Sir Nicolas Browne-Wilkinson VC took the opposite view . . .

Much of the academic discussion to which [*McGhee*] has given rise has focused on the speech of Lord Wilberforce. . . . He said:

> . . . First, it is a sound principle that where a person has, by breach of duty of care, created a risk, and injury occurs within the area of that risk, the loss should be borne by him *unless he shows that it had some other cause*. Secondly, from the evidential point of view, one may ask, why should a man who is able to show that his employer should have taken certain precautions, because without them there is a risk, or an added risk, of injury or disease, and who in fact sustains exactly that injury or disease, have to assume the burden of proving more: namely, that it was the addition to the risk, caused by the breach of duty, which caused or materially contributed to the injury? In many cases of which the present is typical, this is impossible to prove, just because honest medical opinion cannot segregate the causes of an illness between compound causes. And if one asks which of the parties, the workman or the employers should suffer from this inherent evidential difficulty, the answer as a matter in policy or justice should be that it is the creator of the risk who, *ex hypothesi*, must be taken to have foreseen the possibility of damage, who should bear its consequences. (My emphasis)

My Lords, it seems to me that [these dicta] amount to saying that, in the circumstances, the burden of proof of causation is reversed and thereby to run counter to the unanimous and emphatic opinions expressed in *Bonnington Castings Ltd v Wardlaw* [1956] 1 All ER 615 . . . to the contrary effect. I find no support in any of the other speeches for the view that the burden of proof is reversed and, in this respect, I think Lord Wilberforce's reasoning must be regarded as expressing a minority opinion.

The conclusion I draw . . . is that *McGhee v National Coal Board* laid down no new principle of law whatever. On the contrary, it affirmed the principle that the onus of proving causation lies on the pursuer or plaintiff. Adopting a robust and pragmatic approach to the undisputed primary facts of the case, the majority concluded that it was a legitimate inference of fact that the defenders' negligence had materially contributed to the pursuer's injury. The decision, in my opinion, is of no greater significance than that and the attempt to extract from it some esoteric principle which in some way modifies, as a matter of law, the nature of the burden of proof of causation which a plaintiff or pursuer must discharge once he has established a relevant breach of duty is a fruitless one.

Subsequently, though, in *Fairchild v Glenhaven Funeral Services*[86] Lord Bridge's analysis of the law in *Wilsher* was itself the subject of reappraisal. In *Fairchild*, which, like the *McGhee* case, was a negligence action brought by an employee, the evidential problem in relation to causation was that of multiple possible tortfeasors. The claimant was suffering from mesothelioma, which it was accepted had been caused by inhaling asbestos fibres during his employment. However, he had worked for a number of different companies, each of which had negligently exposed him to asbestos, and it was not possible now to say, of any particular one, that the fatal inhalation took place while the claimant was working there.

In allowing recovery, the House of Lords regarded *McGhee* as authority for departing from the normal need to satisfy the 'but for' test on the balance of probabilities on the basis of special policy considerations. Where these applied, the proven creation of a material risk of harm (rather than proof the risk actually materialised) should be treated as sufficient for liability.[87] Nonetheless, their Lordships affirmed the correctness of *Wilsher* on its facts. In his speech in *Fairchild*, Lord Hoffmann was anxious to emphasise that a similar relaxation of causation would not apply in the context of medical negligence:

> **Lord Hoffmann**: [68] The Court of Appeal [in *Wilsher*] treated the causal requirement rule applied in *McGhee* as being of general application...
>
> [69] The House of Lords, in a speech by Lord Bridge of Harwich with which all other noble Lords concurred, rejected this broad principle. I would respectfully agree. The principle in *McGhee*'s case is far narrower and I have tried to indicate what its limits are likely to be. It is true that actions for clinical negligence notoriously give rise to difficult questions of causation. But it cannot possibly be said that the duty to take reasonable care in treating patients would be virtually drained of content unless the creation of a material risk of injury were accepted as sufficient to satisfy the causal requirements for liability. And the political and economic arguments involved in the massive increase in the liability of the National Health Service which would have been a consequence of the broad rule favoured by the Court of Appeal in *Wilsher*'s case are far more complicated than the reasons given by Lord Wilberforce [in *McGhee*] for imposing liability upon an employer who has failed to take simple precautions.[88]

However, subsequently, in *Bailey v Ministry of Defence*,[89] the Court of Appeal was prepared to countenance a relaxation of the 'but for test', allowing a patient to recover damages on the basis of the defendant's material contribution to her injury. The facts were that the claimant was left very weak after surgery, partly due to the defendant's negligent aftercare and partly from developing pancreatitis; she later suffered brain damage after choking on a drink. The experts were unable to say whether, 'but for' the negligence, she would have avoided this outcome; the pancreatitis by itself may have led to it. In nevertheless awarding damages, the court distinguished *Wilsher* as dealing with the problem of fixing responsibility between mutually exclusive (alternative) risks, whereas here the negligence and pancreatitis had cumulatively weakened the claimant. According to Waller LJ:

> **Waller LJ**: [46] If the evidence demonstrates on a balance of probabilities that the injury would have occurred as a result of the non-tortious cause or causes in any event, the claimant will have failed to

---

86 [2002] 3 WLR 89.
87 Subsequently, this exception was put on a statutory footing by s 3 Compensation Act 2006; however, as confirmed by the Supreme Court in *Sienkiewicz v Greif (UK) Ltd* [2011] UKSC 10, it only applies to mesothelioma cases.
88 See also his Lordship's comments, together with those of Lords Scott and Walker, in *Barker v Corus Ltd* [2006] UKHL 20.
89 [2008] EWCA Civ 883.

establish that the tortious cause contributed . . . If the evidence demonstrates that 'but for' the contribution of the tortious cause the injury would probably not have occurred, the claimant will (obviously) have discharged the burden. In a case where medical science cannot establish the probability that 'but for' an act of negligence the injury would not have happened but can establish that the contribution of the negligent cause was more than negligible, the 'but for' test is modified, and the claimant will succeed.

Recently, the application of the 'material contribution' approach in medical negligence was also considered by the Privy Council in its decision in *Williams v The Bermuda Hospitals Board*.

Williams v The Bermuda Hospitals Board[90]

The claimant attended the defendant hospital with a ruptured appendix; due to a breach of duty there was a delay of two to four hours in treating this properly. At some point infected material from the rupture damaged the claimant's heart function, and he required intensive care and endured a difficult recovery. He alleged that timely treatment would have avoided these complications. The scientific evidence on the matter was unclear:

Lord Toulson (delivering the judgment of the Board): [34] [In *Bonnington Castings v Wardlaw*][91] Lord Tucker said, at p 623, that the inference to be drawn from the known facts was that 'the silica dust discharged from the swing grinders contributed to the harmful condition of the atmosphere, which admittedly resulted in the pursuer contracting pneumoconiosis, and was therefore a contributory cause of the disease'. Lord Keith said, at p 626, that the claimant had proved enough to support the inference that the employers' fault had materially contributed to his illness, because prima facie the particles inhaled were acting cumulatively and that the natural inference was that, had it not been for the cumulative effect, he would not have developed pneumoconiosis when he did.

[35] The parallel with the present case is obvious. The Board is not persuaded by Ms Harrison's argument that *Bonnington* is distinguishable because in that case the inhalation from two sources was simultaneous, whereas in the present case the sepsis attributable to the hospital's negligence developed after sepsis had already begun to develop. . . .

[41] In the present case the judge found that injury to the heart and lungs was caused by a single known agent, sepsis from the ruptured appendix. The sepsis developed incrementally over a period of approximately six hours, progressively causing myocardial ischaemia. (The greater the accumulation of sepsis, the greater the oxygen requirement.) The sepsis was not divided into separate components causing separate damage to the heart and lungs. Its development and effect on the heart and lungs was a single continuous process, during which the sufficiency of the supply of oxygen to the heart steadily reduced.

[42] On the trial judge's findings, that process continued for a minimum period of two hours 20 minutes longer than it should have done. In the judgment of the Board, it is right to infer on the balance of probabilities that the hospital board's negligence materially contributed to the process, and therefore materially contributed to the injury to the heart and lungs. . . .

[44] Although not strictly necessary, it may be helpful to comment by way of postscript on two matters which were raised in argument. First, Ms Harrison was critical of the decision,

---

90 [2016] PC 4.
91 [1956] AC 613.

and more particularly the reasoning, of the Court of Appeal in *Bailey*. The starting point is Foskett J's findings of fact, which were set out in close detail in his judgment: [2007] EWHC 2913 (QB). . . .

[46] The judge found on the strength of medical evidence that 'the claimant's generally weakened and debilitated condition on 26 January caused her not to be able to respond naturally and effectively to the emergence of vomit from her gut with the consequence that she inhaled it' (para 54). The question was whether this was too remote a consequence of her negligent treatment following the ERCP, having regard to the fact that her weakened state was partly due to the pancreatitis for which the hospital was not responsible. . . .

[47] In the view of the Board, on those findings of primary fact Foskett J was right to hold the hospital responsible in law for the consequences of the aspiration. As to the parallel weakness of the claimant due to her pancreatitis, the case may be seen as an example of the well known principle that a tortfeasor takes his victim as he finds her. The Board does not share the view of the Court of Appeal that the case involved a departure from the 'but-for' test. The judge concluded that the totality of the claimant's weakened condition caused the harm. If so, 'but-for' causation was established. The fact that her vulnerability was heightened by her pancreatitis no more assisted the hospital's case than if she had an egg shell skull.

As is apparent, the Privy Council, like the Court of Appeal in *Bailey*, in finding liability was content to apply the 'material contribution' approach from cases of industrial injury (*Bonnington* was a case, similar to *McGhee*, where an employer negligently added to the employee's exposure to a noxious workplace substance, and science could not disentangle the relative effect of the 'negligent' and 'innocent' exposures). Rather surprisingly, whereas the Court of Appeal in *Bailey* acknowledged that the application of this approach, allowing damages, involved a departure from the 'but for' test, the Privy Council denied this.

With the greatest respect, had the Board properly isolated the injury in suit in *Williams* – the damage to the claimant's heart, necessitating intensive care and his associated protracted recovery – it would have been clearer that a relaxation of the but for test was indeed involved: the (scientifically unanswerable) issue was simply: but for the additional hours of infection emanating from the rupture, would the claimant have escaped the damage to their heart function, or would this also have occurred if the operation had taken place two hours earlier? Similarly, as we saw, in *Bailey* the question was: did the claimant's extra weakness, stemming from negligent post-operative treatment, make the difference in terms of her choking, or would the weakness induced by pancreatitis alone have led to this?

Certainly one may have sympathy with claimants in such cases, who receive lamentably inadequate treatment, and end up with serious injuries they otherwise might well have avoided.[92] However, to suggest that negligence law – in awarding damages – is here behaving routinely, skates over what is in effect a proof relaxation. As noted, in industrial injury cases the courts are prepared to take such an approach. However, as Lord Hoffmann pointed out in *Fairchild*, there are important policy differences between the two areas, not to mention serious potential resource implications for the National Health Service in adopting it for medical negligence cases. At a more intuitive level too, the 'justice' of the situations may be felt to differ. Thus, in industrial injury cases, the

---

92 See also *Sido John v Central Manchester NHS Foundation Trust* [2016] EWHC 407, where, following *Bailey* and *Williams*, the High Court awarded full damages to the claimant for a significant neurological deficit, following the defendant's culpable delay in treating him for a serious head injury.

defendant's negligence adds actively to the risks to the claimant in an environment, which is under the defendant's overall control. By contrast, a significant number of medical negligence cases – including those of delayed diagnosis or treatment – are essentially 'failures to rescue'. In such cases the causative impact of the defendant's conduct is passive: it is a failure to intervene and halt the progress of the claimant's underlying condition.[93] Here, it is unclear why the claimant should benefit from a proof presumption that the rescue would have been successful.

In any event, it will be interesting to see what the UK Supreme Court does when it has occasion to consider a case with facts similar to *Williams*.

THINK POINT

If the *Barnett* case were decided today following the *Williams v Bermuda* decision, do you think the patient's widow might win damages?

6.4.2.2 Claims for 'loss of chance'?

The recent interest in 'material contribution' has rather overshadowed an earlier, arguably more coherent, approach proposed to cases of intractable evidential causal uncertainty. This was the suggested award of proportionate damages in line with the statistical probability that the defendant's negligence made a difference to the claimant's injurious outcome. It offered itself as an option especially in cases of failed or delayed diagnosis, where there are empirically derived statistics available (based on the observed outcomes for previous patients properly treated for the same condition), which show the chance of recovery that the claimant lost by not receiving proper treatment.

The courts were required to decide whether a claim founded upon such statistical evidence was admissible in the case of *Hotson v East Berkshire AHA*,[94] in which the claimant schoolboy attended the defendant's casualty department after falling from a tree and injuring his hip. The defendant failed, in breach of duty, to carry out an x-ray of the hip and, by the time the true extent of the injury was discovered (when the boy returned to hospital several days later), permanent disability was unavoidable. The medical evidence, based on class statistics, was that, even with immediate diagnosis, 75 per cent of patients with such an injury went on to develop permanent disability.

Rather than suing on the basis that the defendant had caused the disability itself (clearly an impossible task, given the need to satisfy the civil standard of proof by showing *on the balance of probabilities* that the failed diagnosis had played a necessary part in it), the claimant restricted his claim to the loss of the residual 25 per cent chance that proper diagnosis would have resulted in successful treatment. At first instance, Simon Brown J accepted that the loss of a substantial chance of this kind was actionable and awarded damages assessed at 25 per cent of the full quantum in respect of such an injury, and this approach was upheld in the Court of Appeal:

> **Sir John Donaldson MR**: Mr Whitfield, for the defendants, submits that no causal connection between the negligence and the development of avascular necrosis and consequent disability has been established,

---

93 See Stauch, n 83 above.
94 [1987] 1 AC 750.

since a 25% likelihood fails to achieve the requisite standard of proof. Without that causal connection, there can be no liability in damages based upon that development. In more concrete terms, it is all, ie, £46,000, or nothing – £46,000 if the likelihood of the connection exceeds 50% and otherwise nothing. In the instant case it is nothing . . .

As a matter of common sense, it is unjust that there should be no liability for failure to treat a patient, simply because the chances of a successful cure by that treatment were less than 50%. Nor, by the same token, can it be just that if the chances of a successful cure only marginally exceed 50%, the doctor or his employer should be liable to the same extent as if the treatment could be guaranteed to cure. If this is the law, it is high time that it was changed, assuming that this court has power to do so.

However, the health authority appealed successfully to the House of Lords:

Lord Bridge: The plaintiff's claim was for damages for physical injury and consequential loss alleged to have been caused by the authority's breach of their duty of care. In some cases, perhaps particularly medical negligence cases, causation may be so shrouded in mystery that the court can only measure statistical chances. But that was not so here. On the evidence there was a clear conflict as to what had caused the avascular necrosis. The authority's evidence was that the sole cause was the original traumatic injury to the hip. The plaintiff's evidence, at its highest, was that the delay in treatment was a material contributory cause. This was a conflict, like any other about some relevant past event, which the judge could not avoid resolving on a balance of probabilities. Unless the plaintiff proved on a balance of probabilities that the delayed treatment was at least a material contributory cause of the avascular necrosis he failed on the issue of causation and no question of quantification could arise. But the judge's findings of fact . . . are unmistakably to the effect that on a balance of probabilities the injury caused by the plaintiff's fall left insufficient blood vessels intact to keep the epiphysis alive. This amounts to a finding of fact that the fall was the sole cause of the avascular necrosis.

The upshot is that the appeal must be allowed . . .

Although in *Hotson* their Lordships stopped short of saying that there could never be recovery in medical negligence for loss of chance, they gave little clue as to when it might be allowed. Subsequently, in *Gregg v Scott*, the House of Lords had another opportunity to consider the merits of a claim framed in this way:

Gregg v Scott[95]

The claimant, Mr Gregg, consulted Dr Scott in November 1994 about a lump under his arm. The latter assumed it was benign and negligently failed to refer the claimant to hospital for tests. The claimant was subsequently admitted to hospital in January 1996 where it was found that he was suffering from non-Hodgkin's lymphoma. The effect of the 14-month delay in diagnosis was that the cancer had spread and, statistically, Mr Gregg's chance of a 'cure' (defined, medically, as ten-year disease-free survival) had diminished from 42 per cent to 25 per cent. In his action against the doctor, the claimant argued, inter alia, that the lost (or, more accurately, reduced) statistical chance of a cure should itself be compensated for. This basis of the claim would have been allowed by Lord Nicholls:

Lord Nicholls: [21] . . . What the patient loses depends, of course, on the circumstances of the individual case. No doubt in some cases medical opinion will be that, given his pre-existing

95 [2005] UKHL 2.

condition, the patient lost nothing by the delay in treatment because he never had any realistic prospect of recovery. The doctor's misdiagnosis made no significant difference to the patient's prospects of recovery. In other cases medical opinion may be that the patient lost everything. Barring unforeseen complications he would have made a complete recovery had his condition been diagnosed properly and had he then received appropriate treatment.

[22] These two types of case are, in the present context, straightforward. But there are also many cases of serious illness or injury where a patient's existing chances of recovery fall between these extremes. There are occasions where medical opinion will be that, given prompt and appropriate treatment, the outcome was uncertain but the patient's prospects of recovery were appreciable, sometimes exceeding 50%, sometimes not . . .

[24] Given this uncertainty of outcome, the appropriate characterisation of a patient's loss in this type of case must surely be that it comprises the loss of the chance of a favourable outcome, rather than the loss of the outcome itself. Justice so requires, because this matches medical reality. This recognises what in practice a patient had before the doctor's negligence occurred. It recognises what in practice the patient lost by reason of that negligence. The doctor's negligence diminished the patient's prospects of recovery. And this analysis of a patient's loss accords with the purpose of the legal duty of which the doctor was in breach. In short, the purpose of the duty is to promote the patient's prospects of recovery by exercising due skill and care in diagnosing and treating the patient's condition.

However, Lord Hoffmann was in the opposite camp. As foreshadowed in his speech in *Fairchild*,[96] one of his Lordship's concerns related to the effect of permitting such claims upon scarce healthcare resources:

Lord Hoffmann: [84] Academic writers have suggested that in cases of clinical negligence, the need to prove causation is too restrictive of liability. This argument has appealed to judges in some jurisdictions; in some, but not all, of the states of the United States and most recently in New South Wales and Ireland: *Rufo v Hosking* . . . [2004] NSWCA 391; *Philp v Ryan* . . . [2004] 1 IESC 105. In the present case it is urged that Mr Gregg has suffered a wrong and ought to have a remedy. Living for more than 10 years is something of great value to him and he should be compensated for the possibility that the delay in diagnosis may have reduced his chances of doing so. In effect, the Appellant submits that the exceptional rule in *Fairchild* should be generalised and damages awarded in all cases in which the defendant may have caused an injury and has increased the likelihood of the injury being suffered. In the present case, it is alleged that Dr Scott may have caused a reduction in Mr Gregg's expectation of life and that he increased the likelihood that his life would be shortened by the disease.

[85] It should first be noted that adopting such a rule would involve abandoning a good deal of authority. The rule which the House is asked to adopt is the very rule which it rejected in *Wilsher's* case [1988] AC 1074. Yet *Wilsher's* case was expressly approved by the House in *Fairchild* [2003] 1 AC 32. *Hotson* [1987] AC 750 too would have to be overruled. Furthermore, the House would be dismantling all the qualifications and restrictions with which it so recently hedged the *Fairchild* exception. There seem to me to be no new arguments or change of circumstances which could justify such a radical departure from precedent . . .

[90] . . . [A] wholesale adoption of possible rather than probable causation as the criterion of liability would be so radical a change in our law as to amount to a legislative act. It would have enormous consequences for insurance companies and the National Health Service.

---

96 See n 86 above.

Lord Phillips and Baroness Hale agreed with Lord Hoffmann in dismissing the claimant's appeal. However, they appear to have been swayed more by the particular factual complexities of the case at hand, and a distrust of the statistical evidence on offer. As the former commented:

> **Lord Phillips**: [189] There are no doubt cases where it is possible to adopt the simple approach of asking to what extent the negligent treatment has reduced the prospects of curing the patient. There are other cases, and this is one, where that simple question is almost impossible to answer ... The likelihood seems to be that Dr Scott's negligence has not prevented Mr Gregg's cure, but has made that cure more painful.
>
> [190] The complications of this case have persuaded me that it is not a suitable vehicle for introducing into the law of clinical negligence the right to recover damages for the loss of a chance of a cure. Awarding damages for the reduction of the prospect of a cure, when the long term result of treatment is still uncertain, is not a satisfactory exercise. Where medical treatment has resulted in an adverse outcome and negligence has increased the chance of that outcome, there may be a case for permitting a recovery of damages that is proportionate to the increase in the chance of the adverse outcome. That is not a case that has been made out on the present appeal. I would uphold the conventional approach to causation ...

Gregg v Scott is undoubtedly a difficult case, and one may agree with Lord Phillips' assessment that it did not provide a suitable vehicle for recognising 'loss of chance' claims in medical negligence. A fundamental problem, as their Lordships noted, was that the claimant was still alive nearly ten years after the original misdiagnosis. Thus (leaving aside, the more painful treatment he had to undergo)[97] he had quite possibly lost nothing, not even a chance. Although statistically it made a difference for 17 per cent of patients with a similar condition whether diagnosis took place at the earlier stage (when it should have) or only later, it appeared increasingly likely that the claimant was not in that group. Instead, his case was akin to that of someone who is exposed to a hazardous substance, known to increase the risk of a given harm, but where as yet no harm has materialised and no one knows whether it will or not (and where it is generally acknowledged that no recovery lies in negligence).[98] On the other hand, as suggested in a number of recent High Court decisions, there may in appropriate cases be a modest award for reduced life expectancy and/or mental suffering induced by the belief that one has been wrongly deprived of a cure.[99]

However, returning to the more classical loss of chance scenario illustrated by *Hotson* – where the claimant's injury has already occurred – it is submitted that such claims should in fact be permitted. Just as in the *Barnett* case,[100] the basic question is whether or not the claimant's medical condition was untreatable from the outset. Would the illness alone have been sufficient for the injury, or did the lack of proper treatment also play a necessary part? In such cases, it is strongly arguable that class statistics (where available) bring us significantly closer to the truth than adherence to the balance of probabilities standard of proof:

---

97 As Baroness Hale suggested in her speech, had the claimant put this in his claim, he could have obtained some damages for the more painful treatment.

98 See *Grieves v F T Everard & Sons* [2007] UKHL 39 (the pleural plaques test case).

99 See *JD v Mather* [2012] EWHC 3063 (QB); *Oliver v Williams* [2013] EWHC 600 (QB); *Muller v King's College Hospital NHS Foundation Trust* [2017] EWHC 128 (QB).

100 See the text at n 82 above.

Stauch, M, *The Law of Medical Negligence in England and Germany – A Comparative Analysis*[101]

[In loss of chance claims] the statistics at issue are derived empirically by reference to how patients with the claimant's condition generally fare (ie with the proper treatment). It is true that this does not offer certainty in a particular case . . . Nonetheless, the crucial point is that the traditional balance of probabilities test is no different. In finding that a given patient's condition was *probably* untreatable, the court also draws upon past experience as to how other patients with a similar condition respond to treatment (ie that the majority do not benefit). It does not tell us that the *claimant* individually could not have been helped: he might have been one of the (perhaps substantial) minority, whose condition would have responded. In this context, the use of statistics providing an accurate measure of the opportunity lost as a prequel to an award of proportionate damages, appears significantly fairer than the present 'all or nothing' approach.

Similarly, the fear that allowing claims for proportionate recovery would undermine general principles of causation in personal injury cases is not justified. In the first place, such claims, which depend on the availability of empirical statistical evidence, would normally be confined to medical misdiagnosis cases; . . . it is much less likely that such evidence will be at hand where the doctor's mistake actively added to the risks to the patient. Secondly, it is important to reiterate that . . . loss of chance claims arise as a response to factual uncertainty (ie in default of individuating evidence as to what would have happened in the particular case). In this regard, the relevant rules operate on a different plane to the substantive law elements, including 'but for' causation.

Thus, following on from the above, it would remain necessary for the (substantive law) requirement of *actual* injury to the claimant to be satisfied – these cases are not about treating exposure to risk per se as a recoverable form of injury. This, it is submitted, was the key difficulty with *Gregg v Scott*, where the claimant's injury (the lost benefit of a cure) had not yet occurred, and it was uncertain whether it would do so in the future . . . By contrast, in the most scenarios of this type – such as in *Hotson* – this problem does not arise.

Finally, as to the concern that permitting loss of chance claims could lead to a flood of additional litigation against the NHS, we should be clear that, in terms of overall compensation, no more would be paid out in faulty diagnosis claims than before: this is because, logically the use of statistics as a basis for proportionate recovery 'must cut both ways' [*per* Baroness Hale in *Gregg v Scott* [2005] UKHL 2, para 225]. Thus a patient who had, say, a 60 per cent chance of benefiting from wrongfully omitted treatment should only receive 60 per cent of damages in respect of his injury, not 100 per cent as at present. It remains true that the total number of claims may increase, as patients will no longer be deterred, as at present, from litigating in cases where their prospects of successful treatment were low. Arguably, to guard against a proliferation of low-value actions, the law (in a pragmatic vein) should demand that the chance lost was a substantial one.

6.4.2.3 Human agency in the causal chain

Complications of a different kind arise in cases in which resolving the causal inquiry requires us to decide how a human agent would have behaved in the hypothetical circumstances of no original breach of duty. In contrast to the cases considered previously, in which the causal chain consists only of physical events, such as the progress of an untreated disease, it may well be felt that the balance of probabilities standard of proof remains the most acceptable one here (to assert that because, in a given situation, X per cent of persons are observed to do A, a particular individual, P, is X per cent likely to do A, would be to take an unduly mechanistic view of human agency).

As we saw in Chapter 3, a common type of case, which requires us to assess the impact of human agency in the causal chain, is where the doctor fails to advise the patient of a given risk attached to treatment. Here the patient, in order to succeed in his claim, must show that, on the balance of probabilities, if properly advised, he would not have agreed to the treatment, or

---

101 Oxford: Hart Publishing, 2008.
102 On this aspect, see *Webster v Burton Hospitals NHS Foundation Trust* (2017) EWCA Civ 62.

(following *Montgomery*) would have favoured an alternative therapy canvassed.[102] However, in other cases it is the defendant's hypothetical conduct that will be at issue: this is true in particular where a doctor negligently fails to attend the patient. Assuming that treatment is available which would benefit the patient, would the doctor have administered it? If not, so the doctor might argue, the failure by him to attend made no difference.

Here (as with the analogous claim by a patient that, had he known of a risk, he would have refused treatment), the court must first accept the veracity of the doctor's assertion that he would not have given treatment. In *Wisniewski v Central Manchester Health Authority*[103] the court, in holding that the necessary treatment would probably have been carried out, drew an adverse inference from the doctor's non-appearance in the witness box to back up his contrary assertion. If, though, the doctor's testimony is accepted, then, as Lord Browne-Wilkinson made clear in *Bolitho v City and Hackney HA*,[104] that is not the end of the matter. There is a second question that the court must resolve:

Lord Browne-Wilkinson: Where, as in the present case, a breach of a duty of care is proved or admitted, the burden still lies on the plaintiff to prove that such breach caused the injury suffered: *Bonnington Castings Ltd v Wardlaw* [1956] AC 613; *Wilsher v Essex AHA* [1988] AC 1074. In all cases the primary question is one of fact: did the wrongful act cause the injury? ... In a case of non-attendance by a doctor, there may be cases in which there is a doubt as to which doctor would have attended if the duty had been fulfilled. But in this case there was no doubt: if the duty had been carried out it would have either been Dr Horn or Dr Rodger, the only two doctors at St Bartholomew's who had responsibility for Patrick and were on duty. Therefore in the present case, the first relevant question is 'what would Dr Horn or Dr Rodger have done if they had attended?' As to Dr Horn, the judge accepted her evidence that she would not have intubated. By inference, although not expressly, the judge must have accepted that Dr Rodger also would not have intubated: as a senior house officer she would not have intubated without the approval of her senior registrar, Dr Horn ...

However in the present case the answer to the question 'what would have happened?' is not determinative of the issue of causation. At the trial the defendants accepted that if the professional standard of care required any doctor who attended to intubate Patrick, Patrick's claim must succeed. Dr Horn could not escape liability by proving that she would have failed to take the course which any competent doctor would have adopted. A defendant cannot escape liability by saying that the damage would have occurred in any event because he would have committed some other breach of duty thereafter. I have no doubt that this concession was rightly made by the defendants. But there is some difficulty in analysing why it was correct. I adopt the analysis of Hobhouse LJ in *Joyce v Merton, Sutton and Wandsworth HA* [1996] 7 Med LR 1. In commenting on the decision of the Court of Appeal in the present case, he said, p 20:

> Thus a plaintiff can discharge the burden of proof on causation by satisfying the court *either* that the relevant person would in fact have taken the requisite action (although she would not have been at fault if she had not), or that the proper discharge of the relevant person's duty towards the plaintiff required that she take that action. The former alternative calls for no explanation since it is simply the factual proof of the causative effect of the original fault. The latter is slightly more sophisticated: it involves the factual situation that the original fault did not itself cause the injury but that this was because there would have been some further fault on the part of the defendants; the plaintiff proves his case by proving that his injuries would have been avoided if proper care had continued to be taken. In the *Bolitho* case the plaintiff had to prove that the continuing exercise of proper care would have resulted in his being intubated.

103 [1998] PIQR P324.
104 See n 57 above.

There were, therefore, two questions for the judge to decide on causation: (1) 'What would Dr Horn have done, or authorised to be done, if she had attended Patrick?' And: (2) 'If she would not have intubated, would that have been negligent?' The *Bolam* test has no relevance to the first of those questions but is central to the second.

An interesting recent Court of Appeal decision that raised similar issues, but in the context of separate putative defendants, is *Wright (A Child) v Cambridge Medical Group (A Partnership)*.[105] There, the infant claimant, who had a bacterial infection, suffered permanent injury to her hip after a negligent two-day delay by the defendant GPs to refer her to hospital. However, the hospital itself took an unduly long time to diagnose and treat the infection. The defendant argued that, even if it had referred the claimant earlier, the hospital would still probably have negligently failed to deal with the problem in time. In the High Court this argument was accepted, but, as the Court of Appeal noted, an unfortunate feature of the case was that neither party had seen fit to join the hospital itself to the proceedings, so the evidence as to what would have occurred if the claimant had arrived there earlier remained highly speculative.

For its part, the Court of Appeal (Lord Neuberger MR, Dame Janet Smith; Elias LJ dissenting) allowed the claimant's appeal, but the majority equivocated on the question of whether the defendant's argument was admissible in principle. Thus, Lord Neuberger, referring to the earlier Court of Appeal authority, *Gouldsmith v Mid-Staffordshire General Hospitals NHS Trust*,[106] was of the view that (as in the case of a single doctor in *Bolitho*) the defendant was debarred as a matter of law from relying on the later hypothetical negligence of other medical professionals to deny causation. However, *Gouldsmith* had involved the complete failure of a GP to refer the patient to hospital, and Dame Janet Smith, while accepting the principle's application there, was more doubtful that it should extend to a delayed referral as here. She agreed, however, with Lord Neuberger that, in so far as the defendant's argument was admissible, the defendant carried the burden of proof and, on the facts, had not shown sufficiently that the hospital would have failed to treat the claimant's infection properly, had it had two days longer to do so.

Such complexities would clearly have been avoided if the hospital had been joined in the proceedings, in which case the court could have arrived at an equitable apportionment between it and the GPs as to their respective liabilities to the claimant.[107]

6.4.3 Legal causation/remoteness of damage

Legal causation, or 'remoteness', operates as a further limiting device, which may exclude liability even where the defendant's conduct clearly *did* play a necessary part in the claimant's injury (ie the factual causation requirement of the 'but for' test has been satisfied). In negligence, the dominant approach of the courts, following the decision of the Privy Council in *The Wagon Mound (No 1)*,[108] is to begin by considering the nature of the harm in suit (that is, the damage that actually materialised) and ask if it was reasonably foreseeable. In other words, was it the risk of *that* harm occurring that made the defendant's conduct faulty?

It is often said that, once the broad 'type' of harm suffered by the claimant was reasonably foreseeable, the fact that its precise manner of upshot or extent may not have been is immaterial. On the other hand, as cases since *The Wagon Mound* demonstrate, given that any harmful

---

105 [2011] EWCA Civ 669.
106 [2007] EWCA Civ 397.
107 Under the provisions of the Civil Liability (Contribution) Act 1978.
108 [1961] AC 388.

outcome can be described at different levels of detail, the question of its foreseeability – and, hence, the defendant's liability – will turn on the specificity of the description applied by the court in a particular case. This point has led some commentators to regard the whole remoteness enquiry as merely a cover for the concealed policy choices of judges. Arguably, a more cogent approach is to focus not so much on the 'type' of harm that has occurred, but on the further necessary conditions that (together with the defendant's conduct) completed the causal set for harm in the particular case. Was the possible completion of a causal set that included those further conditions a reason for regarding the conduct as a breach of duty?[109]

In principle, remoteness principles may apply in medical negligence (just as in other negligence cases) to defeat the claimant's action. In *Brown v Lewisham and North Southwark HA*[110] the claimant, who had undergone heart surgery, was negligently discharged from hospital while suffering from a chest infection. Later he was found to have an unsuspected thrombosis, which led to the loss of his leg. The court did not accept that, had he remained in hospital, the leg would have been saved (ie it denied factual causation). However, as Beldam LJ noted in the Court of Appeal, the claimant's action would in any event have failed on remoteness grounds:

> **Beldam LJ**: The public policy of limiting the liability of tortfeasors by the control mechanism of foreseeability seems to me as necessary in cases of medical as in any other type of negligence. I do not see on what policy ground it would be fair or just to hold a doctor [liable] who failed to diagnose an asymptomatic and undetectable illness merely because he was at fault in the management of a correctly diagnosed but unrelated condition. In short, it must be shown that the injury suffered by the patient is within the risk from which it was the doctor's duty to protect him.

Subsequently, this *dictum* was approved in the case of *Thompson v Bradford*,[111] in which the Court of Appeal denied the liability of a doctor for vaccine injuries to a child following immunisation for polio. The doctor had failed to advise the parents that a boil the child had was a contra-indication for the vaccination – advice which would have led to the procedure being postponed. In the event, the boil played a factually causative role in the vaccine damage. Nonetheless, the reason the advice should have been given was not the added risk of such damage (which had been unforeseeable), but the discomfort to the child of vaccinating him in those circumstances.

Overall though, cases of medical negligence claims failing for lack of legal causation are the exception. Usually the courts will refuse to draw fine distinctions between the risk which ought to have been foreseen and that which actually materialised. Thus, in *Hepworth v Kerr*[112] a doctor was held liable for using an experimental anaesthetic technique on a patient, which resulted in a spinal stroke. The risk of inducing a spinal stroke was, in fact not known about, but the risk of a cerebral stroke (making the procedure's use negligent) was. Similarly, in *Wisniewski v Manchester HA*[113] the defendant tried to deny liability on the basis that, though the claimant's hypoxia during birth – which he had negligently failed to manage – had been foreseeable, the mechanics of it in the particular case (involving a rare instance of a knot in the umbilical cord) had not been. In the Court of Appeal, Brooke LJ commented that to make such a distinction would be an 'affront to common sense, and the law would look an ass'.

---

109 See further, Stauch, M, 'Risk and remoteness of damage in negligence' (2001) 64 MLR 191.
110 [1999] Lloyd's Rep Med 110.
111 [2005] EWCA 1439.
112 See n 71 above.
113 See n 103 above.

As we saw in Chapter 3, the requirement of legal causation may also be relaxed in the context of 'non-disclosure' cases (leading exceptionally to liability for risks over which the doctor had no control).[114]

6.5 Defences

It must be said that the usual tortious defences are rarely used in medical cases and, for that reason, are dealt with only briefly. The first possibility is a claim by the doctor/hospital of contributory negligence, to the effect that the patient was also at fault in his conduct, in relation to managing his condition, and this contributed to the injury suffered. If this is accepted, the court may reduce the damages awarded, in accordance with the Law Reform (Contributory Negligence) Act 1945. However, as Grubb and Jones note, the defence has an unattractive feel in the context of medical negligence and will seldom be argued:

Grubb, A (ed), *Principles of Medical Law*[115]

> 7.55 Although, in theory, there is no reason why contributory negligence should not apply in a claim for medical negligence, in practice the defence is rarely invoked successfully, and this is reflected in a comparative dearth of cases. It may be that the plea is considered to be inappropriate, given the inequality between the respective positions of doctor and patient. Patients do not generally question the advice or conduct of their doctors, even when they are aware that their condition is deteriorating or not improving. If the patient has ignored the doctor's advice (for example by discharging himself from hospital or failing to return for further treatment) it may be easier to establish the defence. It would have to be shown that a reasonable person would have been aware of the significance of the advice, which will depend on the nature of the advice and whether it was clear to the patient . . .
>
> 7.57 The one English reported case in which the claimant's conduct was held to be negligent is *Pidgeon v Doncaster HA* [[2002] Lloyd's Rep Med 130 (Doncaster County Ct)] where a claimant who developed cervical cancer, having been told that the results of a smear test were negative, was held to have been two-thirds contributory negligent in failing to have a further smear test despite frequent reminders. It would also be possible for a plea of contributory negligence to apply in cases where the claimant attempts suicide and a claim is brought against medical staff on the basis of a negligent failure to prevent the suicide attempt . . .

A second possible defence is that of consent, or *volenti non fit injuria*. This is where the defendant argues that the patient had consented to the risk. In a Scottish medical negligence decision, *Sabri-Tabrizi v Lothian Health Board*,[116] it was said that such consent must normally have occurred prior to, and certainly cannot come after, the defendant's breach of duty. It is arguable that this condition would never be satisfied in the context of medical treatment, and there would appear to be no cases where the defence has been argued successfully.

Finally, the defence of illegality, or *ex turpi causa*, may apply where the background events relied on by the claimant in his negligence action disclose criminal wrongdoing on his part. In such cases, the defendant may persuade the court that, as a matter of public policy, it would not be seemly to allow the action. The doctrine will seldom be of any relevance in the medical negligence context. However, the Court of Appeal had recourse to it in *Clunis v Camden and*

---

114 See further the discussion there of *Chester v Afshar* [2004] UKHL 41.
115 Oxford: OUP, 2nd edn, 2004.
116 (1997) 43 BMLR 190.

Islington HA,[117] where the claimant, a mentally ill man imprisoned for manslaughter, alleged that the defendant authority had negligently failed to detain him in time under the Mental Health Act 1983.

6.6 Liability for defective medicines

Frequently patients may allege that they were injured, not through negligence on a doctor's part, but by medicinal drugs that they were (properly) given during treatment.

Before they are made available for prescription, medicines are subject to comprehensive licensing requirements pursuant to the Medicines Act 1968. However, the fact that such drugs may sometimes give rise to unpredictable and harmful metabolic reactions was brought poignantly to the public consciousness by the Thalidomide tragedy of the late 1960s and, given the difficulty in proving fault on the part of manufacturers (even the most thorough testing may fail to reveal a particular reaction in advance), provoked calls from both the Law Commission[118] and the Pearson Committee[119] for 'no fault' compensation to be introduced for such injury.

In the event, the emergence of a scheme, dispensing with the need to show fault, had to await initiatives at EC level in relation to defective consumer products generally. As a result of the EC Product Liability Directive,[120] the Government passed Pt I of the Consumer Protection Act 1987, which imposes strict liability upon manufacturers in respect of products put into circulation after 1 March 1988:

... 2 Liability for defective products

1 Subject to the following provisions of this Part, where any damage is caused wholly or partly by a defect in a product, every person to whom sub-s (2) below applies shall be liable for the damage.

2 This sub-section applies to –

   a the producer of the product;

   b any person who, by putting his name on the product or using a trade mark or other distinguishing mark in relation to the product, has held himself out to be the producer of the product;

   c any person who has imported the product into a Member State from a place outside the Member States in order, in the course of any business of his, to supply it to another.

...

3 Meaning of 'defect'

1 Subject to the following provisions of this section, there is a defect in a product for the purposes of this Part if the safety of the product is not such as persons generally are entitled to expect, and for those purposes 'safety', in relation to a product, shall include safety with respect to products comprised in that product and safety in the context of risks of damage to property, as well as in the context of risks of death or personal injury.

2 In determining for the purposes of sub-s (1) above what persons generally are entitled to expect in relation to a product, all the circumstances shall be taken into account, including –

   a the manner in which, and purposes for which, the product has been marketed, its get-up, the use of any mark in relation to the product and any instructions for, or warnings with respect to, doing or refraining from doing anything with or in relation to the product;

---

117 [1998] 3 All ER 180.
118 Report 82, Cmnd 6831, 1977.
119 Cmnd 7054, 1978 (the Pearson Report). A limited pocket of 'no fault liability', namely for injuries resulting from vaccination, was introduced by the Vaccine Damage Payments Act 1979.
120 85/374/EC.

b   what might reasonably be expected to be done with or in relation to the product; and

c   the time when the product was supplied by its producer to another,

and nothing in this section shall require a defect to be inferred from the fact alone that the safety of a product which is supplied after that time is greater than the safety of the product in question.

In the 2001 High Court ruling in *A and Others v National Blood Authority*,[121] a class action brought by 114 people who contracted Hepatitis C from contaminated blood supplies, Burton J – in finding for the claimants – took the view that, for a 'defect' to arise under s 3, it was enough that the risk of infection was not one that was known and accepted by society generally. As Deards and Twigg-Flesner comment:

Deards, E and Twigg-Flesner, C, 'The Consumer Protection Act 1987: proof at last that it is protecting consumers'[122]

The High Court drew a distinction between 'standard' and 'non-standard' products. 'Standard' products were those that met the design and standard of safety intended by the manufacturer. A 'non-standard' product was a particular unit of the product that did not meet the standard. In *A and Others*, the court stated that the infected blood products were non-standard, that is to say, differed from the standard product intended by the manufacturer. The standard blood products were not inherently defective. In the case of blood transfusions, it was only 1% of the product that 'failed' in that it had been contaminated with the Hepatitis C virus. The court suggested that it might be easier to prove a defect where the product was non-standard, since it would fall to be compared with the standard product. The problem with this argument is that a product is only non-standard if it is defective, but whether it is defective could be affected by whether it is non-standard. Admittedly the court envisaged that a non-standard product was one that was defective in a non-technical, non-Act sense, but there could be cases where even this was disputed, and then a circular argument would result. In respect of non-standard products, the court stated that the consumers' expectations as to safety depended on whether they accepted the non-standard nature of the product.

The High Court confirmed that the factors for assessing the defectiveness listed in section 3 of the Act were not exclusive, and that all relevant circumstances were to be considered. However, it ruled that avoidability of the risk of infection was not a relevant factor. The possibility of avoiding the harmful characteristics by taking precautionary measures, the impracticality, cost and difficulty of taking such measures and the benefit to society of the product were therefore not relevant. On the facts, the risk was known by doctors but was not known and accepted by society generally. The risk of infected blood could therefore not have been accepted by consumers unless they were warned, which they had not been. The infected blood products were therefore defective.

Recently, though, in *Wilkes v Depuy International Ltd*,[123] which involved a claim under the CPA 1987 by a patient whose artificial hip fractured, Hickinbottom J in the High Court took issue with Burton J's approach to the meaning of defect, including the 'standard/ non-standard' distinction:

Hickinbottom J: [94] In my respectful view, the categorisation of defects into 'standard'/'non-standard', as a classification, is unnecessary and undesirable. It is not, of course, a classification deriving from the

---

121 [2001] 3 All ER 289.

122 (2001) 10(2) Nott LJ 1.

123 [2016] EWHC 3096 (QB); see also *Gee & Others v DePuy International Limited* [2018] EWHC 1208 (QB).

> Directive or Act. In my judgment, whether a particular product is within the producer's specification, and is compliant with relevant standards . . . may be relevant circumstances in relation to whether the level of safety is that to which persons generally are entitled to expect; but to raise the distinction to a rigid categorisation is positively unhelpful and potentially dangerous.

In finding that, in the circumstances, the artificial hip at issue, despite the known (very small) risk of fracture, was of an appropriate level of safety (and hence not defective), his Lordship noted that the product had been tested and approved in line with European and UK safety standards (under medical device regulations):

> [97] It was, rightly, common ground that non-compliance with any appropriate mandatory standards will provide evidence of defect; and that compliance with such standards, whilst not providing a complete defence, will provide evidence that, in respect of the matters to which those standards go, the level of safety required by the Act has been satisfied and the product, in those respects, is therefore not defective.

In fact claims under the 1987 Act involving medical or medicinal products remain very rare. It should also be noted that the payment of compensation is in any event contingent upon causation being shown between the product and injury. Given the frequently opaque nature of causal processes in this area (with plausible causal chains between phenomena often hard to find), this may often be a serious obstacle for claimants. This is especially so in respect of idiosyncratic reactions to a drug on the part of a small minority of users where the degree of regularity between cause (ingesting the drug) and effect (injury), which generally ground causal inferences, will be absent. In the case of *XYZ v Schering Health Care Ltd*,[124] the High Court held that claimants had failed to show the drug they ingested (an oral contraceptive) was capable of causing their injuries, and this has also been the fate of similar actions for medicinal injury at common law.[125]

6.7 Reforming the law

6.7.1 Problems with the medical litigation system

Medical negligence cases are often very expensive to bring, because of the technical and complex nature of the litigation. Moreover, statistically, far fewer such claims succeed – between 25 and 45 per cent – than the average for negligence actions generally (around 80 per cent).[126] Nevertheless, this has not prevented a major upsurge in such claims over the last 30 years or so, with the public generally appearing less deferential, more aware of their rights, and holding higher expectations of what can and should be achieved on their behalf.

---

124 [2002] EWHC 1420 (QB).
125 See *Kay v Ayrshire and Arran Health Board* [1987] 2 All ER 417; *Loveday v Renton* [1990] 1 Med LR 117.
126 *Compensation Culture*, HC Constitutional Affairs Committee, Third Report of Session 2005–06, London: TSO, 2006.

In 1996, the Woolf Report looked critically at medical negligence litigation and found some major problems:

Lord Woolf MR, *Access to Justice: The Final Report to the Lord Chancellor on the Civil Justice System in England and Wales*[127]

Reasons for looking at medical negligence

2   ... [E]arly in the Inquiry it became increasingly obvious that it was in the area of medical negligence that the civil justice system was failing most conspicuously to meet the needs of litigants in a number of respects:

a   The disproportion between costs and damages in medical negligence is particularly excessive, especially in lower value cases.

b   The delay in resolving claims is more often unacceptable.

c   Unmeritorious cases are often pursued, and clear-cut claims defended, for too long.

d   The success rate is lower than in other personal injury litigation.

e   The suspicion between the parties is more intense and the lack of co-operation frequently greater than in many other areas of litigation.

...   5 The difficulty of proving both causation and negligence, which arises more acutely in medical negligence than in other personal injury cases, accounts for much of the excessive cost. The root of the problem, however, lies less in the complexity of the law or procedure than in the climate of mutual suspicion and defensiveness which is still all too prevalent in this area of litigation. Patients feel let down when treatment goes wrong, sometimes because of unrealistic expectations as to what could be achieved. Doctors feel they are under attack from aggrieved patients and react defensively...

...change of culture

21 The extent of patients' mistrust of doctors and other hospital staff is illustrated by the submission I have received from Action for Victims of Medical Accidents (AVMA). They argue that the real reason for defendants' reluctance to investigate complaints where there is a possibility of legal action is a concern that such an investigation might indeed disclose negligence...

22 If that mistrust is to be removed, the medical profession and the NHS administration must demonstrate their commitment to patients' well being by adopting a constructive approach to claims handling. It must be clearly accepted that injured patients are entitled to redress, and that professional solidarity or individual self-esteem are not sufficient reasons for resisting or obstructing valid claims.

23 Patients and their representatives, for their part, must recognise that some degree of risk is inherent in all medical treatment, and that even the best practitioners do sometimes make mistakes. They should not pursue unrealistic claims, and should make every effort to resolve disputes without recourse to litigation.

Since then, the general Woolf reforms (including stricter pre-trial management and more incentives to settle claims) appear to be having a positive impact on medical litigation; thus there has been some reduction in costs, and an increase in claims settled. Nevertheless, tensions in relation to this area of litigation persist, not least in the light of the decision, following the Jackson review of civil litigation, to scrap legal aid for nearly all medical negligence claims.[128] Secondly, recent data has made clear the enormous overall costs of medical accidents to the NHS. Statistics

---

127 London: HMSO, 1996.
128 See the Government Response to Lord Justice Jackson's Recommendations (Cm 8041, March 2011), at: www.gov.uk/government/uploads/system/uploads/attachment_data/file/228974/8041.pdf.

collated by the NHS Litigation Authority (which handles claims against the NHS) showed total annual payments in respect of medical negligence (in settlements, awards, and lawyer's fees) to be £235 million in 1996–97; by 2015–16 this figure had quintupled to around £1,150 million.[129] Equally, though, it has been recognised that claims brought are merely the tip of the iceberg relative to the actual number of 'preventable adverse events' that occur in the health sector. On the basis of international studies (including the 1990 Harvard Medical Practice Study in the US), it has been estimated that 850,000 adverse outcomes occur in the NHS annually, of which around half are 'preventable'. In this regard, the inadequacy of tort law alone as a means for safeguarding treatment quality and safety was starkly illustrated by the events of the Mid-Staffordshire health scandal, as revealed in the 2013 report of the Francis Inquiry.[130]

In response to that inquiry, the Government passed the Health and Social Care Act 2008 (Regulated Activities) Regulations 2014, which is designed to introduce greater transparency into the healthcare environment. *Inter alia*, there are 'specific requirements that providers must follow when things go wrong with care and treatment, including informing people about the incident, providing reasonable support, providing truthful information and an apology when things go wrong'.[131] There is also potential criminal liability for failure to meet patients' nutritional or hydrational needs. It remains debatable how far this is a constructive way to deal with providers, already operating under stressful and difficult conditions, and sometimes with very limited resources.

Another solution that has been proposed over the years, and was reiterated by Professor Ian Kennedy in his 2001 report into the Bristol Royal Infirmary Inquiry,[132] is that we should move away from the common law of tort altogether towards a statutory 'no fault' based system of liability for medical negligence. Some jurisdictions, notably New Zealand and the Scandinavian countries, have been running such schemes for a number of years,[133] with at least some success: certainly, the administration costs are lower than for tort, and it appears that tensions between patients and doctors are reduced; on the other hand, problems remain in designing such schemes equitably (to decide who qualifies for compensation, and who does not), and they may potentially become very expensive.[134] Moreover, the difficulties for the claimant associated with proving causation will in any event remain, and his ability to overcome them will determine whether he comes within the no fault scheme at all.

⌐ THINK POINT

In his 2003 report, *Making Amends* (see below), the Chief Medical Officer proposed a limited no fault scheme to deal with cases of neurologically impaired babies. As an independent research exercise investigate why (so far) this suggestion has not been acted upon.

6.7.2 *Making Amends* and the NHS Redress Act 2006

In 2001, the Department of Health launched a wide-ranging review by the Chief Medical Officer (CMO), Sir Liam Donaldson, into the way the law functions in practice in this area, and options

---

129 See the data on the NHS Litigation Authority website, at: www.nhsla.com/home.htm.
130 See: www.midstaffspublicinquiry.com/report.
131 See: www.cqc.org.uk/guidance-providers/regulations-enforcement/regulation-20-duty-candour.
132 *Learning from Bristol: the report of the public inquiry into children's heart surgery at the Bristol Royal Infirmary 1984–1995*, Cm 5207, July 2001.
133 More recently, the French have introduced such a scheme: see further Taylor, S, 'Providing Redress for Medical Accidents in France: Conflicting Aims, Effective Solutions?' (2011) 1 JETL 57.
134 For an analysis of the New Zealand scheme, including changes made from time to time to the 'eligibility criteria' in respect of medical injury claims, see Oliphant, K, 'Beyond Misadventure: Compensation for Medical Injuries in New Zealand' (2007) 15 Med L Rev 357.

for its reform (including the arguments for and against a general 'no fault' scheme). The CMO's report, *Making Amends*, was published in June 2003:

Chief Medical Officer, *Making Amends: A consultation paper setting out proposals for reforming the approach to clinical negligence in the NHS*[135] – Summary

A vision for a successful alternative to the present system

● Any new system should create a climate where:
  - risks of care are reduced and patient safety improves because medical errors and near misses are readily reported, successfully analysed and effective corrective action takes place and is sustained;
  - remedial treatment, care and rehabilitation are available to redress harm and injuries arising from healthcare;
  - any financial compensation is provided fairly and efficiently;
  - payments of compensation act as financial incentives on healthcare organisations and their staff to improve quality and patient safety;
  - the process of compensation does not undermine the strength of the relationship between patient and healthcare professional; . . .

. . . The case for no fault compensation

● The main arguments in favour of 'no fault' compensation are:
  - fairness;
  - speedier resolution of cases;
  - lower administrative and legal costs than court action;
  - increased certainty for claimants on the circumstances in which compensation is payable and increased consistency between claimants;
  - reduced tension between clinicians and claimants;
  - greater willingness by clinicians to report errors and adverse events.

The case against no fault compensation

● Critics of no fault compensation schemes argue that:
  - overall costs will be higher than under a tort system;
  - it will open the floodgates to compensation payments and fuel a compensation culture;
  - disputes about causation remain, even if 'fault' is removed;
  - disputes about the amount of damages remain, unless there is a tariff-based approach;
  - it is difficult to distinguish injury from the natural progression of the disease in some cases;
  - explanations and apologies are not necessarily provided in a system which focuses on financial recompense alone;
  - a no fault scheme, in itself, does not improve accountability or ensure learning from adverse events.
● The review specifically considered the option of a comprehensive no-fault compensation system. This was rejected because:
  - a true 'no-fault' scheme would lead to a potentially huge increase in claims and overall costs would be far higher than under the present tort system. Initial estimates suggest that the annual bill could reach £4 billion.

---

135 CMO, *Making Amends: A consultation paper setting out proposals for reforming the approach to clinical negligence in the NHS*, London: DoH, 2003. An archived version is available at: www.dh.gov.uk/prod_consum_dh/groups/dh_digitalassets/@dh/@en/documents/digitalasset/dh_4060945.pdf.

- to be affordable, compensation would need to be set at a substantially lower level than current tort awards and would not necessarily meet the needs of the harmed patient;
- it would be difficult to distinguish harm to a patient from the natural progression of a disease;
- no-fault schemes, of themselves, do not improve processes for learning from error or reduction of harm to patients.

The CMO instead recommended establishing what he named the 'NHS Redress Scheme', to provide for extra-judicial compensation of low-value claims against the NHS (in which litigation costs often exceed the size of awards). This proposal formed the basis for the NHS Redress Act 2006, which received Royal Assent in late 2006:

1 Power to establish redress scheme

(1) The Secretary of State may by regulations establish a scheme for the purpose of enabling redress to be provided without recourse to civil proceedings in circumstances in which this section applies.

(2) This section applies where under the law of England and Wales qualifying liability in tort on the part of a body or other person . . . arises in connection with the provision, as part of the health service in England, of qualifying services.

. . . (4) The reference in subsection (2) to qualifying liability in tort is to liability in tort owed –

    a   in respect of or consequent upon personal injury or loss arising out of or in connection with breach of a duty of care owed to any person in connection with the diagnosis of illness, or the care or treatment of any patient, and

    b   in consequence of any act or omission by a healthcare professional . . .

2 Application of scheme

1   Subject to subsection (2), a scheme may make such provision defining its application as the Secretary of State thinks fit.

2   A scheme must provide that it does not apply in relation to a liability that is or has been the subject of civil proceedings.

3 Redress under scheme

. . . (2) A scheme must provide for redress ordinarily to comprise –

    a   the making of an offer of compensation in satisfaction of any right to bring civil proceedings in respect of the liability concerned,

    b   the giving of an explanation,

    c   the giving of an apology, and

    d   the giving of a report on the action which has been, or will be, taken to prevent similar cases arising, . . .

. . . 6 Proceedings under scheme

. . . (3) A scheme must –

    a   make provision for the findings of an investigation of a case under the scheme to be recorded in a report . . .

The 2006 Act is an enabling statute, laying out the framework of the Redress Scheme, while leaving much of the detail to be fleshed out in regulations to be made by the Secretary of State for Health. However, it gives effect to the CMO's intention that lower-value medical negligence claims should be dealt with outside the courts; such claims will be referred to the NHS Litigation

Authority, which will manage the Scheme, for investigation.[136] Where substandard treatment and care is found, it may offer redress (including financial compensation of up to £20,000). The patient is not required to accept this but, if he does, he will be asked to sign a waiver of subsequent legal proceedings.

Besides being designed to relieve pressure on the legal system, the Scheme also aims to promote risk-management and learning from mistakes: thus, as provided by s 6(3), each case arising should be investigated and the subject of a report. In addition, members of the Scheme (ie NHS hospitals) are required under s 10(3) to 'prepare and publish an annual report about cases involving the member that are dealt with under the scheme and the lessons to be learnt from them'.

At present the implementing regulations for the Scheme in England remain subject to a lengthy on-going consultation process, so that (as of 2018) it still remains unclear when it will become operative. By contrast, in Wales, the scheme was introduced (in a pilot phase) in 2011.[137] In fact, Wales has since 2005 been operating a mediation scheme of 'Speedy Resolution for Lower Value Clinical Negligence Claims', with some similarities to NHS Redress. Mari Rosser discusses the experiences made with that scheme, as follows:

Rosser, M, 'The changing face of clinical negligence in Wales'[138]

Like all methods of ADR, the scheme is consensual. In summary, the objectives of the scheme are:

- to provide a procedure for quick, proportionate and fair resolution of low value clinical negligence claims against NHS Trusts in Wales;
- to provide for NHS Trusts in Wales to make apologies to patients where the standard of medical care has fallen below the required standard;
- to encourage NHS Trusts in Wales to give patients an explanation for their treatment and medical state;
- to provide a structure for the negotiation and settlement of clinical negligence claims; and
- to encourage Trusts to learn from mistakes to reduce the incidents of clinical negligence claims in the future.

The basic principles are:

- that both the claimant and defendant have agreed that the case is one that meets the scheme criteria;
- it will work to a timetable ... The maximum period that a claim can take under the scheme is 61 weeks;
- the scheme will provide single jointly instructed experts; ...

... In recommending that the scheme, which was established firstly as a pilot project in February 2005, should be continued as a permanent scheme, the evaluators found that the scheme had been very positively received and was seen as providing a realistic alternative to litigation in the field of clinical negligence. It was seen from the perspective of claimant's solicitors and Welsh Health Legal Services as providing a number of benefits including reduction of costs by the NHS and fixed predictable costs for claimants, access to a relatively inexpensive medical report and a quick resolution of claims ...

Given the undoubted success of the Speedy Resolution Scheme it is difficult to understand why the Welsh Assembly Government has not adopted more of its provisions within the draft NHS Redress Regulation (the Regulations). . . . [I]t is the Minister's intention to allow the Speedy Resolution Scheme to continue for the time being alongside NHS Redress . . .

---

136 The Scheme will apply only to claims arising from hospital care within the NHS, not private healthcare. Also excluded (by s 1(6) of the 2006 Act) are 'primary care' from general practitioners, and dental services.
137 See the National Health Service (Concerns, Complaints and Redress Arrangements) (Wales) Regulations 2011, SI 2011/704.
138 (2010) 3 JPIL 162.

In England there is some concern that, if and when the NHS Redress Scheme does come into operation, the patient's interests may be insufficiently protected. This stems from two main issues: first, the fact that the NHS Litigation Authority, with its interest in keeping costs down, will run the Scheme; and, secondly, the lack of provision for patient legal advice or an appeal procedure.[139] Undoubtedly the Welsh experience will be watched with interest.

Summary of key points

1   Patients who are injured by medical treatment (either through additional 'iatrogenic' harm or a failure to benefit following a misdiagnosis) may potentially have a claim against the doctor and/or hospital in negligence.

2   Medical negligence actions are a species of the general tort of negligence: in this regard for the patient to succeed, the same basic elements must be established, viz. duty of care, breach, and causation of damage.

3   The duty of care element is usually unproblematic, at least where the doctor has accepted the patient for treatment. An exception, deriving from the House of Lords' decision in the *McFarlane* case, relates to the 'loss' occasioned by the birth of a healthy child following negligent contraceptive treatment.

4   In assessing whether a doctor was in breach of duty, his conduct will be measured by the yardstick of a reasonably skilled and experienced practitioner in the relevant field.

5   A controversial question has been how far the doctor may defend himself in such a case by showing that the treatment he gave complied with a practice accepted by other doctors (the so-called '*Bolam* test').

6   In the past, it appeared that such an argument would be conclusive against a finding of negligence. However, in the *Bolitho* case the House of Lords reiterated that ultimately the judge must be satisfied the practice stands up to 'logical analysis'.

7   As with negligence claims generally, the question of the factual causal link will be decided by the 'but for' test. The fact, though, that the patient was exposed to other risks of injury at the time of treatment, often makes the test very difficult to satisfy in evidential terms.

8   In the past, the courts rejected approaches that would relieve the patient of the need to show 'but for' causation to the 'balance of probabilities' proof standard. However, recently, they have begun to apply a relaxation of proof, where it is shown that the defendant 'materially contributed' to the harm.

9   Dissatisfaction has often been expressed with the tort system as a means for compensating medical injury claims. An alternative considered, but so far not taken up in the UK, might be to establish a 'no-fault' compensation scheme for such injury.

10 Following the CMO's 2003 review of medical negligence actions, the Government enacted the NHS Redress Act 2006, laying out the framework for resolving low-value negligence claims against the NHS extra-judicially. At present the scheme in England is still awaiting implementation.

 ## Further reading

Donaldson, Sir L (Chief Medical Officer), *Making Amends: A consultation paper setting out proposals for reforming the approach to clinical negligence in the NHS*, London: Department of Health, 2003.

---

139 See Farrell, A-M, and Devaney, S, 'Making amends or making things worse? Clinical negligence reform and patient redress in England' (2007) 27 Legal Studies 630.

Farrell, A-M, and Devaney, S, 'Making amends or making things worse? Clinical negligence reform and patient redress in England' (2007) 27 Legal Studies 630.

Jones, M, *Medical Negligence*, 5th edn, London: Sweet & Maxwell, 2017.

Mulheron, R, 'Trumping *Bolam*: A critical legal analysis of *Bolitho*'s "gloss"?' (2010) 69 Cambridge Law Journal 609.

Oliphant, K, 'Beyond misadventure: compensation for medical injuries in New Zealand' (2007) 15 Medical Law Review 357.

Quick, O, 'Outing medical errors: questions of trust and responsibility' (2006) 14 Medical Law Review 22.

Stauch, M, 'Causation, risk, and loss of chance in medical negligence' (1997) 17 Oxford Journal of Legal Studies 205.

Stirton, R, 'The Health and Social Care Act 2008 (Regulated Activities) Regulations 2014: a litany of fundamental flaws?' (2017) 80 Modern Law Review 299.

Part 2

Specific areas in medical treatment

Chapter 7

Assisted reproduction and embryo research

7.1 Introduction

In the last decades, medical science has made significant strides in an area previously largely 'off limits', that of human reproduction. The law, in attempting to regulate these developments, has had to balance many competing interests and viewpoints in an area of particular ethical sensitivity. Four years after the birth, in Britain in 1978, of the world's first 'test tube baby', the Government established a Committee of Inquiry led by the moral philosopher, Dame Mary Warnock, to recommend an appropriate legislative response. The Warnock Committee, which reported in 1984, was well aware of the unprecedented and controversial nature of its remit:

Warnock Committee, *Report of the Committee of Inquiry into Human Fertilisation and Embryology*[1]

1.1   The birth of the first child resulting from the technique of *in vitro* fertilisation in July 1978 was a considerable achievement. The technique, long sought, at last successful, opened up new horizons in the alleviation of infertility and in the science of embryology. It was now possible to observe the very earliest stages of human development, and with these discoveries came the hope of remedying defects at this very early stage. However, there were also anxieties. There was a sense that events were moving too fast for their implications to be assimilated. Society's views on the new techniques were divided between pride in the technological achievement, pleasure at the new-found means to relieve, at least for some, the unhappiness of infertility, and unease at the apparently uncontrolled advance of science, bringing with it new possibilities for manipulating the early stages of human development.

1.2   Against this background of public excitement and concern, this Inquiry was established in July 1982, with the following terms of reference:

To consider recent and potential developments in medicine and science related to human fertilisation and embryology; to consider what policies and safeguards should be applied, including consideration of the social, ethical and legal implications of these developments; and to make recommendations.

In the introduction to her 1985 book, *Question of Life*, Mary Warnock noted the stormy reception accorded to the report, and a key problem faced by the Committee:

Warnock, M, *Question of Life: Warnock Report on Human Fertilization and Embryology*[2]

The Times, on 15 December 1984, carried a dramatic headline. It read 'Warnock: Ethics Undermined'. What followed was a denunciation of the Report of the Committee of Inquiry into Human Embryology ascribed to the Chief Rabbi which was, in fact, moderate in tone compared with some of the abuse to which members of the Inquiry had been, and are still, subjected both collectively and individually, since the publication of our report in July 1984. None of the members of the Inquiry had any doubt that they were concerned with moral issues. But we were not perhaps all of us certain how such issues ought to be approached, and especially how they should be approached by a body set up by Parliament to make recommendations which might lead to legislation. Many of our critics (including, I believe, the Chief Rabbi) have not really addressed themselves to this problem either: the problem of legislation, and its relation to morality, in such controversial fields.

The question of how far, and in what manner, legal regulation of human procreation should occur is undoubtedly one of great complexity. In the remainder of the introduction we shall first

---

1 Cmnd 9314, London: HMSO, 1984.
2 Oxford: Blackwell, 1985.

briefly survey the principal parties whose interests stand to be affected, before outlining the legal framework that has been put in place in the UK.

7.1.1 The key interests at stake

7.1.1.1 Potential parents

People who wish to be parents and would otherwise be infertile are the most obvious beneficiaries of fertility treatment. As the Warnock Committee commented:

Warnock Committee, *Report of the Committee of Inquiry into Human Fertilisation and Embryology*[3]

> 2.2   Childlessness can be a source of stress even to those who have deliberately chosen it. Family and friends often expect a couple to start a family, and express their expectations, either openly or by implication. The family is a valued institution within our present society: within it the human infant receives nurture and protection during its prolonged period of dependence. It is also the place where social behaviour is learnt and where the child develops its own identity and feeling of self-value. Parents likewise feel their identity in society enhanced and confirmed by their role in the family unit. For those who long for children, the realisation that they are unable to found a family can be shattering. It can disrupt their picture of the whole of their future lives. They may feel that they will be unable to fulfil their own and other people's expectations. They may feel themselves excluded from a whole range of human activity and particularly the activities of their child-rearing contemporaries. In addition to social pressures to have children there is, for many, a powerful urge to perpetuate their genes through a new generation. This desire cannot be assuaged by adoption.

As is clear from this extract, the general assumption made by Warnock was that demand for treatment would come mainly if not entirely from infertile, heterosexual couples. In fact, while it is true that such couples account for the majority of demand, a striking phenomenon, especially in more recent years, has been the degree to which homosexual couples and single persons have also recognised the possibilities offered by reproductive technologies to experience parenthood. As we shall see further below (in section 7.4), this has the potential significantly to alter the traditional picture of the family, as has indeed been acknowledged in the latest legislative changes.

7.1.1.2 Gamete providers/surrogates

The success of many fertility treatments depends upon the use of gametes (sperm and eggs) and embryos or, in the case of surrogacy, gestational capacity, provided by third parties, that is, persons who, it is envisaged, will not subsequently play any role in rearing the children born as a result of treatment. A key problem for the law in such cases is to determine how best to regulate the involvement of such third parties (who are the child's genetic or gestational parents). Should they receive money in return for their services? Should they be screened? How should they be counselled? In addition, what sort of obligations may such third parties' claims have towards the child? Should they be protected from future contact by a guarantee of anonymity? What, conversely, if a provider later wishes to have contact with the child?

---

3 See n 1 above.

7.1.1.3 Potential children

The answers we give to these last questions clearly have a direct impact on the interests of children who result from infertility treatment involving third party providers. For example, giving gamete providers anonymity will be to deny the child's interest in knowing who one (at least) of its genetic or gestational parents is. In other cases, there may be a conflict between the interests of the potential child and its potential rearing parent(s). A 1989 inquiry into reproductive technologies sponsored by the European Commission, and led by the moral philosopher, Jonathan Glover, commented as follows:

Glover, J et al., *Report to the European Commission on Reproductive Technologies, Fertility and the Family*[4]

The children are those most deeply affected. Their family circumstances may be unusually complicated: like adopted children, they may have to get used to the fact that at least one of their social parents is not their biological parent. Much more importantly, their very existence results from reproductive help. If they are glad to be alive, they are perhaps the greatest beneficiaries. They are the people who have no say at the time the decisions are taken, and their needs and interests have to be given great weight. Their central need is for a certain kind of home and family...

Besides the question of their existence *per se*, another far-reaching issue in respect of the children who result from new reproductive technologies concerns the identities and attributes that they may possess: in particular, some of the new technologies (associated with IVF treatment – see section 7.2) allow for the possibility of selecting between possible children (through choosing which out of a number of embryos to implant) or even of manipulating the characteristics of a given embryo (and hence of the resulting child) that is implanted. As we shall see, these too are matters that have attracted the regulatory attention of the law-maker.

7.1.1.4 Embryos

So far, we have been assuming that a child is born following treatment. The position is complicated when we introduce the human embryo (as a separate entity) into the equation. The procedure of *in vitro* fertilisation (IVF), in particular, involves the manipulation of the early human embryo. To work effectively, the procedure typically requires the creation of more embryos than can ever be implanted in the uterus of the woman receiving treatment. There is therefore the question of what to do with such 'spare' embryos; must we simply let them perish? This, in itself, may be seen as a bad thing. Alternatively, should we store them (there are techniques available for freezing early embryos) and, if so, for how long? More radically, should it be permissible to use them for research purposes and, if so, under what conditions? And once the possibility of research is conceded, is there any reason not to employ IVF technology specifically to create embryos for research?

These last questions are hugely contentious because they turn partly on a debate of a metaphysical character, viz. do early embryos have any interests in the first place? We return to them in sections 7.2.3 and 7.3 below.

---

4 London: Fourth Estate, 1989.

7.1.2 Legal regulation – the Human Fertilisation and Embryology Acts 1990 and 2008

In the light of the interests and putative interests just outlined, how should the law respond? In a liberal democratic state such as the UK, the autonomous activity of individual citizens, each pursuing their own ends, is regarded as of central importance, and this gives rise to a strong presumption in favour of respecting procreative liberty. In *Question of Life*, Mary Warnock had the following to say about the extent to which the law may intrude into the area of assisted reproduction:

Warnock, M, *Question of Life: Warnock Report on Human Fertilization and Embryology*[5]

If the question is what measures to remedy infertility should be permitted in this country, the problem may be put in the following form: why should the law intervene to prevent people using whatever methods are possible to enable them to have children? Why should not everybody be entitled to whatever is currently the best and most efficient treatment for infertility? The issues here are quite closely parallel to the issues raised in the 1960s by the Wolfenden Report on homosexuality between consenting males. Ought the law to intervene to make such conduct criminal or ought it not? The famous view of Lord Devlin (*The Enforcement of Morals*, 1959) was that where there is a consensus of opinion against a certain practice among members of the general public (exemplified by the notorious 'man on the Clapham omnibus') then the law must intervene to prevent conduct which is repellent to that public. A shared moral view . . . was the cement that bound society together. . . .

The drawback with Devlin's view is that, increasingly, we are compelled to accept that 'common morality' is a myth. There is no agreed set of principles which everyone, or the majority, or any representative person, believes to be absolutely binding, and especially is this so in areas of moral concern which are radically and genuinely new . . .

Furthermore, any law enacted to render [donor insemination] a criminal offence, besides going against the moral views of a fair number of the community, would involve, in itself, a disagreeable intrusiveness, for [DI] is something that can relatively easily be carried out at home, without any medical intervention. For a law to be enforceable, there would need to be a band of snoopers or people ready to pry into the private lives of others, which might well itself constitute a moral wrong . . .

In 1990, Parliament enacted the Human Fertilisation and Embryology Act, which followed many of the recommendations in the Warnock Report; perhaps most importantly, it accepted the need to establish a statutory regulatory authority to oversee continuing developments in this area. Some barriers in the form of absolute prohibitions – backed by criminal sanctions – were established. However, the Act is more notable for its flexibility and its willingness to entrust the new regulatory authority, the Human Fertilisation and Embryology (HFE) Authority, with large amounts of discretion. In his assessment of the impact of the 1990 Act, Jonathan Montgomery suggested 'pragmatism' rather than 'principle' was the guiding impulse behind the new legal regime:

Montgomery, J, 'Rights, restraints and pragmatism'[6]

The nature of the forum in which the debates about infertility treatment and embryo research are to be carried out is structured by a complex web of discretion, restraints control and accountability. The Human Fertilisation and Embryology Authority is to be given powers to oversee the activities of individual health practitioners, and will not be limited to applying standards established by Parliament or government. It will be able, indeed required, to develop its own standards of what is acceptable and proper . . .

---

5 See n 2 above.
6 (1991) 54 MLR 524.

Having conferred this considerable flexibility upon the licensing authority, the Government has also reserved a number of powers to reduce it. The boundaries of the power to license may be contracted and expanded by regulations. By requiring annual reports to the Secretary of State, detailing both past activities and those projected for the following 12 months, the Act seeks to ensure that the Authority's practice can be monitored (s 7). The reports are to be laid before Parliament by the minister. Nevertheless, pending the exercise of the power to make regulations, considerable trust is placed in the members of the Authority.

The Act permits the Authority to exercise a high degree of control over practitioners. In addition to the power to grant or withhold licences, the Authority will be able to issue mandatory directions (ss 23 and 24). Failure to comply with these directions will sometimes constitute an offence (s 41(2)), but will always empower the Authority to revoke a licence (s 18([2])(c)). Secondly, a code of practice is to be drawn up to provide guidance as to the proper conduct of licensees. This is less coercive than the power to give directions in that disobedience will not in itself constitute an offence, but it may be taken into account by the Authority when considering revocation (s 25).

In summary, the Human Fertilisation and Embryology Authority has been entrusted with considerable powers to determine what embryo research and infertility treatment will be carried out. A system of checks and balances has been created which will allow for the Authority to be accountable to Parliament, but many of the normative principles to be applied will be established neither by the law nor by democratic discussion. In essence, the creation of the Authority is a pragmatic exercise in facilitating medical advances rather than a principled approach to the vindication of rights.

Subsequently, Lord Bingham, in his speech in *R (on the application of Quintavalle) v Secretary of State for Health*[7] distinguished three levels of control provided for by the 1990 Act:

Lord Bingham of Cornhill: [4] The Act imposes three levels of control. The highest is that contained in the Act itself. As is apparent, for example from section 3(2) and (3), the Act prohibits certain activities absolutely, a prohibition fortified by a potential penalty of up to ten years' imprisonment (section 41(1)). The next level of control is provided by the Secretary of State, who is empowered to make regulations for certain purposes subject (so far as relevant here) to an affirmative resolution of both Houses of Parliament (section 45(1), (4)). Pursuant to section 3(3)(c) the Secretary of State may make regulations prohibiting the keeping or use of an embryo in specified circumstances. The third level of control is that exercised by the Authority. Section 3(1) prohibits the creation, keeping or use of an embryo except in pursuance of a licence, and the Act contains very detailed provisions governing the grant, revocation and suspension of licences and the conditions to which they may be subject: see, among other references, sections 11–22 of and Schedule 2 to the Act. A power is also conferred on the Authority to give binding directions: sections 23–24.

Overall the scheme of regulation introduced in 1990 has proved successful in reassuring the public that advances in reproductive technology are subject to a degree of scrutiny and control, including by non-medical scientists (the majority of the HFE Authority's members are not scientists), so that practices evoking significant ethical concern are not permitted without more. Nonetheless, more recently, in the light both of new scientific developments and changes in social attitudes since 1990, the Government chose to enact further, reforming legislation in the form of the Human Fertilisation and Embryology Act 2008. Unfortunately, the changes have also added significantly to the complexity of the legislation in this area. Marie Fox has commented upon the reform process, and the unwieldy mass of statute it has left in its wake, as follows:

---

7 [2003] UKHL 13.

Fox, M, 'The Human Fertilisation and Embryology Act 2008: tinkering at the margins'[8]

The Human Fertilisation and Embryology Act 2008 . . . received royal assent on 13 November 2008, marking the culmination of a protracted reform process. Most of the changes took effect on 1 October 2009, although the revised definitions of parenthood contained in Part 2 of the Act have been effective since April 2009. A final stage of amendments will give effect to parental orders in 2010. Although, as detailed below, many of the changes are to be welcomed, it is questionable how far-reaching their impact will be . . . In part this was due to the strict parameters the government placed on it. It conceived the legislation as an amending statute which, as McCandless and Sheldon note, ensured that 'the key question was not "what model of law do we want?" but rather "what needs to be changed?"' within the confines of the Human Fertilisation and Embryology Act 1990 . . . The upshot is that a rather clumsy and convoluted mass of legislation now governs the regulation of fertility treatment and embryology research, since the 1990 Act as amended in 2008 must also be read alongside earlier amending legislation. This has led the Department of Health to issue an illustrative amended Act . . ., prompting the question of whether it might not have been preferable to repeal and replace the 1990 Act.

However, it was clear from the outset of the reform process that the government was committed to retaining the core architecture of the 1990 Act. This was unquestionably a landmark piece of legislation which has been emulated elsewhere. Underpinned by the 'twin pillars' of ensuring consent to the use of donated gametes and embryos, and the welfare of children to be born via assisted conception, the 1990 Act established a statutory regulator – the Human Fertilisation and Embryology Authority (the Authority) – to oversee any research or treatment involving creation of human embryos outside the body, or the donation or storage of human gametes. The statutory regime is characterised by a broadly permissive approach to fertility treatment and embryo research, whereby only the most contentious aspects, including human reproductive cloning, are prohibited; other types of treatment and research must be licensed by the Authority.

The 2008 Act is divided into three parts. Part 1 is a purely amending part: it contains a series of provisions that, rather than having stand-alone character, replace and/or add to the terms of the original 1990 Act. In citing the relevant provisions, reference should thus be made to the Human Fertilisation and Embryology Act 1990 (as amended). As noted by Fox, the complexity of these changes prompted the Department of Health to prepare an illustrative consolidated text of the 1990 Act as amended, which is available on its website.[9] By contrast, Part 2, which sets out new rules determining the parenthood of children born as a result of assisted reproduction, is in effect an autonomous statute, and its sections should be cited as the Human Fertilisation and Embryology Act 2008. Lastly, Part 3 contains a number of miscellaneous provisions (without stand-alone character), including changes to the Surrogacy Arrangements Act 1985.

As before, much of the day-to-day supervision exercised by the HFE Authority over fertility clinics up and down the country (currently over 100, the majority within the private sector) occurs by means of the Code of Practice, which it promulgates. This is currently in its eighth edition (2009, with further revisions, most recently in October 2017) and provides detailed guidance on all aspects of the treatment that clinics might wish to provide. Breaches of the Code by a clinic may result in the Authority revoking its licence. Another important function of the Authority is the collection of information pertaining to fertility treatment in the UK. In this regard it has from its inception been required to maintain a register (under s 31 of the HFE Act 1990 (as amended)), recording each case in which a person or persons have received licensed

---

8 (2009) 17 Fem Leg Stud 333.
9 See: www.dh.gov.uk/en/Publicationsandstatistics/Publications/PublicationsLegislation/DH_080205.

treatment services (including, where donor gametes are used, the identity of the donor).[10] At the same time, it should be noted that not every type of fertility treatment is covered by the Act: most significantly, the use of 'fertility drugs' to increase ovulation remains unregulated.

In the rest of this chapter, we shall be exploring in more detail the specific solutions adopted by the law in relation to the key areas of licensed fertility treatment. We shall focus, first, in section 7.2 upon IVF treatment involving the creation of an embryo *ex vivo* to be implanted in a woman's uterus for gestation. Although IVF obviously has wide potential applications (it may be used in conjunction with forms of collaborative reproduction involving donated gametes and surrogacy), at this stage the assumption will be that the recipient couple are also the gamete providers. However, another possibility arising from the technique of IVF is of using the embryos so created as objects of research – the ethics and law in relation to such research is the subject of section 7.3. In section 7.4 we then return to the field of assisted reproduction, but move on to address the additional complexities that arise when third party gamete providers are introduced into the picture by procedures such as artificial insemination by donor ('DI') and egg donation. Here, the law must regulate not only the conditions subject to which donation occurs, but provide for the legal status and rights of the resulting children, as against the rearing parent(s) and gamete provider(s). Finally, in section 7.5 we shall look at one area where such third-party involvement in reproduction has aroused particular controversy, namely surrogacy, in which a woman makes use of her gestational capacity to carry a child for others.

THINK POINT

Why do you think it is that, unlike other forms of fertility treatment, the use of fertility drugs has not been subject to legal regulation in the UK?

7.2 IVF treatment

7.2.1 Background

In its report, the Warnock Committee explained the process of IVF (*in vitro* fertilisation) in the following terms:

Warnock Committee, *Report of the Committee of Inquiry into Human Fertilisation and Embryology*[11]

5.2 – The concept of IVF is simple. A ripe human egg is extracted from the ovary, shortly before it would have been released naturally. Next, the egg is mixed with the semen of the husband or partner, so that fertilisation can occur. The fertilised egg, once it has started to divide, is then transferred back to the mother's uterus. In practice the technique for recovery of the eggs, their culture outside the mother's body, and the transfer of the developing embryo to the uterus has to be carried out under very carefully controlled conditions. The development of laparoscopic techniques during the 1960s made the collection of the egg, in cases where the ovaries were accessible, relatively easy. (Another technique for egg recovery based on ultrasound identification has now been developed.) It was not particularly difficult to fertilise the human egg *in vitro*. The real difficulty related to the implantation of the embryo in the uterus after transfer.

---

10 See the HFE Authority's website at: www.hfea.gov.uk/fertility-treatment-facts.html. The law governing access to the register in DI cases is discussed further in section 7.4.4 below.
11 See n 1 above.

A pregnancy achieved in this way must not only survive the normal hazards of implantation of *in vivo* conception, but also the additional problems of IVF and embryo transfer. More is now known about how best to replicate the natural sequence of events, but undoubtedly achieving a successful implantation is still the most uncertain part of the procedure.

Since the early – 1990s a newer variant of IVF has been available, known as intracytoplasmic sperm injection (ICSI): this technique involves injecting a single sperm into the egg and has proven effective in addressing problems of male infertility, including low sperm count and impaired sperm mobility. Today IVF – including ICSI – is increasingly a mainstream treatment: latest HFE Authority figures show that between 1991 and 2015, would-be mothers underwent more than 1 million IVF treatment cycles, resulting in 281,438 live births.[12]

Pursuant to s 3(1) of the HFE Act 1990 (as amended), IVF is a process which may only be carried out under licence from the HFE Authority. Moreover, s 3(2) straightaway places limits upon the nature of the embryos – and gametes – that are used for treatment (ie by being implanted in a female patient):

3 Prohibitions in connection with embryos

1 No person shall bring about the creation of an embryo except in pursuance of a licence.

. . .

2 No person shall place in a woman –

a an embryo other than a permitted embryo (as defined by section 3ZA), or

b any gametes other than permitted eggs or permitted sperm (as so defined)

The definitions of 'permitted eggs, permitted sperm, and permitted embryos' are found in s 3ZA. As is clear from that section, Parliament's concern has been to prohibit scientific interventions that seek to modify the attributes of embryos and gametes (and hence influence the characteristics of the future child):

3ZA Permitted eggs, permitted sperm and permitted embryos

1 This section has effect for the interpretation of section 3(2).

2 A permitted egg is one –

a which has been produced by or extracted from the ovaries of a woman, and

b whose nuclear or mitochondrial DNA has not been altered.

3 Permitted sperm are sperm –

a which have been produced by or extracted from the testes of a man, and

b whose nuclear or mitochondrial DNA has not been altered.

4 An embryo is a permitted embryo if –

a it has been created by the fertilisation of a permitted egg by permitted sperm,

b no nuclear or mitochondrial DNA of any cell of the embryo has been altered, and

c no cell has been added to it other than by division of the embryo's own cells.

We consider further the law as it bears on the potential, during IVF treatment, for doctors to engage in certain forms of embryonic manipulation, in section 7.2.4 below. First, however, we shall look at matters from the perspective of the would-be recipients of IVF treatment, ie the (as

---

12 See: www.hfea.gov.uk/about-us/news-and-press-releases/2017-news-and-press-releases/the-uk-reaches-new-milestones-for-fertility-treatments/.

will for now be assumed) heterosexual couples, who wish to avail themselves of treatment in order to have a child. What rights do such persons – jointly and singly – enjoy in respect of obtaining treatment, receiving adequate information in relation to it, and controlling the use/disposition of their gametes and any *ex vivo* embryos created with them?

7.2.2 The potential parents

7.2.2.1 Access to treatment

IVF remains an expensive treatment (a single treatment cycle costs £3,000–4,000 in the UK), and, while there are some fertility clinics within the NHS, the treatment they offer is usually rationed to one cycle per couple, and waiting lists are predictably long. Accordingly, an immediate constraint upon a couple's access to treatment may be the lack of resources needed to fund private treatment. Assuming, though, that a couple has the means, the decision whether actually to provide treatment will be for the individual fertility clinic, acting pursuant to the Code of Practice promulgated by the HFE Authority. Where a couple is refused treatment, para 8.17 of the Code makes it clear that reasons should be given to them in writing.

There are two main reasons why treatment might be refused. First, the couple may be medically unsuitable. Secondly, and far more controversially, they may be deemed socially unsuitable as parents. In the latter case, the decision essentially turns on the potential welfare of any child born as a result of treatment. The Glover Report addressed the key arguments in this regard, as follows:

Glover, J et al., *Report to the European Commission on Reproductive Technologies, Fertility and the Family*[13]

It is hard to know who will be a good or bad parent. But children need warmth and love. Some of the worst cases of cruelty to children would make any humane person wish that those parents stayed childless. It is surely unthinkable that anyone would have wished to help them have children. Of course we cannot easily predict such disasters. But, where there seems a risk, there is a strong reason not to help.

... But a distinction has to be drawn between two very different types of case. If it is a question of giving a child to people who will behave with horrifying cruelty, it may be 'a mercy if the child is not born'. On the other hand, perhaps a child with only one parent suffers some disadvantage relative to other children, but few such children would feel life was anywhere near so bad as to wish they had not been born.

A parallel can be drawn with handicap. Some handicaps are so terrible that death can seem a mercy, and it is possible to think it would have been better if the person had not been born. But many handicaps are mild or only moderately severe. No one would think that colour blindness made it better for someone not to have been born. No one would think it wrong to help a couple have a child who would be at risk of colour blindness.

... If the disadvantage is only relative, and the child will come nowhere near regretting having been born, it is hard to see how it can be in the interests of the future child for the potential parents to be denied help.

Although, as Glover notes, it seems far-fetched (save in the most extreme cases) to suppose that the interests of the child should dictate that it never exist at all, the HFE Act 1990 (as amended) requires such an assessment to be made. Section 13(5) provides as follows:

---

13 See n 4 above.

A woman shall not be provided with treatment services unless account has been taken of the welfare of any child who may be born as a result of the treatment (including the need of that child for supportive parenting), and of any other child who may be affected by the birth.

The HFE Authority's Code of Practice elaborates on this requirement in para 8.10. Among the matters to which clinics should have regard in deciding whether to provide treatment are the existence of risk factors for possible abuse of the child, as well as the couple's ability to provide a stable and supportive environment for it.

HFEA Code of Practice[14]

Factors to take into account during the assessment process

8.10 The centre should consider factors that are likely to cause a risk of significant harm or neglect to any child who may be born or to any existing child of the family. These factors include any aspects of the patient's or (if they have one) their partner's:

a   past or current circumstances that may lead to any child mentioned above experiencing serious physical or psychological harm or neglect, for example:
   i   previous convictions relating to harming children
   ii   child protection measures taken regarding existing children, or
   iii violence or serious discord in the family environment

b   past or current circumstances that are likely to lead to an inability to care throughout childhood for any child who may be born, or that are already seriously impairing the care of any existing child of the family, for example:
   i   mental or physical conditions
   ii   drug or alcohol abuse
   iii medical history, where the medical history indicates that any child who may be born is likely to suffer from a serious medical condition, or
   iv   circumstances that the centre considers likely to cause serious harm to any child mentioned above.

In so far as infertility treatment is denied to a couple, what, if any, form of legal redress is available to them? In respect of IVF provided by an NHS-funded clinic, a case predating the HFE Act 1990, that of *R v Ethical Committee of St Mary's Hospital (Manchester), ex p Harriott*, suggests that a challenge may lie in judicial review. At the same time, as we saw in Chapter 2, it will generally be no easy matter for the applicant to pass the '*Wednesbury* unreasonable test', and **See Chapter 2** persuade the court to strike down the relevant refusal decision.

R v Ethical Committee of St Mary's Hospital (Manchester), ex p Harriott[15]

The applicant applied for judicial review after being refused IVF treatment as a result of advice given to her consultant by the hospital's ethical committee. The committee was unhappy with the fact that she and her husband had already been rejected as foster parents on the basis of her alleged poor understanding of parenting and past convictions for prostitution offences:

---

14 London: HFE Authority, 8th edn, 2009 (as last revised, October 2017). The Code is available on the Authority's website at: www.hfea.gov.uk/code.html.
15 [1988] 1 FLR 512.

Schiemann J: Frustrated in her desire to foster and adopt and to conceive by normal means, the applicant wishes to be considered for in vitro fertilisation . . . under the National Health Service. The Health Service – to use an imprecise term for the moment – decided to refuse to give her this treatment. In this application for judicial review she complains of that decision essentially alleging that it was reached by the wrong body: alternatively that she was not given an adequate opportunity to make representations to the decision maker before the decision was taken. . . .

Mr Bell, for the committee, submitted that judicial review does not lie to review any advice given by the committee. As at present advised, I would be doubtful about accepting that submission in its full breadth. If the committee had advised, for instance, that the IVF unit should in principle refuse all such treatment to anyone who was a Jew or coloured, then I think the courts might well grant a declaration that such a policy was illegal . . . But I do not need to consider that situation in this case. Here the complaint is that the committee's advice was that the consultant must make up her own mind as to whether the treatment should be given. That advice was, in my judgment, unobjectionable.

Subsequently, in *R v Sheffield HA, ex p Seale*,[16] a 37-year-old woman failed to persuade the High Court to quash a health authority's decision to exclude her from its IVF programme on the basis of her age.

See Chapter 2 → The judge held that, in view of its limited resources and the lower success rates achieved with older women, the Authority's policy only to treat women below the age of 35 was not irrational.

Increasingly, licensing and other decisions made by the HFE Authority itself have also been the subject of judicial review proceedings. One example is the case of *R v Human Fertilisation and Embryology Authority, ex p Assisted Reproduction and Gynaecology Centre and H*,[17] in which the applicants – a 46-year-old woman and the clinic treating her – challenged the HFE Authority's policy of only allowing a maximum of three embryos to be placed in women during a single treatment cycle (so as to reduce the risk of multiple pregnancy): the clinic would have wished to transfer five embryos into the patient in this case. However, the Court of Appeal, in upholding Ousely J's dismissal of the action, took the view that the court had no part to play in the scientific debate and no power to intervene:

Clarke LJ and Wall J: [65] . . . [This] is an area of rapidly developing science in which judicial review has a limited role to play. Disagreements between doctors and scientific bodies in this pioneering field are inevitable. The United Kingdom, through the Act, has opted for a system of licensing and regulation. The Authority is the body which is empowered by Parliament to regulate. Like any public authority, it is open to challenge by way of judicial review, if it exceeds or abuses the powers and responsibilities given to it by Parliament; but where, as is manifest here from an examination of the facts, it considers requests for advice carefully and thoroughly, and produces opinions which are plainly rational, the court, in our judgment, has no part to play in the debate, and certainly no power to intervene to strike down any such decision. The fact that the appellants may disagree with the Authority's advice is neither here nor there.

We shall encounter further cases where applicants have brought judicial review proceedings in respect of decisions by the HFE Authority below: one area where this has occurred is where the Authority has denied the applicant access to treatment with particular gametes or embryos (see

---

16 (1994) 25 BMLR 1.
17 [2002] EWCA Civ 20; see too *R (on the application of Assisted Reproduction and Gynaecology Centre) v HFE Authority* [2017] EWHC 659 (Admin), where the applicant clinic challenged the Authority's method of presenting information on IVF treatment success rates.

7.2.2.3 below). More generally, the relevance of the Human Rights Act 1998 to this area should also be noted. Thus, as Lord Phillips MR recognised in *R v SS for the Home Department, ex p Mellor*,[18] denying a person access to fertility treatment will engage their rights under Article 8 (right to respect for family life) and Article 12 (right to found a family) of the ECHR, and require to be justified under Article 8(2).

7.2.2.2 Information and counselling requirements

It is important that adequate information and counselling are provided to a couple prior to them consenting to treatment with IVF. This is necessary so that they can make an informed decision regarding ethically sensitive aspects of the procedure, such as the creation of surplus embryos with little chance of ever developing into fully fledged human beings. Similarly, they should be warned of the high risk that the treatment will fail: it has been estimated that only about 25 per cent of IVF procedures will result in a live birth (and then often only after several failed attempts).

Such information and counselling requirements are outlined in s 13(6) in conjunction with Part 1 of Sch 3ZA of the HFEA 1990 (as amended):

> 13(6) A woman shall not be provided with treatment services of a kind specified in Part 1 of Schedule 3ZA unless she and any man or woman who is to be treated together with her have been given a suitable opportunity to receive proper counselling about the implications of her being provided with treatment services of that kind, and have been provided with such relevant information as is proper.
>
> ... SCHEDULE 3ZA
>
> **Part 1 Kinds of treatment in relation to which counselling must be offered**
>
> ... 2 The treatment services involve the use of any embryo the creation of which was brought about *in vitro*.

It is also important that the couple are invited to think through and make provision in their consents for various future contingencies that may arise, such as their relationship breaking down or the death of the male partner. As we shall see in 7.2.2.3 below, the failure in some past instances to do so has led to some difficult and sad cases. Accordingly, the amendments to the 1990 Act include – in s 25(2A) – an increased responsibility upon the HFE Authority in its Code of Practice to offer guidance to fertility clinics, as to the nature of their obligation to patients in respect of information and (the offer of) counselling. In this regard, the present Code of Practice lists the following matters that should be divulged to IVF patients:

HFEA Code of Practice[19]

> **Information for those seeking treatment**
>
> 4.2 Before treatment is offered, the centre should give the woman seeking treatment and her partner, if applicable, information about:
>
> a the centre's policy on selecting patients
>
> b the centre's statutory duty to take account of the welfare of any resulting or affected child
>
> c the expected waiting time for treatment

---

18 [2001] EWCA Civ 472.
19 See n 14 above.

> d fertility treatments available
> e the likely outcomes of the proposed treatment (data provided should include the centre's most recent live birth rate and clinical pregnancy rate per treatment cycle, verified by the HFEA, and the national live birth rate and clinical pregnancy rate per treatment cycle)
> f the nature and potential risks of the treatment, including the risk of children conceived having developmental and birth defects
> g the possible side effects and risks to the woman being treated and any resulting child, including ovarian hyperstimulation syndrome (OHSS)
> ...
> i the availability of facilities for freezing embryos, and the implications of storing embryos and then using embryos
> j the importance of informing the treatment centre about the eventual outcome of the treatment (including if no live birth results)
> k the centre's complaints procedure, and
> l the nature and potential risks (immediate and longer term) of IVF/ICSI with in vitro matured eggs, including reference to the clinic's experience.

7.2.2.3 Control over the use/disposition of embryos/gametes

One of the cornerstones of the 1990 Act (as amended) consists in the great weight accorded to the consents of the gamete providers in determining what may be done with those gametes and/or any embryos created with them. In establishing a regime in which the providers are invited, following proper counselling, to specify the uses to which the material may be put, the Act reflects a commitment to the autonomy of such providers. The key consent provisions are contained in Sch 3 of the Act:

> **Schedule 3 – Consent to use or storage of gametes, embryos . . . etc**
> 1 1 A consent under this Schedule, and any notice under paragraph 4 varying or withdrawing a consent under this Schedule, must be in writing and, subject to sub-paragraph (2), must be signed by the person giving it.
>   2 A consent under this Schedule by a person who is unable to sign because of illness, injury or physical disability (a 'person unable to sign'), and any notice under paragraph 4 by a person unable to sign varying or withdrawing a consent under this Schedule, is to be taken to comply with the requirement of sub-paragraph (1) as to signature if it is signed at the direction of the person unable to sign, in the presence of the person unable to sign and in the presence of at least one witness who attests the signature.
>   3 In this Schedule 'effective consent' means a consent under this Schedule which has not been withdrawn.
> 2 1 A consent to the use of any embryo must specify one or more of the following purposes –
>   a use in providing treatment services to the person giving consent, or that person and another specified person together,
>   . . . and may specify conditions subject to which the embryo may be so used.
>
> *. . . Variation and withdrawal of consent*
>
> 4 1 The terms of any consent under this Schedule may from time to time be varied, and the consent may be withdrawn, by notice given by the person who gave the consent to the person keeping the gametes, human cells, [or] embryo . . . to which the consent is relevant.
>   2 . . . the terms of any consent to the use of any embryo cannot be varied, and such consent cannot be withdrawn, once the embryo has been used –
>   a in providing treatment services . . .

... In vitro fertilisation and subsequent use of embryo

6　1　A person's gametes or human cells must not be used to bring about the creation of any embryo in vitro unless there is an effective consent by that person to any embryo, the creation of which may be brought about with the use of those gametes or human cells, being used for one or more of the purposes mentioned in paragraph 2(1)(a), (b) and (c) above.

　　2　An embryo the creation of which was brought about in vitro must not be received by any person unless there is an effective consent by each relevant person in relation to the embryo to the use for one or more of the purposes mentioned in paragraph 2(1) ...

　　3　An embryo the creation of which was brought about in vitro must not be used for any purpose unless there is an effective consent by each relevant person in relation to the embryo to the use for that purpose of the embryo and the embryo is used in accordance with those consents.

... Storage of gametes and embryos

8　1　A person's gametes must not be kept in storage unless there is an effective consent by that person to their storage and they are stored in accordance with the consent.

　　2　An embryo the creation of which was brought about in vitro must not be kept in storage unless there is an effective consent, by each relevant person in relation to the embryo, to the storage of the embryo and the embryo is stored in accordance with those consents ...

As para 1(1) makes clear, for consent to the storage and/or use of gametes and embryos to be effective, it needs to be made in writing and signed by the gamete provider; an exception to the need for a signature is allowed for in para 1(2) in so far as the provider is physically unable to sign due to illness or injury. In fact, following the 2008 amendments to the 1990 Act, it is possible exceptionally for consent to the storage of gametes to be dispensed with: this is, as specified in paras 9 and 10 of Sch 3, where a child or temporarily incapable adult, respectively, is to undergo treatment that may render them infertile, and a registered medical practitioner has certified that in his opinion such storage is in the patient's best interests. Nonetheless, the gametes may not be used for IVF (or other) treatment unless the person, having (re)gained capacity, subsequently gives consent.

Subsequently, in *Yearworth v North Bristol NHS Trust*,[20] the Court of Appeal held in the context of a negligence claim brought by a number of men against a clinic following the accidental destruction of their sperm, that they could for these purposes be regarded as owning their gametes. As the court noted, a significant factor was the degree of control they had over the material pursuant to the statutory consent provisions, including the right (through withdrawing consent) to compel its destruction. At the same time, in relation to fertility treatment undertaken by a couple, this approach leaves open the question of what, if any, rights to using the genetic material are enjoyed by the other party to the couple.

There have in fact been several high-profile decisions involving challenges by the other party to the consent provisions in the 1990 Act. One of the first was the well-known case of *R v Human Fertilisation and Embryology Authority, ex p Blood*, which concerned the posthumous use of sperm taken from a dying patient.

R v Human Fertilisation and Embryology Authority ex p Blood (1997)[21]

Mrs Blood sought judicial review of the HFE Authority's refusal to license infertility treatment of her with her dead husband's sperm. The sperm had been taken from Mr Blood as he lay in a coma shortly before his

---

20　[2009] EWCA Civ 37; the case is discussed further in Ch 11 below.
21　[1997] 2 WLR 806, CA.

death from meningitis and, consequently, none of the written consents to its storage or use (stipulated in the 1990 Act) had been obtained:

Lord Woolf MR:

The position as to storage

... Parliament has required that [the preserving of gametes] should be ... subject to the control of the licensing process. The result is that in the ordinary way no preservation can take place unless the required written consents exist. This would also apply in the case of the preservation of sperm intended for export unless a particular direction was obtained prior to preservation which permitted the storage to take place notwithstanding that there were not the requisite consents.

It follows that Mr Blood's sperm should not in fact have been preserved and stored. Technically therefore an offence was committed by the licence holder ... There is however no question of any prosecution being brought in the circumstances of this case and no possible criticism can be made of the fact that storage has taken place because Professor Cook of IRT was acting throughout in close consultation with the Authority in a perfectly bona fide manner, in an unexplored legal situation where humanity dictated that the sperm was taken and preserved first, and the legal argument followed. From now on, however, the position will be different, as these proceedings will clarify the legal position. Because this judgment makes it clear that the sperm of Mr Blood has been preserved and stored when it should not have been, this case raises issues as to the lawfulness of the use and export of sperm which should never arise again.

In the special circumstances, it was held that, although Mrs Blood could not be lawfully treated with the sperm in the UK, she was entitled to export it and receive treatment in Belgium pursuant to her rights under Art 59 of the EC Treaty (now Art 56 TFEU).[22] She later had two children as a result.

In so far as gametes are provided and stored pursuant to effective consent, their posthumous use in fertility treatment is allowed for in principle by the Act. In this regard, Sch 3, para 2(2)(b) requires gamete providers to specify what use may be made of their gametes in the event of death, and this may include consent to usage by the other party. However, it is essential that this consent is still effective as at death: a case in point is *Centre for Reproductive Medicine v Mrs U*,[23] where the respondent widow's husband, after initially agreeing to the posthumous use of his sperm to treat his wife in the event of his death, later revoked this consent. The Court of Appeal, having rejected the respondent's argument that the clinic had unduly influenced her husband's change of mind, held that she was not entitled to use the sperm.

By contrast, if there is a formal failure to specify usage, but the deceased provider's wishes can be demonstrated by other evidence, the HFE Authority should be prepared to release the gametes for use in another jurisdiction, not covered by the strict HFEA licensing requirements. The Court of Appeal recently so found in *Mr and Mrs M v HFE Authority*,[24] where it allowed a challenge by the parents of a young woman, who died from cancer, against the Authority's refusal to release her eggs. The parents wanted to export these to the USA to be fertilised by an anonymous donor, and implanted in the mother, so they might have and raise their daughter's child in accordance with her wishes.

---

22 See also the recent, unusual case of *L v HFE Authority* [2008] EWHC 2149, permitting a woman to export sperm from her deceased husband, extracted after his death pursuant to an erroneous court order.

23 [2002] EWCA Civ 565.

24 [2016] EWCA Civ 611.

As the earlier *Mrs U* case illustrates, where the requisite consents were obtained at the outset, they remain inherently revocable at the initiative of either gamete provider. Moreover, even if the gametes have subsequently been mixed with those of the other party to the couple to form an embryo, the effective and continuing consent of both parties are required for its use in treatment. Apart from the death of one of the gamete providers, the other main problem – as regards a party's ability to use such gametes (or embryos created with them) in order to have a child – will be presented by relationship breakdown. Here, the withdrawal of the consent of the other party to the continued storage of any embryo formed with his or her gametes will entail that further storage (and *a fortiori* use in IVF treatment) are impermissible: see Sch 3, paras 4(1) and 6(2). The validity of these statutory provisions was the subject of legal challenge in *Evans v Amicus Healthcare Ltd*.

Evans v Amicus Healthcare Ltd[25]

The claimant, Ms Evans, had a number of eggs harvested from her at the defendant clinic in October 2001 following the diagnosis of ovarian cancer. As, at the time, the cryopreservation of eggs was not yet possible, they were mixed with the sperm of her then partner, Mr Johnston, and the resulting embryos stored by the defendant. In May 2002, the relationship between the claimant and Mr Johnston broke down. The claimant attempted to resist the embryos' destruction by arguing, *inter alia*, that Mr Johnston was estopped from revoking his consent:

Thorpe and Sedley LJJ: [35] In relation to his estoppel ground . . . Mr Tolson [counsel for Ms Evans] sought to develop the submission that Mr Johnston had concealed his ambivalence, thereby inducing Ms Evans to go forward with him into couple treatment. Mr Tolson submitted that had she known his true state of mind and feeling she would have appreciated the risks of his withdrawing consent and, perhaps, elected for fertilisation of her eggs with donor sperm.

. . . [37] [T]he clear policy of the Act is to ensure continuing consent from the commencement of treatment to the point of implant. Consent may be given subject to conditions. Consent may be varied. Consent may be withdrawn. Against that background the court should be extremely slow to recognise or to create a principle of waiver that would conflict with the Parliamentary scheme.

. . . [41] In our judgment therefore, Mr Johnston was entitled by the terms of the Act to withdraw his consent as and when he did. The effect of his withdrawal of consent is to prevent both the use and the continued storage of the embryo fertilised with his sperm. Future treatment of the appellant would not be 'treatment together' with Mr Johnston.

In the alternative, Ms Evans contended that the HFEA 1990, by permitting such revocation, was incompatible with her rights under Article 8 ECHR:

Arden LJ:

Article 8

[108] It is common ground that Article 8, which has already been set out by Thorpe and Sedley LJJ, is engaged because Ms Evans' bodily integrity (private life) is affected. I do not consider that she could assert any right to family life with a future child whose embryo has not yet been transferred to her . . . The assumption made by all parties is that Article 8 is engaged to the extent that the 1990 Act purports to regulate any right they would otherwise have to use an embryo . . .

---

25 [2004] EWCA Civ 727, CA.

[109] The next question is whether the interference is justified under Article 8(2). In the 1990 Act Parliament has taken the view that each genetic parent should have the right to withdraw their consent for as long as possible. It was not inevitable that Parliament should take that view. Subject to the possible effect of the Convention, Parliament could have taken the view that, as in sexual intercourse, a man's procreative liberty should end with the donation of sperm but that, in the light of the woman's unique role in making the embryo a child, she should have the right to determine the fate of the embryo. But Parliament did not take that view. Nor did Parliament take the view that the court should have any power to dispense with the requirement for consent of both parties, even when circumstances occur which were not envisaged when the original arrangements were made.

[110] Like Thorpe and Sedley LJJ, I consider that the imposition of an invariable and ongoing requirement for consent in the 1990 Act in the present type of situation satisfies Article 8(2) of the Convention. . . . As this is a sensitive area of ethical judgment, the balance to be struck between the parties must primarily be a matter for Parliament: see the passage from the speech of Lord Nicholls in *Wilson v First County Trust Ltd (No. 2)* [2004] . . . Parliament has taken the view that no-one should have power to override the need for a genetic parent's consent. The wisdom of not having such a power is, in my judgment, illustrated by the facts of this case. The personal circumstances of the parties are different from what they were at the outset of treatment, and it would be difficult for a court to judge whether the effect of Mr Johnston's withdrawal of his consent on Ms Evans is greater than the effect that the invalidation of that withdrawal of consent would have on Mr Johnston. The court has no point of reference by which to make that sort of evaluation. The fact is that each person has a right to be protected against interference with their private life. That is an aspect of the principle of self-determination or personal autonomy . . .

Ms Evans subsequently appealed to the European Court of Human Rights in Strasbourg. However, in dismissing her action, the court noted that, at the European level too, there was no consensus as to how to resolve the conflicting Article 8 rights of the parties in such a case. In this context, the majority of the court was of the view that the approach adopted in the HFE Act – incorporating the need for their joint consent – was a permissible one.[26]

In the wake of the *Evans* case, the 2008 amendments to the HFE Act have included a change to the relevant consent provisions. Thus Sch 3, para 4A of the 1990 Act (as amended) now provides for a 12-month 'cooling off' period, where one party withdraws consent to the storage of an embryo created with his/her and the other party's gametes. During this time, the embryo may not be destroyed without the other party's agreement. Nor, however, may any other use be made of it.

THINK POINT

Do you think it is appropriate, in the context of assisted reproduction (in contrast to non-assisted conception), for the interests in procreating (or not) of the female and male gamete providers to enjoy equal weight?

---

26 *Evans v United Kingdom* (2006) 46 EHRR 321.

7.2.3 The embryo

7.2.3.1 Status issues

From what has been said above, in relation to the primacy granted to the wishes of gamete providers in determining the use made of the resulting embryos, it might appear that the embryo's own status is an entirely subordinate one. This is partly true; as we have just seen, the consequence of a gamete provider withdrawing consent to storage of an embryo is the latter's inevitable destruction. Nevertheless, as we shall see when we look at embryo research (see section 7.3 below), there are important limits on the freedom of action of medical scientists so far as the treatment of embryos is concerned. The ambivalence of the law on the early embryo was foreshadowed in the Warnock Report. After describing the initial stages of embryonic development, the report side-stepped the question of what moral inferences were to be drawn:

Warnock Committee, *Report of the Committee of Inquiry into Human Fertilisation and Embryology*[27]

The starting point for discussion

11.8 It was the development of IVF that, for the first time, gave rise to the possibility that human embryos might be brought into existence which might have no chance to implant because they were not transferred to a uterus and hence no chance to be born as human beings. This inevitably led to an examination of the moral rights of the embryo.

11.9 Some people hold that if an embryo is human and alive, it follows that it should not be deprived of a chance for development, and therefore it should not be used for research. They would give moral approval to IVF if, and only if, each embryo produced were to be transferred to a uterus. Others, while in no way denying that human embryos are alive (and they would concede that eggs and sperm are also alive), hold that embryos are not yet human persons and that if it could be decided when an embryo becomes a person, it could also be decided when it might, or might not, be permissible for research to be undertaken. Although the questions of when life or personhood begin appear to be questions of fact susceptible of straightforward answers, we hold that the answers to such questions in fact are complex amalgams of factual and moral judgments. Instead of trying to answer these questions directly we have therefore gone straight to the question of how it is right to treat the human embryo. We have considered what status ought to be accorded to the human embryo, and the answer we give must necessarily be in terms of ethical or moral principles.

In the American case of *Davis v Davis*,[28] which involved a custody battle over frozen embryos, the Tennessee Supreme Court was concerned with the question of whether embryos should be categorised as 'persons' or 'property' or as having an interim, *sui generis* legal status. In his judgment, Daughtrey J discussed the position as follows:

Daughtrey J: To our way of thinking, the most helpful discussion on this point is found not in the minuscule number of legal opinions that have involved 'frozen embryos', but in the ethical standards set by the American Fertility Society, as follows:

Three major ethical positions have been articulated in the debate over pre-embryo status. At one extreme is the view of the pre-embryo as a human subject after fertilisation, which

---

27 See n 1 above.
28 842 SW 2d 588 (1992).

requires that it be accorded the rights of a person. This position entails an obligation to provide an opportunity for implantation to occur and tends to ban any action before transfer that
might harm the pre-embryo or that is not immediately therapeutic, such as freezing and some
pre-embryo research.

At the opposite extreme is the view that the pre-embryo has a status no different from any
other human tissue. With the consent of those who have decision making authority over the
pre-embryo, no limits should be imposed on actions taken with pre-embryos.

A third view – one that is most widely held – takes an intermediate position between the
other two. It holds that the pre-embryo deserves respect greater than that accorded to human
tissue but not the respect accorded to actual persons. The pre-embryo is due greater respect
than other human tissue because of its potential to become a person and because of its symbolic meaning for many people. Yet, it should not be treated as a person, because it has not yet
developed the features of personhood, is not yet established as developmentally individual,
and may never realise its biologic potential . . .

We conclude that pre-embryos are not, strictly speaking, either 'persons' or 'property', but occupy an
interim category that entitles them to special respect because of their potential for human life.

The position in England as regards the existence of property rights in embryos remains uncertain.
As noted earlier, in *Yearworth v North Bristol NHS Trust*[29] the Court of Appeal was prepared to
recognise such rights in gametes for the purposes of a negligence action against a clinic, which had
lost them. Though the judgment did not expressly address the position as to embryos, in some
ways its logic could be read as extending to them – at least in a case where a couple jointly wished
to sue a clinic responsible for their destruction. On the other hand, the courts might well recoil
from the symbolic implications of categorising nascent human organisms in terms of property.

What is clear, by contrast, is the embryo's lack of personhood under English law. In *Evans v
Amicus Healthcare Ltd*[30] the Court of Appeal, in denying that the embryo was a legal person for
the purposes of Article 2 of the ECHR, commented as follows:

Thorpe and Sedley LJJ: [19] . . . In our domestic law it has been repeatedly held that a foetus prior to the
moment of birth does not have independent rights or interests: see *Re F (In Utero)* . . . and *Re MB (Medical
Treatment)*. . . . Thus even more clearly can there be no independent rights or interests in stored embryos.
In this respect our law is not inconsistent with the decisions of the ECHR. Article 2 protects the right to life.
No Convention jurisprudence extends the right to an embryo, much less to one which at the material point
of time is non-viable. Mr Tolson was prepared to accept that the Article 2 right would fail if both gamete
providers wanted the embryo destroyed. Yet, as was pointed out to him, the right to life, where it exists,
cannot be waived by its possessor, let alone by others. This simply illustrates the fallacy of invoking
Article 2 in the present argument. Ms Evans' case is not about the right to life; it is about the right
to bring life into being.

See Chapter 8 →

(See also the discussion of the status of the foetus in Chapter 8 below.)

7.2.3.2 The storage of embryos and gametes

As we have already seen, the consent of gamete providers must be obtained in order to continue
to store their gametes/embryos in accordance with the Act. Such storage is possible in relation

---

29 See n 20 above.
30 See n 25 above.

to both embryos and gametes (though egg storage is still in its infancy) by means of 'cryopreservation' (freezing). Nevertheless (assuming that valid consents are in force), should there be any absolute time limit beyond which the material in question may in any event not be kept?

The Warnock Committee recommended the need for an upper time limit to storage, on grounds both of the possible (albeit speculative) risk of physical harm to children born from embryos after extended storage, and the increased risk of gamete providers dying or falling into disagreement over the period in question. The HFEA 1990, as originally enacted, reflected these concerns in stipulating in maximum storage periods of ten years for gametes and five years for embryos. After the expiry of these periods, the clinics storing the material were required to 'allow it to perish'. However, subsequently, it was felt desirable to extend the limit in respect of embryos: this was especially so in cases where gametes were taken from a female provider prior to therapy for cancer, where it is medically preferable to wait for as long as possible after such therapy before implanting her with any embryo formed with them.

Accordingly, s 14(4) of the HFEA 1990 (as amended) now provides – subject to the specification by the gamete providers of a lesser period – for a ten-year storage period for embryos as well. Indeed, pursuant to the Human Fertilisation and Embryology (Statutory Storage Period for Embryos and Gametes) Regulations 2009,[31] the latter limit itself may be exceeded, eg in cases where a woman is due to undergo some other treatment, for example radiotherapy, interfering with her fertility. Here, reg 3 allows for ten-year extensions to storage to be made where the gamete providers' original consents provided this and a medical practitioner certifies in writing that one of them is, or is likely to become, prematurely infertile. This is subject to a long-stop period of 55 years from original storage. In the recent case of *Warren v Care Fertility (Northampton) Ltd and HFEA*,[32] where a clinic failed to advise the donor (who subsequently died of cancer) of the need for written consent to the long-term storage of his sperm, the High Court held that storage could and should nevertheless continue, pursuant to the applicant widow's Article 8 ECHR rights, to allow her more time to decide whether she wished to undergo fertility treatment with the gametes.

7.2.3.3 Embryo testing and selection

As we have seen, the process of IVF treatment consists of two main stages: first, the creation of one or more *ex vivo* embryos; secondly, the implantation of these in the female patient's uterus for gestation to birth. One possibility this separation opens up is of screening embryos in the interim so as to identify those with genetic defects, either of a kind that will prevent a live birth, or as will lead to a future child with a serious genetic disorder. However, other more controversial possibilities also exist, such as screening to identify embryos that would provide a tissue match for an existing sick child ('saviour siblings'), or of identifying and selecting embryos on social grounds, including on the basis of sex. We look in turn at how the law currently deals with these various issues.

7.2.3.3.1 Pre-implantation genetic diagnosis to eliminate disease

The practice of 'pre-implantation genetic diagnosis' (PGD) involves testing embryos for specific genetic diseases – only embryos free of genes associated with the disease will be implanted, while the others are discarded. In 1999, the HFE Authority and Advisory Committee on Genetic Testing published a report, *Pre-Implantation Genetic Diagnosis*, which concluded that the practice was ethically sound, at least in the case of serious genetic diseases such as cystic fibrosis. An

---

31 SI 2009/1582.
32 [2014] EWHC 602 (Fam).

analogy can be invoked here with abortion on grounds of serious foetal handicap, which is also widely regarded as permissible. In fact, in terms of the implications for the 'sanctity of life', not to mention the health of the putative mother, the discard of an embryo prior to implantation may well be thought preferable to the termination of an already existing pregnancy. Indeed, it is clear that some couples (notably, those who have previously had a genetically disabled child) will resort to IVF precisely because of the possibility of testing.

See Chapter 8 →

Arguably more controversial was the HFE Authority's decision in 2006 to license PGD in order to identify embryos with genes that would not cause disability at birth, but significantly increase the child's risk of developing an inherited form of cancer later in life. Here the effect is to 'screen out' persons who potentially could enjoy many years of disease-free existence. Nonetheless, the permissibility of such screening – as well as that designed to eliminate more immediate genetic disabilities – is confirmed by the 2008 amendments to the HFE Act 1990. Schedule 2 of the Act now provides that:

Schedule 2 – Activities that may be licensed under the 1990 Act

Licences for treatment

. . . Embryo testing

1ZA (1) A licence . . . cannot authorise the testing of an embryo, except for one or more of the following purposes –

    a   establishing whether the embryo has a gene, chromosome or mitochondrial abnormality that may affect its capacity to result in a live birth.

    b   in a case where there is a particular risk that the embryo may have any gene, chromosome or mitochondrion abnormality, establishing whether it has that abnormality or any other gene, chromosome or mitochondrion abnormality,

    . . .

(2) A licence . . . cannot authorise the testing of embryos for the purpose mentioned in sub-paragraph (1) (b) unless the Authority is satisfied –

    a   in relation to the abnormality of which there is a particular risk, and

    b   in relation to any other abnormality for which testing is to be authorised under sub-paragraph (1)(b),

    that there is a significant risk that a person with the abnormality will have or develop a serious physical or mental disability, a serious illness or any other serious medical condition.

7.2.3.3.2 'Saviour siblings'

A particular application of PGD, which has evoked controversy, is its use – in conjunction with tissue typing – to try to create a so-called 'saviour sibling' (ie a new child whose tissue is compatible with that of an existing sick child of the same couple). In 2002, the HFE Authority licensed a clinic in Nottingham to carry out treatment designed to enable a couple, Mr and Mrs Hashmi, to produce a child who would be a tissue donor for one of their children, Zain, who suffered from beta-thalassaemia – a serious genetic blood disorder. Subsequently, in *R (on the application of Josephine Quintavalle on Behalf of CORE) v HFEA*,[33] this decision was challenged by the pressure group CORE (Comment on Reproductive Ethics). In arguing that such testing fell outside the scope of the Authority's licensing powers, CORE relied on the (former) wording of Sch 2, para 1 of the 1990 Act, which provided that a licensed activity must be necessary or desirable for the

---

33 [2005] UKHL 28.

purpose of providing 'treatment services'. It contended that these provisions should be construed narrowly as assisting a woman physically to carry a child, but not a child with specific genetic attributes.

Although CORE's argument succeeded at first instance, it was rejected by the Court of Appeal and the House of Lords, which saw the provisions as conferring a discretion upon the Authority in such cases. Following the 2008 amendments to the HFE Act 1990, Sch 2, para 1ZA(1)(d) now expressly provides for the legality of tissue typing to determine an embryo's compatibility to act as a donor for a sick sibling, as follows:

Licences for treatment

... Embryo testing

1ZA (1) A licence under paragraph 1 cannot authorise the testing of an embryo, except for one or more of the following purposes –
... (d) in a case where a person ('the sibling') who is the child of the persons whose gametes are used to bring about the creation of the embryo (or of either of those persons) suffers from a serious medical condition which could be treated by umbilical cord blood stem cells, bone marrow or other tissue of any resulting child, establishing whether the tissue of any resulting child would be compatible with that of the sibling.

Nonetheless, as later made clear in para 1ZA(4), tissue typing will not be permitted in relation to the proposed creation of a child to serve as a whole organ donor for a sibling.

In fact, the HFE Authority has remained cautious in granting treatment licences in such cases; generally it must be satisfied both that the condition of the existing child is serious or life-threatening and that other reasonable possibilities of treatment and/or sources of tissue have been exhausted.[34] Originally, a further requirement imposed by the Authority was that the tested embryos should themselves be at risk of developing the condition affecting the existing child. For this reason it refused, in the summer of 2002, to grant a licence to carry out PGD and tissue-typing in the case of a couple, the Whitakers, who wanted a child to provide a tissue match for their three-year-old son, who had Diamond Blackfan anaemia (the crucial difference between their case and the Hashmis' was that the anaemia was sporadic rather than congenital, so that any further embryos produced by them were not at special risk of having it). However, this requirement – which the Authority attempted to justify by reference to the speculative risk to embryos from PGD itself – was subject to criticism,[35] and was abandoned in 2004.

7.2.3.3.3 Sex selection

Another controversial and significant possibility that has arisen out of developments in reproductive technology is that of testing *ex vivo* embryos (and more recently, sperm alone) in order to determine the sex of the potential child. How far should this practice be permitted for merely social (as opposed to medical) reasons? The Warnock Report had the following to say:

---

34 HFEA Code of Practice, 8th edn (2009) para 10.25.
35 See Sheldon, S, and Wilkinson, S, 'Hashmi and Whitaker: an unjustifiable and misguided distinction?' (2004) 12 Med L Rev 137.

Warnock Committee, *Report of the Committee of Inquiry into Human Fertilisation and Embryology*[36]

Other reasons for sex selection

9.11 – So far we have discussed the use of sex selection in a clinical context, where it would be practised solely for the purpose of avoiding hereditary sex-linked disorders. We see no reason why, if a method of selecting the sex of a child before fertilisation is developed, this should not be offered to couples who have good medical reasons for choosing the sex of their child. But if an efficient and easy method of ensuring the conception of a child of a particular sex became available, it is likely that some couples would wish to make use of it for purely social reasons. Such a practice would obviously affect the individual family and the children involved, and would also have implications for society as a whole. It is impossible to predict, either in the long or the short term, the likely effects of such a practice on the ratio of males to females within society. It is often suggested that a majority of couples would choose that their first child was male, and if this happened, it could have important social implications, since there is considerable evidence that the first born sibling may enjoy certain advantages over younger siblings. It would have particular implications for the role of women in society, although some would argue that these effects would today be less damaging than they might have been 100 years ago. These important considerations make the Inquiry dubious about the use of sex selection techniques on a wide scale, but because of the difficulty of predicting the outcome of any such trend we have not found it possible to make any positive recommendations on this issue. Nevertheless, we consider that the whole question of the acceptability of sex selection should be kept under review.

As originally enacted in 1990, the HFE Act left the possibility of licensing sex selection to the discretion of the HFE Authority. In 1993, following a process of consultation, the Authority decided that such selection for non-medical reasons was unethical and should not be carried out, and later reaffirmed its opposition in its report, *Sex Selection: Options for Regulation*,[37] and in successive Codes of Practice. As noted by the Warnock Report, one concern regarding the practice is the uncertain effects it would have, were it to be widely employed, upon the ratio of the sexes in society. Admittedly, this problem could be sidestepped, were permissible sex selection to be limited to cases of 'family balancing' (where the couple already have one or more child of the other sex). Nonetheless, as Stephen Wilkinson argues in the following extract, an objection that remains here relates to the sexual stereotyping involved:

Wilkinson, S, 'Sexism, sex selection and "family balancing"'[38]

As with 'regular' sex selection, whether 'family balancing' involves stereotyping depends on what exactly it is that the parents are aiming at. If what they want is a 'balance' of plainly biological features (if they want half their children to be capable of beard growth and other half to develop breasts, for example), then (as explained previously) while we may think that this is weird or objectionable in other ways, it does not seem to involve sex-stereotyping, for the desired sex-linked characteristics really are biologically determined. If, on the other hand, the sort of 'balance' that they are after is less clearly related to biology and more to

---

36 See n 1 above.
37 London: HFEA, 2003; available at: www.hfea.gov.uk/docs/Final_sex_selection_main_report.pdf.
38 (2008) 16 Med L Rev 369.

do with character traits that may or may not be determined by physical sex, then there is a significant risk that the parents are guilty of stereotyping. It seems then that such stereotyping is as likely in the case of 'family balancing' sex selection as it is in 'regular' sex selection. Consider these two cases. Family A want all of their children to have aggression and sporting prowess and so select all boys; Family B want half their children to have aggression and sporting prowess, and the other half to be caring and musical, and so use ('family balancing') selection to have half boys and half girls. Whatever the general merits of these choices, it seems clear that, as far as sex-stereotyping is concerned, the families are in the very same position; both are guilty of sex-stereotyping.

In fact, the 2008 changes to the HFE Act 1990 have now removed from the HFE Authority the possibility of licensing social sex selection, and instead contain a statutory prohibition of the practice. Schedule 2, para 1ZB of the 1990 Act (as amended) states:

Licences for treatment

. . . Sex selection

1ZB
(1)   A licence under paragraph 1 cannot authorise any practice designed to secure that any resulting child will be of one sex rather than the other.

. . .

(3)   Sub-paragraph (1) does not prevent the authorisation of any other practices designed to secure that any resulting child will be of one sex rather than the other in a case where there is a particular risk that a woman will give birth to a child who will have or develop –
   a   a gender-related serious physical or mental disability,
   b   a gender-related serious illness, or
   c   any other gender-related serious medical condition.
(4)   For the purposes of sub-paragraph (3), a physical or mental disability, illness or other medical condition is gender-related if the Authority is satisfied that –
   a   it affects only one sex, or
   b   it affects one sex significantly more than the other.

As is apparent from sub para 1ZB(3) (and as previously allowed by the HFE Authority) sex selection remains permissible for medical reasons, in particular to avoid/reduce the risk of transmitting a serious sex-specific genetic disease. For example, where a couple are known to be transmitters of the genes for haemophilia – and assuming testing cannot determine which of their embryos have these – it would be lawful to screen out all the male embryos (as only male children are at risk of actually developing the condition).

7.2.3.3.4 Other bases for embryo selection

So far, the only genes that can be identified with any certainty are those for some genetic diseases and for sex. However, in the future it may become possible to identify genes that contribute to other attributes such as intelligence, musicality, or aggression (assuming they have some genetic as opposed to purely social basis). If this were to occur, should the testing of embryos for the relevant genes – enabling parents to use the information to choose which embryos to have implanted – be permitted? This possibility, leading to the creation of what are popularly termed 'designer babies', was the subject of a report by the Nuffield Council on Bioethics in 2002, which found against the practice, *inter alia*, on the basis that it could negatively affect the attitude of parents towards their children:

Nuffield Council on Bioethics, *Genetics and Human Behaviour. The Ethical Context*[39]

Summary and Recommendations . . .

At present, parents accept their children as they find them in an attitude of 'natural humility' to the unchosen results of procreation. This attitude is an important feature of parental love, the love that parents owe to their children as individuals in their own right; for this is a love that does not have to be earned and is not dependent on a child having characteristics that the parents hoped for. Parental love which includes this element of natural humility is, therefore, incompatible with the will to control. It is not compatible with attempts to interfere in the life of a child except where the interference is in the child's own interest. Equally, it is not compatible with the practice of prenatal selection which seeks to identify, as a basis for choice, genetic predispositions for enhanced abilities or special character traits. For this is an attempt to determine the kind of child one will have – which is precisely not the unconditional, loving acceptance of whatever child one turns out to have.

Given that we are dealing here with only speculative possibilities, and since the likely small effects of individual genes may make accurate predictions of future behaviour very difficult, it is hard to evaluate the disagreement between the contrasting positions. In particular, it may be that the contrast between the affirmation of a right to procreative autonomy and the defence of natural humility is too simple. It might turn out that there are possibilities for modest applications of PGD in relation to the traits considered in this Report which would not seriously undermine the present relationship between parents and their children. *While not entirely persuaded by this conservative line of argument, we do accept that, at present, the case for permitting prenatal selection based on the identification of genetic predispositions for enhanced abilities remains to be made. We recommend, therefore, that the technique of preimplantation genetic diagnosis, which is currently restricted to serious diseases and disorders, should not be extended to include behavioural traits in the normal range such as intelligence, sexual orientation and personality traits* (para 13.78).

On the other hand, other commentators have defended such hypothetical selection on consequentialist grounds. Julian Savelescu argues that it is consonant with the demands of 'procreative beneficence' – which requires parents to select, as between possible children, those with the greatest chance of having the best life (ie containing the most well-being). He goes on to dismiss two objections that are often raised to the approach:

Savelescu, J, 'Procreative beneficence: why we should select the best children'[40]

1. *Harm to the child*: One common objection to genetic selection for non-disease traits is that it results in harm to the child. There are various versions of this objection, which include the harm which arises from excessive and overbearing parental expectations, using the child as a means, and not treating it as an end, and closing off possible future options on the basis of the information provided (failing to respect the child's 'right to an open future').

There are a number of responses. Firstly, in some cases, it is possible to deny that the harms will be significant. Parents come to love the child whom they have (even a child with a serious disability). Moreover, some have argued that counselling can reduce excessive expectations.

Secondly, we can accept some risk of a child experiencing some state of reduced well-being in cases of selection. One variant of the harm to child objection is: 'If you select embryo A, it might still get asthma, or worse, cancer, or have a much worse life than B, and you would be responsible.' . . . [However,] you have

39 (2002); the full report is available at: www.nuffieldbioethics.org/go/browseablepublications/geneticsandhb/report_354.html.
40 (2001) 15 Bioethics 413.

not harmed A unless A's life is not worth living (hardly plausible) because A would not have existed if you had acted otherwise. A is not made worse off than A would otherwise have been, since without the selection, A would not have existed.

2. *Inequality*: One objection to Procreative Beneficence is that it will maintain or increase inequality. For example, it is often argued that selection for sex, intelligence, favourable physical or psychological traits, etc all contribute to inequality in society . . .

. . . Even if the Disability Discrimination Claim were true, it would be a drastic step in favour of equality to inflict a higher risk of having a child with a disability on a couple (who do not want a child with a disability) to promote social equality.

. . . There are better ways to make statements about the equality of people with disability (e.g., we could direct savings from selection against embryos/fetuses with genetic abnormalities to improving well-being of existing people with disabilities).

These arguments extend to selection for non-disease genes. It is not disease which is important but its impact on well-being. In so far as a non-disease gene such as a gene for intelligence impacts on a person's well-being, parents have a reason to select for it, even if inequality results.

As noted, at present it is not possible to link attributes such as intelligence to genes in this way and the HFE Act 1990 (as amended) does not contain any express provisions on the matter – instead, the question of whether to license such practices would remain with the HFE Authority, which, given the public ambivalence towards the idea of 'designer babies', may be expected to act cautiously. Interestingly, in another context the Act (as amended) appears to give some endorsement to Savelescu's more radical approach. This is in relation to a prohibition it contains on selecting on social grounds in favour of embryos (or gamete donors) with genes for conditions that are commonly perceived as disabling (the situations contemplated are of deaf couples who might wish to select embryos with the genes for deafness, dwarf couples those with the genes for dwarfism, etc). Section 13(9) of the HFEA 1990 (as amended) provides:

Section 13 Conditions of licences for treatment

. . . (9) Persons or embryos that are known to have a gene, chromosome or mitochondrion abnormality involving a significant risk that a person with the abnormality will have or develop –

a   a serious physical or mental disability,

b   a serious illness, or

c   any other serious medical condition,

must not be preferred to those that are not known to have such an abnormality.

As Savelescu notes, such a prohibition – which runs counter to the procreative liberty of the couple, as well as arguments based on diminishing inequality in society – cannot easily be justified by reference to the harm to a hypothetical child who is born with the relevant disability, since otherwise (ie in a case where a non-disabled embryo is selected) that particular child would not exist at all. Instead, its justification appears to be based on something akin to procreative beneficence.

7.2.3.4 Embryonic manipulations

In 7.2.3.3 above, we looked at the use of PGD and the selection between embryos with different attributes it makes possible. However, another possibility – as yet in its scientific infancy – concerns the genetic modification of embryos. This may take the form of 'genetic engineering', in which certain genes are added or replaced, resulting in a new individual, possessing new or enhanced genetic characteristics. Another possibility, and so far more scientifically feasible, is that of 'reproductive cloning', in which a child is produced who is the genetic copy of an existing person. We consider the ethical and legal issues in each case below.

7.2.3.4.1 Genetic engineering

The practice of modifying the genetic content of an embryo is often termed 'positive genetic engineering' (in contrast to the more 'negative' process of selecting embryos from a pool, and discarding those without a particular characteristic, looked at in 7.2.3.3). Sometimes, the manipulation may be aimed at enhancing some desired genetic characteristic; alternatively, it may be done to remove defective genes – known as 'gene therapy' – in a case where embryo selection is not available, eg because all a couple's embryos are affected by the defect. In either case such manipulations are generally perceived as ethically problematic. The Glover Report in 1989 commented on the issue as follows:

Glover, J et al., *Report to the European Commission on Reproductive Technologies, Fertility and the Family*[41]

Safe gene therapy is not yet with us. But it is better to start thinking about the implications of likely technological developments before they arrive. The stage when a technology seems too remote to be worth thinking about has been followed so often by abrupt transition to the stage when it is already out of control...

There are real causes for concern about positive genetic engineering, and it is worth bringing them into sharper focus.

One concern is perhaps obvious to any late 20th century European. This is the danger of giving new technological powers to a government with a programme of racist eugenics, or perhaps to one which had some other, not 'race' linked, category of people it regarded as less than fully human. In our countries there is nearly universal revulsion against this kind of outlook. But technology once developed is always available, and it is hard to be sure that such an outlook will never return.

Another cause for concern is not the deliberate use of genetic engineering for perverted ends, but the accidental side effects of well-intentioned uses. One problem is that we may overlook some genetic linkage between different characteristics. In choosing, say, genes for high intelligence, we may find we have inadvertently also chosen genes for high levels of aggression or depression. All technology carries with it the risk of mistakes and unwanted side effects. Here the 'mistakes' will be human beings. There is also the risk of disasters which are irreversible: 'mistaken' genes would be passed on to future generations.

Another problem is that if certain characteristics were frequently selected, those who did not have them might come to be seen as inferior. It may be hard to keep the decent reluctance to see people in terms of some competitive rank ordering, when, in another part of our mind, we are ranking characteristics which may be available for our children.

There are also enormous problems about who would take the decisions. These problems are sometimes gestured at by describing the choice as 'playing God', with the implication that it would take a great deal of presumption to put oneself forward as qualified to choose the genes of another person.

Perhaps, if there were great benefits, we would overcome our reluctance to play God in this way. But there would remain the question of whose decision it should be. Many shudder at the idea of some central government committee taking such decisions. The alternative of parents choosing for their children is much more attractive. But that too has huge unsolved problems. Could parents not sometimes choose disastrously for their children? And suppose too many parents chose the same characteristics? What social limits to their choice would be set, and by what means?

---

41 See n 4 above.

> ... This adds up to a case for saying that positive human genetic engineering is unethical now (or when it becomes available) and will remain so at least until policies have been worked out to cope with the huge problems it raises.

Some of these problems are also present in the case of 'negatively' selecting between embryos on the basis of social characteristics (see 7.2.3.3.4). However, a specific additional one is the risk, noted by Glover, that genetic modifications could have unintended side-effects, damaging the resulting child and/or future generations.

Under the HFE Act 1990 (as amended), genetic engineering (including gene therapy) – assuming it becomes scientifically feasible – remains prohibited pursuant to ss 3 and 3ZA, which only countenance the implantation of 'permitted' (ie non-modified) embryos and gametes:

---

3 Prohibitions in connection with embryos

... (2) No person shall place in a woman –

a   an embryo other than a permitted embryo (as defined by section 3ZA), or

b   any gametes other than permitted eggs or permitted sperm (as so defined).

...

3ZA Permitted eggs, permitted sperm and permitted embryos

1   This section has effect for the interpretation of section 3(2).

2   A permitted egg is one –
    a   which has been produced by or extracted from the ovaries of a woman, and
    b   whose nuclear or mitochondrial DNA has not been altered.

3   Permitted sperm are sperm –
    a   which have been produced by or extracted from the testes of a man, and
    b   whose nuclear or mitochondrial DNA has not been altered.

4   An embryo is a permitted embryo if –
    a   it has been created by the fertilisation of a permitted egg by permitted sperm,
    b   no nuclear or mitochondrial DNA of any cell of the embryo has been altered, and
    c   no cell has been added to it other than by division of the embryo's own cells.

...

7.2.3.4.2 Reproductive cloning

Reproductive cloning entails, first, that an embryo is created which is a genetic copy of an existing individual (through nucleus substitution or cell nuclear replacement) and, secondly, that it is implanted in a woman to be gestated to term. Although in its infancy, such cloning has already successfully been carried out on some mammals. Most famously, 'Dolly' the sheep was produced by CNR cloning at the Roslin Institute, Edinburgh in 1997, and since then other animals have been cloned around the world in the same way.

The notion that human beings might also be cloned in this fashion undoubtedly evokes widespread fear and repugnance. Some of the concerns surrounding reproductive cloning are directly consequentialist in form (relating to the potential well-being, physical or psychological, of the individuals who result from cloning; indeed, the experience with cloned animals, including Dolly the sheep, is that these often suffer from ill-health and die prematurely. Even so – as with embryo selection (though unlike positive genetic engineering) – the invocation of harm in this context may encounter the response that the life of the cloned person is still unlikely to be so bad, for him to prefer (hypothetically) never to have existed at all. Nor are arguments based on the denial of genetic individuality to clones ultimately persuasive, given the widespread existence of identical twins. On the other hand, other objections to the practice of a more intuitive character remain: probably an important aspect, as with other instances of genetic engineering, is the foreboding that, if people were 'manufactured' in this way, deep-rooted notions of human dignity (and perhaps the sanctity of human life itself) might be placed in jeopardy.[42]

As to the law, the HFE Act 1990, as originally enacted, placed a ban on the creation of human clones by nucleus substitution: subsequently, due to doubts whether this ban also covered a newer form of 'CNR cloning' (where a nucleus taken from an adult human is introduced into an unfertilised egg as opposed to an embryo), Parliament enacted a short Act, the Human Reproductive Cloning Act 2001, to make it clear that such embryos could not be used for reproductive cloning. This though was subsequently repealed as part of the 2008 amendments to the HFE Act 1990. This is because, pursuant to ss 3 and 3ZA of the amended HFE Act (see section 7.2.1 above), a CNR-produced embryo is not a 'permitted embryo' and so could not in any event be implanted in a woman.

At the same time, it should be emphasised that the above provisions do not prevent the creation of cloned embryos by CNR for research purposes (so-called 'therapeutic cloning'), a matter looked at further in section 7.3.3 below.

THINK POINT

If it is acceptable for parents to use PGD to prevent a child suffering a significant genetic disadvantage, then (once this is safe) should they not equally have access to techniques of genetic enhancement, to advantage the child?

7.3 Embryo research

7.3.1 Background

The creation of human embryos *ex vivo* opens up significant opportunities for the conduct of medical research. Nevertheless, for many people the possibility of such research is one of the most troubling aspects of the advance in reproductive technology, more so than, for example, simply allowing spare or unwanted embryos – left over from IVF treatment – to perish. Why this should be so is a complex question, which is inextricably linked to our attitudes towards unborn human life in general. In *Question of Life*, Mary Warnock commented as follows:

---

42 See Robertson, J, 'Liberty, identity, and human cloning' (1998) 76 Texas L Rev 1371, for a careful analysis of the various issues.

Warnock, M, *Question of Life: Warnock Report on Human Fertilization and Embryology*[43]

There was, however, a more testing kind of question [than the issue of regulating fertility treatment], infinitely more important, in my opinion.

This was the question of research using human embryos . . . Utilitarianism could . . . by itself, provide no solution, simply because the very question at issue was whether or not embryos count as those whose harms and benefits, pleasures and pains, have to be thrown into the balance to be weighed against the benefits or harms to society as a whole. But here we had, it seemed, an issue on which legislation must be foreseen, and must be enacted quickly. No one felt inclined to argue that the decision whether or not to embark on research with the use of human embryos was a matter of personal conscience, as they might in the case of [donor insemination], surrogacy, or, for that matter, homosexuality between adults. Everyone agreed that this was a matter on which there must be legislation, and that whether and to what extent embryos should be used must be a decision for the law.

It is certainly true that the moral permissibility of embryo research turns upon the issue of the embryo's moral status in a particularly direct way. This is because, unlike the case of 'spare embryos' allowed to perish following IVF treatment carried out for an infertile couple, or that of embryos/foetuses destroyed through abortion, the rights/interests of identifiable, fully fledged individuals are not directly implicated. To the extent that the view of embryo-as-person is rejected, such research may appear acceptable in principle. On the other hand, as argued by John Robertson, other problems – notably the symbolic damage it may cause – remain:

See Chapter 8

Robertson, JA, *Children of Choice: Freedom and the New Reproductive Technologies*[44]

. . . [C]reating embryos for research and then discard deserves protection only if other important interests are served that justify whatever symbolic costs deliberate creation and discard of embryos entails. The purpose here is to increase knowledge of how to treat infertility, improve contraception, and treat or prevent cancer or birth defects. With cryopreservation of extra embryos limiting the number donated for research, a policy against creating embryos solely for research and discard could greatly limit the amount of embryo research. Research with embryos would then occur only with spare embryos created as a by-product of IVF treatment of infertility, which may be too few to meet all research needs, with the result that important research across a range of fields is lost. The symbolic benefits of protecting embryos from being created solely for research purposes does not appear to justify this loss. If the embryo is so rudimentary that research on excess, discarded embryos does not harm them and is permissible, there would appear to be no additional harm to embryos from creating them for this purpose only. In both cases research will occur at the same stage of development, and thus no added harm would occur from deliberate creation of embryos for research purposes.

Opponents, however, would argue that additional symbolic harm arises from creating embryos solely to be vehicles of research and then discarded. Additional symbolic harm results because creating embryos with the intent to discard them demonstrates a profound disrespect for the earliest stages of human life. This practice permits human life to be created, manipulated, and discarded for utilitarian purposes, without regard to the embryo's own interests or potential. The deliberateness of the act – creating new human life only to destroy it – is thus viewed as symbolically more offensive than research on excess embryos created as a by-product of the IVF process of treating infertility.

---

43 See n 2 above.
44 Ewing, NJ: Princeton UP, 1994.

Although, as noted in section 7.2.3.1, the Warnock Committee avoided taking a view as to the personhood or otherwise of the embryo, it concluded that 'the status of the embryo is a matter of fundamental principle which should be enshrined in legislation' (para 11.17). This recommendation was followed in the HFE Act 1990, which in s 3(3)(a) prohibited 'keeping or using' an embryo after the appearance of the 'primitive streak'. According to s 3(4) this was deemed to occur no later than 14 days after the initial creation of the embryo (not counting any periods of storage). The effect of these provisions was thus to outlaw any research on embryos more than two weeks old.

As the Warnock Report had noted, the formation of the primitive streak marks that stage in embryonic development when a new individual entity is first discernible:

Warnock Committee, *Report of the Committee of Inquiry into Human Fertilisation and Embryology*[45]

11.5 The first of these features is the primitive streak, which appears as a heaping up of cells at one end of the embryonic disc on the 14th or 15th day after fertilisation. Two primitive streaks may form in a single embryonic disc. This is the latest stage at which identical twins can occur. The primitive streak is the first of several identifiable features which develop in and from the embryonic disc during the succeeding days, a period of very rapid change in the embryonic configuration. By the 17th day the neural groove appears and by the 22nd to 23rd day this has developed to become the neural folds, which in turn start to fuse and form the recognisable antecedent of the spinal cord.

As for research on embryos within the first 14 days, this could be carried out (with the consent of the gamete providers) subject to the researcher having a research licence from the HFE Authority. In granting a licence the Authority needed to be satisfied that the research was 'necessary or desirable' for one of the purposes specified in Sch 2, para 3 of the 1990 Act. Originally these included promoting infertility treatment, increasing knowledge about congenital diseases, and improving techniques of contraception.

Subsequently, in 2001, several new research purposes were added by statutory instrument,[46] which included increasing knowledge about, and developing treatments for, serious disease. The reason for this change (which followed a report by the Chief Medical Officer's Expert Group, *Stem Cell Research: Medical Progress with Responsibility*)[47] was to allow research into embryonic stem cells, including those generated by the technique of CNR (cell nuclear transfer). Possibly, in the future, this technique could be used, in conjunction with cells taken from particular patients, to clone replacement organs and tissue for them. As the Human Genetics Advisory Commission (HGAC) and the HFE Authority commented in their report, *Cloning Issues in Reproduction, Science and Medicine*:

HGAC and HFE Authority, *Cloning Issues in Reproduction, Science and Medicine*[48]

5.3 The most likely objective of a research project involving the use of CNR would be to create a cultured cell line for the purposes of cell or tissue therapy. People who have tissues or organs damaged by injury or disease (eg, skin, heart muscle, nervous tissue) could provide their own somatic nuclei and, by using these

---

45 See n 1 above.
46 Human Fertilisation and Embryology (Research Purposes) Regulations 2001, SI 2001/188. As discussed in section 7.3.3, the Regulations have now been superseded by the 2008 amendments to the HFE Act 1990.
47 London: DoH, 2000.
48 HGAC & HFEA, London: December 1998.

to replace nuclei in their own or donated eggs, individual stem cells (not embryos) could be produced in culture. These cells could then be induced (by exposure to appropriate growth factors) to form whichever type of cell or tissue was required for therapeutic purposes with no risk of tissue rejection and no need for treatment of the patient with immunosuppressive drugs.

7.3.2 Embryo research following the 2008 amendments to the HFE Act

7.3.2.1 Permissible research purposes

The 2008 changes to the HFE Act have consolidated and extended the purposes for which licensed research may be conducted upon embryos. These are listed in Sch 2, para 3A as follows:

3A 1 A licence under paragraph 3 cannot authorise any activity unless the activity appears to the Authority –

    a   to be necessary or desirable for any of the purposes specified in sub-paragraph (2) ('the principal purposes'),

    b   to be necessary or desirable for the purpose of providing knowledge that, in the view of the Authority, may be capable of being applied for the purposes specified in sub-paragraph (2)(a) or (b), or

    c   to be necessary or desirable for such other purposes as may be specified in regulations.

  2   The principal purposes are –

    a   increasing knowledge about serious disease or other serious medical conditions,

    b   developing treatments for serious disease or other serious medical conditions,

    c   increasing knowledge about the causes of any congenital disease or congenital medical condition that does not fall within paragraph (a),

    d   promoting advances in the treatment of infertility,

    e   increasing knowledge about the causes of miscarriage,

    f   developing more effective techniques of contraception,

    g   developing methods for detecting the presence of gene, chromosome or mitochondrion abnormalities in embryos before implantation, or

    h   increasing knowledge about the development of embryos.

Here, the references in sub-para (2) to research aimed at improving knowledge of and treatments for 'other serious medical conditions' (as well as disease in the narrower sense) makes it clear that new treatments for spinal cord injuries are now a permissible goal of research – this could potentially be an important application for stem-cell replacement therapy. At the same time, as sub-para (1) stipulates, the HFE Authority may only grant a licence in cases where it is satisfied that the proposed research is necessary or desirable for promoting one of the purposes. Indeed, this is augmented by a yet stricter necessity test in Sch 2, para 3(5), which provides that: 'No licence under this paragraph is to be granted unless the Authority is satisfied that any proposed use of embryos or human admixed embryos is necessary for the purposes of the research.'

The effect of this last provision is that the HFE Authority must be satisfied that the research could not be carried out effectively using non-embryonic materials. This condition may become harder to satisfy in the future in the light of recent scientific progress in using adult cells, reprogrammed to behave like embryonic stem-cells, as a substitute for the latter. At present, though, the need in general for recourse to embryonic cells in this area of science remains.

7.3.2.2 The use of 'human admixed embryos' in stem-cell research

The comparative shortage of human eggs has led to pressure to employ eggs from animals (such as cows, mice or rabbits) to create embryos by CNR-cloning for use in stem-cell research. In fact, the resulting embryos will be largely human, since as part of the cloning process, the animal nucleus of the egg is removed and replaced by a human cell. Nonetheless, some mitochondrial animal DNA will remain in the outer membrane of the egg.

The question of whether the creation of such 'hybrid' embryos should be permitted was the subject of fierce public and parliamentary debate in the run-up to the 2008 amendments to the HFE Act. Originally, the Government itself favoured a ban on such creations. However, due to arguments brought to bear by the scientific lobby, it changed its view and accepted an amendment to the Bill as it passed through Parliament.[49] In the result, s 4A of the HFE Act 1990 (as amended) provides for the creation of hybrid embryos for research – which it terms 'human admixed embryos' – as follows:

---

4 A Prohibitions in connection with genetic material not of human origin

(2) No person shall –
- a   mix human gametes with animal gametes,
- b   bring about the creation of a human admixed embryo, or
- c   keep or use a human admixed embryo, except in pursuance of a licence.

...

(6) For the purposes of this Act a human admixed embryo is –
- a   an embryo created by replacing the nucleus of an animal egg or of an animal cell, or two animal pronuclei, with –
  - i   two human pronuclei,
  - ii   one nucleus of a human gamete or of any other human cell, or
  - iii   one human gamete or other human cell,
- b   any other embryo created by using –
  - i   human gametes and animal gametes, or
  - ii   one human pronucleus and one animal pronucleus,
- c   a human embryo that has been altered by the introduction of any sequence of nuclear or mitochondrial DNA of an animal into one or more cells of the embryo,
- d   a human embryo that has been altered by the introduction of one or more animal cells, or
- e   any embryo not falling within paragraphs (a) to (d) which contains both nuclear or mitochondrial DNA of a human and nuclear or mitochondrial DNA of an animal ('animal DNA') but in which the animal DNA is not predominant.

The terms of this provision are in fact of wider application than to CNR-cloned embryos using denucleated animal eggs (covered under s 4A(6)(a)). Thus, as per sub-s (6)(b), it is apparent that other forms of hybrid – this time composed of equal amounts of animal and human DNA – will also qualify as 'human admixed embryos', and may thus be created under licence. On the other hand, what is equally clear is that their only possible use would be in

---

49 See Fox, M, 'The Human Fertilisation and Embryology Act 2008: tinkering at the margins', n 8 above.

research: the placing of such embryos in a woman (or for that matter in an animal) for gestation is expressly forbidden by s 4A(1) and (4), respectively. Nor, for good measure, will such an embryo meet the definition of 'permitted embryo' under s 3ZA of the Act (see section 7.2.3.4 above).

7.3.2.3 Time limits and consent issues

As discussed in section 7.3.1, following the recommendations of the Warnock Report, the original 1990 Act prohibited research upon human embryos that are older than 14 days. This time-limit has been retained in the amendments to the 1990 Act (under s 3(3)), while s 4A(3) also extends it to human admixed embryos:

> **4A** (3) A licence cannot authorise keeping or using a human admixed embryo after the earliest of the following –
> a   the appearance of the primitive streak, or
> b   the end of the period of 14 days beginning with the day on which the process of creating the human admixed embryo began, but not counting any time during which the human admixed embryo is stored.

A final important issue in relation to embryo research concerns the consent of the (human) gamete providers to the use of their genetic material in this way. In line with the generally strict consent requirements that characterise the HFE legislative scheme, here too the 1990 Act (as amended) stipulates in Sch 3, para 2 the need, normally, for fully informed written consent on the part of the providers. In relation to research involving stem cells the HFE Authority's Code of Practice (8th edn) suggests in para 22.7 that providers should be made aware that their consent will allow use to be made of their cells indefinitely (including after their death). Equally, they should appreciate that they personally are extremely unlikely to benefit (either medically or financially) from the research.

Nonetheless the HFE Act 1990 (as amended) provides for an exception to the need for consent in relation to mentally incapacitated persons, where research using their cells may increase knowledge into and/or treatments for a condition or disease from which they suffer. As provided for in Sch 3, para 15B *et seq* this is subject to a number of limiting conditions, including that the research cannot be carried out equally effectively using the cells of competent persons. So too, in the case of child gamete providers, provisions dispensing with the need for consent are found in Sch 3, para 15A, which allow for parental consent instead (subject to similar, stringent conditions).

THINK POINT

Do the consent provisions in the HFE legislation, as regards what kind of research gamete providers permit their genetic material to be used for, serve any real purpose (in terms of protecting some recognisable interest)?

7.4 Collaborative reproduction

7.4.1 Background

The term 'collaborative reproduction' (borrowed from John Robertson)[50] describes situations in which a third party (who will have no parental role in nurturing the child) assists in the production of the child. Such assistance may come either through the donation of gametes and embryos, or (in the case of a woman) the provision of her uterus to gestate the child. The latter practice, known as surrogacy, raises particular problems and will accordingly be dealt with separately in section 7.5 below. For the time being, we shall restrict our discussion to issues centring on gamete/embryo donation; useful summaries of the key techniques can be found in the Warnock Report:

Warnock Committee, *Report of the Committee of Inquiry into Human Fertilisation and Embryology*[51]

I Artificial insemination

4.1 The term artificial insemination (AI) is used to refer to the placing of semen inside a woman's vagina or uterus by means other than sexual intercourse. The principle of this technique has been known for centuries in the veterinary context. The simplicity of artificial insemination contrasts sharply with the technical complexity of more recent developments such as *in vitro* fertilisation. It begins with the collection of semen from the husband or a donor, through masturbation. The semen is either placed in the upper part of the vagina next to the cervix or injected into the uterus through a fine catheter. Insemination is undertaken near the predicted time of ovulation, the time in a woman's menstrual cycle when she has the highest chance of conceiving. The semen used may be fresh or it may have been previously frozen and thawed before use . . .

II Artificial insemination by donor (AID)

4.6 Artificial insemination by donor (AID) may be used when investigations have shown the husband to be sterile or to have significantly reduced fertility, or it may be used for the avoidance of hereditary diseases when these are carried by the male . . . In this procedure the woman is inseminated with semen from a donor. [NB: *Today the more common term for this type of treatment is 'Donor Insemination' (DI).*]

. . .

III Egg donation

6.1 Egg donation . . . may help those women who cannot themselves produce an egg. It may also help those who would be candidates for IVF except that in their case egg collection is impossible because their ovaries are inaccessible. About 5% of infertile couples might benefit from the technique. A mature egg is recovered from a fertile woman donor, for example, during sterilisation, and is fertilised *in vitro*, using the semen of the husband of the infertile woman. The resulting embryo is then transferred to the patient's uterus. If it implants she may then carry the pregnancy to term. There are other situations where eggs might be donated. When a woman is herself undergoing infertility treatment and several eggs have been recovered from her, she may be prepared to donate one or more eggs to another woman whose infertility can be treated only by egg donation.

. . .

IV Embryo donation

7.1 Embryo donation would help the same groups of women who might benefit from egg donation and, more particularly, the even smaller number whose husbands are also infertile. Embryo donation may take two

---

50 See Robertson, JA, *Children of Choice: Freedom and the New Reproductive Technologies*, n 44 above.
51 See n 1 above.

forms. One involves the donation of both egg and semen. The donated egg is fertilised *in vitro* with donated semen and the resulting embryo transferred to a woman who is unable to produce an egg herself and whose husband is infertile. The second method, known as lavage, does not involve removing the egg by surgical intervention. Instead the egg is released naturally from the ovary at the normal time in the donor's menstrual cycle. At the predicted time of ovulation she is artificially inseminated with semen from the husband of the infertile woman (or from a donor if the husband is also infertile). Some three to four days later, before the start of implantation, the donor's uterus is 'washed out' and any embryo retrieved is then transferred to the uterus of the infertile woman. If the embryo implants successfully the recipient carries the pregnancy to term.

According to statistics published by the HFE Authority, licensed donor-assisted conception has to date been responsible for the births of over 23,000 children in the UK. However, the proportion of such births relative to the total number of children resulting from licensed fertility treatment has declined significantly; thus, for example, in 1992 there were 1,703 births involving donated gametes/embryos, and 2,031 live births not involving donation; in 2015, the respective figures were 702 and over 21,000.[52] As the HFE Authority has noted, a key reason for this change has been the development of the newer ICSI variant of IVF treatment (see section 7.2.1 above), which has reduced the need for recourse to donated sperm. Instead it appears that today, where donated sperm is used, this is often to provide children for women in single-sex partnerships (it should be recalled too that donor-assisted conception is often fairly easy to perform on a 'DIY' basis, and some people may prefer this as a cheaper and more informal alternative, even at the cost of losing the greater legal certainty and safeguards afforded by licensed treatment).

The potential for techniques of collaborative reproduction to alter the traditional picture of the heterosexual, two-parent family is one – though not the only – reason why this field of medicine tends to generate controversy. As John Robertson has written:

Robertson, JA, *Children of Choice: Freedom and the New Reproductive Technologies*[53]

Resort to donor gametes or surrogates is not an easy choice for infertile couples. The decision arises after previous efforts at pregnancy have failed, thus confronting the couple with the fact of one or both partners' infertility. A collaborative technique is chosen because it offers an opportunity to have a child who is the biologic offspring of one or, in the case of egg donation and gestational surrogacy, both partners. Yet collaborative reproduction occurs in an uncertain ethical, legal, and social milieu, where social practices and legal rules are still largely unclear.

A basic commitment to procreative liberty – to the freedom to have and rear offspring – should presumptively protect most forms of collaborative reproduction. After all, collaborative reproduction occurs for the same reason as IVF: the couple is infertile and cannot produce offspring. They need donor or surrogate assistance if they are to have children. Even if both rearing partners are not reproducing in the strict genetic sense, at least one partner will have a genetic or gestational relationship with their child. The same techniques may also be sought by a single woman or a same-sex couple that wishes to have offspring. In a few cases, donor gametes are used to avoid genetic handicap in offspring.

Despite its clear link to procreative choice, collaborative reproduction often generates controversy and even calls for prohibition. Collaborative reproduction is problematic because it intrudes a third party a donor or surrogate – into the usual situation of two party parenthood, and separates or deconstructs the traditional genetic, gestational, and social unity of reproduction. A child could in theory end up with three different biologic parents (a genetic mother, a gestational mother, a genetic father) and two separate rearing parents, with various combinations among them. Such collaboration risks confusing offspring about who their 'true' parent is and creating conflict about parental rights and duties.

---

52 See n 12 above.
53 See n 44 above.

In what follows we consider the law on gamete and/or embryo donation as it bears in turn on the interests of the immediate parties to such an enterprise, namely the potential nurturing parent(s), the gamete donor(s), and any child who is born as a result. This is an area of law that has been sensitive to shifting social attitudes, and, as we shall see, there have been some significant changes in recent years – not least in the 2008 amendments to the HFE legislation – which have rebalanced (and to a degree reconceptualised) the key interests at stake.

7.4.2 The potential nurturing parent(s)

7.4.2.1 Access to treatment

Pursuant to s 4(1) of HFEA 1990 (as amended), infertility treatment involving the use of third-party gametes may only be carried out under licence (the same condition applies to donated embryos by virtue of s 3 of the Act). The first major issue is who should be eligible for such treatment? In particular, should it be limited to those in a traditional heterosexual marriage who are unable to reproduce by reason of medical infertility, or may it be given also to single persons or homosexual couples whose 'infertility' results from their lifestyle? The Warnock Committee had the following to say on the matter:

Warnock Committee, *Report of the Committee of Inquiry into Human Fertilisation and Embryology*[54]

2.9 . . . [T]he various techniques for assisted reproduction offer not only a remedy for infertility, but also offer the fertile single woman or lesbian couple the chance of parenthood without the direct involvement of a male partner. To judge from the evidence, many believe that the interests of the child dictate that it should be born into a home where there is a loving, stable, heterosexual relationship and that, therefore, the *deliberate* creation of a child for a woman who is not a partner in such a relationship is morally wrong. On the other side some expressed the view that a single woman or lesbian couple have a right under the European Convention to have children even though those children may have no legal father. It is further argued that it is already accepted that a single person, whether man or woman, can in certain circumstances provide a suitable environment for a child, since the existence of single adoptive parents is specifically provided for in the Children Act 1975.

2.10 In the same way that a single woman may believe she has a right to motherhood, so a single man may feel he has a right to fatherhood. Though the feminist position is perhaps more frequently publicised, we were told of a group of single, mainly homosexual, men who were campaigning for the right to bring up a child. Their primary aim at present is to obtain in practice equal rights in the adoption field, but they are also well aware of the potential of surrogacy for providing a single man with a child that is genetically his. There have been cases in other countries of surrogacy in such circumstances. It can be argued that, as a matter of sex equality, if single women are not totally barred from parenthood, then neither should single men be so barred.

2.11 We have considered these arguments, but, nevertheless, we believe that as a general rule it is better for children to be born into a two-parent family, with both father and mother, although we recognise that it is impossible to predict with any certainty how lasting such a relationship will be.

---

54 See n 1 above.

Although the Warnock Committee stopped short of making specific recommendations on this point, its attitudes were reflected by the insertion into the HFE Act 1990 of s 13(5), which – as originally drafted – required the clinic, in considering the welfare of the future child, 'to have regard to [its] need . . . for a father'. This provision, with its clear bias against lesbian couples, remained controversial, and in practice was ignored by clinics (as noted in 7.2.2.1 above, the general idea underlying s 13(5) that the potential child's welfare may dictate that it should never exist at all, is implausible save in extreme cases, and the marginal disadvantage (if any) of having two female parents is clearly not one of them).

As one of the 2008 changes to the 1990 Act, this aspect of s 13(5) has now been replaced by the requirement on clinics to take account of the child's need for 'supportive parenting'. This has been elaborated on in para 8.11 of the HFE Authority in its Code of Practice as follows:

HFEA Code of Practice

8.11 When considering a child's need for supportive parenting, centres should consider the following definition:

'Supportive parenting is a commitment to the health, well being and development of the child. It is presumed that all prospective parents will be supportive parents, in the absence of any reasonable cause for concern that any child who may be born, or any other child, may be at risk of significant harm or neglect. Where centres have concern as to whether this commitment exists, they may wish to take account of wider family and social networks within which the child will be raised.'

Also pertinent here is the non-discrimination provision contained in para 8.7 of the Code:

8.7 Those seeking treatment are entitled to a fair assessment. The centre is expected to consider the wishes of all those involved, and the assessment must be done in a non-discriminatory way. In particular, patients should not be discriminated against on grounds of gender, race, disability, sexual orientation, religious belief or age.[55]

As was suggested in 7.2.2.1, in respect of a couple seeking fertility treatment for themselves, an action in judicial review may lie against refusal of treatment by an NHS clinic: see *Ex p Harriott* (1988),[56] and this avenue would clearly be available also to a lesbian couple, seeking treatment with donor sperm. As noted too, following the enactment of the Human Rights Act 1998, the right to found a family – including through recourse to fertility treatment – has been recognised by the courts as protected by the European Convention on Human Rights: *R v SS for the Home Department, ex p Mellor* (2002),[57] and a decision to deny treatment will require justification under Article 8(2) ECHR. In principle, a judicial review action could thus be brought by a single woman – in particular if a clinic were to interpret s 13(5), and its invocation of 'supportive parenting', in such a way as to mandate a refusal of treatment. It is arguable that such a 'blanket approach' to what is already a philosophically shaky provision could not be justified; more defensible, given the general importance attached to motherhood, might be such a policy in respect of single or homosexual males – but here too the arguments are by no means clear-cut.[58]

---

55 See n 14 above.
56 See n 15 above.
57 See n 18 above.
58 An added complication for solely male applicants is their need to use a surrogacy arrangement. Surrogacy is looked at in section 7.5 below.

At the same time, a more general, underlying constraint on the ability of persons to procure fertility treatment should not be forgotten, namely the requirement that they can pay for it. At present, only a minority of clinics offering such treatment are financed as part of the National Health Service, and waiting lists are predictably long. In this regard, the main concern of NHS clinics presented with, for example, a single woman desiring fertility treatment, is likely to be whether their limited resources should be expended on those who are 'socially' as opposed to 'medically' infertile.[59]

7.4.2.2 Counselling and information requirements

As in the case of a couple seeking IVF treatment using their own gametes (see 7.2.2.2), those seeking treatment involving donated gametes are required to be offered counselling pursuant to s 13(6) of the 1990 Act. However, in addition, s 13A will apply, which (in conjunction with Part II of Sch 3ZA) sets out specific counselling and information requirements in cases where the husband or partner of the carrying mother will – in agreeing to her treatment – be signalling their willingness to be a legal parent of the child. Arguably, the need for counselling in such a case is particularly pressing. The parents must of necessity accept the fact of their infertility as a couple and, where the infertility is specifically attributable to one partner, the latter's possible reaction to nurturing a child not genetically his or her own must be canvassed.

In respect of egg donation, which commonly occurs within families (eg between sisters), the identity of the donor will often be known to the nurturing parents. In other cases, they will be provided with non-identifying information that nevertheless gives them an idea of the donor's genetic characteristics. According to the HFE Authority Code of Practice:

HFEA Code of Practice

20.1 The centre should give people seeking treatment with donated gametes or embryos:

  a   non-identifying information about donors whose gametes are available to them, including the goodwill message and the pen-portrait (if available),
  b   relevant information about genetic inheritance and, in particular, the likelihood of inheriting physical characteristics from the donor, and
  c   information about the age of the donor and the associated risks of miscarriage and chromosomal abnormalities.

Under paras 20.3 and 20.4, clinics should also inform the prospective parents of the genetic and other screening that has occurred in relation to the donated gametes (including the limitations on such screening).

A key further issue in this field concerns how the parents later approach the subject of the child's genetic identity with the child. Admittedly this problem does not arise in the increasing proportion of cases where same-sex female couples or single women, make use of gamete donation; here it will be clear to the child that its genetic and nurturing parents differ. However, in cases involving heterosexual couples, the evidence since the enactment of the HFE Act 1990 is

---

59 The prioritising of the clinically infertile is presupposed by the relevant NICE guidance; see *Fertility: assessment and treatment of people with fertility problems* (Clinical Guideline 156, February 2013).

that most parents who make use of such treatment do not tell the child; this is arguably no longer a tenable position, given the recent abolition of donor anonymity (see 7.4.3.2 below), as well as the increasing importance for a person's medical treatment of accurate genetic information derived from their family history.

In this regard, the 2008 changes to the 1990 Act stop short of compelling the nurturing parents to inform the child of the use of donated gametes in its conception – that itself might well be thought an intrusive and heavy-handed approach. However, s 13(6C) places clinics under a duty to make clear to the parents the desirability of being open with their children in this matter:

Conditions of licences for treatment

13 (6C) In the case of treatment services falling within paragraph 1 of Schedule 3ZA (use of gametes of a person not receiving those services) or paragraph 3 of that Schedule (use of embryo taken from a woman not receiving those services), the information provided by virtue of subsection (6) or (6A) must include such information as is proper about –

a   the importance of informing any resulting child at an early age that the child results from the gametes of a person who is not a parent of the child, and

b   suitable methods of informing such a child of that fact.

The HFE Authority's Code of Practice elaborates upon this requirement in paras 20.7 and 20.8, as follows:

HFEA Code of Practice[60]

20.7 The centre should tell people who seek treatment with donated gametes or embryos that it is best for any resulting child to be told about their origin early in childhood. There is evidence that finding out suddenly, later in life, about donor origins can be emotionally damaging to children and to family relations.

20.8 The centre should encourage and prepare patients to be open with their children from an early age about how they were conceived. The centre should give patients information about how counselling may allow them to explore the implications of treatment, in particular how information may be shared with any resultant children.

7.4.2.3 Legal status vis à vis child

It is self-evident that a couple (or, indeed, a single person) that seeks fertility treatment, involving the use of third party gametes/embryos, will be concerned about the legitimacy of any child born as a result. Indeed, the attitude of the law towards this issue may be one of the most significant factors taken into account by would-be nurturing parents when deciding whether to opt for treatment in the first place. The original response of the legislature was contained in ss 27–28 of the HFEA 1990, and these provisions continue to remain valid for parents treated with donated gametes or embryos prior to April 2009. As regards treatment after that date, the new rules, set out in ss 33–47 (comprising the self-standing Part II) of the HFE Act 2008, operate. In what follows we shall consider both the old and new legal positions, but with an emphasis on the innovations (and their rationale), contained in the 2008 Act.

---

60 See n 14 above.

7.4.2.3.1 Legal motherhood

First, as regards motherhood, the effect of s 27 of the 1990 Act was that the woman who received the gametes or embryo, and gestated the child to term, was its legal mother. This applied whether or not she had her treatment in the UK or elsewhere. Conversely, in no case was the egg or embryo donor regarded as the mother. The only ways to effect a subsequent change in status were through adoption proceedings or by obtaining a parental order.

This approach has been re-enacted, in respect of post-April 2009 fertility treatment, by s 33 of the HFE Act 2008:

---

33 Meaning of 'mother'

1   The woman who is carrying or has carried a child as a result of the placing in her of an embryo or of sperm and eggs, and no other woman, is to be treated as the mother of the child.

2   Subsection (1) does not apply to any child to the extent that the child is treated by virtue of adoption as not being the woman's child.

3   Subsection (1) applies whether the woman was in the United Kingdom or elsewhere at the time of the placing in her of the embryo or the sperm and eggs.

By contrast, matters are more complex in relation to determining the child's legal father. Here it is useful to consider the 1990 and 2008 Acts separately, as they bear respectively upon pre- and post-April 2009 instances of collaborative reproduction.

7.4.2.3.2 Fatherhood in cases before April 2009

The rules under s 28 of the HFE Act 1990 drew a distinction according to whether or not the woman treated with donated gametes or embryos was married at the time. If so, under s 28(2) the presumption of legitimacy applied, making her husband the legal father of the child, unless it was shown that he had not consented to the treatment. In respect of unmarried women, s 28(3)(a) conferred fatherhood upon the man together with whom the woman sought out fertility treatment. In other cases, eg where she received the treatment alone, the child would remain legally fatherless: s 28(6) expressly made clear that the donor who provided the sperm was not considered the child's legal father.

The original fatherhood provisions in the 1990 Act occupied the courts on more than one occasion. Thus in the well-known case of *The Leeds Teaching Hospitals NHS Trust v Mr A, Mrs A et al.*,[61] the High Court was required to consider the effect of s 28(2) in circumstances – scarcely foreseeable by the parliamentary draftsman – of a mistake at a fertility clinic, which led to a woman, Mrs A, receiving sperm not as planned from Mr A, her husband, but from a Mr B. For his part, Mr B had given his sperm for the treatment of his wife, Mrs B. In determining the paternity of the resulting twins, Dame Elizabeth Butler-Sloss P held that the mistake as to the identity of the embryos vitiated Mr A's consent so that he was not the father under s 28(2). Instead, Mr B was their father at common law (it would have been otherwise if Mr B had been a sperm donor – there s 28(6)(a) would have removed his paternity; however, he had not consented to the use of his sperm to treat anyone but Mrs B).

Difficulty also arose in relation to s 28(3), with its recourse to the concept of 'treatment services provided for [the woman] and a man together' to impute fatherhood to unmarried partners. In *Evans v Amicus Healthcare Ltd*, Thorpe and Sedley LJJ interpreted this to mean 'the couple are united in their pursuit of treatment, whatever may otherwise be the nature of the relationship between them'.[62] However, the case of *Re D (a child appearing by her guardian ad litem)*

---

61 [2003] EWHC 259 (Fam).
62 See n 25 above (para [29]).

(*Respondent*)[63] highlighted the potential for residual uncertainty. Here a woman received IVF treatment, involving donor sperm at a licensed fertility clinic after she and her partner had provided the requisite consents. She later returned for a further course of treatment, accompanied by a man whom the clinic took to be the original partner (and did not ask to re-consent), but who was in fact a different man. When that treatment resulted in the birth of a child, the original partner argued that, as the consent-provider, he was the baby's father under s 28(3). Though it rejected this contention, the House of Lords noted the Act's vagueness here.

7.4.2.3.3 Fatherhood (and female parenthood) in cases after April 2009

As noted, Part II of the HFE Act 2008 introduced key changes to the law governing the fatherhood (or – in the case of a lesbian couple – 'female parenthood') of children conceived/implanted using donated gametes/embryos after April 2009, in favour of a (ostensibly more rigorous) contract-based approach. As before, in cases where the woman (referred to in the new provisions as 'W') is married at the time of the treatment, her husband will be deemed the father of the child unless it is shown that he did not consent to it. This is the case whether or not the treatment occurred in a licensed clinic. Section 35 of the HFE Act 2008 provides:

---

35 Woman married at time of treatment

1   If –

   a   at the time of the placing in her of the embryo or of the sperm and eggs or of her artificial insemination, W was a party to a marriage, and

   b   the creation of the embryo carried by her was not brought about with the sperm of the other party to the marriage,

   Then . . . the other party to the marriage is to be treated as the father of the child unless it is shown that he did not consent to the placing in her of the embryo or the sperm and eggs or to her artificial insemination (as the case may be).

2   This section applies whether W was in the United Kingdom or elsewhere at the time mentioned in subsection (1)(a).

As regards treatment of an unmarried woman, the 2008 Act has replaced the old test that focused on the man with whom she was 'treated together' by a contractual-style approach in which 'the agreed fatherhood conditions' will be satisfied through the signing by both parties of written notices of consent (prior to the treatment cycle) to the man being treated as the father:

---

36 Treatment provided to woman where agreed fatherhood conditions apply

If no man is treated by virtue of section 35 as the father of the child and no woman is treated by virtue of section 42 as a parent of the child but –

a   the embryo or the sperm and eggs were placed in W, or W was artificially inseminated, in the course of treatment services provided in the United Kingdom by a person to whom a licence applies,

b   at the time when the embryo or the sperm and eggs were placed in W, or W was artificially inseminated, the agreed fatherhood conditions (as set out in section 37) were satisfied in relation to a man, in relation to treatment provided to W under the licence,

---

63 [2005] UKHL 33.

c   the man remained alive at that time, and

d   the creation of the embryo carried by W was not brought about with the man's sperm,

then, subject to section 38(2) to (4), the man is to be treated as the father of the child.

37 The agreed fatherhood conditions

1   The agreed fatherhood conditions referred to in section 36(b) are met in relation to a man ('M') in relation to treatment provided to W under a licence if, but only if, –

    a   M has given the person responsible a notice stating that he consents to being treated as the father of any child resulting from treatment provided to W under the licence,

    b   W has given the person responsible a notice stating that she consents to M being so treated,

    c   neither M nor W has, since giving notice under paragraph (a) or (b), given the person responsible notice of the withdrawal of M's or W's consent to M being so treated,

    d   W has not, since the giving of the notice under paragraph (b), given the person responsible –

        i   a further notice under that paragraph stating that she consents to another man being treated as the father of any resulting child, or

        ii   a notice under section 44(1)(b) stating that she consents to a woman being treated as a parent of any resulting child, and

    e   W and M are not within prohibited degrees of relationship in relation to each other.

As is apparent from s 36(a), a prerequisite for the agreed fatherhood conditions to apply in such a case is that the woman receives treatment in a licensed UK clinic. In this regard, the 2008 Act continues the policy of the 1990 Act in discouraging recourse by single women to 'do-it-yourself' methods of donation, where the legal father would remain the sperm provider at common law. Otherwise, though, the provisions are notable in allowing the woman to select any man she wishes to be the child's father (provided he agrees); there is no requirement that they be living together or, indeed, in any form of relationship. The only limitation, as per s 37(1)(e), is that the man must not be within the prohibited degrees of relationship to her, eg the woman could not choose her brother to be her child's father.

A further innovation in the 2008 Act is to allow legal parenthood in DI cases to be conferred on a second woman (typically the mother's lesbian partner). As with heterosexual couples, the 2008 Act distinguishes between cases where the mother and the other woman are in a legal civil partnership (akin to marriage), and those where they are not. In the former situation, s 42 provides (analogously to s 35 for married women) that the mother's civil partner will automatically be the child's second parent, unless it is shown that she (the civil partner) did not consent to the treatment. In other cases, where there is no civil partnership, the second woman may enjoy legal parenthood subject to the fulfilment of the 'agreed female parenthood conditions' in ss 43–44 of the 2008 Act. These mirror the 'agreed fatherhood conditions' for unmarried men in ss 36–37 of the Act in being based on the existence of written notices of consent from both parties. Here too the rules on prohibited degrees of relationship will apply: thus (under s 44(1)(e)) the mother may not choose, eg, her sister to be the child's second parent.

As noted earlier, the evidence nowadays is that increasingly it is lesbian, rather than heterosexual, couples, who are the main recipients of treatment with donated gametes and, in this regard, the 2008 Act may be seen as incorporating timely changes that reflect modern social attitudes. At the same time the legislation holds fast to the traditional idea that a child can have no more than two parents. Julie McCandless and Sally Sheldon have commented upon this aspect as follows:

McCandless, J and Sheldon, S, 'The human fertilisation and embryology act (2008) and the tenacity of the sexual family form'[64]

The two parent model retains a grip on the law which appears to have out lived any inevitable relationship between legal parenthood and either biological fact or marital convention. Significantly, while the reform of section 13(5) ensured that there was sustained attention to the question of whether a child could flourish equally well without a father (either in a single parent family or raised by a same sex couple), this reform process saw no discussion of the question of whether, if two parents are better than one, three parents might be better than (or, at least, as good as) two. In other contexts, family law has developed increasingly flexible and creative ways of recognising a range of adults as of significance to a child. To take just two examples: parental responsibility can be awarded to any number of adults and current adoption practice seeks to maintain links with birth parents alongside those with legal/social parents. Yet it seems that notwithstanding this greater flexibility, there remains something special about the legal status of parent and registration as such on a birth certificate. The question of whether, in certain circumstances, more than two parents might be legally recognised was raised by just one respondent early in the Government consultation process regarding how the 1990 Act should be reformed and, although noted in two consecutive interventions in the House of Lords debates, was not subject to any further elaboration. . . . [T]he Department of Health told us that they had mooted the possibility of a child having three legal parents in the early stages of the reform process and discussed it with the Office for National Statistics. The idea was rejected on the basis that the consequences of such a change were too far reaching and controversial, potentially 'hijacking' the reform process and jeopardising the Bill.

In the context of lesbian relationships, where couples might consider having one partner provide the egg and – following IVF using donated sperm – the other carry the embryo to term, it is apparent from s 33 of the 2008 Act that the latter alone will be the child's mother. As s 47 makes clear, the egg provider may be the second female parent, but only where she is the mother's civil partner, or the agreed female parenthood conditions are met:

47 Woman not to be other parent merely because of egg donation

A woman is not to be treated as the parent of a child whom she is not carrying and has not carried, except where she is so treated –

a   by virtue of section 42 or 43, ...

Unfortunately, despite the aim of the 2008 changes to put the legal relation of the couple having treatment and the resulting child on a more certain footing, in practice it has rather had the opposite effect. In particular, Parliament, in providing for a bureaucratic scheme of multiple consents forms, underestimated the potential for human failure in its day-to-day administration. This came to light following a 2013 HFE Authority audit of UK fertility clinics, showing nearly half of them had failed to keep proper records of the relevant consents. As noted, by the President of the Family Division in the case of *Re A & 7 others (Human Fertilisation and Embryology Act)*,[65] the implications are disturbing:

Sir James Munby P: [3] The question of who, in law, is or are the parent(s) of a child born as a result of treatment carried out under this legislation – the issue which confronts me here – is dealt with in Part 2, sections 33–47, of the 2008 Act. It is, as a moment's reflection will make obvious, a question of the most

64 (2010) 73 MLR 175.
65 [2015] EWHC 2602 (Fam).

fundamental gravity and importance. What, after all, to any child, to any parent, never mind to future generations and indeed to society at large, can be more important, emotionally, psychologically, socially and legally, than the answer to the question: Who is my parent? Is this my child?

... [5] ... [T]he relevant statutory requirements [contain] two fundamental prerequisites to the acquisition of parenthood by the partner of a woman receiving such treatment. First, consents must be given in writing *before* the treatment, both by the woman and by her partner. The forms required for this in accordance with directions given by the [HFE Authority] are Form WP, to be completed by the woman, and Form PP, to be completed by her partner. Secondly, both the woman and her partner must be given adequate information and offered counselling.

[6] ... The alarming outcome [of the Authority's audit] was the discovery that no fewer than 51 clinics (46%) had discovered "anomalies" in their records: WP or PP forms absent from the records; WP or PP forms being completed or dated *after* the treatment had begun; incorrectly completed WP or PP forms (for example, forms not signed, not fully completed, completed by the wrong person or with missing pages); and absence of evidence of any offer of counselling ...

... [8] The picture thus revealed ... is alarming and shocking. ... [It] is one of what I do not shrink from describing as widespread incompetence across the sector on a scale which must raise questions as to the adequacy if not of the [Authority]'s regulation then of the extent of its regulatory powers. That the incompetence to which I refer is, as I have already indicated, administrative rather than medical is only slight consolation, given the profound implications of the parenthood which in far too many cases has been thrown into doubt ...

Following the above decision, there has been a stream of further applications in which the High Court has been asked to exercise its power to make declarations of legal parenthood, so as to make good shortcomings of fertility clinics in observing formalities of the 2008 Act.[66]

7.4.3 The gamete donors

The ethical and legal issues in relation to the third-party donors who provide their gametes in order for others to be treated may conveniently be divided into two parts. First, how should they be treated at the initial point of recruitment and, secondly, what role, if any, should they be accorded after the birth of any child which, genetically, is theirs?

7.4.3.1 Recruitment, screening and information issues

As countenanced by the HFE Act 1990, the recruitment of gamete donors in the UK originally took place under a significant shroud of secrecy, at least as regard sperm donation, whose main source was students in medical schools. The policy of according donors anonymity was based on a recommendation of the Warnock Report, which was concerned that, otherwise, men might be put off from being donors, thus placing the DI programme in jeopardy (as regards egg donation – which entails some discomfort and risk – anonymity has generally been less of an issue: the donor was often someone known to the infertile woman, such as a sister, wishing to help for altruistic reasons).

---

66 See, *inter alia, Re Human Fertilisation & Embryology Act 2008 (Case G)* [2016] EWHC 729 (Fam); *Re Human Fertilisation & Embryology Act 2008 (Case I)* [2016] EWHC 791 (Fam); *Re P & 5 others (Human Fertilisation & Embryology Act 2008) (No 2)* [2017] EWHC 2532 (Fam).

As discussed further under section 7.4.4, the policy of donor anonymity was abandoned in April 2005 as no longer consonant with modern perceptions of the interests of children, conceived in this way, in knowing of their genetic identity. Interestingly, contrary to the original fears, the statistics in relation to gamete donation collected by the HFE Authority show a significant increase since then in the number of registered donors (both male and female).[67] Added to that is the point, noted in section 7.4.1, that today donated gametes play less of a role (both in absolute and relative terms) in fertility treatment, due to scientific advances in helping (heterosexual) couples conceive using their own gametes.

Subject to any lower limit specified by the donor, his or her gametes may be used to conceive children for up to ten families.[68] As regards the matter of paying gamete donors, s 12 of the HFE Act 1990 (as amended) states:

12 General conditions

(1) The following shall be conditions of any licence granted under this Act –

. . . (e) that no money or other benefit shall be given or received in respect of any supply of gametes, embryos or human admixed embryos unless authorised by Directions . . .

In the past, Directions (issued by the HFE Authority) provided for a standard payment of £15 per donation; however, since 2006 this is no longer so.[69] The present Directions merely allow compensation for reasonable out-of-pocket expenses (such as the standard costs of travelling to the clinic). Nonetheless, egg donors may still receive a very considerable benefit in kind, in terms of receiving their own IVF treatment at a reduced rate. The pros and cons of this practice (known as 'egg sharing') were considered in the 'SEED Report', undertaken by the HFE Authority in 2006, which concluded that, though not free from difficulty, it was on balance justified in order to ensure an adequate supply of eggs:

SEED Report – *A report on the Human Fertilisation & Embryology Authority's review of sperm, egg and embryo donation in the United Kingdom*[70]

6.10 Many opponents of egg sharing clearly regard the value of the compensation offered to the egg provider as equivalent to a substantial payment amounting to a significant inducement to her to give up her eggs. One way of stating this argument is that the offer of discounted treatment encourages the egg provider to ignore the consequences and possible risks of donation and therefore invalidates her consent to the procedure. However, if an egg provider's judgement were really obscured by the promise of free treatment, one might expect to find evidence of people complaining about this afterwards, or at least that some egg providers later regret giving up their eggs.

6.11 Such evidence is scant, but even where it does exist this might not be a decisive objection, as long as the majority derive considerable benefit from the procedure (and as long as every effort has been made to ensure that their consent is properly informed and their choice is uncoerced). The argument that almost any adverse consequence is sufficient to prohibit a practice which brings great general benefit seems disproportionate. In any case, subsequent regret is not in itself evidence of vitiated

---

67 See 'new donor registrations 1992–2008', at: www.hfea.gov.uk/3411.html.
68 HFEA Code of Practice 8th edn (2009), para 11.35.
69 Policy changed following the recommendations of the SEED Report, n 70 below.
70 HFEA: London, 2005. The full report is available at: www.hfea.gov.uk/docs/ SEEDReport05.pdf.

> consent (people often freely do things which they later wish they had not done) and may often have more to do with people's changing values than the impairment of their judgement or the constraint of their consent.
>
> ... 6.14 Having debated these and many other arguments at length, it is our view that the opponents of compensated egg sharing have not succeeded in arguing that the alleged harms are proximate, likely or significant enough to amount to a sufficient or compelling reason to prohibit the practice. Having said this, we acknowledge that it will remain necessary to ensure that egg sharing, whether compensated or not, is managed in such a way as to minimise the acknowledged potential for adverse effects for those involved. We intend to keep egg sharing in general under review, in particular evidence of the emotional consequences for women participating in egg sharing arrangements, about which there is as yet little available.

In fact, recently there have been renewed concerns in the light of newspaper evidence that, in certain clinics, exploitative practices may indeed be taking root.[71]

Other significant issues concern the screening and informing of donors. The need for enquiry into the donor's medical history, and testing of the gametes, so as to reduce the risk to the recipient woman and/or potential children from infectious disease or genetic defects is clear, and is the subject of detailed guidance in the current Code of Practice (at paras 11.07–11.14). However, matters are more complex when it comes to the screening/selection of donors for their positive attributes. The Warnock Report in 1984 commented unfavourably upon the practice, in parts of the USA, of offering the nurturing parents a choice of donors, as follows:

Warnock Committee, *Report of the Committee of Inquiry into Human Fertilisation and Embryology*[72]

> 4.19 It is the practice of some clinics in the USA to provide detailed descriptions of donors, and to permit couples to exercise choice as to the donor they would prefer. In the evidence there was some support for the use of such descriptions. It is argued that they would provide information and reassurance for the parents and, at a later date, for the child. They might also be of benefit to the donor, as an indication that he is valued for his own sake. A detailed description also offers some choice to the woman who is to have the child, and lack of such choice can be said to diminish the importance of the woman's right to choose the father of her child.
>
> 4.20 The contrary view, also expressed in the evidence, is that detailed donor profiles would introduce the donor as a person in his own right. It is also argued that the use of profiles devalues the child who may seem to be wanted only if certain specifications are met, and this may become a source of disappointment to the parents if their expectations are unfulfilled.

The Committee instead felt that information provided to the rearing parent(s) should be limited to that needed for their reassurance, such as the donor's ethnic group and genetic health (para 4.21). This is an issue on which the HFE Authority, for its part, has vacillated over the years. In its current Code of Practice, however, it is operating a more liberal policy, advising clinics to 'encourage prospective donors to provide as much other non-identifying biographical information as possible', to pass on to the parents and resulting children.[73]

---

71 See: www.hfea.gov.uk/about-us/news-and-press-releases/2017-news-and-press-releases/hfea-statement-regarding-the-daily-mail-investigation/.
72 See n 1 above.
73 See n 14 above, recommendation 11.09.

For their part, donors should also receive full information at the time of giving their consent to the extraction and use of their gametes (under Sch 3 para 5 of the HFE Act 1990 (as amended)). The HFE Authority Code elaborates upon this requirement at 11.34, listing 15 heads of relevant information, including:

HFEA Code of Practice[74]

11.34 Before any consents or samples are obtained from a prospective donor, the recruiting centre should provide information about:

a   the screening that will be done, and why it is necessary

b   the possibility that the screening may reveal unsuspected conditions (eg, low sperm count, genetic anomalies or HIV infection) and the practical implications

c   the scope and limitations of the genetic testing that will be done and the implications for the donor and their family

d   the importance of informing the recruiting centre of any medical information that may come to light after donation that may have health implications for any woman who receives treatment with those gametes or for any child born as a result of such treatment

e   the procedure used to collect gametes, including any discomfort, pain and risk to the donor (eg, from the use of superovulatory drugs)

f   the legal parenthood of any child born as a result of their donation

. . . .

Where a would-be donor is considered unsuitable to donate, paras 11.28–11.29 of the Code state that they should receive a sensitive explanation as to the reasons, as well as an offer of counselling.

7.4.3.2 Legal status and contact in respect of resulting children

As we saw in section 7.4.2, the effect of the parenthood rules in ss 33–47 HFE Act 2008 (and for pre-2009 births, ss 27–28 of the 1990 Act) is that all parental rights and obligations, in relation to children born out of licensed DI treatment, inhere in the recipient(s) of the gametes, not the donor(s). This is also the default position in cases of non-licensed treatment (where the donors are known to the recipients), so far as the recipients are married or in a civil partnership. However, in the latter case, the gamete data may – with the leave of the court – apply in appropriate circumstances for a parental order under s 8 of the Children Act 1989.[75]

Issues also arise in relation to managing other aspects of the relationship between the donor and the child conceived with his or her gametes. First and foremost, should they be made aware of each other's identity at all? Originally, as noted in 7.4.3.1, the HFE Act 1990 incorporated a policy of donor anonymity: though the HFE Authority has from the outset been required to include information in its register, linking gamete providers with resulting children, the latter's access to this information was previously strictly controlled. As further discussed in section 7.4.4,

---

74 See n 14 above.
75 See *Re G (Children)* [2013] EWHC 134 (Fam).

this changed with the enactment of the HFE (Disclosure of Donor Information) Regulations 2004:[76] for gamete donations prior to April 2005, these allowed detailed information about the donor to be provided to the child, albeit not such as would identify the donor (this reflected s 31(5) of the 1990 Act, which stipulated that regulations could not retrospectively require a donor's identity to be divulged – ie where he had donated under the assumption of anonymity). By contrast, children born from gametes donated after 31 March 2005, were given the right, on reaching 18, to discover the identity of the donor.

These changes have been built upon further in the 2008 amendments to the 1990 Act, which for the first time also accord donors the right to some information concerning children born using their gametes. Pursuant to s 31ZD of the 1990 Act (as amended):

31ZD Provision to donor of information about resulting children

(1) This section applies where a person ('the donor') has consented under Schedule 3 (whether before or after the coming into force of this section) to –

a   the use of the donor's gametes, or an embryo the creation of which was brought about using the donor's gametes, for the purposes of treatment services provided under a licence, . . .

. . . (3) The donor may by notice request the appropriate person to give the donor notice stating –

a   the number of persons of whom the donor is not a parent but would or might, but for the relevant statutory provisions, be a parent by virtue of the use of the gametes or embryos to which the consent relates,

b   the sex of each of those persons, and

c   the year of birth of each of those persons.

As is apparent, the above does not entitle donors to receive identifying information in respect of children conceived with their gametes. The only way they could learn the specific identity of such a child is if the latter (where conceived after March 2005) were later to access the register and initiate contact: this is discussed in section 7.4.4 below.

Finally, it should be noted that the HFE legislation provides that, in certain circumstances, the donor may potentially be liable to the child in a civil action for damages. The details of when this might be the case are considered further under 7.4.4.2.

7.4.4 The child

7.4.4.1 Establishing genetic identity

It is apparent from the foregoing discussion that, while in 1990 the law gave a nod to the interests of prospective children (in s 13(5) of the HFEA 1990), these were until recently largely subordinated to those of the other key players in the collaborative reproductive process, that is the nurturing parents and gamete providers. In particular, the latter parties' interests in preserving anonymity/confidentiality were allowed to prevail over any interest the child might have in knowing of its provenance. In fact, even prior to the original HFE Act, the Glover Report had commented on the potentially deleterious psychological consequences of policy of anonymity for the child as follows:

76 SI 2004/1511.

Glover, J et al., *Report to the European Commission on Reproductive Technologies, Fertility and the Family*[77]

> Our sense of who we are is bound up with the story we tell about ourselves. A life where the biological parents are unknown is like a novel with the first chapter missing. Also there are the marked similarities between children and their biological parents. The child may wonder who is the person, perhaps among those passed in the street, who has that degree of closeness.
>
> On the other hand, for young children who know who the semen donor was, there may be problems about their identity. They may see neither person as being unambiguously their father. This suggests that it may not be in the children's interest to be told who the donor is at an early age, but is not a point against a system of the Swedish type, setting the right to know at the age of 18. And, since the legal right to know need not be exercised, no child loses anything by it. Since some people care so much about their origins, seeing them as an important part of their identity, the interests of the children count strongly in favour of the right to know . . .

In the wake of the enactment of the Human Rights Act 1998, the question also arose more directly as to whether the policy of donor anonymity was compatible with the ECHR rights of children conceived with donated gametes. This was partially tested in the case of *Rose and Another v Secretary of State for Health*,[78] in which two 'DI children' obtained a declaration that their interest in obtaining information about the sperm donor engaged Article 8 of the ECHR. Scott Baker J commented:

> **Scott Baker J**: [47] It is to my mind entirely understandable that [DI] children should wish to know about their origins and in particular to learn what they can about their biological father or, in the case of egg donation, their biological mother. The extent to which this matters will vary from individual to individual. In some instances, as in the case of the Claimant Joanna Rose, the information will be of massive importance. I do not find this at all surprising bearing in mind the lessons that have been learnt from adoption. A human being is a human being whatever the circumstances of his conception and a [DI] child is entitled to establish a picture of his identity as much as anyone else. We live in a much more open society than even 20 years ago. Secrecy nowadays has to be justified where previously it did not.

Though the court was not asked to decide the further question of whether anonymity could be justified under Article 8(2) ECHR (as necessary to protect the donor's rights, etc), the Government decided shortly afterwards to abandon the previous policy. As noted in section 7.4.3.2, this occurred through Regulations enacted in 2004, and this shift has since been cemented (and expanded on) by the 2008 amendments to the HFE Act 1990.

The relevant section of the HFE Act 1990 (as amended) now provides as follows:

> **31ZA Request for information as to genetic parentage etc.**
>
> 1   A person who has attained the age of 16 ('the applicant') may by notice to the Authority require the Authority to comply with a request under subsection (2).
> 2   The applicant may request the Authority to give the applicant notice stating whether or not the information contained in the register shows that a person ('the donor') other than a parent of the applicant

---

77 See n 4 above.
78 [2002] EWHC 1593 (Admin).

would or might, but for the relevant statutory provisions, be the parent of the applicant, and if it does show that –

a   giving the applicant so much of that information as relates to the donor as the Authority is required by regulations to give (but no other information), or

b   stating whether or not that information shows that there are other persons of whom the donor is not the parent but would or might, but for the relevant statutory provisions, be the parent and if so –

    i   the number of those other persons,

    ii   the sex of each of them, and

    iii   the year of birth of each of them.

3   The Authority shall comply with a request under subsection (2) if –

a   the information contained in the register shows that the applicant is a relevant individual, and

b   the applicant has been given a suitable opportunity to receive proper counselling about the implications of compliance with the request.

4   Where a request is made under subsection (2)(a) and the applicant has not attained the age of 18 when the applicant gives notice to the Authority under subsection (1), regulations can not require the Authority to give the applicant any information which identifies the donor.

5   Regulations cannot require the Authority to give any information as to the identity of a person whose gametes have been used or from whom an embryo has been taken if a person to whom a licence applied was provided with the information at a time when the Authority could not have been required to give information of the kind in question.

The effect of these provisions is that children aged 16 or over may request detailed non-identifying information about the donor held by the HFE Authority. For children born using gametes donated after 31 March 2005 (the date specified in the 2004 Regulations), the donor's identity itself can be revealed once they reach the age of 18. By contrast, as s 31ZA(5) makes clear, children conceived with gametes donated before this date will not normally be entitled to identifying information: as noted in section 7.4.3(b) this is to protect the donor's legitimate expectation of anonymity at the time they donated.[79]

It is now also possible, pursuant to s 31ZE of the HFE Act 1990 (as amended), for DI children aged 18 or above to obtain identifying information as to their genetic half-siblings (ie other children conceived using gametes from the same donor), subject to the half-sibling agreeing to the release of this information. Excluded from this section, though, are situations where the half-sibling is the donor's own legitimate child. Clearly, one circumstance in which it will be of particular importance for half-siblings to be aware of each other's identity is where there is otherwise a risk of them entering into an incestuous relationship. This is catered for specifically by s 31ZB (which re-enacts provisions already contained in the original 1990 Act), as follows:

31ZB Request for information as to intended spouse etc.

1   Subject to subsection (4), a person ('the applicant') may by notice to the Authority require the Authority to comply with a request under subsection (2).

2   The applicant may request the Authority to give the applicant notice stating whether or not information contained in the register shows that, but for the relevant statutory provisions, the applicant would or might be related to a person specified in the request ('the specified person') as –

a   a person whom the applicant proposes to marry,

b   a person with whom the applicant proposes to enter into a civil partnership, or

c   a person with whom the applicant is in an intimate physical relationship or with whom the applicant proposes to enter into an intimate physical relationship.

---

79 Though if they wish, pre-April 2005 donors can register themselves as identifiable under s 31ZF of the HFE Act 1990 (as amended).

Here the information may be disclosed (subject to the other party's consent) to applicants from the age of 16 upwards, and may (in contrast to s 31ZE) extend to parties who are the donor's legitimate children. On the other hand, this section – as indeed do the rest of the information access provisions under the Act – presupposes that the DI child is aware he or she was conceived in this way in the first place and, as we saw in 7.4.2.2, this may often not be the case.

7.4.4.2 Redress against the gamete donor

In one situation, even in 1990, it was contemplated that full disclosure (that is, which identifies the individual gamete donor) could occur, namely in prospect of a legal suit by the child against the donor. In this regard, s 35 of the 1990 Act (as amended) provides:

35 Disclosure in interests of justice: congenital disabilities, etc

(1) Where for the purpose of instituting proceedings under section 1 of the Congenital Disabilities (Civil Liability) Act 1976 (civil liability to child born disabled) it is necessary to identify a person who would or might be the parent of a child but for the relevant statutory provisions, the court may, on the application of the child, make an order requiring the Authority to disclose any information contained in the register kept in pursuance of section 31 of this Act identifying that person.

... (2A) In subsection (1) ... 'the relevant statutory provisions' means –

a   sections 27 to 29 of this Act, and

b   sections 33 to 47 of the Human Fertilisation and Embryology Act 2008.

Such disclosure is part of a cluster of provisions designed to afford remedies to children injured prenatally in the course of fertility treatment provided to one or both of their parents. Gillian Douglas explains the effect of these provisions as follows:

Douglas, G, *Law, Fertility and Reproduction*[80]

English law does not usually permit a child to bring an action for 'wrongful life' which is a claim that he or she should never have been born. However, a handicapped child who claims that his or her birth resulted from defective gametes being used, or a defective embryo being wrongly transferred, has now been given a right of action under [s 1A of] the Congenital Disabilities (Civil Liability) Act 1976, which was originally enacted to deal with cases concerning prenatal injury.

That legislation was amended by the 1990 Act, to make clear that a child may sue under it where he or she is born disabled, and the disability results from an act or omission in course of the selection, or the keeping or use outside the body, of the embryo ... or of the gametes used to bring about the creation of the embryo ...

Where the *donor* of the gametes fails to reveal infection or genetic disease, it will be more difficult for the child to bring a claim. Of course, in most cases, there would be no advantage to the child to sue the donor rather than the doctor, who will carry insurance. But where a condition cannot be revealed by testing, so that the doctor would not be at fault, the child might wish to seek redress from the donor. The anonymity of the donor may in such a case be overridden, by the child applying to the court for an order under s 35 ...

---

80 London: Sweet & Maxwell, 1991.

As Douglas notes, the existence of such a remedy is not without its puzzles: in particular affording a remedy to a child who, but for the relevant impugned conduct, would not have been conceived, appears vulnerable to philosophical objections – and the problem of quantifying loss – identified by the Court of Appeal in its 'wrongful life' judgment in *Mackay v Essex AHA*.[81] To date, however, the point remains untested, as a claim using the section has yet to be brought.

See Chapter 8 →

THINK POINT

Are the new parenthood provisions in the HFE Act 2008, really much of an improvement over the rules found in the HFE Act 1990?

7.5 Surrogacy

7.5.1 Background

Surrogacy describes the practice whereby one woman (the 'surrogate mother') agrees to carry a child on behalf of another person or couple ('the commissioning parent(s)'), with the intention that, following birth, it will be handed over to the latter for nurturing. Most often, the commissioning parents will be a heterosexual couple, where the female partner is unable to bear children. However, in principle, a single person or homosexual couple could also make use of the practice. While often the surrogate mother will expect to be paid for her services, this is not always true: sometimes 'altruistic surrogacy' occurs, such as where a woman agrees to carry a child for her infertile sister.

A further distinction that is often drawn is between cases of 'partial' (or genetic) and 'total' (or gestational) surrogacy: in the former, the surrogate mother is inseminated with sperm from the commissioning father, and will thus herself be the genetic mother of the child. By contrast, in gestational surrogacy, another woman's egg will be used, usually from the commissioning mother (if she is able to produce one), which is then implanted in the surrogate following IVF. In this situation, the surrogate will be the gestational mother, but not genetically related to the child.

The number of surrogacy arrangements in the UK remains small (constituting a tiny proportion of licensed fertility treatment overall): figures from the HFE Authority show that, from 2007 to 2012, the annual mean was about 30 live births from surrogacy, around two-thirds of which involved the total or gestational kind.[82] Nonetheless, the practice has long excited a disproportionate amount of ethical and legal controversy. In 1984 the Warnock Report made clear its hostility to surrogacy, including on deontological grounds: 'that people should treat others as a means to their own ends, however desirable the consequences, must always be liable to moral objection' (para 8.17). A few years later Glover, reporting to the EC Commission, provided a summary of the main arguments for and against the practice, as follows:

---

81 [1982] QB 1166; see Ch 8, section 8.4, below.
82 See: http://hfeaarchive.uksouth.cloudapp.azure.com/www.hfea.gov.uk/8492.html. Admittedly, the overall number of such arrangements, including partial surrogacy following (unlicensed) DIY insemination, is likely to be rather higher.

Glover, J et al., *Report to the European Commission on Reproductive Technologies, Fertility and the Family*[83]

1 The case for surrogacy

Part of the case is straightforward. Surrogacy relieves childlessness. For women who have had repeated miscarriages, or who suffer from conditions making pregnancy dangerous, surrogacy may be the only hope of having a child.

Another, more problematic, argument appeals to the interests of the child who would not have existed without surrogacy.

Another argument appeals to liberty. Some strong justification is needed for preventing people from bearing children to help their sisters or friends. And a similar strong justification is needed for preventing people freely contracting to do this for someone for money. This argument relates to the legality of surrogacy, but does nothing to show that surrogacy is a good thing in itself. The central case for that has to rest on relieving the burden of childlessness.

2 The case against surrogacy

(a) *The children*: One line of thought appeals to the rights of the child. It appears in the Catholic document issued by the Congregation for the Doctrine of the Faith, which says that surrogacy 'offends the dignity and the right of the child to be conceived, carried in the womb, brought into the world and brought up by his own parents'.

This case seems to us not overwhelming. Even if the child has a strong interest in being created sexually, to call this a right is to claim that it trumps any interests of the childless couple. This requires that being the child of a surrogate is such an indignity that, by comparison, relieving any degree of the potential parents' misery is to count for nothing. We have not found the powerful supporting argument this would need.

The objection is made even weaker by a further problem. For the potential child, the alternative to surrogacy may be non-existence. It seems unlikely that the child will see surrogacy as so bad as to wish he or she had not been born at all. The 'right' looks like one the child will later be glad was not respected. It is hard to see the case for giving this supposed interest any weight at all, let alone for saying that it justifies leaving people unwillingly childless.

Another argument appeals to the psychological effects of surrogacy on the child. If the surrogacy is paid for there is a danger that the child will think he or she has been bought. Also, it is sometimes suggested that surrogacy breaks a bond formed by the time of birth. Dr John Marks, the chairman of the British Medical Association, has said: 'By the time a baby is born there is a bond between the mother and the child. With surrogacy you break that bond. You are depriving the child of one natural parent. We think that is wrong'. ((1987) *The Guardian*, 8 May) . . .

The surrogate mother may well feel a bond between herself and the child. But is there reason to believe in any bond in the other direction before birth? Or could this be an illusion created by projecting the mother's feelings on to the foetus? If the child's feelings are a reason against surrogacy, the baby has to have, by the time of birth, highly specific feelings towards the particular woman who bears him. The evidence for this can charitably be described as slight.

Suppose, for the sake of argument, that there is such a bond. It is then undesirable to break it. But, where it is broken, is the child so harmed that it would have been better if he or she had not been born? For this is what banning surrogacy on these grounds seems to imply. We do not have such drastic thoughts about people who are adopted. The British Medical Association's Board of Science is quoted as saying that

---

83 See n 4 above.

while adoption may be 'the next best thing' for a child facing an uncertain future, any arrangement where a surrogate mother hands over the child 'dooms it to second best from the start' ((1987) *The Independent*, 8 May). But is it obvious here that no life at all is preferable to 'second best'?

(b) *Conflicts*: The conflicts sometimes arising between the potential parents and the surrogate mother may harm the child, and this is part of the case against surrogacy.

(c) *Effects on the family*: Perhaps introducing a third party so intimately into the process of having children may weaken the institution of the family . . .

(d) *The surrogate mother*: The position of the surrogate mother varies, according to whether she is bearing a child to help a sister or friend, or has made a commercial arrangement. There is the criticism that surrogacy is an invasion of her bodily integrity. This criticism may be weaker if she willingly agreed than if she was forced into it by money problems. Sometimes she may bitterly regret having agreed to give away the baby. As we have seen, there is a danger of her being exploited. Financial pressures may put her in a weak position to resist contractual conditions which give little weight to her interests.

Another important motive for volunteering to act as a surrogate seems to be the desire for friendship with the parents-to-be. As this is usually exactly what the parents-to-be do not want, it is an illusory objective. She wants friendship: she is treated as a provider of a service, and afterwards dismissed . . .

At the same time, it is important to keep the questions of the moral and legal permissibility of surrogacy separate. For its part, the law must distinguish in its response between two different moments in time; it must first determine how far it is legitimate to discourage, or indeed prohibit, the formation of surrogacy arrangements in the first place. Secondly, however, in so far as its strictures at this earlier stage are ignored and a surrogacy arrangement results in pregnancy, the law must attribute rights and duties to the participants and, if they are in dispute, adjudicate between them. In doing so, of course, the position of any resulting child must be resolved. These two distinct stages were recognised by Latey J in one of the first surrogacy cases to reach the English courts:

Re C (A Minor) (Wardship: Surrogacy)[84]

A partial surrogacy arrangement, negotiated by an agency, was entered into between an American commissioning couple and a British woman, Kim Cotton (who was married with three children of her own). Following the successful birth of a child, it was clear that Mrs Cotton was happy to relinquish all parental rights in respect of it. The commissioning father issued a wardship summons in order to obtain custody, which was duly granted:

Latey J: First and foremost, and at the heart of the prerogative jurisdiction in wardship, is what is best for the child or children concerned. That and nothing else. Plainly the methods used to produce a child, as this baby has been, and the commercial aspects of it, raise difficult and delicate problems of ethics, morality and social desirability. These problems are under active consideration elsewhere.

Are they relevant in arriving at a decision on what now and, so far as one can tell, in the future is best for this child? If they are relevant, it is incumbent on the court to do its best to evaluate and balance them.

In my judgment, however, they are not relevant. The baby is here. All that matters is what is best for her now that she is here and not how she arrived. If it be said (though it has not been

---

84 [1985] FLR 846.

said during these hearings) that because the father and his wife entered into these arrangements it is some indication of their unsuitability as parents, I should reject any such suggestion. If what they did was wrong (and I am not saying that it was), they did it in total innocence. . . .

So, what is best for this baby? Her natural mother does not ask for her. Should she go into Mr and Mrs A's care and be brought up by them? Or should some other arrangement be made for her, such as long term fostering with or without adoption as an end?

The factors can be briefly stated. Mr A is the baby's father and he wants her, as does his wife. The baby's mother does not want her. Mr and Mrs A are a couple in their 30s. They are devoted to each other. They are both professional people, highly qualified. They have a very nice home in the country and another in a town. Materially they can give the baby a very good upbringing. But, far more importantly, they are both excellently equipped to meet the baby's emotional needs. They are most warm, caring, sensible people, as well as highly intelligent. When the time comes to answer the child's questions, they will be able to do so with professional advice if they feel they need it. Looking at this child's well being, physical and emotional, who better to have her care? No one.

Clearly, the two stages are often not separate in practice: the anticipated response of the law at the second stage will almost certainly have an impact on the parties' decision to risk entering into the arrangement in the first place. Nevertheless, for expository purposes, it is useful to look at each in turn.

7.5.2 Entering into surrogacy arrangements

Following adverse media reaction to the *Re C* case, and in the light of the recommendations of the Warnock Committee, Parliament enacted the Surrogacy Arrangements Act (SAA) 1985:

1 Meaning of 'surrogate mother', 'surrogacy arrangement' and other terms

1 The following provisions shall have effect for the interpretation of this Act.
2 'Surrogate mother' means a woman who carries a child in pursuance of an arrangement –
    a made before she began to carry the child, and
    b made with a view to any child carried in pursuance of it being handed over to, and the parental rights being exercised (so far as practicable) by, another person or other persons.
3 An arrangement is a surrogacy arrangement if, were a woman to whom the arrangement relates to carry a child in pursuance of it, she would be a surrogate mother.

. . .

1A Surrogacy arrangements unenforceable

No surrogacy arrangement is enforceable by or against any of the persons making it.

2 Negotiating surrogacy arrangements on a commercial basis, etc

(1) No person shall on a commercial basis do any of the following acts in the United Kingdom, that is –
    (a) initiate any negotiations with a view to the making of a surrogacy arrangement;
    (aa) take part in any negotiations with a view to the making of a surrogacy arrangement,
    (b) offer or agree to negotiate the making of a surrogacy arrangement; or
    (c) compile any information with a view to its use in making, or negotiating the making of, surrogacy arrangements,
    and no person shall in the United Kingdom knowingly cause another to do any of those acts on a commercial basis.

(2)   A person who contravenes sub-s (1) above is guilty of an offence; but it is not a contravention of that sub-section –

   a   for a woman, with a view to becoming a surrogate mother herself, to do any act mentioned in that sub-section or to cause such an act to be done; or

   b   for any person, with a view to a surrogate mother carrying a child for him, to do such an act or to cause such an act to be done.

(2A) A non-profit making body does not contravene subsection (1) merely because –

   a   the body does an act falling within subsection (1)(a) or (c) in respect of which any reasonable payment is at any time received by it or another, or

   b   it does an act falling within subsection (1)(a) or (c) with a view to any reasonable payment being received by it or another in respect of facilitating the making of any surrogacy arrangement.

. . . (2C) Any reference in subsection (2A) or (2B) to a reasonable payment in respect of the doing of an act by a non-profit making body is a reference to a payment not exceeding the body's costs reasonably attributable to the doing of the act.

Here s 1A, which provides that a surrogacy arrangement will be void (as a contract in private law), was inserted in 1990 by an amending section in the original HFE Act. Otherwise, though, the main thrust of the 1985 Act – in terms of the criminal prohibitions in s 2 – is against the commercial facilitators of surrogacy arrangements, notably agencies which profit from brokering between the commissioning couple and potential surrogate. In this regard, s 3 of the Act extends liability to the advertisement of their services.

By contrast, under s 2(2), immunity from criminal liability is conferred upon the immediate parties to the arrangement, viz. the surrogate mother and commissioning couple (as per the rules of statutory interpretation, the reference to 'him' in s 2(2)(b) includes 'her'). Moreover, under s 2(3), the payment of monies to the surrogate herself is not unlawful. This reflected the view of the Warnock Committee that it would be undesirable for the birth of a child through surrogacy to be tainted with criminality. In addition, the operation of charitable brokering organisations in this field has not been prohibited. Indeed, their position has recently been strengthened by the insertion of s 2(2A)–(2C) into the Act (by s 59 of the HFE Act 2008), permitting them to charge a fee for their reasonable expenses.

It is important to note too that the 1985 Act is not aimed at doctors (or fertility clinics) who receive a fee for medically facilitating a surrogate pregnancy by carrying out IVF or DI treatment on the surrogate. Accordingly (assuming the clinic has the appropriate licence to carry out such treatment under the HFE legislation), they would commit no offence. Indeed, the provision of medical treatment ancillary to surrogacy has increasingly gained acceptance within the medical profession: thus, the BMA in its report, *Changing Conceptions of Motherhood, The Practice of Surrogacy in Britain*,[85] has recognised surrogacy as 'an acceptable treatment of last resort'. The HFE Authority, in its Code of Practice, has similarly acknowledged the modern-day reality of surrogacy arrangements. The latter in paras 14.2–14.5, places its focus upon the additional information that clinics, involved in surrogacy treatments, should provide to the parties:

---

85 London: BMA, 1996.

HFEA Code of Practice

14.2 The centre should ensure that those involved in surrogacy arrangements have received information about legal parenthood under the HFE Act 2008 and other relevant legislation. This information should cover who may be the legal parent(s) when the child is born, as outlined in guidance note 6.

14.3 The centre should ensure that those involved in surrogacy arrangements have received information about the effect of the Parental Orders provisions in the HFE Act 2008 and in particular the Parental Orders provisions in the Act. These state that parental rights and obligations in respect of surrogacy arrangements may be transferred from the birth parents to those who commissioned the surrogacy arrangement, as long as certain conditions are met.

14.4 The centre should advise patients that surrogacy arrangements are unenforceable and that they should seek legal advice about this.

14.5 The centre should satisfy itself that those involved in surrogacy arrangements have received enough information and understand the legal implications of these arrangements well enough to be able to give informed consent to treatment.

The courts too have changed their attitude towards surrogacy. From an initially censorious stance (in *A v C* from 1978 the Court of Appeal referred to such an arrangement as 'a kind of baby-farming operation of a wholly distasteful and lamentable kind'),[86] judges have since evinced more sympathy towards those having recourse to the practice. In *Briody v St Helen's and Knowsley AHA*,[87] the Court of Appeal was required to consider whether the claimant, who had lost her womb as a result of medical negligence, should also receive damages to fund the costs of a surrogacy arrangement. While rejecting this on the facts (given the claimant's very slim chance of successfully so having a child), the court demonstrated an open-minded approach to surrogacy in general. Hale LJ commented as follows:

Hale LJ: [14] ... [W]hile there is general agreement that commercial agencies and advertising should be banned, that surrogacy for convenience or social rather than medical reasons is unacceptable, and that the agreement should be unenforceable, there is little discernible consensus on anything else. Lord Winston's view was that opinion was turning against surrogacy, and that was certainly his experience at his hospital, but if anything the tone of official publications since Warnock has been more sympathetic. Professor Craft's view was certainly different ...

[16] ... I find it impossible to say that the proposals which the claimant now wishes to pursue are contrary to public policy ... She fulfils the criteria for permissible surrogacy laid down both by the Human Fertilisation and Embryology Authority and the BMA: she has no other way of having a baby because she has no womb. She has found a surrogate mother through perfectly lawful means with whom she proposes to make a lawful, although unenforceable, arrangement.

It is nevertheless true that surrogacy arrangements, and their optimal legal regulation, continue to pose difficult questions. In 1997, the Government commissioned an inquiry (headed by Professor Margaret Brazier) into the arrangements for payments and regulation under the 1985 Act. The ensuing report, *Surrogacy: Review for Health Ministers of Current Arrangements for Payment and Regulation*,[88] recommended a number of changes to the existing law. In particular, it felt that

---

86 [1985] FLR 445, *per* Cumming-Bruce LJ (the case was decided in 1978).
87 [2001] EWCA Civ 1010.
88 Cm 4068, London: DoH, 1998.

payment to surrogate mothers should be more closely controlled to ensure that only genuine expenses were covered and that the (charitable) agencies involved in negotiating surrogacy arrangements should be required to operate in accordance with a code of practice drawn up by the Department of Health. However, the Government subsequently chose not act upon these recommendations.

7.5.3 Resolving surrogacy arrangements

As regards the law's involvement in surrogacy arrangements at the second stage, namely once the child is born, two possibilities need to be considered. First, the parties to the arrangement may have fallen into dispute as to who should nurture it. Secondly, in so far as there is no dispute (that is, the surrogate mother is willing to hand over the child and the commissioning parents are happy to accept it and to pay the agreed fee), there remains the need to legitimate the child.

7.5.3.1 Where the parties are in dispute

Sometimes the surrogate, during the course of her pregnancy, may decide that she is not, after all, prepared to go through with the agreement to hand over the child after birth. In the early case of A v C,[89] the Court of Appeal upheld the trial judge's ruling that the surrogacy agreement providing, *inter alia*, for this handing over was void on grounds of public policy. As noted above, when enacting the HFEA 1990, Parliament also inserted s 1A into the SAA 1985, to reinforce the voidness of such arrangements. Nevertheless, this point will not in itself be determinative of the outcome in a given surrogacy dispute. The reason is that what is now generally at issue is the future of a child: is it to be brought up by the surrogate who gestated it, or the couple who commissioned it (and to whom it may be partly or wholly genetically related)? Thus, in principle, and notwithstanding the voidness of their contractual rights, it might seem that the commissioning parents could win custody.

An analogy could be drawn here with cases of marital break-up in which the custody of a child is at issue. The courts, in dealing with such matters as residence and contact, will, in accordance with the provisions of the Children Act 1989, regard the welfare of the child as paramount. This approach can indeed already be seen at work in the pre-Children Act case of *Re P (Minors)*:

Re P (Minors)[90]

Mrs P, a divorcée with one son of her own, entered into an arrangement with Mr B to bear his child and hand it over to him and his wife, Mrs B. As her pregnancy progressed, she began to have doubts about honouring the agreement and these hardened following the birth of twins. Although upset about disappointing Mr and Mrs B, she ultimately refused to hand the twins over. The latter were made wards of court:

Sir John Arnold P: In this, as in any other wardship dispute, the welfare of the children, or child, concerned is the first and paramount consideration which the court must, by statute, take into account, and that is what I do.

These children have been, up to their present age of approximately five months, with, quite consistently, their mother and in those circumstances there must necessarily have been some bonding of those children with their mother and that is undoubtedly coupled with the

---

89 See n 86 above.
90 [1987] 2 FLR 421.

fact that she is their mother, a matter which weighs predominantly in the balance in favour of leaving the children with their mother, but there are other factors which weigh in the opposite balance and which, as is said by Mr B through his counsel, outweigh the advantages of leaving the children with their mother, and it is that balancing exercise which the court is required to perform . . .

What then are the factors which the court should take into account? I have already mentioned on the side of Mrs P the matters which weigh heavily in the balance are the fact of her maternity, that she bore the children and carried them for the term of their gestation and that ever since she has conferred upon them the maternal care which they have enjoyed and has done so successfully. The key social worker in the case who has given evidence testifies to the satisfactory nature of the care which Mrs P has conferred upon the children and this assessment is specifically accepted by Mr B as being an accurate one. I start, therefore, from the position that these babies have bonded with their mother in a state of domestic care by her of a satisfactory nature and I now turn to the factors which are said to outweigh those advantages, so as to guide the court upon the proper exercise of the balancing function to the conclusion that the children ought to be taken away from Mrs P, and passed over, under suitable arrangements, to Mr and Mrs B. They are principally as follows. It is said, and said quite correctly, that the shape of the B family is the better shape of a family in which these children might be brought up, because it contains a father as well as a mother and that is undoubtedly true. Next, it is said that the material circumstances of the B family are such that they exhibit a far larger degree of affluence than can be demonstrated by Mrs P. That, also, is undoubtedly true. Then it is said that the intellectual quality of the environment of the B's home and the stimulus which would be afforded to these babies, if they were to grow up in that home, would be greater than the corresponding features in the home of Mrs P . . .

Then it is said that the religious comfort and support which the B's derive from their Church is greater than anything of that sort available to Mrs P. How far that is true, I simply do not know. I do know that the B's are practising Christians and do derive advantages from that circumstance, but nobody asked Mrs P about this and I am not disposed to assume that she lacks that sort of comfort and support in the absence of any investigation by way of cross-examination to lay the foundations for such a conclusion. Then it is said, and there is something in this, that the problems which might arise from the circumstance that these children who are, of course, congenitally derived from the semen of Mr B and bear traces of Mr B's Asiatic origin would be more easily understood and discussed and reconciled in the household of Mr and Mrs B, a household with an Asiatic ethnic background, than they would be if they arose in relation to these children while they were situated in the home of Mrs P, which is in an English village and which has no non-English connections . . .

As regards [these] factors, they are, in the aggregate, weighty, but I do not think, having given my very best effort to the evaluation of the case dispassionately on both sides, that they ought to be taken to outweigh the advantages to these children of preserving the link with the mother to whom they are bonded and who has, as is amply testified, exercised over them a satisfactory level of maternal care, and accordingly it is, I think, the duty of the court to award the care and control of these babies to their mother.

This case suggests that there is a presumption that the welfare of the child is best served by leaving it with the surrogate mother. This is all the more so, given the inevitable delay, following the birth of the child, in such disputes coming before the courts, during which time the child may well have bonded with her.

The surrogate's position has since been recognised by the parenthood provisions in the HFE legislation. In this regard, one should recall that at birth it is she – as the gestational mother – who, under s 27 HFEA 1990 and now s 33 HFE Act 2008, is the child's legal mother. This is so whether or not it is a case of partial or total surrogacy (ie whether her own egg or that of the commissioning mother was used). For a while, the HFE Authority also interpreted the rules in such a way that the commissioning father – even where his sperm was used – would not be the legal father of the child on birth (but treated akin to a sperm donor).[91] However, in October 2013, the HFE Authority announced a change of policy, so that (where the surrogate is not married or in a civil partnership, or is, but her spouse did not consent), provided the parties satisfy the mandatory requirements (including necessary consents), the biological commissioning partner will be the male legal parent upon birth.

As suggested by the decision in *Re P*, the court will normally be reluctant to oust the legal parenthood of a surrogate against her will. However, a rare case in which this occurred is *Re N (a child)*.[92] Here the evidence showed that from the beginning, the surrogate had set out to deceive the commissioning couple into believing that she intended to hand the child over to them at birth – in fact she wanted the child for herself. Thorpe LJ noted:

> **Thorpe LJ**: [4] The judge's findings in relation to the history are perhaps largely superfluous for this afternoon's disposal of the appeal, but in very broad terms he rejected the evidence of the P's and commended the responsibility of the J's. In particular, and crucially, he found that the P's had deliberately embarked on a path of deception, driven by Mrs P's compulsive desire to bear a child or further children, and that she had never had any other objective than to obtain insemination by surrogacy, with the single purpose of acquiring for herself, and her family, another child. This was crucially important, since it informed the review of the experts and the review of the judge of the medium and long-term future of N, if the responsibility for his future care were left with the P's.
>
> [5] The judge had the considerable advantage of two reports from Dr Eia Arsen of the Marlborough Day Clinic. His expertise in this field, forensic child and adolescent psychiatry, is second to none, and the judge was clearly guided by him to his ultimate conclusion. Dr Arsen had been instructed by the guardian ad litem, and the guardian ad litem fully supported Dr Arsen's conclusions, as well as expressing her independent expert view that, of the two options that the judge surveyed, the better for N was the future offered by the J's. So, given those ingredients, the judge's ultimate conclusion could not have been surprising to any of the professionals in the case, even if it was unexpected by the P's.

In these circumstances (and despite the fact that by the time of the hearing N, the child, had been living with the Ps for 18 months) the Court of Appeal upheld the order of Coleridge J in the High Court, granting residency to Mr J, the commissioning father (who was also the genetic father) and his wife.

Such exceptional cases aside, it is suggested that the courts will normally prefer to allow the child to remain with the surrogate. For one thing, they would not wish to send out a signal to surrogate mothers who, while pregnant, change their minds about handing over the child, that it could subsequently be taken from them against their will. As the Glover Report argues, this could be bad for the child. Instead, the Report suggests that 'the possibility of the surrogate

---

91 Under ss 35–37 HFE Act 2008; often the child at birth will be legally fatherless, eg where the surrogate is unmarried and the agreed fatherhood conditions do not apply.
92 [2007] EWCA Civ 1053.

mother changing her mind should be accepted by the [commissioning] couple as one of the risks of this way of trying to overcome childlessness'.[93]

7.5.3.2 Where the parties are agreed

On the face of it, things should be simpler where there is consensus between the surrogate and commissioning couple that the child be handed over. However, as we shall see, despite special statutory rules designed to assist the parties in transferring the parentage of the child, in a significant proportion of cases – in particular those involving cross-border surrogacy arrangements – serious difficulties may remain.

Starting with the relevant statutory provision, s 54 of the HFE Act 2008 allows the commissioning couple to apply for a parental order in a non-contentious surrogacy case. This is a swifter and notably less bureaucratic process than the alternative of adopting the child.[94] Nonetheless, for such an order to be granted, a variety of conditions need to be satisfied:

---

54 Parental orders

1 On an application made by two people ('the applicants'), the court may make an order providing for a child to be treated in law as the child of the applicants if –

    a   the child has been carried by a woman who is not one of the applicants, as a result of the placing in her of an embryo or sperm and eggs or her artificial insemination,

    b   the gametes of at least one of the applicants were used to bring about the creation of the embryo, and

    c   the conditions in subsections (2) to (8) are satisfied.

2 The applicants must be –

    a   husband and wife,

    b   civil partners of each other, or

    c   two persons who are living as partners in an enduring family relationship and are not within prohibited degrees of relationship in relation to each other.

3 Except in a case falling within subsection (11), the applicants must apply for the order during the period of 6 months beginning with the day on which the child is born.

4 At the time of the application and the making of the order –

    a   the child's home must be with the applicants, and

    b   either or both of the applicants must be domiciled in the United Kingdom or in the Channel Islands or the Isle of Man.

5 At the time of the making of the order both the applicants must have attained the age of 18.

6 The court must be satisfied that both –

    a   the woman who carried the child, and

    b   any other person who is a parent of the child but is not one of the applicants (including any man who is the father by virtue of section 35 or 36 or any woman who is a parent by virtue of section 42 or 43),

have freely, and with full understanding of what is involved, agreed unconditionally to the making of the order.

7 Subsection (6) does not require the agreement of a person who cannot be found or is incapable of giving agreement; and the agreement of the woman who carried the child is ineffective for the purpose of that subsection if given by her less than six weeks after the child's birth.

---

93 See n 4 above.
94 Under the Adoption and Children Act 2002.

> 8 The court must be satisfied that no money or other benefit (other than for expenses reasonably incurred) has been given or received by either of the applicants for or in consideration of –
>
> a the making of the order,
>
> b any agreement required by subsection (6),
>
> c the handing over of the child to the applicants, or
>
> d the making of arrangements with a view to the making of the order,
>
> unless authorised by the court.

This provision replaces the rules as to parental orders contained in s 30 of the HFE Act 1990. In fact the only significant change (under sub-s (2)) is that, whereas under the 1990 Act, the applicants (ie the commissioning parents) had to be married to one another, now co-habiting couples and homosexual couples are also able to apply. Nonetheless, the fact that, as before, a single person may not obtain such an order led the High Court, in *Re Z (A Child) (No 2)*,[95] to declare the section incompatible with Articles 8 and 14 (the right to non-discrimination) ECHR; indeed, the relevant incompatibility was conceded by the Government, which has recently announced that it will legislate to remedy this.[96]

The requirement in sub-ss (6)–(7) that the surrogate must consent to the order, and that such consent is not valid where given fewer than six weeks after the birth of the child, is clearly there to protect the surrogate's position. Less obviously defensible is the apparent double-standard applied by sub-s (8) requiring on the one hand the court to be satisfied that the surrogate was unpaid, but on the other allowing it retrospectively to authorise any such payment. In practice, given the court will have the child's welfare as its paramount concern, it is difficult to imagine circumstances when – as a prerequisite for making the desired order – it would fail to do this.

The High Court had to consider the effect of the previous (identical) rules in s 30 of the 1990 Act, including the possibility of authorising payment to the surrogate, in the case of *Re Q (Parental Order)*:

Re Q (Parental Order)[97]

> Baby Q was born in the summer of 1995 as a result of a total surrogacy arrangement. The unmarried surrogate, Miss A, received IVF treatment at a licensed clinic, and was paid £8,280 to cover her expenses and loss of earnings. Although she developed a strong attachment to the child she was carrying and equivocated about handing it over, she ultimately decided to go through with the agreement. The commissioning couple applied for a parental order:
>
> **Johnson J**: Turning belatedly to the particular application made to me, I am satisfied that the statutory requirements are all complied with. . . .
>
> The first relates to the consent of the carrying mother. She had entered into the procedure with the best of intentions, but when the time came to relinquish the child that she had carried so devotedly, she was overcome with doubt and at first declined to give her consent. This reaction is natural and was contemplated by parliament in stipulating that the carrying mother is to be given at least six weeks after the birth to make her decision before she can give a binding consent. One of the duties of the guardian *ad litem* under the Family Proceedings

---

95 [2016] EWHC 1191 (Fam).
96 See: www.gov.uk/government/uploads/system/uploads/attachment_data/file/664161/Command_paper_Cm_9525.pdf.
97 [1996] 1 FLR 369.

Courts (Children Act 1989) (Amendment) Rules 1994 is to investigate the circumstance of the carrying mother's consent.

It may be of interest if I quote *verbatim* from the guardian's report:

> I have visited Miss A twice in order to ascertain her wishes in this matter and to try and clarify the issues around her agreement to the order. Miss A explained how she came to offer herself as a surrogate mother due to seeing the anguish of infertile friends and how she had never thought she would have difficulty parting with the baby she bore. When she received details of Mr and Mrs B she immediately warmed to them and these first good impressions were confirmed when she met them. Miss A has two children of her own and they are both aware of this child's whereabouts...; they always knew that the baby would not be living with them. At about 28 weeks Miss A experienced some bleeding and was admitted to hospital. She questioned for the first time what she was doing and feels that it was only at this stage that the baby began to feel like a real person to her and that she began to bond with her. Notwithstanding this first period of questioning she decided to carry through handing over the baby to Mr and Mrs B and remained of this view until after the birth. . . . In talking to Miss A, it is clear that the depth of feeling she experienced towards her baby took her by surprise. She said that she felt no different toward this baby at her birth than she had felt towards her other children and had not really been prepared for this. It is clear that Miss A felt emotionally torn in half by the separation from the baby. With time, however, and as her own body settled after the birth, so she was able to think more clearly about the issues and this is why she decided to give her agreement. I prepared an agreement form for her to sign on my second visit and she did this willingly and in a positive and definite manner. She fully understands the effects of a parental order, understanding that she loses all parental responsibility, and wishes the order to be made as soon as possible. She does not now wish to attend court herself for the hearing.

This account of the feelings of this carrying mother shows the sensitivity and, indeed, difficulty of the task of the guardian *ad litem* in these cases. . . .

Secondly, I had to consider whether or not I should authorise payments totalling £8,280 which had been made to Miss A by Mr and Mrs B.

I hold that such authorisation can be given retrospectively. In so doing I follow the decision of Latey J in *Re Adoption Application (Payment for Adoption)* (1987) . . . which was concerned with a similar provision in the Adoption Act 1976.

The guardian told me that she had at first thought that this amount seemed rather high but on further inquiry she concluded that the payments were understandable. £3,280 was made up of payments to cover clothes, daily trips to the doctor for injections, child care provision of her own children during some of those visits and similar related expenses. A further £5,000 was a payment to compensate Miss A for loss of earnings. Given the circumstances of the pregnancy and her potential earnings of £15,000 [per annum], I joined with the guardian in concluding that the payment was reasonable and, retrospectively, I gave authority for it.

Since this case was decided, the courts have sanctioned the payment of increasingly high sums to surrogate mothers. In *Re C (A Child)*,[98] a payment of £12,000 was authorised by the High Court in similar circumstances; more recently, in *Re X & Y (foreign surrogacy)*,[99] Hedley J granted

---

98 [2002] 1 FLR 1008.
99 [2008] EWHC (Fam) 3030.

a parental order (including the authorisation of payment) in a case in which a British couple paid a Ukrainian woman £23,000 to put down as a deposit on a flat in return for bearing them twins following an IVF surrogacy (using the commissioning father's sperm and a donor egg). In subsequent cases, the courts have granted such orders also in cases where a (foreign) surrogacy agency has made a commercial profit out of the arrangement. Indeed in *Re L (Commercial Surrogacy)*,[100] Hedley J suggested that, only in the clearest cases of abuse of public policy should a court hesitate to make a parental order where it was consistent with the child's welfare interests.

The *Re X & Y* case referred to above was complicated by the fact that, while under Ukrainian law, the British couple were the twins' legal parents at birth, under British law this was not the case: as we have seen, the effect of the HFE Act(s) is that the surrogate was their mother and *her* husband, rather than the commissioning (and genetic) father, their father. The disturbing implications of this case, that children born through a foreign surrogacy may potentially be left both parentless and stateless, are commented on by Theis, Gamble and Ghevaert, as follows:

Theis, L, Gamble, N, and Ghevaert, L, 'Re X and Y (Foreign Surrogacy): a trek through a thorn forest'[101]

Though the facts of this case may seem unusual, the prospect of other children being born into similar complications is worrying. The numbers of British people travelling abroad for fertility treatment (including surrogacy) are growing fast, driven by ease of access to information about foreign fertility services via the internet, cost, the acute shortage of egg donors in the UK, the lifting of anonymity for donors, and public policy restrictions which prohibit commercial surrogacy and advertisements for surrogate mothers. Hedley J acknowledged this trend saying, at para [26]: 'As babies become less available for adoption and given the withdrawal of donor confidentiality (wholly justifiable, of course, from the child's perspective), more and more couples are likely to be tempted to follow the applicants' path to commercial surrogacy in those places where it is lawful, of which there may be many.'

This suggests that some of the problems with the law highlighted by this case (as well as the lack of good quality public information) should be addressed as a matter of urgency. Surrogacy was an issue not looked at in detail as part of the government's review of fertility laws last year, though the government did suggest in Parliament that it was minded to review surrogacy separately. Hedley J noted, at para [29]: 'It is no part of the court's function to express views on that, save perhaps to observe that some of the issues thrown up in this case may highlight the wisdom of holding such a review.'

The language is moderate but Hedley J is right: surrogacy law urgently needs a review. What *Re X and Y* has demonstrated so graphically is how complex and difficult the current law is for British children born through foreign surrogacy, and at the same time how the law fails in practice to uphold the public policy of discouraging payments for childbirth. Parliament needs to take a fresh look at surrogacy and find a more effective legal solution fit for the twenty-first century. In the meantime, anyone contemplating foreign surrogacy (and their legal advisers) should proceed with extreme caution lest they too find themselves on 'a trek through a thorn forest'.

Although, as we have seen, the HFE Act 2008 has added to the parties who are eligible to apply under s 54 for a parental order in cases of surrogacy, the above problem has not been addressed. Similarly, although the HFE Authority Code (in para 14.6) requires couples to be alerted to

---

100 [2010] EWHC 3146 (Fam); see also *Re P-M (Parental Order: Payments to Surrogacy Agency)* [2013] EWHC 2328 (Fam); *Re A, B and C (UK surrogacy expenses)* [2016] EWFC 33.
101 [2009] Fam Law 239.

potential issues with foreign surrogates, this will *ex hypothesi* only benefit those who approach their treatment through a licensed clinic.

Difficulties may also occur in the opposite situation – that is, where a foreign commissioning couple avails itself of the services of a British surrogate. Here the couple will not satisfy the requisite UK residency condition to allow them to apply for a parental order. Instead, as occurred in the case of *Re G (Surrogacy: Foreign Domicile)*[102] – involving a commissioning couple from Turkey – the couple will be forced back upon the more cumbersome alternative of applying for adoption, pursuant to the Adoption and Children Act 2002.

THINK POINT

Has the time now come for wholesale reform of the law in respect of surrogacy and, if so, what form should the main changes take?

Summary of key points

1   The Human Fertilisation and Embryology Act 1990 (as amended in 2008) provides detailed regulation in respect of most aspects of fertility treatment. One of its key achievements was to set up the HFE Authority, responsible for the detailed supervision and licensing of UK fertility clinics.

2   Great importance is attached by the Act both to the consent of the gamete providers and to the welfare of children born as a result of fertility treatment. The stringency of the consent provisions especially has provoked several (in most cases unsuccessful) legal challenges to the Act in recent years.

3   Another concern of the legislation is to rein in the more extreme possibilities of scientific technology (reproductive cloning, genetic engineering, etc), where it is deemed that public opinion is not yet ready for them. Some of the 2008 changes to the 1990 Act address scientific techniques unknown in 1990.

4   One controversial question is how far genetic modifications may be undertaken that will affect the characteristics of the resulting child. At present, some 'selecting out' of embryos is permitted (chiefly on account of genetic defects); by contrast, positive manipulations of the embryo are prohibited.

5   As regards the related issue of embryo research, the law has adopted a compromise position: research is permitted within the first 14 days if necessary for one of the defined statutory purposes (including attempting to develop treatments for serious disease by using embryonic stem-cells).

6   A separate set of complexities emerge in relation to using donor gametes to provide children for infertile persons or couples ('collaborative reproduction'). Here one matter is the need for the law to resolve the question of who, between the donors and the recipients of treatment, are the legal parents.

7   In the light of experience with the 1990 rules, as well as changes in social attitudes (particularly as regards the potential for homosexual couples to use donor gametes to found a family), these parenthood rules have been amended: they are now contained in (the self-standing part of) the HFE Act 2008.

---

102 [2007] EWHC 2814 (Fam).

8   A second issue relates to the degree of contact (if any) that the children should have with the donor. Until 2005, the law pursued a policy of 'donor anonymity'; however, since then the position has changed, so that the child may later access the HFE Authority register showing who the donor was.

9   One especially contentious area of collaborative reproduction is surrogacy, in which a woman agrees to bear a child for others – normally for payment. Here the law (in the 1985 Surrogacy Arrangements Act) attempted to clamp down on commercialisation in this area by banning profit-making agencies.

10   At the same time, the practice itself – as well as the surrogate's ability to charge for her services – remains lawful. Overall, this form of assisted reproduction appears inconsistently regulated; a particular challenge is posed by the increasing number of cross-border surrogacies.

Further reading

Fox, M, 'The Human Fertilisation and Embryology Act 2008: tinkering at the margins' (2009) Feminist Legal Studies 333.

Freeman, M, 'Does surrogacy have a future after Brazier?' (1999) 7 Medical Law Review 1.

Glover, J, *Choosing Children: Genes, Disability, and Design*, Oxford: Clarendon Press, 2006.

Jackson, E, *Regulating Reproduction: Law, Technology and Autonomy*, Oxford: Hart Publishing, 2001.

Robertson, JA, *Children of Choice: Freedom and the New Reproductive Technologies*, Ewing, NJ: Princeton University Press, 1994.

Robertson, J, 'Liberty, identity, and human cloning' (1998) 76 Texas Law Review 1371.

Surrogacy UK (pressure group) report, *Surrogacy in the UK: myth-busting and reform* (November 2015) (available at: www.surrogacyuk.org/Downloads/Surrogacy%20in%20the%20UK%20Report%20 FINAL.pdf)

Chapter 8

Abortion and pre-natal harm

8.1 Introduction

By contrast with the issues examined in Chapter 7, in which the law has had, in the main, to respond to novel problems created by recent advances in medical technology, abortion as a procedure has existed for centuries. In the last few decades with the advent of new, non-surgical techniques, it has though become increasingly routine: indeed in the UK each year some 200,000 abortions (or 'terminations') are performed. Nevertheless, it remains one of the most intractable and emotive topics within the province of medical law.

Broadly speaking, abortion denotes the practice of terminating a pregnancy in such a way as to destroy the life of the foetus being carried by the pregnant woman. In the case of abortions carried out early in pregnancy on non-viable foetuses, the fact that the foetus is expelled from the womb is sufficient for its death. In other cases, where the foetus is more mature (and capable of surviving outside the womb), additional steps are taken to ensure that it dies prior to delivery. Either way, it is apparent that the practice stands in direct opposition to the major forms of fertility treatment considered in the last chapter. There, the intention is normally to produce a pregnancy resulting in a successful live birth. Here, the intention is to bring an existing pregnancy to an end without the live birth of the child. In another sense, however, there is a close relationship between the practices in that they both implicate (albeit in opposing ways) reproductive freedom. As John Robertson notes:

Robertson, JA, *Children of Choice : Freedom and the New Reproductive Technologies*[1]

> An essential distinction is between the freedom to avoid reproduction and the freedom to reproduce. When people talk of reproductive rights, they usually have one or the other aspect in mind. Because different interests and justifications underlie each, and countervailing interests for limiting each aspect vary, recognition of one aspect does not necessarily mean that the other will also be respected; nor does limitation of one mean that the other can also be denied.
>
> However, there is a mirroring or reciprocal relationship here. Denial of one type of reproductive liberty necessarily implicates the other. If a woman is not able to avoid reproduction through contraception or abortion, she may end up reproducing, with all the burdens that unwanted reproduction entails. Similarly, if one is denied the liberty to reproduce . . . one is forced to avoid reproduction, thus experiencing the loss that absence of progeny brings. By extending reproductive options, new reproductive technologies present challenges to both aspects of procreative choice.

Gillian Douglas has explored the background to the right to avoid reproduction claimed for individuals as follows:

Douglas, G, *Law, Fertility and Reproduction*[2]

> Methods, effective or not, for avoiding conception or childbirth are probably as old as civilisation itself, and various remedies to alleviate childlessness are probably of equal antiquity. To what extent have individuals been at liberty to make use of these? The former, certainly, have always been forthrightly condemned by the Roman Catholic Church, drawing originally upon the Jewish view that the duty to procreate through marriage is the first of all commandments. Sex became associated by St Augustine with sin, and could only

---

1 Ewing, NJ: Princeton UP, 1994.
2 London: Sweet & Maxwell, 1991.

be justified by procreation. Aquinas considered that to dissociate sex from procreation was to act against nature and therefore to sin.

The breaking down of this religious influence and the rise of a rights-based political philosophy in the West during the 18th and 19th centuries, utilised first by men and then by women, enabled individuals to challenge these old ideas and control of sexual behaviour. Since women are the central actors in reproduction, it is not surprising to find that the first wave of feminism in the 19th century was in part characterised by a desire to enable women to restrict their childbearing, albeit mainly to ensure that they could be better mothers to a few children, rather than poor mothers to too many. The possibility of a right to control one's reproductive capacity through contraception is more likely to be a female than a male concern because of the consequences for the woman where such a possibility is not permitted. In this century, the modern wave of feminism has demanded such a freedom directly, as an aspect of a general desire to gain autonomy and control over one's own body.

In this chapter, we shall first consider the principal moral arguments for and against abortion, together with the additional factors which influence the legal response to what many regard as an ethical impasse. Next, in section 8.2, the present state of the law will be analysed, including, in section 8.3, the implications for the parties most directly affected by the practice. Lastly, in section 8.4 the discussion will move beyond the question of abortion to address the legal position in relation to other forms of avoidable pre-natal harm.

8.1.1 The moral debate

Traditionally, the debate as to the rights and wrongs of abortion has been couched in terms of the 'right to life' of the foetus versus the pregnant woman's 'right to choose' whether or not to bear a child. In many cases, the position a person takes in this debate will depend upon the underlying moral status they accord to the human foetus. As Rosalind Hursthouse writes:

Hursthouse, R, _Beginning Lives_[3]

The simplest view on the issue of abortion, the one often expressed explicitly or implicitly by non-philosophers in letters to newspapers, discussions on the wireless and so on, is that the moral rights and wrongs of abortion can be unproblematically settled by determining the moral status of the foetus. Hence it is common to find people on the conservative side insisting that the foetus is an unborn baby and hence that abortion is infanticide or murder and absolutely wrong, while people on the opposite side insist that the foetus is just a clump of living cells and hence that abortion is merely an operation which removes some part of one's body and hence is morally innocuous.

Now it is certainly true that the question of the moral status of the foetus is important, for according to what its status is, different arguments will bear upon the rights and wrongs of abortion. If, as conservatives believe, the foetus has the same moral status as a baby, then the mother's moral right to abortion is, to say the least, problematic; if there were any such right, a quite particular case would have to be made out for it. If, on the other hand, the foetus has the same moral status as, say, a kidney, then the argument for the mother's moral right to abortion could proceed, quite generally, as an argument concerning the right, of both women and men, to decide what happens to their own bodies.

3 Oxford: Blackwells, 1987.

The physical attributes of the foetus and the developmental process that it undergoes during pregnancy are, as we saw in the previous chapter, agreed upon. What is controverted is the moral inferences as to its status that should be drawn from the physical facts. The two key contrasting views, the 'theological' and 'personhood' approaches, are discussed by Jane Fortin in the following extract, along with a middle position put forward by Michael Lockwood:

Fortin, J, 'Legal protection for the unborn child'[4]

[M]ost philosophers argue that the point in time when human life begins is quite distinct from and less relevant than when a human 'person' comes into existence. The advantage of this approach is that it avoids the 'speciesism' involved in maintaining that all human life automatically has a greater intrinsic value and right to protection than that of any other species. Instead, it concentrates on those aspects of human life that merit such preferment. Thus whilst few would claim that a human sperm or unfertilised egg merits greater protection than a 10 week old kitten, most would accept without question the automatic right to life of a 10 year old child. This is because the child has become a person and as such, his life has an intrinsic value both to himself and others. Arguably then, there is little reason for extending legal protection to human life until 'a person' comes into existence. If this argument is accepted, it becomes vital to establish a clear definition of 'personhood'; no easy matter when moral philosophers show little accord in their choice of essential attributes to be displayed by a 'person'.

Perhaps the most widely known to the general public is the traditional Roman Catholic approach to the question. This is a metaphysical one which, in its strictest form, maintains that a human person comes into existence at the moment of the ovum being fertilised. At this moment of 'ensoulment', the fertilised ovum becomes infused with a rational soul of its own and this theory of immediate animation is widely believed to embody the official teaching of the Roman Catholic Church . . .

Many moral philosophers reject the metaphysical approach to personhood which is so often associated with the Roman Catholic Church. In their view personhood is not defined by reference to the presence or otherwise of an immaterial human soul but by reference to a complicated combination of mental and or physical properties. . . . Inevitably, many proponents of such a combination of properties, find it impossible to accept that a human foetus can be deemed a person and worthy of protection; consequently, in their view, there can be no moral objection to abortion, however late. Indeed, Michael Tooley lucidly presents the argument that since even a newly born child lacks these properties, infanticide is not morally objectionable.

. . . Although many would find Tooley's conclusion distasteful, its logic cannot be denied. A possible way of avoiding some, but not all, of these problems is to maintain three clear distinctions. Thus Michael Lockwood distinguishes between human organisms, human beings and persons. In this way, depending on the definition of 'human being', a newly born infant might be classified as such, with certain consequential rights, despite its not having attained the status of personhood. Lockwood uses the term 'human being' to describe what 'you and I are essentially, what we can neither become nor cease to be, without ceasing to exist'. Thus, in his view, this concept revolves round that of personal identity, which underlies 'certain discernible continuities' such as memory and personality – those unchanging elements in a human being which establishes his own unique blueprint. Accordingly, the concept of identity is established not by the continuities themselves but by those elements underlying them . . .

In his view, it is only when the brain develops to this extent, that a human embryo can be said to have become a human being. Only then does it become able to sustain distinctively mental processes, thereby justifying certain protection. Lockwood himself feels that it is impossible to be precise over the point in time when this occurs. Nevertheless, on the basis of the existing, albeit sparse, scientific evidence, he suggests that an appropriate marker might be 10 weeks' gestation. Lockwood's analysis is attractively clear and less cold blooded than that of Tooley. Moreover, it has the advantage of allowing both the unborn and the newly born child to have a measure of protection as human beings, without claiming either to be a fully fledged person.

---

4 (1988) 51 MLR 54.

However, it is apparent that all three views described by Fortin require some commitment to unprovable 'metaphysical' premises. As Margaret Brazier has noted:

Brazier, M, 'The challenge for Parliament'[5]

The difficulty is that the dispute is itself incapable of any conclusive resolution. Perception of the status of the embryo derives in many cases from the presence or absence of religious belief. Most, but not all, proponents of the belief that the embryo is from fertilisation a genetically unique individual as fully human as you or I, rest that belief, at least in part, on the embryo's potential possession of an immortal, immaterial soul . . . Many, but again by no means all, proponents of allowing research on embryos deny or doubt the existence of the soul.

Thus the argument on abortion becomes for opponents: 'How can the law permit the wanton destruction of human life?' And supporters of liberal abortion laws respond: 'By what right do you seek to impose your personal unprovable claims about God and the soul on others?' The dispute reaches stalemate . . . The humanity of the embryo is unproven and unprovable. But that acts both ways. Just as I cannot prove that humanity was divinely created and that each and every one of us possesses an immortal soul, so it cannot be proved that it is not so. Admitting the possibility of the soul, the moment of ensoulment cannot be proved. Nothing more or less can be concluded about the full humanity of the embryo save to say that the cases for and against are, to borrow a Scottish term, not proven.

Rather than attempting to found the moral status of the foetus on any particular attribute it possesses as it now is, an increasingly popular approach is to stress the potential (understood in terms of how it would develop naturally, other things equal) that the foetus has to become a person in the future. However, this concept stands in need of significant clarification if it is to bear any real moral weight. As Glover notes:

Glover, J et al., *Report to the European Commission on Reproductive Technologies, Fertility and the Family*[6]

Perhaps what matters is not some property an embryo now has, but what it has the potential to become. This claim seems to imply that disposing of an embryo is wrong because it prevents the existence of a particular developed person, namely the one the embryo would have become. But this argument rules out contraception. You are a particular developed person, and contraception would have prevented your existence. The apparently innocuous word 'potential' turns out to be very slippery.

To avoid ruling out contraception, potentiality has to be interpreted differently. Perhaps the destruction of potential is not just a matter of the loss of a future developed person, but also the loss of something that has got a certain distance on the way there: the programme is already in existence, as all the genes are present. But this leaves some unanswered questions. If the properties an embryo now has do not generate a right to life, and the argument about one less future person does not do so either, why should combining the two considerations give the desired result? Of course a compound can have properties not possessed by its individual ingredients, but in this case some account is needed of the moral chemistry involved.

It is accordingly important to consider whether there may be alternative ways to understand the debate which allow conclusions about the morality of abortion which do not depend on views about the status of the foetus. Two very different, but equally bold, attempts to recouch the abortion debate to precisely this end have been made, respectively, by Judith Jarvis Thomson and

5 In Dyson, A and Harris, J (eds), *Experiments on Embryos*, London: Routledge, 1990.
6 London: Fourth Estate, 1989.

Ronald Dworkin. Taking Thomson's argument first, in a celebrated article 'A defense of abortion', she suggested that, even if, for the sake of argument, we were to grant the foetus equal moral status to adult human persons, abortion would remain morally permissible in a large number of circumstances, given the prior right of the pregnant woman to exercise control over her body:

Thomson, JJ, 'A defense of abortion'[7]

Most opposition to abortion relies on the premise that the foetus is a human being, a person, from the moment of conception . . . .

. . . How, precisely, are we supposed to get from there to the conclusion that abortion is morally impermissible? Opponents of abortion commonly spend most of their time establishing that the foetus is a person, and hardly any time explaining the step from there to the impermissibility of abortion. Perhaps they think the step too simple and obvious to require much comment. Or perhaps instead they are simply being economical in argument. Many of those who defend abortion rely on the premise that the foetus is not a person, but only a bit of tissue that will become a person at birth; and why pay out more arguments than you have to? Whatever the explanation, I suggest that the step they take is neither easy nor obvious, that it calls for closer examination than it is commonly given, and that when we do give it this closer examination we shall feel inclined to reject it.

I propose, then, that we grant that the foetus is a person from the moment of conception. How does the argument go from here? Something like this, I take it. Every person has a right to life. So the foetus has a right to life. No doubt the mother has a right to decide what shall happen in and to her body; everyone would grant that. But surely a person's right to life is stronger and more stringent than the mother's right to decide what happens in and to her body, and so outweighs it. So the foetus may not be killed; an abortion may not be performed.

It sounds plausible. But now let me ask you to imagine this. You wake up in the morning and find yourself back to back in bed with an unconscious violinist. A famous unconscious violinist. He has been found to have a fatal kidney ailment, and the Society of Music Lovers has canvassed all the available medical records and found that you alone have the right blood type to help. They have therefore kidnapped you, and last night the violinist's circulatory system was plugged into yours, so that your kidneys can be used to extract poisons from his blood as well as your own. The director of the hospital now tells you: 'Look, we're sorry the Society of Music Lovers did this to you – we would never have permitted it if we had known. But still, they did it, and the violinist now is plugged into you. To unplug you would be to kill him. But never mind, it's only for nine months. By then he will have recovered from his ailment, and can safely be unplugged from you.' Is it morally incumbent on you to accede to this situation? No doubt it would be very nice of you if you did, a great kindness. But do you have to accede to it? What if it were not nine months, but nine years? Or longer still? What if the director of the hospital says: 'Tough luck, I agree, but you've now got to stay in bed, with the violinist plugged into you, for the rest of your life. Because remember this. All persons have a right to life, and violinists are persons. Granted you have a right to decide what happens in and to your body, but a person's right to life outweighs your right to decide what happens in and to your body. So you cannot ever be unplugged from him.' I imagine you would regard this as outrageous, which suggests that something really is wrong with that plausible-sounding argument I mentioned a moment ago.

In this case, of course, you were kidnapped; you didn't volunteer for the operation that plugged the violinist into your kidneys. Can those who oppose abortion on the ground I mentioned make an exception for a pregnancy due to rape? Certainly. They can say that persons have a right to life only if they didn't come into existence because of rape; or they can say that all persons have a right to life, but that some have less of a right to life than others, in particular, that those who came into existence because of rape have less. But these statements have a rather unpleasant sound. Surely the question of whether you have a right to life at all, or how much of it you have, shouldn't turn on the question of whether or not you are the product of a rape.

7 (1971) 1(1) Philosophy and Public Affairs 47.

Despite its ingenuity, there are a number of difficulties with Thomson's argument. First, while it may well permit abortion in cases of rape (where the woman has not given the foetus a 'right' to the use of her body), it is not clear that it can be extended to pregnancy which results from consensual sex. As Hursthouse notes:

Hursthouse, R, *Beginning Lives*[8]

Thomson asserts it as a premise that a woman cannot be said to have given the foetus the right to use her body if she is pregnant because of rape. Plausibly the pregnancy must result from voluntary intercourse . . . However this still leaves a very large number of cases; does Thomson agree that in all cases of pregnancy due to voluntary intercourse in full knowledge of the facts of life the mother could be said to have given the foetus the right to use her body – that the intercourse, as it were, amounts to an offer to have one's body thus used?

She clearly does not, but her argument at this point depends on two rather unsatisfactory analogies. In one she imagines that children come about by people-seeds taking root in one's carpet; this may happen even if one has gone to great trouble to try to prevent it by putting fine mesh screens over one's windows. In the other analogy, she does not consider children, but how people might acquire a right to use my house, and says it would be absurd to suppose that someone had acquired it by just blundering in, through a window I had happened to open, behind bars I had installed to keep people out which happened to have a defect. In each case I go to some trouble to try to keep people-seeds or people out; in each case there is supposed to be a way that would guarantee keeping them out, say with sealed windows, but it cannot be said that I am responsible for their being in my house and that hence they have a right to it simply because I do not go in for this extreme measure.

These analogies are obviously supposed to be with contraception; despite the woman's efforts not to become pregnant, she does. Given that she was trying not to, her voluntary intercourse cannot count as an offer, conferring a right, to have her body used by the foetus. But the difficulty with the people-seed analogy is that, because it is so far-fetched, it lacks all the background that enables one (sometimes) to make up one's mind. Do these people-seeds just root for nine months? What are the available alternatives to uprooting and killing them – can they be transplanted, can you swap your house for nine months with someone who wants children . . .? The difficulty with the other analogy is that it misses out the crucial aspect of the foetus being dependent on the use of the woman's body for its survival . . .

Secondly, there remains the problem that abortions are typically carried out by a third party, the doctor, and it may be argued that conceiving of abortion in terms of a conflict of maternal–foetal rights cannot settle the question of what would be an appropriate moral response on the part of such a third party. Finally, and more generally, Thomson's narrow focus on rights may be felt to obscure other ways in which an action is morally problematic. In particular, it does not follow, from the mere fact that the foetus lacks a right to use the woman's body, that abortion is morally innocuous. This appears to be recognised by Thomson herself:

Thomson, JJ, 'A defense of abortion'[9]

We surely must all grant that there may be cases in which it would be morally indecent to detach a person from your body at the cost of his life. Suppose you learn that what the violinist needs is not nine years of your life, but only one hour: all you need do to save his life is to spend one hour in that bed with him.

---

8 See n 3 above.
9 See n 7 above.

Suppose also that letting him use your kidneys for that one hour would not affect your health in the slightest. Admittedly you were kidnapped. Admittedly you did not give anyone permission to plug him into you. Nevertheless it seems to me plain you *ought* to allow him to use your kidneys for that hour – it would be indecent to refuse.

In a telling contribution to the abortion debate, Ronald Dworkin attempted to bridge the gap between the 'pro-life' and 'pro-choice' positions by identifying an important piece of common ground between the two camps. In particular, he argued that both conservatives and liberals share a common commitment to the sanctity of human life:

Dworkin, R, *Life's Dominion: An Argument About Abortion and Euthanasia*[10]

Both conservatives and liberals assume that in some circumstances abortion is more serious and more likely to be unjustifiable than in others. Notably, both agree that a late term abortion is graver than an early term one. We cannot explain this shared conviction simply on the ground that foetuses more closely resemble infants as pregnancy continues. People believe that abortion is not just emotionally more difficult but morally worse the later in pregnancy it occurs, and increasing resemblance alone has no moral significance. Nor can we explain the shared conviction by noticing that at some point in pregnancy a foetus becomes sentient. Most people think that abortion is morally worse early in the second trimester – well before sentience is possible – than early in the first one . . . Foetal development is a continuing creative process, a process that has barely begun at the instant of conception. Indeed, since genetic individuation is not yet complete at that point, we might say that the development of a unique human being has not started until approximately 14 days later, at implantation. But after implantation, as foetal growth continues, the natural investment that would be wasted in an abortion grows steadily larger and more significant.

Human and divine

So our sense that frustration rather than just loss compromises the inviolability of human life does seem helpful in explaining what unites most people about abortion. The more difficult question is whether it also helps in explaining what divides them . . .

Suppose parents discover, early in the mother's pregnancy, that the foetus is genetically so deformed that the life it would lead after birth will inevitably be both short and sharply limited. They must decide whether it is a worse frustration of life if the gravely deformed foetus were to die at once – wasting the miracle of its creation and its development so far – or if it were to continue to grow in utero, to be born, and to live only a short and crippled life. We know that people divide about that question, and we now have a way to describe the division. On one view, immediate death of the foetus, even in a case like this one, is a more terrible frustration of the miracle of life than even a sharply diminished and brief infant life would be, for the latter would at least redeem some small part, however limited, of the natural investment. On the rival view, it would be a worse frustration of life to allow this foetal life to continue, because that would add, to the sad waste of a deformed human's biological creation, the further, heartbreaking waste of personal emotional investments made in that life by others, but principally by the child himself, before his inevitable early death.

We should therefore consider this hypothesis: though almost everyone accepts the abstract principle that it is intrinsically bad when human life, once begun, is frustrated, people disagree about the best

---

10 London: Harper Collins, 1993.

answer to the question of whether avoidable premature death is always or invariably the most serious possible frustration of life. Very conservative opinion, on this hypothesis, is grounded in the conviction that immediate death is inevitably a more serious frustration than any option that postpones death, even at the cost of greater frustration in other respects. Liberal opinion, on the same hypothesis, is grounded in the opposite conviction: that in some cases, at least, a choice for premature death minimises the frustration of life and is therefore not a compromise of the principle that human life is sacred but, on the contrary, best respects that principle ...

Although enlightening, Dworkin's inclusive strategy is not likely to satisfy everybody. In particular, in the metaphysical assumptions he makes about the foetus he appears to be far closer to the liberal than the conservative position. Even if he is right that some conservatives oppose abortion on the 'detached' ground that it frustrates life in the abstract, there will inevitably remain others whose opposition is derived from religious beliefs about foetuses which are not amenable to any compromise. Equally, it is likely that some adherents of a liberal-feminist persuasion will not be convinced that the foetus is to be regarded as any more sacred than other parts of the woman's body tissue. Nevertheless, it is probable that Dworkin's view is one that, empirically speaking, accurately reflects a broad consensus of opinion in our society today.

THINK POINT

Which of the arguments considered above do you personally find most persuasive?

8.1.2 Abortion and legislation

The point that questions as to the morality of a practice must be distinguished from the rightness of legislating against the same was noted in Chapter 7. In relation to abortion, the salient arguments are well put by Rosalind Hursthouse:

See Chapter 7

Hursthouse, R, *Beginning Lives*[11]

The confusion of questions about morality and legislation is particularly common in arguments about abortion ... One reason why the questions become readily confused in debate is because of the tactics of opposition. Many people, particularly women, do think there is something wrong about having an abortion, that it is not a morally innocuous matter, but also think that the current abortion laws are if anything still too restrictive, and find it difficult to articulate their position on the morality of abortion without, apparently betraying the feminist campaign concerning legislation. To give an inch on 'a woman's right to choose', to suggest even for a moment that having an abortion is not only 'exercising that right' (which sounds fine) but also 'ending a human life' (which sounds like homicide) or even 'ending a potential human life' (which sounds at least serious) is to play into the hands of the conservatives.

What happens to the conservative and the liberal sides of the debate once the distinction between questions of morality and questions of legislation is drawn? In theory, drawing the distinction opens up the possibility of four different positions.

11 See n 3 above.

Morality of abortion	Laws on abortion	Position
Wrong	Restrictive	Conservative
Innocuous	Restrictive	'Totalitarian'
Innocuous	Liberal	Liberal/radical
Wrong	Liberal	Liberal/moderate

The 'totalitarian' position is of merely theoretical interest. (It might be occupied by someone in an under-populated country, indifferent both to women's rights and to appeals to the sanctity of life, who thought it was necessary to increase the population quickly.) The first position is a familiar one. It is well known that the conservative position on legislation about abortion is based on a corresponding conservative position about its morality. According to the conservative view, abortion is morally wrong because it is the taking of human life, and hence, like any other case of homicide, justifiable in only a restricted range of circumstances, which should be laid down by law.

It is the possibility of two distinct liberal positions, which for want of better labels I will henceforth distinguish as the 'radical' and the 'moderate', which is not so familiar, and much that is said on the liberal side about women's rights leaves it quite unclear which of two views about the morality of abortion its supporters hold. Do they hold that abortion is morally quite innocuous – and hence that to have laws restricting women's access is as absurd and punitive as having laws which decreed, say, that women (though not men) were forbidden to cut their hair or smoke? Or do they agree with the conservatives that it is a morally very serious matter but hold that nevertheless the suffering and lack of freedom that women must at present undergo when abortion is not legally available not only justify but require our having laws which permit this wrong to be done whenever the woman wishes it? Is abortion a necessary evil as things are at present, or not an evil at all?

As this suggests, at a pragmatic level any law maker must consider the likely *effect* of laws which (for whatever reason) straightforwardly prohibited abortion. Experience, in both this country as well as in many others, has indeed tended to show that, rather than curtailing the practice, abortion will simply be driven underground.

8.2 The legal position

8.2.1 Criminal law provisions

Abortion in the UK remains prima facie a criminal offence. Historically, the influence of the canon law of the Christian Church played an important part in the emergent common law on the subject. John Keown has charted this influence as follows:

Keown, J, Abortion, Doctors and the Law: Some Aspects of the Legal Regulation of Abortion in England from 1803 to 1982[12]

... [T]he weight of available authority supports the view that the common law prohibited abortion, at the latest, after the foetus had become 'quick' or 'animated'. Animation was believed to occur when the foetus 'quickened' in the womb. An incident of the second trimester of pregnancy, quickening marks the first

---

12 Cambridge: CUP, 1988.

maternal perception of foetal movement. In associating the origin of life with quickening, the law betrayed both pragmatic and metaphysical influences. The former concerned the need to prove, in any prosecution for abortion, that the woman had been pregnant and that the foetus had been killed by the abortifacient act. Evidence of quickening would clearly facilitate prosecution. The metaphysical influence upon the law was the popular theory, originated by Aristotle and perpetuated by Galen, that human life began at the point of 'animation'. This theory was espoused by the canon law of the Christian Church and thence it found its way into the developing common law.

The criminal law of abortion achieved its modern form only in the mid-nineteenth century. As JK Mason has written:

Mason, JK, *Medico-Legal Aspects of Reproduction and Parenthood*[13]

The recognition of variable foetal rights has fluctuated in British law. The influence of medieval teaching was still apparent in 1803 when procuring the miscarriage of a woman who was 'quick with child' was a statutory offence subject to capital punishment. Abortion at an earlier state of gestation carried a lesser penalty, although it is difficult now to see much advantage to the culprit of a sentence of up to 14 years' transportation; nevertheless, the distinction was clearly meaningful at the time. The law remained the same until 1861 when the Offences Against the Person Act came into being. This introduced two major changes – first, the death penalty was replaced by potential penal servitude for life and, secondly, any distinction as to foetal age was abolished. The 1861 Act remains the definitive law in England, Wales and Northern Ireland . . .

Section 58 of the Offences Against the Person Act (OAPA) 1861 provides as follows:

58 Administering drugs or using instruments to procure abortion

Every woman, being with child, who, with intent to procure her own miscarriage, shall administer to herself any poison or other noxious thing, or shall unlawfully use any instrument or other means whatsoever with the like intent, and whosoever, with intent to procure the miscarriage of any woman, whether she be or be not with child, shall unlawfully administer to her or cause to be taken by her any poison or other noxious thing, or shall unlawfully use any instrument or other means whatsoever with the like intent, shall be guilty of felony, and being convicted thereof shall be liable to be kept in penal servitude for life.

Furthermore, s 59 of the Act prohibits various ancillary acts designed to facilitate the commission of the offence:

59 Procuring drugs, etc, to cause abortion

Whosoever shall unlawfully supply or procure any poison or other noxious thing, or any instrument or thing whatsoever, knowing that the same is intended to be unlawfully used or employed with intent to procure the miscarriage of any woman, whether she be or be not with child, shall be guilty of a misdemeanour, and being convicted thereof shall be liable to be kept in penal servitude.

---

13 Aldershot: Dartmouth, 1990.

It will be noted that the Act does not speak in terms of 'carrying out an abortion', but rather of 'procuring a miscarriage'. This (although it remains undefined) is arguably a narrower concept, which would apparently leave certain forms of foetal killing lawful, namely those where the woman does not 'miscarry' as a result of the procedure. The most startling example would be a situation in which the foetus is destroyed once the woman is already in labour: no miscarriage occurs here, but equally the foetus, even one which has partially emerged from the womb, does not yet enjoy the protection of the criminal law against homicide. The existence of such a legal *lacuna* was deplored by Talbot J in charging a jury at Liverpool in 1928, and his comments led to the passing of a further piece of legislation, the Infant Life (Preservation) Act (IL(P)A) 1929. Section 1(1) of the 1929 Act created a new offence of 'child destruction':

> **1 Punishment for child destruction**
>
> (1)   Subject as hereinafter in this sub-section provided, any person who, with intent to destroy the life of a child capable of being born alive, by any wilful act causes a child to die before it has an existence independent of its mother, shall be guilty of felony, to wit, of child destruction, and shall be liable on conviction thereof on indictment to penal servitude for life:
>
> Provided that no person shall be found guilty of an offence under this section unless it is proved that the act which caused the death of the child was not done in good faith for the purpose only of preserving the life of the mother.

Although, as noted, the primary purpose of this provision was the protection of the foetus during the course of its birth, it is apparent that its effect goes further by extending such protection back in time to the point in the pregnancy at which the foetus became 'capable of being born alive'. By virtue of s 1(2) of the Act, this is rebuttably presumed to be at 28 weeks' gestation:

> 1(2) – For the purposes of this Act, evidence that a woman had at any material time been pregnant for a period of 28 weeks or more shall be *prima facie* proof that she was at that time pregnant of a child capable of being born alive.

Thus, the 1861 and 1929 Acts operate to some extent in overlap: a termination carried out on a foetus capable of being born alive will, in so far as it occurs by way of a miscarriage, be an offence under both statutes. By contrast, only the 1861 Act applies to the younger, non-viable foetus and, conversely, only the 1929 Act to a foetus already in the course of its birth.

8.2.2   Defences to abortion prior to 1967

Section 1(1) of the ILPA 1929 contains an express proviso to the effect that no offence is committed by a person who causes the death of the foetus in order to save the life of the pregnant woman. This provision was included because, before the development of modern Caesarean sections, the craniotomy (crushing the foetus's skull) was a standard medical procedure to deal with cases where normal delivery was not medically possible. It is apparent, however, that no similar defence was provided for in the OAPA 1861 in relation to procuring a miscarriage. A question that long remained open, therefore, was whether a doctor who terminated a pregnancy at this earlier stage in order to save the pregnant woman's life was necessarily guilty of an offence under the 1861 Act. The issue finally came before a court in 1938 in the case of *R v Bourne*.

R v Bourne[14]

A 14-year-old girl became pregnant as a result of a brutal rape. Mr Bourne, an eminent gynaecologist, made public his intention to perform an abortion on the girl and, having obtained the consent of her parents, duly did so. He was charged with procuring a miscarriage contrary to s 58 of the OAPA 1861. In his defence, could a similar proviso to that found in the ILPA 1929 be read into the section and, if so, what was its scope?

Macnaghten J: No such proviso is in fact set out in s 58 of the Offences Against the Person Act 1861; but the words of that section are that any person who 'unlawfully' uses an instrument with intent to procure miscarriage shall be guilty of felony. In my opinion the word 'unlawfully' is not, in that section, a meaningless word. I think it imports the meaning expressed by the proviso in s 1, sub-s (1) of the Infant Life (Preservation) Act 1929, and that s 58 of the Offences Against the Person Act 1861 must be read as if the words making it an offence to use an instrument with intent to procure a miscarriage were qualified by a similar proviso.

In this case, therefore, my direction to you in law is this – that the burden rests on the Crown to satisfy you beyond reasonable doubt that the defendant did not procure the miscarriage of the girl in good faith for the purpose only of preserving her life . . .

What then is the meaning to be given to the words 'for the purpose of preserving the life of the mother'? There has been much discussion in this case as to the difference between danger to life and danger to health. It may be that you are more fortunate than I am, but I confess that I have found it difficult to understand what the discussion really meant, since life depends upon health, and it may be that health is so gravely impaired that death results. A question was asked by the learned Attorney General in the course of his cross-examination of Mr Bourne. 'I suggest to you, Mr Bourne,' said the Attorney General, 'that there is a perfectly clear line – there may be border-line cases – there is a clear line of distinction between danger to health and danger to life'. The answer of Mr Bourne was: 'I cannot agree without qualifying it; I cannot say just yes or no. I can say there is a large group whose health may be damaged, but whose life almost certainly will not be sacrificed. There is another group at the other end whose life will be definitely in very great danger.' And then he adds:

> There is a large body of material between those two extremes in which it is not really possible to say how far life will be in danger, but we find, of course, that the health is depressed to such an extent that life is shortened, such as in cardiac cases, so that you may say that their life is in danger, because death might occur within measurable distance of the time of their labour.
>
> If that view commends itself to you, you will not accept the suggestion that there is a clear line of distinction between danger to health and danger to life. Mr Oliver wanted you to give what he called a wide and liberal meaning to the words 'for the purpose of preserving the life of the mother'. I should prefer the word 'reasonable' to the words 'wide and liberal'. I think you should take a reasonable view of those words.

It is not contended that those words mean merely for the purpose of saving the mother from instant death. There are cases, we are told, where it is reasonably certain that a pregnant woman will not be able to deliver the child which is in her womb and survive. In such a case where the doctor anticipates, basing his opinion upon the experience of the profession, that the child cannot be delivered without the death of the mother, it is obvious that the sooner the operation is performed the better. The law does not require the doctor to wait until the unfortunate woman is in peril of immediate death. In such a case he is not only entitled, but it is his duty to perform the operation with a view to saving her life.

Mr Bourne was acquitted by the jury.

---

14 [1939] 1 KB 687.

Although an important decision, the law still continued to remain in a state of some uncertainty. Unsurprisingly, given the prospect of criminal prosecution and possible conviction, many doctors would only intervene in the clearest cases of risk to the woman's life. In the meantime, the practice of illegal and unhygienic backstreet abortions thrived, leading not infrequently to serious injury to the pregnant woman, or even her death. In the light of this situation, and with the arrival of the more permissive social climate of the 1960s, pressure built up in favour of legislative reform. This culminated in the enactment of the Abortion Act of 1967.

THINK POINT

In Northern Ireland, where the 1967 Act was never enacted, the law is still governed by *R v Bourne*: as a short independent research exercise, examine later developments in the case law there and summarise your findings.

8.2.3 The Abortion Act 1967

It is important to be clear at the outset that the Abortion Act 1967 has not replaced the pre-existing criminal law statutes on abortion. Rather, its effect is to provide a medical practitioner who carries out an abortion within its terms with a statutory immunity to such criminal prosecution. Originally, only liability under the 1861 Act was excluded; however, the Abortion Act was amended in 1990 (by s 37 of the Human Fertilisation and Embryology Act), to also exclude liability for child destruction under the 1929 IL(P)A. The effect was a further liberalisation of the law, as terminations could now be carried out on later, viable foetuses, including where the pregnant woman's life was not at risk – notably for foetal disability.

The relevant terms of the 1967 Act (as amended) are set out in s 1 as follows:

1 Medical termination of pregnancy

1 Subject to the provisions of this section, a person shall not be guilty of an offence under the law relating to abortion when a pregnancy is terminated by a registered medical practitioner if two registered medical practitioners are of the opinion, formed in good faith –

    a   that the pregnancy has not exceeded its 24th week and that the continuance of the pregnancy would involve risk, greater than if the pregnancy were terminated, of injury to the physical or mental health of the pregnant woman or any existing children of her family; or

    b   that the termination is necessary to prevent grave permanent injury to the physical or mental health of the pregnant woman; or

    c   that the continuance of the pregnancy would involve risk to the life of the pregnant woman, greater than if the pregnancy were terminated; or

    d   that there is a substantial risk that if the child were born it would suffer from such physical or mental abnormalities as to be seriously handicapped.

2 In determining whether the continuance of a pregnancy would involve such risk of injury to health as is mentioned in para (a) or (b) of sub-s (1) of this section, account may be taken of the pregnant woman's actual or reasonably foreseeable environment.

3 Except as provided by sub-s (4) of this section, any treatment for the termination of pregnancy must be carried out in a hospital vested in the Secretary of State for the purposes of his functions under the

National Health Service Act 2006 or the National Health Service (Scotland) Act 1978 . . . or in a place approved for the purposes of this section by the Secretary of State . . . .

4   Sub-section (3) of this section, and so much of sub-s (1) as relates to the opinion of two registered medical practitioners, shall not apply to the termination of a pregnancy by a registered medical practitioner in a case where he is of the opinion, formed in good faith, that the termination is immediately necessary to save the life or to prevent grave permanent injury to the physical or mental health of the pregnant woman.

THINK POINT

Why is it that Parliament in 1967 did not simply repeal the earlier criminal law statutes on abortion?

In the following we consider each of the four grounds for termination mentioned in s 1(1) in turn.

8.2.3.1 Risk . . . of injury to the physical or mental health of the pregnant woman or any existing children of her family

This ground is used to justify the great majority of abortions carried out in Britain. It is widest in scope and the suggestion that it permits abortions on 'social' as well as strictly 'medical' grounds is given weight by the fact that, besides risks to the pregnant woman, those to the existing children of her family may also be considered. Similarly, s 1(2) of the Act provides that account may here be taken of the woman's environment. It is apparent that the risks in question need not be substantial; it is enough that they exceed the risk to the woman (and/or her existing children) of carrying out the termination. This has led to an argument that since, statistically, an abortion carried out in the first 12 weeks of pregnancy poses fewer health risks to the woman than carrying the foetus to term, the Act will invariably permit such early terminations. Jonathan Montgomery has commented upon the operation of ground 1(1)(a) as follows:

Montgomery, J, *Health Care Law*[15]

While this ground clearly refers to health matters, it has been described as a 'social' ground, because doctors may take account of the woman's actual or foreseeable environment when they assess the risks involved. This means that the inconvenience of having a child may provide a basis for an abortion. It has been argued that this makes it lawful to terminate a pregnancy on the basis of the sex of the foetus where the social and cultural pressures upon a woman to produce a child of a particular sex are strong.

The majority of induced abortions are performed under s 1(1)(a) . . . This overwhelming pattern of 'social' abortions has led to the 1967 Act being criticised for allowing abortion on demand. This assertion is based on the practice of some doctors who argue that there is statistical evidence that carrying a foetus to term is more dangerous to the woman than terminating the pregnancy in its early stages. This enables them to hold that s 1(1)(a) is made out whenever a woman is pregnant. This argument has never been tested in the courts, but it appears that doctors have given 'pregnancy' as the sole reason for believing that termination is less risky than continuing without being prosecuted.

---

15 Oxford: OUP, 1997.

However, it is apparent that the fact that proceeding to term poses some risk to the woman is not, in itself, a sufficient reason for termination. Rather, the doctor should perform a balancing operation in respect of the patient and determine that termination itself carries a *lower* risk: it is after all possible that, in a particular case, the risks of termination may in fact be greater than those attached to continuance, for example where the woman may subsequently suffer some form of psychological reaction. This need to identify the risks running both ways suggests that the doctor's role requires him to engage in more than mere statistical 'rubber stamping'. In this context, the BMA in its guidance, *The Law and Ethics of Abortion: BMA Views*, comments on the practice, seemingly current among some doctors, of pre-signing abortion certificates (HSA1 forms), as follows:

BMA, *The Law and Ethics of Abortion: BMA Views*[16]

The General Medical Council's (GMC) *Good Medical Practice* makes it clear that doctors are personally accountable for their professional practice, and must be able to justify their decisions and actions and demonstrate that they formed their opinion in good faith. The BMA believes that the practice of pre-signing is always likely to raise questions about whether the decision was made in good faith. However, there may be some circumstances where the pre-signing of HSA1 forms is not necessarily incompatible with the requirement of the Abortion Act for a doctor to have formed an opinion in good faith. For example, a doctor could prepare a stock of pre-signed forms in advance of being away from clinic, which are only used where the doctor verbally authorises their use following a telephone conversation or other communication, during which they decide, in good faith, that the woman's circumstances fit within the statutory grounds. These circumstances, however, should be seen as exceptional, and in the BMA's view, it would be inadvisable to routinely pre-sign HSA1 forms.

Importantly, unlike the other grounds under s 1(1), ground (a) contains a time limit: it may only be invoked in so far as the pregnancy has not exceeded its 24th week. This limit was introduced in the 1990 amendments to compensate for the fact that the same amendments removed the effect of the IL(P)A 1929, which had previously supplied a rough upper time limit to lawful abortions (in terms of the child's viability).[17] The practical difficulties, though, in applying a precise time limit in such cases have been noted by Andrew Grubb:

Grubb, A, 'The new law of abortion: clarification or ambiguity'[18]

Section 1(1)(a) does not specify the point in time which starts the clock running in calculating the 24 weeks. There are four possibilities: (A) the first day of the woman's last period; (B) the date of conception (up to 14 days later); (C) the date of implantation (up to 10 days later); and (D) the first day of the woman's first missed period (about four weeks after (A)).

In England the medical profession calculates the length of gestation of a baby on the basis of (A) because it is the most certain date of any of these alternatives. Options (B) and (C), namely the date of conception and the date the fertilised egg implants into the woman, by contrast, cannot be known for certain. But there are difficulties with option (D), because although the first day of the woman's first missed

---

16 London: BMA, November 2014 (updated June 2017), at p 6; see: www.bma.org.uk/advice/employment/ethics/ethics-a-to-z/abortion.
17 As noted in section 8.2.2 above, the 1929 Act itself allowed for late-term feticide in case of imminent risk to the woman's life.
18 [1991] Crim LR 659.

period is certain, it may be quite misleading to indicate length of pregnancy where, for example, following conception during the last week of a cycle the woman does not miss the next period but only the one that follows. The date calculated on the basis of (D) could be about five weeks after conception has actually occurred.

Consequently, when does time start to run? The law might accept the medical profession's approach because of the certainty it would achieve. More importantly, however, it might be accepted because it is the basis upon which parliament introduced the 24 week time limit in s 1(1)(a) . . . . On that basis, in order to conform to the underlying premise that a foetus which is capable of surviving should not be aborted on the ground in s 1(1)(a), the time limit should actually be 22 weeks or even less.

8.2.3.2 Termination necessary to prevent grave permanent injury to the physical or mental health of the pregnant woman

This ground contains no time limit and, by virtue of s 1(4), may be invoked in an emergency by a single doctor without waiting for a second certificate. Arguably, it simply codifies the common law defence available to the doctor who performs a therapeutic abortion designed to avoid serious harm to the woman, as established in *R v Bourne*. There is, however, one oddity. In speaking of the termination being 'necessary', the ground appears to require foresight by the doctor of such harm as a practical certainty, yet s 1(2) (which applies to this ground as well as (a) above) implies that a mere 'risk' of such injury will be sufficient. While, doubtless, at some point a high enough risk may be treated, analytically, as forming a practical certainty, the term usually denotes something rather less than this.

8.2.3.3 Risk to the life of the pregnant woman, greater than if the pregnancy were terminated

Like ground (b) above, this ground may be used in an emergency by a single doctor. Although ground (c) specifically refers to risk to 'life', in practice a large measure of overlap may be expected between the two grounds. This is because, as was apparent in *R v Bourne*, it may be difficult to say, as a matter of evidence, where grave injury to health ceases and risk to life begins. Moreover, given that – as in the case of ground (a) – the doctor is required to conduct a simple balancing of risks to determine whether a termination is justified, ground (c) may actually be easier to employ: the risk to the woman's life in continuing to term need not be substantial provided that it exceeds the risk involved in abortion. Ironically, the risks at issue are likely to be more readily quantifiable than the somewhat diffuse harms contemplated under ground (a), so it may be here that a 'statistical argument' would have the greatest purchase. For example, suppose that a doctor assesses the risk to the life of the woman in giving birth at one in 8,000. Provided the risk attached to termination is even lower, say, one in 10,000, an abortion would apparently be justified here. Since, in contrast with ground (a), no time limit is placed on terminations under this ground, it appears that an abortion in the circumstances just described could, in theory, take place until birth.

8.2.3.4 Substantial risk that if the child were born it would suffer from such physical or mental abnormalities as to be seriously handicapped

In common with the first three grounds, there are significant difficulties in interpreting the precise application and scope of this ground. On the face of it, however, it differs from the others in being directed to the welfare of the foetus rather than that of the pregnant woman. Derek Morgan argued for a strict interpretation of the ground, allowing its use only in cases of 'foetal euthanasia', that is to say where termination is in the foetus's best interests:

Morgan, D, 'Abortion: the unexamined ground'[19]

Section 1(1)[(d)] requires that the physician decide that there is a 'substantial' risk that the physical or mental abnormalities are such that the child if born would be 'seriously' handicapped . . .

One immediate analogy which could be drawn is that of the severely handicapped neonate who if its condition had been known, might have been aborted under s 1(1)[(d)]. In two recent cases, the Court of Appeal has had to consider in what, if any, circumstances a severely handicapped infant might be allowed to die. In *In Re C* the court was concerned with a baby born with an unusually severe form of hydrocephalus and with a poorly formed brain structure. She was physically handicapped, including generalised spastic cerebral palsy of all limbs, probable blindness and deafness and an inability to absorb food. In the first judgment of its kind, the High Court acknowledged and condoned the paediatric practice of managing some neonates towards their death rather than striving with heroic interventions to save or treat at all costs . . .

Re C amplified the earlier judgment of the Court of Appeal in *Re B*. There, the court had established, first, that these cases could only proceed under a 'best interests' test (in that case of the ward). And secondly, the court held that only in a case where the prognosis established that the child's life was going to be 'demonstrably . . . so awful', and where there was no lingering doubt about that future, could a non-treatment order be contemplated. Lords Justices Templeman and Dunn observed that this would include cases of severe proved damage such that the court would be driven to conclude that non-treatment was appropriate. This would not be the case, however, where the prognosis or information about the damage was 'still so imponderable' that it would be wrong for the baby to be allowed to die.

The attempt to invoke an analogy between the severely disabled foetus (even at term) and the similarly afflicted neonate is weakened, however, by the fact that, in another crucial respect, the law clearly regards the two situations as very different. In particular, whereas the foetus remains vulnerable to active measures to destroy it, the most that is permitted in relation to the neonate is the passive withholding of measures that would otherwise prolong its life. The view that this ground, like the others, in fact goes principally to the parents' interests, is supported by the history behind the 1990 amendments, which removed the time limits restricting the abortion of handicapped foetuses 'capable of being born alive'. The 1988 Select Committee of the House of Lords had the following to say on the issue:

See Chapter 12 →

House of Lords Select Committee, *Report of the Select Committee on the Infant Life (Preservation) Bill*[20]

41 Although abortions on ground 4, that is to say, a substantial risk that the child if born would suffer from such abnormalities as to be seriously handicapped, are only a small proportion of the total abortions, they comprise most of the abortions performed after 24 weeks . . . It is these late abortions which would be made more difficult to obtain if an upper limit of 24 weeks were to be imposed, and they represent in the opinion of the Committee a highly important factor. Whether an abortion is desired or justified in such a case will depend to a large extent on the degree of abnormality which is diagnosed and the circumstances

---

19 [1990] Crim LR 687.
20 HL Paper No 50, London: HMSO, 1987–88.

and attitude of the parents. Although a severely handicapped child is often the cause of crisis and disaster, there are other cases where even severe handicap has been the means of inspiring love and care within the family, and even the strengthening of character and family ties. At its worst, a child severely affected by spina bifida may be not only mentally retarded, but also severely paralysed so as to be unable to walk, doubly incontinent, deaf and blind. It is obvious that the birth of such a child will constitute an immediate crisis for parents and doctors. Although some women elect nevertheless to have severely handicapped children, the Committee have received evidence that the cumulative effect on families of years of caring for a totally dependent child can be devastating, and when the parents die the child must all too often be institutionalised, with traumatic effects. Ante-natal care is rightly directed to the detection of mothers who are subject to these risks, and counselling must always be available, though the choice will be the mother's.

As we have seen, s 1(1)(d) speaks of the foetus suffering from 'such mental or physical abnormalities as to be seriously handicapped'. This undoubted vagueness is compounded by the fact that the section requires only 'a substantial risk' of such abnormalities, which again leaves room for semantic disagreement. Significantly, if the 'parental interests' interpretation of s 1(1)(d) is correct, it suggests these terms should be understood subjectively – ie in the light of the meanings assigned to them by the foetus' mother/parents.

This view arguably finds support in the 2003 case of *Jepson v Chief Constable of West Mercia Police*,[21] which arose after it was revealed that s 1(1)(d) had been used to carry out an abortion at more than 24 weeks upon a foetus with a cleft palate. The claimant, a Church of England curate, sought judicial review of the police's decision not to prosecute the doctors involved, as well as a declaration that a cleft palate was not capable of constituting a serious handicap within the section. Although it eventually gave leave to proceed, the Divisional High Court made it clear that in its view the claimant had little chance of succeeding at trial, and the action was subsequently dropped. Rosamund Scott has commented upon the proceedings as follows:

Scott, R, 'Interpreting the disability ground of the Abortion Act'[22]

The claimant in *Jepson* contended that a key error of law surrounding the abortion in that case was 'that the medical practitioners who signed the certificate . . . took into account the views of the parents involved' and 'that . . . in relation to the decision in question, the parents' views, as a matter of law, could have no weight'. Certainly the Act states that two doctors must be 'of the opinion, formed in good faith' that the impairment is serious. Whether two doctors can decide in good faith that the condition is serious and mean, in so doing, 'serious for this woman or couple' is a crucial question. Doctors could decide that a woman's or couple's views as to seriousness are relevant to their opinion of whether the condition of seriousness is satisfied if they consider that the purpose of the disability section of the Act, at least in some cases, is to protect parents by giving them choice.

. . . [T]he basis of this section has recently been reconsidered by Sally Sheldon and Stephen Wilkinson [(2001) 9 Med L Rev 85]. They argue that, because very few foetuses aborted under this ground would have lives of little or no quality if born, most abortions under this section cannot be seen as protecting the foetus from such a life. Rather, in most cases in which this section is invoked, the real concern is with the woman's or parents' interests. This is a moral argument as to the legal interpretation of this section of the Act.

---

21 [2003] EWHC 3318 (Admin).
22 (2005) 64 CLJ 388.

> The legal objection to this argument, originally explored by Derek Morgan, is that a 'parental interests' interpretation of section 1(1)(d) of the Act would essentially repeat section 1(1)(a) of the Act, making section 1(1)(d) redundant. Sheldon and Wilkinson observe that, from an ethical viewpoint, it may simply be that there is more than one justification for this section . . . .
>
> Of course, section 1(1)(d) can never be entirely redundant in that, unlike section 1(1)(a), it allows terminations up until birth. Apart from this point and more fundamentally, it may be that as a society we have not necessarily been honest about whose interests the disability section of the Act is capable of protecting: it is to some degree taboo to say that parents have an interest in choosing to accept or avoid the birth of an impaired child and those debating the Act in Parliament may well have sensed this.

In its 2010 report, *Termination of Pregnancy for Fetal Abnormality in England, Scotland and Wales*,[23] the Royal College of Obstetricians and Gynaecologists expressed the view that it would be impractical to produce an objective list of conditions constituting serious handicap, given the difficulty of predicting the long-term impact of an abnormality on a child or its family.

THINK POINT

How far could it be argued that the main change to the law made by the 1967 Act was to permit abortion for foetal disability?

8.3 Implications of the law

8.3.1 The involved parties

Given the legal framework sketched above, what rights are enjoyed by the key actors in the abortion process? We begin by considering the position of the pregnant woman.

8.3.1.1 The pregnant woman

The general view is that the 1967 Act gives the pregnant woman no right to demand an abortion. As Jonathan Montgomery notes:

Montgomery, J, *Health Care Law*[24]

> [I]t does not follow from the fact that doctors are in practice usually immune from prosecution that the Abortion Act 1967 provides for abortion on demand. The Act does not provide women with rights to terminate their pregnancy. Instead, it leaves them dependent upon finding a doctor who will co-operate with their wishes. This means that women who can afford to go to private clinics will usually have little difficulty obtaining a legal abortion. Those reliant on NHS provision, however, are faced with considerable variation between the practice of different doctors. Consequently, there is considerable disparity in the degree to

---

23 See: www.rcog.org.uk/files/rcog-corp/TerminationPregnancyReport18May2010.pdf.
24 See n 15 above.

which abortions are readily available both between and within different areas of the country. Official statistics showed that in 1973 only 10% of those seeking an abortion in Walsall were able to get one through the NHS, while in Oxford the figure was 79%.

It is therefore doctors who control access to abortions. Women's access to abortions is dependent on the ethical position of individual doctors and is vulnerable to prejudices of an essentially white middle class profession. Norrie has pointed out that terminations sought because the child is the 'wrong' sex are as justifiable under the Act as those because the pregnancy is inconvenient for economic or career reasons. However, the former is far less likely to be accepted by the medical profession. The Abortion Act 1967 may allow doctors to offer abortion on demand in the early stages of pregnancy, but it does not secure it for women.

It is certainly true that nowhere in the Abortion Act 1967 is there to be found any express right to an abortion and, in this omission, it could be argued that it is a less liberal measure than similar laws in many other jurisdictions. In the USA, for example, the effect of the decisions of the Supreme Court in *Roe v Wade* and *Planned Parenthood v Casey* is that, until viability, state laws placing undue obstacles in the path of abortion will infringe the woman's constitutionally protected right to privacy.[25] However, although English law, thus, inhibits (at least in symbolic terms) a woman's freedom to terminate her pregnancy, it could be asked whether abortion differs in this respect from any other form of medical treatment available in this country. After all, it is well established that a patient cannot insist upon a particular procedure if the doctor does not believe it to be medically indicated as in the patient's best interests.[26]

In fact, in practice, the wishes of the pregnant woman will usually be the principal factor in persuading doctors to certify an abortion's legality within the Act. This is borne out by empirical studies into the way in which women who undergo abortions perceive their experience. Ellie Lee has chronicled the accounts of some young women who sought access to UK abortion services as follows:

Lee, E, 'Young women, pregnancy, and abortion in Britain: a discussion of law in practice'[27]

[M]ost young women made a decision about what the outcome of the pregnancy should be before seeing a doctor. This did not mean there was no perceived need for discussion, 'I made my decision straight away. I didn't really need to think about it . . . She [the GP] talked it over for a while with me so it was good'.

It was quite straight cut, it wasn't the right time . . . the doctor was really helpful . . . he asked me what I wanted to do . . . and we'd spoken for a little bit and I said that I didn't really want it and so he went through the procedure and what I had to do . . . he told me exactly what was going to happen . . . so he made me feel a bit easier, that I didn't have to do it on my own, didn't have to find out about it on my own.

These accounts show that the experience of referral was positive where referrers provided clear information about what obtaining an abortion entails. As another interviewee explained, the GP she saw was, '. . . really good' because, '. . . he did get me referred quick, and he did sit down and say what the risks were, what could happen and what couldn't happen'. Information provision was experienced positively not simply because it meant specific questions were answered and it was made clear how abortion could be obtained. It was also of psychological significance, in that it legitimized and normalized requesting abortion.

---

25 410 US 113 (1976) and 112 S Ct 2791 (1992). See also the US Supreme Court's recent decision in *Whole Woman's Health v Hellerstedt*, 579 US, 136 S Ct 2292 (2016).
26 See, eg, *R v Cambridge HA, ex p B* (1995) 23 BMLR 1, discussed in Ch 2, section 2.4.2.
27 (2004) 18 International Journal of Law, Policy and the Family 283.

As noted under 8.2.3, the grounds under the Abortion Act 1967 (as amended) for a lawful termination are so framed that one or other may relatively easily, or arguably even invariably, be satisfied. This was noted by Laws LJ in *Pro-Life Alliance v British Broadcasting Association*,[28] where his Lordship commented:

> **Laws LJ**: [6] The great majority [of abortions] are performed on the [ground] . . . that the continuance of the pregnancy would involve risk, greater than if the pregnancy were terminated, of injury to the physical or mental health of the pregnant woman. There is some evidence that many doctors maintain that the continuance of a pregnancy is always more dangerous to the physical welfare of a woman than having an abortion, a state of affairs which is said to allow a situation of *de facto* abortion on demand to prevail.

This is also reflected in the high number of abortions that take place in the UK each year. According to Department of Health Statistics, in 2014 there were a total of 184,571 terminations on women resident in England and Wales, and 11,475 on those in Scotland. Of these, 98 per cent were funded by the NHS (including 67 per cent in the independent sector under NHS contract). Ninety-two per cent of abortions were carried out at under 13 weeks of gestation; 80 per cent were at under 10 weeks.[29] However, the picture is distorted by the fact that, as alluded to in 8.2.2, in Northern Ireland the law on abortion, where the Abortion Act 1967 has never applied, remains restrictive. As a consequence, terminations are barely available in that province,[30] and women who wish to have such treatment must instead travel to England for it. This situation formed the background of the recent UK Supreme Court decision in *R (on the application of A and B) v Secretary of State for Health*.

> ### R (on the application of A and B) v Secretary of State for Health[31]
>
> The appellants were a mother and daughter resident in Northern Ireland. After A became pregnant at the age of 15, the two of them travelled to Manchester for her to undergo a termination, involving significant financial outlay as well as the stress of raising the funds without disclosing the purpose. They argued the Health Secretary ought to have used his power to provide NHS-funded abortions in England for Northern Irish women, and not to do so was a breach of their right to private life in conjunction with the right to non-discrimination under Articles 8 and 14 of the ECHR:
>
> > **Lord Wilson (with whom Lords Reed and Hughes agreed)**: [6] Although this court must acknowledge respect for the ethical "pro-life" convictions which inform the law in relation to abortions in Northern Ireland (together, of course, with equal respect for the contrary "pro-choice" convictions), it remains easy to understand why the plight of women who find themselves in unwanted pregnancy there is deeply unenviable.
> >
> > . . . [19] The appellants submit that:
> > (a) A was usually resident in part of the UK and thus, in principle, she was a UK tax-payer and a contributor to the funding of the UK-wide NHS;
> > (b) she was also a UK citizen;
> > (c) all UK citizens usually resident there should, at any rate in this context, be treated alike irrespective of the area within the UK of their usual residence;
> > (d) the respondent chose to provide abortion services in England free of charge under the NHS for women usually resident in England on the basis (which was correct) that they had a reasonable requirement for it;

---

28 [2002] EWCA Civ 297.
29 See: www.patient.co.uk/doctor/termination-of-pregnancy.
30 Ibid., recording 23 terminations in Northern Ireland for the year 2013/14 ; in *In the Matter of an Application by NIHRC* [2018] UKSC 27, a majority of the UK Supreme Court suggested (without making a formal ruling) that this restrictive position is incompatible with the ECHR rights of pregnant women.
31 [2017] UKSC 41.

(e) but women usually resident in Northern Ireland were, as he knew, generally unable to access such services there;

(f) and so the only decision rationally open to him was to provide such services for them in England.

[20] Like the judges in the courts below, I would reject the appellants' submissions set out above. Parliament's scheme is that separate authorities in each of the four countries united within the kingdom should provide free health services to those usually resident there. The respondent was entitled to make a decision in line with this scheme for local decision-making and in accordance with the target reflective of it which was imposed on him by statute.

... [34] The appellants correctly submit that, in interpreting Convention rights, the ECtHR now frequently refers to the text of international conventions and even to the recommendations of committees set up to oversee observance of them by the parties to them. They and the interveners urge the court to assess the fairness (or, as they submit, the unfairness) of the respondent's decision in its application to women who were UK citizens but usually resident in Northern Ireland through the prism of such material. ...

[35] ... [However, the relevant documents] carefully stop short of calling upon national authorities to make abortion services generally available. ... At its highest one can say only that there is a trend in some of the international material to which the current law in Northern Ireland runs counter. The trend adds background colour to the inquiry into fair balance under the Convention. In my view, however, the appellants need material of a far more vivid hue to put into the balance against the respondent's resolve to stay loyal to the overall scheme for separate provision of free health services within each of our four countries and to the democratic decision reached in Northern Ireland in relation to abortion services. In my view the balance struck by his decision was fair.

Lord Kerr (dissenting): [74] Lord Wilson has said that the Secretary of State was entitled to afford respect to the democratic decision of the people of Northern Ireland ... I agree. Indeed I would go further. He was bound to show such respect. But respect for what? The Northern Ireland Assembly had decided that abortion in that jurisdiction should not be provided on the same basis as in England. But it has expressed no view about the ability of women from NI to travel to England to obtain abortions. Assembly members, indeed all informed persons in the entire population of Northern Ireland, are plainly aware of the fact that many women from NI travel every year to England to obtain abortions and have done so for many years. The need for respect on the part of the Secretary of State, on behalf of the British government, did not extend to denying Northern Irish women the means of obtaining abortions in England. It was entirely right that this should be so. Why should affording Northern Irish women abortions on the NHS constitute a lack of respect, when countenancing and permitting such abortions does not?

Lady Hale (dissenting) [92] ... The question ... is whether a policy of not providing the medical service of terminating pregnancies under the Abortion Act 1967 to women who live in Northern Ireland is consistent with the [Health Secretary's] duty to provide (or secure the provision of) such services as are "necessary to meet all reasonable requirements".

[93] In considering what is reasonably required, regard must be had to some of the fundamental values underlying our legal system ... These include autonomy and equality, both of which are aspects of an even more fundamental value, which is respect for human dignity. The right of pregnant women to exercise autonomy in relation to treatment and care has been hard won but it has been won ...

As with other patients who can show that they were improperly denied medical treatment, a pregnant woman prevented from having an abortion through a doctor's failure to certify it under the Abortion Act, may potentially have an *ex post facto* claim in negligence. Though, as we saw in Chapter 6, substantive awards in cases of 'wrongful birth' are no longer available for the birth of a healthy child, the woman remains entitled to damages arising from continued pregnancy, as well as a 'solatium' for the denial of procreative autonomy.[32] In cases where the child is born disabled, significantly higher compensation is payable. Indeed, over the years a number of successful negligence actions have been brought by women who have argued that they should have been given the opportunity to have an abortion on the ground of foetal handicap under s 1(1) (d) of the 1967 Act. An example is the case of *Mackay v Essex AHA*, in which Griffiths LJ expressly suggested that the medical profession is under a duty to advise the pregnant woman of 'her right to have an abortion and the pros and cons of doing so'.[33]

See Chapter 6 ➜

By contrast, in so far as a pregnant woman, who is a competent adult, chooses not to abort her foetus, it is clear that the law will not make her do so. At first glance, this assertion may seem to be a straightforward application of the principle that competent adults must always consent to medical procedures carried out upon them. However, this is to ignore the possible use of indirect legal means to pressurise women to opt for terminations in certain cases. For example, in the context of an action for wrongful birth, might a woman be denied compensation for the costs of raising a disabled child on the basis that her failure to have a termination was 'unreasonable'? This question was at the heart of the case of *Emeh v Kensington and Chelsea AHA*:

Emeh v Kensington and Chelsea AHA[34]

The claimant, who already had four children, underwent a voluntary sterilisation at the defendant's hospital. The operation was negligently performed and the plaintiff subsequently became pregnant, only discovering this fact when her foetus was of 17–20 weeks' gestation. She refused the defendant's offer of an abortion and later gave birth to a disabled child. At first instance, Park J denied her claim for the costs of raising the child, finding that her failure to have the abortion amounted to a *novus actus interveniens*, which eclipsed the defendant's earlier negligence and made her the author of her loss. The claimant successfully appealed:

Slade LJ: The judge, in saying that her failure to obtain an abortion was so unreasonable as to eclipse the defendants' wrongdoing, was, I think, really saying that the defendants had the right to expect that, if they had not performed the operation properly, she would procure an abortion, even if she did not become aware of its existence until nearly 20 weeks of her pregnancy had elapsed.

I do not, for my part, think that the defendants had the right to expect any such thing. By their own negligence, they faced her with the very dilemma which she had sought to avoid by having herself sterilised.

For the reasons which I have attempted to give, I think that they could and should have reasonably foreseen that if, as a consequence of the negligent performance of the operation she should find herself pregnant again, particularly after some months of pregnancy, she might well decide to keep the child. Indeed, for my part I would go even a little further. Save in the most exceptional circumstances, I cannot think it right that the court should ever declare it unreasonable for a woman to decline to have an abortion in a case where there is no evidence that there were any medical or psychiatric grounds for terminating the particular pregnancy. And no such evidence has been drawn to our attention relating to this particular pregnancy of the plaintiff in the present case.

---

32 *Rees v Darlington Memorial Hospital NHS Trust* [2003] UKHL 52; see further, Ch 6 section 6.2.2 above.
33 [1982] QB 1166. The case is further considered in section 8.4.1 in relation to the child's attempt to claim for 'wrongful life', which unlike the mother's action in 'wrongful birth' was not allowed to proceed.
34 [1985] QB 1012, CA.

8.3.1.2 The foetus

Self-evidently, the existence of the regime under the 1967 Abortion Act, permitting legal abortion in a large number of circumstances, means that the foetus has no legal right to life. In this regard, Jane Fortin has written as follows:

Fortin, J, 'Legal protection for the unborn child'[35]

[T]he abortion legislation has contrived a situation whereby a decision to terminate the life of the foetus can be reached by two doctors in consultation only with the mother. There is thus no possibility of anyone intervening on behalf of the foetus, to ensure that adequate consideration has been given to its particular stage of physical and mental development, in order to assess the precise degree of its increasing 'humanness' and whether it warrants protection against its mother's desire for an abortion.

In this context, there is a stark contrast between the legal protection accorded to the unborn and to the newly born. In relation to the latter, however premature, the wardship jurisdiction can be used to cast an immediate cloak of protection over the child, thereby ensuring that fundamentally important decisions relating to the child's future can be considered dispassionately by the High Court. Thus, in the case of *Re B*, the Court of Appeal authorised a life-giving operation on a Down's syndrome child, against the wishes of its parents who had rejected it. By contrast, it is clear from the decisions in *Paton* and *C v S* that although an abortion has a fatal effect on the unborn child, intervention by a third party would be impossible even if in his view the abortion decision has been reached erroneously . . .

Despite the heavy responsibility for interpreting the 1967 Act imposed on the medical profession, it is surprising that the Act contains no guidance to them as to the factors to consider when deciding whether to approve an abortion. The omission of any direction specifically requiring the doctors to consider the interests of the foetus itself, when deciding whether to approve the abortion, implies that the abortion is a purely medical matter relating only to the mother herself and devoid of any moral implications relating to the foetus.

As Fortin notes elsewhere, the perceived need to safeguard the interests of the pregnant woman has led the courts to deny that the foetus, *in utero*, enjoys any legal personality. This important point lay behind the decision of the High Court in the case of *Paton v Trustees of British Pregnancy Advisory Services*.

Paton v Trustees of British Pregnancy Advisory Services[36]

The claimant sought an injunction restraining his wife from having an abortion under the Abortion Act 1967. Although she had obtained the required certificates from two doctors that she satisfied one of the statutory grounds, the plaintiff alleged that she was in fact acting in *male fides*. As a starting point, the plaintiff needed to establish *locus standi* to bring his action, either in his own right or as 'next friend' of the foetus:

Sir George Baker P: The first question is whether this plaintiff has a right at all. The foetus cannot, in English law, in my view, have a right of its own at least until it is born and has a separate existence from its mother. That permeates the whole of the civil law of this country (I except the criminal law, which is now irrelevant), and is, indeed, the basis of the decisions in those countries where law is

---

35 See n 4 above.
36 [1979] QB 276.

founded on the common law, that is to say, in America, Canada, Australia and, I have no doubt, in others.

For a long time there was great controversy whether, after birth, a child could have a right of action in respect of pre-natal injury . . . but it was universally accepted, and has since been accepted, that in order to have a right the foetus must be born and be a child. There was only one known possible exception . . . an American case, *White v Yup* . . ., where a wrongful 'death' of an eight month old viable foetus, stillborn as a consequence of injury, led an American court to allow a cause of action, but there can be no doubt, in my view, that in England and Wales the foetus has no right of action, no right at all, until birth. The succession cases have been mentioned. There is no difference. From conception the child may have succession rights by what has been called a 'fictional construction', but the child must be subsequently born alive: see per Lord Russell of Killowen in *Elliot v Lord Joicey*.

The approach of the High Court in *Paton* was subsequently endorsed by the Court of Appeal, outside the context of abortion, in the case of *Re F (In Utero)*.

Re F (In Utero)[37]

A woman with a history of psychiatric problems was 38 weeks pregnant when she absconded from the residential care home in which she lived. Her local authority, which was responsible for her care, sought to make her unborn child a ward of court as a preliminary to further measures to protect its health at this late stage in the pregnancy:

May LJ: Even though this is a case in which, on its facts, I would exercise the [wardship] jurisdiction if I had it, in the absence of authority I am driven to the conclusion that the court does not have the jurisdiction contended for. I respectfully agree with the dictum from the judgment of Sir George Baker P in the *Paton* case . . .

Secondly, I respectfully agree with the judge below in this case that to accept such jurisdiction and yet to apply the principle that it is the interest of the child which is to be predominant is bound to create conflict between the existing legal interests of the mother and those of the unborn child, and that it is most undesirable that this should occur . . .

Staughton LJ: I agree that this appeal should be dismissed. In their notice of appeal the local authority seek orders as follows:

1   The tipstaff do seek and detain in a suitable place the defendant and do report her whereabouts to the plaintiffs and the court.
2   The defendant do not leave the jurisdiction so long as she remains pregnant and further following the birth of the said child do not remove the said child from the jurisdiction.
3   The defendant do forthwith surrender her passport or other travel document to the court.
4   The defendant do attend forthwith such hospital suitable for the delivery of the said unborn child as the plaintiffs in their discretion direct.

It will be observed that all are orders directed at the mother, as in the nature of things they must be until the child is born.

When the wardship jurisdiction of the High Court is exercised, the rights, duties and powers of the natural parents are taken over or superseded by the orders of the court. Until a child

---

37 [1988] Fam 122.

> is delivered it is not, in my judgment, possible for that to happen. The court cannot care for a
> child, or order that others should do so, until the child is born; only the mother can.

In the wake of the decision in *Paton v Trustees of British Pregnancy Advisory Services*, Mr Paton took his case to Strasbourg; however, he failed to persuade the European Commission on Human Rights that the foetus's right to life is protected under Article 2 of the European Convention on Human Rights (ECHR).[38] The Commission's view was that, given the intimate connection between the foetus's life and that of the pregnant woman, any such right must in any event be limited in cases where the latter's life and health are at stake. More recently, in *Vo v France*,[39] the European Court of Human Rights (ECtHR), after noting the lack of consensus in ECHR signatory states as to the nature and status of the foetus, held that unborn life need not be treated as within the ambit of Article 2 of the ECHR. Thus, the degree of legal protection to be accorded to the foetus (in particular by criminal law) was a matter for each individual state.[40]

On the other hand, it should not be concluded that a foetus enjoys no protection at all in English law. It is rather that its interests are subordinated to those of full legal subjects – ie persons already born. Especially in the context of abortion, where there is a conflict between its interests and those of the pregnant woman, the law will accord priority to the woman (the degree to which the foetus is protected in other circumstances is explored in section 8.4 below).

8.3.1.3 The father

It is well established that, under English law, the father of a foetus cannot prevent a pregnant woman from having an abortion and, indeed, has no right even to be consulted over her proposed course of action. As we have seen, this was made clear in *Paton v Trustees of British Pregnancy Advisory Services*:[41]

> **Sir George Baker P**: The father's case must . . . depend upon a right which he has himself. I would say a word about the illegitimate, usually called the putative, but I prefer myself to refer to the illegitimate father. Although American decisions to which I have been referred concern illegitimate fathers, and statutory provisions about them, it seems to me that in this country the illegitimate father can have no rights whatsoever except those given to him by statute. That was clearly the common law. One provision which makes an inroad into this is s 14 of the Guardianship of Minors Act 1971, s 9(1) and some other sections of that Act which apply to illegitimate children, giving the illegitimate father or mother the right to apply for the custody of or access to an illegitimate child. But the equality of parental rights provision in s 1(1) of the Guardianship Act 1973 expressly does not apply in relation to a minor who is illegitimate: see s 1(7).
>
> . . . [T]his plaintiff must, in my opinion, bring his case, if he can, squarely within the framework of the fact that he is a husband. It is, of course, very common for spouses to seek injunctions for personal protection in the matrimonial courts during the pendency of or, indeed, after divorce actions, but the basic reason for the non-molestation injunction often granted in the family courts is to protect the other spouse or the living children, and to ensure that no undue pressure is put upon one or other of the spouses during the pendency of the case and during the breaking up of the marriage . . .
>
> The law is that the court cannot and would not seek to enforce or restrain by injunction matrimonial obligations, if they be obligations, such as sexual intercourse or contraception (a non-molestation

---

38 *Paton v UK* (1980) 3 EHRR 408.
39 (2004) 2 FCR 577.
40 Subsequently, the ECtHR reiterated this position in *A, B & C v Ireland* [2010] ECHR 2032.
41 See n 36 above.

injunction given during the pendency of divorce proceedings could, of course, cover attempted intercourse). No court would ever grant an injunction to stop sterilisation or vasectomy. Personal family relationships in marriage cannot be enforced by the order of a court. An injunction in such circumstances was
described by Judge Mager in *Jones v Smith* . . . in the District Court of Appeal of Florida as 'ludicrous'.

I ask the question, 'If an injunction were ordered, what could be the remedy?' and I do not think I need
say any more than that no judge could even consider sending a husband or wife to prison for breaking
such an order. That, of itself, seems to me to cover the application here; this husband cannot by law stop
his wife by injunction from having what is now accepted to be a lawful abortion within the terms of the
Abortion Act 1967.

In his action before the European Commission of Human Rights, Mr Paton argued that his right
to 'respect for family life' under Article 8 of the ECHR had been infringed. In dismissing this
claim, however, the Commission noted that Article 8(2) specifically limits that right in so far as
necessary to protect the rights of another person (here the pregnant woman).[42] The view taken
in *Paton* as to the father's lack of status has been endorsed by the courts on a number of occasions
since, including by the Court of Appeal in *C v S*.[43]

8.3.1.4 The doctor/healthcare worker

As will have been apparent in the discussion of s 1(1) of the Abortion Act 1967 above, the Act
gives doctors a very wide discretion in determining whether one of the grounds for lawful termination has been met. Writing in *The Lancet* in 1971, IM Ingram suggested that the wording of
the Act is indeed so wide as to be meaningless, and, though the 1990 amendments to the Act
have moved the key provisions around, it is apparent that they have not introduced any greater
precision. What safeguards are there, then, to prevent a doctor from abusing his discretion? John
Keown has discussed this issue as follows:

**Keown, J, *Abortion, Doctors and the Law: Some Aspects of the Legal Regulation of
Abortion in England from 1803 to 1982*[44]**

During the parliamentary debates on his Bill, Mr Steel [the Act's sponsor] said that it was necessary for
such a measure as his to contain 'safeguards' against abuse, and he pointed to three 'essential and new'
safeguards in his Bill: the requirements of certification of opinions, notification of abortions, and approval
of premises where the operations were to be performed. To what extent have these safeguards, which he
said would prevent abuse of the Act, operated as a check on excessively permissive interpretation of s 1?

. . . The Abortion Regulations 1968 came into effect on the same day as the Abortion Act in discharge
of the statutory duty placed on the minister by s 2(1) of the Act. Section 3 of the Regulations deals with the
certification of the practitioner's opinions . . . .

This Regulation undoubtedly represents a restriction on the practitioner's freedom in that it introduces a formality which he must observe, on pain of a fine. However, certification hardly restricts the
exercise of medical discretion, for although it ensures a second opinion it requires neither the second
practitioner to be of a particular status nor limits the number of practitioners who may be approached for
a second opinion. It does not even require the second practitioner to see the patient . . .

As a safeguard against abuse of medical discretion, therefore, certification is only of limited effectiveness. Its main virtue is in ensuring a second opinion, but this had been standard practice well before the

---

42 See n 38 above.
43 [1988] QB 135; see also the Scottish decision of *Kelly v Kelly* 1997 SLT 896.
44 See n 12 above.

enactment of the Regulations, among both reputable and disreputable practitioners. Although the ostensible function of certification is the protection of the patient, it also serves the interests of the practitioner by helping to protect him from suspicion of impropriety.

If certification is only a limited safeguard against abuse of the Act, what of notification? This safeguard was built into the Act in the form of s 2(1)(b), and its requirements are specified in s 4 of the Regulations. Section 4(1) requires the operating practitioner to notify the abortion to the CMO [Chief Medical Officer] within seven days, including in the notification form such information as is specified in Sched 2 to the Regulations.

Unlike certification, notification did represent a significant innovation in this area of medical practice, for whereas it had long been usual to obtain a second opinion, practitioners had not previously reported the operation to a third party. Moreover, failure to notify might, like failure to certify, involve the practitioner in liability under s 2(3) of the Act, and also in suspicion of illegal abortion.

However, the effectiveness of notification as a safeguard is also limited, for, just as a practitioner could certify an illegal abortion as falling within the terms of the Act, so too could he notify such an operation as having been performed within the Act, and it would be extremely difficult to prove the absence of good faith.

The procedure for certification under the Act as amended is now dealt with in the Abortion Regulations 1991, made under s 2 of the Act. The Regulations provide, in reg 3, as follows:

Certificate of opinion

3   (1) Any opinion to which s 1 of the Act refers shall be certified –

    a   in the case of a pregnancy terminated in accordance with s 1(1) of the Act, in the form set out in Part I of Sched 1 to these Regulations; and

    b   in the case of a pregnancy terminated in accordance with s 1(4) of the Act, in the form set out in Part II of that Schedule.

(2)   Any certificate of an opinion referred to in s 1(1) of the Act shall be given before the commencement of the treatment for the termination of the pregnancy to which it relates.

(3)   Any certificate of an opinion referred to in s 1(4) of the Act shall be given before the commencement of the treatment for the termination of the pregnancy to which it relates or, if that is not reasonably practicable, not later than 24 hours after such termination.

(4)   Any such certificate as is referred to in paras (2) and (3) of this Regulation shall be preserved by the practitioner who terminated the pregnancy to which it relates for a period of not less than three years beginning with the date of the termination.

(5)   A certificate which is no longer to be preserved shall be destroyed by the person in whose custody it then is.

A rare case in which a doctor's performance of an abortion was impugned, on the basis that he had not formed the view in good faith that the termination came within one of the grounds under the 1967 Act, was that of *R v Smith (John)*:

R v Smith (John)[45]

Dr Smith performed an abortion on a young woman, allegedly without either satisfying himself that continuance of her pregnancy would involve a risk greater than termination to her mental or physical health,

---

45 [1973] 1 WLR 1510.

or obtaining the requisite second opinion. The matter came to light because, following the operation, the patient became ill, and it was she who subsequently acted as the main prosecution witness. After his conviction by a jury of procuring a miscarriage contrary to s 58 of the OAPA 1861, Dr Smith appealed:

> **Scarman LJ**: On 28 April 1970 at the Hayward Nursing Home a Miss Rodgers underwent an operation performed by the appellant, the initial purpose of which was to terminate her pregnancy. The prosecution's case is that he was not acting in good faith; he had not formed a *bona fide* opinion as to the balance of risk between termination and continuation of her pregnancy, that is to say, that the continuance would involve risk to her physical or mental health greater than if it were terminated. The appellant's defence was twofold: he said that he formed an honest opinion as to the need for an abortion, but that when he had the girl on the operating table, he found she was starting an inevitable abortion. Thus according to him, his operation became not a termination, but a facilitating and tidying up of an inevitable abortion – a natural process which had already begun. If this be the truth, the prosecution concedes that the operation would be lawful without the need of recourse to the Abortion Act 1967....
>
> The case against the appellant relied on the evidence of Miss Rodgers and of police officers who interviewed the appellant in November and December 1970 and March 1971. Professor Fairweather, a distinguished gynaecologist, gave evidence on the question as to the likelihood of an inevitable abortion when there had been no history of pain or bleeding; he thought it unusual but possible. In reply to the recorder he emphasised the need for careful inquiry when the reason for abortion was injury to mental health and agreed that the 1967 Act could be abused. Both defendants and Dr Davis gave evidence. The trial was a long one and culminated in a lengthy summing up.
>
> Was the verdict unsafe? Counsel for the appellant took a great number of detailed points in his attack on the trial and the summing up. But, as he put it, his central submission was that a finding of bad faith against a doctor, when it relates to the forming of a medical opinion, cannot be safe or satisfactory unless supported by medical evidence pointing overwhelmingly to the lack of good faith ...
>
> Although the 1967 Act has imposed a great responsibility on doctors, it has not ousted the function of the jury. If a case is brought to trial which calls in question the *bona fides* of a doctor, the jury, not the medical profession, must decide the issue. The risk of abuse, by some, of the protection afforded by the Act was recognised as a genuine risk by Professor Fairweather. In the instant case it was for the jury to determine whether the appellant had or had not abused the protection afforded him by the Act. By leaving the ultimate question to a jury, the law retains its ability to protect society from an abuse of the Act.

This case, which is undoubtedly an unusual one, appears, on the face of it, to be at odds with subsequent judicial reluctance – evident in Sir George Baker P's comments in *Paton v British Pregnancy Advisory Services*[46] – to scrutinise the doctor's bona fides in applying the terms of the Abortion Act 1967:

> **Sir George Baker P**: The case put to me ... by Mr Rankin ... is that while he cannot say here that there is any suggestion of a criminal abortion, nevertheless if doctors did not hold their views, or come to their conclusions in good faith, which would be an issue triable by a jury (see *R v Smith (John)* ...), then this plaintiff might recover an injunction. That is not accepted by Mr Denny. It is unnecessary for me to decide that academic question because it does not arise in this case. My own

---

46 See n 36 above.

> view is that it would be quite impossible for the courts in any event to supervise the operation of the Abortion Act 1967. The great social responsibility is firmly placed by the law upon the shoulders of the medical profession: see per Scarman LJ in *R v Smith (John)*....
>
>   ... The two doctors have given a certificate. It is not and cannot be suggested that the certificate was given in other than good faith and it seems to me that there is the end of the matter in English law.

Subsequently, in *R v Dixon*[47] a doctor who continued with a hysterectomy upon a patient whose pregnancy only came to light during the operation, was similarly charged with an offence under s 58 of the OAPA 1861. On this occasion, the doctor's defence that he had acted in good faith to preserve the woman from grave permanent injury to her mental health (within s 1(1)(b) of the Abortion Act 1967) was accepted by the jury. While the doctor's evidence may appear flimsy ('in view of this lady's age, her very recent history of deliberate suicide attempt by overdose ... and her express wish for hysterectomy, we felt an emergency termination of pregnancy would be justified'), the case highlights the reluctance of juries to criminalise the practice of the modern abortion doctor.

In 2012, following an undercover newspaper investigation, appearing to show a doctor agree to perform an abortion on the basis of the foetus' (female) gender, the Crown Prosecution Service considered whether a charge should be preferred under the OAPA 1861 (for an attempt). However, it concluded that this would not be in the public interest, *inter alia* because the GMC was already investigating the matter.[48] In the event, the GMC similarly chose not to impose disciplinary sanctions. The incident led to disquiet among MPs, and the Health Secretary, Jeremy Hunt, wrote to the Attorney General, asking for his views. As discussed in section 8.2.3.1, however, it is arguable that the current law (in particular s 1(1)(a) of the 1967 Act) indeed permits doctors to carry out gender-based terminations where they consider this to be in the interests of the particular patient (including by reference to her cultural and family background). This is clearly a sensitive political and social issue, but, in fact, statistical analysis of birth gender ratios among different UK ethnic communities does not bear out the existence of systematic practices of this kind.[49]

A final and important issue in relation to the doctor is how far he may in fact refuse to participate in an abortion on grounds of conscience. This question is dealt with in s 4 of the Abortion Act 1967:

4 Conscientious objection to participation in treatment

1   Subject to sub-s (2) of this section, no person shall be under any duty, whether by contract or by any statutory or other legal requirement, to participate in any treatment authorised by this Act to which he has a conscientious objection, provided that in any legal proceedings the burden of proof of conscientious objection shall rest on the person claiming to rely on it.
2   Nothing in sub-s (1) of this section shall affect any duty to participate in treatment which is necessary to save the life or to prevent grave permanent injury to the physical or mental health of a pregnant woman.

---

47 *R v Dixon (Reginald)* (1995) (unreported).
48 See: www.cps.gov.uk/news/latest_news/cps_statement_abortion_related_case.
49 See DoH (2016) Birth Ratios in Great Britain, 2010–14: A report on gender ratios at birth in Great Britain, DoH, London.

As is apparent from s 4(2) above, this provision cannot be relied upon by a doctor called upon to perform an abortion in an emergency. The question (in non-emergency situations) of who, apart from the treating doctor, may rely on the conscientious objection clause, came before the House of Lords in 1988 in *Janaway v Salford HA*,[50] in which the claimant, a Roman Catholic, lost her job working as a secretary for the defendant health authority after refusing to type a letter of referral in respect of an abortion patient. She then brought an action for unfair dismissal on the basis that her refusal was protected under s 4(1). This argument, though accepted by a majority of the Court of Appeal, was rejected by House of Lords, which found her actions were too ancillary to the abortion procedure to bring her within the scope of the provision.

More recently, the UK Supreme Court was required to deal with similar questions in the case of *Doogan and another v NHS Greater Glasgow & Clyde Health Board*.

Doogan and another v NHS Greater Glasgow & Clyde Health Board[51]

Two Catholic midwives working at a Glaswegian hospital argued that their refusal to take part in planning/supervising other staff involved in abortions on their ward was protected under s 4(1) of the Abortion Act 1967. Following the success of this argument in front of the Court of Inner Session (the Scottish appeal court), the health authority appealed to the UK Supreme Court:

Lady Hale: [11] ... [T] he question in this case, and the only question, is the meaning of the words "to participate in any treatment authorised by this Act to which he has a conscientious objection". That question was addressed by the House of Lords in *R v Salford Health Authority, Ex p Janaway* ..., a case which all parties accept was rightly decided ... It was held that "any treatment authorised by this Act" meant the process of treatment in hospital for the termination of pregnancy and "participating" meant actually taking part in that process. It did not have the extended meaning given to participation by the criminal law. The House was not concerned, as we are in this case, with what those words mean in the context of hospital treatment.

... [31] ... [T]he petitioners argue that they have the right to object to any involvement with patients in connection with the termination of pregnancy to which they personally have a conscientious objection. The exercise of conscience is an internal matter which each person must work out for herself. It is bound to be subjective. In their case, as practising Roman Catholics, their objections extend to receiving and dealing with the initial telephone call booking the patient into the Labour Ward, to the admission of the patient, to assigning the midwife to look after the patient, to the supervision of the staff looking after the patient, both before and after the procedure, as well as to the direct provision of any care for those patients, apart from that which they are required to perform under section 4(2).

... [34] ... I would agree ... that the course of treatment to which the petitioners may object is the whole course of medical treatment bringing about the termination of the pregnancy. It begins with the administration of the drugs designed to induce labour and normally ends with the ending of the pregnancy by delivery of the foetus, placenta and membrane. It would also, in my view, include the medical and nursing care which is connected with the process of undergoing labour and giving birth ...

... [37] The more difficult question is what is meant by "to participate in" the course of treatment in question. The employers accept that it could have a broad or a narrow meaning. On any view, it would not cover things done before the course of treatment began, such as making the booking before the first drug is administered. But a broad meaning might cover things done in connection with that treatment after it had begun, such as assigning staff to work with the patient, supervising and supporting such staff, and keeping a managerial eye on all the patients in the ward, including any undergoing a termination. A narrow meaning would restrict it to "actually taking part", that is actually performing the tasks involved in the course of treatment.

[38] In my view, the narrow meaning is more likely to have been in the contemplation of Parliament when the Act was passed. The focus of section 4 is on the acts made lawful by section 1. It is unlikely that, in enacting the conscience clause, Parliament had in mind the host of ancillary, administrative and managerial tasks that might be associated with those acts. Parliament will not have had in mind the hospital managers who decide to offer an abortion service, the administrators who decide how best that service can be organised within the hospital (for example, by assigning some terminations to the Labour Ward, some to the Fetal Medicine Unit and some to the Gynaecology Ward), the caterers who provide the patients with food, and the cleaners who provide them with a safe and hygienic environment. Yet all may be said in some way to be facilitating the carrying out of the treatment involved. The managerial and supervisory tasks carried out by the Labour Ward Co-ordinators are closer to these roles than they are to the role of providing the treatment which brings about the termination of the pregnancy. "Participate" in my view means taking part in a "hands-on" capacity.

... [40] Whatever the outcome of the objectors' stance, it is a feature of conscience clauses generally within the healthcare profession that the conscientious objector be under an obligation to refer the case to a professional who does not share that objection. This is a necessary corollary of the professional's duty of care towards the patient. Once she has assumed care of the patient, she needs a good reason for failing to provide that care. But when conscientious objection is the reason, another healthcare professional should be found who does not share the objection.

[41] I would therefore allow this appeal and set aside the declarator made in the Inner House.

As this also makes clear, a GP cannot use s 4 to deny a referral to an abortion clinic. In *Barr v Matthews*[52] Alliott J expressed the view that 'once a termination of pregnancy is recognised as an option, the doctor invoking the conscientious objection clause should refer the patient to a colleague at once'. This is echoed in current GMC guidance, which addresses doctors in the following terms:

GMC, *Personal Beliefs and Medical Practice*[53]

12. Patients have a right to information about their condition and the options open to them. If you have a conscientious objection to a treatment or procedure that may be clinically appropriate for the patient, you must do the following.
    a. Tell the patient that you do not provide the particular treatment or procedure, being careful not to cause distress. You may wish to mention the reason for your objection, but you must be careful not to imply any judgement of the patient.
    b. Tell the patient that they have a right to discuss their condition and the options for treatment (including the option that you object to) with another practitioner who does not hold the same objection as you and can advise them about the treatment or procedure you object to.

---

52 (1999) 52 BMLR 217.
53 GMC (April 2013). See: www.gmc-uk.org/Good_practice_in_prescribing.pdf_58834768.pdf.

c. Make sure that the patient has enough information to arrange to see another doctor who does not hold the same objection as you.

13. If it's not practical for a patient to arrange to see another doctor, you must make sure that arrangements are made – without delay – for another suitably qualified colleague to advise, treat or refer the patient. You must bear in mind the patient's vulnerability and act promptly to make sure they are not denied appropriate treatment or services . . .

THINK POINT

Do you think that the father of the foetus should be accorded greater rights (such as a right to be consulted by the pregnant woman) in cases of abortion?

8.3.2 Forms of termination raising special issues

We continue our examination of abortion by considering a number of procedures, in relation to the practice, that have generated particular legal or ethical concerns.

8.3.2.1 Pre-implantation terminations

What is the legality of a measure which prevents a newly formed embryo from implanting in the woman's uterus in the first place? In particular, is it the case here that a 'miscarriage' is procured contrary to the terms of the OAPA 1861? Margaret Brazier has commented on this question as follows:

Brazier, M, *Medicine, Patients and the Law*[54]

The 1967 Act envisaged that once a diagnosis of pregnancy had been made, the doctor faced with a request for an abortion would then consider and weigh any risk to the woman or the child. But there is a drug approved for general use which will, if taken by a woman within 72 hours of intercourse, ensure that any fertilised ovum will not implant in the womb. This, inaptly named, 'morning after' pill is not the only means by which a fertilised ovum (egg) may be disposed of at a stage before pregnancy can be confirmed. An intra-uterine device (IUD) fitted within a similar time after intercourse will have the same effect.

Are such methods lawful? They raise the question of where the line is to be drawn between contraception and abortion. . . . The crucial legal issue . . . is whether a procedure which prevents implantation is an act done to procure a miscarriage so as to make the doctor liable for criminal abortion . . . The argument that prevention of implantation is no offence runs thus. There is no carriage of a child by a woman before implantation takes place, and so to prevent that event even occurring cannot be an act done to procure a miscarriage. Many fertilised ova fail to implant naturally and no one then suggests that a miscarriage has occurred. The opponents of post-coital birth control reply that the fertilised ovum is present within the body of the woman; she carries it within her . . . .

No successful prosecution has ever been brought in respect of either the 'morning after' pill, or the use of an IUD, as means of post-coital birth control. In 1983 the Attorney General expressed his opinion

---

54 Harmondsworth: Penguin, 2nd edn, 1992.

that prior to implantation there is no pregnancy and so means used to prevent implantation do not constitute procuring miscarriage. In 1991 a judge dismissed a prosecution for criminal abortion based on the insertion of an IUD agreeing with the Attorney General that until implantation there is no pregnancy. The Attorney General's ruling is persuasive, but not binding on his successors. The matter remains unresolved by higher judicial authority. In practice, however, doctors are prescribing the 'morning after' pill without any pretence of applying the criteria laid down in the Abortion Act.

In spring 2002, the Society for the Protection of the Unborn Child brought judicial review proceedings against the decision by the Secretary of State for Health to allow the sale of the morning after pill in chemists, without prescription. In dismissing the application, Munby J held that 'the prescription, supply, administration or use of the morning after pill does not – cannot – involve the commission of any offence under either s 58 or s 59 of the 1861 Act': see *R v Secretary of State for Health, ex p Smeaton*.[55]

8.3.2.2 Selective reduction

As we saw above, in Chapter 7, certain forms of fertility treatment, IVF or (more often) the use of super-ovulatory drugs, may result in a multiple pregnancy in which the woman carries more foetuses than can safely be brought to term. The term 'selective reduction' refers to the practice, in such a pregnancy, of deliberately terminating the lives of some of the foetuses in order to improve the survival chances of those that remain. Andrew Grubb has discussed the legal problems posed by the practice as follows:

See Chapter 7

Grubb, A, 'The new law of abortion: clarification or ambiguity'[56]

Modern medicine has developed techniques whereby a multiple pregnancy may be reduced by killing one or more foetuses *in utero*. This has become particularly important in cases where infertility treatment has led to a multiple pregnancy. The greater the number of foetuses carried by a woman, the greater is the risk to her health during pregnancy and at delivery. Equally, in these circumstances there is the risk of foetal mortality and of foetal handicap, including cerebral palsy, blindness and mental retardation . . . .

It was not clear under the law prior to 1 April 1991 whether selective reduction and selective foeticide were covered by the abortion legislation. It could be argued that in cases where the 'reduced' foetus(es) is not expelled there is not a 'miscarriage' within the terms of s 58 of the Offences Against the Person Act 1861. The better view is, however, that the term 'miscarriage' does not require expulsion of the contents of the womb but merely that some or all of the contents cease to be carried alive within it. This would bring both procedures within s 58 of the 1861 Act. In any event, the argument overlooks the fact that ultimately, the withered and dead products of the foetus will be expelled at the time the remaining foetuses are delivered.

A further complication was raised as to whether selective reduction was a 'termination of pregnancy' within the Abortion Act 1967 because the woman is still pregnant in the sense that one or more of the healthy foetuses remains after the procedure. If there was no termination of pregnancy, then the procedure could never be lawful, because what was being done would not fall within the wording of the Abortion Act. There would be a crime but no possible defence.

---

55 [2002] EWHC 610 (Admin).
56 See n 18 above.

In the light of these uncertainties, when Parliament came to amend the Abortion Act in 1990 a new s 5(2) was introduced specifically to deal with the practice:

5 (2) – For the purposes of the law relating to abortion, anything done with intent to procure a woman's miscarriage (or, in the case of a woman carrying more than one foetus, her miscarriage of any foetus) is unlawfully done unless authorised by s 1 of this Act and, in the case of a woman carrying more than one foetus, anything done with intent to procure her miscarriage of any foetus is authorised by that section if –

a   the ground for termination of the pregnancy specified in sub-s (1)(d) of that section applies in relation to any foetus and the thing is done for the purpose of procuring the miscarriage of that foetus; or

b   any of the other grounds for termination of the pregnancy specified in that section applies.

It is apparent that the effect of this provision is that selective reduction will be lawful either to protect the health or life of the pregnant woman (in which case the foetus(es) for destruction may be randomly chosen) or to terminate the life of a particular foetus on the s 1(1)(d) ground of foetal handicap.

8.3.2.3 Drug-induced abortions

When the Abortion Act 1967 was first enacted, medical abortion invariably necessitated the surgical removal of the foetus by a qualified doctor. For this reason, s 1(1) confers immunity from criminal liability only where abortion is carried out by 'a registered medical practitioner'. Developments in abortion techniques since then, particularly the availability of new 'aborti-facient' drugs, now allow others, besides doctors, to take a much more direct role in terminating pregnancy. How far will they be protected by the terms of the 1967 Act? The issue, in relation to nursing staff, was considered by the House of Lords in the case of *Royal College of Nursing of UK v DHSS*.

Royal College of Nursing of United Kingdom v DHSS[57]

The RCN became concerned over the potential liability of its members in relation to the practice of using the drug Prostaglandin to carry out many abortions. The drug acts by stimulating contractions in the uterus, leading to the expulsion of the foetus. Here, whilst a doctor will perform the initial insertion of a catheter into the pregnant woman's uterus, the drug itself is later fed through the catheter by a nurse. The College sought a declaration that a Department of Health circular authorising the practice was wrong in law:

Lord Keith: Section 1(1) of the Act of 1967 can operate to relieve a person from guilt of an offence under the law relating to abortion only 'when a pregnancy is terminated by a registered medical practitioner'. Certain other conditions must also be satisfied, but no question about these arises in the present case. The sole issue is whether the words I have quoted cover the situation where abortion has been brought about as a result of the procedure under consideration.

The argument for the respondents is, in essence, that the words of the sub-section do not apply because the pregnancy has not been terminated by any registered medical practitioner, but by the

---

57 [1981] AC 800.

nurse who did the act or acts which directly resulted in the administration to the pregnant woman of the abortifacient drugs.

In my opinion this argument involves placing an unduly restricted and unintended meaning on the words 'when a pregnancy is terminated'. It seems to me that these words, in their context, are not referring to the mere physical occurrence of termination. The sidenote to s 1 is 'Medical termination of pregnancy'. 'Termination of pregnancy' is an expression commonly used, perhaps rather more by medical people than by laymen, to describe in neutral and unemotive terms the bringing about of an abortion. So used, it is capable of covering the whole process designed to lead to that result, and in my view it does so in the present context. Other provisions of the Act make it clear that termination of pregnancy is envisaged as being a process of treatment . . . .

[I]t remains to consider whether, on the facts of this case, the termination can properly be regarded as being 'by a registered medical practitioner'. In my opinion this question is to be answered affirmatively. The doctor has responsibility for the whole process and is in charge of it throughout. It is he who decides that it is to be carried out. He personally performs essential parts of it which are such as to necessitate the application of his particular skill. The nurse's actions are done under his direct written instructions. In the circumstances I find it impossible to hold that the doctor's role is other than that of a principal, and I think he would be very surprised to hear that the nurse was the principal and he himself only an accessory. It is true that it is the nurse's action which leads directly to the introduction of abortifacient drugs into the system of the patient, but that action is done in a ministerial capacity and on the doctor's orders. Even if it were right to regard the nurse as a principal, it seems to me inevitable that the doctor should also be so regarded. If both the doctor and the nurse were principals, the provisions of the sub-section would be still satisfied, because the pregnancy would have been terminated by the doctor notwithstanding that it had also been terminated by the nurse.

I therefore conclude that termination of pregnancy by means of the procedures under consideration is authorised by the terms of s 1(1). This conclusion is the more satisfactory as it appears to me to be fully in accordance with that part of the policy and purpose of the Act which was directed to securing that socially acceptable abortions should be carried out under the safest conditions attainable. One may also feel some relief that it is unnecessary to reach a decision involving the very large numbers of medical practitioners and others who have participated in the relevant procedures over several years past should now be revealed as guilty of criminal offences.

While the decision of the House of Lords (by a narrow 3:2 majority) means that nursing staff involved in abortions enjoy the same statutory protection as doctors, the problem of who else might benefit has now arisen following the development of a further abortifacient drug, RU-486 or Mifepristone. This drug is similar in its operation to Prostaglandin but is significantly easier to administer. Indeed, the drug could, in principle, be made available on prescription in tablet form to be taken by pregnant women who remain out-patients. As part of the 1990 amendments to the Abortion Act, a new s 1(3A) was specifically introduced to allow the Health Secretary to authorise GPs' surgeries as a 'class of place' where Mifepristone could be administered (previously, under s 1(3), treatment to terminate a pregnancy could only be given at NHS or other hospitals approved by the Secretary):

1 (3A) The power under subsection (3) of this section to approve a place includes power, in relation to treatment consisting primarily in the use of such medicines as may be specified in the approval and carried out in such manner as may be so specified, to approve a class of places.

Nevertheless, as Kennedy and Grubb point out, a further difficulty remains:

Kennedy, I and Grubb, A, *Medical Law: Text with Materials*[58]

[Mifepristone] is prescribed by a doctor, dispensed by a pharmacist, but administered to herself by the pregnant woman. In this situation who terminates the pregnancy?

There are two possible situations which might arise. First, the termination is only completed after the woman has returned to the hospital some 36 to 48 hours later after the Prostaglandin pessary has been inserted. Here, undoubtedly the termination would be by the doctor even if the Prostaglandin were given by a nurse under his supervision (*Royal College of Nursing* case). This is not problematic for the law. However, the alternative situation that might arise is.

Suppose, instead, the effects of Mifepristone occur before the woman returns to the hospital for the Prostaglandin pessary. In 55% of cases bleeding (and therefore, the potential for a 'miscarriage') occur within 48 hours of administering Mifepristone. In a proportion of cases (about 3%) termination will occur before readmission. In our view, in this situation it must be the pregnant woman and not the doctor who terminates the pregnancy. It is she who does the last voluntary act necessary to effect the termination. Legally, the situation is analogous to a case where a doctor provides the means (eg, pills) for a patient to kill himself. It is the patient who commits suicide . . .

However, an argument which would challenge this view could be mounted on the basis of the *Royal College of Nursing* case. There, the House of Lords . . . extended 'medical practitioner' to include all acts performed by the medical team for whom the doctor is responsible . . .

Could this wider notion of 'termination by a registered medical practitioner covering all action for which the doctor takes responsibility' (or 'charge') help in the case of Mifepristone? In one sense, a doctor does have responsibility for the patient throughout the treatment. However, it is a different kind of responsibility from that contemplated in the *Royal College of Nursing* case. In that case the responsibility denoted the right to control those who acted on his behalf in a professional capacity. In the case of Mifepristone . . . the relationship is neither one of control nor one where the patient (in administering the drug to herself) can be said to act on the doctor's behalf or be in his charge.

The issue was recently tested in *British Pregnancy Advisory Service v Secretary of State for Health*,[59] in which the applicant argued that, where the woman self-administers the drug at home, it would still be the doctor (and not the woman) who had carried out the termination; and this was thus permissible under the 1967 Act. However, Supperstone J disagreed and refused a declaration to that effect. The upshot is that (as had previously been the case) the use of Mifepristone, and of a similar, newer drug, Misoprostol, requires their administration by – or at least under the supervision of – nursing staff in approved hospitals/clinics.

8.3.2.4 Late-term abortions

As noted, in some circumstances the Abortion Act 1967 (as amended) permits termination of pregnancy up until birth, namely under grounds (b), (c) and (d). Such late terminations are extremely rare,[60] and, due to restrictions in the licences granted to private abortion clinics

---

58 London: Butterworths, 2nd edn, 1994.

59 [2011] EWHC 235 (Admin); see further Sheldon, S, 'British abortion law: speaking from the past to govern the future' (2016) 79 MLR 283.

60 The abortion statistics published by the DoH for 2014 show that of the 184,571 terminations carried out on England and Wales residents that year, only 212 involved foetuses of 24 weeks and over. See: www.gov.uk/government/uploads/system/uploads/attachment_data/file/433437/2014_Commentary_5_.pdf.

(imposed by the Secretary of State pursuant to s 1(3) of the Act), may only be carried out in NHS hospitals. In practice, it is the last of the grounds, foetal handicap, which is almost always invoked in such circumstances.

By contrast with early abortions, where abortifacient drugs or vacuum aspiration may be used, late abortions normally require surgical intervention. Of course, the intention of the doctor is that the foetus will not survive the abortion process; however, unless measures are taken to kill the foetus while still inside the womb, there is a real chance that it will be born alive. What is the legal position of the doctor, in such circumstances, where the foetus only dies some time after delivery? In *AG's Reference (No 3 of 1994)*[61] the House of Lords considered a reference in respect of the acquittal for murder (on the directions of the trial judge) of a man who had stabbed his pregnant girlfriend in the abdomen (the woman went into labour soon after the attack and, although the child was delivered alive, it died 120 days later due to its severe prematurity). In reversing the decision of the Court of Appeal that a murder charge could lie in such circumstances, their Lordships were nevertheless extremely cautious to limit their response to the facts in hand (involving an intention by the respondent to harm the pregnant woman). Lord Mustill commented that he 'would wish to proceed with particular care in relation to allegations of murder stemming from an injury to the foetus unaccompanied by any causative injury to the mother'. Given this present lack of certainty in the law, the doctor responsible for a late abortion would be well advised to take the greatest care that the foetus dies while it is still inside the womb.

Another issue in relation to late-term abortions relates to the potential capacity of the foetus to feel pain. Evidence as to this matter is conflicting, but there is reason to think that, by 26 weeks' gestation, the foetal nervous system is sufficiently developed for it to do so.[62] On this basis, one of the arguments the claimant wished to use in the *Jepson* case[63] was that the foetus at this stage should receive protection under Article 3 of the ECHR (right not to be subjected to torture or inhuman or degrading treatment). This argument in itself is problematic, as arguably reliance on Convention rights presupposes that an entity is at least a rights-bearer for the purposes of Article 2 of the Convention, which as we have seen with foetuses is not the case.[64] Nonetheless, as the BMA notes, in ethical terms this is a matter in respect of which abortion doctors certainly should exercise caution:

BMA, *The Law and Ethics of Abortion: BMA Views*[65]

. . . A note on fetal pain

Whether, and at what stage, a fetus feels pain has been a matter of much debate. Interpretation of the evidence on fetal pain is conflicting, with some arguing that the fetus has the potential to feel pain at ten weeks' gestation; others arguing that it is unlikely to feel pain before 26 weeks' gestation; and others arguing for some unspecified gestational period in between.

The Royal College of Obstetricians and Gynaecologists' 2011 report *Fetal Awareness – Review of Research and Recommendations for Practice* concluded that the fetus cannot experience pain prior to 24 weeks' gestation, as prior to this point, the necessary connections from the periphery to the cortex are not present. They also found limited evidence to suggest that fetuses can perceive pain after 24 weeks, and noted increasing evidence to suggest that the fetus never experiences a state of truewakefulness *in utero*.

---

61 [1997] 3 WLR 421.
62 Glover, V, and Fisk, NM, 'Foetal pain: implications for research and practice' (1999) 106 British J of Obstet and Gyn 881.
63 See n 21 above.
64 See section 8.3.1.2 above.
65 See n 16 above.

> The BMA recommends that doctors should give due consideration to the appropriate measures for minimising the risk of pain, including assessment of the most recent evidence. The BMA suggests that even if there is no incontrovertible evidence that the fetus feels pain, the use of fetal analgesia when carrying out any procedure (whether an abortion or a therapeutic intervention) on the fetus *in utero* may go some way in relieving the anxiety of the woman and health professionals.

8.3.3 Moving towards a decriminalised 'counselling model'?

Though, as we have seen, abortion in England and Wales (and Scotland) remains technically subject to medical control, in practice a liberal approach prevails, which comes close in practice to 'abortion on demand'. Although around 90 per cent of terminations take place in the first trimester, the law is more permissive than that in many other countries in respect of later abortions. This, plus the fact of the more than usually restrictive abortion policy operated by its close neighbour, Ireland, has also made Britain subject to a degree of 'abortion tourism'.[66]

At the same time, there appears to be little appetite in Parliament for law reform, which many politicians fear would simply provoke divisive and insoluble debate. On this view, the existing 1967 Act, in treating abortion as a 'medical question' for doctors to rule on, has functioned well in depoliticising the issue, avoiding the polarities ('pro-life' vs. 'pro-choice') that have disfigured abortion discourse in countries such as the US. The downside, though, is a vaguely worded statute, with arguably something of a disjunction between its terms and how it is applied in practice. A further concern is that the Act – in medicalising the issue – remains bound to a paternalistic approach, which fails to treat the pregnant woman sufficiently as the author of her decision.

In the following extract, Sjef Gevers, referring to the comparative law work of Eser and Koch,[67] notes three broad models on which countries around the world have premised their abortion laws:

Gevers, S, 'Abortion legislation and the future of the "counseling model"'[68]

> If there is any medico-legal issue on which it seems virtually impossible to reach consensus, it is abortion. Over the last decades, abortion law has been highly debated in many countries, also in Europe, but it has turned out to be hard to reconcile the opposing views . . .
>
> Whereas – at the normative level – there is the tension between the 'pro life' and the 'pro choice' approach to abortion, at the practical level, the situation is more complex. In all countries, abortions take place, even where the law prohibits them. According to the World Health Organisation, an estimated 46 million pregnancies end in induced abortion each year; as nearly 20 million of these are estimated to be unsafe, safe abortion services with adequate equipment and well trained staff need to be available so that women can have rapid access to these services, at least within the limits allowed by the law.
>
> Often, medicine plays an important role in bridging the gap between 'pro life' and 'pro choice' on the one hand and between normative beliefs and practical necessities on the other. According to the WHO report, most countries allow abortion when pregnancy poses a threat to the woman's physical or mental health (medical indication model), making doctors 'gatekeepers' of abortion. Other countries have taken a further step in liberalising criminal statutes that prohibit abortion, and have enacted laws that allow for it on request of the woman at least in the first term of pregnancy (time limitation model).

---

66 In 2014, 5,521 abortions carried out in England and Wales involved non-residents: see n 60 above.
67 Eser, A, and Koch, HG, *Abortion and the Law: from international comparison to legal policy*, The Hague: TMC Asser Press, 2005.
68 (2006) 13 Eur J Health L 27.

In their important, comparative work on abortion and the law, Eser and Koch observe that a third model of legislation has emerged, i.e. the so-called 'conflict (or emergency) oriented discourse model'. Basically, this refers to regulations in which the law establishes grounds (such as certain emergencies) for allowing abortions but leaves the determination of whether such grounds exist ultimately to the judgment and the discretion of the woman. She is expected, however, to make a careful decision, to weigh the alternatives and to be willing to be counseled in doing so. Because of this latter aspect, this model is also referred to as the 'counseling model'. In their recent book, the authors not only notice that this approach is adopted by legal reformers to a growing extent but also argue that it is the best way to do justice to the conflicting values involved.

Within the above rubric, abortion law in England and Wales currently illustrates – at least on paper – the 'medical indication' approach. Nonetheless, there are some indications of support among the public for decriminalisation of abortion within the first trimester of pregnancy.[69] Indeed, the BMA has recently gone further by mooting that termination of foetuses prior to viability should no longer be criminal: this would be achieved by repealing ss 58–59 of the Offences Against the Person Act 1861, while retaining the 1929 Infant Life (Preservation) Act on the statute book.[70]

At the same time, reform advocates emphasise that decriminalisation would not equate to deregulation of the practice, and that measures to ensure professional oversight should remain, coupled with the availability of impartial counselling and need for properly informed consent from the women concerned. In fact, as Charles Foster argues, these last points are matters on which both those disposed to support and oppose liberalising reforms may find a measure of agreement:

Foster, C, 'A lost opportunity'[71]

1967 is a long time ago. Medicine has moved on. We now know a good deal more about the effect of abortion on the bodies of foetuses, on the bodies and minds of women, on the psyches of doctors and nurses, on the bank accounts of abortion providers, and on the ethics of the medical profession as a whole. It was amended, rather tentatively, by the Human Fertilisation and Embryology Act 1990. Whatever one's view of the ethics, abortion matters. Surely it is hard to contend coherently that it does not deserve a review?

Although [the Abortion Act] 1967 itself made no express provision for it, informed consent is plainly vitally important. Abortion sometimes seems to exist on a tiny island, terribly isolated from the rest of the law of consent. It is a significant procedure. Most would agree that it can cause prematurity in subsequent pregnancies and debilitating guilt: some argue for a link between abortion and lasting depression . . . Whatever one makes of this evidence, the magnitude of the risks and the significance of the possible sequelae would, in any comparable area of medicine or surgery, make detailed counselling mandatory. And yet all the indications are that abortion counselling, if it occurs at all, is generally cursory. . . . The pro-abortionists are right: we do need an informed consent clause in [the Act]. All sensible people should be 'pro-choice' in the sense of being pro-informed-choice.

---

69 See Sheldon, S, 'The decriminalisation of abortion: an argument for modernisation' (2016) 36 OJLS 334.
70 BMA, *Decriminalisation of Abortion: a discussion paper from the BMA*, London (February 2017).
71 (2008) 158 NLJ, Issue 7326.

THINK POINT

See Chapter 7 → Can the relative lack of attention to the patient's consent in relation to abortion, in contrast to that which it receives in cases of assisted reproduction, be rationalised?

8.4 Pre-natal harm beyond the abortion context

8.4.1 General principles

Beyond the context of abortion, it is readily apparent that injuries may be caused to a foetus *in utero* which subsequently lead to it being born disabled. The question of whether a child damaged in this way can, after it is born, bring an action against the person responsible has created a surprising amount of difficulty for the common law. Nevertheless, in respect of children born after 21 July 1976, such a child has been given a statutory right to recover damages under the Congenital Disabilities (Civil Liability) Act 1976. Section 1 of this Act provides as follows:

1 Civil liability to child born disabled

1   If a child is born disabled as the result of such an occurrence before its birth as is mentioned in sub-s (2) below, and a person (other than the child's own mother) is under this section answerable to the child in respect of the occurrence, the child's disabilities are to be regarded as damage resulting from the wrongful act of that person and actionable accordingly at the suit of the child.

2   An occurrence to which this section applies is one which –
     a   affected either parent of the child in his or her ability to have a normal, healthy child; or
     b   affected the mother during her pregnancy, or affected her or the child in the course of its birth,
     so that the child is born with disabilities which would not otherwise have been present.

3   Subject to the following sub-sections, a person (here referred to as 'the defendant') is answerable to the child if he was liable in tort to the parent or would, if sued in due time have been so; and it is no answer that there could not have been such liability because the parent suffered no actionable injury, if there was a breach of legal duty which, accompanied by injury, would have given rise to the liability.

4   In the case of an occurrence preceding the time of conception, the defendant is not answerable to the child if at that time either or both of the parents knew the risk of their child being born disabled (that is to say, the particular risk created by the occurrence); but should it be the child's father who is the defendant, this sub-section does not apply if he knew of the risk and the mother did not.

5   The defendant is not answerable to the child, for anything he did or omitted to do when responsible in a professional capacity for treating or advising the parent, if he took reasonable care having due regard to then received professional opinion applicable to the particular class of case; but this does not mean that he is answerable only because he departed from received opinion.

6   Liability to the child under this section may be treated as having been excluded or limited by contract made with the parent affected, to the same extent and subject to the same restrictions as liability in the parent's own case; and a contract term which could have been set up by the defendant in an action by the parent, so as to exclude or limit his liability to him or her, operates in the defendant's favour to the same, but no greater, extent in an action under this section by the child.

7   If in the child's action under this section it is shown that the parent affected shared the responsibility for the child being born disabled, the damages are to be reduced to such extent as the court thinks just and equitable having regard to the extent of the parent's responsibility.

The effect of s 1(3) is to found the child's action upon the concept of 'derivative liability', ie it may only bring a claim in so far as the occurrence which caused its injuries involved a breach of duty by the tortfeasor to one of its parents. Subsequently, in *Burton v Islington HA*, the Court of Appeal had to tackle head on the problem at common law of how it is that a duty in tort can be owed to an entity which has no legal personality. In finding for the claimant, Dillon LJ relied extensively upon Commonwealth authority, in particular the decision of the Supreme Court of Victoria in *Watt v Rama*.[72]

Burton v Islington HA[73]

The claimant was born disabled as a result of an invasive gynaecological procedure carried out upon her mother early on in the pregnancy: the defendant had negligently failed to carry out a pregnancy test before performing the procedure. As these events occurred prior to the enactment of the 1976 Act, the Court was required to consider the legal position at common law.

Dillon LJ: The main Commonwealth case from a country with a common law jurisdiction is *Watt v Rama* ... which has since been accepted by other appellate courts in Australia as a correct statement of the law, that is to say the common law of Australia. That was a case which arose out of injuries in a motor accident. The leading judgment is that of Winneke CJ and Pape J. It is founded on an analysis – in my judgment, correct – of the tort of negligence by reference to well-known authorities like *Donoghue v Stevenson* [1932] AC 562; *Dorset Yacht Co Ltd v Home Office* [1970] AC 1004; *Bourhill (Hay) v Young* [1943] AC 92 ... After the citations the judgment continues, at pp 360–61:

Those circumstances, accordingly, constituted a potential relationship capable of imposing a duty on the defendant in relation to the child if and when born. On the birth the relationship crystallised and out of it arose a duty on the defendant in relation to the child. On the facts which for present purposes must be assumed, the child was born with injuries caused by the act or neglect of the defendant in the driving of his car. But as the child could not in the very nature of things acquire rights correlative to a duty until it became by birth a living person, and as it was not until then that it could sustain injuries as a living person, it was, we think, at that stage that the duty arising out of the relationship was attached to the defendant, and it was at that stage that the defendant was, on the assumption that his act or omission in the driving of the car constituted a failure to take reasonable care, in breach of the duty to take reasonable care to avoid injury to the child.

With respect, the analysis endorsed by Dillon LJ appears to confuse breach of duty with the damage which is thereby caused. It might be simpler to accept that legal duties can be owed to the unborn child, as a potential person, even though the corresponding right of such an entity to bring a claim remains contingent upon its subsequent birth. Indeed, this seems to have been an unspoken assumption in many medical negligence claims: see, for example, *Whitehouse v Jordan*.[74]

Ultimately, all that is being allowed in these cases is that a damaged child may recover damages where, but for the defendant's negligence, it would have been born undamaged. A claim, on the other hand, by such a child who, but for the defendant's negligence would never

---

72 (1972) VR 353.
73 [1993] QB 204, CA.
74 [1981] 1 All ER 267. This case is looked at in Ch 6, above.

have been born at all, would form an inadmissible action for 'wrongful life'. Such a claim was considered, and rejected, by the Court of Appeal in *Mackay v Essex AHA*:

Mackay v Essex AHA[75]

The claimant's mother was infected with German measles while pregnant with the claimant. The latter claimed, *inter alia*, that the defendant doctor had negligently failed to advise her mother of the desirability of an abortion, and (given that her mother would have accepted such advice) she had consequently suffered damage by 'entry into a life in which her injuries are highly debilitating, and distress, loss and damage':

Stephenson LJ: There is no doubt that this child could legally have been deprived of life by the mother's undergoing an abortion with the doctor's advice and help. So the law recognises a difference between the life of a foetus and the life of those who have been born. But because a doctor can lawfully by statute do to a foetus what he cannot lawfully do to a person who has been born, it does not follow that he is under a legal obligation to a foetus to do it and terminate its life, or that the foetus has a legal right to die . . .

   To impose such a duty towards the child would, in my opinion, make a further inroad on the sanctity of human life which would be contrary to public policy. It would mean regarding the life of a handicapped child as not only less valuable than the life of a normal child, but so much less valuable that it was not worth preserving, and it would even mean that a doctor would be obliged to pay damages to a child infected with rubella before birth who was in fact born with some mercifully trivial abnormality. These are the consequences of the necessary basic assumption that a child has a right to be born whole or not at all, not to be born unless it can be born perfect or 'normal', whatever that may mean. Added to that objection must be the opening of the courts to claims by children born handicapped against their mothers for not having an abortion . . .

   Finally, there is the nature of the injury and damage which the court is being asked to ascertain and evaluate.

   The only duty of care which courts of law can recognise and enforce are duties owed to those who can be compensated for loss by those who owe the duties, in most cases, including cases of personal injury, by money damages which will as far as possible put the injured party in the condition in which he or she was before being injured. The only way in which a child injured in the womb can be compensated in damages is by measuring what it has lost, which is the difference between the value of its life as a whole and healthy normal child and the value of its life as an injured child. But to make those who have not injured the child pay for that difference is to treat them as if they have injured the child, when all they have done is not having taken steps to prevent its being born injured by another cause.

   The only loss for which those who have not injured the child can be held liable to compensate the child is the difference between its condition as a result of their allowing it to be born alive and injured and its condition if its embryonic life had been ended before its life in the world had begun. But how can a court of law evaluate that second condition and so measure the loss to the child? Even if a court were competent to decide between the conflicting views of theologians and philosophers and to assume an 'after life' or non-existence as the basis for the comparison, how can a judge put a value on the one or the other, compare either alternative with the injured child's life in this world and determine that the child has lost anything, without the means of knowing what, if anything, it has gained?

---

75 [1982] QB 1166, CA.

Nonetheless, two points should be made. First, as noted earlier in this chapter, the mother/parents of the child may still be able to claim damages for 'wrongful conception/birth'.[76] Secondly, in one situation, the exclusion of liability in *Mackay* has been statutorily reinstated, namely for children born disabled after licensed fertility treatment. Here the Human Fertilisation and Embryology Act 1990 amended the CD(CL)A 1976 to provide that the child (including one who would not otherwise have existed) has a remedy against the person (the fertility clinic, or possibly a gamete donor), whose negligence led to the disability.[77]

8.4.2 Harm caused by the child's mother

It is important to note that, except in the case of negligent driving (allowed for in s 2 of the Act) no action will lie under the 1976 Act where the pre-natal injuries arose through the negligence of the child's mother. The policy grounds underlying this immunity are discussed by Jane Fortin as follows:

Fortin, J, 'Legal protection for the unborn child'[78]

By making liability to the child depend on liability to the parent, th[e] formula [of derivative liability] excludes a wide range of negligent acts and omissions on the part of the mother. Some would say that circumstances like those arising in the *Berkshire* case indicate quite clearly that the existence of maternal tortious liability would be a useful means of controlling the mother's ante-natal behaviour. Nevertheless, the Law Commission rejected the proposition that a child might sue its mother for pre-natal injuries caused by her negligence, largely on the social policy grounds that the existence of such a right of action would have deleterious effects on family cohesion. In particular, the mother might become vulnerable to litigation brought on behalf of her child, claiming that it was her failure to give up cigarette smoking or alcohol or to follow the latest dietary ante-natal regime that had caused the child's disablement. Moreover, the existence of such a cause of action might well fuel a matrimonial or parental conflict....

Nevertheless, the Law Commission was satisfied that different considerations applied to cases of pre-natal injury caused by a road accident, where the existence of third party insurance would prevent any risk of a child's claim against its mother causing family conflicts. Consequently, despite the unborn child's lack of legal personality, the 1976 Act does impose on the pregnant mother a duty of care in relation to it, but only in the context of driving a motor vehicle....

Despite the inconsistency of the exception relating to maternal liability for negligent driving, the 1976 Act maintains the general principle of the civil law that the unborn child has no legal personality. It is arguable that this principle is acquiring an element of unreality, particularly when the 1976 Act itself and now the *Berkshire* case, clearly adhere to the proposition that a child's development is a continuing process that commences at conception not birth.

In the case of *D v Berkshire CC*,[79] referred to by Fortin, the House of Lords held that events prior to a child's birth (which led to it being born with drug withdrawal symptoms) could properly be taken into account by magistrates when making a care order.

In general, it might seem paradoxical, given the relative ease with which the pregnant woman may dispose of her foetus altogether through abortion, that the law should concern itself with 'lesser harms' it may suffer as a result of her behaviour while pregnant. However, the point

---

76 See text at n 32 above.
77 Congenital Disabilities (Civil Liability) Act 1976, s 1A; see further the discussion in Ch 7, at section 7.4.4.2.
78 See n 4 above.
79 [1987] 1 All ER 20, HL.

is, of course, that in the latter case alone there will be an existing person whose interests have been adversely affected by her conduct. The highly contentious question of whether, in cases of this sort, the criminal law might be invoked to afford protection to the foetus, is addressed by John Robertson:

Robertson, JA, *Children of Choice: Freedom and the New Reproductive Technologies*[80]

Given the foreseeable impact of certain pre-natal acts or omissions on the welfare of offspring, one cannot reasonably argue that women and men have no pre-natal obligation to avoid harm to children they choose to bring into the world. The more contested question is what public policies and legal options should be pursued to prevent pre-natal harm to offspring. The choice ranges from education and access to treatment to post-birth sanctions and pre-natal imposition of treatment on pregnant women. Because procreative liberty is not involved, and because the conduct in question poses serious harm to offspring, coercive sanctions are not in principle excluded. However, as we shall see, the better policy in most cases will be to rely on information, education, and access to treatment ...

Opponents of prosecution also see a grave threat to personal privacy and civil liberties. If illegal drug use during pregnancy is independently punishable, then anything with the slightest pre-natal risk to offspring could be punished as pre-natal child abuse. Women could be prosecuted for smoking or drinking even moderate amounts of alcohol at any time during pregnancy, because even a few drinks might lower IQ points, and smoking increases the risk of prematurity and low birth weight. In the worst-case scenario, special pregnancy police will be commissioned to monitor women for pregnancies, and then surveil their behaviour; if they err, they are then stigmatised, shamed, fined, or incarcerated. Margaret Atwood's *The Handmaid's Tale*, a chilling novel of women forced to serve the needs of a repressive dictatorship, starts sounding much less fanciful than it appears to be ...

All these points deserve considered attention. They explain why prosecutions have been largely unsuccessful, are widely opposed, and are unlikely to be a key factor in preventing pre-natal harm. They also show why education, treatment, and services are the more desirable and most effective avenue for public policy.

Despite the drawbacks of a criminal approach, however, these criticisms do not establish that criminal sanctions should never be imposed on persons who culpably harm offspring by pre-natal conduct. When culpability is established, criminal law theory easily includes pre-natal as well as post-natal conduct that harms offspring. For example, Lord Coke in the 17th century recognised criminal liability for pre-natal actions that caused post-natal death.

In some cases, the only effective means of preventing harm to the future person that a given foetus will become, may take the form of *ex ante* coercive restraint of the pregnant woman. However, this raises even greater problems of civil liberty and sexual equality than *ex post facto* sanctions. As we saw earlier, in *Re F (in utero)*, the Court of Appeal recoiled from the implications of making a foetus a ward of court, in order to allow it to direct restraining orders at the mother.[81]

Admittedly, in *Re F (in utero)*, the risk to the child was not directly quantifiable; it might be argued that different considerations should apply where the mother's conduct, if allowed to continue, is nearly certain to damage her child. A situation of this kind arose in Canada in *Winnipeg Child & Family Services v DFG*,[82] in which the Supreme Court of Canada was required to decide whether to allow restraint against a woman in her fifth month of pregnancy, who was addicted to glue-sniffing. As a result of this addiction, she had already had two severely disabled children:

---

80 See n 1 above.
81 See n 37 above.
82 [1997] 3 SCR 925.

McLachlin J: [41] ... While the law may properly impose responsibility for the consequences of addictive behaviour, like drunkenness, the policy question remains of whether extending a duty of care in tort in this particular situation as the remedy for redressing problems which are caused by addiction is a wise option. Given the lack of control pregnant women have over many of these harmful behaviours, it is doubtful whether recognizing a duty of care to refrain from them will significantly affect their choices. As a result, the general deterrent value of the proposed new duty of care is questionable.

[42] Recognizing a duty of care in relation to the lifestyle of the pregnant woman would also increase the level of outside scrutiny that she would be subjected to. Partners, parents, friends, and neighbours are among the potential classes of people who might monitor the pregnant woman's actions to ensure that they remained within the legal parameters. Difficulty in determining what conduct is and is not permissible might be expected to give rise to conflicts between the interested persons and the pregnant woman or even between the interested persons themselves. This raises the possibility of conflict which may exacerbate the pregnant woman's condition (and thus the fetus') rather than improve it.

[43] If it could be predicted with some certainty that all these negative effects of extending tort liability to the lifestyle choices of pregnant women would in fact diminish the problem of injured infants, the change might nevertheless arguably be justified. But the evidence before this Court fails to establish this. It is far from clear that the proposed tort duty will decrease the incidence of substance-injured children. Indeed, the evidence suggests that such a duty might have negative effects on the health of infants. No clear consensus emerges from the debate on the question of whether ordering women into 'places of safety' and mandating medical treatment provide the best solution or, on the contrary, create additional problems.

Accordingly, the Court refused to issue a restraining order, and it is suggested that in England the outcome of such a case would be the same.[83]

8.4.3 Refusals of obstetric intervention

Perhaps even more controversial are cases in which, rather than doing anything active to harm her foetus, the pregnant woman passively declines medical intervention which her doctors tell her is necessary to prevent serious harm occurring to it. What should the law's approach be here? On the face of things, as we saw in Chapter 3, a capable adult patient must consent to any treatment they undergo (and, as a corollary, has an absolute right to refuse treatment). However, in *Re T (Adult: Refusal of Treatment)* (1992), Lord Donaldson MR expressly left the question open as to whether the presence of a viable foetus may provide an exception to this principle:

Lord Donaldson MR: An adult patient who ... suffers from no mental incapacity has an absolute right to choose whether to consent to medical treatment, to refuse it or to choose one rather than another of the treatments being offered. The only possible qualification is where the choice may lead to the death of a viable foetus. That is not the case here and if and when it arises, the court will be presented with a novel problem of considerable legal and ethical complexity.[84]

---

83 See now also the Court of Appeal decision in *CP (A Child) v First-tier Tribunal (Criminal Injuries Compensation)* [2014] EWCA Civ 1554.
84 [1992] 4 All ER 649, CA.

Very soon afterwards, the issue came squarely before the High Court in the case of *Re S (Adult: Refusal of Treatment)*:

Re S (Adult: Refusal of Treatment)[85]

Mrs S was a 30-year-old 'born-again Christian' in labour with her third child. Her foetus was in a position of 'transverse lie' and it was a practical certainty that, unless an immediate Caesarean section was carried out, her uterus would rupture, killing the child and, very possibly, Mrs S herself. The latter refused the operation, however, on religious grounds:

Sir Stephen Brown P: I have heard the evidence of P, a Fellow of the Royal College of Surgeons, who is in charge of this patient at the hospital. He has given, succinctly and graphically, a description of the condition of this patient. Her situation is desperately serious, as is also the situation of the as yet unborn child. The child is in what is described as a position of 'transverse lie', with the elbow projecting through the cervix and the head being on the right side. There is the gravest risk of a rupture of the uterus if the section is not carried out and the natural labour process is permitted to continue. The evidence of P is that we are concerned with 'minutes rather than hours' and that it is a 'life and death' situation. He has done his best, as have other surgeons and doctors at the hospital, to persuade the mother that the only means of saving her life, and also I emphasise the life of her unborn child, is to carry out a Caesarean section operation. P is emphatic. He says it is absolutely the case that the baby cannot be born alive if a Caesarean operation is not carried out . . .

I have been assisted by Mr Munby QC appearing for the Official Solicitor as *amicus curiae*. The Official Solicitor answered the call of the court within minutes and, although this application only came to the notice of the court officials at 1.30 pm, it has come on for hearing just before 2 o'clock and now at 2.18 pm I propose to make the declaration which is sought. I do so in the knowledge that the fundamental question appears to have been left open by Lord Donaldson MR in *Re T (Adult: Refusal of Medical Treatment)* . . . heard earlier this year in the Court of Appeal, and in the knowledge that there is no English authority which is directly in point. There is, however, some American authority which suggests that if this case were being heard in the American courts the answer would be likely to be in favour of granting a declaration in these circumstances: see *Re AC* (1990) . . . I do not propose to say more at this stage, except that I wholly accept the evidence of P as to the desperate nature of this situation, and that I grant the declaration as sought.

The President referred in his judgment to the American decision of *Re AC*.[86] This was undoubtedly an unfortunate choice of authority. Ian Kennedy has charted the history of that case as follows:

Kennedy, I, *Treat Me Right: Essays in Medical Law and Ethics*[87]

On 10 November 1987, the Court of Appeals of the District of Columbia, in the case of Angela C, approved the lower court's order that a Caesarean section be carried out on a terminally ill woman with hours or days to live, despite her apparent refusal of permission. The child was in its 26th week of gestation. The mother was heavily sedated and in extremis suffering from a metastatic oxygenic carcinoma in her lung. The operation was performed. The child died two hours thereafter. The mother died two days later. The court in upholding the order held that 'the trial judge did not err in subordinating AC's right against bodily intrusion to the interests of the unborn, [but potentially viable] child'. This was particularly so, the court held, because 'Caesarean section would not significantly affect AC's condition because she had, at best, two days left of sedated life'.

---

85 [1992] 4 All ER 671.
86 573 A 2d 1235 (1990).
87 Oxford: OUP, 2nd edn, 1992.

> Obviously, 'significantly' assumes great significance here . . .
>
> [Footnote:] *Re AC* was subsequently reheard *en banc* and the Court of Appeals issued a second judgment on 26 April 1990 . . . The court vacated its prior order on the grounds that there had not been a proper finding of fact whether AC was competent, or, if she was not, how 'substituted judgment' was to be applied. The court did, however, decide that the decision of a competent patient or substituted judgment should prevail, even if surgery was refused, in 'virtually all cases' unless there are 'truly extraordinary or compelling reasons to override them', by taking account, for example, of the State's interest in protecting life. At the same time the court did not dissent from, or overrule, a previous decision (1986) of the Superior Court in *Re Madyun* (unreported: published as Appendix to *Re AC*). In *Madyun*, the court authorised surgery on a woman who objected for religious reasons. 'All that stood between the *Madyun* foetus and its independent existence was, put simply, a doctor's scalpel [*sic*]. In these circumstances, the life of the infant inside its mother's womb was entitled to be protected.'

The issue of whether a court should authorise a Caesarean section against the wishes of the pregnant woman gives rise to considerable ethical and legal dilemmas. On the one hand, a situation in which the doctors stood idly by and allowed a mature foetus to rupture its mother's womb would arguably do serious symbolic damage to the concept of the sanctity of life, which any society must maintain. On the other, the thought of doctors carrying out invasive, and potentially risky, therapy upon unwilling patients is deeply troubling to the concept of individual autonomy, another of liberal society's fundamental values. Moreover, the fact that the patients whose rights are infringed in this way are invariably women, opens up the spectre of gender inequality and domination, a problem exacerbated by the time constraints operating which often mean that the women in question lack adequate legal representation.

In the later 1990s a number of further Caesarean cases came before the English courts. In every case it was declared that the treatment would be lawful. Almost without exception, though, the judges involved based their decisions on a prior determination of fact that the women in question were incapable and could accordingly be treated in their best interests.[88] In one case, *Norfolk and Norwich (NHS) Trust v W*,[89] the patient, who was in labour, denied that she was pregnant at all. Johnson J granted a declaration authorising intervention at common law:

> **Johnson J**: In reliance upon the opinion of the consultant psychiatrist and taking account of the information I had about the statements made by the patient during the course of the day, I held that although she was not suffering from a mental disorder within the meaning of the statute, she lacked the mental competence to make a decision about the treatment that was proposed because she was incapable of weighing up the considerations that were involved. She was called upon to make that decision at a time of acute emotional stress and physical pain in the ordinary course of labour made even more difficult for her because of her own particular mental history.
>
> I held that termination of this labour would be in the best interests of the patient. I was satisfied that unless the patient was delivered of the foetus which she was carrying, whether by way of forceps delivery or by Caesarean section, then her own physical health would be put at risk. This risk would arise if the foetus died because of rupture of the patient's old Caesarean scar or by suffocation in the birth canal. The death of the foetus would have immediate and increasing deleterious effects upon the patient herself leading to serious physical damage and possible death. Termination would end the stress and the pain of her labour, it would avoid the likelihood of damage to her physical health which might have potentially

---

88 See further, the discussion of treating incapable patients in their best interests, in Ch 4, above.
89 [1996] 2 FLR 613.

life-threatening consequences and, despite her present view about the foetus, would avoid her feeling any feeling of guilt in the future were she, by her refusal of consent, to cause the death of the foetus.

Throughout this judgment I have referred to 'the foetus' because I wish to emphasise that the focus of my judicial attention was upon the interests of the patient herself and not upon the interests of the foetus which she bore. However, the reality was that the foetus was a fully formed child, capable of normal life if only it could be delivered from the mother . . .

The preference in these decisions for intervention to be authorised on grounds of the woman's lack of capacity left the principle in *Re S (Adult: Refusal of Treatment)* isolated and doubtful. As we have seen, Sir Stephen Brown P in that case adverted to *dicta* in Lord Donaldson MR's judgment in *Re T* as to the effect the presence of a viable foetus could have upon refusals of treatment. However, when the House of Lords in *Airedale NHS Trust v Bland* [90] came to restate the general treatment-refusal principle, they did not mention any qualification in such a case. The issue was addressed once more at appellate level by the Court of Appeal in *Re MB (An Adult: Medical Treatment)*.

Re MB (An Adult: Medical Treatment)[91]

Miss MB required a Caesarean section in order to save her foetus from death or serious disability. However, although she agreed to the operation, her 'needle phobia' caused her to panic in the operating theatre and refuse the preliminary anaesthetic. Hollis J granted a declaration that, in these circumstances, it would be lawful to provide her with the treatment in her own best interests and this was upheld, the same evening, by the Court of Appeal. Five weeks later, their Lordships handed down a reserved judgment:

Butler-Sloss LJ (delivering the judgment of the court): All the decisions made in the Caesarean section cases to which we have referred arose in circumstances of urgency or extreme urgency. The evidence was in general limited in scope and the mother was not always represented as a party. With the exception of *Re S* . . . in all the cases the court decided that the mother did not have the capacity to make the decision. In these extremely worrying situations, it is important to keep in mind the basic principles we have outlined, and the court should approach the crucial question of competence bearing the following considerations in mind. They are not intended to be determinative in every case, for the decision must inevitably depend upon the particular facts before the court:

. . . A competent woman who has the capacity to decide may, for religious reasons, other reasons, for rational or irrational reasons or for no reason at all, choose not to have medical intervention, even though the consequence may be the death or serious handicap of the child she bears, or her own death. In that event the courts do not have the jurisdiction to declare medical intervention lawful and the question of her own best interests, objectively considered, does not arise . . .

. . . Applying these principles to the facts of this case we find:

1   Miss MB consented to a Caesarean section.
2   What she refused to accept was not the incision by the surgeon's scalpel but only the prick of the anaesthetist's needle. Capacity is commensurate with the gravity of the decision to be taken.
3   She could not bring herself to undergo the Caesarean section she desired because, as the evidence established:

. . . a fear of needles . . . has got in the way of proceeding with the operation . . . At the moment of panic . . . her fear dominated all . . . at the actual point she was not capable of making a

---

90 [1993] AC 789.
91 [1997] 2 FLR 426, CA; see also the discussion of the case in Ch 3, above.

> decision at all . . . at that moment the needle or mask dominated her thinking and made her quite unable to consider anything else.
>
> On that evidence she was incapable of making a decision at all. She was at that moment suffering an impairment of her mental functioning which disabled her. She was temporarily incompetent. In the emergency the doctors would be free to administer the anaesthetic if that were in her best interests.
>
> A feature of some of the cases to which we have referred has been the favourable reaction of the patient who refused treatment to the subsequent medical intervention and the successful outcome. Having noted that, we are none the less sure that however desirable it may be for the mother to be delivered of a live and healthy baby, on this aspect of the appeal it is not a strictly relevant consideration. If therefore the competent mother refuses to have the medical intervention, the doctors may not lawfully do more than attempt to persuade her. If that persuasion is unsuccessful, there are no further steps towards medical intervention to be taken. We recognise that the effect of these conclusions is that there will be situations in which the child may die or may be seriously handicapped because the mother said no and the obstetrician was not able to take the necessary steps to avoid the death or handicap. The mother may indeed later regret the outcome, but the alternative would be an unwarranted invasion of the right of the woman to make the decision.

It is apparent that, though couched in strong terms, the Court of Appeal's endorsement of the principle that, where capable, the woman's autonomy must prevail over her own best interests and those of the foetus, is *obiter*. On the facts, as we have seen, the court accepted Hollis J's finding that MB herself was incapable and thus treatment had been lawful.[92]

Subsequently, in *St George's Health Care NHS Trust v S*,[93] the Court of Appeal dealt with an action in judicial review by a woman who had been sectioned under the Mental Health Act 1983 and then subjected to an enforced Caesarean. The latter was authorised by a trial judge who was misled by the trust into thinking that the patient was already in labour. In ruling that the latter had been subjected to an unlawful battery, the court reiterated many of the principles it had outlined in the *Re MB* case. In cases involving capable women, it is thus clear that the law will refuse to countenance medical interventions on behalf of the foetus in defiance of her wishes. Indeed, this appears an essential guarantee of her autonomy in the light of continuing advances in foetal diagnostics and therapies, from HIV testing to intra-uterine surgery.[94]

Summary of key points

1   Abortion has long been an area of intractable moral debate. The pro and contra positions on the practice are often referred to as 'pro-choice', stressing the pregnant woman's right to decide what happens in her body, and 'pro-life', which appeals to the interests of the foetus.

2   For the law maker, besides trying to find an acceptable middle ground in this debate, there is the need to consider the likely adverse consequences of any law that radically restricted access to abortion, in terms of driving it underground.

---

92 For a criticism of aspects of the decision, see Stauch, M, 'Court-authorised Caesareans and the principle of patient autonomy' (1997) 6 Nott LJ 74.
93 [1999] Fam 26.
94 Cf. *NHS Trust and others v FG* [2014] EWCOP 30, a case of an incapable woman, in which the Court of Protection adverted also to the interests of the unborn child as a reason for intervention.

3   Under current UK law abortion remains an offence under s 58 Offences Against the Person Act 1861 (which criminalises 'procuring a miscarriage'). In addition, the killing of an older, viable foetus is punishable as 'child destruction' under the Infant Life (Preservation) Act 1929.

4   The 1929 Act gave a defence to a doctor who terminated the life of a foetus in order to save the life of the mother; subsequently, the courts held that a doctor who carried out an abortion to protect the mother from a significant risk to life had a similar defence to a charge under the 1861 Act.

5   Since the entry into force of the Abortion Act 1967, the grounds for lawful abortion have been widened. A doctor who terminates a pregnancy under one of these and conforms with the further statutory requirements (including certification by a second doctor) is protected from criminal prosecution.

6   Following amendment in 1990, four such grounds appear in the 1967 Act. The most widely used is the so-called 'social ground', which permits abortion up to 24 weeks where the continuance of the pregnancy poses greater risk to the woman and/or her existing children than its termination.

7   The other grounds encompass situations of serious risk to the woman's health or life, as well as – more controversially – the prospect of foetal disability. These grounds may be used to carry out terminations up to birth (though in practice it is rare for abortions to occur after 24 weeks).

8   Though the effect of the legal position is thus to deny the pregnant woman a right to an abortion (she must persuade the doctor(s) she falls within one of the statutory grounds), in practice she is unlikely to face difficulty in obtaining one: each year around 200,000 abortions take place in England, Wales, and Scotland. Indeed, there have been recent calls to decriminalise early abortions in the UK altogether.

9   Outside the abortion context, the foetus enjoys legal protection, if born alive, but disabled due to a damaging event while *in utero*: here it may bring an action under the Congenital Disabilities (Civil Liability) Act 1976. However, the Act largely excludes the possibility of it suing its mother.

10   More generally, the law, in denying legal personality to the foetus, has shown its unwillingness to curtail the capable pregnant woman's autonomy. This includes cases where the woman engages in activity that poses a risk to the life or health of the foetus, as well as ones where she refuses obstetric intervention.

 ## Further reading

BMA, *The Law and Ethics of Abortion: BMA Views*, London (November 2014, updated June 2017) (available at: www.bma.org.uk/advice/employment/ethics/ethics-a-to-z/abortion)

BMA, *Decriminalisation of Abortion: a discussion paper from the BMA*, London (February 2017) (available at: www.bma.org.uk/advice/employment/ethics/ethics-a-to-z/abortion)

Fortin, J, 'Legal protection for the unborn child' (1988) 51 Modern Law Review 54.

Gevers, S, 'Abortion legislation and the future of the "counseling model"' (2006) 13 European Journal of Health Law 27.

Hursthouse, R, *Beginning Lives*, Oxford: Blackwells, 1987.

RCOG, *Termination of Pregnancy for Fetal Abnormality in England, Scotland and Wales*, London, 2010 (available at: www.rcog.org.uk/files/rcog-corp/TerminationPregnancyReport18May2010.pdf)

Sheldon, S, *Beyond Control: Medical Power, Women and Abortion Law*, London: Pluto Press, 1997.

Sheldon, S, 'The decriminalisation of abortion: an argument for modernisation' (2016) 36 Oxford Journal of Legal Studies 334.

Chapter 9

Mental health law

Chapter contents

9.1 Background

9.1.1 Introduction

Mental disorder cannot be treated like any other form of medical disorder. First of all, there are special difficulties involved in deciding precisely what we mean when we say that someone is mentally 'disordered'. Perhaps this is inevitable, given the nebulous nature of mental disorders and their overlap with antisocial behaviour, the holding of bizarre beliefs, and eccentric lifestyles. In addition, the mentally ill are often stigmatised and misunderstood. Furthermore, the Mental Health Act (MHA) 1983 provides for the compulsory detention of both criminal offenders and non-offenders. It is clear, therefore, that mental health law raises distinct ethical and legal issues.

Leaving aside the special problems that can arise when dealing with the mentally ill criminal offender, it is generally accepted that compulsorily detaining someone who has committed no offence is probably the most serious interference with civil liberties that a state can impose. In consequence, its ethical underpinning must be beyond reproach, and the mechanism which allows this to be done should be open to the most searching scrutiny. We are concerned here with balancing, on the one hand, the rights of the individual, and, on the other hand, both the utilitarian desire to protect the community at large, and the paternalistic impulse to protect the individual from harming himself. This is reflected in the Mental Health Act 1983, by which compulsory civil detention, either for assessment or treatment, is permitted when the patient is suffering from mental disorder and ought to be detained either to protect themselves or others (the latter being a mixture of paternalism and community protection).

9.1.2 European Convention on Human Rights

Although the Human Rights Act 1998 might be used to some effect, where appropriate, in most areas of medical law, it is particularly pertinent to mental health law because of the power of the state to detain, without consent, people who have been diagnosed as suffering from a number of forms of mental disorder. Article 5 is particularly relevant.

Article 5 (right to liberty and security) provides that:

> 1 . . . No one shall be deprived o3f his liberty save in the following cases and in accordance with a procedure prescribed by law:
>
> . . .
>
> (e) the lawful detention of persons for the prevention of the spreading of infectious diseases, of persons of unsound mind, alcoholics or drug addicts of vagrants
>
> . . .
>
> 4 Everyone who is deprived of his liberty by arrest or detention shall be entitled to take proceedings by which the lawfulness of his detention shall be decided speedily by a court and his release ordered if the detention is not lawful.

The European Court of Human Rights, in *Winterwerp v Netherlands*,[1] set out the conditions which a national government has to satisfy in order for detention on the ground of 'unsoundness of mind' to apply:

---

1 (1979) 2 EHRR 387.

1   except in emergency cases, a true mental disorder has been established by objective medical expertise;
2   the detention must be effected in accordance with a procedure prescribed by law;
3   the mental disorder is of a kind or degree warranting compulsory confinement;
4   the validity of continued confinement depends upon the persistence of such a disorder.

In *Aerts v Belgium*[2] the European Court held that the detention of a mentally disordered person will only be lawful in terms of Article 5 if effected in a hospital, clinic or other appropriate institution.

Article 6 (right to a fair trial) has some application if a patient is claiming that his rights have been contravened, for example, under Article 5, and he has not been given the opportunity of putting his case before a court. Article 3 (the prohibition on torture or inhuman or degrading treatment or punishment) has been used successfully in the context of treatment in prison of a suicidal prisoner who was deemed to be vulnerable and who was not given the appropriate care in a medical, as opposed to a penal, context (*Keenan v United Kingdom*).[3] Articles of the Convention will be referred to, where appropriate, below.

The most significant mental health ECHR case in recent times was *HL v United Kingdom*[4] which concerned 'informal patients' under the Act, ie patients who were not compulsorily detained because they were compliant. UK law was found to be incompatible with Article 5. The case is dealt with in detail below at 9.5.3.4 and in Chapter 4 at 4.3.3.

9.1.3 What is mental disorder?

The wording of the original Mental Health Act 1983 referred to mental disorder, mental illness, psychopathic disorder and mental impairment. The new revised Act simply refers to mental disorder. Mental illness is often thought to consist of more serious aspects of disorder such as schizophrenia, but there is no definition of these general phrases, either in the medical or legal literature. There have been a number of writers who have questioned the existence of mental illness, or at least, questioned whether it is a *medical* condition. Interestingly, these views have been harnessed to both right- and left-wing perspectives. The American doctor and writer, Thomas Szasz, is one of the most well-known proponents and approaches it from a libertarian analysis. His view is that *all* illness has a *physical* pathology, and the psychiatrist must be either a malevolent meddler or a benevolent, but misguided, healer; he sees psychiatry as a study of personal conduct. Szasz maintains that psychiatric interventions are directed at moral, rather than medical problems, the view he takes is that of the psychiatrist as malevolent meddler. Szasz's pithy summary of his thesis is uncompromising:

Szasz, TS, *The Myth of Mental Illness: Foundations of a Theory of Personal Conduct*[5]

Summary

The principal arguments advanced in this book and their implications may be summarised as follows.

1   Strictly speaking, disease or illness can affect only the body; hence, there can be no mental illness.
2   'Mental illness' is a metaphor. Minds can be 'sick' only in the sense that jokes are 'sick' or economies are 'sick'.

---

2 (2000) 29 EHRR 50.
3 (2001) 33 EHRR 38.
4 (2005) 40 EHRR 32, ECtHR.
5 New York: Harper and Row, revised edn, 1974.

3   Psychiatric diagnoses are stigmatising labels, phrased to resemble medical diagnoses and applied to persons whose behaviour annoys or offends others.

4   Those who suffer from and complain of their own behaviour are usually classified as 'neurotic'; those whose behaviour makes others suffer, and about whom others complain, are usually classified as 'psychotic'.

5   Mental illness is not something a person has, but is something he does or is.

6   If there is no mental illness there can be no hospitalisation, treatment, or cure for it. Of course, people may change their behaviour or personality, with or without psychiatric intervention. Such intervention is nowadays called 'treatment', and the change, if it proceeds in a direction approved by society, 'recovery' or 'cure'.

7   The introduction of psychiatric considerations into the administration of the criminal law – for example, the insanity plea and verdict, diagnoses of mental incompetence to stand trial, and so forth, corrupt the law and victimise the subject on whose behalf they are ostensibly employed.

8   Personal conduct is always rule-following, strategic, meaningful. Patterns of interpersonal and social relations may be regarded and analysed as if they were games, the behaviour of the players being governed by explicit or tacit game rules.

9   In most types of voluntary psychotherapy, the therapist tries to elucidate the inexplicit game rules by which the client conducts himself; and to help the client scrutinise the goals and values of the life games he plays.

10 There is no medical, moral, or legal justification for involuntary psychiatric interventions. They are crimes against humanity.

Szasz has continued to maintain his basic contentions:

Szasz, T, 'Psychiatric diagnosis, psychiatric power and psychiatric abuse'[6]

Psychiatric practice, as the term implies, is a practical, not a theoretical, enterprise. Accordingly, so long as psychiatrists continue to assign the role of mental patient to persons against their will, that fact will remain a fundamental characteristic of psychiatric practice ...

Art historians, drama critics, musicologists, and many other scholars also make subjective classifications. However, lacking State-sanctioned power over persons, their classifications do not lead to anyone's being deprived of life, liberty, or property. Surely, the plastic surgeon's classification of beauty is subjective. But because the plastic surgeon cannot treat his or her patient without the patient's consent, there cannot be any political abuse of plastic surgery. It is as simple, and inconvenient, as that.

While not doubting the sincerity of Szasz's views, it is easy to see how they might be attractive to those who wish to reduce public spending on the care of those diagnosed as being mentally ill.

The British psychoanalyst, the late RD Laing, whose most well-known publication is *The Divided Self*,[7] took a different approach, and did not deny the existence of mental 'illness', but saw it as the reaction of a normal person to abnormal social pressures, for example oppressive family situations. He related the experience of mental illness very much to being out of kilter with the social norm. It is not difficult to see how this approach might be used in libertarian and even anarchistic arguments against traditional social organisations. It must, however, be said that,

---

6 (1994) 20 JME 135–38.
7 Harmondsworth: Penguin, 1959, reissued 1990.

interesting though theories such as those of Szasz and Laing are, they were never brought into the mainstream of psychiatry.[8]

However, although most people would not dispute the existence of mental illness, there is an inevitable difference between patients who are physically ill, and patients who are mentally ill, in that it is by no means agreed what is meant by *mental* illness. Although there may be some dispute about areas of physical illness, generally, it is acknowledged that one can point to examples of physical 'normality', but clearly it would be futile to attempt to define a psychologically normal person. While it is accepted that there can be desirable deviations from the physical norm (for example, athletic prowess), we are used to thinking of most significant deviations from the physical 'norm' as being undesirable. However, significant deviations from the psychological 'norm' can be *much better* than the norm, for example, in intellectual ability or capacity for forgiveness and compassion. Furthermore, in the case of physical characteristics, it is easier to decide whether the deviation is desirable or not, not least because mental qualities are essentially part of personal identity.

One of the few cases to consider the definitional issue is *W v L*,[9] where the Court of Appeal considered whether a young man was 'mentally ill' following a series of acts of violence and cruelty. He had hanged a puppy, strangled a terrier with wire, made a cat inhale ammonia and then cut its throat, and had put another cat in the gas oven. When he turned his attention away from family pets, and threatened his wife with a knife and offered other forms of violence towards her, he was admitted as an emergency under the provisions of the Mental Health Act 1959. Both Denning MR and Orr LJ accepted the medical evidence that the patient was psychotic, and did not consider the meaning of the expression 'mentally ill'. However, Lawton LJ made these observations:[10]

> **Lawton LJ**: The facts of this case show how difficult the fitting of particular instances into the statutory classification can be. Lord Denning MR and Orr LJ have pointed out that there is no definition of 'mental illness'. The words are ordinary words of the English language. They have no particular medical significance. They have no particular legal significance. How should the court construe them? The answer in my judgment is to be found in the advice which Lord Reid recently gave in *Cozens v Brutus* [1973] AC 854, p 861 namely, that ordinary words of the English language should be construed in the way that ordinary sensible people would construe them. That being, in my judgment, the right test, then I ask myself, what would the ordinary sensible person have said about the patient's condition in this case if he had been informed of his behaviour to the dogs, the cat and his wife? In my judgment such a person would have said: 'Well, the fellow is obviously mentally ill'. If that be right, then, although the case may fall within the definition of 'psychopathic disorder' in s 4(4), it also falls within the classification of 'mental illness'; and there is the added medical fact that when the EEG was taken there were indications of a clinical character showing some abnormality of the brain. It is that application of the sensible person's assessment of the condition, plus the medical indication, which in my judgment brought the case within the classification of mental illness, and justified the finding of the county court judge.

If it is the case that the words 'mental illness' are ordinary words and *have no particular medical significance*, what are the implications of this? In some ways this is an extraordinary conclusion, because if it has no medical significance, what significance does it have? The 'any normal person can see he's ill' definition of mental illness is a worrying one, and it adds fuel to the arguments of people such as Szasz.

---

8 See also Horwitz A and Wakefield J, *The Loss of Sadness: How Psychiatry Transformed Normal Sorrow into Depressive Disorder*, New York: OUP, 2007.
9 [1974] QB 711.
10 At pp 718–19.

On the difficulty of making precise medical classifications of mental disorders, see the House of Lords case of R *(on the application of B)* v *Ashworth Hospital Authority*.[11]

If one looks at the two main psychiatric diagnostic manuals published by the American Psychiatric Association and the World Health Organisation,[12] it will be seen that the symptoms of all known psychiatric disorders are described in some detail, but, not surprisingly, 'mental disorder or mental illness' as such are not considered.

It should also be noted that those with learning disabilities can be brought within the remit of the Act and that the concept of' 'learning disability' has replaced 'mental impairment' in the revised MHA. This is discussed further below.

THINK POINT

Do you think that it would be preferable to define mental disorder in terms of unacceptable behaviour on the part of the patient? If so, how would you decide what is acceptable?

9.1.4 Justifying detention

The Percy Commission, which reported before the MHA 1959, stated that it was wrong to detain someone compulsorily, before they had committed any criminal offence:

Lord Percy of Newcastle, *Report of the Royal Commission on the Law relating to Mental Illness and Mental Deficiency* (the Percy Commission)[13]

> Preventive detention under the ordinary criminal law may only be applied to offenders over a certain age who have a definite criminal record of a certain number of convictions for serious offences; and even preventive detention lasts only for a fixed period, after which the prisoner must be released even if it is almost certain that he will then commit further crimes. If one is to apply preventive control to psychopathic patients under wider conditions than these, one is in effect applying to them preventive detention in hospital in circumstances which would not justify preventive detention in prison under the criminal law. Whether or not special forms of control are justified on these grounds depends on how accurate the diagnosis of the patient's condition and the prognosis of his future behaviour is likely to be, and on the extent to which it is fair to assume that the risks to society from persons suffering from these forms of mental abnormality are greater than the risks which society runs from criminals who are not considered to be mentally abnormal.

Apart from having to be suffering from some form of mental disorder, the person compulsorily detained under the Act for assessment 'ought to be so detained in the interests of his own health or safety or with a view to the protection of other persons' (s 2(2)(b)), and in the case of a person compulsorily detained for treatment, it must be *'necessary* for the health or safety of the patient or for the protection of other persons that he should receive such treatment and it cannot be provided unless he is detained under this section' (s 3(2)(c)). It will be seen that the 'protection' condition is wider in the case of admission for assessment, being 'ought to be so detained in the interests of' as opposed to 'necessary for' and this is hardly surprising. However, it is not clear as to what sort of risks must be involved for patients and/or third parties.

---

11 [2005] UKHL 20.
12 *Diagnostic and Statistical Manual of Mental Disorders*, Washington DC: American Psychiatric Press, 2000 and *The Classification of Mental and Behavioural Disorders*, Geneva: World Health Organisation, 1992: known as DSM IV Revised and ICD – 10, respectively.
13 Cmd 169. London: HMSO, 1954–57, para 348.

The Code of Practice contains no guidance on the safety of the patient; perhaps it is thought to be self-evident, but the assessment of the risk and the probability of the risk turning into reality must surely be of central importance. There is guidance on health risk which states:

Department of Health and Welsh Office, *Code of Practice, Mental Health Act 1983*[14]

Factors to consider – the health or safety of the patient

4.6 Factors to be considered in deciding whether patients should be detained for their own health or safety include:

- The evidence suggesting that patients are at risk of:
  - suicide;
  - self-harm;
  - self-neglect or being unable to look after their own health or safety; or
  - jeopardising their own health or safety accidentally, recklessly or unintentionally;

or that their mental disorder is otherwise putting their health or safety at risk:

- any evidence suggesting that the patient's mental health will deteriorate if they do not receive treatment;
- the reliability of such evidence, including what is known of the history of the patient's mental disorder;
- the views of the patient and of any carers, relatives or close friends, especially those living with the patient, about the likely course of the disorder and the possibility of it improving;
- the patient's own skills and experience in managing their condition;
- the potential benefits of treatment, which should be weighed against any adverse effects that being detailed might have on the patient's wellbeing; and
- whether other methods of managing the risk are available.

Is the desire to protect from self-harm paternalistic and unsustainable? It can be argued that there is no interference with the positive freedom of the individual because there is a competing right held by the patient himself. The argument states that a person in ill health has reduced capacities to act and therefore less ability to make effective choices. In other words, the patient will be *more free* as a result of the paternalistic intervention. Cavadino gives a good account of the civil libertarian and other issues raised by the treatment of the mentally ill.

Cavadino, M, *Mental Health Law in Context: Doctors' Orders*[15]

[L]iberal thinkers such as Isaiah Berlin (1969) have usually adopted the 'negative concept of freedom'. Negative freedom is defined as the absence of coercion or constraint imposed on the individual by other people. (I use the word 'liberty' to mean freedom in this negative sense.) In this sense, everyone who is not prevented from doing so by other people is equally free to run a mile in under four minutes or to dine at the Ritz Hotel, although only some people (those fast enough, or rich enough) actually can.

There is, however, a rival concept of freedom which also has its adherents. 'Freedom in the positive sense' may be defined as 'the ability to make effective choices about one's own life'. In this positive sense, I am not free to run a mile in under four minutes, or to dine at the Ritz in my present financial circumstances. For to be 'positively free' is to be actually able to perform the action in question, not simply to be

---

14 London: HMSO, 2008, para 4.6.
15 Aldershot: Dartmouth, 1989.

unconstrained by other people or by the law. To be sure, negative freedom (absence of constraint) is necessary in order to have positive freedom; but to be positively free additionally requires, first, the physical and psychological capacities to carry out the action or course of action in question; and second, access to any material resources necessary to perform the action. So I am not free to dine at the Ritz if I cannot physically get there or cannot afford it.

Surely liberal theory of any kind – even those which emphasise the importance of 'negative freedom' – must presuppose that 'positive freedom' is of value. For what else is the point of valuing negative freedom (as liberalism does) if this negative freedom does not actually enable people to make real, effective choices? For all that some liberals vehemently insist on employing the negative definition of freedom, it must be 'positive freedom' which is the intrinsically valuable commodity to human beings, with 'negative freedom' only of instrumental value in so far as it is conducive to real ability to choose. In short, if negative freedom is to be valued, this can only be because positive freedom is of more fundamental value.

If we accept that positive freedom is of value, and necessarily is of value to every human being, then any defensible philosophy of morality must accept as a basic principle that every individual has an equal right to maximum positive freedom. This is the 'positive freedom principle' (PFP). I suggest that this principle provides a much more consistent and coherent approach than liberal theories typically do . . .

The presumption in favour of liberty must be a strong one. For as is generally accepted over a wide spectrum of political views, States and other powerful authorities have a distressing tendency to restrict liberty excessively (thereby depriving people of the positive freedom to which they are entitled). Given this, there are good reasons for holding (as liberalism does) that people should not be deprived of substantial liberty without strong justification being adduced. Thus it is indeed right that laws should be framed to protect negative freedom with clear criteria and adequate procedural safeguards.

What should the criteria for deprivation of liberty be? First, it is clear that the protection of others can in principle be a valid justification for deprivation of liberty. The potential victims of violent assault have a right to personal safety which comes into competition with the right to liberty of the potential detainee, since the infliction of injury represents an unjustified diminution of the positive freedom of the victim. The injured person's real abilities to act are diminished by injury and totally extinguished by death, because injury and death reduce or remove a person's physical capacities.

This is not to say, however, that people may be justly deprived of liberty without further ado if there is any evidence or belief, however slight, that they might be dangerous to others. The nature of the risk to others must be assessed together with its likelihood of eventuating. As Dworkin has suggested, we 'should treat a man against his will only when the danger he presents is vivid' [Dworkin, R, *Taking Rights Seriously*, 1978, London: Duckworth, p 11]. It also follows from the strength of the presumption in favour of liberty that cogent evidence of the patient's dangerousness should normally be adduced under conditions of due process before detention can be justified. (And incidentally, as we saw in Chapter 8, a psychiatrist's assessment that a patient is dangerous is by no means always 'cogent evidence'; due process requires that such evidence should be carefully scrutinised to assess its validity.)

What about parentalism [paternalism]? Here again a case can be made for interfering with the individual's (negative) liberty on the ground that there is a more important competing right to be protected. In this case, however, the competing right is not one owned by some other individual, but by the patient, the same person who has the right to liberty. If the intervention results in the preservation or promotion of the health of the patient, this could result overall in the maximisation of the patient's positive freedom. For a person in ill health has reduced capacities to act, and consequently less ability to make effective choices . . .

(Note that this argument is not a utilitarian one. It does not rest on the contention that the patient will be happier or will suffer less if the intervention occurs. It argues that the patient will be more free overall if parentalism is allowed.)

This is a persuasive justification, but it depends upon much sharper definitions of self-harm, and the possibility of accurate diagnoses, which at present we do not have.

As to the protection of others, it may be accepted even on strong libertarian grounds that detention of someone who, for example, violently assaults others, is consistent with the concept of the freedom of the individual as the patient will be seriously interfering with their liberty. However, in the Act itself the requirement regarding harm to others is weak: there is no suggestion that the severity of the harm, and likelihood of the risk are relevant.

The Code of Practice deals with the protection of others, and it is clear from this that, while it includes the protection of others from psychological as well as physical harm, risk to property is not enough:

Department of Health and Welsh Office, *Code of Practice, Mental Health Act 1983*[16]

4.7 In considering whether detention is necessary for the protection of other people, the factors to consider are the nature of the risk to other people arising from the patient's mental disorder, the likelihood that harm will result and the severity of any potential harm, taking into account:

- that it is not always possible to differentiate risk of harm to the patient from the risk of harm to others;
- the reliability of the available evidence, including any relevant details of the patient's clinical history and past behaviour, such as contact with other agencies and (where relevant) criminal convictions and cautions;
- the willingness and ability of those who live with the patient and those who provide care and support to the patient to cope with and manage the risk; and
- whether other methods of managing the risk are available.

4.8 Harm to other people includes psychological as well as physical harm.

Price comments on the notion of dangerous as follows:

Price, DPT, 'Civil commitment of the mentally ill: compelling arguments for reform'[17]

Dangerousness is a social construct, it is not a psychiatric phenomenon and thus not peculiarly within the competence of psychiatrists to assess in individual cases. In any event, the problems in predicting dangerousness are immense. Almost all studies of predictive accuracy show that there are likely to be more false positives than true positives in any defined population. This is hardly surprising in view of the (relative) rarity of violent conduct and the fact that violent or dangerous conduct is at least partly a product of a person's environment (in other words it is situation specific). Some studies have shown very substantial over-predictions of dangerousness by psychiatrists, which is partially due to the understandable tendency to err on what can be considered from one perspective as 'the safe side'. The potential for erosion of civil liberties through the unwarranted removal of liberty is then clear.

In 2000, government proposals for reform of the 1983 Act envisaged more draconian measures for 'dangerous' patients; see below at 9.1.5.

---

16 London: HMSO, 2008, para 4.7.
17 (1994) 2 Med L Rev 321.

9.1.5 History of statutory control

Brenda Hoggett sets out the development of the law relating to the control of mentally disordered people. After describing the provisions of the Lunacy Act 1890 and the Mental Treatment Act 1930, she goes on:

Hoggett, BM, *Mental Health Law*[18]

Until the 1959 Act . . . there were three different types of patient in mental illness hospitals – voluntary and temporary patients under the 1930 Act and patients certified under the various procedures in the 1890 Act. For mental 'defectives' there was a totally different, if rather less complex, set of procedures under the Mental Deficiency Acts of 1913 and 1927. These did not include a voluntary status, but the institutions were not expressly prohibited from taking patients without formality. After 1952, this was officially encouraged for short stays, and the Percy Commission recommended that it could be extended to long stay patients without waiting for legislation. In . . . the 1959 Act, a determined effort was made to break down the rigid legal boundaries and integrate the separate legal systems relating to 'lunacy' and 'mental deficiency'.

Two developments lay behind much of the Percy Commission's thinking. First was the introduction of the National Health Service in 1948 . . . The Commission believed that there was no longer any need for strict legal control over public hospitals. Further, as improvements depend upon the availability of resources, full responsibility should rest with the government department which controlled the allocation of resources within the health service as a whole. The Board of Control could safely be abolished, and with it the legal segregation of mental hospitals from the main stream of hospital development.

Second was the great optimism about the advances in medical treatment for the major mental illnesses, through psycho-surgery, electro-convulsive therapy and above all the new breed of psychotropic drugs, the major tranquillisers. These made it possible for increasing numbers of seriously disordered patients to be discharged into the community or treated on clinical wards in ordinary hospital conditions. It no longer seemed necessary for the law to assume that these patients were inevitably different from the physically sick or injured. For the most part, they could be admitted to hospital in just the same way. Compulsory procedures could be kept only for those for whom they were absolutely necessary. Once in hospital, their treatment and care could be left in the hands of the medical profession. As many as possible would be discharged back into the community just like other patients.

Hence, removing the legal controls over mental patients was inextricably linked with removing the legal controls over their doctors. The 1983 Act was mainly concerned to reimpose some of the latter.

In 1998, the Government set up a 'scoping study review committee' to examine the provisions of the 1983 Act, to take soundings from experts and interested parties and to prepare a report, outlining recommendations for reform. The committee reported in July 1999 (known as the 'Richardson Report') and, in November 1999, the Government issued a Green Paper.[19] Peay describes the Green Paper that followed the Richardson Report which had been patient-focused, as a 'squandered opportunity'.[20]

In 1999, another consultation document was issued by the Department of Health and the Home Office, *Managing Dangerous People with Severe Personality Disorder*. This was largely in response to the public outcry following the murders committed by Michael Stone, an allegedly 'untreatable' personality disordered patient who had been released into the community. Subsequently, a White Paper was issued, *Reforming The Mental Health Act*.[21] In 2002

---

18 London: Sweet & Maxwell, 4th edn, 1996.
19 *Reform of the Mental Health Act 1983: Proposals for Reform*, Cm 4480, London: DoH, 1999.
20 See Peay, J, 'Report of the Mental Health Act 1983: Squandering an Opportunity?' (2000) J Mental Health L 5.
21 Cm 5016–1, London: DoH and the Home Office, 2000.

a draft Mental Health Bill was issued, which gave rise to much criticism that it was too draconian in its measures to deal with people who were classified as personality disordered and dangerous.

Debate continued through Bills that were introduced in 2002 and 2004, which were abandoned, and in 2006 another Bill was produced that subsequently became the Mental Health Act 2007. Essentially, it made some amendments to the 1983 Act in certain key areas, but much of the Act remains the same. Certainly there has been no root and branch reform that had been hoped for by parties on all sides of the debate.

The main changes are as follows.

1   In order to be detained under the Act, patients now have to be suffering from 'mental disorder'; ie the other definitions have gone.
2   The 'treatability requirement' has gone. Previously, in order to justify admitting a patient for treatment under s 3, if the patient was suffering from non-severe mental impairment or psychopathic disorder then there had to be available treatment that was likely to alleviate or prevent a deterioration of his condition. This was controversial because, arguably, such a requirement should apply to all patients. It is also problematic because patients suffering from 'psychopathic disorder' (defined as a 'disorder or disability of mind . . . which results in abnormally aggressive or seriously irresponsible conduct . . .' and which, in terms of the diagnostic manuals, is more properly referred to as 'antisocial personality disorder') are often very difficult patients to deal with, and there could be a temptation to declare them to be untreatable in order to discharge them from hospital. That is not to say that there is no genuine debate as to how far such patients can be treated. However, the interpretation of 'treatment' under the Act has been very wide indeed. Since the changes, the issue has remained very much alive in that now, under s 3 of the Act, which sets out the conditions to be met in order for someone to be detained in hospital for treatment, 'appropriate treatment' has to be available. We shall examine this issue in due course.
3   The Act now provides for compulsory treatment in the community which is an attempt to avoid the 'revolving door' syndrome whereby patients are detained under the Act, treated successfully, released into the community, only to suffer relapse when they fail to take the stabilising medication.
4   The Act also provides for an independent advocacy scheme for detained patients who have no other form of representation.

The main elements of the revised legislation are set out below. For a detailed and exhaustive examination of the statutory provisions, readers are advised to consult Richard Jones's excellent guide to the Act.[22]

It should also be noted that there is a code of practice that gives detailed guidance on the operation of the Act. In July 2014, the Department of Health issued a consultation paper[23] on proposed changes to the Code, which came into force in 2015. The main areas where change is proposed are: the use of restrictive interventions such as physical restraint, medication and seclusion; the use of community treatment orders; and the use of police powers to detain people in places of safety. There are also suggested new chapters on care programmes, equality and human rights, and mental capacity and deprivation of liberty.

In May 2018, the Government published the scope of a review of the Mental Health Act.[24]

---

22 *Mental Health Act Manual*, 20th edn, London: Sweet & Maxwell, 2018.
23 *Stronger Code: Better* Care, London: DoH, 2014.
24 www.gov.uk/government/groups/independent-review-of-the-mental-health-act.

9.2 Detention

9.2.1 Mental disorder

Brief and somewhat unhelpful definitions of mental disorder and the other conditions referred to in the Act are contained within s 1:

1 Application of Act: 'mental disorder'

1   The provisions of this Act shall have effect with respect to the reception, care and treatment of mentally disordered patients, the management of their property and other related matters
2   In this Act –
'mental disorder' means any disorder or disability of mind and 'mentally disordered' shall be construed accordingly ...
...11.5

Under s 1(3) of the Act, definitions exclude alcohol or drug dependency without more. The *Review of the Mental Health Act 1959*, carried out by the Department of Health and Social Security[25] concluded that it was inappropriate to regard such problems as mental disorders. Note that Article 5 of the European Convention provides for detention of persons who are alcoholic or addicted to drugs, although the Act does not permit this, without more. It has been recognised that, where there is a 'dual diagnosis' of people with both mental illness and either drug or alcohol problems, there is a risk that they can fall between the mental health services, and substance misuse services. The Department of Health has issued guidance for both providers on 'dual diagnosis'.[26]

In *St George's Healthcare NHS Trust v S*,[27] there had been an attempt to use the provisions of the Act to detain a pregnant woman and perform a non-consensual Caesarean section. She had attended a GP practice when 36 weeks pregnant, not having previously sought antenatal care. She had pre-eclampsia and was advised that she should be admitted to hospital for an induced delivery. She refused this, wanting her baby to be born naturally. A social worker became involved and an application was made under s 2 of the Act (compulsory detention in hospital for 'assessment'). The Court of Appeal was highly critical of the way in which the case was handled from both the point of view of the law and medicine (even the way in which the court procedure was used was flawed). For example, the hospital sought legal advice because it was erroneously believed that treatment could not be given under a s 2 admission. The doctor assessing the patient found her to have capacity, although subsequently reconsidered this and amended her note to say that her mental state may be affecting her capacity. The mental state referred to was diagnosed as moderate depression. After approval by the court (the judge having been erroneously informed that it was a 'life and death situation' with only minutes to spare), the child was delivered by Caesarean section. The following day the woman was examined again, and the consultant found 'no current abnormalities in her mental state'. The s 2 order was discharged. The Court of Appeal granted judicial review and stated that someone not suffering from mental disorder could not be detained under the MHA 1983 against his will merely because his thinking process was unusual and contrary to the views of the overwhelming majority of the community. It was clear that the purpose of detention was to manage her pregnancy and confinement and not to assess and treat a mental condition.

---

25 Cmnd 7320, London: HMSO, 1978.
26 *Mental health policy implementation guide: Dual diagnosis good practice guide* (DoH, May 2002).
27 [1998] 3 All ER 673.
28 (1979) 2 EHRR 387.

In *Winterwerp v Netherlands*,[28] when referring to the rather quaint expression in Article 5 – 'persons of unsound mind' – the ECtHR held that this term is constantly evolving in the light of developments in psychiatry and in society's attitude to mental illness.

The old expression of 'mental impairment' is no longer used in the Act since the 2007 reforms. The new expression is 'learning disability'.

Mental Health Act 1983

1 Application of Act: 'mental disorder'

(2A) But a person with learning disability shall not be considered by reason of that disability to be –

(a) suffering from mental disorder for [certain purposes]
. . . unless that disability is associated with abnormally aggressive or seriously irresponsible conduct on his part.

The certain purposes referred to above include all compulsory admissions except admission under s 2 for assessment which is for a maximum of 28 days and is non-renewable. For all other compulsory detentions the learning disability must be associated with antisocial behaviour of an 'abnormal' nature.

The question of what constitutes 'seriously irresponsible conduct' was raised in *Re F (Mental Health Act: Guardianship)*.[29] The Court of Appeal held that a 17-year-old's desire to return to her home where she had been severely neglected and sexually exploited was not 'seriously irresponsible'. It was said that the expression should be interpreted as relating to a significant risk of harm to self or others.

THINK POINT

Do you agree with the argument that there should only be compulsory detention if the patient is a risk to the health and safety of others, and not to him/herself?

9.2.2 Key parties involved

The Act refers to a number of key personnel who are empowered to take action in respect of patients liable to be detained. Under s 11 of the Act, applications for compulsory admission may be made either by an approved mental health professional or by the patient's nearest relative.

9.2.2.1 Approved mental health professionals

Under s 114 of the Act, the local authority must appoint a 'sufficient number of approved mental health professionals for the purpose of discharging the functions conferred upon them'. Under the 1959 Act the same functions were carried out by mental welfare officers; under the 1983 Act prior to 2007 the functions were carried out by approved social workers:

13 Duty of approved mental health professionals to make applications for admission or guardianship

[(1) If a local social services authority have reason to think that an application for admission to hospital or a guardianship application may need to be made in respect of a patient within their area, they shall

---

29 [2000] 1 FLR 192.

make arrangements for an approved mental health professional to consider the patient's case on their behalf.

(1A) If that professional is –

a   satisfied that such an application ought to be made in respect of the patient; and

b   of the opinion, having regard to any wishes expressed by relatives of the patient or any other relevant circumstances, that it is necessary or proper for the application to be made by him,

he shall make the application.

(1B) Subsection (1C) below applies where –

a   a local social services authority makes arrangements under subsection (1) above in respect of a patient;

b   an application for admission for assessment is made under subsection (1A) above in respect of the patient;

c   while the patient is liable to be detained in pursuance of that application, the authority have reason to think that an application for admission for treatment may need to be made in respect of the patient; and

d   the patient is not within the area of the authority.

(1C) Where this subsection applies, subsection (1) above shall be construed as requiring the authority to make arrangements under that subsection in place of the authority mentioned there.]

(2) Before making an application for the admission of a patient to hospital an [approved mental health professional] shall interview the patient in a suitable manner and satisfy himself that detention in a hospital is in all the circumstances of the case the most appropriate way of providing the care and medical treatment of which the patient stands in need.

(3) An application under subsection (1A) above may be made outside the area of the local social services authority on whose behalf the approved mental health professional is considering the patient's case.

(4) It shall be the duty of a local social services authority, if so required by the nearest relative of a patient residing in their area, to [make arrangements under subsection (1) above for an approved mental health professional to consider the patient's case] with a view to making an application for his admission to hospital; and if in any such case [that professional] decides not to make an application he shall inform the nearest relative of his reasons in writing.

It will be seen from the following (s 13) that the approved mental health professional's duty is described as being personal to them and not as a functionary of the local authority which has appointed them, ie see the wording of sub-s (1A). See also *St George's Healthcare NHS Trust v S*.[30]

9.2.2.2 Nearest relative

Under some of the early reform proposals, the nearest relative provisions would be abolished in favour of a nominated person, the identity of whom being, to some extent, under the control of the patient. In the European Court case of *JT v United Kingdom*,[31] where the patient alleged that there was an infringement of her Article 8 right as the legislation did not provide for her to 'change' her nearest relative, the UK government responded (to the satisfaction of the court) that this would be reformed. The same point was taken in the case of *R (on the application of M) v Secretary of State for Health*,[32] where the nearest relative provisions (not open to challenge by the patient) were declared to be incompatible with the HRA 1998, Article 8. In consequence,

---

30 [1998] 3 All ER 673, at 694.
31 [2000] 1 FLR 909.
32 [2003] EWHC 1094.

under s 29(3), patients will now be able to apply to the county court to displace their nearest relative on the ground that they are unsuitable to act.

The nearest relative is defined by s 26 of the Act:

---

26. – Definition of 'relative' and 'nearest relative'.

1   In this Part of this Act 'relative' means any of the following persons: –
    a   husband or wife [or civil partner];
    b   son or daughter;
    c   father or mother;
    d   brother or sister;
    e   grandparent;
    f   grandchild;
    g   uncle or aunt;
    h   nephew or niece.

2   In deducing relationships for the purposes of this section, any relationship of the half-blood shall be treated as a relationship of the whole blood, and an illegitimate person shall be treated as the legitimate child of [. . .]
    [(a)   his mother, and
    (b)   if his father has parental responsibility for him within the meaning of section 3 of the Children Act 1989, his father.]

3   In this Part of this Act, subject to the provisions of this section and to the following provisions of this Part of this Act, the 'nearest relative' means the person first described in subsection (1) above who is for the time being surviving, relatives of the whole blood being preferred to relatives of the same description of the half-blood and the elder or eldest of two or more relatives described in any paragraph of that subsection being preferred to the other or others of those relatives, regardless of sex.

4   Subject to the provisions of this section and to the following provisions of this Part of this Act, where the patient ordinarily resides with or is cared for by one or more of his relatives (or, if he is for the time being an in-patient in a hospital, he last ordinarily resided with or was cared for by one or more of his relatives) his nearest relative shall be determined –
    a   by giving preference to that relative or those relatives over the other or others; and
    b   as between two or more such relatives, in accordance with subsection (3) above.

The definition does not include spouses who are separated and provision is also made for cohabitees and other persons with whom the patient has been residing to be treated as relatives (sub-ss (5)–(7)). It is possible for persons who do not come within the ambit of s 26 nevertheless still to act in the capacity of a nearest relative. The nearest relative may forfeit status, and can authorise another person to act, or that person can be appointed by the county court to be the patient's nearest relative, under s 29:

---

29 . . .

(3)   An application for an order under this section may be made upon any of the following grounds, that is to say –
    (a)   that the patient has no nearest relative within the meaning of this Act, or that it is not reasonably practicable to ascertain whether he has such a relative, or who that relative is;
    (b)   that the nearest relative of the patient is incapable of acting as such by reason of mental disorder or other illness;

(c) that the nearest relative of the patient unreasonably objects to the making of an application for admission for treatment or a guardianship application in respect of the patient; [. . .]

(d) that the nearest relative of the patient has exercised without due regard to the welfare of the patient or the interests of the public his power to discharge the patient [. . .] under this Part of this Act, or is likely to do so [; or]

[(e) that the nearest relative of the patient is otherwise not a suitable person to act as such.]

In W v L[33] the Court of Appeal had to consider the meaning of s 29(3)(c), that is when does a nearest relative *unreasonably* object?

Lord Denning MR (p 717): This brings me to the final question: is the wife unreasonable in objecting to the making of an application for the husband's detention? . . . if you look at it from her own point of view, she may not be unreasonable. But I do not think it correct to look at it from her own point of view. The proper test is to ask what a reasonable woman in her place would do in all the circumstances of the case.

9.2.2.3 Doctors

Applications must, of course, be supported by medical recommendations. An application under s 2 (admission for assessment), s 3 (admission for treatment) or s 7 (reception into guardianship) requires two medical recommendations. An application under s 4 (emergency) needs only one recommendation. The doctor in charge of the patient's treatment is referred to as the 'responsible clinician'.

9.2.3 The categories of admission

9.2.3.1 Admission for assessment – s 2

Section 2 of the MHA 1983 states as follows:

2 Admission for assessment

(2) An application for admission for assessment may be made in respect of a patient on the grounds that –

a   he is suffering from mental disorder of a nature or degree which warrants the detention of the patient in a hospital for assessment (or for assessment followed by medical treatment) for at least a limited period; and

b   he ought to be so detained in the interests of his own health or safety or with a view to the protection of other persons.

. . .

(4) Subject to the provisions of s 29(4) below, a patient admitted to hospital in pursuance of an application for admission for assessment may be detained for a period not exceeding 28 days beginning with the day on which he is admitted, but shall not be detained after the expiration of that period unless before it has expired he has become liable to be detained by virtue of a subsequent application, order or direction under the following provisions of this Act.

---

33 [1974] QB 711.

It should be noted that, under s 11(3), if the application is made by an approved mental health professional, he must inform the nearest relative that an application is to be made. There is no requirement in respect of a s 2 admission for the approved mental health professional to have *consulted* with the relative (see s 11(4)), but under s 13(1) the social worker must have regard to any wishes expressed by the relative when deciding whether to make the application. There is no illegality if it subsequently transpires that the patient is not suffering from mental disorder at all (*R v Kirklees Metropolitan BC, ex p C*).[34]

Admission under s 2 is for 28 days only, and s 2(4) states that the patient 'shall not be detained after the expiration of that period unless before it has expired he has become liable to be detained by virtue of a subsequent application, order or direction under the following provisions of this Act'. Clearly, this means that it is not renewable, and it may be argued that no subsequent s 2 application could be made. However, in *R v South Western Hospital Managers, ex p M*,[35] it was held that the discretion of an approved social worker (as they were then called) could not be fettered by the earlier decision of a Mental Health Review Tribunal to discharge a s 2 patient, albeit in this case, to pursue a subsequent application under s 3 (admission for treatment). Laws J stated that such decisions by the social workers, doctors and hospital managers would be amenable to applications for judicial review. It seems therefore that a further s 2 application, made immediately after the expiry of an earlier one, would be judicially reviewable, but, on the reasoning employed by Laws J would not be automatically regarded as unlawful on the face of the statute.

A similar issue came up in *R v East London and City Mental Health NHS Trust, ex p Brandenburg*,[36] in relation to the discharge of a patient by a Mental Health Tribunal following a s 2 admission. The patient was redetained on the day before the discharge was due to take place. The Court of Appeal held that there did not have to be a change of circumstances to justify this under the Act, but the decision to discharge must be given great weight. A decision to redetain, where there was no change of circumstances, would have to be made in the light of facts known to the doctors and not to the tribunal, otherwise the decision of the tribunal would prevail. The House of Lords rejected an appeal, but it was stated by Lord Bingham that an ASW (approved social worker as they were then called) may not lawfully apply for the admission of a patient whose discharge has been ordered by a tribunal unless s/he has formed the reasonable and bona fide opinion that s/he has information not known to the tribunal which puts a significantly different complexion on the case as compared with that which was before the tribunal.[37]

A related point is the question of 'assessment' and when it is appropriate to admit for that reason. In *B v Barking Havering and Brentwood Community Healthcare NHS Trust*[38] it was said that assessment could be an important part of evaluating treatment. This would mean that a patient could be admitted for assessment under s 2 where a diagnosis of his condition had already been made. Admitting someone under s 2, however, and then failing to undertake any form of assessment would be unlawful.[39]

9.2.3.2 Admission for treatment – s 3

Long-term admission is sanctioned under s 3 of the Act.

---

34 [1993] 2 FLR 187.
35 [1994] 1 All ER 161.
36 [2001] EWCA Civ 239.
37 [2003] UKHL 58. See also *R (on the application of Wirral Health Authority and Wirral BC) v Dr Finnegan and DE* [2001] EWCA Admin 312.
38 [1999] 1 FLR 106.
39 See *St George's Healthcare NHS Trust v S* [1999] Fam 26.

3 Admission for treatment

...

(2)   An application for admission for treatment may be made in respect of a patient on the grounds that –
 a   he is suffering from mental disorder of a nature or degree which makes it appropriate for him to receive medical treatment in a hospital; and
 b   it is necessary for the health or safety of the patient or for the protection of other persons that he should receive such treatment and it cannot be provided unless he is detained under this section; and
 c   appropriate medical treatment is available to him.

It can be argued that applications under s 3 are, more often than not, unnecessary. Why should this be the case? Although there is no obligation to do so, an application in respect of a patient who has not been formally sectioned before will usually be under s 2 of the Act. This means that for up to 28 days a patient can be observed, and, if necessary, treated. After the lapse of this period of time, therefore, the patient may be a lot 'better' than when first admitted, and therefore more amenable to remaining as a voluntary patient, rather than by invoking the provisions of s 3.

The use – or abuse – of the wording of s 3 was considered in the case of *R v Hallstrom and Another, ex p W (No 2)*. In that case, an admission under s 3 was made, and almost immediately the patient was discharged under s 17 (a provision of the Act which enables the responsible clinician to grant leave of absence to any patient liable to be detained). The purpose was to allow compulsory treatment within the community. McCullough J said:[40]

R v Hallstrom and Another, ex p W (No 2)[41]

McCullough J: It stretches the concept of 'admission for treatment' too far to say that it covers admission for only so long as it is necessary to enable leave of absence to be granted after which the necessary treatment will begin. 'Admission for treatment' under s 3 is intended for those whose condition is believed to require a period of treatment as an in-patient. It may be that such patients will also be thought to require a period of out-patient treatment thereafter, but the concept of 'admission for treatment' has no applicability to those whom it is intended to admit and detain for a purely nominal period, during which no necessary treatment will be given.

This principle was, in the words of Phil Fennell, distinguished almost to the point of extinction in the case of *R (on the application of DR) v Merseycare NHS Trust*.[42] In that case, the claimant alleged that the renewal of her detention under s 20(2) of the Act was only appropriate when a patient's treatment plan was for treatment as an 'in-patient'. In her case, the proposal was that she be treated as an 'out-patient'. Her application for judicial review was rejected on the basis that 'any distinction between treatment at a hospital and in a hospital was too subtle'. It is also important to note here that, since the 1983 Act was passed, there has been a move away from treatment in hospital to treatment in the community, a change based upon a desire to avoid the institutionalisation of patients and to allow an appropriate degree of autonomy. However, as

---

40 At p 315.
41 [1986] 2 All ER 306.
42 [2002] All ER (D) 28. See Commentary [2003] Med L Rev 382.

demonstrated, in effect, the interpretation of the requirement under the unamended legislation that the patient's condition 'warrants the detention of him in a hospital' has included hospital out-patient treatment, so that treatment can effectively be carried out in the community without the use of the newly introduced community treatment orders.

The interpretation of 'the nature or degree' of the disorder warranting hospital treatment was considered in *R v The Mental Health Review Tribunal for the South Thames Region, ex p Smith*.[43] It was said that this would be satisfied in the case of a patient whose symptoms are adequately controlled by medication, but who has stopped taking medication and whose history is such that a significant deterioration can be expected as a result of this. This not uncommon scenario (and results in what is often described as the 'revolving door' of admission/discharge/admission) was considered by the Court of Appeal in relation to the application of the HRA 1998 in the case of *R (on the application of H) v Mental Health Review Tribunal, North and North East London Region*.[44] It was said that the continued detention of such a patient was not contrary to Article 5(1)(e) of the ECHR (no one shall be deprived of his liberty save in (*inter alia*) the lawful detention of persons of unsound mind and in accordance with a procedure prescribed by law). There was no contravention as long as the detention was a proportionate response having regard to the risks that would be involved in discharge.

9.2.3.3 Admission for assessment in emergencies – s 4

Section 4 of the Act states as follows:

---

4 Admission for assessment in cases of emergency

1. In any case of urgent necessity, an application for admission for assessment may be made in respect of a patient in accordance with the following provisions of this section, and any application so made is in this Act referred to as 'an emergency application'.

2. An emergency application may be made either by an approved mental health professional or by the nearest relative of the patient; and every such application shall include a statement that it is of urgent necessity for the patient to be admitted and detained under s 2 above, and that compliance with the provisions of this Part of this Act relating to applications under that section would involve undesirable delay.

3. An emergency application shall be sufficient in the first instance if founded on one of the medical recommendations required by s 2 above, given, if practicable, by a practitioner who has previous acquaintance with the patient and otherwise complying with the requirements of s 12 below so far as applicable to a single recommendation, and verifying the statement referred to in sub-s (2) above.

4. An emergency application shall cease to have effect on the expiration of a period of 72 hours from the time when the patient is admitted to the hospital unless –

   a. the second medical recommendation required by s 2 above is given and received by the managers within that period; and

   b. that recommendation and the recommendation referred to in sub-s (3) above together comply with all the requirements of s 12 below (other than the requirement as to the time of signature of the second recommendation).

---

43 [1999] COD 148.
44 [2001] EWCA Civ 415.

Although it may be accepted that there will be cases which are genuine emergencies and where a streamlined admission procedure is necessary, some may find cause for concern if such a procedure is used frequently. Further, it is important to keep in mind the wording of the section: it should not be used where it is simply more convenient to admit in this way, and obtain a second recommendation once the patient is in hospital so that the patient can then be admitted under s 2 or s 3. These concerns were considered in the 1978 *Review of the 1959 Mental Health Act*:

Review of the 1959 Mental Health Act[45]

Emergency admission for observation (s 29)

2.3 – Section 29 provides, in a case of urgent necessity, for the compulsory admission to hospital of a patient for observation. Twelve thousand people were admitted in this way in 1976. An application can be made by any relative (as defined by the Act) or by a Mental Welfare Officer, on the basis of a recommendation by any doctor. The section authorises detention for up to 72 hours only, unless the second medical recommendation which is required . . . is obtained within that period. The intention of the 1959 Act was that . . . s 29 should be used only in emergencies when there was not enough time to obtain the second medical recommendation. Section 29 has however been invoked more frequently than originally envisaged, and it has become the most widely used form of compulsory admission. There is also wide regional variation in its use. The Government hopes that the increasing development of the 24 hour crisis intervention services envisaged in the White Paper 'Better Services for the Mentally Ill' will in time reduce the need for such admissions, by enabling some emergencies to be contained without the need for compulsory admission to hospital or alternatively for two medical assessments to be provided. However, given the present constraints on manpower and resources, it is accepted that there is a continuing need for a statutory emergency procedure. While there is a good deal of support in comments on the Consultative Document for developing 24 hour crisis intervention services and for the view that these would reduce the use of s 29, it was also argued that, however fully developed, crisis intervention services could never adequately replace s 29 powers, particularly in rural areas. Comments included the point that s 29 allows for a short assessment or 'cooling off' period which can often lead to discharge within 72 hours or to the person staying in hospital as an informal patient.

It should be noted that treatment cannot be given to a patient admitted under this section under Part IV of the Act (that is, without his consent) so the patient is in the same position as a voluntary patient to whom treatment cannot be given without consent if they have capacity. These emergency powers do not contravene the HRA 1998, because the ECHR's procedural safeguards do not apply in emergency situations (*Winterwerp v Netherlands*).[46]

9.2.3.4 Guardianship – s 7

The requirements of s 7 are such that a patient over the age of 16 can be made the subject of a guardianship order if he is suffering from mental disorder of a nature or degree which warrants his reception into guardianship. The powers of the guardian are to require specified residence; to require attendance for medical treatment, education and training; and to require access to the patient.

---

45 Cmnd 7320, London: HMSO, 1978, para 1.17.
46 (1979) 2 EHRR 387.

A person received into guardianship is not a person who is 'liable to be detained' for the purposes of s 56, and therefore the Part IV provisions as to treatment do not apply; that is, the patient cannot be treated for the mental disorder against his will (see 9.4, below).

Both Article 5 (right to liberty) and Article 6 (right to a fair trial) apply to guardianship. There is no contravention of Article 6 because there is a right to appeal to a Mental Health Review Tribunal. As far as Article 5 is concerned, this applies even though the patient is not directly physically restrained. Restrictions as to dwelling place, etc, are also capable of contravening Article 5 (*Ashingdane v United Kingdom*).[47]

Guardianship is used infrequently (see the House of Commons Health Committee, *Report on Community Supervision Orders*),[48] and, given that substantial resources would be necessary to 'police' the system successfully, there must be doubts as to its usefulness. Mike Fisher, referring to the Social Services Research Group Study, carried out in 1985–86, notes that during that 12-month period, the 63 incidents of guardianship constituted less than 1 per cent of all detentions under the Act.[49] It might be thought that now there is the provision to provide treatment in the community, there would be no need to retain the power to make someone the subject of guardianship. However, guardianship is not about medical treatment, but about general personal care and, in that respect, it can be argued that it still retains a role.

9.2.3.5 The detention of inpatients – s 5

5 Application in respect of patient already in hospital

1   An application for the admission of a patient to a hospital may be made under this Part of this Act notwithstanding that the patient is already an in-patient in that hospital or, in the case of an application for admission for treatment that the patient is for the time being liable to be detained in the hospital in pursuance of an application for admission for assessment; and where an application is so made the patient shall be treated for the purposes of this Part of this Act as if he had been admitted to the hospital at the time when that application was received by the managers.

2   If, in the case of a patient who is an in-patient in a hospital, it appears to the registered medical practitioner in charge of the treatment of the patient that an application ought to be made under this Part of this Act for the admission of the patient to hospital, he may furnish to the managers a report in writing to that effect; and in any such case the patient may be detained in the hospital for a period of 72 hours from the time when the report is so furnished.

. . .

The purpose of s 5 is to enable a hospital to detain a voluntary patient who decides that he is going to leave the hospital. Where the provisions of s 5(2) and (4) are used, the patient cannot be treated without consent; that is, the patient is specifically excluded from the provisions of Part IV by s 56 of the Act.

9.2.3.6 Informal admission – s 131

Patients can be informally admitted under the Act, that is they are voluntary patients, and, as such, are free to leave at any time. As we saw in Chapter 4, following the case of *HL v United Kingdom*[50] in the European Court of Human Rights, the Mental Health Act 2007 amended the

---

47 (1985) 7 EHRR 528.
48 London: HMSO, 1992–93.
49 See Fisher, M, 'Guardianship under the mental health legislation: a review' [1988] J Soc Wel L 316.
50 (2005) 40 EHRR 32.

Mental Capacity Act 2005 by introducing the Deprivation of Liberty Safeguards and, of course, these apply to informal psychiatric patients just as much as they apply to non-psychiatric patients and residents in care homes. Note the relationship between the Mental Health Act and the Mental Capacity Act 2005 (see below 9.8).

9.2.3.7 Miscellaneous powers

Under s 17 of the Act, a detained patient may be granted leave of absence subject to such conditions as the responsible clinician thinks necessary in the interests of the patient or for the protection of others. It should be noted that such a person is still liable to be detained, so that both the consent to treatment provisions of the Act and the HRA 1998 apply.

Finally, it must be noted that there are a number of powers under the Act conferred upon the police and social workers. Under s 115, an approved mental health professional may enter and inspect any premises if he has reasonable cause to believe that a mentally disordered person living there is not under proper care. Under s 136, a police officer may remove a person to a place of safety if he finds, in a public place, a person who appears to be suffering from mental disorder and to be in immediate need of care or control. Such a person can be detained to a maximum period of 72 hours to enable him to be examined by a doctor and interviewed by an approved mental health professional. Section 135 provides for the issue of warrants to search for and remove patients to a place of safety, so that persons believed to be suffering from mental disorder can be removed from private premises too. The power given to approved mental health professionals under s 115 does not enable them to force entry and, in such circumstances, it would be necessary to obtain a warrant under s 135.

9.2.4 Detention via the criminal justice system

A detailed examination of this area would involve consideration of criminological matters and penal policy which are outside the scope of this book. However, it is important to remember that many patients compulsorily detained have arrived in that state via criminal sentences. For an account of the criminal provisions see Bartlett and Sandland.[51]

9.3 Non-medical treatment

Part IV of the Act deals specifically with medical treatment. However, the Act is silent on issues such as the management of difficult patients, the extent to which they can be physically restrained, secluded and searched. In *Pountney v Griffiths*[52] the House of Lords said that detention under the Act (the 1959 Act at that time) necessarily involves the exercise of control and discipline.

Department of Health and Welsh Office, *Mental Health Code of Practice*[53]

Personal and other searches

16.10 Hospital managers should ensure that there is an operational policy on searching patients detained under the Act, their belongings and surroundings and their visitors. When preparing the policy, hospital managers should consider the position of informal patients.

---

51 Bartlett, P and Sandland, R, *Mental Health Law: Policy and Practice*, Oxford: OUP, 2014, Ch 8.
52 [1976] AC 314.
53 London: HMSO, 2008.

16.11 The policy should be based on the following clear principles:

- the intention is to create and maintain a therapeutic environment in which treatment may take place and to ensure the security of the premises and the safety of patients, staff and the public;
- the authority to conduct a search of a person or their property is controlled by law, and it is important that hospital staff are aware of whether they have legal authority to carry out any such search;
- searching should be proportionate to the identified risk and should involve the minimum possible intrusion into the person's privacy; and
- all searches will be undertaken with due regard to and respect for the person's dignity.

This approved use of routine and random searching for no particular reason was considered by the Court of Appeal in *R v Broadmoor Special Hospital Authority and Another, ex p S and Others*.[54] Prior to 1997, Broadmoor's policy had been to search patients only when there had been a reason to do so. However, the policy was changed after a patient had attacked a priest with a heavy object which he had hidden on his person. In consequence, the search policy was amended to permit random searches, without consent or cause and, if necessary, overriding medical opinion against its exercise (presumably such opinion would be based upon the issue of 'trust'). The Court of Appeal confirmed the lawfulness of the policy on the basis that prisoners held in a special hospital such as Broadmoor were there because of their dangerous, violent or criminal propensities, and the policy was necessary in order to maintain a safe therapeutic environment.

Seclusion was considered by the Court of Appeal in *Colonel Munjaz v Mersey Care NHS Trust (1) The Secretary of State for Health and (2) The National Association for Mental Health (MIND), and S v Airedale NHS Trust and (1) The Secretary of State for Health and (2) The National Association for Mental Health (MIND)*.[55] The following principles emerged: the power to seclude is derived from the statutory power to detain and the common law justification of necessity; if the power is exercised in this way it will not amount to the tort of false imprisonment; seclusion is capable of being 'medical treatment'; it can amount to inhuman or degrading treatment or punishment under Article 3 of the ECHR but would have to reach a minimum level of severity; it would infringe Article 8 but could be justified under Article 8(2); if a hospital's actions breached the Code of Practice, an action in judicial review would lie. The Court of Appeal held that this policy governing the seclusion of psychiatric patients detained at its high security mental hospital departed from the Code of Practice issued by the Secretary of State pursuant to the Mental Health Act 1983, s 118(1) and was unlawful. The trust appealed to the House of Lords, where the appeal was allowed by a majority of 3:2. (*R (on the application of Munjaz) v Mersey Care NHS Trust and R (on the application of S) v Airedale NHS Trust (Appeal)*[56]). The appeal was allowed on the basis that the Code provided guidance and not instruction. A hospital had to consider the Code with great care, and departure from any aspect had to be justified. On the evidence, the Code had been very carefully considered by the trust and most parts of it had been reproduced in the policy. Where the policy had departed from the Code (there was provision for less frequent medical review after seven days), the trust had provided very detailed justification for the policy.

The case was then heard by the European Court of Human Rights[57] with submissions that there were violations of Articles 3, 5, 8 and 14. The last one was rejected on the basis that this

---

54 [1998] COD 199.
55 [2003] EWCA Civ 1036.
56 [2005] UKHL 58.
57 *Munjaz v UK* [2012] ECHR 1704.

was not relied on during the domestic proceedings and therefore the patient had not exhausted his domestic remedies. As to breach of Article 3 (the right not to be subjected to torture or inhuman and degrading treatment), this was found to be manifestly ill founded. If the ECtHR were to depart from the findings of fact of the national courts, it required cogent reasons to do so and there were none in this case. What is more, whatever the frequency of review of seclusion provided for by the policy, the risk of physical or psychological deterioration in a patient was significantly minimised as a nurse had to be within sight and sound of the seclusion room, periods of association were allowed and the conditions of seclusion could be adjusted according to the needs of the patient. As to Article 5 (the right to liberty), the patient was not being deprived of his liberty beyond what were already lawful restrictions. It was accepted that Article 8(1) (the right to a private life) had been interfered with by the imposition of the seclusion policy but this was justified under Article 8(2) as being lawful, justified and proportionate. In consequence the ECtHR agreed with the decision of the House of Lords.

Section 134 of the Act permits inspection and withholding of a detained patient's outgoing and incoming mail. Article 8 of the ECHR, which protects the right to respect for private life, specifically refers to protection of correspondence, so would it be possible to use the HRA 1998 to challenge this? First, it must be said that, under the Act, the restrictions on mail are not unqualified. Except in cases where the addressee has requested that communications from the patient to him should be withheld, the restrictions apply only to hospitals at which high security psychiatric services are provided and, secondly, they can only be imposed if it is necessary to do so in the interests of the safety of the patient or for the protection of other persons. This is likely to be proportionate and to satisfy Article 8(2), that is 'to be necessary in a democratic society in the interests of public safety . . . for the prevention of disorder or crime, for the protection of heath or morals, or for the protection of the rights and freedoms of others'. Furthermore, the restriction does not apply to mail sent (*inter alia*) to 'any legally qualified persons instructed by the patient to act as his legal adviser'.[58] Further, this exception should also have the effect of avoiding any potential breach of Article 6, which protects the right to a fair trial.

Article 8 was considered in *R v Ashworth Hospital Authority, ex p E*,[59] where it was held that the decision to refuse the request of a male patient to dress as a woman was lawful. The restrictions on dress were justified in terms of a pressing social need (the risk of disguise to facilitate abscondment was one reason) and it was proportionate.

In *McCann v State Hospitals Board for Scotland*,[60] the Supreme Court had to consider how far restrictions on smoking and on tobacco products breached Article 8 of the European Convention on Human Rights. The patient applied for judicial review of the policy which prohibited patients from smoking or possessing tobacco products in the hospital buildings and grounds, and from smoking during, what are described in the case as home visits, but which must mean during hospital visiting hours. In addition to this prohibition, the policy also permitted both patients and their visitors to be searched for tobacco products, and the confiscation of anything found. The case involved detailed discussion of the various statutory provisions that apply in Scotland, and it was found that the policy of search and confiscation was contrary to the Mental Health (Care and Treatment)(Scotland) Act 2003. However, it is the consideration of Article 8 that concerns us here. It was held that Article 8 was engaged. Even if a finding of interference with the right to a private life were made, it could still be justifiable under Article 8(2).

---

58 See *Valle v Finland* (2000) unreported, 16 March, where restrictions on telephone calls to a psychiatric patient's legal adviser were found to be unjustified.
59 [2002] QBD, Admin Court, Richards J, 19 December 2001.
60 [2017] UKSC 31.

Lord Hodge: 58 As is well known, justification under article 8(2) requires that the measure which interferes with the right (i) is in accordance with the law, (ii) pursues a legitimate objective, (iii) is rationally connected to the legitimate objective and (iv) is proportionate. I have already discussed the requirement that the interference be 'in accordance with the law' and have concluded that the part of the impugned decision relating to the prohibition of possession, searches for and confiscation of tobacco products, did not meet that requirement . . . But because the Board may seek to introduce such measures in accordance with the 2003 Act, I address the other tests.

59 I address first the tests of legitimate objective and rational connection. In the Rampton Hospital case both the Divisional Court and the Court of Appeal cited public documents which recorded (a) that in 1998 it was estimated that smoking in the United Kingdom caused each year 46,500 deaths from cancer and 40,300 deaths from circulatory diseases, (b) that those who smoke regularly and then die of smoking-related disease lose on average 16 years from their life expectancy when compared with non-smokers and (c) that in 2005 second-hand smoking caused at least 12,000 deaths a year in the United Kingdom. Having regard to the adverse effects that smoking can have on the health of smokers and others exposed to tobacco smoke, I have no difficulty in agreeing with the Second Division that the comprehensive smoking ban pursued the legitimate aim of the protection of health which is recognised in article 8(2). The aim is to protect the detained patient from the health risks of his smoking and other people from the health risks of second-hand smoke. The comprehensive smoking ban clearly has a rational connection with the pursuit of that desirable goal.

60 Finally, in order to be 'necessary in a democratic society' in the interests of public health the interference must be proportionate. Again, as is well known, the tests for proportionality (in addition to the tests of the importance of the legitimate objective and the rational connection of the measure to that objective) are (i) whether a less intrusive measure could have been used without unacceptably compromising the achievement of the objective and (ii) whether a fair balance has been struck between the rights of the individual and the interests of the community having regard to (a) the severity of the impact of the measure on the individual's rights and (b) the contribution of the measure to the achievement of the objective: Bank Mellat v HM Treasury (No 2) [2014] AC 700, para 20 per Lord Sumption, para 74 per Lord Reed. No challenge is made to the ban on smoking indoors, where the danger of exposing other patients and supervising staff in designated smoking areas is obvious. The minute (para 12 above) and the document discussed in para 7 above both record that the impugned decision which led to the comprehensive ban resulted from the operational difficulties which the Board faced in operating the partial ban which allowed supervised smoking within the hospital grounds. Those problems threatened to compromise the health of the supervising staff, the welfare of the patients and the security of both. Mr McCann did not challenge the account of events in those documents, which, in my view, this court must treat as the accepted factual background to the impugned decision. Faced with such difficulties, I am satisfied that the Board did not act disproportionately in imposing the comprehensive smoking ban when it did.

61 If there is to be a comprehensive smoking ban, it is likely that the managers of the Board will need to prohibit the possession of tobacco products and also have powers to search for and confiscate such products. As counsel for Mr McCann does not dispute that the introduction of such measures in accordance with the 2003 Act, the Code of Practice, and the 2005 Regulations would comply with the ECHR, it is not necessary further to consider the justification of those measures if they are introduced in that way.

62 Accordingly, but for the illegality under our domestic law of the prohibition of possession of tobacco products, the searches and the confiscation of tobacco products which are part of the impugned decision, I would have held that the decision was not contrary to Mr McCann's article 8 right to respect for his private life.

9.4 Medical treatment

9.4.1 Appropriate treatment is available

Following the 2007 amendments to the Act, an additional condition has been inserted by s 3(2)(c) of the Act, where admission is for treatment. This condition is that there is appropriate treatment available for the patient. In the case of some patients with personality disorder, there is no suitable medication and, in the case of psychological therapies, a degree of co-operation is required from the patient and this is frequently not forthcoming. Does this mean that there is no appropriate treatment available? This issue can arise in the case of patients who are detained under the criminal law arm of the Act, because often certain personality disorders can be linked to criminal behaviour, but it applies equally to those subject to civil detention. Section 145(1) of the Act states that 'medical treatment' includes intervention and specialist mental health habilitation, rehabilitation and care. Section 145(4) states that medical treatment shall be construed as a reference to medical treatment, the purpose of which is to alleviate, or prevent a worsening of, the disorder, or one or more of its symptoms or manifestations. Chapter 6 of the Code of Practice states as follows:

Department of Health and Welsh Office, *Code of Practice, Mental Health Act 1983*[61]

6.4 Purpose is not the same as likelihood. Medical treatment may be for the purpose of alleviating, or preventing a worsening of, a mental disorder even though it cannot be shown in advance that any particular effect is likely to be achieved.

6.5 Symptoms and manifestations include the way a disorder is experienced by the individual concerned and the way in which the disorder manifests itself in the person's thoughts, emotions, communication, behaviour and actions. But it should be remembered that not every thought or emotion, or every aspect of the behaviour, of a patient suffering from a mental disorder will be a manifestation of that disorder.

6.6 Even if particular mental disorders are likely to persist or get worse despite treatment, there may well be a range of interventions which would represent appropriate medical treatment. It should never be assumed that any disorders, or any patients, are inherently or inevitably untreatable. Nor should it be assumed that likely difficulties in achieving long-term and sustainable change in a person's underlying disorder make medical treatment to help manage their condition and the behaviours arising from it either inappropriate or unnecessary.

Appropriate medical treatment test

6.7 The purpose of the appropriate medical treatment test is to ensure that no one is detained (or remains detained) for treatment, or is an SCT [supervised community treatment] patient, unless they are actually to be offered medical treatment for their mental disorder.

6.8 This medical treatment must be appropriate, taking into account the nature and degree of the person's mental disorder and all their particular circumstances, including cultural, ethnic and religious considerations. By definition, it must be treatment which is for the purpose of alleviating or preventing a worsening of the patient's mental disorder or its symptoms or manifestations.

6.9 The appropriate medical treatment test requires a judgement about whether an appropriate package of treatment for mental disorder is available for the individual in question. Where the appropriate medical

---

61 London: HMSO (2008) Chapter 6.

treatment test forms part of the criteria for detention, the medical treatment in question is treatment for mental disorder in the hospital in which the patient is to be detained. Where it is part of the criteria for SCT it refers to the treatment for mental disorder that the person will be offered while on SCT.

...

6.13 Medical treatment must actually be available to the patient. It is not sufficient that appropriate treatment could theoretically be provided.

6.14 What is appropriate will vary greatly between patients. It will depend, in part, on what might reasonably be expected to be achieved given the nature and degree of the patient's disorder.

6.15 Medical treatment which aims merely to prevent a disorder worsening is unlikely, in general, to be appropriate in cases where normal treatment approaches would aim (and be expected) to alleviate the patient's condition significantly. For some patients with persistent mental disorders, however, management of the undesirable effects of their disorder may be all that can realistically be hoped for.

6.16 Appropriate medical treatment does not have to involve medication or individual or group psychological therapy – although it very often will. There may be patients whose particular circumstances mean that treatment may be appropriate even though it consists only of nursing and specialist day-to-day care under the clinical supervision of an approved clinician, in a safe and secure therapeutic environment with a structured regime.

6.17 Simply detaining someone – even in a hospital – does not constitute medical treatment.

6.18 A patient's attitude towards the proposed treatment may be relevant in determining whether the appropriate medical treatment test is met. But an indication of unwillingness to cooperate with treatment generally, or with a specific aspect of treatment, does not make such treatment inappropriate.

6.19 In particular, psychological therapies and other forms of medical treatments which, to be effective, require the patient's cooperation are not automatically inappropriate simply because a patient does not currently wish to engage with them. Such treatments can potentially remain appropriate and available as long as it continues to be clinically suitable to offer them and they would be provided if the patient agreed to engage.

6.20 People called on to make a judgment about whether the appropriate medical treatment test is met do not have to be satisfied that appropriate treatment will be available for the whole course of the patient's detention or SCT. What is appropriate may change over time, as the patient's condition changes or clinicians obtain a greater understanding of the patient's case. But they must satisfy themselves that appropriate medical treatment is available for the time being, given the patient's condition and circumstances as they are currently understood.

The Code of Practice gives guidance in Chapter 35 on people with personality disorders, stating that treatment approaches for personality disorders need to be relatively intense and long term, structured and coherent (at 35.10), and 'people with personality disorders may take time to engage and develop motivation for such longer-term treatment'. But even patients who are not engaged in that kind of treatment may need other forms of treatment, including nurse and specialist care, to manage the continuing risks posed by their disorders, and this may constitute appropriate medical treatment.

The issue was considered in the case of *MD v Nottinghamshire Health Care NHS Trust*.[62] The case concerned a restricted patient who had been detained under s 41 of the Act (i.e. via the criminal

---

62 [2010] UKUT 59 (AAC).

provisions of the Act), and the interpretation of the provision in s 72 of the Act, which provides that a tribunal shall discharge a patient if it is not satisfied that appropriate medical treatment is available to him or her. This also applies to civilly detained patients, and the definition of what is appropriate and available will give rise to the same considerations in both discharge and the original detention under s 3 of the Act. In this case, the patient had been sentenced to five years' imprisonment for violent offences, but had subsequently been transferred to a secure hospital to receive treatment for his personality disorder. He applied for discharge, and the tribunal found that he was at risk of violent re-offending and that, although his psychological defence mechanisms prevented him from co-operating with therapy, he could potentially benefit from the 'milieu' of being on the hospital ward, which had short-term beneficial effects, and that it might result in him eventually taking part in therapy. The patient appealed to the Upper Tribunal (Administrative Appeals Chamber). Counsel for the patient argued that he was not being treated but was merely detained.

MD v Nottinghamshire Health Care NHS Trust[63]

Jacobs J: 30 . . . This distinction is fundamental in our law. Containment is essentially a matter for the criminal courts and prisons . . . Treatment is a matter for hospitals with oversight by the First-tier Tribunal and, on appeal, the Upper Tribunal.

31 Mr Pezzani addressed me at length on this distinction. It was a theme throughout his argument that the treatment provisions must not be operated as a means of containment. I accept that, but it needs to be unpacked. A patient has a right to liberty and to the chance of liberty, but the right is conditional on the statutory criteria. There is no right to liberty for so long as the statutory conditions for detention are met. It is possible that they will always be met and, if they are, the patient has no right to be discharged. Mr Pezzani's argument focused on the meaning of 'medical treatment'. That definition is very wide, but the availability of medical treatment is not a sufficient condition for detention. The test is whether medical treatment is available and appropriate. It may be that medical treatment is still available for a patient but, because of the circumstances of a particular case, it is no longer appropriate. Appropriateness is an important additional criterion for detention; it is not surplus verbiage. There may come a point (I put it no higher) at which continuing treatment for a patient, even viewed in the long term, would no longer be appropriate.

32 A patient also has an additional protection in the tribunal's power to direct a discharge even if the conditions in section 72(1)(b) remain satisfied. The case would have to be exceptional. But it is a possibility that the legislation allows for and it must be considered, however briefly, in each case.

33 Mr Pezzani made two specific arguments.

34 The first argument was this: detention without the possibility of reduction of the risk posed by the patient was containment. I do not accept that. The treatment has to be appropriate, but it need not reduce the risk. Section 145(4) provides that it is sufficient if the treatment is for the purpose of preventing a worsening of the symptoms or manifestations. That envisages that the treatment required may not reduce risk. It is also sufficient if it will alleviate but one of the symptoms or manifestations, regardless of the impact on the risk posed by the patient.

35 The second argument was this: if there was no prospect of the patient progressing beyond milieu, his detention became mere containment. As I have said, if that were the position, there might come a point at which detention was no longer appropriate. However, the tribunal found that there was the potential for the milieu to benefit the patient in both the short and longer term. The facts found by the tribunal show that the patient had not reached the position that formed the premise of Mr Pezzani's argument.

---

63 Ibid.

The appeal was dismissed. In *DL-H v Devon Partnership NHS Trust, Secretary of State for Justice*,[64] Jacobs J was faced with a very similar fact pattern. However, in this case he found that the tribunal had merely recorded that they accepted the expert opinion to the effect that continued treatment in hospital provides alleviation or prevention of a deterioration in the condition of the patient, rather than investigating the substance of assertions, generalisations and standard phrases. Each patient should receive an individualised assessment. A re-hearing was ordered.

9.4.2 Consent to treatment

As we saw in Chapter 3, adult patients in possession of the necessary decision-making capacity have the right to refuse even life-saving medical treatment for any physical condition from which they may be suffering. However, in the case of patients detained under the Act, treatment for the mental disorder itself requires neither their express nor their implied consent (s 63). This is subject to exceptions contained within ss 57, 58 and 58A for certain types of treatment, and subject to s 62, which deals with urgent treatment. Consent, however, is required of voluntary patients (s 56(1) and (2)). These exceptions are examined in detail below but, first, the nature of treatment for mental disorder must be considered.

9.4.2.1 Treatment not needing the patient's consent

> **63 Treatment not requiring consent**
>
> The consent of a patient shall not be required for any medical treatment given to him for the mental disorder from which he is suffering, not being treatment falling within ss 57,58 or 58A above, if the treatment is given by or under the direction of the approved clinician in charge of the treatment.

The implication is that treatment for other purposes, ie the patient's physical disorders, remains governed by the common law. What constitutes medical treatment for the mental disorder from which the patient is suffering has recently been given a very wide interpretation by the courts. As we have seen above at 9.4.1, the Act defines medical treatment at s 145. In the case of *B v Croydon HA* the Court of Appeal interpreted this so as to permit a wide range of acts ancillary to the core treatment. The case concerned a s 3 patient, suffering from a psychopathic disorder, which, it was found, was treatable only by psychoanalytical psychotherapy. The patient made various attempts to harm herself and, when these were discovered and prevented, she decided that she would refuse to eat. The health authority decided to force feed her without her consent, and she applied to the court for an injunction to restrain them. At first instance the court refused this on the basis that it was treatment for the mental disorder and therefore, by reason of s 63, did not require her consent. The Court of Appeal upheld this.

It was accepted that, because of the 'treatability' requirement in s 3 (which has been removed since reform in 2007) (see 9.1.5, above), it would not have been lawful to detain her unless her condition was treatable. However, it was held that it did not follow that every act which formed part of treatment as defined by s 145(1) must, *in itself*, be likely to alleviate or prevent a

---

64 [2010] UKUT 102 (AAC).

deterioration of the disorder. The nasogastric feeding would be a form of concurrent care. Hoffmann LJ said:

B v Croydon HA[65]

Hoffmann LJ: Mr Gordon says that food is a medicine. He draws our attention to the fact that some special foods (for example, gluten-free rice cookies for coeliacs) may be obtained on prescription. In my view, however, this is not relevant to whether food is a medicine within the meaning of s 58. The section is concerned with medicines administered as treatment for mental disorder. The words 'by any means' in the opening phrase show that one identifies a medicine by its chemical composition and not by whether it is administered to the patient through a tube down his throat or by being put before him on a plate. Even gluten-free rice cookies are not administered for mental disorder and in my judgment ordinary food in liquid form, such as would be used in tube feeding, is not a medicine within the meaning of s 58.

That brings one back to the question of whether tube feeding would have been treatment for the mental disorder from which Ms B was suffering. My initial reaction was that it could not be. Ms B suffers from a psychopathic disorder which, according to the evidence, is incapable of treatment except by psychoanalytical psychotherapy. How can giving her food be treatment for that disorder? Mr Gordon says that it cannot. It may be a prerequisite to a treatment for mental disorder or it may be treatment for a consequence of the mental disorder, but it is not treatment of the disorder itself. He draws attention to s 3 of the Act, which specifies the grounds upon which a person suffering from a psychopathic disorder may be detained. It is not enough that the disorder must be 'of a nature or degree which makes it appropriate for him to receive medical treatment in a hospital' (sub-s (2)(a)). The proposed treatment must be 'likely to alleviate or prevent a deterioration of his condition' (sub-s (2)(b)) and it must be 'necessary for the health or safety of the patient or for the protection of other persons that he should receive such treatment' (sub-s (2)(c)). So Mr Gordon says that the patient cannot lawfully be detained unless the proposed treatment will alleviate or prevent a deterioration of his condition. No less should be required of the treatment which can be given without his consent under s 63.

This is a powerful submission. But I have come to the conclusion that it is too atomistic. It requires every individual element of the treatment being given to the patient to be directed to his mental condition. But in my view this test applies only to the treatment as a whole. Section 145(1) gives a wide definition to the term 'medical treatment'. It includes 'nursing, and also includes care, habilitation and rehabilitation under medical supervision'. So a range of acts ancillary to the core treatment fall within the definition. I accept that by virtue of s 3(2)(b) a patient with a psychopathic disorder cannot be detained unless the proposed treatment, taken as a whole, is 'likely to alleviate or prevent a deterioration of his condition'. In my view, contrary to the submission of Mr Francis, 'condition' in this paragraph means the mental disorder on grounds of which the application for his admission and detention has been made. It follows that if there was no proposed treatment for Ms B's psychopathic disorder, s 63 could not have been invoked to justify feeding her by nasogastric tube. Indeed, it would not be lawful to detain her at all.

It does not however follow that every act which forms part of that treatment within the wide definition in s 145(1) must in itself be likely to alleviate or prevent a deterioration of that disorder. Nursing and care concurrent with the core treatment or as a necessary prerequisite to such treatment or to prevent the patient from causing harm to himself or to alleviate the consequences of the disorder are in my view all capable of being ancillary to a treatment calculated to alleviate or prevent a deterioration of the psychopathic disorder. It would seem to me strange if a hospital could, without the patient's consent, give him treatment directed to alleviating a psychopathic disorder showing itself in suicidal tendencies, but not

---

65 [1994] 2 WLR 294, at p 297.

without such consent be able to treat the consequences of a suicide attempt. In my judgment the term 'medical treatment . . . for the mental disorder' in s 63 includes such ancillary acts.

Mr Francis was, I think, right to draw our attention to s 62 as throwing some light upon the question. Sections 57 and 58 place special restrictions upon the use of particular 'forms of medical treatment for mental disorder', surgical operations for destroying brain tissue or implanting hormones (s 57), electro-convulsive therapy and drugs (s 58). There are special procedures which must be followed before these treatments can be given. But s 62(1) says that in certain specified cases of emergency, these special rules need not be complied with. They include:

. . . any treatment –

a which is immediately necessary to save the patient's life; or

b . . .

c which (not being irreversible or hazardous) is immediately necessary to alleviate serious suffering by the patient; or

d which (not being irreversible or hazardous) is immediately necessary and represents the minimum interference necessary to prevent the patient from behaving violently or being a danger to himself or to others.

Mr Francis says, in my view rightly, that these emergency cases are not primarily concerned with a direct alleviation or the prevention of a deterioration of the mental disorder. The danger to the patient's life or the likelihood of serious suffering or the patient being a danger to himself or others are more likely to be the results of symptoms of the disorder. Nevertheless, the treatment of such symptoms is assumed by s 62 to be a 'form of medical treatment for mental disorder', since otherwise it would not have come within ss 57 or 58 in the first place.

I therefore agree with Ewbank J in *In re KB (An Adult) (Mental Patient: Medical Treatment)* (1994) 19 BMLR 144, p 146 when he said of the tube feeding of an anorexic: '. . . relieving symptoms is just as much a part of treatment as relieving the underlying cause.' To similar effect is the judgment of Stuart-White J, quoted by Sir Stephen Brown P in *Riverside Mental Health NHS Trust v Fox* [1994] 1 FLR 614, p 619. The decision in *In re C (Adult: Refusal of Treatment)* [1994] 1 WLR 290, in which a schizophrenic was held entitled to refuse treatment for gangrene, is distinguishable. The gangrene was entirely unconnected with the mental disorder.

Mr Gordon said that if the meaning of 'medical treatment for mental disorder' was wide enough to include ancillary forms of treatment, s 63 would involve a breach of the Convention for the Protection of Human Rights and Fundamental Freedoms, Cmnd 8969, 1953. He referred us to *Herczegfalvy v Austria* (1992) 15 EHRR 437 in which the court said, p 485, that a measure constituting an interference with private life and therefore *prima facie* contrary to Art 8(1) (like involuntary tube feeding) can only be justified under Art 8(2) if, among the other requirements of that article, its terms are sufficiently precise to enable the individual 'to foresee its consequences for him'. This requirement is necessary to prevent such measures from being a source of arbitrary official power, contrary to the rule of law. In my judgment s 63 amply satisfies this test. There is no conceptual vagueness about the notion of treating the symptoms or consequences of a mental disorder, although naturally there will be borderline cases. But there is no question of an exercise of arbitrary power.

This is arguably a disturbing decision, widening as it does the ambit of non-consensual treatment. Note, also, that this case has been followed in *Re VS (Adult: Mental Disorder)*[66] and, even more controversially, in the case of *Tameside and Glossop Acute Services Trust v CH*,[67]

---

66 [1995] 3 Med LR 292.
67 [1996] 1 FLR 762.

where it was held that the performance of a Caesarean section was treatment for mental disorder under s 63:[68]

> **Wall J**: Is the question of inducing the defendant's labour and/or causing her to be delivered of her child by Caesarean section 'entirely unconnected' with her mental disorder? At first blush, it might appear difficult to say that performance of a Caesarean section is medical treatment for the defendant's mental disorder: I am, however, satisfied that on the facts of this case so to hold would be 'too atomistic a view', to use Hoffmann LJ's phrase in the passage from *B v Croydon HA* which I have cited and the reasoning of which I respectfully adopt.
>
> There are several strands in the evidence which, in my judgment, bring the proposed treatment within s 63 of the Act. First, there is the proposition that an ancillary reason for the induction and, if necessary, the birth by Caesarean section is to prevent a deterioration in the defendant's mental state. Secondly, there is the clear evidence of Dr M that in order for the treatment of her schizophrenia to be effective, it is necessary for her to give birth to a live baby. Thirdly, the overall structure of her treatment requires her to receive strong anti-psychotic medication. The administration of that treatment has been necessarily interrupted by her pregnancy and cannot be resumed until her child is born. It is not, therefore, I think, stretching language unduly to say that achievement of a successful outcome of her pregnancy is a necessary part of the overall treatment of her mental disorder. Treatment of C's gangrene was not likely to affect his mental condition: the manner in which the delivery of the defendant's child is treated is likely to have a direct effect on her mental state.

However, the Court of Appeal confirmed in *St George's Healthcare NHS Trust v S*[69] that s 63 cannot be used to force upon patients medical procedures that are totally unconnected with mental disorder. Nevertheless, it was said that s 63 may apply to the treatment of any condition which is integral to the mental disorder, which means that it does not specifically overrule the *Tameside* case. It is arguable that it is still possible for virtually any form of treatment to be given for mental disorder and that the *St George's* case failed from the point of view of s 63, largely because of inadequate diagnosis and assessment of mental disorder, which, in turn, stemmed from the fact that the real purpose of the action was management of the pregnancy. *Nottinghamshire Healthcare NHS Trust v RC*[70] concerned a young man with a serious personality disorder who was detained under the Act. He was a Jehovah's Witness and had made an advance decision to refuse blood products. He was prone to self-harming, which resulted in substantial blood loss because he was on anticoagulant drugs due to a history of thrombosis. The patient had capacity and, if capacity were to be lost at some point, the advance decision was valid. The issue to be decided was whether he could be given blood transfusions in the face of this under the provisions of s 63. Mostyn J held that it would be an abuse of power to do so, and would be a denial of a most basic freedom.

Treatment under s 63 was considered in the case of *R v Collins and Ashworth Hospital Authority, ex p Brady*.[71] It was found that force feeding was treatment under s 63 because the hunger strike was a manifestation or symptom of the patient's personality disorder (the patient was also found to lack capacity so could, in any event, be treated in his best interests). The responsible medical officer had formed the view that the hunger strike was 'a florid example of his psychopathology in action' which stemmed from aspects of his personality such as self-importance and desire to control. The judge was also required to consider the appropriate test for the lawfulness of treatment under s 63. The argument on behalf of Brady had been that the court must be satisfied that the treatment actually was treatment for mental disorder and not just that the doctor had reasonable grounds for considering it to be, that is the test in *Khawaja v Secretary of State for*

---

68 At p 775.
69 [1998] 3 All ER 673.
70 [2014] EWHC 1317 (COP).
71 [2000] Lloyd's Rep Med 355.

the Home Department,[72] rather than '*Wednesbury* unreasonableness' (*Associated Provincial Picture House v Wednesbury Corp*).[73] The court rejected this argument and held that the correct test was the '*super-Wednesbury*' test, that is the more substantial the interference with human rights, the more the court would require by way of justification.[74] However, the judge went on to say:

> **Maurice Kay J**: I am entirely satisfied that [the doctor's diagnosis] satisfies both tests. On any view, and to a high degree of probability, section 63 was triggered because what arose was the need to medical treatment for the mental disorder from which the applicant was and is suffering. The hunger strike is a manifestation or symptom of the personality disorder. The fact (if such it be) that a person without mental disorder could reach the same decision on a rational basis in similar circumstances does not avail the applicant because he reached and persists in his decision because of his personality disorder.

The issue was examined in a slightly different context (where the patient had been detained under the criminal provisions of the Act and was subject to a hospital and restriction order under ss 37 and 41) in the case of *R (on the application of B) v Ashworth Hospital Authority*.[75] The House of Lords held that it was not unlawful for the patient to receive treatment under s 63 for a 'mental disorder' in respect of which he had not been 'classified'. A contrary decision would certainly have sat uneasily alongside the case of *B v Croydon*.[76]

THINK POINT

Do you agree that 'force feeding' can be regarded as 'treatment for mental disorder'?

9.4.3 Exceptional treatment not covered by s 63

9.4.3.1 Section 57 – consent and a second opinion

This section covers the most drastic forms of treatment for mental disorder. It covers psychosurgery and any other form of treatment specified by the Secretary of State (at present the only treatment pursuant to this is surgical implantation of hormones to reduce the male sex drive). It should be noted that, given that consent is necessary as well as a second medical opinion, it is not possible to treat a patient under s 57 who lacks capacity.

9.4.3.2 Sections 58 and 58A – consent or a second opinion

Section 58 specifies treatment which requires consent or a second opinion. The treatment covered by s 58 is medication administered over a period of three months or more. The section empowers the Secretary of State to make regulations to cover other treatment under this section. Section 58A deals with electroconvulsive therapy or any other treatment that is specified by regulations made by the 'appropriate national authority'.

---

72 [1984] 1 AC 74.
73 [1947] 2 All ER 680.
74 *R v Ministry of Defence, ex p Smith* [1996] QB 517.
75 [2005] UKHL 20.
76 [1994] 2 WLR 294.

It must be noted that this section does little to protect the patient's right to refuse treatment; it merely adds a safeguard by requiring that, in so far as the patient refuses, two doctors rather than one must recommend a course of treatment. Phil Fennell reports the results of a survey of second opinions carried out in 1992 (note that SOAD means Second Opinion Appointed Doctor):

Fennell, P, *Treatment Without Consent : Law, Psychiatry and the Treatment of Mentally Disordered People Since 1845*[77]

Concerns of the 1970s and early 1980s led to the introduction of express legal provision for treatment without consent, which had previously been so much taken for granted as part of clinical authority that mentioning it did not even occur to legislators. By the 1980s it was necessary to spell it out. Part IV upheld the position of the RMO as in charge of a detained patient's treatment, and defined powers to treat without consent, subject to a second opinion procedure. If the personnel with power to decide whether or not to treat without consent had changed, did Part IV result in a change in the substance of these decisions? One clear incursion on clinical authority was that psychosurgery would no longer be allowed without valid consent. Another was that the decision of the SOAD to refuse permission was binding on the RMO and there was no appeal to the MHAC. Set against this is the fact that the second opinion is medical. Although there is a duty on the SOAD to consult other professionals, on occasion these are staff in occupations with little to do with patient care, and often nurses and others were brought in to 'get to know' the patient before being consulted. The test for giving the treatment, likelihood of benefit or prevention of deterioration, used in combination with the *Bolam* test, creates a presumption in favour of the RMO's judgment. Not surprisingly, the concordance rate for s 58 opinions is high. The 1992 survey showed that the main cases where authority was withheld for clinical reasons involved ECT or the 'new' antipsychotic Clozaril, because it was felt that other less drastic treatments should be given time to work. There was even one case, the *Pimozide* case, where the second opinion may have been a life saver. The survey also shows the extent of psychiatry's continued reliance on ECT, and in particular the strikingly high numbers of middle aged and elderly women who have the treatment. In this the pattern of the past is being followed, for women have traditionally been in the majority of those receiving radical treatment, whether it be clitoridectomy, ovariotomy, lobotomy, chemical shock, comas or ECT.

Perhaps the most important indicator of the effect on the substance of clinical decisions, and of the resilience of the experimental spirit, is the extent to which SOADs authorised high dose medication. The BNF recommended dose levels, used loosely as a yardstick in the second opinion process, are viewed by some psychiatrists as too low, and resistance to central prescription remains strong. The fact that 12% of medicine second opinions involved doses above [British National Formulary – BNF] limits does not suggest a significant interference with clinical authority. A poignant reminder of psychiatry's limitations were the numbers of patients in the MHAC 1 survey who had been on high doses of medication for years and who showed no improvement, remaining totally inaccessible (61 out of 232). Could it be that their medication contributed to their poor mental state?

Since s 58 offers no real protection to the patient, no real purpose of this provision is discernible.

In *R v Feggetter and Another, ex p Wooder*[78] the Court of Appeal said that a SOAD should give adequate reasons when certifying s 58 treatment and these should be communicated to the patient unless this would be likely to cause serious harm to the physical or mental health of the patient or any other person. In *R (on the application of Wilkinson) v RMO Broadmoor Hospital*,

---

77 London: Routledge, 1996.
78 [2002] EWCA Civ 554.

the Mental Health Act Commission SOAD Doctor and the Secretary of State for Health[79] the Court of Appeal held that a patient who was opposed to treatment under s 58 could apply for judicial review on the question as to whether his rights under Articles 2, 3 and 8 of the Convention were violated, or could raise an action in tort for assault against the special health authority. In order for the court to reach a decision it would be necessary for the doctors concerned to give evidence and be subjected to cross-examination.

9.4.3.3 Urgent treatment under s 62

Under s 62 urgent treatment, normally subject to the additional requirements of ss 57, 58, or 58A, may be given without satisfying those conditions and, if it is a form of treatment for which consent was required and that consent is subsequently withdrawn, treatment can continue under these provisions if it is thought that discontinuance of the treatment would cause serious suffering to the patient:

62 Urgent treatment

1   Sections 57 and 58 above shall not apply to any treatment –
   (a)   which is immediately necessary to save the patient's life; or
   (b)   which (not being irreversible) is immediately necessary to prevent a serious deterioration of his condition; or
   (c)   which (not being irreversible or hazardous) is immediately necessary to alleviate serious suffering by the patient; or
   (d)   which (not being irreversible or hazardous) is immediately necessary and represents the minimum interference necessary to prevent the patient from behaving violently or being a danger to himself or to others.
   (1A)   Section 58A above, in so far as it relates to electro-convulsive therapy by virtue of subsection (1)(b) of that section, shall not apply to any treatment which falls within paragraph (a) or (b) of subsection (1) above.
   (1B)   Section 58A above, in so far as it relates to a form of treatment specified by virtue of subsection (1)(b) of that section, shall not apply to any treatment which falls within such of paragraphs (a) to (d) of subsection (1) above as may be specified in regulations under that section.
2   Sections 60 and 61(3) above shall not preclude the continuation of any treatment or of treatment under any plan pending compliance with s 57 or 58 above if the approved clinician in charge of the treatment considers that the discontinuance of the treatment or of treatment under the plan would cause serious suffering to the patient.
3   For the purposes of this section treatment is irreversible if it has unfavourable irreversible physical or psychological consequences and hazardous if it entails significant physical hazard.

Where the treatment is ECT (s 58A) urgent treatment can only be given if either of the grounds in paras (a) or (b) apply. In practice, it will only be treatment under s 58 and s 58A to which this section will apply, as the nature of s 57 treatments (at present psychosurgery and surgical implantation of hormones to reduce the male sex drive) are unlikely to comply with sub-s (1)(a)–(d) in terms of hazard and/or irreversibility. The section would therefore be most likely to be used in the administration of medicine under s 58, when the three-month period was about to elapse, and a second opinion could not be obtained. These occasions should be rare, genuine emergencies.

79   [2002] 1 WLR 419.

However, in practice the situation may be very different as treatment may be given to those who lack capacity as consent does not have to be obtained and this section can apply to patients who have been admitted under s 4 of the Act as an emergency.

Bickle et al.[80] carried out an audit of urgent treatment administered at Rampton High Security Hospital from 2000 to 2005, in total 107 occasions. They reviewed the treatment against the standards from the then relevant Code of Practice and found compliance with this. The other standard they reviewed it against was the recommendation from the Mental Health Act Commission which said that generally a second opinion should be obtained, and there was around 50 per cent compliance with this. However, they found this to mean that the standard was close to being met.

9.4.4 Community treatment orders

Community treatment orders (CTOs) were introduced by the Mental Health Act 2007. They were designed to tackle the well-known 'revolving door' problem whereby patients enter hospital, are stabilised and discharged, then go on to no longer take medication, become ill again and return to hospital.

17A Community treatment orders

1   The responsible clinician may by order in writing discharge a detained patient from hospital subject to his being liable to recall in accordance with section 17E below.

2   A detained patient is a patient who is liable to be detained in a hospital in pursuance of an application for admission for treatment.

3   An order under subsection (1) above is referred to in this Act as a 'community treatment order'.

4   The responsible clinician may not make a community treatment order unless –

    a   in his opinion, the relevant criteria are met; and

    b   an approved mental health professional states in writing –

        i   that he agrees with that opinion; and

        ii   that it is appropriate to make the order –

5   The relevant criteria are –

    a   the patient is suffering from mental disorder of a nature or degree which makes it appropriate for him to receive medical treatment;

    b   it is necessary for his health or safety or for the protection of other persons that he should receive such treatment;

    c   subject to his being liable to be recalled as mentioned in paragraph (d) below, such treatment can be provided without his continuing to be detained in a hospital;

    d   it is necessary that the responsible clinician should be able to exercise the power under section 17E(1) below to recall the patient to hospital; and

    e   appropriate medical treatment is available for him.

6   In determining whether the criterion in subsection (5)(d) above is met, the responsible clinician shall, in particular, consider, having regard to the patient's history of mental disorder and any other relevant factors, what risk there would be of a deterioration of the patient's condition if he were not detained in a hospital (as a result, for example, of his refusing or neglecting to receive the medical treatment he requires for his mental disorder).

---

80 Bickle, A et al., 'Audit of statutory urgent treatment at a high security hospital' (2008) J Mental Health L 66.

CTOs can only be made in respect of patients who have been discharged from hospital having been detained under s 3 or the criminal provisions of the Act, so they do not apply to voluntary patients or s 2 patients. The approved mental health professional (AMHP) and the responsible clinician (RC) have to be satisfied that the patient is suffering from a mental disorder of a nature or to a degree that makes it appropriate for them to receive medical treatment, and that it is necessary for the patient's health or safety, or for the protection of others, that the patient should receive such treatment, and that, subject to the powers of recall, the treatment can be provided in the community. The power of recall must be *necessary*, and, self-evidently, appropriate medical treatment is available. There are two compulsory conditions and these are that, where necessary, the patient makes themselves available for examination by the RC when/if the RC is considering whether to remove the CTO; and, secondly, that, where necessary, the patient makes themselves available for examination by a second opinion doctor.

Other conditions can be imposed, but only if they are necessary or appropriate to ensure the patient receives treatment that prevents harm to self or others. A residence requirement for example might be imposed. Although the patient does not have to agree to a CTO, it is unlikely that they would be discharged from hospital without this.

The order is initially for six months but is renewable. If it is renewed the patient has to be examined and the AMHP has to agree to renewal.

Hoyer and Ferris examine CTOs (they refer to the process as 'outpatient commitment' (OC)) and refer to two models: those that are imposed as a condition of leave and those that are invoked as an alternative to hospitalisation. The model under the 1983 Act is the former. Hoyer and Ferris, however, cite some empirical evidence in support of the latter model being the most successful. Referring to this distinction, they state that 'a wide interpretation' of the legal requirements for OC can muddy the waters:

Hoyer, G, and Ferris, R J, *Outpatient commitment. Some reflections on ideology, practice and implications for research*[81]

> The legal criteria are such that OC can only be imposed on patients suffering from a 'Serious mental disorder', usually understood as synonymous with a psychotic condition. In a Supreme Court verdict of 1993, however, the courts ruled that patients who were taking antipsychotics would have manifested psychotic symptoms if they were not taking medication. Thus they were legally to be regarded as still suffering from a serious mental disorder so long as they were taking antipsychotic medication(s), and could accordingly be placed under an OC order, in spite of a lack – for the time being – of any sign of psychotic symptoms. Thus the patient is being coerced to receive continuing treatment with medication in the absence of overt psychotic symptoms, because of a presumption that serious mental disorder persists, and despite the fact that most patients will have retained competency to accept or refuse treatment. This problem is not unique to Norway, but represents a fundamental problem regarding OC legislation and its implementation.

Certainly, the assumption of the court in this case that without the medication the patient would have been psychotic is worrying, as that could result in OC or CTOs in perpetuity.

In *R (on the application of H) v Mental Health Review Tribunal*[82] it was held that a conditional discharge, conditional upon complying with medication, did not amount to a compulsion that interfered with a patient's right to refuse medication (as he would have that right when not detained under the Act). Of course, now that CTOs are available a refusal to agree to a treatment regime that was a condition of the CTO could result in the patient's recall.

---

81 (2001) J Mental Health L 56, at 60.
82 [2007] EWHC 884.

Note the case of *PJ (a patient) v Local Health Board*[83] discussed in Chapter 4, and the application of the Deprivation of Liberty Safeguards to community treatment orders.

9.4.5 Human rights and treatment without consent

Psychiatrists, as has been seen, have very wide powers to treat without consent. The interests of the wider community may justify detention, but can they justify treatment? It is arguable that most treatment will be consented to because, after the initial treatment, the patient is compliant and will therefore consent to subsequent treatment. But in the case of a refusal, why should we make treatment compulsory?

Given that a patient can refuse life-sustaining treatment for physical illness, if mentally competent, what is the argument for saying that the mentally ill patient cannot refuse treatment of mental illness? The 1959 Mental Health Act did not deal with the issue of consent to treatment, and it was thought that detention was sufficient to suspend the need to obtain a patient's consent.

During the passage through Parliament of the 1983 Mental Health Act, a justification for being able to treat without consent was given by the Minister of Health in the debate on the proposal in parliamentary committee:

Special Standing Committee on the Mental Health (Amendment) Bill (Parliamentary Session 1981–82), 29 June 1982

… those who looked after them (those forcibly detained) would have to gaze on them knowing perfectly well that some treatment could be given to alleviate their suffering and distress and enable them eventually to recover their liberty. Hospitals are places of treatment …

This reasoning relies upon the fact that, by detaining someone against their will on the ground that they are ill, means that it is in the interests of them regaining their liberty that they receive treatment to enable them to do just this. It has to be admitted that this argument has a certain force. What is clear is that the reason cannot be that, *by definition*, the mental patient is incompetent because of the vagueness of the definition of mental illness and, indeed, case law confirms that a long-term mental patient can refuse life-sustaining treatment for a physical condition. The question is whether the patient has the capacity to understand the particular form of treatment.

THINK POINT

If a patient is capable of consenting to treatment, they should also be able to refuse treatment. Why should this be different for mental health patients?

---

83 [2015] UKUT 480 (AAC)

9.5 Safeguarding the patient

9.5.1 Discharge of the patient under s 23

Section 23 states:

23 Discharge of patients

. . .

(2)   An order for discharge may be made in respect of a patient –
    a   where the patient is liable to be detained in a hospital in pursuance of an application for admission for assessment or for treatment by the responsible medical officer, by the managers or by the nearest relative of the patient;
    b   where the patient is subject to guardianship, by the responsible medical officer, by the responsible local social services authority or by the nearest relative of the patient.

It should be noted that, under s 23, these are powers, and not duties, and therefore a patient cannot claim that, for example, once he ceased to be a danger to self, or others, he should be discharged under s 23.

In *Johnson v United Kingdom*[84] the European Court of Human Rights held that, even if there is no longer justification under the Act for detention, this does not mean that the patient must be discharged immediately if he still poses a risk to others. Discharge can be delayed until aftercare facilities have been put in place. But, see *R v Camden and Islington HA, ex p K*,[85] and s 117 of the Act, see 9.6, below (see also *R v Nottinghamshire Healthcare NHS Trust and Others, ex p IH*[86] and *R v Mental Health Review Tribunal, North and East London Region, ex p H*).[87]

There can be no doubt that the powers of civil detention under the Act have great potential for abuse. The importance of protective procedures, therefore, cannot be over-estimated.

9.5.2 The Care Quality Commission

Section 120 of the Act deals with the general protection of patients:

120 General protection of relevant patients

1   The regulatory authority must keep under review and, where appropriate, investigate the exercise of the powers and the discharge of the duties conferred or imposed by this Act so far as relating to the detention of patients or their reception into guardianship or to relevant patients.
2   Relevant patients are –
    a   patients liable to be detained under this Act,
    b   community patients, and
    c   patients subject to guardianship.

---

84   (1997) 27 EHRR 296.
85   [2001] EWCA Civ 240.
86   [2001] EWHC Admin 1037.
87   (2001) unreported, 28 March.

3   The regulatory authority must make arrangements for persons authorised by it to visit and interview relevant patients in private –

   a   in the case of relevant patients detained under this Act, in the place where they are detained, and

   b   in the case of other relevant patients, in hospitals and regulated establishments and, if access is granted, other places.

4   The regulatory authority must also make arrangements for persons authorised by it to investigate any complaint as to the exercise of the powers or the discharge of the duties conferred or imposed by this Act in respect of a patient who is or has been detained under this Act or who is or has been a relevant patient.

5   The arrangements made under subsection (4) –

   a   may exclude matters from investigation in specified circumstances, and

   b   do not require any person exercising functions under the arrangements to undertake or continue with any investigation where the person does not consider it appropriate to do so.

6   Where any such complaint as is mentioned in subsection (4) is made by a Member of Parliament or a member of the National Assembly for Wales, the results of the investigation must be reported to the Member of Parliament or member of the Assembly.

7   For the purposes of a review or investigation under subsection (1) or the exercise of functions under arrangements made under this section, a person authorised by the regulatory authority may at any reasonable time –

   a   visit and interview in private any patient in a hospital or regulated establishment,

   b   if the authorised person is a registered medical practitioner or approved clinician, examine the patient in private there, and

   c   require the production of and inspect any records relating to the detention or treatment of any person who is or has been detained under this Act or who is or has been a community patient or a patient subject to guardianship.

...

The body charged with carrying out these functions is the Care Quality Commission. The Commission appoints medical practitioners and other persons for the purposes of providing second opinions and verifying consent to treatment under Part IV of the Act and examines reports on that treatment; submits proposals for inclusion in the Code of Practice; and submits proposals in relation to s 57 treatments. For further details of the Commission's functions, visit www.cqc.org.uk.

It is important to note that the Commission's powers do not extend to voluntary patients, but only to those who are formally detained under the Act. Note the decision in *R v Bournewood Community and Mental Health NHS Trust, ex p L*[88] and the discussion in Chapter 4.

9.5.3 Challenging detention

The powers of the Commission are not designed to provide a mechanism for challenging the validity of the compulsory admission itself. There are, however, a number of ways in which a compulsorily detained patient may gain his liberty, both under the Act itself, and by the use of the common law.

---

88   [1998] 3 All ER 289.

9.5.3.1 Mental health review tribunals

A statutory framework for challenging compulsory admissions was first introduced by the 1959 Act following the recommendations made by the Royal Commission (the Percy Commission 9.1.4 above, see para 438). Under s 66, patients, including those admitted for assessment, can apply to a tribunal for a review of their case. The nearest relative also has a right to apply. There is also an automatic review process, under s 68, whereby hospital managers must refer to a tribunal any patient admitted for treatment who has not exercised his right to apply within the first six months. They must also refer any patient admitted for treatment if his detention is renewed and three years have gone by since the case was last considered by a tribunal.

Mental health review tribunals consist of at least one 'legal member', one 'medical member' and the third must be neither a legal nor a medical member. Procedures are governed by the Mental Health Review Tribunals Rules.

Decisions of mental health review tribunals are susceptible to the judicial review test if no reasonable tribunal would come to such a decision (*R v Mental Health Review Tribunal for West Midlands and North West, ex p Ashworth Hospital Authority and Others*).[89]

In *R (Von Brandenburg) v East London and the City Mental health NHS Trust and another*,[90] the claimant had been discharged by a tribunal but with a delayed discharge date, in order for accommodation to be found. The day before he was due to be discharged, he was further detained under s 3 of the Act. He sought judicial review. The House of Lords held that a social worker, as in this case, who made an application for detention under the Act, being aware of the decision to discharge, would be acting unlawfully unless he reasonably, and in good faith, considered that he had information that was not before the tribunal, which put a different complexion on the case. Further, if the social worker was not aware of the decision of the tribunal, as long as appropriate inquiries had been made before taking the decision to detain under the Act, there was no wider obligation to try to ascertain whether there had been an earlier tribunal decision to discharge the patient.

9.5.3.2 Habeas corpus

It may be thought that, since the introduction of the right to apply to a Mental Health Review tribunal, this ancient remedy would have little application. However, it has continued to be used, and was given approval as, in certain circumstances, *the* only remedy for an unlawfully detained patient.[91] Nevertheless, challenges are more likely to be made by way of judicial review, particularly since the enactment of the HRA 1998.

In *M v South West London & St George's Mental Health NHS Trust*[92] the appellant was a woman who had been detained under s 2 of the Act, suffering from a number of psychiatric conditions. While in hospital she was found to need treatment for a physical disorder and was transferred to a general hospital for treatment. It was thought by her psychiatrist that she should be detained under s 3 of the Act because she was a danger to herself and others, and a social worker and another psychiatrist went to the hospital to examine and interview her. The patient was unco-operative but it was decided to detain her under s 3. The patient applied for a writ of habeas corpus on the basis that the formal requirements for detention under the Act had not been met and that the court should determine this by hearing evidence about disputed matters of fact. The judge rejected this argument and concluded that the 'interview' with the patient had been sufficient to comply with the statutory requirements, and dismissed her application for habeas corpus. The Court of Appeal upheld this and also confirmed that there was nothing in the legislation that

---

89 [2001] EWHC Admin 901.
90 [2003] UKHL 58.
91 See *Re S-C (Mental Patient: Habeas Corpus)* [1996] 1 FLR 548.
92 [2008] EWCA Civ 1112.

required co-operation on the part of the patient. This must be the case because, by its very nature, compulsory detention is primarily there to deal with unco-operative patients.

9.5.3.3 Judicial review

Although Gunn's views were expressed some time ago, judicial review remains an important remedy.

Gunn, M, 'Judicial review of hospital admissions and treatment in the community under the Mental Health Act 1983'[93]

The right to apply for judicial review forms, along with an application for a writ of habeas corpus, a vital way in which the patient can complain about the original admission. Indeed, they form the only way, if it is right that a Mental Health Review Tribunal cannot consider the validity of the initial admission to hospital, as one member of the Court of Appeal, Ackner LJ, said in passing. It is important, therefore, to emphasise that a Mental Health Review Tribunal apparently can only decide whether a person should continue to be detained in hospital by considering whether the conditions justifying detention exist at the time the Tribunal sees the patient. Although judicial review and habeas corpus do permit consideration of the original admission decision, neither provide a form of appeal on the merits of the decision: neither can question whether the decision was right or wrong. Instead they concentrate on whether the doctors, social workers and nearest relatives had the legal power to admit the patient; they consider whether the discretion that the professionals have was exercised in a proper manner; for example, did they take all relevant factors into account?

See too the cases of *R v Hallstrom and Another, ex p W*[94] and *R v Gardner and Another, ex p L*.[95]

In *R v Mental Health Review Tribunal and Another, ex p KB and Others*,[96] it was held that commonplace delays in hearings before the Mental Health Review tribunal breached the right to a speedy hearing under Article 5(4) of the ECHR.[97]

9.5.3.4 Article 5 of the European Convention on Human Rights

One of the issues in the *Bournewood* case was the adequacy or otherwise of the judicial review (and habeas corpus) procedures to safeguard the patient's Article 5 rights:

HL v United Kingdom[98]

...

Lawfulness and protection against arbitrary detention

...

136 The Government mainly argued that an application for leave to apply for judicial review of the decision to admit and detain, including a writ of habeas corpus, constituted a review fulfilling the requirements of Art.5(4) of the Convention. The applicant disagreed.

---

93 [1986] J Soc Wel L 290.
94 [1986] 2 All ER 306.
95 [1986] 1 QB 1090.
96 (2002) 152 NLJ 672.
97 See also *R v Mental Health Review Tribunal South West Region, ex p C* [2002] 1 WLR 176.
98 (2005) 40 EHRR 32, European Court of Human Rights.

137 The Court considers that the starting-point must be the above-cited X v United Kingdom judgment where the Court found that the review conducted in habeas corpus proceedings was insufficient for the purposes of Art.5(4) as not being wide enough to bear on those conditions which were essential for the 'lawful' detention of a person on the basis of unsoundness of mind since it did not allow a determination of the merits of the question as to whether the mental disorder persisted. The Court is not persuaded by the Government's argument that the X case can be distinguished because it concerned detention pursuant to a statutory power: no authority has been cited and no other material adduced to indicate that the courts' review of detention based on the common law doctrine of necessity would indeed have been more intrusive.

138 Nor does the Court find convincing the Government's reliance on the development of the 'super-Wednesbury' principles of judicial review prior to the entry into force of the Human Rights Act 1998 in October 2000. Those principles were outlined and applied in the domestic judgment in the above-cited case of R v Ministry of Defence Ex p Smith. In the subsequent application to this Court by the same applicant, it was found that, even if his essential complaints under Art.8 of the Convention had been considered by the domestic courts, the threshold at which those courts could have found to be irrational the impugned policy prohibiting homosexuals from the armed forces had been placed so high that it effectively excluded any consideration by the domestic courts of the question whether the interference with the applicants' rights answered a pressing social need or was proportionate to the national security and public order aims pursued, principles which lay at the heart of the Court's analysis of complaints under Art.8 of the Convention. The Court concluded that the remedy of judicial review, even on a 'super-Wednesbury' basis, could not therefore constitute an effective remedy (within the meaning of Art.13) for a breach of Mr Smith's rights under Art.8.

139 The Court considers that it can be equally concluded for the purposes of Art.5(4) (the lex specialis vis-à-vis Art.13 in terms of entitlement to a review of the lawfulness of detention) that, even with the application of the 'super-Wednesbury' principles on judicial review, the bar of unreasonableness would at the time of the applicant's domestic proceedings have been placed so high as effectively to exclude any adequate examination of the merits of the clinical views as to the persistence of mental illness justifying detention. This is indeed confirmed by the decision of the Court of Appeal, in a case where the necessity of medical treatment was contested by the patient, that pre-incorporation judicial review of necessity in accordance with 'the super- Wednesbury' criteria was not sufficiently intrusive to constitute an adequate examination of the merits of the relevant medical decisions.

140 For these reasons, the Court finds that the requirements of Art.5(4) were not satisfied, as suggested by the Government, by judicial review and habeas corpus proceedings. It is not necessary therefore to examine the applicant's additional submissions that those proceedings did not satisfy the requirements of that Article because, inter alia, the burden of proof was on the detainee or because such proceedings did not provide 'speedy' and 'periodic control' at 'reasonable intervals'.

141 The Government also contended, without elaboration, that a dissatisfied patient could bring a civil claim for damages for negligence, false imprisonment and for trespass to the person (technical assault consequent on detention for treatment) which actions would be 'likely' to cause the hospital to justify its treatment of the patient without consent. The Government then proposed, without further detail, that the applicant could have invoked the declaratory jurisdiction of the High Court. However, the applicant did not allege that the relevant health professionals were negligent but rather that they had been incorrect in their diagnoses. His own action in false imprisonment and assault did not involve the submission of expert evidence by each of the parties or any assessment by the courts of that expertise and no case, decided at or around the relevant time, has been cited where such expertise was requested or such a merits review was carried out. As to seeking declaratory relief from the High Court, the Government has not cited any case decided around the relevant time where the High Court accepted that there was a 'serious justiciable issue'

to be examined by it in a case such as the present one where the patient was readmitted and detained for assessment and treatment (which treatment was not of an exceptional nature) on the basis of a consensus amongst the health professionals that admission was necessary.

142 In such circumstances, the Court concludes that it has not been demonstrated that the applicant had available to him a procedure which satisfied the requirements of Art.5(4) of the Convention. There has been therefore a violation of this provision.

In *R (H) v Secretary of State for Health*[99] the respondent (M), who was severely mentally disabled, had been detained in hospital under s 2 of the Act. She had not applied to the mental health review tribunal within the first 14 days, as was her right. The hospital wished to arrange for M to be received into guardianship under s 7 of the Act but M's mother, as her nearest relative, objected. An application was made to the county court to displace her mother and appoint an acting nearest relative under s 29 of the Act. The county court proceedings took longer than expected, which meant that M was detained under the s 2 order well beyond the usual 28 days. The issue before the House of Lords was whether this meant that s 2 was incompatible with Article 5(4) of the Convention where a patient had a right to apply to a tribunal but did not have the capacity to do so, and whether s 29(4), which has the effect of extending the s 2 detention until it is resolved, is incompatible with the Convention. The Court of Appeal had held that there was incompatibility.

The House of Lords granted the appeal and held that there was no authority that implied into Article 5(4) the requirement of judicial review in every case where the patient was unable to make his own application. Hospital managers had a statutory duty to take steps to ensure that a patient understood their rights under the provisions of their detention. Even if a patient's nearest relative had no independent right of application there was much that they could do to put the patient's case before a judicial authority. In this case, M's mother had been able to challenge every important decision. She had also initiated the reference (under s 67(1) of the Act) to the Secretary of State after it became clear that her daughter was to be kept in hospital longer than 28 days. A mental health review tribunal was best suited to determining the merits of a patient's detention, and doing so in a way that was convenient to the patient, readily accessible and comparatively quick.

R (H) v Secretary of State for Health[100]

Baroness Hale of Richmond

32 . . . while judicial review and/or habeas corpus may be one way of securing compliance with the patient's article 5(4) rights, this would be much more satisfactorily achieved either by a speedy determination of the county court proceedings or by a Secretary of State's reference under section 67. Either way, however, the means exist of operating section 29(4) in a way which is compatible with the patient's rights. It follows that the section itself cannot be incompatible, although the action or inaction of the authorities under it may be so.

Conclusion

33 For these reasons, my Lords, I would decline to hold that either section 2 or section 29(4) is incompatible with article 5(4) of the Convention in the respects identified by the Court of Appeal. I would therefore allow this appeal and set aside the declarations.

99 [2005] UKHL 60.
100 Ibid.

This unsatisfactorily vague approach to protection illustrates the point that Richardson and Machin make when they suggest that there is something anti-therapeutic about the judicial review process and that the latter's emphasis on procedure creates an uneasy conflict.

Richardson, G and Machin, D, 'A clash of values? Mental Health Review Tribunals and judicial review'[101]

If the classic conflict between law and psychiatry, between autonomy and welfare, were to be reflected in the judicial review case law we might expect to see the reviewing courts assiduously protecting those aspects of patient autonomy which had not been unambiguously restricted by statute. The case law relating both to the discharge criteria and to tribunal powers denies that expectation.

For other comments as to judicial review of Human Rights Act challenges, see *R v Responsible Medical Officer Broadmoor Hospital and Others, ex p Wilkinson*[102] and *Lee-Hirons v Secretary of State for Justice*.[103] Judicial review also applies to private psychiatric hospitals: *R v Partnerships in Care Ltd, ex p A*.[104]

9.6 A right to treatment for mental disorder?

Because of the civil liberty issues that it raises, much of the concern surrounding patient rights is to do with the patient's right to liberty unless there are compelling reasons to the contrary. However, it can also be asked whether a mentally ill patient has a right to be treated.

In terms of medical treatment generally, there have been a number of attempts over the years to persuade courts to intervene when limited healthcare resources within the UK National Health Service have resulted in the denial of treatment to physically ill patients.[105] The conclusion to be drawn from these cases is that unless there is irrationality or procedural impropriety, the courts will not intervene. There is, therefore, very limited scope in making a challenge, and none in respect of *clinical* judgment.

However, the element of public protection in mental health law means that treatment for physical illness and treatment for psychiatric illness are not exactly comparable. There have been a number of recent incidents when members of the public have been injured and even killed by ex-psychiatric patients, and there has been something of an outcry that the persons concerned were not receiving treatment, or not receiving in-patient treatment.[106] However, in this regard, note the case of *Clunis v Camden and Islington HA* (the *Jonathan Zito* case),[107] where the Court of Appeal held that there was no liability of a discharging health authority towards a patient who subsequently killed a member of the public. This was based upon the fact that the action was grounded in the patient's own illegal act, so that *ex turpi causa non oritur actio* applied, and upon the court's decision that the obligation under s 117 of the Act to provide patient after care did not give rise to an obligation at common law.[108]

---

101 [1999] J Mental Health L 3, at 11.
102 [2002] 1 WLR 419.
103 [2016] UKSC 46.
104 [2002] EWHC 529.
105 See Ch 2 and, for example, the cases of *R v Secretary of State for Social Services, ex p Hincks* (1980) 1 BMLR 93; *R v Central Birmingham HA, ex p Walker* (1987) 3 BMLR 32; and *R v Cambridge HA, ex p B* [1995] 2 All ER 129.
106 See, for example, newspaper reports in (1994) *The Independent*, 16 September; and (1995) *The Guardian*, 28 July; and (1997) *The Guardian*, 30 May.
107 [1998] 2 WLR 902.
108 See Jones, MA, 'The violent mentally disordered patient: who cares?' (1998) 14(2) Professional Negligence 99.

Judicial review was brought to allege a violation of the patient's rights under Article 5 in the case of *R v Secretary of State for the Home Department and another, ex p IH*.[109] A mental health review tribunal had been satisfied that the patient should be discharged, but subject to suitable s 117 supervision within the community. There were difficulties in finding suitable supervision and discharge was deferred. The patient made an application for judicial review and, at the suggestion of the court, the case went before another tribunal. The decision of this tribunal was that it was appropriate for the patient to be detained in hospital. The allegations of the patient were two-fold: first that his rights under Article 5(4) had been violated (this requires a speedy review of lawfulness of detention). He succeeded in this respect. However, the more interesting aspect of his application concerned Article 5(1)(e), which provides for detention of patients of unsound mind. The patient argued that this should be interpreted as providing for detention *only in circumstances in which the level of security represents a proportionate response to the risk posed by the patient*. In other words, he was asking for a gloss to be placed on the provision to reflect the European law concept of proportionality. The House of Lords rejected this, and distinguished the ECtHR case of *Johnson v UK*,[110] where an applicant's discharge had been delayed because suitable accommodation could not be found and, in circumstances where there was no doubt that the patient was no longer ill. Here, the difficulty in finding suitable aftercare was based upon the fact that the psychiatric services who would have been responsible for aftercare disagreed with discharge into the community as 'being clinically inappropriate'.

A patient is unlikely to request to be compulsorily detained under the Act, but could request to be informally admitted (s 131). For the purposes of this, the patient would have no more rights than a patient who demanded to be admitted to hospital for the treatment of physical illness. The decision would be based upon clinical judgment and, in the absence of judicially reviewable procedural irregularity, the courts would not intervene.

After the discharge of a patient detained under s 3 (or under certain criminal provisions, under ss 37, 47 or 48 of the Act, for detention), there is a duty on both the local health authority and the local social services authority to provide, in co-operation with the relevant voluntary agencies, after-care services until both are satisfied that the patient no longer needs them (s 117): this is a duty in respect of the individual patient rather than to the mentally disordered generally.

Given the concern about the discharge of potentially dangerous patients mentioned above, it is interesting to speculate on the nature of this duty and whether it does impose a heavier onus on healthcare providers in the field of mental health than on their counterparts who are providing treatment for physical illnesses. This was considered in the case of *R v Ealing District HA, ex p Fox*,[111] where a health authority refused to provide psychiatric supervision for a patient who had been conditionally discharged by a mental health review tribunal subject to receiving psychiatric supervision in the community. In this case, the judge held that the health authority had erred in law in not attempting with all reasonable expedition and diligence to make arrangements so as to enable the patient to comply with arrangements '*required by a Mental Health Review Tribunal*'.[112] However, does this mean that if tribunals are prepared to attach such conditions to discharge orders that they will be enforceable? The answer to this is in the negative. In *Fox*, it was said that there should have been a reference back to the tribunal, presumably with a view to amendment, and that duties owed to the patient could only be enforced by alleging procedural defectiveness through the mechanism of judicial review, which, as we have seen, are

---

109 [2003] UKHL 59.
110 (1997) 27 EHRR 296.
111 [1993] 3 All ER 170.
112 *Per* Otten J, emphasis added.

important, but limited in scope. In *R v Mental Health Review Tribunal, ex p H*,[113] the Court of Appeal confirmed that a tribunal does not have the power to make orders against local and health authorities compelling them to implement any particular s 117 after-care plan. Furthermore, in *R v Camden and Islington HA, ex p K*,[114] the Court of Appeal confirmed that s 117 does not impose an absolute obligation on authorities to satisfy any conditions imposed by a tribunal on the discharge of a patient.

In other words, as with treatment for physical illness, the courts will defer to clinical judgment and will not compel treatment to be given, as long as the decision to refuse to treat has been taken in a procedurally sound way. In this particular case the authority's consultant psychiatrist was doubtful that supervision in the community would work. However, the judge said that the health authority is bound to continue to seek to provide the necessary treatment, either from its own resources or from elsewhere and, if it cannot do so, then the matter should be referred back to the mental health review tribunal to reconsider the discharge condition. However, suppose there was not clinical doubt, but simply lack of the appropriate resources to provide the treatment? After all, the reason for the failure to provide medical treatment is more likely to be lack of financial resources than anything else (although in the case of *R v Cambridge HA, ex p B*[115] resources were in issue, but the stress was upon the likelihood of success of the treatment). The question of resources was raised in the case of *R v Hertfordshire CC, ex p Three Rivers DC*.[116] This was about the level of provision in the community under the National Health Service and Community Care Act 1990, which imposes a duty upon the local social services authority to assess the needs of, *inter alia*, discharged mental patients. It was held in that case that identifying the level and nature of the service to be provided may be constrained by available resources and that these constraints could properly be taken into account when identifying the appropriate level of service provision.

The conclusion is, therefore, that ultimately there is no 'right' to treatment for the psychiatrically ill any more than there is for the physically ill. The only right is to be considered for treatment and given the appropriate clinical assessment.

THINK POINT

Do you think that psychiatric patients should have some entitlement to treatment that other patients should not have?

9.7 Liability towards patients

9.7.1 Criminal liability

The ordinary criminal law does, of course, apply to psychiatric patients, and in addition there are a number of specific statutory offences relating to ill treatment of patients and forgery of documentation for the purposes of detention, and these can be found in Part IX of the Act.

---

113 [2000] 1 WLR 1323.
114 [2001] EWCA Civ 240.
115 [1995] 2 All ER 129.
116 (1992) 90 LGR 526.

9.7.2 Civil liability

9.7.2.1 False imprisonment

In addition to the remedies discussed above, a patient unlawfully detained may pursue a civil claim for false imprisonment, and, if successful, obtain an award of damages. In the case of *Furber v Kratter*,[117] the patient succeeded despite the fact that the original detention was lawful. It was held that the substitution of a harsher regime than at first prescribed could constitute false imprisonment.

9.7.2.2 Battery and negligence

The same principles of common law negligence apply to the treatment of psychiatric patients. If it can be shown that those treating a potentially suicidal patient failed to supervise and treat in accordance with the appropriate standard of care, then the claimant will succeed: see *Selfe v Ilford and District Hospital Management Committee*.[118] *Kirkham v The Chief Constable of the Greater Manchester Police*[119] concerned a successful suicide in police custody. The widow of the person concerned succeeded in her claim. The Court of Appeal rejected the argument that the defence of *volenti* could apply: it was held that, as the person was clinically depressed, his judgment was too impaired in order for this to succeed. The latter point is of some interest: it is accepted that mental disorder itself does not mean that a patient is incapable as far as medical decision-making is concerned. Refusal of life-saving treatment by such a patient, unless it can be shown that the treatment is for the mental disorder *itself*,[120] is acceptable. However, a positive act of suicide in *Kirkham* should have been prevented on the basis of clinical impairment of judgment. Is there an illogicality here, or are we simply back to the distinction between positive acts, and omissions to take certain courses of action?

The liability of doctors and nurses to supervise suicidal patients was considered in the case of *Selfe v Ilford Hospital Management Committee*, where damages were awarded when there was found to be an unacceptable level of supervision. The clinical judgment of a psychiatrist was examined by the Supreme Court of Canada in the case of *Villemure v l'Hôpital Notre-Dame et al*. where a '*Bolam*' argument as to what other doctors would have done was rejected. The majority decision approved the following finding of the trial judge:

Villemure v l'Hopital Notre-Dame et al[121]

> The court is unable to accept the opinion of Drs Fortin and Saucier. It may be that they would have done exactly what Dr Turcot did. Had they done so, in the opinion of the court they would have been wrong and negligent. It is no answer to say it is impossible absolutely to prevent a person from committing suicide unless he is placed in a straitjacket. This of course is obvious. But it is surely possible to prevent him from committing suicide for 30 hours and until a sufficient investigation has been made into his condition to be able more accurately to diagnose his true situation. The court also rejects Dr Saucier's view that there were many factors which indicated that the patient's condition was not nearly as serious as might at first have been thought. The facts as proven of what happened prior to the entry into the hospital, coupled with the incidents in the hospital, indicate to the court rather a situation which should have made both Dr Turcot and the nurses take particular care of the deceased.

---

117 (1988) *The Times*, 21 July.
118 (1970) 114 SJ 935.
119 [1990] 2 QB 283.
120 See the case of *B v Croydon HA* [1994] 2 WLR 294, 9.4.1.2, above.
121 (1972) 31 DLR (3d) 454.

In the context of civil liability, mention must be made of a form of statutory immunity contained within s 139(1) of the Act:

> **139 (1)** No person shall be liable, whether on the ground of want of jurisdiction or on any other ground, to any civil or criminal proceedings to which he would have been liable apart from this section in respect of any act purporting to be done in pursuance of this Act or any regulations or rules made under this Act, or in, or in pursuance of anything done in, the discharge of functions conferred by any other enactment on the authority having jurisdiction under Part VII of this Act, unless the act was done in bad faith or without reasonable care.

It will be seen that the reference to 'without reasonable care' means that this section gives no immunity against an action in negligence. However, under s 139(2), leave of a High Court judge is required to bring an action in the first place. Gunn concludes that, in order to bring an action for judicial review, a patient does not have to allege bad faith or lack of reasonable care.[122]

9.7.2.3 A violation of Article 2 of the European Convention on Human Rights?

In *Savage v South Essex Partnership NHS Foundation Trust (MIND and others intervening)* the House of Lords had to consider the application of Article 2 of the Convention with regard to a situation where a detained mental patient absconded from hospital and killed herself:

Savage v South Essex Partnership NHS Foundation Trust (MIND and others intervening)[123]

Lord Rodger of Earlsferry

19 Fundamentally, article 2 requires a state to have in place a structure of laws which will help to protect life. In *Osman v United Kingdom* 29 EHRR 245, 305, para 115, the European court identified the 'primary duty' of a state under the article as being:

> to secure the right to life by putting in place effective criminal law provisions to deter the commission of offences against the person backed up by law-enforcement machinery for the prevention, suppression and sanctioning of breaches of such provisions.

But, as the parties in Osman's case recognised, the state's duty goes further, and article 2: 'may also imply in certain well defined circumstances a positive obligation on the authorities to take preventive operational measures to protect an individual whose life is at risk from the criminal acts of another individual'.

...

68 In terms of article 2, health authorities are under an over-arching obligation to protect the lives of patients in their hospitals. In order to fulfil that obligation, and depending on the circumstances, they may require to fulfil a number of complementary obligations.

69 In the first place, the duty to protect the lives of patients requires health authorities to ensure that the hospitals for which they are responsible employ competent staff and that they are trained to a high professional standard. In addition, the authorities must ensure that the hospitals adopt systems of work which

---

122 Gunn, M, 'Judicial review of hospital admissions and treatment in the community under the Mental Health Act 1983' [1986] J Soc Wel L 290.
123 [2009] 2 WLR 115.

will protect the lives of patients. Failure to perform these general obligations may result in a violation of article 2. If, for example, a health authority fails to ensure that a hospital puts in place a proper system for supervising mentally ill patients and, as a result, a patient is able to commit suicide, the health authority will have violated the patient's right to life under article 2.

70 Even though a health authority employed competent staff and ensured that they were trained to a high professional standard, a doctor, for example, might still treat a patient negligently and the patient might die as a result. In that situation, there would be no violation of article 2 since the health authority would have done all that the article required of it to protect the patient's life. Nevertheless, the doctor would be personally liable in damages for the death and the health authority would be vicariously liable for her negligence . . .

71 The same approach would apply if a mental hospital had established an appropriate system for supervising patients and all that happened was that, on a particular occasion, a nurse negligently left his post and a patient took the opportunity to commit suicide. There would be no violation of any obligation under article 2, since the health authority would have done all that the article required of it. But, again, the nurse would be personally liable in damages for the death and the health authority would be vicariously liable too.

72 Finally, article 2 imposes a further 'operational' obligation on health authorities and their hospital staff. This obligation is distinct from, and additional to, the authorities' more general obligations. The operational obligation arises only if members of staff know or ought to know that a particular patient presents a 'real and immediate' risk of suicide. In these circumstances article 2 requires them to do all that can reasonably be expected to prevent the patient from committing suicide. If they fail to do this, not only will they and the health authorities be liable in negligence, but there will also be a violation of the operational obligation under article 2 to protect the patient's life. . . .

In *Rabone v Pennine Care NHS Foundation Trust*,[124] the Supreme Court considered liability under Article 2 of the Convention, following the suicide of an informal patient. The patient had been granted two days' home leave and during this time hanged herself. Her parents issued proceedings, alleging negligence and a breach of Article 2. The trust admitted negligence and a settlement had been made with the patient's parents, but they had not admitted liability for a breach of Article 2. Lord Dyson, who gave the main judgment, set out the six issues before the court, and these were as follows:

Rabone v Pennine Care NHS Foundation Trust[125]

Lord Dyson: 14 The six issues that arise in this appeal are: (i) whether the operational obligation under article 2 can in principle be owed to a hospital patient who is mentally ill, but who is not detained under the MHA; if the answer to (i) is yes, (ii) whether there was a 'real and immediate' risk to the life of Melanie on 19 April 2005 of which the trust knew or ought to have known and which they failed to take reasonable steps to avoid; if the answer to (ii) is yes, (iii) whether Mr and Mrs Rabone were 'victims' within the meaning of article 34 of the Convention; if the answer to (iii) is yes, (iv) whether they lost their victim status, because the trust made adequate redress and sufficiently acknowledged its breach of duty; if the answer to (iv) is no, (v) whether their claims are time-barred by section 7(5) of the HRA; and if the answer to (v) is no, (vi) whether the Court of Appeal erred in holding that they would have awarded £5000 each to Mr and Mrs Rabone if their claims had been established . . .

---

124 [2012] UKSC 2.
125 [2012] UKSC 2.

23 When finding that the article 2 operational duty has been breached, the ECtHR has repeatedly empha-sised the vulnerability of the victim as a relevant consideration. In circumstances of sufficient vulnerability, the ECtHR has been prepared to find a breach of the operational duty even where there has been no assumption of control by the state, such as where a local authority fails to exercise its powers to protect a child who to its knowledge is at risk of abuse as in Z v United Kingdom Application No 29392/95 (10 May 2001)

. . .

29 Although informal patients are not 'detained' and are therefore, in principle, free to leave hospital at any time, their 'consent' to remain in hospital may only be as a result of a fear that they will be detained

. . . .

33 . . . These factors, taken together, lead me to conclude that the ECtHR would hold that the operational duty existed In this case.

Lord Dyson examined the situation with regard to the second question, which was whether there was a 'real and immediate' risk to the life of Melanie; he concluded that, on the facts, there was risk, in as much as it was not remote or fanciful. On the third issue Mr and Mrs Rabone were clearly 'victims' of an unlawful act as required by s 7(1) of the Human Rights Act, as the ECtHR has stated in many cases that family members can bring claims in their own right. On the fourth issue the question was whether Mr and Mrs Rabone lost their victim status as a result of the settlement of their negligence claim.

Lord Dyson: 49 It is common ground that a person ceases to be a victim within the meaning of arti-cle 34 of the Convention if two conditions are satisfied. These are that the domestic public authority has (i) provided 'adequate redress' and (ii) 'acknowledged, either expressly or in substance, the breach of the Convention'

. . . .

57 I do not find it easy to extract from the Strasbourg jurisprudence a clear statement of the effect of the settlement of a domestic law claim on the ability of an individual to pursue a corresponding Con-vention claim. The court does not, however, seem to adopt a strict approach to the interpretation of a settlement . . .

58 To return to the facts of the present case, I do not accept that by settling the 1934 Act negligence claim on behalf of Melanie's estate, Mr Rabone renounced an article 2 claim on behalf of himself and Mrs Rabone for damages for non-pecuniary loss for their bereavement. No such claim had been made in the negligence proceedings because such a claim was not available in English law. That is because section 1A of the Fatal Accidents Act 1976 provides that a claim by parents for damages for bereavement for the loss of a child (currently fixed by section 1A(3) at £11,800) shall only be for the benefit of the parents of a minor and Melanie was more than 18 years of age at the date of her death. In these circumstances, the settlement of the 1934 Act claim did not amount to an implied renuncia-tion of any article 2 claim. In the absence of an express renunciation, the settlement of itself had no legal effect on the status of Mr and Mrs Rabone as victims for the purpose of their article 2 claim. It remains to be considered whether (as the Court of Appeal held) the sum of £7,500 was nevertheless 'adequate redress'.

Lord Dyson concluded that the compensation was not 'adequate redress' because it consisted of a statutory sum, which did not provide for compensation for the non-pecuniary damage suffered by Mr and Mrs Rabone as a result of the breach of Article 2.

The fifth issue was whether the claim was out of time. Section 7(5) of the HRA provides that proceedings under s 7(1)(a) (a claim that a public authority has acted in a way which is incompatible with a Convention right) must be brought within one year of the date that the act took place, but gives discretion to a court to extend this period if it is equitable to do so. Here, the claim was brought almost four months beyond the first anniversary of Melanie's death. The Supreme Court, exercising discretion afresh, found that Mr and Mrs Rabone had made a formal complaint within five months of Melanie's death and they had been advised that their claim would be put on hold until the report, following a formal investigation, had been completed. The report took many months to complete and, while proceedings could have been issued within the one-year period, Mr and Mrs Rabone had acted reasonably in waiting for the report and the trust had not been prejudiced by the delay. The appeal was allowed and Mr and Mrs Rabone were awarded £5,000 each (the sum suggested by the Court of Appeal).

9.7.2.4 The United Nations Convention on the Rights of Persons with Disabilities (2011)

Although the Convention is not formally incorporated into law in the UK, it has been ratified and it is arguable therefore that legislation should be compatible with its provisions. Bartlett and Sandland argue that deficiencies in the care of people with mental disabilities can amount to a violation of Article 25 of the Convention, which protects the right to health. Article 17 states that '[e]very person with disabilities has a right to respect for his or her physical and mental integrity on an equal basis with others', and Bartlett and Sandland argue that the use of coercion in imposing 'treatment' upon mentally disabled people should amount to a violation of this, but because of its vague wording, Article 17 lacks definition and scope.[126]

9.8 Mental health law and mental capacity

We looked at the operation of the Mental Capacity Act 2005 in Chapter 4. The capacity and mental health regimes are separate, and patients who are 'incapable' under the MCA can be treated in their best interests for both physical and mental illness. Szmukler, Daw and Dawson maintain that there should be new legislation that would govern all non-consensual treatments. Dawson is a New Zealand academic, and they acknowledge that the current discrete approaches to capacity and to mental health are also reflected in schemes in Australasia as well as the UK. They believe that the best of both approaches should be fused:

Szmukler, G, Daw R and Dawson J, 'A model law fusing incapacity and mental health legislation'[127]

The 'fusion' framework

The alternative approach that we advocate is to abandon the two-track approach, and, instead, to fuse the two together into a single comprehensive involuntary treatment scheme, which preserves the strengths of each. A major strength of non-consensual treatment schemes that are based on incapacity principles is the respect shown for the autonomy of those patients who retain their capacity; but these schemes

---

126 Bartlett, P and Sandland, R, *Mental Health Law: Policy and Practice*, 4th edn, Oxford: OUP, 2014.
127 [2010] special edn J Mental Health L 11, 12.

are, nevertheless, often weak on the regulation of emergency treatment powers, detention in hospital, and forced treatment. These are the areas, in contrast, in which civil commitment schemes are strong. The use of force, and the detention and involuntary treatment of objecting patients, is clearly authorised and regulated by mental health legislation. We therefore advocate a legal regime that retains the strengths of both, but still relies squarely on the incapacity of the person to make necessary care or treatment decisions as the primary justification for intervention in their life.

Our proposed 'fusion' legislation deals with all persons who lack capacity who may require treatment or care; compulsory powers will only affect a subset of those covered. Provisions for the treatment and care of informal patients include safeguards for those requiring 'serious medical treatment', protections for informal patients in residential care, and requirements for informal patients lacking capacity who need to be 'deprived of their liberty' in their best interests. A single regime is thus provided that specifies the conditions for both treatment under compulsion and treatment under circumstances amounting to a 'deprivation of liberty'.

... The basic criterion for intervention under 'fused' legislation is incapacity to make necessary treatment decisions.

... [the patient] enters a staggered compulsory assessment process ...

... Comprehensive review and accountability mechanisms ... apply. All involuntary patients must have ready access to rights advice and to independent review of their status before a court or tribunal. A substitute decision-maker for treatment is appointed.

... involuntary treatment is restricted to patients who lack capacity. This does not preclude involuntary treatment for the protection of others, which is permitted ... first, where treatment for the protection of others is in the patient's best interests, and second, where in the course of providing treatment in the best interests of the patient, there arises a risk of harm to others.

Certainly, this proposal demonstrates coherence of approach. However, is it satisfactory that capable patients who would currently be detained under a mental health regime, who pose a danger to themselves or others, can only be treated without consent if it is in their best interests to be so treated? It is effectively saying that their refusal of consent can be overridden in their best interests if they are a danger to others, which is roughly how the current scheme operates, albeit that the words 'best interests' are not explicitly used. Undoubtedly, supporters of the current scheme would say that it would be unthinkable to be providing treatment that is not in the best interests of the patient.

The relationship between the Mental Health Act and the Mental Capacity Act was considered in the case of *GJ v Foundation Trust*.[128] Charles, J held that the Mental Health Act has primacy, and that medical practitioners, social workers and others who are involved cannot pick and choose between the two regimes. In *AM v South London & Maudsley NHS Foundation Trust*,[129] Charles J clarified this approach and held that in cases where the patient was compliant but lacked capacity, it was generally more appropriate to rely upon the Deprivation of Liberty Safeguards under the Mental Capacity Act, but there could be circumstances where the Mental Health Act regime was more appropriate. What has to be done is to make a comparison of the impact of each regime respectively. Any reference to the Mental Health Act having primacy, therefore, had to be case specific.

---

128 [2009] EWHC 2972 (Fam).
129 [2013] UKUT 365 (AAC).

Summary of key points

1   Mental health law is considered a discrete area of medical law for two main reasons. First, there are difficulties in defining 'mental health' or defining 'mental disorder', as these are inextricably bound up with personality, and 'norms' are much harder to find. Secondly, some forms of mental disorder can result in behaviours that are socially unacceptable and sometimes dangerous, and in consequence the general medical principle that patients can only be treated with their consent or in their best interests if they lack the ability to give consent has not been applied to cases where the patient is a serious risk to themselves or others.

2   There has been much debate surrounding the above issues, ranging from asserting that some, if not all, mental illness is a fiction, to more moderate concerns about how compulsory detention of mentally disordered patients can be justified, particularly if they have the capacity to make treatment decisions.

3   Mental health law raises important human rights questions, particularly in relation to Article 5 of the European Convention on Human Rights, and the deprivation of liberty. Under Article (5)(1)(e) lawful detention of persons of unsound mind is permitted in principle, and case law has refined the requirements that must be fulfilled in order to be compliant with the Convention.

4   There are statutory schemes in many parts of the world that permit detention by reason of mental disorder if there is a risk of harm to self or others, and in England and Wales the Mental Health Act 1983 (as amended in 2007) is such a scheme. It provides for compulsory detention for assessment in hospital, for treatment, detention in an emergency, detention of an informal in-patient and also for treatment within the community.

5   Mental health hospital regimes raise special considerations both in terms of general treatment with regard to respect for privacy and the provision of a therapeutic environment, and in terms of medical treatment itself. As far as the latter is concerned the Mental Health Act 1983 provides, in certain circumstances, for treatment without the consent of the patient.

6   Ways of challenging detention under the Act include statutory mental health review tribunals and common law remedies of judicial review and habeas corpus.

7   Patients might argue that they have a right to treatment if they are liable to be detained in hospital against their will as a result of their disorder.

8   Special issues can arise in relation to the prevention of suicide and other self-harm.

Further reading

Bartlett, P and Sandland, R, *Mental Health Law: Policy and Practice*, 4th edn, Oxford: Oxford University Press, 2014.

Fennell, P, *Treatment Without Consent: Law, Psychiatry and the Treatment of Mentally Disordered People since 1845*, London: Routledge, 1996.

Jones, R, *Mental Health Act Manual*, 17th edn, London: Sweet & Maxwell, 2014.

Laing, JM, 'Perspectives on monitoring mental health legislation in England: a view from the front line' (2015) 23 Medical Law Review 400.

Journal of Mental Health Law, special edition, 2010.

Peay, J, *Decisions and Dilemmas*, Oxford: Hart Publishing, 2003.

Richardson, G, 'Autonomy, guardianship and mental disorder: one problem, two solutions' (2002) 65 Modern Law Review 702.

Chapter 10

Medical research

10.1 Introduction

10.1.1 Background

New therapies are constantly being developed in the battle against sickness and disease, and advances are not merely desired, but expected by society at large. However, their achievement inevitably involves carrying out previously untried treatment upon human subjects, with attendant uncertainty as to the treatment's capacity to harm rather than benefit the subjects in question.

In this chapter, we are concerned with the legal and ethical issues presented by medical research. To this end, we look first at the scientific methodology of research, and examine the key ethical dilemmas raised by such practices. The remaining sections then consider the legal and quasi-legal constraints that operate upon the researcher; in particular the need for research to be subject to independent ethical review: the requirement that the subject consent to research; the various voluntary codes which seek to impose further safeguards in this field; and the issue of *ex post facto* compensation for those injured during the course of research.

It should be borne in mind that medical research gives rise to issues that have been discussed in other chapters such as confidentiality and privacy (see Chapter 5 at 5.4), human tissue and assisted reproduction.

10.1.2 The importance of scientific advancement

There is a school of thought that says there is an obligation to carry out research, for the advancement of society generally or, even if there is no such positive obligation, there is a right not to be unduly fettered in pursuing that scientific enquiry. Medical research is just one form of scientific enquiry which is generally thought to be a good thing. However, there is a particular resonance in the field of medicine because of the impact and potential impact upon the control of disease and pain and discomfort. The personal benefits to patients therefore make endorsement of this form of scientific enquiry rather different from the benefits that can be obtained from advances in, say, civil engineering techniques, however important these might prove to be for society as a whole.

John Harris is typically robust in his advocacy of the importance of medical research, to the extent that he argues that we have a moral duty to participate in medical research:

Harris, J, 'Scientific research is a moral duty'[1]

> Let me present the question in its starkest form: is there a moral obligation to undertake, support and even to participate in serious scientific research? If there is, does that obligation require not only that beneficial research be undertaken but also that 'we', as individuals and 'we' as societies be willing to support and even participate in research where necessary? Thus far the overwhelming answer given to this question has been 'no', and research has almost universally been treated with suspicion and even hostility by the vast majority of all those concerned with the ethics and regulation of research.
>
> ...
>
> Two separate but complementary lines of argument underpin a powerful obligation to pursue, support, and participate in scientific research.
>
> ...
>
> The first is one of the most powerful obligations that we have, the obligation not to harm others. Where our actions will, or may probably prevent serious harm then if we can reasonably (given the balance

---

of risk and burden to ourselves and benefit to others) we clearly should act because to fail to do so is to accept responsibility for the harm that then occurs. . . .

Because medical research is a necessary component of relieving [medical needs] in many circumstances furthering medical research becomes a moral obligation. . . . Second, the obligation also flows from an appeal to basic fairness. This is sometimes expressed as an appeal to the unfairness of being a 'free rider'. We all benefit from the existence of the social practice of medical research. Many of us would not be here if infant mortality had not been brought under control, or antibiotics had not been invented.

. . .

[There is a concept of] 'mandatory contribution to public goods'. All British citizens between 18 and 70 are liable for jury service. They may be called, and unless excused by the court, must serve. This may involve a minimum of 10 days but sometimes months of daily confinement in a jury box or room, whether they consent or not. However, although all are liable for service only some are actually called. If someone is called and fails to appear they may be fined. Participation in, or facilitation of, this public good is mandatory. There are many senses in which participation in vaccine or drug trials involve features relevantly analogous to jury service.

THINK POINT

Is Harris's view merely treating human beings as means to further the interests of others, and does this fit in with our more conventional view of medical ethics?

10.1.3 Defining 'research'

Scientific research may be defined, very broadly, as any systematic inquiry aimed at discovering new facts about the way things in the world around us behave. In the case of medical research, the object of such inquiry is usually improving the efficacy of medical treatments. This includes the development of new forms of treatment and the ways in which medical treatments can be more effectively administered. The scope of research is wider than might be thought. Often people think only about the testing of new drug treatments, but, for example, research is often carried out in the field of preventative medicine where lifestyle choices might be the subject of medical research, where research can be carried out by simply observing doctor/patient interactions, or by the use of questionnaires and interviews with healthcare professionals or patients, and so on. Frequently methodologies give rise to minimal risk to the participants, but they can raise quite sensitive issues, and even if the questions do not raise such issues, they will almost always give rise to ethical matters such as privacy and confidentiality of information which must be considered in the ethical review process.

It is important to emphasise the deliberate and systematic nature of the research enterprise. Plomer comments as follows:

Plomer, A, *The Law and Ethics of Medical Research: International Bioethics and Human Rights*[2]

The distinction between experimental treatment and research is particularly significant in respect of the specification of the legal obligations imposed on researchers, with the risk that the categorisation of an intervention or procedure as innovative or experimental 'treatment', 'therapy' or 'practice' could be used to

---

2 London: Cavendish Publishing, 2005.

justify a lower level of legal protection on levels of information and disclosure of risks than those appropriate for research, notwithstanding the fact that the effects and risks of an innovative or experimental procedure by definition are yet to be proven. Undoubtedly, the recipient of an innovative or experimental treatment or therapy, like a participant in a therapeutic medical research program, potentially stands to derive a health benefit from the intervention *if* the anticipated, unproven health benefits materialise.

Plomer refers to the case of *Simms v Simms*[3] which concerned proposed invasive brain surgery on a young person with CJD. The procedure had never been tested on humans but there was no other possible treatment for this condition. The High Court authorised the surgery, simply as a form of experimental treatment. Although this form of experiment needs to be controlled in the sense that there must be fully informed consent or court authorisation, and it must be used in quite specific circumstances (mostly as a measure of last resort), it is not controlled by the regulatory frameworks of research ethics. However, experience with such treatment (often referred to as 'innovative therapy') may subsequently form the 'jumping off point' for proper research (especially if it turns out to be highly effective), but it lacks the necessary systematic and repetitive quality to count as research; equally its level of scientific probity remains fairly low.

Significantly, from the doctor's point of view, the desire in such cases is solely to benefit the individual patient being treated in this way. Of course, he may foresee the likelihood of gaining new knowledge in the process, but this merely equates to a wider intention on his part to acquire it (contrast therapeutic research where it is part of his desire). The upshot is that there is no conflict between the doctor *qua* doctor and *qua* scientist: he acts as the former alone. In such a case, it is also submitted that (subject to gaining proper consent) the doctor may also run higher risks on the patient's behalf than those permissible in the context of research. This is because the intended beneficiary of the treatment is the patient alone; he is not being used as a means to any further end.

The key components to 'research' that requires some form of ethical approval is that there is either some form of risk to the participant, and/or that the procedure requires consent in the knowledge that it is a research project.

Without the emphasis on the systematic aspect of research, one might be inclined to regard all medical treatment as constituting 'research', given that our store of knowledge will inevitably increase in the course of providing it. As John Marshall comments:

Marshall, J, 'The case against experimentation'[4]

[In] one sense any medical intervention is research. Giving an aspirin to a patient, though done thousands and thousands of times, may on the thousand-and-oneth [sic] occasion produce some unexpected, unpredictable result because of idiosyncrasies in that patient. Therefore, when people talk on the one hand about certain orthodox procedures which they do without thinking and, on the other hand, about unorthodox procedures, it is clear that there is a difference in degree but never a difference in kind. Anything that is done, any intervention in another person, can have unexpected and unpredictable results. But it is not about that that we are really talking in this context.

The other area which ought to be distinguished is that of improving therapy. Again, people think that there is a certain standard way of doing appendectomies, or coronary bypass procedures, that there is a certain standard way of treating people with respiratory failure. But medicine is always engaged in the business of improving therapy, and improving therapy is often on a research basis. When you try to modify some procedure because you think it might work better in a different way, you are engaged in a form of research, a form of inquiry.

---

3 [2003] 2 WLR 1465.
4 In Dyson, A and Harris, J (eds), *Experiments on Embryos*, London: Routledge, 1989.

It is generally accepted that, in scientific terms, randomised control trials (RCTs) represent the ideal form of medical research. The basic idea is that subjects are randomly divided into different groups. One will be offered the treatment under research, and another (the 'control group') will not. As is evident from the following extract written by Charles Fried in 1974, many therapies that are considered standard today were once the subject of RCTs to establish their efficacy:

Fried, C, *Medical Experimentation: Personal Integrity and Social Policy*[5]

Coronary bypass surgery

In recent years techniques have been developed for bypassing regions of serious atherosclerotic blockage in the major coronary arteries . . . There have, however, been serious questions raised regarding the efficacy of this technique in certain cases of coronary artery disease

In order to evaluate the claims for coronary bypass surgery in various categories of disease, a number of hospitals throughout the country have instituted randomised clinical trials. In one trial, participants are referred by their physician to cardiologists in the participating hospital. The participants are told that a study is being conducted in which they are involved, that they will receive the best available treatment for their case, and that they are free not to join in or stay in the study. Although they know of the alternative therapies, only if they ask are they told that the choice is determined by a randomising scheme.

The scientific utility of randomisation is derived from the elimination, through the randomisation process, of potential bias in observing and interpreting the results of the treatment. In particular, some patients will not be receiving any active drug at all, but will be randomised into a group that is receiving a placebo. The term 'placebo' used here refers to an inert substance, such as a 'dummy' pill, which is given to a subject so that he is unaware that he is in the control group not receiving the therapy under research. Patients are normally aware that they might be receiving the active treatment or a placebo. This is meant to deal with the beneficial effects of a patient simply believing that they are, or might be, receiving a genuine therapy designed to make them better. Indeed the placebo affect can influence the interpretation of trial outcomes, so a lot of clinical trials take place 'double blind' so that the researcher does not know which control groups are which. The use of placebo drugs has been well established over many years as a good research tool, but, of course, other treatments might be subject to placebo use. There are instances of research being carried out involving placebo surgery, where the patient undergoes some form of surgical intervention (cutting open the body and suturing it without doing anything further, for example). The ethical issue with the use of placebo drugs is that the patient might benefit from an active drug, but at least the placebo is not actively harmful. In surgery (even under local anaesthetic only) there is a form of harm taking place.

As Sarah Hewlett notes, from the point of view of participants in clinical trials, a measure of inconvenience and, indeed, risk will be entailed:

Hewlett, S, 'Consent to clinical research – adequately voluntary or substantially influenced?'[6]

The scientific gold standard for clinical research is the randomised controlled trial (RCT) which attempts to establish statistically the risk-benefit ratio of the drug by reducing bias and controlling for variables. This it does by controlling the selection of well characterised groups of patients, randomising them into treatment groups, using standardised outcome measurements performed by blinded assessors, and stipulating

---

5 Amsterdam: North-Holland Publishing, 1974.
6 22 JME 232.

a population size powerful enough to answer the question being asked. Although not without criticisms the RCT is a credible test of safety and efficacy within the medical world and some would say it would be unethical to introduce a new drug without RCT data.

Patients participating in an RCT will usually need to attend hospital regularly for safety and efficacy assessments ... Such visits may take several hours and their frequency varies from every few days to every month, as does the duration of the RCT (from a few days to several years). Neither the safety nor the efficacy of the drug is yet proven and in addition the patient may receive a placebo during the course of the study. When taken together these are not inconsiderable inconveniences for the patient and although hopefully kept to minimum impact, there is sometimes an element of risk.

It should also be noted that clinical trials do not necessarily involve the use of placebos as a standard treatment might be being compared with the trial drug where the standard treatment is inadequate in some way.

THINK POINT

Is there something inherently unethical about the use of placebos?

Concern has been expressed about patient understanding of RCTs:

Ames, J and Thurston, M, 'Trials and treatments: some reflections on informed consent and the role of research ethics committees'[7]

Key features of the methodology of RCTs are:

- There is uncertainty about which of two, or more treatments is most effective in treating a particular condition, a circumstance likely to occur when at least one of the treatments is new or has been amended in some way;
- The trial is designed to discover which of the treatments in the trial is most effective;
- The method of allocating patients to one of the treatments is based on randomization, rather that clinical judgement.

Patients who have participated in RCTs, however, have produced somewhat different accounts of their methodology.

...

The authors of an influential study (Snowden C, Garcia J, Elbourne D. Making sense of randomization: responses of parents of critically ill babies to random allocation of treatment in a clinical trial. Soc Sci Med 1997; 45(9): 1337–1355) identified four areas where the accounts of 37 parents, who had consented to their seriously-ill babies participating in a neonatal RCT, differed from the rationale for RCTs outlined above.

Firstly, the word trial was portrayed by some parents to refer to a treatment that was being tried-out. Opportunities for the treatment to be tried out were stated by some to be limited and, hence, randomization was used in order to decide which babies would receive the treatment. In these accounts, the term 'trial' was employed as a synonym for 'treatment'. Secondly, some parents expressed the belief that their babies were being chosen for a treatment, rather than for inclusion in a trial comparing two treatments. The

---

7 4(3) Research Ethics Review 95–100.

issue for them was whether their baby would be selected as suitable for the specified treatment. Thirdly, some parents said that they knew that the experimental treatment was available in other countries and, hence, their accounts did not display an understanding of the principle of uncertainty surrounding the two treatments in the trial. Fourthly, for parents whose child was not responding to the standard treatment, the authors argued that the hope afforded by the experimental treatment made it desirable for its own sake. To be included in the trial, yet randomized out of receiving the experimental treatment, was described as difficult for these parents . . .

Parents' reported expectations were that clinicians would offer the best treatment suitable for their baby. This was inaccurate in the context of a randomized controlled trial.

Research proposals can be quite complex, particularly with regard to justifying the research methodology and providing suitable statistical analysis. The question arises as to how far the scientific validity of the research can be challenged. In this chapter we are concerned with the regulation of research from the point of view of ethics. The questions that are important for people carrying out an ethical review of scientific projects normally relate to such things as fully informed consent, the level of risk to the participants that is acceptable, the amount of protection afforded to the identities and personal information of the participants. The question of whether the science makes it a worthwhile project in the first place is outside the remit of ethical review, except in cases where the science is so flawed the project will be a waste of the time of participants, or where there is another way of achieving the same results without the level of risk and/or intrusion involved in the proposal under consideration.

THINK POINT

Do you think that people should be paid to take part in medical research?

10.1.4 Therapeutic and non-therapeutic research

The distinction between therapeutic and non-therapeutic research is central to any discussion of the ethical and legal issues surrounding medical research. This does not go to the methodology of the research process (RCTs may equally be used for both), but derives from the two main classes of research subject on whom research may be carried out, and to what end. Both, of course, must be contrasted with experimental treatment or innovative therapy, as discussed above. Despite this well-used distinction, there are circumstances in which 'therapeutic' can mean benefit to patients in general rather than the individual.

10.1.4.1 Therapeutic

This type of research is defined as that which is carried out on patients with the direct potential for beneficial results in respect of their illness. The researcher (who is in a doctor–patient relationship with the subject) will commonly be attempting to establish whether a new treatment is more effective than existing therapy that is available for that condition. It is significant here that the doctor/researcher has what is termed a 'dual intention': he desires both the attainment of new knowledge *and* benefits for the individual patient/subject, although, as far as the latter is concerned, in many cases it might be more accurate to say that the benefit might be for patients suffering from that condition as a whole.

10.1.4.2 Non-therapeutic

In contrast to the therapeutic form, non-therapeutic research denotes that which is carried out on volunteers (either drawn from the public or, perhaps, those hospitalised with unrelated conditions) and offers no hope of benefiting them personally. It often takes place in relation to new drug treatments in order to establish toxicity levels or any side effects. Here, the researcher is in the position of scientist alone: he does not owe duties to the research subject *qua* patient, and intends only the gaining of knowledge.

Although these two categories may admit of some blurring, they have been recognised for legal and ethical purposes as distinct and are addressed separately in Codes such as the Declaration of Helsinki.

Non-therapeutic research can take place in the context of all forms of medical treatments, but it is in the field of clinical drug trials that the most risk lies and which can give rise to considerable controversy. Trials of new drugs are divided into a number of phases. Prior to human testing, drugs are tested on animals to ascertain minimum safety levels. Although this gives rise to considerable emotional responses and protestation, this chapter is not concerned with non-human aspects of research. The first phase for our purposes is the 'first in human' phase, where the new drug is tested on healthy volunteers. This phase of a clinical trial has been highlighted in the UK by the tragic events that occurred at Northwick Park Hospital, London, in 2006. The drug concerned, TGN1412, was an anti-inflammatory drug developed at a German university, which had set up a biotechnology company, TeGenero, to develop it, and this company contracted with Parexel to conduct the clinical trial on this drug in the UK. Parexel carries out a number of functions with regard to servicing the pharmaceutical industry. This structure is described in detail because TeGenero subsequently became insolvent. Questions arise as to liability and ability to pay compensation for injury, and this will be discussed further at 10.5 below.

As a result of their participation in this trial six young men suffered serious adverse reactions to the drug, which resulted in multiple organ failure. Five of them were able to be discharged from hospital after two months, but the sixth suffered pneumonia and septicaemia, as well as organ failure. One of the volunteers had several toes and fingers amputated as a result of gangrene. It was, in short, a catastrophe, and they commenced proceedings against Parexel for compensation.

Prior to this trial Pamela Ferguson had carried out research to try and ascertain the motivations of healthy volunteers who participate in such trials. She obtained data from 65 volunteers and the seven potential motivations specified were: that it was 'something to do'; curiosity; helping others; a way to obtain health checks; the social contact involved; being part of a team; and financial reasons. On this last reason, Ferguson comments as follows:

Ferguson, Pamela R, 'Clinical trials and healthy volunteers'[8]

Twenty years ago, the [Royal College of Physicians] warned that financial incentives 'may overpersuade individuals, including students, who have low incomes, and may promote the "professional volunteer"'. Several newspaper reports of the TGN1412 trial emphasised that the men were to be paid £2,000 for their participation, and that some people were able to earn £13,000 a year by volunteering for drug studies. One author has warned of the dangers of 'inappropriate rewards or inducements', concluding: 'It may be very difficult for the poor . . . to say no to a risky project if they are offered valuable commodities in exchange for participating'. As Table 2 shows, money was indeed the main motivating factor in the Tayside study, with 80% of volunteers regarding 'financial reasons' as relevant (35%) or highly relevant (45%). One might have expected that the percentage of volunteers who regarded payment as irrelevant to be very low, yet almost one-fifth of participants claimed that the money they would be paid was of no relevance in their

---

8 Spring Med L Rev, 16m.

decision to take part. Some of these volunteers claimed that they were unaware of the amount of their fee, or indeed that any payment was involved.

. . . In the Tayside study, the fees ranged from £185/£200 to £650/£750. Interestingly, four volunteers mis-stated the amount they were to be paid: one of those in a trial with a fee of £200 stated that he believed that he would be paid £100, and another in the same trial thought he would be paid only £50. A participant who was to be paid £375 thought she would be given £350, whereas another thought the fee was £400 when it was actually £750. . . . Somewhat surprisingly, three of these had rated financial reasons as a 'highly relevant' motivation. Participants were asked to state whether they thought the fee they were getting was 'a reasonable amount', 'too much' or 'too little' . . . the majority (77%) thought that the fee they were to be paid was a reasonable one, 12% thought that it was too little and 6% thought that they were being paid too much money.

10.1.5 The concept of risk

As already mentioned, medical research, at least where its focus is on invasive forms of therapy, exposes the human research subject to a degree of *additional* risk. Additional, that is to say, to the risks attendant upon receiving treatment where no research is being carried out. Why is this, and what meaning may be ascribed to the concept of risk itself, in this context?

We may begin by recognising that there is always a residual uncertainty, when carrying out any invasive medical procedure, as to whether the patient may in fact be harmed in the process. Given the complexity of each individual human metabolism, we can never be 100 per cent sure in advance that a particular drug will not react with some feature (perhaps of a highly idiosyncratic order) in that metabolism, perhaps with disastrous consequences. Nevertheless, the more often we give the treatment in question, the better the picture we build up of the drug's causal properties, including any such propensity to do harm, and, if so, with what frequency and magnitude.

Clearly, in the case of research involving novel treatment, we will lack this (relative) certainty: the very fact that a particular treatment is untried means that we have no databank of experience as to how the treatment in question has acted upon patients in the past. Although, by the very nature of things, the precise degree of risk presented to a research subject through their participation is thus difficult to quantify, the following rough categories have been proposed:

Nicholson, RH (ed), *Medical Research with Children: Ethics, Law and Practice*[9]

Table 5.6 Risk equivalents

British definition	Negligible	Minimal	More than minimal
American definition	Minimal	Minor increase over minimal	Greater than minor increase over minimal
Risk of death	Less than 1 per million	1 to 100 per million	Greater than 100 per million
Risk of major complication	Fewer than 10 per million	10 to 1,000 per million	Greater than 1,000 per million
Risk of minor complication	Less than 1 per thousand	1 to 100 per thousand	Greater than 100 per thousand

Despite their tentative character, as we shall see, these categories are often considered ethically significant in furnishing acceptable parameters within which research may take place.

9 Oxford: OUP, 1986.

10.2 The ethics of good research practice

10.2.1 Human rights

Although, as we have seen, nearly all medical research involves some extra degree of risk to the research subject, without it medical science would be unable to progress properly. This raises a classic dilemma (similar to that in relation to the use of body tissue and organs from live donors): under what conditions and to what extent is it permissible to treat a person (the research subject) as a means to an end (here, greater medical knowledge)?

The need for some form of response, at an international level, to this question became dramatically apparent in the wake of the Second World War when, at the Nuremberg Trials, Nazi doctors were revealed to have performed a catalogue of horrific medical experiments on inmates of concentration camps, causing terrible suffering and death.

In the course of their judgment, the judges at Nuremberg articulated a set of parameters within which they felt research might acceptably take place. This has become known as the Nuremberg Code. This was followed, in 1964, by the World Medical Association's Declaration of Helsinki, which deals with the issues in a lengthier and more systematic fashion. As will be seen, the Declaration consists of a preamble followed by two parts: Part B sets out basic principles which apply to all forms of medical research and Part C applies specifically to medical research combined with medical care, that is therapeutic research. Three themes dominate: the research must be scientifically sound, it must satisfy the proportionality test (that is, risks to the subject should be commensurate with the expected benefits of carrying the research out), and there must be the greatest possible respect at all times for the integrity of the research subject:

Declaration of Helsinki (1964) (as amended – most recently in October 2013 at the 64th Assembly of the World Medical Association in Brazil)

Preamble

1   The World Medical Association (WMA) has developed the Declaration of Helsinki as a statement of ethical principles for medical research involving human subjects, including research on identifiable human material and data.
   The Declaration is intended to be read as a whole and each of its constituent paragraphs should be applied with consideration of all other relevant paragraphs.
2   Consistent with the mandate of the WMA, the Declaration is addressed primarily to physicians. The WMA encourages others who are involved in medical research involving human subjects to adopt these principles.

General Principles

3   The Declaration of Geneva of the WMA binds the physician with the words, 'The health of my patient will be my first consideration,' and the International Code of Medical Ethics declares that, 'A physician shall act in the patient's best interest when providing medical care.'
4   It is the duty of the physician to promote and safeguard the health, well-being and rights of patients, including those who are involved in medical research. The physician's knowledge and conscience are dedicated to the fulfilment of this duty.
5   Medical progress is based on research that ultimately must include studies involving human subjects.
6   The primary purpose of medical research involving human subjects is to understand the causes, development and effects of diseases and improve preventive, diagnostic and therapeutic interventions

(methods, procedures and treatments). Even the best proven interventions must be evaluated continually through research for their safety, effectiveness, efficiency, accessibility and quality.

7   Medical research is subject to ethical standards that promote and ensure respect for all human subjects and protect their health and rights.

8   While the primary purpose of medical research is to generate new knowledge, this goal can never take precedence over the rights and interests of individual research subjects.

9   It is the duty of physicians who are involved in medical research to protect the life, health, dignity, integrity, right to self-determination, privacy, and confidentiality of personal information of research subjects. The responsibility for the protection of research subjects must always rest with the physician or other healthcare professionals and never with the research subjects, even though they have given consent.

10   Physicians must consider the ethical, legal and regulatory norms and standards for research involving human subjects in their own countries as well as applicable international norms and standards. No national or international ethical, legal or regulatory requirement should reduce or eliminate any of the protections for research subjects set forth in this Declaration.

11   Medical research should be conducted in a manner that minimises possible harm to the environment.

12   Medical research involving human subjects must be conducted only by individuals with the appropriate ethics and scientific education, training and qualifications. Research on patients or healthy volunteers requires the supervision of a competent and appropriately qualified physician or other healthcare professional.

13   Groups that are underrepresented in medical research should be provided appropriate access to participation in research.

14   Physicians who combine medical research with medical care should involve their patients in research only to the extent that this is justified by its potential preventive, diagnostic or therapeutic value and if the physician has good reason to believe that participation in the research study will not adversely affect the health of the patients who serve as research subjects.

15   Appropriate compensation and treatment for subjects who are harmed as a result of participating in research must be ensured.

Risks, Burdens and Benefits

16   In medical practice and in medical research, most interventions involve risks and burdens.

     Medical research involving human subjects may only be conducted if the importance of the objective outweighs the risks and burdens to the research subjects.

17   All medical research involving human subjects must be preceded by careful assessment of predictable risks and burdens to the individuals and groups involved in the research in comparison with foreseeable benefits to them and to other individuals or groups affected by the condition under investigation.

     Measures to minimise the risks must be implemented. The risks must be continuously monitored, assessed and documented by the researcher.

18   Physicians may not be involved in a research study involving human subjects unless they are confident that the risks have been adequately assessed and can be satisfactorily managed.

     When the risks are found to outweigh the potential benefits or when there is conclusive proof of definitive outcomes, physicians must assess whether to continue, modify or immediately stop the study.

Vulnerable Groups and Individuals

19   Some groups and individuals are particularly vulnerable and may have an increased likelihood of being wronged or of incurring additional harm.

     All vulnerable groups and individuals should receive specifically considered protection.

20   Medical research with a vulnerable group is only justified if the research is responsive to the health needs or priorities of this group and the research cannot be carried out in a non-vulnerable group. In addition, this group should stand to benefit from the knowledge, practices or interventions that result from the research.

Scientific Requirements and Research Protocols

21   Medical research involving human subjects must conform to generally accepted scientific principles, be based on a thorough knowledge of the scientific literature, other relevant sources of information, and adequate laboratory and, as appropriate, animal experimentation. The welfare of animals used for research must be respected.

22   The design and performance of each research study involving human subjects must be clearly described and justified in a research protocol.

   The protocol should contain a statement of the ethical considerations involved and should indicate how the principles in this Declaration have been addressed. The protocol should include information regarding funding, sponsors, institutional affiliations, potential conflicts of interest, incentives for subjects and information regarding provisions for treating and/or compensating subjects who are harmed as a consequence of participation in the research study.

   In clinical trials, the protocol must also describe appropriate arrangements for post-trial provisions.

Research Ethics Committees

23   The research protocol must be submitted for consideration, comment, guidance and approval to the concerned research ethics committee before the study begins. This committee must be transparent in its functioning, must be independent of the researcher, the sponsor and any other undue influence and must be duly qualified. It must take into consideration the laws and regulations of the country or countries in which the research is to be performed as well as applicable international norms and standards but these must not be allowed to reduce or eliminate any of the protections for research subjects set forth in this Declaration.

   The committee must have the right to monitor ongoing studies. The researcher must provide monitoring information to the committee, especially information about any serious adverse events. No amendment to the protocol may be made without consideration and approval by the committee. After the end of the study, the researchers must submit a final report to the committee containing a summary of the study's findings and conclusions.

Privacy and Confidentiality

24   Every precaution must be taken to protect the privacy of research subjects and the confidentiality of their personal information.

Informed Consent

25   Participation by individuals capable of giving informed consent as subjects in medical research must be voluntary. Although it may be appropriate to consult family members or community leaders, no individual capable of giving informed consent may be enrolled in a research study unless he or she freely agrees.

26   In medical research involving human subjects capable of giving informed consent, each potential subject must be adequately informed of the aims, methods, sources of funding, any possible conflicts of interest, institutional affiliations of the researcher, the anticipated benefits and potential risks of the study and the discomfort it may entail, post-study provisions and any other relevant aspects of the study. The potential subject must be informed of the right to refuse to participate in the study or to

withdraw consent to participate at any time without reprisal. Special attention should be given to the specific information needs of individual potential subjects as well as to the methods used to deliver the information.

After ensuring that the potential subject has understood the information, the physician or another appropriately qualified individual must then seek the potential subject's freely given informed consent, preferably in writing. If the consent cannot be expressed in writing, the non-written consent must be formally documented and witnessed.

All medical research subjects should be given the option of being informed about the general outcome and results of the study.

27 When seeking informed consent for participation in a research study the physician must be particularly cautious if the potential subject is in a dependent relationship with the physician or may consent under duress. In such situations the informed consent must be sought by an appropriately qualified individual who is completely independent of this relationship.

28 For a potential research subject who is incapable of giving informed consent, the physician must seek informed consent from the legally authorised representative. These individuals must not be included in a research study that has no likelihood of benefit for them unless it is intended to promote the health of the group represented by the potential subject, the research cannot instead be performed with persons capable of providing informed consent, and the research entails only minimal risk and minimal burden.

29 When a potential research subject who is deemed incapable of giving informed consent is able to give assent to decisions about participation in research, the physician must seek that assent in addition to the consent of the legally authorised representative. The potential subject's dissent should be respected.

30 Research involving subjects who are physically or mentally incapable of giving consent, for example, unconscious patients, may be done only if the physical or mental condition that prevents giving informed consent is a necessary characteristic of the research group. In such circumstances the physician must seek informed consent from the legally authorised representative. If no such representative is available and if the research cannot be delayed, the study may proceed without informed consent provided that the specific reasons for involving subjects with a condition that renders them unable to give informed consent have been stated in the research protocol and the study has been approved by a research ethics committee. Consent to remain in the research must be obtained as soon as possible from the subject or a legally authorised representative.

31 The physician must fully inform the patient which aspects of their care are related to the research. The refusal of a patient to participate in a study or the patient's decision to withdraw from the study must never adversely affect the patient-physician relationship.

32 For medical research using identifiable human material or data, such as research on material or data contained in biobanks or similar repositories, physicians must seek informed consent for its collection, storage and/or reuse. There may be exceptional situations where consent would be impossible or impracticable to obtain for such research. In such situations the research may be done only after consideration and approval of a research ethics committee.

Use of Placebo

33 The benefits, risks, burdens and effectiveness of a new intervention must be tested against those of the best proven intervention(s), except in the following circumstances:

Where no proven intervention exists, the use of placebo, or no intervention, is acceptable; or

Where for compelling and scientifically sound methodological reasons the use of any intervention less effective than the best proven one, the use of placebo, or no intervention is necessary to determine the efficacy or safety of an intervention and the patients who receive any intervention less effective than the best proven one, placebo, or no intervention will not be subject to additional risks of serious or irreversible harm as a result of not receiving the best proven intervention.

Extreme care must be taken to avoid abuse of this option.

Post-Trial Provisions

34   In advance of a clinical trial, sponsors, researchers and host country governments should make provisions for post-trial access for all participants who still need an intervention identified as beneficial in the trial. This information must also be disclosed to participants during the informed consent process.

Research Registration and Publication and Dissemination of Results

35   Every research study involving human subjects must be registered in a publicly accessible database before recruitment of the first subject.

36   Researchers, authors, sponsors, editors and publishers all have ethical obligations with regard to the publication and dissemination of the results of research. Researchers have a duty to make publicly available the results of their research on human subjects and are accountable for the completeness and accuracy of their reports. All parties should adhere to accepted guidelines for ethical reporting. Negative and inconclusive as well as positive results must be published or otherwise made publicly available. Sources of funding, institutional affiliations and conflicts of interest must be declared in the publication. Reports of research not in accordance with the principles of this Declaration should not be accepted for publication.

Unproven Interventions in Clinical Practice

37   In the treatment of an individual patient, where proven interventions do not exist or other known interventions have been ineffective, the physician, after seeking expert advice, with informed consent from the patient or a legally authorised representative, may use an unproven intervention if in the physician's judgement it offers hope of saving life, re-establishing health or alleviating suffering. This intervention should subsequently be made the object of research, designed to evaluate its safety and efficacy. In all cases, new information must be recorded and, where appropriate, made publicly available.

Comment should be made on para 2 of this latest version of the Helsinki Declaration that recognises the fact that, although the primary concern of the World Medical Association is the behaviour of doctors, medical research involves people from many other disciplines, and that these principles also apply to them. The Declaration has acted as a template for the various domestic codes, which have subsequently been drafted in respect of particular areas of research practice worldwide. In Europe the Convention on Human Rights and Biomedicine (CHRB) (note that the UK is not a signatory to this at the moment), drawn up by the Council of Europe, states the following on the subject of scientific research:

Comment should be made on para 2 of this latest version of the Helsinki Declaration that recognises the fact that although the primary concern of the World Medical Association is the behaviour of doctors, medical research involves people from many other disciplines, and that these principles also apply to them. The Declaration has acted as a template for the various domestic codes, which have subsequently been drafted in respect of particular areas of research practice worldwide. In Europe the Convention on Human Rights and Biomedicine (CHRB) (note that the UK is not a signatory to this at the moment), drawn up by the Council of Europe, states the following on the subject of scientific research:

**Convention for the Protection of Human Rights and Dignity of the
Human Being with regard to the Application of Biology: Convention
on Human Rights and Biomedicine (Council of Europe, 1997):
Chapter V – Scientific research**

Article 15 – General rule

Scientific research in the field of biology and medicine shall be carried out freely, subject to the provisions of this Convention and the other legal provisions ensuring the protection of the human being.

Article 16 – Protection of persons undergoing research

Research on a person may only be undertaken if all the following conditions are met:

i   there is no alternative of comparable effectiveness to research on humans;

ii   the risks which may be incurred by that person are not disproportionate to the potential benefits of the research;

iii   the research project has been approved by the competent body after independent examination of its scientific merit, including assessment of the importance of the aim of the research, and multidisciplinary review of its ethical acceptability,

iv   the persons undergoing research have been informed of their rights and the safeguards prescribed by law for their protection;

v   the necessary consent as provided for under Article 5 has been given expressly, specifically and is documented. Such consent may be freely withdrawn at any time.

Article 17 – Protection of persons not able to consent to research

1   Research on a person without the capacity to consent as stipulated in Article 5 may be undertaken only if all the following conditions are met:

    i   the conditions laid down in Article 16, sub-paragraphs i to iv, are fulfilled;

    ii   the results of the research have the potential to produce real and direct benefit to his or her health;

    iii   research of comparable effectiveness cannot be carried out on individuals capable of giving consent;

    iv   the necessary authorisation provided for under Article 6 has been given specifically and in writing; and

    v   the person concerned does not object.

2   Exceptionally and under the protective conditions prescribed by law, where the research has not the potential to produce results of direct benefit to the health of the person concerned, such research may be authorised subject to the conditions laid down in paragraph 1, sub-paragraphs i, iii, iv and v above, and to the following additional conditions:

    i   the research has the aim of contributing, through significant improvement in the scientific understanding of the individual's condition, disease or disorder, to the ultimate attainment of results capable of conferring benefit to the person concerned or to other persons in the same age category or afflicted with the same disease or disorder or having the same condition;

    ii   the research entails only minimal risk and minimal burden for the individual concerned.

Article 18 – Research on embryos *in vitro*

1   Where the law allows research on embryos *in vitro*, it shall ensure adequate protection of the embryo.

2   The creation of human embryos for research purposes is prohibited.

10.2.2 The duty of doctor/researcher

Our concern in this section is the duties of an *ethical* nature that the doctor/researcher may be held to owe to the research subject. In accordance with the central distinction, outlined above, between therapeutic and non-therapeutic research, we shall deal separately with the duties which exist in each case.

10.2.2.1 Duties to patients

Can therapeutic research, and the additional risks it entails, be reconciled (and, if so, how far) with the doctor's pledge under the Hippocratic Oath to do the best for each of his patients? In itself, this question admits of an affirmative answer: the higher risks can be balanced against the hope that a new therapy will bring increased benefits for the patients so treated. However, matters are complicated by the use, in randomised control trials, of randomisation to determine the treatment given to each patient. For here it might well be argued that the doctor has abdicated his duty to tailor the treatment he provides to the latter's individual needs. The question of how far the patient's fully informed consent could provide a justification is analysed by Charles Fried:

Fried, C, *Medical Experimentation: Personal Integrity and Social Policy*[10]

> Should [the patient] be told that he is receiving that therapy which in the judgment of his physicians is the best available in his case, or should he be told more fully that his therapy is being determined by some randomising device in furtherance of a medical experiment? In the case where the choice between the two treatments is not in equipoise, the failure to disclose the existence of the RCT adds insult to injury since it plainly withholds information which any patient should find relevant and indeed the basis for considering a change of doctors. The non-disclosure is deceptive because it fails to reveal that the patient's interests are, to some extent, being sacrificed for the sake of the experimental design and thus, the wider social good. That sacrifice might be the overt one of exposing the patient to the risk of a treatment which in the present state of knowledge is somewhat less favoured, or the less overt one of not inquiring fully into his particular circumstances (including his particular value system) in order to determine whether the balance of probabilities is in equipoise in his particular case. There are two justifications for non-disclosure frequently offered: (1) that the distress this would cause the patient would be therapeutically undesirable; and (2) that the disclosure would endanger the experiment by introducing a disturbing element or even by causing the patient to withhold his consent. Both justifications are inadequate to show that non-disclosure does not sacrifice some interest of the subject. Both justifications beg this question, since they assume that the choice by randomisation is proper, and thus they assume that limiting disclosure in order to facilitate this kind of experimentation is proper.

However, Fried does not acknowledge that it is in the interests of the researcher to tell the patient that the trial is 'blind', because knowledge of the treatment arm into which the patient has been placed can influence the outcome of the trial itself. Furthermore, as already noted, a lot of trials are 'double blind', in the sense that neither researcher nor patient has this knowledge.

10.2.2.2 Duties to volunteers

As previously noted, the researcher who carries out non-therapeutic research on volunteers has no doctor–patient relationship with his subject. Nevertheless, this does not entail the absence of ethical duties on his part towards the latter. In some ways, indeed, it may heighten the ethical obligation.

---

10 Amsterdam: North-Holland Publishing, 1974.

Exceptionally a doctor may rely on the doctrine of 'therapeutic privilege'[11] to avoid informing a patient of his participation in therapeutic research; no such argument is admissible in relation to volunteers.

10.3 Consent to research

Whereas research upon embryos may only be carried out under licence pursuant to the Human Fertilisation and Embryology Act 1990,[12] and that upon animals is regulated by the Animals (Scientific Procedures) Act 1968, there are no similar statutory safeguards operative in respect of research upon (full) human beings. Perhaps the major reason for this is that the human research subject is thought able to protect himself adequately against abuse by the researcher through the mechanism of consent at common law. How far is this really so? Although we have examined consent to treatment in some detail,[13] medical research gives rise to some special considerations. For example, in relation to general treatment, consent may sometimes simply be inferred from the surrounding circumstances, as when a patient submits to a medical examination. In the context of therapeutic research, the additional (and cloaked) intention of the doctor/researcher means that the subject's consent cannot be so inferred.

It will be recalled that the three elements to a valid consent are capacity, voluntariness and information, and each will be examined in relation to therapeutic and non-therapeutic research, respectively.

10.3.1 Therapeutic research

10.3.1.1 The competent patient

The first issue here is to determine whether the subject has genuine capacity to consent. In this regard, could it be argued that the latter must possess a more sophisticated understanding than someone who is receiving 'ordinary' medical treatment? In one sense, the answer is 'yes', because the issues in a research project may be quite complex, but there is no real difference of criteria. Consent to general treatment requires an ability to understand the nature of the treatment and this general principle applies equally to therapeutic research.

More problematic, however, may be the requirement for such consent to be free from coercion. This is because there is a danger that pressure (real or perceived) may be placed upon a patient to agree to participate in a clinical trial for fear of not receiving the best treatment in the face of a refusal. Sarah Hewlett comments on this problem as follows:

Hewlett, S, 'Consent to clinical research – adequately voluntary or substantially influenced?'[14]

Influences or controlling influences?

So strong is [the trust in doctors] that patients may agree to anything the doctor suggests and even the invitation to participate may be viewed as a recommendation rather than a request. Patients may feel flattered by the request and under an obligation to help because of past care received.

For many patients the relationship is an unequal one, with the doctor being perceived as a powerful figure on whom they depend, making it difficult for them to take an unnaturally dominant role and refuse

---

11 See Ch 3, above.
12 See Ch 7, above.
13 See Ch 3, above.
14 22 JME 232.

the doctor's request. Patients may fear that if they do so, the doctor will be displeased and their future care will be jeopardised. Patients may view clinical research as a means of access to care (which may be true for patients in countries where many people do not have healthcare insurance) and may also equate the frequent safety visits with improved care.

She suggests that one way of dealing with this is to introduce a system of patient advocates, funded by the NHS and trained and supervised by research ethics committees. The problem with this is the cost of such an exercise. In particular, members of research ethics committees are not paid, and to give them the additional responsibility of training and supervising patient advocates would bring a call for payment and have an adverse effect on recruitment of members of such committees.

The Royal College of Physicians confirms in its Guidance[15] that patients must feel free to decline to participate and assured that the refusal will not put them at a disadvantage (paras 7.4 et seq). Note, below, the provisions of s 33 of the Mental Capacity Act 2005 which reflect this, as do the Medicines for Human Use (Clinical Trials) Regulations 2004.

There is concern that certain groups in particular may be vulnerable to exploitation in the field of research. It will be recalled that this was examined in Chapter 3, above.[16] In relation to prisoners, Mason and McCall Smith comment as follows:

Mason, JK and McCall Smith, RA, *Law and Medical Ethics*[17]

[T]he use of prisoners exposes many ethical issues essentially based on the arguments that some advantage, even if only imagined, must accrue to the prisoner participating in a trial; that advantage may be so great as to induce the prisoner to volunteer for research which involves greater discomfort or risk than would be accepted by a free man and, in particular, it may compromise his inalienable right to withdraw from the experiment. The arguments are not, however, entirely one way – it is possible to be paternalistic in an attempt to preserve people's autonomy. Thus, prisoners could well resent protective attitudes on the grounds that it is their right to dispose of their bodies and to take such risks as they please that is being compromised. This could be the subject of lengthy debate, but we would suggest that the conditions in today's prisons are such that any process which provides some relief deserves, at least, a sympathetic evaluation and, secondly, that many prisoners might be therapeutically benefited through helping society. But it is also felt that experiments on prisoners should be particularly rigidly controlled by ethical committees which should always contain lay members with experience in criminology.

However, given the concerns we address later about the lack of sanctions given to ethics committees, it may be doubted as to whether they really can 'rigidly control' such a situation. The Declaration of Helsinki at para 17 states that research involving a disadvantaged or vulnerable population can only be justified if it is responsive to the health needs of that particular population.

A further major issue in respect of therapeutic research carried out upon competent patients concerns the amount of information to which they are legally entitled. We have seen that a battery will be committed if the patient is not informed of the broad nature of an intended medical procedure. Kennedy and Grubb comment as follows:

---

15 *Research Involving Patients*, London: RCP, 1990.
16 See the cases of *Freeman v Home Office* [1984] 1 All ER 1036 and *Kaimowitz v Michigan Department of Mental Health* 42 USLW 2063 (1973).
17 London: Butterworths, 3rd edn, 1991.

Kennedy, I and Grubb, A, *Medical Law*[18]

One view, and it is ours, is that where there is a dual intention on the part of the doctor, ie, to treat and to conduct research, any failure to inform the patient concerning *both* of these intentions and their possible consequences would amount in law to a battery. This is because in the absence of such knowledge the patient will have assented to a procedure which is materially different in its nature from that which the doctor intends to carry out. To put it another way, research adds a further component to the quality of the consent that the law requires.

... A court may insist on the patient being informed of three particular matters in addition to this generalised intention. Each of them is an aspect of those interests of the patient which the law of battery seeks to protect. The patient must be informed: (1) that he may refuse to take part in the research project or may at any time withdraw from the research and that in either case if he does so he will suffer no adverse consequences in terms of the treatment he will then receive; (2) that the nature of the research may be such that he may be a member of a control group in a trial which is intended to evaluate the efficacy of a new therapy; (3) that the trial is a randomised controlled trial (RCT) if it be such.

As regards (2), one consequence of being a member of a control group could be that the patient does not receive the form of treatment which subsequently proves to be the more efficacious. To meet this ethical difficulty researchers ordinarily would be expected to provide for periodic examination of the emerging data. It is our view that a patient's consent is not informed for the purpose of the tort of battery unless he is made aware of this periodic review.

As regards (3), randomisation means that a treatment regime is assigned to a patient randomly without regard to the particular circumstances of that patient, his needs, his preferences or the preferences of his doctor. Again, it is our view that a patient may volunteer for such a trial but his consent is only valid if he is given the opportunity of knowing it is randomised and he is aware of what this means.

As redrafted over the years, the Declaration of Helsinki has placed greater emphasis upon informed consent (see paras 24–26, 34) than it did in the 1964 version which provided for circumstances in which the physician might consider it essential not to obtain informed consent (para II (5)), but even so the 2008 version does not expressly refer to disclosure of the precise nature and use of an RCT. There could be circumstances in which therapeutic privilege could be used to avoid giving full details to patients of the precise nature of the trial. However, as Kennedy and Grubb point out, if the patient would be caused distress by the knowledge that he is in a clinical trial, this is an argument for excluding him from the trial, not for including him without his knowledge. As yet, however, the position has not been tested in the courts. The cases of *Sidaway v Board of Governors of the Bethlem Royal Hospital and the Maudsley Hospital*[19] and *Chester v Afshar*[20] are pertinent here. As we have seen in Chapter 3, *Chester* confirmed that the patient has a right to be informed of any risks that would have affected the decision of the reasonable patient in his/her circumstances. The same conclusion must be drawn, even more forcibly, in a case where there is an objective (here, research) other than the well-being of the patient. However, even in *Chester* it was acknowledged that there could be circumstances where therapeutic privilege might apply, and in *Sidaway* Lord Scarman had stated the same thing. In the USA, where there is Federal law that regulates medical research, the doctrine of therapeutic privilege is acknowledged.[21] Given that, at least in part, the purpose of therapeutic research is to offer some benefit to the patient, is it not inevitable that something akin to therapeutic privilege will exist?

---

18 London: Butterworths, 3rd edn, 2000.
19 [1985] AC 871.
20 [2004] UKHL 41.
21 See Myers, D, *The Human Body and the Law: A Medico-Legal Study*, Edinburgh: Edinburgh UP, 1990.

A report from Peter Hamilton, the Sheriff in Aberdeen, however, highlights a case, where the patient had been positively misled:

Hamilton, P (Sheriff), 'Sheriff's Report, Aberdeen'[22]

28 January 1997

In 1993, while recovering from a fractured hip, Mrs Phyllis Moffit was recruited into a clinical trial after receiving the following revised patient information sheet:

Dear...

We are asking patients who have had a hip fracture in the past if they will take part in a research project. The aim is to try to prevent their unaffected hip from breaking at a later date.

In order to do this, we would like to have the opportunity to inject your unaffected hip (the one you have not broken) with a material which we think would actually strengthen the bone. It is composed of crystals of calcium, very like bone, and a protein which is known to stimulate bone growth.

We know there is a one in five chance that you might break the other hip within four years, and therefore there would be great benefits if the injection were to be successful. We are not aware of any significant risks associated with this injection.

If you agree to this injection, you will be admitted to Woodend Hospital. It will be done under a local anaesthetic in the operating theatre. It will involve having a small cut (about half an inch) made in your unaffected hip and the material being injected into your hip bone. This is not a painful procedure and should not inconvenience or incapacitate you in any way. This will not affect your mobility...

Mrs Moffit died in August 1994 of heart failure while under sedation for the experimental hip surgery. The heart failure was caused by an unsuspected aneurysm of the coronary artery. In this case, the statistic quoted in the information sheet as to the likelihood of a second hip fracture was based upon inconclusive evidence and had indeed been changed from an earlier sheet in which the chance was described as 'one in 10 over two years'. The victim's daughter gave evidence that the alarm her mother had felt on reading this was the chief reason she had agreed to participate in the research. Moreover, the research proposal approved by the local research ethics committee (LREC) had not mentioned the need for sedation of subjects as initially it had not been thought that the procedure would be painful. While the researchers had become aware that this would in fact be required some time prior to recruiting Mrs Moffit, they failed either to amend the information sheet or to inform the LREC. Finally, although the patient here was recovering from a fractured hip, it may be queried whether this was really *therapeutic* research at all.

10.3.1.2 The incapable patient

Both the Declaration of Helsinki and the European Convention on Human Rights permit a limited amount of research on those patients who are not capable of giving a valid consent.[23] Some would argue that this is ethically unacceptable, on the basis that without consent the incapable are being used as a means to the ends of others unless there are direct benefits to the incapable patient. Garwood-Gowers uses a 'slippery slope' argument.

---

22 Bulletin of Medical Ethics 22.
23 See principles 24–26 above, at 10.2.1.

**Garwood-Gowers, A, 'Vindicating the right to bodily security
of the incapable in research' – Part 2**[24]

Of course it might in theory be possible to argue that if it is legitimate to trade off the right to bodily security vis-à-vis the needs of others in extreme circumstances then participation of incompetent adults in medical research is one such extreme circumstance. However, for common arguments to the effect that we need to dilute protection to make progress in relation to conditions like Alzheimer's disease, one could substitute the argument that we need to dilute protection of all classes of person to facilitate greater extraction of bodily material to help meet the need for transplantation and general biotechnological advancement. Or, more specifically, we could substitute the argument that we need to dilute protection of insensate dying persons to facilitate the need to prepare their body for use in transplantation, medical research or medical education after their death.

It is suggested that this argument breaks down in the way that all slippery slope arguments do by taking something that is fairly innocuous (such as allowing incapable adults who suffer from Alzheimer's disease to participate in a risk-free observation exercise), and concluding this will mean that society is, in consequence, incapable of preventing this leading to wholescale involuntary euthanasia and organ-harvesting. However, writers such as Garwood-Gowers might rightly argue that such an observation exercise, while not interfering with bodily integrity, is not innocuous, because it is a breach of privacy. As we have seen in Chapter 5, the legal right to privacy is subject to a number of wide exceptions, and this might well fall into the 'protection of health' exception, but there is still an argument that, from an ethical point of view, it is an unacceptable breach. It goes to whether one is prepared to use a consequentialist argument or not. Undoubtedly such an argument is powerful in the need to investigate serious illness such as Alzheimer's disease.

10.3.1.2.1 Children

Does s 8 of the Family Law Reform Act 1969[25] apply to research? The section refers to 'any surgical, medical or dental treatment', and it has been argued[26] that this does not cover treatment which includes a research component. This would mean that the age of 16 would have no significance as far as consent of the child is concerned, but presumably the concept of *Gillick* competence would apply. The guidelines issued by the professional bodies such as the Royal College of Paediatrics and the British Medical Association acknowledge that children can consent to *therapeutic* research. The European Directive on Clinical Trials[27] acknowledges the necessity of carrying out research on children, but only when the research in question cannot be carried out on adults. It is important to note that there is a real need for research on children, because even if a clinical trial has found a drug to be effective and safe in adults, it does not mean to say that it will be safe or efficacious in children. Frequently medicines are prescribed for children 'off label', which means that they have not been licensed for use in children. However, children are not just small adults; they have different physiological and psychological characteristics, and there are certain diseases that are specific to childhood.

In the House of Lords case of S v S[28] the court had to consider whether it was appropriate to order a blood test on a child for the purposes of establishing paternity when the mother of the child was refusing to consent. Lord Reid said that it was 'not against the interests of the child' for

---

24 J Mental Health L 17.
25 See Ch 3, above.
26 By, for example, Kennedy and Grubb in *Medical Law*, 3rd edn, London: Butterworths, 2000.
27 See below, at 10.4.
28 [1970] 3 All ER 107.

this to be done. The implication for therapeutic research appears to be that the therapeutic aspect of the treatment means that it would not be contrary to the child's interests. However, if we consider randomised control tests, where the child may be getting no treatment at all, and where the choice as to whether the child is treated is not made on clinical grounds, can it still be argued that this is not contrary to the interests of the child?

10.3.1.2.2 Incapable adults

As we have seen, until the enactment of the Mental Capacity Act 2005 there was no provision in English law for proxy decision-making in medical and personal welfare matters. However, the new legislation not only applies to bona fide medical treatment but also extends to providing for medical research to be carried out on incapable adults. The Law Commission had recommended that research on incapable adults should be permitted[29] but this recommendation was not followed up in the Mental Incapacity Bill. It was however taken up again when the Mental Capacity Bill was drafted following the pre-legislative scrutiny of the Joint Committee.[30]

Mental Capacity Act 2005

30   Research

1   Intrusive research carried out on, or in relation to, a person who lacks capacity to consent to it is unlawful unless it is carried out –

   a   as part of a research project which is for the time being approved by the appropriate body for the purposes of this Act in accordance with section 31, and

   b   in accordance with sections 32 and 33.

2   Research is intrusive if it is of a kind that would be unlawful if it was carried out –

   a   on or in relation to a person who had capacity to consent to it, but

   b   without his consent.

3   A clinical trial which is subject to the provisions of clinical trials regulations is not to be treated as research for the purposes of this section.

4   'Appropriate body', in relation to a research project, means the person, committee or other body specified in regulations made by the appropriate authority as the appropriate body in relation to a project of the kind in question.

5   'Clinical trials regulations' means –

   a   the Medicines for Human Use (Clinical Trials) Regulations 2004 (S.I. 2004/1031) and any other regulations replacing those regulations or amending them, and

   b   any other regulations relating to clinical trials and designated by the Secretary of State as clinical trials regulations for the purposes of this section.

6   In this section, section 32 and section 34, 'appropriate authority' means –

   a   in relation to the carrying out of research in England, the Secretary of State, and

   b   in relation to the carrying out of research in Wales, the National Assembly for Wales.

31   Requirements for approval

1   The appropriate body may not approve a research project for the purposes of this Act unless satisfied that the following requirements will be met in relation to research carried out as part of the project on, or in relation to, a person who lacks capacity to consent to taking part in the project ('P').

---

29 Law Commission Report 231 (1995).
30 Reports HL Paper 189-I & HC 1983-I.

2   The research must be connected with –

a   an impairing condition affecting P, or

b   its treatment.

3   'Impairing condition' means a condition which is (or may be) attributable to, or which causes or contributes to (or may cause or contribute to), the impairment of, or disturbance in the functioning of, the mind or brain.

4   There must be reasonable grounds for believing that research of comparable effectiveness cannot be carried out if the project has to be confined to, or relate only to, persons who have capacity to consent to taking part in it.

5   The research must –

a   have the potential to benefit P without imposing on P a burden that is disproportionate to the potential benefit to P, or

b   be intended to provide knowledge of the causes or treatment of, or of the care of persons affected by, the same or a similar condition.

6   If the research falls within paragraph (b) of subsection (5) but not within paragraph (a), there must be reasonable grounds for believing –

a   that the risk to P from taking part in the project is likely to be negligible, and

b   that anything done to, or in relation to, P will not –

i   interfere with P's freedom of action or privacy in a significant way, or

ii   be unduly invasive or restrictive.

7   There must be reasonable arrangements in place for ensuring that the requirements of sections 32 and 33 will be met.

Section 32 provides for consultation with carers.

The following are some observations on these provisions. First, it will be seen that 'intrusive' research is research that would constitute a battery if it were carried out without consent, so that mere observation of a mentally incapacitated person would not constitute intrusive research. Secondly, the Act does not apply to clinical trials as these are covered by the Medicines for Human Use (Clinical Trials) Regulations 2004 (see below). Secondly, the key provisions of s 31(1)–(4) should be carefully noted. The research must be connected with either an impairing condition which affects the incompetent patient, or its treatment, and the condition must be one which causes some impairment or functioning of the mind or brain. In other words, the research could not be on a physical condition that affects the patient, as such a physical condition might affect those who are competent to provide the necessary consent. Nevertheless although we are referring to patients here, there is no requirement that the 'patient' is 'suffering' or acutely ill, merely that they have an impairment, so it is not strictly speaking correct to think of them as 'patients'. Interestingly this neatly conflates the patient/healthy volunteer distinction, arguably to the detriment of the research subject, whether described as a patient or not.

Further, under s 31(5) the research must either have the potential to benefit the patient (without imposing a disproportion burden), or to be beneficial to other persons affected by the same or similar conditions. It is arguable that the second part of the justification is unethical as it means that research which is not of benefit to the incapable person can be carried out. However, this might be countered by s 31(6) which states that, in these circumstances, there must be reasonable grounds for believing that the risk is negligible and that it will not interfere with the patient's 'freedom of action or privacy in a significant way' or 'be unduly invasive or restrictive'. The key ethical point here is whether these provisions are sufficient to justify actions which might well constitute a battery upon a capable person who refused consent. For the protection of the patient it is important that s 31(6)(b) is construed so that both (i) and (ii) have to be satisfied and not be construed as justifiable alternatives. The explanatory notes to the Bill did indicate that the type of research typical to sub-s (6) might include indirect research on medical notes, or on human tissue already taken for other purposes, or may include interviews or questionnaires about health or social care with the patient or his carers or limited observation of him. This is interesting given the views expressed by the Law Commission, see 10.3.2.2.2 below, and the Commission's acknowledgement of the risk to the dignity and privacy of the research participant when they were incapable and the research was non-therapeutic. Here we have a situation where provision is made quite clearly for this sort of research to be carried out on participants when it is not of benefit to them, ie it is non-therapeutic.

Section 33 provides additional safeguards and s 34 deals with loss of capacity during a research project:

33 Additional safeguards

1 This section applies in relation to a person who is taking part in an approved research project even though he lacks capacity to consent to taking part.

2 Nothing may be done to, or in relation to, him in the course of the research –
    a to which he appears to object (whether by showing signs of resistance or otherwise) except where what is being done is intended to protect him from harm or to reduce or prevent pain or discomfort, or
    b which would be contrary to –
        i an advance decision of his which has effect, or
        ii any other form of statement made by him and not subsequently withdrawn,
    c of which R is aware.

3 The interests of the person must be assumed to outweigh those of science and society.

4 If he indicates (in any way) that he wishes to be withdrawn from the project he must be withdrawn without delay.

5 P must be withdrawn from the project, without delay, if at any time the person conducting the research has reasonable grounds for believing that one or more of the requirements set out in section 31(2) to (7) is no longer met in relation to research being carried out on, or in relation to, P.

6 But neither subsection (4) nor subsection (5) requires treatment that P has been receiving as part of the project to be discontinued if R has reasonable grounds for believing that there would be a significant risk to P's health if it were discontinued.

34 Loss of capacity during research project

1 This section applies where a person ('P') –
    a has consented to take part in a research project begun before the commencement of section 30, but
    b before the conclusion of the project, loses capacity to consent to continue to take part in it.

2 The appropriate authority may by regulations provide that, despite P's loss of capacity, research of a prescribed kind may be carried out on, or in relation to, P if –
    a the project satisfies prescribed requirements,
    b any information or material relating to P which is used in the research is of a prescribed description and was obtained before P's loss of capacity, and
    c the person conducting the project takes in relation to P such steps as may be prescribed for the purpose of protecting him.

3 The regulations may, in particular, –
    a make provision about when, for the purposes of the regulations, a project is to be treated as having begun;
    b include provision similar to any made by section 31, 32 or 33.

THINK POINT

Would you wish to restrict non-therapeutic research being carried out on people who lack capacity and, if so, how would you do this?

10.3.2 Non-therapeutic research

10.3.2.1 The capable volunteer

Given that we are not considering *treatment* at all, should the test of capacity to consent be different in this context? The test, it is suggested, will be the same. The volunteer will still be required to understand the nature of the procedure and any risks involved, and weigh up the risks of the procedure with the advantage of participating (either financial, or psychological well-being because of the potential benefits to others).

However, just as there may be a temptation for a doctor, who wishes to treat a refusing patient in the latter's own interests, to regard such a patient as *incapable*, here, where a researcher needs healthy volunteers to assist in what he believes to be valuable research, the opposite temptation may arise: that is to say, the researcher may be over-ready to find an assenting volunteer capable. It is clear that vigilance is needed to protect individuals from unwarranted physical interference in both cases.

Difficulties also arise in the context of ensuring that consent to participate is truly voluntary. This is especially true of volunteers, who are already in hospital for unrelated treatment, and who may feel unable to refuse 'secondment' into a trial if approached by their doctor. Another potential group of research subjects, vulnerable in a somewhat different way, are the poor. Although the financial inducements are relatively modest, the sums may tempt those on low incomes. For example, advertisements in *The Big Issue* (a publication sold on the streets by the homeless) invite volunteers for medical research (stating that they are 'all approved by ethics committees'), for £100. See the extract from Ferguson at 10.1.4.2 above.

The next requirement, once again, is that the research subject be properly informed of the risks attendant upon participating in the research. Clearly, therapeutic privilege can have no part to play in research on healthy volunteers. In the Canadian case of *Halushka v University of Saskatchewan*[31] it was stated:

> **Hall JA**: The example of risks being properly hidden from a patient when it is important that he should not worry can have no application in the field of research. The subject of medical experimentation is entitled to a full and frank disclosure of all the facts, probabilities and opinions which a reasonable man might be expected to consider before giving his consent.

To what extent would the UK courts similarly distinguish non-therapeutic from therapeutic research in this context? In the post-*Sidaway* case of *Gold v Haringey HA*[32] the Court of Appeal held that disclosure, in the context of non-therapeutic treatment, was just as much governed by the *Bolam* test (as now refined by the cases of *Bolitho v City and Hackney Health Authority*[33] and *Chester v Afshar*)[34] as advice given in the course of therapy. However, it is probable that this

---

31 52 WWR 608.
32 [1987] 2 All ER 888.
33 [1998] AC 232.
34 [2004] UKHL 41.

question is of theoretical interest only since, as noted earlier in our discussion of therapeutic research, the *Bolam* test itself would surely impose the duty to obtain fully informed consent upon the researcher (all guidance, including the Declaration of Helsinki, is unanimously to this effect).

10.3.2.2 The incapable volunteer

The expression 'incapable volunteer' is, of course, a contradiction in terms. If the person is incapable, then, by definition, he is unable to volunteer. However, others may 'volunteer' on his behalf, and this undoubtedly generates some of the most contentious ethical and legal issues in medical research. Indeed it may be felt that there is an argument for prohibiting any form of non-therapeutic research on those who lack the capacity to consent.

10.3.2.2.1 Children

It is generally thought ethically acceptable, in certain circumstances, to carry out non-therapeutic research upon children. That is certainly the view taken by such bodies as the Royal College of Paediatricians[35] and the Royal College of Physicians,[36] whose guidelines offer very similar advice here to that covering therapeutic research on patients. In the case of mature minors, there is an assumption that *Gillick* competence will apply (clearly, s 8 of the Family Law Reform Act 1969 will not apply to 16 and 17-year-olds in this context). However, should children really be able to consent at all to non-therapeutic measures on *Gillick* principles? It is suggested here that the answer is 'yes', at least where the risks involved are negligible or minimal. After all, mature minors are capable of giving consent to major medical interventions, such as surgery, which may require them to comprehend and balance much higher risks.

Interesting issues arise when the child is incapable of consenting, and the parent consents on the child's behalf. Robert Redmon tackles arguments which state that children in such research are being used merely as 'ends' and sees participation as part of the child's wider development as a moral being, even though the research is not for the benefit of the child's immediate health:

Redmon, R, 'How children can be respected as "ends" yet still be used as subjects in non-therapeutic research'[37]

If the child is old enough, she may enjoy seeing how this aspect of science functions, and her participation may aid her education. Also, this participation can be seen as part of her moral education.

However, these particular benefits – scientific and moral education – are of a different nature from most others (money, health, prestige, etc). To aid in the development of intellectual and, especially, moral abilities (or sensitivities) is to aid in the development of the individual's autonomy. For Kant, a person was only free when she was doing the morally praiseworthy thing (acting from 'a good will'). A development of a 'good will' (notwithstanding Kant's view that such a will is 'non-empirical' and thus, in some sense, innate) is a step towards being an ultimate 'end'.

Citing a piece by Hans Jonas ('Philosophical reflections on experimenting with human subjects' (1969) *Daedalus* (Spring) 219), Redmon favours the approach whereby, if the goals of the subject are the same as the researcher, then the subject is not being merely used. This he refers to as an 'identification of interests':

---

35 *Child Health: Ethics Advisory Committee Guidelines for the ethical conduct of medical research involving children* (2000) 82 Archives of Disease In Childhood 177.
36 *Guidelines on the Practice of Ethics Committees In Medical Research with Human Participants*, 4th edn, RCP: London, 2007.
37 12 JME 77.

Redmon, R, 'How children can be respected as "ends" yet still be used as subjects in non-therapeutic research'[38]

It does make sense . . . to ask how a person with a particular moral outlook, particular values, virtues and vices, would act. Thus the prediction of how the child will later view his participation must be made by those in the child's family, in particular by his parents. Their consent should be based upon their own values and the expectation that the child will share, to some extent, in them. They might reasonably expect, for example, that their child may later, as an adult, have an interest in the welfare of children whom the research may benefit. Their child will probably be a parent himself. They should also . . . be present during all stages of the research, and be involved in it as much as possible. This will help confirm their judgment that their child will later 'identify' with the research project.

My 'Kantian deliberations' thus lead to a tentative conclusion: if we can reasonably expect this child to 'identify' (in Jonas' sense) with the goals of the research when she is an adult, and that the identification will be strong enough to outweigh the harm of the knowledge of being used by her parents, and if the child (if old enough) assents, and if the possibility of harm is slight ('minimal risk'), then such research is permissible.

Could it be argued, in the light of this (and echoing the approach taken in the case of *S v S*),[39] that parental consent to enter their child into non-therapeutic research involving minimal risk is not contrary to the child's best interests? In the US case of *Curran v Bosze*[40] it was suggested that 'individual altruism in an abstract theoretical sense' was an insufficient basis for regarding a non-therapeutic procedure as in a child's best interests.[41] Significantly, in that case, however, the children's mother opposed the procedure in issue.

10.3.2.2.2 Adults

It is arguable that non-therapeutic research on the incapable adult is always wrong, both morally, and in law, as it constitutes a battery (contrast the position of children, where at least a parent may (and must) consent on their behalf). At the very least, additional safeguards should be necessary. The Law Commission in its report, *Mental Incapacity*, commented as follows:

Law Commission, *Mental Incapacity*, report no 231[42]

6.29 'Non-therapeutic' research . . . does not claim to offer any direct or immediate benefit to the participant. Such procedures may well be scientifically and ethically acceptable to those who are qualified to decide such matters. If, however, the participant lacks capacity to consent to his or her participation, and the procedure cannot be justified under the doctrine of necessity, then any person who touches or restrains that participant is committing an unlawful battery. The simple fact is that the researcher is making no claim to be acting in the best interests of that individual person and does not therefore come within the rules of law set out in *Re F*. It was made abundantly clear to us on consultation, however, that non-therapeutic research projects of this nature are regularly taking place. We were told of a research project into the organic manifestations of Alzheimer's disease which involves the administration of radioactive isotopes to sufferers, followed by extensive testing of blood and bodily functions. Another project was said to involve the examination of written patients' records, although they are unable to consent to

---

38 12 JME 77.
39 [1970] 3 All ER 107.
40 566 NE 2d 1319 (1990).
41 See Ch 11, below.
42 London: HMSO, 1995.

this examination. In some cases relatives are asked to 'consent' to what is proposed, and do so. It appears that some funding bodies and ethics committees stipulate for consent by a relative where the research participant cannot consent. As a matter of law, such 'consent' is meaningless. It appears that the question of the legality of non-therapeutic research procedures is regularly misunderstood or ignored by those who design, fund and approve the projects.

6.30 A number of our respondents expressed concern about non-invasive research based on observations, photography or videoing of participants (sometimes covertly). We accept that questions of dignity and privacy arise in such situations where the project is not designed to benefit the research participant.

6.31 We suggested in our consultation paper that the balance of expert opinion favours the participation of people unable to consent in even non-therapeutic research projects, subject to strict criteria. The majority of our consultees argued that there is an ethical case for such participation. This case turns on the desirability of eradicating painful and distressing disabilities, where progress can be achieved without harming research subjects ...

We recommend that research which is unlikely to benefit a participant, or whose benefit is likely to be long delayed, should be lawful in relation to a person without capacity to consent if (1) the research is into an incapacitating condition with which the participant is or may be affected and (2) certain statutory procedures are complied with. (Draft Bill, cl 11(1).)

The Commission, therefore, took the view that one of the essential conditions of non-therapeutic research taking place on an incapable person is that the person has the condition which the research is seeking to alleviate. Nevertheless, as the Law Commission's report noted, non-therapeutic research on incompetent patients does occur and, indeed, the Medical Research Council's guidelines, *The Ethical Conduct of Research on the Mentally Incapacitated*, 1991, in this respect mirror its Guidance on incompetent minors: such research may be carried out provided the hoped-for knowledge is unprocurable by other means and risk to the subject is no more than minimal. Furthermore, para 24 of the Declaration of Helsinki (see above) expressly acknowledges that this may take place as it is contained within section B, which is not restricted to therapeutic research. It is also anticipated by Article 17(2) of the European Convention on Human Rights and Biomedicine, which states that exceptionally, and under conditions that are protectable by law, non-therapeutic research can be carried out on incapable adults. Nevertheless, it is still pertinent to ask how such research can satisfy the 'best interests' requirement laid down in *Re F*. Admittedly, the courts have been prepared to construe best interests quite widely in some cases (see especially the discussion of *Re Y (An Adult Patient) (Transplant: Bone Marrow)*),[43] but only to the extent that some form of benefit can be shown to accrue directly to the individual concerned. The problem stems from the issue discussed above at 10.4.1 where we acknowledged that the therapeutic/non-therapeutic divide is not a distinct dichotomy. Certainly under the MCA 2005 the patient has to have been diagnosed with the condition concerned, but the research does not have to benefit the research subject personally (see s 31(5)(b) MCA, 10.3.1.2.2 above).

10.4 The regulation of research in the UK

Until relatively recently, medical research has been subject to the common law, and clinical trials have been subject to the Medicines Act 1968. However, the enactment of the European Clinical

---

43 BMLR 111.

Trials Directive 2001/20 EC prompted the government to issue regulations to govern the conduct of clinical trials. Not all research, however, is concerned with the investigation of medicinal products and research that lies outside this ambit will still be governed by a mixture of the common law, any constraints imposed by ethics committees, and any quasi-statutory guidance from the relevant bodies (see below).

10.4.1 Common law

10.4.1.1 Contract

There are two contractual relations that are relevant to medical research. First, there is the contract between the research subject and the researcher and, secondly, the contract between the sponsor of the research (for example a drug manufacturer), and the researcher, or investigator. Ian Dodds-Smith comments as follows:

Dodds-Smith, I, 'Clinical research'[44]

The sponsor's obligations to the investigator

The contract between the sponsor/manufacturer and the investigator will govern the legal relationship between them. Ideally, to avoid uncertainty and possible unnecessary dispute, the agreement should be in writing and clearly expressed. There is no model format for such contracts – they may be and often are contained in a letter. The overriding concern, however, is that they should be unambiguous and contain all the crucial details relating to the protocol to be adopted, information to be made available about the test product, reporting of adverse drug reactions, the duration of the study, the maintenance of patient confidentiality, the publication of results, liability for injury to subjects and the fee for the study. Under English law, certain conditions are implied additionally into any contract for services. These include that the service will be performed with reasonable care and skill and in a reasonable period. There are also rules under statute which may restrict the ability of the parties to exclude their liability for damages for personal injury caused by negligence.

The sponsor's obligations to the research subject

Contract

The Declaration of Helsinki does not address the matter of how the subject/sponsor relationship might be structured or recorded. In general, the sponsor and a patient subject do not enter into a direct contractual arrangement. However, where studies are to be conducted upon healthy volunteers, a form of contract may and usually will exist. In 1970 the Association of the British Pharmaceutical Industry (ABPI) published a report to which a simple form of written contract was appended. In 1986 the Royal College of Physicians issued a report on healthy volunteer studies in which it advocated the use of a 'simple form of contract' mainly to ensure that the subject would be compensated for any injury occurring during a trial. In the appendix to the report the college provided a checklist of matters which should be considered when drawing up such a contract. In 1988, the ABPI published revised Guidelines for medical experiments in non-patient human volunteers which contained both a model patient information form and draft provisions for a volunteer agreement and consent form and stated that all volunteers 'must sign a simple form of agreement'. . . with the sponsor or outside research establishment.

---

44 In Dyer, C (ed), *Doctors, Patients and the Law*, Oxford: Blackwell Science, 1992, p 146.

As Dodds-Smith states, in relation to the contract between sponsor and investigator, certain terms are implied into the contract. These terms will also apply to any contract between sponsor and research subject. Although when the patient is receiving NHS treatment, there will not be a contract, a contractual situation must arise, within the NHS as well as elsewhere, in the case of healthy volunteers (in the context of non-therapeutic research), as they are not being treated pursuant to a statutory obligation. Clearly, s 2(1) of the Unfair Contract Terms Act 1977 would prevent any such contract excluding liability for damages for negligently caused death or personal injury, and there would be an implied term that the research would be carried out with reasonable skill and care.

Although, for the purposes of the research subject bringing an action for injuries suffered, the contents of the contract may well be important, in the context of the research subject failing to participate, or withdrawing part way through the research, would a court enforce such a contract? The answer must surely be that it is unenforceable from the point of view of the researcher. Damages would be unquantifiable, and an order for specific performance repugnant.

10.4.1.2 Tort

The torts of battery and negligence will apply to those who participate in medical research. These have already been considered in relation to consent, and will be looked at again, in the context of recovering compensation for injuries: see 10.5.

10.4.1.3 Criminal law

It is important to recall that battery is a crime as well as a tort, and that statutory criminal offences may apply in the appropriate circumstances. While, in the normal course of medical research, the criminal law would be unlikely to be invoked, note the US case of *Hyman v Jewish Chronic Disease Hospital*,[45] where doctors injected live cancer cells into 22 patients, not only without their consent, but by leading them to believe that the injections were part of their normal treatment. The Medical Association Review Board found the doctors guilty of fraudulent and deceitful conduct, but no criminal proceedings were taken. There is some precedent in English law in the case of *R v Burdee*,[46] where a doctor who had prescribed cold water foot baths and a three-day fast for a sick patient who subsequently died, was convicted of manslaughter (as has previously been noted, however, something which is experimentation at best, and quackery at worst, is not research in the accepted sense of the term).

10.4.2 Statutory provisions in relation to clinical trials

The European Clinical Trials Directive 2001/20 EC governs the regulation of clinical trials of medicines and has been transposed into UK law by the Medicines for Human Use (Clinical Trials) Regulations 2004 which replace the clinical trial provisions of the Medicines Act 1968 and regulations made thereunder. These came into force on 1 May 2004. The Medicines and Healthcare Products Regulatory Agency is the regulatory body that oversees the operation of the Regulations (note that the 2001 Directive will be replaced by the Clinical Trials Regulation 536/2014, in 2019).

The aim of the Directive is to simplify and harmonise the regulation of clinical trials. There are two main aspects to this: the establishment of a clear procedure for dealing with clinical trials and the facilitation of effective co-ordination of clinical trials throughout Europe. While the protection of trial participants is given importance it seems that the advancement of medical

---

45 251 NYS 2d 818 (1964).
46 25 Cox 598.

research and the promotion of the internal market in medicinal products are key to the impetus behind the Directive. As well as the regulation of research it also deals with manufacturing standards. For our purposes the important part of the Regulations is Sch 1 (implementing Article 3(2) of the Directive) and this deals with consent to participation. As far as capable adults are concerned, the conditions are: that the subject has had an interview with the investigator, or another member of the investigating team, in which s/he has been given the opportunity to understand the objectives, risks and inconveniences of the trial and conditions under which it is to be conducted; that he has been informed of his right to withdraw from the trial at any time; that he has given his 'informed consent' to participating and that this can be withdrawn at any time without resulting in detriment; and that he has been given a contact point for further information.

As far as children are concerned, the Schedule provides for a hierarchy of consent on behalf of the child, commencing with a parent or person with parental responsibility. The others are personal legal representatives and professional legal representatives (ie someone nominated by the relevant healthcare provider) but consent can only be taken from these in emergencies. There are similar provisions for incapable adults. Obviously a parent has no relevance in the latter case, *qua* parent, but the personal legal representative is someone suitable to act as the legal representative by virtue of their relationship with the adult concerned, and who is not connected with the conduct of the trial. The following provisions contained within Sch 1 relate to the principles of good clinical practice and the protection of clinical trial subjects:

PART 2

CONDITIONS AND PRINCIPLES WHICH APPLY TO ALL CLINICAL TRIALS

Principles based on International Conference on Harmonisation GCP Guideline

1   Clinical trials shall be conducted in accordance with the ethical principles that have their origin in the Declaration of Helsinki, and that are consistent with good clinical practice and the requirements of these Regulations.

2   Before the trial is initiated, foreseeable risks and inconveniences have been weighed against the anticipated benefit for the individual trial subject and other present and future patients. A trial should be initiated and continued only if the anticipated benefits justify the risks.

3   The rights, safety, and well-being of the trial subjects are the most important considerations and shall prevail over interests of science and society.

4   The available non-clinical and clinical information on an investigational medicinal product shall be adequate to support the clinical trial.

5   Clinical trials shall be scientifically sound, and described in a clear, detailed protocol.

6   A trial shall be conducted in compliance with the protocol that has a favourable opinion from an ethics committee.

7   The medical care given to, and medical decisions made on behalf of, subjects shall always be the responsibility of an appropriately qualified doctor or, when appropriate, of a qualified dentist.

8   Each individual involved in conducting a trial shall be qualified by education, training, and experience to perform his or her respective task(s).

9   Subject to the other provisions of this Schedule relating to consent, freely given informed consent shall be obtained from every subject prior to clinical trial participation.

10   All clinical trial information shall be recorded, handled, and stored in a way that allows its accurate reporting, interpretation and verification.

11   The confidentiality of records that could identify subjects shall be protected, respecting the privacy and confidentiality rules in accordance with the requirements of the Data Protection Act 1998 and the law relating to confidentiality.

12 Investigational medicinal products used in the trial shall be –

    a   manufactured or imported, and handled and stored, in accordance with the principles and guidelines of good manufacturing practice, and

    b   used in accordance with the approved protocol.

13 Systems with procedures that assure the quality of every aspect of the trial shall be implemented.

Conditions based on Article 3 of the Directive

14 A trial shall be initiated only if an ethics committee and the licensing authority comes to the conclusion that the anticipated therapeutic and public health benefits justify the risks and may be continued only if compliance with this requirement is permanently monitored.

15 The rights of each subject to physical and mental integrity, to privacy and to the protection of the data concerning him in accordance with the Data Protection Act 1998 are safeguarded.

16 Provision has been made for insurance or indemnity to cover the liability of the investigator and sponsor which may arise in relation to the clinical trial.

PART 3

CONDITIONS WHICH APPLY IN RELATION TO AN ADULT ABLE TO CONSENT OR WHO HAS GIVEN CONSENT PRIOR TO THE ONSET OF INCAPACITY

1 The subject has had an interview with the investigator, or another member of the investigating team, in which he has been given the opportunity to understand the objectives, risks and inconveniences of the trial and the conditions under which it is to be conducted.

2 The subject has been informed of his right to withdraw from the trial at any time.

3 The subject has given his informed consent to taking part in the trial.

4 The subject may, without being subject to any resulting detriment, withdraw from the clinical trial at any time by revoking his informed consent.

5 The subject has been provided with a contact point where he may obtain further information about the trial.

PART 4

CONDITIONS AND PRINCIPLES WHICH APPLY IN RELATION TO A MINOR

Conditions

1 Subject to paragraph 6, a person with parental responsibility for the minor or, if by reason of the emergency nature of the treatment provided as part of the trial no such person can be contacted prior to the proposed inclusion of the subject in the trial, a legal representative for the minor has had an interview with the investigator, or another member of the investigating team, in which he has been given the opportunity to understand the objectives, risks and inconveniences of the trial and the conditions under which it is to be conducted.

2 That person or legal representative has been provided with a contact point where he may obtain further information about the trial.

3 That person or legal representative has been informed of the right to withdraw the minor from the trial at any time.

4 That person or legal representative has given his informed consent to the minor taking part in the trial.

5   That person with parental responsibility or the legal representative may, without the minor being subject to any resulting detriment, withdraw the minor from the trial at any time by revoking his informed consent.

6   The minor has received information according to his capacity of understanding, from staff with experience with minors, regarding the trial, its risks and its benefits.

7   The explicit wish of a minor who is capable of forming an opinion and assessing the information referred to in the previous paragraph to refuse participation in, or to be withdrawn from, the clinical trial at any time is considered by the investigator.

8   No incentives or financial inducements are given –

  a   to the minor; or

  b   to a person with parental responsibility for that minor or, as the case may be, the minor's legal representative, except provision for compensation in the event of injury or loss.

9   The clinical trial relates directly to a clinical condition from which the minor suffers or is of such a nature that it can only be carried out on minors.

10   Some direct benefit for the group of patients involved in the clinical trial is to be obtained from that trial.

11   The clinical trial is necessary to validate data obtained –

  a   in other clinical trials involving persons able to give informed consent, or

  b   by other research methods.

12   The corresponding scientific guidelines of the European Medicines Agency are followed.

Principles

13   Informed consent given by a person with parental responsibility or a legal representative to a minor taking part in a clinical trial shall represent the minor's presumed will.

14   The clinical trial has been designed to minimise pain, discomfort, fear and any other foreseeable risk in relation to the disease and the minor's stage of development.

15   The risk threshold and the degree of distress have to be specially defined and constantly monitored.

16   The interests of the patient always prevail over those of science and society.

PART 5

CONDITIONS AND PRINCIPLES WHICH APPLY IN RELATION TO AN INCAPACITATED ADULT

Conditions

1   The subject's legal representative has had an interview with the investigator, or another member of the investigating team, in which he has been given the opportunity to understand the objectives, risks and inconveniences of the trial and the conditions under which it is to be conducted.

2   The legal representative has been provided with a contact point where he may obtain further information about the trial.

3   The legal representative has been informed of the right to withdraw the subject from the trial at any time.

4   The legal representative has given his informed consent to the subject taking part in the trial.

5   The legal representative may, without the subject being subject to any resulting detriment, withdraw the subject from the trial at any time by revoking his informed consent.

6   The subject has received information according to his capacity of understanding regarding the trial, its risks and its benefits.

7   The explicit wish of a subject who is capable of forming an opinion and assessing the information referred to in the previous paragraph to refuse participation in, or to be withdrawn from, the clinical trial at any time is considered by the investigator.

8   No incentives or financial inducements are given to the subject or their legal representative, except provision for compensation in the event of injury or loss.

9   There are grounds for expecting that administering the medicinal product to be tested in the trial will produce a benefit to the subject outweighing the risks or produce no risk at all.

10   The clinical trial is essential to validate data obtained –

   a   in other clinical trials involving persons able to give informed consent, or

   b   by other research methods.

11   The clinical trial relates directly to a life-threatening or debilitating clinical condition from which the subject suffers.

Principles

12   Informed consent given by a legal representative to an incapacitated adult in a clinical trial shall represent that adult's presumed will.

13   The clinical trial has been designed to minimise pain, discomfort, fear and any other foreseeable risk in relation to the disease and the cognitive abilities of the patient.

14   The risk threshold and the degree of distress have to be specially defined and constantly monitored.

15   The interests of the patient always prevail over those of science and society.

A comparison should be made between the conditions placed upon clinical trials concerning adults who lack capacity and the conditions that are contained in the Mental Capacity Act 2005. Put simply, conditions are much more stringent in relation to clinical trials, notably in the case of clinical trials the requirement that the trial relates directly to a 'life-threatening or debilitating clinical condition from which the subject suffers'.[47] While conditions such as Alzheimer's disease would be covered by this, mere mental impairment would not.

10.4.3 UK-specific regulation

This is governed by the Medicines for Human Use (Clinical Trials) Regulations 2004, SI 2004/1031 and, in England, the *Governance Arrangements for NHS Research Ethics Committees* and the Research Governance Framework for Health and Social Care, 2001, as amended in 2005. There are very similar framework documents for Northern Ireland, Scotland and Wales. The ethics of medical research is regulated via independent research ethics committees (RECs) in accordance with the Declaration of Helsinki which states, as one of its basic principles, that the design and performance of all research trials should be subject to scrutiny by 'a specially appointed ethical review committee which must be independent of the investigator, the sponsor or any other kind of undue influence' (para 15 at 10.2.1 above). In addition to these, the REC must consider other regulatory conditions such as the Mental Capacity Act 2005 and the Human Tissue Act 2004.

In 2015, the Health Research Authority took over from the Department of Health the role of issuing a research governance framework. The current 2001 guidance deals with the composition of a REC as follows:

---

47 See para 11 above.

Department of Health, *Governance Arrangements for NHS Research Ethics Committees*, 2001

6 Composition of an REC

6.1 An REC should have sufficient members to guarantee the presence of a quorum (*see* 6.11) at each meeting. The maximum should be 18 members. This should allow for a sufficiently broad range of experience and expertise, so that the scientific, clinical and methodological aspects of a research proposal can be reconciled with the welfare of research participants, and with broader ethical implications.

6.2 Overall the REC should have a balanced age and gender distribution. Members should be drawn from both sexes and from a wide range of age groups. Every effort should also be made to recruit members from black and ethnic minority backgrounds, as well as people with disabilities. This should apply to both expert and lay members.

6.3 RECs should be constituted to contain a mixture of 'expert' and 'lay' members. At least three members must be independent of any organisation where research under ethical review is likely to take place.

Expert members

6.4 The 'expert' members of the committee shall be chosen to ensure that the REC has the following expertise:
   relevant methodological and ethical expertise in:
   - clinical research;
   - non-clinical research;
   - qualitative or other research methods applicable to health services, social science and social care research,
   clinical practice including:
   - hospital and community staff (medical, nursing and other);
   - general practice,
   statistics relevant to research.

Lay members

6.5 At least one third of the membership shall be 'lay' members who are independent of the NHS, either as employees or in a non-executive role, and whose primary personal or professional interest is not in a research area.

6.6 The 'lay' membership can include non-medical clinical staff who have not practised their profession for a period of at least five years.

6.7 At least half of the 'lay' members must be persons who are not, and never have been, either health or social care professionals, and who have never been involved in carrying out research involving human participants, their tissue or data.[48]

THINK POINT

Do you think that research participants should be able to sue REC members if they suffer damage as a result of participating in medical research that has been approved by a REC?

---

48 London: DOH, 2001.

It can be questioned as to exactly what sort of experience is required of an REC member, as it raises the question of the very function of the committee. The Department of Health guidance states baldly that the purpose of the committee is 'to consider the ethics of proposed research projects within the NHS'. Matters that they should have regard to, as a minimum, in doing so are as follows:

Department of Health, *Governance Arrangements for NHS Research Ethics Committees,* **2001**

Requirements for a favourable opinion

9.12 Before giving a favourable opinion, the REC should be adequately reassured about the following issues as applicable:

9.13 *Scientific design and conduct of the study*

    a   the appropriateness of the study design in relation to the objectives of the study, the statistical methodology (including sample size calculation where appropriate), and the potential for reaching sound conclusions with the smallest number of research participants

    b   the justification of predictable risks and inconveniences weighed against the anticipated benefits for the research participants, other present and future patients, and the concerned communities

    c   the justification for use of control arms in trials, (whether placebo or active comparator), and the randomisation process to be used

    d   criteria for prematurely withdrawing research participants

    e   criteria for suspending or terminating the research as a whole

    f   the adequacy of provisions made for monitoring and auditing the conduct of the research, including the constitution of a data safety monitoring committee (DSMC)

    g   the adequacy of the research site, including the supporting staff, available facilities, and emergency procedures. For multi-centre research, these locality issues will be considered separately from the ethical review of the research proposal itself

    h   the manner in which the results of the research will be reported and published.

9.14 *Recruitment of research participants*

    a   the characteristics of the population from which the participants will be drawn (including gender, age, literacy, culture, economic status and ethnicity) and the justification for any decisions made in this respect

    b   the means by which initial contact and recruitment is to be conducted

    c   the means by which full information is to be conveyed to potential research participants or their representatives

    d   inclusion criteria for research participants

    e   exclusion criteria for research participants.

9.15 *Care and protection of research participants*

    a   the safety of any intervention to be used in the proposed research

    b   the suitability of the investigator(s)'s qualifications and experience for ensuring good conduct of the proposed study

    c   any plans to withdraw or withhold standard therapies or clinical management protocols for the purpose of the research, and the justification for such action

    d   the health and social care to be provided to research participants during and after the course of the research e   the adequacy of health and social supervision and psychosocial support for the research participants

f   steps to be taken if research participants voluntarily withdraw during the course of the research

g   the criteria for extended access to, the emergency use of, and/or the compassionate use of study products

h   the arrangements, if appropriate, for informing the research participant's general practitioner, including procedures for seeking the participant's consent to do so

i   a description of any plans to make the study product available to the research participants following the research

j   a description of any financial costs to research participants

k   the rewards and compensations (if any) for research participants (including money, services and/or gifts)

l   whether there is provision in proportion to the risk for compensation/treatment in the case of injury/disability/death of a research participant attributable to participation in the research; the insurance and indemnity arrangements

m   the nature and size of any grants, payments or other reward to be made to any researchers or research hosts

n   circumstances that might lead to conflicts of interest that may affect the independent judgement of the researcher(s).

9.16   *Protection of research participants' confidentiality*

a   a description of the persons who will have access to personal data of the research participants, including medical records and biological samples

b   the measures taken to ensure the confidentiality and security of personal information concerning research participants

c   the extent to which the information will be anonymised

d   how the data/samples will be obtained, and the purposes for which they will be used

e   how long the data/samples will be kept

f   to which countries, if any, the data/samples will be sent

g   the adequacy of the process for obtaining consent for the above.

9.17   *Informed consent process*

a   a full description of the process for obtaining informed consent, including the identification of those responsible for obtaining consent, the time-frame in which it will occur, and the process for ensuring consent has not been withdrawn

b   the adequacy, completeness and understandability of written and oral information to be given to the research participants, and, when appropriate, their legally acceptable representatives

c   clear justification for the intention to include in the research individuals who cannot consent, and a full account of the arrangements for obtaining consent or authorization for the participation of such individuals

d   assurances that research participants will receive information that becomes available during the course of the research relevant to their participation (including their rights, safety and well being)

e   the provisions made for receiving and responding to queries and complaints from research participants or their representatives during the course of a research project.

9.18 *Community considerations*

  a   the impact and relevance of the research on the local community and on the concerned communities from which the research participants are drawn

  b   the steps which had been taken to consult with the concerned communities during the course of designing the research

  c   the extent to which the research contributes to capacity building, such as the enhancement of local healthcare, research, and the ability to respond to public health needs

  d   a description of the availability and affordability of any successful study product to the concerned communities following the research

  e   the manner in which the results of the research will be made available to the research participants and the concerned communities.[49]

Some might argue that the 'expert' committee members will tend to dominate discussion and be instrumental in the final decision.[50]

Regulation 12 of the Medicines for Human Use (Clinical Trials) Regulations 2004 prohibits anyone from commencing or conducting a clinical trial, recruiting subjects or advertising to recruit subjects to be in a trial unless certain conditions are met. Specifically, such a trial can only be started or conducted if it has been authorised by the Medicines and Healthcare Products Regulatory Agency and approved by an ethics committee.

What would be the legal consequences of a breach of the above guidelines? Certainly, any researcher employed by the NHS who was in breach would be liable to dismissal or other form of discipline, but would a patient or healthy volunteer have any right of redress? It is likely that the breach would be akin to a breach of statutory duty, in the sense that it would not necessarily give rise to a private law right in itself. However, if the patient suffered injury, then failure to obtain REC approval might point towards negligence, although the problem of causation would remain. Another problem, highlighted by the case involving Mrs Moffit,[51] arises where, though initially obtaining approval in the proper way, a researcher fails to keep the REC apprised of changes in the execution of a project.

As will be seen from para 3.1, ethical approval for non-NHS research is not specifically required. However, even if the private sector can, in theory, ignore RECs, in practice, because of the effect upon insurance and legal liability generally (not to mention publication), researchers will want to obtain approval of their projects, and para 3.2 makes provision for this. Furthermore, as far as clinical trials are concerned, reg 12 of the Medicines for Human Use (Clinical Trials) Regulations 2004 applies to non-NHS trials.

In *R (on the application of Richmond Pharmacology Ltd) (Claimant) v Health Research Authority (Defendant) & Sense about Science (Interested Party)*[52] the claimant carried out clinical trials. These proceedings concerned phase 1 trials, ie the first trials to be carried out on human beings, but the case was essentially about a requirement by the Health Research Authority (HRA) to register a trial on a publicly accessible database. The challenge was whether this was a legal requirement, or a matter of good clinical practice. The challenge to the HRA was upheld on the basis that the requirement of registration was misleading as it gave the impression that it was a legal requirement. The Medicines for Human Use (Clinical Trials) Regulations 2004, as

---

49 London: DoH, 2001.
50 See McNeill, PM, *The Ethics and Politics of Human Experimentation*, Cambridge: Press Syndicate of the University of Cambridge, 1993.
51 See 10.3.1.1, above.
52 [2015] EWHC 2238 (Admin)

amended in 2006, refers to the Declaration of Helsinki and the reference in Sch 1 Pt 2 para 3 to 'ethical principles in all their aspects' which should guide all clinical trials, but does not mean that sponsors (normally pharmaceutical companies) and researchers are bound to register trials. As a result of this, since the wording did not make it clear that registration was a principle of good clinical practice or a legal requirement, it failed the public law tests of certainty and transparency.

Members of RECs are indemnified by the NHS in respect of any action brought by a research subject alleging that they have been damaged as a result of the decision of the REC, as long as they have not acted in bad faith, or been deceitful or grossly negligent. Damage can of course include damage that has occurred as a result of breach of, say, confidentiality. In the vast majority of cases, any injury they have received will be as a result of the execution of the research, eg wrong dosages, keeping patients in the research when they have experienced an adverse reaction, inadequate monitoring and so on. However, it is possible that approval is given to research that does not have sufficient safeguards attached to it, eg specific 'stopping rules' that require the participant to be taken out of a trial at clinically appropriate times, and if damage results the REC might be liable. Of course, in order to show that the REC has been negligent, there has to be a duty owed to the research participants in the first place, and the usual tort considerations apply, which principally relate to the proximity of the relationship and the issue of whether it is just and reasonable to impose a duty in the first place. Given the protective remit of the REC it would be hard to argue that no duty was owed. Pattinson endorses this view but goes on to say:

Pattinson, SD, *Medical Law and Ethics*[53]

[T]he majority of REC approvals of research protocols are not straightforwardly analogous to those situations where assumptions of responsibility have previously been imposed, as protocols do not usually identify specific individual participants and the participants might not even be aware of the existence of the REC. Consider, for example, *Kent v Griffith* [2001] QB 36, where the ambulance service was held to owe a duty to provide an ambulance for the claimant within a reasonable time *because* it had accepted a call dealing with a *named individual* and had thereby *discouraged others* from providing alternative means of transport to the hospital. Thus, while there are clearly circumstances where a duty of care will be owed, the courts are unlikely to impose a blanket duty. In any event . . . proving breach and causation are onerous obstacles to overcome.

It has been stated by Christopher Roy-Toole that, under the European Clinical Trials Directive, RECs have an obligation to ensure the *legality* of the proposed trial as well as giving ethical approval:

Roy-Toole, C, 'Illegality in the research protocol: the duty of research ethics committees under the 2001 Clinical Trials Directive'[54]

There is no value in an ethics committee unless it can and does protect the research subject from the illegality of research, and especially if the legal rights of the subject are violated by it. The expression of a legal opinion by an ethics committee would be the clearest way of protecting these rights. Instead, if that committee has concerns about the legality of the research, [the Governance Arrangements for Research

---

53 London: Sweet & Maxwell, 2006.
54 4(3) Research Ethics Review 111–16.

Ethics Committees] seems to contemplate a situation in which it can merely recommend that a researcher obtain legal advice in order to clarify the matter . . . If the committee gives a favourable opinion before the researcher has obtained that legal advice, it has expressly endorsed research that might be illegal. Furthermore, what is the committee supposed to do if a researcher resumes his application armed with a sponsor's legal advice that the committee knows to be wrong?

. . . if an ethics committee rejects a protocol for its illegality, paragraph 9.11 [of the Governance Arrangements] would expose the committee to the allegation that it had gone beyond its proper function in providing what is, in effect, a legal opinion.

. . .

Article 2 of the 2001 Directive defines the legal duty of the REC. It stipulates that it is their responsibility to protect the rights, safety and wellbeing of human subjects involved in a trial. It is obvious and unassailable from the context in which it appears that this reference to 'rights' includes the legal rights of the subject. What else could it mean?

Arguably, Roy-Toole overstates the case. The phrase in the Directive could be referring to the rights of the patient in terms of the right to have any research in which s/he participates subjected to ethical scrutiny. The expression 'rights' is much more likely to mean rights under the various international and national agreements such as the Declaration of Helsinki which constitute general statements and the rights which a REC are meant to safeguard when they ethically review the research. In any event, Roy-Toole does not adequately distinguish between the rights of the participant, even if these are interpreted as all-encompassing legal rights, and the general concept of 'legality' which is much wider. For example a piece of research could be ethical but for a reason relating to, say, the terms of a lease the research could not lawfully be carried out on the premises where it is proposed to do it (clinical trials in non-NHS establishments have to be approved by a REC). The fact that research can be entirely lawful but unethical just reinforces this point. A good example of this is the availability of insurance to provide compensation if the participant is injured. Biggs states:

Biggs, H, *Healthcare Research Ethics and Law: Regulation, Review and Responsibility*[55]

Under the Clinical Trials Regulations it is a requirement that all clinical trials include provision for 'insurance or indemnity to cover the liability of the investigator and sponsor which may arise in relation to the clinical trial'... This is incorporated into reg15(5) of the Clinical Trials Regulations which stipulates that:

In preparing its opinion, the committee shall consider, in particular, the following matters:

. . .

(i)   provision for indemnity or compensation in the event of injury or death attributable to the clinical trial;

(j)   any insurance or indemnity to cover the liability of the investigator or sponsor . . .

Clearly, it is easy for an REC to establish the existence of insurance (but not, of course, that it will be renewed if it expires before the research has been completed), but not so easy to satisfy

---

55 London: Routledge, 2010.

itself that the insurance is adequate. In the case of the large pharmaceutical companies this is not of great concern because they will have the resources to pay regardless of insurance, but some of the companies are relatively small. As was seen above in relation to the Northwick Park research, the company set up to develop the drug became insolvent (see section 10.1.4.2 above).

THINK POINT

Do you think that the regulation of medical research might stifle innovation that could result in much needed medical advances?

10.4.4 The EU General Data Protection Regulation 2016/679

This has been discussed in Chapter 5, but it is worth re-examining it in the context of research. One well-known element of the Regulation is that it gives data subjects the 'right to be forgotten', more formally the right to erasure of personal data (Article 17). However, research (including medical research) is exempt from the right of erasure obligation if it is likely to render impossible or seriously impair the achievement of the research objectives (Article 17(3)(d)). Article 21 states that the data subjects still have a right to object to further data processing, but this too can be overridden by the researcher in the public interest (Article 21(6).

The researcher must in any event show a lawful basis for the processing. Besides the use of subject consent (Article 9(2)(a)), the Regulation (in Article 9(2)(j)) also permits processing health data for research without consent, subject to safeguards for the rights of the subject being adopted under Article 89(1), including data minimisation and technical and organisational measures. This may be especially relevant where organisations engage in 'secondary processing' of personal data originally collected for a different purpose (eg diagnosis) for research (Article 6(4); Recital 50). In such cases, as long as they implement appropriate safeguards, these organisations also may override a data subject's right to object to processing and to seek the erasure of personal data (Article 6(4); Recital 50). However, where research is planned all along, researchers may often prefer for ethical reasons to seek consent. Here the Regulation improves on the previous rules (in the 1995 Directive) by making clear that broad consent may suffice (ie the subject need not be told every detail as to the research use – which in the case of further, future research is not yet known) provided this also accords with recognised research ethics (Recital 33).

Elsewhere the Regulation distinguishes between anonymisation and pseudonymisation of personal data. Whereas anonymous data – which is not reasonably linkable back to the data subject – falls outside the scope of the Regulation, pseudonymous data remains personal. However, pseudonymisation means that it is stored in a way that subjects can no longer be identified without the use of additional information, and that information is stored separately (and the organisation has taken technical and organisational measures to ensure this separation) (Article 4(3b)). According to the 'data-minimisation' principle (Article 5(1)(c)) the personal data processing must be 'limited' (ie not excessive) by reference to the processing purpose. This requires that the purpose aimed at cannot be achieved by processing less personal data: in this regard, the onus will be on the researcher to show (if it be the case) that achieving the research purpose requires use of identifying rather than pseudonymised (or, better still, anonymous), data.

10.5 Compensation for injuries arising from research

10.5.1 Compensation at common law

A patient who is entered in a clinical trial without giving his properly informed consent may arguably have an action against the doctor in battery; this would perhaps be most likely in the case of a volunteer involved in non-therapeutic research. Failing an action in battery, however, an action in negligence may lie and could arise in two main ways, albeit in both cases the subject must show some tangible injury. In the first case, the trial itself may be properly conducted, but the doctor/researcher (while providing enough basic facts to escape an action in battery) falls below his duty of care in the amount of information he divulges to his subject, and the latter is able to show that, if properly informed, he would not have participated in the trial.

In the second case, the trial itself, in terms of design or execution, may turn out to be defective in some way. An additional issue which arises here is whether, to the extent that the defect was something which the REC, in approving the trial, should have noticed, the members of that committee could be joined as defendants in any action. The standard terms and conditions of appointment of REC members now state that the strategic health authority who will take full responsibility for members' actions in the course of the performance of their duties as members of the REC excepting actions taken in bad faith, wilful default or gross negligence.

10.5.2 'No fault' compensation?

Whatever form his action takes, the injured research subject (like his 'pure' patient counterpart) will have substantial hurdles to overcome, both in relation to the breach of duty question and causation. However, an ethical argument for treating research subjects more favourably than other patients injured in the course of treatment is that, just as society at large stands to benefit from any advances in medical knowledge that the research may secure, so it should bear the costs of mishaps along the way. Accordingly, it has frequently been urged that those injured in the course of medical research should be compensated on a 'no fault' basis. A direct analogy can be invoked here with persons injured in the course of a community-wide vaccination programme, who are entitled to 'no fault' compensation under the Vaccine Damage Payments Act 1979:

1 Payments to persons severely disabled by vaccination

1   If, on consideration of a claim, the Secretary of State is satisfied –

   a   that a person is, or was immediately before his death, severely disabled as a result of vaccination against any of the diseases to which this Act applies; and

   b   that the conditions of entitlement which are applicable in accordance with s 2 below are fulfilled,

2   he shall in accordance with this Act make a payment of the relevant statutory sum to or for the benefit of that person or to his personal representatives.

In its 1978 Report, the Royal Commission on Civil Liability and Compensation for Personal Injury (the Pearson Committee) recommended that a similar scheme of compensation be established for injuries in the course of medical research. While this recommendation has not been acted upon by Parliament, the DoH's REC Guidelines mention the existence of provision for *ex gratia* compensation as a relevant factor in the sanctioning of trials (para 9.15(1)).

In every case, of course, it remains necessary for the research subject to demonstrate that his injuries were caused by participation in the trial. This may be by no means easy to do: after all, research will be taking place precisely because the causal properties of the new treatment (including its propensity to do harm) are unclear. Sometimes, to be sure, the claimant's case will be a strong one, for example where everyone in the trial is similarly affected. However, where the claimant's injury is a more isolated occurrence, a court may well take the view that some unknown, independent cause was, just as likely, at work.[56]

10.5.3 Drug-induced injury

One area in which the use of research subjects has attracted particular attention is in relation to the testing of new drugs and pharmaceutical products. There is a heightened sense here (engendered both by the power imbalance between subject and drug company and by the latter's pre-eminently economic motivation), that volunteers and patients participating in such trials require protection.

In fact, the Association of the British Pharmaceutical Industry has issued Guidelines that recommended that *ex gratia* compensation should be paid in cases where injury results. These ABPI Guidelines are echoed by guidance at EU level.[57]

Finally, in cases of drug-induced injury, the subject may also wish to bring an action under the Consumer Protection Act 1987. The issues in relation to the use of this Act have been addressed in Chapter 6, above.

Summary of key points

1   The need to scrutinise medical research must be examined in the light of the importance of scientific research and the public expectation of medical advances.
2   The nature of medical research methodologies is important in deciding on what is ethically permissible, in particular the use of placebos and randomised controlled trials.
3   Human rights play a central role in medical research, in particular in the Declaration of Helsinki.
4   It is important to examine the distinctions between therapeutic and non-therapeutic research and innovative treatment.
5   Legal duties are owed to research participants, and these will vary according to whether the research is therapeutic or non-therapeutic.
6   The consent aspects of research must be examined in relation to research on children and incapable adults and also the differences between consent in therapeutic and consent in non-therapeutic research.
7   Medical research is heavily regulated at both the European and the domestic level, and in the composition and functions/duties of research ethics committees (RECs).
8   There are difficulties in awarding compensation for injuries caused by research if it is not caused by general negligence principles.

---

56 See, in this regard, the case of *Loveday v Renton* [1990] 1 Med LR 117 referred to in Ch 6, above.
57 See *Detailed Guidance for the Request for Authorisation of a Clinical Trial on a Medicinal Product for Human use to the Competent Authorities, Notification of Substantial Amendments and Declaration of the End of the Trial* (2010).

Further reading

Biggs, H, *Healthcare Research Ethics and Law: Regulation, Review and Responsibility*, London: Routledge, 2010.

Cheung, P, *Public Trust in Medical Research? Ethics, Law and Accountability*, Oxford: Radcliffe, 2008.

Foster, C, *The Ethics of Medical Research on Humans*, London: Cambridge University Press, 2001.

Morrison, D, 'A holistic approach to clinical and research decision-making' (2005), 13 Medical Law Review 45.

Plomer, A, *The Law and Ethics of Medical Research: International Bioethics and Human Rights*, London: Cavendish Publishing, 2004.

Chapter 11

Organ transplantation

11.1 Introduction

Organ transplantation is undoubtedly one of the triumphs of modern medicine. The procedure has become increasingly routine as a means of saving and improving the quality of the lives of thousands of people each year. The history of this programme, and the manner in which it has expanded to encompass an increasing variety of organs and other body tissue, has been chronicled by David Lamb:

Lamb, D, *Organ Transplants and Ethics*[1]

The idea of taking bone, skin, or organs from one person and transplanting them into another has been a subject of fascination and intrigue since earliest times. Yet until the 20th century the dream of creating a healthy whole person by transplantation remained in the realm of mythology and the miraculous. Early attempts at blood transfusion met with no success until knowledge of different blood types and their mutual compatibility or incompatibility was discovered. This meant that many attempts at blood transfusion during the 18th century resulted in charges of homicide before several European courts outlawed the practice. However, blood transfusion was widely used in the 1914–18 war when blood banks were created to store blood. This, perhaps, was one of the most important features in the early stages of the history of transplantation. . . .

Transplantation of non-vital organs has steadily increased during the 20th century. Skin grafts began in the late 1920s. This procedure is usually applied as a temporary measure in cases of burns. Recent experiments with cultured skin, however, suggest that procurement from donors may one day be unnecessary. Under appropriate conditions skin can be stored and there are now skin and bone banks, where bone is stored for treatment of the skeletal system. . . .

The modern transplant era, however, began with the transplantation of non-regenerating vital organs in the 1950s, but its antecedents can be traced back to the turn of the century when Dr Alexis Carrel and Dr Charles C Guthrie developed the technique of suturing blood vessels. Then, in 1902, an Austrian surgeon, Dr Emmerick Ullman, removed a kidney from a dog and kept it functioning in the body of another dog for a few days. The eventual failure of this transplant revealed the problem of rejection, and it was discovered in further experiments that successful transplants depend on a close genetic resemblance between donor and recipient . . .

The major breakthrough in understanding rejection had to wait until Dr Peter Medawar, winner of the 1960 Nobel Prize, explained how the body's immunisation system recognises foreign bodies that enter it by means of markers or antigens, and then rejects foreign matter by means of the production of antibodies. This knowledge led to the development of tissue-typing, where the donor's and recipient's tissues are examined with a view to compatibility. . . . Throughout the 1960s and 1970s drugs were developed which lessened the organism's ability to develop antibodies. But many of these had the unfortunate effect of weakening the recipient's immune system. However, a major breakthrough occurred in 1983 when a Swiss pharmaceutical company produced Cyclosporin, which selectively inhibits the rejection of foreign tissues without damaging their ability to combat viruses and bacteria. The ability to control tissue rejection marks the transition from the era of transplantation as an experimental therapy to the era of organ transplantation as routine therapy.

However, despite compelling evidence that such transplants are not only of significant therapeutic benefit to the majority of recipients but highly cost effective (in allowing savings in other, more expensive forms of treatment, for example dialysis), this is an area which remains fraught with ethical difficulty. This is especially so as the demand for donor organs continues markedly to outstrip supply. As New et al. note:

---

1 London: Routledge, 1990.

New, B, et al., *A Question of Give and Take: Improving the Supply of Donor Organs for Transplantation*[2]

The transplanting of organs from one human to another is a medical intervention which 50 years ago would have seemed a suitable topic for a science fiction novel. And yet, in the 1990s, kidney transplants are the treatment of choice for end-stage renal disease, and heart and liver transplants offer the only chance of life for thousands of people across the world with chronic heart or liver failure. It is an operation which attracts intense media attention, particularly when children's lives are at stake. However, the reason for such attention is often particularly poignant, involving a race against time for a suitable donor.

The legal framework within which transplantation takes place – the general law as to the removal, retention and use of human materials – was subject to important review and change in the form of the Human Tissue Act 2004, which entered force in 2006. The background to the Act, which again illustrates the sensitivity of this whole area of medical activity, is set out in the explanatory notes issued by the Department of Health:

Explanatory Notes to the Human Tissue Act 2004[3]

4.   The purpose of the Act is to provide a consistent legislative framework for issues relating to whole body donation and the taking, storage and use of human organs and tissue. It will make consent the fundamental principle underpinning the lawful storage and use of human bodies, body parts, organs and tissue and the removal of material from the bodies of deceased persons. It will set up an over-arching authority which is intended to rationalise existing regulation of activities like transplantation and anatomical examination, and will introduce regulation of other activities like *post mortem* examinations, and the storage of human material for education, training and research. It is intended to achieve a balance between the rights and expectations of individuals and families, and broader considerations, such as the importance of research, education, training, pathology and public health surveillance to the population as a whole.

5.   The Act arose from concern raised by events at Bristol Royal Infirmary and the Royal Liverpool Children's Hospital (Alder Hey) 1999–2000. The *Kennedy* and *Redfern* inquiries at these hospitals established that organs and tissue from children who had died had often been removed, stored and used without proper consent. A subsequent census by the Chief Medical Officer for England (2000) and the *Isaacs Report* (2003) showed that storage and use of organs and tissue from both adults and children without proper consent has been widespread in the past. It also became clear that the current law in this area was not comprehensive, nor as clear and consistent as it might be for professionals or for the families involved . . .

In this chapter our main focus will remain the law as it pertains to organ transplants (although at times we shall touch upon wider issues arising from the use of human material). In sections 11.2 to 11.4, we look at the various sources from which organs may be obtained, including live donors and deceased human donors, and the ethical and legal issues raised in each case. In section 11.5 we then consider the (relatively novel) legal problem of what status to accord to extracted body parts, before addressing the rights of the donee of such material in section 11.6. Lastly, in section 11.7, we examine possible measures of law reform that aim to increase the number of organs available for transplantation.

---

2 London: Kings Fund Institute, 1994.
3 London: DoH, Crown copyright, 2004.

11.2 Transplants from living donors

11.2.1 Background

The world's first successful kidney transplant, which took place in Boston in 1954, involved a live donation between identical twins. Indeed, until the development of powerful new immuno-suppressant drugs in the early 1980s, live donation between close relatives was preferred in order to reduce the chance of organ rejection by the donee. Although, since then, live donations have decreased as a proportion of total organ transplants (2015–16 statistics from 'NHS Blood and Transplant' show that in the UK live donors accounted for just over a fifth of solid organ transplants), the numbers have been rising in actual terms: that year there were 1,075 live transplants, mostly involving kidneys.[4] Moreover, certain tissues, such as bone marrow and skin, are invaria-bly obtained from live donors.

The major ethical issue here is similar to that considered in the last chapter in relation to medical research, ie how far is it permissible to expose a person to harm, or the risk of harm, in order to benefit another? Just as in the case of research, the question exposes a conflict between two differing systems of moral philosophy. As Price and Garwood-Gowers observe:

Price, DPT and Garwood-Gowers, A, 'Transplantation from minors: are children other people's medicine?'[5]

By virtue of the fact that removal of the material from the donor is primarily for the prospective benefit of another individual, the whole issue of living donation of body materials for transplantation raises starkly the conflict between the two fundamental philosophical theories, deontological theory and consequen-tialist theory. Few areas of law highlight this conflict as keenly as deontological theory, of which Immanuel Kant is the prime exponent, which seeks to guide our actions by reference to overriding moral imperatives and insists that as part of a respect for persons their intrinsic moral worth dictates that they should not be used merely as a means to another's ends. By contrast, consequentialist approaches, of which utilitarian-ism is the pre-eminent example, attempt to judge the rightness or wrongness of an action according to the consequences which flow from it. The action which maximises happiness and minimises suffering is the preferred one. Clearly, on a utilitarian calculus the pendulum swings further in favour of donation than on a deontological approach in so far as the risks from donating even a paired organ are generally fairly modest, whereas transplanting such an organ has the potential to improve the quality (and duration) of life of the recipient dramatically.

The Kantian approach, with its emphasis on the primacy of human autonomy, may well be pre-ferred here. On the other hand, as suggested in Chapter 1, the conflict between the two systems largely disappears once it is realised that any plausible form of utilitarianism must also accord great weight to individual autonomy (albeit as an instrumental rather than intrinsic value): a society in which persons could have their organs forcibly extracted for the benefit of others would be a perilous and miserable one indeed.

That having been said, an interesting question concerns how far autonomy in this area should be completely unfettered. This is relevant where a person actively wishes to donate an organ even though the consequences to them will be serious harm or death. The Nuffield Coun-cil on Bioethics has expressed its conclusions on this matter as follows:

---

4 See: https://nhsbtdbe.blob.core.windows.net/umbraco-assets-corp/1452/activity_report_2015_16.pdf.
5 (1995) 1 Contemporary Issues in the Law 1.

Nuffield Council on Bioethics, *Human Tissue: Ethical and Legal Issues*[6]

6.4   We identify the avoidance and limitation of injury as a basic requirement for any type of use of human tissue to be ethically acceptable. Avoidance and limitation of injury can be seen as expressing a central element of the undefined, yet widely endorsed, demand for respect for the human body and for respect for human dignity. In paras 6.7–6.16 we identify and elaborate this basic requirement which makes types of use of human tissue ethically acceptable.

6.5   We note, however, that the avoidance and limitation of injury is a complex requirement, and that in certain circumstances, injury can be avoided or limited only by inflicting injury. In our view, the only circumstance in which inflicting injury is acceptable is when it is done to avoid greater injury. It is this that justifies much medical treatment, and action taken in self defence and in other situations. This principle is also useful in evaluating proposed uses of human tissue.

6.6   Although we identify the avoidance and limitation of injury as basic to acceptable use of human tissue, there are other important considerations. For example, consent of those from whom tissue is taken (patient, donor) or of relatives (post mortem) is important. Consent, however, is not the primary consideration. In particular, consent cannot justify injury: for example, killing or maiming cannot be justified by the victim being willing . . .

Avoidance and limitation of injury

6.7   It is not easy to state the underlying rationale for viewing these and other sorts of action as unacceptable. The difficulty is in part that many people see these actions as wrong, repugnant or repellent for multiple reasons, about some of which there is no agreement. The most widely accepted reasons, however, often stress that these sorts of action fail to respect others or to accord them dignity, that they injure human beings by treating them as things, as less than human, as objects for use. Although all these phrases are vague, there is considerable agreement about a central range of injurious activity that would constitute disrespect for human beings and for human dignity . . .

A related issue, touched upon in section 11.7 below, is how far a person should be entitled to benefit financially from the provision of his or her body parts?

11.2.2   The position at common law

11.2.2.1   The capable donor and the limits of consent

As a minimum, the donor must, where adult and capable, always consent to the removal of an organ. This is simply an application of the general rule that the consent of such a person is needed to any medical procedure. In this context, however, there may well be doubts about one of the preconditions for valid consent being present, namely freedom from coercion or undue influence. This is especially so in the vast majority of cases where the donation is between two members of the same family. As we saw in Chapter 3, the Court of Appeal was obliged to consider the effect of institutionalised power relationships upon the reality of consent in the case of *Freeman v Home Office (No 2)*.[7] Nevertheless, there is a suspicion that, in the case of related live transplants, the courts do not wish to get involved in determining such matters, and are instead leaving the question to the doctors.

Be that as it may, a further question long unresolved at judicial level was whether the removal of an organ for transplant by a surgeon would in any event remain a criminal assault, ie

---

6   London: Nuffield Council on Bioethics, 1995.
7   [1984] 1 All ER 1036.

notwithstanding the donor's consent. Writing in 1970, Gerald Dworkin commented on this issue as follows:

Dworkin, G, 'The law relating to organ transplantation in England'[8]

> [M]any surgical operations are *prima facie* unlawful. Without further justification not only would operations be criminal acts, but they would also be unlawful in the civil law and surgeons might be liable to pay compensation for the consequences of their acts, even though they had exercised all reasonable care. What are the criteria, then, which convert unlawful acts into lawful surgical operations? In some countries the criminal codes absolve from responsibility persons who perform in good faith and with reasonable care and skill a surgical operation upon another person, with his consent and for his benefit, if the performance of the operation is reasonable in the circumstances. No such provision appears in any United Kingdom legislation but it is clear, of course, that surgery, within limits, is a perfectly legal activity. Sir James Fitzjames Stephen formulated the general proposition that 'everyone has a right to consent to the infliction of any bodily injury in the nature of a surgical operation upon himself' and stated that although he knew of no authority for this, the existence of surgery as a profession assumed its truth.

Dworkin suggested four conditions that would need to be satisfied for surgery in general, and donor-organ removal in particular, to be lawful:

> (i)   *The patient must give a full, free and informed consent.* The importance of consent cannot be overemphasised ... It is clear that, in any common law jurisdiction, the general principle is that a patient should be informed of all the material facts relating to the operation which would enable a reasonable person to weigh up the risks and benefits and arrive at a rational decision whether or not to undergo the operation. Also, there should be no unfair pressure upon the patient which induces him to give his consent in spite of all the risks.
>
> (ii)   *The operation must be therapeutic: it must be expressly for the patient's benefit.* The major distinguishing feature between surgical operations and unlawful mutilation is, of course, that all surgical operations are allegedly in the medical interests of the patient. Coke refers to a case in 1603 where 'a young and lustie rogue prevailed upon a friend to cut off his left hand, so that he might be better able to beg'. Both were found guilty of the crime of maim; today, they would also be criminally liable. In the criminal codes of some countries, the provisions concerning surgical operations expressly state that they must be for the patient's benefit; in other countries this, until recently, has been accepted as being obvious.
>
> (iii)   *There must be lawful justification.* This is a relatively unexplored and open ended requirement. Ethical and social questions are more relevant here and the courts may occasionally use this rubric to extend the law to meet new circumstances. Most surgical operations are lawful ... There are other surgical operations, only arguably of therapeutic benefit to the patient, where the courts nevertheless may be tempted to emphasise their lawful justification. It is unlikely that the courts would condemn circumcision as unlawful. No doubt the ritual circumcision of Jewish infants could be upheld on grounds of religious toleration, although circumcision for non-religious reasons would have to be accepted on wider public policy grounds.
>
> (iv)   Generally, the operation must be performed by a person with appropriate medical skills ...

It is suggested that, rather than each being necessary in its own right, condition (ii) would tend now to be regarded as a particular application of the more general principle contained in (iii). In the present context (as opposed to therapeutic surgery), it is all-important to look at the reason why the operation is taking place: removal for transplantation is a socially recognised good and

---

8 (1970) 33 MLR 353.

is lawfully justified; removal for other purposes, for example because the person whose organ it was wanted to taste it, would remain a battery. A further requirement, given that no therapeutic benefit will accrue to the donor, appears to be that such removal must not expose the donor to an unreasonable amount of harm (or a significant risk thereof). In this regard, the media reported in February 1996 that doctors had refused the request of a father that his remaining kidney be transplanted into his chronically ill son and he be placed on dialysis instead. He had previously given up his first kidney to his other son.

It follows *a fortiori* from what has just been said that the law will not sanction the removal of vital organs where the consequence for the donor will be death. In his above article Gerald Dworkin cites the comment, made extra-judicially by Edmund Davies LJ to the effect that he would:

> be surprised if a surgeon were successfully sued for trespass to the person or convicted of causing bodily harm to one of full age and intelligence who freely consented to act as donor always provided that the operation did not present unreasonable risk to the donor's life or health. That proviso is essential. A man may declare himself ready to die for another, but the surgeon must not take him at his word.[9]

In such a case, the surgeon would be guilty of murder (or, at the very least, manslaughter). For this reason, transplants involving live donors are generally limited to tissues such as bone marrow, blood, and (more recently) liver lobes, which are all capable of regenerating; or kidneys, of which most people have a 'spare'. The only exception relates to so called 'domino transplants' of hearts which may occur following the donor's own receipt of a heart-lung transplant.

11.2.2.2 The incapable donor

The legal position, until relatively recently, was less clear in relation to the lawfulness of using incapable adults as donors. Such persons are by definition incapable of giving their consent; rather, as the House of Lords made clear in its decision in *Re F (Mental Patient: Sterilisation)*,[10] they may be subjected to medical intervention only in so far as the procedure is in their best interests. Can donating an organ be regarded as in the donor's (as opposed to the donee's) best interests? An important US case in point is *Strunk v Strunk*,[11] where an affirmative answer was given by the Kentucky Court of Appeals: it authorised a kidney transplant from Jerry, a 27-year-old man with a mental age of six, to his 28-year-old brother after hearing psychiatric evidence of the 'extremely traumatic effect' his brother's death would have upon him.

The question subsequently arose for determination by an English court in the case of *Re Y (An Adult Patient) (Transplant: Bone Marrow)*:

Re Y (Adult Patient) (Transplant: Bone Marrow)[12]

> Miss Y was 25 years old and had been severely mentally and physically disabled from birth. She had lived in care since the age of 10. Her sister, aged 36, who suffered from pre-leukaemic bone marrow disorder, sought a declaration that it would be lawful to perform blood tests and possible bone marrow extraction upon Miss Y, despite the latter's inability to consent:
>
> > **Connell J**: The taking of blood tests and the harvesting of bone marrow from the defendant who is incapable of giving informed consent would amount to assaults upon the defendant and would therefore be illegal unless shown to be in the best interests of the defendant and therefore lawful.

---

9 'A Legal Look at Transplants' (1969) 62 Proc Roy Soc Med 633.
10 [1990] 2 AC 1; this case is discussed in Ch 4.
11 445 SW 2d 145 (1969).
12 [1997] 2 WLR 556.

> The test to be applied in a case such as this is to ask whether the evidence shows that it is in the best interests of the defendant for such procedures to take place. The fact that such a process would obviously benefit the plaintiff is not relevant unless, as a result of the defendant helping the plaintiff in that way, the best interests of the defendant are served.
>
> The approach is as set out in the case of *Re F (Mental Patient: Sterilisation)* [1990] 2 AC 1 ... a non-therapeutic sterilisation case. Thus, the giving of medical treatment to mentally disordered adult patients is, save as to treatment for their mental disorder under the Mental Health Act 1983, governed by common law. The lawfulness of the action depends upon whether the treatment is in the best interests of the patient ...
>
> This case is different from the case of *Re F* because it involves the concept of donation of bone marrow by a donor who is incapable of giving consent where a significant benefit will flow to another person. There was no other person in *Re F* who would have benefited directly as a result of the declaration sought, the benefits of sterilisation attaching solely to the mentally incapacitated subject of the application.
>
> Nonetheless, I am satisfied that the root question remains the same, namely, whether the procedures here envisaged will benefit the defendant and accordingly benefits which may flow to the plaintiff are relevant only in so far as they have a positive effect upon the best interests of the defendant ...
>
> The information provided by those who now care for the defendant in the residential home make it apparent that the defendant benefits from the visits which she receives from her family and from her occasional involvement in family events, for example, the wedding of one of her sisters, particularly because these visits maintain for her a link with the outside world which is helpful to her and which would otherwise be lost to her. . . .
>
> If the plaintiff dies, this is bound to have an adverse effect upon her mother who already suffers from significant ill health. One lay witness took the gloomy view that this event would prove fatal to the mother, but in any event her ability to visit the defendant would be handicapped significantly, not only by a likely deterioration in her health, but also by the need which would then arise for her to look after her only grandchild, E.
>
> In this situation, the defendant would clearly be harmed by the reduction in or loss of contact to her mother. Accordingly, it is to the benefit of the defendant that she should act as donor to her sister, because in this way her positive relationship with her mother is most likely to be prolonged. Further, if the transplant occurs, this is likely to improve the defendant's relationship with her mother who in her heart clearly wishes it to take place and also to improve her relationship with the plaintiff who will be eternally grateful to her.

This case shows the court adopting a wide interpretation of 'best interests'; it is not somatic health alone which is relevant, but the wider interests a person has as part of the social community (this approach is also in line with decisions relating to sterilisation discussed in Chapter 4). Nevertheless, there are important limits on invoking the test in order to justify organ extraction, especially where the organ is non-regenerative. As Andrew Grubb has commented:

Grubb, A, 'Commentary on *Re Y*'[13]

> Of course, the judge recognised that it was insufficient for him merely to identify a 'benefit' to Miss Y without weighing against this any detriment that she might suffer by undergoing the procedures. However, the risks inherent in the procedures – the general anaesthetic and the removal of two pints of bone

---

13 (1996) 4 Med L Rev 204.

marrow – were regarded as 'very small' (one in 10,000 risk of death) and non-existent (as bone marrow is regenerative) respectively. Further any pain that might arise from the harvesting could be controlled by morphine. And, of course, there could be a detriment by not undergoing the procedure . . . In *Re Y*, Connell J referred to the 'harm' Miss Y would suffer (directly and indirectly) from the death of her sister although the evidence never elevated this to the level of psychiatric injury.

Limitations in future cases. Given the weaknesses in the evidence which have been suggested above, *Re Y* could be seen as giving a 'green light' to support donations by [incapable] adults and children in the future. This would, I think, be a misreading of the case and not Connell J's intention for a number of reasons.

First, the case is probably an unusual one in that it concerned a procedure which does have minimal risks for the donor. Given the need to weigh the benefits of the procedure against the risks of doing it, it is not likely that a court would contemplate donation of non-regenerative tissue such as a kidney. Connell J suggested as much when he remarked that his decision should not be considered 'a useful precedent in cases where the surgery involved is more intrusive.' While the long term risks of having one kidney are not great, they do exist and the nature of the procedure suggests that it would be difficult to satisfy the 'best interests' test . . .

Secondly, the courts will undoubtedly look for evidence of a 'close relationship' which will be damaged if the donee patient dies. It is most unlikely, therefore, that the court would contemplate even a minimally risky procedure if the donor's mental disability or if the child's age prevented them forming such a relationship. Donations by babies and the severely mentally disabled may thus be out of court.

The common law position is left broadly intact by the statutory framework for the mentally incapable, introduced by the Mental Capacity Act 2005. Thus, while the Code of Practice under the Act states that proposed cases of organ or bone marrow extraction should be referred to the Court of Protection, it expressly leaves the door open for court approval of such procedures, as follows:

Mental Capacity Act 2005 Code of Practice[14]

8.20 Cases involving organ or bone marrow donation by a person who lacks capacity to consent should also be referred to the Court of Protection. Such cases involve medical procedures being performed on a person who lacks capacity to consent but which would benefit a third party (though would not necessarily directly or physically benefit the person who lacks capacity). However, sometimes such procedures may be in the person's overall best interests. . . . For example, the person might receive emotional, social and psychological benefits as a result of the help they have given, and in some cases the person may experience only minimal physical discomfort.

11.2.2.3 Child donors

In contrast to the position with incapable adults, there is no English authority directly on the question of live organ donation by minors. Moreover, this issue raises a number of further complications. First, in the case of older children who satisfy the test of '*Gillick* competence', can they consent in their own right to act as donors? The answer, in principle, would appear to be yes. As Lord Donaldson MR noted, *obiter*, in *Re W (A Minor) (Medical Treatment)*:[15]

Lord Donaldson MR: [Section 8 of the Family Law Reform Act 1969 establishing the presumption that a minor of 16 years can consent to medical treatment] extends not only to treatment, but also to diagnostic

---

14 London: TSO, 2007; see: www.gov.uk/government/publications/mental-capacity-act-code-of-practice.
15 [1992] 3 WLR 758; the case is discussed in Ch 4.

procedures (see sub-s (2)). It does not, however, extend to the donation of organs or blood since, so far as the donor is concerned, these do not constitute either treatment or diagnosis. I cannot remember to what extent organ donation was common in 1967, but the Latey Committee expressly recommended that only 18 year olds and older should be authorised by statute to consent to giving blood. . . . It seems that parliament accepted this recommendation, although I doubt whether blood donation will create any problem as a *Gillick* competent' minor of any age would be able to give consent under the common law.

Organ transplants are quite different and, as a matter of law, doctors would have to secure the consent of someone with the right to consent on behalf of a donor under the age of 18 or, if they relied upon the consent of the minor himself or herself, be satisfied that the minor was *Gillick* competent' in the context of so serious a procedure which would not benefit the minor. This would be a highly improbable conclusion. But this is only to look at the question as a matter of law. Medical ethics also enter into the question. The doctor has a professional duty to act in the best interests of his patient and to advise accordingly. It is inconceivable that he should proceed in reliance solely upon the consent of an under-age patient, however *Gillick* competent', in the absence of supporting parental consent and equally inconceivable that he should proceed in the absence of the patient's consent. In any event he will need to seek the opinions of other doctors and may be well advised to apply to the court for guidance, as recommended by Lord Templeman in a different context in *Re B (A Minor) (Wardship: Sterilisation)* . . .

Lord Donaldson MR suggests here that it would be 'inconceivable' both that extraction would go ahead without parental consent *and* that it could occur solely on the basis of the latter (a necessary caveat in the light of his Lordship's 'flak jacket' approach to consent in his decision in the case).

In the case of children who lack capacity, it is apparent that the parents must normally give proxy consent to any form of medical intervention upon them. Indeed, in the American case of *Bonner v Moran*[16] a doctor who failed to obtain parental consent was held liable in battery after taking skin grafts from a 15-year-old boy to treat the latter's badly burnt cousin. On the other hand, it is clear that parental authorisation of such an intervention will not guarantee that it is lawful. Rather, as Lord Scarman made clear in *Gillick v W Norfolk and Wisbech HA*,[17] the parent's power to consent is one they should exercise exclusively for the child's benefit.

In its April 2017 Code of Practice on guiding principles and consent, the Human Tissue Authority offers the following guidance where the involvement of a child donor is contemplated:

Human Tissue Authority, *Code of Practice A – Guiding Principles and the Fundamental Principle of Consent*[18]

Children

128.   The HT Act allows children to consent to activities for scheduled purposes if they are competent to do so . . .

129.   Where the child has died and the child had not made a decision to give or withhold consent, the HT Act allows a person with parental responsibility for him or her immediately before he or she died to consent. Where the child is alive and has not made a decision and is either:

   a)   not competent to do so; or
   b)   competent to do so, but is unwilling to make that decision a person who has parental responsibility for the child may consent on their behalf

---

16 126 F 2d 121 (1941) (USCA DC).
17 [1986] 1 AC 112.
18 See: www.hta.gov.uk/sites/default/files/files/HTA Code A.pdf. The role of the Authority is discussed in section 11.2.3.

...131.   The HT Act is silent on how to assess a child's competence. The responsibility for assessing competence rests with the person seeking consent. The *Gillick* test . . . is considered to be the appropriate benchmark for assessing a child's competence.

132.   Where there is any dispute between people with parental responsibility or any doubt as to the child's best interests, the matter should be referred to court for approval . . .

133.   Where a child has capacity to consent, and agrees to the sharing of their information, it is good practice to consult the person (or people) who have parental responsibility for the child and to involve them in the process of the child making the decision. However, it should be emphasised that, if the child has capacity to consent, the decision to consent and to share their information must be the child's. It is also essential to make sure that a child has consented voluntarily and has not been unduly influenced by anyone else.

In fact, it appears that bone marrow donation between minor siblings occurs fairly routinely on the basis of parental consent. In relation to more intrusive and risky procedures, such as solid organ donation, it is much less likely that this would suffice. Rather, as suggested by the HTA Code of Practice, the matter would almost certainly be brought before the court for a declaration of lawfulness. In the USA, there have been a number of cases where such declarations have been granted: see, for example *Hart v Brown*,[19] which concerned a kidney transplant between seven-year-old identical twins. By contrast, the Illinois Supreme Court refused to make one in the case of *Curran v Bosze*:

Curran v Bosze[20]

The plaintiff was the former wife of the defendant and mother of three-and-a-half-year-old twins by him. The defendant's 12-year-old son from a previous marriage was dying from leukaemia and the defendant brought a petition requiring her to submit the twins to a blood test to establish compatibility with the 12-year-old with a view to a subsequent bone marrow transplant:

Calvo J: In each of the foregoing cases where consent to the kidney transplant was authorised, regardless whether the authority to consent was to be exercised by the court, a parent or a guardian, the key inquiry was the presence or absence of a benefit to the potential donor. Notwithstanding the language used by the courts in reaching their determination that a transplant may or may not occur, the standard by which the determination was made was whether the transplant would be in the best interest of the child or incompetent [incapable] person.

The primary benefit to the donor in these cases arises from the relationship existing between the donor and recipient. In *Strunk* [*v Strunk*], the donor lived in a State institution. The recipient was a brother who served as the donor's only connection with the outside world. In both *Hart* [*v Brown*] and *Little* [*v Little*], there was evidence that the sibling relationship between the donor and recipient was close. In each of these cases, both parents had given their consent . . .

We hold that a parent or guardian may give consent on behalf of a minor daughter or son for the child to donate bone marrow to a sibling, only when to do so would be in the minor's best interest.

The evidence reveals three critical factors which are necessary to a determination that it will be in the best interests of a child to donate bone marrow to a sibling. First, the parent who consents on behalf of the child must be informed of the risks and benefits inherent in the bone marrow harvesting procedure to the child.

---

19 289 A 2d 386 (1972).
20 566 NE 2d 1319 (1990).

Second, there must be emotional support available to the child from the person or persons who take care of the child. The testimony reveals that a child who is to undergo general anaesthesia and the bone marrow harvesting procedure needs the emotional support of a person whom the child loves and trusts. A child who is to donate bone marrow is required to go to an unfamiliar place and meet with unfamiliar people. Depending upon the age of the child, he or she may or may not understand what is to happen. The evidence establishes that the presence and emotional support by the child's caretaker is important to ease the fears associated with such an unfamiliar procedure.

Third, there must be an existing, close relationship between the donor and recipient. The evidence clearly shows that there is no physical benefit to a donor child. If there is any benefit to a child who donates bone marrow to a sibling it will be a psychological benefit. According to the evidence, the psychological benefit is not simply one of personal, individual altruism in an abstract theoretical sense, although that may be a factor.

The psychological benefit is grounded firmly in the fact that the donor and recipient are known to each other as family. Only where there is an existing relationship between a healthy child and his or her ill sister or brother may a psychological benefit to the child from donating bone marrow to a sibling realistically be found to exist. . . .

This court shares the opinion of the circuit court that Jean Pierre's situation evokes sympathy from all who've heard [it]. No matter how small the hope that a bone marrow transplant will cure Jean Pierre, the fact remains that without the transplant, Jean Pierre will almost certainly die. The sympathy felt by this court, the circuit court, and all those who have learned of Jean Pierre's tragic situation cannot, however, obscure the fact that, under the circumstances presented in the case at bar, it neither would be proper under existing law nor in the best interests of the three and a half year old twins for the twins to participate in the bone marrow harvesting procedure.

THINK POINT

Given the primacy of autonomy in other contexts (eg a patient's right to reject life-saving treatment), is the law not unduly paternalistic in its refusal to countenance a person's considered decision to donate, say, their heart in order to save their dying child?

11.2.3 Statutory limitations on live organ donation

11.2.3.1 'Appropriate consent' to storage and use of organs and tissue

The Human Tissue Act 2004 has introduced a new statutory regime of consent (termed by the Act 'appropriate consent') needed before human organs and tissue may be used and/or stored, including for transplantation. Nominally, the Act leaves it to the common law to determine the lawfulness of the prior *removal* of such material from live donors. However, in practice the new regime will already operate – in duplication with the common law – at the point of removal. Not only does removal here precede the material's use for transplantation but, as noted earlier, in legal terms such an intended use is essential. In other words, the failure to have obtained statutory consent (to subsequent use and/or storage) before removing an organ will render the removal itself unlawful at common law.

The relevant consent provisions of the 2004 Act, so far as they relate to live donors, are as follows:

Human Tissue Act 2004

2 'Appropriate consent': children

1   This section makes provision for the interpretation of 'appropriate consent' in section 1 in relation to an activity involving the body, or material from the body, of a person who is a child or has died a child ('the child concerned').
2   Subject to subsection (3), where the child concerned is alive, 'appropriate consent' means his consent.
3   Where –
    a   the child concerned is alive,
    b   neither a decision of his to consent to the activity, nor a decision of his not to consent to it, is in force, and
    c   either he is not competent to deal with the issue of consent in relation to the activity or, though he is competent to deal with that issue, he fails to do so,
'appropriate consent' means the consent of a person who has parental responsibility for him. . . .

3 'Appropriate consent': adults

1   This section makes provision for the interpretation of 'appropriate consent' in section 1 in relation to an activity involving the body, or material from the body, of a person who is an adult or has died an adult ('the person concerned').
2   Where the person concerned is alive, 'appropriate consent' means his consent. . . .

6 Activities involving material from adults who lack capacity to consent

Where –

a   an activity of a kind mentioned in section 1(1)(d) or (f) involves material from the body of a person who –
    i   is an adult, and
    ii lacks capacity to consent to the activity, and
b   neither a decision of his to consent to the activity, nor a decision of his not to consent to it, is in force,

there shall for the purposes of this Part be deemed to be consent of his to the activity if it is done in circumstances of a kind specified by regulations made by the Secretary of State.

As previously noted, these provisions operate on top of the existing common law requirements in relation to the lawful removal of material, and simply add a further safeguard. Thus, for example, as regards the use of material from an incapable child, s 2(3), providing for consent by a person with parental responsibility, in duplicating the common law requirement, in no way detracts from the requirement at common law for the removal procedure (and hence the consent thereto) also to be in the child's best interests.

Section 6 of the Act provides for the Health Secretary to make regulations to address the issue of consent in relation to incapable adults. This was done in 2006 in the form of the Human Tissue Act 2004 (Persons who Lack Capacity to Consent and Transplants) Regulations 2006,[21] which introduce special procedural requirements for such cases. These are discussed further in 11.2.3.3 below.

---

21 SI 2006/1659.

11.2.3.2 The prohibition on organ (and tissue) trafficking

Following a well-publicised scandal in the late 1980s, in which it was revealed that a Harley Street clinic was paying impoverished Turkish donors up to £3,000 for their spare kidneys, Parliament enacted the Human Organ Transplants Act 1989. This prohibited commercial dealings in organs (which were defined by the Act to include non-regenerative body parts, such as kidneys, but not regenerative tissues such as bone marrow or blood). The 1989 Act was repealed by the 2004 Human Tissue Act, which, in re-enacting the salient prohibitions, extended them to cover other forms of human tissue too. Section 32 provides as follows:

Human Tissue Act 2004

Trafficking

32   Prohibition of commercial dealings in human material for transplantation

(1)   A person commits an offence if he –
   a   gives or receives a reward for the supply of, or for an offer to supply, any controlled material;
   b   seeks to find a person willing to supply any controlled material for reward;
   c   offers to supply any controlled material for reward;
   d   initiates or negotiates any arrangement involving the giving of a reward for the supply of, or for an offer to supply, any controlled material;
   e   takes part in the management or control of a body of persons corporate or unincorporate whose activities consist of or include the initiation or negotiation of such arrangements.
(2)   Without prejudice to subsection (1)(b) and (c), a person commits an offence if he causes to be published or distributed, or knowingly publishes or distributes, an advertisement –
   a   inviting persons to supply, or offering to supply, any controlled material for reward, or
   b   indicating that the advertiser is willing to initiate or negotiate any such arrangement as is mentioned in subsection (1)(d).
. . .(6) For the purposes of subsections (1) and (2), payment in money or money's worth to the holder of a licence shall be treated as not being a reward where –
   a   it is in consideration for transporting, removing, preparing, preserving or storing controlled material, and
   b   its receipt by the holder of the licence is not expressly prohibited by the terms of the licence.
(7)   References in subsections (1) and (2) to reward, in relation to the supply of any controlled material, do not include payment in money or money's worth for defraying or reimbursing –
   a   any expenses incurred in, or in connection with, transporting, removing, preparing, preserving or storing the material,
   b   any liability incurred in respect of –
      i   expenses incurred by a third party in, or in connection with, any of the activities mentioned in paragraph (a), or
      ii   a payment in relation to which subsection (6) has effect, or
   c   any expenses or loss of earnings incurred by the person from whose body the material comes so far as reasonably and directly attributable to his supplying the material from his body.
(8)   For the purposes of this section, controlled material is any material which –
   a   consists of or includes human cells,
   b   is, or is intended to be removed, from a human body,
   c   is intended to be used for the purpose of transplantation, and
   d   is not of a kind excepted under subsection (9).

> (9) The following kinds of material are excepted –
>
> a   gametes,
>
> b   embryos, and
>
> c   material which is the subject of property because of an application of human skill . . .

Gametes and embryos are excepted on the basis that they are subject to their own regulatory regime under the Human Fertilisation and Embryology Act 1990 (as amended). However, otherwise it is apparent that the definition of controlled material under sub-s (8) is very wide and will encompass all cellular matter, including blood used for transfusions. It should also be noted that the immediate participants in the arrangement, ie the donor and donee of the material, are also caught by the section (contrast other statutes, such as the Surrogacy Arrangements Act 1985, where on public policy grounds, the immediate parties, are granted an immunity: in the case of trading in organs, clearly it was felt there were no such grounds). However, as stated in s 32(7) (c), the donor's reasonable expenses and/or loss of earnings as a result of donating will not count as a 'reward', and thus can lawfully be paid.

Section 32(4) and (5) provide for offences under the section to be punishable by stiff penalties, including (in the case of a breach of sub-s (1)) by a term of imprisonment of up to three years.

11.2.3.3 Further restrictions on live transplants – the role of the Human Tissue Authority

In addition to prohibiting commercial dealings, Parliament, when it passed the 1989 Human Organ Transplants Act, evinced a general concern about live donations between persons not genetically related. Accordingly, it created a special authority, the Unrelated Live Transplants Regulatory Authority, and provided that, to be lawful, such transplants had first to be approved by this authority. Nonetheless, the basis for singling out the unrelated donor for special protection in this way was never very convincing: arguably it is, if anyone, the related donor who may be vulnerable to illicit pressure to donate. As Kennedy and Grubb pointed out in their analysis of the 1989 legislation:

Kennedy, I and Grubb, A, *Medical Law: Text with Materials*[22]

Parliament was concerned that the donation be entirely altruistic and presumes that this will be so in the case of those who are 'genetically related' whereas it may not be otherwise. It is fair to ask, however, if the key to altruism is close family ties, why should a spouse be treated as a stranger? Furthermore, grandparents and grandchildren are genetically related and may surely be presumed to act as altruistically as those included within the Act, yet they too are excluded as if they were strangers. It cannot be that a grandparent is necessarily too old to be a donor because someone may be a grandparent at 40!

By contrast, if altruism is the key, why should parliament restrict unregulated donation to the genetically related? It could be said that intrafamily donations may well be the product of severe social pressure ('coercion') rather than altruism . . . In some jurisdictions, consequently, legislation prohibits the removal of non-regenerative tissue from a minor for the purpose of transplantation, recognising the danger of pressure within the family (see, for example, s 14(1) of the Human Tissue Act 1982 in Victoria, Australia).

---

22 London: Butterworths, 2nd edn, 1994.

Under the Human Tissue Act 2004, while special safeguards in relation to live transplants remain, the distinction between genetically related and unrelated donors has been largely removed. Instead, all proposed transplants – related and unrelated alike – must be referred for approval to the Human Tissue Authority.[23] The relevant provision of the 2004 Act, s 33, is as follows:

Human Tissue Act 2004

Transplants

33 Restriction on transplants involving a live donor

(1) Subject to subsections (3) and (5), a person commits an offence if –

    a   he removes any transplantable material from the body of a living person intending that the material be used for the purpose of transplantation, and

    b   when he removes the material, he knows, or might reasonably be expected to know, that the person from whose body he removes the material is alive.

(2) Subject to subsections (3) and (5), a person commits an offence if –

    a   he uses for the purpose of transplantation any transplantable material which has come from the body of a living person, and

    b   when he does so, he knows, or might reasonably be expected to know, that the transplantable material has come from the body of a living person.

(3) The Secretary of State may by regulations provide that subsection (1) or (2) shall not apply in a case where –

    a   the Authority is satisfied –

        i   that no reward has been or is to be given in contravention of section 32, and

        ii   that such other conditions as are specified in the regulations are satisfied, and

    b   such other requirements as are specified in the regulations are complied with.

(4) Regulations under subsection (3) shall include provision for decisions of the Authority in relation to matters which fall to be decided by it under the regulations to be subject, in such circumstances as the regulations may provide, to reconsideration in accordance with such procedure as the regulations may provide.

(5) Where under subsection (3) an exception from subsection (1) or (2) is in force, a person does not commit an offence under that subsection if he reasonably believes that the exception applies. . . .

(7) In this section –

    . . . 'transplantable material' means material of a description specified by regulations made by the Secretary of State.

The regulations referred to, the Human Tissue Act 2004 (Persons who Lack Capacity to Consent and Transplants) Regulations 2006 (which notwithstanding their title cover both capable and incapable donors)[24] were introduced in September 2006. After defining 'transplantable material' in reg 10 to include organs or part organs,[25] as well as – in the case of children and incapable adults – bone marrow and peripheral blood stem cells, reg 11 goes on to provide:

---

23 The Authority was set up under s 13 ff of the HTA 2004. For details of its work (which extends to the licensing of virtually all activities involving the use human tissue, not just organ donation), including the codes of practice it operates, see: www.hta.gov.uk.

24 See n 21 above.

25 Reg 10(2) makes an exception for 'domino transplants' (see 11.2.2.1 above), which accordingly do not require approval by the Authority.

Human Tissue Act 2004 (Persons who Lack Capacity to Consent and Transplants) Regulations 2006

Cases in which restriction on transplants involving a live donor is disapplied

11 – (1) Section 33(1) and (2) of the Act (offences relating to transplants involving a live donor) shall not apply in any case involving transplantable material from the body of a living person ('the donor') if the requirements of paragraphs (2) to (6) are met.

(2) A registered medical practitioner who has clinical responsibility for the donor must have caused the matter to be referred to the Authority.

(3) The Authority must be satisfied that –

    a   no reward has been or is to be given in contravention of section 32 of the Act (prohibition of commercial dealings in human material for transplantation), and

    b   when the transplantable material is removed –

        i   consent for its removal for the purpose of transplantation has been given, or

        ii   its removal for that purpose is otherwise lawful.

(4) The Authority must take the report referred to in paragraph (6) into account in making its decision under paragraph (3).

...

(6) Subject to paragraph (7), one or more qualified persons must have conducted separate interviews with each of the following –

    a   the donor,

    b   if different from the donor, the person giving consent, and

    c   the recipient,

and reported to the Authority on the matters specified in paragraphs (8) and (9).

(7) Paragraph (6) does not apply in any case where the removal of the transplantable material for the purpose of transplantation is authorised by an order made in any legal proceedings before a court.

(8) The matters that must be covered in the report of each interview under paragraph (6) are –

    a   any evidence of duress or coercion affecting the decision to give consent,

    b   any evidence of an offer of a reward, and

    c   any difficulties of communication with the person interviewed and an explanation of how those difficulties were overcome.

(9) The following matters must be covered in the report of the interview with the donor and, where relevant, the other person giving consent –

    a   the information given to the person interviewed as to the nature of the medical procedure for, and the risk involved in, the removal of the transplantable material,

    b   the full name of the person who gave that information and his qualification to give it, and

    c   the capacity of the person interviewed to understand –

        i   the nature of the medical procedure and the risk involved, and

        ii   that the consent may be withdrawn at any time before the removal of the transplantable material.

As well as needing to be satisfied that no payment has occurred, the Authority is thus directed to pay close attention to the consent aspects of the arrangement. In this regard it will require an independent assessor to carry out interviews with both the donor and recipient of the organ, covering such matters as possible coercion, the donor's knowledge of the risks and ability to understand them, etc. The decision to allow the transplant will then normally be taken by a 'HTA transport approvals team'; however, under reg 12, a panel of at least three Authority members is required to decide cases involving children or incapable adults, as well as ones of 'non-directed altruistic', 'paired' or 'pooled' donations. The meanings of the latter terms are elucidated in reg 12(5) of the 2006 Regulations:

> **12** – (5) In this regulation –
> 'non-directed altruistic donation' means the removal (in circumstances not amounting to a paired or pooled donation) of transplantable material from a donor for transplant to a person who is not genetically related to the donor or known to him;
> 'paired donations' means an arrangement under which –
> a   transplantable material is removed from a donor ('D') for transplant to a person who is not genetically related or known to D, and
> b   transplantable material is removed from another person for transplant to a person who is genetically related or known to D;
> and
>   'pooled donations' means a series of paired donations of transplantable material, each of which is linked to another in the same series (for example, transplantable material from D is transplanted to the wife of another person ('E'), transplantable material from E is transplanted to the partner of a third person ('F') and transplantable material from F is transplanted to D's son).

Paired live donation arises as an option where one person (D1) would like to donate to a specific person (R1), but is prevented from doing so by tissue incompatibility. In such a case, the solution is to find another similar couple (D2 and R2) and – assuming their respective compatibility – for D1 to donate to R2 in return for D2 donating to R1; pooled donation involves the same process with more than two couples. In 2006, NHS Blood and Transplant began setting up a paired/pooled donation matching scheme,[26] and the Human Tissue Authority has since approved a number of such arrangements, including the first pooled kidney donation in 2009.[27]

> **THINK POINT**
>
> In the light of the need for the donor to provide valid consent to extraction at common law, do the further consent formalities in the 2004 Act, including the requirement of HT Authority approval, serve any purpose?

11.3 Transplants from deceased donors

11.3.1 Background

As noted earlier, the development of new immuno-suppressant drugs within the last 30 years has diminished the importance of donor–recipient compatibility and permitted the increased use of cadaveric transplants. Currently, around two-thirds of kidneys transplanted in the UK are obtained in this way and the practice enjoys a number of practical advantages. Most obviously, there is no difficulty in terms of exposing the dead donor to harm (or the risk of harm) and a total harvesting of organs is therefore possible, including the heart, lungs, pancreas, and corneas. On the other hand, some distinct problems are also created, notably the need for the organs to be

---

26 See further: https://nhsbtdbe.blob.core.windows.net/umbraco-assets/1430/27514-uk-living-kidney-sharing-schemes.pdf.
27 See: www.telegraph.co.uk/news/health/news/7375616/First-three-way-kidney-transplants-carried-out-in-Britain.html.

removed fairly rapidly after death, if they are to be of any use. This raises the issue not only of who may authorise such removal, but also the larger question of how it is proper to treat the recently deceased human corpse. David Lamb has commented on this latter issue as follows:

Lamb, D, *Organ Transplants and Ethics*[28]

Although respect for the deceased takes different forms in different cultures, for the most part violation of the body's integrity for therapeutic purposes, such as organ transplantation, is not regarded as disrespect. At least no Western Church has adopted an unfavourable stance towards organ removal. Jewish, Christian, and Buddhist countries, despite prohibitions on the mutilation of corpses, permit cadaveric transplants provided prior consent of the deceased – or family consent – has been obtained.

The respect accorded to dead bodies in the Muslim faith rules out the study of anatomy on indigenous corpses. Post mortems are rare in Islamic countries. But in 1982 organ donation after death was declared *halal* (permissible) by the Senior 'Ulama' Commission, the highest religious authority in such matters, in Saudi Arabia . . .

Nevertheless, there are sources of resistance to organ transplantation which deserve consideration. An important aspect of resistance to routine harvesting of cadaveric organs is the symbolic role which is assigned to the dead body. This role should not be underestimated, even though the interests of the living may outweigh those of the dead. Joel Feinberg . . . cites a case which brings out the importance of such symbolism. In 1978 the Department of Transport in the USA contracted with several university laboratories to test designs for automobiles in actual crashes at varying velocities. Dummies had proven unsatisfactory. Some researchers – with the consent of the relatives – had substituted human cadavers. After a public outcry the tests were stopped, despite the Department of Transport's protest that such a decision would set back progress on safety protection for years. The grounds for the prohibition of these tests were that 'the use of human cadavers for vehicle safety research violated fundamental notions of morality and human dignity' . . .

The issue at stake appears to concern the symbolic role of the human cadaver. Violent assault on a cadaver is an assault on the important symbolic role assigned to the newly dead.

According to Feinberg, symbolic fears of this kind, though culturally significant, should not outweigh the imperative to save lives. Certainly objections to the routine salvaging of cadaveric organs based on symbolic fears should not impede research to improve life expectancy. To drive home this point Feinberg draws an analogy with William James' story of a Russian aristocrat who wept over a fictional tragedy in a theatre while her coachman froze to death outside in her carriage. In such cases the symbolic has outweighed the real.

There is merit in Feinberg's argument. But in reply it must be stressed that symbols are important to the very fabric of society. A society with no symbolic values for the dead is little short of savagery. Moreover, a body is not just a symbol. The newly dead continue as a presence, which is why they are referred to as deceased. The absence of the life that once existed has a very real presence . . .

Arguably, such symbolic concerns contributed to the furore in the wake of the revelations at Bristol and Alder Hey as to the non-consensual retention of organs from deceased children. As noted earlier, a result of these scandals has been the Human Tissue Act 2004, which aims to clarify the law governing the treatment of human materials generally. We shall look at the effect of the 2004 Act in relation to cadaveric organ transplants shortly. First, though, we consider two residual matters of common law that remain important.

---

28 See n 1 above.

11.3.2 Dealing with the recently deceased

11.3.2.1 Establishing death

Traditionally, death was defined in terms of cessation of cardiovascular function, that is the person had no pulse, was not breathing, etc. Advances in medical technology have rendered this approach obsolete: the features in question, though closely aligned with death, are no longer either sufficient or necessary for it (a person may be revived from the above state or, conversely, have the relevant functions sustained mechanically in the absence of all brain activity). Accordingly, a new definition of death was put forward in Guidelines issued by the Medical Royal Colleges in 1976.[29] Death is now equated with irreversible loss of brainstem function: the brainstem, which is the last part of the brain to die off, is necessary both for any possibility of awareness (the upper brainstem) and for spontaneous reflexes such as respiration (lower brainstem).

Although this new concept of death (referred to interchangeably as 'brainstem death' or simply 'brain death') has not been incorporated into legislation, it was accepted by the High Court in the 1992 case of *Re* A:

Re A[30]

A was a 19-month-old infant who was admitted to hospital with serious head injuries following a domestic incident. He was placed upon a ventilator but showed no signs of recovery. The hospital, after carrying out the diagnostic tests laid down by the MRC Guidelines, was satisfied that A was dead and applied for a declaration allowing his removal from the ventilator:

Johnson J: On 20 January – that is last Monday – the consultant removed A briefly from the ventilator to see whether he was capable of supporting himself without the ventilator. When she did so she heard slight gasping noises which led her to believe that A was not brainstem dead according to criteria now generally accepted in medical circles.

The precise definition of death has been the subject of recommendations by both the Royal College of Surgeons and the Royal College of Physicians and a working party of the British Paediatric Association. Applying the criteria laid down by her profession the consultant concluded on 20 January that A was not then brainstem dead. On the following day she again carried out the tests which are necessary to determine whether the necessary criteria are satisfied. The consultant described those tests to me and she explained to me that each one was satisfied. The tests lasted overall about half an hour. . . .

On the same day the consultant had arranged for a colleague consultant paediatric neurologist to carry out the same tests that she had, herself, carried out the previous day with a view to confirming or otherwise the validity of her own professional conclusion. Under professional guidelines it was not necessary for her to seek a second opinion in that way, but she decided that in the particular circumstances of the case it would be a wise thing for her to do. Accordingly, the tests were carried out again on Wednesday of last week, 22 January, by this colleague who reached the same conclusion as had been reached by the first consultant. Both doctors were at pains to exclude other possibilities for A's state, including the possibility of his suffering from extreme hypothermia or some abnormality of his biochemistry. Moreover, they tested for drugs, lest his brainstem function should have been suppressed by the administration of some drug of which they had not been aware . . .

Both doctors concluded that A was brainstem dead . . .

It is now Monday 27 January. I have no hesitation at all in holding that A has been dead since Tuesday of last week, 21 January.

---

29 (1976) 2 BMJ 1187.
30 [1992] 3 Med LR 303 (Fam).

The current Code of Practice in relation to diagnosing brain stem death, issued by the Academy of Medical Royal Colleges in 2008,[31] reiterates the earlier Medical Royal Colleges guidance.

11.3.2.2 Elective ventilation

The ability to establish the fact of death swiftly, but nevertheless with an appropriate degree of certainty, is important in the context of transplanting organs where, to maximise the chances of success, removal should generally take place as soon as possible. Before death is positively verified, the removal cannot of course come into question; even so, once the doctors are certain that a patient will not survive, there are other, earlier steps they might wish to take in order to preserve his organs pending their removal after death has been confirmed.

The problem here is that the patient will be – if not already dead – in an irreversible coma, and thus can, as an incapable person, only be treated in his own best interests. Concerns as to the legality of medical interventions upon patients in this situation led to the halting of a technique for organ retrieval previously deployed in the south west of England with some success. The background to the procedure in question, known as 'elective ventilation', and the debate it aroused, are described by David Price:

Price, DPT, 'Organ transplant initiatives: the twilight zone'[32]

In 1988 the Royal Devon and Exeter Hospital became the first British hospital to develop an E[lective] V[entilation] protocol. Patients in deep irreversible coma and believed to be dying imminently of intracranial haemorrhage were transferred to intensive care, with relatives' consent, so that artificial ventilation could be commenced immediately respiratory arrest occurred and until brain (stem) death tests could be satisfied. However, in October 1994, the Health Departments of England and Wales issued guidelines stating that EV for transplantation purposes constituted an unlawful battery – being non-therapeutic and not done in the best interests of the individual. This . . . is probably an accurate perception of the present common law. Although an alternative 'not against the interests of the individual' test has been occasionally employed in relation to non-therapeutic procedures performed on minors, such a standard has yet to be legally employed in respect of a mentally incompetent [incapable] adult person in a similar context . . .

The meaning of death

By contrast with the majority view across all disciplines, the clinicians who developed the Exeter protocol argue that the process of dying is not prolonged by EV, as the patient is already dead – one is ventilating a corpse . . . Riad, from Exeter, has said, 'The procedure causes no harm to the patient as ventilation is instituted at the time of respiratory arrest which is the consequence of brain death . . . Therefore it is important not to institute EV before respiratory arrest' . . .

Supporters of the Exeter protocol argue that cessation of respiration is (necessary and sufficient) evidence that the patient has already succumbed to brain death – the question is whether this is so . . .

Judicial acceptance

. . . [A]lthough there is no definition of death in English law, brain stem death established in accordance with the agreed criteria incorporated in the code of practice of the medical royal colleges has been accepted as establishing legal as well as 'medical' death. However, whilst this constitutes judicial acceptance of these tests, it does not necessarily indicate that this is the sole criterion for the determination of death in law . . .

---

31 See: http://aomrc.org.uk/wp-content/uploads/2016/04/Code_Practice_Confirmation_Diagnosis_Death_1008-4.pdf.
32 (1997) 23 JME 170.

> *Re A* illustrates that death can be legally declared to have occurred according to brain death criteria before two sets of tests have been completed and death has been confirmed. . . . The code of practice, although highly influential, does not have the force of law . . .

In effect, proponents of the Exeter protocol argued that in some cases (where patients had received direct injury to the brain stem) brain stem death should be recognised as preceding – and causing – cessation of respiration, rather than vice versa: accordingly, ventilation could already begin at that point simply to facilitate organ harvesting. Nonetheless, the diagnostic uncertainties involved, plus evidence of a risk of putting patients with residual brain-stem function into a PVS, have meant that 'elective ventilation', in terms of *commencing* ventilation of comatose and dying patients with a view to subsequent organ extraction, is no longer practised.

What, by contrast, is regarded as ethically and legally acceptable is the *continuing* life-support of patients initially placed on the ventilator on therapeutic grounds, in order to prolong the dying process until the transplant team is on hand (extraction will then take place once brain-stem death has been diagnosed, including – in an increasing number of cases – after cessation of ventilation as a 'non-heart-beating donation').[33] In these cases, where the incapable, dying patient previously expressed the wish to be an organ donor, such measures may be considered in their best interests, which, as per the 2005 Mental Capacity Act, may be influenced by the patient's previous wishes and values.[34] In this context, the Department of Health's Organ Donation Taskforce, in its 2008 Report, *Legal issues relevant to non-heartbeating donation*, advises as follows:

DoH, *Legal issues relevant to non-heartbeating donation*[35]

Maintenance of life-sustaining treatment

. . . 6.11   Decisions to carry out such interventions must be made in line with the MCA. If a person wanted to be an organ donor and such steps facilitate donation, then this will mean that these steps may be considered to be in that person's best interests. However, these considerations must be weighed against any significant risk of harm in maintaining each treatment and any distress that may be caused to the family by certain procedures, before determining if such steps would be in their best interests.

. . . 6.14   Anything that places the person at risk of serious harm . . . or distress . . . is unlikely ever to be in the person's best interests in this situation. A clinician would need strong and compelling reasons to consider these types of actions and would be recommended to seek a declaration from the Court of Protection in relation to the person's best interests before doing so.

. . . Timing and location of withdrawal of treatments

6.15   Decisions about the timing of withdrawal of treatment must be made in the person's best interests. It is generally understood and accepted that there is some flexibility in timing, for example to allow family members to be present or to make sure the relevant health professionals are available to oversee the donation process . . .

---

33   According to the statistics from NHS Blood and Transplant – see n 4 above – organs from non-heart-beating donors ('DCD donor organs') accounted for 1,267 of the 3,899 deceased donor solid organs transplanted in 2015/16.

34   MCA 2005, s 4(6); see further the discussion in Ch 12, section 12.4.3.

35   London: DoH, 2008, Crown copyright.

6.16 It is necessary to begin organ retrieval very soon after death has been declared. In practice this means that the surgical retrieval team must be ready and an operating theatre available before cardio-respiratory support is withdrawn. Because it commonly takes some hours for arrangements for retrieval to be completed, this requires withdrawal of cardio-respiratory support to be delayed if NHBD is to be possible. For similar reasons, local circumstances may necessitate moving the patient to a different location within the hospital ...

6.17 Again, it will be necessary for clinicians to assess whether such actions are in the best interests of the potential donor. If the person wanted to donate, then in many cases, because these steps facilitate donation, they may be considered to be in that person's best interests. The decision-maker must therefore consider whether this is something the person wanted to happen, whether the actions would cause any harm or distress to the person, or whether there was any significant risk of such an occurrence ...

As regards the Human Tissue Act 2004, this specifically allows, in s 43, for doctors to take steps to preserve cadaveric organs for transplantation. However, this provision is directed to potential donors whose death has already been confirmed: it relates to the legality of measures taken after this point, but before 'appropriate consent' has been obtained to the organs' removal and use: see further 11.3.3.2 below.

11.3.3 Authorising the removal and use of organs

11.3.3.1 Historical background

In 1970 Gerald Dworkin commented upon the shortcomings in previous law in this area, and the consequent need for more recent statutory intervention, as follows:

Dworkin, G, 'The law relating to organ transplantation in England'[36]

a   *Common law.* The common law position concerning corpses is curious but relatively well established. A corpse cannot ordinarily be the subject of ownership. Usually the executor or next of kin will have lawful possession of the body and there is a duty to arrange for burial at the earliest opportunity. It follows that, at common law, a man cannot by his will, or otherwise, legally determine what shall happen with his body after his death, although in most cases his wishes concerning the disposal of his body will be observed. That does not, of itself, authorise organs to be taken from corpses for the purpose of transplantation.

b   *Statute.* The need for human bodies for medical purposes is not new: bodies have always been required for anatomical teaching and research. But any attempt on the part of persons in possession of a body to sell it, even for the purpose of dissection, was unlawful; the bodies of persons convicted of murder were alone capable of being used for dissection. The scandals of body snatching and the publicity of the murder trial of Burke and Hare led to the passing of the Anatomy Act 1832, which enabled bodies to be supplied legally to medical schools for the purpose of anatomical examination. The demand for corpses was then successfully met for over a century.

It is only in recent times that the medical profession realised that the law relating to cadavers was far too restrictive. The successful development of the corneal graft operation focused attention on the lack of supply of eyes and the inability of potential donors to bequeath their eyes for such purposes. In a

---

36 See n 8 above.

little debated, but carefully prepared, piece of legislation the Corneal Grafting Act 1952 (the wording of which to some extent followed the Anatomy Act 1832) was passed authorising the use of eyes of deceased persons for therapeutic purposes. This Act quickly proved to be too narrow, for it did not enable any other part of the body to be removed. However, once this kind of provision was on the statute book, it was much easier to extend it. The Human Tissue Act 1961 replaced the 1952 Act and authorised, in certain circumstances, 'the use of the body or any specified part of the body after death for therapeutic purposes or for purposes of medical education or research'.

The Human Tissue Act 1961 allowed organs to be removed by the hospital (in lawful possession of the body) for transplant where the deceased had made an express request to that effect. Alternatively, in the absence of such a request, removal was authorised where reasonable inquiry revealed no objection to the same either by the deceased or by his spouse/surviving relatives. Nonetheless, significant vagaries remained in the statutory provisions, including as to the scope of 'any surviving relative', and what amounted to the making by the hospital of 'such reasonable inquiry as may be practicable'. More seriously, even if a breach of the statute could be demonstrated – eg the parents of the deceased were present but simply not asked if they objected to organ removal – the Act failed to provide for any offence to be committed.[37]

The lack of effective legal penalties for taking cadaveric organs without reference to the relatives may well have contributed to the Alder Hey scandal in the late 1990s, in which it was revealed that organs of deceased children had routinely been taken and stored without their parents' knowledge. The subsequent public inquiry into those events accordingly recommended urgent amendment of the 1961 Act to provide for criminal, and possibly also civil law sanctions:

The Royal Liverpool Children's Inquiry Report[38]

We respectfully recommend that:

- The Department of Health, the Royal Colleges and medical schools shall instruct members of the medical profession in the precise terms and provisions of the Human Tissue Act 1961, on the basis of our analysis, and the need for strict compliance.
- The Human Tissue Act 1961 shall be amended to provide a test of fully informed consent for the lawful post mortem examination and retention of parts of the bodies of deceased persons. While we have concluded that there has been little difference between 'lack of objection' and 'informed consent' in practical terms for the next of kin, it is important that the law and future practice are brought into line and updated.
- The class of persons relevant to the obtaining of fully informed consent shall be defined as the 'next of kin'.
- The class of 'any surviving relative' shall no longer be relevant to post mortem examination.
- There shall be a programme of health education for the public relevant to the medical need for continued post mortem examination and access to organs and samples for therapeutic, educational and research purposes.

---

37 Subsequently, in *AB v Leeds Teaching Hospital NHS Trust* [2004] EWHC 644 – an action brought by parents affected by the Alder Hey Scandal – the High Court recognised a remedy in negligence (in the form of damages for psychiatric injury).
38 London: HMSO, 2001.

- The Department of Health, the Royal Colleges and medical schools shall provide training for all those involved in obtaining fully informed consent.
- The Human Tissue Act 1961 shall be amended to impose a criminal penalty by way of fine for breach of its provisions in order to encourage future compliance.
- Guidelines relating to the requirements of the Human Tissue Act 1961 and the obtaining of fully informed consent shall be drawn up and provision made for breach to result in disciplinary proceedings which could lead to suspension, dismissal or financial penalty.

The Human Rights Act 1998 makes provision for an effective remedy other than in criminal proceedings. If breaches of the Human Tissue Act 1961 amount to breaches of the Human Rights Act 1998 consideration shall be given to incorporating a financial remedy with the Human Tissue Act 1961 itself. If necessary, reference should be made to the Law Commission.

In the event, Parliament opted to repeal the 1961 Act altogether, and include cadaveric organ transplantation as one of the matters covered in the Human Tissue Act 2004, which entered force in 2006.

11.3.3.2 The effect of the Human Tissue Act 2004

As noted earlier, the 2004 Act establishes a comprehensive regulatory regime in relation to the removal, storage and/or use of human tissue, with wider implications than for transplantation alone (indeed, the Alder Hey scandal itself did not involve any issues of transplantation). However, transplantation is one of the scheduled purposes caught by the Act, in respect of which 'appropriate consent' will now be required. We have already examined the relevant sections as they bear upon live donors. As regards cadaveric donors, the salient terms of the Act are as follows:

Human Tissue Act 2004

2 'Appropriate consent': children

(1) This section makes provision for the interpretation of 'appropriate consent' in section 1 in relation to an activity involving the body, or material from the body, of a person who is a child or has died a child ('the child concerned') . . .

(7) Where the child concerned has died . . . 'appropriate consent' means –

  a   if a decision of his to consent to the activity, or a decision of his not to consent to it, was in force immediately before he died, his consent;

  b   if paragraph (a) does not apply –

    i   the consent of a person who had parental responsibility for him immediately before he died, or

    ii   where no person had parental responsibility for him immediately before he died, the consent of a person who stood in a qualifying relationship to him at that time.

3 'Appropriate consent': adults

(1) This section makes provision for the interpretation of 'appropriate consent' in section 1 in relation to an activity involving the body, or material from the body, of a person who is an adult or has died an adult ('the person concerned') . . .

(6) Where the person concerned has died . . . 'appropriate consent' means –

a if a decision of his to consent to the activity, or a decision of his not to consent to it, was in force immediately before he died, his consent;

b if –

i paragraph (a) does not apply, and

ii he has appointed a person or persons under section 4 to deal after his death with the issue of consent in relation to the activity,

consent given under the appointment;

c if neither paragraph (a) nor paragraph (b) applies, the consent of a person who stood in a qualifying relationship to him immediately before he died.

(7) Where the person concerned has appointed a person or persons under section 4 to deal after his death with the issue of consent in relation to the activity, the appointment shall be disregarded for the purposes of subsection (6) if no one is able to give consent under it.

(8) If it is not reasonably practicable to communicate with a person appointed under section 4 within the time available if consent in relation to the activity is to be acted on, he shall be treated for the purposes of subsection (7) as not able to give consent under the appointment in relation to it.

4 Nominated representatives

(1) An adult may appoint one or more persons to represent him after his death in relation to consent for the purposes of section 1.

(2) An appointment under this section may be general or limited to consent in relation to such one or more activities as may be specified in the appointment.

(3) An appointment under this section may be made orally or in writing . . .

These requirements are elaborated upon in the Human Tissue Authority's Code of Practice F on solid organ and tissue donation. As regards the position of deceased donors, the latter states:

Human Tissue Authority, *Code of Practice F – Donation of Solid Organs and Tissue for Transplant*[39]

117. A legally valid decision from the donor him or herself is sufficient to allow organs and tissue to be retrieved for transplantation where they have decided to donate. Similarly, in circumstances where they have decided not to donate, donation cannot proceed. There is no legal right for anyone in a qualifying relationship to revoke a legally valid decision to give or withhold consent.

. . . 120. Where valid consent has been given by the donor, but relatives object to organ or tissue donation proceeding, then they should be sensitively supported to respect the prospective donor's consent to ensure his or her wishes are fulfilled. A relative's objection does not nullify appropriate, valid consent from the prospective donor.

121. The existence of appropriate, valid consent permits an activity to proceed, but does not mandate that it must. The final decision about whether to proceed with the activity rests with the medical practitioner . . .

---

39 See: www.hta.gov.uk/sites/default/files/files/HTA%20Code%20F.pdf. For a case applying the relevant HTA provisions outside the organ donation context, see *CM v Estate of EJ* [2013] EWHC 1680 (Fam).

... 128.   If the deceased person's decision is not known and they were an adult who had nominated a person to deal with the use of their body after death, then consent can be given by that nominated representative ...

129.   If the deceased person's decision is not known, and they had not appointed a nominated representative, consent can be given by a person who was in a qualifying relationship when death has been declared by the caring team ...

130.   An approach should be made to the deceased person's spouse or partner, relatives or close friends ... by a [Senior Nurse for Organ Donation]. Best practice recommends that the approach to the deceased person's relatives should be made together by the SN-OD and a member of the team who is caring for the person to establish any known decision of the potential donor.

As the Code notes, where the deceased did not consent (or refuse), then there are two mechanisms through which their organs may nevertheless be taken; the first is if the deceased appointed a nominated representative under s 4 of the 2004 Act, and the latter consents.[40]

Secondly, in the absence of a nominated representative, appropriate consent may be given by someone in a 'qualifying relationship'. Such persons are defined in s 54(9) of the Act as 'spouse, partner, parent, child, brother, sister, grandparent, grandchild, child of a brother or sister, stepfather, stepmother, half-brother, half-sister and friend of long standing'. In practice a ranking is applied: in this regard the 2004 Act enjoined the Human Tissue Authority to provide in its Code of Practice as follows:

Human Tissue Act 2004

27   Provision with respect to consent

(1)   The duty under section 26(3) [viz, to deal with consent issues in its Code of Practice] shall have effect, in particular, to require the Authority to lay down the standards expected in relation to the obtaining of consent where consent falls by virtue of section 2(7)(b)(ii) or 3(6)(c) to be obtained from a person in a qualifying relationship ...

(4)   The qualifying relationships for the purpose of sections 2(7)(b)(ii) and 3(6)(c) should be ranked in the following order –

    a   spouse or partner;

    b   parent or child;

    c   brother or sister;

    d   grandparent or grandchild;

    e   child of a person falling within paragraph (c);

    f   stepfather or stepmother;

    g   half-brother or half-sister;

    h   friend of longstanding.

(5)   Relationships in the same paragraph of subsection (4) should be accorded equal ranking.

(6)   Consent should be obtained from the person whose relationship to the person concerned is accorded the highest ranking in accordance with subsections (4) and (5) ...

---

40   The role of nominated representatives is elaborated on in HTA: *Code of Practice A*, paras 79–85.

In the case of deceased children, the rules are similar: if capable, the deceased would himself have been able consent; if he did not do so, a person with parental responsibility should be asked and, failing such a person, then somebody in a qualifying relationship.[41]

Unlike the Human Tissue Act 1961, which failed to provide any sanction for non-compliance, the 2004 Act makes clear that the use of material without 'appropriate consent' is a criminal offence. Section 5 provides as follows:

Human Tissue Act 2004:

5 Prohibition of activities without consent etc

(1) A person commits an offence if, without appropriate consent, he does an activity to which subsection (1), (2) or (3) of section 1 applies, unless he reasonably believes –

    a   that he does the activity with appropriate consent, or

    b   that what he does is not an activity to which the subsection applies . . .

(7) A person guilty of an offence under this section shall be liable –

    a   on summary conviction to a fine not exceeding the statutory maximum;

    b   on conviction on indictment –

        i   to imprisonment for a term not exceeding 3 years, or

        ii   to a fine, or

        iii to both.

THINK POINT

What would the position be if the doctors, in taking an organ, ignore the ranking in s 27(4) of the 2004 Act, and obtain the consent of the deceased's half-brother, rather than of his wife: will they have committed an offence or be otherwise liable?

11.3.3.3 Further issues – conditional and directed donation

In general, it should be noted that, under s 1(1) of the 2004 Act, the presence of 'appropriate consent' merely makes it lawful for the hospital to remove material from the deceased and use it for a stipulated scheduled purpose, including for transplantation. There is, however, no obligation upon it to do so. Most obviously, the organs in question may not be medically suitable for donation; more problematically, even where the deceased expressed the wish to donate in a donor card, the relatives in their distress may voice objections, and the doctors then feel unable ethically to proceed: this appears to have occurred quite often under the (in this respect identical regime of the) 1961 Human Tissue Act. Indeed, while the HTA, in its previous Code of Practice under the 2004 Act, was here robust (advising doctors to tell the relatives they have no veto rights,)[42] this advice has been dropped from the 2017 Code.

In 1998, media reports into an incident in the north of England highlighted a somewhat different concern, namely the practice of 'conditional donation' in which the relatives, or indeed the deceased, have sought to impose conditions upon the donation of the deceased's organs – in

---

41 See too the HTA Code of Practice F, at paras 135 ff.
42 HTA Code of Practice 2 (2009), para 102.

that case that they should only go to a white person. In its subsequent report into the incident, the Department of Health rejected as unethical the possibility of any such conditional donation:

Department of Health, *An Investigation into Conditional Organ Donation: The Report of the Panel*[43]

6.1   This was a very unfortunate incident. It should not have happened. In the Panel's view to attach any condition to a donation is unacceptable, because it offends against the fundamental principle that organs are donated altruistically and should go to patients in the greatest need. The Panel consider that racist conditions are completely abhorrent, as well as being unacceptable under the Race Relations Act ...

6.4   In saying this, the Panel are conscious that one consequence of a decision not to accept organs might be that seriously ill potential recipients might die before other organs become available. This is therefore a hard judgement to make. The Panel are, however, convinced that it is the right one, morally as well as legally. The Panel have been interested to discover that the vast majority of those they have talked to in the course of their investigation, patient groups as well as clinicians, take the same view.

6.5   This is not true of everyone, however. Some very strongly believe that the overriding principle should be the saving of lives. In their view any conditions should be accepted if the consequence is that more organs become available than would otherwise be the case. The Panel do not accept this argument.

In this case, the racist nature of the donor's condition made it relatively easy for the DoH Panel to reject this form of donation as unethical.[44] However, in other circumstances, the ethics of the situation may be more complex: in particular, what of a case where the deceased attaches as a condition of donation that one or more of their organs should be used to treat a particular person or persons? As we saw in section 11.2, this kind of 'directed' donation is the norm in the context of transplants from living donors; however in relation to cadaveric donation, the default position is of 'unconditional' donation, according to an ethic of disinterested altruism, ensuring that organs are allocated purely on the basis of greatest medical need. Two questions are how far this ethical position is open to challenge, particularly in the light of the quite different approach to living donation; and, secondly, whether the recent change to the law (in the form of the 'appropriate consent' requirements in the 2004 Act) may unwittingly have served to undermine it?

As regards the first issue, controversy was generated in 2008 by media reports into the case of Laura Ashworth, a young woman who, prior to her sudden death from asthma, intended to apply to the Human Tissue Authority to act as a living kidney donor for her mother, who had suffered renal failure. Ms Ashworth had also registered as a deceased donor and, following her death, her organs were in fact given to anonymous recipients on the basis of medical need. This was despite her family telling the hospital staff she would have wanted a kidney to go to her mother. The incident prompted the Authority to issue a statement in response:

Human Tissue Authority, *Statement on directed donations of organs after death*[45]

The central principle of matching and allocating organs from the deceased is that they are allocated to the person on the UK waiting list who is most in need and who is the best match with the donor. This is regardless of gender, race, religion or any other factor. The ethics of this position have long been supported by the government and professionals working in the field.

---

43 London: DoH, 2000.
44 See also the HTA Code of Practice F (April 2017), at para 23.
45 HTA Statement 14 April 2008.

> In line with this central principle, a person cannot choose to whom their organ can be given when they die; nor can their family. However, the HTA recognises that there may be exceptional situations when this rule might be reconsidered, but the importance of maintaining the central principle means that such exceptional situations would need to be considered with the greatest care before any part of the current rules were to be changed.

Subsequently, NHS Blood and Transplant, together with the HTA, have adopted a more flexible approach, acknowledging that exceptionally, the previous wishes of the deceased to donate to a specified individual could be taken into account: this is subject though to the donor having registered to donate on an unconditional basis and, secondly, that no one else is in 'desperately urgent clinical need' of the organ.[46]

As to the effect of the Human Tissue Act 2004, it is arguable that, with its new regime of appropriate consent, it has actually (if unintentionally) put greater power in the hands of deceased donors and/or their relatives to attach conditions to donation, which – if not adhered to – may lead to the potential liability of the medical staff. This argument is explored by Cronin and Douglas as follows:

Cronin, AJ, and Douglas, JF, 'Directed and conditional deceased organ donations: laws and misconceptions'[47]

[P]aragraph 105 [of the HTA Code] states:

Consent can be:

- General, i.e. if someone consents to the use of tissue for research, it need not be limited to a particular object
- Specific, i.e. a person limits their consent – a sample can only be used for research into a particular condition
- Both general and specific, i.e. a general consent subject to specific exceptions.

It is true that the examples given by the 2006 Code seem to refer to cases of proposed tissue retention for research: but both the 2004 Act and the Code make it clear that, in section 3, 'general provision is made for adults to consent to the use of their material for a range of purposes, including research and organ transplantation'. If consent is not required to be unrestricted, or 'generic' in the context of donations for research, the same *must* apply to consent for deceased organ donation for transplantation since neither the 2004 Act nor the Codes make any distinction as to the nature of the consent involved in these two situations. In 2009, a Revised Code of Practice not only restated the difference between generic and specific consent but also emphasized that it should be *valid*, i.e. given voluntarily by an 'appropriately informed' and [capable] person . . .

The conclusion from this interpretation of consent is clear but disconcerting. If a donor's consent has been limited to specific situations, it follows that any allocation of organs contrary to such limitations vitiates that consent and amounts to dealing with the organs without consent . . . [In such a case] [NHS Blood and Transplant, Organ and Transplantation Directorate] (or any other organ user) is *not* free to accept the donation while ignoring the restriction . . . To do so would be an offence under section 5 of the Act. It has been argued already that conditional and directed donations have never been illegal per se, as they are not prohibited by any law. But, even if a restriction were held to be illegal (e.g. under the Race Relations Acts), it

---

46 See: http://odt.nhs.uk/pdf/introduction_to_selection_and_allocation_policies.pdf (POL200/3, Appx 1).
47 (2010) 18 Med L Rev 275.

> does not follow that it could then be disregarded for the purposes of establishing consent to unconditional donation. On the contrary, like any other qualification, it would tend to vitiate the donor's consent, raising the prospect of criminal liability as a result.

A further, interesting, question that follows on from this is whether, in such circumstances of a conditional directed donation (ie where the deceased consents to donate a given organ to a specified individual only), the medical staff/organ procurement agency would remain free simply to refuse to use the organ on those conditions. For, at least where the organ would have been medically suitable for the nominated recipient, such a refusal could arguably expose them to a civil law action by the latter in negligence. This possibility is considered further in section 11.6.1 below.

11.4 Other sources of organs/tissue

As well as living and deceased human donors, there are a number of other possible sources of supply of organs and tissue that may offer themselves. As transplant technology continues to advance, some of these can be expected to assume increasing importance in the future.

11.4.1 Foetal tissue transplants

Recent developments in medical science have revealed the possibility of using live brain cells, harvested from aborted foetuses of 10–14 weeks' gestation, to treat certain degenerative brain disorders, notably Parkinson's and Alzheimer's disease. In the future, foetal pancreatic cells may also be used in the treatment of some forms of diabetes. In contrast to the issue of embryo research looked at in Chapter 7, the focus here is on the usage of *in vivo* foetuses. The ethical difficulty that this gives rise to, and the entanglement of this issue with the abortion debate, is explored by David Lamb:

Lamb, D, *Organ Transplants and Ethics*[48]

> What are the chief ethical objections to foetal tissue research and transplants? There are three closely related objections. First, it is argued that killing and then dissecting a foetus is an abuse to the developing human being. The second objection is that engaging in such practices will brutalise those who perform this work, and the third objection is that it will encourage abortions and even motivate conceptions with the express intention to abort . . . In addition to these objections are ethical problems concerning the authorisation of embryo tissue research and transplantation.
>
> The . . . objections are so closely related that they can be dealt with together. The issue they relate to is the morality of voluntary termination of pregnancy. . . . In short, if voluntary termination is wrong, then so are actions which depend on it, and at least some degree of guilt by association is incurred by those who seek to benefit from the killing of a foetus. Moreover, an assurance that no foetus is ever dissected prior to death would be of no consequence. For on these terms the issue turns on the rightness or wrongness of killing the foetus in the first place . . .
>
> On these terms, it would seem that if the arguments against voluntary terminations are persuasive, then the only scope for ethical discussion on foetal tissue transplantation is whether it is morally

---

48 See n 1 above.

acceptable to use material from spontaneous abortions. The problem is that material from the latter is less reliable than from voluntary abortions. This is because the possibility of foetal abnormality is too high, and because of various problems concerning the time lag between the actual death of the foetus and its expulsion from the uterus. In any case, most miscarriages occur too early for viable transplantation.

But given the obvious benefits of foetal cadaver research and transplantation, can these virtues be separated from what some people see as the immorality of elected abortion? According to the foregoing discussion the rights and wrongs of abortion and foetal tissue research and transplantation stand or fall together. Yet despite an obvious causal relationship between them, this is not necessarily the case. It could be argued that even if abortion is regarded as wrong, discussions concerning the ethical status of research on embryos and possible transplantation of foetal tissue are an independent issue. The UK Committee, chaired by John Polkinghorne (1989), outlined a 'separation principle' according to which there must be 'a separation of the supply of foetal tissue from its use'. This is to ensure that the need for foetal tissue does not influence decisions to have abortions. One consequence of this principle was the recommendation that whilst informed maternal consent is required for the use of foetal tissue, the woman concerned should have no knowledge of what happens to it.

What is the ethical basis of a separation principle? [John] Robertson, who maintains that the abortion issue and the ethics of foetal research can be treated separately, suggests an analogy with transplant organs taken from homicide victims. If consent is obtained, then the victim's organs can be retrieved and distributed to recipients without any suggestion that the surgeon who has received the heart, lung, or kidneys, was an accomplice to murder, even if he or she was aware of the source. By the same token medical students, who use cadavers of murder victims in anatomy, cannot be associated with a crime. Moreover, research on legally obtained cadavers of murder victims cannot, in any way, be said to be responsible for the brutalisation of the researchers or contribute to an increase in the homicide rate. 'One may benefit from another's evil act without applauding or approving of that evil', says Robertson . . .

The Polkinghorne Report referred to here was presented in 1989 by a committee of inquiry, chaired by the Revd John Polkinghorne, into the research use of such foetuses. It set out its 'separation principle' as follows:

Polkinghorne Committee, *Review of Guidance on the Research Use of Foetuses and Foetal Tissue*[49]

4.1   We have taken the view that, whatever one's ethical opinion about abortion itself, it does not follow that morally there is an absolute prohibition on the ethical use of foetuses or foetal tissue from lawful abortion. We have argued that the termination of pregnancy and the subsequent use of foetal tissue should be recognised as separate moral questions and we regard it as of great importance that the separation of these moral issues should be reflected in the procedures employed. Accordingly, we have recommended that great care should be taken to separate the decisions relating to abortion and to the subsequent use of foetal material. The prior decision to carry out an abortion should be reached without consideration of the benefits of subsequent use. . . .

4.2   It has been argued that knowledge of the use of foetal tissue could influence mothers' decisions to have their pregnancies terminated. It has been suggested that the use of foetal tissue could place women under pressure when reaching a decision or result in more abortions taking place. It has even been put to us that someone could become pregnant in order to make a foetus available for medical use. In our

---

49 Cm 762, London: HMSO, 1989.

view, pregnancy undertaken to such an end would be an ethically unacceptable use of the foetus as an instrument (treating it as a 'thing'). It is not possible fully to discern people's motivations, but it is possible to limit the degree to which morally dubious wishes can be implemented. To this end we recommend, not only the separation of the decisions relating to abortion and the subsequent use of foetal tissue, but also procedures which will make it impossible for a mother to specify that foetal tissue, which she makes available, should be used in a particular way.

A related question is whether the consent of the mother of the foetus should in fact be sought in these circumstances. David Lamb comments on this as follows:

Lamb, D, *Organ Transplants and Ethics*[50]

It might be argued that having decided to terminate her pregnancy, she has foregone any rights concerning the foetal disposal. [John] Harris argues that there is no moral basis for seeking the mother's consent over what happens to an aborted foetus. 'Has she not already abdicated responsibility for the foetus by opting for abortion?' asks Harris . . . Moreover, when the aborted foetus cannot live, or is already dead, Harris sees no moral requirement to seek maternal consent:

> If experimenters ask her for, and are given, permission to experiment on the foetus this permission will not absolve them from the responsibility of deciding for themselves whether such a course of action is ethically sound. And if she withholds permission, we must ask what gives her the right to decide that others should not benefit from the research or from transplantation . . .

Harris is equally dismissive of the view that the mother has quasi property rights by virtue of the fact that the foetus is growing inside her. Deadly and infectious viruses may grow in someone's body without any claim that they are in some way 'owned' by the being who plays host to them. Furthermore, if it were established that a foetus were a person, then prohibitions against slavery would rule out property rights over the foetus . . .

In contrast Robertson argues that the case for denying the mother's control is not persuasive: 'As a product of her body and potential heir that she has for her own compelling reasons chosen to abort, she may care deeply about whether foetal remains are contributed to research or therapy to help others' . . . Thus, although:

> . . . she cannot insist that foetal remains be used for transplant because no donor has the right to require that intended donees accept anatomical gifts, but she should retain the existing legal right to veto use of foetal remains for transplant research or therapy. Her consent to donation of foetal tissue should be routinely sought.

Now the case for giving the woman control, on Robertson's terms, seems to rest on the analogy with organ donation, such as live kidney donation. But this analogy is complicated by the suggestion that, by undergoing voluntary termination for family planning purposes, her interest in the foetus ceases with its removal. In electing an abortion, she is, on these terms, expressing an overriding interest in a premature separation from the foetus, consequently terminating any potential interest which could apply to the foetus. Having fulfilled her primary interest, further interest in the foetus would be foregone . . .

---

50 See n 1 above.

For its part, the Polkinghorne Committee took the view that the woman's informed consent should always be obtained:

Polkinghorne Committee, *Review of Guidance on the Research Use of Foetuses and Foetal Tissue*[51]

2.8 ... The use of foetal tissue from terminations of pregnancy has been justified by analogy with the use of human organs which have become available as a result of morally questionable circumstances, such as careless accident or even murder. However, it has been suggested that this analogy is imperfect, since in the case of abortions the one who consents to the use of the material (the mother) is also the one who has brought about its availability by her decision to seek the termination of the existence of her foetus. Some have argued that this decision abrogates the mother's subsequent rights in relation to her foetus. Again, this is an opinion to which the Committee has given careful consideration, but once more it is one that we are unable to accept. Because abortion is a decision of moral ambiguity and perplexity for many, reached only through a conflict of considerations, it seems too harsh a judgment of the mother's relation to her foetus to suppose that she is no longer in a special position with regard to it, following an abortion.

The position that the pregnant woman must consent to the use of aborted foetal tissue is also that reflected in the Human Tissue Authority's Code of Practice on guiding principles and consent:

Human Tissue Authority, *Code of Practice A – Guiding Principles and the Fundamental Principle of Consent*[52]

141. The law does not distinguish between fetal tissue and other tissue from the living; fetal tissue of fewer than 24 weeks gestation is considered to be the mother's tissue, as are non-fetal products of conception (i.e. placenta, membranes, umbilical cord, amniotic fluid). Consequently, fetal tissue and non-fetal products of conception are subject to the same consent requirements under the HT Act as all other tissue from the living ... However, because of the sensitivity surrounding pregnancy loss, consent should always be sought, even where it might not be lawfully required.

142. It should be noted that the reference to fetal tissue within this Code does not include stillbirths (babies born dead after 24 weeks gestation) or neonatal deaths (babies or fetuses of any gestational age which are born showing signs of life and die before the age of 28 days). Seeking consent for the removal, storage or use of the tissue of babies from stillbirths or neonatal deaths should be handled in accordance with provisions for seeking consent for use of the tissue of the deceased ... It is recommended that, whenever possible, the consent process for the examination of stillbirths and neonatal deaths involves the mother, and that, where appropriate, both parents are involved.

THINK POINT

Could it be lawful for a woman to enter into and terminate a pregnancy, with a view to the foetal tissue being used to treat a particular person, eg her sick husband?

---

51 See n 49 above.
52 See n 18 above.

11.4.2 Xenotransplantation

Recently, significant research effort has gone into the possibility of xenografting, literally the use of organs and tissue taken from non-human animals. Previously, though such transplants were occasionally tried (a well-known case from 1984 concerned a Californian infant, baby Fae, who survived for three weeks with a baboon's heart), there was a formidable difficulty in the way of lasting success in the form of inevitable tissue rejection by the donee. However, there now seem real prospects of overcoming this problem by genetically engineering certain breeds of animals specifically for transplant purposes.

The Nuffield Council of Bioethics, in its 1996 report, *Animal to Human Transplants: The Ethics of Xenotransplantation*, charted some of the obstacles in the way of carrying out such transplants on a wide scale:

Nuffield Council on Bioethics, *Animal to Human Transplants:
***The Ethics of Xenotransplantation*[53]**

10.9 Even if some use of animals for medical purposes can be justified in principle, their use for xenotransplantation raises specific issues that need further consideration. Particular concerns are raised by the use of primates, such as baboons ... The high degree of evolutionary relatedness between human beings and primates both suggests that xenotransplantation of primate organs and tissue might be successful and also raises questions about whether it is ethical to use primates in ways that it is not considered acceptable to use human beings. Certainly, any harm suffered by primates should be given great weight. This position is reflected in the principles underlying current practice in the UK. *The Working Party endorses the special protection afforded to primates used for medical and scientific purposes. ...*

10.12 Given the ethical concerns raised by the use of primates for xenotransplantation, attention has turned to developing the pig as an alternative source of organs and tissue. As discussed below, in the view of the Working Party, the use of pigs for xenotransplantation raises fewer ethical concerns. To develop the use of primates for xenotransplantation, when there is an ethically acceptable alternative, would not be justifiable. *The Working Party recommends that non-primate species should be regarded as the source animals of choice for xenotransplantation.* However, possibilities for alleviating the organ shortage which do not involve the use of animals, such as increased donation of human organs, and the development of artificial organs and tissue, should be actively pursued. ...

Transmission of infectious diseases

... 10.25 It is not possible to predict or quantify the risk that xenotransplantation will result in the emergence of new human diseases. But in the worst case, the consequences could be far-reaching and difficult to control. The principle of precaution requires that action is taken to avoid risks in advance of certainty about their nature. It suggests that the burden of proof should lie with those developing the technology to demonstrate that it will not cause serious harm. *The Working Party concluded that the risks associated with possible transmission of infectious diseases as a consequence of xenotransplantation have not been adequately dealt with. It would not be ethical therefore to begin clinical trials of xenotransplantation involving human beings ...*

In 1997 a government inquiry, chaired by Professor Ian Kennedy, also took the view that, because of the unknown risks associated with infectious diseases passing from animal to human, clinical trials should be delayed. Subsequently the Government established the Xenotransplantation Interim Regulatory Authority to keep the situation under review, but this body was wound up in 2006 in favour of regulation by Department of Health guidance. The latter, while allowing the

---

53 London: Nuffield Council on Bioethics, 1996.

possibility of xenotransplantation as part of a controlled research project, stipulates strict conditions designed to minimise the attendant risks:

Department of Health, *Xenotransplantation Guidance*[54]

The Department of Health considers that further development of xenotransplantation should take place in line with international recommendations and guidance. It is recommended that anyone considering xenotransplantation be familiar with these.

Key recommendations include those from the Council of Europe, the European Medicines Agency (EMEA), the Food and Drug Administration (FDA), and the World Health Organisation (WHO).

Common themes across all the international recommendations are that:

- Xenotransplantation should only take place when there is an adequate regulatory framework in place;
- Risks of transmission of known or unknown infections from animal to human should be minimised;
- Traceability and ongoing surveillance of patients is essential;
- Public debate in this area should be encouraged.

The major issue around xenotransplantation is one of public safety, particularly the risk that infectious disease/agents might be transmitted from the animal tissue to the recipient and potentially to the wider population. Much attention is focused on the possibility that [porcine] endogenous retroviruses (which exist harmlessly in animals) may be transferred into humans and become activated – potentially spreading new diseases to the human population. Investigators/researchers will need to bear this in mind as a key factor for consideration by any authorising committee and the regulator.

Concerns in respect of animal–human infections have increased still further in the wake of the recent emergence of avian flu, not to mention the 2009 swine flu pandemic. In the light of this, it is unsurprising that at present there appear world-wide to be no clinical trials involving xenotransplantation.[55] Indeed, it could be argued that, given the unquantifiable risks of proceeding, and the availability of reasonable alternatives, the time has now come for xenotransplantation trials to be prohibited. As Forvargue and Ost write:

Forvargue, S, and Ost, S, 'When should precaution prevail? Interests in (public) health, the risk of harm, and xenotransplantation'[56]

Given the impossibility of measuring the risks of xenotransplantation and the 'histories of lentiviruses and prions have taught us about the untameable distances between the laboratory, the spread of infectious diseases and public health', a better approach would be to avoid taking the risk to ensure that needless harm is not created. This may seem unnecessarily precautionary but as there are alternatives to xenotransplantation including reforming the existing allotransplant recovery systems and structures and the promise of stem cells, there is no need to create this risk in the first place. In the light of the limited pre-clinical survival times, uncertainty as to the ability of genetically engineered pig organs to support human life, the potentially catastrophic risks, and the difficulties in identifying, managing, and controlling those risks, it is unclear why some still view xenotransplantation as a viable solution to the shortage of organs. In this environment, the public interest in health and state obligations to protect public health require the state to prohibit clinical xenotransplantation.

---

54 London: DoH, 12 December 2006; see: http://webarchive.nationalarchives.gov.uk/+/www.dh.gov.uk/ab/Archive/UKXIRA/index.htm.
55 Though this may be about to change; see: http://science.sciencemag.org/content/357/6358/1338.
56 (2010) 18 Med L Rev 302.

In a recent briefing paper, *Taking Organ Transplantation to 2020: A UK Strategy*,[57] NHSBT stated its view that 'Xenotransplantation is unlikely to have any impact within the next 20 years, because it will take time to address issues such as immunological and physiological differences and the potential for infection with Porcine Endogenous Retrovirus and other infections.'

11.4.3 Mechanical organs

While artificial implants and other devices have long been a mainstay of modern medical science (for example, hip replacements, pacemakers, etc) in terms of organs, the successful design and manufacture of full organs has proven more difficult. Until very recently, the only organ that it appeared feasible to reproduce in mechanical form was the heart. David Lamb chronicles the history of such devices, and the ethical problems to which their use gives rise, as follows:

Lamb, D, *Organ Transplants and Ethics*[58]

The idea of a totally implantable artificial heart was first mooted in 1964, when the USA National Heart Institute drew up a plan for the construction of a prototype and obtained financial support from Congress for the project. The researchers were unrealistically optimistic, for they looked forward to the mass production and implantation of artificial hearts by 1970 . . . Despite some limited success with animals, artificial implants into humans did not achieve any significant results. One major problem is the high incidence of strokes and chronic infections, which has not been overcome. The first human implantation of an artificial heart was performed in Texas in 1969 on a dying patient, Haskelle Karp, who survived for a further 65 hours with it before receiving a human heart. He died shortly after. In 1977 a woman in Zurich survived for two days with an artificial heart . . . The initial belief that an artificial heart might function as a permanent replacement has given way to more realistic therapy. Artificial hearts are presently used, in a limited sense, as 'bridges' to assist survival until a donor becomes available. As of January 1987, some 17 US transplant centres were using artificial heart 'bridges', and 63 patients had been implanted with such a device . . . The number of artificial hearts and ventricular assistance devices currently functioning as bridges is 200 worldwide . . .

The deeper ethical and philosophical aspects of artificial heart implants surfaced in the widely discussed case of Dr Barney Clark, a retired American dentist who received an artificial heart in 1982. Dr Clark's own defective heart was replaced with a device made of polyurethane. The motor driving the heart was too large to be implanted, so it was placed in a cart which the patient had to push around. He lived for 112 days, and his death was caused by the failure of most of his other organs, but not by the failure of the heart, which went on pumping blood to a mass of dead organs, thus demonstrating the separability of the heart function from the mechanism of death. The longest survivor with an artificial heart was William Schroeder, who lived for 620 days, but during that time he suffered four strokes and developed chronic infections which sapped his strength . . .

The suffering endured by Barney Clark and William Schroeder and their families certainly raises ethical problems concerning the extent to which doctors should strive to maintain life. But this limited success may bring hope for the future; hope that an artificial heart is not an impossible dream, and that with sufficient technological improvements artificial implants could reduce waiting lists for human organs.

In the wake of technological developments, increasing use is now made of artificial hearts, either as bridging devices until a donor of a natural heart is found, or to supplement the workings of the

---

57 See: https://nhsbtdbe.blob.core.windows.net/umbraco-assets-corp/4240/nhsbt_organ_donor_strategy_long.pdf.
58 See n 1 above.

patient's own damaged heart. In general the therapeutical results have been very positive: a ten-year pilot study published in the US in 2004 showed that patients who receive such devices have a much higher chance of surviving to transplant and beyond.[59]

Advances in this field continue apace. Thus scientists in France in 2013 began clinical testing of a permanent artificial heart; the trial was suspended for a while in 2016 after a number of patient deaths, but has since resumed.[60] Previously in September 2010, scientists in San Francisco unveiled a prototype model for an artificial kidney that in the future could eliminate the need for dialysis, and which is expected to be ready soon for clinical trials.[61]

11.5 The status of extracted material

11.5.1 The requirements of the Human Tissue Act 2004

As noted, the 2004 Act established a new authority, the Human Tissue Authority, to be responsible for licensing various activities in relation to extracted human material (whether taken from the living or the deceased). Section 16 provides as follows:

Human Tissue Act 2004

Licensing

16 Licence requirement

(1) No person shall do an activity to which this section applies otherwise than under the authority of a licence granted for the purposes of this section.

(2) This section applies to the following activities –

a the carrying-out of an anatomical examination;

b the making of a post-mortem examination;

c the removal from the body of a deceased person (otherwise than in the course of an activity mentioned in paragraph (a) or (b)) of relevant material of which the body consists or which it contains, for use for a scheduled purpose other than transplantation;

d the storage of an anatomical specimen;

e the storage (in any case not falling within paragraph (d)) of –

i the body of a deceased person, or

ii relevant material which has come from a human body,

for use for a scheduled purpose;

f the use, for the purpose of public display, of –

i the body of a deceased person, or

ii relevant material which has come from the body of a deceased person . . .

(7) In subsection (2) –

a references to storage do not include storage which is incidental to transportation, and

b 'relevant material', in relation to use for the scheduled purpose of transplantation, does not include blood or anything derived from blood.

59 Copeland, JG, et al., 'Cardiac Replacement with a Total Artificial Heart as a Bridge to Transplantation' (2004) 351 New England Journal of Medicine 859–67.

60 See: www.massdevice.com/carmat-gains-french-approval-resume-artificial-heart-trial/.

61 See: https://pharm.ucsf.edu/kidney/device/faq.

Organ transplantation is a scheduled purpose (under Sch 1 of the Act). The effect of this provision, so far as relevant to that purpose, is that, while the organs' removal need not be licensed, their storage will need to be (although this excludes storage in the course of transportation). This will admittedly have little impact in relation to 'organs' in the narrower sense of solid matter, such as kidneys, etc, which are not presently capable of storage in any event, but will affect holdings of tissue including bone marrow. Licensees will be required to adhere to good practice guidelines issued by the Human Tissue Authority, which will in due course incorporate EU-wide standards of quality assurance and safety, as laid down in the EC Tissues and Cells Directive (2004/23/EC). The storage of blood for transfusion is excluded, being subject to its own regulatory regime pursuant to a separate EC Directive (2002/98/EC).

The framework of regulation instituted by the 2004 Act, and especially its creation of a special authority with responsibility for licensing and disseminating codes of practice, is clearly modelled upon the regime established in relation to reproductive medicine by the Human Fertilisation and Embryology Act 1990. In fact, for a time the Government planned to merge the Human Tissue Authority with the Human Fertilisation and Embryology Authority; in the event though this idea was abandoned as overly complicated.

11.5.2 The question of property rights

The phenomenon of organ and tissue transplantation, and the practice of removing tissue for medical purposes including donation, give rise to interesting questions as to the status of such material. Is it susceptible of ownership, and, if so, who enjoys the relevant property rights? It is convenient to look at the position in relation to deceased persons first, and then move on to look at ownership of body parts taken from living persons.

11.5.2.1 Rights in the body of a deceased person (or parts taken therefrom)

Traditionally, English law took the view that there were no property rights in the human corpse.[62] The origins of this rule, as well as the development of an exception for cases where the corpse, or body parts taken therefrom, is subject to alteration through human skill, were recently analysed by the Court of Appeal in its decision in *Yearworth v North Bristol NHS Trust*:[63]

> **Lord Judge CJ** (delivering the judgment of the Court): [31] In his Institutes of the Laws of England, mostly published in 1641, after his death, Sir Edward Coke wrote . . . that the 'buriall of the Cadaver is nullius in bonis [in the goods of no one] and belongs to Ecclesiastical cognizance'. In his Commentaries on the Laws of England, published in 1765, Sir William Blackstone wrote . . . that:
>
>> . . . though the heir has a property in the monuments and escutcheons of his ancestors, yet he has none in their bodies or ashes; nor can he bring any civil action against such as indecently at least, if not impiously, violate and disturb their remains, when dead and buried. [But] if any one in taking up a dead body steals the shroud or other apparel, it will be felony; for the property thereof remains in the executor, or whoever was at the charge of the funeral.
>
> There were at least three reasons for the rule that a corpse was incapable of being owned. First, in that there could be no ownership of a human body when alive, why should death trigger ownership of it? Second, as implied by Coke and Blackstone, the body was the temple of the Holy Ghost and it would be sacrilegious

---

62 *Williams v Williams* (1882) 20 Ch D 659.
63 [2009] EWCA Civ 37.

to do other than to bury it and let it remain buried: see for example, *In Re Estate of Johnson 7 NYS 2d 81* (1938) .. Third, it was strongly in the interests of public health not to allow persons to make cross-claims to the ownership of a corpse: in the words of Higgins J in his dissenting judgment in *Doodeward v Spence* in the High Court of Australia [(1908) 6 CLR 406], there was an 'imperious necessity for speedy burial'.

...

[33] ... [I]in *Doodeward* ... [t]he body of a still-born two-headed baby was preserved in spirits by the doctor who had been attending its mother; upon the doctor's death it was sold and later came into the possession of C, who exhibited it for profit as a curiosity. D, a police officer, seized it with a view to its burial. C's action for detinue succeeded. Griffith CJ said:

> '[W]hen a person has by the lawful exercise of work or skill so dealt with a human body or part of a human body in his lawful possession that it has acquired some attributes differentiating it from a mere corpse awaiting burial, he acquires a right to retain possession of it ...'

Although evidently disgusted by C's exhibition of a 'dead-born foetal monster', Barton J agreed. Higgins J dissented on the footing that there could be no ownership of a human corpse.

Parts of a human corpse

[34] In relation to parts of a human corpse our courts have recently built upon the exception, recognised in *Doodeward*, to the principle that there can be no ownership of a human corpse.

[35] First there was the decision of this court in *Dobson v North Tyneside Health Authority and Another* [1996] 4 A ll ER 474 [in which] Peter Gibson LJ held ... that the decision in *Doodeward* was (at least arguably) correct. ...

[36] The issue was also addressed in the Court of Appeal, Criminal Division, in *R v Kelly and Lindsay* [1998] 3 All ER 741. The defendants appealed against their conviction (and sentence) for theft of human body parts which had been preserved or fixed and had come into the possession of the Royal College of Surgeons, by which they had been used in training surgeons. Their appeals against conviction, founded upon a submission that body parts could not be property and thus the subject of theft, were dismissed. In giving the judgment of the court Rose LJ said in a valuable passage. ...:

> 'We accept that, however questionable the historical origins of the principle, it has now been the common law for 150 years at least that neither a corpse nor parts of a corpse are in themselves and without more capable of being property protected by rights ...
>
> ... [But] parts of a corpse are capable of being property within section 4 of the Theft Act 1968 if they have acquired different attributes by virtue of the application of skill, such as dissection or preservation techniques, for exhibition or teaching purposes ...
>
> Furthermore, the common law does not stand still. It may be that if, on some future occasion, the question arises, the courts will hold that human body parts are capable of being property for the purposes of section 4, even without the acquisition of different attributes, if they have a use or significance beyond their mere existence. This may be so if, for example, they are intended for use in an organ transplant operation, for the extraction of DNA or, for that matter, as an exhibit in a trial ...'

11.5.2.2 Rights in body parts taken from the living

We now need to consider the problem of body parts taken from a living person. Here matters are complicated by the fact that the latter, himself, may be felt to have a prima facie claim upon such material. This indeed was the question at issue in the *Yearworth*[64] case itself, which involved a

---

64 Ibid.

compensation claim brought by a number of men whose frozen sperm was negligently destroyed by the defendant fertility clinic. In finding that, for the purposes of their negligence action, the men had property in their sperm, the Court of Appeal held:

Lord Judge CJ: [45] We conclude:

a   In this jurisdiction developments in medical science now require a re-analysis of the common law's treatment of and approach to the issue of ownership of parts or products of a living human body, whether for present purposes (viz. an action in negligence) or otherwise.

b   The present claims relate to products of a living human body intended for use by the persons whose bodies have generated them. In these appeals we are not invited to consider whether there is any significant difference between such claims and those in which the products are intended for use by other persons, for example donated products in respect of which claims might be brought by the donors or even perhaps by any donees permissibly specified by the donors.

. . .

(f)   In our judgment, for the purposes of their claims in negligence, the men had ownership of the sperm which they ejaculated:

(i)   By their bodies, they alone generated and ejaculated the sperm.

(ii)   The sole object of their ejaculation of the sperm was that, in certain events, it might later be used for their benefit . . . It is true that, by confining all storage of sperm and all use of stored sperm to licence-holders, the [Human Fertilisation and Embryology Act 1990] has effected a compulsory interposition of professional judgment between the wishes of the men and the use of the sperm . . . For two reasons, however, the absence of their ability to 'direct' its use does not in our view derogate from their ownership. First, there are numerous statutes which limit a person's ability to use his property – for example a land-owner's ability to build on his land or to evict his tenant at the end of the tenancy or a pharmacist's ability to sell his medicines – without eliminating his ownership of it. Second, by its provisions for consent, the Act assiduously preserves the ability of the men to direct that the sperm be not used in a certain way: their negative control over its use remains absolute.

. . .(v) In reaching our conclusion that the men had ownership of the sperm for the purposes of their present claims, we are fortified by the precise correlation between the primary, if circumscribed, rights of the men in relation to the sperm, namely in relation to its future use, and the consequence of the Trust's breach of duty, namely preclusion of its future use.

In the upshot, there now appear two separate bases for acquiring property rights in body parts. The first, which applies to material from the deceased and living alike, is where the material is subject to some process or application. Here, third parties in lawful possession, such as medical personnel, may acquire rights in the material; indeed, this principle receives statutory recognition in s 32(9)(c) Human Tissue Act 2004, which excludes from the prohibition on commercial dealings, 'material which is the subject of property because of an application of human skill'. Secondly, as regards material from living persons, this may, as held in *Yearworth*, be regarded as the property of the donor of the tissue, in so far as he retains a legitimate interest in its use for his own benefit.

The difficult question remains, though, of what happens when such third party and first party claims are in conflict? This is a matter of huge practical significance given the scope for the commercial exploitation of human tissue, including through its use to develop cell-lines with lucrative future applications. The problem of how to balance the interests of the parties, as well as take account of wider social interests, underlay the well-known decision of the Supreme Court of California in *Moore v Regents of University of California*.[65] In that case, the plaintiff had his

---

65 793 Pd 479 (1990).

spleen removed during treatment for leukaemia. Unbeknown to him, the doctors then used it to generate a cell line from which a highly profitable drug was produced. Moore subsequently brought a claim, *inter alia*, in conversion (on the basis that he retained ownership) in order to secure a share of the profits. However, the court rejected this head of the claim, essentially for policy reasons:

Panelli J (for the majority): Research on human cells plays a critical role in medical research. This is so because researchers are increasingly able to isolate naturally occurring, medically useful biological substances and to produce useful quantities of such substances through genetic engineering. These efforts are beginning to bear fruit. Products developed through biotechnology that have already been approved for marketing in this country include treatments and tests for leukemia, cancer, diabetes, dwarfism, hepatitis-B, kidney transplant rejection, emphysema, osteoporosis, ulcers, anemia, infertility, and gynecological tumors, to name but a few. . . .

    The extension of conversion law into this area will hinder research by restricting access to the necessary raw materials. Thousands of human cell lines already exist in tissue repositories, such as the American Type Culture Collection and those operated by the National Institutes of Health and the American Cancer Society. . . . At present, human cell lines are routinely copied and distributed to other researchers for experimental purposes, usually free of charge. This exchange of scientific materials, which still is relatively free and efficient, will surely be compromised if each cell sample becomes the potential subject matter of a lawsuit . . .

Mosk J (dissenting): [O]ur society acknowledges a profound ethical imperative to respect the human body as the physical and temporal expression of the unique human persona. One manifestation of that respect is our prohibition against direct abuse of the body by torture or other forms of cruel or unusual punishment. Another is our prohibition against indirect abuse of the body by its economic exploitation . . . for the sole benefit of another person. The most abhorrent form of such exploitation, of course, was the institution of slavery. Lesser forms, such as indentured servitude or even debtor's prison, have also disappeared. Yet their specter haunts the laboratories and boardrooms of today's biotechnological research-industrial complex. It arises wherever scientists or industrialists claim, as defendants claim here, the right to appropriate and exploit a patient's tissue for their sole economic benefit – the right, in other words, to freely mine or harvest valuable physical properties of the patient's body . . .

The decision in the *Moore* case remains controversial and, following the Court of Appeal decision in *Yearworth*, it is possible the courts in England might take a different view of the claimant's rights.[66] Nonetheless, as Herring and Chau argue, it is far from clear that according the donor property in his material offers the best solution:

Herring, J, and Chau, P-L, 'My body, your body, our bodies'[67]

To some, *Moore* shows the problem with not adopting the property approach. Vast sums of money were made by the scientists, but the person who made 'everything possible' was left with nothing. A property approach would ensure he was adequately rewarded. The difficulty is that the property approach might

---

66 See n 63 above. In the post-*Moore* US case of *Greenberg v Miami Children's Hospital*, 264 F Supp. 2d 1064 (2003), the Florida Southern District Court – while denying the donor's property in extracted material – suggested that they could pursue a claim against the profiting researchers for unjust enrichment.
67 (2007) 15 Med L Rev 34; for a different view, see Nwabueze, R, 'Donated organs, property rights, and the remedial quagmire' (2008) 16 Med L Rev 201.

ensure he was over-rewarded. On the facts, if we regarded the DNA sequence as his and therefore accept he has a claim to the money produced from his property, then in theory he should be entitled to all the proceeds. There is a danger that valuable research into stem cell lines and DNA will be hindered if patients are able to claim an interest in the products ... The door might be opened to a lawyer's goldmine as weeks are spent in the courtroom attempting to ascertain whose bodily material was used in the creation of a particular product. It may be that the *Moore* decision is complicated by the fact that the research on Moore's body parts was carried out without his consent and permission. The decision left this deception without any form of sanction. ...

The real issue is money. To some, to give an individual whose body by chance carries a useful DNA sequence a share in millions of dollars is iniquitous. On the other hand, is it any less iniquitous that the money should end up in the hands of the scientists who may have put little effort into the discovery? And some people are able to make large sums of money from their outward appearance which may simply be an accident of DNA. Some have suggested that genetic information that creates a useful product should be seen as owned by the community and the money put to projects that benefit the community ...

We all benefit from the existence of the social practice of medical research. Many of us would not be here if infant mortality had not been brought under control, or antibiotics had not been invented. Most of us will continue to benefit from these and other medical advances (and indeed other advances such as clean drinking water and sanitation). Since we accept these benefits, we have an obligation in justice to contribute to the social practice which produces them.

It could be argued that, just as it was unlucky chance that Moore contracted leukemia, requiring his (successful) treatment, it was lucky chance that exploitable material was inside *him*. Here, a financial reward to the patient may well appear inconsistent. After all, a fundamental aim of any equitable system of healthcare – from which Moore himself benefited – is to even out, not encourage, inequalities arising from the 'natural lottery'.

THINK POINT

If body parts were recognised generally as the property of the person whose body they come from, would this mean persons could sell their organs and tissue on the open market? If so, is this a prospect we should embrace or reject?

11.6 The interests of the organ recipient

11.6.1 The putative recipient

We begin by looking at the position of the potential recipient of a transplant organ, prior to the transplant actually taking place. First it is clear that, even if he desperately needs the organ to survive, and a compatible donor is identified, he cannot require the latter to submit to non-consensual extraction. A well-known case in point is *McFall v Shimp*,[68] discussed in Chapter 3 above. In that case an American court refused to compel a man to undergo a bone-marrow transplant in order to save his dying cousin. While Flaherty J took the view that the man's refusal to

---

68 10 Pa D & C (3d) 90 (1978).

submit voluntarily was morally indefensible, he was not prepared to recognise a legal duty to donate, which would fly in the face of the stress placed by liberal society on the inviolability of the individual. It is virtually certain that an English court, faced with a similar predicament, would come to the same conclusion.

The legal position is less clear, however, in cases where the organ has already been removed from the donor. In such cases, it is arguable that, as discussed in section 11.5.2, the organ may enjoy the status of property. This possibility was alluded to by Rose LJ in *R v Kelly and Lindsay*,[69] and Remigius Nwabueze has argued such an approach would offer the best means of addressing problems relating to damaged or misdirected organs:

Nwabueze, R, 'Donated organs, property rights, and the remedial quagmire'[70]

Transplantation technology brought with it a significantly different dimension to property claims over the human body and body parts. Unforeseen problems may arise in the course of moving organs across state and local borders and through several authorised hands en route to the recipient. Although people within the organ transfer network (physicians, nurses, administrators and technicians) appreciate the need for optimal levels of care and competence, human fallibility remains an undermining factor with enormous potential for injury. For instance, an organ donated and prepared for transplantation might be damaged by poor preservation techniques or inefficient handling. Likewise, an organ donated by A for transplantation to B might be intentionally or negligently redirected to C . . . Such challenges have exacerbated with the development of organ transplantation as a routine medical procedure. It is important that a legal system should have clear rules for dealing with such problems . . . A claim in negligence is surely one of the possible causes of action, though problems relating to causation and proof of damage remain formidable. The focus here, however, is on the property liability of a defendant in the above hypothetical scenario.

Property claims to body parts donated for transplantation are qualitatively different from other contexts in which property rights have been asserted with respect to the human body and parts of it . . . More than emotional pain, a misdirected organ causes some real, physical deprivation. The claimant will complain about not only his or her mental agony but also the loss of a physical organ directed to him or her . . . The claimant has lost something whose physical embodiment shares some of the characteristics of ordinary forms of property and would, accordingly, be reasonable to expect a proprietary redress.

In the US, a claim by a disappointed putative recipient (after the organ earmarked for him by the deceased donor was given to another person) was the subject of litigation in *Colavito v New York Organ Donor Network*.[71] In *Colavito (No 2)*, the court dealing with the matter expressed a preference for a property-based analysis; however in *Colavito (No 3)*, this approach was rejected by the New York Court of Appeals, which saw the remedy in such a case as lying in negligence. On the facts, though, the plaintiff's claim failed as he would not in any event have been a compatible recipient for the material.

As discussed in 11.3.3 above, in the UK the practice of directed donation from deceased (as opposed to living) donors is currently opposed by guidelines maintained by NHS Blood and Transplant, which see it as contrary to the desired ethic of altruism. However, as suggested in the article by Cronin and Douglas, this policy may no longer be consonant with the regime of 'appropriate consent' under the 2004 Human Tissue Act. In a case where a donor opted for directed donation, and the procurement agency failed to abide by his wishes (eg by allowing the organ to perish), it is quite possible that – subject to establishing compatibility – the English courts would

---

69 [1999] QB 621.
70 (2008) 16 Med L Rev 201.
71 *Colavito v New York Organ Donor Network (No 2)* 438 F 3d 214 (2006); *Colavito (No 3)* 8 NY3d 43 (2006).

grant the putative recipient a remedy in negligence.[72] Such a claim appears even stronger in the case of a misdirected live transplant.

11.6.2 The actual recipient

11.6.2.1 Redress for injury against the surgeon/procurement agency

As we have seen, some organ transplant therapy (especially that involving animal or artificial implants) remains highly experimental in nature. It has been argued by JK Mason that, just as the donor cannot consent to the extraction of an organ if it is likely to cause them serious harm, 'it is equally unlawful to consent to accept an organ in the certainty or near certainty that it would be fatal to do so'.[73] We respectfully doubt whether, so far as a 'near certainty' is involved, this is correct: a one in 1,000 chance of life is surely better – other things equal – than no chance at all. At the same time, problematic questions of consent may arise, at least at an ethical level. As Forvargue and Ost note in the context of possible participation in a xenotransplantation trial:

Forvargue, S, and Ost, S, 'When should precaution prevail? Interests in (public) health, the risk of harm, and xenotransplantation'[74]

In order to fulfil the positive obligation of autonomy, which requires '[r]espectful treatment in disclosing information and actions that foster autonomous decision making', the surgeon performing the xenotransplant must provide the necessary information for a person to make an informed decision. This will not be easy given the limited information available on xenotransplantation. And an individual consenting to participate in a xenotransplant trial might not be truly exercising individual autonomy because it will lead to such a severe infringement of their personal autonomy in the future. Is it possible to give fully informed consent to as-of-yet unexperienced severe liberty limiting measures which could include a lifelong surveillance and monitoring regime, remaining within it, refraining from having children, and compulsory post-mortems?

Similar doubts surrounding consent may arise in respect of the unknown psychological effects of participating in recently developed transplant procedures affecting the outward appearance of the recipient, such as face or hand transplants.

What is, by contrast clearer is that in so far as a transplant surgeon performs the operation without due care and, in so doing, causes harm to the recipient, the standard principles of negligence will apply to afford the latter a remedy. An allegation of negligence may also be framed against the agency or authority which procured the organ for transplantation. This will be so if the organ itself turns out to be defective in some way, notably if the donee is exposed to a virus, such as HIV or hepatitis, that the donor was carrying. The Nuffield Council on Bioethics has considered some of the special problems that might face a recipient claimant in such a case as follows:

Nuffield Council on Bioethics, *Human Tissue: Ethical and Legal Issues*[75]

12.53   Standards of care change from time to time: what was not negligence in 1990 may well be negligence in 1995. As knowledge, and the perception of risks and their avoidance, improve, so too do the

72 With due respect to Nwabueze (n 70 above), it is unlikely causation and damage would pose any real problem: the putative recipient will generally be quantifiably worse off than if he had received the organ.
73 In Dyer, C (ed), *Doctors, Patients and the Law*, Oxford: Blackwells, 1992, 122.
74 See n 56 above.
75 See n 6 above.

obligations imposed upon those who work in these areas. For example, at one time far less was known than today about the various contaminants in blood products: HIV, hepatitis, syphilis, malaria and toxo-plasmosis; and methods of screening or heat treating blood products were not so prevalent. There may have been no negligence liability on the supplier of defective blood had a person then been contaminated with an HIV virus. The situation would be different today, when the norm is to test for such viruses. But what of other viruses? Does an obligation to screen for all known viruses arise as soon as the risk of their presence becomes known? The view has been expressed that as:

> . . . more and more minor contaminants of recombinant DNA derived human growth hormone are being identified which are biologically active and pose no safety problem . . . the effort and expense in identifying them and then measuring them on a batch-to-batch basis may be out of proportion to the public health risk.

– As long as no adverse consequences follow, that argument may appear to be sound. But what happens if a virus which is deliberately neglected turns out to be far more potent than was anticipated? This has been an issue with hepatitis C: could it be said to be negligent to take a professional, and considered, decision not to screen for this virus even when its presence but not its full potency were known? And what of such bodies as the Committee on the Safety of Medicines and the Licensing Authority . . . should they be liable for failure to act earlier to impose higher standards of care? In the last resort, it will be for the courts to weigh up all the factors and decide whether the balance struck was reasonable . . .

The Nuffield Council also considered whether a claimant might be able to bring an action under the Consumer Protection Act 1987:

12.57 A product is 'defective' when it does not provide the safety which a person is entitled to expect, taking all the circumstances into account. Thus, instructions for use, contraindications and warnings and supplied information in one form or another may in some cases assist in determining whether the product was 'defective'. Contaminated blood supplied to patients, or a defective organ used for transplantation, are likely to be regarded as 'defective products' regardless of the information which is given to patients.

12.58 Liability is imposed upon producers, including manufacturers, importers and suppliers of such products. It is likely that human tissue would be regarded as 'products' for these purposes. This was rec-ommended by the Pearson Royal Commission in 1978. Human tissue used for medical purposes, although not strictly manufactured, would possess the 'essential characteristics attributable to an industrial or other process'.

12.59 Although these strict liability provisions are an improvement on the negligence action, there are still many difficult hurdles which an injured person has to face before liability can be established. The two most difficult are the so called 'development-risk' defence and, once again, causation.[76]

Lastly, it should be noted that other forms of action, besides those just mentioned, may be available against the procurement agency in appropriate cases. In the American case of *Ashcraft v King*,[77] the plaintiff recovered in battery after receiving HIV-infected blood from an anonymous donor; she had stipulated that she wanted blood obtained only from members of her immediate family. Equally, in France the director of a procurement agency was charged with manslaughter after a patient, who had received an infected corneal graft, died of rabies.

---

76 See further on these residual hurdles, the discussion in Ch 6, section 6.6.
77 278 Cal Rptr 900 (1991).

11.6.2.2 Redress against the organ donor

Because of limitations in current screening techniques, it is possible for infected tissue to fail to be identified even though the procurement agency took all reasonable precautions. In such a case a donee, injured through the use of such tissue, would have an action, if at all, only against the original donor of the material: it may be that the latter was (or should have been) aware of their infected status and/or failed to reply honestly to the inquiries of the procurement agency.

In a number of US and Commonwealth cases, the courts have been unsympathetic to the donee's cause. In *Rasmussen v South Florida Blood Service*,[78] in which the plaintiff became infected with HIV following a blood transfusion, public policy in favour of the preservation of donor anonymity was said to outweigh the donee's rights in the matter:

> **Barkett J**: The threat posed by the disclosure of the donors' identities goes far beyond the immediate discomfort occasioned by a third party probing into sensitive areas of the donors' lives. Disclosure of donor identities in any context involving AIDS could be extremely disruptive and even devastating to the individual donor. If the requested information is released, and petitioner queries the donors' friends and fellow employees, it will be functionally impossible to prevent occasional references to AIDS . . .
>
> We wish to emphasise that although the importance of protecting the privacy of donor information does not depend on the special stigma associated with AIDS, public response to the disease does make this a more critical matter. By the very nature of this case, disclosure of donor identities is disclosure in a damaging context. We conclude, therefore, that the disclosure sought here implicates constitutionally protected privacy interests.
>
> Our analysis of the interests to be served by denying discovery does not end with the effects of disclosure on the private lives of the 51 donors implicated in this case. Society has a vital interest in maintaining a strong volunteer blood supply, a task that has become more difficult with the emergence of AIDS. The donor population has been reduced by the necessary exclusion of potential blood donors through AIDS screening and testing procedures as well as by the unnecessary reduction in the donor population as a result of the widespread fear that donation itself can transmit the disease. In light of this, it is clearly 'in the public interest to discourage any serious disincentive to volunteer blood donation'. Because there is little doubt that the prospect of inquiry into one's private life and potential association with AIDS will deter blood donation, we conclude that society's interest in a strong and healthy blood supply will be furthered by the denial of discovery in this case.

A similar conclusion was reached in the Scottish case of *AB v Scottish National Blood Transfusion Service*.[79] However, in other cases some relaxation of this strict anonymity requirement has been allowed in favour of a rule of 'cloaked disclosure'.[80] Even so, the point of doing this is to assist a plaintiff where there is a suspicion that the *procurement agency* may have been negligent in allowing the blood through. Indeed, as one of the conditions for receiving such information, the plaintiff has had to undertake not to sue the donor directly.

THINK POINT

Could it not be argued against the recipient (in at least some cases) that he is in any event better off than if he had not received the organ/tissue at all, and accordingly has not suffered any damage?

---

78 500 So 2d 533 (1987).
79 1993 SLT 36.
80 See *Snyder v Mekhjian* 593 A 2d 318 (1991); *PD v Australian Red Cross Society (NSW Div)* (1993) 30 NSWLR 376.

11.7 Tackling the shortage in organs

Transplant activity is increasingly constrained by the shortage of organs, a phenomenon affecting every country which has developed the ability to undertake this form of surgery. Quite possibly uniquely, doctors and surgeons are prevented from alleviating suffering and avoiding death by the shortage of a particular physical resource – a human organ. Figures from NHS Blood and Transplant[81] show that in December 2017, there were over 6,500 persons on the National Transplant 'active' waiting list for a transplant (the active list only includes persons with a reasonable chance of receiving an organ; the overall number of persons who could benefit from the procedure is significantly higher). Given the poignant consequence of a significant number of avoidable deaths, often of quite young people, it is natural that much attention has been focused on the possibility of remedying this shortfall through legal reform. In terms of the possible sources of organs and tissue identified above, cadaveric transplants seem prima facie to be the type where such reform may have the greatest chance of achieving positive results.

11.7.1 Addressing the shortfall in cadaveric organs

The system, under the Human Tissue Act, with its emphasis on 'appropriate consent', either from the deceased or someone else empowered by the Act to give it, may be described as an 'opt-in' scheme: in default of 'appropriate consent', material may not be taken or used. The reason for this approach, which is stricter than the regime it replaced under the 1961 Human Tissue Act (which simply required enquiry of relatives who could be reasonably located, to check they did not object) may be understood in the context of the scandals that formed the background to the new Act.

Nonetheless, a move to a more liberal 'opt-out' approach to organ donation, based on the presumed consent of the donor unless he made known his objections while alive, has long been advocated by the BMA and, both during and after the passage of the 2004 Act, several MPs pressed for such a scheme. Key questions remain, though, as to the degree of public support such a move would enjoy, and whether it would actually increase organ donation rates. One should also be aware that, as the 1994 Kings Fund Institute report notes by reference to practices in other jurisdictions, 'presumed consent' itself is not a single approach, but comes in alternative forms:

New, B, et al., *A Question of Give and Take: Improving the Supply of Donor Organs for Transplantation*[82]

Changing the law on gaining consent

Of particular interest to policy makers has been the various legal frameworks within which procurement takes place. The UK, along with Germany, the Netherlands, Italy, Canada, Australia and New Zealand, have what might broadly be termed 'opting in' legal systems. Two other systems have generated much interest in the literature: presumed consent – also known as opting out – and required request.

Presumed consent

Presumed consent schemes have been introduced into many countries, although attempts to enact such legislation in the UK have always failed, the latest being the Transplantation of Human Organs Bill 1993. The international legislation falls into several categories. The purest version of the law allows automatic

---

81 NHS Blood and Transplant publishes weekly statistics, including numbers of persons registered for a transplant, and operations taking place, at: https://nhsbtdbe.blob.core.windows.net/umbraco-assets/1730/weekly_stats.pdf.
82 See n 2 above.

removal except in a situation in which the deceased has expressed an objection during his or her lifetime. This 'strict' type of presumed consent procedure applies in Austria where organs can be removed provided in his or her life, the person concerned has not expressed an objection. The views of close relatives are not taken into account ...

A slightly less strict version of presumed consent operates in Belgium where, if there is no explicit objection by the deceased, the relatives are allowed to object but the medical profession are under no obligation to seek their views. The relatives must initiate the process under these circumstances ...

Other, still weaker, schemes allow removal unless the deceased has made an explicit or informal objection at any time. Such a formulation of the law effectively requires that the relatives are consulted in order to glean the wishes of the deceased. Although it is formally the views of the deceased whilst alive which are being sought, such schemes allow the relatives to object on the deceased's behalf. France and Spain operate presumed consent legislation of this kind ...

Finally, a scheme in operation in Singapore provides for the automatic exclusion of certain categories of potential donor, including non-citizens and Muslims ... Muslims can, however, donate their organs if they wish, by pledging their organs whilst alive or if their relatives consent ...

In fact, as discussed further below, within the UK, Wales has recently introduced an autonomous system of 'deemed consent'.[83] In 2009, a research review carried out for NICE by the Health Technology Assessment programme found notably higher rates of cadaveric transplants in countries with presumed consent approaches, such as Belgium and Austria,. Interestingly, the country with the highest rate (with 34.3 donors per million of population annually, compared to 20.9 in the UK for 2015/16) was Spain: the latter has a 'soft' version of presumed consent, which allows the relatives to object, but apparently in practice only around 20 per cent do so. As the HTA programme review concludes:

Rithalia, A, et al., *A Systematic Review of Presumed Consent Systems for Deceased Organ Donation*[84]

1. Presumed consent alone is unlikely to explain the variation in organ donation rates between different countries. A combination of legislation, availability of donors, transplantation system organisation and infrastructure, wealth and investment in healthcare, as well as underlying public attitudes to and awareness of organ donation and transplantation, may all play a role, although the relative importance of each is unclear. The between-country comparison studies overall point to presumed consent law being associated with increased organ donation rates (even when other factors are accounted for) although it cannot be inferred from this that the introduction of presumed consent legislation per se leads to an increase in donation rates. The before-and-after studies suggest an increase in donation rates following the introduction of presumed consent legislation; however, it is not possible to rule out the influence of other factors on donation rates ....

Implications for policy

... The available evidence suggests that presumed consent legislation is associated with an increase in organ donation rates, although the size of the association varied between studies. Other factors also appear to be associated with organ donation rates, such as transplant capacity and GDP and health

---

83 See the discussion at n 88 ff.
84 (2009) 13(26) Health Technology Assessment. The review can be accessed at: www.hta.ac.uk/fullmono/mon1326.pdf.

expenditure per capita. It is therefore important to consider such factors when attempting to predict the impact of changing to a presumed consent system. It is also important to take into account the likely public response to presumed consent should legislation be changed. The limited and incomplete evidence available from surveys suggests variable levels of support. In addition, consideration needs to be given to potential variation in attitudes between different socio-demographic subgroups.

Arguably, in this area, legal change unaccompanied by any corresponding change in cultural values (notably the pre-eminence accorded to the views of relatives), or commitment of greater technical resources to organ retrieval, is unlikely to decrease appreciably the shortfall in donor organs. As Bernard Teo has observed:

Teo, B, 'Strategies of organ procurement'[85]

What strategy of organ procurement a society ought to adopt depends on its willingness to expend resources for its transplant programme(s), ie, after the requirements of social priorities have been considered. If it chooses to ration resources for these programme(s), then it is arguably wiser to adopt a less efficient but ethically preferable strategy of expressed consent or its variants. The system would most likely yield a limited quantity of organs which would probably remain comfortably within the resources allocated for the programme(s). What would be the purpose of adopting a more efficient organ procurement policy when the number of procedures capable of being performed would be constrained by limitations in other resources? ...

Perhaps France is a case in point. In his report on the French organ transplant and procurement programmes, Arthur Caplan noted that concerns for the rising costs of healthcare have created a less than enthusiastic commitment of its scarce medical resources to its transplant programmes. Restrictions in the availability of resources for transplants have placed '... severe limits both in terms of personnel and hospital space on the number of transplants of all types that can now be performed'. ... Thus, it is arguable that France ought not to have adopted presumed consent without prior consideration of the extent to which it is prepared to support its transplant programmes. ...

Even as a society contemplates the adoption of presumed consent, it ought to consider another important factor: political feasibility. ... The French people hold a strong belief in the rights of families relative to cadaver disposal. French doctors find it 'psychologically intolerable to remove tissues from a body without obtaining the permission of the next of kin' ... In practice, France's presumed consent policy, ie of not requiring familial consent, exists only on paper.

A similar conclusion was reached by the Organ Donation Taskforce (an arm of NHS Blood and Transplant) in its 2008 Report, *Organs for Transplant*.[86] While rejecting the adoption of a 'presumed consent' model, it outlined various recommendations directed to organisational and logistical aspects of organ retrieval, including UK-wide co-ordination and improved education of medical personnel and the public; these served to produce a 50 per cent increase in deceased donors and a more than 30 per cent rise in transplants by April 2013, a success the latest NHS Blood and Transplant Strategy, *Taking Organ Transplantation to 2020*, aims to build upon. The latter incorporates a number of targets, including the achievement of an 80 per cent consent figure in respect of the use of cadaveric organs by 2020 (compared to 57 per cent in 2013).[87]

---

85 (1992) 6 Bioethics 113.
86 London: DoH, January 2008.
87 See: www.nhsbt.nhs.uk/tot2020/.

In the meantime the Welsh National Assembly has chosen the more radical option of moving to a soft opt-out scheme. In particular, the Human Transplantation (Wales) Act 2013 (which entered force in December 2015)[88] now provides that – in default of a specific objection – deceased patients aged 18 and above, who were resident in Wales for 12 months, may be deemed to have consented to donate.[89] Two years into the new regime, the effect in increasing organ donations remains unclear,[90] but its continued progress will undoubtedly be monitored with interest from elsewhere in the UK.

11.7.2 Creating a market in organs?

The shortfall in organs could probably be eradicated at one stroke if we were prepared to sanction commercial dealings in them. However, such a possibility undoubtedly arouses widespread repugnance. The main arguments against permitting a market in organs are explored by Wilkinson and Garrard, who find them less convincing than often supposed:

Wilkinson, S and Garrard, E, 'Bodily integrity and the sale of human organs'[91]

There seem to us to be four standard objections to permitting organ sale, each of which we regard as ultimately unconvincing:

Pain and risk

The first is simply that the organ seller is subjected to an extremely high level of pain and risk. This in itself, though, can't be sufficient to justify a ban on organ sale, since we don't in general think that it's wrong to pay people for doing dangerous things (there are numerous examples of this: firefighters, astronauts, miners and divers, to name but a few). Common forms of 'risky labour' are often more dangerous than organ sale, but are regarded as heroic, rather than condemned; it is seen as quite proper to reward those who do them. And this difference in attitude can't be justified in terms of the good consequences that 'risky labour' produces, since the consequences of an organ sale (typically, saving a life) may be just as good or better.

Exploitation and commodification

The second worry is that the relationship between the buyer and seller is likely to be exploitative and to either cause or constitute an unacceptable *commodification* of the seller and/or her body. Brecher, for example, describes trading in human kidneys (along with many other practices) as 'exploitation based on making a commodity of human beings'.

There are two problems with this objection. First, although organ sale does necessarily involve treating a human body part as a commodity, there is no reason to suppose that this is *necessarily exploitative*. Would we really regard it as exploitative if the organ seller were wealthy, educated, rational and well informed and got paid £1,000,000 for her organ? Second, we do, in fact, permit many practices which are at least as exploitative and 'commodifying' as organ sale (for example, poorly paid labour). Of course, this doesn't show that exploitation and commodification are acceptable. But it *does* show that they aren't a special problem for organ sale and that they alone can't explain why organ sale is seen as more offensive than (say) low wages. . . .

---

88 See: www.legislation.gov.uk/anaw/2013/5/section/3/enacted.
89 The UK HTA has published a code of practice on the new Act, available at: www.hta.gov.uk/sites/default/files/Code-Human Transplantation Wales Act 2013-v.July 2017_0.pdf.
90 See: http://gov.wales/statistics-and-research/evaluation-human-transplantation-wales-act/?lang=en.
91 22 JME 334.

Undermining the practice of free donation

Another objection to permitting organ sale is that to do so would undermine the practice of free dona-tion. Abouna *et al.*, for example, claim that there is 'considerable evidence to indicate that marketing in human organs will eventually deprecate and destroy the present willingness of members of the public to donate their organs out of altruism'. There are two distinct worries here. The first is a purely practical one. If payment is allowed, then virtually all donors will begin to expect payment and so voluntary donations will cease. The second is that allowing payment for organs would deprive people of an opportunity to participate in 'giving' relationships with one another: relationships which have some ethical or social value, independently of their practical consequences.

Taking the second worry first, it is sufficient to point out that the mere permissibility of sale doesn't itself prevent people from donating (although it might, of course, encourage them to sell rather than donate). Organ givers are at liberty to waive their fee and, in a sense, the possibility of sale allows the (free) donor to be even more generous than she could otherwise have been; for not only does she give up her organ, but she gives up her fee as well.

As regards the first worry, it seems that there's no compelling reason to believe that organ sale would undermine the practice of free donation. After all, professional social work and charitable social work co-exist. Also, if organ sale led to a significant overall increase in the supply of organs, this would more than compensate for the reduced number of free organs. But in any case, it is far from clear that there is a significant practice of free donation to be undermined . . . Given the high level of pain and risk involved, free donation (except by relatives, who might well waive the fee, if it were offered) is very unlikely to take place anyway.

Concerns about autonomy and consent

It is generally agreed that the absence of coercion and manipulation is required for genuine consent. And the final objection we consider is that no one could ever be in a position autonomously to consent to selling an organ such as a kidney, since the process would be so unpleasant and/or dangerous that only someone who was coerced or manipulated would agree to it. One virtue of this objection is that it would explain why we're more concerned about organ selling than the selling of blood and certain other body products. In the case of the latter, the level of pain and/or risk is very low, and so the need for coercion and manipulation is much less.

This objection does, indeed, raise a serious practical worry about the possibility of organ sellers being coerced, and it is certainly true that, were organ sale to be permitted, rigorous safeguards aimed at ensuring fully informed consent in every case would be required. But does organ sale necessarily involve coercion or manipulation? It seems not, since even a wealthy, informed and rational agent might consent to it (without coercion or manipulation) if the price were high enough. Would we want to say, in such a case, that the person hadn't really consented? (Of course, with a broad enough con-ception of manipulation, the answer to this question might be 'yes', but we would question whether so broad a conception would be able to do any ethical work, since too many things would be counted as manipulative.)

Also, given that organ sale is less unpleasant and dangerous than many accepted forms of 'risky labour', were we to take this objection seriously, then a wide range of accepted practices should be con-demned on similar grounds.

Ultimately, our reluctance to treat irreplaceable bodily parts as commodities which may be the subject of buying and selling seems to be grounded both in an intrinsic sense of respect for persons as ends in themselves, and in fears as to the moral climate of any society in which organised trading in organs became the norm. As Bernard Teo writes:

Teo, B, 'Strategies of organ procurement'[92]

[T]he human body is not like other things. Since human bodiliness is intrinsically tied to human person-ality and identity, it follows that respect for the human person would also be intrinsically tied to respect for the human body and its parts. In every culture and society, the instinctive revulsion and strong moral aversion toward treating the human body as property and commodity in both religious and secular atti-tudes is shown by the special respect accorded to the body in elaborate ceremonies and rituals surround-ing death and burial. They are signs of respect and reverence for the person who lived. There seems to be that intuitive instinct that the human body has a special moral significance that cannot be equated with other things or commodities. Leon Kass, a physician and philosopher, has warned against trivialising human embodiment. Because human dignity is intrinsically linked to human embodiment, treating the body and its parts as commodities would be to strip the human body of its proper dignity. It would be morally intolerable therefore if human body parts are treated as objects for payment and as commodities of exchange in the market place. Thus it is arguable that placing a monetary value on human body parts would be ethically unacceptable.

Furthermore, in a society where cherished communal values such as altruism and giving are encour-aged and cultivated, legalising a commercial market for organs and paying for them would dissolve communal bonds and relationships based on goodwill and altruism. It would transform them into one of contractual buying and selling. . . . The wisdom of paying for organs and allowing commercialisation is therefore highly questionable even for the lofty purpose of saving lives.

As noted earlier, under the law in the UK as it stands, commercial dealing in organs (both from live donors and cadavers) is a criminal offence under s 32 of the Human Tissue Act 2004.

Summary of key points

1   Organ transplantation, particularly since the development of modern immuno-suppressant drugs, is a technique with great potential for saving and improving the quality of human lives. However it is subject to a number of ethical and legal doubts and qualifications, which have partly contributed to the shortage of transplant organs.

2   At present the main sources of organs are live or deceased human donors. As regards the former, the key issues at common law concern the validity of the donor's consent, including how far a person is entitled legally to expose himself to harm or the risk of harm.

3   In relation to organs taken from deceased donors, the main common law questions relate to how far patients who are near death may already be treated with a view to taking their organs after death. Subsequently, their death must also be established in legal terms.

4   For both types of transplant, the common law has been significantly supplemented by statute, now in the form of the Human Tissue Act 2004. The Act established the Human Tissue Authority to oversee transplants (and other activities involving the use of human tissue).

---

92 See n 85 above.

5   The 2004 Act re-enacts previous statute law prohibiting commercial dealings in organs ('organ trafficking'). Those engaging in such practices (including the donor and recipient directly involved) may be liable to imprisonment for up to three years.

6   A further, key requirement introduced by the 2004 Act is the need for 'appropriate consent' by the donor. In the context of deceased organ donation this also addresses the need, where the donor himself did not express a wish, for the surviving relatives to consent instead. Failure to obtain such consent is made a criminal offence.

7   The 2004 Act has not resolved every issue: one area of uncertainty is the enforceability of conditional or directed donations from deceased donors. As regards living donors, directed donations are the norm, but the Human Tissue Authority, together with NHS Blood and Transplant, oppose them in relation to the deceased.

8   A further, controversial issue concerns the status of organs and tissue following extraction from the donor. Does such material amount to property and, if so, to whom does it belong? These questions, which may have significant commercial implications, were addressed (though not fully clarified) by the Court of Appeal in the *Yearworth* case.

9   There remains a significant shortfall in transplant organs in the UK. Given the cost in human lives, there is an overriding social imperative to address this, including through law reform. Possibilities include moving from the current 'opt-in' system for deceased donation (in the Human Tissue Act 2004) to a system based on presumed consent.

10   At present, though a shift to a presumed consent model remains off the political agenda in England, it has recently occurred in Wales. By contrast, it is unlikely that commercial dealings in organs would ever be legalised. This is a prospect most people view with apprehension, given the dangers of exploitation and commodification of the human body.

Further reading

Cronin, A, and Douglas, J, 'Directed and conditional deceased donors organ donations: laws and misconceptions' (2010) 18 Medical Law Review 275.

Herring, J, and Chau, P-L, 'My body, your body, our bodies' (2007) 15 Medical Law Review 34.

Hoppe, N, *Bioequity – Property and the Human Body*, Farnham: Ashgate, 2009.

Journal of Medical Ethics (2003) Vol 29, no 3, special issue on organ donation (June 2003).

Lamb, D, *Organ Transplants and Ethics*, London: Routledge, 1990.

NHS Blood and Transplant, *Taking Organ Transplantation to 2020: A detailed strategy* (London 2013) (available at: https://nhsbtdbe.blob.core.windows.net/umbraco-assets-corp/4240/nhsbt_organ_donor_strategy_long.pdf)

Price, D, 'The Human Tissue Act 2004' (2005) 68 Modern Law Review 798.

Chapter 12

Treatment at the end of life

12.1 Introduction

12.1.1 End-of-life decisions and euthanasia

Treatment decisions that result in the ending of a patient's life are sometimes characterised as euthanasia. The latter term (literally 'an easeful death', from the Greek) describes the practice of bringing about death in a manner that causes the least amount of suffering to the patient. At the same time, it is somewhat ambiguous: it can be used narrowly to refer only to the taking of life by active means, for example the giving of a lethal injection to a patient whose life is full of unbearable pain or, more widely, it can also encompass situations in which a doctor, intending his or her patient's death, omits to provide life-prolonging treatment. In this wider use, one would distinguish between 'active' euthanasia and 'passive' euthanasia (the latter involving such an omission). While this is ultimately a matter of semantics, the reader should be alert, especially when reading judgments, as to whether the narrower or wider usage has been adopted in a particular instance. In addition to the active/passive distinction, the practice of euthanasia may also be characterised as 'voluntary' or 'non-voluntary', depending on whether the patient was mentally capable to request it or not.

12.1.2 Ethical background: the value of human life

12.1.2.1 Sanctity of life

What makes the withdrawal/withholding of treatment to allow the patient to die (let alone active euthanasia) so morally contentious is the enormous value which we place upon human life. In the following extract, Helga Kuhse charts the historical framework in which respect for individual human life attained centrality in Western thought, as well as noting the difficulties encountered by the view in an increasingly secular age:

Kuhse, H, *The Sanctity-of-Life Doctrine in Medicine: A Critique*[1]

Every society known to us subscribes to some principle or principles involving respect for human life. As Georgia Harkness puts it:

> In every society there appears to be an elemental reverence for life which makes the deliberate killing of another person a punishable offence. In all societies there are exceptions . . . yet aversion to murder is probably the most universal of all moral attitudes.

But if aversion to murder, or wrongful killing, is universal, there have been great variations between cultural traditions as to what constitutes wrongful killing.

If we turn to the roots of our Western tradition, we find that in Greek and Roman times not all human life was regarded as inviolable and worthy of protection. Slaves and 'barbarians' did not have a full right to life, and human sacrifices and gladiatorial combat were acceptable at different times. Spartan law required that deformed infants be put to death; for Plato, infanticide is one of the regular institutions of the ideal State; Aristotle regards abortion as a desirable option; and the Stoic philosopher Seneca writes unapologetically: 'Unnatural progeny we destroy; we drown even children who at birth are weakly and abnormal.'

. . . And whilst there were deviations from these views . . ., it is probably correct to say that such practices as abortion, infanticide, suicide, and euthanasia were less proscribed in ancient times than they

---

1 Oxford: Clarendon Press, 1987.

are today. There has been a gradual expansion of the circle protecting human life, outlawing not only the killing of slaves or 'barbarians', gladiatorial combat, and human sacrifice, but also abortion, infanticide, and euthanasia.

Most historians of Western morals agree that the rise of Judaism and even more of Christianity contributed greatly to the general feeling that human life is valuable and worthy of respect.

WEH Lecky gives the now classical account of the sanctity of human life in his *History of European Morals*:

> Considered as immortal beings, destined for the extremes of happiness or of misery, and united to one another by a special community of redemption, the first and most manifest duty of the Christian man was to look upon his fellow men as sacred beings and from this notion grew up the eminently Christian idea of the sanctity of human life ... it was one of the most important services of Christianity that besides quickening greatly our benevolent affections it definitely and dogmatically asserted the sinfulness of all destruction of human life as a matter of amusement, or of simple convenience, and thereby formed a new standard higher than any which then existed in the world ... This minute and scrupulous care for human life and virtue in the humblest form, in the slave, the gladiator, the savage, or the infant, was indeed wholly foreign to the genius of Paganism. It was produced by the Christian doctrine of the inestimable value of each immortal soul.

... Whilst it is today no longer generally believed that life has sanctity in the religious sense, the ethical attitudes to which these religious beliefs gave rise still find expression in the deep-seated belief that human life, irrespective of its quality or kind, is absolutely inviolable and equally valuable; and that we must never take life – either our own or that of anyone else – because life is not ours to do with as we see fit.

Kuhse here associates the 'sanctity of life' doctrine, in its strongest form, with the view that human life is of absolute value and should, where possible, be maintained at any cost, including the cost to the individual whose life it is. Thus, it is impermissible to shorten (or fail to extend) life, by however small an amount and irrespective of any suffering endured by the person concerned.[2]

12.1.2.2 Quality of life

A number of contemporary philosophers have argued that, in making decisions about ending life, we should instead be prepared to deploy overt quality of life considerations.[3] Human life is no longer to be regarded as possessing intrinsic value *per se*; rather, what makes life valuable is, crudely, the life-holder's capacity for pleasurable states of consciousness. As Kuhse notes, this value is enhanced where the individual in question is a person with a sense of existing over time and capable of valuing their existence:

Kuhse, H, *The Sanctity-of-Life Doctrine in Medicine: A Critique*[1]

... [W]hat is it that gives value to human life, but not – or not to the same degree – to the lives of other living things? Two answers are possible. The first answer is that human life has sanctity simply because it is human life, that is, because it is the life of a member of the species *Homo sapiens*. The second answer is that human life has special value because humans are self-aware, rational, autonomous, purposeful, moral

---

2   For an argument that the 'sanctity of life' approach is in reality more flexible, see Keown, J, 'Restoring moral and intellectual shape to the law after *Bland*' (1997) 113 LQR 481.

3   See, eg, Glover, J, *Causing Death and Saving Lives*, Harmondsworth: Penguin, 1977; Harris, J, *The Value of Life: Introduction to Medical Ethics*, London: Routledge & Kegan Paul, 1985.

beings, with hopes, ambitions, life purposes, ideals, and so on . . . Any of these qualities, or a combination of them, could serve as a basis for a moral distinction between human beings and lettuces or chickens. That such distinguishing qualities are needed is clear: for if the value of life were based on 'mere life', rather than on one or more of the above characteristics, then every life including the earthworm's or the lettuce's would be equally valuable.

It is not difficult to see that the second answer does point to a morally relevant difference between some lives and others. For example, it is quite plausible to hold that the life of a self-aware, rational, purposeful being that sees itself as existing over time is more valuable than the life of an entity or being who lacks these characteristics. But if one takes this approach, then one is not saying that human life has sanctity, but rather that rationality, the capacity to be self-aware, moral or purposeful, and so on, have 'sanctity'. Of course, one may still hold . . . that human life has sanctity or special worth, but only in so far as it is a precondition for rationality, purposiveness, or whatever else one takes the valuable characteristic to be. One would not, on this view, be able to argue that the lives of all members of the human species have special value – for example, the lives of the irreversibly comatose, or the lives of severely brain-damaged new-born infants. The second approach, then, does not give us a reason for preserving all human lives, and cannot serve as the basis for the view that all human lives, irrespective of their quality or kind, are equally valuable . . .

In cases where the individual whose life is at stake is mentally capable, there is also the argument that it should be for them alone to decide if and when the quality of that life is so low that it should end; this is consistent with respecting their autonomy. In this context an appeal is often made to a capable person's (moral) 'right to die', and this has underpinned campaigns to have 'active voluntary euthanasia' legalised. As Margaret Otlowski writes:

Otlowski, M, *Voluntary Euthanasia and the Common Law*[4]

The main argument in support of the legalisation of active voluntary euthanasia is based on the principle of autonomy or the right of self-determination. According to this principle, each person has value and is worthy of respect, is the bearer of basic rights and freedoms, and is the final determinant of his or her destiny . . .

Proponents argue that the maintenance of the current legal prohibition on active voluntary euthanasia is an unjustifiable infringement of the liberty of those persons who would choose to be killed. It has been argued that to deny active voluntary euthanasia is a form of tyranny; an attempt to control the life of a person who has his or her own autonomous view about how that life should go, and that this constitutes an ultimate denial of respect for persons. According to proponents of euthanasia, in order to uphold the patient's interest in self-determination, doctors should be free to act upon the request of an informed and mentally capable patient for active voluntary euthanasia without fear of criminal liability.

12.1.2.3 The 'qualified' sanctity of life approach

We now turn to a position which may be regarded as a compromise between the sanctity and quality of life approaches. This 'qualified' sanctity doctrine agrees with the fully fledged sanctity approach that there is something special about human life, such that it is not reducible to the sum of the life-holder's states of consciousness. The respect due to such life is reflected in a

---

4   Oxford: Clarendon Press, 1997.

(virtual) prohibition on active steps by third parties, including doctors, to terminate it. This prohibition extends to cases where a capable patient requests help in dying. On the other hand, the doctrine is more relaxed about allowing quality of life considerations to determine when third parties need not act to prolong life, ie allowing death by omission. This attitude can be broadly summed up by reference to the Victorian poet AH Clough's sardonic lines: 'thou shalt not kill, but need'st not strive officiously to keep alive'.[5]

It is this position that has been adopted by English law. In the Court of Appeal in *Airedale NHS Trust v Bland*,[6] Hoffmann LJ articulated it in the following terms:

> **Hoffmann LJ**: In my view the choice which the law makes must reassure people that the courts do have full respect for life, but that they do not pursue the principle to the point at which it has become almost empty of any real content and when it involves the sacrifice of other important values such as human dignity and freedom of choice. I think that such reassurance can be provided by a decision, properly explained, to allow Anthony Bland to die ... Is this answer affected by the proposed manner of his death? Some might say that as he is going to die, it does not matter how. Why wait for him to expire for lack of food or be carried off by an untreated infection? Would it not be more humane simply to give him a lethal injection? No one in this case is suggesting that Anthony Bland should be given a lethal injection. But there is concern about ceasing to supply food as against, for example, ceasing to treat an infection with antibiotics. Is there any real distinction? In order to come to terms with our intuitive feelings about whether there is a distinction, I must start by considering why most of us would be appalled if he was given a lethal injection. It is, I think, connected with our view that the sanctity of life entails its inviolability by an outsider. Subject to exceptions like self-defence, human life is inviolate even if the person in question has consented to its violation. That is why although suicide is not a crime, assisting someone to commit suicide is. It follows that, even if we think Anthony Bland would have consented, we would not be entitled to end his life by a lethal injection.
>
> On the other hand, we recognise that, one way or another, life must come to an end. We do not impose on outsiders an unqualified duty to do everything possible to prolong life as long as possible. I think that the principle of inviolability explains why, although we accept that in certain cases it is right to allow a person to die (and the debate so far has been over whether this is such a case), we hold without qualification that no one may introduce an external agency with the intention of causing death.

12.1.3 The acts/omission distinction

The qualified sanctity approach relies heavily upon the acts/omissions distinction, which underpins much of common-sense morality: it generally strikes people as worse to bring about a bad result by acting, as opposed to failing to prevent the same thing from occurring 'naturally'. Nonetheless, the distinction has attracted criticism from ethicists and philosophers. As John Keown has observed: 'There is surely no significant moral difference between a doctor intentionally killing a patient by, say, choking the patient, and by deliberately failing to stop the patient from choking, when the doctor could easily do so, precisely so that the patient should die.'[7] Similarly,

---

5 Clough, AH, *The Latest Decalogue*.
6 [1993] AC 789.
7 *Euthanasia, Ethics and Public Policy: An Argument Against Legalisation*, Cambridge: CUP, 2002.

James Rachels has produced a pair of well-known (and colourful) hypothetical cases to deny the relevance of whether death is caused by action or inaction:

Rachels, J, 'Active and passive euthanasia'[8]

One reason why so many people think that there is an important moral difference between active and passive euthanasia is that they think killing someone is morally worse than letting someone die. But is it? Is killing, in itself, worse than letting die? To investigate this issue, two cases may be considered that are exactly alike except that one involves killing whereas the other involves letting someone die. Then, it can be asked whether this difference makes any difference to the moral assessments. It is important that the cases be exactly alike, except for this one difference, since otherwise one cannot be confident that it is this difference and not some other that accounts for any variation in the assessments of the two cases. So, let us consider this pair of cases:

In the first, Smith stands to gain a large inheritance if anything should happen to his six-year-old cousin. One evening while the child is taking his bath, Smith sneaks into the bathroom and drowns the child, and then arranges things so that it will look like an accident.

In the second, Jones also stands to gain if anything should happen to his six-year-old cousin. Like Smith, Jones sneaks in planning to drown the child in his bath. However, just as he enters the bathroom Jones sees the child slip and hit his head, and fall face down in the water. Jones is delighted; he stands by, ready to push the child's head back under if it is necessary, but it is not necessary. With only a little thrashing about, the child drowns all by himself, 'accidentally', as Jones watches and does nothing.

Now Smith killed the child, whereas Jones 'merely' let the child die. That is the only difference between them. Did either man behave better, from a moral point of view? If the difference between killing and letting die were in itself a morally important matter, one should say that Jones's behavior was less reprehensible than Smith's. But does one really want to say that? I think not.

It is certainly true that, in many cases, the intention of an agent and the consequences of his or her conduct, in the context of bringing about the death of another individual, will be the same whether active or passive means are adopted. However, a residual difference can be found in the causal relationship between the agent and the death. Arguably, the causal authorship of the doctor who actively kills a patient makes his or her conduct problematic in a sense not shared (at least where the duty to treat has ceased) by the doctor whose non-intervention results in a patient's death. The problem resides in the first doctor's breaching of the 'equality principle':

Stauch, M, 'Causal authorship and the equality principle: a defence of the acts/omissions distinction in euthanasia'[9]

The failure to provide someone with medical assistance cannot by itself cause that person's death: he must first be in need of life-saving treatment through illness or otherwise. In fact, the agent who fails, through omission, to prevent death is allowing the completion (his non-intervention is *necessary* for this) of a pre-existing causal set for that outcome. By contrast, the agent who causes death by an act, for example by administering a lethal injection, typically instigates a causal set for the same result: his act is *sufficient* to produce it in conjunction with normal background conditions alone . . .

---

8 (1975) 292 New England Journal of Medicine 78.
9 (2000) 26 J Med Ethics 237.

According to [the equality principle], the life of each individual has an equal claim to a minimum respect by possessing irreducible value (ie, a value that cannot be fully cashed out in terms of the life-holder's own states of consciousness, pleasurable or otherwise). An agent who engages in active euthanasia (even at the behest of the 'victim') fails to show this respect, for, in assuming authorship over that other's death, he automatically accords his own life an ontological priority: he draws upon his own resources (for which his life is, of course, a precondition) in such a way as to extinguish the life of the other. This breaching of the equality principle amounts, it is submitted, to a prima facie reason against any killing, and one which persists even if, in all the circumstances, we are disposed morally to excuse a *particular* killing. Consider, for example, the following hypothetical case proposed by Dan Brock:

> A patient is dying from terminal cancer, undergoing great suffering that cannot be relieved without so sedating him that he is unable to relate in any way to others. This patient prepared an advance directive at an early stage of his disease indicating that in circumstances like this he wanted to have his life ended either by direct means or by withdrawing life-sustaining treatment. In a recent lucid moment he reaffirmed the directive. The attending physician and the patient's family are in agreement that the patient's desire to die ought now to be granted.

Brock offers two alternative conclusions to this case. In the first, the man's wife places a pillow over his face and asphyxiates him while he is asleep. In the second, the man develops breathing problems (while unconscious) and needs placing on a respirator to prolong his life. His wife, who is present and knows this, fails to alert the medical staff and the man dies. Brock goes on to ask if there is 'any reason why what the wife does in the first instance is morally (as opposed to legally) worse or different to what she does in the second instance?' The answer (and remember we are not being asked whether, in the first instance as well, we should not morally excuse her action) is surely simply that in the first instance, by assuming authorship over the man's death, she infringes the equality principle. In the second instance she does not.

This may admittedly be thought a rather thin distinction, standing in need of further argument as to why the equality principle itself matters. On one view the latter is linked to an outmoded theological picture of the world. As David Price noted:

Price, D, 'What shape to euthanasia after *Bland*? Historical, contemporary and future paradigms'[10]

People ... commonly feel that death should be 'natural', not controlled nor contrived by human agency. But whilst a theological or spiritual account of the world shaped by a higher force counsels against interventions interfering with the natural design, a secular view finds difficulties in the notion of the sanctity of the natural order. On a Darwinian, evolutionary plane, nature lacks a harmony or purpose of its own shaped by any intelligent force, and thus to speak of 'interfering' with nature is vacuous. It has, moreover, nothing to do with the right or the good. Radcliffe-Richards nevertheless observes that 'there is still a strong tendency for non-religious people to think of nature as taking the place of God in specifying how the world should be, and of evolution as producing progress of all kinds'; 'vestigial religion' as Rachels refers to it.

---

10 (2009) 125 LQR 142.

Leaving aside the question of whether the acts/omissions distinction is philosophically coherent, it is apparent that policy arguments play an important part in the law's prohibition of active euthanasia. Jonathan Glover has commented on this point as follows:

Glover, J, *Causing Death and Saving Lives*[11]

One [objection to abandoning the prohibition] is the suggestion that, if voluntary [active] euthanasia were known to be an option, people might put pressure on their burdensome relations to volunteer. It is hard to evaluate this objection. It seems to me rather implausible, but perhaps I am being too optimistic. In advance of trying a voluntary euthanasia policy, we do not know how people would behave. (Is there any evidence of such pressures in a country where voluntary euthanasia is not illegal?)

A related objection is that, even without pressure being brought by relations, people who felt they were a burden might think that, although they had lives worth living, they ought to volunteer for euthanasia. This gains some support from the fact that there have been cases of suicide by people whose motive was a reluctance to be a burden on others. Part of the difficulty of evaluating this objection is that it is hard to predict how widespread such feelings would be. Another difficulty is the more fundamental uncertainty about whether it is right in such a case to override the person's autonomy. Where he is wrong in thinking he is a burden, he should not be given euthanasia, but should be persuaded of the truth. (It seems possible that, with so much talk of old people almost as though they were members of another species, many old people who are loved and wanted members of a family do have unnecessary fears that they are a nuisance to the others.) But there are sometimes cases where a person who is old or ill does put a great strain on a family, and where he sees this and would rather die than have the situation continue, it is not obvious that a paternalist refusal to carry out his wishes is justified.

Another possible bad side effect of voluntary euthanasia concerns the treatment of dying patients. Is there a danger that allowing such a policy would hamper the development of the kind of terminal care which would make euthanasia unnecessary? The policy of total rejection of euthanasia may have the advantage of strengthening people's commitment to developing more humane and imaginative forms of terminal care. Certainly some of the most sensitive and impressive work here, such as that of Cicely Saunders and others, has been done in the context of a principled refusal to comply with euthanasia requests. But it is not clear that voluntary euthanasia would seem an alternative rather than a supplement to better terminal care. A hospital with a voluntary euthanasia policy could still have a staff that did all they could to make euthanasia requests unnecessary. The view that voluntary euthanasia would be accepted as an easy alternative to improved care underrates the deep revulsion against killing which most people have, and which often seems especially strong among those in professions like nursing. (Perhaps this is again too optimistic. Is there any clear evidence relevant to this?)

However, if pragmatic policy reasons, rather than any fundamental ethical principle, are seen as underlying the present law, then, as Glover implies, this turns the evaluation of the law into an essentially empirical question: would the consequences of changing the present rules be worse than the ills that such reform is designed to cure?

We shall return to the question of whether the law in respect of end-of-life treatment rests on tenable foundations in section 12.5, when we address arguments and initiatives in favour of law reform. First, though, we shall consider the law as it currently stands. We begin in section 12.2 by further examining the prohibition on doctors (and others) on being actively involved in ending life, including how far it is always adhered to in practice. We then go on to

---

11 See n 3 above.

consider the law's approach to cases of 'letting die' by withholding life-sustaining treatment – first, in section 12.3, in respect of capable patients; and then, in section 12.4, in respect of the incapable: in what circumstances are doctors permitted to take such a course?

> **THINK POINT**
>
> If the quality of life approach were to inform the law in this area, might it mean that doctors would be required to kill their patients on demand?

12.2 Active euthanasia and assisted suicide

12.2.1 The prohibition on taking life

The intentional taking of a patient's life by a doctor, including as a response to the patient's wishes, will amount to the crime of murder. In this context the doctor's motive for acting (to spare the patient pain), as distinct from his intention (to cause death) will be irrelevant. A well-known case illustrating this point is that of *R v Cox*:

R v Cox[12]

Dr Cox injected a 70-year-old patient, Lillian Boyes, with the lethal poison potassium chloride, after she pleaded with him to put her out of her misery; she was *in extremis*, suffering from the terminal stages of rheumatoid arthritis, and her pain was beyond the control of analgesic drugs. He was charged only with her attempted murder on the basis that, given her condition, Mrs Boyes' death at that time could in fact have been due to her illness rather than the poison (her body had been cremated without a post-mortem):

Ognall J (directing the jury): This is a sad and testing case for all of us involved. The reason is obvious. A distinguished professional man of unblemished reputation and character is now on trial, and the allegation is that he behaved in a way which is a clear repudiation of a doctor's lifelong professional duty, namely to save and not to take life.

Even the prosecution case acknowledged that he did so only because he was prompted by deep distress at Lillian Boyes' condition; by a belief that she was totally beyond recall and by an intense compassion for her fearful suffering. Nonetheless, members of the jury, if he injected her with potassium chloride for the primary purpose of killing her, of hastening her death, he is guilty of the offence charged. You are therefore tested to the utmost, members of the jury, for you must do your best to put emotion to one side. You must try this case impartially and objectively. You 12 ladies and gentlemen represent the public interest in ensuring that, where it is surely proved, no man of whatever situation or in whatever circumstance can place himself above the law . . .

You must understand, members of the jury, that in this highly emotional situation, neither the express wishes of the patient nor of her loving and devoted family can affect the position. Lillian Boyes was fully entitled to decline any further active medical treatment and to specify that thereafter she should only receive painkillers. She did that on 11 August. That was her absolute right and the doctors and nursing staff were obliged to respect her wishes. A young senior

---

> house officer, Dr Byrne, gave evidence before you. He told you that on that day when Lillian Boyes had said 'no more active intervention, please, only painkillers from now on', he had said to her, in effect: 'Thus far and no further. We will stop your positive medical treatment, we will confine ourselves to giving you only analgesics, only painkillers, but we cannot accede to your request that we give you something to kill you'.
>
> Dr Cox was convicted of attempted murder. However, he did not receive a jail sentence, and also escaped a ban from the GMC, instead being placed under supervision for 12 months.

That this represents the state of the law was confirmed by the House of Lords in the case *Bland*,[13] although not without some misgivings:

> **Lord Goff**: I must however stress, at this point, that the law draws a crucial distinction between cases in which a doctor decides not to provide, or to continue to provide, for his patient treatment or care which could or might prolong his life, and those in which he decides, for example by administering a lethal drug, actively to bring his patient's life to an end ... [T]he former may be lawful, either because the doctor is giving effect to his patient's wishes by withholding the treatment or care, or even in certain circumstances in which ... the patient is incapacitated from stating whether or not he gives his consent. But it is not lawful for a doctor to administer a drug to his patient to bring about his death, even though that course is prompted by a humanitarian desire to end his suffering, however great that suffering may be: see *R v Cox* (1992) ... So to act is to cross the Rubicon which runs between on the one hand the care of the living patient and on the other hand euthanasia – actively causing his death to avoid or to end his suffering.
>
> **Lord Browne-Wilkinson**: Finally, the conclusion I have reached will appear to some to be almost irrational. How can it be lawful to allow a patient to die slowly, though painlessly, over a period of weeks from lack of food but unlawful to produce his immediate death by a lethal injection, thereby saving his family from yet another ordeal to add to the tragedy that has already struck them? I find it difficult to find a moral answer to that question. But it is undoubtedly the law and nothing I have said casts doubt on the proposition that the doing of a positive act with the intention of ending life is and remains murder.

In fact, it seems that doctors in practice not infrequently aid the incurably ill to die, but that most cases are never investigated, let alone prosecuted, because of lack of evidence and/or any prospect of obtaining a conviction. As David Price commented:

Price, D, 'What shape to euthanasia after *Bland*? Historical, contemporary and future paradigms'[14]

> Whilst the medical profession continues to maintain its traditional resistance to the legalisation of both physician-assisted suicide and voluntary euthanasia, not only is there considerably less unanimity amongst members of its representative organisations than at any point in time, but a British Social Attitudes survey conducted in early 2007 revealed that 80 per cent of the public would support doctors assisting terminally

---

13 See n 6 above.
14 See n 10 above.

ill patients to die if they so requested. The debate becomes increasingly urgent. It has been claimed that approximately 18,000 people in Britain are medically assisted to die annually in any event, and that the deaths of approximately 2,800 patients are a consequence of either voluntary euthanasia or the ending of life without an explicit request from the patient. Moreover, the number of clinical decisions bearing on this estate is expanding rapidly due to substantial demographic trends towards a larger elderly and potentially infirm population . . .

12.2.2 Medicines which shorten life

One reason doctors treating the terminally ill in practice have significant discretion in taking measures that shorten life is due to the existence of the so-called 'Adams defence'. According to this, a doctor is entitled to administer powerful analgesic (pain-killing) drugs, such as diamorphine, to such patients, even though these drugs, ingested in large doses, have the known side-effect of accelerating death.

The existence of this exception (that is, the fact that a doctor who prescribes such drugs to control pain, though foreseeing his patient's earlier death, will not be guilty of murder) was established in the case of *R v Bodkin Adams*:

R v Bodkin Adams[15]

Dr Bodkin Adams was charged with murder after increasing the dosage of opiates for an elderly stroke patient, who left him a Rolls-Royce and a chest of silver in her will. Devlin J, commenting upon the doctor's defence that his primary purpose had been to dull the patient's sensation of pain, gave the following direction to the jury:

Devlin J: [A] doctor who is aiding the sick and the dying [need not] calculate in minutes, or even in hours, and perhaps not in days or weeks, the effect upon a patient's life of the medicines which he administers or else be in peril of a charge of murder. If the first purpose of medicine, the restoration of health, can no longer be achieved there is still much for a doctor to do, and he is entitled to do all that is proper and necessary to relieve pain and suffering, even if the measures he takes may incidentally shorten life. That is not because there is any special defence for medical men; it is not because doctors are put into any category different from other citizens for this purpose. The law is the same for all, and what I have said to you rests simply upon this: no act is murder which does not cause death. 'Cause' means nothing philosophical or technical or scientific. It means what you 12 men and women sitting as a jury in the jury box would regard in a common sense way as the cause . . . If, for example, because a doctor has done something or has omitted to do something death occurs, it can be scientifically proved – if it could – at 11 o'clock instead of 12 o'clock, or even on Monday instead of Tuesday, no people of common sense would say, 'Oh, the doctor caused her death'. They would say the cause of her death was the illness or the injury, or whatever it was, which brought her into hospital, and the proper medical treatment that is administered and that has an incidental effect of determining the exact moment of death, or may have, is not the cause of death in any sensible use of the term. But it remains the fact, and it remains the law, that no doctor, nor any man, no more in the case of the dying man than of the healthy, has the right deliberately to cut the thread of life.

---

15 [1957] Crim LR 365.

The notion that, in such a case, the doctor may be regarded as not having caused the patient's death is, with respect, difficult to accept: after all, usually it is clear that 'but for' the administration of morphine, the patient would have lived somewhat longer, and nor will legal causation (in terms of foreseeability) be in issue. Subsequently, in the *Cox* case,[16] Ognall J preferred to concentrate upon the doctor's intention as providing the key to his possible exculpation:

> **Ognall J**: We all appreciate that some medical treatment, whether of a positive, therapeutic character or solely of an analgesic kind – by which I mean designed solely to alleviate pain and suffering – some treatment carries with it a serious risk to the health or even the life of the patient. Doctors are frequently confronted with, no doubt, distressing dilemmas. They have to make up their minds as to whether the risk, even to the life of their patient, attendant upon their contemplated form of treatment, is such that the risk is, or is not, medically justified. If a doctor genuinely believes that a certain course is beneficial to his patient, either therapeutically or analgesically, then even though he recognises that that course carries with it a risk to life, he is fully entitled, nonetheless, to pursue it. If in those circumstances the patient dies, nobody could possibly suggest that in that situation the doctor was guilty of murder or attempted murder . . .
>
> There can be no doubt that the use of drugs to reduce pain and suffering will often be fully justified notwithstanding that it will, in fact, hasten the moment of death. What can never be lawful is the use of drugs with purpose of hastening the moment of death.
>
> And so, in deciding Dr Cox's intention, the distinction the law requires you to draw is this. Is it proved that in giving that injection, in that form and in those amounts, Dr Cox's primary purpose was to bring the life of Lillian Boyes to an end?
>
> If it was, then he is guilty. If, on the other hand, it was, or may have been, his primary purpose in acting as he did to alleviate her pain and suffering, then he is not guilty. That is so even though he recognised that, in fulfilling that primary purpose, he might or even would hasten the moment of her death.

The apparent reliance of this way of regarding the *Bodkin Adams* defence on the principle of double effect (a Catholic doctrine, which has the support of advocates of the full sanctity of life position, but is rejected by other commentators), has given rise to much debate. Normally, intention in the criminal law is established through straightforward foresight that a given outcome will be the likely effect of one's act.[17] In this situation, though, the law is exceptionally prepared to limit its focus to the primary intention of the doctor, that is to say the desire to relieve the patient's pain.

The upshot is that, provided the doctor administers life-ending drugs that at the same time have some analgesic effect (*cf* Dr Cox, who used potassium chloride, a drug with no such effect), he or she would seem, as a practical matter, to be safe from criminal liability. As Suzanne Ost notes:

Ost, S, 'Euthanasia and the defence of necessity: advocating a more appropriate legal response'[18]

> Undoubtedly, the physician is likely to know what his primary intent was in administering the drug in question, yet how can the jury truly know whether the intent was to relieve suffering rather than cause death? When a certain act can be carried out with more than one intent, perhaps the most we can ascertain as objective actors is what these different intents could be, rather than what the primary intent actually is . . .

---

16 See n 12 above.
17 *R v Woollin* [1999] 1 AC 82.
18 (2005) Crim L Rev 355.

Significantly, in the light of such concerns, the question of whether the doctrine provides an effective means of establishing the physician's intent has been addressed by a recent study involving 683 Australian general surgeons. Two hundred and forty-seven of these surgeons stated that when administering drugs in order to relieve a patient's suffering, they had administered a greater dosage than they felt necessary to relieve symptoms with the intention of hastening death. Interestingly, the authors of the study raise the question of whether the only distinction between these surgeons and the other participants in the study is that they reported their own mental state differently. This leads to a further related criticism of the utilisation of the doctrine of double effect in English law. The legal application of the doctrine undoubtedly requires reliance upon physicians to truthfully report their primary intent. Yet, if a physician did administer lethal treatment with a primary intent to cause death, can we really expect him to reveal this truth, given the legal consequences of this revelation?

As Ost goes on to ask, 'by utilising the doctrine . . . are we not skating around the issue of the intent behind administering lethal doses of pain-alleviating treatment towards the end of life instead of tackling it head on?' In her view, it would be preferable to see the doctrine as affording a defence (based on necessity) to the doctor, notwithstanding his intention to cause death. In its 2005 paper, 'A New Homicide Act for England and Wales' the Law Commission appears to go along with this, endorsing Kennedy and Grubb's suggestion that in such cases the doctor indeed intends the patient's death, but 'the intention is not culpable . . . because the law permits the doctor to do the act in question'.[19]

Leaving aside its precise doctrinal justification, there is no doubt that the *Adams* defence forms an established part of the common law; as Lord Sumption recently stated in *Nicklinson v Ministry of Justice*:[20]

Lord Sumption: [255] . . . (4) Medical treatment intended to palliate pain and discomfort is not unlawful only because it has the incidental consequence, however foreseeable, of shortening the patient's life: *Airedale NHS Trust v Bland* [1993] AC 789, 867D (Lord Goff), 892 (Lord Mustill), *R (Pretty) v Director of Public Prosecutions* [2002] 1 AC 800, 831H–832A (Lord Steyn).

At the same time, the defence's limited ambit should be remembered; it applies to cases where the patient in any case (without analgesia) only has a comparatively short time to live, and would otherwise experience significant suffering. The latter will ordinarily be physical in nature; however, in a case brought in 1997 by a woman, Annie Lindsell, dying from motor neurone disease, Sir Stephen Brown, President of the Family Division of the High Court, confirmed that the defence protects doctors who prescribe such analgesics to ease their patients' mental torment (although this was not made the subject of a formal declaration).[21]

12.2.3 The separation of a non-viable conjoined twin

In 2001, a further inroad was made into the distinction between active and passive euthanasia to the extent that, in one particular set of circumstances, the Court of Appeal sanctioned an act (separation surgery) whose inevitable consequence was to terminate a patient's life. This step was taken in the well-known case of the conjoined twins, *Re A (Children)*.

---

19 Law Commission, Consultation Paper No 177, para 4.87. See: www.lawcom.gov.uk/docs/cp177_web.pdf.
20 [2014] UKSC 38.
21 *Lindsell v Holmes* (1997) *The Guardian*, 29 October.

Re A (Children) (Conjoined Twins: Surgical Separation)[22]

Jodie and Mary were conjoined twin girls who were born joined at the pelvis. The medical evidence was that Jodie sustained the life of Mary (whose own heart and lungs did not function) by circulating oxygenated blood through a common artery, and that, if they were not separated, Jodie's heart would eventually fail and they would both die within a few months. The hospital wished to perform separation surgery, which would enable Jodie to lead a relatively normal life (though Mary would die almost immediately), but the parents refused to consent on religious grounds. In the High Court, Johnson J granted a declaration that the hospital could lawfully carry out the surgery in both twins' best interests. The parents appealed:

Robert Walker LJ: Every member of the court has been deeply troubled by this case, but we have to decide it in accordance with the principles of existing law as we perceive them to apply to this unprecedented situation. I will summarise my conclusions as to the applicable principles as simply as I can.

i   The feelings of the twins' parents are entitled to great respect, especially so far as they are based on religious convictions. But as the matter has been referred to the court the court cannot escape the responsibility of deciding the matter to the best of its judgment as to the twins' best interests.

ii   The judge erred in law in equating the proposed surgical operation with the discontinuance of medical treatment (as by disconnecting a heart-lung machine). Therefore the Court of Appeal must form its own view.

iii Mary has a right to life, under the common law of England (based as it is on Judaeo-Christian foundations) and under the European Convention on Human Rights. It would be unlawful to kill Mary intentionally, that is to undertake an operation with the primary purpose of killing her.

iv   But Jodie also has a right to life.

v   Every human being's right to life carries with it, as an intrinsic part of it, rights of bodily integrity and autonomy – the right to have one's own body whole and intact and (on reaching an age of understanding) to take decisions about one's own body.

vi   By a rare and tragic mischance, Mary and Jodie have both been deprived of the bodily integrity and autonomy which is their natural right. There is a strong presumption that an operation to separate them would be in the best interests of each of them.

vii In this case the purpose of the operation would be to separate the twins and so give Jodie a reasonably good prospect of a long and reasonably normal life. Mary's death would not be the purpose of the operation, although it would be its inevitable consequence. The operation would give her, even in death, bodily integrity as a human being. She would die, not because she was intentionally killed, but because her own body cannot sustain her life.

viii Continued life, whether long or short, would hold nothing for Mary except possible pain and discomfort, if indeed she can feel anything at all.

ix   The proposed operation would therefore be in the best interests of each of the twins. The decision does not require the court to value one life above another.

x   The proposed operation would not be unlawful. It would involve the positive act of invasive surgery and Mary's death would be foreseen as an inevitable consequence of an operation which is intended, and is necessary, to save Jodie's life. But Mary's death would not be the purpose or intention of the surgery, and she would die because tragically her body, on its own, is not and never has been viable.

I would therefore dismiss this appeal.

---

22 [2001] Fam 147, CA.

The Court of Appeal's judgment runs to over 100 pages, and the three Lord Justices, while agreeing in the result, justify their conclusions in different ways. Thus, whereas Robert Walker LJ (relying on the doctrine of 'double effect') suggested that the doctors who performed the operation would not intend Mary's death, both Ward and Brooke LJJ applied the criminal law approach to intention set out by the House of Lords in *R v Woollin*,[23] and found that there would be intent.

For his part, Ward LJ thought that an argument based on self-defence could be used to justify the doctors' intervention on behalf of Jodie, but was not supported in this by Brooke or Robert Walker LJJ. Moreover, although all three members of the Court took the view that Mary's killing could be justified on the basis of the doctrine of necessity, they appear to have differed as to the precise ambit of this doctrine in the criminal law. Ward LJ, in particular, was careful to limit his decision to the particular circumstances of the case:

> **Ward LJ**: In my judgment, the appeal must be dismissed. Lest it be thought that this decision could become authority for wider propositions, such as that a doctor, once he has determined that a patient cannot survive, can kill the patient, it is important to restate the unique circumstances for which this case is authority. They are that it must be impossible to preserve the life of X without bringing about the death of Y, that Y by his or her very continued existence will inevitably bring about the death of X within a short period of time, and that X is capable of living an independent life but Y is incapable under any circumstances, including all forms of medical intervention, of viable independent existence. As I said at the beginning of this judgment, this is a very unique case.

An extensive academic literature has been generated by this case: for a selection, see the special edition of the Medical Law Review devoted to it.[24] Subsequently, in the Court of Appeal in *Nicklinson v Ministry of Justice*,[25] counsel for the applicants argued that the case opened the way towards a more general acceptance of necessity as a defence in cases of active euthanasia. However, this was rejected by the court:

> **Lord Dyson MR and Elias LJ**: [62] Mr Bowen also relies heavily on the case of *Re A (Children) (Conjoined Twins: Surgical Separation)* [2001] Fam 147 where the Court of Appeal held that doctors could operate on twins joined at birth notwithstanding that it would necessarily lead to the immediate death of one of them who was surviving off the metabolism of the other. Mr Bowen says that this is a case where, to use the language of Lord Goff in *Bland*, the judges crossed the Rubicon and allowed the deliberate taking of life. But the justification in that case was that the operation would in all probability save the life of the other twin who would otherwise have died within months.
>
> [63] Furthermore, the court emphasised that this was an exceptional case and that their judgments should have no wider significance. In any event, there is a world of difference between taking a life to save one and taking a life because the deceased wishes it to end. This case is too slender a thread on which to hang such a far-reaching development of the common law.

---

23 See n 17 above.
24 (2001) 9(3) Med L Rev.
25 [2013] EWCA Civ 961.

That *Re A* should be seen as an isolated response to a very unusual fact situation was reiterated by Lord Neuberger when *Nicklinson* reached the UK Supreme Court:[26]

> **Lord Neuberger:** [25] As Hoffmann LJ said in *Bland* . . ., 'Modern medicine . . . faces us with fundamental and painful decisions about life and death which cannot be answered on the basis of normal everyday assumptions'. The accuracy of this observation was subsequently demonstrated by the decision of the Court of Appeal *In re A (Children) (Conjoined Twins: Surgical Separation)* [2001] Fam 147. . . . This decision took the law further in that the court authorised surgeons to separate conjoined twins, a positive act rather than omission, which would inevitably hasten the death of one twin in order to improve very considerably the life expectancy of the other.

12.2.4 Assisted suicide

In respect of patients who are not already dying, or though dying are not in pain, the doctor is clearly not permitted to do anything that directly shortens life. How far, though, may he furnish the means to allow such patients to kill themselves? It is evident that a doctor who acts thus is not guilty of murder; even one who, say, in the case of a paralysed patient, places a lethal pill in the latter's mouth will (provided the patient knows what is in the pill) at most have assisted in the patient's suicide. The reason is that the latter's voluntary and informed action of swallowing the pill operates as a *novus actus interveniens* which 'breaks the chain of causation' between the doctor's previous act of providing the pill and the patient's death.

Here, notwithstanding that suicide itself is not a crime, the doctor will be guilty of the offence of 'assisting suicide' contrary to s 2 of the Suicide Act 1961 (as re-enacted by s 59(2) of the Coroners and Justice Act 2009):

> **2 Criminal liability for complicity in another's suicide**
>
> 1   A person ('D') commits an offence if –
>
>   (a)   D does an act capable of encouraging or assisting the suicide or attempted suicide of another person, and
>
>   (b)   D's act was intended to encourage or assist suicide or an attempt at suicide.
>
>   . . .
>
>   (1C)   An offence under this section is triable on indictment and a person convicted of such an offence is liable to imprisonment for a term not exceeding 14 years.
>
>   . . . . (4)[N]o proceedings shall be instituted for an offence under this section except by or with the consent of the Director of Public Prosecutions.

The key reason for retaining the offence of assisted suicide is to protect the lives of the vulnerable and the weak, in particular those who might otherwise be placed under (real or perceived) pressure to end their lives to relieve others from the burden of caring for them. In this regard, the House of Lords Select Committee on Medical Ethics (1994), set up after the *Bland* case, commented that 'the message which society sends to vulnerable and disadvantaged people should not, however obliquely, encourage them to seek death, but should assure them of our care and support in life'.[27]

---

26 See n 20 above.
27 *Report of the Select Committee on Medical Ethics*, HL Paper No 21, 1994, para 239.

Nonetheless, this is an issue that has remained firmly on the political and judicial agenda, particularly in the light of European human rights law after the enactment of the Human Rights Act 1998. The English courts were first required to rule on the compatibility of the provisions of the Suicide Act 1961 with the rights of the putative suicide under the European Convention on Human Rights (ECHR) in *R (on the application of Pretty) v DPP*:

R (on the application of Pretty) v DPP[28]

Dianne Pretty was suffering from the terminal stages of motor neurone disease. Rather than await death through suffocation or starvation (the natural outcome of the disease), she wished to commit suicide, but, due to her condition, needed help to do so. Her husband was willing to assist her, provided that the Director of Public Prosecutions undertook not to prosecute him under s 2 of the Suicide Act 1961. When the DPP refused to do so, Mrs Pretty brought an action in judicial review proceedings, arguing that s 2 of the 1961 Act contravened her ECHR rights, in particular those under Article 2 (the right to life), Article 3 (the right not to suffer inhuman or degrading treatment) and Article 8 (the right to private and family life):

Lord Steyn: [59] . . . Counsel for Mrs Pretty argued that article 2 and in particular its first sentence acknowledges that it is for the individual to choose whether to live or die and that it protects her right of self-determination in relation to issues of life and death. This interpretation is not sustainable. The purpose of article 2(1) is clear. It enunciates the principle of the sanctity of life and provides a guarantee that no individual 'shall be deprived of life' by means of intentional human intervention. The interpretation now put forward is the exact opposite viz a right of Mrs Pretty to end her life by means of intentional human intervention. Nothing in the article or the jurisprudence of the European Court of Human Rights can assist Mrs Pretty's case on this article.

[60] . . . The core of counsel's argument [under Art 3] is that . . . the state's obligations are to take effective steps to ensure that no one shall be subjected to inhuman or degrading treatment. For my part article 3 is not engaged. The word 'treatment' must take its colour from the context in which it appears. While I would not wish to give a narrow interpretation to what may constitute degrading treatment, the concept appears singularly inapt to convey the idea that the state must guarantee to individuals a right to die with the deliberate assistance of third parties. So radical a step, infringing the sanctity of life principle, would have required far more explicit wording

[61] . . . Counsel submitted that [Art 8] explicitly recognises the principle of the personal autonomy of every individual. He argues that this principle necessarily involves a guarantee as against the state of the right to choose when and how to die. None of the decisions cited in regard to article 8 assist this argument. It must fail on the ground that the guarantee under article 8 prohibits interference with the way in which an individual leads his life and it does not relate to the manner in which he wishes to die.

. . . [68] . . . The logic of the European Convention does not justify the conclusion that the House must rule that a state is obliged to legalise assisted suicide. It does not require the state to repeal a provision such as section 2(1) of the 1961 Act. On the other hand, it is open to a democratic legislature to introduce such a measure. Our Parliament, if so minded, may therefore repeal section 2(1) and put in its place a regulated system for assisted suicide (presumably doctor assisted) with appropriate safeguards.

---

28 [2002] 1 AC 800.

The other Law Lords agreed with Lord Steyn in dismissing Mrs Pretty's application. Subsequently, she appealed to the European Court of Human Rights in Strasbourg, which agreed with the House of Lords that Articles 2 and 3 had no application to the case. However, it endorsed the minority view of Lord Hope (on this point) that Mrs Pretty's right under Article 8 of the ECHR was engaged:

> [65] The very essence of the Convention is respect for human dignity and human freedom. Without in any way negating the principle of sanctity of life protected under the Convention, the Court considers that it is under article 8 that notions of the quality of life take on significance. In an era of growing medical sophistication combined with longer life expectancies, many people are concerned that they should not be forced to linger on in old age or in states of advanced physical or mental decrepitude which conflict with strongly held ideas of self and personal identity.[29]

At the same time, the European Court of Human Rights held that the interference in this right – in terms of the prohibition on assisted suicide – ultimately lay within the margin of appreciation of individual states, and could be justified under Article 8(2) of the ECHR, namely as necessary in order to protect the rights of others – ie vulnerable persons who might otherwise feel pressure to agree to suicide. In this regard, the court noted that s 2(4) of the 1961 Act already provides for some flexibility in genuinely 'hard cases' (involving circumstances such as those in *Pretty*), by making prosecution under s 2 subject to the consent of the DPP.

While the court thus dismissed Mrs Pretty's action against the UK Government, the legal position in such cases remained dangerously uncertain from the point of view of those contemplating helping others to commit suicide: when would the DPP exercise his discretion under s 2(4) not to prosecute them, and when not? Against this background the House of Lords was required to rule again on the compatibility of the law in this area with the ECHR in the case of *R (on the application of Purdy) v DPP*.

R (on the application of Purdy) v DPP[30]

> Debbie Purdy was suffering from incurable, progressive multiple sclerosis. She wished to be able to end her life at a point when she judged it no longer bearable, by travelling to a country such as Switzerland, where assisted suicide is lawful; however, she would need the assistance of her husband to make the journey. Unlike Mrs Pretty, she did not seek an undertaking from the DPP that her husband would not be prosecuted under the 1961 Act; but she argued that, pursuant to Art 8 of the ECHR, she at least had a right to more detailed information from the DPP as to the factors that would influence his decision whether to prosecute.
>
> > **Lord Hope:** [26] It must be emphasised at the outset that it is no part of our function to change the law in order to decriminalise assisted suicide. If changes are to be made, as to which I express no opinion, this must be a matter for Parliament . . . We do not venture into that arena, nor would it be right for us to do so. Our function as judges is to say what the law is and, if it is uncertain, to do what we can to clarify it . . .
> >
> > [28] Lord Pannick Q.C. for Ms Purdy directed his argument to s.2(4) of the 1961 Act, which provides that no proceedings shall be instituted for an offence under that section except by or with

---

29 *Pretty v United Kingdom* (2002) 35 EHRR 1.
30 [2009] UKHL 45.

the consent of the Director of Public Prosecutions, and to her right to respect for her private life under art.8(1) of the European Convention for the Protection of Human Rights and Fundamental Freedoms ... He submits, first, that the prohibition in s.2(1) of the 1961 Act constitutes an interference with Ms Purdy's right to respect for her private life under art.8(1) of the European Convention on Human Rights; and, second, that this interference is not 'in accordance with the law' as required by art.8(2), in the absence of an offence-specific policy by the Director of Public Prosecutions which sets out the factors that will be taken into account by him and Crown Prosecutors acting on his behalf in deciding under s.2(4) of the 1961 Act whether or not it is in the public interest to bring a prosecution under that section ...

[46] ... Consistency of practice is especially important here. The issue is without doubt both sensitive and controversial. Many people view legally assisted suicide as an appalling concept which undermines the fundamental human right to life itself. On the other hand there are those, like Ms Purdy, who firmly believe that the right to life includes the right to end one's own life when one can still do so with dignity. Crown Prosecutors to whom the decision-taking function is delegated need to be given the clearest possible instructions as to the factors which they must have regard to when they are performing it ...

... [56] I would therefore allow the appeal and require the Director to promulgate an offence-specific policy identifying the facts and circumstances which he will take into account in deciding, in a case such as that which Ms Purdy's case exemplifies, whether or not to consent to a prosecution under s.2(1) of the 1961 Act.

Following this decision, the DPP in February 2010 issued guidance on his policy in respect of prosecuting cases of assisted suicide.[31] Among the public interest factors mentioned as militating against prosecution are that the victim had a settled and informed wish to die, and that the assisting person was motivated wholly by compassion. In contrast, a factor in favour of prosecution is that the assisting person was acting in his or her capacity as a medical doctor, nurse, or other healthcare professional.[32]

In fact, this last aspect of the guidance was challenged in the recent UK Supreme Court case of *Nicklinson v Ministry of Justice*, a decision which also invited a general reconsideration of whether (notwithstanding the earlier House of Lords decisions in *Pretty* and *Purdy*) s 2 of the Suicide Act 1961 should still be regarded as compatible with the specific application of Article 8 ECHR in UK law.

R (on the application of Nicklinson and Another) v Ministry of Justice; R (on the Application of AM) v DPP[33]

Tony Nicklinson was left almost totally paralysed, but mentally unimpaired, after a stroke and able to communicate only through eye blinks. He considered his life in this state no longer tolerable and applied initially for a declaration that his Article 8 ECHR rights required he be provided with lawful third party assistance to die (given his physical inability to commit suicide except by self-starvation). Mr Nicklinson died soon after the rejection of this argument by the High Court, but his action was pursued by his widow,

---

31 DPP, 'Policy for Prosecutors in Respect of Cases of Encouraging or Assisting Suicide', available at: www.cps.gov.uk/publications/prosecution/assisted_suicide_policy.html.
32 Ibid., para 43: 14; in October 2014 the DPP announced that this factor would apply only where the doctor was in a pre-existing care relationship with the patient: see the text at nn 38–39 below.
33 See n 20 above.

together with a new applicant, Paul Lamb, who was in a similar position to Mr Nicklinson. As noted, in *Pretty v UK* the ECtHR had found the regulation of assisted suicide to be a matter within a state's margin of appreciation, ie it required domestic determination. In this regard much of the argument in the Supreme Court was taken up with the constitutional and institutional propriety of an unelected court using its powers under the Human Rights Act 1998 to declare the 1961 Act incompatible. In view of its importance the case was heard by no fewer than nine UKSC Justices, and, as summarised in Lady Hale's speech, there was a division of opinion on this point:

> **Lady Hale:** [299] … [Lord Neuberger] has shown that, even if the Strasbourg court would regard the issue before us as within the margin of appreciation which it accords to member states, it is within the jurisdiction accorded to this court under the Human Rights Act 1998 to decide whether the law is or is not compatible with the Convention rights recognised by UK law. … Hence both he and Lord Wilson accept that, in the right case and at the right time, it would be open to this court to make a declaration that section 2 of the Suicide Act 1961 is incompatible with the right to respect for private life protected by article 8 of the European Convention on Human Rights. Understandably, however, they would prefer that Parliament have an opportunity of investigating, debating and deciding upon the issue before a court decides whether or not to make such a declaration. Lord Mance is also prepared to contemplate that possibility, although he too thinks Parliament the preferable forum in which any decision should be made (paras 190–191)). Together with Lord Kerr and I, who would make a declaration now, this constitutes a majority who consider that the court both can and should do this in an appropriate case. Lord Clarke (para 293) and Lord Sumption (para 233) might intervene but only if Parliament chooses not to debate the issue; otherwise, they, and Lord Reed and Lord Hughes, consider that this is a matter for Parliament alone.

For her part, Lady Hale (along with Lord Kerr) would have made an immediate declaration of incompatibility:

> **Lady Hale:** [311] The only legitimate aim which has been advanced for [the prohibition on assisted suicide] is the protection of vulnerable people, those who feel that their lives are worthless or that they are a burden to others and therefore that they ought to end their own lives even though they do not really want to. In terms of article 8.2, this could be put either as the 'protection of health' or as the 'protection of the rights of others', the right in question being the most important right of all, the right to life protected by article 2. …
>
> [312] Is it then reasonably necessary to prohibit helping *everyone* who might want to end their own lives in order to protect those whom we regard as *vulnerable* to undue pressures to do so? I can understand the argument that it is: how does a person judge which pressures are undue and which are not? We can all understand why people placed in the situation of Mr Nicklinson, Mr Lamb, Martin or Ms B might wish an end to their suffering. But (as I ventured to point out in *Purdy*, at para 66) there are many other reasons why a person might consider it a sensible and reasonable thing to do. On what basis is it possible to distinguish some of those pressures from others?
>
> [313] That problem is certainly enough to justify a *general* ban on assisting suicide. But it is difficult to accept that it is sufficient to justify a *universal* ban, a ban which forces people like Mr Nicklinson, Mr Lamb and Martin to stay alive, not for the sake of protecting themselves, but for the sake of protecting other people. In *Pretty*, the Strasbourg court rejected the argument that Mrs Pretty was suffering inhuman and degrading treatment contrary to article 3. But no-one who has read the appellants' accounts of their lives and their feelings can doubt that they experience the law's insistence that they stay alive for the sake of others as a form of cruelty.
>
> [314] It would not be beyond the wit of a legal system to devise a process for identifying those people, those few people, who should be allowed help to end their own lives. There would be

four essential requirements. They would firstly have to have the capacity to make the decision for themselves. They would secondly have to have reached the decision freely without undue influence from any quarter. They would thirdly have had to reach it with full knowledge of their situation, the options available to them, and the consequences of their decision. . . . And they would fourthly have to be unable, because of physical incapacity or frailty, to put that decision into effect without some help from others. I do not pretend that such cases would always be easy to decide, but the nature of the judgments involved would be no more difficult than those regularly required in the Court of Protection or the Family Division when cases such as *Aintree University Hospitals NHS Trust v James* . . . or *Re B (Treatment)* come before them.

However, the other Justices held that a declaration would not be appropriate at the present time. As noted by Lord Sumption, this was especially so given that the issue remained under active consideration by Parliament itself:

Lord Sumption: [231] . . . Parliament has made the relevant choice. It passed the Suicide Act in 1961, and as recently as 2009 amended section 2 without altering the principle. In recent years there have been a number of bills to decriminalize assistance to suicide, at least in part, but none has been passed into law. Lord Joffe introduced two bills on the House of Lords in 2004 and 2005. The 2005 bill went to a second reading in May 2006, but failed at that stage. Lord Falconer moved an amendment to the Coroners and Justice Bill 2009 to permit assistance to a person wishing to travel to a country where assisted suicide is legal. The amendment also failed. The Assisted Dying Bill, sponsored by Lord Falconer, is currently before the House of Lords. In addition to these specific legislative proposals, the issue of assisted suicide has been the subject of high-profile public debate for many years and has been considered on at least three occasions since 2000 by House of Lords Select Committees. Sometimes, Parliamentary inaction amounts to a decision not to act. But this is not even an issue on which Parliament has been inactive. So far, there has simply not been enough Parliamentary support for a change in the law. The reasons why this is so are irrelevant. That is the current position of the representative body in our constitution. As Lord Bingham observed in *R (Countryside Alliance) v Attorney-General* . . . at para 45, '[t]he democratic process is liable to be subverted if, on a question of moral and political judgment, opponents of the Act achieve through the courts what they could not achieve in Parliament.'

Subsequently, the applicants unsuccessfully petitioned the European Court of Human Rights.[34] In the meantime the UK Parliament has further debated the issues surrounding assisted dying, but no majority in favour of relaxing the current prohibitions has emerged. Against this background, in *Conway v Secretary of State for Justice*, there was a recent, new attempt to obtain a judicial declaration that the law here is incompatible with human rights.

Conway v Secretary of State for Justice[35]

Noel Conway suffered from incurable progressive motor neurone disease, with a limited life expectancy. He wished to be assisted to commit suicide at a time of his own choosing and argued that, in the light of Parliament's continued refusal to decriminalise assisted suicide, it was now time for the courts to make the incompatibility declaration that the UK Supreme Court had mooted, but drawn back from, in *Nicklinson*.

---

34 *Nicklinson and Lamb v United Kingdom* [2015] ECHR 783.
35 [2017] EWHC 2447 (Admin).

As an aspect of the his argument, the claimant (drawing on suggestions in some of the speeches from *Nicklinson*),[36] also presented the text of a possible statute he claimed would adequately safeguard the weak and vulnerable from being pressured into assisted suicide, while permitting it in cases of medical necessity such as his own; *inter alia*, this would require all applications for such assistance to be reviewed by a High Court judge:

> **Lord Justice Sales (giving the judgment of the Divisional Court):** [91] ... [T]here is an issue between the parties regarding the aim or aims which section 2 [of the Suicide Act] seeks to pursue. Mr Gordon [Counsel for Mr Conway] submits that the only aim of any significance is the protection of the weak and vulnerable. Mr Strachan [Counsel for the Secretary] submits that even if that is correct, section 2 is still objectively justified under Article 8(2) [ECHR]; but in fact the legitimate aims of the provision are wider than that, encompassing protection of the weak and vulnerable but also protection of the sanctity of life and promotion of trust and confidence between doctor and patient, which encourages patients to seek and then act upon medical advice... In our view, Mr Strachan has properly identified wider aims which section 2 seeks to promote and this serves to reinforce his submission that it is a provision which is objectively justified under Article 8(2)....
>
> [98] Mr Gordon submits that the proposed legislative regime which Mr Conway has outlined would be adequate to address concerns regarding the protection of the weak and vulnerable. In particular, the involvement of the High Court to review any application for permission to provide assistance to a person wishing to commit suicide would ensure that he or she was free of any pressure and had full capacity to make the decision to die, as can already happen when a person wishes to have life sustaining support switched off: see *In re B (Adult: Refusal of Medical Treatment)*. Therefore the blanket prohibition against assistance for suicide in section 2 cannot be regarded as necessary to meet the legitimate aim in issue.
>
> [99] As mentioned above, Mr Strachan makes two submissions in response. First, he says that even if the legitimate aim promoted by section 2 is confined to protection of the weak and vulnerable, there is nonetheless a clear and proper case that the provision is necessary to promote that aim. Secondly, he submits that the justification of the prohibition in section 2 is clearer still when the other legitimate aims referred to above are taken into account.
>
> [100] We agree with both these submissions. As to the first, the involvement of the High Court to check capacity and absence of pressure or duress does not meet the real gravamen of the case regarding protection of the weak and vulnerable. Persons with serious debilitating terminal illnesses may be prone to feelings of despair and low self-esteem and consider themselves a burden to others, which make them wish for death. They may be isolated and lonely, particularly if they are old, and that may reinforce such feelings and undermine their resilience. All this may be true while they retain full legal capacity and are not subjected to improper pressure by others....
>
> [107] Parliament has considered the matter with the benefit of the judgments of the Supreme Court in *Nicklinson* and has decided to maintain section 2 in place, after taking all relevant countervailing arguments into account.
>
> [108] In those circumstances, we consider that there are powerful constitutional reasons why Parliament's assessment of the necessity of maintaining section 2 in place should be respected by this court....

---

36 See Lady Hale at [314], cited above; see also Lord Neuberger at [123] and Lord Wilson at [205].

[112]. . . . As the conscience of the nation, Parliament is entitled to maintain in place a clear bright-line rule which forbids people from providing assistance to an individual to commit suicide. Parliament was and is entitled to decide that the clarity of such a moral position could only be achieved by means of such a rule. Although views about this vary in society, we think that the legitimacy of Parliament deciding to maintain such a clear line that people should not seek to intervene to hasten the death of a human is not open to serious doubt. Parliament is entitled to make the assessment that it should protect moral standards in society by issuing clear and unambiguous laws which reflect and embody such standards.

Accordingly, the Court declined to make a declaration of incompatibility. In January 2018, the Court of Appeal granted Mr Conway leave to appeal against this decision.

Returning to the conjoined proceedings in *Nicklinson*, of *AM v DPP*,[37] there the applicant, known as Martin, did not attack the prohibition on assisted suicide as such, but – as Ms Purdy had done before him – argued that the DPP's discretion in prosecuting made the offence too vague to satisfy the rule of law. As noted above, in February 2010 the DPP drafted a policy, as required by the House of Lords in the *Purdy* case, listing relevant factors pointing in favour of and against a prosecution.[38] One factor in favour (under para 43(14) of the policy) was that the assister was a doctor or other professional. Martin claimed, though, that the failure to explain either the rationale or the relative weight of this factor meant that the policy remained an insufficient guide for such assisters.

A majority of the Court of Appeal accepted this contention and ordered the DPP to clarify the policy. By contrast, the Supreme Court held it was not appropriate to make a formal order of this kind, but signalled its expectation that the DPP would consider how to make the relevant paragraph clearer. Accordingly, in October 2014 (following public consultation) the DPP issued a revised, expanded version of paragraph 43(14), stating as a factor in favour of prosecution that:

the suspect was acting in his or her capacity as a medical doctor, nurse, other healthcare professional, a professional carer [whether for payment or not], or as a person in authority, such as a prison officer, *and the victim was in his or her care; [1]*

. . .

Footnote [1]: For the avoidance of doubt the words "and the victim was in his or her care" qualify all of the preceding parts of this paragraph [43.14]. This factor does not apply merely because someone was acting in a capacity described within it: it applies only where there was, in addition, a relationship of care between the suspect and the victims such that it will be necessary to consider whether the suspect may have exerted some influence on the victim.

The effect of this is that a doctor brought in from the outside to assist with medical aspects of the suicide would not be at a heightened risk of being prosecuted. Subsequently, in *R (Kenward) v DPP*,[39] this revision was itself subject to a judicial review challenge by applicants who

---

37 [2014] UKSC 38.
38 See n 31 above.
39 [2015] EWHC 3508 (Admin).

argued it went too far in the direction of enabling physician-assisted suicide. In dismissing the application, though, Sir Brian Leveson in the Divisional Court commented:

> **Sir Brian Leveson**: [53] . . . The gradation between circumstances in which it is appropriate to prosecute and those in which it is not will always involve a very detailed consideration of all the facts and, ultimately, a balanced judgement: it is for that reason that I set out all the factors set out in the policy that fall to be considered. Neither does the policy impact on the view which professional regulatory bodies are entitled to take about the obligations and responsibilities of those whom they regulate: the criminal law identifies minimum standards of behaviour and professional requirements may well be set at a higher level. Thus, although I recognise that Mr and Mrs Kenward hold very strong views, I do not accept that this policy provides support for the proposition that those views will not be respected by all with whom they come into contact.

THINK POINT

If a doctor, intending to end a patient's life, were to inject him with a massive dose of morphine, how likely, as a practical matter, is a conviction for murder?

12.3 Withholding treatment: capable patients

12.3.1 Background

Our concern here is with the more flexible attitude taken by the qualified sanctity of life doctrine in respect of omissions to provide life-sustaining treatment (reflected in the 'need'st not strive officiously' part of AH Clough's couplet).

A preliminary question is what conduct, in the context of providing medical care, will be regarded in law as an *omission* rather than an *act*? For example, a common means of sustaining the life of a critically ill patient in hospital is to place him on a ventilator. If, in a given case, a doctor decides that there is no hope of recovery and switches the machine off, could he not be said to have acted to bring about the patient's death? Lord Goff, however, forcefully rejected this possibility in the *Bland*[40] case:

> **Lord Goff**: Why is it that the doctor who gives his patient a lethal injection which kills him commits an unlawful act and indeed is guilty of murder, whereas a doctor who, by discontinuing life support, allows his patient to die, may not act unlawfully – and will not do so, if he commits no breach of duty to his patient? Professor Glanville Williams has suggested (see his *Textbook of Criminal Law* . . .) that the reason is that what the doctor does when he switches off a life support machine 'is in substance not an act but an omission to struggle', and that 'the omission is not a breach of duty by the doctor, because he is not obliged to continue in a hopeless case'.
>
> I agree that the doctor's conduct in discontinuing life support can properly be categorised as an omission. It is true that it may be difficult to describe what the doctor actually does as an omission, for example where he takes some positive step to bring the life support to an end. But discontinuation of life support is, for present purposes, no different from not initiating life support in the first place. In each case,

---

40 See n 6 above.

the doctor is simply allowing his patient to die in the sense that he is desisting from taking a step which might, in certain circumstances, prevent his patient from dying as a result of his pre-existing condition; and as a matter of general principle an omission such as this will not be unlawful unless it constitutes a breach of duty to the patient. I also agree that the doctor's conduct is to be differentiated from that of, for example, an interloper who maliciously switches off a life support machine because, although the interloper may perform exactly the same act as the doctor who discontinues life support, his doing so constitutes interference with the life-prolonging treatment then being administered by the doctor. Accordingly, whereas the doctor, in discontinuing life support, is simply allowing his patient to die of his pre-existing condition, the interloper is actively intervening to stop the doctor from prolonging the patient's life, and such conduct cannot possibly be categorised as an omission.

It is apparent that, for these purposes, the description of a given piece of conduct by the doctor as an *act* turns not upon a narrow criterion of voluntary physical movement, but rather upon whether what he has done amounts to an interference with the natural course of events. Whereas the doctor, in stopping life support, simply brings to a close his own previous and continuing interference in nature, the malicious interloper does interfere in (and hence 'acts' relative to) the life-sustaining regime – a sort of second 'nature' created and maintained by the doctor.

The principle that conduct engaged in by the medical staff in the process of withdrawing treatment will not amount to an act in legal terms, is implicit in the High Court decision in the case of *Ms B v An NHS Hospital Trust*,[41] in which a hospital was held to be acting unlawfully in continuing to ventilate a capable patient, who was paralysed from the neck down, and no longer wished to be kept alive. At the same time, the President of the Family Division acknowledged the psychological difficulties faced by the treating team in the case:

Dame Elizabeth Butler-Sloss P: [58] It was clear from their evidence that both the treating clinicians were deeply distressed by the dilemma which had faced them over the year that Ms B had spent in the ICU. They knew her well and respected and liked her. They considered her to be capable to make decisions about her medical treatment. They could not, however, bring themselves to contemplate that they should be part of bringing Ms B's life to an end by the dramatic, (my word), step of turning off the ventilator. As I listened to the evidence of each of them I had the greatest possible sympathy for their position.

Accordingly, the hospital was ordered to arrange for Ms B's transfer to another facility where the medical staff would be prepared to switch off the ventilator sustaining her life.

For similar reasons it makes no difference whether the doctors decide to withhold medical treatment from the outset or, having begun to treat the patient, elect to withdraw it at a later stage: in both cases what is at stake is an omission. As Lord Lowry commented in *Airedale NHS Trust v Bland*:[42]

Lord Lowry: I do not believe that there is a valid legal distinction between the omission to treat a patient and the abandonment of treatment which has been commenced, since to recognise such a distinction could quite illogically confer on a doctor who had refrained from treatment an immunity which did not benefit a doctor who had embarked on treatment in order to see whether it might help the patient and had abandoned the treatment when it was seen not to do so.

---

41 [2002] EWHC 429 (Fam); the case is discussed in Ch 3.
42 See n 6 above.

At the same time, it certainly does not follow that, provided his conduct can be characterised as an omission, the doctor has a free hand in allowing death to occur. The reason why this is not so, and the manner in which the doctor's position differs in this respect from that of the average citizen, is evident from the following passage from Lord Browne-Wilkinson's speech in *Bland*:

> **Lord Browne-Wilkinson**: It is the submission of the Official Solicitor that the withdrawal of artificial feeding would constitute murder. The Official Solicitor has been criticised for using emotive language in this case. In my judgment this criticism is misplaced: much the most difficult question is indeed whether the proposed course of action is, in law, murder notwithstanding the best motives from which everyone concerned is acting.
>
> Murder consists of causing the death of another with intent so to do. What is proposed in the present case is to adopt a course with the intention of bringing about Anthony Bland's death. As to the element of intention or *mens rea*, in my judgment there can be no real doubt that it is present in this case: the whole purpose of stopping artificial feeding is to bring about the death of Anthony Bland.
>
> As to the guilty act, or *actus reus*, the criminal law draws a distinction between the commission of a positive act which causes death and the omission to do an act which would have prevented death. In general an omission to prevent death is not an actus reus and cannot give rise to a conviction for murder. But where the accused was under a duty to the deceased to do the act which he omitted to do, such omission can constitute the actus reus of homicide, either murder (*R v Gibbins* (1918) 13 Cr App R 134) or manslaughter (*R v Stone* [1977] QB 354) depending upon the *mens rea* of the accused . . .

It is apparent, then, that the lawfulness of withholding life-sustaining treatment revolves around the question: 'When is the doctor released from his normal duty to treat?' In answering this, we shall look first, in the remainder of this section, at the position of those patients who remain capable to decide whether or not they wish to receive such treatment, or who have codified their previous capable wishes in an advance directive. In section 12.4 we then go on to consider the question of permitting death through non-treatment in the case of those incapable patients who have never expressed a capable and/or sufficiently clear view on the subject.

12.3.2 The patient who wishes to be kept alive

In so far as a capable patient wishes to receive life-sustaining treatment, then the doctor will virtually always be obligated to provide it, at least where the treatment is one that is medically established. This principle lay at the heart of the case of *R (on the application of Burke) v* GMC:

R (on the application of Burke) v GMC[43]

> Mr Burke suffered from a cerebellar ataxia, a terminal degenerative condition that at some point would require him to receive artificial nutrition and hydration (ANH) to prolong his life: he would thereupon remain conscious and capable for a considerable time until the disease reached its final stages. He was concerned by the tenor of the GMC's Guidance to doctors, which implied that unless the patient was actively *refusing* ANH, its continuation was a matter of medical discretion, and challenged the Guidance's legality in relation both to the common law and his rights under the ECHR.
>
> At first instance, Munby J agreed that the Guidance had attached too little weight to the patient's right, reinforced by ECHR considerations, to require life-prolonging ANH, and ruled it unlawful in a number

---

43 [2005] EWCA Civ 1003.

of respects. However, this ruling was reversed by the Court of Appeal, which emphasised that the patient was amply protected by the existing common law, and that nothing in the GMC's Guidance should be read as detracting from this:

> **Lord Phillips MR** (delivering the judgment of the Court): [31] . . . Autonomy and the right of self-determination do not entitle the patient to insist on receiving a particular medical treatment regardless of the nature of the treatment. Insofar as a doctor has a legal obligation to provide treatment this cannot be founded simply upon the fact that the patient demands it. The source of the duty lies elsewhere.
>
> [32] So far as ANH is concerned, there is no need to look far for the duty to provide this. Once a patient is accepted into a hospital, the medical staff come under a positive duty at common law to care for the patient. The authorities cited by Munby J at paragraphs 82 to 87 under the heading 'The duty to care' establish this proposition, if authority is needed. A fundamental aspect of this positive duty of care is a duty to take such steps as are reasonable to keep the patient alive. Where ANH is necessary to keep the patient alive, the duty of care will normally require the doctors to supply ANH. This duty will not, however, override the competent patient's wish not to receive ANH. Where the competent patient makes it plain that he or she wishes to be kept alive by ANH, this will not be the source of the duty to provide it. The patient's wish will merely underscore that duty.
>
> [33] Insofar as the law has recognised that the duty to keep a patient alive by administering ANH or other life-prolonging treatment is not absolute, the exceptions have been restricted to the following situations: (1) where the competent patient refuses to receive ANH and (2) where the patient is not competent and it is not considered to be in the best interests of the patient to be artificially kept alive. It is with the second exception that the law has had most difficulty. The courts have accepted that where life involves an extreme degree of pain, discomfort or indignity to a patient, who is sentient but not competent and who has manifested no wish to be kept alive, these circumstances may absolve the doctors of the positive duty to keep the patient alive. Equally the courts have recognised that there may be no duty to keep alive a patient who is in a persistent vegetative state ('PVS'). In each of these examples the facts of the individual case may make it difficult to decide whether the duty to keep the patient alive persists.
>
> [34] No such difficulty arises, however, in the situation that has caused Mr Burke concern, that of the competent patient who, regardless of the pain, suffering or indignity of his condition, makes it plain that he wishes to be kept alive. No authority lends the slightest countenance to the suggestion that the duty on the doctors to take reasonable steps to keep the patient alive in such circumstances may not persist. Indeed, it seems to us that for a doctor deliberately to interrupt life-prolonging treatment in the face of a competent patient's expressed wish to be kept alive, with the intention of thereby terminating the patient's life, would leave the doctor with no answer to a charge of murder.

Mr Burke's subsequent application to the European Court of Human Rights was ruled inadmissible. The Court found that he had not shown a real and imminent risk that ANH would be withdrawn, thereby infringing his right to life under Art 2 ECHR.[44]

Accordingly, where straightforward treatment such as ANH is at issue, the doctor has a near-absolute duty to provide it as part of his duty to treat his patients in their best interests: the interests in question will be strongly coloured by the patient's wish to be kept alive. However, as

---

44 ECtHR: Application 19807/06.

the Court of Appeal in *Burke* recognised, there could exceptionally be cases, eg where a patient asks for treatment that will marginally prolong his life but at the cost of severe suffering, where the doctor may legitimately refuse to administer the treatment. This proposition was recently approved by the UK Supreme Court in *Aintree University Hospitals Foundation Trust v James*:[45]

> **Lady Hale**: [18] [I]n *R (Burke) v General Medical Council*..., Lord Phillips MR accepted the proposition of the General Medical Council that if a doctor concludes that the treatment which a patient wants is 'not clinically indicated he is not required (ie he is under no legal obligation) to provide it' (para 50), and 'Ultimately, however, a patient cannot demand that a doctor administer a treatment which the doctor considers is adverse to the patient's clinical needs' (para 55).

At the same time, as clarified by the Court of Appeal in *R (David Tracey) v Cambridge University Hospitals NHS Foundation Trust & Ors*,[46] the patient has a strong prima facie right to be involved in any such decision. There the defendant's failure to tell a terminally ill patient that it had placed a DNR order on her was held to have infringed her right to respect for private life under Article 8 ECHR:

> **Lord Dyson MR**: [53] ... [S]ince a DNACPR decision is one which will potentially deprive the patient of life-saving treatment, there should be a presumption in favour of patient involvement. There need to be convincing reasons not to involve the patient.
>
> [54] There can be little doubt that it is inappropriate (and therefore not a requirement of article 8) to involve the patient in the process if the clinician considers that to do so is likely to cause her to suffer physical or psychological harm....
>
> [55] Lord Pannick [for the NHS Trust] submits that it is also inappropriate to involve the patient if the clinician forms the view that CPR would be futile even if he considers that involvement is unlikely to cause the patient harm. I would reject this submission for two reasons. First, a decision to deprive the patient of potentially life-saving treatment is of a different order of significance for the patient from a decision to deprive him or her of other kinds of treatment. It calls for particularly convincing justification. Prima facie, the patient is entitled to know that such an important clinical decision has been taken. The fact that the clinician considers that CPR will not work means that the patient cannot require him to provide it. It does not, however, mean that the patient is not entitled to know that the clinical decision has been taken. Secondly, if the patient is not told that the clinician has made a DNACPR decision, he will be deprived of the opportunity of seeking a second opinion ...

A further, complicating feature in some cases where a capable patient requests a particular form of treatment to prolong his life for as long as possible is of possible resource constraints in the background. For here the doctor's accession to the wishes of one patient will necessarily impact upon the treatment of other patients. The problem of limited resources – and its interaction, in the case of potentially life-prolonging treatment, with the patient's right to life – has been discussed above in Chapter 2, in relation to the public law applications of patients to receive the cancer drug, Herceptin.[47] We shall also return to the issue in section 12.4.5, in relation to the issue of keeping alive incapable patients, with no or minimal awareness.

---

45 [2013] UKSC 67.
46 [2014] EWCA Civ 822.
47 See Ch 2, section 2.4.2.

12.3.3 Refusals of life-sustaining treatment

As we saw in Chapter 3, it is a cardinal principle of medical law that, in respect of a capable adult patient, treatment may generally not be administered without consent; this is so even in a situation in which, without the treatment, the patient will die.[48] In this regard, Lord Goff commented in *Airedale NHS Trust v Bland* that:

> [I]t is established that the principle of self-determination requires that respect must be given to the wishes of the patient, so that if an adult patient of sound mind refuses, however unreasonably, to consent to treatment or care by which his life would or might be prolonged, the doctors responsible for his care must give effect to his wishes, even though they do not consider it to be in his best interests to do so ... To this extent, the principle of the sanctity of human life must yield to the principle of self-determination ...

Subsequently, the principle formed the *ratio* in the High Court decisions in *Re C (Adult: Refusal of Treatment)*[49] and *Secretary of State v Robb*.[50] Indeed, in *Ms B v An NHS Hospital Trust*[51] it underlay the decision, referred to earlier, that a capable, paralysed woman had the right to require her life-sustaining ventilator to be switched off.

As was noted by Lady Hale in the UK Supreme Court in *Aintree University Hospitals Foundation Trust v James*,[52] the matter can also be usefully approached from the other direction, namely from the consideration that it is the act of providing treatment (including to sustain life) that actually requires legal justification:

> **Lady Hale:** 19 . . . [A]ny treatment which the doctors do decide to give must be lawful. As Lord Browne-Wilkinson put it in *Airedale NHS Trust v Bland* ...,'... the correct answer to the present case depends upon the extent of the right to continue lawfully to invade the bodily integrity of Anthony Bland without his consent. If in the circumstances they have no right to continue artificial feeding, they cannot be in breach of any duty by ceasing to provide such feeding.'.... Generally it is the patient's consent which makes invasive medical treatment lawful. It is not lawful to treat a patient who has capacity and refuses that treatment. Nor is it lawful to treat a patient who lacks capacity if he has made a valid and applicable advance decision to refuse it: see 2005 [Mental Capacity] Act, sections 24 to 26. Nor is it lawful to treat such a patient if he has granted a lasting power of attorney (under section 10) or the court has appointed a deputy (under section 16) with the power to give or withhold consent to that treatment and that consent is withheld; but an attorney only has power to give or withhold consent to the carrying out or continuation of life-sustaining treatment if the instrument expressly so provides (section 11(8)) and a deputy cannot refuse consent to such treatment (section 20(5)).

12.3.4 Advance decisions

As referred to in the *Aintree* decision, one situation in which the doctor is not permitted to provide the patient with life-sustaining treatment is where the latter has made a binding advance decision to refuse it. This involves a declaration by the patient, while still capable, that specifies in advance what forms of treatment he or she would or would not accept in the event of his or her future incompetence.

---

48 See Ch 3, section 3.2.1.
49 [1994] 1 All ER 819.
50 [1995] 2 WLR 722.
51 See n 41 above.
52 See n 45 above.

The use of advance decisions (often also referred to as 'advance directives' or 'refusals', and colloquially known as 'living wills') to refuse future treatment began in North America; a good illustration of their operation is provided by the decision in the Canadian case of *Malette v Shulman*:

Malette v Shulman[53]

The claimant was a Jehovah's Witness who was admitted to hospital unconscious following a road accident. She was found to be carrying a card which (translated from French into English) read as follows:

No blood transfusion! As one of Jehovah's Witnesses with firm religious convictions, I request that no blood or blood products be administered to me under any circumstances. I fully realise the implications of this position, but I have resolutely decided to obey the Bible command:'Keep abstaining . . . from blood' (Acts 15:28, 29). However, I have no religious objection to the use of non-blood alternatives, such as Dextran, Haemaccel, PVP, Ringer's Lactate or saline solution.

However, the defendant doctor carried out a life-saving blood transfusion:

Robins JA: On the facts of the present case, Dr Shulman was clearly faced with an emergency. He had an unconscious, critically ill patient on his hands who, in his opinion, needed blood transfusions to save her life or preserve her health. If there were no Jehovah's Witness card he undoubtedly would have been entitled to administer blood transfusions as part of the emergency treatment and could not have been held liable for so doing. In those circumstances he would have had no indication that the transfusions would have been refused had the patient then been able to make her wishes known and, accordingly, no reason to expect that, as a reasonable person, she would not consent to the transfusions.

. . . Here, the patient, anticipating an emergency in which she might be unable to make decisions about her healthcare contemporaneous with the emergency, has given explicit instructions that blood transfusions constitute an unacceptable medical intervention and are not to be administered to her. Once the emergency arises, is the doctor nonetheless entitled to administer transfusions on the basis of his honest belief that they are needed to save a patient's life?

The answer, in my opinion, is clearly no. A doctor is not free to disregard a patient's advance instructions any more than he would be free to disregard instructions given at the time of the emergency. The law does not prohibit a patient from withholding consent to emergency medical treatment, nor does the law prohibit a doctor from following his patient's instructions. While the law may disregard the absence of consent in limited emergency circumstances, it otherwise supports the right of capable adults to make decisions concerning their own healthcare by imposing civil liability on those who perform medical treatment without consent.

The claimant was awarded C$20,000 in damages.

Malette involved a patient suffering from temporary incapacity; however, the same principles would apply to those patients who become permanently incapable. In at least some cases, a tension may be felt between the interests of the capable maker of the decision and the incapable person they later become. Thus, there may be patients who lose capacity through moderate brain injury or illness, but continue to derive significant pleasure from their existence. Here it does not seem self-evidently right that the latter, incapable patient should be denied life-saving treatment on the basis of previous wishes made when, mentally, the patient was a significantly different

---

53 (1990) 72 OR (2d) 417 (Ontario Court of Appeal).

person. As the following extract makes clear, it is at least an approach whose justification involves accepting arguments of some philosophical complexity:

Kuczewski, MG, 'Whose will is it, anyway? A discussion of advance directives, personal identity and consensus in medical ethics'[54]

Living wills are attempts by the capable person to make treatment decisions for her future based upon her present, rather than future, interests. It may be wrong to base how we treat a patient on interests the person previously possessed rather than her current ones. As [John] Robertson states, 'The values and interests of the capable person no longer are relevant to someone who has lost the rational structure on which those values and interests rested.' Robertson wishes his critique to apply only to situations that involve an incapable conscious patient. This limitation occurs, presumably, because permanently unconscious patients do not possess significant enough interests to generate a morally weighty conflict with their previous wishes ...

We need to keep in mind that this is not a mere abstract philosophical word game ... It is not empirically obvious why interests in dignity, the financial well being of one's family, bodily integrity, and so on, should be said to survive and be applicable to a person who either no longer exists or cannot cognise and presently appreciate these values. Although present practices regarding the use of living wills may go on despite the failure to justify their employment philosophically, such failure would mean that the consensus was forged on a fictitious account of self-determination. Thus, those who argued in the pre-consensus years for the primacy of the best interest standard as the sole standard of decision-making would actually be correct ...

Kuczewski goes on to argue that the interests of the formerly capable person do survive, not in a personal, but rather in a communal or institutional sense. Accordingly, that person's advance decision should be respected:

[A]n individual's interest in dignity, privacy, and bodily integrity is encoded in his living will, in the memory of others, and even in their perceptions of the situation at the time of one's incompetence. . . . The body that belongs to the incapable patient at t2 is in some sense 'mine' because other persons will call it by my name and make the story of what happens to it a chapter of the story they tell about 'me'. As such, I attempt to make that chapter embody the values which are presently mine. Through the same type of act of will by which I commit to live today in accordance with dignity, so also, I commit that my final chapter shall embody those values ...

In England, the concept of advance decisions was supported by the Court of Appeal in *Re T (Adult: Refusal of Medical Treatment)*,[55] where Lord Donaldson MR commented as follows:

Lord Donaldson MR: There seems to be a view in the medical profession that in such emergency circumstances the next of kin should be asked to consent on behalf of the patient and that, if possible, treatment should be postponed until that consent has been obtained. This is a misconception because the next of kin has no legal right either to consent or to refuse consent. This is not to say that it is an undesirable practice if the interests of the patient will not be adversely affected by any consequential delay. I say this because contact with the next of kin may reveal that the patient has made an anticipatory choice which, if clearly established and applicable in the circumstances – two major 'ifs' – would bind the practitioner.

---

54 (1994) 8 Bioethics 27.
55 [1992] 4 All ER 649.

Subsequently, the High Court upheld the binding effect of the wishes of a patient not to receive future treatment at a time when no longer capable in *Re C (Adult: Refusal of Treatment)*.[56] In that case, as discussed in Chapter 3,[57] Thorpe J granted an injunction, preventing doctors from amputating the gangrenous leg of a paranoid schizophrenic (who was nevertheless adjudged capable), which was drafted so as to include the period after the patient had lost competence. Another example is furnished by the case of *Re AK (Medical Treatment: Consent)*.[58] Here the patient suffered from a neuro-muscular disease causing rapid muscle degeneration; at the time of the court application he was only able to communicate with the doctors treating him by blinking one of his eyes. Hughes J upheld his wish that, once this last means of communication had disappeared, his artificial ventilation should cease and he be allowed to die. Indeed the judge suggested that the law (in favour of such a step) was sufficiently clear that a formal declaration may not have been necessary.

In its 1995 report, *Mental Incapacity*,[59] the Law Commission recommended that the legal effect of advance decisions be enshrined in legislation and this has occurred by virtue of ss 24–26 of the Mental Capacity Act 2005:

Mental Capacity Act 2005

24 Advance decisions to refuse treatment: general

(1)   'Advance decision' means a decision made by a person ('P'), after he has reached 18 and when he has capacity to do so, that if –

   a   at a later time and in such circumstances as he may specify, a specified treatment is proposed to be carried out or continued by a person providing healthcare for him, and

   b   at that time he lacks capacity to consent to the carrying out or continuation of the treatment, the specified treatment is not to be carried out or continued.

. . .

25 Validity and applicability of advance decisions

(1)   An advance decision does not affect the liability which a person may incur for carrying out or continuing a treatment in relation to P unless the decision is at the material time –

   a   valid, and

   b   applicable to the treatment.

. . .

(5)   An advance decision is not applicable to life-sustaining treatment unless –

   a   the decision is verified by a statement by P to the effect that it is to apply to that treatment even if life is at risk, and

   b   the decision and statement comply with subsection (6).

(6)   A decision or statement complies with this subsection only if –

   a   it is in writing,

   b   it is signed by P or by another person in P's presence and by P's direction,

   c   the signature is made or acknowledged by P in the presence of a witness, and

   d   the witness signs it, or acknowledges his signature, in P's presence.

. . .

---

56   See n 49 above.
57   See Ch 3, section 3.4.1.
58   [2001] 1 FLR 129.
59   (1995) Law Com No 231.

26 Effect of advance decisions

(1) If P has made an advance decision which is –

    a   valid, and

    b   applicable to a treatment,

    the decision has effect as if he had made it, and had had capacity to make it, at the time when the question arises whether the treatment should be carried out or continued.

(2) A person does not incur liability for carrying out or continuing the treatment unless, at the time, he is satisfied that an advance decision exists which is valid and applicable to the treatment.

(3) A person does not incur liability for the consequences of withholding or withdrawing a treatment from P if, at the time, he reasonably believes that an advance decision exists which is valid and applicable to the treatment.

(4) The court may make a declaration as to whether an advance decision –

    a   exists;

    b   is valid;

    c   is applicable to a treatment.

(5) Nothing in an apparent advance decision stops a person –

    a   providing life-sustaining treatment, or

    b   doing any act he reasonably believes to be necessary to prevent a serious deterioration in P's condition,

    while a decision as respects any relevant issue is sought from the court.

Broadly, these provisions echo the previous position at common law. An advance decision to refuse treatment may be made by a person aged 18 or over at a time when he is capable, which binds the treating team beyond the onset of incompetence (and thus stops them from providing treatment), just as a contemporaneous, capable refusal would. However, in s 25 of the Act, the operation of the decision in this way is made subject to two significant requirements, namely that the decision is 'valid' and that it is 'applicable' in the relevant circumstances.

In this regard, an advance decision will not be valid if, subsequent to it, the patient confers authority upon another person (the 'donee') under a lasting power of attorney to make decisions in relation to his medical treatment. The general manner in which LPAs operate in relation to the treatment of the incapable has been discussed in Chapter 4.[60] Here, though, it is important to emphasise that the donee does not thereby gain the power, previously enjoyed by the patient (as encoded in the decision), to refuse treatment that the doctors regard as objectively indicated. Rather, the donee must at all times make treatment decisions that accord with the incapable person's best interests.

Moreover, an advance decision will be invalid under s 25 MCA 2005 if the patient has subsequently behaved inconsistently with the beliefs that underlay the decision. An example of this occurring is in the pre-MCA 2005 case of *HE v A Hospital NHS Trust and AE*.[61] There, a young woman was unconscious with serious heart problems, and required surgery including the use of blood products in order to survive. She had been brought up a Muslim, but – together with her mother – subsequently became a Jehovah's Witness and, at that time (in February 2001), signed an advance directive rejecting the use of blood products. Although by the time of the proposed surgery (in April 2003) all the indications were that she had reverted to the Muslim faith, her mother insisted that the hospital abide by the directive 'despite the greatly increased risk of death'. In declaring the use of blood products during surgery lawful, Munby J held that the

---

60 See Ch 4, section 4.3.2.2.
61 [2003] EWHC 1017 (Fam).

burden of proof was on those asserting the continued applicability of a directive and that, given that life was at stake, the evidence offered would need especially close and anxious scrutiny.

Section 26 of the Act details the effect that the existence of an advance decision has upon the rights and duties of the doctors treating the patient. Provided the decision is valid and applicable, then, as noted, it will bind the doctors just like a capable, contemporaneous refusal. Accordingly, continued treatment would amount to a battery,[62] and possibly also lead to a charge of criminal assault. What about, however, where there is uncertainty in the minds of the doctors as to whether the decision really is valid and/or applicable? This is addressed in s 26(2), which states that the doctor will not be liable for giving treatment unless he is satisfied that it meets the relevant tests. Equally, under s 26(3) he will not be liable for withholding treatment (in accordance with the advance decision) where he reasonably believes that the decision is valid and applicable.

In *Briggs v Briggs*[63] Charles J in the Court of Protection commented on the thrust of these provisions, as follows:

Charles J: [20] *Advance decisions.* It has been said (see *Re M (Adult Patient) (Minimally Conscious State: Withdrawal of Treatment)* [2012] 1 WLR 1653 at paragraph 226) that the MCA provides stringent conditions that have to be complied with in respect of an advance decision relating to life-sustaining treatment. In my view this is overstating what is provided. The decision has to be accompanied by a statement that it is to apply even if life is at risk and has to be made in writing and witnessed. What is not provided is that the person making it has have any particular knowledge or have had any particular advice. In that context what is provided is less stringent than what the common law requires for the signing of a bank guarantee.

[21] Importantly, the advance decision also has to identify with clarity the treatment to which, and the circumstances in which, it is to apply which go a long way to identifying what the person who has made it has considered and taken into account.

[22] A safety net is provided by both s. 25(2)(c) and s. 25(3). Section 25(2)(c) does not specify whether to qualify the inconsistent act must take place when the person has capacity. Section 25(3) provides a test in fairly general terms. But it seems to me that an interpretation of these safety nets based on the sanctity of life or anything else (e.g. the detail of prognosis and alternatives at the time when the question about the treatment arises) that sets a low threshold to rendering an advance decision invalid or inapplicable would run counter to the enabling intention of ss. 24 to 26 of the MCA. In any event, if those provisions did found the view that an advance decision was invalid or inapplicable, and so a best interests test became determinative, I consider that the court would have to take into account the impact of that removal of that person's right of self-determination that he or she has sought to exercise by making an advance decision.

In cases of dispute as to the validity and/or applicability of an advance decision, the matter may (albeit not 'must') be referred to the Court of Protection to make a declaration on the issue, and in the meantime treatment to sustain life or prevent a serious deterioration in health remain permissible under s 26(5). In a case from late 2007, which attracted media concern, it was reported that doctors had felt obliged to respect the written advance refusal of life-saving treatment by a young woman, Kerrie Wooltorton, who attended hospital after poisoning herself. In fact, it is not clear if her written refusal complied with the statutory formalities to be a binding decision within the MCA 2005; indeed the doctors appear to have been swayed more by the

---

62 In December 2017, it was reported that a Nuneaton hospital paid £45,000 to settle a case where it treated a patient for two years contrary to her advance decision (which it mislaid); see: www.bbc.com/news/uk-england-coventry-warwickshire-42240148.
63 [2016] EWCOP 53 (CP).

contemporaneous oral refusal of Ms Wooltorton, who on attendance remained conscious and, in the doctors' view, capable.[64]

An interesting recent case, where – in the context of a patient detained under the Mental Health Act – Mostyn J held that clinicians would be 'well advised' to apply for a judicial declaration before acceding to the refusal of life-saving treatment contained in an advance decision, is *Nottinghamshire Healthcare NHS Trust v RC*.[65]

Finally, in so far as an advance decision is found not to be binding, this does not mean that it will lose all significance: rather, as stated in para 9.45 of the MCA 2005 Code of Practice,[66] (and highlighted by Charles J in the *Briggs* case) it may still be regarded as an expression of the patient's former wishes and, as such, relevant in determining his best interests. The paragraph also reminds health professionals not to 'assume that because an advance decision is either invalid or not applicable, they should always provide the specified treatment (including life-sustaining treatment) – they must base this decision on what is in the person's best interests'.

THINK POINT

Will a doctor who switches off a life support machine have performed active euthanasia? If it by contrast qualified as a passive withdrawal of treatment, could the doctor still be guilty of murder anyway?

12.4 Withholding treatment: incapable patients

12.4.1 Background

In this section we address the question of when life-saving treatment may be withheld or withdrawn from the incapable patient (in the absence of a valid and applicable advance decision). As already noted, the crucial issue here is the extent of the doctor's duty to employ life-prolonging measures in respect of his patient. It is clear that common sense has never regarded this duty as an absolute one. Nevertheless, the first significant English authority in point is a Court of Appeal decision from 1981:

Re B (A Minor) (Wardship: Medical Treatment)[67]

B was a baby girl born with Down's syndrome and also suffering from an intestinal blockage. Without an operation to remove the blockage, she would die within a few days. Her parents, however, refused to consent to the treatment and B was made a ward of court. The judge at first instance initially authorised treatment, but revoked his order after speaking to the parents and also hearing that the surgeon appointed to the case was unwilling to operate contrary to their wishes. The health authority appealed:

Templeman LJ: There may be cases, I know not, of severe proved damage where the future is so certain and where the life of the child is so bound to be full of pain and suffering that the court might be driven to a different conclusion, but in the present case the choice which lies before the court is this: whether to allow an operation to take place which may result in the child living

---

64 See Szawarski, P (2013) 14 Journal of the Intensive Care Society 211. The question whether in such a case the doctors could be justified in overriding a patient's treatment refusal is considered in Ch 3, section 3.3.1.2.
65 [2014] EWHC 1317 (COP).
66 London: TSO, 2007, referring to s 4(6) MCA 2005.
67 [1981] 1 WLR 1421, CA.

for 20 or 30 years as a mongoloid or whether (and I think this must be brutally the result) to terminate the life of a mongoloid child because she also has an intestinal complaint. Faced with that choice I have no doubt that it is the duty of this court to decide that the child must live. The judge was much affected by the reasons given by the parents and came to the conclusion that their wishes ought to be respected. In my judgment he erred in that the duty of the court is to decide whether it is in the interests of the child that an operation should take place. The evidence in this case only goes to show that if the operation takes place and is successful then the child may live the normal span of a mongoloid child with the handicaps and defects and life of a mongol child, and it is not for this court to say that life of that description ought to be extinguished.

Accordingly the appeal must be allowed and the local authority must be authorised themselves to authorise and direct the operation to be carried out on the little girl.

This decision is an important one, not least because it renders doubtful a well-known criminal case of about the same time, *R v Arthur*,[68] in which a doctor was acquitted of attempting to murder a Down's syndrome baby (whose parents did not wish it to live) after ordering treatment to be withheld: the effect of *Re B* is that, whatever the parents' views, doctors will generally be obliged to treat babies with the standard disabilities associated with Down's syndrome. However, although Templeman LJ recognised *obiter* the possibility that, in other cases of more drastic disability, treatment could be withheld, it remained unclear in what circumstances this would be so.

Subsequently, some light was shed on this problem in *Re C (A Minor) (Wardship: Medical Treatment)*,[69] where the Court of Appeal authorised the withdrawal of treatment from a severely brain-damaged baby said to be 'dying' in any event. The decisive step, in favour of a more open endorsement of allowing death by omission in extreme cases, came shortly afterwards in the seminal case of *Re J*:

Re J (A Minor) (Wardship: Medical Treatment)[70]

J was a five-month-old baby who suffered severe brain damage as a result of his grossly premature birth. He was profoundly disabled, both mentally and physically, and was unlikely to develop even the most basic functions. He had collapsed on a number of occasions since his birth and the court, pursuant to its wardship jurisdiction, was asked to decide if mechanical ventilation of J should occur in the event of a further collapse:

Lord Donaldson MR: Of the three neonatalogists who have been concerned with [J's] care, the most optimistic is Dr W. His view is that J is likely to develop serious spastic quadriplegia, that is to say, paralysis of both his arms and legs. It is debatable whether he will ever be able to sit up or to hold his head upright. J appears to be blind, although there is a possibility that some degree of sight may return. He is likely to be deaf. He may be able to make sounds which reflect his mood, but he is unlikely ever to be able to speak, even to the extent of saying Mum or Dad. It is highly unlikely that he will develop even limited intellectual abilities. Most unfortunately of all, there is a likelihood that he will be able to feel pain to the same extent as a normal baby, because pain is a very basic response. It is possible that he may achieve the ability to smile and

---

68 (1981) 12 BMLR 1.
69 [1989] 2 All ER 782, CA.
70 [1991] 1 Fam 33, CA.

to cry. Finally, as one might expect, his life expectancy has been considerably reduced, at most into his late teens, but even Dr W would expect him to die long before then . . .

The issue here is whether it would be in the best interests of the child to put him on a mechanical ventilator and subject him to all the associated processes of intensive care, if at some future time he could not continue breathing unaided . . .

The basis of the doctors' recommendations, approved by the judge, was that mechanical ventilation is itself an invasive procedure which, together with its essential accompaniments, such as the introduction of a nasogastric tube, drips which have to be re-sited and constant blood sampling, would cause the child distress. Furthermore, the procedures involve taking active measures which carry their own hazards, not only to life but in terms of causing even greater brain damage. This had to be balanced against what could possibly be achieved by the adoption of such active treatment. The chances of preserving the child's life might be improved, although even this was not certain, and account had to be taken of the extremely poor quality of life at present enjoyed by the child, the fact that he had already been ventilated for exceptionally long periods, the unfavourable prognosis with or without ventilation and a recognition that if the question of reventilation ever arose, his situation would have deteriorated still further.

The Court of Appeal accordingly upheld the decision of the High Court that further ventilation aimed at prolonging J's life should not occur.

12.4.2 The role of the court

In both the *Re B* and *Re J* cases, the final decision – in the first case to authorise treatment, in the second to withhold it – was taken by the court pursuant to its wardship jurisdiction in relation to minors under the age of 18 years. As regards incapable adults, it increasingly became good practice for the doctors to apply to the High Court for a declaration confirming (*ex ante*) that the proposed course of treatment (or its withdrawal) would be lawful. In some cases, failure to do so could expose the doctor to a charge of serious professional misconduct.[71] Thus, according to the House of Lords in *Airedale NHS Trust v Bland*, a declaration should always be obtained prior to withdrawing ANH from a patient in PVS (see further 12.4.4 below).

As discussed in Chapter 4,[72] since the coming into force of the Mental Capacity Act 2005, the new Court of Protection has been invested with jurisdiction to make (as opposed to merely confirm the lawfulness of) decisions as to the medical treatment of incapable adults: under s 17(1)(d) MCA the Court's powers extend to 'giving or refusing consent to the carrying out or continuation of a treatment by a person providing medical care for P'. Nonetheless, the preliminary question as to when exactly the responsible carers are required to approach the court for a decision – as opposed to taking it themselves – is arguably no clearer than before. The MCA Code of Practice, after reiterating the need to seek court approval in cases where it is proposed to withdraw ANH from patients in PVS, has the following to say:

---

71 See the guidance contained in the Court of Protection's Practice Direction 9E, at: www.hmcourts-service.gov.uk/cms/files/09E_-_Serious_Medical_Treatment_PD.pdf.
72 See Ch 4, section 4.3.4.6.

Mental Capacity Act 2005 Code of Practice[73]

Serious healthcare and treatment decisions

8.18 Prior to the Act coming into force, the courts decided that some decisions relating to the provision of medical treatment were so serious that in each case, an application should be made to the court for a declaration that the proposed action was lawful before that action was taken. Cases involving any of the following decisions should therefore be brought before a court:

- decisions about the proposed withholding or withdrawal of artificial nutrition and hydration (ANH) from patients in a permanent vegetative state (PVS) . . .
- all other cases where there is a doubt or dispute about whether a particular treatment will be in a person's best interests.

8.19 The case law requirement to seek a declaration in cases involving the withholding or withdrawing of artificial nutrition and hydration to people in a permanent vegetative state is unaffected by the Act and as a matter of practice, these cases should be put to the Court of Protection for approval. . . .

8.23 Other cases likely to be referred to the court include those involving ethical dilemmas in untested areas (such as innovative treatments for variant CJD), or where there are otherwise irresolvable conflicts between healthcare staff, or between staff and family members.

8.24 There are also a few types of cases that should generally be dealt with by the court, since other dispute resolution methods are unlikely to be appropriate . . . This includes, for example, cases where it is unclear whether proposed serious and/or invasive medical treatment is likely to be in the best interests of the person who lacks capacity to consent.

It appears then that, following the Act, the expectation remains that in most cases, the decision to withdraw life-prolonging treatment will be made by the doctors in consultation with the relatives. In this regard, as the High Court confirmed in *Winspear v City Hospitals Sunderland NHS Foundation Trust*, the relatives have a specific right to be consulted, pursuant to their rights under Article 8 ECHR.[74] However, provided there is consensus between the parties, there will usually be no formal need for court proceedings: see M (*Withdrawal of Treatment: Need for Proceedings*).[75] It is only exceptionally, where the factors telling in favour and against the decision are finely poised and/or a sharp conflict of views arises between the doctors and relatives that the matter should go to the Court of Protection. Even so, as Lady Hale noted in the *Aintree* decision,[76] where the dispute concerns potential future treatment, then, so far as the patient's condition and prognosis remain uncertain, the court may decline to make any declaration:

Lady Hale: [47] . . . [I]f the clinical team are unable to reach agreement with the family or others about whether particular treatments will be in the best interests of the patient, they may of course bring the question to court in advance of those treatments being needed. But they may find, as here, that the court is unable to say that when they are needed, they will not be in the patient's best interests.

---

73 See: www.justice.gov.uk/downloads/protecting-the-vulnerable/mca/mca-code-practice-0509.pdf.
74 [2015] EWHC 3250 (QB).
75 [2017] EWCOP 19 (CP).
76 See n 45 above.

12.4.3 Reaching the decision: the best interests test

As already implied, in resolving the substantive question – should life-sustaining treatment be provided to a particular incapable patient? – the decision-maker (be they the doctors or a judge) must consider the best interests of the patient. We have previously encountered the 'best interests' test in the context of decisions to provide incapable patients with treatment of a non-life-saving nature, most notably in sterilisation cases involving mentally disabled women.[77] In itself the test lacks substance: it is merely a direction that, in reaching the decision whether to treat, the decider should objectively weigh up the factors in favour of treatment against those which militate against it. The factors themselves, and their respective weighting, clearly stand in need of further specification.

An initial question, however, is whether such a balancing exercise can be meaningfully performed at all in a context in which one of the options (non-treatment) leads to death. This point was taken by counsel for the Official Solicitor in the *Re J* case:[78]

> **Lord Donaldson MR:** [James Munby QC's] first, or absolutist, submission is that a court is never justified in withholding consent to treatment which could enable a child to survive a life-threatening condition, whatever the pain or other side effects inherent in the treatment, and whatever the quality of the life which it would experience thereafter. . . .
>
> In support of this submission, Mr Munby draws attention to the decision of this court in *McKay v Essex HA* . . . There a child suffered severe and irreversible damage before birth, as a result of her mother contracting rubella (German measles). She sued the health authority [inter alia] . . . on [the] basis . . . that her mother should have been advised to seek an abortion and that, if this advice had been given and accepted, she would never have been born at all. The damages claimed under this head were necessarily based upon a comparison between her actual condition and her condition if, as a result of an abortion, she had never been born at all.
>
> . . . I do not regard this decision as providing us with either guidance or assistance in the context of the present problem. The child was claiming damages, and the decision was that no monetary comparison could be made between the two states.
>
> **Taylor LJ:** Despite the court's inability to compare a life afflicted by the most severe disability with death, the unknown, I am of the view that there must be extreme cases in which the court is entitled to say: 'The life which this treatment would prolong would be so cruel as to be intolerable.' If, for example, a child was so damaged as to have negligible use of its faculties and the only way of preserving its life was by the continuous administration of extremely painful treatment such that the child either would be in continuous agony or would have to be so sedated continuously as to have no conscious life at all, I cannot think Mr Munby's absolute test should apply to require the treatment to be given. In those circumstances, without there being any question of deliberately ending the life or shortening it, I consider the court is entitled in the best interests of the child to say that deliberate steps should not be taken artificially to prolong its miserable lifespan.

Assuming that a balancing exercise is possible, it will nevertheless be somewhat different in nature from the comparative assessment of benefits and burdens (the patient's *life with treatment* against her *life without treatment*) familiar from decisions dealing with such matters as sterilisation. In the latter type of case, one can imagine that decisions may sometimes be finely weighted, ultimately turning on apparently marginal differences. By contrast, where without treatment

---

77 Ch 4, section 4.5.2.
78 See n 71 above.

death will occur, the courts will brook no such ambiguity: not only must a life be truly awful for death to seem preferable, but the residual force of the (qualified) sanctity of life principle here asserts itself:

> **Taylor LJ**: Three preliminary principles are not in dispute. First, it is settled law that the court's prime and paramount consideration must be the best interests of the child . . .
>
> Secondly, the court's high respect for the sanctity of human life imposes a strong presumption in favour of taking all steps capable of preserving it, save in exceptional circumstances. The problem is to define those circumstances.
>
> Thirdly, and as a corollary to the second principle, it cannot be too strongly emphasised that the court never sanctions steps to terminate life. That would be unlawful. There is no question of approving, even in a case of the most horrendous disability, a course aimed at terminating life or accelerating death. The court is concerned only with the circumstances in which steps should not be taken to prolong life.

What, then, will be the substantive factors relevant to a decision that it is not in a patient's best interests to have his or her life prolonged? Lord Donaldson MR suggested that 'the critical equation . . . cannot be done with mathematical or any precision'. Balcombe LJ also commented as follows:

> **Balcombe LJ**: . . . I would deprecate any attempt by this court to lay down . . . an all-embracing test, since the circumstances of these tragic cases are so infinitely various. I do not know of any demand by the judges who have to deal with these cases at first instance for this court to assist them by laying down any test beyond that which is already the law: that the interests of the ward are the first and paramount consideration . . .

On the other hand, Taylor LJ was prepared to be more expansive:

> **Taylor LJ**: I consider the correct approach is for the court to judge the quality of life the child would have to endure if given the treatment, and decide whether in all the circumstances such a life would be so afflicted as to be intolerable to that child. I say 'to that child' because the test should not be whether the life would be tolerable to the decider. The test must be whether the child in question, if capable of exercising sound judgment, would consider the life tolerable. This is the approach adopted by McKenzie J in *Re Superintendent of Family and Child Service and Dawson* . . . It takes account of the strong instinct to preserve one's life even in circumstances which an outsider, not himself at risk of death, might consider unacceptable. The circumstances to be considered would, in appropriate cases, include the degree of existing disability and any additional suffering or aggravation of the disability which the treatment itself would superimpose. In an accident case, as opposed to one involving disablement from birth, the child's pre-accident quality of life and its perception of what has been lost may also be factors relevant to whether the residual life would be intolerable to that child.

Subsequently, Taylor LJ's approach was applied by the High Court in *Re R (Adult: Medical Treatment)*.[79] There the patient was a 23-year-old man who had been born with a serious malformation of the brain and cerebral palsy. He was described as being in a 'low-awareness state' with roughly the perception and cognitive faculties of a new-born infant. During 1995 he was

---

79 [1996] 2 FLR 99.

admitted to hospital on no fewer than five occasions and his weight dropped to five stone. The NHS trust responsible for his care sought a declaration that it would be lawful to withhold cardio-pulmonary resuscitation if he collapsed and, subject to the views of his doctors and parents at the relevant time, antibiotics in the face of a life-threatening infection. In granting the declaration, Sir Stephen Brown P commented:

> **Sir Stephen Brown P:** The principle of law to be applied in this case is that of the 'best interests of the patient' as made clear by the Court of Appeal in *Re J (A Minor) (Wardship: Medical Treatment)* . . . In the course of his judgment . . . Taylor LJ said:
>
> > I consider the correct approach is for the court to judge the quality of life the child would have to endure if given the treatment, and decide whether in all the circumstances such a life would be so afflicted as to be intolerable to that child.
>
> Although this present case concerns a handicapped adult and not a child who is a ward of court the overriding principle in my judgment is the same.

At first instance in *R (on the application of Burke) v* GMC,[80] Munby J (who as James Munby QC had acted as counsel in the *Re J* case) favoured the recognition of 'intolerability' as providing the general touchstone of best interests in the context of withdrawing medical treatment from a sentient incapable patient. However, in reversing that judgment, the Court of Appeal[81] was critical of the attempt to define best interests in such cases by means of a single test:

> **Lord Phillips MR:** [58] There are tragic cases where treatment can prolong life for an indeterminate period, but only at a cost of great suffering while life continues. Such a case was *In re J (a Minor) (Wardship: Medical Treatment)*. . . . There are other cases, and these are much more common, where a patient has lost competence in the final stages of life and where ANH may prolong these final stages, but at an adverse cost so far as comfort and dignity are concerned, sometimes resulting in the patient's last days being spent in a hospital ward rather than at home, with family around.
>
> . . .
>
> [62] . . . The suggestion that the touchstone of 'best interests' is the 'intolerability' of continued life has, understandably given rise to concern. The test of whether it is in the best interests of the patient to provide or continue ANH must depend on the particular circumstances. The two situations that we have considered above are very different. As to the approach to be adopted in the former, this court dealt with that in *Re J* and we do not think that it is appropriate to review what the court there said in a context that is purely hypothetical.
>
> [63] As to the approach to best interests where a patient is close to death, it seems to us that the judge himself recognised that 'intolerability' was not the test of best interests. At paragraph 104 he said:
>
> > 'where the patient is dying, the goal may properly be to ease suffering and, where appropriate, to "ease the passing" rather than to achieve a short prolongation of life.'
>
> We agree. We do not think it possible to attempt to define what is in the best interests of a patient by a single test, applicable in all circumstances . . .

---

80 [2004] EWHC 1879 (Admin).
81 See n 43 above.

In its 1995 *Report on Mental Incapacity*, the Law Commission had recommended an approach in which significant weight should also be attached to the past and present attitudes of the incapable person, and those close to him or her, in determining best interests:

Law Commission, *Mental Incapacity*[82]

3.28 – We recommend that in deciding what is in a person's best interests regard should be had to:

1   the ascertainable past and present wishes and feelings of the person concerned, and the factors that person would consider if able to do so;
2   the need to permit and encourage the person to participate, or to improve his or her ability to participate, as fully as possible in anything done for and any decision affecting him or her;
3   the views of other people whom it is appropriate and practicable to consult about the person's wishes and feelings and what would be in his or her best interests;
4   whether the purpose for which any action or decision is required can be as effectively achieved in a manner less restrictive of the person's freedom of action. (Draft Bill, cl 3(2).)

Wishes, feelings and putative factors

3.29 – This first element in the checklist establishes the importance of individual views. Realistically, the former views of a person who is without capacity cannot in every case be determinative of the decision which is now to be made. Past wishes and feelings may in any event conflict with feelings the person is still able to express in spite of incapacity. People who cannot make decisions can still experience pleasure and distress. Present wishes and feelings must therefore be taken into account, where necessary balanced with past wishes and feelings. One of the failings of a pure 'substituted judgment' model is the unhelpful idea that a person who cannot make a decision should be treated as if his or her capacity were perfect and unimpaired, and as if present emotions need not also be considered.

These recommendations are broadly reflected in the Mental Capacity Act 2005. As part of the exercise to determine an incapable person's best interests under s 4(6), the decision-maker is required to consider, 'so far as is reasonably ascertainable (a) the person's past and present wishes and feelings (and, in particular, any relevant written statement made by him when he had capacity), (b) the beliefs and values that would be likely to influence his decision if he had capacity, and (c) the other factors that he would be likely to consider if he were able to do so'.

Even so, the application of the test in the context of treating severely mentally and physically incapacitated patients at the end of life has often proven contentious in practice, leading to disputes between on the one side, the doctors treating the patient and, on the other, the latter's family. Moreover, in resolving these disputes, the courts have not always taken a consistent line. Thus, notwithstanding the Court of Appeal's warning in *Burke* cited above, other judges have continued to flirt with the prospect of refining the test into a single formula, invoking concepts such as intolerability and futility. The issues were recently revisited by the UK Supreme Court in the case of *Aintree University Hospitals NHS Foundation Trust v James*:

---

82 See n 59 above.

Aintree University Hospitals NHS Foundation Trust v James[83]

David James, who was aged 68, was admitted to hospital in May 2012 due to of a problem with a stoma, fitted during previous, successful cancer treatment. Unfortunately he acquired an infection and also developed serious kidney and cardiovascular problems. After admission to the ICU his condition deteriorated further, and following a stroke in July he was assessed as in a low awareness state and no longer mentally capable. His family and friends continued to visit him regularly and reported that he obtained pleasure from this and was able to interact to a limited degree.

The Trust brought an application before the Court of Protection for a declaration (under section 15 MCA 2005) that it would be lawful to withhold certain life-prolonging measures, including invasive circulatory and renal support and CPR should these become necessary. This application was resisted by Mr James' family, and was dismissed by the CoP in December 2012. However, (following a further worsening of the patient's condition) the Court of Appeal allowed the Trust's appeal and Mr James died at the end of December. The matter proceeded to the Supreme Court for it to resolve the different approaches taken towards the best Interests test by the trial judge (Peter Jackson J) and Court of Appeal:

Lady Hale: [28] The [2007] Mental Capacity Act Code deals with decisions about life-sustaining treatment in this way:

> 5.31 All reasonable steps which are in the person's best interests should be taken to prolong their life. There will be a limited number of cases where treatment is futile, overly burdensome to the patient or where there is no prospect of recovery. In circumstances such as these, it may be that an assessment of best interests leads to the conclusion that it would be in the best interests of the patient to withdraw or withhold life-sustaining treatment, even if this may result in the person's death. The decision-maker must make a decision based on the best interests of the person who lacks capacity. They must not be motivated by a desire to bring about the person's death for whatever reason, even if this is from a sense of compassion. Healthcare and social care staff should also refer to relevant professional guidance when making decisions regarding life-sustaining treatment.

[29] . . . Paragraph 5.31 gives useful guidance, derived from previous case law, as to when life-sustaining treatment may not be in the patient's best interests. Both the judge and the Court of Appeal accepted them as an accurate statement of the law and so would I. However, they differed as to the meaning of the words in italics. The Code is not a statute and should not be construed as one but it is necessary for us to consider which of them was closer to the correct approach.

. . . . [35] The authorities are all agreed that the starting point is a strong presumption that it is in a person's best interests to stay alive. As Sir Thomas Bingham MR said in the Court of Appeal in *Bland*, at p 808, 'A profound respect for the sanctity of human life is embedded in our law and our moral philosophy'. Nevertheless, they are also all agreed that this is not an absolute. There are cases where it will not be in a patient's best interests to receive life-sustaining treatment.

[36] The courts have been most reluctant to lay down general principles which might guide the decision. Every patient, and every case, is different and must be decided on its own facts. As Hedley J wisely put it at first instance in *Portsmouth Hospitals NHS Trust v Wyatt* [2005] 1 FLR 21, 'The infinite variety of the human condition never ceases to surprise and it is that fact that defeats any attempt to be more precise in a definition of best interests' (para 23). There are

---

83 See n 45 above.

cases, such as *Bland*, where there is no balancing exercise to be conducted. There are cases, where death is in any event imminent, where the factors weighing in the balance will be different from those where life may continue for some time.

. . . [40] In my view, therefore, Peter Jackson J was correct in his approach. Given the genesis of the concepts used in the Code of Practice, he was correct to consider whether the proposed treatments would be futile in the sense of being ineffective or being of no benefit to the patient. . . . He was also correct to say that 'recovery does not mean a return to full health, but the resumption of a quality of life which Mr James would regard as worthwhile'. He clearly did consider that the treatments in question were very burdensome. But he considered that those burdens had to be weighed against the benefits of a continued existence. He was also correct to see the assessment of the medical effects of the treatment as only part of the equation. Regard had to be had to the patient's welfare in the widest sense, and great weight to be given to Mr James' family life which was 'of the closest and most meaningful kind'.

. . . [43] It follows that I respectfully disagree with the statements of principle in the Court of Appeal where they differ from those of the judge. Thus it is setting the goal too high to say that treatment is futile unless it has 'a real prospect of curing or at least palliating the life-threatening disease or illness from which the patient is suffering' . . . A treatment may bring some benefit to the patient even though it has no effect upon the underlying disease or disability. . . .

[44] I also respectfully disagree with the statement that 'no prospect of recovery' means 'no prospect of recovering such a state of good health as will avert the looming prospect of death if the life-sustaining treatment is given'. . . It was accepted in *Burke* (as it had been earlier) that where the patient is close to death, the object may properly be to make his dying as comfortable and as dignified as possible, rather than to take invasive steps to prolong his life for a short while (see paras 62–63). But where a patient is suffering from an incurable illness, disease or disability, it is not very helpful to talk of recovering a state of 'good health'. The patient's life may still be very well worth living. Resuming a quality of life which the patient would regard as worthwhile is more readily applicable, particularly in the case of a patient with permanent disabilities. As was emphasised in *Re J* (1991), it is not for others to say that a life which the patient would regard as worthwhile is not worth living.

[45] Finally, insofar as Sir Alan Ward and Arden LJ were suggesting that the test of the patient's wishes and feelings was an objective one, what the reasonable patient would think, again I respectfully disagree. The purpose of the best interests test is to consider matters from the patient's point of view. That is not to say that his wishes must prevail, any more than those of a fully capable patient must prevail. We cannot always have what we want. Nor will it always be possible to ascertain what an incapable patient's wishes are. Even if it is possible to determine what his views were in the past, they might well have changed in the light of the stresses and strains of his current predicament. In this case, the highest it could be put was, as counsel had agreed, that 'It was likely that Mr James would want treatment up to the point where it became hopeless'. But insofar as it is possible to ascertain the patient's wishes and feelings, his beliefs and values or the things which were important to him, it is those which should be taken into account because they are a component in making the choice which is right for him as an individual human being.

[46] However, in my view, on the basis of the fresh evidence which was before them, the Court of Appeal were correct to allow the appeal and make the declarations they did (which were in the present tense). There had been such a significant deterioration in Mr James' condition that the prospect of his regaining even his previous quality of life appeared very slim. The risk

> that cardiovascular resuscitation would make matters even worse appeared great. The time had indeed come when it was no longer premature to say that it would not be in his best interests to attempt to restart his heart should it stop beating. Indeed, had the judge been asked to reach a decision on the basis of the evidence then available, it seems clear on the basis of his reasoning that he would have done the same.

As *Aintree v James* makes clear, determinations of best interests will inevitably be extremely fact sensitive. One distinction that may be drawn, though, is between patients who once enjoyed capacity, but have now lost this due to accident or illness, and those – infants or adults mentally disabled from childhood – who never attained it. The difference is relevant in terms of s 4(6) of the MCA 2005, which, as noted above, requires the decision-maker to take account of the patient's past wishes, beliefs and values, and can only apply to the first category of person. Another relevant distinction (reflected in the need in s 4(6) MCA also to consider *present* wishes) is between patients who, though mentally disabled, remain able to express wishes or beliefs, and more seriously mentally impaired patients who cannot.

Looking first at patients who are still able to express contemporaneous wishes, it is evident that a high weight may be accorded to such wishes, even where they involve rejection of life-saving treatment. A recent decision in point is *Wye Valley NHS Trust v B*,[84] in which a 73-year-old man, who had a longstanding mental illness that deprived him of capacity, refused a life-saving amputation of his infected leg. In refusing to authorise the operation, Peter Jackson J, in the Court of Protection, stated:

> **Peter Jackson J**: [10] On behalf of the Trust in this case, Mr Sachdeva QC submitted that the views expressed by a person lacking capacity were in principle entitled to less weight than those of a person with capacity. This is in my view true only to the limited extent that the views of a capacitous person are by definition decisive in relation to any treatment that is being offered to him so that the question of best interests does not arise. However, once incapacity is established so that a best interests decision must be made, there is no theoretical limit to the weight or lack of weight that should be given to the person's wishes and feelings, beliefs and values. In some cases, the conclusion will be that little weight or no weight can be given; in others, very significant weight will be due.
>
> [11] This is not an academic issue, but a necessary protection for the rights of people with disabilities. As the [Mental Capacity] Act and the European Convention make clear, a conclusion that a person lacks decision-making capacity is not an *"off-switch"* for his rights and freedoms. To state the obvious, the wishes and feelings, beliefs and values of people with a mental disability are as important to them as they are to anyone else, and may even be more important. It would therefore be wrong in principle to apply any automatic discount to their point of view.
>
> [12] In this case, the Trust and the Official Solicitor consider that a person with full capacity could quite reasonably decide not to undergo the amputation that is being recommended to Mr B, having understood and given full thought to the risks and benefits involved. However, the effect of their submissions is that because Mr B himself cannot balance up these matters in a rational way, his wishes and feelings are outweighed by the presumption in favour of life. It is, I think, important to ensure that people with a

---

84 [2015] EWCOP 60 (CP); see also *An NHS Foundation Trust v X* [2014] EWCOP 35 (CP).

disability are not – by the very fact of their disability – deprived of the range of reasonable outcomes that are available to others. For people with disabilities, the removal of such freedom of action as they have to control their own lives may be experienced as an even greater affront that it would be to others who are more fortunate.

[13] In some cases, of which this is an example, the wishes and feelings, beliefs and values of a person with a mental illness can be of such long standing that they are an inextricable part of the person that he is. In this situation, I do not find it helpful to see the person as if he were a person in good health who has been afflicted by illness. It is more real and more respectful to recognise him for who he is: a person with his own intrinsic beliefs and values.

Secondly, as noted, there is a category of patients who, while no longer able to express wishes in respect of the life-sustaining treatment they are receiving, were previously capacitous and expressed relevant wishes or values at that earlier point. *Aintree v James* was a case of this kind where, as we saw, the patient's relatives opposed the medical decision to withdraw treatment on the basis that, on a holistic view of Mr James' best interests, incorporating reference to his past preferences, it was appropriate to continue.[85]

On other occasions it may be the doctors who wish to provide treatment – including life-prolonging treatment – to an incapable patient, in the face of objections from the patient's relatives.In such cases, the doctors may point to the presumption in favour of taking steps to preserve life. Originally, the Mental Capacity Bill 2004 proposed to incorporate this into the 'best interests' test: cl 4(5) stated that, '[the decision-maker] must, where the determination relates to life-sustaining treatment, begin by assuming that it will be in the person's interests for his life to continue'. However, this clause was altered during the Bill's passage, and s 4(5) of the 2005 Act as enacted reads differently:

Mental Capacity Act 2005

4 Best interests

... (5) Where the determination relates to life-sustaining treatment [the person making the determination] must not, in considering whether the treatment is in the best interests of the person concerned, be motivated by a desire to bring about his death.

This is an odd provision. On the one hand it acknowledges that removal of life-sustaining treatment may sometimes be in a person's best interests. On the other, it attempts to exclude wrongly motivated determinations by the decision-maker. It is hard to see though what the decision-maker's motivation has to do with the fact (if established) that treatment is no longer in a given patient's interests.[86] In the event, the courts have also not made any detailed attempt to interpret the subsection. Nonetheless, a significant recent case, which looked at the wider relevance of the patient's previous wishes and attempted to weigh these against the default presumption in favour of life, is *Briggs v Briggs*.

---

85 See also *St George's Healthcare NHS Trust v P* [2015] EWCOP 42 (CP).
86 See Coggon, J, 'Ignoring the moral and intellectual shape of the law after *Bland*: the unintended side-effect of a sorry compromise' (2007) 27 Legal Studies 110.

Briggs v Briggs[87]

Paul Briggs suffered serious brain injuries in a motorcycle accident and was in a minimally conscious state, receiving clinically assisted nutrition and hydration (CANH). The medical evidence was that he might recover limited cognitive functioning to the extent of being able to choose which colour t-shirt to wear, and he would be unlikely to be depressed, due to lack of insight into his condition; however, he would remain severely physically impaired and require 24-hour care for the rest of his life.

The trust caring for him wished to continue with rehabilitative treatment, but Mr Brigg's family applied for a declaration that CANH should cease, as he would not have wished to survive in such a condition:

Charles J: (27) The involvement of the treating team has been with Mr Briggs after the accident and so a Mr Briggs who has serious and permanent brain injuries and who is and will be totally dependent on others for his day to day physical care. And so with the severely disabled Mr Briggs who lacks capacity. The involvement of his family and friends has been with Mr Briggs as a . . . loving husband, father, son and brother, popular colleague and very physically active outdoors [man] as well as with the seriously disabled Mr Briggs who now lacks capacity.

(28) These different involvements have clear links to the central clash of principles that arises in this case, namely:

a   The sanctity of life and so the preservation and prolongation of Mr Briggs' life. Understandably this lies at the heart of the strongly held and consistent view of Mr Briggs' treating consultant that it would be unethical to withdraw his treatment by CANH and so deprive him of the opportunity of leading a life of value.

b   Autonomy and so self-determination which enables a person with capacity to do so to refuse life-sustaining treatment and so as a consequence to choose the side-effect of death. That decision can be made for any reason including that in existing or defined future circumstances that person considers that his or her life is or would be intolerable or has or would have no value and so not worth living. Understandably, the family want to achieve the result that they are convinced Mr Briggs would have wanted and decided on. . . .

[53] In this context it must be remembered that:

i)   issues relating to life-sustaining treatment are intensely personal,

ii)   a fundamental principle is that a person with capacity can make decisions that determine what is to happen to them in the future and so "an earlier self can bind a future and different self" with the result that the principle of self-determination outweighs the sanctity of life, and so

iii)   if persons who do not have the relevant capacity (Ps) are treated as individuals, just as in the case of individuals who consider whether or not to make an advance decision concerning the giving of life-sustaining treatment based on their own predictions and assessments, in the circumstances that exist for them some Ps would, if they were able to, consent to life-sustaining treatment and others would not.

It is confirmed by the Supreme Court in the *Aintree Hospitals* case, which concerned life-sustaining treatment that the correct approach to the application of the MCA and its best interests test is to see P as an individual and consider what P would have done if he or she had capacity. . . . .

[57] . . . [I]t is clear and important to stress that a conclusion on what P would have done is not determinative of the MCA best interests test and so, by stating that the MCA enables the court to do for the patient what he could do for himself if of full capacity, the Supreme Court is not

---

87 See n 64 above.

saying that a conclusion on what the patient would have done is decisive. The test is not a "what P would have done test", it is a best interests test and so a test that requires the decision maker to perform a weighing or balancing exercise between a range of divergent and competing factors. . . .

[62] But, in my view when the magnetic factors engage the fundamental and intensely personal competing principles of the sanctity of life and of self-determination which an individual with capacity can lawfully resolve and determine by giving or refusing consent to available treatment regimes:

i) the decision maker and so a judge must be wary of giving weight to what he thinks is prudent or what he would want for himself or his family, or what he thinks most people would or should want, and

ii) if the decision that P would have made, and so their wishes on such an intensely personal issue can be ascertained with sufficient certainty it should generally prevail over the very strong presumption in favour of preserving life.

[98] . . . After the oral medical evidence Mr Briggs' wife and mother were recalled to address the point that had been made that the extent of Mr Briggs' brain damage meant that he was now a different person who would not appreciate how he had been before his accident.

[99] They confirmed that they had not altered their views and in doing so they did not try to embellish their evidence. It is clear that they know that as a result of his brain damage Mr Briggs is now a different person who will not have insight into his previous wishes, feelings, beliefs, values, approach to life and the impact on him of his brain injury but that to them he still also remains the husband, father and son they loved and love.

Briggs is a striking instance of what has arguably been a sea-change since the enactment of the MCA 2005, with the courts now increasingly favouring the presumed wishes of the incapacitated person, also where these run counter to sanctity of life concerns. Another relevant decision is M v N,[88] in which the Court of Protection authorised discontinuance of CANH from an advanced multiple sclerosis patient (in a minimally conscious state) on the basis of her family's evidence as to her previous values. That case may be contrasted with the older authority of *W Healthcare NHS Trust v H*,[89] where – in a very similar fact situation – the courts refused to countenance treatment withdrawal.

It such cases it is also interesting to consider the relevance of the patients not having made an advance decision, which as discussed at 12.3.4 above, offers a formal way for a capacitous person to bind the doctors in terms of the treatment they may provide to his future, incapacitous self. In fact, a point based on the non-existence of such a decision was raised by the trust in the *Briggs* case:

Charles J: [68] It was submitted . . . that the fact that a person had not made an applicable advance decision . . . indicated a decision or wish that life-sustaining should be carried out. This was in effect a submission that it is only when a person has made a decision that, if it had been signed, would have been valid and applicable under ss. 24 to 26 of the MCA that the court can conclude that the giving or continuation of life-sustaining treatment is not in P's best interests . . . I do not agree. . . .

88 [2015] EWCOP 76 (CP).
89 [2004] EWCA Civ 1324.

[71] I acknowledge and urge that the evidence and reasoning relied on to reach a conclusion that P would not have given consent to the relevant life-sustaining treatment, and then to rely on it as a weighty or determinative factor to depart from the default position that P's best interests are promoted by preserving his or her life, require close and detailed analysis which founds a compelling and cogent case that this is what the particular P would have wanted and decided and so considered to be in his or her best interests.

[72] It is also obvious that the existence of a relevant written statement (referred to in s. 4(6)(a)) would be helpful and so of particular relevance in the way that an advance directive or living will was before the MCA was enacted. But it is also obvious that in real life many if not most relevant expressions of wishes and feelings will not be in writing.

In the third place, as suggested earlier, there is a category of incapable patients who have never enjoyed capacity, as exemplified by cases of seriously disabled infants. Some of the key early cases on withdrawal of life-sustaining treatment involved such patients, eg *Re B* and *Re J*.[90] Nonetheless, they continue to be among the most challenging and emotive cases, particularly where the doctors and the infant's parents are in disagreement. In 2005, in *Wyatt v Portsmouth NHS Trust*,[91] the Court of Appeal was required to rule in a dispute between the doctors, who did not wish to mechanically ventilate a seriously premature and disabled baby girl if she suffered an infection, and the baby's parents, who wanted every effort to be made to prolong her life. In its judgment, the court gave the following advice to trial judges deciding such cases:

Wall LJ (giving the judgment of the Court): [87] In our judgment, the intellectual milestones for the judge in a case such as the present are ... simple although the ultimate decision will frequently be extremely difficult. The judge must decide what is in the child's best interests. In making that decision the welfare of the child is paramount, and the judge must look at the question from the assumed point of view of the patient (In re J [1991] Fam 33). There is a strong presumption in favour of a course of action which will prolong life, but that presumption is not irrebuttable (In re J). The term 'best interests' encompasses medical, emotional, and all other welfare issues (In re A [2000] 1FLR 549). The court must conduct a balancing exercise in which all the relevant factors are weighed (In re J) and a helpful way of undertaking this exercise is to draw up a balance sheet (In re A).

[88] Inevitably, whilst cases involving the treatment of children will fall into recognised categories, no two cases are the same, and the individual cases will inevitably be highly fact-specific. In this context any criteria which seek to circumscribe the best interests tests are, we think, to be avoided. As Thorpe LJ said in In re S [2001] Fam 15: 'it would be undesirable and probably impossible to set bounds to what is relevant to a welfare determination.'

In the *Wyatt* case, the courts agreed with the medical view that, given the baby's serious disabilities and limited capacity to develop, it would not be in her best interests to subject her to further invasive treatment.

As discussed in Chapter 4, where disputes arise over what is best for incapable children, the medical opinions of the doctors will generally carry the day.[92] However, there have been decisions the other way. A case in point is *An NHS Trust v MB*,[93] which concerned an 18-month-old

---

90 See n 68 and n 71 above.
91 [2005] EWCA Civ 1181.
92 See Ch 4, section 4.4.3; see also Morris, A, 'Selective Treatment of Irreversibly Impaired Infants' (2009) 17 Med L Rev 347.
93 [2006] EWHC 507 (Fam).

boy with spinal muscular atrophy, a degenerative muscle-wasting disease. By the time of the hearing, he was completely paralysed and reliant on mechanical ventilation to breath. It was unclear to what extent he was impaired mentally, but, on the basis of the parents' evidence, Holman J was prepared to assume that he derived pleasure from activities such as listening to stories or watching DVDs. His Lordship applied the 'balance sheet' approach to determining MB's best interests, endorsed by the Court of Appeal in *Wyatt*, and made the following observations:

> **Holman J**: [58] The test is one of best interests, and the task of the court is to balance all the factors. The Court of Appeal have suggested that the best and safest way of reliably doing this is to draw up a list on which are specifically identified, on the one hand, the benefits or advantages and, on the other hand, the burdens or disadvantages of continuing or discontinuing the treatment in question. At a relatively early stage of this hearing I therefore asked each advocate to draw up and submit to me their respective proposed lists, and they kindly did so. It has been an enormously useful discipline, both during evidence (when the lists were used as a kind of check list), the argument and now as I reach my decision and prepare this judgment. I would like, as an aside, to suggest that in similar cases each party should prepare such lists as part of their preparation of the case. The lists can always be added to, or amended, in the light of the evidence, as happened in this case.
>
> . . .
>
> [102] It is impossible to put a mathematical or any other value on the benefits. But they are precious and real and they are the benefits, and only benefits, that M was destined to gain from his life. I do not consider that from one day to the next all the routine discomfort, distress and pain that the doctors describe (but not the ones I have now excluded) outweigh those benefits so that I can say that it is in his best interests that those benefits, and life itself, should immediately end. On the contrary, I positively consider that as his life does still have benefits, and is his life, it should be enabled to continue, subject to excluding the treatment I have identified.

The treatments excluded by the judge were radical, painful interventions to prolong life, such as cardio-pulmanory resusciation.

In 2015, the Royal College of Paediatrics and Child Health issued specific guidance to doctors working in the field,[94] but this has not decreased the number of such cases requiring determination by the courts. A poignant and well-known recent case, in which the parents tried every legal avenue to enable their child to receive further treatment, was *Yates v Great Ormond Street Hospital NHS Foundation Trust*.[95]

Yates v Great Ormond Street Hospital NHS Foundation Trust[96]

> Charlie Gard, who was aged nine months at the time of the hearing, had been born with a rare genetic mutation that caused the progressive loss of muscular function. He had been unable to breathe unaided since the age of two months and, in the doctors' view, had already suffered irreversible brain damage; they wished to end the artificial ventilation as no longer in his best interests. However, this was contested by Charlie's parents who disputed the diagnosis of irreversible brain damage and wished to take him to the USA for novel genetic therapy.

---

94 *Making decisions to limit treatment in life-limiting and life-threatening conditions in children: a framework for practice* (March 2015).
95 [2017] EWCA Civ 410; see also *Re Jake (A Child)* [2015] EWHC 2442 (Fam); *Bolton NHS Foundation Trust v C* [2015] EWHC 2920 (Fam); *Re A (a child)* [2016] EWCA Civ 759.
96 Ibid.

The High Court (Francis J) ruled in favour of the trust, and the parents appealed to the Court of Appeal:

Lord Justice McFarlane: [95] When thoughtful, caring, and responsible parents are putting forward a viable option for the care of their child, the court will look keenly at that option, in the same way that a court in family proceedings, when it gets to the welfare stage of any case, looks at the realistic options that are before it. The court evaluates the nitty-gritty detail of each option from the child's perspective. It does not prefer any particular option simply because it is put forward by a parent or by a local authority. The judge decides what is in the best interests of the child by looking at the case entirely through eyes focused on the child's welfare and focused upon the merits and drawbacks of the particular options that are being presented to the court.

[96] If one option is favoured by a parent, that may give it weight, or as Lord Justice Waite put it [in *Re T (Wardship: Medical Treatment) [1997] 1 WLR 242*], incline the court to be "influenced by a reflection that in the last analysis, the best interests of every child, include an expectation that difficult decisions affecting the length and quality of its life will be taken for it by the parent to whom its care has been entrusted by nature". Notwithstanding that that is the case, in the end it is the judge who has to choose the best course for a child. Where, as in the case of *Re King [[2014] EWHC 2964 (Fam)]*, there really was nothing to choose as between the benefits and detriments of the two forms of radiotherapy, the court readily stood back and allowed the parents to make their choice.

[97] Where, however, as in this case, the judge has made clear findings that going to America for treatment would be futile, would have no benefit and would simply prolong the awful existence that he found was the current state of young Charlie's life, he was fully entitled, on the basis of those findings to conclude as he did. The consequence of that conclusion is that the proposal for nucleoside therapy was not a viable option before the court.

[The UK Supreme Court dismissed the parent's application to appeal, and their final petition to the European Court of Human Rights was ruled inadmissible.][97]

12.4.4 The problem of patients in PVS

So far our concern has been with patients who have been sentient (ie capable of sensory experience) but severely impaired. Here it has arguably made sense to conduct a form of comparative exercise in which their (intolerable) quality of life is measured against death (conceived of as permanent unconsciousness). We must now consider a further category of patient for whom no such exercise appears possible, viz. those who, while still alive, become permanently insensate. As Jonathan Glover remarks, citing the idealist philosopher Arthur Schopenhauer, in subjective terms such patients are already dead:

Glover, J, *Causing Death and Saving Lives*[98]

I have no way of refuting someone who holds that being alive, even though unconscious, is intrinsically valuable. But it is a view that will seem unattractive to those of us who, in our own case, see a life of permanent coma as in no way preferable to death. From the subjective point of view, there is nothing to choose between the two. Schopenhauer saw this clearly when he said of the destruction of the body:

---

97 See the Court's Press Release ECHR 222 (2017) of 27 June 2017.
98 See n 3 above.

> But actually we feel this destruction only in the evils of illness or of old age; on the other hand, for the *subject*, death itself consists merely in the moment when consciousness vanishes, since the activity of the brain ceases. The extension of the stoppage to all the other parts of the organism which follows this is really already an event after death. Therefore, in a subjective respect, death concerns only consciousness.

Legally, of course, such patients are alive: as we saw in Chapter 11, death is regarded in law as occurring only when the whole of an individual's brainstem has perished. The brainstem is divided into upper and lower parts, the former, together with the cerebral cortex, being necessary for consciousness while the latter controls the body's automatic functions such as breathing, swallowing and other basic reflexes. When the brain is starved of oxygen, the lower brainstem is the last part of it to die, a fact which may give rise to a permanently insensate condition known, medically, as a permanent (formerly 'persistent') vegetative state or 'PVS'. Although there are no precise figures, it has been estimated that in the UK there are around 850 patients with this condition, and a further 2,500 who are in a minimally consciousness 'near PVS' state.[99]

The issue of whether a patient diagnosed as being in PVS should be subject to a life-sustaining regime of treatment and care fell to be decided by the House of Lords in the landmark case of *Airedale NHS Trust v Bland*:

Airedale NHS Trust v Bland[100]

Tony Bland suffered massive and irreversible brain damage in the Hillsborough football disaster in April 1989. He had lain in a PVS for more than three years and the medical evidence was unanimous that he would never regain any form of awareness. The trust caring for him applied, with his parents' approval, for a declaration that it would be lawful to withhold further life-prolonging treatment and care (artificial nutrition and hydration as well as antibiotics) from him, thus, allowing him to die. The declaration was granted by the High Court, and this was unanimously affirmed by the Court of Appeal and by the House of Lords:

Lord Keith of Kinkel: The broad issue raised by the appeal is stated by the parties to be: 'In what circumstances, if ever, can those having a duty to feed an invalid lawfully stop doing so?' The immediate issue, however, is whether in the particular circumstances of Anthony Bland's case those in charge of it would be acting lawfully if they discontinued the particular measures, including feeding by nasogastric tube, which are now being used to maintain Anthony Bland in his existing condition . . .

It is argued for the respondents, supported by the *amicus curiae*, that his best interests favour discontinuance. I feel some doubt about this way of putting the matter. In *Re F (Mental Patient: Sterilisation)* [1990] 2 AC 1 this House held that it would be lawful to sterilise a female mental patient who was incapable of giving consent to the procedure. The ground of the decision was that sterilisation would be in the patient's best interests because her life would be fuller and more agreeable if she were sterilised than if she were not. In *Re J (A Minor) (Wardship: Medical Treatment)* [1991] Fam 33 the Court of Appeal held it to be lawful to withhold life-saving treatment from a very young child in circumstances where the child's life, if saved, would be one irredeemably racked by pain and agony. In both cases it was possible to make a value judgment, as to the consequences to a sensate being, of in the one case withholding and in the other case

---

99 Jennett, B in Laureys, S (ed), *The Boundaries of Consciousness*, Amsterdam: Elsevier, 2005, 537.
100 See n 6 above.

administering the treatment in question. In the case of a permanently insensate being, who if continuing to live would never experience the slightest actual discomfort, it is difficult, if not impossible, to make any relevant comparison between continued existence and the absence of it. It is, however, perhaps permissible to say that to an individual with no cognitive capacity whatever, and no prospect of ever recovering any such capacity in this world, it must be a matter of complete indifference whether he lives or dies. . . .

Given that existence in the persistent vegetative state is not a benefit to the patient, it remains to consider whether the principle of the sanctity of life, which it is the concern of the State, and the judiciary as one of the arms of the State, to maintain, requires this House to hold that the judgment of the Court of Appeal was incorrect. In my opinion it does not. The principle is not an absolute one. It does not compel a medical practitioner on pain of criminal sanctions to treat a patient, who will die if he does not, contrary to the express wishes of the patient. It does not authorise forcible feeding of prisoners on hunger strike. It does not compel the temporary keeping alive of patients who are terminally ill where to do so would merely prolong their suffering. On the other hand it forbids the taking of active measures to cut short the life of a terminally ill patient. In my judgment it does no violence to the principle to hold that it is lawful to cease to give medical treatment and care to a PVS patient who has been in that state for over three years, considering that to do so involves invasive manipulation of the patient's body to which he has not consented and which confers no benefit upon him . . .

My Lords, for these reasons, which are substantially the same as those set out in the speech delivered by my noble and learned friend, Lord Goff of Chieveley, with which I agree, I would dismiss the appeal.

As we have seen, there is a philosophical problem in applying the best interests approach to a patient who will never again enjoy any form of experience. For such patients, rather than offering any prospect of release from suffering, death must, as Lord Keith recognised, be a matter of pure indifference. Thus, it might well be argued, it cannot be in their best interests. In the Court of Appeal in *Bland*, Hoffmann LJ, drawing on Ronald Dworkin's work, *Life's Dominion*,[101] addressed this difficulty by suggesting that patients in PVS do in fact retain certain interests (*critical* – as opposed to *experiential* – interests in Dworkinian terms) and that these are served by allowing them to die:

Hoffmann LJ: Counsel for the Official Solicitor argued that however vestigial Anthony Bland's life might be, one could not assume that he would choose to die. Being unconscious, he felt no pain or humiliation and therefore had no interests which suffered from his being kept alive. Anthony Bland was in fact indifferent to whether he lived or died and there was nothing to put in the balance against the intrinsic value of his life.

I think that the fallacy in this argument is that it assumes that we have no interests except in those things of which we have conscious experience. But this does not accord with most people's intuitive feelings about their lives and deaths. At least a part of the reason why we honour the wishes of the dead about the distribution of their property is that we think it would wrong them not to do so, despite the fact that we believe that they will never know that their will has been ignored. Most people would like an honourable and dignified death and we think it wrong to dishonour their deaths, even when they are unconscious that this is happening. We

---

101 Dworkin, R, *Life's Dominion: An Argument About Abortion and Euthanasia*, New York: Knopf, 1993.

> pay respect to their dead bodies and to their memory because we think it an offence against the dead themselves if we do not. Once again I am not concerned to analyse the rationality of these feelings. It is enough that they are deeply rooted in our ways of thinking and that the law cannot possibly ignore them. Thus I think that counsel for the Official Solicitor offers a seriously incomplete picture of Anthony Bland's interests when he confines them to animal feelings of pain or pleasure. It is demeaning to the human spirit to say that, being unconscious, he can have no interest in his personal privacy and dignity, in how he lives or dies.

This argument has a slightly metaphysical flavour and was not adopted in the House of Lords. Instead, as reflected in Lord Keith's judgment, their Lordships preferred to look at the question from the opposite direction and ask if *treatment* was a benefit to the patient. As noted earlier, this way of approaching matters (viz. from the starting point that it is the continued treatment, not its cessation, that requires justification) was recently reiterated by the UK Supreme Court in its *Aintree* decision.

An apparent implication of this approach, which the courts have noted in passing but have tended not to stress, is that the continuing treatment of a PVS patient (at least one with a confirmed diagnosis) will actually be an unlawful battery.[102] At the same time, it may be doubted if doctors and relatives involved in the care of such patients would accept any interpretation of the law that required them to cease treatment (as opposed to sometimes permitting them to do so). Indeed, as noted in section 12.4.2 above, following a recommendation in *Bland*, such cases are subject to a special safeguard, requiring a judicial hearing as to the lawfulness of withdrawing treatment (typically ANH). This requirement was originally included in a Practice Note issued by the Official Solicitor. Since the coming into force of the Mental Capacity Act 2005, and as specified in Practice Direction 9E of the Court of Protection,[103] it also applies to patients not strictly in PVS, but who are in a state of minimal consciousness.

In the 25 years since the *Bland* decision, there has been a small but steady trickle of applications to court in such cases. In some of these the relatives were divided and/or opposed to the view of the doctors as to whether treatment should continue;[104] in other cases doubts were raised as to whether the patient's diagnosis really conformed to a PVS.[105] Nonetheless, in so far as medical opinion supported such a course, the courts in such cases have invariably approved the proposed withdrawal of treatment as in the patient's best interests. Recently, though, new doubts have surfaced as to the accuracy of diagnosing PVS, fuelled by the discovery that the administration of a drug, Zolpidem, may in some cases allow patients, previously thought to be in PVS, to recover some level of consciousness. This development was acknowledged by the High Court in the case of *An NHS Trust v J*,[106] which concerned a woman who had been in a PVS for some three years after suffering a stroke. Here, Sir Mark Potter P agreed with the Official Solicitor (but against the wishes of J's family) that, before finally withdrawing ANH, a short course of Zolpidem should be tried upon her. In the event, though, the drug did not have any positive effect, and the court thereupon authorised the withdrawal of ANH to allow her to die.

Another recent development, adding to the difficulty in resolving PVS cases, relates to research done with functional magnetic resonance imaging (fMRI), which may open up the possibility of communicating with patients ostensibly in PVS. The implications of this are discussed by Skene et al. in the following article:

---

102 Dicta to this effect can also be found in the speeches in *Bland* of Lords Browne-Wilkinson and Lowry.
103 See n 72 above.
104 See, eg, *Re G (Persistent Vegetative State)* [1995] 2 FCR 46; *An NHS Trust v D* [2005] EWHC 2349 (Fam).
105 See, eg, *Frenchay Healthcare NHS Trust v S* [1994] 2 All ER 403.
106 [2006] EWHC 3152 (Fam).

Skene, L, et al., 'Neuroimaging and the withdrawal of life-sustaining treatment from patients in vegetative state'[107]

[R]ecent research by Professor Adrian Owen suggests that some patients in VS may be able to follow instructions leading to a pattern of brain activity that can be observed by fMRI . . . Two of [his] patients . . . manifested characteristic changes on brain scanning after being instructed to imagine playing tennis. Both . . . had been diagnosed as being in VS at the time, but both subsequently improved clinically to the point where they inconsistently manifested behavioural responses to stimuli and thereby met the criteria for M[inimally] C[onscious] S[tate] . . .

It is at least conceivable that future research will show that some patients who respond to fMRI may be able to use this or a similar technique to communicate and make their wishes known, though it seems unlikely on the basis of what we know about the nature of the global brain injury in patients in VS. If such a form of communication were established with some brain-damaged patients, it would certainly be relevant, especially if the patient wanted treatment to be stopped. However, it would probably not be determinative, even concerning the withdrawal of treatment, as the meaning of a response to fMRI and its significance in assessing the competence of the patient are so uncertain . . .

Courts have held in a number of cases that it is lawful not to provide life-sustaining treatment if it is 'futile', justifying this on the ground of the patient's best interests. As Lord Goff said in Bland, 'if the treatment is futile . . . it is no longer in the best interests of the patient to continue it' . . . While there is reasonable consensus among health professionals and in the case law about the permissibility of withdrawing life-sustaining treatment from patients in VS, there is much less agreement about MCS . . .

One might question whether the possibility of a very small change in the patient's condition . . . is sufficient to warrant the continuation of treatment that would otherwise be withdrawn, given the remote chance that the patient will ever make a reasonable recovery. Also, as argued above, it should not be assumed that minimal consciousness would give us more reason to keep such patients alive; the reverse may be true. In such a life, unlike in VS, a patient clearly has interests, including an interest not to suffer, that might be compromised by continued existence, something not true of other patients in VS.

In the High Court decision of *W v M and others*,[108] where an application was made for the withdrawal of ANH from a patient initially thought to be in PVS, but whom tests then revealed was in a minimally conscious state, Baker J emphasised the importance of a full prior diagnosis being performed. He also noted the desirability, given the fundamental public interest of such cases, for them to be heard openly and (subject to privacy protections for the patient and relatives) freely reported.

12.4.5 Non-medical reasons for the withdrawal of life-sustaining medical treatment – scarce resources and/or impracticability

The discussion in this chapter has so far ignored the fact that, in keeping alive patients who enjoy a low (or, in the case of someone in PVS, non-existent) quality of life, there is an 'opportunity cost', in the sense that scarce resources are expended which might otherwise be utilised upon people with a greater capacity to benefit from them. In *Re J (A Minor) (Wardship: Medical*

---

107 (2009) 17 Med L Rev 245.
108 [2011] EWHC 2443 (Fam); see also *St George's Heathcare NHS Trust v P* [2015] EWCOP 42 (CP).

Treatment),[109] the Court of Appeal quashed the trial judge's order that the health authority treat a severely disabled baby. Balcombe LJ stated:

> **Balcombe LJ**: I would also stress the absolute undesirability of the court making an order which may have the effect of compelling a doctor or health authority to make available scarce resources (both human and material) to a particular child, without knowing whether or not there are other patients to whom those resources might more advantageously be devoted. Lord Donaldson MR has set out in his reasons the condition of J and his very limited future prospects. The effect of the order of Waite J, had it not been immediately stayed by this court, might have been to require the health authority to put J on a ventilator in an intensive care unit, and thereby possibly to deny the benefit of those limited resources to a child who was much more likely than J to benefit from them. At the very least it would in those circumstances have required the health authority to make a further application to the court to vary or discharge the injunction.

In *Airedale NHS Trust v Bland*[110] the fact that resource allocation is ultimately an issue that must be faced up to was noted by Lord Mustill:

> **Lord Mustill**: Threaded through the technical arguments addressed to the House were the strands of a much wider position, that it is in the best interests of the community at large that Anthony Bland's life should now end. The doctors have done all they can. Nothing will be gained by going on and much will be lost. The distress of the family will get steadily worse. The strain on the devotion of a medical staff charged with the care of a patient whose condition will never improve, who may live for years and who does not even recognise that he is being cared for, will continue to mount. The large resources of skill, labour and money now being devoted to Anthony Bland might in the opinion of many be more fruitfully employed in improving the condition of other patients, who if treated may have useful, healthy and enjoyable lives for years to come.
>
> This argument was never squarely put, although hinted at from time to time. In social terms it has great force, and it will have to be faced in the end. But this is not a task which the courts can possibly undertake. A social cost-benefit analysis of this kind, which would have to embrace 'mercy killing' to which exactly the same considerations apply, must be for parliament alone, and the outcome of it is at present quite impossible to foresee. Until the nettle is grasped, we must struggle on with the existing law, imperfect as it is.

In his speech, Lord Browne Wilkinson similarly stated that 'it is not legitimate for a judge in reaching a view as to what is for the benefit of the one individual whose life is in issue to take into account the wider practical issues as to allocation of limited financial resources'. Rather, as he suggested, the inclusion of scarce resources as a permissible basis for withdrawing treatment would have to be a matter for Parliament. So far, Parliament has (not surprisingly) steered clear of the issue. As discussed in Chapter 2,[111] resource considerations will play a part earlier, in deciding, at the macro-level, whether a particular form of treatment should be made available on the NHS. At the micro-level, by contrast, the 2013 Neuberger Review into the Liverpool Care Pathway – a controversial initiative aimed at easing the suffering of patients deemed to have entered the dying process – stressed the unacceptability of financial incentives for hospitals to move patients off further active treatment and onto the Pathway.[112]

---

109 [1992] 4 All ER 614; this case should not be confused with the slightly earlier CA decision of the same name.
110 See n 6 above.
111 See Ch 2, section 2.4.1 above.
112 See Neuberger, J et al., 'More care, less Pathway' (July 2013), available at: www.gov.uk/government/uploads/system/uploads/attachment_data/file/212450/Liverpool_Care_Pathway.pdf.

As to impracticability as a reason for withdrawing life-sustaining treatment, this was alluded to at first instance in *R (on the application of Burke) v GMC*.[113] There, Munby J suggested that this may comprise a further category (besides the PVS type of case, where continued treatment may be said to be futile, and the class of case looked at in section 12.4.3, of sentient incapable patients, in which continued treatment will be disproportionately burdensome). By way of illustration, he posited a case in which 'the patient, although incapable, strongly objects and is not prepared to submit to the relevant procedure . . .'.

This type of situation occurred in the case of *Re D (Medical Treatment: Mentally Disabled Patient)*,[114] where a long-term psychiatric patient required ongoing dialysis treatment for renal failure. The patient was refusing to co-operate and sometimes had to be anaesthetised for the treatment to take place. In the circumstances, the High Court ruled that the continued imposition of dialysis was not in the patient's best interests. However, a stricter approach may be found in the subsequent case of *An Hospital NHS Trust v S and others*.[115] Here, the question for the High Court related to the medical care of an 18-year-old with serious mental disabilities, who had suffered end-stage renal failure. In holding that further, invasive treatment (possibly including a kidney transplant) should not be ruled out on 'non-medical grounds', Dame Elizabeth Butler-Sloss P commented as follows:

> **Butler-Sloss P**: [64] The medical situation cannot, of course, be considered in isolation. There is no doubt that S's severe learning disability militates against explanations other than the simplest. I recognise the complexity of the operation and the probability of emergency recall to hospital on more than one occasion. I recognise the real concerns about the risk of infection and the likely need for one, or possibly even several, biopsies and the added difficulties for S to have an immediate biopsy, since he is on warfarin. The very real concerns of the Hospital Trust are, however, mainly based upon the consequences of emergency surgery on an autistic boy without any preparation of any kind. However, an emergency admission to hospital followed by life-saving surgery and treatment would be a traumatic experience for anyone. For an autistic boy, as I have set out above, it must have been extremely distressing and he reacted accordingly . . . With some preparation and with the support of a person or people in whom he had trust, in my view, and despite the opposite conclusions of the medical and nursing team at the Hospital Trust, S ought to be manageable post operation. The need for blood tests, the use of needles and the likelihood of several returns to hospital post operation, do not seem to me to be insuperable obstacles. On balance, however, if the medical reasons for a kidney transplantation are in his favour, and alternative methods of dialysis are no longer viable, in my judgment, a kidney transplantation ought not to be rejected on the grounds of his inability to understand the purpose and consequences of the operation or concerns about his management.

THINK POINT

Why do patients in PVS and minimally conscious states receive more protection from the law (in terms of the need for the withdrawal of treatment to be judicially sanctioned) than other incapable patients?

---

113 See n 81 above.
114 [1998] 2 FLR 22; see also *An NHS Foundation Trust v X* (2014) EWCOP 35 (CP).
115 [2003] EWHC 365 (Fam).

12.5 Reforming the law

12.5.1 Introduction

As discussed in 12.1 above, the 'qualified sanctity of life' approach taken by English law draws heavily upon the so-called 'acts/omissions distinction'. Doctors are accorded some flexibility in allowing death to occur (through removing treatment), but – leaving aside the special case of palliative care for the terminally ill, as well as the unique problem posed by the *Re A (Children)* case[116] – are not permitted to take positive measures to shorten life. We have seen too that, so far, assisted suicide (by physicians or others) also remains a criminal offence in the UK.

In the final part of this chapter, we address the issue of whether there should be legal change in this area to permit greater physician involvement in death. The most radical option would be to allow doctors to kill their patients (where the patient requested this), for example by lethal injection; another possibility would at least be to allow doctors to assist in suicide, for example by supplying drugs for the patient to take himself or herself. In section 12.5.2, we consider the experience of some other jurisdictions where these options have been tried, before returning in 12.5.3 to the current debate in the UK. As noted, in its 2014 *Nicklinson* decision, the Supreme Court evinced significant sympathy for legalising physician assisted suicide; indeed some members went to some lengths in suggesting to Parliament how a suitable Act (incorporating necessary safeguards) might look.

12.5.2 Experience in other jurisdictions

12.5.2.1 The Netherlands – active voluntary euthanasia

In the Netherlands, active voluntary euthanasia has been permitted in cases of 'unbearable suffering' since the 1970s. This was initially made possible by the courts, which developed guidelines for doctors to follow in such cases, compliance with which would foreclose prosecution under Dutch criminal law. In 2001 the position was formalised by the Termination of Life on Request and Assisted Suicide (Review Procedures) Act. Under s 2 of this Act, a doctor will be protected from prosecution where – following consultation with another doctor – he is satisfied that the patient: is in a state of lasting and unbearable suffering; is fully informed as to his condition, prospects and options; and has an enduring and voluntary wish to die. The Act also establishes certain safeguards, notably that the doctor be present at the death and report it to the municipal coroner for assessment by a regional review committee (as to whether the relevant criteria were satisfied).

The effects and implications of the Dutch law in this area have sparked an intense (if ultimately inconclusive) debate among commentators, who have vied to produce statistics showing that abuse (in terms of non-compliance with all of the eligibility requirements and/or reporting safeguards) is/is not occurring. In fact, the significance accorded to instances of non-compliance will inevitably be influenced in part by the commentator's underlying views as to the rights and wrongs of active euthanasia. Moreover, as Otlowski observes, failure to comply with the formal law on euthanasia is just as likely to occur – if not more so – in countries where the practice remains prohibited:

---

116 See sections 12.2.2 and 12.2.3 above.

Otlowski, M, *Voluntary Euthanasia and the Common Law*[117]

[C]oncern regarding the adequacy of safeguards must be interpreted in the light of current practice. As was noted in an earlier chapter, there is incontrovertible evidence to suggest that active voluntary euthanasia is to some extent already being performed, but in a totally unregulated fashion. Thus, the current situation inevitably involves some risk of abuse, and there is good reason to believe that the legalization of the practice, with appropriate regulatory procedures, would in fact reduce the possibility of covert improper practices. It would, however, be naive to suggest that a proposal for the legalization of active voluntary euthanasia would be completely free of risk. All existing laws are potentially open to abuse, and a law permitting the practice of active voluntary euthanasia would be no exception. Looking at the situation realistically, the aim of legislation legalizing active voluntary euthanasia would be to minimize the risk of abuse by the imposition of stringent safeguards regulating the practice.

Overall, the number of deaths occurring in the Netherlands as a result of active euthanasia appears to have remained fairly constant (thus in 2005 there were around 8,400 requests for active euthanasia, of which some 2,400 were granted).[118] Arguably, more noteworthy is the change in social attitudes that appears to have occurred since (or because of?) the legal acceptance of active voluntary euthanasia. A survey carried out in the wake of the 2002 *Brongersma* case,[119] in which a physician was convicted of assisting the death of a former politician, who was 'tired of life' (but did not satisfy the 'unbearable suffering' test in the 2001 Act), found that nearly half of the population supported the doctor's actions. In early 2010 it was reported that a citizens' initiative, 'Out of Free Will', whose members include prominent figures from politics and the arts, has begun to campaign for the right of all Dutch citizens aged over 70, who are 'tired of life', to have the legal right to be helped to die.

A further point to note is that, while primarily concerned with active voluntary euthanasia, in one category of case Dutch law also permits active non-voluntary euthanasia: this is in relation to severely disabled neonates in respect of whom it has been decided to withdraw life-prolonging medical care (ie they have already been selected for passive euthanasia). As Suzanne Ost explains, by reference to the discussion of this practice found in Griffiths et al.

Ost, S, review of Griffiths, J, Weyers, H and Adams, M, *Euthanasia and the Law in Europe: With Special Reference to the Netherlands and Belgium*[120]

The Dutch approach to this matter has been discussed by the Nuffield Council on Bioethics' Working Party on Critical Decisions in Fetal and Neonatal Medicine, who unreservedly rejected 'the active ending of neonatal life even when that life is "intolerable"'... The most crucial requirements in order for such practice to be lawful in the Netherlands are that there must have already been a legitimate decision made to withdraw or withhold life-sustaining treatment and that both parents must agree to the termination of life on the basis of the baby's current unbearable and hopeless suffering ... Termination of life is justifiable because following the withholding or withdrawal of treatment, death is not going to take place immediately. The doctor must comply with 'due care norms'... The authors refer to research studies that indicate that almost all neonatal end-of-life practice that occurs in the Netherlands is in the form of withholding and withdrawing treatment and that the active termination of life is very rare, although the statistics from national

117 See n 4 above.
118 Pasman, HR et al., 'Concept of unbearable suffering in context of ungranted requests for euthanasia: qualitative interviews with patients and physicians' (2009) 339 BMJ b4362.
119 Dutch Supreme Court, 24.12.2002; NJ 2003/167.
120 (2009) 17 Med L Rev 118.

surveys indicate higher figures . . . It is of note that in 2007, a national committee of experts was created specifically to advise the prosecutorial authorities on the matter of the active termination of neonatal life, to receive doctors' reports of cases where such practice has occurred and pass its conclusions on to the authorities . . . One of the conclusions that the reader can draw from the authors' analysis here is that a country moving towards legalisation of euthanasia must also be prepared to reassess the reasons for prohibiting other even more sensitive forms of [medical behaviour that potentially shortens life]. It must be decided whether it is possible to justify placing a dividing line between euthanasia and the termination of neonatal life, for instance, so that the former becomes lawful while the latter does not. The answer to this question will depend, in large part, upon the legitimating values and principles that lie behind the proposals to decriminalise euthanasia within that particular society.

Subsequently, Belgium (in 2002) and Luxembourg (in 2009) have legislated to permit active voluntary euthanasia in circumstances similar to those recognised by Dutch law. However, in almost every other country in the world the prohibition on active euthanasia currently remains.

12.5.2.2 Switzerland and Oregon – assisted suicide

As is well known, assisted suicide for the ill and dying is lawful in Switzerland. Indeed, in recent years a small but increasing number of British citizens have been travelling there to end their lives in this way (it will be recalled that the background to the *Purdy* case was the applicant's wish for her husband to be able to accompany her on the journey without risk of prosecution under the 1961 Suicide Act). Here, it should be noted that there is no specific Swiss legislation on the matter: it is simply that the Swiss Criminal Code only prohibits cases of 'selfish' assisted suicide (ie where the assister will gain personally in some way from the death).[121] Accordingly, in other cases, where the assister can show that they acted from motives of altruism, no offence will have been committed.

It also follows that in Switzerland physicians do not have any privileged role in relation to assisting suicide – in principle, any person may do so. Nor are there any qualifying conditions that the person to be assisted must satisfy, in terms of being terminally ill or subject to unbearable suffering. It is enough that the patient has expressed the capable wish to die. In a decision in 2006, the Swiss Federal Supreme Court confirmed that assisted suicide would be lawful in the case of those suffering from mental illness, provided that this was not due to temporary and treatable factors, but reflected a 'rational and well-considered' decision to put an end to their further suffering.[122] In such cases, this would need to be established by a full psychiatric evaluation.

The implications of the relatively unregulated situation in Switzerland, as well as the attitudes of doctors there to assisting in suicide, are explored by Hurst and Mauron in the following extract:

Hurst, SA and Mauron, A 'Assisted suicide and euthanasia in Switzerland:
allowing a role for non-physicians'[123]

The Swiss Academy of Medical Sciences states in its ethical recommendations that assisted suicide is 'not a part of a physician's activity'. This statement is ambiguous. It has usually been understood to mean that physicians should not assist suicide and was paraphrased in 2002 in a joint statement by the Swiss Medical Association and the Swiss Nurses Association. But the statement from the Swiss Academy of Medical

---

121 § 115 Swiss Criminal Code.
122 Federal High Court of Switzerland, Decision 2A.48/2006 (3 November 2006).
123 (2003) 326 BMJ 271.

Sciences has also been understood to place assisted suicide outside the purview of professional oversight, and to refer physicians, as citizens, to the law. This allows them, like other citizens, to altruistically assist suicide. In fact, even if it is understood to discourage physicians from assisting suicide, legally it leaves physicians with the same discretion as any citizen to altruistically assist suicide.

In practice, many physicians oppose assisted suicide and euthanasia, and hospitals have barred assisted suicide from their premises. Some physicians, however, do assist suicides and some advocate the decriminalisation of euthanasia. The arguments advanced are the same as in other countries. Opponents argue that killing patients violates physicians' professional integrity and endangers the doctor patient relationship. Proponents see assisted suicide and euthanasia as part of a caring response to intractable human suffering. In 2001, the Swiss parliament rejected a bill that would have barred physicians from assisting suicide ...

Assisted suicide is a controversial topic in Switzerland, but data on public attitudes ... are scarce ... In a 1999 survey of the Swiss public, 82% of 1000 respondents agreed that 'a person suffering from an incurable disease and who is in intolerable physical and psychological suffering has the right to ask for death and to obtain help for this purpose.' Of these, 68% considered that physicians should provide this help ...

No validated statistics exist for assisted suicides in Switzerland. These deaths are not differentiated from unassisted suicides in official records. According to the president of one of the Swiss right to die societies, around 1800 requests for assisted suicides are made each year. Two thirds are rejected after screening. Half of the remaining people die of other causes, leaving about 300 suicides assisted by these societies annually. This constitutes around 0.45% of deaths in Switzerland ... Individuals outside these societies may assist additional suicides. In comparison, reported assisted suicide in Oregon represents 0.09% of deaths ...

In recent years, a number of assisted dying associations have established themselves in Switzerland, which help persons who wish to commit suicide by arranging a consultation with a doctor (to obtain the required drugs) and for the persons to ingest the drugs in a supervised environment. Nonetheless, the activities of such groups remain controversial, not least because of their willingness to arrange suicide for those who are simply tired of life, as opposed to seriously ill or suffering – it has been estimated that around a quarter of cases fall into this category; also striking is the over-representation of women among applicants for suicide.[124]

In 1994, the US state of Oregon legislated to permit physician-assisted suicide in the Death With Dignity Act, which entered into force in 1998. The Act, which is limited to residents of Oregon, allows terminally ill patients with a likely prognosis of fewer than six months to live to obtain a prescription of a lethal drug. The process is subject to numerous safeguards, including the following responsibilities that are imposed on the patient's doctor by s 3 of the Act:

The Oregon Death With Dignity Act 1994, s 3

1   The attending physician shall:
   a   Make the initial determination of whether a patient has a terminal disease, is capable, and has made the request voluntarily;
   b   Request that the patient demonstrate Oregon residency ...;
   c   To ensure that the patient is making an informed decision, inform the patient of:
      A   His or her medical diagnosis;
      B   His or her prognosis;

---

124 Fischer, S et al., 'Suicide assisted by two Swiss right-to-die organisations' (2008) 34 J Med Ethics 810.

C   The potential risks associated with taking the medication to be prescribed;

D   The probable result of taking the medication to be prescribed; and

E   The feasible alternatives, including, but not limited to, comfort care, hospice care and pain control;

d   Refer the patient to a consulting physician for medical confirmation of the diagnosis, and for a determination that the patient is capable and acting voluntarily;

e   Refer the patient for counseling if appropriate . . .;

f   Recommend that the patient notify next of kin;

g   Counsel the patient about the importance of having another person present when the patient takes the medication . . . and of not taking the medication in a public place;

h   Inform the patient that he or she has an opportunity to rescind the request at any time and in any manner, and offer the patient an opportunity to rescind at the end of the 15 day waiting period . . .;

i   Verify, immediately prior to writing the prescription for medication . . . that the patient is making an informed decision;

j   Fulfill the medical record documentation requirements . . .;

. . .

An interesting perspective on the way the Act operates in practice, including the type of patient making use of it, can be found in the annual reports on it published by the Oregon state government. The 2016 report provides the following snapshot:

Death With Dignity Act – 2016 Annual Report: Summary[125]

During 2016, 204 people received prescriptions for lethal medications under the provisions of the Oregon DWDA, compared to 218 during 2015. . . As of January 23, 2017, the Oregon Public Health Division had received reports of 133 people who had died during 2016 from ingesting the medications prescribed underDWDA, compared to 135 during 2015.

Since the law was passed in 1997, a total of 1,749 people have had prescriptions written under the DWDA, and 1,127 patients have died from ingesting the medications. During 2016, the rate of DWDA deaths was 37.2 per 10,000 total deaths.

. . . Of the 204 patients for whom prescriptions were written during 2016, 114 (55.9%) ingested the medication and died without regaining consciousness while 36 (17.6%) did not take the medications and subsequently died of other causes . . .

Of the 133 DWDA deaths during 2016, most patients (80.5%) were aged 65 years or older. The median age at death was 73 years. As in previous years, decedents were commonly white (96.2%) and well-educated (50.0% had a least a baccalaureate degree). Patients' underlying illnesses were similar to those of previous years. Most patients had cancer (78.9%), followed by amyotrophic lateral sclerosis (ALS) (6.8%) . . .

Similar to previous years, the three most frequently mentioned end-of-life concerns were loss of autonomy (89.5%), decreasing ability to participate in activities that made life enjoyable (89.5%), and loss of dignity (65.4%).

A total of 102 physicians wrote 204 prescriptions during 2016 (1–25 prescriptions per physician). During 2016, no referrals were made to the Oregon Medical Board for failure to comply with DWDA requirements. During 2016, five patients were referred for psychological/psychiatric evaluation.

---

125 See: www.oregon.gov/oha/PH/PROVIDERPARTNERRESOURCES/EVALUATIONRESEARCH/DEATHWITHDIGNIT-YACT/Documents/year19.pdf.

In 2008, Washington became the second US state to legislate to allow physician-assisted suicide, based on the Oregon model, and Vermont enacted a similar law in 2013. In Montana, following a 2009 ruling of its Supreme Court,[126] a physician charged with assisting suicide has a judicially recognised defence of consent.

In 2015 the Canadian Supreme Court in *Carter v Canada (Attorney General)*[127] held that a ban on assisted dying was incompatible with rights under the Canadian Charter of Rights and Freedoms. Following this decision, the Federal Government passed a statute in June 2016, which permits physician-assisted dying (encompassing both active euthanasia and assisted suicide) for competent patients who have a 'grievous and irremediable medical condition'.[128] The early evidence is that more persons than expected have availed themselves of the new regime – the vast majority opting for active euthanasia – and it will be interesting to see how matters develop.[129]

12.5.3 Current developments in the UK

In the wake of the *Bland* case, a Select Committee of the House of Lords was established to look into the current state of English law in relation to euthanasia. While endorsing steps to facilitate the withholding of unwished for further treatment, such as by the greater use of advance directives, the Committee in its 1994 Report recommended that both assisted suicide and active euthanasia should remain offences, the latter continuing to be treated as murder:

House of Lords Select Committee, *Report of the Select Committee on Medical Ethics*[130]

236 The right to refuse treatment is far removed from the right to request assistance in dying. We spent a long time considering the very strongly held and sincerely expressed views of those witnesses who advocated voluntary [active] euthanasia. Many of us have had the experience of relatives or friends whose dying days were less than peaceful or uplifting, or whose final stages of life were so disfigured that the loved one already seemed lost to us, or who were simply weary of life. Our thinking must inevitably be coloured by such experience. The accounts we received from individual members of the public about such experiences were particularly moving, as were the letters from those who themselves longed for the release of an early death. Our thinking must also be coloured by the wish of every individual for a peaceful and easy death, without prolonged suffering, and by a reluctance to contemplate the possibility of severe dementia or dependence. We gave much thought too to Professor [Ronald] Dworkin's opinion that, for those without religious belief, the individual is best able to decide what manner of death is fitting to the life that has been lived.

237 Ultimately, however, we do not believe that these arguments are sufficient reason to weaken society's prohibition of intentional killing. That prohibition is the cornerstone of law and social relationships. It protects each of us impartially, embodying the belief that all are equal. We do not wish that protection to be diminished and we therefore recommend that there be no change in the law to permit euthanasia. We acknowledge that there may be individual cases in which euthanasia may be seen by some to be appropriate. But individual cases cannot reasonably establish the foundation of a policy which would have such serious and widespread repercussions. Moreover dying is not only a personal or individual affair. The death of a person affects the lives of others, often in ways and to an extent that cannot be foreseen. We believe that the issue of euthanasia is one in which the interest of the individual cannot be separated from the interest of society as a whole.

---

126 *Baxter v Montana*, 2009 MT 449.
127 2015 SCC 5 (Sup Ct (Can)).
128 Bill C-14, at: www.parl.ca/DocumentViewer/en/42-1/bill/C-14/royal-assent.
129 See: www.canada.ca/en/health-canada/services/publications/health-system-services/medical-assistance-dying-interim-report.
130 See n 27 above.

In 2003, however, in the wake of developments in the Netherlands, Belgium and Oregon, and the public debate at home unleashed by the *Diane Pretty* case,[131] the issue of law reform once again appeared on the UK parliamentary agenda. In that year the Labour peer, Lord Joffe, introduced a private member's bill, the Assisted Dying for Terminally Ill Bill, modelled on the Oregon Death with Dignity Act. Subject to various qualifying conditions being satisfied, terminally ill patients experiencing unbearable suffering would have access to 'assisted dying': this was defined as a doctor providing the means for the patient to commit suicide or, if the patient was physically unable to do so, directly ending the patient's life. Subsequently the Bill was considered by a House of Lords Select Committee under the Chairmanship of the former Lord Chancellor, Lord Mackay.

In its Report the Committee – while accepting that there had been a shift in UK public opinion, with more people open to the idea of medical assistance in dying – was critical of the Bill's merging of assisted suicide and voluntary active euthanasia, which it felt would encourage a higher take-up on assisted death than needed as a genuine last resort:

Select Committee on the Assisted Dying for the Terminally Ill Bill[132]

243 Lord Joffe's Bill seeks to legalise not only medical assistance with suicide but also, in cases where self-administration of lethal medication is not possible, voluntary euthanasia. We have visited two places – Oregon and The Netherlands – which have gone down different roads in this regard and which show widely different death rates from this source. In Oregon less than 1 in 700 deaths is currently attributable to assisted suicide, whereas in The Netherlands the figure is more than 1 in 40, less than 10% of which are from assisted suicide while over 90% are as a result of voluntary euthanasia . . .

Subsequently Lord Joffe introduced an amended version of the Bill so that, as in the case of Oregon, it was restricted to allowing cases of physician-assisted suicide. However, at its second reading in 2006, the House of Lords voted against its progression.

More recently, in 2012 the former Lord Chancellor, Lord Falconer of Thoroton, set up and chaired a committee into assisted dying, whose report again recommended legislation in order to permit physician-assisted suicide for the terminally ill. At the time of writing, a relevant bill is before the House of Lords, but it has already drawn criticism for arguably lacking sufficient protections for the vulnerable. As the pressure group, Living and Dying Well (made up of peers, including the former President of the Family Division, Baroness Butler-Sloss), comments:

Another 'assisted dying' bill – does it pass the public safety test?[133]

Lord Falconer's Assisted Dying Bill [HL Bill 24] is the fourth of its kind to come before the House of Lords in the last ten years. None of its predecessors has made progress and the last one (Lord Joffe's Assisted Dying for the Terminally Ill Bill) was rejected in May 2006. This latest bill is little different from Lord Joffe's – it seeks to license doctors to supply lethal drugs to terminally ill patients to enable them to end their lives.

The bill contains no safeguards, beyond stating eligibility criteria, to govern the assessment of requests for assisted suicide. It relegates important questions such as how mental capacity and clear and settled intent are to be established to codes of practice to be drawn up after an assisted suicide law has been approved by Parliament. This is wholly inadequate for a bill, such as this, with life-or-death consequences.

---

131 See n 28 above.
132 HL Paper 86-I, London: TSO, 2005.
133 See: www.livinganddyingwell.org.uk/publications/our-reports/another-assisted-dying-bill-does-it-pass-the-public-safety-test.

Parliament cannot responsibly be asked to approve such a radical piece of legislation without seeing the nature of the safeguards that would accompany it. On this measure alone the bill is not fit for purpose.

Like its predecessors, the bill places responsibility for assessing applicants for assisted suicide and supplying them with lethal drugs on the shoulders of the medical profession. Only a minority of doctors would be willing to participate in such acts if they were to be made lawful. An inevitable consequence, as evidence from the US State of Oregon has shown, is that many of those seeking physician-assisted suicide would find themselves being assessed by doctors to whom they had only recently been introduced and who could know little of them beyond their case notes. The implications of such 'doctor shopping' for thorough and proper assessment are obvious.

The bill also ignores expert medical evidence given to Parliament in recent years regarding the unreliability of prognoses of terminal illness at the range it envisages.

As discussed in Part 12.2.4 above, in the *Nicklinson* case in 2014,[134] the UK Supreme Court invited Parliament to reconsider the area of assisted suicide and the possibility of legislating to achieve a regime to permit this in extreme cases, subject to sufficient safeguards to protect important public interests. The ensuing Parliamentary debates though have been inconclusive, which has occasioned renewed legal challenge, Thus, as we saw in the *Conway* case,[135] the courts are once more being invited to declare the prohibition on assisted suicide incompatible with human rights. Whatever the final outcome of that case,[136] there is little doubt the delicately poised issues in this area will continue to take up political and legal attention.

THINK POINT

Especially in the light of 'suicide tourism' within Europe, would it now be preferable for the UK to legalise assisted suicide? If so, what are the key provisions that should be included in any relevant statute?

Summary of key points

1   Treatment decisions at the end of life (euthanasia) are typically aimed at bringing about an easeful death for the patient. In principle, this might involve the use of means to cause death (active euthanasia). Alternatively, the patient may be 'allowed to die' (passive euthanasia), where the doctor deliberately withholds or withdraws life-sustaining treatment.

2   Under English law as it stands, active euthanasia is unlawful, and generally treated as murder. This prohibition on killing, which persists even where the patient himself wishes to die, reflects the (qualified) sanctity of life principle, which treats human life as inviolable.

3   However, by way of an important qualification, doctors are permitted to prescribe powerful analgesic drugs to terminally ill patients, even though they foresee that such drugs will

---

134 See n 20 above.
135 See n 35 above; the Divisional Court details Parliament's post-*Nicklinson* consideration of the issues at para 51 of its judgment.
136 The Court of Appeal hearing of the case began at the end of April 2018.

shorten the patient's life. This common law exception was recognised in 1957 in the case of *R v (Bodkin) Adams*.

4   In other cases where, rather than acting directly to cause death, the doctor provides the means for the patient to kill himself, the doctor will be liable for the offence of assisted suicide. This remains punishable under the Suicide Act 1961, with up to 14 years' imprisonment.

5   The legal position in respect of passive euthanasia is generally more flexible: as confirmed by the House of Lords in 1993 in *Airedale NHS Trust v Bland*; in so far as the prima facie duty to treat has lapsed, the doctor may withdraw life-sustaining treatment to allow the patient's death.

6   One such situation is where a capable patient refuses consent to further treatment. Here the doctor who continues to prolong the patient's life will commit a battery. Nor does it matter if, in discontinuing treatment, the doctor 'acts' (in the narrow sense), eg by detaching a tube. Legally this will count as an omission.

7   As set out in the 2005 Mental Capacity Act, a formerly capable patient may encode a treatment refusal in an advance decision. Provided the decision is found to be both valid and applicable, it will bind the doctors to cease maintaining the life of the (now incapable) patient.

8   In respect of incapable patients, where there is no binding advance decision, life-sustaining treatment may be withdrawn in so far as it is no longer in the patient's best interests. In some cases, notably where the decision relates to a patient in PVS, an application should be made to the Court of Protection under the Mental Capacity Act.

9   In other cases, concerning sensate and suffering incapable patients, and where there is no dispute between the doctors and the relatives, the decision may be taken without court involvement.

10   In recent years, particularly given the lawfulness of active euthanasia and assisted suicide in certain other countries, there has been pressure in the UK in the direction of law reform. Following the UK Supreme Court decision in *Nicklinson v Ministry of Justice*, the legalisation of assisted suicide in certain circumstances remains under intense debate.

Further reading

Adenitire, J, 'A conscience-based human right to be "doctor death"' (2016) Public Law 613.

Birchley, G and Huxtable, R, 'Critical decisions for critically ill infants' in Stanton, C et al. (eds), *Pioneering Healthcare Law: Essays in Honour of Margaret Brazier*, New York, Routledge, 2016.

Greasley, K, '*R (Purdy) v DPP* and the case for wilful blindness' (2010) 30 Oxford Journal of Legal Studies 301.

Huxtable, R, *Euthanasia, Ethics and the Law: From Conflict to Compromise*, Abingdon: Routledge-Cavendish, 2007.

Keown, J, *Euthanasia, Ethics and Public Policy: An Argument Against Legalisation*, Cambridge: Cambridge University Press, 2002.

Lewis, P, 'Euthanasia in Belgium five years after legalisation' (2009) 16 European Journal of Health Law 125.

Otlowski, M, *Voluntary Euthanasia and the Common Law*, Oxford: Oxford University Press, 1997.

Price, D, 'What shape to euthanasia after *Bland*? Historical, contemporary and future paradigms' (2009) 125 Law Quarterly Review 142.

Index